W9-BPO-844

The
New Dictionary
of
Theology

The
New Dictionary
of
Theology

• EDITORS •

Joseph A. Komonchak

Mary Collins   **Dermot A. Lane**

Michael Glazier, Inc. • **Wilmington** • **Delaware**

Second Printing, 1988

First published in 1987 by Michael Glazier, Inc., 1935 West Fourth Street, Wilmington, Delaware 19805. • International Standard Book Number 0-89453-609-5 • Library of Congress Card Number 87-82327 • ©Michael Glazier, Inc. All rights reserved. No part of this publication may be copied, reproduced or transmitted, in any form or by any means, without written permission of the publisher. • Typesetting and design by Connie Runkel, Laura Burke, Sandy Almeida Kelly. • Printed in the United States of America.

Editorial Preface

The New Dictionary of Theology appears as the Roman Catholic Church observes the twenty-fifth anniversary of the opening of the Second Vatican Council. That remarkable event was made possible by the "return to the sources" carried out by scholars in the decades before. By focusing on the two-fold goal of renewal in the light of the gospel and reform in the light of the demands of the times, the Council in turn inspired a widespread and profound set of changes in Catholic theology.

The *Dictionary* represents the first collaborative attempt in English to take stock of the remarkable developments in the church and in theology since the Council, a purpose which determined the structure, authorship, and intended audience of this work.

Vatican II drew attention to a "hierarchy of truths" drawn up on the basis of the varying relationship between church doctrines and "the foundation of the Christian faith" (U.R. 11). Similarly, this *Dictionary* is constructed around twenty-four topics which the editors believe constitute the principal themes of the christian vision of faith. The longest and the most important articles are devoted to these themes, which provide the center around which all the other articles revolve and from which they derive their own meaning and relationship to the whole. Cross-references at the end of the articles will aid the reader in making the associations with the interpretative center.

Since the *Dictionary* makes no claim to be an exhaustive encyclopedia of theology, we realize that others might have made different choices about the structure and the topics, but we hope that we have supplied in this volume a reference work which any student will find to be an intelligent and critical introduction to Catholic theology in our day.

As the list of contributors will indicate, articles were solicited from all over the English-speaking world, a choice which reflects the increased recognition that theology must be carried out locally, that is, in a renewed effort of "faith seeking understanding" with the help of the resources and in response to the challenges of varying social and cultural situations.

The New Dictionary of Theology was conceived as an aid to preachers and teachers of the faith. The contributors assumed the difficult task of presenting serious scholarly research in such a way as to be useful for those engaged in secondary and college-level teaching or in ordinary preaching.

The contributors were asked to review the biblical, traditional, liturgical, and

v

magisterial foundations of their topics, to summarize the contribution of Vatican II, and to indicate the present state of theological understanding. Although our aim was not to present personal theological developments of the topics, we are pleased that so many of our authors brought to their work a good measure of theological insight and creativity.

Apart from the guidelines mentioned above, the contributors were left free to develop their topics as they wished, and the editors did not seek either to favor any theological school or to impose any single editorial direction. We believe that the result is a variety of approaches, methods, languages, and interpretations which itself rather faithfully reflects the development of theology since the Second Vatican Council.

While this is a dictionary of Catholic theology, we are pleased that the articles manifest an acute ecumenical sensitivity.

Credit for the idea of this *Dictionary* goes to the publisher, Michael Glazier. The editors wish to express their gratitude to him for his patient and gentle encouragement, and especially to Eileen Daney Carzo, the publisher's Chief Editor, who bore the burden of the day-to-day responsibilities of a complicated task and whose attentiveness and diligence greatly facilitated the work of the editors.

Joseph A. Komonchak
Chief Editor

Abbreviations

A.A.	*Apostolicam actuositatem:* Vatican II, Decree on the Apostolate of the Laity
Adv.Haer.	Against Heresies (St. Irenaeus)
A.G.	*Ad gentes:* Vatican II, Decree on the Church's Missionary Activity
AmER	American Ecclesiastical Review
Apost. Trad.	Apostolic Tradition (Hippolytus)
C.D.	*Christus Dominus:* Vatican II, Decree on the Pastoral Office of Bishops in the Church
C.I.C.	*Codex Iuris Canonici:* The Code of Canon Law
Cod. Theod.	Codex Theodosianus
C.S.E.L.	*Corpus Scriptorum Ecclesiasticorum Latinorum.*
D.	H. Denzinger, *Enchiridion Symbolorum,* 31st edition, 1957
D.H.	*Dignitatis humanae:* Vatican II, Declaration on Religious Liberty
Did.	*Didache*
D.S.	New edition of Denzinger, edited by A. Schönmetzer, 32nd edition, 1963
D.T.C.	*Dictionnaire de théologie catholique*
D.V.	*Dei verbum:* Vatican II, Dogmatic Constitution on Divine Revelation
Enc. Bib.	*Enchiridion Biblicum*
G.E.	*Gravissimum educationis:* Vatican II, Declaration on Christian Education
G.I.R.M.	General Instruction on the Roman Missal
G.S.	*Gaudium et spes:* Vatican II, Pastoral Constitution on the Church in the Modern World
JB	Jerusalem Bible
JBC	Jerome Biblical Commentary
JEH	Journal of Ecclesiastical History
L.E.	*Laborem Exercens* (Pope John Paul II)
L.G.	*Lumen gentium:* Vatican II, Dogmatic Constitution on the Church

L.G.G.	*Die Religion in Geschichte und Gegennwart*
LXX	Septuagint
N.A.B.	New American Bible
O.E.	*Orientalium ecclesiarum:* Vatican II, Decree on the Catholic Oriental Churches
Oss. Rom.	*Osservatore Romano*
P.C.	*Perfectae caritatis:* Vatican II, Decree on the Up-to-date Renewal of Religious Life
P.G.	J.P. Migne, *Patrologia Graeca,* 1857-1865
P.L.	J.P. Migne, *Patrologia Latina,* 1878-1890
P.O.	*Presbyterorum ordinis:* Vatican II, Decree on the Life and Ministry of Priests
Paed.	*Paidagogos* (Clement of Alexandria)
Protrep.	*Protrepticus* (Clement of Alexandria)
Quodl.	*Quodlibetales*
R.C.I.A.	Rite of Christian Initiation of Adults
R.J.	Rouët de Journel, ed., *The Enchiridion Patristicum*
R.S.V.	Revised Standard Version
S.C.	*Sacrosanctum concilium:* Vatican II, Constitution on the Sacred Liturgy
Sc.G.	*Summa Contra Gentiles* (St. Thomas Aquinas)
S.Th.	*Summa Theologiae* (St. Thomas Aquinas)
Strom.	*Stromata* (Clement of Alexandria)
Th. Inv.	Theological Investigations (Karl Rahner)
Thom.	The Thomist
U.R.	*Unitatis redintegratio:* Vatican II, Decree on Ecumenism
Vulg.	Vulgate

A

ABBA

Jesus was one who had a serene relationship with God. Without self-consciousness he spoke of "Father" and "Son"; he turned with direct confidence to that Father in prayer. The gospel evidence points to Jesus' consistent use of the term Abba in speaking of God and especially in prayer to God. Admittedly, in the gospels, this Aramaic word is met with only once (Mk 14:36)—not surprisingly in documents written in Greek. But the term stands behind "the Father," "Father" or "my Father" in all strands of the gospel tradition. *Abba,* originally an infant-word, was, in Jesus' day, a familiar designation of one's father; it carried a note of tenderness combined with a recognition of benign authority. That Jesus regularly addressed his God as Abba shows his unconventional regard towards and intimate communion with God. Because he really knew his God he could dare to call him Abba. And because he expected his disciples really to get to know God—not any God but the Father *he* knew—he wanted them, too, to address prayer to the Father in the same manner—*audemus dicere*. This is clearly present in Luke's version of the Lord's Prayer: "When you pray, say: Father (i.e. Abba)" (11:1-2).

That early Christians did pray so we know from Gal 4:6 and Rom 8:15 (the only places in the NT, apart from Mk 14:36, where the Aramaic word appears). Evidently, they did not regard Jesus' use of the term as pointing to the uniqueness of his sonship—otherwise they could never have addressed the Father in the same manner as he. What does follow is that they, rightly, recognized in Jesus' use of the title evidence of his religious experience of deep intimacy with God. They recognized that he knew God as no one ever had known him. And if indeed Jesus had taught his disciples to pray in the same manner as he, it was precisely his disciples whom he so taught. For that matter it is, Paul tells us, the Spirit of the Son sent by God into the heart of the Christian who cries "Abba."

Consideration of the title *Abba* leads us to look to Jesus' sense of sonship. Did Jesus think of himself as *the* Son? A key text is Mt 11:27—"All things have been delivered to me by my Father; and no one knows the Son except the Father, and no one knows the Father except the Son and anyone to whom the Son chooses to reveal him" (cf. Lk 10:22). The question is, could Jesus have spoken of his relationship with God in such an absolute and exclusive manner? Jesus *prayed* to God as Father; here he claims to know God. One must recall that, in a Hebrew context, to speak of knowledge in a setting of personal relationship is to

1

imply intimate relationship. In God-man relationship it describes the love and surrender stirred by the gracious love of God. It is the same I-Thou relationship expressed by Abba. Jesus relates to God with the warmth and intimacy of a son towards his father.

Where should one seek the ground of Jesus' Abba-experience? It would seem that we should seek and find it in his humanness—in a humanness always immediately related to God. The eternal and self-sufficient God had freely and from eternity willed to be for another. In pursuance of this desire God summoned forth the human race and, one day, out of that race which looked in hope to something beyond itself, came one who would be like him and would respond to him wholly. In Jesus of Nazareth God met his own counterpart, the image and likeness of himself. To Jesus he could say, "My Son" and hear the spontaneous response "Abba." Jesus' was the answer to God's eternal decision not to be alone. In Johannine language, the Word became flesh and dwelt among us.

See **God**

J. Jeremias, *The Prayers of Jesus,* London: SCM, 1967, 11-65. E. Schillebeeckx, *Jesus,* N.Y.: Crossroad, 1981, and London: Fount Books, 1983, 256-271.

WILFRID HARRINGTON, OP

ABORTION

Abortion is the induced termination of pregnancy before the fetus is capable of surviving outside the womb. As a human phenomenon abortion is as old as recorded human history and has been sought for numerous reasons and by a variety of methods. While no society has ever regarded abortion as something good or neutral in terms of ethical evaluation, its acceptance as an alternative to unwanted or risky pregnancy has an uneven history among civilized peoples.

In the Greco-Roman world abortion was used to hide the fact of a promiscuous adulterous lifestyle, to save a woman's life or even her feminine figure, and to prevent having too many children. Often a caution was expressed to abort before there is "sensation and life" (Aristotle), or before the person is formed. Even today the status of the human embryo and fetus continues to be a disputed issue despite advanced knowledge of human development made available by modern science. The moral issue of abortion revolves principally around the value and rights accorded to the human fetus; whether the values of human dignity, sacredness of life, and inalienable rights are possessed by the unborn, and if so, whether there is a discernible point in development at which the unborn make claim for protection upon the already born.

Attempts to root a clear condemnation of abortion in the Jewish or christian scriptures will discover that there is but one OT text which explicitly mentions abortion (Exod 21:22-25) and no NT text. The Exodus text containing a Jewish legal code prescribed that, in the event a woman miscarries as a result of a fight between two men, the responsible party must pay a fine set by the woman's husband. Should she be injured or die, a corresponding punishment was to be exacted, including "life for life." The fact that capital punishment was not required for the fetus's death would suggest that the fetus was not considered to be a human person as was the woman. A later translation of this same text in the Septuagint notes that if the miscarried fetus "be perfectly formed" the defendant "shall give life for life." This reflects development of thought regarding the status of the fetus encountered also in later writings, like those of Aristotle, which taught that the fetus became a human person when it was fully formed so as to be apt material for the infusion of the human soul. Certain other OT texts testify to the Israelites' appreciation for God's work in forming each new life in the womb (Gen 4:1; Job 31:15; Isa 44:24; 49:1, 5; Jer 1:5), but there is no mention of abortion and no specific law in Jewish writings treating of it until into the christian era in the Mishnah compiled around 200 A.D.

The NT is equally silent, if not more so, regarding abortion. That life in the womb is acknowledged and esteemed is evident in the synoptic infancy narratives. Some writers point to a passage in the Pauline literature and in Revelations where the authors condemn the giving of certain drugs (*pharmakeia*), interpreting this to mean abortifacient potions (Gal 5:20; also, Rev 9:21; 21:8). The Greek word, however, can mean a number of things and it is unlikely that Paul, or others, would have used such a word to condemn something as specific as abortion. Two first-century documents are more specific in their condemnation of abortion: the *Didache* or *Teachings of the Apostles,* and the *Epistle of Pseudo-Barnabas.* The *Didache* states flatly that "you shall not kill the fetus by abortion, or destroy the infant already born." Following the virtual silence of the NT on abortion and the existing cultural context of the gentile world where both practices were fairly common as a way to hide the fruits of promiscuity, the starkness of this command suggests an already developed and operative ethical stance against abortion and infanticide by early Christians. In fact, the christian teaching opposing the killing of the unborn ran counter to a culture marked by general indifference to fetal and infant life.

There are notable examples in christian theology attesting to the fact that abortion was repudiated among christian believers. Clearly the reason for the condemnation was a christian commitment to living the commandment of neighborly love. The fetus was considered to be a neighbor,

and any direct attack upon its life was an attack upon one whom God has made and loved. "You shall love your neighbor more than your own life. You shall not slay the child by abortions. You shall not kill what is generated" (*Pseudo-Barnabas 19:5*). What was not always so clear was the species of the crime: homicide, or something less. Tertullian spoke of the potential human person: "He who is man-to-be is man, as all fruit is now in the seed." He called upon the mother ("there is no more fitting teacher") to verify the humanity of the child in her womb. In later centuries, Jerome and Augustine, while condemning abortion, wrestled with the question of ensoulment (at forty-six days for Augustine) and the formed and unformed fetus, concluding that there was no solution to this, but that the killing of either was to be condemned. Others allowed the distinction of "formed and unformed" to influence the punishment visited upon the perpetrator of abortion. By 450 A.D. the position of the christian world, East and West, was clearly one opposed to abortion. Note that often there was little distinction made between contraception and abortion because of primitive biological knowlege which believed that the tiny new person (the *homunculus*) was in the male semen and any act which wasted semen also wasted this new life.

Thomas Aquinas, following Aristotle's philosophy, held that ensoulment did not occur at conception but at a later time, at forty days for the male and ninety for the female (*Commentary on Book 3 of the Sentences of Peter Lombard*). Yet Thomas taught that it was a "grave sin against the natural law" to kill the fetus at any stage, and a graver sin of homicide to do so after ensoulment. Thomas even believed that intercourse during pregnancy was mortally sinful as it posed a risk of causing an abortion.

In the ensuing centuries the question of

ensoulment or animation continued to influence the species of crime or sin entailed in abortion and the punishment and penances to be assigned. There was also discussion and disagreement about values which might be equal to or greater than the value of the life of the fetus, for example, the physical life or health of the mother. Some permitted aborting prior to ensoulment in a lesser-evil calculation. In the eighteenth century, Catholic teaching argued for protection of the fetus from conception since from that point the human person was considered to be present *in potentia*. Pius IX in 1869 (*Apostolicae sedis*) condemned abortion from the moment of conception as homicide and attached to the crime an excommunication. Terminating fetal life would be justifiable only in situations termed "indirect abortion" (Double Effect principle) when the loss of the fetal life is a secondary effect of some therapeutic procedure done to save the life of the mother, e.g., the removal of a cancerous but pregnant uterus or the excision of a fallopian tube containing an ectopic pregnancy.

Protestant theologians from the Reformation on into the twentieth generally reflected the same negative stance toward abortion as did their Catholic counterparts, even to the disagreements over the time of ensoulment and the possible practical implications of this distinction. Abortion was customarily grouped with other sins of sexual immorality.

In the twentieth century a combination of scientific advancement in understanding and controlling human reproduction and some modified appreciation of certain value conflicts surrounding abortion culminated in significant departures from the traditional christian ethic. Embryology, fetology and genetics provided a wealth of information about early life stages and the autonomy of the human fetus following fertilization. They demon-strated that from the time of the union of sperm and egg a human life is biologically a continuum with its developmental stages arbitrarily demarcated and labeled, e.g., zygote, embryo, fetus, infant, etc. Certain significant events involving cell differentiation and organ development give the fetus an increasingly more human appearance, but these events were already preprogrammed into its genetic code. Genetic evaluation of the fetus *in utero* through amniocentesis and sonography techniques permit detection of many genetic and accidental abnormalities and allow for decisions to be made about terminating a pregnancy. Justification for abortion in such cases is premised on the belief that it is in the best interests of the abnormally developing fetus and his or her family and society which otherwise will be forced to bear the burdens of mental anguish, lifestyle disruptions and financial cost. Dissenters claim that such argumentation should logically be extended to justify infanticide, unless morally significant differences can be demonstrated between the born and the unborn.

Altered ethical positions on the purpose or ends of human sexuality have also contributed to changing attitudes among many in society regarding abortion. The procreational bias in traditional sexual ethics, modified to give equal weight to the *unitive* and *affective communication* components of sexual intercourse, no longer offers them compelling reason to accept an unwanted pregnancy resulting from intercourse engaged in without procreative intent.

The women's movement which has realized important and necessary gains for women in social and personal autonomy often posits a claim to reproductive rights which would encompass the right to terminate an unwanted pregnancy. The claim of an inalienable right to life on the part of the fetus conflicts with the woman's reproductive right and raises, again, the disputed question of the moral status of the fetus: human person, or something less.

A variety of theories present themselves regarding the value and the moral and legal status of the developing fetus. The question "When does a subject with the rights of a human person come into existence?" cannot be decided by the biomedical sciences and is likely to be the subject of philosophical, theological, and legal deliberation for the course of human history. In a sense, the ancient query about "ensoulment" and "formed" and "unformed" fetuses is still at the heart of the matter. Most agree that "human life" is initiated at fertilization, but there is wide speculation concerning when, at what stage of development, that human life becomes personalized or individualized so as to be deserving of the respect and protection accorded to any infant.

Official Roman Catholic teaching maintains that, since it is not possible to discover the precise moment of animation or ensoulment, if one truly respects and values human personal life, the benefit of any doubt must be given to the earliest possible stage when such life could be present, and that, the teaching maintains, is at fertilization. "(F)rom the moment of conception life must be guarded with the greatest care, while abortion and infanticide are unspeakable crimes" (G.S. 51). Again, "respect for human life is called for from the time that the process of generation begins. From the time that the ovum is fertilized, a life is begun which is neither that of the father nor of the mother; it is rather the life of a new human being with his own growth. It would never be made human if it were not human already.... Divine law and natural reason, therefore, exclude all right to the direct killing of an innocent man" (*Declaration on Procured Abortion,* 1976). This condemnation of abortive acts extends even to such birth control agents as the intrauterine device and the so-called "mini pill," both of which have as their primary effect inhibiting implantation of the newly fashioned human embryo into the uterine wall. Official Roman Catholic moral teaching remains unalterably opposed to all direct abortion for whatever reason. In a contemporary society where abortion has been legalized the church insists that "a Christian can never conform to a law which is in itself immoral, and such is the case of a law which would admit in principle the liceity of abortion" (*Declaration,* 1976).

Some christian ethicians, including a number of Catholic moralists, find cause to acknowledge "personhood" at a time later than fertilization for reasons related to fetal development or even in the way the fetus is perceived by the human community in terms of individualization and community belonging. Entrance into participation in human "rights" is viewed as a gradual process. Some even claim that the fullness of human personal status is not achieved until after birth when parents accept the newborn as a member of the human community with a right to life and the full protection of the law. This position goes beyond abortion to embrace moral justification for infanticide. In a Judeo-Christian ethic human biological life has never been considered an absolute or supreme value. Killing has been justified, even while regretted as an *objective evil.* The preservation of values of equal or greater importance has allowed for killing in self defense, "just war," and capital punishment. Some moral systems (e.g., Roman Catholic) view such killing "indirect" because the intention is to sustain or preserve the other value held to be proportionally equal or greater. Those who do not accord the fetus the full status and value of a human person, even while granting it some value, will find it less difficult to justify abortion when other values are in conflict, e.g., freedom from an unwanted pregnancy; securing and exercising one's reproductive rights; escaping the burden of severe handicap or the stigma attached to being conceived through rape or incest. The value one attributes to the fetus at any gestational stage will largely determine the offsetting value which would justify abortion.

In summary, the christian tradition has maintained a generally negative and condemnatory stance towards abortion for reasons rooted in the tradition's understanding of human sexuality and the dignity and sacredness of human life. Arguments and disagreements about the status of the human fetus will likely remain and will be influenced by the prevailing state of scientific knowledge of early human development. Philosophical and theological perspectives will continue to help shape the ethical controversy as will legal decisions in the civil sector (e.g., *Roe et al. v. Wade,* the U.S. Supreme Court decision of 1973 legalizing abortions is also ethical). In more recent times sociological phenomena, e.g., the women's movement, sociopolitical and demographic concerns, have tended to produce a climate more accepting of abortion. Those opposed warn of a significant potential for devaluing all human life in an abortion accepting society. They judge abortion to be a symptom of a greater systemic illness in a society which uses and oppresses persons for commercial gain, neglects the elderly and the handicapped, exhibits gender and sexual discrimination, and spends proportionally more for defense than it does to alleviate the societal educational, medical, and employment needs which lessen the quality of life for many. The presence of these social ills in a society suggests a lack of commitment to the Judeo-Christian ethic which values equally every human person regardless of age, condition, or developmental stage.

D. Callahan, *Abortion: Law, Choice, and Morality,* 1970. J. Connery, *Abortion: The Development of the Roman Catholic Perspective,* 1977. *Declaration on Procured Abortion,* 1976. *Gaudium et Spes,* 51. G. Grisez, *Abortion: The Myths, the Realities, and the Arguments,* 1970. B.W. Harrison, *Our Right to Choose: Toward a New Ethic of Abortion,* 1983. J.T. Noonan, Ed., *The Morality of Abortion: Legal and Historical Perspectives,* 1970. *A Private Choice: Abortion in America in the Seventies,* 1979.

ROBERT M. FRIDAY

ABSOLUTE

That which exists without any dependence on another being and without any conditions In christian theology, the term applies only to God.
See **God**

ABSOLUTION

In reference to the sacrament of penance, "absolution" is used in two ways: the absolution of sins and the absolution, or remission, of censures. The absolution of sins is an essential part and the completion of the sacrament of penance; in scholastic terminology, it is the "form" of the sacrament. The words of absolution imparted by the priest in the name of Christ are a sign of God's pardon of the sinner and they obtain the forgiveness of sins and reconciliation with God and the Church. (Cf. Rite of Penance, 6d; Code of Canon Law, canon 959.) In the Latin rite the formula of absolution is: "God, the Father of mercies, through the death and resurrection of his Son has reconciled the world to himself and sent the Holy Spirit among us for the forgiveness of sins; through the ministry of the church may God give you pardon and peace, and I absolve you from your sins in the name of the Father, and of the Son, and of the Holy Spirit." The formula indicates that the reconciliation of penitents comes from God's mercy; it shows the connection between reconciliation and the paschal mystery; it stresses the role of the Holy Spirit in the forgiveness of sins; and it underscores the ecclesial aspect of the sacrament (Rite of Penance, 19). The final words beginning with "I absolve you" are necessary for validity but do not suffice for liceity except in danger of imminent death.

According to the Council of Trent, the absolution is like a judicial act whereby the sentence is pronounced by the priest as a judge (D., 1685, 1709). The 1974 Rite of Penance (nn. 6b, 10a) and the 1983 Code of Canon Law (canon 978) recall the judicial nature of absolution, but it is balanced by describing the confessor as a healer placed by God as the minister of divine mercy and salvation who reveals the heart of God and shows the image of Christ the Good Shepherd.

Ordinarily absolution is given after individual confession, but in exceptional circumstances general absolution can be imparted to a number of penitents without previous individual confession. Canon law allows this in two cases: (1) in danger of death when there is not time for the priest or priests to hear the confessions of all the individuals present; and (2) in a case of serious necessity when there are insufficient confessors readily available rightly to hear individual confessions within a suitable time. The diocesan bishop can determine general cases of necessity in view of criteria agreed upon by the episcopal conference. For the validity of general absolution, the penitents must be suitably disposed and intend to confess their serious sins later in individual confession. (See canons 961-962.)

The remission of a penalty, as opposed to the absolution of sins, is an act of the external forum and is usually reserved to a competent ecclesiastical authority, but canon law allows for two exceptions. (1) A person in danger of death can have any censures absolved by any priest (canon 976). (2) If it would be hard on the penitent to remain in a state of serious sin during the time needed to receive a remission from the competent authority, any confessor can remit in the internal sacramental forum any undeclared, automatic censure of excommunication or interdict, observing the stipulations of canon 1357. The formula for the remission of censures in such cases is the same as the words of absolution of sins, provided the minister intends to remit the censure by means of these words. When a priest absolves a penitent from a censure outside the sacrament of penance, or if during the sacrament he remits the censure before he absolves the sins, the following formula is used: "By the power granted to me, I absolve you from the bond of excommunication (suspension, interdict). In the name of the Father, and of the Son, and of the Holy Spirit."

See **Reconciliation**

John Huels, *The Pastoral Companion: A Canon Law Handbook for Catholic Ministry,* Part V. Chicago: Franciscan Herald Press, 1986. Frederick McManus, "The Sacrament of Penance," in *The Code of Canon Law: A Text and Commentary.* New York/Mahwah: Paulist Press, 1985.

JOHN M. HUELS, OSM

ACOLYTE

Formerly one of the four minor orders, the acolyte today is one of the two official "lay ministries" established in 1972. An acolyte assists the deacon and priests at the altar, may distribute Holy Communion both at Mass and to the sick as an auxiliary minister, and may expose the Blessed Sacrament for adoration but not give the benediction. Under present canon law, only men may be installed as acolytes.

STEPHEN FUNK

ADOPTION

See **Grace, Justification.**

ADOPTIONISM

The view that Jesus was simply a human being, especially favored or "adopted" as the Son of God at some point, usually either at his baptism or at his resurrection. Adoptionist views were espoused by some early Jewish-Christian groups, by Elipando of Toledo in the eighth century, and by Abelard in the twelfth.

STEPHEN FUNK

ADORATION, EUCHARISTIC

The worship in private devotion or public cult of Christ present in the eucharistic elements of the Mass and in the reserved sacrament.

Eucharistic adoration is intimately connected with eucharistic reservation and the evolution of the eucharistic liturgy itself.

It is clear from very early on and perhaps even from the time the gospels were written that the bread and wine of christian community meals were held in special regard and handled with care and reverence. Such regard would only increase as the eucharistic ritual with bread and wine was distinguished more and more from the meal of the community and finally separated from it. The eucharistic food was also brought to those who had been absent (Justin, 1 Apol. c. 150 at Rome), and it was reserved for the communion of the sick and dying. Respectful care for the eucharist brought home for private communion during the week was enjoined by Hippolytus at Rome c. 215 (*Apost. Trad.* 37): "Let everyone take care that no unbeliever eats of the eucharist, nor any mouse or other animal, and that none of it falls and is lost. For it is the body of Christ, to be eaten by believers, and not to be despised."

During the first millennium, the permanent reservation of the sacrament for the communion of the sick and dying became established in the western church. Though signs of respect (and at times a kind of superstitious awe) might attend the sacrament especially in its use for the sick and dying, there are no indications of external worship, private or public, given to the sacrament as such.

In the same thousand years, the liturgy of the Mass evolved, becoming a largely clerical ritual observed by the people who could not understand its language and who rarely received communion. Their attention and devotion were focused more and more on viewing the bread and wine, but most especially the host, not as food to be eaten but as object to be adored. Centuries-old attitudes and gestures of reverence for the sacrament within the liturgy were enhanced, emphasized and supplemented. Controversies about the nature of Christ's presence in the eucharist and long-established allegorical interpretations of the Mass as a kind of drama of Jesus' life, death and resurrection stressed sharply the reality of the body and blood to be adored in the sacrifice of the Mass.

It is largely out of acts of reverence and adoration paid the sacrament within the liturgy that private and public cult of the reserved sacrament began, grew, and flourished after the year 1000. Controversy about the real presence was ignited again by Berengarius (+1088); theological discussion (twelfth century) dealt with the moment of consecration, the concomitant presence of body and blood in each species, and the legitimacy of intinction—and all of this reinforced the worship of Christ substantially (twelfth- and thirteenth-century scholastics) present on the altar and in the sacrament now reserved on or near the principal altar in most European churches.

Visits to the blessed sacrament were recommended for personal devotion. This practice probably stemmed from the general desire to see or at least be in the presence of the sacred host and from priestly and popular salutations of the sacrament which entered the Mass liturgy (eleventh through thirteenth centuries).

A procession with the sacrament, long a part of Triduum liturgies, appeared on Palm Sunday in some churches (eleventh century), the sacrament replacing the cross or gospel book. A procession, often with the sacrament exposed in a monstrance for public view, became a key element in the Corpus Christi liturgy (approved in 1264 by Pope Urban IV) and then a recurring devotion on other solemn occasions, churchly or civil.

From various showings and elevations of the sacrament within the Mass and its "portable" exposition on Corpus Christi came the practice of exposing the sacrament for private devotion for short or long periods or even permanently in some types of sacrament houses. Later still, customs of shared devotion before the sacrament exposed came into being: Mass before the sacrament exposed (fourteenth century); short exposition with Benediction following Mass or Vespers (fourteenth century); Forty Hours Devotion (sixteenth century); Holy Hours, nocturnal, or perpetual adoration before the sacrament (seventeenth century).

Benediction, which sprang from the practice of blessing the faithful with the sacrament at the stations and end of the Corpus Christi procession (fourteenth century) became a common final blessing at other liturgical services or popular devotions and eventually stood alone (sixteenth-seventeenth centuries).

Signs of honor once shown to persons, altar, cross, or relics—bows, genuflections, incense, lights, bells—were transferred to the sacrament as signs of worship, first within Mass and then in services of communal devotion for the reserved sacrament.

Eucharistic Congresses, begun in 1881, have been marked by eucharistic liturgies and devotions and by the study of theological and pastoral issues, including the relationship of the eucharist with mission, justice and peace.

As an aspect of liturgical and spiritual renewal following Vatican II, eucharistic reservation and adoration were frequently treated in Roman documents, culminating in *Holy Communion and Eucharistic Devotion outside Mass* (1973). The documents enunciate general principles and norms for eucharistic adoration.

The celebration of the eucharistic liturgy is the center of christian life, and communion within Mass is the norm. Still, the sacrament is rightly reserved for communion outside Mass and for the adoration of the faithful, though these are secondary motives for reservation. Since the celebration of the eucharist is both the origin and the goal of the worship of Christ in the sacrament reserved, such worship extends the grace of the eucharistic sacrifice and must be in harmony with the eucharistic liturgy, flowing from the liturgy and leading people back to it. Adoration is always directed toward sacramental and spiritual communion and a deeper participation in the paschal mystery of Christ.

All of the rites for communion, viaticum and worship outside of Mass include a gathering of the church (no matter how small in some situations) and a proclamation of the biblical word with prayer.

Visits to the blessed sacrament are encouraged, and the place of reservation should be conducive to private prayer and devotion.

Norms are provided for the exposition of the sacrament in monstrance or ciborium for short or longer periods of time. Exposition may not occur during Mass or in the same place where Mass is being celebrated because of the dynamic and multiple modes of Christ's presence in the eucharistic action itself. Communal adoration during exposition must include Bible lessons, song, prayer, and silence, and be in harmony with the eucharistic liturgy. Though an annual, longer period of exposition is recommended, the Forty Hours Devotion is not mentioned. Perpetual adoration is limited to those religious communities or other groups devoted to it by their constitutions.

Benediction with the sacrament may occur within periods of exposition, i.e., after a suitable period of reading, prayer, and adoration. Exposition exclusively for giving Benediction is forbidden.

The appropriateness of processions with the sacrament in contemporary situations is left to the judgment and guidelines of the local bishop. The Corpus Christi procession is encouraged, and it ends, traditionally, with Benediction.

Guidelines for Eucharistic Congresses view them as local, regional or international. In addition to expressing eucharistic faith and exploring theological and pastoral themes, such congresses are to put great stress on the promotion of social undertakings for human development and right distribution of property.

In short, eucharistic adoration as a sign of Catholic faith is entirely dependent on the eucharistic liturgy and communion with the Lord in the church. Adoration must foster a hunger for eucharistic worship and communion, for conversion in faith, and for ministry to the world.

See **Eucharist; Reservation, Eucharistic; Viaticum**

N. Mitchell, *Cult and Controversy: The Worship of the Eucharist Outside Mass.* New York 1982.

ALLAN BOULEY, OSB

AGAPE

The Greek word most commonly used in the NT (see especially 1 Cor 13) for the love of God for humanity and for the love which ought to characterize Christians.

See **Love**

AGNOSTICISM

The view that only what can be experienced or empirically verified can be known and that, therefore, ultimate reality is unknown and unknowable. Agnosticism may be found either in the form of skepticism about religious claims or as the view that all religious faith represents a "leap" which may neither be justified nor disqualified by reason.

See **Apologetics, Faith, Proof for the Existence of God**

STEPHEN FUNK

ALLEGORY
See **Senses of Scripture**

ALTAR

The meaning of the altar is fundamentally dependent on the theology of worship. As the theology of worship developed, four images came to dominate the christian understanding. These occur at varying times and with varying degrees of intensity. Generally, however, all four share in the continuing meaning of the altar.

First is the tendency to dematerialize or spiritualize the altar, so that the Hebrew meaning of the altar is subsumed by the person of Christ. A second tendency is the mirror opposite, in which temple worship and its altar become types of christian worship and altar. The third image describes the altar as the table of the Lord. Fourth, the altar is associated with the burial place of martyrs whose deaths are icons of Jesus' sacrificial death.

The Spiritualized Meaning

During the apostolic period many of the connotations associated with temple sacrifice were spiritualized so that Christ himself takes on these qualities. The classical Hebrew sense of the altar as the meeting place between heaven and earth, or its image as the place of sacrifice and communion are the qualities of Christ. He is the new temple (Jn 2:21), the altar (Heb 13:10), the sacrificial victim (Heb 9:12) and the priest (Heb 9:11). This tendency spiritualizes and dematerializes the physical altar. It disassociates it with a specific place (Jerusalem) and removes it as the focus of the sacral priesthood's action in the name of the people.

This spiritualized sense of the altar parallels the earliest christian understanding of sacrifice which was solely that of Christ and by analogy associated with the life of Christians. Likewise the christian altar is only analogously the place of Christ's sacrifice for he himself and his cross are the primordial referents. The most radically spiritualized image associated with the temple and therefore sacrifice, is found in Rev 21:22 in which the city itself becomes the dwelling place for God and there is no temple, no altar, and no sacrifice. Now all is penetrated by the tangible glory of God for the new creation had done away with the old symbols. God's self has replaced them.

This spiritual image of the altar is part of the earliest christian understanding. It occurs also during the Reformation and again during the Second Vatican Council.

The second major image like the first understands that the altar is Christ. But the image also depends on a typological sense of the Hebrew temple and its sacrifice. These sacrificial overtones associated with the altar are especially strong during the Carolingian reforms of the ninth century.

This second image transfers much of the spiritual meaning associated with Christ to the physical altar and the actions of the liturgy. Now the physical altar becomes the place of meeting between God and humanity; it is the place of sacrifice and of communion. Such imagery is strong during the times when eucharistic theology stressed sacrificial aspects, the role of priests as other Christs and the general typology completing Hebrew temple sacrifice. Such imagery remained strong among Roman Catholicism until the mid-twentieth century. Attempts to secure the sacrificial imagery as the sole image of the altar are found in Pope Pius XII's condemnation as in error the image of the altar as a table (Mediator Dei No. 62).

The Lord's Table

The earliest christian imagery associates the altar with the table of the Lord (1 Cor 10:21). This image is neither spiritualized nor typological; it is a functional image which evolved from the Lord's supper and the agape. Although the temple and its sacrificial imagery are absent, the table remains a place of encounter between God and humanity and a place of communion. We see this clearly in the resurrection account describing the Emmaus experience (Lk 24:13ff). Jesus sits with them to eat and in the breaking of bread he is revealed in their midst. Like the previous images the table is understood as a place of action and of convergence where the christian faithful gather for the broken bread and filled cup.

The meal aspect of the eucharist was supported by many of the reforms in the sixteenth century in their attempts to emphasize the biblical grounding of the Lord's supper. The Council of Trent (Session 22, Chapter 1) continued to stress the sacrificial aspects of the eucharist. Because of this the imagery of the table did not develop in the Roman Church until a theology of the paschal banquet and holy table were explored. There are clear indications of such a trend when Pope Pius X invited frequent communion at the holy table.

Since the beginning of the twentieth century, there has been a growing affection in Roman Catholicism for the image of the altar as the table of the Lord. Because the table's focus is the meal rather than sacrifice, there has been some tension in selecting the most appropriate term to describe this object. Ultimately the conciliar document embraced both images of sacrifice and banquet (S.C. 47).

The General Instruction on the Roman Missal (259) states: "The altar where the sacrifice of the cross is made present under sacramental signs is also the table of the Lord. The people of God are called together to share in this table. Thus the altar is the center of thanksgiving accomplished in the eucharist."

The Rite of Dedication of a Church and Altar embraces many of the other ancient images as well. The altar is described in the spiritual sense in which both Christ and the Christian people are God's altar. The sacrificial table and the banquet table are also cited. It was fulfilled on the tree of the cross. The altar is proclaimed the place of sacrifice, the Lord's table, a place of nourishment and strength. It is a table of joy, a place of communion and peace, a source of unity and friendship. The altar is the center of praise and thanksgiving until all arrive at the eternal tabernacle. (48).

The Martyrium Altar

A recurring but less central image describes the altar as a place of memorial at a martyr's tomb. Because martyrdom was an image of Christ's death, the early church quickly hallowed the graves of martyrs. The altar was often placed over the grave. The purpose of this altar was to be a memorial of the martyr's death. Its dignity was still eucharistic rather than sepulchral.

This image of the altar shares in the previous images only in so far as Christ remains the prime referent. The martyr's imitation of Christ's sacrifice is an essential part of the altar's authentic image. "It is not to any of the martyrs but to God of the martyrs, though in memory of the martyrs, that we raise our altars" (Augustine, Contra Faustum 20, 21). Augustine's observation concurs with present legislation, since relics are no longer required and small fragments are discouraged. Further the martyrium imagery is absent from the prayer of dedication.

The Problem of Form

Although one normally assumes that form follows function, it is not necessarily true here. The earliest christian altars were portable not simply because they were tables but because the spaces were necessarily flexible. Clear evidence exists that some first century Roman sacrificial altars were table-like and portable.

Solidity does not necessarily indicate a sacrificial connotation. Fixed cubic altars began to appear in the fourth century after the Constantinian accord because special rooms could now be set aside exclusively for the eucharistic liturgy and the need for flexibility of the altar and lectern was not as central. The altar's shape was designated by the gifts placed on it and the scale of the building. During the Byzantine period, even in the west, smaller apses had smaller altars. In the Theodosian basilica of Hagia Sophia the altar was two meters square.

Even during the Reformation, not all reformers who advocated the table actually changed the shape of their altars, One cannot conclude, therefore, that the historical shape always expressed a particular theology. All theological images were present during the twenty centuries, although some dominated during one or another period.

What criteria exist for a contemporary altar? The conciliar legislation has retained both the sacrificial altar and banquet table images, while at the same time weakening the sense of martyrium. *Sacrosanctum Concilium* (22, 128) allows competent ecclesiastical authority to establish norms for church furnishings. This is the prime guideline. The altar's freestanding and focal position as well as the insistence on a single altar are other criteria. Appropriateness and dignity are to mark the design of both the fixed and movable altars.

Above all, the altar table is a place for the gathering of the church. It is a place where the mystery of Christ unfolds and where in the church's banquet, we plead for the world's salvation. There is even a wider perspective in which the church building, and the altar as one of its central focuses, becomes a place for the poor to find justice; the victims of oppression true freedom; and the whole world is invited into God's city of peace.
See **Dedication of a Church, Eucharist, Liturgy**

JAMES NOTEBAART

AMERICANISM

Roman Catholic Americanism was a movement within the American Catholic Church of the late nineteenth century in which some Catholics expressed their acceptance of the fundamental cultural assumptions of American society, assumptions which were rooted in New England Puritanism and the Enlightenment, and then sought to export their convictions, on the wings of American expansionism, to the universal church.

Archbishop John Ireland of St. Paul, Minnesota, Bishop John Keane of Richmond, Virginia, and Msgr. Denis O'Connell, rector of the North American College in Rome, were the center of this reform movement. While in Rome in late 1886, they reinterpreted the old Puritan vision of a divinely bestowed mission of the American people to be a lighthouse to the world into a mission of the American Catholic Church to guide the universal church into its accommodation to the modern age.

The mood of this movement was "liberal" in the sense that it involved a broad openness to American and modern culture, to people of other religious faiths, to the social and labor movements of the day, to science and education. All of its advocates wanted to see the Vatican accept the principle of religious liberty, the separation of church and state, and to refrain from condemnations of innovators. In addition each Americanist had his own personal agenda. John Ireland's central concern was to engage the church in a manly way in the social, political and economic problems of the day. Keane, who sought to make the Catholic University of America, of which he was founding rector, the intellectual center of this reformed Catholicism, wanted the reunion of the christian churches, and thus went out of his way to encourage public contacts with Protestants, and even led a contingent of Catholics into participation in the World Parliament of Religions held in Chicago in 1893. O'Connell proposed a new Code of Canon Law based on the English Common Law tradition, with its due process provisions, rather than the old Roman Law tradition. By 1898, when this movement reached its peak, a large number of people in the U.S. and in Europe had come to conceive of themselves as reformers and many were using the name "Americanism" for their proposals, meaning by the term anything that was "new." It is true, however, that when compared to what is known as liberal Protestantism or Modernism of the same era, Roman

Catholic Americanism was quite moderate in its reformatory goals and its assumptions about the basis of religious truth claims. Its openness to the modern age, to religious liberty, social concerns, relations with other Christians, and the like was later embraced by the Second Vatican Council.

While their goals were moderate, the methods of the Americanists were not. Their desire to Americanize the church in the U.S. frequently led to policies of suppressing ethnic language and customs; the meetings of the episcopate were soon filled with contention, and it was necessary for Rome to intervene on several occasions. Most significantly the Americanists gained access to the semi-official Vatican newspaper, *Le Moniteur de Rome,* and thus began the international propagation of the Americanist platform. Articles began to appear portraying the Americanists as apostles sent by God to revive a dying European church. By 1891 the Americanists even had control of the international cable lines across the Atlantic, providing them with the ability to manipulate the major source of newspaper news in the Western world. News stories and reports portraying these men in larger than life form and their reform proposals as ingenious inventions circulated freely through the press and arrived in millions of homes with the morning newspaper.

The Vatican was at first tolerant of this development, as it coincided in the early 1890's with the direction of its policies in Europe, especially vis-à-vis France, but as it shifted its policies later in the decade and the Americanists became bolder, attempts were made to curtail their activities. O'Connell and Keane were removed from their positions. When a biography of deceased American convert Isaac Hecker was translated into French in 1897 and welcomed as reflective of the model saint of the "new" era, and Amer-

ican military invaded Cuba, Puerto Rico and Guam in the spring of 1898 in connection with the Spanish-American War, Vatican patience with the young and expansionist new nation was over. A papal condemnation of Americanism was issued in January 1899, which, with the exception of its warning that the church rather than individuals update the church, did not address the issues, including religious liberty, advocated by the Americanists, but instead focused on certain subjectivist inclinations in the spirituality of Fr. Hecker, which he brought into the church with his conversion from New England Transcendentalism. The papal action, to which Ireland and Keane submitted, divided the Americanists and killed their reform movement, and also had the effect of splitting Americanism off from the larger crisis known as Modernism which was to occupy the church in the following decade.

The standard but now outdated survey of Americanism is Thomas T. McAvoy, C.S.C. *The Great Crisis in American Catholic History 1895-1900,* Chicago: H. Regnery Co., 1957. See also Thomas Wangler, "The Birth of Americanism: 'Westward the Apocalyptic Candlestick'" and "American Catholic Expansionism: 1886-1894," both in *The Harvard Theological Review,* 65 (July 1972) 415-436, and 75 (July 1982) 369-393.

THOMAS E. WANGLER

ANALOGY

Recent work on analogy concurs that it does not represent a theory nor a metaphysical contention, so much as a fact about language and the way we use language. Thus it is more proper to speak of analogous uses of language, and hence to focus on the analogical potential of certain expressions. Indirectly, of course, these observations reflect the structure of a mind inquiring into the structures of the universe, so the fact that our use of language seems to be irreducibly analogous will have metaphysical implications.

But the focus of the tradition has been on terms and expressions, and especially on their use in attributing features to God. So while contemporary discussion underscores analogy as a pervasive fact of our discourse (esp. McInerny and Ross) theologians have a particular need for clarity regarding analogous expressions. And especially so among Jews, Christians and Muslims, for whom the *distinction* of God from the world is fundamental to their shared faith in a creator.

Yet the first explicit treatment is found in Aristotle, who identified a useful subset of ambiguous terms by the Greek word *analogia,* meaning "proportion." For he noted that some expressions—ordinary ones like "wise," "powerful," and "living," as well as the most intractable one "being"—functioned in a peculiar way. He identified their peculiarity with a proportional similarity compatible with dissimilar features—as with a powerful dictator and a powerful saint, or a wise mathematician and a wise mother. This allowed him to link apt analogies with good metaphors (Poetics 1459a5)—a point to be remembered since medievals tended rather to distinguish properly analogous expressions from metaphor, while current discussion returns to emphasize their connection (Martin, McFague).

Aristotle profited, certainly, from Plato's dialectical exploration of analogous terms, like "love"(in the *Symposium)* and "good" (in the *Republic*). While Plato was concerned to develop ways of using such terms responsibly to help explore what lies beyond our ken and yet is nonetheless reflected in the arrangements native to human understanding, Aristotle was more directly concerned with their utility in argument. The concern was a technical one connected with his preoccupation with the form of argument (or syllogistic): the terms employed need to be sufficiently similar to allow the argu-

ment to carry through from one premise to another. So by adopting the mathematical scheme of proportion (a:b::c:d), he was able to display how certain expressions could retain enough similarity through some of their various uses to allow them to be used in syllogistic constructions, and hence be part of our reliable knowledge. (One begins to see how this preoccupation would lead medievals concerned to develop theology as a form of *knowledge* to contrast analogy with metaphor, more commonly associated with poetic expression.)

Yet Aristotle also recognized another pattern in analogous expressions, whereby many uses could be referred to one, and so the different senses of a term might be traced by their relation to a single paradigmatic use (Owen). And it is this pattern to which he has recourse in the *Metaphysics* (1016b6-10) to illustrate how all uses of the pervasive expression "to be" must be traced to that sense exemplified by substances (i.e., what exists in itself and not in another). It is this pattern for identifying properly analogous expressions and for monitoring their responsible use which formed the basis for medieval discussions of the "analogy of being" (*analogia entis*). The Arab philosophers —Alfarabi(870?-950), Avicenna (980-1037), Algazali (1058-1111), and Averroes (1126-1198)— employed this pattern for analogous expressions, generally classifying them by the alternate Greek word *amphibolous* (Wolfson). Moses Maimonides (1135-1204) knew of such a strategy from their writings, but could not see how to employ it to gain a positive understanding of things divine (*Guide for the Perplexed* 1.56).

It was Thomas Aquinas (1225-1274) who exploited Aristotle's discussion of this peculiar feature of predication, linking it with the neo-Platonic treatment of pseudo-Dionysius (between 450 and

550), to develop a fruitful account of ways in which creatures may responsibly speak of their creator (Booth). He was quite beholden as well to those speculative grammarians in the century preceding his own who had classified diverse ways in which the sacred scriptures employed language, and so developed an art for relating different senses of the same term as it is put to different use. Their discussions offered Aquinas useful ways of moving from creation to creator, while acknowledging and even underscoring the infinite difference between the two. It was indeed this attention to the art of recognizing and distinguishing among analogous uses which prevented Aquinas from developing a *theory* of analogy. Later scholastics—notably Cajetan (1469-1534)—had no such scruples, however, and it is their work which tended to further separate analogy from metaphor, and also set the stage for a strongly negative reaction, notably among the reformers.

For Cajetan's propensity to turn the art of employing certain expressions analogously into a "theory of analogy" made it look as though theologians had found a way of extending human language to expound the properties of God. The reaction was at once philosophical and theological, with philosophers insisting that no linguistic strategy could extend human meanings to a divine level, and theologians objecting to one's pretending to do so, since God's transcendence must be sustained above all. Thus Karl Barth protested against the theory which he took *analogia entis* to represent, although subsequent discussion with von Balthasar showed that he had no objection to analogy in its classical form—as presented here—and that in fact his own work presupposed it. For having distinguished the question as it developed from Aristotle to Aquinas from later codifications (notably Cajetan), one may discern the issue clearly: how is it that discourse which must transcend our ordinary categories may proceed in a rational manner, and so lead to a form of knowledge?

Philosophers will differ as to *how* such a thing is possible, but all those who allow that our engagement in discourse about divinity is a responsible activity will find themselves attending to a specific set of notions whose internal structures turn out to match what Aristotle identified as analogous. Our use of such notions, especially of God, will involve a moment of affirmation as well as one of negation. Taken together—as analogous expressions allow—they form what Aquinas called the *via eminentiae*. What baffles theologian and philosopher alike is the lack of clear rules for correct "eminent use" of notions like *wise* and *just,* yet practice can distinguish better use from worse, as faithful hearers of the word of God—Jews, Christians, or Muslims—can distinguish fruitful preaching from sterile commentary.

See **God**

E. Booth, *Aristotelian Aporetic Ontology in Islamic and Christian Thinkers,* Cambridge, 1983. D. Burrell, *Analogy and Philosophical Language,* Yale, 1973. J.S. Martin, *Metaphor and Religious Language,* Oxford, 1986. S. McFague, *Metaphorical Theology,* N.Y., Seabury, 1983. R. McInerny, *Logic of Analogy,* The Hague, Nijhoff, 1961. G.E.L. Owen, "Logic and Metaphysics in some Earlier Works of Aristotle," in During and Owen (eds), *Aristotle and Plato in mid-Fourth Century, Goteborg, 1960.* J. Owens, *Doctrine of Being in the Aristotelian Metaphysics,* Toronto, Pontifical Institute of Medieval Studies, 1963. J. Ross, *Portraying Analogy,* Cambridge, 1983. R. Sokolowski, *The God of Faith and Reason,* Notre Dame, 1981. H. Urs von Balthasar, *Karl Barth,* Koln, Hegner, 1962. H.A. Wolfson, "Amphibolous Terms in Aristotle, Arabic Philosophy, and Maimonides," in *Studies in History and Philosophy of Religion* I, Harvard, 1973.

DAVID B. BURRELL, CSC

ANAMNESIS

A Greek word meaning: calling to mind, remembrance, or memorial (cf. 1

Cor 11:24, do this in my remembrance, or in memory of me). In its strict, technical sense, anamnesis names that part of a eucharistic prayer which follows the account of institution and mentions succinctly the principal saving events of Christ's life: "Father, calling to mind the death your Son endured for our salvation, his glorious resurrection and ascension into heaven, and ready to greet him when he comes again . . ."(Roman Euch. Prayer 3).

In a much wider sense, anamnesis is an essential dimension of all of christian liturgy. It is always in memory of Christ that the church assembles, the biblical word is proclaimed, prayer is offered, sacraments celebrated, and all of the story of Christ remembered anew in the course of the liturgical year. In the liturgical actions of remembrance, Christ is rendered truly present in the assembly, and in word, prayer, and sacrament, especially in the eucharistic bread and wine. Christ's presence through anamnesis grounds the church's hope both now and for the future until he comes in glory.

Liturgical anamnesis, therefore, is not the mere mental recall of something past, over and done with, nor is it the fond recollection of something or someone absent. Rather, in the church's liturgical anamnesis before God, Christ is truly present now. Anamnesis in this sense has no adequate English equivalent; "remembrance" or "calling to mind" may translate the word but cannot do justice to the reality.

How anamnesis and the real presence of Christ in the liturgy are to be understood in relation to each other is a matter of continuing theological discussion. There is a movement away from two positions now considered unsatisfactory: 1) an older position that sacraments make present for us the grace and merits won by Christ and now stored up in heaven—considered quite apart from the events of

his life; 2) a more recent position that sacraments make present now for our salvation the very saving events of Christ's life which the liturgy remembers. Contemporary liturgical theology stresses that it is the person of Jesus Christ in his glorified humanity who is present for us in the acts of anamnesis. The events of his life, in their space and time particularity cannot be made present again. Still, the essential core which gave rise to those acts—Jesus' perfectly faithful and obedient self-giving-over to his Father and his total, sacrificial self-giving-over for us and for the world—perdures in the glorified Christ who even now is priest and victim, the Lamb with glorious wounds. In this sense, the events of Jesus' life exist now in the risen Christ and are present in Christ in the liturgical remembrance. The events themselves must ever be recalled before God in worship for they reveal who Christ is for us and offer us his death and resurrection as the pattern which brings grace and salvation to the pivotal moments and to the whole of our lives in him.

See **Liturgy, Memorial**

ALLAN BOULEY, OSB

ANAPHORA

A Greek noun from the verb *anapherein* meaning to bring or carry up, to lift, to offer. It is the usual Greek term for a eucharistic prayer, commonly used today by liturgiologists to designate eucharistic prayers of the eastern rites. In its stricter sense, the word names the eucharistic prayer proper, from its opening dialogue between priest and people to its closing doxology and amen. It is the principal prayer of the eucharist in which the church gives thanks and praise to God, commemorates the last supper, the sacrificial death and entire saving work of Christ, invokes the Holy Spirit, and makes intercession, thus consecrating bread and wine as the body and blood of Christ given in sacrifice for the salvation and communion of his people. In its broader sense, the anaphora in the eastern liturgies may include additional ritual and verbal elements before and/or after the eucharistic prayer. Some historical Roman equivalents of anaphora are: prayer of offering, or simply *the* prayer, or canon (of the Mass). The 1969 Roman *Order of Mass* uses *prex eucharistica,* eucharistic prayer.

See Eucharist

ALLAN BOULEY, OSB

ANATHEMA

The Greek word for "that which is accursed." Introduced into christian language by St. Paul ("If anyone preach to you a gospel other than what you have received, let him be anathema" [Gal 1:9]), it became a standard term in conciliar condemnations of heterodox positions, indicating that those who held them were to be regarded as excommunicated.

STEPHEN FUNK

ANGELS

In christian, as well as Jewish and Islamic belief, angels are immaterial spirits or pure intelligences created by God prior to human creation to regulate the order of the world and specifically to serve as messengers (Latin *angeli*, from Greek *aggeloi*) to human persons with respect to the divine plan of salvation.

In the earliest writings of the OT, *mal'ak* ("messenger") was used to indicate a divine envoy, often barely distinct from God, who appeared to inform, guide, protect, or warn men and women individually or the Chosen People as a whole (Gen 16:3, 7ff.; 21:17ff., etc.). Only rarely

was the term used in the plural (Gen 19:1ff.; 28:12; 32:2). As a personification or sensible manifestation of the divine word or action, the use of the term "angel" maintained the transcendent sovereignty of God while affirming God's direct intervention in human affairs. The Hebrews did not think of angels as "pure spirits," however, but portrayed them as ordinary if unusual human beings or merely a heavenly voice.

Angels also appear in the OT as the divine retinue, "heavenly court," or host of heaven (e.g., Deut 4:19; Josh 5:14; 1 Kgs 22:19); the "Holy Ones" or "Sons of Elohim" (Pss 29:1; 89:6-7; Job 1:6; 2:1; 5:1; 38:7; Dan 8:13); guardians of persons and places (Ps 91:11; Dan 10:12; Tob 12:15); and worshippers of God (Pss 103:20; 148:2). They were important as mediators between God and the prophets, including Moses (Exod 3:2; Judg 6:14; 13:22; Zech 1:7—6:15; Dan 8:16ff.; 9:21ff.; 10:13, 21). While mainly protective and benevolent (Gen 19:1ff.; Exod 14:19; 23:20; 33:2; etc), "destroying" angels sometimes executed the wrath, judgment, or vengeance of God (Exod 12:23; Num 21:6—8; 2 Sam 24:16ff.; 2 Kgs 22:19; etc.).

Influenced by Mesopotamian religious beliefs and folklore, the canonical writings and apocryphal literature of later Judaism tended to magnify the role of the angels in the drama of salvation, particularly with regard to the rebellion of part of the heavenly host against the sovereignty of God, their role in the temptation and fall of human beings, and the struggles of the last times, a theme alluded to in Jude 6 and developed in Rev 5:2; 11; 7:1, etc.

NT teaching generally follows that of the OT and apocrypha. Angels serve as messengers (Mt 1:20; 2:13, 19: Lk 1:11ff., 26ff.; 2:9ff; Gal 3:19; Heb 1:4ff.; 2:2), guardians and protectors (Mt 4:11; 18:10; Mk 1:13; Lk 22:43; Acts 5:19; 12:7), the divine court (Mt 24:36; Lk 12:8ff.; 15:10), and companions of Christ as judge (Mt 13:41—49; 16:27, 24:31; Mk 8:38; 13:27; Lk 9:26; 2 Thess 1:7; 1 Tm 5:21). They also bear witness to events of salvation, especially the resurrection of Jesus (Mt 28:2; Lk 24:23; Jn 20:12; Acts 8:26; 10:3 ff.; 27:23; 1 Cor 4:9), bring healing (Jn 5:4) as well as destruction (Acts 12:23), and offer worship to God (1 Cor 11:10).

Pauline teaching (and the Petrine epistles) connected the angelic order with cosmic and social forces, some of them hostile to the gospel. These "principalities and powers" were clearly subordinated to Christ, however, a theme also developed in Col 1:16, 2:18, Eph 1:21 and Heb.

In later christian doctrine, angelology gradually acquired a more systematic character, achieving in the sixth century biblical speculations of Pseudo-Dionysius and St. Gregory the Great the rank and order of choirs passed on to the Middle Ages and subsequent periods. In the thirteenth century, Thomas Aquinas' synthesis of Aristotelian and Neo-Platonic metaphysics with scriptural and patristic sources gave definitive expression to the classical theological interpretations. In recent times, Karl Rahner has clarified and deepened the theology of angels as a subordinate area of christology.

Strictly speaking, the existence of angels is not a matter of divine revelation, but is presupposed by both the biblical witness and church teaching (see D.S. 800). Angels are less the subject or content of revelation than its medium. In that respect, they can be viewed as real and dynamic mediations of human consciousness of the divine, i.e., through them we apprehend the presence, knowledge, and will of God for us in terms of both the general providence and specific circumstances of our lives. Theologically, angels are also cosmological principles, dynamic and mysterious structures of extra-mental reality that pervade and order the universe

as the expression of God's creative knowledge and purpose beyond all human concerns. In either respect, angels are manifestations of suprahuman wisdom and power that operate within time and space but are not confined to historical existence as we know it.

They are not, for instance, living beings (organisms), since they are not embodied, and so cannot die. Nor are they subject to sickness, fatigue, hunger, or illusion. Activities such as knowing, willing, and remembering, while sufficiently analogous to human experience to permit communication, are also fundamentally different. Finally, insofar as angels are bodiless, individuals are distinguished from one another functionally rather than materially, each angel being a species or class in itself which expresses a specific relationship between God and the natural and human world.

RICHARD WOODS, OP

ANHYPOSTASIA

A term used in the christological controversies of the fifth and sixth centuries to refer to the view that the human nature of the Incarnate Word does not possess its own metaphysical subsistence or *hypostasis* but subsists in the *hypostasis* of the Son of God.

See **Enhypostasia**, **Hypostasis**, **Person**

ANNULMENT

Annulment is the popular term to signify an official declaration by an ecclesiastical authority that a marriage contract was null and void from the beginning. It is not the termination of an existing marriage but the judicial recognition of the fact that a marriage has never come into being notwithstanding the appearances to the contrary, such as an externally correct celebration of the wedding.

During the first christian millennium such problems were handled informally by priests, bishops and popes, but by the end of the tenth century formal judicial structures and procedures began to emerge and then kept developing both in Rome and in provincial and diocesan centers. They became standardized in the eighteenth century and finally reached an unusual height in complexity with the promulgation of the first Code of Canon Law in 1917. The second Code in 1983 brought some relief; more importantly it recognized the need for a more pastoral approach, for a greater simplicity and for a speedier administration of justice. Thus, at the end of the second millennium we are experiencing the beginning of a new trend.

The church has no tribunals specifically established to handle marriage cases. Every tribunal is entitled to hear all types of cases, but when they accept a petition for a declaration of nullity, they must follow a special procedure. Ideally each diocese would have its own court, but for good reasons and with the approval of the Holy See, several dioceses can establish one single court serving them all.

A petition for annulment can be accepted by a tribunal only if there is a "semblance" of a marriage; that is, there is *prima facie* evidence that a marriage has taken place, and at the same time there is a serious doubt whether or not all the conditions for its validity were fulfilled.

There are three potential sources of invalidity and consequently three main reasons for which an annulment can be sought: (a) an impediment which was not cleared by an appropriate dispensation (there are twelve well-defined impediments in canon law); (b) the internal consent of one or of both of the parties was either missing or vitiated (such a lack or defect of consent may originate in a substantial misapprehension about the marriage, in a disturbed psyche, or in an incapacity to carry out the marital obligations); (c) the so-called canonical form was not observed at the celebration of the marriage (a lawfully designated priest must accept the consent of the parties in the presence of two witnesses).

If there is clear documentary evidence that the invalidity was caused by the presence of an impediment or by the nonobservance of an essential formality, a declaration of nullity is usually speedily granted by a local authority through a simple "summary" procedure. If the validity of marriage is contested on the basis of a lack or defect of consent, the case must go through a carefully structured judicial process. Ordinarily the diocesan tribunal of the place where the marriage was contracted, or where the parties reside is competent. Such a "trial" can be time-consuming.

In the beginning of the process the suspected grounds for nullity must be defined. The trial then turns around those grounds, with arguments for both sides: the petitioner bringing forth proofs for their existence, and the defensor of the bond (designated by the court) arguing, as far as justice permits it, for the initial validity of the marriage. The judges (ordinarily a panel of three, exceptionally one), helped also by experts as needed, pronounce their sentence with the traditional words "nullity is (*or* is not) established."

In order to be effective, the decision of the first instance must be confirmed by an appeal court, either after a summary review of the case, or, after a retrial if the same court sees a need for it. Since without two concurring judgments the freedom to marry cannot be restored to the parties, the appeals may go on for some time and the case may reach the highest courts of the church, which are the Roman Rota and the Apostolic Signatura.

Not even the final judgment is, however, infallible; if new evidence emerges a marriage case can always be reopened before a competent court.

The annulment process has been often criticized as abounding in legalities but lacking in pastoral sensitivity. Although the Code of Canon Law promulgated in 1983 brought some reforms and introduced a new trend, many problems remain with both the theoretical conception of "marriage trials" and the practical operation of the tribunals. Outdated medieval psychological theories still influence (in fact, dominate) the definition of the grounds of nullity, and the impersonal machinery of justice displays little concern for the spiritual well-being of the parties, mostly in need of help after a disastrous attempt to marry. A better balanced concern would be required.

Overall, in the universal church, the tribunals do not perform well. In the third world few dioceses are in position to appoint qualified persons to their courts and to provide the material means for their efficient operation. In the second world oppression and government interference reduce their functioning to a minimum; in some places to nil. In the first world, apart from exceptions (mostly but not exclusively in the U.S. and Canada), the "marriage courts" have acquired a reputation of being excessively slow in handling their caseload, often keeping the faithful, who are seeking an official determination of their marital status, in uncertainty for years, creating an obviously unhealthy situation. Furthermore, the administration of justice does not appear even-handed; the tribunals may vary widely in their understanding of the grounds of nullity. Reforms are undoubtedly indicated.

In the practical order, if there are reasons for the initiation of an annulment, the best course of action is to approach directly the competent diocesan tribunal, since correct information requires a great deal of specialized knowledge.

The majority of christian churches and communities who are not in communion with Rome, recognize divorce and remarriage; consequently, outside of the Roman Catholic Church there is only a limited interest in the specific problem of annulment.

See **Canon Law, Divorce, Marriage**

The source for the canonical norms about annulments is the *Code of Canon Law*, especially its part on "Processes," canons 1400-1716. An expert commentary on the procedural rules is Lawrence Wrenn, "Processes" in *The Code of Canon Law: A Text and Commentary*, New York: Paulist Press, 1985, pp. 943-1022. For law of impediments and consent on which many claims of invalidity are based, see Laclislas Orsy, *Marriage in Canon Law*, Wilmington, DE: Glazier, 1985. A good introductory guidebook for the lay person concerning the process is Geoffrey Robinson, *Marriage, Divorce and Nullity: A Guide to the Annulment Process in the Catholic Church*, Melbourne: Dove Communications, 1984, and London: Geoffrey Chapman, 1985. A highly technical work used by tribunals is Lawrence Wrenn, *Annulments*, Fourth ed., Washington, DC: Canon Law Society of America, 1984.

LADISLAS ORSY, SJ

ANOINTING

"Anointing" is the touching of persons or things with a substance to achieve some effect either within the person or thing itself or in the way the community will later perceive that person or thing. Various substances have been used (oil, water, blood, mud, fat, saliva) in various cultures. The result can be a change in the person physically (health, strength, fertility) or in the relationship one has with the community (priest, king, adult, prophet).

Anointing is a cosmic sign related to cleansing and touching in anthropological studies as well as in classical literature of ancient Greece and Rome. Oil, which corresponded to soap (usually with perfume of some kind) seems to have been the most popular substance for anointing. It was used for washing, for athletic events, for religious rites, for designation of special persons. Very primitive religions may have seen the virtue and power of a sacrificial animal pass to the one anointed with the fat of that sacrifice.

In the OT a person or thing was anointed to make it sacred. Moses anointed the meeting tent, the ark, the table, the lamp stand, the altar, Aaron and his sons as priests (Exod 30:27-30). The oil mixture was to be considered sacred in itself and could never be used for secular purposes (Exod 30:36-38). Kings were anointed by prophets and priests. Emphasis is given to the anointing of Saul (1 Sam 10:1); David (1 Sam 16:13); and Solomon (1 Kgs 1:39). Prophets became charismatic persons by anointing and their mission was given impulse by the Spirit. Is 61:1 is quoted by Christ as his mission: "The spirit of the Lord God is upon me, because the Lord has anointed me...."

Christ comes from *Messiah,* a Hebrew term which means the *anointed one.* It is a title for Jesus rather than a name. The church has understood the baptismal account of Mark (1:9-11) as the "Messianic anointing" of Jesus by the Holy Spirit. This anointing has been extended to each Christian in the ritual of baptism down through the centuries in the post-baptismal anointing with chrism.

The christian church has a long tradition of anointing with oil. Three oils are used in the Catholic tradition at the present time: oil of catechumens, oil of the sick, and chrism.

The oil of catechumens is used only prior to baptism. It relates to the anointing of athletes for combat and appears in every baptismal liturgy until the sixteenth century. A person was at one time anointed all over the body but now only the breast, hands or if it seems desirable other parts of the body (RCIA no 194).

This anointing is a type of exorcism; it symbolizes the candidates' need for God's help and strength as they approach the sacraments of initiation. The oil may be blessed by the priests but is usually blessed by the local bishop at the Chrism Mass. Children are anointed in the rite of baptism itself but adult candidates early in the day of Holy Saturday. It symbolizes the candidates' need for God's help and strength as they approach baptism.

The oil of the sick is used in the sacrament of anointing of the sick which has its roots in James 5 and a long tradition in the church of interceding for the sick. By the grace of the sacrament the whole person is helped, strengthened against temptation, ready to face the anxiety of death. Physical healing may result and even sins may be forgiven. The oil may be blessed by the priest in the celebration, but it is also blessed by the local bishop during the Chrism Mass. The head and hands are anointed by the priest.

Chrism is used in the sacrament of baptism, confirmation and the ordination of priests and bishops. This oil can be blessed only by a bishop. Until 1970, all the oils had to be from the olive and chrism was a mixture of olive oil and balsam. The church now merely requires that the oils be from plants and chrism has a perfume additive to give a pleasing fragrance. Just as priests, prophets and kings were anointed with consecrated oil in the OT and these prefigured *Christ* the anointed one, so Christians share in the kingly, prophetic and priestly ministry of Christ by their baptism. In the Roman rite, persons are anointed on the crown of the head with chrism after baptism when confirmation does not follow immediately. Those confirmed are sealed with the Holy Spirit on the forehead with chrism. Priests are anointed on the hands and bishops on the head in ordination celebrations. Churches and altars are anointed with chrism in their dedication but other objects such as chalices are no longer anointed.

The Holy Spirit has long been associated with anointing in the tradition of the church. One is sealed with "the Gift of the Holy Spirit" in the present rite of Confirmation. The *Rushma* or seal reflects early christian concepts about anointing. Also, the laying on of hands usually accompany rites of anointing in both the eastern and western traditions.

Leonel L. Mitchel *Baptismal Anointing,* Notre Dame, 1978 *The Rites of the Catholic Church, (ICEL) "Rite of Anointing and Pastoral Care of the Sick" and "Rite of Christian Initiation of Adults,"* New York: Pueblo, 1976.

JOSEPH L. CUNNINGHAM

ANOINTING OF THE SICK

The pastoral care of the sick and dying has always been an integral part of the church's mission entrusted to it by its founder: "I was sick and you visited me" (Mt 25:36). This ministry finds sacramental expression in the rites of anointing and viaticum. In the words of the Second Vatican Council, "By the sacred anointing of the sick and the prayer of the priests the whole Church commends those who are ill to the suffering and glorified Lord that he may raise them up and save them. And indeed she exhorts them to contribute to the good of the People of God by freely uniting themselves to the passion and death of Christ" (L.G. 11). The Council also called for a revision of the liturgies for the sick and the dying. The *Constitution on the Sacred Liturgy* (S.C. 73-75) suggested first of all a change of name from "extreme unction" to "anointing of the sick" and urged that the time of its administration be not delayed. Second, the order of the continuous rites was to be revised so that viaticum would be clearly perceived as the sacrament of the dying. Third, considerable freedom was granted to the commission which would eventually revise the rites so that they might "correspond to the varying needs of the sick." These provisions attempted to recover the authentic tradition of anointing and viaticum.

Tradition of Anointing

According to the Council of Trent, the sacrament of anointing was alluded to in Mark and recommended and promulgated to the faithful by James. Mk 6:13 has to do with the apostolic ministry of healing: "And they cast out many demons, and anointed with oil many that were sick and healed them." Jas 5:13-15, in keeping with the parenetic purpose of the letter, applies the unifying theme of prayer to three existential situations: suffering, joy and sickness. "Is any one among you suffering? Let him pray. Is any cheerful? Let him sing praise. Is any among you sick? Let him call for the elders of the church, and let them pray over him, anointing him with oil in the name of the Lord: and the prayer of faith will save the sick man, and the Lord will raise him up; and if he has committed sins, he will be forgiven." A balanced exegesis would suggest that on the one hand the subject is a sick, not necessarily a dying, Christian. On the other hand, the ministration is not simply medicinal. Hebrew anthropology saw no strict distinction between body and soul; there was also thought to be some, however obscure, relationship between sin and sickness. The anointing was carried out in the name of the Lord with particular efficacy ascribed to the prayer of faith. The presbyters are official ministers of the local church; hence the passage is not an instance of charismatic healing as such.

For 800 years the church practiced anointing as a rite for the sick. Liturgical sources and patristic and hagiographical texts yield the following evidence. A primordial importance was invested in the blessing of the oil, whereby Pope Innocent I deemed it a *sacramentum*. The blessed oil could be applied not only by the ordained ministers but also by the faithful. Although the use of fixed formulas for blessing oil is very ancient in the Latin Church (*Apostolic Tradition,* Gelasian Sacramentary), liturgies for the actual anointing only begin to appear in the middle of the eighth century. Christians could anoint themselves or anoint one another; the oil could be applied externally to the body or imbibed internally. The expected results were a wholeness of body, mind and spirit; the anointing does not appear as a rite preparatory for death.

The oldest extant full ritual for the actual anointing of the sick dates from between 815-845. A small community is on hand for a liturgy concelebrated by priests. At one point the sick person is invited to kneel down, a provision scarcely possible for someone in their last agony. The sick person is anointed amply with sanctified oil, including the place where the pain is most pronounced. The service of anointing and communion may be repeated for the following seven days. During this same Carolingian period, however, a change occurred in pastoral practice and liturgy which was to profoundly alter the meaning of anointing from a rite for the sick into a sacrament for the dying. Various local synods attest that as a result of a reform movement seeking to renew the priestly ministry, lay anointing was abandoned and the anointing of the sick henceforth reserved to priests. Rituals for applying the oil were at this time created; previously the only liturgical sources had to do with the episcopal blessing of oil. The rituals for anointing came to be associated with the rites of death-bed penance, which was the usual occasion for sacramental reconciliation at that time. According to the tradition going back to Pope Innocent, a sick person had first to be reconciled and in the good graces of the church before the anointing could take place. From this time onward two tendencies begin to color the sacrament: a spiritualizing tendency associated with the penitential anointing of the five senses and a growing perception of anointing as a rite for the dying. By the twelfth century the original order of penance, anointing, viaticum had been altered to penance, viaticum, anointing. Anointing had become quite literally extreme unction, the "last anointing."

This change in pastoral practice set the stage for the sacramental systematization of the scholastic theologians. Anointing was numbered among the seven sacraments. Sacraments confer a spiritual grace which occurs *ex opere operato*. Although some early scholastics (Hugh of St. Victor, d. 1141, still maintained anointing was a sacrament for the sick, the consensus ultimately considered it impossible for the recovery of health to be a promised result infallibly bestowed. From its close association with deathbed reconciliation, anointing had to do with the forgiveness of sin. Since baptism removes original sin and penance remits actual personal sins, the sacramental grace of anointing was thought to pertain to the removal of either venial sins (Franciscan school of Bonaventure and Scotus) or the remnants of sin (Dominican school of Albert the Great and Thomas Aquinas). The purpose of the sacrament was to prepare the dying Christian for the beatific vision, an anointing unto glory.

The Council of Trent (1551) in refuting the Protestant Reformers affirmed unction as a sacrament instituted by Christ with an enduring salvific meaning which did not contradict the scriptural passage of James and had the priest as its ordinary minister. But Trent refused to completely endorse the medieval approach to anointing as a sacrament of the dying. The original draft spoke of extreme unction as a sacrament to be administered "only (*dumtaxat*) to those in their final struggle and who have come to grips with death and are about to go forth to the Lord." The definitive text made a decisive alteration: "This anointing is to be used for the sick, but especially (*praesertim*) for those who are dangerously ill as to seem near to death." Three times the recipients of anointing are described as sick (*infirmi*), not dying. The Council taught that the specific effect of anointing was the grace of the Holy Spirit with spiritual, psychological, and physical ramifications. The post-Tridentine era saw a progressive leniency concerning the interpretation of the danger of death required for unction and a gradual re-assertion of anointing as a sacrament for the sick. Such teaching was reflected in the teaching of the catechism of the Council of Trent and the Encyclical Letters of Popes Benedict XV and Pius XI, who in the twentieth century urged the administration of unction at the beginning of a "probable danger" of death.

In addition to the scriptural, traditional, and pastoral reasons leading to the recovery of anointing as a sacrament for the sick, there is also a fourth one of ecumenical convergence. Both the Eastern Orthodox and the Anglican Communion provide services for anointing the sick. The euchelaion or "prayer oil" is found in the Eastern Orthodox *Euchologion* and, when fully implemented, is an elaborate service involving seven priests, seven readings from epistles and gospels, seven prayers, and seven anointings of the sick. The 1549 Book of Common Prayer retained an order for anointing in its office of the visitation of the sick. Although the rite of anointing was deleted in the 1552 Prayer Book and subsequent revisions, reform movements advocated the revival of anointing as a rite for the sick until the present century when it has been restored to the Prayer Books of most of the member churches of the Anglican Communion.

Revised Rites for the Sick and Dying

With an Apostolic Instruction Paul VI promulgated the Latin typical edition *Ordo Unctionis infirmorum eorumque pastoralis curae* in 1972; the International Commission for English in the Liturgy translated this rite in a provisional manner for use in 1974, *Anointing and the Pastoral Care of the Sick*. On the basis of a wide-ranging consultation, ICEL in 1982 prepared a more definitive text better adapted to pastoral needs. *Pastoral Care of the Sick: Rites of Anointing and Viaticum* was approved by Rome and implemented in 1983. The revised rites for the sick and the dying highlight the pastoral ministry to the sick, recover the original tradition of anointing the sick, and make a clear differentiation between pastoral care of the sick and pastoral care of the dying.

The very title of the revision indicates its overall pastoral thrust. *Pastoral Care* is enriched with insightful pastoral intro-ductions which expand upon the original Roman *praenotanda*. Prayer services are provided for visiting the sick, sick children as well as adults. The communion of the sick envisions the ailing Christian united in the sacrament with the other brothers and sisters of the eucharistic assembly. Adaptations are made to a hospital setting, although the ideal and normative celebration continues to be the full rite of anointing with a community of believers. Many parishes now celebrate communal anointing services several times a year, a provision which has also found en-dorsement in Canon 1002 of the new Code of Canon Law and has met with much pastoral success. Throughout the rite the terms given for the various ministries are to be used advisedly. For example, "priest" means the minister of the sacraments of penance, anointing, or viaticum within Mass. "Priest or deacon" refers to liturgies where a deacon may preside as well. "Minister" includes priests, deacons, and other ministers to the sick in such wise that the proper non-ordained minister to the sick may administer virtually all the rites except penance and anointing.

The original meaning of anointing the sick is recovered: nowhere are the misleading terms "extreme unction" or "last rites" used to describe the sacrament. The condition set forth for its reception is anyone of the faithful whose health is "seriously impaired by sickness or old age" (para. 8). "The celebration of this sacrament consists especially in the laying on of hands by the priests of the Church, the offering of the prayer of faith and the anointing of the sick with oil made holy by God's blessing" (para. 5). The oil is olive oil, or if needed, other oil derived from plants. The oil is ordinarily blessed by the bishop at the Chrism Mass during Holy Week; in case of necessity any priest may do the blessing. The priest anoints the forehead and hands or other suitable parts of the body together with the following sacramental form: "Through this holy anointing may the Lord in his love and mercy help you with the grace of the Holy Spirit. Amen. May the Lord who frees you from sin save you and raise you up. Amen."

The organization of the ritual makes a clear distinction between *Pastoral Care of the Sick (Pt I)* and *Pastoral Care of the Dying (Pt II)*. Just as anointing has been recovered as a sacrament for the seriously ill, so also has viaticum (literally "food for the journey"), holy communion with special prayers for a Christian departing this life, been restored as the sacrament for the dying. Already the first ecumenical council of Nicaea in 325 mandated that a dying Christian "is not to be deprived of the last and necessary provision for the journey, viaticum." In view of the encouragement to celebrate viaticum within Mass, the baptismal profession of faith, the sign of peace, and communion under both kinds, the church seems to be suggesting an earlier time for viaticum when the patient and family may have arrived at a stage of acceptance. All traces of fatalism are removed and this much-neglected sacrament may be received on successive days.

Various images pervade the church's tradition of praying for the dying: death as sleep and eternal repose, death as birth, death as a journey to the Lord. Indeed, the vision of the commendation rite is that of a procession in which the earthly church accompanies its dying members as far as it can go before entrusting them to the care of the angels and saints of heaven who escort them to the Lord. The short scripture texts, readings, litany of the saints, and prayers are a consolation and support in this critical moment when Christians complete their journey and are reborn into the fullness of everlasting life with God.

The Prayers for the Dead are a welcome addition for a priest called upon to minister to a Christian who has already died so that the anointing of the sick would not be permitted. The minister concludes the prayers with a blessing of the body. The Rites for Exceptional Circumstances are to be treated as such: continuous rites of penance, anointing and viaticum, rite for emergencies, christian initiation for the dying. Part III with readings, responses and verses from sacred scripture with which the pastoral minister should be conversant, completes the revised rites.

Remaining Questions

Who may be anointed? *Pastoral Care* answers this question (para. 8-15): Christians seriously impaired by sickness or old age: before surgery occasioned by a serious illness, elderly people "notably weakened," children with sufficient use of reason, even sick people who have lapsed into unconsciousness when deemed appropriate. The sacrament may be repeated in the course of a progressive sickness. New is the possibility of anointing the mentally ill. The priest is not to administer the sacrament to someone who is already dead. Indiscriminate anointing of people not seriously ill is to be avoided. The criterion should be not so much the medical condition, but rather the spiritual powerlessness brought on by the illness.

Who may anoint? Present discipline permits only a bishop or priest (*sacerdos*) in keeping with the teaching of the council of Trent, although the anointing of the sick has experienced a long evolution and the doctrinal arguments could be re-examined. Furthermore, precedents exist for the extension of the presiding ministry in other sacraments, e.g., priests confirming adult converts and children of catechetical age. A conflict results from the Vatican Council's encouragement to receive the sacrament yet an insufficient number of priestly ministers to make it available.

What does the anointing do? The emphasis is not on healing, nor on forgiving, nor on preparing for death as such. The sacrament has to do with the discovery and revelation of the saving mystery of God within a serious illness. The rich ambiguity of sacramental grace is expressed in para. 6:

"This sacrament gives the grace of the Holy Spirit to those who are sick: by this grace the whole person is helped and saved, sustained by trust in God, and strengthened against the temptations of the Evil One and against anxiety over death. Thus the sick person is able not only to bear suffering bravely, but also to fight against it. A return to physical health may follow the reception of this sacrament if it will be beneficial to the sick person's salvation. If necessary, the sacrament also provides the sick person with the forgiveness of sins and the completion of Christian penance."

The scholastic theologians during the Middle Ages viewed unction as a sacrament for the dying and taught that its sacramental grace was to prepare the soul for immediate entrance into heaven, a purpose which now appears to pertain more to the Apostolic Pardon found in the rites for the dying. The present rediscovery of anointing as a sacrament for the sick challenges contemporary theology to develop a more holistic understanding of its sacramental grace which does full justice to the entire tradition of the church.

Pastoral Care of the Sick: Rites of Anointing and Viaticum, Washington D.C.: ICEL, 1982. James Empereur, *Prophetic Anointing;* Wilmington: Michael Glazier and Dublin: Gill and Macmillan, 1982. Charles W. Gusmer, *And You Visited Me: Sacramental Ministry to the Sick and the Dying,* New York: Pueblo, 1984.

CHARLES W. GUSMER

ANONYMOUS CHRISTIANITY

A term made popular by Karl Rahner to deal with the question of the salvation of those who, without fault, never become Christians. On the basis of the universal salvific will of God and his own theory of transcendental revelation, Rahner argued that every person is given an opportunity in the ordinary course of his life to make fundamental choices about his own existence whose self-constituting reality has the same quality, if not content, as the choice about explicit faith in Christ.

ANTHROPOLOGY, CHRISTIAN

Christian anthropology is the articulation of the christian understanding of human existence. This understanding is grounded in Jesus Christ as the revelation of the meaning of humanity in relation to God. Thus christian anthropology flows from christology, specifically from that part of christology wherein Christ is portrayed as the paradigm of the human as intended by the creator. God created humanity to become his "image and likeness" (Gen 1:26). In the NT Jesus Christ is presented (especially by Paul and John) as the definitive fulfillment of the divine creative intentionality. In the Pauline tradition the universal significance of Jesus Christ for all humanity is expressed in the symbols of the "New Adam," the "Wisdom" of God, indeed, *the* Image of God. The fundamental meaning of these protological symbols is the same: Jesus is the eschatological revelation of God's plan or purpose in the creation of the world. In him is revealed "the secret hidden from the ages" (Col 1:26). The Johannine symbol of the "Word" of God is similar in meaning. As God's final "Word," Jesus is the enfleshment of the divine immanence, the divine ordering of the universe, dynamically creating the meaning of the world. Without this ordering divine presence the world is chaos; with it the world becomes cosmos, the ordered, intelligible whole. Thus, the universalist thrust of these biblical symbols disclose Jesus as the archetypal Christ, God's "definition" of what humanity and the world are all about.

Christian anthropology is the pneumatological extension of christology. In the third article of the creed Christians confess the Holy Spirit as the personal power of God in the world whose presence is focused in Christ and through Christ given to all. Thus, christian anthropology expresses the self-understanding of those who in faith have received the self-communication of God through Christ and in the Spirit. As the symbol, Christ, is employed to express the uniqueness of Jesus, so the symbol, Spirit, is used to express the universal grace of Christ whence Christians "live, move, and have their being"(Acts 17:28). Where the Spirit of Christ is, there is christian anthropology, and it is only in the Spirit that one can confess that Jesus is the Christ. Thus, the relationship between christology and christian anthropology is the noetically reflective form of the mutually conditioning relationship between Christ and the Spirit. As the universal presence of God in the world, the Spirit is the prevenient grace whose definitive epiphany in history is the Christ. Christ mediates the Spirit as the divine power effective through him for the salvation of all humanity.

A very important hermeneutical key for the interpretation of both the OT and the NT is the intrinsic connection between creation and redemption, or between their reflective formulations, protology and eschatology. Biblical speech about origins (protology) is always in light of the future (eschatology). Creation is for redemption; redemption is the fulfillment of creation. This hermeneutical key is especially important for interpreting the classical themes of christian anthropology. The protological dimension of christian self-understanding finds its traditional expression in the words, creature and sinner. The eschatological dimension of this same self-understanding is traditionally expressed in the words, grace and hope.

As a religious understanding of origins, the doctrine of creation in the OT is set in a soteriological context. Only in the Wisdom literature of late Judaism does creation become a matter of focal interest in itself. For the rest of the OT Yahweh is primarily Savior, who through the events of the Exodus and the Sinai covenant both constituted the Israelites as a people and promised them a blessed future. Most probably the people of Israel, together with the other peoples of the

Near East, originally understood the divine in terms of the origin of the world. But when the events of their salvation history became for them *the* epiphany of God, their understanding of God as creator was contextualized within their historical traditions. Thus, the creation of the world was understood by Israel in terms of the divine purposes of election: God created for the sake of his covenant with Israel.

Constituted by the freedom of a gracious God, the finite world is good. As finite, human beings are good. As image and likeness of God, the human being is graced with a unique nobility. Different from the cosmocentrism of Greek anthropology wherein the human being is understood as the highest grade of finite being within the cosmic order, the bible relates humanity directly to God. Like God, the human person is a being of freedom and creativity. But this special ennoblement of humanity is misinterpreted when it gives rise to that pathetic hubris which is the denial of creatureliness. The goodness of being human is identical with that humility (literally, "being down to earth") which accepts the truth that we are finite creatures in radical dependence on our creator for everything we are or have.

A distinctively Catholic way of putting together the biblical understanding of the human person as both creature and *imago dei* is the traditional theme (from the nature-grace discussions) of the *finitum capax infiniti* (the finite open to the infinite). The fundamental goodness of creation (despite the enormity of evil in the world) has always been the point of departure for the Catholic understanding of grace and redemption. In accord with this understanding of the affinity between the human and the divine, Jesus Christ, as the New Adam, is the divinely wrought fulfillment of the basic potential of the human creature. As for us, and "for our salvation," Jesus becomes the effective paradigm of human fulfillment in grace.

Before moving to the heart of christian anthropology which is focused on the grace of Christ a word must be said on the surd of sin. According to the protological myth of Genesis the first human beings, created good by God, separated themselves from their creator by their pride, their pernicious pretension to parity with God. They could not accept the truth of their finitude. Not avowing their creatureliness, they could not allow the creator to be creator. Thus, their infinite potential became infinite disorientation. They "fell" from the future God had ordained for them, and they initiated human history as the story of universal deviation.

This experience of sin, guilt, and alienation was intensified through the preaching of the prophets. In the name of Yahweh, the Faithful One, the prophets indicted the faithlessness of Israel. They intensified the sense of guilt and responsibility, while they slowly came to realize the powerlessness of the people to obey the moral demands of God. Their "ethical monotheism" created a terrible tension between the clarity of the divine command and the human incapacity to fulfill it. Jeremiah longed for a "new covenant," written by God on the heart, a new divine empowerment from within the human spirit (Jer 31:33) Similarly, Ezekiel hoped for a new heart, a heart of flesh to replace the heart of stone, when God would put his Spirit within the people (Ezek 11:19). The prophetic indictment of sin yields to the language of hope for redemption and renovation.

With the experience of the "quenching of the Spirit" and the end of prophecy in late Judaism, obedience to the Torah becomes the sign of the faithful Jew. Pessimism about the prospects of "this age" increases, the prophetism gives way to apocalypticism—a visionary language of hope for "the age to come" with the final establishment of the kingdom of God and the resurrection of the dead. The human problems of sin and death await an eschatological resolution.

The NT is the proclamation of precisely this eschatological resolution, fulfilled in the resurrection of the crucified Jesus, the eschatological prophet. In resonance with the yearning of the prophets for God's final salvific act for his people, Paul translates the death and resurrection of Jesus into a soteriological anthropology. Through faith in the presence of the vivifying Spirit of Christ the Christian is enabled to die with the Lord to that self-destruction which is sin and to rise with the Lord to a new life of discipleship. In the seventh chapter of the Epistle to the Romans Paul portrays the hopeless impotency of people without Christ, our universal solidarity in sin. But this universal solidarity in sin is for Paul the primitive presupposition for the good news of universal deliverance from sin and death through Christ (Rom 8). Human incapacity to fulfill the divine command is overcome through faith in divine empowerment in the Spirit of the Risen Christ.

The Pauline experience of the redemptive grace of Christ is formulated in the language of doctrine by Augustine in the context of his controversy with Pelagius. For Augustine, Pelagianism was a moralistic reductionism for which Christ was at most the final facilitator of human free will. To combat this heretical distortion of the good news of redemption Augustine insisted with Paul on our universal need of redemption. To express this universal need Augustine radicalized the doctrine of original sin. Born of the race of Adam, all inherit both sin and death. Because of this universal corruption no one can be saved without the internal efficacy of the grace of Christ, the utterly gratuitous gift of God.

This hamartiologically contextualized teaching of Augustine became the official doctrine of the western church on grace at the Councils of Carthage in 418 (against Pelagianism) and Orange (against Semipelagianism) in 529. The doctrine of original sin was formulated at Carthage with the biological metaphor of "generation." This same metaphor was retained by the Council of Trent in the form of "propagation." While this biological language obviously asserts universal human solidarity in sin, it is, precisely as a *biological* metaphor, open to serious misunderstanding. It seems to assert that original sin is a "sin of nature." But sin is not a structural defect of human nature. Sin is a contingency of history whose source is not nature but disoriented freedom. Contemporary efforts responsibly to retrieve the doctrine of original sin for contemporary human self-understanding carefully distinguish nature and history without, however, separating them. If it is the "nature" of being human to become human, then history is the (always ambiguous) self-enactment of the human race. History is the realm where sin appears, and christian faith avers that in history God through Christ is reconciling the world to himself in the Spirit (2 Cor 5:18).

Grace

The central theme of christian anthropology is the reality of grace. In many ways the entire theology of the west can be viewed as a long commentary on the theology of grace. At times this commentary became passionate controversy— even to the point of the division of the western church in the sixteenth century. While the doctrines of God and Christ had received their classical formulation in the great ecumenical councils of the eastern church, western christianity found its center of gravity in the issue of the new understanding of the human person as the beneficiary of God's reconciling work through Jesus Christ. The biblical point of departure for this sustained western absorption with christian anthropology was the Pauline theology of grace. But prior to the development of this distinctively western theology, the Greek Fathers had developed their own understanding of christian existence under the influence of what might broadly be called Johannine mysticism.

The incarnate Word of the Johannine tradition was the distinctive focus for eastern theology. Accordingly, the new christian self-understanding was explored with the heuristically evocative Johannine themes of "life" and "light." For the eastern Fathers the sin of Adam was the source not of human guilt but of mortality. Death "the wages of sin," was the destructive inheritance of the human race. Thus, the redemptive efficacy of Christ was understood in terms of his victory over death. In accord with the biblical (and specifically Johannine) insistence that only God has life and separation from God means death, the redemption of humanity is realized in principle at the very moment of the incarnation when the divine Word brings life to the world of darkness and death.

In resonance with the Hellenistic language of 2 Pet 1:4 the eastern theology of grace is centered on the doctrine of the divinization (or deification) of the Christian. God became a human being so that human beings might become divine. Here we find the classical illustration of that emphasis on divine immanentism so characteristic of eastern christianity. Divinization means that the Christian shares by grace in everything God is by nature. Christians are images (icons) of God through the deifying grace of the Image incarnate. Recalling Ps 82:6 and Jn 10:34, the doctrine of divinization proclaims: "You are gods, and all of you are sons of the Most High."

While the eastern theology of grace is a clear celebration of divine immanence, it is also most insistent on divine transcendence. God in his quintessential being remains inaccessible (1 Tm 6:16). To protect the transcendent majesty of God the eastern tradition employed the notion of the divine "energies" (energeiai). Distinct from the divine essence or nature, the divine energies are eternal, uncreated forces or powers whereby God creates and divinizes the world. This theology of the divine energies received its classical development in the work of the fourteenth century Byzantine thinker, Gregory Palamas. Western theology has no category cognate to that of divine energy. Its speech about the "divine attributes" would be a rather pale similarity. The eastern themes of divinization and energy reflect both the Platonic doctrine of participation and the biblical teaching on the necessity of communion between God and his creatures. Perhaps the contemporary notion of panentheism comes closest to the realism of the divine divinizing energies.

The *Filioque* controversy between the eastern and western churches is related to the theology of grace. The east has with reason suspected the west of a practical subordinationism of the Spirit to the Christ. Their insistence on the Spirit's procession from the Father (God) protects the universal efficacy of the Spirit in the world. The west, however, can justify the *Filioque* by a complementary insistence that for the Christian Christ is the ultimate criterion for assessing the authenticity of the Spirit's empowerment of human *praxis*.

For the western church Augustine is the "Doctor of Grace." Perhaps because of the pragmatic legacy of imperial Rome the central issue of western reflection has been human action (*praxis*), its range and its limits. Thus grace becomes associated with action or "works." This practical bent, however, in no way obviated the contemplative posture of christian mysticism, the form of spirituality congenial to Catholic immanentism. Augustine's broad theology of grace resonates with the immanentist theme of divinization, especially in his explorations of christian interiority, the ground of which is that gracious divine presence that is *intimior intimo meo* (closer to me than I am to myself). To the west Augustine mediated the biblical emphasis on the conative or erotic structure of the human person: "What are we but wills?" The God of Augustine is primarily the One who is found within as the driving ground of the vital restlessness of the human heart for eternal fulfillment. Augustine appears quite "modern" in his understanding of the trinitarian God not as the object but as the very condition of human consciousness. In an explicitly religious sense Augustine anticipated the modern "turn to the subject" with his heuristic language of interiority: memory, illumination, inspiration, etc.

The context for the development of the western doctrine on grace was set by the Augustinian-Pelagian controversy. To destroy Pelagianism Augustine insisted that the grace of Christ as the internal working of the Holy Spirit illuminating the mind and inspiring the will was absolutely necessary for salvation and an absolutely gratuitous gift of God. This teaching was embraced by the Council of Carthage in 418, and the subsequent papal approbation of this provincial synod rendered Augustine's teaching on grace the official doctrine of the western church. Augustine's peculiar interpretation of the gratuity of grace in terms of the pessimistic doctrine of predestination became part of the theological tradition, but it was not canonized by the official teaching. Emphatically insisting on the utter dependence of sinful humanity on the grace of God, Augustine constructed

the vocabulary that was to inform the entire subsequent history of reflection on grace. Augustinianism became synonymous with the thesis that God alone presides over the entire process of the salvation of those whom he has elected. This primacy of grace is clearly reflected in the doctrine of "operating grace"— "what God does in us without us." But Augustine did not forget his apologia for the reality of free will against Manichean fatalism. While according the primary efficacy to grace, Augustine did not omit consideration of the necessity of human cooperation with God's grace. He became indeed the "Father of Catholicism" with his balancing formulation of the notion of "cooperating grace"— "what God does in us with us."

Another doctrinal victory for Augustinianism occurred at the Council of Orange in 529. Augustine's teaching on "prevenient grace" was employed to condemn what is known today as Semipelagianism, the doctrine that people can initiate the process of conversion by turning to God. The teaching of Orange on prevenient grace also gained subsequent papal approbation and thus became part of the church's official doctrine. To rule out any form of Pelagian moralism the church proclaimed the gracious efficacy of God in saving his people. In this context the role of human cooperation is obviously a matter of secondary concern. The lesson to be learned from the condemnation of Semipelagianism is that any description of divine-human "cooperation" which portrays such cooperation as a concurrence on the same level is an heretical deviation from the gospel. In this way the official doctrine on grace implicitly endorsed the later theological distinction between primary and secondary causality.

Until the thirteenth century the western theology of grace was dominated by the Augustinian categories. In his famous "opinion" Peter Lombard, author of *the* medieval textbook, summed up the Augustinian heritage on grace by identifying grace with charity and both grace and charity with the Holy Spirit. All grace is the "uncreated grace" of the Spirit. New questions, however, continued to arise. One of them was concerned with the issue of grace and infant baptism. The Augustinian categories were most useful for exploring the divine efficacy in the justification and the sanctification of adults, but the "actualism" of this understanding of grace rendered it less helpful for answering the question whether or not infants were graced by the sacrament of Baptism. A new vocabulary was needed, and this new language of grace was supplied by Thomas Aquinas.

Aquinas disagreed with the Lombard's identification of grace with the Holy Spirit. For Thomas, the word, grace, more properly describes the renovation or regeneration of the human being as a "new creature." This "anthropocentric turn" in Thomas must be understood within the architectonic structure of his thought.

The "catholicity" of Thomas's theology is evident in his choice of creation rather than redemption as its focal symbol. Like the sapiential literature of the bible and like the cosmocentric orientation of Greek philosophy, Thomistic theology seeks to disclose the meaning of all reality "in the light of eternity." Through faith Thomas has access to the divine mind, and in his *Summa Theologiae* he elucidates the basic structure of all creation as from God unto God. For Thomistic "intellectualism" the intrinsic intelligibility of creation is assured by its origination from the divine wisdom. The structure of the world betrays the sagacity of its Author. Inheriting from Greek thought the thesis that the world is cosmos, an ordered, intelligible, harmonious whole,

Thomas was convinced that christian faith "proved" this thesis. The *nous* of Aristotle is clarified by the *logos* of christianity. The supernatural is *above* the natural only that the former might be the fulfillment and the perfection of the latter. With the vision of Thomas Aquinas the medieval synthesis finds its definitive legitimacy.

St. Thomas' theology of grace is the clearest illustration of a christian anthropology articulated in the substantialist categories of Greek philosophy. The interest of this theology is the formulation of the essential structure of grace as the regeneration of human nature. The universalism of the philosophical notion of human nature is its presupposition. The Latin noun, *natura*, is rooted in the verb, *nasci* "to be born." An imaginative etymology of *natura* could further note its dynamic quality by interpreting its verbal form as the future active participle of *nasci*, an interpretation which would note the importance of "active becoming" for that which was born. Indeed, the active or operative connotation of "nature" over against the static connotation of "essence" was never completely overlooked by the scholastic use of the term in its theological anthropology. While nature and essence were often used synonymously, nature was essence precisely as the principle of operation. Thus, when Thomas describes the metaphysical structure of the human being, rendered God's friend through the grace of Christ, he speaks of the elevation of human nature as the grace-enabled principle of a new human *praxis* on a level of parity with God, the supernatural goal of human action. The realism of this understanding of grace as the radical restructuring of human nature leads to that positive evaluation of grace-enabled action unto God expressed in the term, merit. Correctly understood, the term, merit, does not describe the subjectivity of christian motivation. It realistically asserts the objective value of human deeds done in grace. Thus, a contemporary retrieval of Thomas's theology of grace would underscore the dynamic meaning of nature as becoming and merit as the self-determination of the human person, empowered by grace.

Thomas's christian anthropocentrism stretched the substantialist cast of Greek thought to its limit. But Thomas did not overcome the basic restrictions of Greek cosmocentrism. A metaphysics of substance tends naturally toward reification, and later scholasticism bears witness to this reductionism. For christian faith the human person is not merely the "highest thing" in the world. A new language more appropriate to the exploration of the uniqueness of the human as the image and likeness of God was necessary, and christian anthropology subsequent to Thomas Aquinas began to develop that language as a prelude to the "turn to the subject" characteristic of modern thought.

Reaction to Thomistic intellectualism begins forcefully in the voluntarism of Duns Scotus. Influenced by the Augustinianism of the medieval Franciscan tradition, Scotus opted for the primacy of the will over the intellect for the proper exposition of christian anthropology. But this voluntarism was not restricted to anthropology. It became the key for modern theology as well. The God of Thomistic intellectualism was the Supreme Intelligence who in fidelity to his wisdom had created an intrinsically intelligible world. The God of Scotistic voluntarism reflected the biblical accent on the freedom of the God who revealed himself primarily as Will. Thus was the precarious synthesis of the medieval (especially Thomistic) blending of the biblical God and philosophical cosmic order undermined. When God is understood primarily as Will, and when that Will takes on the character of incom-prehensible omnipotence, the connection between world order and its divine author becomes arbitrary in principle. The famous Scotist distinction between the divine "ordinary power" and "absolute power" does indeed protect the divine freedom, but the price to be paid for the subsequent radicalization of this distinction was the emergence of modern atheism. Indeed, the utter transcendence of divine omnipotence evokes dehumanizing terror in the believer, while its irrationality renders such a divinity pragmatically otiose for the atheist or agnostic.

Despite its subtle theological dangers, however, Scotistic voluntarism marks a definite advance for christian anthropology. With his focus on the will Scotus asserts the primacy of *praxis* over theory. As Nicholas Lobkowicz in *Theory and Practice: History of a Concept from Aristotle to Marx* (Lanham, MD: University Press of America, 1967) observes regarding Scotistic thought: "the christian emphasis upon charity and love as opposed to mere knowledge has resulted, and from now on even more radically will result, in an emphasis upon practice as opposed to theory until eventually practice will become the sole source of meaning and salvation"(p.74). Thus does Scotistic voluntarism initiate the modern recovery in the west of the biblical understanding of the human being as person.

The radicalization of Scotistic voluntarism is completed in the nominalism of another Franciscan, William of Occam. The absolute freedom of the divine will is now celebrated in the language of extreme arbitrariness. The natural order is separate from the supernatural which is unknowable outside the pale of positive divine revelation. The natural "point of contact" between the human and the divine cedes to biblical or ecclesiastical positivism. In the religious realm the principle of authority replaces reason. The basic identity of grace and future glory in the Thomistic system yields to a frustrating extrinsicism which for some nominalistic theologians found expression in Semipelagian slogans. Fideism becomes the final expression of this basically pessimistic religious anthropology.

But this religious pessimism which drastically reduced the range of humanity's theological horizon is uncannily combined with a rather optimistic naturalism. While the heavenly pretensions of the human mind are abandoned, the earthly potential of human intelligence is enhanced. Theoretical contemplation of abstract universals is replaced as the highest human ideal by a new interest in the concrete particular. The theological ideal of the "ancient way," to understand everything "in the light of eternity," gives way to the new ideal of exploring the world of nature and history intramurally.

Despite its obvious theological ambiguities nominalism, like voluntarism, did further the christian anthropological recovery of personalism. Indeed, both voluntarism and nominalism evince a clear, albeit ambiguous, affinity with the biblical cast of mind. In many ways the "modern way" can be understood as the modern emergence of a way of thinking which is rooted not in Greek cosmocentrism but in the historical horizons of biblical thought. With the "modern way" historical consciousness advances, as history itself becomes the object of philosophical study—something inconceivable for the Greek mind.

At the beginning of the modern era unresolved issues in christian anthropology led to the division of the church in the west. The official doctrine of the church was the Augustinian teaching that sinners are justified by the grace of Christ. Salvation is the gratuitous work of God for helpless humanity. But the question of the relationship between human action and salvation remained unanswered. Aquinas had essayed an answer to this question with his notion of created grace, but his metaphysical language was often misinterpreted as a reification of grace. Some nominalistic schools, as noted above, publicly taught a Semipelagian answer to the question of the salvific efficacy of human action. The Augustinian friar, Martin Luther, loudly denounced this answer as heresy and identified the gospel with the Pauline doctrine of justification by grace alone. Luther developed a new, biblically inspired, language for christian anthropology. He replaced the scholastic notion of human nature with the biblical notion of personhood. For Luther the christian person is one who has found through faith in Christ a new relationship with God, a relationship of trust, confidence, and acceptance. Luther's answer to the question of the salvific import of human action was a radical form of Augustinianism—grace alone saves, good works at most attest to the authenticity of personal conversion.

Luther's insistence on the immediacy of each person's access to God in faith was a massive contradiction of the essence of Catholicism, the principle of mediation. The Council of Trent was summoned to respond to Luther, but it failed to do so for two basic reasons. The new language of Luther's christian anthropology was not really understood by most of the Tridentine Fathers, steeped as they were in scholastic categories (e.g., Luther understood faith in the biblical sense of trust, while Trent understood faith as belief). And in terms of the central issue of the theological evaluation of human action vis-á-vis salvation, they were unable to clarify the relationship between uncreated and created grace. Luther rightly rejected the notion of created grace in its nominalistic interpretation as an intermediate being or separate entity. Perhaps he would have been helped by

Bonaventure's precise interpretation of created grace: "to possess grace is to be possessed by it." However, the tragedy of a divided church was the result of Luther's new christian anthropology.

While Trent failed to heal the divisions in the church, it did present a positive doctrinal exposition of the Catholic position on grace and justification. Its content is basically a synthesis of Augustine and Aquinas, and its language is scriptural and patristic rather than scholastic. Post-Tridentine Catholic theology of grace was focused polemically on created grace as against the forensically formulated Protestant position. Catholic theologians themselves were divided on the question of actual grace. These debates yielded little positive fruit, and today they are generally regarded as side issues. However, because these disputes were contextualized within the doctrine of predestination, they tended to construct an antithesis between divine grace and human freedom. Together with the pervasive presence of the nominalist understanding of divine transcendence, this disastrous tendency to conceive of God as contending with human freedom created a fateful theological mortgage for modern christianity.

Contemporary Christian Anthropology

The modern history of western thought is generally characterized by a turning away from the primacy of the cosmocentric category of substance and a turning to the primacy of human subjectivity. A whole new vocabulary has been forged to explore human experience, its ground or conditions, its range and its limits. The anthropocentrism of the Renaissance set the tone for this entire era. The Cartesian *cogito* signals its reflective philosophical emergence, its optimistic pretentiousness and its tragic pathology. Against the religious indictment of the Reformation's cry, "God alone," modernity answered, "Man a-lone." The foundation for the christian understanding of human existence is implicitly rejected by the Cartesian discovery of the self alone. For there is no basis for a christian anthropology when one turns within and finds only the self and not the self and "More" of christian spirituality. Thus, modernity is the pseudo-legitimation of individualism, which is the radical distortion of christian personalism. The "private self" of the modern secular west is *not* the "interior self" of christian anthropology. (Cf. Charles Davis, *Body as Spirit* (New York: The Seabury Press, 1976), pp. 59-86.)

Contemporary christian anthropology can be understood as an attempt to overcome modern deism and its consequence, anthropological reductionism. Deism aptly describes the God of the Enlightenment, modernity's reflective self-appropriation. But the cultural pervasiveness of this deism was contagious. It cryptically, and hence destructively, affected modern christianity as well. While Christians continued in their "dogmatic slumbers," it was genius of the philosopher, Hegel, to sound the alarm. Among modern thinkers Hegel is perhaps the clearest illustration of the philosophical contention that history is intelligible because it is constituted by meaning.

For Hegel a religion based on transcendence without immanence is the major cause of human alienation from self, from others, and from nature. He decried the authoritarian positivism of the ecclesiastical christianity of his day. Convinced that he had divined the absolute truth of christianity, he interpreted the doctrine of the Trinity in a way that brought God and world together in an historical process of becoming. For Hegel the trinitarian God cannot be a God of distant, aloof transcendence. Trinity means radical divine immanence, the divine evacuation of heaven to make the world the sacred temple. History becomes the history of God's self-determination, and as such history becomes the eminently intelligible process constituted by the divine meaning. The Incarnation reveals the affinity between the human and the divine, the finite and the infinite. The presence of the Spirit assures the historically enacted reconciliation of all otherness between God and the world. Hegel, "the owl of Minerva," flew at the dusk of world history and alighted on the final elucidation of the meaning of the whole of reality.

Hegel did not become the Aquinas of Lutheranism. But the significance of his philosophical translation of the intrinsic rationality of christianity had an enormous impact on subsequent christian theology. Crypto-deism, illustrated in the various authoritarian claims of ecclesiastical positivism, began to yield to a theological recovery of christian immanentism. This new emphasis on the divine immanence in the world is characteristic both of liberal Protestantism and of modern Catholicism. Despite the Barthian indictment of the former and the Pian condemnation of the latter, contemporary theology maintains a critical insistence on God's immanence in the whole of creation. Indeed, this critically retrieved immanentism is *the* theological presupposition behind the salient features of contemporary christian anthropology: the universality of grace, grace as experienced, grace and spirituality, and grace as the ground of *praxis*.

Significant developments in christian anthropology for Catholic theology in the present century began with the now well known "turn to the subject." A pioneer in this new direction for Catholic thought was the christian philosopher, Maurice Blondel. Blondel constructed a philosophical anthropology explicitly to serve as a propaedeutic to theology. His apologetics of immanence focused on the

traditional western concern with human action. In line with the Augustinian type of the philosophy of religion Blondel produced a phenomenology of the heart wherein he discovered an insatiable conative drive as the energy grounding the erotic momentum of all human living. For Blondel this ineluctable elan of the human spirit bore witness to the prevenient grace of the Spirit. Because of this presence human beings will infinitely, and the gospel meets this infinite need with the invitation to will the Infinite. Thus did Blondel's anthropocentrism anticipate the subsequent Catholic theological exploration of the intrinsic relationship between nature and grace.

The employment of a philosophical anthropology as a prolegomenon for theology implies universalism. To move from philosophical anthropology to christian anthropology is to move from an understanding of humanity as such structurally open to God to humanity universally graced by God. The universal salvific will of God is a theme central to contemporary christian anthropology wherein it is translated in different linguistic forms of universal prevenient grace. The documents of Vatican II are permeated by this universalism, and in the Council's official recognition of non-christian religions *as religions* the universality of grace is presupposed. Given the blood bath that has been the twentieth century, it is rather startling to note the consistent presence in christian anthropology of this optimism of grace.

The theological turn to the subject is clearly illustrated in the contemporary exploration of grace as experienced. Against the extrinsicist understanding of the relationship between the natural and the supernatural characteristic of post-Tridentine Catholic theology, much recent thought has reflected on the experience of grace as the basis for christian discipleship. In transcendental theologies inspired by Karl Rahner the distinction is often drawn between what might be called the habitual experience of grace in the ordinary christian life and the focal experience of grace *as grace*. This theology of the experience of grace has been most significant for the contemporary study of the structure of christian spirituality. In this context a distinction is frequently made between mystical and prophetic types of spirituality. Broadly construed, mysticism is understood as a universal form of spirituality found in all religious traditions, while prophetism is seen as the form of spirituality distinctive to religious traditions nourished by the Bible. Dissatisfied by the former tendency to subordinate action (prophetic spirituality) to contemplation (mystical spirituality), theologians have sought to relate the two classical types of spirituality dialectically. Accordingly, mysticism becomes the vivifying ground of prophetism, while prophetism becomes the concrete realization of mysticism. Love of God and love of neighbor become one love wherein the latter becomes the criterion or the effective expression of the former. The ideal of personal immediacy to God receives an intrinsically christian modification in the contemporary insistence on the notion of "mediated immediacy."

The notion of mediation is central to Catholicism's characteristic emphasis on divine immanence together with the principle of sacramentality. But this notion can be and has been misused. When it is detached from the christian experience of the divine immediacy, it is misused to support (albeit unintentionally) that vague deism which has infected modern ecclesiastical christianity so deleteriously. Improperly employed, the notion of mediation promotes a non-christian understanding of the divine transcendence as distant aloofness. Properly understood, the notion of mediation appositely affirms the divine immanence which grounds the incarnational realism of Catholic sacramentalism.

As a result of the contemporary "linguistic turn" in theology Christians are becoming more critically aware of the formative power on both consciousness and practice of effective tradition. Prior to and pervasively affecting all theological reflection is the fact that Christians are always already formed by the linguistic power of their received religious tradition. Recognition of this fact has led some theologians to seek some Archimedean point of neutrality to distance themselves from the tradition in order more critically to appropriate its meaning and truth. Other theologians question the validity of this search for a non-historical foundation for the theological project of the critical appropriation of the christian tradition. Given recent developments in the field of hermeneutics, the latter are convinced that the only way critically to appropriate the tradition is from within the tradition itself. As an historically grounded and historically mediated understanding of human existence, christian anthropology must be appropriated historically by a critically hermeneutical retrieval of its identity. The remainder of this article will attempt to illustrate the salient features of such a retrieval with the hope to overcome at least partially some of our inherited insidious pseudo-antinomies such as that between divine sovereignty and human freedom in grace.

Christian Anthropology: A Hermeneutical Retrieval

Christian existence is human existence as disclosed in the life of Jesus and enabled by the Spirit or grace. It is a new structure of existence, born of a distinct understanding of God. It is first and foremost a theocentric anthropology, and only because it is theocentric is it simultaneously anthropocentric. It is based not on some general notion of God but on the special character of the God revealed in the bible. To speak responsibly of the grace of God as empowering a particular way of being human demands that we specify the content or meaning of the word, God, from within the language of our religious tradition. To become the "image of God" the Christian must know what God is like.

The covenant traditions of the OT celebrate the fidelity of God, a God actively involved with and passionately pursuing the salvation of the people, Israel. For Israel this God, Yahweh, is the primary agent of their communal history. Through their salutary association with Yahweh the people of Israel discovered history as divine epiphany. When, however, their sacred history turned into the terror of national destruction, their confidence in the fidelity of Yahweh was shaken. To meet this challenge to Yahwism the prophets proclaimed the divine freedom. This prophetic insistence on the freedom of God served to highlight the divine personhood. In response to the call to conversion by the personal God through the preaching of the prophets, there emerged in Israel what we understand today as the personal structure of human existence. The "ethical monotheism" of the prophets engendered a recognition of the human being as a morally responsible self or as a person in relation to the personal God.

Thus, personhood describes an anthropology whose roots are in the religious soil of the bible. It is different from the philosophical anthropology of the Greek tradition with its emphasis on reason as the highest human power. Personhood is an anthropology which accentuates the conative dimension of the human being over the cognitive. Will, freedom, and history constitute the vocabulary of personhood, while intellect, knowledge, and nature describe the anthropology of

Greek philosophy. The distinctive content of the word, person, defines the biblical understanding of the human being as "image of God." While the Greeks specified what Karl Jaspers termed the "axial" emergence of the individual in the millennium before Christ in terms of the self as reason, the Hebrews discovered the self as person called to freedom by their personal God.

The NT furthered the development of biblical personalism. The Incarnation is the ultimate radicalization of the biblical discovery of God, dynamically present in human history. The God of Jesus is the God who becomes historical in order to become *Deus pro nobis* (God for us). While Greek philosophy described the divine nature over against the world as eternal, immutable, and necessary, the NT continues the biblical testimony to the fidelity and freedom of the personal God. The only glory sought by this God is humanity fully alive (Irenaeus). The only power possessed by this God is the power of love, revealed in the folly of the Cross. The words, deeds, and destiny of Jesus, God's self-deed, constitute the definitive revelation of what God has willed to be for humanity. The divine freedom is revealed as the redemptively victorious divine fidelity. The grace of *this* God, the Gift of the Spirit, which is the basis for Christian anthropology, cannot be a coercive overwhelming of the human spirit. The proper notion of grace, hermeneutically retrieved from within the biblical tradition, means divine enabling, divine empowerment, divine companionship, divine liberation. As Paul so aptly stated the essence of christian anthropology: "Where the Spirit of the Lord is, there is freedom" (2 Cor 3:17).

The God of absolute omnipotence who has predetermined in detail the entire course of world history while himself remaining in sublime, immutable transcendence over the world is not the

God of Jesus. This deistic God who sometimes intervenes in the world to effect salvific adjustments has been rejected by atheistic humanism in the name of human freedom. Contemporary christian anthropology must also and very clearly reject this alienating divinity in the name of the God of freedom revealed in Jesus. The God who redeemed humanity through Christ is not only in no way inimical to human freedom; this God is the source, the ground, the energy that makes freedom possible. The grace of God, the Spirit of Christ means freedom!

For Paul and Augustine freedom is the grace-enabled ability to do the good; it is the liberation of the heart turned in on itself. This christian freedom is not to be reduced to the narrow notion of "free will." With the intensification over the past several centuries of "historical consciousness" reflective people have discovered a new meaning of time. History is now understood as human time; time has become the material of human freedom. Thus, freedom means much more than discrete self-determination in acting. Freedom is the ability to determine the self as a temporal process of self-creation. For christian faith freedom is the grace-enabled *praxis* of a person who in and through this *praxis* produces a self-identity destined for eternity.

Recent reflection on the ramifications of the religious significance of human freedom in grace has overcome in principle the traditional dualism often referred to as "other-worldliness." Time is no longer understood as a transient image of an over-arching eternity. Appropriated by the consciousness of freedom, time is now exalted as the very content of eternity. Grace means that freedom is not the ever-revisable possibility of change in a process of perpetual perishing. Freedom is the promise of the achievement of permanence, because the God of the promise fulfills its ever precarious movement by becoming its source and goal. In this way christian anthropology dares to aver that the kingdom of God is the fruit of human history which is simultaneously the history of God.

These observations on grace and freedom must not be interpreted as a new christian idealism which becomes a kind of "consolation of theology," relieving the believer of the burden of responsibility for history. They are intended to be a corrective of a traditional misunderstanding of what christian anthropology understands by personhood. As a religious path to self-identity personhood is constituted by listening and speaking to the personal God. Augustine's *Confessions* is a superb illustration of christian interiority as the route of self-discovery. But when the God discovered within is identified as an other-worldly Being, the true self of the Christian will tend to be identified as equally other-worldly. This tendency of religious idealism can be corrected only by a conscious appropriation of the "worldly" God of Jesus. This God is salvifically involved in and for the world, and by "cooperating grace" Christians are invited to partnership in the pursuit of the divine plan of love and justice for all, men and women.

No christian anthropology today can be silent on the issue of feminism. Theology and anthropology are always in correlation when the human is understood as the image of the divine. Thus, there is a not very subtle connection between modern deism and modern androcentrism. The image of the absolute God of omnipotence in modern culture is the dominating male in control of nature. Patriarchal power produces not personalism but the ugly fragmentation of human society that is individualism. The feminist movement is a prophetic indictment of the androcentric threat to all human beings, male and female. While the terms, male and female, can be taken to refer to the sexual identity of men and women, the terms, masculine and feminine, name archetypal psychic energies common in different ways to both men and women. The repression of the feminine is thus a repression of the human as such. The liberation of women is a necessary condition for the liberation of the feminine dimension of all human beings. Androgyny is the call to everyone to a new imagination, a new vision of interconnection, interrelation, and interdependence among all. This creative appropriation of the feminine energies of all human beings is vitally necessary to overcome the androcentric domination of nature which is the cause of our contemporary ecological crisis.

In consequence of the appropriation of the christian tradition on grace and freedom outlined above, christian anthropology today insists on the primacy of *praxis* over theory. This "praxiological turn" is most evident in contemporary political and liberation theologies. If the vision of christian anthropology is a world of persons living together in the freedom of grace, then this vision must be translated into responsible *praxis* in a world so massively distorted as to render the christian vision incredible. To the personalist, existentialist, and transcendental theologians we are indebted for the christian recovery of the theology of freedom. They have all contributed to the elucidation of the christian claim that authentic freedom is always theonomously grounded. But a personalist theology of freedom by itself is open to the charge of idealism. Concretely, the basic human value of freedom is historically and socially mediated. Freedom remains merely an ideal if it is not supported by social, political, and economic structures. Persons are free in a society of freedom. Hence, the christian appropriation of the ideal of human autonomy so powerfully

promoted by the tradition of "the modern history of freedom" (Kant, Hegel, Marx, *et al.*) cannot be merely the construction of an apologia for the christian roots of the western ideal of freedom. The theology of freedom in grace must become the theology of liberation, wherein the disclosure of the vision of freedom becomes a call to a grace-enabled transformation of human society. It is ultimately christian *praxis* that will validate the christian claim that heteronomy is overcome by autonomy only when autonomy is grounded in theonomy. Christian anthropology can no longer merely *interpret* history as the mediation of freedom in grace; christian *praxis* must *change* the terror of present history into provisional anticipations of the eschatological realm of freedom.

See **Grace, Feminist Theology, Freedom**

James D.G. Dunn, *Jesus and the Spirit*, Philadelphia: Westminster Press, and London: S.C.M., 1975. John Cobb, *The Structure of Christian Existence*, Philadelphia: Westminster, Press, 1967. Roger Haight, *The Experience and Language of Grace*, New York: Paulist Press, and Dublin: Gill and Macmillan, 1979. Wolfhart Pannenberg, *Anthropology in Theological Perspective*, Philadelphia: Westminster Press 1975. Karl Rahner, *Foundations of Christian Faith*, New York: Seabury Press, and London: Darton, Longman and Todd, 1978. Edward Schillebeeckx, *Christ: The Experience of Jesus as Lord*, New York: Seabury Press, and London: S.C.M., 1980.

MICHAEL J. SCANLON, OSA

ANTICHRIST

The mysterious figure or figures mentioned in the Johannine Epistles (1 Jn 2:18-22; 4:3; 2 Jn 7) as denying Christ. In later tradition, Antichrist is often identified with the Beast described in the Book of Revelation and with the "man of sin" of 2 Thess 2:3-10 who will appear during the great apostasy which must precede the return of Christ. The term has been interpreted as a single person, as several persons, and as the personification of all the forces hostile to Christ.

STEPHEN FUNK

APOCALYPTIC

"Apocalyptic" is properly an adjective, derived from the title of the Apocalypse of John, but it is widely used as an abbreviation for "apocalypticism." The word "apocalypse" means "revelation" and is the name of a genre of revelatory literature which became popular in Judaism in the last two centuries before Christ. The revelation presented in an apocalypse is mysterious in nature and requires the mediation of an angel or other supernatural figure. The recipient is usually a famous ancient figure (e.g., Enoch in Jewish circles, the apostles in Christianity), who is the pseudonymous or fictitious author of the book. (The Apocalypse of John is an exception in this regard, since there is no reason to doubt that John of Patmos was the real author.) The content of an apocalypse deals with heavenly mysteries, conspicuously including foreknowledge of eschatology, i.e., the end of history and the judgment of the dead.

Broadly speaking, there are two types of apocalypses. The first may be called historical. The revelation is usually given in the form of a symbolic vision, interpreted by an angel. It provides an overview of history, divided into periods, and culminating with a great crisis followed by judgment and resurrection. The classic prototype is the Book of Daniel. The Apocalypse of John is also basically of this type although it does not have a developed division of history into periods. The second type of apocalypse may be labeled "mystical." Here the visionary is typically taken on a tour of heaven or hell, guided by an angel. He is shown the mysteries of creation, including the abodes of the dead and places of judgment. The prototype of this sub-genre is found in the Ethiopic Book of Enoch (chaps. 1-36) where Enoch is taken on a tour by the angels. This composition probably dates from the early second century B.C., shortly before the Book of Daniel (164 B.C.). These two types of apocalypse are closely related to each other. Both types are attested within the Ethiopic Book of Enoch.

The adjectival use of "apocalyptic" most often refers to the "historical" type of apocalypse and is often equated with the expectation of cosmic catastrophe. Apocalypses of this type flourished especially in time of crisis, most notably the persecution of the Jews by Antiochus Epiphanes (168-164 B.C.) and the aftermath of the destruction of the Jerusalem temple by the Romans (70 A.D.). Similar ideas and expectations were widespread in Judaism in this period. The Essene community at Qumran, by the Dead Sea, conceived of an ongoing struggle between the cosmic forces of light and darkness which would culminate in a final battle. Distinct but related eschatological ideas were propagated among Greek-speaking Jews in the form of Sibylline Oracles.

Apocalyptic expectations played a crucial role in the development of early Christianity. Scholars are divided as to whether Jesus was an apocalyptic preacher, but there is no doubt that his resurrection was conceived as part of an apocalyptic scenario. According to St. Paul Christ was "the first fruits of those who have fallen asleep" (1 Cor 15:20), the forerunner of the general resurrection. The Gospels identified Jesus with the Son of Man foretold in Daniel's vision, who would come on the clouds of heaven for the final judgment (Mark 13 and parallels). The culmination of early christian apocalypticism is found in the Apocalypse of John, written in the last decade of the first century.

After the first century A.D. apocalypticism became less prominent in Judaism, although it did not disappear. The tradition of the ascent apocalypses was taken up in the Jewish mystical writings. The historical eschatology found a place in the exegetical writings, but was no longer the subject of independent apocalypses. This decline is often thought to have been a result of disillusionment with apocalyptic hopes after the wars against Rome. The genre flourished in Christianity and apocalypses were ascribed to Peter, Paul, Mary, etc., (primarily of the mystical, or ascent, type). It is also to Christianity that we owe the preservation of most of the Jewish apocalypses—in Ethiopic, Syriac, Latin and Old Church Slavonic. The mystical apocalypses had a broader impact on western culture through their influence on Dante's Divine Comedy. A medieval example of the historical type of apocalypticism is found in the twelfth-century Calabrian abbot, Joachim of Fiore.

See **Eschatology**

J.H. Charlesworth, ed., *The Old Testament Pseudepigrapha Vol. 1. Apocalyptic Literature, Testaments,* Garden City: Doubleday, 1983. J.J. Collins, *The Apocalyptic Imagination,* New York: Crossroad, 1984. J.J. Collins, ed., Apocalypse, The Morphology of a Genre, Semeia 14, Chico, Scholars, 1979. B. McGinn, *Apocalyptic Spirituality,* New York: Paulist, 1979 and London: S.P.C.K., 1980.

JOHN J. COLLINS

APOCRYPHA

The term "apocrypha" means "hidden things" but it is used to refer to those books which are found in the OT of the Latin Vulgate but not in the Hebrew Bible. Traditionally, the designation has been applied to 15 books or parts of books: 1 and 2 Esdras, 1 and 2 Maccabees, Tobit, Judith, Wisdom of Solomon, Ecclesiasticus (Ben Sira), Baruch, The Letter of Jeremiah, Prayer of Manasseh, the Additions to Esther and the Additions to Daniel (the Prayer of Azariah and the Song of the Three Young Men, Susanna, Bel and the Dragon). The latest edition of the Oxford Annotated Apocrypha also includes 3 and 4 Maccabees and Psalm 151, which are found in manuscripts of the Greek Bible. The Psalms of Solomon, which are also found in the Greek Bible, are not included in the Apocrypha.

The Roman Catholic Church accepts the Latin Apocrypha as canonical, with the exceptions of 1 and 2 Esdras and the Prayer of Manasseh, which are less firmly supported by tradition. This position was officially taken at the Council of Trent in 1546. The Reformers had not condemned the apocryphal books, but had denied that they had divine authority or could be used to establish doctrine. The status which these books had enjoyed in the early church is still a matter of dispute. The Jewish canon was closed at the end of the first century A.D. (Some scholars hold that it was already closed before the turn of the era, but the evidence is ambiguous.) The christian church inherited from Judaism a larger corpus of authoritative writings than what was included in the Hebrew canon. (Some of these, e.g., the Wisdom of Solomon, 2 Maccabees, were composed in Greek in the first case). There was uncertainty on the extent of the OT canon among second-century Christians. When Melito of Sardis, in the late second century A.D., was asked for an accurate list, he had to send to Palestine for an answer. His list was confined to the Hebrew canon, but without Esther. Tertullian, on the other hand, accepted the authority of Enoch, although he knew it was not in the Jewish canon. Clement of Alexandria cited Tobit, Ecclesiasticus and the Wisdom of Solomon as scripture. Origen accepted Susanna (as part of Daniel) and Tobit, although he knew they were not in the Hebrew Bible.

St. Jerome was committed to the *Hebraica veritas* in canon as well as in text. He called attention to the apocryphal status of the additional books and passages in his prefaces. Yet since he included these books in his translation, and since his prefaces were not always read or copied, the Western Church came to accept all books of the Vulgate as canonical. The Gelasian Decree at the end of the fifth century affirmed all except 1 and 2 Esdras and the Prayer of Manasseh. The Reformation did not lead to suppression of the Apocrypha. They were included in the King James Version of 1611, but were omitted with increasing frequency in later printings. The disputed books are sometimes referred to as "deutero-canonical." The Greek and Russian Orthodox Churches accept slightly larger canons than the Roman Catholics.

Regardless of their canonical status, the books of the Apocrypha are an important part of the religious heritage of both Christianity and Judaism. They represent a sampling of Jewish literature from the last two centuries B.C. and the first century A.D. (A more extensive sampling can be found in the category of Pseudepigrapha.) Two of the major examples of wisdom literature fall in this category—Ecclesiasticus and the Wisdom of Solomon. The latter composition is especially important as it provides an early illustration of the fusion of Hebrew faith and Greek culture which would shape the christian theological tradition. The stories of the Maccabees, Susanna and Judith have inspired operas and works of art. Columbus is said to have been inspired by a verse from 2 Esdras (6:42) which says that waters occupy one-seventh part of the earth. Most important, perhaps, is the fact that the existence of this category serves to remind us that the boundary between canonical and non-canonical literature is not a firm one and does not necessarily indicate a qualitative difference.

B. Metzger (ed.) *The Oxford Annotated Apocrypha,* New York, Oxford, 1977. G.W. Nickelsburg, *Jewish Literature Between the Bible and the Mishnah,* Philadelphia: Fortress and London: S.C.M., 1981. A.C. Sundberg, *The Old Testament of the Early Church,* Cambridge, Mass: Harvard, 1964.

JOHN J. COLLINS

APOLOGETICS

"Apology" is a formal written or oral defense of some ideas, viewpoint, religion, philosophy. Apologetics refers to that discipline of theology that is concerned with the defense of or proofs for Christianity. Whereas apologies for Christianity have existed as long as Christianity itself, apologetics as an independent theological discipline has come into existence only in modern times.

Classical Apologies

Early Church. During the second century christian theologians, called the apologists, wrote apologies for Christianity: Justin Martyr's *First and Second Apology* and *Dialogue with Trypho the Jew,* Aristides' *Apology,* Athenagoras' *Supplication for Christians* and *On the Resurrection of the Dead,* and others such as those of Quadratus and Tatian. Their apologies for Christianity followed the pattern of apologetics that Hellenistic Jews had already developed. They stressed the moral superiority and antiquity of monotheism. They applied the contemporary philosophical criticism of Greek and Roman popular myths against the religions themselves. Against the Jews, the apologists argued that Christ had fulfilled the prophecies.

In the third century Christians had to face serious intellectual criticisms of Christianity. Clement of Alexandria's *Protrepticus* and Origen's *Contra Celsum* give a defense of Christianity that appeals to Hellenistic culture and philosophy. In the West, Tertullian's *To the Pagans* and *Apology,* Lactantius' *Divine Institutes,* Minucius Felix's *Octavius,* and Arnobius' *Case against the Pagans* continue the apology for Christianity. In the fourth century, Eusebius' *Preparation of the Gospel* and *The Proof of the Gospel* respond to philosophical and historical criticisms brought against Christianity by Porphyry. Eusebius advocates a political theology and argues for the Christianization of the Roman Empire.

If Eusebius combined apologetics and political theology, Augustine's *De civitate Dei* offers a critique of political theology. The fall of Rome led to the accusation that the conversion to Christianity and refusal to give homage to the Roman gods were responsible. Since Eusebius had linked the success of Constantine and the empire with christian conversion, the charge affects such a christian political theology. Although Augustine planned the work before the fall of Rome, he answers the charge in part through an alternative political theology. The notion of the two cities underscores the transcendent eschatology of christian faith.

Medieval Church. In medieval theology, the chief apologies were directed against Islam and against Judaism. Unfortunately, the apologies against Judaism are extremely disparaging. Abelard's *A Dialogue between a Philosopher, a Jew and a Christian,* much less polemic than most, argues not so much from visible miraculous signs or from faith alone, but rather from rational defense of Christianity and of its moral superiority, especially in its ethic of charity.

Aristotle's influence within Islam (Averroes) makes him a resource to whom one could appeal. Thomas Aquinas' *Summa Contra Gentiles* (which in some manuscripts has the descriptive title (*On the Truth of the Catholic Faith against the Errors of the Unbelievers*) is often considered such an apology against

the Saracens, but it embraces a host of challenges from the scientific Greco-Arabic world.

Apology as Controversial Theology

The post-Reformation period constitutes a decisive change from the medieval apologetic because the post-reformation apologetic became a controversial theology about disputed issues of christian faith within Christianity. The Roman Catholic-Protestant controversies led to the emergence of new theological tracts. The focus was primarily on issues of church, papacy, sacraments, justification, anthropology, and theological method, especially the relation between scripture and tradition. The outstanding example is Cardinal Robert Bellarmine's *Disputations concerning the Controversies of the Christian Faith against the Heretics of this Age.*

Modern Apologetics

The fifteenth, sixteenth, and seventeenth century also give rise to apologetical treatises that do not simply focus on controversial theological issues, but become increasingly comprehensive. This comprehensiveness is a characteristic of modern apologetics and its many distinct creative developments. Some of the distinctive modern approaches are as follows:

Christianity as True Religion. Marsilio Ficino's *On Christian Religion* argues for the truth of Christianity as the true religion. His characterization of true religion influenced Abbé Pierre Charon. *The Three Truths* is primarily a response to Phillip du Plessis-Mornay's *Treatise on the Church.* These treatises influenced the shape of apologetics as integral to fundamental theology insofar as they influenced eighteenth-century apologetic defenses against Deism of religion as revealed. The division into a defense of revealed religion, christian religion, and Catholic religion becomes standard in traditional apologetics and it forms the grid of much nineteenth-century apologetics and especially of the neo-scholastic and manual handbooks of apologetics.

Distinctive Essence. Schleiermacher developed the notion of apologetics as a part of philosophical theology. It does not proceed as an *a priori* rational argument or historical argument from miracles but as the presentation of the essence or distinctive configuration of religion and of Christianity, especially Protestant Christianity. Apologetics establishes the distinctive historical mode of christian faith in relation to other religious communities, whereas polemics analyzes deviations from the historically established essence.

Similar in approach is the development of symbolics as an apologetical discipline. Johann Adam Moehler's *Symbolics*, as a prime example, presents the complete doctrinal system of Roman Catholicism and Protestantism as an organized whole expressing contrasting principles of Christianity and representing distinct visions of Christianity's essence. This apologetic replaced piece-meal philosophical and historical arguments with arguments about a distinctive essence or vision.

Foundation of Revelation. Johann Sebastian von Drey, known as the Father of the Tübingen School, sought to establish apologetics as a distinct academic discipline. His three volume *Apologetics* sought to be more than an apology, and to demonstrate the revealed foundation of Christianity. Although he first followed Schleiermacher's view of apologetics as elucidating the distinctiveness of the christian faith, his *Apologetics* developed the foundation of Christianity as a philosophy of revelation that could be correlated with history and human subjectivity.

*"New Apologetics" as Political The-*ology. The Enlightenment and French Revolution led to the development of an apologetical political theology called the "new apologetics." Abbé Felicité de Lamennais' *Essay on Indifference in Matters of Religion,* Joseph de Maistre's *On the Pope,* Juan Donoso Cortes' *Essay on Catholicism, Authority, and Order,* and Louis de Bonald defended Christianity by stressing the social and functional utility of religion. Advocating the interrelation between religious beliefs and political practice, they argued for the human need for authority, tradition, and divine revelation.

This political theology was essentially a conservative apologetic insofar as it not only argued for tradition and authority, but also for royalist and ultramontane causes. In the 1960's Johann Baptist Metz revived the conception of political theology in responding to the challenge of Marxism. This new political theology sharply contrasted with the integralism of traditional political theology. It underscored the eschatological proviso and the memory of suffering as a constant critical corrective of existing ideologies and distortions of societal institutions. It thereby provided an apologetic defense of Christianity against the charge of Marxism that religion was ideology.

Apologetics and "Method of Immanence." In a lengthy essay, "Letter on the Requirements of Contemporary Thought in the Field of Apologetics," Maurice Blondel developed what is called a "method of immanence"—a title easily open to misunderstanding. This method opposes the extrinsicism of the traditional arguments from miracles. Instead it shows a correspondence between human desire and need and the objects of faith. Although Blondel's method was viewed with some suspicion, it has significantly influenced twentieth-century Roman Catholic apologetics. Pierre Rousselot sought to show the importance of human subjectivity in the discernment of the signs and evidences of credibility. The attempt to overcome the neo-scholastic dualism between the natural and supernatural became characteristic of the theological movement in the 1950's known as *la nouvelle théologie*.

Transcendental Apologetics. Karl Rahner's *Foundations of the Christian Faith* seeks to relate the basic tenets of christian faith to human existential subjectivity. He thereby continued the apologetical direction of Blondel, Rousselot, and *la nouvelle théologie*. Rahner's conception of human nature as historically conditioned by God's salvific will (supernatural existential) avoids the criticisms that have been brought against the Blondelian approach.

Current Issues

The nature and function of apologetics stands very much open to debate. The very name "apologetics" has fallen into disuse. Nevertheless several major issues are at the center of discussion and current hermeneutical theory offers important insights for the reformulation of apologetics.

Apologetics as Internal. The truthfulness and meaning of Christianity have become questionable for many within Christianity. Individuals may have been baptized and educated as Christians, but their adherence to Christianity is often external and formal. The distance between historical scriptures and creed and contemporary culture is such that Christianity appears foreign to many. Many belong to Christianity and yet are estranged from Christianity.

If traditionally apologetics was directed toward non-believers or non-Christians, apologetics has to be reconceived today. It should seek to communicate Christianity's claims to Christians themselves. Apologetics is becoming increasingly hermeneutical insofar as its task is to so interpret the christian truth so as it make its truths meaningful and relevant to contemporary human life and practice.

Ground of Apologetics. A second issue is the basis of an apologetics. Traditionally one sought to argue for the christian faith from an independent or neutral standpoint shared by one's opponents: human reason, a particular philosophy, allegedly neutral historical arguments, etc. This approach is questionable. First, the pluralism of current world views precludes appeals to a commonly accepted philosophical basis. Second, if a neutral criterion or standard is selected, then the danger exists that a foreign or reductionistic criterion becomes the standard to measure christian beliefs rather than a standard expressing the inner logic of these beliefs themselves. Current hermeneutical theory seeks to show that the world of religious language and texts does not simply explicate experience, but opens a vision and a world that should influence and form experience.

Apologetical Demonstration. For the above reasons many argue that apologetics and systematic theology should not be separated from one another. It is not possible to argue for one's faith conviction from a neutral standpoint; instead, such arguments have to be made hermeneutically with retrospective and retroductive arguments from life practice (Fiorenza). Others, accepting the hermeneutical role of communities of discourse, prefer to emphasize the public nature of apologetical discourse (Tracy).

Apologetics and Ecumenical Dialogue. Today there is a great deal of interest in ecumenical dialogue among the diverse christian churches and with non-Christians and non-Western religions. Does ecumenical dialogue obviate apologetics? What is at stake here is the interrelation between truth and the discovery of truth. Through open conversation and dialogue one discovers truth. Such ecumenical dialogues lead diverse religions to clarify the distinctiveness of their beliefs and truth claims and to show how religions deal with the ever transcending problems and crises of human life. Thus the apologetic concern for truth is not surrendered but is opened to a mutual search and learning.

Maurice Blondel, *The Letter on Apologetics and History and Dogma*, New York: Holt 1965. Henri Bouillard, *The Logic of Faith*, New York: Sheed & Ward, 1967. Avery Dulles, *A History of Apologetics*, New York: Corpus 1971. Francis Schüssler Fiorenza, *Foundational Theology; Jesus and the Church*, New York: Crossroad, 1984. Karl Rahner, *Foundations of the Christian Faith: An Introduction to the Idea Of Christianity*, New York: Seabury 1978. Friedrich Schleiermacher, *On Religion: Speeches to the Cultured Despisers of Religion*, New York: Harper & Row, 1958.

FRANCIS SCHÜSSLER FIORENZA

APOPHATIC THEOLOGY

Negative theology, that is, theology which is so conscious that God transcends all created conceptions that it limits itself to statements about what God is not rather than making any claims to know God in himself.

See **Mysticism, Theology**

APOSTASY

The notion of apostasy entered Christianity from the OT where it referred to Israel's turning away from Yahweh. For example, Jer 2:19 reads: "Your own wickedness is punishing you, your own apostasies are rebuking you: consider carefully how evil and bitter it is for you to abandon Yahweh your God and not to stand in awe of me—it is Yahweh who speaks."

In the NT, apostasy was attributed by the Jews to those Jewish-Christians who had ceased observing the Jewish law (Acts 21:21). Since the apostolic period, apostasy has always referred to the total repudiation of the faith by one who had formerly believed (see C.I.C., c. 751).

The question of the imputation of guilt for the act of apostasy divides Catholic theologians. There are those who maintain there is never sufficient reason for one to deny the faith. Such a denial, they maintain, is always sinful because it implies a rejection of grace that is always available to one authentically seeking the truth. There are other theologians, however, who hold that whereas apostasy is always objectively sinful, one must admit the possibility of conditions existing within the mind and heart of a person which preclude the imputation of guilt. One such condition would be the degree of freedom with which one is acting.

See **Faith**

NANCY C. RING

APOSTLE

1. Concept

The Greek word *apostolos*, "someone (-thing) sent," is the nominal cognate of *apostellein*, "to send." The word had an extremely meager history in pre-christian Greek, largely unrelated to its christian meaning. It appears eighty times in the NT, in most of its books, with concentration in Paul (authentic letters twenty-eight times; deutero-Paulines seven times), and Luke (Luke six times; Acts twenty-eight times), otherwise eleven times. Related is "apostleship," four times. It is a designation for figures of crucial importance in the NT Church.

The origins of the concept are disputed. Earlier and now later study tends to see it as derivative from the commissioning convention of OT and rabbinic Judaism. The Hebrew root *slh*, "to send," rendered in the LXX as *apostellein*, is often used in the OT to express the commission of an agent sent by a principal to act in his stead. In the rabbinic period this usage developed into a formal convention involving "sent-men," as in the axiom "The-one-whom-a-man-sends [*sālîaḥ*] is like the man himself." This commissioned agent, who might act in private or institutionalized capacity, was regarded as the surrogate, the authoritative representative of the principal within the limits of the commission given. Third and fourth century christian/Roman texts translate the Hebrew term as *apostolos/apostolus*. It is conjectured that this convention was known in Jewish circles of NT times and that it provides the formal background for NT usage. Its phenomenological content would, of course, be derived from christian experience. Documentary evidence from contemporary non-christian sources is lacking, but texts from the NT itself appear to provide evidence, e.g., Jn 3:16 "nor is a messenger [*apostolos*] greater than the one who sent him"; and see the Q saying preserved by Matt 10:40 par.; 2 Cor 8:23; Phil 2:5 (Rengstorf, Roloff). Sketchy documentary evidence and phenomenological disparity of rabbinical sentiment and NT apostles led at mid-twentieth century to a denial of this theory by many. They regard apostleship as a new phenomenon generated by the new experience of Christians (Cerfaux, Klein, Müller). One of this group (Schmithals) has proposed a theory of gnostic derivation. The first position, which incorporates the significant observation of the second, is better argued. The theory of gnostic derivation has been generally rejected. (For survey, see Agnew).

2. *Range, sense, and ambiguity of NT usage*

All recognize that NT usage shows some range of meaning. All would agree that the word appears sometimes with the sense "messenger," as in the texts cited above, perhaps also in Mk 6:30; Lk 11:49, though already with christian coloration in the Pauline and synoptic texts. Some see only this and the solemn theological usage (Klein, Schmithals). Most others, probably with better reasons, maintain a range of meanings between these usages. They refer to such texts as 1 Thess 2:6; 1 Cor 4:9; 9:5; Acts 14:4, 14; and perhaps some others, where the word appears to describe or include missionary figures to whom the respective authors do not assign the title in its full sense, see also *Did.* 11:3-6. The solemn usage, "apostle of Jesus Christ," as Paul puts it, is discussed below. Hebrews 3:1 uses the word of Jesus. Though they differ in content all these uses can be seen as variations on the sending convention discussed above.

The solemn usage is very old, clearly pre-Pauline, see Gal 1:17, 19, and must have arisen in the Jerusalem community but under circumstances which can no longer be clearly traced. It is now generally agreed that the NT writers present no entirely consistent view of apostleship and, to some extent, disagree in describing it (see Schnackenburg). The major witnesses, Paul and Luke, show significant differences, though they both ascribe common factors to the apostle which should not be minimalized in a spirit of hyper-criticism.

Two major constituents appear in their descriptions. First, the apostle is one who has seen a vision of the risen Lord, so becoming his witness, see 1 Cor 9:1; 15:1-11; Gal 1:15-16; Lk 24:47-48; Acts 1:2, 7-8, 21-26. Second, the apostle has a commission from God/Christ to preach in a way fundamental to the spread of the gospel, see 1 Cor 1:1; Gal 1:1, 11-12, 15-16; Rom 1:1; and the Lukan texts cited above.

But the differences between Paul and

Luke are also obvious. Luke introduces the qualification that the apostle must have been a witness to Jesus from the earliest days of his ministry, Acts 1:21-22. This would, of course, exclude Paul and though Paul is the hero of the second half of Acts, he is only once called apostle, 14:4, 14, in what may be a semi-technical use of the term. Clearly, Paul would be unwilling to admit such a qualification. Given the facts of NT history with its contrasting theologies, respondent to different problems in different places and at different times, the disagreements on this subject are hardly surprising, nor are they problematical for a realistic view of inspiration.

It follows from what has been said that apostleship is a phenomenon of the post-resurrection period. An older scholarship traced it to the earthly Jesus on the basis of such synoptic texts as Mt 10:2; Lk 6:13. But a firmer grasp of gospel as a literary type allows for the view that synoptic usage is a retrojection of post-Easter terminology. However, many claim that the apostolic commission is anticipated in the choice and sending of the twelve (see Rengstorf, Freyne, Roloff).

3. More specific NT usage

Paul provides the most vigorous descriptions of apostleship and its activities. This description is obviously bound up with his own experience of vocation and may not always be applicable to the phenomenon in a general way. For him, apostleship is a charism and the first of the charisms, 1 Cor 12:28, 29. It consecrates solemnly for the service of the gospel in a way that recalls the vocation of the OT prophet, Gal 1:15; Rom 1:1. It is the result of a revelation from God, 1 Cor 15:8; Gal 1:16, which made Paul, the persecutor, a preacher of the gospel, 1 Cor 5:9; Gal 1:13-14; Phil 3:6. It obviously involves missionary activity but in an eminent way that has to do with the origin of the church, so that while every apostle is a missionary, not every missionary is an apostle in the fullest sense. This is the implication of Paul's claim to be apostle to the gentiles as Peter is apostle to the circumcised, Gal 2:7; Rom 1:5; 11:13. It is clear that there were those who questioned Paul's right to use the title. This is already suggested in the remarks of 1 Thess 2, becomes more explicit in 1 Cor 9, and reaches a point of intensity or even bitterness in 2 Cor 2-6; 10-13. Against this background, he is very insistent on the fact that his call is from God/Christ as contrasted to any merely human source, Gal 1:1, and the notion lies behind the whole "autobiographical" section of Gal 1-2. Against any effort to view apostleship in terms of human appearances or enthusiast manifestation, Paul stresses the suffering of the apostle as the servant of the gospel, especially in the above mentioned chapters of 2 Corinthians.

The Lukan notion of apostleship is bound up with the group designated by the evangelists as "the twelve." According to the synoptics they were chosen by Jesus from among his disciples, served as a kind of inner circle of adherents, and were at one point sent on mission by him. Synoptic literary study has shown that this group is, for the most part, named in redactional passages. But, the recollection of their choice, Mk 3:13-14 par., and the list of twelve names, repeated four times in the NT with only slight variation, Mk 3:16-19 par., appear to be solid fragments of historical tradition. There is no serious reason for doubting their choice by Jesus or, though with admittedly less solid evidence, their mission, Mk 6:7-13, 30 par. Significant in this respect is the very old pre-Pauline fragment of 1 Cor 15:3b-5. (On all of which, see Rigaux.) The tendency observable at mid-century to question their origin in the life of Jesus (Klein, Schmithals) has been generally abandoned.

The twelve become the apostles of Acts, see 1:26, and appear frequently in its first fifteen chapters. The number is obviously significant as the account of the replacement of Judas, 1:15-26, shows. It is generally agreed that, as twelve, they symbolize the continuity of salvation-history from the OT with its twelve-tribe people of God to the NT. Something of the kind is also implied in the Q saying preserved in Lk 22:30 par. There is no suggestion that James, brother of John, who died a martyr's death, Acts 12:2, be replaced. Though several among the group undertake missionary activity in Samaria and greater Judea, see Acts 8:14-25; 9:32-11:18, the twelve appear rather as a board or college seated in Jerusalem, providing a widely diversified pastoral leadership. Included in their activities are teaching, 2:42; miracle working, 2:43; witnessing, 4:33; administering the financial resources of the community, 4:35-5:2; laying on of hands, 6:6, 8:18; directing missionary activity, 8:14; and arbitrating doctrinal dispute, 15:1-33. It may be readily admitted that Luke's presentation involves theological stylizing in the interest of the unified flow of salvation history, and this may account for his reluctance to give Paul the title of apostle. But this is not adequate reason for denying apostleship to the twelve in any historical sense (Schmithals, Klein) or for ascribing their description as such to the theological inventiveness of Luke (Klein). The expression "twelve apostles" is also attested by Mt 10:2 and Rev 21:14 (perhaps by Mk 6:30; 1 Cor 15:5) which can hardly be traced to Luke. Still, beyond Peter, members of the group play no very significant role in the canonical literature and appear to have disappeared quickly from the early Christian scene. A considerable body of pseudepigraphical literature, canonical and post-canonical is connected with the group as a whole and with individual members, especially Peter, John, and Thomas.

The greetings of the deutero-Paulines all use the title in sterotyped fashion. For those of the captivity group, the apostles appear first among the charismatics (Eph 4:11), and with the NT prophets as the foundation of the church (Eph 2:20). The pastorals regard them as the source of authority vested in the developing primitive hierarchy of overseer/presbyter, deacon. This idea is carried farther in the famous text of 1 Clem 42:1-2.

The greetings of the Petrines and Jude also use the title in stereotyped fashion. So does Rev 18:20 which recalls Eph 2:20 and Rev 21:14 which have been mentioned above.

Who were the apostles?

Most scholars think that the group was closed. Paul never gives the title to the twelve in a quite unequivocal way, but most take this to be the implication of 1 Cor 15:5, and especially of Gal 1:17, 19. He clearly regards the group as more extensive than himself and the twelve, see 1 Cor 15:7 where, in a list of witnesses including himself and the twelve, he names "all the apostles." But who the others were is not clear. Texts which might imply that James, 1 Cor 15:7; Gal 1:19, or Barnabas, 1 Cor 9:6, or others Rom 16:7 are so designated turn out to be ambiguous. As noted, Luke never gives the title to Paul in an unequivocal way, and a case might be made for the notion that he restricted it to the twelve, though the argument is hardly inevitable. That the group included others than Paul and the twelve is further suggested by the fact that there were false claimants to the title, see 2 Cor 11:13; 11:5 (?); 12:11 (?); 12:11 (?); Rev 2:2

F. Agnew, "The Origin of the NT Apostle-Concept: A Review of Research" *JBL* 105 (1986) 75-96. C.K. Barrett, *The Signs of an Apostle,* Philadelphia: Fortress, 1972, London: Epworth Press, 1970. G. Klein, *Die zwölf Apostel Ursprung und Gehalt einer Idee,* FRLANT 59, Göttingen; Vandenhoeck & Ruprecht, 1961. D. Müller, et al., "Apostle,"

NIDNTT 1, 127-137. K.H. Rengstorf, *"apostolos,"* *TDNT* 1, 398-447. B. Rigaux, "The Twelve Apostles," *Concilium* (34), 5-15, 1968. J. Roloff, *Apostolat-Verkündigung-Kirche,* Gütersloh: Gerd Mohn, 1965. W. Schmithals, *The Office of Apostle in the Early Church,* Nashville: Abingdon, 1969. R. Schnackenburg, "Apostolicity-The Present Position of Studies," *One in Christ* 6 (1970), 243-273.

FRANCIS H. AGNEW, CM

THE APOSTOLIC FATHERS

"The Apostolic Fathers" is a collective term used since the seventeenth century for a disparate group of writings whose authors "came after the Apostles." These are traditionally: the letters of Ignatius of Antioch, the letter of Clement of Rome, the so-called second letter of Clement which is actually a homily and not by Clement, the "Shepherd" of Hermas, the letter of Polycarp of Smyrna as well as the account of his martyrdom, the *Didache* or Teaching of the Twelve Apostles, the letter of Pseudo-Barnabas, the fragments of Papias and, sometimes, the Letter to Diognetus which is actually an apology and more correctly should be listed under that other collective title "the Apologists."

The content of these works usually concerned problems within the church: church authority and structure; the relationship to Judaism and the interpretation of the OT; the disposition of the cases of Christians who had sinned seriously after baptism. During the more fluid period of the NT canon, some of these works, notably the letter of Pseudo-Barnabas and the "Shepherd" of Hermas were accepted in some places as part of the NT.

ROBERT B. ENO, SS

APOSTOLICITY

The four essential marks or dimensions of the church are interdependent realities which overlap one with the other. So the church can be one, holy and catholic only if it is also apostolic. Apostolicity is related to the notion of "apostle" which in the synoptics underwent a redactional process which gives no evidence that Jesus ever used the term. Apostleship is grounded on a witness to the resurrection and to Pentecost. However, the evidence is clear that Jesus did choose from among the first disciples a group of twelve (Mk 3:13 f., Mk 14:10-42, Acts 1:25-26, 1 Cor 15:5-7). Later based on reflection on the structures of the church issued from Pentecost and the activities of Paul, Luke defined an institutional apostleship, identifying the apostles and the Twelve and linking Paul and the churches founded by him among the gentiles to this fundamental institution. Paul himself spoke of his apostleship with different nuances but confirmed in the defense of his own apostleship the basic characteristics of the Twelve to which he was assimilated. But historically and critically, one cannot further identify "the apostles" and "the Twelve."

In Paul's use of the word it can be concluded that, firstly, apostles are those who are witnesses of the risen Christ, to whom the crucified Lord had revealed himself as living; and secondly, those who had been commissioned by the Lord for missionary preaching (Gal. 1:15-17; 1 Cor 9:1 f., 15:5-12). Further the choice of the Twelve is understood in the light of Jesus' eschatological message in which the Twelve signify a renewed Israel understood in relation to the consummation of the kingdom of God. The fundamental significance of the apostles for the church as expressed by Paul, the Synoptics and Acts is that the apostle is a messenger appointed by Christ (Gal 1:15, Acts 9:27, Mk 3:4; Mt 28:19) and through Christ by the Father (Mt 10:40), and therefore stands with authority in the church. He is the authorized representative of Christ and not only a witness to the crucified and risen Christ. But as an authorized ambassador of the Lord, he is also a justified sinner among sinners. The apostles as messengers, witnesses and authorized representatives of the crucified and risen Christ have primacy of place in the church (1 Cor 12:28). The church is founded on their witness and ministry. The church is "built upon the foundations of the apostles and prophets, Christ Jesus being their chief cornerstone" (Eph 2:20).

In the choice of the Twelve corresponding to the twelve tribes of Israel the eschatological dimension of apostolicity is pointed up. Just as the catholicity, this attribute has its origin in Christ, the Alpha and the Omega, the fullness of salvation communicated through the apostles in the new and eternal covenant. Apostolicity seeks to realize and serve the plenitude of salvation present in Christ. Its interior principle is the Holy Spirit who leads the church in faith to its absolute fulfillment.

Apostolicity, then, pertains to the time between the first coming of Christ and his return in glory. In this time of the church, apostolic succession, which must be understood within the broader context of apostolicity, bespeaks a relationship between the apostles and the episcopacy. On the one hand, the apostles witnessed the resurrection, were given authority to govern the churches they founded and were given the charism through which they constituted a normative tradition. On the other hand, the episcopacy is subject to this Tradition but as a college has the fullness of authority over the universal church, always in relation to the bishop of Rome as head, whenever the college formally teaches truth pertaining to the deposit of revelation. Apostleship and the episcopacy both have a common mission: the authority to communicate the Lord Jesus, Source of grace and truth. With the disappearance of the apostles, bishops actualize the presence of the apostolic ministry. "Apostolic succession entails a confrontation of the church with the testimony of the apostles, in a living continuation of the apostolic ministries, with all their various forms of expression" (Küng).

Apostolic succession does not signify the simple, uninterrupted occupation of an episcopal seat because apostolic succession as such resides in the college of bishops and can be actualized anew wherever such is needed in the concrete situation, whether that be in establishing new dioceses or filling vacancies. Nor does it involve a pure fact of sacramental validity, but rather an identity of function based on faith in the service of a community. This responsibility for a community demands communion with the whole church which is realized in each local church. As Congar states in reflecting on the words of Cyprian: "Communion with the whole church, through communion with the undivided episcopate which each realizes wholly in the communion of the college, just as each church is church in the communion of the *Catholica,* is the guarantee that a particular bishop is approved and ordained by God." This includes communion with the center, the bishop of Rome, who is a condition and criterion of communion.

Apostolic succession is constituted as apostolicity by the safeguarding of teachings handed down from the apostles. The essential element in apostolic succession is unity of mission and the core of mission is unanimity in teaching. This is so because the church is essentially the assembly of the faithful whose identity consists in a oneness in faith. The teaching of bishops is a guide for the faithful. But their teaching is conditioned by its fidelity to the Tradition of the apostles living and actualized in history by the Holy Spirit. Apostolicity in ministry and apostolicity in doctrine condition and guarantee one another.

The teaching of Vatican II on the church as the people of God has opened up a significant dimension of apostolicity in recognizing more clearly that the whole church is apostolic and that in a certain sense the laity too are successors of the apostles: "The Spirit is for the Church and for each and every believer, the principle of their union and unity in the teaching of the apostles and fellowship, in the breaking of the bread and in prayer" (L.G. 13). The mission of spreading the Gospel is confided to the whole church in which the laity has its responsibility (D.V. 10).

The whole church as the people of God is the universal sacrament of salvation. The apostolicity of the whole church is realized in an identity of faith and in the communication of this faith. This is true both for the church as a whole and for an apostolicity of ministry which cannot exist without this element. Universal apostolicity is fundamentally apostolicity of faith but it also includes such elements as service, witness, suffering and struggle. Apostolic succession in the technical sense must be placed within the context of this universal apostolicity which represents a communion with the apostles, and with and through them with the Father and Christ. The Holy Spirit is the principle of this communion (2 Cor 13:13) and "to each is given the manifestation of the Spirit for the common good" (1 Cor 12:7). The Holy Spirit keeps the church faithful to the apostles and to the structures of the new covenant and enables it to act with indefectibility so that in an ultimate sense error will not prevail (Mt 16:18).

Hans Küng, *The Church,*, New York: Sheed and Ward, 1967.

TIMOTHY MACDONALD

APPROPRIATION

The attribution to a single divine Person of attributes or activities that are common to all three Persons of the Trinity, as, for example, omnipotence or justice to the Father, wisdom to the Son, love to the Holy Spirit. Such attribution is quite common in the scriptures, tradition, and worship. The insistence of the Catholic tradition that all activities of God towards the world are common to all three Persons represents a concern to avoid turning belief in the Trinity into Tritheism.

See **God, Trinity**

ARCHITECTURE, CHURCH

The scope of this study is limited to post-World War II Roman Catholic churches in the United States. There are four periods to be considered: preconciliar influences, conciliar legislation, the development of national guidelines and current trends.

Preconciliar Influences

Prior to the Second World War, Roman Catholic churches throughout the United States imitated historical forms such as gothic, romanesque or colonial. At the end of the war the reconstruction of Germany became a significant influence on American building. In 1947 the German bishops published "Guiding Principles for Designing and Building a Church in the Spirit of the Roman Liturgy." This document advocated the ancient Byzantine plan for churches which made the place for liturgy part of a wider ecclesial complex with education, hospice, administration etc. Thus the worship space was not isolated from other church functions. The ideal liturgical space was the Constantinian basilica with a centrally located altar, lectern and presiding platform.

Two factors made this document important: it took a functional approach to the design of churches based on the celebration of the eucharist, and it did not restrict the design to classical forms but allowed technology to determine the structure.

This functional approach brought an end to the long period of historic imitations. One of the first buildings following these guidelines was St. John's Abbey Church (1954) (Collegeville, Minnesota). It was designed by Marcel Breuer, a German architect from the Bauhaus. The building is constructed of poured concrete and natural materials with exposed folded construction. Its design is an enclosure for the assembly as it gathers around the word and altar.

The next major architectural influence was the publication of research on protoChristian house churches. Although the research had been done thirty years before, it was not until Fredric Debuyst published "Modern Architecture and Christian Celebration" (1968) that the house church had an impact on design. His study suggested that the Constantinian basilica should not be the model but rather the house church. While Debuyst's approach did not change the emphasis on functional design or the idea that the worship space was part of a larger complex; it changed a sense of scale.

These two publications began to challenge assumptions about what a church should look like and how it should relate to its local environment. Previously many Roman Churches were monuments, now they were challenged to become part of their environment in service of local needs.

The Second Vatican Council

With the publication of the "Constitution on the Sacred Liturgy"(Sacrosanctum Concilium, 3 Dec 1963) a formal mandate to revise the Roman liturgy was endorsed.

The Constitution called for a restructuring of the rites to express more profoundly the mysteries which they celebrated. Liturgical values gave form and direction to the architectural development which followed the Council.

The Constitution devotes chapter seven to sacred art and sacred furnishings. Although the term "sacred" is not defined, article 122 speaks about art as oriented towards the infinite beauty of God; this is a classical approach to beauty. Two criteria are established for art: it should be worthy and serve the dignity of worship. With these the Council advocated true quality and appropriate design.

The Constitution acknowledges that the church has not accepted any particular style (S.C. 123) but supports the natural talents of the peoples of various regions. It also suggests (128) that architecture should be adapted to regional aesthetics. Such a direction would allow a truly indigenous architecture to evolve based in sound liturgical practice (S.C. 124).

The General Instruction on the Roman Missal (1970) describes the central focuses of liturgy. Paramount in the placement of any furnishing is the assembly's participation (S.C. 124; G.I.R.M. 257ff). Church design starts with the assembly not the sanctuary. There are also various levels of priority in arranging liturgical furnishings. The altar, lectern and presiding chair are central. There is also concern for the proper placement of ministers, especially the choir, which takes on a greater role of supporting the assembly's song and sharing in the fundamental action of liturgy.

The baptistry and chapel of reservation

are important although secondary considerations. Finally art and devotional images must contribute rather than distract from the liturgical action (cf. G.I.R.M. 259, 271, 272, 276, 278, 279).

The conciliar and post-conciliar decrees establish a pattern for and principles of church design rather than demand rigid stylistic uniformity.

The Development of National Guidelines

The council directed competent territorial authorities to establish guidelines for the building of churches. Bishops were encouraged to monitor and support artists (S.C. 129). Ireland was the first country to establish such guidelines when it published the "Building and Reorganization of Churches: The Pastoral Directory"(1972). In addition to a care for new construction, this directory established norms for preserving truly historic or artistic spaces. Its lasting value, however, comes in its recognition that the church stands in the midst of a society which is still struggling for redemption. The guidelines call for an authentic sense of poverty in which everything should be true to its material and form, but also representative of the church's detachment from wealth (Introduction). This document was the immediate precursor of the American guidelines.

In 1978 the Bishops' Committee on the Liturgy (a committee of the National Conference of Catholic Bishops) published "Environment and Art in Catholic Worship." The document seeks to bridge the tension between transcendence and hospitality (11, 12), between historical form and contemporary expression, between tradition and vision.

"Architecture," the document states, "responds to the demands of liturgy "(cf. G.I.R.M. 254). Whatever the style or type, no art has a right to a place in liturgical celebration if it is not of high quality and it is not appropriate (12).

The human condition makes other demands: "When the assembly gathers with its own varied backgrounds, there is a commonness demanded which stems from our human condition. The commonality here seeks the best which people can bring together rather than what is compromised or less noble" (32).

Current Trends

During the mid 1970's architectural design met two challenges: to understand multifunctional spaces and to adapt older buildings to meet conciliar values. In the mid-1970's many multipurpose churches were built. Their success depended on the care with which additional activities were defined. Where compatible activities took place, the design had integrity. The tendency toward flexible furnishing still continues, although the totally multifunctional church has begun to decline.

The second challenge of the 1970's was the renovation of classical forms to meet contemporary liturgical needs. The primary goal of renovation was to make the assembly an integral part of the celebration of liturgy while at the same time respecting the architectural integrity. These projects often involved the simplification of spaces, a refinement of the architectural form as well as a highlighting of natural elements such as exposed trusses and stonework. Also during the 1970's there was a growing secular interest in the restoration of the cities. Where such secular interests occurred, they helped define the parameters for church renovation and helped develop guidelines for preserving the architectural form. Among the positive effects of this movement was the insistence on considering all factors in restoration, not merely interior perspectives. Landscape architecture, exterior additions and interior spaces became part of comprehensive planning.

Accompanying the secular interest in renovation and preservation was the broadening of architectural design. The early 1980's marked the decline of the International Style which had dominated architectural design since World War II. Architects began to explore classical forms with a new sense of scale, circulation, materials, and so on. This development widened design possibilities for church architecture.

Although its impact is not yet clear, wider design options in the hands of gifted architects will yield a rich variety of architectural forms; it may also be one step toward indigenous architectural expression.

Conclusion

The conciliar legislation and post-conciliar guidelines have clearly indicated that churches are more than monuments; they are places where the church lives, grows, prays and hopes, finds challenge and responds to the cry of the poor (Rite of Dedication of a Church and Altar, 62). No future direction will be authentic unless these values remain an inherent part of planning. Ultimately the success of any building can only be measured by its authentic representation of the church. Form, materials and space all serve the household of the church.

See **Dedication of a Church, Liturgy**

JAMES NOTEBAART

ARIANISM

A set of beliefs, originating with the Alexandrian presbyter Arius (d. 336), which so stressed the unity and transcendence of God that Christ could not be considered to be the Son of God except in some subordinate and inferior sense. The Son was not the same in substance as the Father and "there was a time when the Son was not." Arius's views were condemned by the Council of Nicaea which proposed a Creed in which is asserted that Christ is "true God from true God," "of the same substance (*homoousios*) as the Father." Despite this condemnation, Arianism enjoyed powerful support throughout the fourth century, much of whose theological debate was taken up with the dispute between the defenders of Nicaea and several forms of Arianism, which ranged from the Anomeans, who maintained that the Son is unlike the Father, through the Homoeans, who held that he is similar to the Father, to the Homoiousians, who taught that he was of like substance to the Father.

See **Jesus Christ; Nicaea, Council of**

ARISTOTELIANISM

Aristotelian doctrines have been commonplaces in Western learning since the first centuries of Christianity and some of these doctrines figure already in early patristic writings, though they have been much less studied than the Platonic borrowings. To survey all the appearances of Aristotelianism in theology would be to recount very nearly the whole history of theology. What is more useful is to distinguish the various layers of Aristotelianism and their different entries especially into the development of Latin theology.

The most coherent influence of Aristotle on patristic authors came through the logical works. This reflected the neo-Platonic use of Aristotle, who was regarded as a good guide for the preparatory studies within the hierarchy of knowledge. It was also the logical works that were first translated into Latin during the fourth and early fifth centuries. Other Aristotelian doctrines were carried in philosophical and medical teaching, but were most often conflated with their later elaborations or the teaching of other schools. The same imbalance was preserved in Boethius' decisive mediation of Aristotle to the Latin West (c. 500). Boethius made his own the neo-Platonic ideal of reconciling Plato and Aristotle, but his translations into Latin and his commentaries cover in fact only the logical works. Moreover, some of these translations never seem to have been read, while others effectively passed out of sight until the twelfth century, so that only a portion of the logic passed into the early medieval West. Of course, Aristotle was read more nearly whole in Byzantium, where there was something of an Aristotelian renaissance in the ninth century; he had been studied with growing interest in Islamic centers since the late eighth century. Both Byzantine and Arabic writers elaborated the Aristotelianisms that were to reenter the West. Important Byzantine uses of Aristotle would come in Nemesius of Emessa (c400-450) and John Damascene (+c753); the most famous of the Arabic Aristotelians were Avicenna (980-1037) and Averroes (1126-1198).

Beginning with the second quarter of the twelfth century, the forgotten works of the logic recaptured Latin attention, in part because of new translations from the Greek at Italian centers. They contributed greatly not only to the development of logical theory, but to the reformulation of the techniques and presuppositions of learning. By mid-century, the works of Aristotelian physics, biology, and metaphysics made their first appearance in Latin versions taken from the Greek. At the same time, the immense erudition of Arabic Aristotelianism was being rendered into Latin by translators at Toledo and other Spanish centers. Some parts of this learning can be found in twelfth-century encyclopedias or physical and medical texts. But the work of translating Aristotle and his Arabic commentators carried on to the middle of the thirteenth century, while translations of Aristotelian materials from the Greek lasted for several decades beyond that. The reflective appropriation of so much material would also take decades and would not happen without conflict.

The most famous conflicts occurred in the thirteenth century at the new "universities" of Paris and Oxford. The first stage occurred at Paris during the period 1210-1235. In 1210, the provincial council of Sens prohibited public or private lecturing at Paris on the Aristotelian books "of natural philosophy." The prohibition was reiterated in 1215 by the papal legate and augmented to cover the *Metaphysics*. The motive for the condemnation seems to be the suspicion that the new Aristotelian works had contributed to certain pantheistic and materialistic heresies. In 1231, the pope appointed a committee to examine and correct the censured Aristotelian works. The committee never completed its task and the prohibited books found their way into official university curricula by mid-century. The second and much fiercer stage in the conflict came in the years 1270-1285 at Paris and Oxford. In 1270, the bishop of Paris condemned a list of propositions drawn from a contentiously literal reading of Aristotle on the soul, the cosmos, and the divine. The same bishop condemned in 1277 a much longer list of some 219 propositions. This second condemnation was matched at Oxford. The motives behind these condemnations are disputed. They arose not only from general apprehensions about the theological use of Aristotle, but from competing traditions of Aristotelian interpretation, not to speak of particular abuses of teaching authority in the faculty of Arts.

Some historians have argued that the condemnations had a chilling effect on theological speculation, and it may well be true that they served to make later thinkers more careful about unreflective appropriations of Aristotle. But it must immediately be added that late thirteenth- and fourteenth-century Aristotelianisms were richly varied and that particular events at Paris and Oxford could neither capture nor control the whole of it. Thus, for example, the northern Italian universities had already begun to develop a characteristic Aristotelianism much more engaged with Averroes and with the physical or biological treatises. Again, the tradition of Albertists at Cologne offered a syncretistic Aristotelianism close to the neo-Platonizing tendencies in Avicenna.

The complexities of theological Aristotelianism are only compounded by the Renaissance. There is, first, a humanist assault on the mingling of Aristotelian philosophy with the Gospel. Second, there comes a philological drive towards the purer representation of original Aristotelianism, with philosophical consequences in Pomponazzi and Zabarella. Finally, the whole use of Aristotle felt increasingly the blows of modern physics and modern philosophy. So far as the language of Latin Aristotelianism had been permanently embedded in Tridentine theology and its various elaborations, the Church seemed increasingly the defender of an untenable philosophy. This charge was to spur the development of nineteenth-century neo-Thomism and its attempts to be reconciled with modern science.

See Theology

Paul Moraux, D'Aristote à Bessarion: Trois exposés sur l'histoire et la transmission de l'aristotèlisme grec, Quebec: Universitè Laval, 1970. Bernard G. Dod, "Aristoteles latinus," In Cambridge History of Later Medieval Philosophy, ed. Norman Kretzmann et al., Cambridge: Cambridge University Press, 1982, 45-79. Fernand van Steenberghen, Thomas Aquinas and Radical Aristotelianism, Washington: Catholic University of America Press, 1980. Charles B. Schmitt, Aristotle and the Renaissance, Cambridge, MA: Oberlin College/ Harvard University Press, 1983.

MARK D. JORDAN

ART

Art is defined as the application of skill, dexterity, knowledge, and taste to the aesthetic expression of beauty, feeling, and emotion through the media of color and form. The work of art is a product of the human intellect and imagination. For the purposes of this entry, art will be discussed in general terms. An in-depth discussion of the role of the arts (architecture, dance, drama, manuscript illumination, music, painting, poetry, prose, sculpture, stained glass, and textiles) in the church is not possible here. However, their intrinisic importance in the history and development of the church is recognized.

Throughout the history of the church, art has manifested itself in the faith development and life of christian believers. Art has functioned in several ways throughout this history: symbolic, didactic, devotional, decorative, or a combination thereof. When the images in a work of art can be said to engage and/or transform the viewer through a minimal use of forms or in a cryptic fashion, that art may be called symbolic, like the images in the catacombs. Where the visual images relate a narrative or an event in an edifying manner, the art is didactic like Leonardo's Last Supper (1495-8). When the imagery leads the viewer into prayer, religious experience, or spiritual engagement, the work of art is devotional like Michelangelo's Vatican Pieta (1497). When the visual images are pleasing to the viewer's aesthetic sensibilities but otherwise incomprehensible because of their abstract or geometric nature, the artwork is decorative like the calligraphic lettering of medieval manuscripts.

Historical Overview: Art and the Church

From its very beginning, the relationship between art and the church has been a focus of action and controversy. The eventual acceptance and intrinsic role of art in the early church assisted in the differentiation of Christianity from Judaism. The initial discussion of the role and purpose of art in Christianity revolved around the Hebraic injunction against images and the constant threat of idolatry in religious worship. In several documents of the early church fathers, we find the problem of images dealt with from the two foundations of Christianity: the Hebraic and the Greco-Hellenistic traditions. In his eulogy for Theodore the Martyr, Gregory of Nyssa recognized that the beauty of the places of worship is an element of great importance to religious experience.

The early church recognized the importance of the visual not only as a prime modality of human and faith development, but as a vehicle for religious education. The early church's attitude towards art might best be described as receptive, and one which led to a mutually beneficial relationship. Artistic images were eventually interpreted as visually narrating events in order to edify the soul of the observer with examples, not as presenting divinity directly (as this would have been idolatry). Thus one became initiated into and nurtured in the christian faith not simply by the word, but through the eyes and the human sensibilities aroused and pleased by visual images.

However, the history of the role of art in Christianity has never been simple, clear, or consistent. As the christological and liturgical controversies of the fourth through the eighth centuries brought about creedal and doctrinal definition, the role of images was at the center of the discussion. For images were to visually narrate events like the nativity or the crucifixion in an appropriate and acceptable manner for theologians and the laity alike. If the doctrinal definition of an event was unclear or subject to controversy, then how was the artist to fashion a visual image, or which image was the artist to make? The power of the visual image gave art a crucial role in the formative period of Christianity.

The iconoclastic controversies of the eighth and ninth centuries were the most critical period for art. At the heart of these tensions were the dialectical foundations of the christian tradition: the Hebraic injunction against images and the Greco-Hellenistic appreciation of the beautiful. The added element in the discussion was the emerging influence of Islam, especially its ban against veneration of images. These controversies which disrupted the church, eventually were resolved by the Second Council of Nicaea (787) and an Eastern Church Synod of 843 in which the distinction between idols and images made by John Damascene was accepted in conjunction with regulations as to the choice of subject and style of execution of visual images. As a result, the canonical role of the visual was clearly stated and restored within the daily life of the church. However, the "image-destroying" tendency within Christianity would re-surface sporadically throughout the history of the church.

During the medieval period, the visual arts were nurtured and flourished in their relationship to and with the church. This was the "Age of Cathedrals" which were simultaneously the cultural, economic, political, religious, and social centers of cities. Visual modality played a major role in the medieval christian theology of such figures as Bernard of Clairvaux, Bonaventure, and Abbé Suger. It is significant to note that the development of major pilgrimage churches and the Black Plague gave rise to a christian devotionalism which found a helpmate in the visual arts such as the didactic visual narratives that adorned the walls of a cathedral, the mystical piety of devotional images, and the glorious enameled cases which preserved treasured pilgrimage relics. In terms of the arts, the medieval synthesis reflects the most complete integration of the arts when architecture, dance, drama, music, painting, poetry, sculpture, and textile arts all worked in unison to produce aesthetic settings that opened the way to religious experience. During the medieval period, all art was created "for the greater glory of God." In medieval Europe, God and therefore Christianity was the center around which the world revolved. Art was interpreted by christian theologians like Thomas Aquinas as a handmaiden of theology.

With the development of the Renaissance in fifteenth-century Italy, the center of the world began to shift away from God to the human person, and as a result the role of art was no longer that of a handmaiden. During the Renaissance the arts flourished and many of the finest works of Renaissance art were created for the church, such as Michelangelo's *Sistine Ceiling* (1508-1513). However, the revival of classical Greek and Roman philosophy led to a revival of interest in classical art and mythology. The styles and themes of the visual arts changed dramatically, and even much religious art created for the church was criticized as being too "humanistic" or "secular" or "pagan," and therefore not christian. As an example of this tendency within Renaissance art consider Michelangelo's *David* (1504), which is as much a study in the beauty of the human body as it is a representation of a scriptural story. The church was both benefactor of these developments in the arts through the patronage and support of Julius II (1443-1513), and critic through the sermons and writings of Savonarola (1452-1498). The medieval synthesis was shattered in the Renaissance, and a new way of understanding the role of art in the church emerged.

Among the causes of the Reformation was hostility to the Italian Renaissance and its arts, The celebration of beauty in nature and the human body which the Renaissance fostered and introduced into christian worship was incompatible with the Reformers' emphasis on original sin and human finitude. The Reformers also sought a purification of the church, and the mediation of visual images in liturgical worship and devotional piety was seen as a hindrance to direct contact with God. Again, the Hebraic fear of images resurfaced. The Reformers' rejection of images "cleansed" the walls of their churches, changed the role of art and artist in their society, and led to the emphasis in liturgical worship on the Word. Therefore, music and poetry flourished in the Protestant traditions and their liturgical worship just as they had done in the Hebraic tradition.

The Counter Reformation Church responded to the Reformers' "image smashing" by defending and re-defining the role of art in the christian faith. In the Twenty-fifth Session of the Council of Trent (December 3, 1563), a decree was promulgated with the official rulings concerning liturgical art. This decree had both positive and negative effects upon the future of the visual arts in the church. It is important to note that the next official documents issued on the role and purpose of art in the church would be in the middle of the twentieth century.

The Decree of the Council of Trent indicated that images were to be created by christian artists and placed in the church for didactic purposes. This type of liturgical art had two functions: first as a visual narration through images whose significance lay not in themselves but in the event they depicted; and, secondly, as instruction in the articles of faith through images whose meaning lay outside of themselves. Thus, the intrinsic value of the work of art as art was negated. The decree also listed a series of criteria for art appropriate to a religious environment, for example, the use of the nude human figure was banned, and many Renaissance masterworks were "corrected" by Baroque artists. On a more positive note, it must be recognized that the Counter Reformation gave rise to a revival of christian symbolism in the arts. In point of fact, a new christian iconography developed as a visual expression and defense of the teachings of the Church of Rome, most especially of those teachings criticized by the Reformers such as the seven corporal works of mercy, the sacrament of penance, and specific images of the Virgin Mary.

Until the middle of the twentieth century, the role of art in the church remained confined to the guidelines of the Tridentine Decree. There was not much room for artistic creativity to flourish in terms of religious art and/or commissions. As a result from the Baroque period until the 1940's and 1950's, the finest artists created art for patrons others than the church. And the art which abounded within the church for this two hundred year period might best be categorized as sentimental and imitative.

Art and the Church in the Twentieth Century

In his encyclical, *Mediator Dei* (1947), Pius XII urged a qualified acceptance of the modern arts within the church. The artists needed to steer a middle course between the exaggerations of contemporary realism and symbolism, and traditional christian art. The building and decoration of several "modern" churches in France such as Notre-Dame-du-Toute-Grace at Assy, Notre-Dame-du-Haut at Ronchamp, and the Chapel of the Rosary at Vence, stirred a controversy within the church. In 1952, the Supreme Congregation of the Holy Office issued the *Instructio de arte sacra* which summarized existing laws, and gave direction on the building of churches and their ornamentation, but did not set styles for art. Nevertheless, this Instruc-

tion was a retreat to the Tridentine strictures and guidelines.

The role of art in the church was reviewed by the Second Vatican Council. The Council's document on the church and culture, *Gaudium et Spes,* issued in 1965, opened the door for the acceptance of "modern" art in the church. The celebration of a Special Mass for Artists on May 7, 1964 by Paul VI was a singular event in the church's history. In his sermon, "The Friendship of Artists and the Church," the Pope called for a renewal and revival of the Renaissance relationship between artists and the church. In 1973, Paul VI established the Museum of Modern Art in the Vatican Museums with the gift of his own personal collection of twentieth century art. The Bishops' Committee on the Liturgy issued *Environment and Art in Catholic Worship* in 1978 which established a series of guidelines for art in the worship environment and a receptive attitude towards contemporary art.

The current discussion and role of the arts in the church has reached an impasse. The focus of the discussion has shifted away from the creative dialogue urged by Paul VI to one which features a pragmatic and an ethical dimension. The pragmatic questions of decoration and/or redecoration of the worship environment are based upon a nostalgia for pre-Vatican II representational arts which were comfortable to the eye and non-threatening to the religious psyche. The ethical issue revolves around the appropriateness of both the cost and the aesthetic pleasures of the worship environment in light of the plight of mass suffering and starvation in the modern world. The fundamental issues of the role and purpose of the arts in the church, or the development of an aesthetic understanding within the church community have retreated once again from the forefront of the discussion and contemporary activity.

Jan Dillenberger, *Style and Content in Christian Art*, New York: Crossroad Publishing, 1986 [1965]. Walter Lowrie, *Art in the Early Church*, New York: Norton, 1969 [1947]. Emile Male, *Religious Art from the Twelfth to the Eighteenth Centuries*, Princeton: Princeton University Press, 1982 [1949]. Margaret R. Miles, *Image as Insight: Visual Understanding in Western Christianity and Secular Culture*, Boston: Beacon Press, 1985. Pie-Raymond Regamey, *Religious Arts in the Twentieth Century*, New York: Herder and Herder, 1963.

DIANE APOSTOLOS-CAPPADONA

ASCENSION OF CHRIST

The ascension is primarily a metaphor, reflecting an ancient and psychically deep-seated cosmology, used to express the real transcendent destiny of Jesus. It also serves to explain the paradoxical character of the present relationship between Jesus and his church, his supremacy over the created universe, his sending of the Holy Spirit, his role as revealer, his heavenly priesthood and the expectation of his second coming or parousia. Being the ascension of the man Jesus, it is also the basis of the hope of all humankind.

Jesus' Transcendent Destiny

According to the OT, heaven is the inaccessible private home of God, a symbol of his transcendence (Isa 66:1; Ps 115:16). For humans even to aspire to scale its heights is consummate arrogance (Gen 11:4ff), although, by God's gift, chosen ones: Enoch (Gen 5:24; Sir 44:16; 49:14) and Elijah (2 Kgs 2:11; Sir 48:12; 1 Macc 2:58) are "taken up" to be with God.

Implicit in all of the NT references to Jesus' ascension, together with those concerning his "elevation," his "glorification" and his session at God's "right hand," is the affirmation that he—the one who died on the cross—is now not merely alive with a life which he enjoyed before his death but is also in the possession of an entirely new kind of existence—with God.

Thus while the metaphor of resurrection expresses the reality of Jesus' triumph over death and the identity between the Risen Lord and Jesus, that of ascension brings out the God-ward or divine aspect of Jesus' destiny. The believing reader of Lk 24:50-52; Acts 1:6-11 and Mk 16:19 is left in no doubt that Jesus is now in God's presence. The account in Acts, coming just after the mention of Jesus' having "presented himself alive after his passion" (1:3), expresses very pointedly the transcendent nature of the end of Jesus' suffering and death.

Jesus Absent From and Present to His Church

The accounts of Jesus' ascension (Lk 24:0-52; Acts 1:6-11 and Mk 16:19) explain why the appearances of the risen Jesus ceased: they came to an end because Jesus, finally, entered into a new kind of existence. Thus, even if Jesus appears to be absent from his church, in one sense, he is, in fact, more profoundly and intimately present to the church, in another sense. For he is now in "heaven" with God—in the heaven which, according to the biblical tradition, is a symbol not only of God's transcendence and inaccessibility but also of God's omnipresence. Paradoxically, being in heaven with God, Jesus is also present in the world in the way that God is present. The words of the risen Jesus to Mary Magdalen (Jn 20:17) pinpoint this paradoxical character of his ascension.

The Supremacy of Jesus over the Created Universe

The image of Jesus having ascended "into the heavens" explains why Jesus is now at God's "right hand" and, therefore, lays claim to a unique messiahship (Acts 2:34-35). Jesus' ascension is a revelation of his status as Lord and Christ. Moreover, through his ascension above creation and his entry into heaven, he has achieved dominion over the whole of this creation (Eph 1:20-23; 4:8-10), filling the whole universe with his presence. Having ascended into heaven and being seated at God's "right hand," he reigns supreme over all things, thus accomplishing the idea of both Pss 8:6 and 110:1.

The Sending of the Holy Spirit

According to Acts, Jesus' ascension is the prelude to his sending of the Holy Spirit upon his disciples at the feast of Pentecost (Acts 1:4, 8; 2:1-4, 33). The mediator of the New Covenant, Jesus has ascended not a mere mountain but that which the mountain represents—heaven—and from there he has "poured out" (Acts 2:33) the Holy Spirit, the principle of the New Covenant.

Jesus the Heavenly Revealer

It is precisely because Jesus, having ascended into heaven and now being with God, is in heaven that he is able to reveal "heavenly things" (Jn 3:12-15; 6:62; 1:18). For the author of the Fourth Gospel, Jesus' elevation on the cross is the sign of his heavenly exaltation, the climax of a revelation which affords eternal life to all those who receive it (Jn 3:14; 8:28; 12:32, 34).

Jesus the Heavenly High Priest

The Letter to the Hebrews exploits the image of Jesus' ascension to demonstrate that the faithful have a high priest who has penetrated not the mere material "holy of holies" of the Jerusalem temple but that "sanctuary" of which the temple was but a symbol: heaven itself (Heb 4:14; 6:19; 9:24). Moreover, being in heaven, Jesus—the heavenly advocate (1 Jn 2:1)—continually intercedes for his faithful (Heb 7:25; 9:24; Rom 8:34).

The Parousia of the Heavenly Jesus

Jesus' present and active existence with God in heaven is the guarantee that he can and will "come again" to accomplish fully the history of salvation. The Jesus who will return at the end of time is the same Jesus who "was taken up into heaven"—the exalted, glorified, heavenly Jesus (Acts 1:11; 3:21; 1 Thess 1:10; 4:16; 2 Thess 1:7; Rev 1:7). It is through his ascension that he has become the heavenly Son of Man and, as such, is ready to bring God's plan for creation to an end.

Jesus' Ascension and Human Destiny

Jesus' ascension into heaven reveals the destiny which God intends for the rest of humankind. The faithful know that their true country is a heavenly one (Heb 11:16), that their homeland is heaven itself (Phil 4:20). Moreover, united with their exalted Lord through faith and baptism, they are encouraged to look beyond this present life to their final destiny which is to appear with Christ in glory.

Conclusion

"He ascended into heaven"—the reality of Jesus' ascension into heaven is a truth which provides the key to an understanding of many different aspects of our faith, ranging from the affirmation of Jesus' own destiny to the revelation of a spirituality and a morality which correspond to this affirmation in the lives of those who make it.

P. Benoit, "The Ascension," in: Jesus and the Gospel vol. I, London, 1973, pp. 209-253. J.G. Davies, He Ascended into Heaven. A Study in the History of Doctrine, New York, 1958. B.M. Metzger, "The Meaning of Christ's Ascension," in: Search the Scriptures, New Testament Studies in Honor of Raimond T. Stamm, Gettysburgh Theological Studies 3, Leiden, 1969, pp. 118-128. S.G. Wilson, "The Ascension: A Critique and an Interpretation." ZNW 59, 1968: pp. 269-281.

LIONEL SWAIN

ASCETICISM

This article will describe christian asceticism, establish its foundation, and survey its practice.

Christian asceticism

The christian life has two aspects, one ascetical, the other mystical. Both terms can describe the whole spiritual journey, but usually they are used in a restrictive sense. The word "ascetical" comes from the Greek *askesis,* which means exercise, training, discipline. Accordingly, ascetical life is either the whole project of appropriating the divine gift of grace or, more frequently, the work of purification. Ascetical practices are methods and programs designed to restrain the influence of sin and maximize union with God. The whole work is under grace, and grace is the mystical element of christian life. Mysticism is the experience of grace, especially those acts which are consciously beyond ordinary initiative and control, such as contemplation or miraculous powers.

Christian life is radically and ultimately mystical. But it is received and fostered in the personal engagement and struggle of asceticism. Ascetical practices are human strategies for spiritual living. They have elements of effort and method, deprivation, and voluntary suffering. Asceticism addresses the effects and vagaries of sin, which in turn are the source of further sins. Concupiscence in both blatant and subtle forms as well as systemic sin that infects social reality are encountered in the world, the flesh and the devil. The ensuing struggle involves effort and pain, though the difficulty or suffering do not determine the spiritual value of the enterprise. Effective asceticism is the work of grace, not heroic will power or high tolerance of pain. Salutary collaboration with God is often an experience of human weakness, poverty, and defeat after the manner of the cross of Jesus.

Foundations

Christian asceticism is concerned with obstacles to the life of grace, but it is not negative in the same way as classical non-christian systems like Stoicism or Buddhism. Historically certain christian movements have looked deceptively like these and similar self-denying or world-denying philosophies and religions. But

biblical Christianity is not dualistic, as if the body or the world were evil and only the immaterial spiritual soul were good. The world that is the enemy is the flawed world in function of sin as portrayed in John's gospel. The flesh is not the human body or sexuality as such, but the human person acting apart from grace; the spirit is that same person under the Holy Spirit. The devil is "the enemy of human nature" (Ignatius of Loyola).

Christian asceticism, therefore, is not anti-human, or anti-body or anti-world, though these qualities have sometimes surfaced in history. Such spiritual movements take these mistaken directions from alien sources and sometimes go to the extreme of heresy, as with Gnosticism, Montanism, or Manichaeism. The primary reason for asceticism is not the natural constitution of the world, but the kingdom, the call to transcendence, the demands of the eschatological reality of the gospel. Sin is the refusal of this divine offer. Once it has entered the scene, the infection spreads to every level of human life; there is progressive fragmentation and division in individuals, society, and the world itself. Christ alone is the antidote; he is savior and redeemer. But he calls human beings to collaborate with him and the cooperation is christian asceticism. Sometimes the strategy is to fight, sometimes flight, and contemporary wisdom emphasizes that all potential obstacles, whether from within, like concupiscence or pride, or from without, like sinful social structures or demonic forces, must be recognized and dealt with in whatever way is wise and prudent.

The climate in the post-Vatican II church is incarnational, not apocalyptic or excessively eschatological. The goodness of things rather than the transitory quality of life or the pervasive presence of sin is emphasized. Today's asceticism looks to total, human development, the human and the divine coinciding; the goal is the integration of all life, personal and social, in Christ Jesus. The language of denial and mortification is unpopular today, because ascetical choices are seen as giving life, not hurt or punishment or suffering for its own sake, as if to compensate for guilt or put oneself down. Christian asceticism never attacks or denies what is already integrated in Christic redemption. Such integration, however, must be full and complete, since it means that the object is sought totally in God.

The positive approach is the new asceticism of our time. The American bishops in their 1985 pre-synodal statement called for an "elaborating of a new asceticism and spirituality for Christians who are in but not of the world." Such a this-worldly spirituality does well to follow the balanced formula of the ancient church, which saw its life expressed in prayer, fasting and almsgiving. The formula comes from Judaism, which had no doctrine of original sin, hence no penchant for negative asceticism. The formula summed up the christian vocation in key, symbolic acts that expressed the triple relationship to God, self, and others. Today the formula is most frequently used as the call to renewal and penance in the season of Lent. It is a formula that aptly expresses the meaning of christian asceticism.

Practice

The gospels call for total renunciation for the sake of the kingdom (e.g. Mk 8:34-35) in absolutes that have never been superseded by subsequent schools or authors. The original call to repentance (*metanoia;* see Mk 1:15) is as thorough-going as the beatitudes (Mt 5:3-12). The repentance-kingdom image of the gospels becomes the dying and rising of the paschal mystery in Paul. The paschal mystery subsumes all of life's vicissitudes (2 Cor 11:23-33) and places both suffering and consolation at the service of the community (2 Cor 1:4-7). Paul's comparison of the athlete (1 Cor 9:24-27) relates particularly well to the word "ascetic." His images of flesh warring against spirit (Rom 8:5-13), the old man versus the new man (Eph 4:22-24) and the demonic struggle (Eph 6:12) are vivid dramatizations of ascetical struggle.

In early Christianity physical martyrdom was the first recognized form of christian perfection. A spiritual form of martyrdom developed among celibates in the local communities who were called virgins or ascetics and lived an austere lifestyle of prayer and penance. Later this group moved away from pagan society and became the fathers and mothers of the desert. They cultivated specific ascetical practices, such as vigils, fasts, exposure to heat and cold, deprivation of human comforts, silence and solitude, and spiritual combat with demonic powers. After the peace of Constantine (311) cenobitic communities gradually replaced the hermitages, and the common life, expressed in service inside and outside the monastery and celebrated in liturgy, gave balance to the asceticism. This monastic mode became the paradigm of fervent christian living, no doubt with some prejudice to lay life in the world. But a lay model took shape in its own right in the form of an elaborate catechumenate and post-baptismal training; the experiences in question have been repossessed, put back into practice in our own time in the *Rite of Christian Initiation of Adults* (RCIA).

Medieval asceticism added a few new elements to this basic perspective, notably, a deeper sense of the humanity of Christ, a desire to imitate his suffering, and the wish to retrace his earthly steps in pilgrimage. St. Francis of Assisi (d. 1226), troubadour of creation but bearer of the stigmata as the first recorded case in history, illustrates the bursting of new life that could no longer be contained in the monastic structures from the past. He is a penitent, though not given to the excesses of the flagellants, an apostolic missioner who would bring the good news to the poor, a warm human being whose ascetical rigor and apostolic zeal left intact his amiable simplicity, joy and fraternal spirit. With Dominic, too, there was a similar conjunction of rigorous asceticism in the form of study and a full community and apostolic life.

At the beginning of modern times the great harbingers of contemporary spirituality—Ignatius of Loyola, Teresa of Avila, John of the Cross, Francis de Sales—continued the strong tradition of asceticism. Protestant reformers downplayed asceticism and rejected some traditional forms, notably celibacy and monasticism, in order to proclaim the pure gratuity of grace. The above leaders in the Counter-Reformation, while eminently mystical persons themselves, asserted the necessity of asceticism and taught a rigorous practice. In the context of their own times they were moderates, who disapproved of foolish extremes in mortification and self-denial, but at the same time taught the value of suffering. Suffering was a grace, not for its own sake, but as a sign of identification with Jesus and a proof of pure love of God. Later teachers perhaps exaggerated this doctrine into a now discredited mysticism of suffering.

An enlightened contemporary spirituality attempts to keep continuity with the past but also to relate the knowledge explosion in the human and sacred sciences into a viable practice. Today ascetical practice searches especially for growth in human authenticity and the achievement of human community, especially through the promotion of justice and peace. Asceticism comes out of life's circumstances; it is less prepackaged and more the response of love. But it hopes to assimilate the wisdom of the past. Vatican II in its secular, human, and social thrust has promoted, not only a new anthropology and theology, but a new way of living out the christian life. The formation of the new asceticism is ongoing.

See **Anthropology, Christian; Conversion; Initiation, Christian; Monasticism; Mysticism; Sin**

Rosemary Rader, "Asceticism," in *The Westminster Dictionary of Christian Spirituality*, Philadelphia: Westminster Press, 1983, pp. 24-28. Jean Gribomont and Jean Leclercq, "Monasticism and Asceticism," in *Christian Spirituality*, eds., Bernard McGinn and John Meyendorff, New York: Crossroads 1985, pp. 89-131. John Francis Kavanaugh, *Following Christ in a Consumer Society*, Maryknoll: Orbis Books, 1982.

ERNEST E. LARKIN, O.CARM.

ASSEMBLY

The notion of assembly has foundational significance for anyone attempting to understand the church, the liturgy, or the relationship between the two. Recognition given in the documents of the Second Vatican Council to the significance of local churches and to their realization in liturgical assemblies bears witness to a recovery of an ancient understanding of assembly.

The word "assembly" comes from the Greek *ekklēsia* and when it appears in the NT it is often translated as "church" or "congregation." *Ekklēsia* was one of the words chosen by early Christians to designate themselves and it has a long heritage. In its secular meaning the word referred to an assembly of citizens summoned for the purpose of making a decision. In the Septuagint it was the word most frequently chosen to translate the Hebrew *qahal* which meant both a summons to an assembly and the act of assembling. *Qahal* had gradually assumed religious significance as the Israelites came to understand themselves as people who had been assembled by God.

Those who have studied the use of

ekklēsia in the NT indicate how Paul used it in a variety of ways. He used it in the singular to refer to Christians gathered in a house (Phlm 2), for Christians assembled for worship (1 Cor 11:18), or to designate a number of house churches in one city (1 Thess 1:1). He also used the word in the plural to refer to several churches (1 Thess 2:14). The idea that the christian assembly is one which has been gathered by God in and through Christ appears when Paul refers to "congregations of God in Christ" (1 Thess 2:14) or the "church of Christ" (Gal 1:22).

The idea of an assembly which has been gathered in Christ is also expressed by the Greek word *koinōnia*, another term used to describe the early christian congregations. It is an important term for it expresses the relationship which gives the assembly its identity. *Koinōnia* means a "common share" or "participation in" and Paul's use of the word suggests that Christians actually participate in or share in the life of Jesus Christ (1 Cor 1:9). Those who share in Christ's life are in communion with God and one another through participation in the one Spirit.

It is clear from Paul's letters that the gift of *koinōnia* was meant to be expressed and realized in a variety of concrete ways. Those who shared spiritual gifts were expected to share their material goods in order to alleviate the sufferings of the poor (Rom 15:25-27). The most complete expression and intensification of the *koinōnia* established in baptism took place in the celebration of the Lord's Supper when the assembly renewed its communion in the body and blood of Christ (1 Cor 10:16-17). Here, the assembly disclosed its identity as one body.

The church is most clearly visible as an assembly in Christ when it gathers for a liturgical celebration. The Second Vatican Council's recovery of the ancient principle that the assembly is the subject of liturgical action is based on a renewed appreciation of the intimate union that exists between Christ and all who are baptized. The assembly is subject because of its communion in Christ who is the ultimate subject of any liturgical celebration.

Although *Sacrosanctum Concilium* does not use the phrase "assembly as subject," the principle is operative in a number of statements. For example, full, conscious, and active participation in the liturgy is set out as the primary goal of the liturgical reform and this participation is recognized as something which is the right and obligation of Christians because of their baptism (S.C. 14). Furthermore, the liturgy is identified as an exercise of Christ the priest and his body, the church (S.C. 7), and liturgical services are identified as celebrations of the church (S.C. 26).

Accompanying this strong recognition of the role of the whole assembly in the liturgy is a second principle which emphasizes the ordered nature of any assembly. *Sacrosanctum Concilium* 28 indicates that there are a variety of roles within a liturgical assembly and that each "minister or layperson who has an office to perform, should do all of, but only, those parts which pertain to that office by the nature of the rite and the principles of liturgy." In *Lumen Gentium* an essential distinction is made within the assembly between the priesthood of all the baptized and the ministerial or hierarchic priesthood (L.G. 10).

This dual recognition of the assembly's role as liturgical subject and the variety of roles operative within any assembly appears in the rites of the Roman Catholic Church as they were revised in the years following the Second Vatican Council. The *General Instruction of the Roman Missal* (G.I R.M.) can serve as an example. There, the celebration of Mass is described as "the action of Christ and the people of God arranged hierarchically"

(1). The goal of conscious, active, full participation is set out as something desired by the church, demanded by the nature of the celebration, and given as a right and duty to christian people by reason of their baptism (3). The celebration of the Mass is identified as "the act of a community" which is made clear by the active participation of the gathered faithful (14-15). The eucharistic prayer is described as one in which "the entire congregation joins itself to Christ in acknowledging the great things God has done and in offering the sacrifice" (54). The point is made that places in which the people of God worship should be arranged to ensure their active participation (253).

The various roles exercised by members of the assembly are described as different ways of participating which are in accord with the different orders and ministries in the church (58). The General Instruction identifies three different categories of people who are active within the eucharistic assembly. The first consists of those who exercise the "offices and ministries of Holy Orders," and they are the bishop, presbyter, and deacon (59-61). Then there are the faithful who carry out "the office and function of the people of God" (62-64). The choir and cantor or choir director are included within this category. Finally, there are those who exercise "special ministries" including: the acolyte, reader, cantor of the psalm, special ministers of communion, those who carry the missal, cross, candles, bread, wine, water, and thurible, those who meet the people and seat them, the commentator, those who take up the collection, and the person who has responsibility for planning services and seeing that they are carried out properly (65-69).

A certain tension is evident in the document between the unity of the whole assembly because of its common participation in Christ through baptism and the distinctions that are made within the assembly. One example appears in the statement that laymen may perform all the functions below those reserved to deacons while, at the discretion of the rector of the church, women may be appointed to ministries that are performed outside the sanctuary (70). An appendix to the General Instruction for dioceses in the United States modifies this distinction by admitting women to the exercise of the liturgical ministries with the exception of service at the altar (Appendix I:66). The role of place and the arrangement of space in establishing or expressing distinctions within the assembly is also apparent in the direction that, although the place of worship should be such that "it conveys the image of the gathered assembly" which has an organic unity, it should also clearly express the hierarchical arrangement of the assembly and the diversity of offices within it (G.I.R.M. 257).

The Second Vatican Council's recognition of assemblies as subjects of liturgical action is closely related to its affirmation of the significance of local churches. The council's statement that "this Church of Christ is truly present in all lawful, local congregations of the faithful, which, united with their pastors, are themselves called Churches in the New Testament" (L.G. 26), is its strongest recognition of the fact that the church is realized in local assemblies. The council describes these churches as the faithful gathered by the preaching of Christ's gospel and joined in communion through their celebrations of the Lord's Supper and their sharing in the body and blood of Christ.

Since local assemblies are constituted by men, women, and children gathered in a great diversity of geographical places and sociocultural contexts, such an affirmation of these assemblies as the locus of the church's self-realization carries with it the acceptance of the task of inculturation. Both the gospel message and the *koinōnia* which is at the heart of any christian assembly must be made incarnate, embodied in the language, liturgy, and life of that assembly. The implications of such a task for the post-conciliar church have only begun to be perceived.

See **Church, Liturgy, Worship**

Colin Brown, Ed., *The New International Dictionary of New Testament Theology,* Michigan: Zondervan, 1975. Gerhard Kittel, Ed., *Theological Dictionary of the New Testament,* Michigan: Eerdmans, 1965. Joseph Lecuyer, "The Liturgical Assembly: Biblical and Patristic Foundations," in *The Church Worships* (Concilium 12), pp. 3-18, New York: Paulist Press, 1966. Michael McDermott, "The Biblical Doctrine of *Koinōnia,"Biblische Zeitschrift* 19 (1975): pp. 64-77; 219-233. J.M.R. Tillard, O.P., "What is the Church of God?", *One in Christ* 20 (1984): pp. 226-242.

MARGARET MARY KELLEHER, OSU

ASSUMPTION OF MARY

Dogmatic Content

On Nov. 1, 1950, Pope Pius XII solemnly defined Mary's bodily Assumption into heaven as a dogma of faith in the following words of the apostolic constitution, *Munificentissimus Deus* (M.D.): "We pronounce, declare, and define it to be a divinely revealed dogma: that the Immaculate Mother of God, the ever Virgin Mary, having completed the course of her earthly life, was assumed body and soul into heavenly glory." (D.S. 3903). The dogmas of her Immaculate Conception, Motherhood of God, and Perpetual Virginity, are all contained in the subject of this definition. By using the phrase, ". . . having completed the course of her earthly life . . . .," Pius XII clearly indicated his intention of leaving open the theological and historical question of whether or not Mary actually experienced death before being taken up into glory. ". . . was assumed . . ." signifies that Mary, a mere creature redeemed by her Son, was "taken up" into heaven by

divine power, and did not "ascend" as Christ did through that power within him. The mystery of her Assumption is quite distinct from that of his Ascension. ". . . body and soul . . ." means that Mary has been glorified in her total personhood, and does not define a dualistic anthropology as the church's official teaching. And finally, ". . . into heavenly glory." refers to the mysterious mode of existence beyond the limits of space and time in the intimate presence of the triune God and our risen Lord.

The various aspects of this mystery are to be found in related doctrines of the Church about general eschatology, particularly the beatific vision and bodily resurrection of all the just. Its essential meaning, as outlined above, can be accepted only by the grace of divine faith. Although nothing definitive has yet emerged in the Tradition concerning such questions, the testimony seems to favor the theological opinions that she did undergo death in the Lord, was probably buried near the Garden of Gethsemane in Jerusalem, and, in the likeness of her Son's resurrection, Mary's body did not decompose after her death and burial, but she was gloriously assumed intact.

Dogmatic Development

In M.D. Pius XII referred to the close association between the New Eve (Mary) and the New Adam (Christ) in that struggle, "which, as foreshadowed in the *protoevangelium* (Gen 3:15), would finally result in that most complete victory over sin and death that are always mentioned together in the writings of the Apostle of the Gentiles (Rom 5 and 6; 1 Cor 15:21-25; 54-57)" (D.S. 3901). Reasoning theologically on the basis of such biblical texts, the Pope concluded that it was most fitting for the New Eve, who had such a significant role in the struggle, to be given by God a special share in the New Adam's resurrection through her glorious Assumption. He considered the sacred scriptures to be the "ultimate foundation" for any arguments advanced by the Fathers and theologians in favor of the dogma (cf. D.S. 3900). Just how any divine insinuations about the Assumption in the bible may have inspired its gradual unfolding and explicitation in the tradition is not itself a matter of faith or dogma, but a complex question of theology in formulating a theory of dogmatic development.

The most influential factor in the development of this dogma seems to have been the *sensus fidelium,* i.e., the beliefs of the faithful, especially as they have been manifested in liturgical devotion. As early as the 5th century, the Christians of the East were already celebrating a feast called the "Memorial of Mary" on Aug. 15. It was patterned after the "birthday into heaven" of the martyrs' anniversaries, and eventually came to be called the *koimesis* (Gk.) or *dormitio* (Lat.), i.e., the "falling asleep" of the Virgin Mary. This expressed the deep faith of early Christians in the resurrection of the body which falls asleep at death. During the reign of Mauricius Flavius (582-602), the feast of Mary's Dormition was decreed to be celebrated on Aug. 15 throughout the Byzantine Empire. After this preachers began to speak more clearly about her bodily Assumption. Rome adopted the feast during the 7th century, and under Pope St. Adrian I (772-795), the title "Assumption" replaced "Dormition."

Among the Fathers one of the earliest testimonies to the doctrine came from Theoteknos, Bishop of Livias on the left bank of the Jordan between 550 and 650, who speaks of the feast as the Assumption (*Analepsis*). By the eighth century the doctrine was completely accepted in the East and taught by St. Germanus of Constantinople and St. John Damascene, the great Doctor of the Assumption.

After auspicious beginnings in the West, the belief and devotion met with some difficulty on account of the Pseudo-Jerome during the ninth century, a spurious letter falsely attributed to St. Jerome, which did not deny the doctrine but called it into doubt. Its negative influence upon the dogmatic development of the Assumption in the West was intensified by the fact that it became one of the readings in the Divine Office. The Pseudo-Augustine of the early eleventh century, however, provided some sound doctrinal reasons for the Assumption and countered its influence. By the middle of the thirteenth century, the devotion regained its former vigor in the West, and was supported both by liturgical celebration and the teaching of Sts. Albert the Great, Bonaventure, and Thomas Aquinas. The outstanding saints and scholars of the ensuing centuries promoted the doctrine and devotion. Between 1849 and 1950 a great number of petitions for its dogmatic definition were sent to Rome from various members of the Roman Catholic Church. On May 1, 1946, Pius XII issued an encyclical, *Deiparae Virginis,* asking his brother bishops whether they considered the doctrine definable and whether their clergy and laity desired its dogmatic definition. The response was overwhelmingly in favor of defining the Assumption, which he regarded as firm proof that it is divinely revealed. Vatican II referred to Mary's Assumption as "... a sign of certain hope and comfort to the pilgrim People of God" (L.G. 68). Her glorification helps deepen our confidence in the bodily resurrection of us all.

K. Healy, *The Assumption of Mary,* Wilmington, DE., 1982. F.M. Jelly, *Madonna - Mary in the Catholic Tradition,* Huntington, IN., 1986. M. O'Carroll, "The Assumption of Our Lady", *Theotokos: A Theological Encyclopedia of the Blessed Virgin Mary,* Wilmington, DE., 1983.

F.M. JELLY, OP

ATHEISM

Historically, "atheist" has been a term of opprobrium. Identifying persons or positions as "godless" or "atheist" has been sufficient reason to persecute and suppress them. Socrates was executed for atheism and corrupting the young. Early gentile Christians were identified as atheists by some Roman authorities because those Christians would not pay expected tribute to the divinities of the state. Christian authorities identified some freethinkers as atheists. Through the nineteenth century, some "Christian" governments persecuted those atheists and forbade publication of books advocating atheism because atheism was alleged to be a threat to social order. Yet Pope Paul VI ("Ecclesiam Suam") recognized some atheists as well-motivated. More recently, Vatican authorities have opposed theologians' use of Marxian categories for social analysis because using them allegedly entails their accepting an atheistic Marxist metaphysics.

Atheism can be defined as the refusal to acknowledge a god. Atheism is as various as are the gods people believe in multiplied by the ways to deny those gods. Confusion about atheism reigns insofar as "atheism" is taken as having a single meaning. What follows only applies to atheism relative to God as understood in the christian tradition. Although the different types of atheism are sometimes found together in an atheistic system, the procedural forms of atheism do not entail substantial forms of atheism. A "methodological" atheist (no matter what method used) is not necessarily committed to an "existential" or "evidential" atheism.

Methodological atheism brackets the existence of God for the purposes of inquiry. Natural and social sciences are methodologically atheistic because the supernatural cannot count as an explanation of the phenomena they investigate.

Methodological atheists neither deny nor affirm the existence of God, as God is outside the purview of their work. A. Flew has argued that philosophical inquiry should use a version of methodological atheism. His "presumption of atheism" calls for the believer to bear the burden of proving the existence of God, as the prosecution bears the burden of proof in criminal court cases against the presumption of innocence. A more appropriate analogue would be to civil cases, where both sides have an equal burden of proof to bear, for theists and atheists both bear the burden of warranting their ultimate claims.

Reductionist atheisms claim that religion can be fully explained without reference to the supernatual once one recognizes the genesis of religion in human nature, human society or human desire.

L. Feuerbach argued that what Christians attribute to God is merely a projection of human nature onto a supersensible being. Christian doctrines about God, he claimed, could be reduced without remainder into doctrines about humanity. Moreover, projections of human nature into the abstract and ideal realm alienate what is truly human from its real locale in concrete humanity. What is worthy of human worship and the center of human value is not a God upon the clouds external to and opposed to humanity, but humanity itself.

K. Marx extended Feuerbach's critique of religion. His doctrines that religious devotion is the cry of the oppressed and that religious consolation is the opiate of the people are well known. Theorizing in a context where religious sanction was often used to legitimate practices which led to the concentration of capital in the nineteenth century, Marx thought religion would disappear once its cause, the pain of the oppressed caused by their alienation from the fruits of their labors, disappeared. Marxists often oppose religion because of its utility for supporting an unjust social order which keeps people alienated from each other and unable to realize their true spiritual potential, which is to be found only in this material world, not in an imaginary afterlife with an imaginary God.

S. Freud claimed on the basis of his psychological investigations that religion was an illusion. Humans create God, replacing a fallible father who fails to fulfill their desires with an infallible eternal Father who never fails. Freud found religion particularly pernicious because it kept humanity in an abased state of infantile dependence. Religion works against distinguishing fantasy from reality and keeps humanity infantile. Once people escaped from their powerless infantile stage, religious belief would collapse.

Existential atheism is a rejection of God because believing in God prohibits people from becoming fully human. Epitomized in F. Dostoevsky, *The Brothers Karamazov* (in the character of Ivan and in the story of the confrontation of Christ and the Grand Inquisitor), rejecting God means affirming human value and freedom. A. Camus portrays authentic human morality as atheistic in *The Rebel* and especially in the character of Dr. Rieux in *The Plague,* who is the exemplar of practical humanistic atheism (as distinguished from nihilism).

Christian atheism. Some christian atheists (T. Altizer, A. Jennings) make moves similar to existential atheism in rejecting God as portrayed in philosophical theism since the beginning of the Enlightenment. They provocatively suggest new ways in which Christians and others can approach the Ultimate. In contrast to reductionist and existental atheism, D. Cupitt curiously denies the reality of God but claims we need God as a myth to support our quests to overcome evil and to become autonomous. These

forms of atheism reject one doctrine of God, but may each support different doctrines of God.

Evidential atheism is a theoretical philosophical position which claims that there is good reason not to believe in God and thus denies God's existence. Agnosticism (there is no good reason to believe in God), uses similar arguments and is similar in practice, but is technically different because it neither affirms nor denies God's existence. First, arguments for the existence of God are undermined. For example: Atheist: "The world exists. Who made it? No one. It just is." Theist: "The world exists. Who made it? God. Who made God? No one. God just is." Both explanations end in the inexplicable. Each explains as much of the world as the other. So there is no good reason to prefer one over the other. Second, neither science nor law accept "miracle" as an explanation. These, our paradigms of rationality and responsibility, presume that all events have a "this-worldly" explanation. Hence, neither rationality nor responsibility supports postulating causes from outside the world for effects within the world. Third, the problem of evil is raised. Does it make any sense to believe that an all-powerful and all-loving being created the world and sustained it for billions of years in the face of all the evils in it? As God neither explains the world nor events in it, there is no need to believe in God. The reality of evils count against existence of God. On the basis of the evidence, there is at least no good reason to believe in God and maybe good reason not to believe in God.

See **God, Proof of the Existence of God**

B. Russell, *Why I Am Not a Christian,* New York, 1957; J. Mackie, *The Miracle of Theism,* Oxford, 1982; H. Küng, *Does God Exist?* New York, 1980.

T.W. TILLEY

ATONEMENT

See **Redemption**

ATTRITION

Sorrow for one's sins for some motive short of the love of God, for example, fear of punishment. It is regarded as an imperfect form of repentance, but one which suffices for the reception of the sacrament of reconcilation, in the course of which it can be brought to its fulfillment in genuine or "perfect" contrition.

See **Contrition, Reconciliation**

AUTHORITY IN THE CHURCH

Like any other human sociological group, the christian community requires some authority to maintain its identity, its unity, and to resolve internal conflicts. But, from the beginning, the christian community recognized that the exercise of authority among its members was to be distinct from other human groups. Authority in the christian community should not be exercised like that of the "Gentiles" but rather as "one who serves" (Lk 22:24-27) and in imitation of the master who washes the feet of his disciples (Jn 13:1-17). Authority in this community is based on the authority of Jesus himself and his commission to his disciples: "All authority in heaven and on earth has been given to me. Go therefore and make disciples of all nations, baptizing them in the name of the Father and of the Son and of the Holy Spirit, teaching them to observe all that I have commanded you; and lo, I am with you always, to the close of the age." (Mt 28:18-29), as well as on the authority of the "Spirit of truth" (Jn 16:12-15). Authority in the early church was understood to be more than a mere sociological necessity; it was *spiritual* authority.

This Spirit-based authority was found in a variety of gifts and a variety of forms of service—apostles, prophets, teachers, workers of miracles, healers, helpers, administrators, speakers of tongues (1 Cor 12:4-31, Eph 4:11, Rom 12:6-8). Whatever gifts were the basis for authority, they were all in service to the community and were not in terms of domination over others (1 Cor 4:5). The apostles, because of their close association with the Lord, were clearly the leaders whether resident in one city or traveling about the empire as Peter and Paul. There were also close associates of the apostles, such as Timothy or Titus, who derived their authority directly from them. But with the death of the apostles, there was great diversity in the way the various local churches structured themselves. (Brown).

In the period from the apostles until Constantine, authority in the church developed with three features: a strong insistence on authority, a very close link with the christian community, and a marked charismatic or spiritual character. As the present division of offices into bishops, priests and deacons developed, the charismatic gifts were not confined to these offices, but bishops were chosen as the men possessing the most spiritual gifts. The bishops also had authority because of their apostolicity, i.e., their continuity with the apostolic teaching.

With the establishment of the church in Constantine's reign, the bishops became public men of rank, administrators of justice, defenders of the poor, widows, etc. The authority in the church became more secular and juridical and tended to become authority for its own sake. The more charismatic or spiritual elements were kept alive by the growth of monasticism. Spiritual authority was separated to some extent from the hierarchical structure, although many of the bishops were monks or men trained in a monastic setting and who lived accordingly. It was really the Gregorian reform of the eleventh century, Congar argues, which, in its attempt to free the church from its identification with the political society and domination by local rulers, gave rise to a more juridical notion of authority and the development of canon law. Pope Gregory VII claimed for the church a completely autonomous and sovereign system of rights proper to a spiritual society, including papal authority over kings and their kingdoms. From this time on, spiritual authority came to be almost completely identified with the structured offices in the church. Although the medieval theologians and canonists made a distinction between *potestas ordinis* and *potestas juridictionis,* both spiritual and legal power resided in the same offices.

The growth of papal authority during the middle ages deserves special note. Although a primacy of honor was accorded to the Bishop of Rome from the patristic period, the great popes of the middle ages such as Leo I, Gelasius, and Gregory the Great, enhanced the papal claims to supremacy and fullness of power over the universal church. While asserting the legitimate autonomy and rights of the church from the secular powers, the medieval papacy simultaneously adopted many of the insignia, vocabulary, style and ideology of the imperial court so that it took on the appearance of a worldly power itself.

Although the centralizing and juridicizing of authority in the church was the dominant trend from the eleventh to the fifteenth centuries, there were countercurrents. There were a series of spiritual protest movements such as the Franciscans, the Lollards and the Hussites. The movement known as conciliarism which was spurred on by the Avignon papacy and the Great Western Schism (1378-1418) argued that ultimate authority in the church lay with a council rather than in the papacy. These protests culminated in the Protestant Reformation in the sixteenth century.

The challenge to authority posed by the Reformers was a very basic one since it was not just a questioning of authority in the historical form then existing, but a challenge to ecclesiastical authority in principle. The cry of *sola scriptura* denied that ultimate authority in the christian community could be located in structured offices. The response of the Roman Catholic Church at the Council of Trent and thereafter was to reemphasize the unwritten traditions handed down from the apostles as complementing the canonical scriptures. Subsequently, however, post-tridentine theologians moved "away from a conception of tradition as content and deposit received from the apostles, to one of tradition considered from the point of view of the transmitting organism, seen as residing above all in the magisterium of the Church" (Y. Congar, *Tradition and Traditions*). Since the sixteenth century, Congar says, the Catholic Church has practiced a veritable "mystique" of authority which may be characterized as the notion of a complete identification of God's will with the institutional form of authority. In the latter it is God himself whose voice we hear and heed.

This mystique of authority reached its highwater mark with the definition of papal infallibility in 1870 at the First Vatican Council. Since that council was unable to complete its work, an unbalanced emphasis on papal authority remained until Vatican Council II.

Although Vatican II reiterated the teaching of Vatican I on papal sovereignty and infallibility (L.G. 25), it also stressed that all hierarchical authority in the church is a "true service" and is rightly called *diakonia* or ministry (L.G. 24) and situated papal authority in the wider context of the college of bishops as successors of the apostles (L.G. 22, 23).

Vatican II also praised the variety and diversity of local churches which "enjoy their own discipline, their own liturgical usage, and their own theological and spiritual heritage." (L.G. 23). Thus, this council laid the groundwork for some developments in the exercise of authority in the church since 1965.

The ecumenical thrust of Vatican II gave rise to a series of bi-lateral theological discussions between Roman Catholic theologians and Anglican, Lutheran, Orthodox, etc. These discussions have made substantial progress toward agreement on the exercise of authority in the church. A balance between primatial and conciliar aspects of authority, between the authority of scripture and the Spirit working through the community (tradition and magisterium) has resulted (e.g., *The Anglican-Roman Catholic Agreement on Authority*, 1976). A restructuring of authority as the churches move toward unity can take place on the basis of the principles of legitimate diversity, collegiality, and subsidiarity—all recognized by Vatican II (Fries and Rahner).

The emphasis of Vatican II on the collegiality of the bishops and on the local church has led to increased authoritative activity on the part of regional and national episcopal conferences such as that of CELAM at Puebla (1968) and Medellin (1979), and the pastoral letters on national issues of the United States Conference of Catholic Bishops. There has been some question raised as to the authority of these conferences to exercise a magisterial function *qua* conferences, but there certainly has developed an awareness of the responsibility to exercise solicitude for the whole church on a basis broader than within their individual diocesan jurisdictions as urged by Vatican II (L.G. 23).

Further the recognition of diversity and pluralism within theology and ecclesiastical practice has eventuated in a greater freedom and willingness to take issue with magisterial statements of a less than infallible character which come from a centralized authority (e.g., diverse evaluations of Latin American liberation theologies).

Finally, the spiritual and charismatic character of authority in the christian community has reemerged to counterbalance the heavily juridical aspect which had dominated the theology and practice of authority in the Roman Catholic community for the last several hundred years (K. Rahner).

See **Bishop, Church, Pope**

Raymond Brown, *The Churches the Apostles Left Behind*, 1984. Y. Congar, "The Historical Development of Authority," 1962. Y. Congar, *Tradition and Traditions*, 1967. Fries and Rahner, *Unity of the Churches*, 1985. K. Rahner, *The Spirit in the Church*, 1979.

T. HOWLAND SANKS, SJ

B

BAPTISM

The word is derived from the Greek *bapto,* meaning "to dip" or "to immerse."

Ritual washings were common religious practices in the first century C.E. These were external rites of purification, signifying what they effected—death to an old way of life; rebirth into a new community.

Pre-Christian Rituals

The Jewish community had many different purification rituals, but only one baptismal ritual. Proselyte baptism was administered to gentiles who sought membership in the Jewish community. After their motives had been tested and sufficient instructions had been given, candidates were baptized, often during the days of Passover. Candidates confessed their sins, were immersed in flowing water, and given a new name.

The Essene community at Qumran had a similar religious practice. After three years of instructions and testing, the baptism took place. Candidates, after praising God and confessing their sins, were blessed by the community and immersed in the water. Unlike other baptismal rituals, however this ritual was repeatable. All members of the community would renew their membership through such a purification ritual annually.

John the Baptizer was so named be-cause a purification ritual formed part of his prophetic call (Mk 1:4-6). To symbolize their conversion, his followers were immersed in flowing water. Although he did not need a sign of conversion, Jesus participated in John's ritual baptism (Mk 1:9-11; Jn 1:32-34). In this way Jesus signified acceptance of his own mission, and established a connection between his ministry and John's prophecy.

Christian Sacrament of Baptism

Sacraments, as they are understood in the christian religious tradition, could not have existed before the death and resurrection of the Lord. Jesus' disciples apparently did baptize along with the prophet John (Jn 3:22; 4:2) but this was a purification ritual rather than the sacrament of baptism.

Since none of its books purports to be an historical account, the NT contains scanty references to the sacrament of baptism. At most, it provides us with allusions to a theological understanding of baptism that was later ritualized when the liturgy of baptism began to take a specific shape. NT authors regarded baptism as a passage, uniting one with Christ in the life of the Spirit (1 Cor 12:12-13). Following the proclamation of the word, people responded with a confession of faith and were baptized (Acts 8:26-40).

Liturgy of Baptism

Although the NT gives no exact account of the ritual of baptism, it is possible to make some assumptions by examining the metaphorical language used by the writers in the light of prechristian rituals and coupling that with what we know of later christian practice.

We can conjecture, for example, primarily from the writings of St. Paul, that there was a special relationship established between the instructor and the individual called to faith (Gal 6:6), that the early church probably practiced baptism by immersion (Rom 6:1), that the newly baptized person wore a special garment to symbolize the new life (Gal 3:27), and that the ritual included some type of anointing (Eph 1:13ff).

As the church expanded, there was a growing need for some standardization of catechetical instruction. Both the *Didache* (c. 90) and the Epistle of Barnabas (c. 100) give an indication of what was contained in this primitive form of religious instruction, but little information as to how the catechetical process occurred. It was not until the *Apostolic Tradition* (AT) of Hippolytus (c. 215) that a highly developed rite of initiation, replete with a serious catechumenate was described.

It is in the AT that we find written evidence for the first time that not everyone was eligible for admission to the christian community. In order to guard against pagan infiltration in an age of persecution, stringent requirements governed candidacy.

The person seeking admission had to be introduced to the teachers by a reputable member of the community. Thorough questioning of the candidates was intended to reveal their mode of life as well as the integrity of their intention to become Christians. Upon being accepted by the teachers, the candidates were enrolled in the order of catechumens in a public ceremony.

Ordinarily the catechumenate was of three years' duration, during which time the catechumens were thoroughly instructed in doctrinal, moral, and ascetical principles. Catechumens were permitted to attend the Liturgy of the Word, but they were dismissed before the Liturgy of the Eucharist began. Only the fully initiated Christians could participate in that sacred meal.

On the first Sunday of the Lent preceding their baptism, the catechumens entered a special period of preparation as *illuminandi.* The culmination of this final preparatory stage occurred at the Easter Vigil when the catechumens were baptized and sealed with the Spirit, and shared fully in the eucharistic celebration for the first time.

Once the persecutions ended and greater numbers of people sought baptism in the Constantinian church, it was virtually impossible to retain the former structure of the catechumenate. With the exception of receiving eucharist, catechumens were entitled to most of the benefits of belonging to the christian community, without being held accountable for sin. Many were content to remain in the order of catechumens until they were near death, rather than subjecting themselves to the possibility of prolonged public penance should they fall into sin.

The triumph of Christianity over paganism meant that fewer sought entrance into the community as adults, since it was increasingly common for infants and young children to be baptized. Augustine's teaching on original sin had made the practice of early baptism emotionally if not theologically, mandatory. There was not, however, an accompanying ritual for the baptism of infants. Instead, the baptismal ritual originally intended for adults was simply "telescoped." The *Ordo Romanus* XI (eighth century) reflects this change.

The pre-baptismal rites were divided for symbolic reasons into seven sections, known as *scrutinia,* which bore nothing in common with the previous system, except the name. These included: 1) imposition of name, basic catechesis, act of aversion from error and conversion to God, first solemn signing; 2) ceremony of tasting salt; 3-5) solemn exorcisms (repeated three times); 6) solemn entrance, bestowal of the Creed and the Lord's Prayer, final exorcism, the rite of opening the ears, anointing with the oil of catechumens after the renunciation of Satan; 7) baptism. Rather than critical examinations, these were simple pieces of a ritual, derived from the *Gelasian Sacramentary* (sixth century) and severely compressed.

The Middle Ages witnessed the complete demise of adult initiation into the christian community, since infant baptism had become almost universal.

During the sixteenth century there was considerable disdain among some reformers for the continuing practice of infant baptism. The Anabaptists, as such reformers came to be known, believed Christianity to be an adult religion, and therefore administered "believers baptism" only to adults. In reaction to the reform movement, the Council of Trent (1545-1563) reaffirmed the medieval practice of baptizing infants. The Ritual of Paul V (1614) remained the official ritual of baptism until the reforms of the Second Vatican Council (1963-1965), which mandated the development of a ritual of baptism for children, restoration of the catechumenate for adults, and revision of the rites of baptism for adults (S.C. 64-70).

Reforms of Vatican II

As the liturgical movement gained impetus in the decades preceding Vatican II, pressure was continually exerted on the Sacred Congregation of Rites to initiate some type of reform of the baptismal ritual. This pressure took two forms: liturgical scholars were anxious to implement a rite which would be more in line with the principles and practices of the early church; bishops in mission countries found that the catechumenal model provided more adequately for the needs of their communities, and were insistent on the development of a ritual which would incorporate that model. What both groups sought was a longer period of initiation, accompanied by suitable intermediary rites. The results of the reform are the *Rite of Baptism for Children* (1969) and the *Rite of Christian Initiation of Adults* (1975).

Theology of Baptism

"Baptism incorporates us into Christ and forms us into God's people. This first sacrament pardons all our sins, rescues us from the power of darkness, and brings us to the dignity of adopted children ..." (*Christian Initiation,* General Introduction, 2). Baptism establishes a relationship between the individual and God, and incorporates the individual into the community of believers, the priesthood of the faithful. Baptism also confers on the soul a permanent character, designating a permanent relationship with Christ and his church, even though one might later cease to be an active member of the community. All of the other christian sacraments, therefore, derive their meaning from baptism.

Bishops, priests and deacons are the ordinary ministers of baptism, although in the case of imminent danger of death, anyone with the right intention may administer the sacrament of baptism. The words for conferring baptism in the Latin Church are: "I baptize you in the name of the Father, and of the Son, and of the Holy Spirit."

See **Catechumen; Initiation, Christian; Liturgy; Sacrament**

J.D.C. Fisher, *Christian Initiation: Baptism in the Medieval West,* London: SPCK, 1965. J.D.C.

Fisher, *Christian Initiation: The Reformation Period,* London: SPCK, 1970. Alexander Ganoczy, *Becoming Christian: A Theology of Baptism as the Sacrament of Human History,* Trans. John C. Lynch, New York: Paulist Press, 1976. Aidan Kavanagh, *The Shape of Baptism: the Rite of Christian Initiation,* Studies in the Reformed Rites of the Catholic Church, 1, New York: Pueblo Pub. Co., 1978. Mark Searle, *Christening: The Making of Christians,* Collegeville: Liturgical Press, 1980.

JULIA UPTON, RSM

BASIC COMMUNITIES

The term "basic communities" gained currency in the church during the 1960's and 1970's. The English expression has its origin in the Spanish and Portuguese phrases *comunidades de base.* In English the term is variously rendered "basic communities," "base communities," or "grassroots communities." Usually it is modified as "basic christian communities" or "basic ecclesial communities" to specify the religious character of the communities and, in some contexts, to emphasize the adhesion of the communities to the institutional church.

The basic christian communities in Latin America are small groups of Christians, numbering from a few people to perhaps thirty families. They are found especially in the countryside, but also in the poor areas of the major urban populations.

The members gather regularly to read and discuss the Bible, to pray, to celebrate, and to discuss and plan for action in the community. An essential characteristic of the group is the christian fellowship, or *koinonia.* As the members of the group reflect on the significance of the scriptural texts for their own lives, new insights are developed, often startlingly and refreshingly different from conventional ways of reading the Bible.

The "base" refers to the bottom of the social—and ecclesiastical—pyramid. The members of the basic communities are usually of the lower classes. For this reason the basic communities are often referred to as "an oppressed and believing people" (Gustavo Gutierrez, Leonardo Boff). The basic communities are a church of the poor and express the church's "preferential option for the poor."

Leadership in the basic communities is primarily lay, although there is often a priest, sister, or other pastoral agent who serves as a chaplain and advisor, or *asesor,* to the community. At the beginning stages, especially, the basic community is often dependent on outside leadership and organizational skills. As the community develops, however, leadership passes into the hands of the local community members, variously called *coordinadores, responsables, animadores,* or *delegados de la palabra.*

There are thousands of these communities throughout Latin America, some estimates running to 200,000, with 100,000 in Brazil alone. Exact estimates are difficult, since the defining line between a basic community and any informal gathering of Christians is not always easy to make.

Small groups of Christians gathering together are, of course, not only a recent phenomenon. The Twelve Apostles were a kind of basic community, as were the house churches referred to in the NT. In Acts 2:44-47 we see a classic definition of such a community: "And all who believed were together and had all things in common; and they sold their possessions and goods and distributed them to all, as any had need. And day by day, attending the temple together and breaking bread in their homes, they partook of food with glad and generous hearts, praising God and having favor with all the people" (JB).

Monastic communities throughout church history shared many of the characteristics of modern basic communities as did many of the small communities and congregations in various Protestant movements.

Contemporary factors involved in the rise of the basic communities in Latin America include grassroots organizations occurring in the non-religious sphere; the European experience of worker-priests and Catholic Action, which many of the Latin American clergy were exposed to during their European studies; the impact of Vatican Council II, with its increased emphasis on the role of the laity, on Bible reading, on an accessible, meaningful liturgy, and on commitment to action for justice; the conscientization, or conscious-ness-raising, methods of literacy educa-tion pioneered by Paulo Freire in Brazil; unmanageably large parishes and a short-age of priests.

The Latin American bishops gathered at Medellín, Colombia, in 1968 referred to the basic communities as "the first and fundamental ecclesial nucleus ... the initial cell of the ecclesial structures and the focus of evangelization" ("Joint Pastoral Planning," no. 10).

Eleven years later at the Third General Conference of the Latin American Bish-ops at Puebla, Mexico, the bishops stated: "In small communities, particularly those that are better organized, people grow in their experience of new interpersonal relationships in the faith, in deeper ex-ploration of God's word, in fuller partic-ipation in the eucharist, in communion with the pastors of the local church, and in greater commitment to justice within the social milieu that surrounds them" (no. 640).

The bishops pointed out the danger that such communities could fall prey to "organizational anarchy or narrow-minded, sectarian elitism" or that they could foster a parallel church, with a parallel magisterium, independent of the institutional Catholic church (nos. 261-62); nonetheless, stated the bishops, the basic christian communities "are one of the causes for joy and hope in the Church" (no. 96).

The basic community phenomenon is not confined to Latin America. In Africa, where the term "small christian commu-nities" is commonly used, Christians relate the communities to traditional African values of communal sharing and celebra-tion. Analogous kinds of communities can be found in Asia as well, especially in the Philippines, and in Western Europe and North America, especially among the marginated groups of society.

The experience of the basic christian communities has been the seedbed for the theology of liberation. All of the major theologians of liberation have some connection with a basic christian commu-nity, and it is that experience, they assert, that provides the "praxis" for the critical reflection that constitutes theology.

The understanding of church that has developed in the basic christian commu-nities has important implications for ecclesiology: the church as people of God (Vatican II); the relationshp between the community and the hierarchy; new forms of lay ministry; the relationship between the particular church and the universal church.

See **Church, Community, Liberation Theology**

Leonardo Boff *Ecclesiogenesis: The Basic Christian Communities Reinvent the Church,* Maryknoll, Orbis Books, 1985. Edward Cleary, *Crisis and Change: The Church in Latin America Today,* Maryknoll, Orbis Books, 1985. *Puebla and Beyond: Documentation and Commentary,* Eds., John Eagleson and Philip Scharper, trans., John Drury, Maryknoll, Orbis Books, 1979.

JOHN EAGLESON

BEATIFIC VISION

Beatific Vision

In technical theological language, the essential joy of heaven is called *beatific vision.* By this is meant the immediate, face-to-face experience of God in which the human person finds ultimate fulfillment after death.

Scripture

Scripture uses many metaphors to speak of the mystery of heaven. The OT offers little textual basis for the notion of *beatific vision*. In the NT there are a number of significant texts. In Mt 5:8 Jesus assures us that the pure of heart are blessed "for they shall see God." Mt 18:10 describes heaven as "beholding the face of the Father, and 1 Jn 3:2 speaks of a future state in which we shall see the mystery of the divinity as it is. In 1 Cor 13:11ff Paul draws a sharp contrast between our present knowledge of God and the future, heavenly knowledge: "For now we see in a mirror dimly, but then face to face. Now I know in part; then I shall understand fully, even as I have been fully understood." The vision of God for which the human person is destined is more intimate than any experience of God while on earth. According to John, the person who enjoys such vision will be transformed into the likeness of God (1 Jn 3:2).

Teaching of the Magisterium

The most important papal text is the constitution *Benedictus Deus* of Benedict XII (D.S. 1000-1001). This document speaks of seeing the divine essence by an "intuitive vision and face-to-face" without the mediation of any creature. The divine essence will manifest itself "plainly, clearly, and openly." The principal conciliar text, which is much less explicit in its language, comes from the Council of Florence (D.S. 1305): "The souls of those who have committed no sins at all after the reception of baptism, and the souls of those who have committed sin but have been purged either while in the body or after they have left the body behind ... are taken immediately into heaven and clearly see God himself, one and three, as he is; some more perfectly than others in accordance with the diversity of their merits." This teaching is reaffirmed with no additions in more recent documents, such as Pope Paul VI's *Credo of the People of God* (1968) and the "Letter on Certain Questions Concerning Eschatology" of the Congregation for the Doctrine of the Faith (1979). From this it is clear that the magisterium teaches that the essential object of heavenly joy is the very mystery of the divinity in its triune reality in as far as this is known immediately and intuitively by the blessed. This knowledge and the joy flowing from it are proportionate to the merit of each individual.

Theological Reflection

All other details in the understanding of the beatific vision are derived from various forms of theological speculation. While the term *vision* in itself would seem to place great emphasis on the intellectual dimension of our relation with God, this ought not to be understood in a one-sided rationalistic way. This vision is not some sort of theoretical knowledge, nor a simple apprehension of the divine. However the beatific vision is to be understood in particular, it must be kept in mind that the final fulfillment of humanity does not reside in the fulfillment of one faculty alone but in the fulfillment of the whole of the person including the full activation of all the person's spiritual faculties. The concept of beatific vision is best understood if we think of it in terms of a living, personal exchange between God and the human person. God offers the mystery of the divine presence to the creature. The human person, on the other hand, is freed from self-seeking and stands before God in total openness. The acts which constitute the heavenly beatitude are knowledge, love, and joy. The basic, unifying act for those who follow Thomas Aquinas is that of the intellect (= vision). For those following Scotus, on the other hand, the basic unifying act is that of the will (= love). Scholastic theology emphasized the totally supernatural character of the beatific vision. From this it was concluded that a supernatural elevation of the intellect was required to make the beatific vision possible. This preparation for vision is called the "light of glory." Scholastic theology commonly distinguished between the primary and the secondary object of the beatific vision. The primary object is the triune mystery of God. The secondary object is the reality of created things, which are known as they are in God, their creative source. Contemporary theologians take this to mean that our final destiny with God is not a matter of leaving the world of created reality, but of entering into a new and deeper relation to all created things at the deepest source of their being and meaning. As the degree of knowledge of God differs in correspondence with the individual person's merit, the knowledge of created things differs in a corresponding way. While the beatific vision is said to be an immediate, intuitive knowledge of God, it remains a conviction of the magisterium's teaching as well as that of Scholastic theology that God remains always incomprehensible. The blessed never possess a full or comprehensive knowledge of the divine reality. The finite spirit can understand the infinite only in a finite manner (cf., S.Th. I, 12, 7, ad 3).

See **Eschatology**

ZACHARY HAYES, OFM

BEAUTY

1. Biblical Context

Beauty does not seem to be an important theological theme in the Bible; the word is virtually absent from the NT. It is simply observed and enjoyed in creation and celebrated in the arts. The psalmist seems to have a special eye for those things everywhere which because of their color, proportion, and marvelous work-ings, are able to fascinate and to elicit wonder and praise. In Psalm 27 we find a reference to the beauty of the Lord, which by poetic parallelism may be connected with the temple and its cult. References to the beauties of creation often function metaphorically in other poetic passages of the OT, especially the prophets, which speaks of the wonderful deeds which God will perform. Even though the Bible does not speak about the nature of the beautiful as such, it reflects eloquently on an awesome and fascinating cosmos, on the reality of human delight and desire and of the manifestations of divine glory. These must form the background of a theological consideration of beauty.

2. Philosophical Background

After two thousands years, from the Greeks to Thomas to the German Idealists and into our own century, philosophy is still hard pressed to give a universally persuasive answer to the question about the nature of the beautiful and the possibility of a science of aesthetics. Common sense might suggest that in order to answer such questions, we must reflect upon the ordinary experience which people have of beauty. Beauty, after all, is not primarily a concept, but something which we meet in the concrete things of our experience. What is it that makes us call some of the objects of our ordinary experience: flowers, figures and faces, buildings, paintings and music, beautiful? Perhaps it is their ability to fascinate us, to demand our attention. What fascinates first of all is the very harmony, proportion and organizational integrity of the things we see. The beautiful has a material comprehensibility, a kind of inner cohesiveness or necessity. Everything fits together. Beauty (formosus) is a mystery of form (forma). But reflectively we are aware of a deeper fascination: the very fact that we have been moved and are drawn. We experience a power or radiance other than ourselves which does not fall from above and outside upon the form, but which reveals itself to us, breaking forth from within. The beautiful is not something which can be predicted or manipulated. In nature and in great works of art its inner radiance and power surprises. It comes as something of a gift, bears the marks of freedom and seems inexhaustible. The visible form not only points to an invisible mystery. It is the real presence of this mystery, precisely as inexhaustible mystery, and so, as hidden. This is why the beautiful has the capacity to sustain its power to evoke wonder. The mystery of beauty is the union of outward form and inner mysterious radiance.

Where does the power come from, which shines out of the beautiful form in such a way that it draws us closer in wonder, both convinced by its necessity and awed by its unexpectedness? The scholastic thinkers of the High Middle Ages, drawing on the foundational insights of classical Greek philosophy, recognized this power to be the manifestation of the hidden depths of being itself. They considered beauty to be more than just an accidental characteristic of the diverse objects of our perception. They held beauty to be a transcendental characteristic of being in its essential unity, together with truth and goodness.

Perhaps Thomas was the one who brought this to classical expression as part of his whole ontology. Beauty, he suggested, has two essential elements: harmonious form and splendor. It is the appearance of the mysterious and inexhaustible depths of being expressing itself in the sensible form of concrete beings. It has the power to fascinate and convince us because the delight it arouses in us is based on the fact that, in it, something of the ultimate truth and goodness of reality becomes visible and communicates itself to us. Such an understanding locates the beautiful objectively in the structure of reality rather than subjectively in the spontaneity of reason. If artistic taste is to be more than arbitrary *eisegesis* of the observer, it must be the capacity to perceive beauty as an inherent, transcendental quality of the observed (*exegesis*). This integrated ontology, however, has had little or no significance for theology since the crisis of nominalism and the demise of metaphysics. In our own time, largely due to the work of the Swiss theologian Hans Urs von Balthasar, some of these important insights are being retrieved. Beauty is becoming an important theological concept once more.

3. Theological Considerations

If, metaphysically, beauty is the gracious appearance of being in concrete form, is there an analogous way of speaking theologically about the reality of God's self-revelation using the category of the beautiful? This is precisely what Balthasar argues in his monumental work *Herrlichkeit* (ET *The Glory of the Lord*). The aesthetic dimension of reality is the vessel within which the infinitely free, invisible God graciously becomes visible. In a way analogous to the worldly beautiful, the visible form of God's revelation not only points to the invisible mystery, it is the real expression and presence of this mystery (*mysterion, sacramentum*), precisely as inexhaustible mystery, and so as hidden. Without simply equating the transcendental beauty of divine revelation with inner-worldly natural beauty, which could only lead to the sort of aesthetical theology which Kierkegaard rightly condemned, Balthasar develops a specifically theological aesthetics.

Focused upon salvation history culminating in Jesus Christ as the concrete form of God's self-revelation, Balthasar meditates upon what God's beauty and glory really is. This cannot be deduced in advance from previous notions or reduced to them. It can only be recognized in the form of Jesus Christ, which brings its own evidence, its own power to convince. Our experiences of natural beauty, precisely as the art work of the creator, are capable of revealing something of God's beauty. But the beauty and glory proper to the God who graciously communicates God's own self to the human world as its truest fulfillment may be seen fully only in God's personal appearance in the form of Jesus Christ. In his cross, no form of beauty for worldly eyes, and hidden in its opposite, the sin of the world, God reveals what God's beauty and glory are really about. For eyes which look at the cross in the light of the resurrection, God's beauty appears as the glorious love which has extended its reign to include and transform what had been a kingdom of darkness and sin. The ultimate beauty of being, its last truth and goodness, is seen to be the gracious love of God for God's creation.

Corresponding to the two moments of the beautiful, form and splendor, Balthasar's aesthetics has two phases. First, a theory of vision (fundamental theology), a treatment of faith as the perception of the form of God's self-revelation. Then, a theory of rapture (dogmatic theology), a treatment of the incarnation of God's glory in the form of Jesus Christ and the transforming power of this form to glorify human flesh in the mystery of grace. This is the beauty which theology has as its theme. This is the beauty, the ultimate truth and good, which fulfills human desire and so brings the creation to its final union with God. "The last of the transcendentals, Beauty guards and sets her seal on the others: in the long run the True and the Good do not exist without this luminosity which is both graced and *gratis*. And if Christianity, following the modern trend, were to embrace merely the True (faith as a system of correct propositions) or merely the Good (faith as the subject's greatest advantage and benefit), it would have fallen from its true eminence. If the saints interpreted their existence as being for God's greater glory, they were also always the guardians of the Beautiful" (Balthasar, "Transcendentality" 12).

See **Glory, God, Revelation**

Hans Urs von Balthasar, *The Glory of the Lord: A Theological Aesthetics* (6 vols.), San Francisco, 1982; and "Transcendentality and *Gestalt*" in *Communio* XI/1 (Spring 1984), pp. 4-12.

JOHN R. SACHS, SJ

BENEDICTION, BLESSING

Blessing (or benediction) is a sign which has God's word as its foundation and which is placed in the context of faith. It is a *sacramental,* instituted in imitation of the sacraments. A blessing is a sign especially of a spiritual effect which has been achieved through the church's intercession.

God is the source of all blessings seen especially in his creation and redemption. He communicates life. To share in life with strength, health, success is a blessing from God. God allowed persons of authority to invoke his name in blessing. Kings, prophets, priests and even parents offered blessings in praise of God to bring about good things for the persons in their charge. The OT mentions many blessings of fertility—the promise made to Abraham that he will be the Father of many nations (Gen 12:2) is itself a blessing. The authority of God stands behind his elect: "I will bless those who bless you and curse those who curse you" (Gen 12:3). Whether God blessed the people himself or whether others invoked blessings in his name, the blessing was an invocation of his favor and loving mercy in keeping with the covenant.

Blessings in the OT are irrevocable as in the case of Esau and Jacob (Genesis 27). They were often accompanied by an imposition of hands so the sense of touch was the means of communicating the good from the one invoking to the one blessed.

Jewish prayer forms indicate that God is also blessed by creatures—the Psalms use the expression "Blessed be God." This is in fact offering praise and thanks to God for the good things he has done for his people. The two-way communication between God and his people is one of blessing: God blesses by giving good things but creatures bless God by thanks, worship, service and praise.

Jesus blessed children, food, the apostles and the bread and wine at the last supper. *Berakoth* in Hebrew and the Greek eucharistia mean basically the same thing: blessing, thanksgiving. The Eucharist is the great act of thanking God but is, in fact, blessing, praising, and worshipping God.

The church has established many forms of blessing in order that its members may praise, thank and glorify God who ultimately blesses. The blessings are perceived by the senses in their invocation usually by the sign of the cross over a place, object or person; often by the sprinkling of holy water or incensation with fire; frequently by the imposition of hands and touch. Prayer formularies have retained the Jewish tradition of: praising God for the good things he has done for his people, asking for the favor requested and warding off the power of evil.

Blessings are liturgical rites in the church and the *Book of Blessings* was one of the final revisions after Vatican II, having been published in 1985. Ideally their celebration should take place in an assembly. The ritual book recognizes the rights of lay people to invoke blessings in light of the universal priesthood of baptism and in virtue of the office one holds. Reading of the Word of God is the first part of the Blessing ritual.

Ritual of Blessing

Benediction of the Blessed Sacrament is a liturgical celebration in which the sign of the cross is made with the consecrated host (either in the monstrance or in a ciborium) over assembled believers. This popular devotion developed in the fourteenth century in connection with the conclusion of vespers or compline. The sacrament in the monstrance was moved in blessing over the congregation as an ending rite for the office. During the same century, the monstrance carried in the Corpus Christi procession was used to bless people at various stations along the way. While originally not a rite in itself, Benediction developed as a separate ritual wherein the sacrament was exposed during the singing of *O Salutaris,* incensed during the singing of *Tantum Ergo,* followed by the blessing, divine praises and reposition. The ritual *Holy Communion and Worship of the Eucharist Outside Mass* regulates this liturgical service. Exposition of the sacrament must be accompanied by readings and prayers but cannot be done for Benediction alone. Deacons and priests can bless with the monstrance but acolytes and persons so designated may expose and repose the sacrament.

JOSEPH L. CUNNINGHAM

BIBLE: NEW TESTAMENT

The *New* Testament—the very name expresses the christian conviction that the collection of twenty-seven writings which Christians acknowledge as inspired writings is not the full christian scripture. The whole Bible, and nothing less, is christian scripture. The common term "testament" is an acknowledgment that the specifically christian part is not wholly distinct from the Hebrew Scriptures, the "Old Testament". This is not just a factual observation; it firmly sets the NT in its true context. Despite the fact that before the end of the first century A.D. Christians had come increasingly to regard themselves as the new Israel, over against Judaism, it would seem that Paul had the clearer vision in his admonition to Gentile Christians: "Remember it is not you that support the root, but the root that supports you" (Rom 11:18). What is remarkable is that while Christians came to stress the distinction between their religion and that of the Jews, and while they claimed that their cult had made obsolete all aspects of the religion of Judaism, they held to the sacred scripture of Judaism. True, they began to read it in a distinctive way as, broadly-speaking, a prophecy of Jesus Christ or as a promise which found its fulfillment in him. The fact remains: that precious body of the sacred scriptures of Israel is essential to a proper evaluation of the sacred scriptures of Christianity.

The NT writings themselves did not arise in a vacuum: they came out of living christian communities. And those communities in turn were a response to Jesus and to all he stood for. The sub-title of Edward Schillebeeckx's book *Jesus,* is, in its Dutch original, The Story of a Living One; it could well serve as a descriptive title of the NT. Those writings are inspired by the life and death of a man who lived 2,000 years ago—and who lives more fully today. Jesus of Nazareth wrote not a word of that twenty-seven volume library; every single word is there only because of him. Yet, if it is a story of him, only four of the writings might be called story; the rest come in varied packages.

The letters of Paul are the earliest NT writings and it might seem logical to begin with them. The fact is, while there is broad scholarly consensus on the dating of the NT writings, we cannot be sure that we have got it right. It seems sensible to follow, where feasible, the traditional order—where feasible, because there are some necessary adjustments. The traditional order, after all, is arbitrary; it should not be made to carry more weight than it can bear.

The Synoptic Gospels and Acts

Mark. Our first adjustment is in presenting Mark as our earliest gospel and the evangelist Mark as the pioneer of this literary form. Traditionally, Mark has been dated to c. 65 A.D. and was said to have been written in Rome. While Roman origin, far from certain, may stand, it becomes increasingly clear that our earliest gospel was written shortly after 70 A.D. A main argument is that chapter thirteen is best understood against the background of the traumatic event of the Roman destruction of Jerusalem and the Temple in 70 A.D. What really matters is the purpose and message of the gospel. Underestimated from early times because of its brevity (almost all of Mark is found in Matthew and Luke) and because of the relative poverty of its Greek, in our day Mark has come into its own. Above all, this evangelist stands side by side with Paul as a stalwart proclaimer of a *theologia crucis*—a theology of the cross. And, congenial to modern christology, the Marcan Jesus is the most human of all. Mark sets the pattern of a gospel: it is concerned with christology and discipleship. Jesus is firmly Son of God, that is, God-appointed leader of the new covenant people; he is the "son of man," the human one who came to serve, the one faithful unto death. One who has come to terms with the cross (the meaning of his death) can know him and can confess him—like the centurion (15:39). His disciples did not understand him before Calvary. The christian reader of the first century and of today is being challenged to come to terms with the love of God manifest in the cross of Jesus.

The gospel of Mark is built up of two complementary parts. The first (1:14-8:30) is concerned with the mystery of Jesus' identity; it is dominated by the question, "Who is Jesus?". The emphasis in this first part of Mark is on Jesus' miracles; the teaching is largely parabolic. The second part (8:31-16:8) is concerned with the messianic destiny of Jesus: a way of suffering and death. The emphasis in this second half of Mark is on Jesus' teaching which, now directed to his disciples, builds upon their recognition of him as Messiah and is concerned mainly with the nature of his messiahship and with the suffering it will entail both for himself and for his followers.

If Mark has presented his christology in terms of the life of Jesus, he has presented his teaching on discipleship in terms of the disciples of Jesus. They are painted in their fragile humanness. "The disciples" are a reflex of Mark's community. They are caricatures, starkly drawn, as through them Mark stresses the vital importance of coming to know Jesus and bluntly states his conviction that, without coming to terms with the cross, there is no hope at all of knowing the Lord. It is this concern that accounts for the unbelievable obtuseness of Peter and the rest. In contrast, the minor characters, the "little people"—many of them women—are models of true discipleship.

Matthew. In the decade 80-90 an unknown christian theologian—we name him "Matthew"—made a synthesis of Mark and "Q" (a collection of Jesus' sayings); he had access to other material proper to him (M). His community (likely based in Antioch) was in a crisis situation. It had been a wholly Jewish community, tolerated by Judaism. But now, after the destruction of Jerusalem in 70 A.D. and the reorganization of a shattered Judaism, it had broken with the synagogue and stood in a state of cold war with official Judaism. Besides, more and more Gentiles had joined. The author solves his two-fold problem of Jewish expulsion and Gentile inclusion by dividing salvation history into three periods: "all the

prophets and the law" up to the Baptist (11:13), the public ministry of Jesus restricted to Israel (10:5-6; 15:24), and the mission to all nations made possible by the death-resurrection of Jesus (27:51-54; 28:16-20). Thus, the church, formed by God's Son, is the true people of God, the fulfiller of the law and the prophets.

The structure of Matthew 3-25, the public ministry of Jesus, is precise: five sections, each containing a narrative part and a discourse. Each of the discourses has a brief introduction (5:1-2; 10:1-5; 13:1-3; 18:1-2; 24:1-3) and is closed by a stereotyped formula (7:28; 11:1; 13:53; 19:1; 26:1). The discourses are the pillars of the gospel the sermon on the mount (chaps. 5-7), the missionary discourse (chap. 10), the parables (chap. 13), the church-life discourse (chap. 18) and the discourse on the End (chaps. 24-25). These five central parts of Matthew are not so many disconnected units; there is a close link between them. The narratives indicate the progressive movement of events while the discourses illustrate parallel progress in the messianic concept of the kingdom of heaven. The climax comes in the death-resurrection (chaps. 26-28), a climax which is foreshadowed by the introductory infancy-narrative (chaps. 1-2).

In the first discourse of the gospel, the Sermon on the Mount, Matthew presents Jesus as Messiah in word (chaps. 5-7). The purpose of the narrative section which follows (chaps. 8-9) is to propose Jesus as Messiah in deed, because this section is entirely made up of miracle stories. Then follows the Missionary Discourse addressed to the Twelve (chap. 10) which is succeeded by another narrative section beginning with the question raised by the Baptist, "Are you he who is to come, or shall we look for another?" (11:3). The evangelist manifestly expects his readers to ask themselves the same question. But Matthew believed that a decision regarding Jesus necessarily involved a decision concerning his church. An authentic commitment to Jesus was possible only within the context of membership in his community.

We may particularly well catch something of the flavor of Matthew's gospel from a glance at its closing words, the great commission (Mt 28:16-20). The glorious Son of Man, in the apt setting of a "mountain", a place of revelation, commissions his church. We are rather taken aback to read (v 17) that, of the eleven disciples, "some doubted." Matthew is drawing for his community a picture of every christian community—believers caught between faith and doubt. Jesus solemnly declares that through his death-resurrection he has been granted, by the Father, total power (v 18); he is therefore, in a position to launch a universal mission. During his ministry Jesus limited his mission to Israel (10:5-6; 15:24); in the new era the good news is for all. Consequently, he duly commissions his representatives and sends them into the world to make disciples of "all nations." It is important to be clear that this solemn commission, so theologically significant, is not historically a command of Jesus to his church at its beginning. Acts 15 and Galatians 2 shows that the reception of Gentiles and the mission to them were bitterly resented. This commission reflects the experience of a church that had become open to all, a church tranquilly convinced that it had become what its Lord had meant it to be.

Luke-Acts. It is unfortunate that an understandable desire to group the four gospels meant the separation of Acts of the Apostles from the gospel of Luke. The fact is, Luke and Acts belong together, as two parts of a single work, and each can be properly assessed only in relation to the other. The gospel begins in Jerusalem, more specifically in the temple, with the message of the angel to

Zechariah; it closes with the disciples of Jesus at prayer in the temple (Lk. 24:53). The plan of Acts is firmly sketched in Acts 1:8—"You shall be my witnesses in Jerusalem and in Judea and in Samaria and to the end of the earth." There are few more dramatic endings in literature than the picture of Paul, in Rome (the Roman Empire, remember, is the "world" of the NT), under house-arrest, "preaching the kingdom of God and teaching about the Lord Jesus Christ quite openly and unhindered" (Acts 28:31).

Luke (in his gospel) follows closely the order of Mark. He breaks with Mark in what are known as the "great omission"—the dropping of Mk 6:45 - 8:26—and the interpolations: Lk 6:20 - 8:3 and 9:51 -18:14. The latter, the "great interpolation," witnesses to his skill and his literary independence. Mark did have a rather hurried journey of Jesus to Jerusalem; Luke turned it into a leisured stroll during which his Jesus had ample time to fit in varied teaching and a host of parables, most of them proper to Luke. It does seem that the first draft of the gospel began with the present chapter 3; the prologue, the infancy-gospel (chaps. 1-2) was Luke's brilliant afterthought.

Luke was a second-generation Christian who wrote about 80-85 A.D. Though a Gentile convert (for such, it appears, he was) he was concerned with Israel and acknowledged the place of Israel in God's salvation history. He did not look to an imminent parousia; his two-volume work was written for Christians who lived in the post-apostolic age. "Today," "now" is the time of salvation; *now* life is poured out in the Holy Spirit. But now, too, is the period of *ecclesia pressa*, a church under stress. Luke has shown what may be made of Jesus' deeds and words in a time after the era of Jesus. For us in the twentieth century, conscious of a gap of two millennia between the first proclamation of the christian message and our own striving to assimilate that message, Luke's form of the kerygma may be more congenial than others.

For Luke salvation-history has three phases: a) period of Israel, from creation to the appearance of John the Baptist: the time of the law and the prophets (1:5 -3:1); b) period of Jesus, from the baptism to the ascension of Jesus: the time of Jesus' ministry, death and exaltation (3:2 - 24:51); c) period of the church: the time of the spread of the word of God (Lk 24:52 - Acts 28:31). If creation is the beginning and if the spread of the word will persist to the close of time, then Luke's understanding of salvation history is emphatically universalist. The new inbreaking of divine saving activity into human history includes the extension of salvation to persons outside of God's chosen people of old. The change involves a distinctive view of Israel. God has not replaced his chosen people with a new one. The church is not a new Israel but a reconstituted Israel with Gentiles taking their place beside Jews who had accepted the message of Jesus.

For Luke the word of God was made flesh in Jesus but in another manner than for John. It is not the Johannine pre-existent Word but the word of God formerly addressed to the prophets that has taken flesh in Jesus (Acts 10:36-37). One may equally well say that in Jesus the flesh becomes word: the messenger becomes the message. In their turn the apostles carry on the incarnation of the word as they become the human and suffering bearers of God's message. They carry the word differently from Jesus—in his name, not in their own.

Since Acts is the second volume of one work it should be taken for what it is: more correctly a sequel to Luke's gospel than a history of the early church. Given this close relationship, we are not surprised to find that the structure of gospel and Acts runs along parallel lines. The narrative of the ministry of Jesus is formed of two more or less equal parts: the first, covering the preaching in Galilee, centers in the Twelve and ends with the mission confided to the Twelve; the other part, the journey to Jerusalem, begins with the mission charge to the Seventy, and has material not found in Mark and Matthew. Similarly, Acts has two parts: one in which Peter has a leading role and which looks to Jerusalem (1:1 - 15:35); the second, centered in Paul, breaks out of this geographical framework and turns towards Rome (15:36 - 28:31).

In Acts, Luke is concerned with showing the progress of the Good News throughout the whole known world (1:8). He is especially interested in the passing of the preaching from Jews to Gentiles and in the progress of the Gentile mission. Behind the continuous spread of the Gospel throughout the provinces of the Empire he sees the power of the Holy Spirit. Luke was aware that the Gentile mission had been set on foot before Paul had begun to play his part and he knew that Paul was not the only architect of the Gentile church. But since his purpose was to portray the spread of the church, he could not have chosen a more dramatic and effective way of doing so. For it is true that Paul the missionary and Paul the theologian has set his stamp on Christianity.

The Pauline Corpus

Traditionally, fourteen writings have been attributed to Paul. Perhaps the first thing to get clear is that there are three NT "Pauls": the real Paul of his authentic letters; the hagiographical Paul of Luke (Acts); the "Paul" of the deutero-pauline letters. It is widely acknowledged today that the authentic pauline letters are: 1 Thessalonians; 1, 2 Corinthians; Galatians; Romans; Philippians; Philemon. There is no reasonable doubt that the Pastorals (1, 2 Timothy; Titus) are pseudepigraphical. Increasingly, 2 Thessalonians, Colossians and Ephesians are held to be by another than Paul. And Hebrews is certainly not pauline.

The Pauline Letters. The letters of Paul are the earliest NT writings. On the whole, they are occasional writings, that is to say, written by the apostle in view of special circumstances affecting the particular church to which he wrote.

2 Thessalonians. Paul visited Thessalonica for the first time probably in 50 A.D. His stay was short—a matter of a few months. Later, in Corinth, being assured by his emissary Timothy that the young community was thriving, he gave expression to his relief in a letter to it. He seized the occasion to draw attention to certain shortcomings and to issue instructions. This first (extant) letter set the pattern for the subsequent pauline letters. A principal reason for a second letter (2 Thessalonians) was to set right erroneous views on the parousia. One practical issue was that some Thessalonians, expecting an imminent End, no longer saw any point in work. Because of the language of apocalyptic drama in 2:1-10 and because phrases have been copied from 1 Thessalonians, many scholars question pauline authorship of 2 Thessalonians.

The Major Epistles. Four of Paul's writings—Galatians, 1, 2 Corinthians, Romans (likely in that chronological order) are known as the Major Epistles. We shall take Galatians in close connection with Romans. Galatia had been evangelized by Paul early in his second missionary journey (50-52) and Galatians was most likely written during his stay in Ephesus (54-57). The purpose of the letter is clearly defined: to refute the error of judaizers who had come to disturb the faith of the Galatians by teaching the need for observance of the Mosaic law and, positively, to vindicate Paul's "gospel": justification through faith in Christ and not through observance of works of the Law.

In Gal 2:15-21 Paul gives a resumé of his gospel; much of the doctrine of Galatians and Romans is compressed into these few verses. The Jerusalem leaders he names were able to accept his stance because they too believed that salvation was from Christ alone. Nor did Paul object to the fact that the Judeo-Christians of Palestine remained faithful to the Mosaic observances. Yet he saw the inherent danger and realized that the full christian doctrine involved freedom from the Law in theory and in fact. We cannot win salvation by our own observances; we must accept it as free gift from Christ. The same basic teaching, in different terms—redemption by the death and resurrection of Christ—runs through the letter.

The issue raised in a polemical atmosphere in Galatians was taken up again by Paul in a letter which was meant to prepare his way for a visit to Rome (Romans, written in Corinth, winter 57/58). Paul is concerned to expound his gospel, his manner of preaching the good news of Christ: his emphasis on the central truth of salvation. He proclaims that salvation, necessary for all and offered to all, is indeed presented to all by the preaching of the gospel. In Romans 1-3, Paul paints a gloomy picture indeed: the whole of humankind, Jew no less than Gentile, is in a situation of total helplessness. He has two, closely-related reasons for his emphasis. He is sure that salvation is God's deed: it cannot be earned; and he is sure that salvation can be ours by means of a faith that is openness to God's gift. Paul envisaged a human world in slavery to the tyrants *Thanatos, Hamartia* and *Nomos* (that is, Death, Sin and Law). The tyrant Sin had gotten a firm grip on *sarx* ("flesh"), the human condition of weakness. Paradoxically, this weakness is the fatal human illusion of independence, of being able to go it alone. That was the first sin recorded in scripture: humankind tried to snatch at the wisdom that could only be gift from God (Gen 3:1-7). Reference to Genesis is not irrelevant because Paul explicitly refers to the Adam story (Rom. 5:12-20).

The passage 5:6-11 presents a favorite Pauline theme. God showed his love for men and women while they were still incapable of doing anything to help themselves. At the appropriate moment in the history of salvation he sent his Son who died on behalf of the sinful and the ungodly—those estranged from God. This was the measure of God's love. To paraphrase v 8: the proof of God's amazing love is that, while we were yet sinners and adrift from God, Christ the Son of God died for us, the ungodly.

Paul's moving peroration at the close of the third major section of the letter (8:31-39) is a summary of the whole first part of Romans and of Paul's gospel in general. From 6:6 to 8:30 his preoccupation has been to demonstrate to the believer God's love for humankind. He wants to show that redemption, what God has done for the world in Christ, is a work of God's love, that is, of his total self-giving in his Son. Nothing, he concludes, in all creation, will separate us from that love of God in Christ Jesus.

One may find that Romans 9-11 do not represent the easiest and clearest part of Paul's writings. But one cannot fail to be moved by the passion behind these chapters. Paul will simply not accept that God has rejected his people (11:1). At the end, he puts his trust in God and can declare, in words that have nothing to do with the logic of his argument up to now: "and so all Israel will be saved" (11:26). Indeed Paul is going to take a giant step: "For God has consigned all men to disobedience, that he may have mercy upon all" (11:32). His declaration has to

be seen in contrast to the unrelieved picture he has painted in chaps. 1-3. But then, that backdrop was meant to highlight the incredibly gracious saving gift of God.

1 and 2 Corinthians. Paul, while at Ephesus (54-57), was informed of rival parties and of scandals in the Corinthian church; and the Corinthians, in a letter to him, had submitted a number of questions. Notable features of his reply (1 Corinthians) consider the christian attitude to marriage and celibacy, the authentic doctrine of the eucharist, and the first appearance of his teaching on the body of Christ. He uncompromisingly rejects the wisdom of the world, the foolish self-sufficiency of human thought. It is foolish because it ignores humankind's complete dependence on God; that is why he is desirous of knowing nothing except "Jesus Christ and him crucified."

While it may be that his experience of dismal failure at Athens just before his departure for Corinth (Acts 17:32-33) had influenced Paul's approach, it must be that the real motivation of his uncompromising preaching of Christ crucified was because he had come to a profound understanding of the cross. He realized that here the ornate language of Greek rhetoric would be wholly out of place. The gospel message, in its starkness, would speak for itself: God redeemed the world through the death of his Son on a cross and he, Paul, was sent by Christ to preach the Good News of this redemption. By human standards it is foolishness: it is folly to look for redemption to one who could not save himself from death. "Theology of the cross" sounds grim. Yet, theology of the cross, as preached by Paul, is positive and full of hope. That is because his starting point is the graciousness of God—or, as he calls it, the "foolishness" of God. This foolishness of God, expressed in the cross of Jesus, shows God's commitment to humankind;

he is indeed a God bent on the salvation of humankind.

In Macedonia, towards the close of 57, Paul learned that the turbulent Corinthian community, in the meantime shaken by further crises, was at last reasonably tranquil. Second Corinthians expresses his satisfaction at this turn; but it is also very much of an apologia. The writing is, in large measure, a defense of the apostolic ministry and reveals the deeper human side of Paul. In 1 Corinthians (1:18-30) Paul had spoken of the folly of the cross; the same idea runs through 2 Cor 4:6-11—God works through human weakness so that the success of the apostolate and the advance of the kingdom of God will be seen as the work of God not of humankind. The message is preached by weak "servants of the word" like himself to show that it is the power of God and not anything in themselves that brings it to fruition.

Our appreciation of Paul will be increased when we understand that what is central to him is not so much a doctrinal position as his experience of the boundless love of Christ. This is the driving force behind his passionate, at times polemical, interest in the christian communities for which he feels himself responsible. The passage 5:11-21 brings us close to the heart of Paul. The love of God stirs him and he, in his turn, proclaims Christ, dead and risen again. Here he gives the reason for Jesus' death not in cultic terms (as sacrifice for sin) but in terms of human existence: Christ died so that we should live a Christ-centered and no longer a self-centered life. Paul mentions one result of this new life in his own case; he no longer judges anyone by worldly standards and conventions. This goes, supremely, for his understanding of Christ (v 16). Before his conversion Paul would have looked upon Jesus as a man among men, "according to the flesh." On the Damascus road he encountered the risen Savior.

Both chapters 8 and 9 are concerned with the collection for the Jerusalem church. The matter of a collection in favor of the "saints" was of great importance in Paul's eyes. It was a facet of his theology of unity developed in face of differences between Judeo-Christians and Gentile converts. Chapters 10-13 is Paul's letter written "out of much affliction and anguish of heart and with many tears" (2:4)—a stirring and emotional defense of his apostolate and gospel. The Lord has called him to the apostolic ministry; this is approbation and praise enough; self-praise would sound foolish beside it (chap. 10). Much of chapter 11 is bitingly sarcastic. Paul had been called a "fool"; let them put up with his "folly" then! He had been driven to self-defense by the fickleness of the Corinthians who were ready to accept a different gospel. Although boasting about visions is out of place, Paul is compelled to recall an extraordinary experience: he had found himself caught up to the divine presence (12:1-4). A keen reminder of his human weakness kept him from being carried away by the experience. He regarded his infirmity as an impediment to the effectiveness of his ministry and prayed to be rid of it. This was not to be and Paul realized that God's mysterious ways of salvation were at work in his own person.

What was important to him above all was the Lord's answer to his prayer: "My grace is sufficient for you, for my power is made perfect in weakness." The human limitation and disabilities of the sincere and generous apostle are not an obstacle to apostolic work because the power of Christ within "is able to do far more abundantly than all we ask or think" (Eph 3:20). Indeed, insult, persecution, even calamity, may be vehicles of that power, a power all the more manifest because it works through the frailty of the apostle.

Philippians and Philemon. The four letters, Philippians, Philemon, Colossians, and Ephesians are called the Captivity Letters because they are, or purport to have been, written in prison. Paul visited Philippi for the first time in 50 A.D., later in 57, and for a third time, on his way back from Corinth in 58. The church of Philippi, predominantly Gentile, was the one dearest to the heart of Paul, and Philippians is remarkable for its spirit of joy. The unity (not the authenticity) of the letter has been questioned. Recent studies plausibly distinguish three letters: A. 4:10-20; B. 1:1 -3:1; C. 3:2 - 4:1; the ending 4:21-23 may belong to any of the three. When the fusion of these letters took place is a matter of conjecture; it may have been at the moment when the Philippians passed on their Pauline correspondence to another church. With some confidence Philippians (or the three letters) may be dated in 56-57 with Ephesus as place of origin. Of special interest and importance is the hymn (2:6-11) quoted by Paul—a passage of major christological reference. Traditionally, this hymn has been taken to portray Christ in his pre-existence, his role as servant and his exaltation as Lord. Recent studies suggest that there is no reference to pre-existence and incarnation. Rather, we have to do with an Adam-Jesus comparison: Jesus, in total obedience to God (in contrast to Adam's disobedience) becomes the perfect exemplar of a true servant of God. This is why he was given the power-title "Lord" and universal dominion.

In the little letter to Philemon Paul, with notable delicacy, urges Philemon to welcome back as a brother in Christ his runaway slave Onesimus now, too, a Christian. The onus is firmly on Philemon. A true christian response must be free, not a matter of duress.

The Deutero-pauline Letters

Pseudonymity (the attribution of a writing, by the author, to another than himself) was a well-known and accepted literary convention in NT times—in both Hellenistic and Jewish circles. More and more it is being accepted that Colossians is pseudonymous. This means that a disciple of Paul, one who revered the great apostle, faced up to the problem and difficulties of his later age in the manner he believed Paul would have done in his own day. Colossae, a hundred miles east of Ephesus, seems never to have been visited by Paul. Approximate date of the letter: 60 A.D. The author wrote this letter because of a dangerous error which threatened to disrupt the Colossian community. What the disturbers propose to the Colossians, in the first place, are observations touching the calendar (2:16b), dietary laws (2:16a, 21-23) and circumcision (2:11-13); the Jewish character of these observances is manifest. Besides, behind it all stands the Jewish law (2:14) with its obsolete air of "shadow of things to come" (2:17). Then, too, the "cult of angels" (2:18) refers to ideas about celestial or cosmic powers common among Jewish groups such as the Essenes. In contrast, the author's one concern is to maintain the absolute supremacy of Christ; his interest in the "powers" is secondary.

Today it is widely held that Ephesians is the work of a disciple of Paul (and not necessarily an immediate disciple) who sought to develop the ideas of his master in a markedly ecclesiological direction. It is agreed that the writing cannot be by Paul himself because of the direction of its theology, its unusual vocabulary, and its curious literary contacts with other NT epistles and with Colossians in 'particular. The title "to the Ephesians" is not original; it seems likely that the letter was, in fact addressed not to one church but to a group of churches. A date about 90 A.D. has been proposed.

The leading themes of Ephesians are

the cosmic dimension of Christ's salvation, the church, and the divine mystery (in their measure, too, the themes of Colossians). The cosmic supremacy of Christ, head of the universe and master of the angels, had been so firmly established in Colossians that Ephesians does not have to dwell on it at length. At most, the theme is recalled in some striking formulas (Eph 1:10, 21; 4:10). What is truly specific in Ephesians is that the idea of Christ's cosmic supremacy has influenced the notion of the church. The church is not only the body of Christ, it is his *plerōma,* his "fullness" (1:23). Beyond Christians who are the "body" properly so called, the church embraces, in some manner, all the forces of the new creation. The cosmic breadth of view of Colossians is maintained in Ephesians but always in relation to the concept of the church. Contemplation of cosmic salvation, which embraces Jews and Gentiles alike and touches the whole of creation, leads the author to see here the "mystery", that is, a secret long hidden in God but now revealed; he insists on the need for supernatural wisdom in order to attain true knowledge of the divine plan (Col 1:26-28; Eph 1:3-14). For the author, the whole structure of the church is founded in unity and leads to unity (4:1-6). And he has brought out, more clearly than in Colossians, the distinction of Head and Body (seen in the subjection of one to the other) and their union (achieved through love) when he presents the church as the Spouse of Christ (5:23-32).

The Pastorals. The two letters to Timothy and the letter to Titus have, since the eighteenth century, been known as the Pastoral Epistles. 1 Timothy and Titus are of an essentially similar literary character; 2 Timothy has a more personal tone than the others. All three have been written by the same author, a man of the third christian generation, who wrote c. 110 A.D. He had invoked the names of the well-known disciples to deal with the problems of the community, or communities, of his concern. Paul is, for him, the ideal apostle. And the pastoral directives, needful for his situation, found greater weight when they were presented as issuing from Paul. The Pastorals differ from the pauline letters not only on the ground of different authorship but more fundamentally because they reflect a greatly changed church. A feature of Paul's outlook is his eschatological expectation; he can contemplate the parousia of the Lord happening in his own lifetime. In Pastorals the view clearly is that the church must make adjustments for a prolonged stay in the world. This involves a preoccupation with institution and with orthodoxy. Natural enough, too, is a concern with "good citizenship." Christians are expected to be model exponents of the moral and social virtues. In this way it was hoped that they would win respect and acceptance among their contemporaries in the Roman world (contrast Revelation). Despite the emphasis on structure no clear structural pattern emerges—certainly no obvious hierarchical institution. Indeed, one man stands out: Paul—he is the real figure of authority. As for doctrine, a clear tendency runs through: traditional teaching is not interpreted but is firmly inculcated as an existing and permanent norm. The Pastorals present a church coming to terms with life: an eminently sensible church concentrating on structure, orthodoxy and respectability. It is a sort of church with which we are familiar because, historically, the christian church has followed the Pastoral model.

Hebrews. The magnificent letter to the Hebrews was written by an unknown, immensely gifted, Hellenistic Christian to encourage Jewish Christians who, in face of difficulties and persecution, were tempted to drift from Christianity. The author exhorts them to cling to the Word of God as unveiled in Christ and to persevere in faith. The force of the argument rests altogether on the person and work of Jesus: Son of God, eternal high priest, offering a perfect sacrifice. It is most likely a document of the second christian generation and may be reasonably dated in the 80's.

The central theme of Hebrews, the priesthood of Christ, is formulated by reference to Jewish theological categories: Christ is superior to angels, to Moses, to the levitical priesthood and Christ's sacrifice is superior even to the high-priestly liturgy of the Day of Atonement. Such OT concepts were well appreciated by first-century Jewish converts though not, even then, by all; inevitably, they lose something of their relevance after twenty centuries. Despite this, we meet throughout the letter religious truths of perennial validity. The author intended his treatise to be "a word of exhortation" (13:22). The whole is a splendid statement of the saving work of Christ and constitutes for us today a moving word of exhortation in a time when we may be tempted to "fall away from the living God" (3:12).

A special worth of Hebrews is its contribution to christology. For the author Jesus is Son of God; but he is the son who "had to be made like his brethren in every respect" (2:17), a Son who "in every respect has been tempted as we are, yet without sinning" (4:15). He is the human being who stands in a relationship of obedient faithfulness towards God (3:16) and who stands in solidarity with human suffering. Thereby he is a mediator: a true priest who can bring humankind to God. If he bears "the very stamp of God's nature" (1:3) it is because we see in him what makes God God; he shows us that God is God of humankind.

The consistently negative evaluation of the whole levitical system might suggest that, for the author of Hebrews, the OT holds nothing of value for Christians. Not so: there is, among other things, the inspiring example of the faith of the great men and women of Israel, with the reminder that faith is necessary for those who would move onward to draw close to God. Faith is the firm assurance of the fulfillment of our hope. For, faith is oriented to the future and reaches out to the invisible. Grounded on the word of God, it is a guarantee of heavenly blessedness; it persuades us of the reality of what is not seen as yet and enables us to act upon it.

The realization that the saints of the OT, their noble ancestors in the faith, are witnesses of the great race which Christians must run, will give them heart and encourage them to persevere. Nor are these merely interested onlookers. As in a relay race, the first runners have passed on the baton of faith—they are deeply involved in the outcome of this race of Christians. But the example that is best calculated to sustain the patience and courage of Christians is that of their Lord who was humiliated and crucified only to rise again and enter into his glory. Jesus is the "pioneer"—that is, chief and leader—offering the example of a faith strong enough to enable him to endure the sufferings of his whole life.

The Johannine Writings

It does not take long to recognize that the Johannine Jesus is, in many respects, very different from the Jesus of the synoptists. It is not only a question of style but of content and, especially, of christology. True, John and the synoptists tell the same story, but they tell it differently. While already in Matthew and Luke there is a tendency to stress what one might call the other-worldliness of Jesus, in John he seems something of a sojourner from another world. In the synoptics Jesus' message concerns "the kingdom of God," the benevolent rule of

God. In John, what Jesus preaches, what he reveals, is himself. Jesus is still concerned to make the real God known, but now who God is can be known and seen in Jesus himself. True, it is in and through Jesus we come to know God, but the Johannine emphasis is distinctive: "No one has ever seen God, the only Son who is in the bosom of the Father, he has made him known" (Jn 1:18). There is a whole series of "I am" sayings (e.g. 6:35; 10:11; 11:25). This reaches its height in the four absolute "I am" sayings (8:24, 28, 58; 13:19). Each time there is a conscious echo of the divine name of Exod 3:14. We should not, however, lose sight of the fact that, throughout the Fourth Gospel, Jesus' subordination to the Father is just as clearly expressed (e.g. 5:19; 5:26). And 14:28 states bluntly: "The Father is greater than I." This qualifying aspect of Johannine christology has rarely been given its proper weight.

The Fourth Gospel had a complex genesis and grew in stages. Yet, it shows signs of having been molded by a dominant figure who shaped the traditional material to a particular theological cast and expression. We can be sure that for the Johannine community another than he, the "Beloved Disciple" (cf Jn 13:23; 19:26-27; 20:2-9; 21:7, 20-23), a disciple of the ministry and source of the tradition, was the greatly venerated link with Jesus; he stands, in contrast to Peter, as the father-figure of the Johannine group. The gospel may have taken its final shape in Ephesus (where the Letters, too, would have been written). Its likely date: 90-100 A.D.

The Fourth Gospel falls into two parts: the Book of Signs (1:19 - 12:50)—the public ministry of Jesus wherein sign and word he shows himself to his own people as the revelation of his Father, only to be rejected, and the Book of Glory (chaps. 13-20)—to those who accept him Jesus shows his glory by returning to his Father in the "hour" of his crucifixion, resurrection and ascension; fully glorified he communicates the Spirit of life. The Prologue (1:1-18) is an early christian hymn, stemming from Johannine circles, adapted to serve as an overture to the Gospel. An Epilogue (chap. 21) adds a series of post-resurrection appearances in Galilee.

In the narrative matter, the structure of the gospel as a whole displays a notably dramatic element. This skillfulness of presentation is also present in the longer individual episodes, such as the Samaritan woman, the cure of the blind man, the raising of Lazarus. In these episodes the reader is brought stage by stage to the full self-revelation of Jesus. And the reader, too, comes to an increasing certainty of his faith. The longer narrative complexes illustrate the conflicts of opinion, the antagonism between belief and unbelief. At the same time, these episodes serve to present the great struggle between light and darkness, a struggle in which, seen from the outside, the powers of darkness and unbelief appear to be gaining the upper hand. Even in the shorter passages such as the marriage of Cana, the cleansing of the temple, and the healing of the official's son, dramatic presentation is not lacking. Here, too, one finds the moment of suspense before the liberating vision of faith.

An aspect of the dramatic in John is present in the emphasis placed on "signs"; the signs are mighty works, performed in the sight of Jesus' disciples, miracles. Still it is by contrasting "miracle" and "sign" that we can best understand John's intention. The restoring of sight to a blind man is a sign of the spiritual light that Christ, who is Light, can give, because he viewed such actions of Jesus as pointers to a deeper, spiritual truth. We are not always left to work out these hidden meanings for ourselves, because, in many cases, they are brought out in the discourses that accompany the signs; we are also thereby provided with a criterion for judging other passages where such comment is lacking. The signs are closely linked to the work of Jesus on earth; the purpose is to bring out the deeper dimension of his works, to reveal the glory of the incarnate One.

Nowhere does the difference between John and the synoptic gospels strike one more forcefully than in the discourses of Jesus: the discourses of the fourth gospel are quite distinctive. John does not reason in our western manner: he testifies, he affirms. He does not set out to prove a thesis by building up consecutive arguments until the conclusion is reached. Instead, his thought moves around a central point. John 14:1-24 can be taken as an example, of how the thought "circles," repeating and insisting, while, at the same time, moving forward and upward to a higher level. Again, one may instance the two great "parabolic discourses" in John—the Shepherd and the flock (10:1-18) and the Vine and the branches (15:1-10). Both passages are built on similar lines: first a presentation of the matter, the "parable"(10:1-5; 15:1-2), followed by the strictly Johannine development: a method of concentric thinking which progresses in new circles. It is a meditative way of thought which, instead of proceeding by arguments delves further into its subject to gain a deeper and higher understanding of it. This distinctive Johannine movement of thought seems to have no direct parallels. It is a personal style, achieved by meditation on the revelation of Jesus Christ and used to clarify this revelation.

The Johannine Letters

The Fourth Gospel shows sign of turmoil within the community, largely about christology. Already, the original Johannine Christians, Jewish all of them, had been expelled from the synagogue (9:22, 34; 12:42; 16:2)—expelled because of their claims on behalf of Jesus. It emerges in chapter 6 that some within the community found the claim that Jesus was a descended heavenly being too much to take—they left (6:61-66). The Johannine Letters tell of a further schism—again over the christological issue. In 1 Jn 2:18 the author, using apocalyptic language, asserts that the appearance of "antichrists" signals the "last hour"—the "antichrists" being those Johannine Christians who have broken with the author's party. In 2 Jn 7 we have the equivalent of the "antichrist" text of 1 Jn 2:19—the "deceivers and antichrists" will not acknowledge "the coming of Jesus Christ in the flesh" (1 Jn 4:2-3). In contrast, true believers "confess that Jesus Christ has come in the flesh"(1 Jn 4:2-3). Manifestly, the issue is "come in the flesh." This does not at all mean a denial of incarnation—the "secessionists"(a convenient term for the breakaway group) are not docetists. The trouble with the secessionists is that they had pushed high christology a stage further. For them the entry of the heavenly figure into our world—the Word-made-flesh—was, in itself, the saving event; the life and death of Jesus had no saving significance. They took their stand on an interpretation of the Johannine tradition, which the author of the letter regarded as misinterpretation. He insists on the saving importance of the life and death of Jesus (1 Jn 1:7; 2:2; 4:9-10; 5:6).

Christology, of course, is not the sole concern. 1 John has been aptly described as: "A work consisting of comments on Johannine tradition as it is known to us in the Fourth Gospel. These comments were written to protect the author's adherents within the Johannine Community from further inroads by secessionist teachers whose slogans, christological and ethical, the author refutes" (R.E. Brown). The brief 2 John is a letter to a particular church warning against secessionist teachers. 3 John urges a certain Gaius to continue, and extend, his hospitality to "true" Johannine missionaries—Demetrius is, plausibly, one of them. Diotrephes, host of a Johannine house-church, has decided to take strong action against *all* visiting missionaries. The author, evidently, does not like this show of authority. An intriguing feature of the Johannine communities is that they had no authority structure. Their authority was the Paraclete, the Spirit (cf 1 Jn 2:27). The three Johannine letters, by the one author, were written in Asia Minor around 100-110 A.D.

Revelation. While apocalyptic themes emerge here and there in the NT (in Mk 13, for instance) there is only one wholly apocalyptic writing. Apocalyptic is crisis literature. A small, vulnerable group can have a real experience of crisis in circumstances that are far from earth-shattering. Such was the situation of a circle of christian communities in towns of the Roman province of Asia (the western part of modern Turkey). The elements of crisis were: conflict with Jews; conflict with Gentiles; conflict over wealth—as part of a general resistance (especially in the East) to Roman rule. By this time sharply distinct from the synagogue, these Christians could no longer shelter under the Jewish umbrella and avail themselves of Roman tolerance of a *religio licita.* Emperor worship was an aggravating factor. Because they refused to pay token reverence to a deified emperor they were classed as disloyal citizens and made to suffer accordingly. An eloquent commentary on the breadth of NT pluralism is the contrast between the Pastoral author's concern with good citizenship and our author's call for speedy divine judgment on the satanic Empire. Revelation is disturbing, but it carries its own christian message. It is a reminder, however radically expressed, that God has the last word, that the empires of the world, by themselves, can never bring true peace. And there is in it the salutary warning that justice, without love, is not wholesome. Revelation is long on justice—short on love.

On the plus side, we may regard the writing as a commentary on the reassuring words of Jesus to his disciples: "In the world you have tribulation; but be of good cheer, I have overcome the world" (Jn 16:33). Christians facing imminent persecution and possible martyrdom need their Lord's word that their very death means a share in their Lord's victory. They need the assurance that their response to a call for "the endurance and faith of the saints" (Rev 14:2) will win them a share in his resurrection. Each needs the assurance that, although one be assaulted or martyred by the forces of evil, still one will not have given one's life in vain. "The Lamb *will* conquer ... for he is Lord of lords and King of kings, and those with him are called and chosen and faithful" (17:14). The author of Revelation, called John (it is unusual for the author of an apocalypse to name himself) wrote, obviously in Asia Minor, about 95 A.D.

The Catholic Epistles

In addition to the collection of Pauline letters, the NT contains another group of seven letters: James; 1, 2 Peter; 1, 2, 3 John; and Jude. But these letters differ so widely among themselves that the mere fact of not being "Pauline" seems to be the only reason for grouping them. Their title Catholic Epistles is meant to imply the "general" character of these writings: they are addressed to Christians in general (and not to individual churches like the letters of Paul). In view of their close relationship with the Fourth Gospel it was proper to take 1, 2, 3 John with the

Johannine writings.

James. It was traditionally accepted that the James named in the address as author of this writing is James "the brother of the Lord," leader of the Jewish Christian community of Jerusalem. Against that, there is the excellent Greek style and the remarkable affinity of James with the first epistle of Clement (c. 96-98). James, then, is a pseudonymous writing and dates from the last decade of the first century.

James is addressed to a milieu in which social differences are marked. There are the rich who expect, and receive, deferential treatment even in the liturgical assemblies (2:1-3), men who are prodigal of generous words that cost them nothing (2:16). Wholly absorbed in business affairs (4:13-17) they do not hesitate to cheat their employees and to squeeze the poor (5:1-6). These same poor receive scant attention even from those who are supposed to be their shepherds and ought to be their servants (2:2-6).

Of special interest is the passage 2:14-26 where, on the issue of faith and works, James appears to be in flat contradiction of Paul. In point of fact, while both use the same terms, they do not give them quite the same meaning. When Paul uses the word "faith" he implies a trust in God, a commitment; for James, "faith" is belief—even the demons believe in God (Jas 2:19). For Paul "works" are works of the Law as means of salvation; for James they are works of charity. Whereas Paul (Rom 4:2-3; cf Gen 16:6) argues that Abraham was justified by faith and not by works, James (2:21)—referring to readiness to sacrifice Isaac (Gen 22:4), the culmination of the trial of Abraham— argues that the patriarch was justified by his good works. There is polemic, but Paul is not James' target; he is aiming at misinterpretation of Paul's teaching. Paul himself (cf. 1, 2 Cor) had been painfully conscious of potential and actual mis-representation.

1, 2 Peter and Jude. The fact of several pseudonymous Pauline writings is manifest evidence of the continuing influence of Paul in the early church; the parallel fact of two pseudonymous Petrine letters witnesses to the prominence of Peter. Both Petrine letters seem to have emanated from a Petrine group at Rome (a group also imbued with Pauline ideas). Both letters are concerned with unity and with sound doctrine—shades of the Pastorals. The significant factor is that Roman Christians, invoking the name of Peter, should have written to christian communities in Asia Minor. Already a "Petrine office" is beginning to emerge.

1 Peter. "1 Peter is a startling blend of joy and suffering. Few biblical books can match its sense of cosmic optimism, its evident enthusiasm for life; yet the letter refers to the sufferings of Jesus more than any other New Testament book" (D. Senior). One might say that concentration on the passion of Jesus is the key to the letter's message. The "aliens" of Asia Minor to whom the letter is addressed (1:1) are Christians who suffer an exile of the spirit, out of step as they are with the pervading culture. They are the new diaspora: Christians exiled from their true homeland. They can console themselves by recalling that Jesus Christ, too, was rejected by the world (2:4).

The passage 3:16 - 4:6 has to do with conduct of Christians in face of persecution. It seems to preserve elements of a baptismal creed: death of Christ (3:18), descent into Sheol (3:19) resurrection (3:21), session at God's right hand (3:22), judgment of living and dead (4:5). The theme of 3:18 is echoed in 4:1-2—the example of the suffering Christ. Persecution and suffering are taken up again in 4:12-19, a passage which might well be seen as a synthesis of the epistle. The "fiery ordeal" of persecution ought not come as a surprise for it is a feature of christian life in this world. It not only tests the genuineness of the faith of Christians but also is a sharing in Christ's sufferings; it is even a cause for joy as pledge of a part in his glory. While they should do nothing that deserves punishment, to suffer on the ground that one is a Christian is not something to be ashamed of. Those who patiently endure suffering are in the care of a faithful Creator—only here in the NT is God so designated.

Jude. The author of the short letter of Jude takes issue with false teaching and unmasks some who would pervert the traditional doctrine and put the faith of the community at risk. The author names himself: "Jude, a servant of Jesus Christ and brother of James" (v 1). By now one should suspect that the letter is, in fact, pseudonymous and was written in the decade 80-90—perhaps even later. The author, desirous of writing to the faithful on the matter of christian salvation, finds that he must urge them to contend for their traditional faith. He writes as he does because he had become aware that heretical teachers had infiltrated the community. Consequently, despite his initial optimistic intention, he ends up as a prophet of gloom, with dire threats for the "false teachers."

2 Peter. The author of 2 Peter is concerned that his readers should not forfeit their promised entry into the eternal kingdom of Jesus Christ and he writes to strengthen them in the traditional faith—taking to task teachers who might lead them astray. Though the writer assumes the name of Peter and refers to 1 Peter (1:1; 3:1) he wrote long after the time of Peter. It is of particular significance that in 3:15-16 he sets the writings of Paul ("in all his letters") on a par with "the other scriptures." Already the canon is, in practice, taking shape and a collection of Pauline letters is regarded as "canonical." This could scarcely have happened before the end of the first century. On the whole, it would seem that 2 Peter is not only among the later NT writings: it is the latest NT writing, perhaps about 125 A.D. The author, by identifying himself with Peter, shows that his intention is to transmit apostolic teaching. In the same spirit, he has made use of the letter of Jude and appealed to the authority of Paul.

The threat faced in 2 Peter is not that of a hostile environment as in 1 Peter: it is a threat from within. Members of the community were propounding false doctrine and living a counterfeit christian life. In chapter 2 the antinomianism of these false teachers emerges; in this respect they are quite like those envisaged in Jude. But 2 Peter gives us to understand that they have progressed in error and have now become deriders of hope in a parousia—because there is no final destiny for the world or its history. From their fundamental error others flow: they disown the Lord of the parousia (2:1, 10) and, discounting the expectation of judgment, they set the moral order aside (3:3). In short, these people have been affected by the prevailing religious skepticism. Against these mistaken views the author, in concepts and language of his culture and theirs, insists on the reality of the day of the Lord, the culmination of God's design (1:4, 8, 11; 3:10, 14). He proclaims the Lordship of Jesus (1:2, 16-17, 3:10, 14) and insistently urges moral living (1:4-11; 3:11, 14, 17). In his final word he entreats his readers to "grow in the grace and knowledge of our Lord and Savior Jesus Christ" (3:18). This puts in a nutshell the purpose of the whole NT.

Conclusion

In conclusion we recall that the NT, like the scriptures of Israel, grew out of the life and experience of a people. In both cases the people, not the book, came first. And the book must ever find its setting in the ongoing life of a people.

Only in the midst of a believing people does the Bible come alive. A truly christian reading of Scripture is "in church"—in the context of a living community. At the same time and all the while this word of God stands as inspiration and norm of christian living and is a perennial challenge to the values and conduct of the community.

See **Jesus Christ; Judaism; Bible, Old Testament**

R.E. Brown, *The Gospel According to John,* N.Y.: Doubleday and London: Geoffrey Chapman, 1966, 1971. *The Epistles of John,* N.Y.: Doubleday, 1982. W. Harrington and D. Senior, Eds, *New Testament Message,* 22 vols. Wilmington, DE: Michael Glazier and Dublin: Veritas, 1979 - 1981. W. Harrington, *Key to the Bible,* Vol. 3, N.Y.: Doubleday, 1976. D. Guthrie, *New Testament Introduction,* Downers Grove, IL: Inter-Varsity Press, 1970. H.C. Kee, F.W. Young, K. Froelich, *Understanding the New Testament,* N.J.: Prentice-Hall, 1973. W. G. Kümmel, *Introduction to the New Testament,* N.Y.: Abingdon Press, 1975. N. Perrin, *The New Testament. An Introduction,* N.Y.: Harcourt Brace Jovanovich, 1974. E. Schillebeeckx, *Jesus,* An Experiment in Christology, N.Y.: Crossroad, 1981. *Christ,* The Experience of Jesus as Lord, N.Y.: Crossroad, 1981.

WILFRID HARRINGTON, OP

BIBLE: OLD TESTAMENT

Sacred books accepted by Jews and Christians as word of God for worship and private prayer, as well as for inspiration and guidance in personal and public morality. Disagreements surround such questions as the name of the collection, the number of books and their arrangement as well as their interpretation and immediate binding force upon conscience. Basic data in Part I cover the external form of the OT: 1) arrangement of books; 2) names for the collection; 3) division into chaps. and vv; 4) languages; 5) types of literature. These provide the setting for discussing the theological questions in Part II (1, canon; 2, origin of OT; 3, interpretation).

Part I—External Format.

1. *Arrangement of Books*

Because the OT in the days of Jesus and the very early church was not a closed collection but open to new additions, variations exist between Jewish and christian editions of the OT as well as between Roman Catholic and Orthodox Churches on the one hand and Protestant Churches on the other. In the long and complex history of the formation of the OT, we witness differences even in the system of combining or separating books and therefore of arriving at their total number. The Council of Trent, which authoritatively defined for Roman Catholicism the larger collection or canon of OT books, did not explicitly mention Lamentations but considered it under the name of Jeremiah.

2. *Names for the Collection*

The names for many individual biblical books will be spelled differently in older Catholic editions of the Bible. The Septuagint background of the Catholic canon and the Greek spelling of names in the NT explain why the Latin Vulgate and the Rheims-Douay translation follow a Greek spelling for proper names: i.e., Isaias instead of Isaiah; Abdias instead of Obadiah, Elias instead of Elijah. The Septuagint used 1-2-3-4 Kings instead of 1-2 Samuel & 1-2 Kings; and in place of 1-2 Chronicles we find 1-2 Paralipomenon.

The name for the entire collection is a still more sensitive issue; OT is hardly a preferred title among Jewish people! For Christians OT gives the impression that the Hebrew Scriptures have been replaced by the new and are helpful only for academic, historical reasons. This judgment sometimes appeals to such texts as: Mt 5:21-22, "You have heard that it was said to your ancestors, ... [but now] what I say to you is ..."; or Rom 7:6, "But now we are discharged from the law, dead to that which held us captive, so that we serve not under the old written code but in the new life of the Spirit." Yet in each case other viewpoints are provided: in Mt 5:17, "Think not that I have

Jewish Canon	Roman Catholic	Protestant
I) Torah	I) The Pentateuch	
1. Gen	1. Gen	1. Gen
2. Exod	2. Exod	2. Exod
3. Lev	3. Lev	3. Lev
4. Num	4. Num	4. Num
5. Deut	5. Deut	5. Deut
II) Nebiim-Prophets	II) Historical Books	
Former Prophets	6. Josh	6. Josh
6. Josh	7. Judg	7. Judg
7. Judg	8. Ruth	8. Ruth
8. 1-2 Sam	9. 1 Sam	9. 1 Sam
9. 1-2 Kgs	10. 2 Sam	10. 2 Sam
Latter Prophets	11. 1 Kgs	11. 1 Kgs
10. Isa	12. 2 Kgs	12. 2 Kgs
11. Jer	13. 1 Chr	13. 1 Chr
12. Ezek	14. 2 Chr	14. 2 Chr
13. The Twelve	15. Ezra	15. Ezra
Hos	16. Neh	16. Neh
Joel	17. Tob	---
Amos	18. Jdt	---
Obad	19. Esth (+Add Esth)	17. Esth
Jonah		--
Mic	III) Wisdom Books	
Nah	20. Job	18. Job
Hab	21. Pss	19. Pss
Zeph	22. Prov	20. Prov
Hagh	23. Eccl	21. Eccl
Zech	24. Cant	22. Cant
Mal	25. Wis	---
	26. Sir	---
III) Kethubim	IV) Prophets	
(Writings)	27. Isa	23. Isa
14. Pss	28. Jer	24. Jer
15. Job	29. Lamen	25. Lamen
16. Prov	30. Bar (+Ep Jer)	---

Megilloth-Scrolls	31. Ezek	26. Ezek
17. Ruth	32. Dan (+ Pr Azar;	
	Sus; Bel)	27. Dan
18. Cant		---
19. Eccle (or Qoh)		---
20. Lam	33. Hos	28. Hos
21. Esth	34. Joel	29. Joel
22. Dan	35. Amos	30. Amos
23. Ezra & Neh	36. Obad	31. Obad
24. 1-2 Chr	37. Jonah	32. Jonah
	38. Mic	33. Mic
	39. Nah	34. Nah
	40. Hab	35. Hab
	41. Zeph	36. Zeph
	42. Hag	37. Hag
	43. Zech	38. Zech
	44. Mal	39. Mal
	45. 1 Macc	---
	46. 2 Macc	

come to abolish the law and the prophets; I have come not to abolish them but to fulfill them"; and in Rom 9:4-5, "[To] Israelites belong the sonship, the glory, the covenants, the giving of the law, the worship, and the promises; to them belong the patriarchs, and of their race, according to the flesh, is the Christ, who is God over all, blessed for ever. Amen." Finally, Paul concludes to "this mystery" of Judaism, for "the gifts [to them] and the call of God are irrevocable" (Rom 11:25, 29).

The designation OT did not become common among Christians till almost two centuries after Jesus. This term, in fact, would have been meaningless in the days of Jesus and even during the preaching of Paul and the other apostles. The NT as a collection of sacred books did not exist, to make the other collection "old"! "Old," therefore, is to be understood as ancient and venerable rather than as antiquated and dead.

Jews today speak of *The Holy Scriptures* or of the *TaNaK*. The latter is an acronym from the first letters of Torah (Law), Nebiim (Prophets) and Kethubim (Writings)—cf., the Prologue to Sirach, where the grandson, translating the work of "my grandfather Jesus [ben Eleazar, ben Sirach—50:27]," refers three times to "the law, the prophets and the other books of our ancestors"; and Lk 24:44 where Jesus calls attention to "the law of Moses and the prophets and the psalms," the latter being the first book in the Writings. For Jewish people up to and beyond the time of Jesus, the OT was a collection, with paramount attention given to the Law of Moses (Sirach wrote, according to his grandson, in order that people "should make ever greater progress in living according to the law"), with a closed series of prophetical books, and with a third area of Writings open to new additions. The Writings eventually included prophecies like Daniel, historical narratives like Ezra and Nehemiah, and collections of prayers as in the Psalms.

In the OT itself references to sacred writings or traditions at first were generic and referred mostly to the Law: Deut 31:24, "Moses had finished writing on a scroll the words of the law in their entirety"; 2 Kgs 22:8, "I have found the scroll of the Law in the temple of the Lord." Up to and during the exile biblical writers seldom referred to earlier prophets, yet the practice begins to surface with Jer 26:17-18, where the elders vindicated Jeremiah by recalling what "Micah of Moresheth prophesied." Such allusions become more prominent with Zechariah's reference to "the former prophets" (Zech 1:4, 6; 7:7; 8:9). Gradually, other phrases came into use, like "the books" (Dan 9:2) or "holy books" (1 Macc 12:9; 2 Macc 8:23). Books or codices, as we know them, were not in use among the Jews; the Hebrew word *sepher* is better translated "scroll," even though there is another, more technical word for scroll, *megillah*. The root for *sepher* actually means to announce orally (Ps 19:1; 22:22; 44:1), so that the more normal way of transmitting the sacred message was orally in religious assemblies, rather than through written documents. Even after referring to "Moses' ... writing the words of this law in a book," the text declares: "Assemble to me all the elders of your tribes, and your officers, that I may *speak these words in their ears ...*" (Deut 31:24, 28). The understanding of Israel as a "religion of the book" is a misnomer for the first seven or eight hundred years after Moses. Oral presentations of sacred traditions lent themselves to explanations and modifications (Neh 8:8), and gave rise to other types of literature among the Jewish people.

The NT never uses a word for the entire "Bible" but follows the OT style of references to the Scriptures. It begins a quotation from the OT simply: "it is written in Isaiah the prophet" (Mk 1:2); or "the Lord had spoken by the prophet" (Mt 1:22); or "spoken by the prophet Jeremiah" (Mt 2:17) or "by the prophet Isaiah" (Mt 8:17); or "it is written" (Mt 11:10; 21:13); "spoken by the prophet Joel" (Acts 2:16) or "David says" (Acts 2:25) "written in the book of the prophets" (Acts 7:42); or again "Holy Spirit . . . was saying . . . through Isaiah the prophet"; or according to Paul's custom, "as it is written" (Rom 3:10; 8:36; 11:8). If there is a preferred phrase, it would be: "the law and the prophets," (Mt 5:17; 11:13; 16:16; Acts 13:15; 24:14; Rom 3:21) affirming that the first two sections are closed and settled, while the "writings" are open to new entries. Even the name for the third section is not set.

The word *testament* provides a new insight into the meaning of the term OT. The Septuagint already adopted for "testament" a special Greek word, *diatheke,* instead of the more ordinary, *suntheke.* The former word does not require the death of the testator for the last will or testament to become effective. It also insists upon the independent declaration of a person's intention rather than upon a mutually agreed treaty. God's supreme, generous and eternal love, consequently, lies behind the biblical appreciation of this word.

When Jer 31:31-34 refers to "a new covenant" or testament, the "new" emphasizes the interior spirit with which the ancient covenant is to be followed. Jeremiah was seeking a renewal of the ideals of Deut 6:4-9, which asks that God be loved with all one's heart, soul and might and that God's words "be [inscribed] upon your heart." Jesus too insisted upon this interior attitude of love in obeying the ancient law and traditions (Lk 10:26-27). Old and new in this case connote the continuously new way of keeping the word of God alive in one's daily life.

The term OT was first used by Melito of Sardis (c. A.D. 180), and set more firmly in place by the popular theologians, Tertullian (A.D. 160-230) and Origen (A.D. 185-254). It is based upon passages like 2 Cor 3:14, "When they read *the old covenant,* that same veil remains unlifted, because only through Christ is it taken away"; and Heb 8:7, "if that first covenant had been faultless, there would have been no occasion for a second." Yet these passages do not abrogate the ancient scriptures but rather affirm the light of Christ to appreciate their full meaning. The theological writers who fixed the term OT in christian tradition clearly argued for the value of the OT against such persons as Marcion, the first major anti-Semitic writer in christian tradition (c. A.D. 150).

The term *Bible* derives from the seaport town of Byblos in Lebanon, named after the papyrus which was imported here from Egypt. *Biblia* originally was the Greek neuter plural, indicating the many books in the sacred collection. Because of the christian usage, common by the fourth century, to bind biblical books in a single codex, the Greek word evolved into a Latin equivalent, *biblia,* a feminine singular noun, indicating the single book of the Bible. Theologically it is helpful to remember that "Bible" is a collection of many books or literary traditions, transmitted orally for many centuries, edited and grouped into small units, dictated and written down especially in times of crisis, lest the word be lost, or in times of religious reform, to assure strength and clarity (2 Kgs 22:1–23:25; Jer 36:32). Some books, like those of Moses or the gospels, received much greater veneration. The Septuagint translates the Torah more literally and cautiously than the prophets and the Writings. The fact that other series of books were added to Torah or gospels, like prophecy & writings, epistles & revelation, points up not only the primary importance of the former but also the need of explaining or adapting even these most sacred parts of the Bible.

3. *Division into Chapters and Verses* This process began quite early; our present system again shows the many stages of biblical tradition. In almost every book of the OT we detect breaks and transitions in style or subject: the new introductions at Deut 1:1; 4:44; 27:1; 29:1 31:1; 31:30; 33:1; or in the prophecy of Amos the smaller collections of sermons with similar stylistic details: Amos 1:3–2:16; 3:1 + 4:1 + 5:1; or the visions in 7:1–8:3. These books began as small collections, orally transmitted, which were preserved and expanded by disciples, and only later gathered into a single unit. We call attention to the fact that Greek translation tended to divide material that the Hebrew kept intact as a single book, like 1-2 Samuel or the "Book" of the Twelve (minor prophets).

The manuscripts at Qumran (250 B.C.—A.D. 68) as well as the Talmud (third to fifth centuries A.D.) witness to a division of the entire Hebrew Bible except Psalms into open and closed sections, depending on whether a new line begins or not. Another system divided the Torah into weekly selections for the liturgy (*sedarim*); the division of the Babylonian Jews into a yearly cycle of fifty-three or fifty-four lessons prevails even today. An earlier three year cycle was current in Palestine. Most probably Jesus knew and followed the one year cycle. Already in the seventh century AD, probably still earlier, marks were added to manuscripts for distinguishing verses, but these were never permitted on synagogal scrolls. Stephen Langton, d 1228, Archbishop of Paris, separated the books of the Bible into chapters for christian readers, making use of the Jewish and possibly other earlier attempts. Verse numbers were added to christian editions of the Bible first by Sanctes Pagnini, O.P., in 1528, and secured in place by the Protestant Robert Etienne in 1555. Jewish editions of the Bible for study and private devotions adopted many of these divisions from printed copies of the Latin Vulgate. While the rabbis divided the Bible into sections principally for liturgical proclamation (adding many indicators in private manuscripts for pauses and accents to prepare well for the synagogal reading), Christians tended to divide into chapters and verses more for study and research.

Though always very close and generally identical, notable differences as to chapters and verses still show up between Jewish and christian editions. The variations appear, for instance, in the psalms in which the opening titles are not included in the versification (except the *New American Bible*) and are printed (if at all) in small letters in christian Bibles. For the Jews the titles constitute the opening verse(s) and are equally a part of the inspired text. The data in the titles about melodies for singing the psalms or about feasts or religious attitude belong to the original text. In commenting upon the psalms, rabbis always devote much attention to the titles. For them the community's way of singing or reciting the psalm is an integral part of the sacred text and its inspired tradition. Again we see theologically how the Bible presumes interpretation and absorption into contemporary life, especially at times of worship and instruction.

4. *Languages of the OT*

Books common to all three canons (Jewish, Roman Catholic & Protestant) were composed and preserved in Hebrew, with the exception of Aramaic in Gen 31:47 (two words); Ezra 4:8–6:18; 7:12-26; Jer 10:11; Dan 2:4b–7:28. Of the deuterocanonical books, Sirach was composed and most of it still survives in Hebrew; the manuscripts were discovered in 1896 in an ancient synagogue in Cairo and later among the scrolls of the Dead Sea and at the fortress of Masada. The Greek translation of Sirach exists in shorter and expanded editions; the latter is received into the Greek Church, while the *New American Bible* prefers the shorter form as inspired and canonical. Other books like Judith, Baruch, Prayer of Azariah, and 1 Maccabees were originally composed in Hebrew but have survived only in Greek; 2 Maccabees, Wisdom and Prayer of Azariah, Bel and the Dragon, and Susanna were composed in Greek.

It is not, therefore, that any single language is essential for canonical status, though Hebrew is certainly preferred. Pastoral purposes for the sake of intelligibility in liturgical assemblies, or literary grounds when an Aramaic phrase or document was incorporated, or apologetic reasons so as to be understood by the non-Jewish population in Alexandria, Egypt, generally dictated the langage to be used. Language has a great deal to do with culture, and we see an outreach to be inculturated in local areas while preserving the sacred books within worship and instruction.

The standard Hebrew text goes by the name *masoretic,* just as the official liturgical Latin text for the Roman Catholic Church remained the Vulgate up till the time of Pope Pius XII (*Divino Afflante Spiritu,* n. 14-16). This Hebrew text is verified among the Dead Sea Scrolls as the preferred form of the OT. Yet it has reached us again like other aspects of the OT through a complex history. The word *masoretic* comes from a root, meaning either "to bind" as in Ezek 20:37 (yet itself a disputed passage) or "to hand down," a post-biblical form. Scholars will even dispute whether it should be spelled with the single or double "s"! The Hebrew text was handed down in various rabbinical schools of the east in Babylon or of the west in Palestine.

Notes or corrections were added, called the little masora on the margin of manuscripts and the large masora at the end. The Masoretic notes, for instance, calculated the number of times letters, words and verses, plus the combinations of words occurred (in the Torah 5,845 verses, 167 paragraphs, 79,856 words and 400,945 letters), the middle verse (i.e., of the Book of Psalms—Ps 78:38) and even the middle letter (the letter *ayin* which was elevated in the word "forest," Ps 80:13), variant readings, a system of *Kethib-Qere,* indicating what was to be written and what was to be read in its place (Jer 3:2 because of a later sexual crudeness; Ps 42:2, lest one should be said to look on the face of God); or *tiqqune sopherim* or "corrections of the scribes" (Gen 18:22, lest it be said inappropriately that God stood before someone). Our translations do not always follow these corrections.

Each masoretic tradition developed a system of points to indicate vowels: the Tiberian, below the consonantal letter, still in use; and the Babylonian above the consonant. These continued to evolve from the seventh to the ninth centuries A.D. In Palestine two families maintained their own tradition of consonantal texts, the ben Asher reaching back in documented history till at least AD 895, and the ben Naphtai, less well documented. By a decree of Moses Maimonides in the twelfth century the ben Asher manuscript tradition was declared the standard text. This exists today in the Aleppo Codex, being used for a new critical edition by the Hebrew University, Jerusalem, and the Leningrad Codex, the basis for the Kittel and Stuttgart editions. This long exposition of the Hebrew text verifies the extraordinary care with which it was transmitted and also the various attempts, with alternate readings and corrections, to sustain a pastoral purpose of devotional and intelligent listening to the word.

Part II — Theological Questions

While theological issues have been surfacing in our discussion of the external form of the OT, we now highlight several more important ones.

1. Canon

"Canon" (from the Hebrew *qanah* meaning a reed, growing in swampy areas, cut and used as a measuring rod, carried over in the Greek *kanon*) is the technical word for measuring off the exact number of books in the Bible and their proper arrangement. Books common to all groups are called "protocanonical" or first-canon; those restricted to the Roman Catholic and Orthodox churches are called "deuterocanonical" or second-canon; Protestants designate them "apocrypha" or "obscure and secret" books. Still other books, sometimes venerated in the ancient church but eventually eliminated by all groups, are named "apocrypha" by Roman Catholics, "pseudepigraphy" or "false writings" by Protestants.

In the three-fold arrangement of the Jewish canon we note the paramount place of the *Torah. Prophecy* like Torah was a closed section already in the days of Sirach (190 B.C.) It was considered much less prediction of the future and more as a commentary upon and application of Torah. For this reason in the postexilic age the reading of the Torah in worship was always followed by a selection from the prophetical books, the former (Joshua, Judges, 1-2 Samuel, 1-2 Kings) or the latter (3 major; 12 minor). This second reading was called "the Haphtaroth" (from *patar*, "to interpret" or "explain"). Because the prophetical books not only recounted Israel's history from Joshua to the fall of Jerusalem but also included the preaching of Israel's great reformers, the haphtaroth showed the many ways by which the people were blessed or punished dependent upon their obeying or disobeying the Torah. Prophecy also kept law and worship from degenerating into lifeless legalism. If Torah was certainly the instrument of survival, the prophetical books showed how it was both possible and worthy of survival, by remaining alive and relevant in each current age.

Kethubim or *Writings,* the final section, was open to new additions and therefore most versatile in subject and style. Just as law and worship dominated Torah, we find the same controlling factor in the final editing and sequence of books in the Writings. This section begins with Psalms, where liturgical concerns become ever more apparent, especially in the collection of Korah and Asaph psalms in the second and third sections (Pss 42-72, 73-89), and the small liturgical booklets in the fifth section (Pss 107-150), like the Egyptian Hallel for major feastdays (Pss 113-118), the Great Hallel for sabbaths (Ps 136), and the pilgrimage psalms (120-134). The Writings and therefore the Jewish canon concludes with 1-2 Chronicles which focus upon the Jerusalem temple. The Jewish canon was arranged primarily for worship, so that *lex orandi lex credendi,* the law for praying is the law for believing.

The Jewish canon, as mentioned already, ended up shorter by seven books and several sections in Esther and Daniel than the Roman Catholic canon. The Orthodox churches have a still slightly larger canon. Judaism began to restrict its canon only after the tragic split with Christianity. The Dead Sea Scrolls and several other Palestinian pieces of evidence witness to the acceptance of the larger canon of the Septuagint in the land of Israel in the days of Jesus and the earliest period after Pentecost. In cave four at Qumran, where almost 400 manuscripts have been identified, all books of the Hebrew canon have been found except Esther, probably because it never mentions the name of God. Other books, recognized as sacred in the

Septuagint, were represented: Tobit, Jubilees, Enoch. Qumran caves also included copies of the Epistle of Jeremiah and Sirach.

Even though the rabbis attempted to settle the issue of canonicity after AD 70 at their school in Jamnia, west of Jerusalem, Sirach was still read for several centuries and is referred to in the Talmud as sacred; other books remained controversial, like Ezekiel, Canticles and Ecclesiastes. This variation in the number of sacred books did not touch the doctrinal essence of Judaism, for the latter depended basically upon the Torah, which in the Septuagint as in all Hebrew manuscripts remained the most holy of all. We should add that Judaism never lived immediately or directly from the Torah, but from Haphtaroth (readings from prophecy), the Writings, and other rabbinical works like the Targum, Midrash and Talmud.

Turning to the Septuagint and the christian canon of the OT, we find that biblical books are arranged in such a way as to stress the historical character in the first section. This system tends to play down the religious or mystical instruction hidden within events and to highlight the more rational or observable elements and to emphasize the sequence of time. Theologically for Christians, Torah was superseded by prophecy, so that each epoch of time was leading up to a divine fulfillment in the Messiah Jesus. The final section of the christian canon was prophecy, and the last of the prophets was Malachi, in which chapter three announces the coming of the messiah into the temple. The first of the gospels begins with this text to proclaim the presence of the promised messiah (Mk 1:1-3). Events and preaching, therefore, do not look forward to the Israelite pilgrimage to the Jerusalem temple (as in the final verses of the Jewish canon, 2 Chr 36:22-23) but to the future messiah

within that temple. Roman Catholic bibles tended to add 1-2 Maccabees at the very end, to bridge the time of Malachi with that of Jesus. The major theological difference then between the Jewish and christian arrangement of books meant that Torah as complete and definitive gave way to prophecy, and prophecy was no longer considered a commentary on Torah but a preparation for the future messiah.

For quite some time Christians were content with an open-ended canon, so that other books were sometimes included, like 3-4 Maccabees, Enoch and Jubilees, and still others of a NT character. It is only when fringe groups began to circulate books, to propagate false doctrine under the name of ancient biblical personages of OT and NT times, that the church responded with a closed canon. Especially in the eastern part of Christianity, under pressure of the Jewish closure of the canon within the second century A.D., a conservative effort was made to restrict the church to the Jewish canon. By the Council of Trullo II (A.D. 692) a larger list became standard in the eastern church. The Orthodox churches not only venerate all books within the canon of Roman Catholicism but they also include: 3-4 Maccabees; Prayer of Manasseh; Psalm 151; and in Russia, 2 Esdras. Ethiopia, which was distant from these controversies, has held on, even to this day, to the largest number of books of any church, this in spite of a strong Jewish influence on the Ethiopian Church. This fact indicates a very early Jewish presence, reaching Ethiopia through Egypt.

The western church, already in the councils of Hippo (A.D. 393) and III Carthage (A.D. 397) and in a decree attributed to Pope Damasus (A.D. 366-384), affirmed a larger canon. This canon, by now traditional, was solemnly decreed by the Council of Trent (A.D. 1546) because of the long usage of the Vulgate in the church. Even though Jerome, the translator of the Vulgate from the Hebrew, vigorously opposed the inclusion of these books, church practice and tradition maintained their role and insisted upon their place in the OT.

The Protestant reformers decided to go behind many church practices and to draw their faith and devotion more directly from the Scriptures. For the OT this meant a return to the Hebrew text. Because the Hebrew canon no longer contained the extra books of the Roman Catholic and Orthodox canons, the reformers at first relegated these to an appendix (devotional books, but not basic for doctrine) while their successors eventually rejected them from the Bible. Protestants, however, did not adopt the overall arrangement of the Jewish Bible.

Both in OT times and later in church history the books of the Bible came into place over a long period by use especially in liturgical assemblies. Throughout history there was a tendency to save only what was more precious and more faithful, consonant with tradition and with the faith of devout Jews. The OT refers quite often to other documents from which it drew some material: like the "Book of the Wars of the Lord" in Numbers 21:14, or the "Book of Jashar" in Joshua 10:13 and 2 Samuel 1:18. Through "much sweat and sleepless nights" the author of 2 Maccabees made a condensation of the five books of Jason (2 Macc 2:23, 26). Theologically the question of canonicity was not settled simply by determining the divinely inspired quality of a work. Many inspired compositions have been lost and those which are preserved manifest various degrees of religious spirit and conformity to orthodox doctrine, two characteristics somewhat lacking, e.g., in Deut 7:1-5; 2 Sam 21:1-14; 1 Kgs 18:30. Ultimately long, consistent use in liturgical assembly seems to have been the major theological criterion of canonicity both in ancient Israel and in the long centuries of the Vulgate. While the inspiration of individual books is presumed in this explanation, the inspiration of the community and the guidance of its religious leaders are equally crucial to the theological question of canonicity.

2. *Origin of the OT*

We have seen the salient role of the liturgical assembly in deciding which of the many books in Israel belonged in their sacred collection. We now ascertain the function of the liturgy in the formation of a biblical book.

Some of the most important biblical events, presented in the Scriptures as world-shattering to Israelites and other people and as fundamental to faith and worship, are hardly granted even a brief notice in non-Israelite evidence. We possess enormous documentation from Mesopotamia and Syria as well as from Egypt. Yet we have yet to locate an absolutely secure reference to Abraham. He fits into the general pattern of migrations in the nineteenth and eighteenth centuries B.C., lost in a crowd of Asiatics, without racial purity or social status, eventually called *abiru* (origin of our word Hebrew). Israel's exodus out of Egypt, from the biblical account, upset every aspect of Egypt's family, politics or economy—death of every firstborn, farm disasters, discrediting of priests, humiliation of Pharaoh—yet not a whisper of all this turmoil is recorded in a single Egyptian document.

Following the lead of such scholars as R. de Vaux, O.P., we offer this schema to explain the background of Israel's major religious positions and of the biblical literature that accompanied their liturgical celebration:

a) The initial episode (of the exodus; or the crossing of the River Jordan) was viewed by non-participants as an insignificant, secular, non-religious event. The exodus was part of many flights out of Egypt by Asiatics, some of whom were expelled, others fled. The crossing of the Jordan was one of many incursions into the land by nomadic bedouins from the southern and eastern deserts. Some of the Israelites, like Moses, Aaron and Miriam proceeded out of Egypt under God's inspiration, many others in the group were what the Bible calls mixed-up riffraff, leaving Egypt for selfish, personal reasons. See Exod 6:1; 10:27-29; 12:31-39; 14:5, Num 11:1-6.

b) The strike for freedom under Moses led initially to celebrations on a small scale (Exod 15:20-21) which quickly collapsed into grumbling and revolt (Exod 15:22-23; 17:1-7). Again a few like Moses sustained their religious spirit.

c) When time and life-experiences separated a new generation from the initial events and when the religious spirit of Moses became the dominant reason for understanding Israel's freedom from slavery, it became necessary to draw up accounts that would memorialize the flight from Egypt as an act of God's providential care. Statements of faith would point out the continuous impact of the event for later generations (Deut 5:21-25; 26:1-11). Sacred objects like the ark and sacred places like sanctuaries and temple became necessary to rally the people together in God's presence and to contain the ever larger number of participants. Because it was no longer possible to return to the actual site of the exodus and the crossing through the sea, symbols and ceremonies became important ways of reliving the event. The pellmell flight for freedom was transformed into an orderly sanctuary procession, as in Ps 68 or Exod 15:1-18. Ordained personnel were required to compose, preserve and transmit the traditions, creeds and prayers and to preside over ceremonies. At this point religion formally begins. De Vaux speaks of the Mosaic age as the pre-religion stage which offered the key events and the major intuitions about God. Later ages put these intuitions into songs, narratives and creeds, into processions and sacred meals. With the origin of religion, the traditions and books of the Bible begin to take shape. In this sense liturgical celebrations transformed seemingly insignificant events into history with impact even into our own day. The Bible, therefore, presents us with the original event narrated principally according to the manner or details of its later celebration.

d) When liturgy lost touch with its origins and was more concerned about rubrics or finances or social status than about God's compassionate concern for people in slavery, need and sorrow, then prophets arose to challenge and condemn this liturgy and its personnel (Micah 3; Isaiah 1; Jeremiah 7).

e) Eventually prophetic condemnations of liturgy became part of the liturgy, for it was the sanctuary which was principally responsible for editing and preserving prophetic sermons, as we notice, for instance, from the arrangement of the entire book of Micah, balancing condemnation with blessing. Psalms 22, 49 and 95 are other examples of prophecy transformed into liturgical celebrations.

Theologically the biblical traditions and books resulted from God's inspiring presence: a) with great heroic leaders like Moses and the prophets; b) with all the people as they reflected upon events and recognized the continuous need of God's saving intervention; c) with people gathered in worship under prophets, priests and levites; d) with prophets and their successors as religion underwent continuous reform.

The inspiration and canonicity of biblical books were ascertained by this complex of factors over long, at times difficult, even chaotic or ambiguous periods of time. The Bible originated in the ability of holy men and women to detect God's presence within crucial events of world and national politics. Through wise religious leaders it continued to be a light for detecting God's holy presence in daily life outside of synagogue and sanctuary. While the temple or sanctuary was the principal focus of pilgrimage and worship before God's mysterious presence in the Holy of Holies, liturgy was intended to lead people to live godly lives in the non-religious spheres of their daily existence. Finding God's word in the sacred literature of the Bible was to enable people to detect God's will once again amid the hopes and problems at home and work.

3. The Interpretation of the OT

Already in OT times there were several major ways for presenting and explaining God's redeeming presence in Israel. The office of priest and levite would emphasize temple and sanctuary, the prophets acted as representatives of small religious communities (1 Sam 11:9-13; 10:5-8; 2 Kgs 2-8) and as champions of the poor against the wealthy establishments of royalty and priesthood (Amos 4; 8:4-8; Mic 2-3). The Wisdom movement with Proverbs, Ecclesiastes and Job reveals wise individuals, well-off, conservative, rather indifferent to temple and salvation history, yet thoroughly dedicated to God's presence within the normal interactions of daily life. The Bible, according to its principal institutions of priest, prophet and sage, offers at least three principal ways of interpreting life and of applying sacred traditions to life.

Still another important difference in interpreting religious norms and creeds appears in representatives of northern and southern tribes. The former is associated with the less centralized government of the kingdom of Israel, with its variety of sanctuaries and with its high-lighting of the mosaic covenant and the exodus tradition—as in Deuteronomy, Hosea, Jeremiah, Isaiah 40-55 and 56-66. The southern tradition was located at Jerusalem with its centralized government and place of worship, eternal covenant of David, and the Zadokite priesthood—as in Isaiah 1-39, Ezekiel, and most post-exilic books.

Along with these larger norms of interpretation already in the OT, many smaller explanations appear already in the Hebrew Bible. In Gen. 14:17 and Ezek 1:2 words are added to clarify earlier statements. Lev 19:19 is expanded in Deut 27:9-11. Different motivations are appended to the Ten Commandments: compare Exod 20:8-11 with Deut 5:12-15. The call for peace in Isa 2:2-5 has a different ending in Mic 4:1-5, and both are seriously modified, even reversed, in Joel 4:9-10 (RSV 3:9-10). Scribal corrections in 1 Sam 3:13 and Job 2:9, generally not found in our Bibles, make sure that God was being blessed, not cursed, an idea abhorrent to the rabbis. For still other corrections, compare 2 Sam 8:18 with 1 Chr 18:17; or 2 Sam 24:1 with 1 Chr 21:1; or Ps 29:1-2 with Ps 96:7-9. In all of these corrective or modifying interpretations, it is not so much a question of removing error as of preventing the wrong impression with a later age. The Bible shows within its own pages many examples that for centuries it was not transmitted verbatim but with a keen sense of intelligent interaction with the vocabulary and customs of later ages.

Many more incidental interpretations from ancient times were gathered by the Masoretes (see above) and placed in the margins of biblical manuscripts.

Another form of interpretation is evident in the vowels associated with the consonantal text. The proclamation and public reading of the sacred text depended upon memory and oral tradition for the vowels and correct pronunciation. Different sets of vowels within the same consonants could modify the meaning of words. For instance the two readings for Ps 110:3, represented now in the Septuagint (followed by the *NAB*) and in the Hebrew text (followed by the *RSV*), generally keep the same consonants but insert different vowels. Even when the written text was set in its sacred form, it was still open to various readings and interpretations.

The Aramaic Targums, explanatory translations in the vernacular of the people in the postexilic age, offer another form of interpretation. The Targum made significant accommodations when a text seemed too radical or too open to misunderstanding: e.g., Isa 19:25, "Blessed be my people Egypt and the work of my hands Assyria, and my inheritance, Israel." With adroit additions it is translated in the Targum much less universally: "Blessed be my people whom I brought forth out of Egypt. Because they sinned before me, I carried them into exile to Assyria, but now that they have repented, they shall be called my people and my inheritance, even Israel."

The Septuagint will frequently interpret as it translates into Greek. Its scholars often consider the Hebrew too blunt in speaking about God or about Israel's position before God, as in Exod 24:10, where the italicized words are added in the Septuagint: "And they beheld *the place where* the God of Israel *stood*." The Greek translation of Ps 16:8 heightens the sense of happiness after death and the resurrection of the body and so brings the Hebrew up to date with later theological developments. In Amos 9:12 no longer is Edom conquered but instead Edom is read as the Hebrew word *adam* (humankind) who now "earnestly seek me," the Lord.

Still another form of ancient interpretation is detected in explanations gathered in a body of literature called

midrash (from *darash*, "to search, inquire"). In the Midrash on the Psalms, Ps 68:18 is drastically remodeled. Originally it described a triumphant military procession, with slaves being offered to the temple: "Thou didst ascend the high mount [of Zion], leading captives in thy train, and receiving gifts from men." The rabbis evidently did not consider it fitting that God needed gifts from men and women, much less slaves, and so they reread the passage to declare that a man, namely Moses, ascended Mount Sinai to receive the gift of the Torah from God. The Epistle to the Ephesians follows this midrashic interpretation but applies it to Jesus, ascending to heaven after his death and sending various gifts upon the church in the form of pastoral ministries (Eph 4:8-11). Biblical interpretation is thus a blend of ancient texts, later revelations and popular appreciation of its meaning in people's own lives.

Qumran scrolls, devoted to interpreting the sacred text, will read them in terms of their own origins with the Teacher of Righteousness, most evident in the commentary on Habakkuk. Quoting first from Hab 2:2, it reads: "*so he may run who reads it,*" their interpretation concerns the Teacher of Righteousness, to whom "God made known all the mysteries of the words of his servants the prophets" (1QpHab 7:1-5). This teacher is generally considered to have been the founder of the community who was persecuted and even martyred. Qumran interpretation clearly did not seek to remain within the original meaning of a passage but rather through new events and developments in their own day and age to peer more profoundly into God's intentions.

Jesus not only venerated the Sacred Scriptures, our OT, but also knew them as his only "Bible." He is seen frequently in the gospels drawing upon the sacred writings, both for disputation (Mk 12:28-

37), preaching (Lk 4:18-19), and personal consolation (Mk 15:34).

There are over 200 quotations of the OT in the NT, at least 118 in the epistles of Paul. Of the 350 or more references, at least 300 are in accordance with the reading of the Septuagint. The NT draws upon the OT, not only to show the universality of salvation, but also to indicate the scriptural witness to Jesus as messiah. It is likely that early christian preachers had memorized or carried written scrolls of selected OT passages.

In early Christianity two major schools of interpretation arose: the Antiochene, founded by Theodore of Mopsuestia (d. A.D. 429), which stressed the historical sense and the human consciousness of the inspired writer as well as the divine insight of *teoria* with the OT message; and the School of Alexandria, founded by Origen (A.D. 185-254), which recognized diverse meanings in the same text: the corporeal or obvious sense; the moral or ethical; and most important of all the allegorical or mystical. This latter always pointed to Christ and the mystery of salvation. The Alexandrian school was favored by such theological giants as Jerome and Augustine. After Jerome, unfortunately, competent knowledge of Hebrew disappeared. Most of biblical interpretation was allegorical or accommodated. Because all of theology (in fact, all sciences) were taught as biblical interpretation, many texts had to be stretched considerably.

The great light of the Middle Ages was Hugh of St. Victor (c. A.D. 1118) who reintroduced the study of Hebrew and synthesized the medieval system of interpretation: besides the literal sense, there was the typical which was subdivided into: messianic about Jesus; anagogical about heavenly realities; and tropological for moral guidance.

While church documents, especially since the *Divino Afflante Spiritu* of Pius XII (1943), have affirmed the importance of the scientific study of the bible, they equally stress the pastoral and devotional value of the scriptures. Vatican II emphasized five important areas of lasting value in the OT: 1) the living sense of God's personal presence in human life; 2) sublime instruction on God; 3) wisdom that is normative and brings salvation; 4) treasure-house of prayer, especially Psalms; and 5) mysterious realization of our salvation (D.V. 14). It further declared that God is "the inspirer and author of both testaments" (16). Vatican II, moreover, expressed this hope in the forthcoming reform of the liturgy: "The treasures of the Bible are to be opened up more lavishly, so that a richer share in God's word may be provided for the faithful. In this way a more representative portion of holy Scripture will be read to the people in the course of a prescribed number of years" (S.C. 51).

It has been evident throughout the history of OT interpretation that OT texts were seen to convey mysteries of faith frequently beyond the obvious sense of their words, brought to light at times only through combination with NT passages. This fact is recognized in the introduction to the *Lectionary for Mass* which states: "The best harmony between the OT and NT readings occurs when it is one that Scripture itself suggests, ... when the teachings and events recounted in texts of the NT bear a more or less explicit relationship to the teachings and events of the OT" (*Documents on the Liturgy, 1963-1979*, no. 1845). The Lectionary, therefore, provided that "each [Sunday] mass presents three readings, the first from the OT, the second from the writings of the apostles ..., and the third from the Gospels. This arrangement best illustrates the basic unity of both Testaments and of the history of salvation in which Christ is the central figure, commemorated in his paschal mystery" (*ibid*).

The OT has an added ecumenical value, an important feature of Vatican II, according to a statement of Pope Paul VI to a congress of OT scholars: the OT is "where Christian theologians, both Catholic and Protestants, as well as scholars of the Jewish religion, can meet and work together . . . We can go even further: they can pray from the same texts."

On a more scholarly or scientific level, according to statements in 1955 by A. Miller and A. Kleinhans, secretary and sub-secretary of the Pontifical Biblical Commission, we note that earlier decrees of the Biblical Commission have been abrogated in so far as they refer to matters of history, geography, or literary questions like the name of the author or the time of composition or the fact of one or multiple human authors. In so far as they state doctrinal positions, enunciated through the voice of tradition, they are still to be respected and followed. In the revised program for the examination for the licentiate in scripture before the Biblical Commission, point four mentions only papal encyclicals on scripture and drops the previous inclusion of decisions of the Biblical Commission (A.A.S. 43 [1951] 747-51; *CBQ* 14[1952] 69). Important statements for the study of the OT, and particularly of the early chapters of Genesis, are to be found in a letter to Cardinal Emanuel Suhard of Paris, 1948 (*Rome and the Study of Scripture,* 148-151, *EB* 577-581). Since no passage of the OT has been defined by the church as to its exact, single meaning, exegetes are free to work scientifically. By the analogy of faith they are not to arrive at a conclusion which contradicts the faith otherwise held by the community of the church and expounded by its teaching authority; but neither are they obliged to locate any single doctrine of the faith in any individual text of the OT.

E. Achtemeier, *The Old Testament and the Proclamation of the Gospel,* Philadelphia: West-minster Press, 1973. J. Barton, *Oracles of God,* London: Darton, Longman and Todd, 1986. *Tradition and Interpretation,* Ed. by G.W. Anderson, Oxford: Clarendon Press, 1979. T.A. Collins, and R.E. Brown, "Church Pronouncements," *Jerome Biblical Commentary,* Englewood Cliffs, NJ: Prentice-Hall, 1968, chap. 72. N.K. Gottwald, *The Hebrew Bible,* Philadelphia: Fortress Press, 1985. S.M. Mayo, *The Relevance of the Old Testament for Christian Faith,* Washington, DC: Catholic U. of America Press, 1982. J.A. Megivern, *Bible Interpretation,* Wilmington, NC: Consortium Book, 1978. B.J. Roberts, *The Old Testament Text and Versions,* Cardiff: U. of Wales Press, 1951. D. Senior and C. Stuhlmueller, *The Biblical Foundations for Mission,* Maryknoll, NY: Orbis Books, 1983. B. Smalley, *The Study of the Bible in the Middle Ages,* 2nd ed., New York: Philosophical Library, 1952. *The Use of the Old Testament in the New and Other Essays,* Ed. by J.M. Efird, Durham, NC: Duke U. Press, 1972. E. Wurthwein, *The Text of the Old Testament,* Grand Rapids: Eerdmans, 1979. R.N. Soulen, *Handbook of Biblical Criticism,* 2nd ed., Atlanta: John Knox Press, 1981. *Rome and the Study of Scripture,* 6th ed., St. Meinrad, IN: Grail Publications, 1958.

CARROLL STUHLMUELLER, CP

BIBLICAL CRITICISM

The term refers to the complex of methods for studying biblical writings in order to establish their text, understand their context and style, and determine their origin and authenticity. The techniques of biblical criticism can be applied to the study of any kind of literature and were frequently developed outside of biblical research. Their goal is to enable the reader to know as much as possible about the meaning of the text in its original historical setting; that is, what the original author was trying to communicate to his original audience. Though there is a legitimate debate whether this goal can ever be fully attained, biblical critics seek to come as close to the goal as is humanly possible.

The text of a biblical document is established by means of textual criticism. We no longer have direct access to the manuscripts written by the biblical authors. Their works have been handed on by copyists through the centuries. With each copying, the possibility and the likelihood of errors or changes entering the manuscript tradition grows. The aim of textual criticism (sometimes called "lower criticism") is to reconstruct a text as close to the autograph (the original text written by its author) as possible.

The initial task for the textual critic is to make an inventory of the ancient manuscript evidence in order to determine where variant readings exist. The earliest complete manuscripts of the Hebrew Bible are dated to the tenth and eleventh centuries A.D. The most important NT Greek manuscripts come from the fourth and fifth centuries. Evidence is also drawn from the ancient versions (Greek, Latin, Coptic, Syriac, etc.), which may preserve important variants behind their translation. The discoveries of biblical materials among the Dead Sea scrolls and of NT fragments among the Greek papyri have allowed textual critics to go further back in history than the date of the major manuscripts might lead one to suppose.

After assembling the evidence, the textual critic must decide which was the original reading and explain how the other readings arose. The original reading must be consistent with the style and content of the document being studied as well as with the rules of philology and good sense. The rejected variants may have been unconscious errors (e.g., omitting words or phrases, confusing similar letters, including marginal comments in the text), or deliberate changes (e.g., "correcting" the author's grammar or style, harmonizing the text with parallel passages, removing potentially offensive material). The rules about preferring the more difficult text and the shorter text can help in determining the original reading.

In addition to establishing the best text, biblical criticism also seeks to understand the content and style of the document by means of literary criticism.

In its broad sense, literary criticism refers to the systematic analysis of a text with regard to its words and images, characters, progress of thought or structure, form, and meaning.

With the help of lexicons, concordances, and encyclopedias, it is possible to chart the development of a biblical word (e.g., "love") or motif (e.g., "covenant"), and situate a particular occurrence within such a framework, though caution must be exercised lest the whole history of the term be read into each instance. Words and motifs are used to describe characters involved in an action (narrative), or to make an argument, or to share a message or an emotion. So it is usually possible to outline the literary structure of a biblical text in terms of the interactions between the major characters (either in the text or supposed by the discourse situation) and to chart the progress of the plot or argument. Some biblical writers apparently like chiastic patterns (ABCB'A') and forms of logic that are foreign to Westerners in our time.

Determining the literary form can be carried out either for the writing as a whole (genre) or for its parts (forms). The OT contains narratives, law codes, prophecies, psalms, collections of proverbs, love poetry, and visions. The NT presents stories of Jesus' words and deeds (gospels), the exploits of some apostles (acts), letters (epistles), and visions (revelation). Within these larger forms, the writers made use of smaller forms. For example, in his gospel, Luke used the forms of the historian's preface, hymns, commissionings, miracles, sayings, and so forth. The literary form is intimately related to the writer's message, for we must assume that, if he wished simply to state a theological truth, our Bible would consist only of theological propositions or theses. It seems that the biblical writers deliberately sought to convey their truth in artistically appealing and memorable literary forms.

The third major task of biblical criticism is historical. It concerns the origin and authenticity of the biblical documents. The literary-critical task of form criticism (determining the genres and smaller forms) suggests that some biblical writers had at their disposal already existing sources in written or oral form. For example, it seems that Matthew and Luke had independent access to Mark's gospel and a collection of Jesus' sayings (known in modern times as Q). Mark in turn appears to have used blocks of controversy stories, miracle accounts, parables, and other sources. According to the classic documentary hypothesis, the Pentateuch consists of four major sources (Yahwist, Elohist, Priestly, Deuteronomist) put into their present form around 550 B.C.

The literary analysis of biblical texts has a historical dimension. Form criticism deals with the range of literary devices used in communicating the message and tries to determine the historical settings in which the forms were employed before they became part of the biblical books. Source criticism seeks to establish where already existing material has been incorporated, either by following explicit statements that a source has been used or by arguing on the basis of literary style and content. Redaction criticism considers how the final author or editor used the sources to address the concerns and problems facing his audience in their historical setting. Thus the biblical critic is concerned with the historical setting of the document itself (redaction criticism) and of the small units (form criticism) or sources (source criticism) contained in the document.

The historical study of biblical writings demands that they be set in their broader historical context. Archaeological excavations and textual discoveries (Dead Sea scrolls. Ugaritic texts, inscriptions, papyri, etc.), have greatly illuminated the material culture and spiritual atmosphere in which the biblical books were written. Extrabiblical texts pertinent to the OT have contributed greatly to understanding the creation stories in Genesis, the biblical narratives from the patriarchs to post-exilic times, and the language and literary forms of biblical poetry. Texts related to the NT world have cast light on the eschatological consciousness of the early Christians, the development of the church, and the problems and challenges that it encountered. These parallels to the biblical writings enable us to know what ideas and modes of expression were current and to appreciate the extent to which biblical writers followed or deviated from their cultural patterns.

The term "historical criticism" is sometimes used in a narrow sense to refer to the event behind the text; that is, to determine what really took place in ancient Israel's escape from Egypt or on the first Easter Sunday. The goal is to describe the event exactly as it happened, not necessarily as the writers have described it. But there are some serious obstacles in the way: since the biblical writers did not distinguish events and their significance, it is hard to untangle them now in our sources. Also, historical critics often proceed on the basis of philosophical assumptions that rule out divine intervention and the miraculous, and hold negative views about the faith-communities that transmitted the biblical sources.

Connected with the historical origin of the biblical writings is the question of authenticity. The classic introductions to the OT and NT describe individual books in terms of their author, date, original audience, language, purpose, content, structure, and theology. Many biblical books are anonymous, with no indication of authorship. Some are presented as the teachings of a prophet that have been compiled by his followers. A few books like Paul's own letters were clearly written by an identifiable individual, though recognition must be given to the contributions of secretaries in composing the text. Still others appear to be pseudonymous; that is, put forth under the name of a famous figure (Paul, Peter, James, etc.,). The problem is that ancient people approached the question of authorship more casually than we do in our day. Although the customary ascriptions and the traditions connected with biblical books should be taken seriously, they too are to be studied in their historical context and weighted alongside other evidence pertaining to the historical setting of a biblical book. At any rate, whatever their precise origin, all the biblical books belong to the canon of Sacred Scripture and thus are part of the norm of christian faith.

Biblical criticism involves textual, literary, and historical methods. The individual operations arose at different times and in different places. Textual criticism goes back to antiquity and is routinely used in establishing the text of classical and other writings. Literary criticism is the set of questions that are customarily put to texts by secular critics. The techniques of and the enthusiasm for historical criticism arose mainly in the German universities of the nineteenth and twentieth centuries.

Vatican II's Dogmatic Constitution on Divine Revelation (D.V. 12) gave its endorsement of biblical criticism (without necessarily endorsing everything that is stated in the name of biblical criticism). Following the lead of Pope Pius XII's 1943 encyclical *Divino afflante Spiritu,* the constitution urged Catholic scholars to pay attention to the literary forms in which divine revelation is expressed, to look for the meaning intended by the biblical writer in his own historical situa-

tion and culture, and to take account of the patterns of perception, speech, and narrative prevailing at that time.

Biblical criticism has had many critics in recent years. They argue that it is often speculative and pastorally disturbing, tells only a small part about the Bible, reflects the assumptions and concerns of the Enlightenment, or does not address the important theological issues raised by the Bible. Although there is some truth in these complaints, it is fair to say that the textual, literary, and historical operations involved in biblical criticism remain basic and indispensable to any serious treatment of Scripture.

See **Canon of Scripture**

R.F. Collins, *Introduction to the New Testament,* Garden City, NY: Doubleday, and London: S.C.M., 1983. D.J. Harrington, *Interpreting the New Testament. A Practical Guide,* Wilmington: Michael Glazier, 1979, and Dublin: Veritas, 1980. W.G. Kümmel, *Introduction to the New Testament,* Nashville: Abingdon, 1975, and London: S.C.M., 1977.

DANIEL J. HARRINGTON, S J

BIBLICAL THEOLOGY

There would seem to be several possibilities open for a discipline called biblical theology. The first is a setting of the various religious ideas which emerge in each testament in an ordered relation with the others, calling that internal dialogue a theology. The difficulties inherent in doing the same thing with two distinct bodies of literature, one describing the life of Israel over seventeen centuries and written in the course of perhaps seven, and the other a shorter collection written within a seventy-year period and descriptive of the events of perhaps one hundred, are evident. In any case the products will be the systematizing of two sets of religious ideas, largely overlapping, as they were lived out in two religious communities which had much in common. A bolder venture than either of the two above is to elicit one biblical theology from both testaments, as Christians reckon them in their largely identical "canons" of scripture.

A second option is to isolate the thought patterns that predominate in the Hexateuch, the Chronicler, the Deuteronomist, the eighth to seventh-century prophets and so on, doing the same with the prevailing ideas in Mark-Matthew, the two Lucan books, the Johannine gospel and epistles, the Pauline corpus, and so on. This would yield clusters of biblical theologies, valid in that the various authors/editors did indeed stress certain convictions and themes over others, but invalid in that they were not themselves systematic (although highly intelligent) thinkers, nor could they envision any thought structures suitable for reflection by individuals isolated from a communal life of worship.

Still a third possibility, and one that has been realized more frequently than the first two, would be to begin with the results of centuries of theology (a peculiarly christian way of conceiving the divine-human relation), and search the Bible for the ways it contains in germ the later theologies of matters like God one and triune, as the Creator of all, Jesus as the Christ and Son of God, God's gracious action on humanity's behalf, sin and reconciliation, and so with the other mysteries of human and divine existence. This theology of roots or origins would legitimately look for data later systematized, often in a fashion quite unlike that of their original appearance in the Bible, but it would illegitimately give the impression that they are present there awaiting the intellectual treatment that the christian centuries later gave them. This type of biblical theology would impose a thought structure on the Bible largely alien to the one found there, even though the translation from biblical to non-biblical categories might have been found necessary for comprehension in earlier times.

A fourth mode of biblical theology would study the Scriptures historically and critically to learn what the Bible meant to the peoples who wrote and received it, adopting insofar as possible their many "horizons" and then, from the horizon of the modern Western Christian, seeing how the two might be fused to yield a single vision. In this attempt, "what the Bible meant" would contribute to "what the Bible means." Indeed, modern biblical theologians tend to maintain that no other approach to Bible study than this last is valid. An emerging few hold that fruitful interpretation must at the same time take into account the history of christian interpretation augmented by Jewish. But at present not many are willing to acknowledge this need. The latter process is immeasurably complex. Most authors are impatient with the intermediate step because they think that doctrinal structures deduced from the Bible will interfere with the construction of a modern biblical theology. Christians in the Protestant tradition are prone to set aside biblical interpretation of the patristic and medieval periods entirely on a *sola scriptura* principle, although they somewhat inconsistently allow the interpretations of the Reformers and of any since them who do systematize but not in the scholastic mode. Catholics of this century in scripture studies, coming abreast of the meanings the biblical books probably had for their authors, tend to be just as ready as their Protestant colleagues to proceed directly from the ancient world to the meanings the Bible can have for this generation. Only slowly are both coming to see that the move is potentially unproductive of the best results if absolutely no account is taken of interpretations of the canonical books and noncanonical books by the church councils, fathers and doctors. The reason is that neither wisdom nor insight into meaning requires sophistication in the realm of history as its sole condition. Both may arise from other sources.

Some Protestants and Catholics alike have grown discouraged at the possibility of constructing truly biblical theologies. Enthusiasm for eliciting them from either testament or the whole Bible has declined from its high point before and after World War II. Facing the project's difficulties squarely, however, does not mean that it has no bright future. It is simply that awareness of its limitations has given momentary pause. To paraphrase Paul, real biblical theology is not always such as appears to be outwardly, nor is a true theology of the Bible something external and physical. This is not to say that what it is essentially and within has yet been arrived at. The present decades are at work on the problem.

Christians of the second century and those following heard their sacred writings read out publicly, both those inherited from Israel and the writings of the apostolic age, and they tried to live by these scriptures. They did not have the theoretical problem of whether it was possible to do so. They were convinced that it was. Largely setting aside the problems of the Lord's continued non-appearance (although the late third-century repudiation of chiliasm indicates for how long a time Christians continued to wrestle with the problem), they lived as they were enjoined to do by the ethics of the Bible, setting aside its prescriptions on ritual and purity. They did not concentrate on adhering to the Law as the great symbol of their belonging to a covenanted community but sought, rather, fulfillments of the promise the Jewish scriptures held out to them. These they found in the typologies the NT writers offered. At the same time the early christian writers provided others of their own. The perceived "harmonies of the two testaments" was the biblical theology of the early centuries.

As early as the book of Acts, Paul's letters, and the other epistolary literature, creedal fragments appeared which indicated that extracts were being made from the vast literature of the Bible. These extracts from the Hebrew scriptures were understood as testifying proleptically to the saving events which had happened among believers in Jesus Christ in recent times. The Qumran community and the later *tannaim* (authors of the Mishnah) would do something quite similar on the basis of their different sets of contemporary experiences. As Christians framed their "books of testimonies" and their creeds, they were convinced they were drawing from the Scriptures their true meaning, not imposing a new one upon them.

All the creedal formularies were presumably liturgical in origin and all were thought to be faithful to history. They were not a theology, any more than the evangelists or Paul set themselves to write theologies. They were an immediate deduction that what had happened in fulfillment of promise was "according to the Scriptures." In isolating Jesus' conception and birth, teaching and example, death and resurrection, followed by his gift of the Spirit from the Father, and setting them in relation, the creeds provided the data for a needed theological exploration. The second-century apologists' comparison of pagan religions with Christian, Clement's marshaling of biblical types to illustrate the hospitality and respect for authority which should characterize the Corinthian community, and Ignatius' inchoate theology of universal salvation in the blood of Christ who "was God," all set the stage for an organization of biblical affirmations in structured fashion. The structure would give intellectual satisfaction to believers who questioned the consistency of the teaching. Doctrinal convictions could also be presented to Jews and pagans as, at the very least, not contradictory or absurd. Thus was the stage set for Irenaeus' pretheological exercise in *Five Books against Gnosis Falsely So Called.*

Irenaeus devised a theory of recapitulation which amplified Paul's paralleling of Adam and Christ to the extent of finding in Mary a new Eve as a means of guaranteeing Jesus' true humanity. The whole history of the race from the start was summed up anew, he held, in a mother and Son from whom a new progeny was born. This basically apologetic work "against [gnostic] heresies" made it possible for Origen in Greek and Tertullian in Latin to cull the Bible and emerge with fairly thoroughgoing systematized presentations, viz., theologies of the mysteries Christians believed in. The liturgical lives being lived by all were strengthened by an intellectual approach to the Scriptures which only the educated few experienced a need of, but which the whole church thenceforth had placed at its service.

The Bible was not itself a theology but it provided the possibility of numerous theologies. One of these came to predominate, that of the second Adam. A proclamation (*kērygma*) and exposition (*didachē*) had marked the original apostolic deliverance. These of themselves provided insufficient assurance that wrong constructions would not be put on their content. Attack would come from without, for which theology's apologetic function was necessary. It would also come from within, which meant that heresies could be identified and defeated only by this same means, theology. A church without a theological tradition is one which, from early times, had no existence. The question is, was this tradition ever one of a biblical theology in any strict sense?

To start at the beginning, did the early church develop an independent theology of the Hebrew scriptures? It did not, as its early use of the Pauline term "new testament" in favorable contrast to one enshrined in written letters (2 Cor 3:6) testifies. It willingly accepted these writings in Greek translation, the so-called Septuagint version (LXX) of the Bible, viewing them as Sacred Scripture and using them for two purposes chiefly. One was to find in them a justification for the belief, already held, that Jesus was Israel's Messiah, the fulfillment of the earliest covenantal promise to Abraham in his seed. The other was to employ them for the ethical formation of candidates recruited from the pagan world for baptism.

The first purpose dictated the mode of the scriptures' use by the early church. This faith community was not interested in the emergence or development of ethical monotheism, as the Wellhausen school of the late nineteenth century held it should have been. The religious history of Israel detained it not at all. Neither was there any curiosity about what contemporaneous Israel made of its own scriptures. Starting with Justin's *Dialogue with Trypho,* the Christians told the Jews what things they should have been concerned with. The early church did not cheer the prophetic movement on in retrospect, as it supposedly dislodged the temple priesthood or concentration on the fulfillment of Mosaic precepts. All these enthusiasms of the eighteenth and nineteenth centuries arose on the European continent. Liberal theology under Romantic influence did battle with Protestant dogmatism by this means, as earlier the Reformers had done with the Roman Church. The Hebrew scriptures, newly discovered under their historical aspect, provided a ready-to-hand arsenal for the battle.

Did the Church fathers view the OT narratives as history and, if so, did they have any hermeneutical principles to deal with them? Or were they only concerned to find in this well-stocked cupboard doctrines they previously held about God and Christ, grace and salvation? They very well knew the Bible as history, but of the kind that Homer wrote, later Herodotus and Thucydides and later still Polybius, Josephus and Tacitus. The narratives described great heroes out of Israel's past (including the line from Adam to Abram's father Terah, a reckoning the Jews who viewed the primordial history as pre-Israelite did not make). The stories of patriarchs and priests, prophets and kings were viewed by Christians as linear history told by the prophetic Spirit for a twofold reason: to chronicle the human stock from which Jesus "descended from David according to the flesh" and "son of God in power according to the spirit of holiness" would come (Rom. 1:3-4; cf. Rom 9, which traced the patriarchal line from which Jesus sprang); and to provide heroes and heroines for emulation in the mold of Jesus Christ, the apostles and the martyrs. The interpretive principle was simple and direct: so it was of old, so it was fulfilled in Jesus and must be in those who believe in him. The chief understanding was one of type and antitype, promise and fulfillment. Matthew's eleven formula quotations which began, "that it might be fulfilled as it was written," were enlarged to the hundreds and thousands.

When people like Justin and Jerome encountered rabbis who thought that these stories had a plain meaning in the context of Israel's ongoing history, the Christians accused them of having a "carnal" (viz., literal) mentality. Alexandrian allegory was the sustained typology of christian interpretation gone wild. Origen, who had engaged in allegory in good measure himself, proved to be its corrector through an exegesis which we would call remarkably scientific for his

day. Jerome did something similar but never managed to let his historical and philological studies overcome the rich symbolisms of Augustine. The latter's interpretations prevailed for more than 1300 years. As to viewing the Hebrew scripture as a descriptive narrative of the ongoing life of a people which produced laws and prophetic oracles and wise sayings along the way, the Christians never engaged in it. They were too busy tracing the golden thread of Jesus Christ, who Jerome said was to be found on every page of scripture.

The christian view of the apostolic writings, later called the "new testament," was quite like that of the old. It was the history of Jesus of Nazareth and of the apostolic age. But it was history of the same two-dimensional kind as that of the Hebrew Bible. The best evidence that the late second century came to think of the gospels as chronicles of Jesus' career rather than the four distinct proclamations of his significance they were was Tatian's *Diatessaron* ("as through four") of ca. 175. This continuous narrative went on the assumption that recording the events of Jesus' life was the main contribution of the four evangelists. It disregarded the special emphasis of each which was the reason for his writing because it probably was not aware of them. In this sense Tatian testified to a historical interest in the gospels which set their theological intent at naught.

Similarly, the "historical Paul" of the Lucan account in Acts and the Paul of the paraenetic section in each epistle became the church's Paul. His transmitted traditions on the Eucharist (1 Cor 11:17-34), the Resurrection of Christ as paradigm for that of the faithful (15:3-57) and his contrast of the folly of the cross with the wisdom of the world (1:18-25) were treasured, but the Apostle was shortly "domesticated" in Maurice Wiles' penetrating phase. A biblical theology of

Paul never emerged, only a misconceived hailing of his preference for the gentiles over the Jews by a gentile church. This came about as a result of a careless reading of Romans which missed its main thrust. The church was looking for other things from Paul than his theology of Israel, such as the sins of gentiles and Jews alike or the triumphant declaration that nothing could separate the Christian from the love of Christ (Rom 8:31-39).

The disciple of Paul who wrote Ephesians did produce a Pauline theology of the community or church composed of Jews and gentiles, although one would need to be a gentile Christian to praise it unreservedly. Whoever wrote the epistles to Timothy and Titus likewise provided a pastoral theology of Paul, if in a totally revisionist spirit. But the whole patristic and medieval eras did not produce a treatise on Pauline thought which saw him as the innovative genius he was. Paul's chief insight was to find a place for gentiles in the religion of Israel without discerning divine repudiation of the adoption, the covenants, the Law and the promises made to it (see Rom 9:4). Instead it was left to Luther to discover and rehabilitate Paul (on erroneous terms) as one who perceived that God had set a gospel of grace in opposition to a burdensome Law. In fact, what Paul did was hail the possibility of the one Jewish and gentile faith in God's deed in Christ. The epistle to the Hebrew and, later, the scholastics would call this same firm adherence "hope." This Pauline faith served to relativize the perfectly acceptable works righteousness of Israel which had been in place, as the fact of Christ relativized all that had gone before. Luther found the gospel testified to in all of scripture to be that of justification by faith through grace and not works. He hailed the scriptures as alone containing all that one needed to know and do for salvation. He did not thereby present the christian world with its first biblical theology. He proposed yet another key to open the treasure-house which Christians call the Bible. There had been many such keys. In centuries to come there will presumably be many more.

The biblical theology movement of the last two hundred years is a key of this sort. Its Protestant initiators were familiar with the inconsistency involved in a *solā scripturā* claim while relying on a theological edifice deriving from the creeds and councils of the patristic period, supplemented by the seventeenth-century evangelical scholastics rather than the repudiated Catholic medievals. They feared that the purity of the Bible had been adulterated by philosophical ways of thinking, and meant to go back to the source. The attempt was made, consequently, to fashion a theology directly from the Bible rather than resort to the Bible for justification of inherited theological positions. An important question is, was the Church's theology not a biblical theology in the sense envisioned by J. Semler and others who went in search of one in the eighteenth century? Had the resort to terms like *homooúsion* or Augustine's "relations of opposition" among the *personae* of the trinity introduced concepts unworthy of a biblical faith? If the charge was unfounded the effort to overcome it could have been ill-conceived. Perhaps all that the early practitioners of the art intended was to mine the Bible for its direct yield in the interest of a new theological structure without turning their backs on the theologies of creation, redemption and sanctification already in place, whatever their history. Perhaps, however, some thought that all christian theologies were in some measure debased and that a fresh start had to be made. If so, what is important is that they thought a purely biblical theology was possible.

Not until the sixteenth century did

Trent define 45 books as the church's canonical Hebrew scripture. The Reformers in the same period chose by a consensus of the learned the Massoretic canon of 39 books (grouped as 22 by the rabbis). Certain second-century writings which were not ultimately canonized were read publicly in more churches than some of those which were (e.g., *The Didache, The Shepherd,* 1 Clement and the epistles of Ignatius). Of these, all but Hermas' *Shepherd* bristled with sayings of Jesus from collections which probably preceded the writing of the canonical gospels. A biblical theology in the sense of one based on the Bible was, therefore, not possible before the year 200. The canonization of scripture in practice ca. A.D. 400 did not remove the continuing ambivalence over the deutero-canonical books nor say anything to the problem of which books were inspired. A great many more were reckoned to be inspired than the designated 27 of the NT, which seemed to be apostolic teaching and hence dependable because each had some claim to relation to an apostle.

All through this time church life was going on. Justin's report from ca. 155 that in Rome the "memoirs of the apostles and the writings of the prophets were read" on the Lord's day (1 *Apol.* 67) could probably have been duplicated in the major cities. When people were baptized it was done interrogatively in terms of the local creed, always triune and always by way of selected phrases featuring the divine creative power, the sufferings, death and resurrection of Jesus Christ and hope of his return, and final mention of belief in the Holy Spirit. The baptismal creeds were thus pertinent summaries of biblical, largely NT, highlights. The creeds drawn up at Nicea and Constantinople known to us from Ephesus and Chalcedon had another purpose. They were meant to catch heretical bishops, who presumably could not recite defined formulas in good conscience if they disagreed with them. It is well known why the conciliar creeds contained non-biblical language. Certifiable heretics were quite content to state their belief in the mysteries of God and Christ in biblical terms, when it was well known that they departed from the traditional understanding the church had of them.

Some of the language resorted to in the creeds looks philosophical but represents no turning to human learning to "explain" the meaning of revealed religion. It was the language of the highly literate which could not be mistaken in its intent at a time when the Bible could. Nowadays terms like ' serially," "mutually acceptable" and "without undue hardship" are used in laws and contracts because their meaning, within certain understood limits, is agreed on in the culture. It was the same with the Greek words for "essence," "the same substance" and "like substance." The well-educated in the populace would know what was intended in every case. A desertion of dynamic or functional Semitic language for static or ontic Hellenistic language was not intended. Absolute clarity of expression was, so that the heretic could not continue to work against the community's faith from within. Speech which was not characteristically biblical was turned to in order to ensure that biblical faith would be held. The principle underlying this move was of utmost importance: believers can only believe through their own cultural context; they cannot believe through another, either out of the present or the past. The largely Semitic outlook of the NT writers, despite their use of Greek, resulted in language clearly understood by Semites or early non-Semites from the same universe of *mythos* nurtured on the Bible. As Jews disappeared from the church and Greek intellectual thought gained the ascendancy, and as pagans who had lived the myths grew fewer, Christians had increasing difficulty in understanding their own faith. They could hear it proclaimed in another cultural mold and get much from it, to be sure, but in order to comprehend all that they heard they had to hear it on their own cultural terms. Only first-century Hellenized Jews, in other words, could do without a christian theology of cultural transformation derived from the scriptures. And even they needed a theology of probe and challenge by putting questions to the Bible which the Bible, in the terms of their own cultural experience, did not raise.

There is the possibility and the necessity of theology—faith seeking understanding—at the first moment there is the claim of a revelation transmitted orally. The need is heightened as soon as the oral tradition becomes written text. Theology's roots are the story contained in the Bible, culminating in the death and resurrection of Jesus Christ, which must be mastered by adult candidates for baptism. This story is far more extensive than the baptismal creed. Irenaeus called it, in the extant Latin translation of *Against Heresies,* the "rule of truth." He never spelled it out, supplying only portions here and there. He obviously meant to equate it with the catechesis given to candidates. It was at no point a digest of the history of Israel but a story of human salvation, governed as to its OT telling by the career of Jesus and the infant church. This narrative was retold by way of detachment from its various *Sitze im Leben* through a selection process, not a polemical or philosophical treatment. This meant that the retelling of the OT would be both recognizable and unrecognizable to a late second-century rabbi.

When, in the next phase, Origen told the biblical story as if the middle Platonist philosophy of his Alexandrian education had been part of the same revelation, he would doubtless have maintained (with Justin and Athenagoras) that of course it was. The same God had revealed all truth, thereby assisting in a special way the learned who could absorb biblical truth best in Plotinian categories. The notion that the gospel had been adulterated by the use of language or concepts foreign to the Bible, such as Origen's famed *apokatástasis* or "recycling" of souls until they were ready to share in the glory of Christ, would have thoroughly distressed this christian intellectual. He thought of himself as a teacher of the Bible, quite simply. He taught what was clearly stated and, to his mind, just as clearly implied by the sacred text.

This brings to light the fact that the problem of any theology's derivation from the Bible is twofold. There is the necessary translation of the biblical language and story into a variety of cultural idioms (e.g., the Greek, Syriac, Coptic, Latin and Armenian worlds, and those of all the peoples whose second languages these were). There is the further problem of employing thought systems other than the Semitic to aid in saying basically Jewish things. This meant that the gospel became, in fact, a distinct Alexandrian, Antiochene, Athenian and Roman reality (as well as of many subgroups), although the appearance was given of a single transformation into Greek categories. The fathers of Nicaea through to the various councils of Constantinople battled over a seemingly common vocabulary but were actually saying different things about a common biblical faith. Throughout these struggles, which seemed to be theological, the matter at stake was the understandings various peoples had of the liturgical formularies and supportive catecheses they were familiar with, as interpreted by their bishops who spoke for them. Various theologies were thus developed to ensure that a traditional understanding of the Bible was being adhered to. It was not so much that the ancient faith was being transposed into Greek philosophical categories, as is often said, as that it was expressed in ways that guarded against betrayal of its traditional understanding. There emerged, therefore, a "biblical theology" in that the primary biblical data as they were perceived governed the discourse and not vice versa.

Such continued to be the case throughout the patristic, Carolingian and medieval periods. Simple folk were informed by a catechesis and preaching which derived fairly directly from the Bible. Indirectly biblical was the creedal material proposed for commitment to memory or the summary formulations which derived from the Church Fathers—chiefly Augustine in the West and the Cappodocians in the East. All such conclusions of the theological process were meant to be protective of biblical truth, not a threat to it. The rise of the twelfth-century logicians in the West brought a new phase of the discussion. They did not claim that the biblical revelation was dispensable but that much of its content could be arrived at by the philosophical process. The Schoolmen of the next century like Albert and Thomas, Bonaventure and Scotus restored the Bible's directive function while retaining the theological language of Augustine—the Thomist school employing Aristotle to feature the intellectual in Augustinianism as primary, the Scotists developing the volitional as primary. All would have claimed that their theology was biblical. But the appearance given was of a series of disputed questions which derived remotely rather than immediately from the biblical data.

The challenges of the rabbis, Islam and the Albigensian heresy resulted in some of the responses of the Schoolmen. But in general they were interested in creating in theology a queen at the apex of all the branches of knowledge. They thought that the church had already extracted the deepest treasures of the Bible, the data of revelation on which they were called to speculate.

The growing ascendancy of process over substance in the fourteenth and fifteenth centuries is well known. Nominalism was the corruption of the voluntarist strain in theology, vain speculation the pathology of the intellectual strain. A variety of contemplative and ascetical theologies arose to fill the vacuum caused by the jejune character of much of late scholasticism. It was the restoration to the West of the Greek and Hebrew tongues by the Renaissance humanists which opened vistas on a biblical theology not previously dreamed of. Aquinas had taught that the literal sense of the Bible was the only one on which theologians could base their work, as Andrew of St. Victor (cf. 1175) had done before him. They thereby denied that the spiritual senses of scripture—the allegorical (doctrinal), anagogic (contemplative) and moral—were useful in the project. Aquinas put forward in theological argument only what he thought was the intention of the biblical authors, without however turning his back on patristic exegesis. The Franciscan friar Nicholas of Lyra (d. 1340), who controlled the Hebrew Bible and contemporary Jewish and Arabic literature, rejected any unfounded traditional exegesis if he thought the text, with or without the support of the Fathers, did not support it. He and Andrew paved the way for humanists like Colet (d. 1519), and Erasmus (d. 1536) in Greek and Reuchlin (d. 1522) in Hebrew. These Renaissance men gave the Reformers the possibility of grounding their theological arguments on a dependable biblical exegesis.

While Luther and Melanchthon, Calvin and Zwingli availed themselves of the new learning, they did not depart from the tradition of doing theology under the influence of certain controlling ideas. In Luther's case it was justification by grace through faith, in Calvin's the total sovereignty of an all-just God. The shape of theology was left undisturbed, namely a consideration of God as origin and creator of all, of the incarnate Son as redeemer, and of the Holy Spirit as sanctifier of the church and of individuals. New stresses, however, were placed on the roles of Son and Spirit in human salvation and much greater use was made of the Bible as the source of the church's doctrines. In all this, the scriptures continued to illumine the trinitarian creedal structure as before, rather than resulting in a new conception of theology's coming directly from the Bible.

The eighteenth-century Protestants, A. Busching (1755) and J. Semler (1771-76), attempted to judge the scholasticism of their tradition by a biblical standard. It was left to J.P. Gabler (1787) and G. L. Bauer (1800-02) to produce works which viewed biblical theology as a historical science distinct from the theologies that had gone before. Bauer proposed the Enlightenment canon of reason and morals as sufficient for distinguishing essential from time-conditioned teaching in biblical history. W. de Wette used the best critical approach his age was capable of to produce a volume of biblical theology for each testament (1813, 1816) in which historical development was the prevailing category. The influence of Hegel was evident in the OT work of W. Vatke (1835) and in the NT of F.C. Baur (published after his death in 1860), both of whom posited dialectical struggle within the testaments which resulted in a synthesized settlement. With the published researches of K. Graf (1866), J. Wellhausen (1878, 1895) and R. Smend (1893), things went in a historical rather than a theological direction. NT theologies produced from Baur's time until an essay of W. Wrede in 1897 tended to be histories of NT thought, beginning with Jesus and ending with the latest canonical writings or the non-canonical second-century material. A. Schlatter tried to turn the tide (1909) by calling for a relation of NT studies to the church's life, hence a biblical theology.

Karl Barth in his multi-volume *Kirchliche Dogmatik* produced a systematic theology which explored the great theological questions (God, creation, sin, grace, redemption) by exploring in first place what the Bible had to say about them and establishing in persuasive rhetoric the meanings they might have for modern Christians. Critical questions are largely set aside. The chief reliance is on intuition. The meaning of the ancient writers in their day is available to modern readers because the subject matter that both are interested in is the same. Any gap of the centuries is bridged by the transcendent character of the revelation made about God, Christ, or the life of grace. It is not bound by time and history. Barth, like Luther and Calvin, thought that it was relatively easy to discern the plain meaning of scripture. Any tension between what the text meant and what it means can be resolved by the determination to expound its ancient meaning in modern terms. The desire to proclaim the gospel modernly carries all before it.

Bultmann was adept at reconstructing historically (often by vivid imagination) those parts of the NT he was most interested in. He opted, however, for a dehistoricizing process which would bring him to the core of the NT message. This was human self-understanding, an existential living out of the kerygma's call to authentic existence. In the Bultmann project the NT writings are of little use in reconstructing a picture of primitive Christianity, whereas the presupposition is that "they have something to say to the present" (*Theology of the New Testament,*

Vol. II, "Epilogue," [p. 251]). His dehistoricizing is important as a way to clear the ground for fidelity to the overall intent of the NT.

Oscar Cullman finds in NT theology a religious philosophy of history which has time as its main category and Christ as the center of time. His translation of biblical themes, which he captures and describes quite accurately, into the present age does not face the hermeneutical task directly or especially successfully. It is much easier to criticize him, however, than to improve on him. Joachim Jeremias lived to produce one volume of a projected NT theology (1971) of Jesus Christ's call and human response. Krister Stendahl stands for many when he says that the key to a satisfactory biblical theology is not to lose enthusiasm for the descriptive task in a critical mood, as Barth does in part, and the later Bultmann almost entirely. He wants the "original" meaning of Bible texts spelled out on their own terms without the imposition of a Kantian, Hegelian or Ritschlian grid. (He would probably also say patristic, conciliar or scholastic.) Stendahl is alerted to the complexity of the task, recognizing the layers of meaning which both testaments acquired in the course of time, the OT over centuries and the gospels and Acts over decades.

The controlling theme of the Hebrew Scriptures is the ongoing life of the people Israel conscious of its history, which is a history of election sealed by covenant. This people proceeds toward an unknown future with its God, the LORD, ready for whatever resolution of its history this God may have for it. The distinct Jewish and christian interpretations of these events arise from two quite different faith positions. Both groups can profit greatly, however, from trying to reconstruct the situations in the life of the people Israel out of which came the

sacred history their bards and their prophets composed. The earliest reminiscences of events were modified by subsequent traditions, but every effort should be made to recapture them rather than yielding to the pressure of a "generalizing sweep of sacred history as though that sweep constituted the entire content of the OT" (Stendahl). Viewing the NT writings as the products of time and history will similarly be the only way to evaluate them on their own terms. Once it is seen that faith in the risen Christ became for the Christians the key both to understanding the entire Hebrew biblical collection and the reason behind the writing of gospels, epistles and apocalypse, it is easier to grasp their christian sense. It does not become automatically easier to know the meanings these many books had for those who composed them, but at least struggling for their original meanings will provide a grounding for the faith interpretation the church has put on them.

Once the crucial task of biblical theology, namely its descriptive function, has been faced there remains the task of seeing what contemporary believers can make of first-century belief, assuming that its general outlines have been arrived at. This is the hermeneutical challenge. The Bible's content must be translated into today's ways of expressing faith. It is true that earlier biblical, functional theologies of history have been supplanted by ontological theologies of God, Christ and the divine-human relation. The way forward is not the way back however; in other words, a simulation of earlier historical naïvetés. This is impractical for the basic reason that it is impossible. Indeed, from the second century apologists onward it was not attempted. Theology freed itself from its historical matrix as soon as Greek philosophy was put in its service; there was no awareness that biblical theology had been deserted. This means that the hermeneutical bridge which needs to be constructed between the biblical past and the christian present will have to be one aware of the theology of successive christian ages on a variety of topics. The concept of grace can be taken as an example. How was anything resembling it conceived in Israel's successive periods of self-understanding, in the various books of the NT, and in high points of the life of the church of East or West? The project is daunting when one considers how many different things have been held theologically about the Incarnation, or the symbols of public christian worship, or any topic one could name.

"Canon theology" seems to be a promising short-cut but it is no more than that. It only describes what the synagogue and the churches took at various times to be the sources of their religious faith, and a theology of those sources can certainly be constructed.

The biblical theology yet to be written cannot content itself with conflating historical horizons, an ancient and a modern. It must try to reveal a modern theology from the many theologies that have surfaced in the church, starting with NT times. This requires the conviction that the church is a living body which is busy reflecting upon its Israelite and christian origins in every age; that its traditions are forever continuous with and not cut off from its primordial period by the canonization of its scriptures.

Brevard Childs, *Introduction to the Old Testament as Scripture*, Philadelphia: Fortress, 1979. Reginald Fuller, "Theology, Biblical" in *Interpreter's Dictionary of the Bible*, Supplementary Volume, Nashville: Abingdon, 1976. E. Schillebeeckx, *Jesus: An Experiment in Christology*, New York: Seabury, 1979 and *Christ, The Experience of Jesus as Lord*, New York: Seabury, 1980.

GERARD S. SLOYAN

BINITARIANISM

Belief that there are only two persons in God, usually because the Holy Spirit is either denied or identified with the Word.
See **Holy Spirit, Trinity**

BIRTH CONTROL

Birth control is commonly understood as referring to any voluntary or intentional act or calculation designed to prevent the birth of a new person. Perceived in this way birth control includes total abstinence, "natural family planning" (NFP) methods, contraception, sterilization, and abortion. Total abstinence from sexual intercourse achieves the goal of preventing pregnancy and birth, but forfeits the value of genital sexual expression within a loving marital relationship in realizing that goal. NFP methods, e.g., the calendar "rhythm" method, the Billings Ovulation method, the Sympto-thermal System or cervical mucus-basal body temperature (CM-BBT) method, all attempt to decode nature's plan built into the physiological and hormonal system of the woman to determine when ovulation will occur. Accuracy in determining this phenomenon with precision would allow the couple to limit genital expression to infertile times in the woman's cycle to prevent the possibility of pregnancy. Modern NFP methods demand periodic abstinence and are rated highly effective (97%), depending largely on user diligence and competency.

Contraceptive birth control, often termed the "artificial" methods, includes chemical and barrier approaches to preventing fertilization of the ovum. Male contraceptives are limited at present to condoms which prevent the ejaculate from being deposited in the vaginal tract and some hormonal implants which curtail sperm production. A wider range of contraceptives have been designed for the female to suppress ovulation, e.g., the traditional "pill," or to prevent sperm from gaining access to the ovum, e.g., the diaphragm, cervical sponge, spermicides, etc. Their effectiveness varies considerably, with "the pill" being the most effective. Some female "contraceptives" are more accurately regarded as abortifacients since their action is to prevent uterine implantation of the fertilized ovum, e.g., the "mini-pill" and the intrauterine device (IUD). Sterilization procedures, a vasectomy for the male or a tubal ligation for the female, produce their contraceptive effects by surgically removing a section of the tubes (the male vas and the female fallopian) through which sperm and ovum must pass toward their goal of fertilization. Unless the body overcomes or bypasses in some way this surgically produced obstruction, sterilization is 100% effective as a birth control measure. Abortion prevents births by terminating the life of the early embryo or fetus. Ethical discussion of abortion involves values considered in a separate article.

Among christian peoples birth control practices have become increasingly more acceptable in recent times. Some theological traditions, e.g., Roman Catholic, have maintained a more restrictive ethical position on all methods other than abstinence and "natural family planning." Historically, attitudes toward the dignity of human life, the importance of perpetuating oneself in and through one's children, an aversion to practices common to prostitutes, and some questions about ensoulment shaped an early christian rejection of birth control practices. While some strands of christian thought advocated celibacy, and others championed freedom in matters of sexuality, a more centrist position prevailed which combined a natural law perspective with a trust of God's provident goodness: pro-

creation accords with the nature of sexual expression and God will not give new life beyond one's abilities to nurture. The resulting ethic rejected all forms of birth control.

In the fourth century, Augustine, reacting against Manichean disdain for procreation, taught that only procreation justified marital intercourse. Augustine's influence perdured through subsequent christian centuries and shaped a rather general ethical attitude rejecting of all forms of birth control. Thomas Aquinas and others of his school postulated arguments against contraceptive acts as being sins against nature. Abortion in all instances was judged to be ethically wrong, although there were arguments as to when ensoulment took place, a consideration affecting penitential and even civil law penalties. Terminating the life of the unborn to prevent birth was consistently held to be a violation of human dignity and a refusal to love one's neighbor. The solid christian front opposing birth control endured through the Reformation and even survived the subsequent and rather general attacks mounted by the Enlightenment philosophers against so much of christian doctrine.

In the twentieth century a gradual and significant erosion of this accord is detected. Social, political, and financial exigencies began to suggest the need for population control. Individual couples, in the years of the Great Depression, found themselves unable or unwilling to simply trust in God's providence. Societal forces combined with higher educational levels and a sense of new found personal freedom to find expression in a desire or commitment to "responsible parenting." The first documented and significant break from the traditional christian rejection of birth control, especially by contraceptive practices, occurred in the Church of England at the 1930 Lambeth

Conference. By a vote of 193 to 67 the bishops resolved that "where there is a clearly felt moral obligation to limit or avoid parenthood, the method must be decided on Christian principles." Complete abstinence from sexual intercourse was cited as the primary and obvious method, but in the event that "morally sound reason for avoiding complete abstinence" is present, "the conference [agreed] that other methods may be used, provided that this is done in the light of the same Christian principles." Strongly condemned by the bishops were motives of "selfishness, luxury, or mere convenience" for justifying methods of birth control. Statistical studies showing falling birth rates in western Europe prior to this Lambeth Conference suggest that the people had already begun to decide for themselves on the issue of birth control and family limitation.

The Roman Catholic Church, reacting against the growing acceptance of birth control among the general populace and the direction taken by the Church of England, responded in December of 1930 with the encyclical of Pope Pius XI, *Casti Connubii,* which condemned "any use ... of matrimony exercised in such a way that the act is deliberately frustrated in its natural power to generate life." Such acts were held to be contrary to the "law of God and of nature, and those who indulge in such are branded with the guilt of grave sin." Even so-called natural methods, e.g., rhythm, were seen as unworthy of persons who truly trust in God's providence, but permission to use such methods could be granted by one's confessor for grave reasons. The principal argument against birth control was rooted in a natural law ethic. Supportive evidence was found in sacred scripture in the proposition that God intended for human sexuality, expressed genitally and heterosexually, both procreative and unitive ends. A direct appeal was also made to

the Genesis 38 passage where Onan spilled his seed and the Lord, being displeased, took his life.

Mainstream Protestant churches followed the lead of the Lambeth Conference and gradually accepted the use of contraception in marriage as ethically acceptable for Christians. In 1959 the World Council of Churches stated that there was "no moral difference between use of the infertile period, artificial barriers to the meeting of sperm and ovum, and drugs regulating ovulation."

In 1963 Pope John XXIII established the Pontifical Study Commission on Family Population and Birth Problems to examine the United Nations policies on the population question and to recommend to the Holy See the course of action that the church should pursue in the light of the increased acceptance of contraceptive birth control in western society. Meanwhile, Vatican Council II, while not addressing the contraceptive issue directly (Pope Paul VI had in June, 1964, indicated his intention to issue a formal papal statement on this issue), did acknowledge in *Gaudium et Spes,* (49-51) an equality of "ends" for marriage and the conjugal act which stood in contrast to former teachers emphasizing the primacy of a procreative finality (e.g., *Casti Connubii,* 43, 84; see *Code of Canon Law, c. 1013.7*). In May, 1966, the pope received but did not make public the concluding position papers of the papal commission. In April, 1967, these "majority" and "minority" reports, together with a third more pastoral document on responsible parenthood, were published. The "majority" report and the pastoral document, while excluding a contraceptive mentality that would "egoistically and irrationally" oppose fruitfulness, called for a reassessment of Catholic teaching to allow for contraceptive intervention in marital intercourse. The "minority" report continued to argue the traditional condemnation of contraceptive acts from a classical natural law perspective. Pope Paul VI responded with the encyclical *Humanae Vitae (H. V.)* on July 29, 1968. This document of the ordinary magisterium teaches that "each and every marriage act *(quilibet matrimonii usus)* must remain open to the transmission of life," and appeals to "the inseparable connection, willed by God and unable to be broken by man on his own initiative, between the two meanings of the conjugal act: the unitive meaning and the procreative meaning." This encyclical does not reflect the stern moralism of *Casti Connubii,* nor does it repeat that encyclical's insistence on the primary and secondary purposes of marriage. Instead, a more personalist approach to the marriage relationship is endorsed and the role of conjugal love is highlighted. Responsible parenthood is presented as an important and ethically imperative element in married life.

Various national Catholic hierarchies reacted differently to *Humanae Vitae,* some finding in it absolute prohibition, others discovering certain nuances which justified not only the use of calculated infertile periods, but also a personal conscience decision to use contraception when deemed necessary to preserve values other than and equal to the procreative end of the marital act. Many contemporary Catholic moral theologians continue to maintain that "responsible parenting" does not mean that each and every act of marital intercourse must be open to the act's life and love giving potential, but that the preservation of the marital *consortium,* the love and unity "end" of the marital act, as a value proportional to that of the procreative, may be chosen with moral justification in the context of a contraceptive act. This position is explicitly rejected by *H. V.* 14, which argues that "it is not licit, even for the gravest reasons, to do evil so that

good may follow therefrom; . . . to make into the object of a positive act of the will something which is intrinsically disordered . . . even when the intention is to safeguard or promote individual, family or social well-being."

Birth control, or "responsible parenting," is recognized as a moral imperative by all mainstream christian churches, including the Roman Catholic church. What is rejected is any mentality or strategy which denies the giftedness and sacredness of human life in its initiation, or which threatens marriage and family. Directly contraceptive acts continue to be viewed by the church's magisterium as such a denial and threat.

G.P. Avvento, *Sexuality: A Christian View,* 1982, chaps. 5-9. A Guindon, *The Sexual Language,* 1976. *Humanae Vitae,* 1968. J.T. Noonan, Jr., *Contraception A History of Its Treatment by the Catholic Theologians and Canonists,* 1965. W.H. Shannon, *The Lively Debate: Response to Humanae Vitae,* 1970.

ROBERT M. FRIDAY

BISHOP

The problem of the origin, mission and nature of episcopacy is one of the most difficult issues of the so-called catholic ecclesiology. It is also one of those problems which needs to be seen in a new perspective if one tries to be in tune with the main insights of Vatican II. For, many affirmations of the Dogmatic Constitution on the Church imply a return to the patristic ecclesiology according to which each local church (that is, each community celebrating an authentic eucharist) is the Catholic Church (L.G. 26, C.D. 11). The universal Church is the *communion* of all these local churches, the *koinônia* of all the Catholic Churches.

This is crucial for the theology of episcopacy. Where the dogmatic constitution *Pastor aeternus* of Vatican I sees the church in its earthly form starting from its "head" the bishop of Rome, Vatican II sees it starting from the bishops who, taken together as a whole, comprise the foundation of the universal church (L.G. 19). The local bishops are the authentic vicars and legates of Christ for the life of the church: "The bishops, as vicars and legates of Christ, govern the particular Churches assigned to them by their counsels, exhortations and example, but over and above that also by the authority and sacred power which indeed they exercise exclusively for the spiritual development of their flock in truth and holiness, keeping in mind that he who is greater should become as the lesser, and he who is the leader as the servant (cf. Lk 22:26-27). This power, which they exercise personally in the name of Christ, is proper, ordinary and immediate, although its exercise is ultimately controlled by the supreme authority of the Church and can be confined within certain limits should the usefulness of the Church and the faithful require that. In virtue of this power bishops have a sacred right and a duty before the Lord of legislating for and of passing judgment on their subjects, as well as of regulating everything that concerns the good order of divine worship and of the apostolate.

The pastoral charge, that is, the permanent and daily care of their sheep, is entrusted to them fully; nor are they to be regarded as vicars of the Roman Pontiff; for they exercise the power which they possess in their own right and are called in the truest sense of the term prelates of the people whom they govern. Consequently their authority, far from being damaged by the supreme and universal power, is much rather defended, upheld and strengthened by it, since the Holy Spirit preserves unfailingly that form of government which was set up by Christ the Lord in his Church." (L.G. 27)

Accordingly, the bishops are the "heads" of the Church (L.G. 18), the pontiffs (L.G. 21), the "shepherds" (L.G. 20). The fullness of the ministry which builds, leads and guides the whole church belongs to the college of bishops as such, following in the wake of the mission entrusted to the apostles as a group (L.G. 20, 21).

I. The Role of the Bishop in the Local Church

1) It is impossible to find in the NT a clear view and even a definition of the precise function of the person designated as *episkopoi* (bishops). The word occurs only five times (Acts 20:28; Phil 1:1; 1 Tim 3:2; Tit 1:7, 1 Pet 2:25), and it seems to be interchangeable with the title of *presbyteroi* (elders) used for the same persons (cf. Acts 20:17, 28; 1 Tm 3:2, 5:17; Tit 1:5, 7; 1 Pet 5:1-3 in many manuscripts). *Episkopos* means supervisor. It is then possible that only some of the *presbyteroi* (elders) assumed the function of supervisor. The *presbyteroi* seem to have formed a council (as did the *Zeqenim* of the pharisaic judaism) and this ruling body may have entrusted some of its members with the specific task of supervising.

It is also difficult to know what exact meaning is given in this context to the verb *episkopein* (1 Pet 5:2) and to the noun *episkope* (Acts 1:20; 1 Tm 3:1). Nevertheless it is possible to collect many indications which, together, help us to sketch at least the main outlines of this "supervision" during the first decades of the church. Even if it is probably in some ways concerned with material issues, like the management or administration of the funds and the handling of the common goods (cf. Acts 4:35; 6:3-6), this watching-over was mainly centered on the spiritual values of christian *koinônia*. Its principal goal was to keep all the baptized in the communion of the same faith, that is the faith proclaimed by those who have been the witnesses of the life, death and glorification of Christ Jesus. But this communion of faith had to be embodied in a communion of life; hence the necessity of decisions affecting life style or of regulations concerning the community. Moreover, the multiplication of communities not only in the same area but also in many regions of the world created the necessity to watch over the way the various preachers were announcing the gospel. All the local churches needed to be in communion in the same faith and united through the same baptism.

This question of leadership became certainly a major concern after the passing away of the apostolic group and the death of the second generation of *episkopoi* or *presbyteroi* acting according to what they had received from this apostolic group or its immediate associates. For even if there is no evidence that any of the Twelve ever served as head of a local church, it is nevertheless clear that they were the foundation of the faith of every local church.

2) Ignatius of Antioch (around 105) is the first of the old writers we know who attributes to the bishop (*episkopos*) the key office in the life of the local church. But his understanding of the service (*episkopè*) that this bishop is supposed to accomplish is coherent with the view we find in the other documents of the immediate post-apostolic period.

For two essential elements of the christian *koinônia* had to be preserved in every local church:

a. The apostolic teaching (grounded in the apostolic witnessing) appeared to be so fundamental that the whole life of the community was dependent on a faithful preservation and transmission of what had been "received" since the beginning. In other words, the local church had to remain in the faith of the departed apostolic generation. This faith was indeed the faith of those who had seen the Lord, "received" and understood his teaching. But it was now entrusted to the various local churches.

In these churches the bishop was chosen (and ordained) in order to keep the community in *its* authentic apostolic faith. He was *the vicar of the Apostles* in one of the churches founded on their witness. This explains why Irenaeus affirms that the bishop receives from the Spirit of God the charisms of truth, enabling him to explain rightly the scriptures (*Adv. Haer.* IV, 26, 5). From the beginning the bishop appears as the guardian of the apostolic tradition in his local church. He has the mandate to help his church to remain in the faith it recognized in him when it chose him to be its pastor.

b. But from the beginning the local church had also to be kept in a real communion of life and mission. This need was crucial especially for two reasons. The first of these reasons was the great variety of charisms given by the Spirit to different members of the community. All these gifts were for the service and the common good of the local church. They needed to be tested, coordinated, kept in harmony. The other reason was the presence in the community of members of diverse social classes, ages, races, professions, sexes, cultures. Being baptized they had to be one, in order to live concretely as reconciled children of God.

Given the evident link between the essential message of the apostolic tradition and the life in communion—grounded in the fact that Christ Jesus had been at the same time the one who preached the gospel of God and the one who gathered together in unity the scattered children of God—it was normal to have the same person as guardian of the apostolic faith in the local church and focus of its life in reconciliation and unity.

c. In the concrete life of the local church this role of the bishop has always been clearly expressed in the celebration of the eucharist. In the first centuries, the bishop was the one who, surrounded by the presbyters and helped by the deacons, presided at the synaxis, that is, at the gathering of the community. And this community was made of the Christians he instructed, baptized, confirmed. There is only one *true* eucharist: the one over which the bishop (or one of his delegates) presides (cf. Ignace, *Smyrn* VIII, 2; *Magn* VII, 2; *Philad* IV, 1). For where the eucharist is celebrated, the true nature and structure of the local church is manifested, this church which is the *koinônia* in the Body of Christ of all the Christians of this place, with their gifts and their differences.

This role of the bishop in the eucharist is so important that, during the first centuries, when the Sunday eucharist was presided over in a parish by one of the presbyters, a portion of the eucharistic bread consecrated by the bishop in his cathedral (and sent to this parish) was put into the chalice. Even today the name of the bishop has to be mentioned in the Canon.

It was clear that being the one presiding at the eucharist—the memorial of the Lord—the bishop was acting in the community in the name of Christ Jesus as his vicar. This also is in tune with the relation of the office of bishop with the apostolic mandate. The bishop is the *vicar* of the apostles not only because he is the one who echoes their teaching, but also because in a certain way he is also what the NT calls a *shaliah,* that is a servant in whom one has to receive and hear Christ, "the one who sent him" (cf. Jn 13:20; Lk 10:16), because he represents his person.

3) In the course of history, especially because of the growing number of small communities (called parishes) within the local churches (called dioceses) and of the reorganization of the whole "pastoral" life this new situation entailed, many changes occurred. For instance, it became impossible for the bishop to be the president of all the eucharistic celebrations of his diocese. The presbyters assumed this key function. In the western churches, the only functions specifically reserved to the bishop were the ordination of other ministers and the confirmation (chrismation) of the newly baptized members of the local church. But this last function is no longer exclusively his own (cf. canons 883-888). Moreover the local bishop is no longer the only one having the right to ordain the presbyters, deacons and other ministers of his diocese. Another bishop can ordain these presbyters and deacons, a major superior can perform the installation of acolytes and readers.

In the past, a bishop was forever the pastor of the local church for which he had been ordained. It was impossible to leave it for the leadership of another church. It was even impossible for him to ordain his successor (cf. Council of Nicaea, canon 15; Eusebius, *Hist. Eccles.* VI, 43,11; Leo, *Epist.* 14.8; etc.). It is clear that it is no longer the case. Another important change has been the creation of the so-called auxiliary bishops. The new canon law considers them as fully bishops, having the right and duty to be at the councils (ecumenical, plenary, provincial) with a deliberative vote (can. 339, 443). They are also members of the episcopal conference usually with a deliberative vote (can. 454). They even ordain priests and can be co-consecrators of other bishops. It is clear that their status is now the status of true sharers of the function of the diocesan bishop. But this creates an ecclesiological situation which is no longer entirely coherent with the important (and essential) principle of the first centuries: one bishop in one local church. The possibility to mention the names of the auxiliary bishops (and in some dioceses they are numerous) during the Canon of the Mass would have been for the Councils of the undivided Church a grave anomaly, probably condemned.

Nevertheless, the three essential functions of the local bishop remain substantially what they have been at least since the end of the second century. We discovered that the bishop always had an office of teacher (in preaching, explaining, keeping the apostolic faith), of leader (keeping the local Church one in spite of the diversity of its members), of sanctifier (holding the responsibility of giving the Church everything which makes it "the chosen race, the royal priesthood, the consecrated nation, the people set apart to sing the praises of God" (1 Pet 2:9). They are still the functions that the ritual of the ordination and the documents of Vatican II affirm to be those of a bishop.

II. The Relationship of the Bishop to the Universal Church

1) The church of God existing in each local church, and this church being necessarily the same everywhere in spite of the diversity of races, tongues, cultures, urgencies, each bishop has to be solicitous for all the churches (cf. C.D. 6). And he has to act in communion with all the other bishops, in order to keep his own local church in the *koinônia* of all the churches. What his church is, the catholic church has to be.

It is because of this presence of the one and indivisible church of God (the apostolic and catholic church) in each local church that the bishops form together an indivisible group, a college. The college is for the maintaining and strengthening of the *koinônia* of the churches. Each local church, indeed, has to recognize its own faith in the life and praxis of its sister church, to see in the *synaxis* of this other church the same apostolic church it sees in its own gathering. This is why the major decisions concerning the interpretation of apostolic faith or the orientations of christian life cannot be taken by a bishop in isolation; the missionary activity of one church cannot be planned without a reference to what the other bishops are planning for their own church; and especially the answers to the burning questions challenging christian doctrine or praxis cannot be given by one local church only. A substantial disagreement on crucial issues of faith would break the *koinônia* and make impossible eucharistic concelebration. And a realistic *koinônia* implies that as soon as a local church is facing great difficulties, other churches help it. It is the duty of the bishop to detect this need and provide the help.

2) When a bishop is ordained, he is at the same time given to his local church and inserted within the unbreakable solidarity of the so-called episcopal college. He cannot be a bishop without both (and this explains why even the titular or auxiliary bishops are—thanks to a very strange juridical fiction—ordained for a local church which had existed somewhere). In this collegial solidarity the bishops are acting according to the historical prerogatives and charisms of their own local church. For they are in the college not only as pastor of their church but also as its representative. In some important situations—such as the consultation for a dogmatic definition—they have to express, together with their own opinion, the *sensus fidelium* of their local church. In other words they are not the group dominating the church of God; they are the group which is in the whole church the "vicar" of the apostolic community (with its faith, its witness, its mission, its pastoral responsibility). The nuance is crucial. It is in this sense that the episcopal college has its origin in the apostolic group.

3) It is because of the charism and of the prerogatives of his local church—the church in which Peter and Paul died, giving the supreme witness of their martyrdom—that the bishop of the local

church of Rome has a specific role concerning the solidarity of the episcopal college. To be in communion with him means to be one with the faith of Peter and Paul, and of all the churches who confess, have confessed, and will confess this faith. Vatican I says that his mission is unity in faith "in order that really (*ut vero*) the episcopate itself be one and undivided," and consequently the churches (D.S. 3050). He is the first among the bishops precisely because he is the servant of the local church which is the guardian of the supreme confession of the apostolic faith. And this faith is the ultimate ground of christian *koinônia*.

A local bishop, then, is not the vicar of the bishop of Rome. He is, strictly speaking, a member of the episcopal college, serving his local church in full fidelity to the apostolic faith confessed by Peter and Paul and over which the bishop of Rome has to watch in order to preserve and foster christian *koinônia*.

4) The episcopal solidarity is for the sake of the universal church. However it is exercised principally at the provincial or national level. Since the first centuries, bishops have met in local or provincial councils to solve together the doctrinal and canonical problems of their region. It is important to recall that, according to the oldest liturgical customs, at the bishop's ordination the bishops of the same region are present and lay on their hands. The solidarity starts within the region. Today the episcopal conferences are an actualization of this first (and essential) level of the episcopal collegiality. And when bishops meet in general or ecumenical councils, they bring with them the mind and the needs of their region. Their college cannot be considered like a sum of consecrated ministers, among which some have been chosen as heads of the local churches (and may be easily transferred from a diocese to another one). The college is a college of

local bishops, and it is thanks to a concession (not entirely in tune with the ecclesiology of the great Tradition) that the auxiliary and titular bishops receive in this college the same rights as the residential local bishops.

III. The Office of Bishop in Protestant Churches

During the turmoils of the Reformation, the traditional doctrine of episcopacy was challenged and sometimes refused. Some churches (especially the churches of the Anglican communion, the Lutheran churches of Sweden and Finland until 1884) proclaimed their intention to remain in the Apostolic Succession and exercise the functions deriving therefrom (see J.G.H. Hoffmann, *La réforme en Suède, 1523-1572 et la succession apostolique,* Neuchâtel-Paris 1945). Some groups retained the title bishops but without retaining all its traditional implications (Lutheran, Episcopal Churches of Norway, Denmark and of some regions of Germany, Methodist Episcopal Churches of America and Africa, Moravians). Calvin, confronted with the non-evangelical style of life of many prelates of his time, tried to transfer to the pastor of the parish the responsibilities then attributed to the bishop.

For the reformers, the question of episcopacy is only one aspect of the problem of ministry. While for Luther and Calvin the pastoral office is of divine institution, for nearly the whole of the reformed traditions it is seen as an actualization of the priesthood of all the believers. Many affirm that the minister derives his authority from the congregation. For instance, the English Free Churches want to grant to all the baptized members of their community "equal rights" in the government of the church (cf. Horton Davies, *The English Free Churches,* London 1952, 89, 199; W.L. Lumpkin, *Baptist Confessions of Faith,* Valley Forge 1983, 288). In this context, the traditional role of the ordained bishop disappears.

The discussions provoked by the statement of Faith and Order on *Baptism-Eucharist-Ministry* (Lima 1982) show that the churches are still deeply divided on this issue, even if some Protestant groups are ready to us the title "bishop" to designate their most important ministers. But some bilateral discussions show, on the other side, that at least the theologians are more and more convinced that significant convergences are possible.

See **Church, Pope, Collegiality**

Raymond E. Brown, *Priest and Bishop, Biblical Reflections,* New York, 1970. K.E. Kirt, *The Apostolic Ministry,* London 1946 (especially Gregory Dix), "The Ministry in the Early Church," 183-304. A. Lemaire, *Les ministères aux origines de l'Église,* Paris 1971 (English translation). R. McBrien, "Collegiality: the State of the Question," in *The Once and Future Church,* ed. by J.A. Corinden, New York, 1971. P. Moore, *Bishops but What Kind? Reflections on Episcopacy,* London, 1982. K. Morsdorf, "Decree on the Bishop's Pastoral Office," in H. Vorgrimler, *Commentary on the Documents of Vatican II,* T. 2, New York, 1968, 165-300. J. Ratzinger and K. Rahner, *Episcopate and Primacy,* New York, 1962. N. Sykes, *The Church of England and Non-Episcopal Churches in the Sixteenth and Seventeenth Centuries,* London, 1948. J. Zizioulas, *L'être ecclésial,* Genève, 1981 (English translation *Being as Communion,* New York, 1985).

J.M.R. TILLARD, OP

BLACK THEOLOGY

The Origin of the Term

While no precise account of its coinage has been established, the phrase "black theology" emerged in the late 1960's. It surfaces, perhaps, for the first time, in the preparatory process of a report presented in the Fall of 1968 by the Theological Commission of the National Conference of Black Churchmen (NCBC), a predominantly Protestant group then known as the National Committee of Negro Churchmen. The Commission, chaired by Gayraud S. Wilmore, received responses to its questionnaire from black church scholars and theologians including Preston Williams, Henry H. Mitchell, Grant Schockley, Lawrence E. Lucas, C. Shelby Rooks, and Frank T. Wilson. It is clear, however, that "black theology" drew its intellectual content from the social, pastoral, and theological concerns of such scholars. And the phrase "black theology" gave voice to the dissatisfaction and disillusionment of black clergy and laity with the appropriation of the christian gospel by their white counterparts and offered a new reading of the black socio-political condition in light of God's revelation in Christ Jesus.

Stages of Development

Wilmore has divided the development of black theology into three stages: the first, from 1964 to 1969; the second, from 1970 to 1976; and the third, from 1977 to the present (Wilmore and Cone, pp. 1-21).

The first period is bracketed by two seminal works, *Black Religion* by Joseph R. Washington, Jr., and *Black Theology and Black Power* by James H. Cone, and is dominated by the civil rights movement. Washington's controversial thesis argued a distinctive black religion, parallel to rather than identical with European-American forms of Christianity. Black religion was folk religion; black congregations were not churches, but religious societies; black religion was not "genuine" Christian religion. Black clergy rejected this contention: pointing out the betrayal of the gospel in the racist behavior of white churches and insisting on the distinction between Sacred Scripture as the word of God and Sacred Scripture as it had been manipulated to serve the social and economic interests of those churches.

When Stokely Carmichael shouted the slogan, "black power," he ushered in a movement that splintered the precarious harmony blacks and whites had enjoyed under the aegis of Martin Luther King,

Jr. Black clergy, rather than denounce this disavowal of King's absolute commitment to nonviolence, published the "Black Power Statement" in *The New York Times,* 31 July 1966. Their affirmation of black power is a benchmark in the development of black theology: inaugurating a radical religious movement among black Christians and preparing the ideological and theological ground for the appearance of *Black Theology and Black Power.* Cone's intent in that first book was "to demonstrate that the politics of black power was the gospel of Jesus to twentieth-century America, for black power was concerned with the liberation of the black poor from oppression, and Jesus had shown just such concern for the liberation of the poor during his earthly ministry" (Cone, *For My People,* p. 32). Cone's work provoked angry responses from white and black critics who charged him with distorting Christianity. But others, white and black, found a springboard for further analysis and reflection.

The second stage may be characterized as a "turn to the academy." A small group of seminary and university professors, black and white, explored the meaning of black theology in monographs and articles and organized conferences and seminars. This period also witnessed the founding of the learned association, the Society for the Study of Black Religion (SSBR) which, under the leadership of Rooks, resumed the dialogue begun by the NCBC with African theologians during the 1960's.

The NCBC Theological Commission's second statement brings this stage to a close. In this document, "Black Theology in 1976," the Theological Commission attempted to relocate black theology within the framework of the institutional black church, and to identify black culture and folk tradition as the primary resources for black theological reflection. This statement charted a program that asserted black theology's independence from white christian liberalism and from the new conservatism; that confessed Jesus as the Black Messiah; that affirmed black ecumenicity and black spirituality; and that committed black theology to a liberating political praxis

The third stage, which dates from 1977, is being shaped by black theology's dialogue with a number of groups, and chief among these are Latin American liberation theologians. This encounter was facilitated by the Theology in the Americas (TIA), an interracial and predominantly Roman Catholic process-organization led by Chilean priest, Sergio Torres, and Filipino Maryknoller, Virginia Fabella. TIA sponsored a conference in Detroit in August of 1975 that brought together theologians, church workers, and activists from Latin America and the U.S. Out of this assembly came several working groups with participants bonding around professional or racial cultural-ethnic or gender or class concerns. These "affinity groups" continued the study and reflection that had been central to the preparation for the Detroit gathering and sought strategies for collaboration in combating structures of injustice in the U.S.

The Black Theology Project, chaired by Charles Spivey and staffed by Muhammad Kenyatta, a Baptist minister, and M. Shawn Copeland, O.P., sponsored in August of 1977 in Atlanta an ecumenical consultation on "The Black Church and the Black Community." Conference attendees included not only pastors, priests, nuns, church executives, and bishops, but also "the so-called 'street people' and representatives of left-wing political organizations" and was less preoccupied simply to react to the criticisms and questions coming from the white churches (Wilmore and Cone, p. 9).

In the keynote address to the conference, James Cone set out new priorities and categories for black theology in the future. Having come under the influence of black philosopher Cornel West, Cone called for a reappraisal of the Marxist analysis of U.S. capitalism in the shaping of the political praxis of black theology. Cone rejected any form of dogmatic Marxism that reduced every contradiction to class analysis, thus ignoring race as a category in the process of liberation. Simultaneously, he insisted that "liberation knows no color bar; the very nature of the gospel is universalism...a liberation that embraces the whole of humanity"(Wilmore and Cone, p. 358). Finally, Cone called explicitly for black theology to assume a global perspective—broadening its horizon and situating black demands for justice within the U.S. in structural relation to the demands for justice by all the world's victims.

Themes and Questions

The point of departure for black theology is the African-American experience in the United States, with particular weight given to the historical situation of chattel slavery and its pervasive influence even into the twentieth century—shaping all manner of cultural, educational, political, legal, economic, and social relations between blacks and other groups, but especially whites; and affecting the transmission, practice, and role of Christianity in U.S. culture.

The term theology in the phrase "black theology" does not connote a finished theological system in which terms and their relations are permanently established, all major doctrines treated. And despite attention to common themes and questions, black theologians do not form a "school." In summary, key black exponents of black theology and its themes are: a) Gayraud S. Wilmore—black religion as a source for black radicalism; b) James H. Cone, Olin P. Moyd, J. Deotis Roberts—black theology as liber-

ation theology as political theology; c) Harold A. Carter, James H. Cone, Cyprian Davis John Lovell—spirituals as a key source of the prayer and social praxis of African-Americans; d) Leonard A. Barrett, Henry H. Mitchell, Albert J. Raboteau, Joseph R. Washington, Jr.—anthropological and historical treatment of ritual, cult, sect, and role of religio-racial heritage for Africans of the diaspora; e) C. Eric Lincoln, Charles H. Long—sociology of religion; f) William Jones—theodicy or the attempt to justify God's goodness in view of the evil of racism; g) Eulalio R. Balthazar—criticism of color symbolism in white Western theology; h) Cornel West—the significance of Marxist categories in shaping an Afro-American revolutionary Christianity; i) Albert B. Cleage, Jr.—black Christian nationalism; j) Major J. Jones—black theological ethics based on Christian agape; k) Frances Beale, Katie G. Cannon, Jacquelyn Grant, Theresa Hoover, Pauli Murray, Delores Williams—black women and ministry in the church, black theology and feminist theology; l) Alfred G. Dunston, Jr., Robert A. Bennett—black theology as biblical theology; m) Edward K. Braxton, Toinette Eugene, Nathan Jones, Joseph Nearon, Jamie Phelps, Clarence Rivers—theological, catechetical, liturgical reflection from black Catholic perspective; n) Kofi Appiah-Kubi, Allan A. Boesak, Noel Erskine, Priscilla Massie, Basil Moore—the relation of Caribbean and African theologies to black theology.

See **Liberation Theology**

James H. Cone, "Black Theology Perspectives," Document no. 4, Theology in the Americas Documentation Series, New York: The Secretariat, Theology in the Americas, 1978. James H. Cone, "Black Theology and Third World Theologies," *The Chicago Theological Seminary Register*, vol. 73, no. 1 (Winter 1983), pp. 3-12. James H. Cone, *For My People: Black Theology and the Black Church*, Maryknoll: Orbis, 1984. Warner R. Traynham, *Christian Faith in Black and White: A Primer in Theology from the Black Perspective*,

Wakefield, Mass: Parameter Press, 1973. Gayraud S. Wilmore and James H. Cone, *Black Theology: A Documentary History, 1966-1979*, Maryknol.: Orbis, 1979.

M. SHAWN COPELAND, O P

BLASPHEMY

Any thought, speech, or act which dishonors God or persons or objects associated with God.

BODY OF CHRIST, BLOOD OF CHRIST

"Body of Christ" and "Blood of Christ" have become familiar liturgical formulas which evoke a ready "Amen" as communicants receive the eucharistic bread and wine in the communion rite of the renewed liturgy of Vatican II. The meaning and purpose of these phrases seem obvious. *Body* and *blood* refer to the physical realities of Christ's humanity, now in glory. The formulas serve to proclaim the communicants' faith that the risen Christ (body, blood, soul, and divinity) is present and offered to them under the sacramental signs of bread and wine. This straightforward understanding, while correct, fails to capture the rich overlay of meanings these phrases have in scripture and tradition.

Body and Blood

In the biblical vocabulary, the most important Hebrew word for our corporeal dimension is *basar;* it can be translated as either *body* (*soma* in Greek) or *flesh* (*sarx* in Greek). In scriptural usage the words *body* and *blood* (*dam* in Hebrew, *haima* in Greek) have several layers of meaning.

The first, most basic meaning differs considerably from contemporary English, where body and blood are physical parts of a human. In the biblical view, each of these words refers to the entire living human being. The living person expresses him/herself through the body/flesh,

which thus becomes the outward manifestation of the personality and life within. The human person is not an incarcerated soul, but an animated body. The person not only *has* a body, but *is* a body. Similarly, blood refers to the entire living being, but with stress on the life force within. In biblical thought God breathes life into the bodily creature, and that breath of life resides in the blood. It is because "blood is life" that human consumption of blood is forbidden (Dt 12:23); the breath of life belongs to God alone.

The second layer of meaning highlights human creatureliness, frailty and mortality. To call humans "flesh and blood" is simply another way of saying that they are perishable creatures (Sir 14:18; Mt 16:17; Jn 1:13), unable to inherit the kingdom of God (1 Cor 15:50).

The third level of meaning stresses the human solidarity found in various relationships. For Adam, Eve is "flesh of my flesh;" husband and wife become "one body" (Gen 2:23-24). Laban acknowledges that his nephew Jacob is "my flesh;" Judah tells his brothers that Joseph is "our own flesh" (Gen 29:14; 37:27). "Israel according to the flesh" (1 Cor 10:18) is one people, descended from "Abraham our ancestor according to the flesh" (Rom 4:1). God and Israel are bonded together as covenant partners in a blood-rite at Sinai (Exod 24:3-8). Unlike Greek and western thought, where the body is a principle of individuation and separation, in Hebrew thought body and blood imply a fundamental solidarity among humans, and, indeed, with the rest of creation.

The fourth layer of meaning adds sacrificial overtones. Body/flesh and blood are separated in sacrifice. The purpose is less to secure the death of a victim than to achieve a redeeming, life-giving union with God. Flesh may be offered to God (burnt offerings) or shared in a communion sacrifice. Blood is a particularly powerful sacrificial symbol. Blood that is spilled, especially innocent blood, "cries out" to God (Gen 4:10); blood that is shed serves to cleanse and save (Heb 9:22). Life is given for life.

Whatever their primary meaning in a particular context, body and blood are never without this layered cluster of meanings. These same layers of meaning carry over into the phrases, *body of Christ* and *blood of Christ*. To sketch these two images, we will gather themes that cut across various NT traditions.

The Body of Christ

In NT usage this phrase can refer to the human body of the historical Jesus, his sacramental presence in the eucharist, and his body which is the church.

The NT normally presents the bodily reality of the historical Jesus as a matter of fact, although John uses strongly realistic language to counteract those who would deny the human reality of Jesus (esp. Jn 6). Jesus not only came *in* the flesh and *has* a body (1 Jn 4:2; Heb 5:7; 10:5), the Word also *became* flesh (Jn 1:14). His body bonds him to his people and, indeed, to all peoples. He was born into the Davidic line and the Israelite race "according to the flesh" (Rom 1:3; 9:5); God sent him to us "in the likeness of sinful flesh" (Rom 8:3). His earthly body, like ours, was a mortal body (Col 1:22). Given up in death, his body was buried (Mk 15:43-46), to be later accorded the customary Jewish reverence for a corpse (Lk 23:55-24:1). Raised from the tomb, his body remains a real body able to be touched (Jn 20:27) and capable of taking nourishment (Lk 24:42-43), but it is a glorified body no longer subject to the constraints of space and time (Jn 20:19, 26) or to the dominion of death (Acts 2:24). But in all these passages the physical reality of the human body of Christ is never the main concern. Rather, his body/flesh is the effective symbol of salvation. Enfleshed, the Word of God

spoke "words of eternal life" (Jn 6:68); when he reached out his hand to cast out demons and heal, the "finger of God" (Lk 11:20) was at work enacting the reign of God. And when he "suffered in the flesh" (1 Pet 4:1), he conquered death's sting and opened the way to life.

This saving meaning of Christ's body is summed up in the second NT usage, in the words Jesus spoke at the Last Supper: "This is my body to be given for you" (Lk 22:19; 1 Cor 11:24). The layers of meaning are richly nuanced. He gives up not just a part of himself, or a body he possessed; rather, he gives his whole body/person, himself. He is completely "given up" in sacrifice. And that self-gift is "for you." These supper words, like his act of washing the disciples' feet (Jn 13:1-17), accurately name and sum up the inner attitude of service (Mk 10:45) that shaped his entire ministry and now brings him to his imminent death. The bread of life discourse records the same attitude, in another wording: "the bread I will give is my flesh, for the life of the world" (Jn 6:51); "those who feed on me have life because of me" (Jn 6:57). The realistic words used in the discourse only serve to underline the reality of his self-gift as food for life. The command to "do this as a remembrance of me" (Lk 22:27) ensures that whenever his followers repeat the supper actions of the Lord in his memory—taking bread, giving thanks over it, and sharing it—Christ's self-gift, finalized in death, for the life of the many is proclaimed and really offered to them until he comes again (1 Cor 11:26).

The third NT usage, Paul's image of the church as the body of Christ, preserves the eucharistic image from a narrowly individualistic interpretation of the life-union offered. Though contemporary stoic writers commonly used Aesop's fable comparing a society to a body, Paul's use of the body-image fits well with a cluster of experiences and ideas in his own background, such as the Adam-Christ parallel (1 Cor 15:22, 45; Rom 5:12-19), with its clear overtones of human solidarity, and the community as the temple/building in which God dwells (1 Cor 3:16-17; see Eph 2:20-22). Paul first develops the idea of the church as the body of Christ (1 Cor 12:4-27; also in Rom 12:4-8) in writing to the Corinthian community which is deeply divided at eucharist. The point of the body of Christ image in 1 Corinthians and Romans is the unity of Christians among themselves in the local church. The union of the wider church with Christ as her head and life-giving source will be stressed in the later Pauline epistles (Col 1:18; Eph 2:11-18; 4:1-16). In 1 Corinthians, the ecclesial body of Christ and the eucharistic body of Christ are not separated. Partaking of the one loaf is a sharing in the body of Christ so that the many who eat are one body (1 Cor 10:16-17). To miss this connection, to fail to discern the body of Christ in this twofold sense, is to eat unworthily and bring judgment on oneself (1 Cor 11:27-29). In Paul the three meanings of the body of Christ form one total symbol. "In his body Christ claims us in our body for his body which is the church" (Käsemann).

In later history St. Augustine was particularly adept at maintaining the multiple richness of Paul's usage. "If then you are the body of Christ and his members," he explained to those who had just been baptized and shared in the eucharistic meal for the first time, "it s your sacrament that reposes on the altar of the Lord. It is your sacrament which you receive. You answer 'Amen' to what you yourself are and in answering you are enrolled. You answer 'Amen' to the words 'The body of Christ.' Be, then, a member of the body of Christ to verify your 'Amen'" (*Sermon* 272). Later theology was unable to hold those meanings together. Beginning in the ninth century,

theological debates about the real presence gradually transformed the phrase "the true body of Christ," which had been used for the church, into a technical phrase affirming the real presence. At the same time, the phrase "the mystical body of Christ," which had been used for the eucharistic presence with strong ecclesial resonances, faced from eucharistic theology and eventually came to stand for the church alone. This reversal and separation of the two meanings took place during the early medieval period, when liturgical practice had made that same separation. The assembly participated in the eucharist by watching and by adoring the host; they received communion only very rarely. During that same period an extensive popular cult of the eucharistic body of Christ developed, and the feast of *Corpus Christi* spread to the whole church during the thirteenth century. The "Mystical Body" ecclesiology reached full development over the past century, culminating in the encyclical of Pius XII in 1943. Vatican II reintroduced the biblical image of the "People of God" into ecclesiology to balance the other images of church. It also restored full participation of the assembly in a vernacular liturgy, reopening to people a full share in the supper actions of the Lord Jesus. As a result people are now able to recover the fuller meaning of the ritual exchange, "The Body of Christ," "Amen."

The Blood of Christ

This phrase shows a somewhat more limited range of use in the NT. It can refer to the earthly Jesus and to his eucharistic presence.

The blood of Jesus is always linked, whether explicitly or implicitly, with the idea of its being shed. Drawing on the OT life symbolism of blood, the NT consistently used the image of Christ's blood to speak about his death and its saving meaning. Yom Kippur serves as a point of comparison for rather extensive development of that meaning (Heb 9:11-28). Various NT traditions also name the meaning through other OT themes: his blood is the purchase price (Acts 20:18, Rev 5:4) and means of redemption (Eph 1:7; Heb 9:12); it is the means of expiation (Rom 3:25), forgiveness (Eph 1:7), cleansing (Heb 9:14; 1 Jn 1:7), purification and deliverance (1 Pet 1:2); in a more positive vein, it sanctifies (Heb 13:12) and justifies (Rom 5:9). The unifying motif is that Jesus' sacrificial handing over of his life has the power to cleanse from sin and restore to life. The note of solidarity sounds here, too; through the blood of Jesus' cross God brings together those who were far apart (Eph 2:13), makes peace and reconciles everyone and everything (Col 1:20) to God.

These statements of the saving meaning of Christ's blood are perhaps nothing more than an unfolding of the meaning contained in the words attributed to Jesus at the Last Supper: "This cup is the new covenant in my blood, which will be shed for you" (Lk 22:20). It is not just his blood that is poured out, but his life, himself. It is "shed" in sacrifice, like the poured-out life of the suffering servant (the "blood of the covenant" formula in Mk 14:24 and Mt 26:28 shifts the sacrificial image to parallel the ritual sealing of the covenant on Sinai in Exod 24:8). Shed "for you," Christ's blood restores solidarity to the people and their covenantal union with God.

The ecclesial dimension is not absent; the cup of blessing is a "sharing in the blood of Christ" (1 Cor 10:16). But unlike the body of Christ, the blood of Christ is never used, in scripture or later tradition, as a way to name the church. The reason may lie in the prohibition against consuming blood and in the ambiguous meaning of blood in those cultural and religious contexts.

Later history shows little concern to dwell on the theological meaning of the blood of Christ. The loss of the lay chalice in the fourteenth century led to controversy with the Hussites and later reformers, triggering the medieval development of the theory of concomitance (the whole Christ—body, blood, soul, and divinity—is present under each species). Given the infrequent use or reservation of eucharistic wine, there was little popular devotion to the blood of Christ until the last century, though devotion to the Sacred Heart did grow in the Middle Ages. In mid-nineteenth century Pius IX established the feast of the Precious Blood for the whole church. The liturgical reforms initiated by Vatican II have restored the communion cup and reunited the feast of the Precious Blood with that of *Corpus Christi* (the English title of the feast retains only the latter title). The way has thus been cleared to recover not only the traditional link between the body and blood of Christ, but also a full and mutual enrichment of meaning for both, as communicants respond "Amen" to "The Body of Christ" and "The Blood of Christ."

See **Epiclesis, Eucharist, Memorial**

L. Cerfaux, *The Church in the Theology of St. Paul,* N.Y.: Herder & Herder, 1963, 262-286; J.A.T. Robinson, *The Body. A Study in Pauline Theology,* London: SCM, 1952. See also the entries under body/blood and Body/Blood of Christ in standard dictionaries such as X. Léon-Dufour (ed.), *Dictionary of Biblical Theology,* N.Y.: Seabury, 1973; *The Interpreter's Dictionary of the Bible,* N.Y.: Abingdon, 1962; and *The New Catholic Encyclopedia,* N.Y.: McGraw-Hill, 1967.

GILBERT OSTDIEK, OFM

BUDDHISM

"Buddhism" designates a set of traditions flourishing at one time or another, in the past two and a half millennia, in south, southeast, central, and east Asia and now also at numerous centers in Hawaii, North America and Europe. Encompassing a diversity of beliefs, practices, and cultures, buddhist traditions result directly or indirectly from the life and teachings of a major historical personality who lived on the Indian subcontinent 2500 years ago and who is regarded as a *buddha*—an "awakened one" or "enlightened one." To name his spiritual descendants merely as buddhists is insufficient. They should be distinguished by: the geographical or cultural regions with which their particular traditions are identified (e.g., Tibet, China, or Thailand); their general practices (e.g., Theravāda, Zen, or Pure Land); or the lineages of buddhist teachers who have initiated them or have simply guided their lives.

Wherever there are buddhists, one finds a *sàngha*, or community of monks (and infrequently nuns), who have taken vows from a particular teacher or elder. They are supported to some degree by a larger body of adherents, some of whom may have taken lay vows and may have lived in the monastery as part of their own spiritual development.

There is no single collection of buddhist scriptures in a universally accepted canonical language. Pāli, is the canonical language of Theravāda buddhists and has remained their liturgical language. Sanskrit, the language of the original Mahāyāna canon, has been preserved and serves a liturgical function largely through vernacular translations such as Tibetan and Chinese. In east Asia certain revered Mahāyāna texts also assumed special importance. The scriptures include the *buddha's* words (*sūtra*) and authorized commentary (*śāstra*) as well as monastic rules (*vinaya*). Although Pāli was the first canonical language, scholars often give Indic terms in Sanskrit, as is the case here. With so rich a diversity of thought, practice, and cultural expression, it is difficult to make general assertions about buddhist traditions with credibility except as general guidelines for inquiry.

All buddhists agree that their doctrines (*dharma*), though eternal, can be lost and that through the ages of cosmic history rare individuals have recovered and retaught these same essential teachings. The important *buddha* in recent times, also called "the historical *buddha*," is identified by name as Siddhartha Gautama and by title as *śākyamuni*. Hagiographical accounts contain episodes of his birth, princely life, renunciation of wealth, defeat of his own ignorance, decision to become an itinerate teacher, and nearly fifty years of public life painted in grand and glorious strokes of heroic legend. The consensus among scholars is that he taught in the northeast area of the Indian subcontinent probably between 563-483 B.C.E. Selecting a number of ideas, principally the inherent causal power of action (*karma*), reincarnation, renunciation and detachment, and release (*nirvāṇa*) from the rounds of sorrow and rebirth (*saṃsāra*), rejecting other ideas, especially the effectiveness of the gods for absolute release and the enduring reality of personal existence (*ātman*), and offering explanations based on insights gained in meditation, he established a middle way between self-indulgence and self-mortification. Thus buddhists take refuge in the *buddha,* the *dharma* which he taught, and the *sàngha* entrusted with passing on and living fully those teachings. These are called the three jewels or triple treasure (*triratna*). *Dharma* also serves as the buddhist term for "buddhism."

Offering membership in the *sàngha*, regardless of social status or ethnicity and a remedy for inescapable sorrow and pain, buddhist monks from a growing variety of traditions spread their teachings throughout Asia. They formed the first great missionary movement in history. The transformation of buddhist thought and expression from a largely Indo-European cultural milieu in India, through the caravan-traversed settlements of central Asia, and into China was singularly remarkable for its creativity and impact on east Asian life and history. Wherever buddhist traditions developed, they gradually took on local features. Today, certain traditions, in particular, some forms of Tantra, Pure Land, Zen, and Nichiren are being tailored to American lifetsyles.

In Asia, the Theravāda tradition is the only surviving form of what other buddhists called Hīnayāna but which Theravādins sometimes call "southern buddhism." It is still prominent in Śri Lanka, Burma, Thailand, Laos, and Kampuchea, although its future under communist regimes is not clear. Tibetan traditions survive in communities of exiles in neighboring regions to Tibet as well as in North America and Europe, and their return and future in Tibet is still being decided. Chinese traditions continue among "overseas Chinese" whereas in China and Mongolia lineages and traditions have not fared well. Korea and Japan have the greatest diversity of Mahāyāna—what Theravādins may also call "northern buddhism." In India, certain forms have arisen after the disappearance of all buddhist traditions from there less than a thousand years ago during the Islamic invasions.

Buddhist teachings are often repeated in enumerations (the three marks, the four stages of sanctification, the five aggregates, and so on), the most famous of which are the four noble truths: all existence is suffering (duḥkha); suffering is caused by craving (tṛṣṇā); suffering can be ended; and suffering is ended through the eightfold path (right understanding, right intention, right speech, right action, right livelihood, right effort, right mindfulness, and right contemplation). The indispensability of meditation and an emphasis upon personal effort for the experience of nirvāṇa are generally char-

acteristic of buddhist traditions though varying spiritual methods and expressions of wisdom have appeared. The earliest texts manifest both a borrowing from the developing yoga tradition of interior meditation practices, which produce deepening states of trance and result in the cessation of mental activities, and a buddhist innovation of exterior meditation, namely, objectively directed practices leading to insight.

Buddhist traditions can be viewed as: spiritualities with elaborate instructions on meditation and accompanying psychologies; thought traditions with rich developments in logic and epistemology, challenging opposing theological and philosophical speculations, and an ethics based upon compassion and similar self-emptying virtues; or cultural traditions with artistic, literary, and social achievements in Asian history. In their way of seeing reality, buddhists generally speak of two levels of truth: conventional truth and ultimate truth. The former is circumscribed by the terminology, logic, and knowledge based on ordinary experience; the latter is equivalent to the essential meaning of dharma, the experience of nirvāṇa and true insight. Whereas conventional truth has pragmatic value in the ceaseless flux of day-to-day existence, ultimate truth dispels the illusions and ignorance which bind persons to such sorrowful existence and leads to its cessation.

Related to this view are the doctrines of the bodies of the buddha, which further differentiate buddhist traditions. The earliest formulation, still held by Theravāda buddhists today, is that the buddha possessed a physical body (rūpakāya), corresponding to the non-eternal and purely nominal character of day-to-day existence, and a dharma body (dharmakāya). Aside from the phenomenal world, the buddha is one with the unconditioned reality which is nirvāṇa and is identical with the truth he taught. This is his *dharma* body. This view was expanded later to the three-body doctrine (*trikāya*). Principally the *buddha* is the *dharma* body, but to account for the numerous glorious appearances of *buddhas* and *buddhas*-to-be (*bodhisattvas*) Mahāyāna buddhists spoke of the enjoyment body (*saṃbhogakāya*). This second body encompasses this multitude of great beings who preached the *mahāyāna sūtras* and who use all sorts of skillful devices (*upāya*) to make their difficult teachings understandable. Finally, the third body, according to Mahāyāna traditions, is the magical-appearance body (*nirmāṇakāya*) of the *buddha* as a human being. Later, in the Vajrayāna (Tantra) tradition, which is notably practiced by Tibetan buddhists today, a fourth body or essence body (*svabhāvikakāya*), constituting the essential unity of the other three, was posited. It represents the diamond (*vajra*) essence of the absolute, nondifferenced voidness of ultimate reality.

The Second Vatican Council's *Declaration on the Relation of the Church to Non-Christian Religions* mentioned "buddhism" among those religious traditions worthy of high regard. The newly formed Secretariat for Non-Christians issued a two volume set *Towards the Meeting with Buddhism* in 1970 with articles on the background and contemporary situation of buddhist traditions as well as these suggested topics for dialogue: detachment from this world, the way of salvation, meditation and prayer, worship, community, and the search for the absolute. In addition to papal audiences with buddhist groups both in the Vatican and in their homelands, many international, national, and local meetings, dialogues, and prayer services between Roman Catholic and buddhist representatives have occurred since the council.

See **Religions**

William Theodore de Bary, *The Buddhist Tradition in India, China and Japan,* New York: The Modern Library, 1969. Walpola Rahula, *What the Buddha Taught,* New York: Grove Press, 1959. Richard L. Robinson, and Willard L. Johnson, *The Buddhist Religion: A Historical Introduction,* Belmont, CA: Wadsworth Pub., 3rd ed., 1982. Donald K. Swearer, *Dialogue: the Key to Understanding other Religions,* Philadelphia: Westminster, 1977. Tenzin Gyatso. *The Buddhism of Tibet and the Key to the Middle Way,* New York: Harper and Row, 1975. Hans Waldenfels, *Absolute Nothingness: Foundations for a Buddhist-Christian Dialogue,* Trans. by J W. Heisig, New York: Paulist Press, 1980. Henry Clarke Warren, Ed. and Trans., *Buddhism in Translation,* Cambridge: Harvard University Press, 1896; repr., New York: Atheneum, 1962 and subsequently.

JOHN BORELLI

C

CALENDAR, LITURGICAL

The christian liturgical calendar is the result of centuries of development. Based upon a combination of the Jewish lunar calendar, which sets dates according to the cycles of the moon, and the more generally employed solar calendar, the christian calendar arranges feasts and seasons of the year according to two types of cycle. The first is the Temporal cycle, which is determined by the (lunar) moveable date of Easter, the first Sunday after the first full moon following the spring equinox. The Easter and Lenten seasons as well as the Sundays of the Year are reckoned according to this cycle. The second is the Sanctoral cycle which is arranged according to calendar dates. Christmas and its associated feasts as well as the feasts and memorials of the saints are determined by this method.

It is impossible to date the origins of a christian liturgical year with anything like exactitude. Earliest christian practice may well have known only Sunday as a day of worship, rendering a weekly rather than a yearly cycle. However, among some christian communities there well may have been a yearly celebration of Easter corresponding to the Jewish Passover, during which the Paschal Mystery had been accomplished. By the late second century the Roman church had adopted a yearly celebration of Easter on a particular Sunday in the spring.

From the setting of Easter flowed a fifty day festal period (Pentecost) as a unitive celebration of Christ's redemptive event. As Easter became the date for annual baptism around the beginning of the third century, a special time of preparation by prayer and fasting was developed to precede this event. By the fourth century this had become what we know as Lent, although the forty day Lent may have originated in the Alexandrian church's practice of a forty day fast following Epiphany imitating the gospel chronology of Jesus' forty day fast in the desert after his temptation.

In the fourth century another cycle of feasts developed around the celebration of Christ's incarnation. Christmas, a nativity feast celebrated on December 25, the Roman pagan feast of the Birth of the Unconquered Sun, and Epiphany an eastern feast of the baptism and/or birth of Christ, celebrated on January 6, were both adopted by most parts of the christian world by the end of the century. Advent is a western liturgical season of preparation for Christmas, which began to develop in the sixth century.

In addition to these two cycles there developed a cycle of saints' days and particular celebrations of Christ. As early as the second century *Martyrdom of Polycarp,* we know of yearly celebrations at the graves of martyrs. At first strictly local celebrations of a locale's own martyrs, these saints' feasts were gradually accepted throughout the christian world. In addition, after the period of persecution other holy men and women besides martyrs were added to the calendars of various churches. Among the latest feasts to develop were those honoring the Virgin Mary. These were latecomers since there were no relics of her body. Another category of feasts were the anniversaries of the dedication of important churches and shrines. A final category, devotional feasts, developed in the course of the Middle Ages and focussed on ideas like the importance of the Trinity or the Precious Blood of Christ, rather than person or specific events.

During the Protestant Reformation there was a strong reaction to the liturgical calendar flooded with saint's days and other feasts. Luther and Cranmer retained the traditional season and the saints of the NT, but pruned the calendar of all other celebrations. A more radical solution was attempted by the Sabbatarians (Scots Presbyterians and English Congregationalists) who allowed only the celebration of Sunday (the new Sabbath) as such with no other feast days including Christmas. A few national days of fasting were the exception to this rule.

The post-Vatican II calendar reform of 1969 simplified the Roman Calendar considerably. The temporal and sanctoral cycles were retained. The numerous categories of feasts (double, greater doubles, large numbers of octaves and the like) were simplified to three categories: solemnities, feasts, and memorials (subdivided into obligatory and optional). The number of saints in the General Roman Calendar was reduced to those saints of universal importance. Many devotional feasts were excised, and provisions were made for particular calendars in national and diocesan churches and religious orders. The number of octaves was reduced to two: Easter and Christmas.

More important, Sunday was recognized as the original feast day, with few celebrations taking precedence over it; the unitive nature of the Easter season (Pentecost) was stressed; the Paschal Triduum was considered the crown of the liturgical year; and Lent was arranged to express its original character as the preparation for Easter baptism as well as a penitential season.

See **Easter Triduum, Liturgy, Paschal Mystery**

Adolf Adam, *The Liturgical Year,* New York: Pueblo, 1981. A.G. Martimort, Ed., *The Church at Prayer, Vol.4: The Liturgy and Time,* Collegeville: Liturgical Press, 1985. Adrian Nocent, *The Liturgical Year,* 4 vols. Collegeville: Liturgical Press, 1977. United States Catholic Conf., *The Liturgical Year,* (Study Text 9), Washington: DC: USCC, 1985.

JOHN F. BALDOVIN, SJ

CANON LAW

Canon law is ecclesiastical law as distinguished from civil law, especially from the Roman and common laws. The word "canon" derives from the Greek meaning a "rule" used by masons or carpenters; it was a standard by which things were measured. For Christians "canon" came to mean an enactment of a council, a "norm" by which one's actions were measured. The word was also applied to the official list of scriptural books and to the list of clergy belonging to a particular church. Later "canonization" designated the process by which an individual was formally placed on the list of saints.

From apostolic times the church has found it necessary to introduce laws over and above the gospel teaching of Christ. Today unfortunately, "there exists a widespread confusion between what is legalistic and what is juridical. In other words, people wrongly identify the exaggerated importance sometimes assigned to the legal element in the life of the Church with her social and organic structure. It is a structure which cannot be conceived (nor can it function) without a common norm, that is to say without *some form of law.*

"When it is conceived as an ordering of the Church's life, law is a fact which needs no justification. Indeed, it is a fact which at every moment of history has found and continues to find an adequate place in the sacramental, pastoral, and social structure of the Church. . . .

"In a sense, the mystery of the Incarnation is reflected in the fact that the Mystical Body at every moment in human history is an organized society, 'one complex reality [as the Second Vatican Council says] in which the divine and the human element are fused . . . *sancta simul et semper purificanda*' ['at once holy and always in need of purification' L.G. 8]. It is a perfect society in the philosophical sense but one which calls for ever-greater perfection in its living reality. In other words, it is a society which over and above the bond of love requires also positive social norms. In this sense it needs a juridical element" (Kuttner 145-146).

Canon law is most developed and significant in the Roman Catholic Church (upon which this article will concentrate) but it also plays an important role in the Orthodox and Anglican Churches. Other churches, such as the United Methodist Church, have their constitution and particular regulations in *The Book of Discipline* or a similarly titled collection.

Although the earliest series of canons that have come down to us do not antedate the fourth century, elements of ecclesiastical legislation are found in the pseudo-apostolic church orders beginning about the year 100. These documents which purport to come from the apostles are manuals of liturgical and disciplinary regulations in force in the early communities. The *Didache,* for example, treats the administration of baptism (infusion is permitted in emergencies), fasting, and prayers at ritual meals. The *Apostolic Tradition of Hippolytus* c.225, a rudimentary sacramentary, provides valuable information on the ordination of bishops, priests and deacons. *The Apostolic Constitutions,* the largest and most inclusive of the church orders, may be dated in the last quarter of the fourth century.

By that time, however, church orders were anachronistic. Christians had begun to look for guidance to the decisions of bishops meeting in council. Five regional councils held in Asia Minor and Syria during the first half of the fourth century contributed what would become the nucleus of canon law. Bishop Meletios of Antioch (c. 380) made a compilation of the canons of the councils of Ancyra, Neocaesarea, Gangra, Antioch and Laodicea known as the *Corpus canonum* of Antioch. Later were added the enactments of the ecumenical councils: Nicaea, Constantinople and Chalcedon. Upon this enlarged foundation all the collections of antiquity were based. Cardinal Gasparri in the preface to the 1917 Code of Canon Law refers to it as the *principium et fons* (origin and source) of almost all the ancient collections.

The range of the legislation may be illustrated from the canons of the Council of Nicaea held in 325 which treat: church structures, the dignity of the clergy, public penance, liturgical rules and the readmission of schismatics. A bishop is to be chosen by all the bishops of the province or at least by three. Metropolitans, bishops of provincial capitals, preside over a number of dioceses united in an eparchy (province). The bishops of Rome, Alexandria and Antioch enjoy a certain customary role of supervision over other bishops. Clerics who do not maintain an exemplary standard of conduct are to be deposed. Christians who apostatize must undergo public penance for twelve years in order to be reconciled. On the Sundays from Easter to Pentecost prayers are to be said while standing. In all, the first ecumenical council enacted twenty canons.

Though Latin versions of the Eastern corpus of canons began to circulate almost immediately in the West, it remained for Dionysius Exiguus, a monk called to Rome by Pope Gelasius I (492-496), to provide a more accurate and complete translation. Dionysius also made a collection of papal decretals from Siricius (384-399) to Anastasius II (496-498). Decretals are letters embodying a ruling of the Roman pontiff on some matter of ecclesiastical discipline. Such a letter or rescript was a response occasioned by a question posed to the pope. It was preceptive in tone and demanded compliance. Papal directives were thus placed on a level with enactments of councils and would in the Middle Ages become the most voluminous part of canon law. Dionysius contributed to the influence of decretals by his parallel collection. His collections of the conciliar canons and the papal decretals were combined in the *Dionysiana collectio,* the most important body of church law during the first millennium.

With the dissolution of the Western Roman Empire toward the end of the fifth century the classical canon law was overlaid and corrupted by Frankish and Anglo-Saxon influences. The Celtic monks, for instance, had supplanted public or canonical penance with a private system similar to what is practiced today. The marriage law had been weakened in some instances by the toleration of remarriage. Charlemagne attempted a reform and to that end received from Pope Hadrian in 774 an enlarged version of the *Dionysiana.* The program of Charlemagne failed as Europe succumbed to a second wave of invasions and feudalism settled in. The process of disintegration, so far as the church is concerned, was not reversed until the Gregorian Reform inaugurated with the pontificate of Leo IX in 1049. The efforts of the popes to secure a measure of independence in the appointment of bishops and other ecclesiastical concerns precipitated spectacular conflicts with feudal rulers. The conflicts were destined to continue through the Middle Ages and on into the early modern period with the emergence of the national states.

These struggles had an important ideological component with both sides seeking a propaganda advantage based on historical precedent and rational argument. The twelfth century proved to be particularly stimulating in the areas of theology and law. Previous centuries had been devoted to collecting and preserving the accomplishments of the past. Now the heritage had to be critically analyzed and developed. The scriptures, the writings of the Fathers, and the church's legal tradition did not present a completely coherent picture. Inconsistencies, if not outright contradictions, had to be reconciled. To this end, churchmen, such as the monk Bernold of Constance and Ivo, bishop of Chartres, drew up rules for the interpretation and harmonization of texts. Peter Abelard (c. 1130) in *Sic et Non* brought together patristic opinions on various theological issues. He assembled over 150 quotations with arguments for and against.

The methodology of Abelard was applied by Gratian in the area of law. About 140 he published the work that has earned him the sobriquet "Father of Canon Law." He sought to collect in one volume the whole legal tradition and to reconcile the apparent discrepancies to be found there. With good reason his work is called the *Decretum* or the *Concordia discordantium canonum.* His practice was to proceed dialectically, citing all the texts on one side of an issue and then those on the other side, concluding with his own solution. In Distinction 63, for example, dealing with the election of bishops by the laity, Gratian gathers all the relevant canons from the nuclear Council of Laodicea (c. 343-380) to the II Lateran Council (1139). He presents eight texts stating that the laity are to have nothing to do with the election followed by seventeen texts recognizing lay influence, especially on the part of kings. Gratian responds that lay participation is limited to acclamation and consent to the election which properly belongs to the clergy alone. The king's role as noted in the texts was a temporary privilege in a crisis situation which no longer exists.

Gratian did not make this collection of texts independently but borrowed heavily from his predecessors, especially Ivo of Chartres, Anselm of Luca and Burchard of Worms. Included in the *Decretum* are texts from Sacred Scripture, writings of the Fathers, canons of many councils and synods, letters of the Roman pontiffs, and citations from the civil law. Roman law had recently been revived at Bologna where the "rediscovered" *Digest* of Justinian was studied with great eagerness. Gratian who was also working at Bologna was therefore able to incorporate a number of Roman law texts in his collection, though possibly not in its first redaction. Roman law was destined to profoundly influence canon law in its subsequent history.

When the *Decretum* appeared, it immediately dominated the field of canon law. Canonists appreciated the richness of its content; almost all the established law was to be found there. The texts were treated in a far more scholarly or scientific way than heretofore. The distinctions that Gratian made and his attention to context and chronology introduced order into the discipline. No wonder, then, that the *Decretum* became the preferred book in the schools as well as in the law courts.

The appearance of the *Decretum* was largely responsible for canon law being separated from theology and taught as a separate subject. While some canonists continued as professional theologians, many more developed an interest in civil law, often obtaining a university degree in both laws. Commentators, called *decretists,* soon glossed or explained every part of Gratian's work. The most notable were Paucapalea, Rolando Bandinelli (later Alexander III, 1159-1181), Rufinus, Stephen of Tournai, and Huguccio of Pisa. Joannes Teutonicus c.1215 produced the ordinary gloss which was transmitted with the *Decretum* itself and which appears in all the early printed editions.

As the *Decretum* was progressively analyzed and the church's court system developed, it became apparent that Gratian was incomplete and did not meet all contemporary needs. The election of several skilled canonists to the papacy (especially Alexander III and Innocent III, 1198-1216) soon brought relief. Hundreds of papal decretals were issued settling disputed points of law or providing for situations not contemplated in Gratian. The decretals recognized as the *ius novum* as distinct from the *ius antiquum* of Gratian were taught in the schools and commented upon by scholars known as *decretalists.* These decretals were compiled in numerous collections referred to as *Decretales extravagantes* (i.e. "wandering around outside" or circulating apart from Gratian). Gradually five collections made between 1191 and 1226 achieved eminence and are known as the *Quinque compilationes antiquae. The Compilatio prima* of Bernard of Pavia is particularly notable for its organization of material in five books headed: *iudex* (law, law on persons, ordination), *iudicium* (procedural law, trials), *clerus* (duties and rights of the clergy, ecclesiastical goods etc.); *connubia* (marriage laws); and *crimen* (derelicts and criminal procedure ending with excommunication).

As the number of decretals multiplied, it became increasingly difficult to determine just what law was in effect on a given issue. The legislation was scattered over several volumes which were not complete. Some laws had been modified or canceled by subsequent enactments. In other instances the decretals were too verbose. Pope Gregory IX, therefore, commissioned the Dominican Raymond of Peñafort to prepare a coherent collection of all ecclesiastical law since the time of Gratian. Raymond organized almost two thousand items into five books, each subdivided into titles and chapters (*capitula*). He followed the plan of Bernard of Pavia in the distribution of material. In 1234 the pope then promulgated this volume which became known as the *Extravagantes* of Gregory IX, "extravagant" because of circulating outside the *Decretum* of Gratian. It remained the most fundamental part of church law until 1917.

As a living society the church needs constantly to update its legislation as new circumstances arise. In addition to numerous papal decretals in the thirteenth century, the two general councils of Lyons (1245 and 1274) issued a series of constitutions. This legislation was eventually gathered and promulgated by Pope Boniface VIII in 1298 as the *Liber sextus* (the sixth book after the five of Gregory IX). It, too, followed the earlier arrangement of five books divided into titles and 359 *capitula*. Within a brief period another official collection appeared in 1317, the *Constitutiones Clementinae*. (Clement V was the first of the Avignon popes). This collection was again divided into five books broken down into titles and 106 *capitula*.

Two private collections brought the medieval body of canon law to a close.

About 1500 Jean Chappuis, a Parisian legist, organized the *Extravagantes Ioannis Papae XXII,* twenty capitula which had previously been gathered together, and the *Extravagantes communes,* seventy-four papal decretals up to Sixtus IV (1471-84). Between 1499-1502 the *Decretum* of Gratian, the three official collection (Gregory IX, Boniface VIII, Clement V) and the two private *Extravagantes* were printed at Paris under the title *Corpus Iuris Canonici*. Pope Gregory XIII adopted the title when he approved in 1530 an edition of these six collections made by the *Correctores Romani* as textually authentic. The most recent edition of these collections was made by A. Friedberg, *Corpus Iuris Canonici* in 2 volumes (1879-81), but it is not a critical text.

Though the *Corpus Iuris Canonici* remained the basis of church law until 1917, it had to be supplemented by subsequent legislation. The Council of Trent (1545-63) in its reform decrees touched upon almost every area of ecclesiastical discipline, especially with regard to the clergy and religious. The decrees on marriage were to profoundly affect canon law. The Congregation of the Council was established in 1564 to give authentic interpretations of the Tridentine decrees. Popes continued to enact legislation, but Benedict XIV is the only one to have had his decrees collected and published as authentic sources of canon law (1751). He also wrote important treatises on the canonization of saints and the diocesan synod. In addition to papal acts, decrees and single decisions there were innumerable directives flowing from the dicasteries of the Roman Curia. When these sources were later compiled (1923-1939), exclusive of the medieval *Corpus Iuris Canonici*, the decrees of Trent, and liturgical law, they filled nine thick volumes.

By the time of the First Vatican Council

(1869-70), therefore, many bishops were convinced that something had to be done to clear up the maze of law in which the operative could hardly be distinguished from the obsolete. Recognizing that it would be a task exceedingly difficult (*opus sane arduum*), they petitioned Pope Pius IX to undertake the preparation of a new code of canon law. Due to the troubled political situation in Rome the project was delayed until 1904 when Pius X entrusted it to Cardinal Gasparri. For almost fourteen years he directed the research of a large group of collaborators. Finally on Pentecost 1917 Pope Benedict XV promulgated the *Codex Iuris Canonici* to take effect the following Pentecost.

The new *Codex* was modeled on the nineteenth-century civil codes of Europe beginning with the *Code Napoléon*. For the first time all previous legislation was completely absorbed and all earlier collections abolished. Traditionally, canonical material had been incorporated at least in the substance of its original form as a sort of case law. But now "with an absolute trust in the ideal of the abstract formula, jurists sought to arrive at an almost mathematically constructed, impeccable system of legislation; a rational aggregate of all juridical norms, each reduced to the most absolute formulation and conceived as completely set apart from the concrete social situations which in life are the mainspring of law itself" (Kuttner 140).

The 1917 *Codex Iuris Canonici* is divided into five books, all except the first of which are subdivided into parts and the parts into titles. The canons are consecutively numbered from 1 to 2414, and nine documents are appended. The *fontes* or footnotes, which indicate the former law from which the canons are taken, are not strictly speaking part of the authentic Code. Book I "General Norms" includes: the application of the Code, custom, the computation of time, rescripts, privileges and dispensations. Book II "On Persons" is divided into three parts: clerics, religious and laity. The part on the clergy considers, first, matters pertaining to all clergy, then takes up the various offices from the Roman pontiff down to the rectors of churches. The treatment of religious includes the foundation of institutes, their government, the training of candidates, dismissal of members, and societies of men and women living in common without public vows. The third part on the laity deals with associations and confraternities of the faithful. Book III "On Things," the largest book, includes the seven sacraments, sacred places and times, divine worship, the teaching authority of the church, benefices and church property. Book IV "On Procedure" is concerned with trials, cases of beatification and canonization, and special procedures involving the clergy. Book V "On Crimes and Penalties" deals with punitive matters.

Just as after the Council of Trent, a special commission was established to give authentic interpretations of the Code. In addition, certain declarations made by offices of the Roman Curia had the force of law when issued with specific papal approval. Over the next forty years church law continued to grow. Five volumes of post-Code legislation (up through 1962) were compiled in *The Canon Law Digest* series. Many changes had taken place in society since World War II and the law of the church needed an updating.

At the time Pope John XXIII announced his intention to convoke an ecumenical council (January 25, 1959), he indicated he would appoint a Pontifical Commission to revise the Code of Canon Law. It was soon realized, however, that the Council had first to chart the direction of church renewal before the revision process could get underway. Accordingly, the Commission for the revision of the Latin Code did not formally begin its work until November 29, 1965, just a few days before the conclusion of the Council.

The Commission established a number of study groups, composed of canonical experts from all over the world, to formulate new canons for the various sections of the Code. A central committee identified ten principles (later approved by the 1967 Synod of Bishops) to guide the work of revision. Among those principles the following may be singled out: the essential end of canon law is to define and protect the rights of individuals with respect to the rights of others and to the community as a whole; while not merely exhortative or overly prescriptive, the Code should avoid excessive rigidity and allow for a certain discretionary application by those charged with pastoral care; bishops are to have power to dispense from the general law of the church except in those matters specifically reserved to the Holy See; the principles of subsidiarity must be recognized, leaving as much latitude as possible for local and regional legislation; ecclesiastical penalties should be kept to a minimum; and, finally, the Code should be restructured in conformity with the decrees of the Second Vatican Council.

With these principles as guidelines the study groups prepared provisional norms. As drafts of a particular part of the Code were completed, they were sent for evaluation to all the episcopal conferences of the world and to pontifical universities and faculties. The consultative process was far more extensive than that employed in developing the 1917 Code. By the end of 1978 this phase of the process was completed.

On the basis of the consultation the original drafts were amended and co-ordinated into a single volume which was then given to the cardinal members of the Commission (June 1980). They were requested to submit written comments in view of a final meeting. The meeting of the full Commission was held during October 1981. At its conclusion, after almost a quarter-century of continuous labor the Commission presented its final draft of the entire Code to Pope John Paul II. The Holy Father studied the text for over a year, made several changes, and then on January 25, 1983, the anniversary of Pope John XXIII's historic announcement, promulgated the new Latin Code to take effect on the First Sunday of Advent 1983.

A parallel Pontifical Commission for the revision of law for the Eastern Catholic Churches was established in 1971. As of 1986, drafts of an entire Code had circulated to the hierarchies of those churches for comment, but a Code had not yet been put in finished form for submission to the Pope.

Pope Paul VI proposed in 1965 to have a constitutional law or *Lex ecclesiae fundamentalis* which would apply to the universal church. Delineating the essential theological and juridical character of the church, it would serve as a common basis for the Latin and Eastern Codes. Never before had an attempt been made to define the essential reality of the church in juridical terminology. It is not surprising, therefore, that successive drafts of the *Lex ecclesiae fundamentalis* were severely criticized. Eventually about half of its canons, most notably those dealing with the rights and obligations of Christians, were incorporated in the Latin Code.

In his apostolic constitution promulgating the 1983 Latin Code, Pope John Paul II noted that it "could be understood as a great effort to translate" the doctrine of the Second Vatican Council, especially its ecclesiological teaching, "into canonical language." "If, however, it is impossible to translate perfectly into canonical language the conciliar image of the Church, nevertheless the Code must always be referred to this image as the primary pattern whose outline the Code ought to express insofar as it can by its very nature." It follows that "what constitutes the substantial newness [*novitas*] of the Second Vatican Council, in line with the legislative tradition of the Church, especially in regard to its ecclesiology, constitutes likewise the newness of the new Code." (The apostolic constitution accompanies all printed editions of the Code).

The new Code treats all the structures introduced or reemphasized by the Council: the college of bishops, the synod of bishops, conferences of bishops, episcopal vicars, presbyteral and pastoral councils. The Code represents, for the most part, a systematization or codification of the very extensive legislation through which Pope Paul VI sought to implement the conciliar mandates. In fact, the ordinary lay person or parish priest would hardly have been aware of any sudden change when the new Code took effect. The Congregation for the Sacraments and Divine Worship, however, did have to publish a list of minor emendations to bring the liturgical books into conformity with the new law.

The 1983 Code of 1,752 canons is considerably shorter than the 1917 Code which had 2,414 canons. The sections on ecclesiastical penalties, judicial processes and the sacraments have been considerably reduced, while those on benefices and the canonization of saints have been eliminated. The most striking overall difference in the two Codes is to be found in their organization. The 1917 Code was divided into five books, influenced by the classical Roman law scheme of "persons, things, and actions." The 1983 Code has seven books. Book II, "The People of God, is based on the second chapter of the conciliar Dogmatic Constitution on

the Church, *Lumen Gentium*. The structure of the rest of the Code is modeled largely on the threefold *munera* or functions of the church: the teaching, sanctifying and governing roles.

Just as after the promulgation of the first Code, a Pontifical Commission has been established to give authentic interpretations of its meaning. "But if on account of the excessively swift changes in contemporary human society certain elements of the new law become less perfect and require a new review the church is endowed with such a wealth of resources that, not unlike prior centuries, it will be able to undertake the task of renewing the laws of its life" (Preface to the 1983 Code).

See **Law, Vatican II**

Canon Law Society of America, *Code of Canon Law: Latin-English Edition*, Washington: Canon Law Society of America, 1983. James A. Coriden, Thomas J. Green, Donald E. Heintschel, eds., *The Code of Canon Law: a Text and Commentary*, New York: Paulist Press, 1985. R.C. Mortimer, *Western Canon Law*, London: Adam and Charles Black, 1953. Harold J. Berman, *Law and Revolution: the Formation of the Western Legal Tradition*, Cambridge: Harvard University Press, 1983. Stephen Kuttner, *The History of Ideas and Doctrines of Canon Law in the Middle Ages*, London: Variorum Reprints, 1980.

JOHN E. LYNCH, CSP

CANON OF SCRIPTURE

A *kanōn* in Greek (*qāneh* in Hebrew) is a reed or measuring stick. When used in connection with the Bible, the word "canon" refers to the collection of books that are acknowledged to be authoritative in the church and by which the church's faith can be measured.

The christian canon of Scripture contains the OT and NT. All Christians today acknowledge the authority of the books in the Hebrew Bible. The traditional Jewish canon consists of twenty-four books divided into three categories: Torah (Genesis, Exodus, Leviticus, Numbers, Deuteronomy), Prophets

(Joshua, Judges, 1–2 Samuel, 1–2 Kings, Isaiah, Jeremiah, Ezekiel, Twelve Minor Prophets), and Writings (Psalms, Job, Proverbs, Ruth, Song of Songs, Ecclesiastes, Lamentations, Esther, Daniel, Ezra-Nehemiah, Chronicles). Jews refer to these books as "Tanak," which is an acronym formed from the first letters in the Hebrew words for the three categories. The content of the Protestant OT is identical with that of the Jewish canon, but the material is divided into thirty-nine books and arranged in a different order.

The canon of OT books traditional in Catholicism contains all the books of the Hebrew Bible along with seven more books that were part of the Greek translation known as the Septuagint (and the Latin Vulgate): Judith, Tobit, Baruch, 1 Maccabees, 2 Maccabees, Sirach/Ecclesiasticus, and Wisdom of Solomon. Also included are some additions to Esther and Daniel. The forty-six books are divided into four categories: Pentateuch (=Torah), Historical Books, Wisdom Writings, and Prophets. Catholics and Protestants usually refer to these books as the "Old Testament," though in recent years some have begun calling them the "Hebrew Scriptures" or the "Jewish Scriptures." The additional books in the Catholic canon are sometimes called the Apocrypha (the "hidden books") or the Deuterocanonicals (a "second canon"). The canons of the various Orthodox churches contain some material beyond what appears in the Catholic canon.

All Christians today share the same canon of twenty-seven NT books. The first division of the NT contains the gospels of Matthew, Mark, Luke, and John, along with the Acts of the Apostles. The thirteen epistles ascribed to Paul are divided into letters written to communities (Romans, 1 Corinthians, 2 Corinthians, Galatians, Ephesians, Philippians, Colossians, 1 Thessalonians, 2 Thessalonians) and letters addressed to individuals (1 Timothy, 2 Timothy, Titus, Philemon). Within both categories of Pauline epistles the letters are arranged according to their physical length from longest to shortest. The letter to the Hebrews, which has some connections with the Pauline corpus, is followed by the seven catholic or general epistles: James, 1 Peter, 2 Peter, 1 John, 2 John, 3 John, and Jude. There is a dispute about whether "catholic" means accepted by all the churches or having content appropriate for the whole church. The Revelation of John, or the Apocalypse, concludes the NT canon.

Although it is not possible to write a complete history of the canon's development, it is possible to single out some decisive moments in that history. The instructions to Ezra from the Persian king that he should act "according to the law/wisdom of your God, which is in your hand" (Ezra 7:14, 25) suggests that the Torah was in final form and regarded as authoritative in the fifth century B.C. The preface to the Greek version of Sirach/Ecclesiasticus distinguished three categories of authoritative writings: "the law and the prophets and the other books of our fathers." This statement indicates that in the late second century B.C. even Diaspora Jews had a concept of canonical writings, though there is no way of knowing what they included among the prophets and the other books. Writing in late first century A.D., Josephus (*Against Apion* 1:37-43) limited the authoritative books to twenty-two. He may have counted Ruth as part of Judges and Lamentations as part of Jeremiah. Or he may reflect the debates about the canonical status of Esther and Qoheleth/Ecclesiastes. But by the second century A.D., the number of twenty-four books was fixed (see *4 Ezra* 14:44-48). Although there is no ancient explanation of criteria for including books in the canon of

Jewish Scriptures, one can assume that alleged antiquity (up to the Persian period), traditional usage by communities, correctness and coherence of teaching and belief in their divine inspiration contributed to their acceptance. The period between A.D. 70 and 100 (after the destruction of the Second Temple) was decisive in the development of the Jewish canon. But the idea that the content and shape of that canon was authoritatively determined at the Synod (or Council) of Yavneh (or Jamnia) at some specific date in that period is not at all certain.

The early Christians recognized as authoritative the Torah, the Prophets, and other writings. The Bible of the early church was the Greek version known as the Septuagint. But Christians did not take over from Judaism the tripartite division of books or the idea of a closed canon of twenty-four books. Rather, the history of the christian canon was independent of developments in rabbinic Judaism. The limits of the christian canon were fluid. The author of the letter of Jude alluded to an episode in the *Assumption of Moses* and referred to a prophecy in *I Enoch* 1:9 (see Jude 14-15). The early manuscripts of the Septuagint contain not only the so-called apocryphal or deuterocanonical works but also other writings. Jerome urged that Christians follow the canon of Hebrew Scriptures. Nevertheless, the inclusive canon (now the Catholic canon) championed by Augustine was adopted in the West and ratified at local church councils held in Hippo (A.D. 393) and in Carthage (A.D. 397, 419).

The inclusive canon prevailed up to the Reformation, though the idea of *Hebraica veritas* ("Hebrew truth") had its advocates through the centuries. In part because of the use of 2 Maccabees 12:46 as a proof-text for the existence of purgatory, Martin Luther advocated the acceptance of only the Hebrew Scriptures as canonical books. He relegated the other books to an appendix in his 1534 German translation and described them as "Apocrypha, that is, books that are not held to be equal to Holy Scripture and yet are profitable and good to read." In response to Luther and other Reformers, the Council of Trent in 1546 declared canonical all the books in the Latin Vulgate (the inclusive canon) but placed in an appendix 1-2 Esdras and Prayer of Manasseh.

The Holy Scriptures of the earliest Christians were the books contained in the Greek version of the OT. Only gradually did the idea of a NT alongside the OT arise. At the end of the first century A.D. or at least by the beginning of the second century, a collection of Pauline letters was in use (see 2 Peter 3:15-16; Ignatius' Letter to the Ephesians 12:2). In the mid-second century A.D., the gospels were being read publicly and regarded as authoritative. Marcion's attempt around A.D. 140 at limiting the canon to Luke and ten Pauline letters shows that the process of defining the NT canon was becoming an issue for Christians. By the late second century A.D. there was widespread agreement that the NT canon contained the four gospels, Acts, the thirteen Pauline letters, 1 Peter, and 1 John. There were continuing disputes about the canonical character of the other catholic epistles, Hebrews, and Revelation. The uncertainty about the extent of the NT came to an end in the East with Athanasius' Easter letter of A.D. 367. He designated as canonical the twenty-seven books contained in our NT today. He also gave the name "canon" to this collection. From the fifth century onward, this same canon was fixed in the West.

Since the NT developed over several centuries, it is impossible to be certain about the precise criteria by which books were accepted as canonical. Some factors that may have contributed to the recognition of christian writings as canonical were their traditional use in the churches, their orthodox content, connection with the apostles, relevance to the whole church, and belief in their inspiration. The external or historical factors affecting canonicity included the natural development of a religious movement toward codification, the threat posed by Marcion's limited canon, and the claims by gnostics and other groups to possess secret revelations in written form.

The complicated history of the biblical canon raises important theological issues: the relation between canon and church, the authority of the canonical books, and the task of canonical criticism as an approach to reading Scripture in the church.

The historical development of the canon in both Judaism and Christianity manifests a symbiosis between sacred text and community. Catholics have usually interpreted this relationship to prove that the Bible is the church's book, for the individual books arose out of experience within the christian community and were declared canonical by the church. Protestants have maintained that the Bible is the rule by which the life of the church is to be guided and measured in all ages. These traditional formulations contain some truth, though they oversimplify the development of the canon. Today there is a tendency to bring Scripture and tradition together more closely as in Vatican II's Dogmatic Constitution on Divine Revelation (D.V. 9-10). There Scripture and tradition are viewed as constituting one source of divine revelation, and the ecclesiastical magisterium is described as "not superior to the Word of God, but its servant."

Whether all canonical books have the same theological authority is a second issue. Luther maintained that the core of Scripture was found in those books that most effectively "promoted Christ" (was Christum treibet in his German formula); that is, in Paul's letters to the Romans and Galatians, John's Gospel, and 1 Peter. The Council of Trent insisted that all the NT books were of equal value. Nevertheless, it is possible to discern in Catholic history a preference for certain canonical writings (Matthew, Pastoral epistles) over others. Whether the "canon within the canon" should be made an explicit theological principle or not, is a matter of debate.

Canonical criticism is a newly formulated approach to biblical interpretation in the church. It is more a theological program than an exegetical method. The first task of the canonical critic is to describe the theological shape of the final canonical form of the biblical book. The second task is to explore the theological implications of the final canonical form of the book for the community of faith in the past and today. Its positive contributions in focusing on the final forms of biblical books, exploring their theological significance, and reflecting on their role in the believing community then and now are obvious. The approach runs into problems on account of the different text-types, canons, and communities in which the Bible is read.

B.S. Childs, *Introduction to the Old Testament as Scripture*, Philadelphia: Fortress, 1979. London: S.C.M., 1983. H.Y. Gamble, *The New Testament Canon: Its Making and Meaning*, Philadelphia: Fortress, 1985. H. von Campenhausen, *The Formation of the Christian Bible*, Philadelphia: Fortress, 1972.

DANIEL J. HARRINGTON, S J

THE CAPPADOCIAN FATHERS

The phrase "Cappadocian Fathers" is a traditional collective name given to three outstanding fourth century bishops and theologians from the province of Cappadocia in Asia Minor. They were St.

Basil, bishop of Caesarea in Cappadocia (c. 330-379) his brother, Gregory of Nyssa, (c. 331-395), and Basil's friend, Gregory of Nazianzus, briefly bishop of Constantinople (329-389). Each in his own way contributed to the formulation of the classical trinitarian theological synthesis, culminating in the final defeat of Arianism and the definition of the divinity of the Holy Spirit at the council of Constantinople in 381, the second ecumenical council. Basil was the more practical leader and organizer; Gregory of Nyssa, more mystically inclined; Gregory of Nazianzus, poet and preacher, known in the Eastern tradition as "the theologian." A minor figure, Amphilochius, bishop of Iconium, and a cousin of Gregory of Nazianzus, is sometimes included in this group.

ROBERT B. ENO, SS

CASUISTRY

The word comes from the Latin *casus* meaning "what happens," or "a case." It refers to a method of interpreting general principles and applying them to particular circumstances. In English, the word has the pejorative sense of overly subtle argument to justify otherwise reprehensible acts. While it had negative features, casuistry must be understood in its historical context. The teaching of the NT addresses "cases," e.g., Sabbath observance (Mk 2:23-28) and the paying of taxes (Lk 20:20-26). In such instances, however, Jesus does not merely interpret and apply the law, but moves beyond the letter to open up a new vision and a corresponding call to a deeper obedience. St. Paul dealt with specific issues, e.g., eating sacrificial food, (1 Cor 8); marriage and virginity, (1 Cor 7). The church fathers, for example, Tertullian, Origen, Clement of Alexandria, Ambrose and Augustine, developed a kind of casuistry in treating such questions as military

service, persecution, wealth, dress, and lying. The origins of casuistry cannot be explained merely as an intrusion into Christianity of alien elements from Stoicism and the Jewish law.

The history of casuistry is linked with the discipline of confession. Between the sixth and eleventh centuries, in response to the introduction of private confession, a casuistry of sins and penances was developed in the Penitential Books. The Fourth Lateran Council (1215) made annual confession and communion obligatory. Clerics were instructed in the complexities of cases of conscience by the *Summae Confessorum*, which went beyond the Penitentials in providing a relatively brief, practical account of morality. The third stage was introduced by the Council of Trent (1551) which required the penitent to confess sins according to number, species and circumstances and insisted on the pastoral formation of clerics. As a result, a new genre of literature was produced known as the *Institutiones Theologiae Moralis*. Among the most important authors were Hermann Busenbaum (1668) and St. Alphonsus Liguori (1787). Texts included a treatment of human acts, conscience, sin, law and an extended study of particular cases. The method followed was to pose a practical question, assemble authorities for one side and the other, and then provide a solution supported with brief argument. Where there was a statement by ecclesiastical authority, this was decisive. This was the model for textbooks of moral theology up to the Second Vatican Council.

Casuistry met strong criticism, notably from Blaise Pascal in his *Provincial Letters* (1656-57). It has been challenged by some Catholic theologians for legalism, minimalism and individualism. Outside the Roman Catholic tradition, casuistry has generally not been favored, although Joseph Fletcher's "situation ethics" has some affinity with it. Some contemporary moral philosophers, especially in the fields of biomedical ethics and business ethics, find the study of cases a helpful method of analysis.

An assessment of the role of casuistry in moral theology calls for a discernment of its positive and negative elements. An ethic founded on faith in God who rules over all, generates a reverential obedience concerned to discover the concrete divine call in all the complex circumstances of life. However, this concern could be subverted into a legalistic attempt to define the minimum necessary. The collection of cases, in the body of literature, may function as the formation of a community ethic in which models are developed from shared experience, and refined by continual exploration, so as to assist personal conscience. On the other hand, this could become an instrument of clerical control, which accords insufficient respect to the conscience and prudence of christian persons. Again, the process could be a way of grappling with new questions which arise, particularly in times of profound historical change, and which are not addressed in the more traditional moral doctrine. It could provide models to guide conscience and a structure for the development of moral insight. But, insofar as the process is conducted as a relatively autonomous, quasi-legal discipline, cut off from the deeper perspectives provided by scripture and theology, it fails to embody the full range of Christian and human values.

See **Moral Life, Christian; Confession**

Raphael Gallagher, "The Manual System of Moral Theology," *The Irish Theological Quarterly* 51 (1985): 1-16. Edward Leroy Long, Jr. *A Survey of Recent Christian Ethics,* New York: Oxford U.P., 1982.

BRIAN V. JOHNSTONE, CSSR

CATECHESIS, CATECHETICS

Nature and Purpose of Catechesis

The Second Vatican Council, in defining catechesis as a ministry of the word, (D.V. 24) restored the oldest and best elements of the catechetical tradition. The word "catechesis" is rooted in the Greek verb *katechein,* to resound or echo. Luke/Acts uses the verb as instruction in the way of the Lord. In St. Paul, *katechein* refers to oral instruction, a handing on of all that has been received in and through Christ.

Christus Dominus (14) stated that the purpose of catechesis is to develop in believers "a living, explicit and active faith enlightened by instruction." Catechesis is to be based on scripture, tradition, liturgy and on the teaching authority and life of the church. It is to be imparted not only to children and adolescents but also to young people and even adults. Catechesis must always be adapted to the age, ability and circumstances of life of the listener. This basic understanding of catechesis is appropriated and extended by the 1971 *General Catechetical Directory* (GCD) and the 1979 U.S. National Catechetical Directory, *Sharing the Light of Faith* (SLF). Catechesis is a life-long process of conversion for the individual and a continual and concerted effort for the christian community (GCD 22). SLF delineates the tasks of catechesis: to share and foster community, to proclaim the message of faith, to motivate to service and to lead to worship and prayer (32, 39, 213). The role of the community is highlighted in c. 773 of the 1983 Code of Canon Law, which emphasizes the experience of christian living as the way in which faith is nurtured. The Code also stresses the responsibility of the whole community for catechesis (c. 774).

Catechetics is the systematic study of the history, nature, goals, principles and process of catechesis. Catechetics is interdisciplinary in that it draws on other disciplines such as theology, biblical studies, learning theory and social sciences for the development of norms and criteria to evaluate its activity. Catechesis is concerned with the process of growth in faith; catechetics is concerned with the nature of the catechetical task, its relationship to the church's overall mission and its place in the pastoral ministry. Catechetics studies practice in order to formulate and test theory.

History of Catechesis

The Catechumenate. In the second and third centuries when the catechumenate structure developed, the word "catechesis" became identified with the preparation of the adult candidate for baptism and eucharist and with the post-baptismal instruction of the neophyte in the mysteries of the faith (*mystagogia*). Some of the greatest catechetical homilies and treatises, such as those of Cyril of Jerusalem, St. Ambrose and St. Augustine, are illustrations of mystagogical reflection on the sacramental experience. The catechumenate consisted of several stages that allowed for the nature of conversion as a process and for the understanding of faith as a way of living in the world. At each stage of initiation, catechesis took place in a liturgical framework. From the beginning, the motivating force of the candidate's conversion was the Word proclaimed, reflected upon and lived out in the community. The conversion process was further supported by the life, prayer and witness of the christian community.

With the decline of the catechumenate in the fourth and fifth centuries, the catechetical situation shifted from adult initiation to the baptism of infants, from pre-baptismal to post-baptismal instruction, and from a catechesis out of a biblical and liturgical context to a formation derived primarily from a christian environment. Catechesis meant the elementary instruction given by parents or sponsors to their baptized child. For the faithful, the homilies on Sundays and holy days centered on moral exhortation. Some memorization of prayers and doctrinal formulas was required but the devotions, processions, mime, songs, sacred verse and art assimilated from the milieu were the most influential forms of instruction.

In the early Middle Ages, the apathy that resulted from lack of effective instruction necessitated legislation with regard to the sacraments. The Fourth Lateran Council (1215), acting on the decrees of local councils, made sacramental confession and communion at least once a year a universal obligation for all those who had reached the years of discretion (c. 21). The pastoral crisis impelled church leaders to find a means of instruction. Out of this need, pulpit materials, manuals and other texts written in question and answer form began to be produced, writings that heralded the advent of the catechism.

The Catechism. Until the end of the fifteenth century, catechesis remained oral and experiential; but the invention of the printing press affected the history of catechesis in a radical way. The focal point of religious education became the printed page and the recitation of doctrinal questions and answers. Although there were a variety of authors and catechisms, the framework generally followed the medieval sequence of catechesis based on creed, commandments, and prayer and did not differentiate between the hierarchy of truths. The catechism reduced catechesis to instruction, to memorization, and to use by children.

Martin Luther's publication of the German catechism in 1529 established the catechism genre as a means of religious instruction. Catholic authors adopted the genre for their own purposes. The most influential of these were the Roman Catechism commissioned by the Council of Trent (1566) as a source book for the use of parish priests and those produced by the Jesuits Peter Canisius in Germany (1555) and Robert Bellarmine in Italy (1597) for both adults and children. The catechisms of Canisius and Bellarmine became the model for the development of many subsequent Catholic catechisms.

In the sixteenth and seventeenth centuries, religious orders of women and men dedicated to education increased in number and the school steadily established itself as the primary setting for catechesis. The catechism remained the basis of instruction, although methodologies such as the "Method of St. Sulpice" organized by Jean Jacques Olier (1608-1657), the treatise of Claude Fleury (1640-1723) and the pedagogy of St. John Baptist de la Salle (1651-1715) adapted the catechism to the age level of the child and placed emphasis on the preparation of teachers.

Concurrent with the development of schools, societies of pious lay teachers, as early as 1536, founded "schools of Christian Doctrine" for poor children in Milan. From this foundation, the movement grew; and the Confraternity of Christian Doctrine was formally organized in Rome in 1560 to instruct children and adults in the rudiments of their faith. In 1905, Pius X ordered the Confraternity of Christian Doctrine to be established in every parish of the world.

The number of catechisms proliferated and it was not uncommon for a diocese to have its own catechism, often written by or attributed to the bishop. The multiplication of catechisms prompted Napoleon I to commission an "imperial catechism" for use in all the dioceses of France (1806). The same situation of pluriform catechisms in the U.S. led the American bishops at the Third Plenary Council of Baltimore in 1829 to author-

ize a uniform catechism for the dioceses of the United States. *A Catechism of Christian Doctrine, Prepared and Enjoined by the Order of the Third Plenary Council of Baltimore* was published in 1885. It contained 421 questions-answers and followed the sequence of creed, sacraments, commandments. For the next seventy-five years the Baltimore catechism was both memorized verbatim and used as a syllabus for Catholic textbooks and religion programs.

The need for a universal catechism was the topic of lengthy debate at the First Vatican Council (1869-70). The recommendation was made to model the universal catechism on the text of Robert Bellarmine and to make the catechism, once approved, mandatory world wide. The idea of "A single faith, a single catechism" equated unity and uniformity. Opposition to the proposal stemmed from the practical difficulty of implementation and of adaptation to local regions; but the primary cause of polarization was the underlying issue of the relationship of the bishops to the Holy See. In the end, although the proposal for a uniform catechism was accepted by the majority of the council fathers, it was never implemented.

The question of a universal catechism arose in the preparatory stages of Vatican II but instead the council mandated a common directory for the universal church (C.D. 44). The directory is not legislation but offers basic principles of theological and pastoral orientation in order to provide assistance for the production of national catechetical directories and catechisms. The extraordinary Synod of Bishops in Rome in 1985 called for a "a catechism or compendium of all Catholic doctrine" that will become a point of reference for all national and regional catechisms.

Modern Catechetical Movement

Pope Pius X (1903-1914), in his effort

"to restore all things in Christ," was instrumental in restoring catechesis to a recognized position of importance in the pastoral life of the church. Through his decrees on frequent communion and liturgical reform Pius X encouraged liturgical and catechetical renewal.

In 1935 in the U.S., a National Center of Religious Education-CCD was established that served as a vehicle for the implementation of many of the reforms of Pius X. The center provided leadership for the organization of parish CCD and disseminated Confraternity information and publications, initiated congresses, priest's institutes and summer training sessions for religious sisters and brothers who in turn prepared the lay catechists.

The liturgical movement was also a significant influence on catechetical renewal in the U.S. In the pages of *Orate Fratres* (*Worship*) Dom Virgil Michel, O.S.B., and his associates continually drew attention to the privileged role of liturgy in the formation of active Christians. In 1929, they collaborated with the Dominican Sisters of Grand Rapids, Michigan on the preparation of *The Christ-Life Series* (1934), graded textbooks for elementary schools based on the liturgy and the liturgical year. The series attempted to restore the early catechetical tradition of progressive initiation into the christian life through the liturgy and to reestablish the intrinsic relationship between catechesis and liturgy.

The authors of the Christ-Life Series anticipated the principles inherent in the kerygmatic renewal initiated by the publication of Josef Jungmann's seminal work, *Die Frohbotschaft und Unsere Glaubensverkündigung* (The Good News and Our Proclamation of the Faith) in 1936. Jungmann (1889-1975), an Austrian Jesuit professor of pastoral theology at the University of Innsbruck, believed that a change in methodology alone would not bring about catechetical renewal; there must be a return to the essential and central elements of the christian faith, the good news of salvation in Jesus Christ.

The kerygmatic renewal called for a cohesive and unified presentation of the christian faith by an integration of the sources of revelation: liturgy, scripture, doctrine and christian witness. This wholistic approach to catechesis is the key to Jungmann's catechetical theory. The Word of God is proclaimed as a word spoken to people in their actual life situation. This anthropological basis of catechesis is central to Jungmann's thought and remains one of the main characteristics of the modern catechetical movement.

Johannes Hofinger (1905-1984), also an Austrian Jesuit, a student of Jungmann's at Innsbruck and director of the East Asian Pastoral Institute in Manila (1957-1965), is most responsible for disseminating the insights and principles of the kerygmatic movement in catechetics. Hofinger lectured extensively and in the 1950's, together with other European scholars, brought new life to the catechetical movement in the U.S. The kerygmatic approach gradually gained wide acceptance, and the publication of text materials based on its principles began to replace the catechism as the means of instruction.

Hofinger initiated the International Catechetical Study Weeks (Nijmegen 1959, Eichstätt 1960, Bangkok 1962, Katigondo 1964, Manila 1967, Medellin 1968), which were important focal moments in the evolution of catechetics. The international character, missionary emphasis, and influence on worldwide church events made the study weeks key events in the development of catechetics; in their totality the study weeks represent a continuity and progression in defining the nature and purpose of catechesis.

The first years after the Vatican Council

were years of unparalleled change, creativity and enthusiasm that quickly became laced with discontent and criticism. Catechesis, which implemented and reflected these changes, became the focal point of much of the dissatisfaction. "Crisis" and "polarization" were words frequently used to describe the situation.

The *General Catechetical Directory* (1971) was an important step in providing direction for catechesis. The GCD, incorporating the insights on culture in the documents of Vatican II and also the political perspectives of the Medellin Study Week, carefully noted that the mission of the church is to proclaim and foster faith in contemporary human society. The GCD identifies the reading of "the signs of the times" and the discerning of the implications of the cultural situation for catechesis as a major task of each national directory committee. Renewal in catechesis is effective when there is renewal in the church and in society as a whole. The GCD exhibited a genuine openness to varying theological and pedagogical viewpoints; specific application of the general principles was left to the national conferences of bishops.

Rite of Christian Initiation of Adults

The publication of the *Rite of Christian Initiation of Adults* (RCIA) in 1972 shifted the focus back from children to adult catechesis, from instruction on individual sacraments to initiation as a process of faith and conversion. The RCIA identifies the community as the context and the means by which catechumens are initiated into the christian way of life. The liturgical year is the framework of the catechesis, and the lectionary readings enable the catechumens to reflect on the word and to integrate it into their lives. The stages within the ritual emphasize that conversion is a process and mark important phases within the spiritual journey of each individual. The RCIA restores the integral relationship between liturgy and catechesis and relates both of these to the life experience of the Christian.

Documents of the American Bishops

In 1973, the Bishops of the U.S. published two documents that had relevance for catechesis. The pastoral message on Catholic education, *To Teach as Jesus Did* (TTJD), identified education as a ministry and broadened the concept of educational ministry to works other than schools. The document stated that the educational mission of the church is an integrated ministry with three interlocking dimensions: message, community and service. The use of the concepts of community and service to communicate the meaning of Catholic educational ministry in *TTJD* was a major contribution to the developing understanding of catechesis.

Basic Teachings for Catholic Religious Education (BT) is a pastoral response to the criticism of religious education programs and textbooks. The purpose of BT is to "prepare a positive statement of irreducible doctrinal principles to serve as a guide" for parents, catechists, writers and publishers of catechetical texts. An edited version of the document is incorporated into *Sharing the Light of Faith*.

Fourth General Assembly of Bishops, 1977

The 1977 Synod of Bishops on "Catechesis in Our Times," described catechesis as word, memory and witness. The bishops stated that the model of all catechesis is the baptismal catechumenate and is the responsibility of all in the church. The Synod affirmed the direction taken by the modern catechetical movement, stating that it has produced excellent results for the renewal of the entire community of the church.

The Apostolic Exhortation of Pope John Paul II in 1979, *Catechesi Tradendae*

(CT), "Handing on the Teaching," affirming the work of the synod, discusses the nature and needs of catechesis. The pope notes that "the primary object of catechesis is the 'mystery of Christ'" and exhorts all catechists to transmit by their teaching and behavior the teaching and life of Jesus. This teaching is not a body of abstract truths but the "communication of the living mystery of God" (CT 7). CT emphasizes that catechesis is the responsibility of the entire community and delineates the specific roles of all members of the church.

The National Catechetical Directory

The National Conference of the U.S. Catholic Bishops endorsed *Sharing the Light of Faith* in 1977, and the Sacred Congregation for the Clergy approved it in 1978. With the publication of the Directory in 1979, the most extensive consultation process ever conducted in the North American church was completed. Thus the document represents not only the positions of the bishops and Directory committee but of a large segment of the American Catholic community. The characteristics of the Directory that make it unique and appropriate for the church of the U.S. are its emphasis on the role of the whole community in catechesis, its identification of the four primary tasks of catechesis, the acknowledgement of adult catechesis as normative and its attention to the ecumenical aspect of catechesis. The publication of the National Catechetical Directory marks the coming of age of the catechetical movement in the United States. It reflects and renews the tradition in its emphasis on catechesis as pastoral ministry, as a ministry of the word that interprets experience, as intrinsically related to liturgy, as a process of growth in faith, as taking place in and through the community, as critical reflection on culture and as awareness of "the vocation to service." All of these aspects reflect the primary goal of catechesis, "the mystery of Christ."

See **Catechumenate; Faith; Initiation, Christian**

Michael Warren, ed., *Sourcebook for Modern Catechetics,* Winona, MN: St. Mary's Press, 1983. Berard Marthaler, *Catechetics in Context,* Huntington, IN: Our Sunday Visitor, 1973.

CATHERINE DOOLEY, OP

CATECHUMENATE

Three documents of the Second Vatican Council called for the restoration of the Rite of Christian Initiation of Adults (RCIA). They are: The Constitution on the Liturgy, nos. 64-66; Decree on the Pastoral Office of Bishops, no. 14; Decree on the Church's Missionary Activity, no. 14. On January 6, 1972, the Congregation for Worship published the provisional Latin text of the RCIA. The English translation of the rite was approved for use in the USA in 1974.

Meant to be a process for initiating new members into the church by nurturing their conversion in the christian way of life and belief, the RCIA is divided into four time periods and provides three transitional rites. The first period, of variable length, is called the pre-catechumenate. It is a time for nurturing conversion through evangelization. Whenever a candidate can be said to have acquired "first faith" and "initial conversion" (RCIA no. 42), it is time to celebrate the first of the transitional rites, the rite of acceptance into the order of catechumens. By this rite one becomes a member of the church as a catechumen and enters the second period.

Usually the longest period of the RCIA, and the period which gives its name to the whole process in many places, the catechumenate is also of variable length. During this time the catechumens are formed in the Catholic christian way of life through catechesis. The RCIA intends catechesis to be more than classroom learning of Catholic teachings. Based on the rhythms of the church's life of worship, particularly the lectionary cycle of readings, catechesis consists of examination of church teachings, engagement in the life of the whole community as it struggles with significant moral and ethical issues, participation in the community's prayer, especially the Sunday Liturgy of the Word, and active involvement in the community's apostolic life (RCIA no. 75). When a candidate can be said to have acquired "enlightened faith" and a "conversion in mind and in action" (RCIA no. 107), it is time to celebrate the rite of election, the second transitional rite. Usually celebrated at the beginning of Lent, preferably by the bishop of the diocese, the rite of election constitutes the church's recognition that these candidates have been chosen by God to be fully initiated into the church at the upcoming Easter Vigil.

During the season of Lent, the candidates for full initation, now called the elect, undergo a process of purification and enlightenment which is prayerfully acknowledged by the community in the three Sunday celebrations of the scrutinies. The scrutinies are prayers for healing, liberation and forgiveness offered on behalf of the elect by the assembled community on the third, fourth and fifth Sundays of Lent. The RCIA also provides others prayers of blessing and purification to be used during Lent, including presentations of the Lord's Prayer and of the Creed.

At the Easter Vigil the Elect are fully initiated into the church as members of the order of the faithful by the sacraments of baptism, confirmation and eucharist. This most important of the transitional rites begins the final period of the RCIA, the post-baptismal catechesis. During the fifty days of Easter the newly initiated join with the entire christian community in reflecting on the meaning of the paschal event all have experienced by "meditating on the Gospel, sharing in the eucharist and doing the works of charity" (RCIA no. 234).

Throughout the entire process of the RCIA, the catechumens are joined by sponsors who act as their witnesses and guides. The RCIA also presumes that the whole parish concern itself with the initiation of new members (RCIA no. 9).

See **Catechesis; Initiation, Christian**

James Dunning, *New Wine, New Wineskins,* New York: William H. Sadlier, Inc., 1981. Robert Duggan, ed. *Conversion and the Catechumenate,* Ramsey, NJ: Paulist Press, 1984. Aidan Kavanagh, OSB, *The Shape of Baptism: the Rite of Christian Initiation,* New York: Pueblo Publi., 1978. Raymond B. Kemp, *A Journey in Faith: an Experience of the Catechumenate,* New York; William H. Sadlier, Inc., 1979. James T. Morgan, ed., *Christian Initiation Resources Reader,* vols. 1-4, New York: William H. Sadlier, Inc., 1984. The Murphy Center for Liturgical Research, *Made, Not Born: New Perspectives on Christian Initiation and the Catechumenate,* Notre Dame: Univ. of Notre Dame Press, 1976. William Reedy, ed. *Becoming a Catholic Christian,* William H. Sadlier, Inc., 1978.

JAMES LOPRESTI, SJ

CATHOLICISM

The basic meaning of the term is universality, comprehensiveness. Historically Catholicism has come to mean the traditions, beliefs, way of life, institutional allegiance and coherence, worship and moral standards of those communities of Christians which maintain full institutional communion with Rome, though the term is sometimes used more broadly to include Anglican and other churches whose structure, worship and beliefs are close to the church of Rome.

The word and the idea of Catholicism have a long history in christian usage. In the second century Ignatius of Antioch used it to mean the whole church in contrast to a local church (*Letter to the Church in Smyrna,* Ch. 8). But later Church Fathers began to use the term in a normative as well as a descriptive sense.

Cyril of Jerusalem instructed his cate-chumens that the church was called Catholic because it extended to all parts of the world, taught all doctrines that people needed to know for their salvation, and had a mission to the whole human race (*Catecheses,* 18). In the West the word "Catholic" became the more usual way of designating the true church in contrast to heretical groups. When the word is used in the ancient creeds, it seems to carry all three meanings: the descriptive, the normative and the distinctive.

In the schism between eastern and western churches which became definitive in 1054, the eastern churches more usually called themselves Orthodox while the western church favored the term Catholic. Through the activities of the monk Hildebrand, who became Pope Gregory VII, the western church at this time became more tightly organized and cen-tralized about the see of Rome which had been the only western partriarchal see. In this way the church of the west acquired some of those traits of strict disipline and sharply defined teachings which later came to be associated with Catholicism. The schism of the sixteenth century, which was mainly a division between the northern and southern sections of the western church, came to focus on this issue of the role of the Roman see and the way that role was exercised. Catholicism came to be defined in strictly institutional terms, describing those in sacramental communion with Rome, accepting the doctrinal, moral and disciplinary au-thority of the Roman see.

Nevertheless, Catholicism is a tradition and style of christian life and community which is more deeply rooted than such institutional definitions express. Charac-teristic of Catholicism as a way of being christian are the following aspects: an assumption about the relation between faith and reason, a respect for the cumu-lative wisdom of experience, a deep appreciation of the sacramental principle, an explicit commitment to avoid elitism, a sense of the corporate nature of sin and redemption, and a broadly inclusive approach to church membership which allows for infant baptism and makes efforts to retain those who are not strongly committed. These characteristics are not exclusive to Catholicism but they are constitutive of it as a phenomenon in history.

Compared with most Protestant posi-tions, Catholicism emphasized the role that reason plays in relation to faith. Reason provides grounds of credibility for that further leap of commitment which is faith, and it is readily harnessed for faith seeking deeper understanding. It is an acceptable exercise both of faith and reason to seek the inner coherence of christian beliefs and teachings, and also to seek a unified world view harmonizing what is observed in the world, and under-stood through science, history and philosophy, with the tenets of the faith. Hence Catholicism has respected the systematizing efforts of the scholastic theologians of medieval and later times, and has approved speculative theology in general. In modern times this has made possible an emerging consensus on dif-ficult questions raised by science as in the case of theories of evolution and psycho-logical and sociological discoveries, thus providing an alternative to fundamen-talism, but avoiding a shift to rationalistic rejecting of faith.

This has been due in part to a con-servative trend in Catholicism based on a deep respect, even reverence, for the cumulative wisdom of the past—a rever-ence which has been institutionalized in various ways referred to globally as Tradition. Tradition, as distinct from traditions, is a normative concept in Catholicism. It represents the outcome of a discernment process of the community.

In the course of the centuries an acceptable pattern for this process has developed: teachings or rituals or community structures become official when they have been observed for a long time, never successfully challenged, and taught as part of the heritage (a process known as the ordinary *magisterium* of the church); they also become official when explicitly so declared by a general council of the church or in later centuries by the Pope (a process known as the extraordinary *magisterium*). The reverence for the cumulative experience and reflection of the past is not exhausted by the process of shaping the official and normative Tradition. Such reverence is also evidenced in the way in which Catholic theology is done, in the way Catholics interpret Scripture and in the way they worship. In all of these, there is a tendency to treasure what has been handed down not only in Scripture but as the product of the centuries of Christianity.

This general trait of reverence for what has been handed down from the past is closely related to appreciation and practical implementation of the sacramental principle. Our communication with God is not direct but mediated by creatures. In the sin-distorted history in which we live this mediation is not universal and spontaneous, but must be cultivated. It is necessary to treasure and cherish moments, places, memories of persons and events, and things in which God's presence and providence has been glimpsed with a certain transparency. Around these grow stories and attitudes out of which the symbolism of encounters with the sacred is constructed very slowly through the course of centuries. This is the basis of the sacramental celebrations, of the formulae and language of faith and prayer, of the church calendar, of the consecration and dedication of certain people for special roles in the church, and of the building of churches and the inclusion of sanctuaries, tabernacles and baptismal fonts. It is also the basis of shrines and pilgrimages and special devotions, and is expressed in the honoring of saints and in seeking their intercession. Because of its commitment to the sacramental principle, Catholicism has been known among christian traditions for its more elaborate rites, church furnishings and appointments, sacred vessels and vestments, representational art and multidimensional expressions of piety.

This has been accompanied by an explicit, though not always completely successful, commitment to avoid elitism. There has been a continuous concern to overcome divisions among rich and poor, peoples of different nations, languages and races, and the acknowledged class distinctions of various societies by an insistence on equality of welcome and participation in the church's gatherings and activities. This has been the basis, for instance, of the insistence until recent times on universal attendance at Sunday Eucharist in the territorial parish, and an avoidance of special-interest congregations on Sundays. In some cases it involved a long struggle, as with slavery and racial segregation in the United States, and with the continuance of national churches side by side in the same city. To this time the principle of non-elitism has not reached as far as allowing leadership roles in worship and church government to women.

A further significant and constitutive trait of Catholicism is its view of sin and redemption as corporate issues for the human community. Original sin is understood not only as a certain distortion in each individual, but as distortion of relationships, social structures, values, expectations and generally accepted standards of law and social order and justice. Society as such is in need of redemption and it is the task of the

church to extend the redeeming grace of
Christ into all aspects of human society,
for the transformation of the large
economic, political and social structures
as well as the smaller patterns of personal
relationships. Catholicism is not concerned with the saving of souls out of the
world, but with the redemption of the
world in all its complexity. It is this
understanding that has led to a long
struggle to come to a theologically
appropriate and practically feasible doctrine of the relationship between church
and state—a process which at some times
yielded strange and unfortunate alliances.

It is also this understanding of the
corporate nature of the redemption that
has led to the development of a critical
social teaching expressed, for instance, in
the papal social encyclical letters since
the late nineteenth century, and in pastoral letters of bishops or bishops'
conferences in different parts of the world.
Such teachings have not only been
formulated in words but have led to the
formation of church structures intended
to implement them, such as apostolic
religious communities, the Catholic Action Movement, the Young Christian
Workers' Movement, the Catholic
Worker Movement, all of which are
mainly lay organizations, as well as papal,
national and diocesan Offices and De-
partments of Justice and Peace, usually
with a staff of ordained and religious
persons. One of the more recent popular
expressions of Catholic understanding of
the corporate nature of the redemption
has been the emergence of Basic Christian
Communities which combine community
worship, mutual help and social, economic and political action on behalf of
the poor and oppressed sectors of the
community. Liberation theology is a
theoretical expression of this movement.

The corporate or community nature of
redemption is also reflected in the role
which the saints play in Catholicism. As

is well known, this role is far more
prominent in popular religious life and
worship than it is in the official teaching
or liturgy of the church. Yet it provides a
certain parallel to the hierarchic structure
of the church. It suggests an order of
intercession in which Jesus is the key and
central figure but in which Mary, the
mother of Jesus, also plays a universal
role, and in which apostles and early
martyrs stand in a superior position to
later saints who play the role of local and
particular patrons, not to mention the
uncanonized dead who are also seen in
an intercessory role. This hierarchy of
intercession seems to reflect in some
degree the social structures of medieval
European society, especially in the period
in which feudalism held sway. In that
society there was a regular pattern of
protection in exchange for services, and a
petitioner would not go directly to the
highest authority but would address the
authority immediately above which owed
this particular petitioner protection and
patronage. The religious form of this has
been expressed in the dedication of special
shrines, pilgrimages, festivals and particular devotional practices. In the present
age this tradition of the intercession of
the saints is manifested most strongly in
peasant communities, among emigrants
trying to maintain a national tradition in
a new environment, and in a more general
way among the peoples of Mediterranean
origin.

One of the more interesting but more
troublesome characteristics of Catholicism is its broadly inclusive approach to
church membership. Drawing on the
experience of centuries, Catholicism
resolutely practices infant baptism, followed by extensive catechesis during
childhood. This extends the invitation to
christian faith to many more people than
would otherwise be confronted by it, but
it also has some disadvantages, because it
results in a church community some

(perhaps many) of whom have not personally made a faith commitment, but follow the tradition because they were raised in it. This is accentuated by the forceful way in which those baptized in the Catholic Church were exhorted and persuaded in recent centuries to attend the Sunday Eucharist every week, frequent the sacraments, and not to abandon the Catholic tradition into which they had been initiated. The dangers of building the church community this way have been recognized, but it is characteristically Catholic to see the benefits of the wider invitation as outweighing the disadvantages.

Catholicism is widely dispersed throughout the world in modern times and has experienced the tension inherent in the need for adaptation to different cultures while maintaining the particularly tightly knit and strongly centralized church structure and teaching. Shaped historically in Mediterranean and European patterns of life, worship and organization, Catholicism is nevertheless committed to accommodating itself to African, Asian and North and South American cultures. Until the Second Vatican Council (1962-1965) the tendency was towards the more rigid patterns envisaged by the Council of Trent (1545-1563) and the First Vatican Council (1869-1870). The Second Vatican Council, however, incorporated into its account of the church, of its role in the secular world, its ecumenical relationships and concern with other faiths, and its task of evangelization, an awareness of history, of the development and variety of contemporary cultures, of the complexity of global economic and political issues, and of the contribution of the social sciences to the understanding of the tasks of redemption in the concrete.

In consequence of this, there have been some shifts in the traditional preoccupation with missionary outreach beyond the boundaries of the established church.

The inaugural encyclical letter of Pope Paul VI, *Ecclesiam suam*, 1963, refocused the missionary outreach from one simply seeking conversion to Catholicism to a concern primarily with dialogue in quest of greater depth and breadth in the understanding of the truth of revelation. The shift to a focus that is more directly on dialogue than proselytizing has issued in the appointment of commissions to enter into bilateral consultations with other christian bodies, and delicate exchanges with Jewish and other non-christian communities about matters of practical as well as theoretical concern to them.

In consequence, also, of the wider perceptions of the Second Vatican Council, questions about the local inculturation of Catholicism in formerly colonial and in other Third World countries have become more insistent. These concern, for instance, family life in traditionally polygamous cultures, patterns of worship in countries where a sufficient number of celibate candidates for ordination is culturally unlikely, the use of indigenous symbolism in christian prayer, more communitarian or democratic structures of leadership and decision making, and economic and political aspects of christian values and behavior patterns. The issue of inculturation raises critical questions about the relationship of local initiative to centralized control. It also raises sensitive questions about the right of lay and grass roots associations to state their position and undertake action on their own initiative in the name of the Catholic Tradition, and about the claim of lay voices to be taken into account in the shaping of church teaching. That, in turn, raises further questions about the relation of the church to political matters—who may speak for the church and act in the name of the church, and on what issues, judged by what criteria, and to what degree of concrete particularity.

As is evident, the character of Catholicism is such that at one and the same time it offers considerable stability but also necessarily generates arguments over interpretation and application of the tradition.

See **Church**

Thomas Bokenkotter, *Essential Catholicism*, N.Y.: Doubleday, 1985. Karl Adam, *The Spirit of Catholicism*, Revised edition. N.Y.: Macmillan, 1929. Henri de Lubac, *Catholicism: a Study of Dogma in Relation to the Corporate Destiny of Mankind*, N.Y.: Longmans, Green, and London: Barnes and Oates, 1950. Monika K. Hellwig, *Understanding Catholicism*, N.Y.: Paulist Press, 1981. Richard McBrien,*Catholicism*, Minneapolis: Winston, 1980 and London: Geoffrey Chapman, 1981.

MONIKA K. HELLWIG

CATHOLICITY

Catholicity, as applied to the church, means the quality of being universal, complete, or all-embracing. The term is not a biblical one, though the idea is well rooted in the NT, which speaks of the church as "the fullness of him [Christ] who fills all in all"(Eph 1:23). Because of its relationship to Christ, the church has a mission to all nations and to all generations (Mt 28:19-20). The Pauline and deutero-Pauline letters repeatedly celebrate the capacity of Christianity to overcome the division between rich and poor, free and slave, male and female, Jew and Gentile, Greek and barbarian.

Christians confess in the Apostles' Creed, "I believe in the holy catholic Church," and in the Nicene-Constantinopolitan Creed, "I believe...in the Church, one, holy, catholic, and apostolic." The Fathers of the Church, who frequently speak of the church as catholic, use the term in somewhat different senses. In some cases they are contrasting the whole church, as catholic, with the local or particular churches, which participate in the catholicity of the whole. In other cases they designated the true church as catholic in contrast to the heretical sects, which have broken off from it. Cyril of Jerusalem, in his *Catechetical Lectures* (c. 347 A.D.) gives a concise discussion of the catholicity of the church, by which he understands its dissemination throughout the whole world, its possession of the totality of saving truth, its mission to all kinds of people, its capacity to heal all kinds of sin, and its abundance in every kind of virtue and spiritual gift. Augustine, in his polemical writings against the Donatists, emphasized the geographical and ethnic universality of the Catholic Church in opposition to the particularism of the sects, which are confined to certain localities and ethnic groups.

In the Middle Ages the various dimension of catholicity were kept in view. Thomas Aquinas holds that the church is catholic in three respects: it has unlimited spatial extension; it includes men and women of every condition of life, and it transcends all limits of time. The idea that the church was already present in the time of Adam or Abel and that it will continue to exist even beyond the end of history, was a regular feature of the concept of catholicity as understood by Augustine and the medieval writers. Later theologians, however, preferred to treat "catholicity in time" under the heading of apostolicity.

In the Roman Catholic apologetics of the sixteenth through the nineteenth centuries catholicity was understood as a mark of the true church in contradistinction to all heretical or schismatic bodies. The assertion in the creed that the church is "one, holy, catholic, and apostolic" was interpreted as offering four criteria. The concept of catholicity consequently had to be reinterpreted so as to apply to Roman Catholicism as a visible institution, and not to any other christian body. Some Catholic apologists recognized that certain other christian bodies were rather widely diffused throughout the world, but they argued that these other communities did not have the same degree of universality as the Roman Catholic Church, which therefore excelled them in "relative catholicity." Some apologists made the further point that catholicity could not be properly understood apart from unity, since a church that was not one could not be catholic. The Protestant churches, even though widely disseminated, were held to lack catholicity because they were deficient in unity. This lack of catholic unity, in turn, was traced to the lack of apostolicity. Any churches that were not governed by a united body of bishops in communion with the successor of Peter, it was contended, lacked visible unity and were for that reason deficient in catholicity.

While this institutional and apologetical concept of catholicity was predominant in certain Roman Catholic circles, other concepts of catholicity were also current. Eastern Orthodox theologians, relying on certain patristic sources, understood the church's catholicity as adherence to the full apostolic heritage of truth and holiness, as expressed in the liturgies, creeds, and dogmatic teaching of the ancient church. Many Anglicans tended to look upon catholicity as a matter of preserving the patristic heritage, including the canon of Scripture, the early creeds, the sacraments of Baptism and Eucharist, and the apostolic ministry. This last feature consisted in a body of bishops standing in the historic apostolic succession. For many Protestants the church was catholic insofar as it continued to profess the gospel as witnessed by the scriptures and as accepted by the faithful of every generation.

Even in Roman Catholic theology the institutional-apologetic concept of catholicity did not hold exclusive sway. Under the influence of nineteenth-century theologians such as Johann Adam Moehler, many twentieth-century theologians came to regard Counter Reformation apologetics as overconcerned with the external, visible, and quantitative aspects of catholicity. An effort was made to recover the more qualitative and theological features of catholicity as it had been understood in the first millennium of Christianity. Catholicity thus came to be understood as a mystery of grace not fully accessible to empirical sociology. According to this view, catholicity is rooted in the triune God and in Jesus Christ as universal mediator. The church, as the sacramental prolongation of him in whom all things hold together (cf. Col 1:17), has the capacity and obligation to exercise a universal reconciling ministry. It must overcome all human oppositions and conflicts and bring about dynamic unity. The catholicity of the church, viewed in this light, is a synthesis of opposites. According to the plan of God, the church is to take into itself the riches and talents of every people and present them to Christ, to whom the nations were given as an inheritance (Ps 2:8).

This renewed understanding of catholicity is vividly set forth in the documents of Vatican Council II. According to the Constitution on the Church, "This attribute of universality which adorns the People of God is that gift of the Lord whereby the Catholic Church tends efficaciously and constantly to recapitulate the whole of humanity with all its riches under Christ the head in the unity of his Spirit. In virtue of this catholicity each individual part brings its particular gifts to the other parts and to the whole Church, so that the whole and the individual parts are enriched by the mutual sharing of gifts and the striving of all for fullness in unity...." (L.G. 13).

Thanks to this vision of catholicity, Vatican II was able to present the church as a diversified unity, made up of distinct local and regional churches, each having its own proper characteristics and gifts to contribute to the whole. The pope, as bishop of Rome, was described as presiding over the whole assembly of charity, so as to protect legitimate differences and to prevent those differences from becoming divisive (L.G. 13). The cooperation of all the local churches, under their respective bishops, was seen as "particularly splendid evidence of the catholicity of the undivided Church"(L.G. 23). This vision of catholicity made it possible for Vatican II to propose a more realistic and appealing concept of christian unity than had been current in preconciliar ecumenism. The goal of ecumenical action was now seen as a "reconciled diversity" in which the uniting churches would retain their distinct traditions and customs, enjoying a measure of autonomy within the catholic communion of churches (U.R. 14-18).

The vision of missionary activity set forth by Vatican II was likewise shaped by this richer concept of catholicity. The church, in proclaiming and promoting the rule of Christ, acts out of "the inmost requirements of her own catholicity" (A.G. 1). Missionary activity is held to "perfect her [the church's] catholic unity by expanding it" (A.G. 6). It heals, ennobles, and perfects all the authentic values present in the traditions and cultures of various peoples (A.G. 9). Missionary expansion thus enables the church to offer to Christ as his inheritance the riches of all the nations (A.G. 22).

The catholicity of the church, we may conclude, is the diversified unity enabling it to reconcile in itself the contrasting values of diverse peoples and cultures, to elevate these through the gifts of grace, and thus to achieve an unexcelled plenitude through mutual enrichment. Theologically, catholicity is rooted in Christ, the universal reconciler. The Holy Spirit, as the bond of loving union between the mutually opposed persons of the Father and the Son in the godhead, is poured out upon the church as the seal and consummation of its catholicity. The diverse gifts of the spirit contribute to the multisplendored unity of the body of Christ. The triune God, who communicates himself in the Incarnate Word and in the Holy Spirit, is the source and ground, the norm and exemplar, of all catholicity.

See **Church, Mission**

Wolfgang Beinert, *Um das dritte Kirchenattribut,* 2 vols. Essen: H. Wingen, 1964. Yves Congar, *L'Eglise une, sainte, catholique, et apostolique,* Vol. 15 of *Mysterium Salutis,* Paris: Cerf, 1970. Avery Dulles, *The Catholicity of the Church,* Oxford: Clarendon, 1985. Gustave Thils, *Les notes de l'Eglise dans l'apologétique catholique depuis la Réforme,* Gembloux: J. Duculot, 1937.

AVERY DULLES, SJ

CELIBACY

Celibacy is the religious practice of non-marriage or the choice of a commitment to the single life for specifically religious reasons. The word comes from the Latin "caelebs" which means "single" or "alone." Someone may be single or choose to be single for other than religious reasons, but the practice of celibacy, strictly speaking, implies religious motivation. A marriage may be considered "celibate" by analogy if the couple chooses to abstain from genital sexual activity for religious reasons. A further distinction must be made between celibacy as an ascetical or spiritual practice, celibacy in the history of christian monasticism and religious life, and clerical celibacy in the Roman Catholic Church.

1. Celibacy as an ascetical or spiritual practice manifests itself in some form in several of the great religious traditions and is not specifically christian, for example, the *brahmacarin* or *sannyasin* in the Hindu tradition, the *bodhisattva* in the Buddhist tradition, and the less

common practice among some Jewish rabbis and in the Essene sect of early Judaism. In these cases the specific motivation may not be the same although the practice of non-marriage or genital sexual abstinence is present. The rabbi who separated for a number of years from his wife for the sake of the study of Torah is not the same as the Hindu *sannyasin*, whose religious ideal culminates in a life of solitude.

2. Celibacy in the history of Christianity is not completely different from the practice of celibacy in the other religious traditions. It also has ascetical and monastic roots as well as apostolic origins. The origins of christian monasticism are traced back to Antony of Egypt (d. 356) and Pachomius (d. 346). Celibacy was a natural part of both eremitical and cenobitic monasticism. The life of the solitary, the monk, or the nun was seen as a radical commitment to Jesus Christ, and such expressions of discipleship particularly flourished after the age of the martyrs came to a close. Virginity and life-long asceticism were interpreted as another form of martyrdom.

The history and theology of celibacy thus partially parallels the history and theology of monasticism and the emergence of the mendicant and active religious orders. In addition to the ascetical and mystical motives for celibate life, there also developed the apostolic motives associated with lives of service, evangelical witness, and itinerant preaching. Celibacy cannot be understood univocally or as simply one thing in the life of the christian church. It is rather an expression of a multiplicity of motives.

Within Eastern Orthodoxy, celibacy exists in conjunction with Eastern monasticism but is not a requirement for priesthood. In the West there developed a clerical celibacy in addition to the celibacy as practiced in religious life. In modern Anglicanism and Protestantism

celibacy has emerged in conjunction with forms of community life. Noteworthy here is the ecumenical community of Taize.

3. Clerical celibacy is a Roman Catholic practice and refers to the obligation of celibacy required of candidates for the priesthood. Since the Second Vatican Council, Roman Catholicism has re-instituted a married diaconate but still requires celibacy of priests.

In the first centuries marriage was not considered an impediment to priesthood. The Synod of Elvira (c. 306), a Spanish synod, provides the earliest legislation. Canon 33 did not forbid marriage but decreed that bishops, presbyters, and deacons abstain sexually from their wives. The ecumenical Council of Nicaea in 325 did not impose celibacy on all priests but forbade marriage after the diaconate. In the tenth century there were still married clergy. The first ecumenical council to require celibacy of all the clergy was the First Lateran Council in 1123.

Since the Second Vatican Council the practice of clerical celibacy has been continued at the same time that it is being called into question for various theological and pastoral reasons. Theologically, some argue that celibacy is not intrinsic to the nature of priesthood itself, that celibate chastity can no longer be interpreted as a more complete perfection of the virtue of chastity than is conjugal chastity, that the practice of obligatory celibacy is historically influenced by a faulty, neo-Platonic understanding of sexuality, and that celibacy is by nature a charism that cannot be imposed. Some also argue against the practice of clerical celibacy for ecumenical reasons.

Pastoral arguments include that celibacy is an unnecessary burden imposed upon clergy, that ministry in the church benefits from the experience of a married clergy, that the present shortage of priestly vocations in many parts of the world is partially a consequence of an obligatory celibacy, and that ministry and even the opportunity for Eucharist suffer as a result of the priest shortage.

The Second Vatican Council in its decree on the priesthood (*Presbyterorum Ordinis,* 1965) encouraged continuing the practice of clerical celibacy (par. 16). In the encyclical letter *Sacerdotalis Caelibatus* (1967), Paul VI reaffirmed the practice. The revised code of canon law (1983) continues to require celibacy of the clergy (canons 277, 1037).

4. From a biblical perspective, the NT foundations for celibacy as a christian way of life include the example of Jesus, Mt 19:10-12, and 1 Cor 7:7-9, 25-38. Whether the Matthean text refers to celibacy as such is disputed today. Some exegetes argue that the word "eunuch" does not refer to someone unmarried but rather to someone whose spouse has been unfaithful and who must live "as a eunuch" since divorce and remarriage were not acceptable according to Jesus' teaching. The Pauline text makes it clear that Paul is expressing his own teaching and not that of Jesus and also that Paul is expressing his opinion in the context of an eschatological perspective that the end is near at hand.

5. From a theological perspective, the reasons for celibacy vary, as has already been stated. They include: the experience of a union with God that is understood as a "spiritual marriage," the spiritual desire for such a union, intimacy with God, a form of asceticism, a sign of the total consecration of one's life to God, an eschatological sign of living for eternal life, freedom from family responsibilities for the sake of giving oneself to the reign of God, apostolic availability and a life of service, and a counter-cultural witness to a christian value system. Celibacy ought not be interpreted over against christian marriage. Both are profoundly christian vocations, as are other forms of the single life.

Roman Catholic theology speaks of celibacy particularly as a gift and as a way of loving. It is a gift from God that is intended to be shared; the celibate person lives "for others." Celibate love is a pursuit of holiness, an expression of love for God, a sign of God's love and grace, a gift of one's self to others in community or through ministry.

6. From a psychological perspective, the motivation for celibacy has also been studied. Modern psychology has explicated unconscious factors as operative in decision making as well as conscious factors. Psychological factors do not necessarily invalidate a commitment to celibacy but rather can clarify a level of motivation that enhances one's freedom. The operative psychological factors can be a question of grace at work in human nature. God's presence in one's life and the human condition are not exclusive.

One can speak of three levels of motivations: the theological level at which celibacy is seen consciously as a christian ideal and way of life, the psychological level at which personal and unconscious factors are also operative, and finally the existential level at which a choice and commitment are made. A danger is focusing on either the first or second level to the exclusion of the other. At the existential level, the decision for a celibate life or a life of which celibacy is a part involves theology, spirituality, psychology, social awareness, and is ultimately experienced as God's call and one's response.

See **Monasticism, Priest, Religious Life**

P. Delhaye, "History of Celibacy," *The New Catholic Encyclopedia,* III (1967), 369-74. D. Goergen, *The Sexual Celibate* (1975). A. Greeley, *The Catholic Priest in the United States—Sociological Investigations* (1972). R. Gryson, *Les origines du célibat ecclésiastique* (1970). E. Kennedy and V. Heckler, *The Catholic Priest in the United States—Psychological Investigations* (1971). C. Kiesling, *Celibacy Prayer and Friendship* (1978). E. Schillebeeckx, *Celibacy* (1968); *The Church with a Human*

Face, (1985). S. Schneiders, "Non-Marriage for the Sake of the Kingdom," *Widening the Dialogue* (1974). M. Thurian, *Marriage and Celibacy* (1969).

                    DONALD J. GOERGEN, O P

CHALCEDON, COUNCIL OF

Convened by the Emperor Marcian with the reluctant consent of Pope Leo I, the Fourth Ecumenical Council met from October 8-31, 451, initially at Nicaea and then at Chalcedon, across the Bosporus from Constantinople. Ecclesiastical, political, and doctrinal concerns converged on its agenda. Ecclesiastically, the Council sealed the reversal of the so-called Robber Synod of Ephesus conducted two years previously by Dioscorus, Patriarch of Alexandria. Politically, the Council acceded to the Emperor's wish for a definition of faith with which to promote religious uniformity within his realm, although the outcome failed to fulfill this desire. Doctrinally, the Council continued the process of articulating the mystery of the Incarnation, a process that began at Nicaea (325) and would extend through III Constantinople (680); Chalcedon's contribution lay in formulating the dogma of the hypostatic union, which would provide subsequent christological reflection with its starting point, terms, and framework until the present century.

The Council Fathers initially resisted the Emperor's request for a new definition of the faith, citing Canon VII of the Council of Ephesus (431), which forbade composing or proffering to converts a creed other than that of Nicaea. In their early sessions they found it sufficient to approve two of the letters written by Cyril of Alexandria in his controversy with Nestorius and the Tome composed by Leo I ratifying Flavian's condemnation of the monk Eutyches at Constantinople. Acquiescing to continued imperial pressure, in their fifth session they approved a text to which the Roman legates took strong exception because of an ambiguity which it preserved; only after this had been revised was a final version approved.

The conciliar definition (D.S. 300-303) opens by linking doctrinal uniformity with Christ's gift of peace, citing John 14:27, and praises the Emperor's zeal. It states as the Council's purpose the expulsion of error and renewal of the faith of the Fathers, acknowledging the primary authority of the definition of Nicaea as well as the authority of I Constantinople. It cites in full both the creed and anathemas of Nicaea and I Constantinople's creed.

While the latter's exposition of the Trinity and Incarnation ought to be sufficient, the definition proceeds to specify the heresies which provide its own occasion. On the one hand are those who deny Mary the title Mother of God and thus reduce Jesus to a mere man; against them the Council has approved the synodical letters of Cyril. On the other hand are those who conceive the Incarnation as a mixture of the divine and the human resulting in a single nature in Christ and thus a passible divinity; against these the Council has acclaimed Leo's Tome.

There follows, finally, the Council's own contribution. Drawing its language from Cyril, Flavian, Leo, and others, it predicates of the Son, Jesus Christ, both complete divinity and complete humanity, balancing each affirmation of the former—that he is truly God, consubstantial with the Father and begotten of the Father before all ages—with an equally full affirmation of the latter—that he is truly man, composed of a rational soul and a body, consubstantial with us and born of the Virgin Mary, the Mother of God. At this point the definition moves beyond Nicaea's "consubstantial" to introduce two further non-biblical terms. Summing up the duality of divine and human attributes it has been confessing, it acknowledges that Christ exists in two "natures," each of which retains its own characteristics; because, however, Christ remains one, the definition proceeds to assert that each nature comes together in one "person." for the latter term it uses the Greek words *prosopon* and *hypostasis,* whence the phrase "hypostatic union."

In its immediate context the conciliar definition sought to respect the valid concerns of both parties, whose quarrels had been tearing apart the church in the East. With the Alexandrians it affirmed the strict unity of Christ as the agent of divine salvation; the Antiochene insistence on the integrity of that salvation as guaranteed by Christ's full humanity found expression in its confession that the natures, while inseparable, were in no way mixed or confused. At the same time it rejected the extremist distortions of the respective parties represented by Eutyches and, as it was thought, Nestorius. More broadly, the Council recapitulated the conciliar development which preceded it, incorporating Nicaea's confession of Christ's full divinity, I Constantinople's rejection of Apollinarius' truncation of Christ's full humanity, and Ephesus' accordance to Mary of the title Mother of God. With its dogma of the hypostatic union Chalcedon effected a restatement, not an explanation, of traditional belief in the mystery of the Incarnation.

Chalcedon's restatement with its key terms of substance, nature, and person was developed systematically into a metaphysical christology which served the church's needs into the modern period. Under the condition of contemporary culture, however, the conciliar definition appears not as the end of doctrinal development but as one moment, albeit privileged, in an ongoing christological process, while the historical and hermeneutical retrieval of its intelligibility constitutes one among the tasks of christology today.

One of the Council's disciplinary decrees deserves mention. Canon XXVIII ratified I Constantinople in according the city of Constantinople the rank of New Rome in the East and extended to the see jurisdiction over several provinces. This decree was not accepted by Pope Leo when he promulgated the works of the Council.

See **Jesus Christ**

A. Grillmeier, *Christ in Christian Tradition, Vol. I. From the Apostolic Age to Chalcedon (451),* 2nd ed., rev., Atlanta: John Knox, 1975. K. Rahner, "Current Problems in Christology," *Theological Investigations I,* New York: Seabury, 1974, pp. 149-200 (The original title of this essay was "Chalcedon—End or Beginning?"). R.V. Sellers, *The Council of Chalcedon,* London: S.P.C.K., 1953.

WILLIAM P. LOEWE

CHARACTER, SACRAMENTAL

The magisterium describes the nature of sacramental character in two places. The substance of the first statement from the *Decree for the Armenians* of the Council of Florence (1439) is contained in the second description from the Council of Trent (1545). In the face of Luther's assertion that sacramental character does not exist Trent affirmed that in baptism, confirmation and orders "a character is imprinted on the soul, a certain spiritual and indelible mark, and for this reason those sacraments cannot be repeated" (D. 1609). This text combines the assertion of the existence of character with the statement of the irrepeatability of three sacraments. The non-repeatability of these sacraments was taught as early as St. Augustine; descriptions of the specific term "sacramental character" arise only in the twelfth century.

In response to the third-century controversy about the rebaptism of heretics in which Cyprian (d. 258) and the Donatists held that heretical baptisms should be repeated, Augustine countered that they should not be repeated because despite involvement in heresy or sin, once baptized a person is never deprived of the sacrament (*De Bapt. contra Donat.* 5, 15, 20). Augustine maintains that it is Christ who baptizes, not the individual minister (*Contra Epistolam Parmeniani* II, 13, 28); hence whether the minister is a heretic or not does not affect the permanent and lasting value of the sacrament administered. To describe the permanent effect of baptism Augustine does not use the term "character" but rather the words *sacramentum* (sacrament), *sanctitas* (sanctity), *consecratio* (consecration), *baptismus* (baptism), and *ordinatio* (ordination). Where he uses the term "character" it is in connection with the invocation of the Trinity in the baptismal formula.

The notion of "seal" in the Tridentine definition recalls the Greek term *sphragis* which is used in Greek patristic authors to signify what is produced in the soul by the sacrament. Authors refer to Rev 7:2-8, 2 Cor 1:22, and Eph 1:13, 4:30 as scriptural background for this term. The baptismal *sphragis* is a mark of the Holy Spirit that designates a person as part of the flock of Christ; hence it is a sign of divine protection. In the Latin West at this period parallel discussions take place about *spiritale signaculum* but these are much less frequent than in the East.

In the thirteenth century theologians clearly assert the presence of "sacramental character" itself. In 1201 Pope Innocent III (d. 1216) distinguished between sacramental character and the grace bestowed in these sacraments. The character remains independent of the subjective dispositions of the recipient. His successor, Pope Gregory IX (d. 1241), mentions the character of ordination. Alexander of Hales (d. 1245) systematizes his teaching by asserting that baptism, confirmation and orders confer sacramental character and that character is an ontological reality adhering logically to the soul. For Alexander, and Bonaventure after him (d. 1274) it is a *habitus* which marks the soul and disposes the baptized to receive grace.

Thomas Aquinas' (d. 1274) treatment is the best known. Contrary to Alexander before him, Aquinas teaches that character is a *potentia* not a *habitus*, and as a spiritual power it deputes the recipient to engage in acts of divine worship (S.Th. 3a, 63, 2). Character also imparts a share in the priesthood of Christ to those so marked. Appealing to 2 Cor 1:21-22 Aquinas states that character means nothing else than the imparting of a certain kind of sign. Therefore ... through the sacraments God imparts his own character upon us" (S.Th. 3a, 63, 1). For him the emphasis is placed not on the sign itself but the purpose for which it is used, that is a relationship to the church and a commission to participate in its acts of worship. Duns Scotus (d. 1308) on the other hand, held that character was a mere relation extrinsically created by God between the soul and the family of Christ. Yet, for Scotus character is a relation that has an ontological reality as its foundation.

In 1439 the Council of Florence did not refer to (but did not deny) an extrinsic understanding of character; rather it spoke of character as an "impress" on the soul. It declared that among the seven sacraments baptism, confirmation and orders "imprint a character on the soul, that is, a certain indelible sign which distinguishes these from others" (D. 1313). This statement clearly led to Trent's assertions about character.

Modern writing on sacramental character separates what derives from baptism and confirmation from what derives from orders. In *Mediator Dei* Pius XII encouraged development on the association between the character of baptism and the "priesthood of the laity."

Contemporary theologians speak of sacramental character in christological and ecclesiological terms. Edward Schillebeeckx argues that the sacraments which impart a character incorporate one into the body of Christ (baptism), give one a commission to take part in the church's activity of witnessing to and bestowing her Spirit particularly through worship (confirmation) and of holding an office in the church (orders), which office is understood in relation to all other charisms which express Christ's saving power and presence. Karl Rahner describes character in terms consonant with his understanding that all sacraments are phases in the process of the church's self-realization as the primordial sacrament.

See **Baptism, Confirmation, Orders, Sacrament, Worship**

KEVIN W. IRWIN

CHARISM

The Greek word *charisma* means free gift, favor. It is Paul who introduced the term into religious language: the word means a free gift of grace. To be more precise, it is a supernatural gift bestowed by the Holy Spirit for building up the body of Christ. A charism is a gift which has its source in the *charis*—grace or favor—of God and which is destined for "the common good" (1 Cor 12:7). This being so, charisms are many and are related to various services and functions. For our purpose it will suffice to look to Paul's treatment of them.

Paul's lists of charismatic gifts do not presume to be exhaustive. Some of those he lists are a constant feature of the life of the church, while others are conditioned by particular circumstances. For the most part the charisms take the form of services within the christian communities. In 1 Cor 12:4-11, which is his fullest classification of charisms, Paul groups them in categories of intellectual gifts, miraculous works, and works of service; and he refers the first to the Holy Spirit, the second to God, and the third to the Lord (12:4-5). He gave a higher place to the service of teaching than to the gifts of tongues. To teach the mystery of Christ in an enlightened and enlightening way one must be specially equipped with the gift of wisdom. The gift of exhortation enables the pastor to speak the admonishing and consoling word. But the gift of prophecy easily holds the foremost place. The prophet speaks to people "for their upbuilding and encouragement and consolation" (14:3). He is the one who reveals the "mystery" of the divine economy of salvation in Christ.

Not surprisingly the christian mission is a privileged area of charisms. If there are apostles it is because God has designated them (1 Cor 12:28, 30), and God's designation always carries with it the apposite endowment. The gift strengthens the apostle to proclaim boldly the good news of the glorified Lord. Paul himself bases his preaching of the message of salvation on the power of the Spirit (2:4-5, 13). Since the characteristic of christian life is (or ought to be) *agapē*, one would expect to find charisms in the service of love. The Spirit gives the grace of *diakonia,* of loving service (Rom 12:7). The charismatic gift of assistance is present at the birth of every notable charitable work of the church. In general, the gift inspires and makes fruitful the love and labor of christian men and women who courageously and generously spend themselves for others. Paul has a complementary list of charisms in Rom 12:6-8; there are parallel lists in Eph 4:11-12; 1 Pet 4:10-11. We may sum up the NT data as follows: because a charism is a gift of the Spirit for the building up of the church it is always meant for the common good; it has upon it the stamp of service. Needs vary and charisms are many and varied. Broadly speaking, we may specify the areas of teaching, of mission and of fraternal love. Accordingly, there are gifts of wisdom and of prophecy, gifts of the apostolate, the gift of *diakonia*. And there are those who have received the gifts: apostles, prophets, teachers, healers, helpers, administrators, and speakers in tongues.

Assessment

The whole long section of 1 Cor 12:4 -14:10 is devoted to the relative merits of the spiritual gifts. The significant—and no doubt for Paul's readers disturbing— point of his analysis is his insistence that not only is there a variety of gifts but that there is a variety of *service* and that the gifts are, essentially, gifts of service. It is not likely that the Corinthians had so regarded them. Their predilection for tongues had led to dissension and Paul is determined to stress unity. It is evident that Paul is replying to a query of the Corinthians and it is not difficult to guess what they would have liked his answer to be. They valued the gift of tongues above all others. Paul does not think it enough to declare that they are mistaken: he wants them to understand why they are mistaken. Tongues is but one of a great variety of gifts—all of which, he is careful to insist, come from one and the same Spirit. And all of these gifts are for the building up of the christian community. Just as the human body is an organic structure with many members having different functions, so the body of Christ is complex and has many Spirit-inspired ministries. No one person or no one group can function for the whole body.

The Corinthians' question to Paul had been: which is the highest gift or, more precisely, it seems to have been whether prophecy or tongue-speaking is the higher gift. Paul is not content to settle the matter on this level, to set off one against the other. There is "the more excellent way" (12:31) of love in the light of which

all the other gifts may be evaluated. At first sight 1 Cor 13 seems an intrusion, interrupting the natural flow of chap. 12 into chap. 14. These two chapters are concerned with the charisms; it might appear that this turn to *agapē* is a digression. In fact the treatment of *agapē* is vital to Paul's argument. He sketches his "more excellent way" in terms of the example of Jesus, in sharp contrast to the behavior of the Corinthians (cf 1 Cor 1-3). Christian love bears the stamp of one who came not to be served but to serve; it is a love that is all-embracing and shows itself in deeds of love. And unlike the charisms which are transient, love will not pass away. The highest gift is nothing other than love—and it is the measure of all others. By his chap. 13 Paul has paved the way for an answer to the question: which spiritual gift does one prefer? And his answer is, firmly, that gift which contributes most fruitfully to the life of the community. Prophecy takes a foremost place.

Prophecy

We know from Acts that prophetism was a feature of the early church (Acts 11:27-28; 13:1-2; 15:32; 21:8-9; 21:11). In general the emergence of NT prophets might be said to constitute a true awakening of OT-style prophetism. Paul lets us have some idea of its nature and its scope. In 1 Thess 5:19 he urges: "Do not quench the Spirit, do not despise prophesying"; prophecy is not to be despised because it is nothing short of word of the Spirit spoken through the prophet to the church. The prophet is one who "speaks to men for their upbuilding and encouragement and consolation"; he is one who "edifies the church" (1 Cor 14:3-4).

There can be little doubt that in at least some of the early communities the prophet held a recognized and respected place. However, there were dangers, especially in a Hellenistic environment like that of Corinth. While Jewish

Christians would spontaneously associate the new christian prophets with their OT predecessors, Gentile Christians, in areas like Corinth, would have been more familiar with the oracular features of pagan cults. Paul is conscious of the need for a "discernment of spirits." He proposes a basic criterion in 1 Cor 12:3—to make the profession "Jesus is Lord" is to prophesy; whereas the denial of Jesus is patently not due to the Holy Spirit. In other words, the yardstick by which prophecy may be measured is faith in Christ and the unqualified profession of that faith. Furthermore, "the spirits of prophets are subject to the prophets" (14:32): the authentic prophet will be able to discern what is truly of God. Just as the OT prophet could confidently declare *koh amar Yahweh* ("Thus says Yahweh"), the christian prophet, sensitive to the Spirit, will be quite sure that he speaks truly in the name of the Lord Jesus.

Tongues

Luke, in Acts, several times refers to speaking in tongues; and always he associates the gift with an initial outpouring of the Spirit. When the Spirit fell upon the Twelve at Pentecost they began to speak in tongues (2:4-12). He represents them as speaking in various specific languages. Indeed, as Luke describes the situation, it would be more accurate to think of a gift of *hearing*. At any rate, what we have here is Luke's own interpretation of the gift of tongues: it marks the dramatic opening of the apostles' world-mission. The statement in 4:31— "And they were all filled with the Holy Spirit and spoke the word of God with boldness"—while not referring to glossolalia, represents, for Luke, a situation not very different from the Pentecost one.

Paul takes the gift of tongues to be a regular occurrence at the christian assemblies—at least it was so at Corinth. In 1 Cor 14 he describes this rather perplexing gift. The Christian who speaks in tongues addresses God and not humans (14:2)—it is a gift of prayer. Further he observes (14:2) that there is a notable strangeness about this gift and this strangeness raises obvious difficulties. In contrast to the gift of prophecy, which directly contributes to the building up of the church, tongues may help the individual but is of no use to the congregation (14:4). Paul firmly sets glossolalia last of all in the train of *agapē*. He does not despise the gift; he himself speaks in tongues. The fact remains that when measured by the standard he has invoked throughout—the building up of the community—it is found wanting. Speaking in tongues is mysterious prayer— more often than not mysterious even to the one who prays. A parallel gift of interpretation is needed if one is to be understood. If there is to be prayer in tongues in a christian assembly, it should be properly ordered: the Spirit is a Spirit of peace and harmony, not of confusion. "So, my brethren, earnestly desire to prophesy, and do not forbid speaking in tongues; but all things should be done decently and in order" (14:39-40).

In our day, with the emergence of the charismatic movement, there has been a fresh interest in the charisms. The importance of Paul is paramount. One might say that 1 Cor 12-14 should be required reading for all involved with or interested in the movement. There we find a critique of charisms by one who acknowledges himself to be a charismatic. Besides, the various lists of charisms, not only in Paul but elsewhere in the NT, none of which purports to be exhaustive, is a salutary reminder that, while there has been a later tendency to limit charisms to more unusual manifestations, the early christian view was to see *charisma,* gifts of the Spirit, in every gift or endowment that contributed to the "building up" of a christian community, the building up of the body of Christ.

See **Charismatic Movement, Grace, Love**

J.D.G. Dunn, *Jesus and the Spirit,* London: SCM, 1975. G.T. Montague, *The Holy Spirit,* N.Y.: Paulist 1976, pp. 145-184. W. Harrington, *Spirit of the Living God,* Wilmington, DE: M. Glazier, 1977, pp. 141-171.

WILFRID HARRINGTON, OP

CHARISMATIC MOVEMENT

The charismatic renewal movement is a comparatively unstructured current in christian spirituality, without membership lists, dues, or specific obligations. It consists in an experience of an intimate personal relationship with Jesus Christ and in a spiritual empowering by his Holy Spirit. This empowering takes the form of a strong appreciation for the ways of the Lord working in the church and for God's word in the Bible, graces of prayer and especially of contemplative prayer, praying in tongues, and witnessing to the faith with courage. In addition, the Lord's way is illustrated in the use of charisms such as prophecy, intercessory prayer, praying with great efficacy for healing, spiritual leadership, evangelization, the discernment of spirits, spiritual combat, and other gifts of the Spirit.

This spiritual experience begins with a new outpouring of grace, often called the "baptism in the Holy Spirit." Not a sacrament, nor even a sacramental, the baptism in the Holy Spirit is the Lord's answer to prayer, usually to the prayer of a group who lay hands on the person asking God for a new outpouring of the Holy Spirit and who pray that the Spirit come to that person in a new way. Catholic teaching holds that everyone in the state of grace has the Holy Spirit, but that on some rare occasions, the Holy Spirit can come to a person in a great fullness and in a life-transforming way; this is the baptism in the Holy Spirit, a Pentecostal experience on the pattern of the first Pentecost when the Spirit descended on the disciples gathered with Mary in the upper room.

Many Pentecostal churches hold the baptism in the Spirit "invalid," not to have taken place, unless accompanied by speaking in tongues, and that may be true for those churches. For Catholics, however, the baptism in the Spirit can authentically take place with or without the person praying in tongues at the time. Frequently, the gift of tongues comes later. This gift, sometimes received as a gift of prophesying in tongues (and any prophecy in tongues needs interpretation), is more commonly received as a gift of prayer, for use in personal prayer especially and also in group worship (for example, in a prayer group or at a "charismatic Mass"). Praying in tongues is a kind of contemplation, vocalized contemplative prayer.

Charisms common in charismatic renewal are prophecy, preaching, teaching, spiritual combat and deliverance from demonic influence, praying for healing, inspired prayer, intercessory prayer, and evangelization. Each of the charisms is a gift given to some persons, not to all, to be used in the power of the Spirit for some useful purpose. (See especially 1 Cor 12-14; Rom 12:4-8; Eph 4:4-13).

The charismatic movement is a major current in the overall Pentecostal movement. "The charismatic movement" or "the charismatic renewal" is the name usually given to Pentecostalism as it has taken shape in the main Protestant Churches and in the Orthodox and Roman Catholic Churches.

Pentecostalism began in the United States at the beginning of the twentieth century, but it has strong roots in the nineteenth-century American revivalism and in the Holiness movement in the Methodist Church in the United States.

The Methodist Holiness movement preached the need for a second conversion, a "second blessing," and called it a Pentecostal experience, a "baptism in the Holy Spirit." Evangelical revivalism also held a second conversion experience and called it a baptism in the Holy Spirit for an empowerment to live a full and vigorous christian life and to give witness to Jesus Christ.

In the first few days of 1901, Charles F. Parham and several of his students, after several days of fervent prayer that the Holy Spirit would come upon them, experienced a "baptism in the Holy Spirit" and spoke in tongues. In 1906, one of Parham's former students began to preach a Pentecostal revival in an old church on Azusa Street in Los Angeles. The revival went on without interruption, day and night, for over three years. Thousands prayed in tongues, were healed, were freed from demonic influence, prophesied, and praised God "in the Holy Spirit." The Azusa Street revival sent ripples all across the United States, and to Canada, Latin America, Europe, and Asia.

Many of the participants in the early Pentecostal movement belonged to the Methodist, Baptist, and Presbyterian Churches. These churches, however, found themselves unable to assimilate the typical Pentecostal religious behavior: tongue speaking and singing, healing, deliverance from evil spirits, prophecy, and comparatively unrestrained enthusiasm in worship. Pentecostal groups broke off from these churches and formed independent sects. Several of these groups joined in 1914 to create the Assemblies of God; other sects came together to form other churches. But sects proliferated and, in fact, new Pentecostal churches even today come into existence from groups that have broken away from already constituted Pentecostal bodies. The Pentecostal churches, particularly in Latin America and in Africa, have for several decades had a phenomenal growth rate that shows no signs of abating.

The charismatic renewal, or charismatic movement, in its early years often called neo-Pentecostalism, began in 1960 in Van Nuys, California, when an Episcopalian priest, the Reverend Dennis Bennett, received the baptism of the Holy Spirit. Forced to resign from his post as rector of his church, he moved to Seattle and had great success in parish ministry as well as in helping the Pentecostal current to spread, through clergymen with whom he prayed, to various Protestant churches.

The Catholic charismatic renewal began at Duquesne University, Pittsburgh, in February 1967, when two Catholic professors received the baptism in the Holy Spirit at a prayer meeting of Episcopalian participants in the charismatic movement. The two Catholics then took part with several Duquesne students in a weekend retreat during which the retreatants experienced the power of God's love, found themselves praising God and speaking in tongues, and were overwhelmed by a great outpouring of grace. Some of these soon prayed with other Catholics. And in early April 1967, about one hundred students from the University of Notre Dame and from Michigan State University, along with several other laypersons and some priests, met at Notre Dame to pray and to share their experiences of the preceding few weeks in which they had received the baptism in the Holy Spirit and various charismatic gifts. From this meeting, the Catholic charismatic renewal spread rapidly, at first on university campuses, and soon after to parishes, monasteries, and convents. Within a year, most American cities with large Catholic populations had a predominantly Catholic prayer group that met at least weekly to sing, to pray in tongues, and to use the charismatic gifts. These prayer groups attracted other Catholics, who in turn received the baptism in the Holy Spirit together with charisms of worship and ministry.

Within a few years, Catholic charismatic prayer groups met weekly or more often not only in North America but also in Europe, Africa, Asia, and Latin America. Within twenty years, there were according to a Vatican estimate about thirty million Catholic "charismatics" all over the world. In May, 1987, representative leaders from well over one hundred countries met in Rome where Pope John Paul II, as he had in 1981 and in 1984, encouraged them and praised the charismatic renewal in the Catholic Church.

See **Charism, Holy Spirit, Prayer**

Walter J. Hollenweger, *The Pentecostals,* trans. by R.A. Wilson, Minneapolis: Augsburg Pub. House, 1972. Kilian McDonnell, *Presence, Power, Praise: Documents on the Charismatic Renewal* (3 vols.), Collegeville, Min.: Liturgical Press, 1980. Watson E. Mills, *Charismatic Religion in Modern Research: A Bibliography,* Macon, Ga.: Mercer Univ. Press, 1985. Richard Quebedeaux, *The New Charismatics,* New York: Doubleday, 1976. Francis A. Sullivan, *Charisms and Charismatic Renewal,* Ann Arbor: Servant Books, 1982. Vincent M. Walsh, *A Key to Charismatic Renewal in the Catholic Church,* St. Meinrad, Ind.: Abbey Press, 1974.

ROBERT FARICY, SJ

CHARITY
See **Love**

CHASTITY
See **Evangelical Counsels, Sexuality**

CHRISM

Chrism is the oil of olives (or of some other plant) mixed with a perfume to give a pleasing fragrance which is blessed by the bishop at the Chrism Mass every year and used in the post-baptismal anointing, confirmation, ordination of priests and bishops, and dedication of churches and altars. It is a sacrament which has always been given great reverence by the church. It is often reserved in a special place in the sanctuary along with oil of the sick and catechumens. The strengthening effect and fragrance of the oil reflect the presence of the Holy Spirit when one is anointed with it.

See **Anointing**

JOSEPH L. CUNNINGHAM

CHRISTENING

Christening is the way one is incorporated into Christ by means of the sacraments of Initiation. *Christ* means *anointed* and through baptism and confirmation one is anointed with water and oil. By ritually imitating the dying (through drowning) and the rising to new life with Christ, one becomes like him. Each baptized person shares the priestly, prophetic and kingly roles of Christ in this conformity. One is initiated into and becomes a member of the church by this ritual. "Christening" is frequently used as a synonym for "baptism" alone. Christening also refers to naming a person in the ceremony of baptism.

See **Initiation, Christian**

JOSEPH L. CUNNINGHAM

CHURCH
I. The Word
  A. Etymology and Meaning.
    1 *"Church."* the English word "church," like its equivalents in the other Germanic languages, derives from the Greek adjective *kuriakos,* meaning "belonging to he Lord." It would have been shorthand originally for *kuriakon doma* or *kuriakos domos*—meaning "the Lord's house."

So its first reference would be to the building in which Christians met for worship—and perhaps that is still the first and dominant reference in ordinary English.

But it was always used in versions of the scriptures to translate the Greek word *ekklesia,* and the first reference of this word is not to a building but to an official assembly of people. So that becomes the secondary, and for the purposes of this article the most important, reference of the word "church." We shall throughout treat is simply as the equivalent of *ekklesia.*

2. Ekklesia. This Greek word is derived from the verb *ekkaleo,* "to summon" or "to call out." Its closest equivalent in Latin and hence in English is *convocatio,* "convocation"—"a calling together," "an assembly." It was the official term for the citizens' assembly of the Athenian democracy. It is used in this secular sense in Acts 19:32, 39 and 41 (RSV "assembly") in the account of the stirring events at Ephesus.

But the NT use of the word is controlled almost entirely by its employment in the OT LXX to translate, with remarkable consistency, the hebrew *qahal,* which has much the same basic meaning of "a convoked assembly." In the strongest sense the *qahal* is the assembly of Israel convoked by God (e.g., Deut 5:19, 23:2-9, 1 Chr 28:8, Num 16:3, 20:4, Mic 2:5).

A synonymous term is *'edah,* which LXX usually translates by *sunagoge.* After the exile this becomes the regular, almost technical word for the sabbath day meeting of Jews for prayer and study of the *torah,* and hence secondarily for the building in which the meeting took place. This secondary reference is the only one found for *sunagoge* in the NT, with the exception of Rev 3:9.

This left the way open for the first christian communities to take over *qahal/ ekklesia* to denominate their own meet-

ings or assemblies. And thus in the course of polemical centuries "church" and "synagogue" became a classic contrasting pair.

B. *References of* Ekklesia. 1) It comes eventually, like "church," to be used to refer to the building in which Christians meet for worship. But it is never used with this kind of reference in the NT—no doubt because Christians at that time did not have any special buildings for worship. This is in any case a use or reference of the word which we shall not be considering further in this article. So here is the place to say something about the theological interest of this reference before closing the subject.

The connection between "church" as building and "church" as community of worshippers goes a little deeper than simple metonymy. The building is spontaneously seen as a symbol of the community; and since the church community is the body of Christ (see below, II, a, 4), churches come to be built deliberately to represent, in a variety of ways, Christ himself. The most obvious way is by their common cruciform ground-plan. Then again, the church community is also the temple of God or of the Holy Spirit (see below, II, b, 1); so christian churches, especially the more prestigious cathedrals and basilicas, take on some of the aura of the Israelite temple in Jerusalem. Thus christian architecture becomes a means, not only of "sermons in stones," but also of increasingly assimilating the religion and church of the NT to the religion and people of the OT. Christian communities began by being, so to say, little nodes of secularization in an excessively sacral pagan world. Eventually, with their churches as so many houses of God, encrusted with the richest sacramental symbolism, holy places and shrines of saints and martyrs, they found themselves committed to resacralizing that world.

2) The primary reference of *ekklesia* in the NT is to the actual assembly meeting for worship (1 Cor 11:18, 14:19, 35). But from this use it is immediately extended to refer to the community of the faithful in any given place, to the local community (e.g., Mt 18:17, though the reference here could be to the actual meeting of the faithful; Acts 5:11, 8:1, 3, 15:22, all these being references to the church in Jerusalem; Acts 13:1, Rom 16:1, 1 Cor 4:17, Col 4:16, 1 Thess 1:1, etc). This is by far the most common use of the world in the NT. One could thus define a church as a community of Christians established in a particular locality and accustomed to meet regularly together for worship; something very like a Jewish synagogue, and indeed almost certainly modeled on it.

3) Much less often the word has a more general reference to the community of the faithful at large. One hesitates to say that it is used to refer to the universal church, because that suggests a universally organized society, if only in embryo; and nothing like that existed, or was even envisaged by the first christian generations. The reference is rather to the church as a mystical idea, not tied down to any particular place (Mt 16:18, though possibly the reference here is to the *qahal* of a renewed and restored Israel; Eph 1:22, 3:10, 5:23-24, Col 1:18). There are a number of passages where *ekklesia* is commonly interpreted as having this universal reference, but this is a matter of reading our contemporary assumptions into the text. For us "the church," unless otherwise qualifed, is always assumed to be the universal church. But this is unlikely to have been the assumption of NT writers. Thus it would seem that all instances of *ekklesia* in Paul's reflections on the body of Christ, 1 Cor 12-14, are making reference to the local community.

4) After the NT the universal reference does gradually become more concrete in ecclesiastical texts. The adjective "catholic" first appears attached to *ekklesia* in Ignatius of Antioch about 109 (*Smyrn.* 8). From then on this reference becomes more and more common and eventually dominant, though perhaps in the creeds ("in the holy catholic church," "in one, holy, catholic and apostolic church") it remains at the level of the church as a mystical idea, rather than of the church as a specific world-wide society.

The use of the word with reference to local communities, of course, continues in frequent use. But complications set in. It is not always, as in the NT, a reference to a local community in one place, presided over by a bishop. From this level of local particularity it gets extended to regions, provinces, and eventually nations (even continents nowadays), so that one may talk about the Syrian or Numidian church, and later on of the French, English or Irish church, and nowadays of the Latin-American or African church. Thus the use of the word with a local reference is very elastic. But whether the word is primarily given a local or a universal reference is of definite theological significance.

5) As a result of schisms and divisions among Christians the word "church" has come to be used frequently with a denominational reference, as in "the Methodist Church," "the Lutheran Church," "the Roman Catholic Church," "the Orthodox Churches," etc. Such denominational reference is sometimes coterminous with a kind of local reference, as with "the Church of Scotland," "the Church of England," "the Russian Orthodox Church," etc. So the denominational reference, while clearly unavoidable in the actual condition of the christian world, may be said to have an anti-theological significance, in that it only serves to obscure the true value and significance of applying the word both to local communities and to the total

community of believers in Christ.

II. New Testament Images of Church

A. Images of the Kingdom of God. In the gospels, especially in the so-called parables of the kingdom, a number of images are employed to illustrate the mystery of the kingdom of God—mustard seed, leaven, hidden treasure, a field of wheat and its sowing, a fishing net or boat, a flock of sheep and a sheepfold, and so on. In the church's exegetical and homiletic tradition these images are all applied to the church itself. The question arises how far this is legitimate; that is to say, how legitimate is it to identify the church with the kingdom of God.

To say without qualification that the church is the kingdom and the kingdom is the church is indeed bad exegesis and bad theology, especially when "the church" in this equation is taken to refer, denominationally, to the Roman Catholic Church (or to any other denomination). This is the vice of "triumphalism," and is possibly what was being criticized in the *bon mot* of Loisy that Jesus came proclaiming the kingdom of God, and what resulted was the church.

But the NT itself authorizes a qualified identification of the church with the kingdom, and a sound exegesis of the parables requires it. A key text is Exod 19:6, "You shall be to me a kingdom of priests and a holy nation," applied to the christian community by 1 Pet 2:9 and Rev 1:6, 5:10. The church, local or universal, represents the inauguration of the kingdom, the sowing of the seed, the casting of the net, the calling of the sheep. It is the kingdom in process, *in fieri*. And as such it is full of tares, and bad fish, and goats, and scandals; it is *ecclesia semper reformanda*. It is not, in other words, the kingdom in its perfection or completion, though it is directed towards the kingdom in that sense. It is only the church of the ultimate future that may be fully identified with the kingdom of God, the church

already realized in the angels and the saints (the church triumphant of a later terminology), to which perhaps reference is made in Heb 12:23 as "the *ekklesia* (RSV assembly) of the first-born who are enrolled in heaven" (see below, b, 2).

B. Images of the Church in the rest of the NT.

1. The Church as Temple. Long before Christians had buildings they called churches, which they could treat as symbols of their proper identity, their first apostles and teachers had seized on God's temple in Jerusalem as a fitting image of the *ekklesia* (local or universal, but chiefly local). Perhaps this statement is not quite accurate: rather they had seen the *ekklesia* as replacing the temple, as the new house or dwelling-place of God, once his presence had departed from the temple when the veil was torn in two from top to bottom (Mk 15:38).

Indeed, this image has its origins in the gospels and in a well known saying of Jesus about destroying the temple and building another in three days, which was made one of the charges against him at his trial (Jn 2:19; Mk 14:58, 15:29, cf 13:1). What it tells us about the church is not only that it is to be the dwelling-place of God, and therefore a holy and innocent community, intimately associated with Jesus Christ the cornerstone (1 Pet 2:1-7; cf Mk 12:10), but also that it may in a sense be identified with Christ, since he too is the new temple (Jn 2:21). And furthermore there is also possible an identification of the individual believer both with Christ and with the church. For Paul tells us that individually we are the temple of the Holy Spirit (1 Cor 6:19), as well as the christian community being God's temple (1 Cor 3:16, 2 Cor 6:16, Eph 2:21).

2. The Church as Zion or Jerusalem. This image seems to have no connection with the previous one, though on the face of it they look similar. This one derives

from the visions of a restored Jerusalem in Second Isaiah, and gives us a plainly eschatological view of the church; the church as the perfect kingdom of God of the future, or as the present anticipation of that final future. This is most clear in the vision of "the holy city, new Jerusalem, coming down out of heaven from God" at the end of Revelation (21:2). But it is also implicit in the "heavenly Jerusalem" and the "Jerusalem above" of Heb 12:22 and Gal 4:26. In all these cases the reference is clearly to the church in general, not in this or that locality, but to the church as a mystical idea, which is however anticipated in any christian community. A point of interest about this image is that because of a prominent feature of the Isaian imagery, taken up in Rev 21:2, it is closely connected to our next image, and leads into it (See Isa 54, 61, 62).

3. The Church as the <u>Bride of Christ</u>. Besides the text just quoted, this image occurs in 2 Cor 11:2 and Eph 5:22-32. In the first instance the reference is to the local church of Corinth, and is supporting an appeal to them for fidelity; in the second it is vaguer, to the church in general, and is introduced to back an exhortation to husbands and wives to love each other, like Christ and his church. There is no strong eschatological overtone, as when the image is combined with that of the heavenly Jerusalem.

What these two images do have in common, though, is their continuity with the OT. The church is heir, not only to the symbolic values of Jerusalem, but also to Israel's symbolic marital relationship with the Lord. So these two images have a close affinity with the concept of the church as the new "Israel of God" (Gal 6:16).

4. The Church as the <u>Body of Christ</u>. This is undoubtedly the most important of the images applied to the church in the NT. It clearly proclaims the closest pos-

sible identification of the church with Jesus Christ, and in this respect it is related to the image of the church as temple. The two in fact get mixed, as in Eph 4:12, "for building up the body of Christ." The idea of a temple somehow representing the body of the deity for whom it was constructed is very ancient and widespread. The concept may well have come into Israel from the Phoenicians who provided Solomon with the model for his temple of Yahweh.

The image is not found in the gospels, but its inspiration is there in Jesus' identification of himself with the least of his brethren (e.g. Mt 25:40, 45). In the two chief *loci* for the image, Romans 12 and 1 Corinthians 12, the reference is very concretely to the members of the local community. It is to be noted that in neither passage does the word "church" actually occur; in the first we have the expression "we, though many, are one body in Christ" (Rom 12:5), and in the second "Now you are the body of Christ, and individually members of it" (1 Cor 12:27). In the next verse, it is true, Paul does mention "the church": "And God has appointed in the church first apostles, second prophets," etc. Given the context, and the very personal tone of his letter to the Corinthians, the reference here too is best understood as being to the local community.

In 1 Cor 10:16-17 the image of the community as the body of Christ is implicitly connected with the eucharist: "The bread which we break, is it not a participation in the body of Christ? Because there is one loaf, we who are many are one body, for we all partake of the same loaf." This connection will be of great significance for St. Augustine's theology of the eucharist—and indeed of the church.

In Eph 1:22-23 and in the related texts Col 1:18, 24 the reference seems to be to the church as mystery or mystical idea—

or the church in general. The same is probably the case with Eph 4:12, though here the reference could be more concrete and local. But the chief difference between the texts in Romans and 1 Corinthians on the one hand, and Ephesians and Colossians on the other, is that the latter make a clear *distinction* between Christ as the head and the church as his body, whereas the former pronounce an *identification* of Christ with his body (head and all) the church. And so in Ephesians 5 the writer can, so to say, merge the image of the church as Christ's body (vv 23, 30) with that of the church as his bride (vv 25-27, 31-32). In both cases the dominant concept is that of Christ the head. And so the practical lesson drawn is one of obedience, whereas in Romans and 1 Corinthians it is one of mutual respect, forebearance and co-operation.

III. Theological Models of the Church

For the category of "models of the church" I am indebted to Avery Dulles' book of that name. But I shall use only three models, and perhaps I am not using the term in altogether the same sense as he. By a model I simply mean a way of envisaging the church. There are, of course, many legitimate ways of doing this. Below I choose the three most important and inescapable ways. I shall try to trace the first model through the course of the church's history. For perhaps the most significant thing about the church (churches) is its (their) involvement in human history.

A. *Church as People of God: i.e., As Observable Social Reality, Institutionally Structured.* This is a rather clumsy formulation of a model. Many prefer "church as institution." But what they mean by that (or what I suggest they should mean) is something like the formulation I have proposed. It is not strictly accurate to call the church an institution, any more than a nation or even a state can be called an institution.

These are all social entities which contain many institutions, and are organized or structured by means of various institutions. So too the church. It is true that in this section our attention will be mainly focused on the institutions by which the church is structured as a visible society; as what Bellarmine called "a perfect society"; as what I prefer to call, following the lead of *Lumen Gentium* 9-17, "the people of God." But "institution" is not, as I am using the term, my model.

We shall briefly sketch the changes that the institutional structures of the church have undergone in the course of its history. It should constantly be born in mind that the word "church" can have a double reference, either to the local or to the universal christian community (see above, I, b, 2 & 3). In general, there is a shift from the predominance of the local reference in the early centuries to the universal in the second millennium.

1. c. 30-330: The Church of the Apostles to the Age of Constantine. Throughout this period the dominant reference of the word is to the local community, just as we have seen that it was in the letters of the NT. It is true, the word "catholic" makes its first appearance as a qualification of the church fairly early on in this period, in the letter of Ignatius of Antioch "to the church of God the Father and of the beloved Jesus Christ which is at Smyrna in Asia" (*Smyrn.* 1)—that is a characteristic use of "church" with a local reference. In *Smyrn.* 8 he writes, "Wherever the bishop appears, there let the people be; as wherever Jesus Christ is, there is the catholic church." Even here, however, the reference is to the general mystery of the church, as embodied or localized in any local community. It is not a reference to a world-wide, universal, organized society such as we mean nowadays when we talk about the catholic church—for the simple reason that such an

organized, universal society scarcely existed.

What manifestly existed were many local communities or churches, like those to which Ignatius wrote his letters, which were united by bonds of fraternal fellowship (were "in communion" with each other), but by few if any institutional links. From the beginning there seems to have been very great variety among these churches in custom, liturgy and organization; e.g., between the Pauline, Johannine, Petrine and Matthaean churches. (See Raymond E. Brown, *The Community of the Beloved Disciple* and *The Churches the Apostles Left Behind*). By the middle of the second century all the churches appear to have shaken down to a common order of an *episkopos, presbyteroi* and *diakonoi* in each church. I refrain from giving them their usual English equivalents of "bishop, priests and deacons," because at that time they had few if any of the hierarchical and sacerdotal connotations that they have acquired since. They were simple secular titles: the *episkopos* was overseer or superintendent of the community, the *presbyteroi* were its elders (a derivation from the synagogue), and the *diakonoi* its servants. It was only gradually that first the *episkopos* came to be thought of as the *hiereus, sacerdos* or priest of the community (third century), and then that several centuries later the presbyters came to be regarded sacerdotally as priests—until from medieval times on they have been assumed (quite wrongly) to be the *primum analogatum* of the concept of priesthood.

By the third century institutional links between the local churches were already extensively developed on a regional basis. Their bishops would meet regularly in regional synods or councils, and in some regions the church of the provincial metropolis, e.g., Carthage in the province of Africa or Caesarea in Palestine, acquired a certain primatial authority over the other churches of the province. Presumably in this century the development was already taking place on which the Council of Nicaea set the seal in 325 by naming Rome, Alexandria and Antioch as enjoying respectively the first, second and third places of honor among the churches. It was the churches of these cities rather than the sees or the bishops occupying them that were at first so ranked. It was as presiding over and representing primatial churches that the bishops of Rome, Alexandria and Antioch possessed a wider prestige and authority than any other bishops.

Though there were few or no structural links between the different regional churches or groups of churches—one could scarcely call the one catholic church of the first three centuries a federation of local churches—nonetheless their unity, their mutual communion was prized very highly, and maintained informally by constant travel and correspondence. It was participation in this communion that was in fact most usually signified by the epithet "catholic." One concrete institutional expression of communion was the ordination of a new bishop of a church by the bishops of neighboring churches. There is not much definite evidence about how bishops were appointed. It is to be presumed that they were chosen somehow by the local community; a later quasi-canonical expression is "elected by the clergy and people of a church." But of the particular procedures we know very little.

These strong, though for the most part informal, bonds of communion produced a very definite sense of catholic identity in the churches, by which they defined themselves, so to say, as such against heretical and schismatical communities, like Gnostics of all kinds, Montanists and Novatianists. This sense of catholic identity and unity, as yet quite uncrimped by any urge to uniformity, was expressed most clearly in three common treasures shared by all the churches: (1) baptismal creeds, varying widely in details, but all with the same trinitarian structure and content; (2) the canonical writings of the NT, the earliest list of them being the so-called Muratorian canon dating from the middle of the second century—though the NT canon was not definitively settled with universal assent until the end of the fourth century; (3) the succession of bishops in the more eminent churches from the apostles, as Irenaeus testifies (*Adv. Haer.* III, 3, 1-2). All the baptismal creeds contained a phrase about "the holy church," which came to be expanded, in the version of the Nicene Creed completed at the Council of Constantinople in 381, into the "one, holy, catholic and apostolic church." Again, it is the universal mystery of the church, visibly embodied in each local church, that is being referred to, rather than a centrally structured world-wide organization.

However, the unique primatial status of the Roman church among the churches, which was to provide the basis, much later on, for a centralized organization of the universal church, was already evident in these first centuries. The first testimony to it is the so-called letter of Clement to the Corinthians, about 90. I say "so-called," because it is written as a letter from the Roman church, and Clement's name is nowhere mentioned, though in the eyes of a later tradition he was the bishop of Rome at that time. There are, however, fairly strong grounds for supposing that the Roman church was not yet episcopally structured at that time, but still conservatively retained the older presbyteral (presbyterian) organization which we see attested in Acts 20:17 & 28. Be that as it may, there is no doubt that the Roman church did not hesitate to send a letter to the Corinthian church in the tone of an elder brother—or even of a Dutch uncle. Ignatius (Rom. 1) and Irenaeus (*Adv. Haer.* III, 3, 3) also bear witness to the primacy of the Roman church, Ignatius talking about a primacy of love, Irenaeus about one of faith. Thus it seems they saw the Roman community as a model or touchstone for other churches. And indeed, whenever in these centuries the Roman tradition conflicted with that of other churches, it was the Roman that won the day; whether in the quartodeciman dispute with the churches of Asia over the correct date of Easter c. 190, or the dispute with the churches of Africa over the rebaptism of converts from heretical or schismatic bodies, c. 255.

But one cannot talk about the Roman church or its bishop, in these centuries, exercising any kind of government over other churches (except, no doubt, over the neighboring churches of central and southern Italy). When Victor, the bishop of Rome during the quartodeciman controversy, proposed to excommunicate the Asian churches for not coming into line with all the others, he was constrained to desist by a very firm protest from Irenaeus, following Paul's example of withstanding Peter to the face (Gal 2:11). And the controversy between Stephen of Rome and Cyprian of Carthage over baptism did not lead to any such exercise of authority.

It may in fact truly be said that not only did the church not have any world-wide administrative institutions in these centuries, but that it could not afford to have them. Had it been as highly centralized in its structures of authority as the Roman Catholic Church is today, its chances of surviving the systematic persecutions of the third and early fourth centuries would, humanly speaking, have been almost nil. Strike the head of such a body, and the body disintegrates. But the church of the martyrs presented to its persecutors the daunting spectacle—in their kind of imagery—of a many-headed hydra. This lack of any but local and regional organization also meant that the missionary expansion of Christianity, though quite unplanned, was perennially effective, the way being open to innumerable initiatives.

2. c. 330-1054; the Age of Constantine to the Schism between Rome and Constantinople. Twelve years after issuing the Edict of Milan, which made Christianity a *religio licita* for the first time in its history, Constantine was presiding at the Council of Nicaea in 325. Sixty years later, under the direction of the Emperor Theodosius, Catholic Christianity had become the official, and only lawful, religion of the Roman Empire.

Such a dramatic change of fortune for the christian communities of the Roman Empire was bound to revolutionize their self-image, their spontaneous "ecclesiology." From now on, for one thing, the word "church" begins to have a more frequent reference to the universal, worldwide church, thought of structurally and organically. This kind of reference does not, indeed, overshadow the reference to local communities for many centuries yet; but it steadily becomes more and more prominent. The universal church from this time on has an organized structure, however loose and intermittent, in the form of general or ecumenical councils.

The most momentous result, however, was that Christians were subjected to enormous cultural, social and political pressures to identify, if not the church with the state, then the ecclesial with the civil society. Before Constantine's conversion the empire had been a sacral society, its rulers sacred and in fact divine persons, and likewise its institutions. In the minds of Constantine and his successors this was in no way changed by their becoming Christians; it simply meant that now Christianity instead of traditional paganism supplied the legitimating sacredness. The empire becomes christian;

it becomes the church; it becomes the people of God, with no more perceptible distinction between church and state or church and world, than there had been in the Israel of the Davidic monarchy.

The resultant ideo-theology received its clearest—and its most appalling—expression in *The Life of Constantine* by Eusebius of Caesarea, the church historian, who was a close associate of the emperor. Its most concrete expression is to be seen in the rapid transformation of the insignificant little church of Byzantium (as it was in 325) into the ecumenical patriarchate of Constantinople, having precedence over the ancient sees and churches of Alexandria and Antioch.

The total symbiosis of Byzantine church and Byzantine Empire has been dubbed, not entirely fairly, "caesaropapism." Emperors, notably Justinian in the sixth century, did sometimes attempt to exercise a quasi-papal authority over the church in matters of doctrine as well as administration. But it must also be said that they were as often fiercely opposed, and successfully so, by hierarchs, monks and laity of the Byzantine church—most notably in the protracted iconoclastic controversy of the eighth and ninth centuries.

Nonetheless, empire and church were so closely knit together that it was virtually impossible to conceive of one without the other. So it will be instructive to jump ahead of our period here in a digression, and consider what happened to the Byzantine or Greek church after the empire was destroyed by the Turks in 1453. To some extent the tradition of ecclesial-civil symbiosis was continued in tsarist Russia. Hardly so in the Ottoman Empire—but even there the Moslem sultans not only supervised the appointment of the patriarchs of Constantinople, but also employed them in the administration of the civil affairs of their Greek christian subjects. But since the *démise* of all these empires, what we now call the orthodox churches have developed a system of autocephalous churches, linked together only by common doctrine and mutual communion. Here the word "church" once more regains its predominant local reference, this time, though, on a national rather than a smaller "diocesan" scale.

To return to the post-Constantinian period: another consequence of the coalescence of ecclesial and civil society was the "hieratization" of the church. Bishops became what in feudal times would be called magnates. They also, somehow, became more sacred. It is from this period that the word "hierarchy" and related words come into regular use to designate the christian ministry. The church comes to be seen as essentially hierarchical both in structure and in nature: this under the influence of a curious and thoroughly unhealthy combination of OT and neoplatonic models. For Pseudo-Dionysius (whose influence was immeasurable) the ecclesiastical hierarchy is a reflection of the celestial hierarchy—part of the grading of all being in terms of proximity to the divine source of being. So, gone is the evangelical notion of the basically equal brotherhood of all Christians in Christ. At the same time the "hierarchy" of bishop, priests and deacons is more and more assimilated to the (late) OT model of high priest, Aaronic priests, and levites. So the christian clergy, without actually becoming a hereditary caste, still become a sacred and highly privileged class, which is frequently just identified with "the church." Thus by an odd paradox the church is being sacralized in the very same process by which it is being secularized or contaminated by "the world." Monasticism arose and its institutions flourished from this time on as a counter-balance and indeed a protest against this assimilation of church to

world. But inevitably as the monastic movement was institutionalized (and endowed with property), it too was drawn into the system.

From the very beginning, however, there was resistance in various forms to this process of identifying church and empire. In the fourth century bishops from all quarters of the empire, led by Athanasius and the church of Alexandria, were resisting the arianizing policies of Constantine and his immediate successors. This conflict, coming right at the beginning of this era, was a godsend for Christianity and the church. It effectively prevented the full realization of what we could call the Eusebian dream.

In the next century resistance came in a different form and with sadder results. Whole churches broke off communion with what they regarded as the imperial church, ostensibly on dogmatic grounds because they rejected the christological definitions, first of Ephesus, 431 (the Nestorians), and then of Chalcedon, 451 (the Monophysites); but more profoundly and emotionally in fact because they resented the hegemony of Constantinople in ecclesiastical as well as imperial administration. What we have here is some of the earliest manifestations of what could be called christian nationalism. The Egyptian or Coptic church, the Armenian, Georgian, and Syriac Churches, whether monophysite or nestorian refused any longer to be dominated by the imperial Greek Church. They were resisting an identification of church with empire; but perhaps at the same time they were illustrating an equally ambiguous development—the identification of church with local, national culture.

The most significant resistance of all to the identification of church and empire, or the Eusebian dream, came from quite a different source and with no immediate consequence of schism—from the Church of Rome. From the middle of the fourth century, from the episcopate of Pope Damasus I (366-384), the bishops of Rome (who from now on may properly be called popes to designate the uniqueness of their position) begin with their chancery to elaborate both the theological grounds of their primacy and its practical application and consequences. They base it on their being the successors of Peter, the prince of the apostles; their see is now "the apostolic see" *par excellence.* Their primacy is in no way due to their presiding over the church of the empire's capital city. They do, however, borrow from the legal traditions of the imperial city the forms and techniques for asserting a universal jurisdiction which they consider to be consequent on their Petrine primacy—a "solicitude for all the churches" (2 Cor 11:28). Just as imperial law was largely made and promulgated by means of *rescripts,* i.e., answers to formal questions or pleas presented by subjects or imperial officials, so now we have the beginnings of a papal canon law formulated in rescripts which were answers to questions sent to Rome from other churches (almost always Latin churches of the West).

By the time of Pope Leo the Great (440-461) the doctrine of the papal primacy and *plenitudo potestatis* (fullness of authority) over all churches—or the whole Catholic Church—was formulated with an amplitude and precision to which the decree *Pastor Aeternus* of the First Vatican Council (1870) would add little of substance, except perhaps the formal statement of papal infallibility. Thus the papacy ensured *in principle* for the future the freedom of the Church of Rome, and all other churches which accepted its primacy and authority, from complete control and domination by political powers. Basically, it was asserting the essential freedom in Christ of every Christian, and every christian conscience, from any such totalitarian domination.

But it must be clearly understood that the popes of these centuries did not exercise their Petrine primacy by actually governing other churches. Even churches founded on the initiative of popes, like the English Church from the seventh century, almost immediately achieved a degree of autonomy that they certainly do not have today. It would be the second millennium that would see the administrative centralization of church government in the papacy and its Roman curia.

3. 1054-1965: The Schism Between East and West to the Second Vatican Council. That the church did not depend for its well-being on a central Roman administration before this date is well illustrated by the fact that from 885 to 1049 the papacy underwent an almost continual degradation as the plaything of powerful Roman families, a kind of dark age Mafia. And yet elsewhere local churches flourished during this period, e.g., the English Church of the tenth century, and new churches were founded without any papal initiatives by missionaries among the Slavs, the Hungarians and the Scandinavians.

But after 1049 things began to change and change rapidly. The papacy was rescued from its degradation by the devout German emperors Henry II and Henry III. There was a distinct possibility of its becoming in relation to these christian sovereigns what the patriarchate of Constantinople had become in relation to the Byzantine emperors. It was saved from this fate by a series of highminded and strong-minded pontiffs making use of the canonical material amassed for them by their predecessors from Damasus I to Nicholas I (858-867). Thus began, under the aegis of Hildebrand (Gregory VII, 1073-1085) the accumulation of a centralized and almost exclusive authority in the hands of the papacy that has continued in the Catholic Church from that day to this.

One thing that made possible this rapid development and extension of papal authority, and also distorted it and its effects on the church from the beginning, was the schism between east and west which became definitive in 1054. This meant that from now on Christians in Rome and the west identified for all practical purposes the Catholic Church with the Latin Church. For all practical purposes most Latin Christians in Rome and the rest of the world still do. And the result of this was that they also identified or confused (and still do) the pope's divinely bestowed Petrine primacy and authority within the whole Catholic Church, and his purely customary and canonical authority over the Latin Churches as "patriarch of the west."

The inflated extension and exaltation of the exercise of papal authority has dominated the institutional history of the Catholic (Latin) Church from 1054 to the present day. It has taken different forms in three main periods, the medieval (1054-1564), the post-Tridentine (1564-1870), and the modern (1870-). In the first the claims were the most inflated, claims to a universal and absolute sovereignty over all other authorities, secular as well as ecclesiastical; claims in virtue of which, for example, Alexander VI (1492-1503) divided the whole world, not yet under the jurisdiction of christian sovereigns, between the monarchs of Spain and Portugal in 1493.

These claims, like a great deal of medieval political and legal theory, were hardly realistic, and the attempt to put them into practice involved the papacy in continuous wrangles and wars with secular rulers. More unfortunately, after an initial 150 years in which the Holy See was indeed a power for reform in the church, culminating in the pontificate of Innocent III (1198-1216), the increasing centralization of administrative authority in the Roman curia led to ever deepening ecclesiastical corruption. Such an administration needed financing; the easiest, perhaps the only, way of raising the necessary funds was by turning the papal jurisdiction over the other local churches into a source of income, for example by the system of the "provision" of lucrative benefices (sometimes even bishoprics and abbacies) to officials of the curia. It was against this kind of abuse that the great bishop of Lincoln, Robert Grosseteste, protested in the thirteenth century, "Obediently I disobey." The most visible signs of this institutional corruption of the papacy and, through the papal grip on the central power ganglions, of the whole Latin Church, were in turn, the Avignon periods of almost seventy years (a significant number) ending in 1377; the great schism lasting forty years (another symbolic number) from 1377-1417, during which there were never less than two and sometimes three rival popes; and finally the scandalous worldliness of the Renaissance popes from 1471 (Sixtus IV) to 1521 (Leo X).

These developments did not take place without ecclesiastical and theological opposition. By the time of the great schism the kind of conservative opposition voiced by Grosseteste had yielded to what is known as the *conciliarist* movement, whose leading figures were theologians in the University of Paris. They proposed what may be called a "parliamentary" (conciliar) form of government for the universal church (in fact for the Latin Church. They dominated the Council of Constance (1414-1418), which succeeded in terminating the great schism, and legislated for regular and frequent general councils, to which the papal curia and the pope himself would be responsible. The scheme was even more unrealistic than the pretension of papal absolutism it sought to control, and broke down within a few years.

The next serious opposition to papalist claims and practices came with the Protestant Reformation, which simply rejected them altogether and established new forms (or variations on old ones) of ecclesiastical organization which we cannot discuss here. From the Catholic point of view it led to the Council of Trent and the counter-reformation. A radically reformed and re-organized curia—the present structure of Roman congregations dates from this period— and a practical limitation to the ecclesiastical sphere of papal claims to universal authority tended in themselves to make papal control of the whole of church life and of local churches and missionary ventures much more absolute than it had ever been in the Middle Ages.

But it was also checked by a far more powerful opposition than the medieval conciliarist movement. This was what came to be known as *gallicanism,* which also had its center in France, though more at Versailles than in the Sorbonne at Paris. Gallicanism had a very high notion of the identity and rights of the local church, but now in the sense of the national church—in this case the Church of France. And since this was the era of absolute monarchies, of which the French was the most prestigious, the rights and privileges of the French Church, *ecclesia gallicana,* meant the rights of the king of France over that church. The Hapsburgs did not lag behind the Bourbons in the assertion of royal rights, and in the eighteen century variations on the theme of gallicanism arose in Germany and Austria known as *Febronianism* and *Josephism.* The idea was the same in all cases: severely to restrict the application of papal authority in these territories. It was a contest between a papal absolutism (or pretension to it) and royal absolutisms. Thus the gallican opposition to extreme papalism was even more compromised by its political motivations than concili-

arism had been.

In any case, gallicanism received its death wound with the French Revolution, and though it still had its following in the nineteenth century, it was given the final *coup de grâce* by the First Vatican Council in the constitution *Pastor Aeternus* on papal primacy and infallibility in 1870. From now on extreme papalism (though not actually underwritten dogmatically by the definitions of 1870) held the field unopposed in the Catholic Church until the Second Vatican Council, 1962-1965.

Since the nineteenth century it has been known as *ultramontanism.* To all intents and purposes it identifies church with papacy. Even if Pius IX did not say *"L'Eglise c'est moi,"* he could very well have done so. Now that the entirely secular states of the modern world were no longer interested in running the church, the papacy had a free hand in controlling, very tightly indeed, all appointments and activities in the local churches that constitute the Latin Church throughout the world. Indeed the concept of "local church" has virtually disappeared. It has been replaced by that of "diocese," which is purely an administrative term borrowed from the Byzantine Empire; and most Catholics, most priests and religious, and even many bishops still think that the bishop is no more than the pope's agent or representative in the diocese, in spite of the Second Vatican Council having expressly stated that this is not so *(L.G.* 27). That the council found it necessary to deny this manifest error shows how far ultramontanism, or extreme papalism, has succeeded in infecting and distorting the modern Catholic mind.

B. Church as Mystery and Sacrament.

So the church, as a visible or empirical society, as the organized people of God, has in the course of its history passed through many institutional forms, and none of them, certainly not the current one of excessively centralized papacy, may be regarded as definitive. In this respect the church as the people of God does not differ essentially from any other people, e.g., the people of China or the people of Italy.

What distinguishes the church, at least in its own self-estimation, from all other empirical societies is that it is also a mystery or sacrament. To call it this is to state that it has a unique relationship with God, and therefore also a unique relationship with the world, or at any rate with the human world which God has created. As Israel in the OT, it was uniquely chosen by God in the ancestors and created or begotten by him at the exodus and Mt. Sinai. As the church, the fulfillment of Israel, the people God has taken for himself from all nations (Acts 15:14), it enjoys a quasi-divine filial relationship with the Father by being identified with his Son, by being the body of Christ endowed with the Spirit of the Father and the Son. Thus the mystery of the church is inseparably linked with the mystery of the Trinity, and indeed is the concrete, visible effect of the revelation of the supreme divine mystery.

This derivation of the church from the revelation of the mystery of the Trinity through the divine missions of the Son and the Holy Spirit means that the mission of the church is an element in its aspect of mystery, and derives from the mission of the Son and of the Holy Spirit. "As the Father has sent me, so I send you" (Jn 20:21; cf also such texts as Jn 13:20, "He who receives anyone whom I send receives me; and he who receives me receives him who sent me"). Now this mission is, of course, to all nations (cf Mt 28:18). So the church shares in Christ's role of being mediator between God and mankind—naturally so, since it is as it were identified with him and shares in all his roles and offices. The function of the church with respect to the world is best expressed in the words of *Lumen Gentium*

1, calling it "a kind of sacrament or sign and instrument of intimate union with God and of the unity of the whole human race." And it is in the light of this description that the constitution goes on to declare the church's "universal nature and mission."

Now since the unity of mankind and its intimate union with God will only be perfectly realized in the fullness of the kingdom when Christ comes again, it follows that both nature and mission of the church have an essentially eschatological dimension to them. Like all the sacraments (in the strict sense), the church in itself has a future reference to eternal glory as well as a past reference to the saving paschal event of Christ's death and resurrection and pentecostal gift of the Spirit and a present reference to the grace of the sacrament. And its mission to proclaim the good news of the kingdom must be seen as preparing the human race for its ultimate destiny and leading it towards it.

Christians have always had a vivid sense of the church as a mystery, though not always expressed in these terms. But the church which is perceived as a mystery has, as we have seen, passed through many institutional forms, and it makes a great difference which of these forms one identifies as mystery and sacrament. In the early church it was primarily the local christian community which was perceived, for example, as the heavenly lady (*Shepherd of Hermas*), and it was this profound sense of constituting in their communities the sacrament of the presence of the divine mystery on earth that gave those Christians their resilience and perseverance in times of persecution.

After the Constantinian revolution it was the hierarchically structured church that was seen as participating in the divine mystery. The sense of mystery and sacredness was concentrated on the hierarchy, and the laity became profane, unmysterious, unless they lived under monastic discipline. They also came to participate much less, if indeed at all, in the mission of the church.

Finally, since the church has come to be perceived as a centralized absolute papal monarchy, it is this papal institution that has been overwhelmingly, not to say suffocatingly vested with the aura of divine mystery; and *pari passu* it has come practically to monopolize at least the direction of the church's mission of evangelization and its task of bearing witness—it has been only what the pope says or teaches that really matters.

The Second Vatican Council came providentially just in time to release the Catholic Church from the hopeless unreality of this posture in the circumstances of the twentieth century world. In his encyclical *Mystici Corporis* Pius XII identified the body of Christ (church as mystery) precisely and exclusively with the Roman Catholic Church, which is as much as to say with the papal system of government. In *Lumen Gentium* 8 the council states more sensitively that this church (the church as mystery) *subsists in* the Catholic Church governed by the pope and the bishops in communion with him, but adds that many elements of sanctification and truth are to be found outside its fabric.

This is in effect to commit the Catholic Church to working, as an integral part of its mission and in function of its being a kind of sacrament of unity for mankind, for the unity of all Christians in the ecumenical movement. Quite inconsistent with this ecumenical commitment is any interpretation of the church as mystery in the terms of ultramontane papalism.

C. Church as Communion and Brotherhood. The concept of communion or fellowship (*koinonia* in the NT) dominates the *Statement on Authority* put out by the first Anglican—Roman Catholic International Commission (ARCIC

1). It is indeed a concept that is crucial to the progress of ecumenical understanding among Christians of distinct traditions who are not yet "in communion" with one another. The basic meaning of the word is "sharing" or "having in common." As an aspect of the church it signifies a community of people who share with one another. What they share most obviously is faith. They have a *common* faith, and therefore a *common* hope and (ideally) a *common* charity. This amounts to their sharing a common life, which is in fact the life of Christ, the life of the Spirit, the life of God himself, as "partakers (sharers) of the divine nature" (2 Pet 1:4). As C.H. Dodd puts it, "These metaphors (of branches and parts of the body) make it clear that the "partnership" of christians is not a mere pooling of their own individual resources...; for neither tree nor body is constituted by an association of separately living parts; the life that is shared exists only as shared; and in the application of the metaphors it is made clear that the life of the church is the divine life disclosed ... in the incarnate Christ and communicated through his spirit" (Hamer, p. 163).

Brotherhood may be seen as both the context and the consequence of communion; it is as a brotherhood that Christians share these things, and it is sharing them that makes them brothers. It is of great significance that in Acts and the NT letters the faithful are always addressed by the apostles, and address them in turn, as "brothers." They took Christ's injunction in Mt 23:8 very seriously indeed.

Lumen Gentium uses this model in a number of ways. The most prominent is its introduction into church theory of the principle of *collegiality,* by which it intends to re-assert the proper authority of the bishops, exercised in a fraternal communion; this, not over against the proper primatial authority of the pope as defined in *Pastor Aeternus,* but certainly over against the exaggerated distortions of ultramontanism that marked the exercise of that authority before the Second Vatican Council.

But it would be a mistake to limit collegiality to the fraternal communion between bishops. *Mutatis mutandis* it should apply to all levels of church order and between all levels, to the fraternal communion of clergy with each other and their bishops, and the fraternal communion of the laity with each other and the clergy.

For besides its stress on collegiality (L.G. 22f), the constitution also emphasized the participation of all members of the people of God (their communion) in all the roles and offices of Jesus Christ, notably in his roles of prophet, priest and king, and in his mission (L.G. 9, 10, 12). An implication of this common sharing of all the faithful in the divine sonship of Christ is that *all* members of the church share in his authority; authority in the church is *not* something simply confined to the hierarchy or the so-called "magisterium."

It is evident then that there is bound to be tension, though not contradiction, between the model of the church as a communion and brotherhood and the model of it as a hierarchically structured society. What does contradict communion and brotherhood is the authoritarianism, the élitism and absolutism to which the concept of hierarchy has all too easily lent itself. And we should not forget that it is the fraternal communion model, not the hierarchical one, that is explicitly presented in the NT.

So if this model is to be taken seriously it will have practical consequences. It will mean that the hierarchical view of the ordained ministry will yield precisely to a *ministerial* view of it—i.e., to a view of bishops and clergy as the *servants* of the

people. It will mean that the pope's title of "servant of the servants of God" must be given a *practical* precedence over such titles as "sovereign pontiff," "head of the church" and "holy father." And since servants are not only expected but also legally obliged to ascertain and execute the intentions of their employers, it will mean that the laity are acknowledged to have a divinely given constitutional right to a say in the management of church affairs and the formulation of christian doctrine.

Again, it will have to mean that the church as local community must come into its own once more, having a certain priority over the church as universal. For sharing and brotherhood can only be fully realized among people who know each other; and then, given this basic achievement of fraternal communion in basic communities, at a further but rarer consistency among people who already share the same culture, language, regional concerns; and only finally and for the most part only in principle at the worldwide level.

With this priority of reference given to the local church the universal Catholic Church does not disappear. As a mystery it is realized in every local community; as institutionally organized it becomes a communion of communities, presided over in charity by the local Church of Rome and its bishop, the servant of the servants of God. What does have to disappear, gradually making way for something better, is the Latin Church with its rather constricted cultural inheritance and its ingrained passion for uniformity. The something better will be the wonderful variety of regional churches spontaneously developing their own local genius in diverse customs and liturgies, contributing to the full catholicity of the one, holy, catholic and apostolic church without detriment to its unity. Thus the words of the psalm will be fully realized:

Astitit regina a dextris tuis ... circumdata varietate—The queen stands at your right hand ... girded with variety (Ps 45:10, LXX & Vulg.).

R. Brown, *The Community of the Beloved Disciple*, New York, 1979. Y. Congar, *The Mystery of the Church*, London, 1960. H. De Lubac, *The Church: Paradox and Mystery*, Shannon, 1969. Dodd, C.H., *The Johannine Epistles*, London, 1953. A. Dulles, *Models of the Church*, Dublin, 1976. J. Hamer, *The Church is a Communion*, London, 1964. H. Küng, *The Church*, London, 1968.

EDMUND HILL, OP

CHURCH AND CULTURE

The relation between the church and culture depends on an understanding of culture, of the church, and of the ideal and actual interactions between the two.

Culture

A culture is a complex but integrated and interacting dynamic whole. (a) The following are *constitutive elements* of a culture: a common worldview or vision of life; common meanings, values, and goals; common categories and patterns of thought; a common tradition and common patterns of behavior; common organization of relationships and roles; with religion, spirituality, and mysticism supplying the transcendent and in-depth dimension.

(b) These elements are acquired, embodied, and transmitted through *symbols*, which also serve as media of communication at all levels, personal, social, and global. Under symbols are included: signs, languages, techniques and technology, status and role systems, knowledge systems (philosophy), economic organizations, social customs and habits, political institutions, modes of behavior, religious practices, artifacts, and lifestyles.

(c) In such elements and by such symbols, cultures emerge and develop only through a *tradition* of at least several generations. Thus cultures are three-dimensional realities, linking the past, the present, and the future. They continue to survive and thrive only if capable of influencing society today in the face of contemporary situations and challenges.

In short, culture is the way of life, ethos, or life-style of a people. The essential element is the value-system. Cultures are both human products and producers of human persons. People create cultures and cultures influence and mold their growth and behavior.

There is a diversity and plurality of cultures both at the global level and within regions and countries. The encounter of cultures, while to some degree a factor in human history from the beginning, has today, because of modern technology, been multiplied and intensified.

The shock this produces can tempt one to a mono-cultural attitude, which can take two extreme forms. Out of a feeling of insecurity, one can try to shield oneself by retreating into cultural isolation. Or one may attempt to impose one's own particular culture on other races and peoples. This cultural neo-colonialism often accompanies, consciously or unconsciously, social, economic, political, and military systems of power. The imposition of an alien culture can lead the members of the subordinated cultures to a profoundly dehumanizing alienation.

What is required today is instead a pluralistic attitude, which appreciates and welcomes the variety of cultures. Other cultures are acknowledged not only as a fact to be tolerated, but also as so great a value that one promotes the growth of other cultures and seeks to be enriched by them, even while valuing and promoting one's own culture. Through such an attitude, cultures will interact and influence one another, change and be changed. Only such an attitude permits peoples at once to be enriched by other peoples and to preserve their distinctive identities.

Though cultures have always undergone change, the pace and depth of this change have greatly increased as the world's continents have entered the modern era. Among the most important characteristics of modernity are: the ideology of the nation-state, with a whole complex of political institutions and administrative machinery; modern economic developments within the capitalist system linking small scale, self-reliant economies with a worldwide market system; industrialization and urbanization; the growth of science and the applications of technology to every sphere of life, particularly to industry, transportation, and communication; new systems of education; the values implicit in secularity, humanism, rationality, and science.

Third World countries have undergone great change during the last two centuries as they have come under the direct influence of the colonizing expanison of western nations. European colonization and political domination often meant adding to and overlaying the already existing cultures. The effect often was a dual culture or cultural dichotomy, with the traditional, local culture coexisting and interacting with the imported western culture. These cultural influences have sometimes been considerable and sometimes not serious or radical, especially on the majority of the population.

The modern values mentioned above are sometimes misleadingly considered "western" values. But in themselves these values are neither eastern nor western; and traditional local values do not necessarily conflict with them. But this modernization, especially through modern transportation and mass media, are producing an international culture as all societies are becoming part of a worldwide network of economic and political, military and strategic, ideological and cultural relationships. This process is called *globalization*. This process and the world culture it is producing need not dispense with or submerge national cultures; it can presuppose and require the preservation and growth of the latter as the necessary condition for a people to be able to relate to other cultures, to participate in the world culture, to make original contributions to it, and to benefit from it creatively.

Local national cultures, usually and basically stable, have been deeply affected and seriously challenged by modern technology. It has triggered radical challenges hitherto unknown. Such change becomes critical when it affects the relationship between a culture's value system and its traditions and tools. The result can be stagnation, a rigid adherence to traditions and inability to assimilate new values; on the other hand, both cultures can move in different directions, working at cross purposes. In both cases conflicts arise and solutions can become critical. These critical challenges do not guarantee progress. They become positive when the existing value system finds new and appropriate ways of self-expression. Real progress takes place when the value system puts itself to the test and opens itself to new values. Thus, while technology is indispensable for material prosperity and human progress and for that reason should be available to and shared by all people, technology without cultural values, especially religion and spirituality, will be a reality without a soul.

While culture and religion are distinct and autonomous, they are not independent and separate. They are related dynamically and influence each other, leading to mutual transformation and enrichment. In First World countries today, cultures are being secularized and desacralized, while the socialist countries tend to promote an atheistic culture. The cultures of Third World countries, in contrast, have continued to be basically religious, although they too have been affected by the worldwide phenomenon of secularization.

Within the complex mechanisms of societies and especially when confronted by an unjust social, economic, and political system, people can adopt either a reform or a radical stance. Religions and cultures, education and life-styles constitute an ideology, provide a meaning-system, and play both covert and overt roles. They can either become subservient to the system and support, maintain, and perpetuate it through rationalization, justification, legitimation, social control, and compensation, or they can play a revolutionary role and perform a prophetical function, challenging the existing system and calling for radical social change.

The Church

The church is the community of Christ's disciples, the new People of God. It is a communion in the Spirit of the Risen Lord, the sacrament or sign and instrument of union between God and man and of unity among men (L.G. 1). It is the Body of Christ which makes visible Christ's presence and action in the world through his Spirit. As such the church is the historical and social prolongation of Christ in space and time. Its mission is to gather, reconcile, and unify all people and all things in Christ and to make them belong to God so that God may be all in all (see Eph 1:3, 14; Col 1:15-20; 1 Cor 3:23; 15:20-28). Having experienced the Father's saving love in the Spirit of the Risen Lord, Christians devote themselves to the proclamation of the Word, to the celebration of the eucharist which makes possible for all the paschal experience, and to promote fraternity and communion among themselves, with other Christian communities, and with people at large. They do so in an openness to the world and to society in the dynamics of history and life through powerful history and humble service in love. All this is animated and guided by the various ministries, coordinated by the unifying ordained leadership.

Such a christian community becomes a church when it is incarnated in a place. The church can become visible and fulfill its mission only by being local. The local church is the realization by which the whole mystery of the church is incarnated and actually present in each place. It expresses itself and operates through the social, cultural, and religious realities of a place, time, and people. The local church is not a division or administrative unit of the universal church. Its ecclesial character is derived from the Spirit: where the Spirit is, there the church is. On this understanding, all the local churches are equal. Every church has its own autonomy and freedom, viability and competence. It is resourceful and fully equipped for its life and mission, is responsible for it, and can undertake initiatives to fulfill it. Originality and creativity are the imperatives by which to meet the needs of church and society. Unity in variety and universality through particularity become the axioms.

The presence and action of the church require visible, concrete, and effective media. This requires the integration of the church in its social, cultural, and religious milieu, that incarnation of the church in a place, time, and people which today is called "inculturation." Inculturation is what results from the interaction and transformation of the gospel and particular cultures. Each christian community should be not only a community of faith, proclaiming and living the gospel, but also a community fully integrated in its culture, social milieu, and religious heritage, expressing its life and mission through them (see A.G. 10, 11).

Church and Culture: Inculturation

The relationship between gospel or church and culture has been a problem since the beginning of Christianity, when

Paul championed the cause of inculturation, affirming the universality of the
gospel, the reality of christian freedom,
and the equality of cultures (see Gal 2-4;
Acts 15). The issue, which remained a
perennial question, has become more acute
in recent decades when many African and
Asian countries have become independent
and decolonization has led to a revival of
nationalism and the renaissance of indigenous cultures. Theologians have vigorously taken up the challenge this has posed
to the church. Vatican II recognized and
confirmed the state of theological discussion at the time. Since then the debate has
continued, and something of a climax was
reached when the issues were clarified and
the implications articulated during the
1974 Synod of Bishops devoted to evangelization in the modern world.

Inculturation, or adaptation, which once
was considered a problem only for the
"missions" in the Third World, now is
recognized to be a universal problem,
challenging all the churches on all continents to achieve a meaningful presence in
their respective societies. The universal
challenge was powerfully stated by Pope
Paul VI: "The split between the Gospel
and culture is without doubt the drama of
our time, just as it was at other times.
Therefore every effort must be made to
ensure a full evangelization of culture, or,
more correctly, of cultures. They have got
to be regenerated by an encounter with the
Gospel. But this encounter will not take
place if the Gospel is not proclaimed"
(E.N. 20).

Two traditions have been at work in
the history of the church. According to
the more ancient tradition, wherever the
church preached the gospel and formed a
community of Christians, it identified
itself with and communicated through
the culture of the people evangelized. But
from the sixteenth century onward, after
the discovery of new continents and in
the context of economic and political

colonization, Christians transplanted in
the new lands the church as it had already
been inculturated in the western European culture of the Greco-Roman tradition.

As a result, the churches of the Third
World often faced a dilemma. On the one
hand, because christianization has meant
westernization, to become a Christian
has meant to adopt the culture and
traditions of the missionaries. Since the
gospel bears the trademark of western
Christianity, its adoption has meant the
alienation of people from their own
culture, social milieus, and religious
traditions, an evasion of their historical
adventure, and a drifting away from the
mainstream of national life. On the other
hand, because of that same identification,
any effort at adaptation or indigenization
was feared as a falsification of Christianity. To involve the church too much
in a particular culture risked losing its
identity. For these reasons, inculturation
was looked on with caution and suspicion.

In addition, it was often considered a
peripheral concern, a secondary and non-
essential dimension of evangelization,
something which could be postponed to
a later stage of missionary activity. Meantime, of course, evangelization continued
under the form of the imposition of
"christian culture," that is, western Christianity, with in fact the effect of alienating
many of the people in the young churches
from their own cultures. Even today,
after a generation of political independence, many Christians of the Third
World are still hostile to any effort at
indigenization.

Today there is a widespread belief that
the more recent tradition was not fully in
accord with the principle of incarnation.
This tradition is now being criticized and
the effort at indigenization is being
promoted in the name of the more ancient
and venerable tradition, which can be
traced back to Christ and the early

church. Vatican II, far from teaching a new doctrine or initiating a new tradition, in fact reaffirmed the age-old christian principle of incarnation and relaunched a new process of inculturation.

Opposition to inculturation is sometimes expressed in the myth that, after all, we already have christian culture, so that there is no need to borrow from the secular or religious culture of a people. But there is no such thing as *the* christian culture, and what is referred to by that phrase simply means the particular christian culture of western Europe. We should speak instead of many "christian cultures," that is, the indigenous cultures of every country and region insofar as they have been permeated by the Spirit of Jesus Christ and purified, enriched and fulfilled by gospel values. Thus there can be as many christian cultures as there are cultures in the world.

Inculturation must be seen as a total process. Some people who defend inculturation wish to limit its scope to the non-religious elements of a culture, as, for example, when in India it is said, "Indigenization, yes; but hinduization, no!" But religion and culture so influence one another that it is difficult to find one without the other. In Asian countries, for example, the cultures are both secular and religious. A global understanding of God's creative and redemptive plan, of Christ's incarnation, and of the church's mission and universality should help overcome any effort to compartmentalize and should extend the scope of inculturation to include all elements of a culture, including the religious.

A theological justification of this point is based on the plan of God to bring everything under Christ the Head (Eph 1:9-10). Through the mystery of incarnation, he assumes the whole of creation in order to redeem it and unify it. Nothing is saved unless it is assumed, and everything that has been created must be saved. The recapitulation of all things in Christ includes not only souls but the whole person and all people, all that is human, not only cultures, but religions also. The church, which continues the mission of Christ as "the universal sacrament of salvation" (L.G. 42), cannot save anything unless she assumes it in order to transform it. As the documents of Vatican II make clear, all truth, goodness, beauty, purity, and holiness should be recognized by the Church as gifts of God and Christ's inheritance (Ps 2:6). Everything belongs to us, we belong to Christ, and Christ himself belongs to God, so that God may be all in all (1 Cor 3:25).

Because cultures and religions are ambivalent, they require a prophetic critique and a christian interpretation. They must be subjected to christian scrutiny and interpretation if they are to participate in Christ's paschal mystery. Inculturation, therefore, has a double task of discernment and interpretation: liberating them from sin, evil, and error and giving them a true christian meaning, orientation, and fulfilment.

The church is meant to be universal. It should be an all-inclusive movement, an ever-widening fellowship, a dynamism towards catholicity. Catholicity is at once a note of the church, and something towards which she stretches. "Many elements of sanctification and of truth can be found outside her visible structure. These elements, as gifts properly belonging to the church of Christ, possess an inner dynamism towards Catholic unity" (L.G. 8). The dynamism of the church towards Catholicity is made operative and effective through evangelization and inculturation, which represent the double movement by which the church preaches the gospel but also receives into itself the riches of the various cultures and religions (see A.G. 22).

Inculturation must cover the total reality of the church's life and mission. As *Ad* gentes made clear, it should affect the formation of local communities of Christians and the training of clergy and religious, their life-styles, every sphere of personal and family life, social and civic activities, economic and political systems, and cultures. It concerns the domains of art, architecture, sculpture, painting, music, dance, and drama. It must be displayed in theology and spirituality, in the exercise of the threefold ministry of word, worship, and service, and in the formation and organization of christian community.

Finally, mission and indigenization are not successive but simultaneous actions. Evangelization does not come first, followed by inculturation, as if the former were essential and the latter secondary. Although historically there has often been a divorce between the two, in fact they are so intimately related that they constitute a single whole. Inculturation should be part and parcel of the very process of evangelization.

On a practical level, the creativity and originality needed for genuine inculturation require that it not proceed from above but from below. It is the local churches which will have to assume the responsibility and take the initiative, using their imaginations to invent relevant forms and patterns, structures and institutions. This will call for a correct understanding of the relationship between the universal church and the particular churches. The autonomy preserved in the oriental churches can provide a model. The church's administrative structures will have to be decentralized and the principle of subsidiarity acknowledged. This will require changes in the relations between the mission societies, church unions, and dioceses, between the Holy See, episcopal conferences, and dioceses.

See **Church, Evangelization, Inculturation, Mission**

Robert J. Schreiter, *Constructing Local Theologies,* Maryknoll, Orbis Books, 1985. Charles M. Murphy, "The Church and Culture Since Vatican II: On the Analogy of Faith and Art," *Theological Studies* (Jun 1987) vol 48, no. 2: 317-331. Paul Tillich, *Theology of Culture,* New York: Oxford University Press, 1959. Paul J. Surlis, "Faith, Culture, and Inculturation According to John Paul II," *Living Light* (Jan 1987) 23: 109-115. Edmund Hill, "Christianity and Cultures," *New Blackfriars* (Jul-Aug 1986) 67: 324-9.

D.S. AMALORPAVADASS

CHURCH AND STATE

The problem of church-state relations must be understood institutionally and analogically. It is a distinct issue from religious freedom, which is primarily a matter of human rights which individuals have to believe, to worship, and to express their beliefs without coercive intervention by the state or society. Thus a nation like Great Britain can have two established churches (Anglican in England and Presbyterian in Scotland) along with complete religious freedom for Catholics, Methodists, Jews, Muslims, and non-believers. In the early federal period of the United States, some states had religious establishments; but none denied the free exercise of religion guaranteed by the First Amendment.

The primary focus of policy discussion and legal debates is the proper form of relationship between two institutions, church and state, which exists within a larger society. These institutions themselves are central but incomplete embodiments of the religious and political concerns of human beings. Church and state are structured differently, and religion and politics are conceived somewhat differently in different societies and different religious traditions. This fact should lead us to be skeptical of generalizations and appreciative of the pragmatic adjustments which different societies have made to resolve conflicts in this area. There is a continuing need to avoid the imposition of the norms and expectations of one culture or one historical period.

But the central pattern or paradigm case for the discussion of church-state relations has been Christianity and Western European society (which also gave rise to the nation-state system). Christianity has long been marked by internal divisions in which different conceptions of the church have played a prominent part. Western European society has spread many of its institutions (religious, political, economic, intellectual) and its sense of rationality both to new colonial societies in the Americas and Australasia and to significant non-Western areas as well. Both Christianity and Western European society have been nourished by cultural roots in Graeco-Roman or "classical" society and by religious roots in Judaism, which both differ in their institutional patterns and normative expectations from the paradigm case. The prevailing pattern in classical antiquity and in ancient Israel was that the one society had religious and political aspects which were interwoven. Kingship was a sacral reality, and all members of the political community participated in religious rituals honoring the divine powers protecting the state. But in both these societies and in the ancient Near East generally, there were specialized religious functionaries, even though not a church conceived as a body distinct from the political community.

Once the early christian community understood that it would be a continuing body distinct from the Jewish people and subject to persecution by the Roman state (as well as having adherents outside the Roman Empire), it had to develop its own account of its relationship to the dominant political powers. Already in the NT, there were contrasting tendencies: obedience to the Roman Empire coupled with an appreciation of its contribution to order and a hope of toleration (Romans

13; Acts) and a conviction that Rome, the worshipper of idols and persecutor of the saints, was soon to be destroyed by divine judgment (Rev 13; 17-18). The conversion of Constantine, the establishment of Christianity as the religion of the Empire by Theodosius, and the endorsement of religious coercion by Augustine created a new set of possibilities. Western Catholicism still had to undergo persecution from Arian Germanic monarchies in the early Middle Ages. Byzantine Christianity was subject to imperial regulation and intervention in both doctrinal and disciplinary disputes. But medieval Europe became, except for a Jewish minority which was shut off from political power, a christian society in which ecclesiastical leaders exercised political power either in their own right or as officials of the developing monarchies. The papacy came to have supreme political authority over most of central Italy, and a state was established which lasted until 1870. From the mid-eleventh century on the papacy engaged in a prolonged struggle with the Holy Roman Empire and to a lesser extent with the kings of western Europe for "the liberty of the church" and resisted efforts to turn bishops and abbots into political functionaries completely subordinate to the monarchs.

During and after the Reformation, three different tendencies developed. The first was the assertion of royal control over the church. This was explicit in England, where Henry VIII was declared to be the "supreme head" of the church, as well as in Scandinavia and the Lutheran parts of Germany. But this pattern was also present in a more veiled form in such Catholic countries as France, Spain, and Portugal. The second tendency was establishment of a christian commonwealth, as in England after the Civil War or Calvinist Geneva or Puritan Massachusetts. The third tendency, which can be found in some religious radicals and in sectarian groups was to develop voluntary christian communities which would be removed from the exercise of political power. But the prevalent assumption was that the political community would be religiously homogeneous and that freedom of worship and expression for dissident groups, whether Catholic recusants in England or Huguenots in France or Lutherans and Calvinists in the domains of the Habsburgs, would be severely restricted. The decline of religious influence among European elites in the eighteenth century and the demands of Enlightenment philosophers for religious toleration and intellectual freedom prepared the way for a general easing of these restrictions and for the emancipation of such marginalized and oppressed groups as the Jews in the aftermath of the French Revolution. The French Revolution also brought with it open attacks on Catholicism. But some form of religious establishment survived in most of Europe into the twentieth century and was endorsed in papal teaching into the twentieth century.

The First Amendment to the U.S. Constitution, which prohibited Congress from making laws "respecting an establishment of religion or prohibiting the free exercise thereof" set up the classic American pattern of separation of church and state. This built on earlier colonial experiments in religious toleration, particularly in Rhode Island, Maryland, and Pennsylvania. But several of the states, notably Massachusetts and Connecticut, retained their existing congregational religious establishments until the 1830's. There has, however, been a continuing need for judicial interpretation of what constitutes an establishment of religion and what social or government practices restrict the free exercise of religion. Particular areas of controversy have been religious symbols and exercises in public

contexts, especially prayer in the public schools, and government aid to religious schools. American political life has remained open to strong religious influences and American levels of religious practice and belief are among the highest in the industrialized world. Catholicism flourished in the United States, and American Catholic leaders became articulate exponents of the principles of religious liberty, preparing the way for the eventual acceptance of this fundamental right of persons in Vatican II's Declaration on Religious Liberty, *Dignitatis humanae* (1965).

The affirmation of religious liberty for all does not, however, entail the rejection of religious establishment, which has continued in many countries, both Catholic and non-Catholic. Many practices related to religious establishment, such as the payment of salaries to religious functionaries, continue even under anti-religious regimes. Religious liberty is a universal norm applying to individuals and the groups in which they assemble, whereas the relationship between church and state is a complex institutional reality which exhibits considerable variety in different polities and which is given definite form by social practices and legal enactments.

Possible relationships can include: separation of church and state, subordination of the state to the church (theocracy), subordination of the church to the state, (as in much of eastern Europe, where westerners rejected it as caesaropapism, or as in the monarchies of western Europe, where it was called Erastianism), persecution or restriction of the church by the state, rejection of or opposition to the state by the church (as in some forms of sectarian or possibly in some forms of liberation theology). Relationship may be significantly different in theory and practice, e.g., an anti-religious regime may seek support from a church, or a sectarian group may disapprove of civil disobedience, or a government with an established church may support the schools of other churches. There can also be a difference between judgments about the state or the church as such and particular states and churches. The general typology sketched here has to be modified to apply to religious groups that are significantly different in organization and scope from christian churches, and to cultures where Christians are a small minority. In particular, countries where the Islamic tradition is dominant have often been governed by a religious legal system and have provided religious toleration for christian and Jewish communities, while at the same time forbidding conversions from Islam and persecuting heretical or pagan groups (e.g., the Bahais in contemporary Iran).

The theological assessment of the different arrangements between church and state should be based on two primary criteria: whether the arrangement respects human rights, particularly the right to religious liberty, and whether it respects the internal liberty of the church, which needs freedom to choose its own officials, to set its internal policies and laws, to engage in missionary and evangelizing activity, to cooperate across national boundaries, to minister to oppressed or dissident groups, and to proclaim its moral and social teaching. Both persecution by the state and some forms of religious establishment fail these criteria.

See **Liberty, Religious**

John Courtney Murray, *We Hold These Truths,* Kansas City: Sheed & Ward, 1986. *Church and State Through the Centuries,* eds. Sidney Ehler & John Morrall, London: Burns & Oates, 1954. T.M. Parker, *Christianity and the State in the Light of History.* London: Adam & Charles Black, 1955. John Lord Acton, *Essays on Freedom and Power,* ed., Gertrude Himmelfarb, Boston: Beacon Press, 1948. *Essays on Church and State,* ed. Douglas Woodruff, London: Hollis & Carter, 1952. *Journal of Church and State.*

JOHN LANGAN, SJ

CIRCUMCISION

Circumcision, the Sign of Belonging to the People of God

Of very ancient origin and still widely practiced as a rite of passage, circumcision acquired its real meaning for Israel as an exterior mark or entry into the community of God's people by the acceptance of the covenant. As such, it is associated with Abraham (Gen 17:9-14; 21:4) and prescribed by the law (Lev 12:3). It is the precondition to the participation in the Passover meal, clearly distinguishing the Israelites from all others (Ex 12:44, 48). Circumcision became the hallmark of Judaism, the very word "circumcision" being a synonym for the covenant.

Circumcision of the Heart

While being an external sign in the flesh, circumcision, precisely as a *sign,* relates to the commitment of the whole person to God in the covenant. This is evident from both the prophets (Jer 4:4; 9:24; Ezek 44:7-9) and the law (Lev 19:23; 26:41; Deut 10:12-22; 30:6). Without the corresponding spiritual "circumcision of the heart," that of the flesh is ineffectual and meaningless.

Baptism and Circumcision

The emphasis on the profoundly spiritual nature of real circumcision, found within the OT, facilitated the relativization of the external rite of circumcision—and, indeed, its replacement by baptism—within the christian church. Two other factors in this shift from circumcision to baptism were undoubtedly the inconvenience of the former for the increasingly large number of Gentiles accepting the gospel and the suitability of the latter as a rite of initiation not only for men but also for women.

The actual practice of admitting Gentiles into the community of the New Covenant on the basis of their faith and baptism (Acts 10:44-48; 11:1-18), followed especially by Paul (Acts 13:48), led to the Council of Jerusalem (Acts 15:1) at which it was decided not to impose circumcision upon gentile converts (Acts 15:28-29). Continuing controversies within the churches—especially those of Galatia—over the need for the external sign of circumcision, however, inspired Paul to insist upon both the interior, faith character of true circumcision (Rom 2:25-29; 4:9-12) and the fact that this circumcision is achieved or, rather, transcended in Christ (Gal 5:6; 6:15; Col 3:11). For Christ's faithful, baptism is the true circumcision (Col 2:11-15). Consequently, to wish to be circumcised physically in order to belong (even more fully) to Christ is to revert from the Spirit to the flesh—worse, it is to annul the cross of Christ, which spelled the end to the external observance of the law, of which circumcision was the epitome (Gal 5:1-12). Devoid of the spiritual significance, which is found only in Christ, circumcision is a mere mutilation of the flesh (Phil 3:1-10). Given this spiritual meaning of faith, however, the external rite of circumcision becomes redundant, giving way to the practice of love (Gal 5:6), the hallmark of the members of the community of the new covenant (Jn 13:35).

R.F. Stoll, "The Circumcision," *Am ER* 110 (1944): pp. 31-42.

LIONEL SWAIN

COLLEGIALITY

Collegiality as both a doctrine and an attitude is one of the distinctive features of the ecclesiology of Vatican II. In the strict sense collegiality refers to the doctrine that all bishops, by virtue of their episcopal consecration and their hierarchical communion among themselves and with the head of the college, the pope, have a corporate responsibility for the unity of faith and of communion in the universal church. Since the council

this has sometimes been spoken of as "effective" collegiality. In a derived sense collegiality also refers to the attitude of mutual interaction and collaboration within the college of bishops, head and members, on the international, national, and regional levels. The council itself speaks of this as the "collegial spirit"; since the council this has been spoken of as "affective" collegiality. A spirit of collegiality can also be reflected in the local church or diocese through presbyteral and pastoral councils.

Roman Catholic interest in collegiality emerged as an outcome of 20th-century liturgical, biblical, and historical studies. The emphasis of Vatican I on the papacy led naturally to an interest in the role of the episcopacy. It was in this context that the expression "collegiality of the bishops" came into being. The understanding of collegiality was seen to be based on the collegial character of office in the ancient church. In the early centuries each bishop was understood to have his episcopacy only in communion with the other bishops, even as each church, while being fully church existed in communion with all other local churches. Historical studies showed that even if over the centuries a universalist outlook, with a corresponding emphasis on the role of the papacy, became predominant in ecclesiology, the ecclesiology of the church as communion and a recognition of the universal responsibility of bishops as a group were never lost from view. Studies of Vatican I showed that even if the role of the bishops was never formally addressed when the council took up the issue of the papacy, the idea of collegiality was not infrequently introduced into the conciliar debates.

The topic of collegiality was debated at length at Vatican II. Some of the bishops were opposed to the idea because they did not see that it could be reconciled with the teaching of Vatican I. The bishops of the council wanted to be faithful to the teaching of Vatican I and to relate the notion of collegiality with the earlier council's dogmatic teaching on the papacy. As a result Vatican II did not give a systematic treatment of the principle of collegiality in all aspects of the church's life; it confined its teaching on collegiality to the universal church and left to later development the application of this principle to other areas.

It is the teaching of Vatican II that the twelve apostles were constituted by Christ in the form of a college or permanent assembly and that the bishops as a college are their successors. One is constituted a member of the episcopal college by sacramental consecration and by hierarchical communion with the head and members of the college. Together with the head of the college and never apart from him the college of bishops has by divine right supreme and full authority over the universal church. The council explicitly speaks of two ways in which episcopal collegiality may be exercised: in an ecumenical council and, in a less solemn way, by a collegiate action of all the bishops throughout the world in union with the pope.

In the years after the council attention has focused on the relationship between the papal primacy and the episcopacy and on other possible expressions of collegiality. The first issue centers on the relationship between the pope as "chief pastor" of the whole church and the pope as "head of the college." This matter was taken up briefly in the "Note of Explanation" added to the text of Vatican II's Dogmatic Constitution on the Church. Since the council many theologians reason that the pope, even when he acts as supreme pastor, is also acting as head of the college and that the primacy of the pope is a primacy within the college and not apart from it. The basis for this position is the view that there is in the

church but one supreme authority which is exercised in different modes and forms of activity. This theological understanding, however, is not universal and some reason that the pope's role as chief pastor can be distinct from his role as head of the college.

A related line of thought looks at the collegial acts of each individual bishop. Based on the doctrine that the college of bishops is a permanent and indivisible reality, each act of a bishop which teaches the apostolic faith and maintains the fundamental communion of the church has universal significance and may be said to be a collegial act.

A second matter centers on the expressions of collegiality, most especially on the synod of bishops and on national conferences of bishops. The synod of bishops was established by pope Paul VI in 1965. Episcopal conferences were encouraged by Vatican II in its *Decree on the Pastoral Office of Bishops in the Church*. While some theologians see the synod of bishops as an expression of non-conciliar collegial action, many theologians regard the synod as an expression of the collegial spirit, though not strictly a collegial act. The revised Code of Canon Law (1983) and the Final Report of the extraordinary Synod of Bishops in 1985 give support to the latter view. Episcopal conferences, too, are seen as important realizations of the collegial spirit, even if, again, they are not strictly collegial actions. The Synod of Bishops in 1985 endorsed this understanding.

Collegiality, both as a doctrine and as a mode of collaboration, must be seen in the context of the history of Roman Catholic ecclesiology. From the anti-conciliar and anti-Protestant polemics of the 15th and 16th centuries to the ultramontane victory at Vatican I, the church has largely been seen in light of a universalist perspective with a strong emphasis on a central papal authority. The ecclesiology of Vatican II maintained much of that perspective and reaffirmed the teachings of Vatican I. But it explicitly added to those teachings an understanding of church as a communion of churches and taught clearly the collegial role of bishops in the church. In so doing it pointed to a theoretical balance between church as universal church and as communion of local churches and between the papacy and the episcopacy. In this light collegiality is not only a contribution to the understanding of the role of bishops in the church; it is also seen by many as a model for participation and co-responsibility among other members of the church. It is in this perspective that one can also speak about a spirit of collegiality being reflected on the local level through presbyteral and pastoral councils.

See **Bishop, Church, Council, Pope**

Y. Congar *et al., La collégialité épiscopale: Histoire et théologie* (Unam Sanctam, 52), Paris, 1965. Y. Congar and B.D. Dupuy, eds., *L'épiscopat et l'église universelle* (Unam Sanctam, 39), Paris, 1962. R.P. McBrien, "Collegiality: State of the Question," in *The Once and Future Church,* ed. J.A. Coriden, Staten Island, 1971.

FREDERICK J. CWIEKOWSKI

COMMANDMENTS OF THE CHURCH

Tradition has accepted certain "commandments of the Church" in addition to the "ten commandments of God" to guide the faithful in their duties as members of the church. There has never been any official pronouncement about their number or content. From as early as the ninth century, prayer books listed such duties to help people examine their conscience in preparation for confession. The principal obligations included attendance at Sunday Mass, observance of fast days, payment of tithes to the church and Easter communion. Through time the "commandments of the Church" were given more and more prominence and

they were given special attention under this heading in the moral theology textbooks of the thirteenth century.

In the fifteenth century St. Antoninus listed ten as binding on all the faithful. In the following century St. Peter Canisius listed five and St. Robert Bellarmine opted for six. German catechisms tended to follow Canisius, whereas Italian and French catechisms followed Bellarmine. A nineteenth-century catechism used in England also listed six, and it was this list that was adopted by the Third Plenary Council of Baltimore (1886) for all U.S. catechisms. The same list seems to have been accepted by practically all the catechisms of the English-speaking world until the Second Vatican Council.

Neither the 1917 code of canon law, the Second Vatican Council, or the new 1983 code speak of the commandments or precepts of the church. Indeed the obligations of the faithful (including clerics) are more numerous than the traditional six, and the new code often speaks of them in association with the "rights" of Christ's faithful. Thus, the faithful "have the right and the obligation" to make the message of salvation known to all people, to manifest views on matters which concern the good of the church, to educate their children, to acquire a knowledge of christian teaching, to preserve communion with the church, to lead a life of holiness and contribute to the holiness of the church, to respect and work for the common good of the church. It can hardly be claimed that these are less important than the traditional six summarized in catechisms for easy recall.

However, the traditional six are still to be found as part of the church's law, but scattered here and there throughout the 1983 code as follows: 1) Attend Mass on Sundays and Holydays (can. 1247). Instead of a ban on "servile work" the faithful are asked to abstain from any work or business "that would inhibit the worship to be given to God, the joy proper to the Lord's Day, or the due relaxation of mind and body." 2) Fast and abstain on specified days (can. 1250); leaving episcopal conferences free to specify this further (can. 1253). 3) Annual confession, if serious sin has been committed (can. 989). 4) Easter Communion (can. 920). The obligation is to receive once a year, preferably during the Easter season, but for a good reason it may be fulfilled at another time. 5) To contribute to the support of the church (can. 222), not just of "the clergy." The obligation to observe and promote social justice is presented as part of this precept, something not mentioned so explicitly before. 6) To observe the church's laws concerning marriage (can. 1055-1165). There have been a number of changes in this area, e.g., instead of forbidding marriage during certain times of the year, the code refers to the recommendations of the approved liturgical books.

Whether future catechisms will continue the tradition of summarizing some basic norms for memorizing and easy recall remains to be seen. In the past they were a useful reminder of the minimum requirements demanded of members of the church. They may still serve that purpose, but they should never be separated from the broader context of the more basic rights and obligations outlined in the Vatican II documents and spelled out more explicitly in the new code of canon law.

See **Canon Law; Moral Life, Christian**

SEÁN FAGAN, SM

COMMUNICATIO IDIOMATUM

A technical term in Christology, meaning the interchange or communication of properties whereby, because of the hypostatic union, the properties of both natures are predicated of the one Person of Christ and sentences are possible in which what strictly is true of only one nature is attributed to the other. This permits one to say, for example, that "the Son of God suffered on the cross" or that "Jesus is the one through whom the world was created."

See **Jesus Christ**

COMMUNION OF SAINTS

The Latin phrase, *communio sanctorum,* can be translated either as "the communion of saints" or as "communion in holy things." This underlying ambiguity in meaning is evident in the history and interpretation of the phrase in the creed.

Article of the Creed

It is not until the end of the fifth century that one finds *communio sanctorum* ("Communion of Saints") part of a christian creed. This insertion apparently begins in the West, particularly in southern Gaul. Nicetas of Remesiana (D.S. 19) speaks of *communio sanctorum* in a way which scholars conclude implies a stabilized creed. Faustus of Riez (d. 490) and Caesarius of Arles (d. 542), both of southern Gaul, clearly attest to it as part of the creed in their area. In the seventh century it is found in Ireland; the Gallican Sacramentary of the same century evidences it, and traces of it are found in England in the ninth century. Nicholas I (856-867), it seems, brought about the adoption of *communio sanctorum* in Rome. Nonetheless, even in the twelfth century some creeds in Italy do not have *communio sanctorum* as an article. Eastern creeds do not contain *communio sanctorum,* so that one must conclude that it is clearly a western addition to the creed.

Two theories have been proposed by scholars for the appearance of *communio sanctorum* in southern Gaul: (a) *communio sanctorum* originated in the East [probably Dacia] and was brought to the West. Harnack and De Morin have been leading advocates of this interpretation. Nicetas is eastern, i.e., Bishop of Dacia (presently Yugoslavia), and his instruction to the catechumens needs to be explained. (b) The second view is that its origin is western (southern Gaul) and was passed on to Nicetas, perhaps through Hilary (Kelly). Probably the exact origin of *communio sanctorum*'s admission into the creed will never be established.

Harnack also notes that the Gallican Church at that time was concerned about the "righteous dead," which would account for the appearance of *communio sanctorum* in southern Gaul. Others counter that *communio sanctorum* is not clearly denotative of the dead and a defense of a cult of the dead would have required a more precise term.

The position of Rufinus that each apostle contributed one of the twelve articles of the Apostles Creed, and therefore *communio sanctorum*, is totally unfounded, even though Sermon 240 of Pseudo-Augustine attributes *communio sanctorum* to Matthew, and Sermon 241 of Pseudo-Augustine attributes *communio sanctorum* to Simon the Zealot.

History of the Article

Even though the inclusion of *communio sanctorum* is late as an addition to some western creeds, and even though it did not become a part of the eastern creeds, *communio sanctorum* as a theological concept does indeed antedate its inclusion into the creeds and does have an eastern as well as a western base. However, in Greek, *communio sanctorum* is not a common expression. Still, in 388 one finds it in a rescript of the emperors Gratian, Valentinian and Theodosius (Cod. Theod. 16, 5, 14). It seemingly refers to eucharistic communion. Later Eastern writers spoke of *ta agia* but also in reference to the eucharist. Basil, Isidore of Pelusium, Athanasius, and Pseudo-

Basil, refer *communio sanctorum* to a communion *with* the saints, i.e., holy persons.

In the western church *communio sanctorum* is rare prior to the end of the fourth century. Augustine, applies it to the eucharist. In Africa, during the time of Augustine, *sancta* (holy things) had frequent reference to the eucharist. However, Augustine also uses the term "communion of the sacraments." The Councils of Vienne (394) and of Nimes (396) use *communio sanctorum* in reference to the eucharist.

In the creed, *communio sanctorum* is associated with the Holy Spirit. Already in Hippolytus we find: "Do you believe in the Holy Spirit, and the holy Church and the resurrection of the body?" In doing this Hippolytus attests to the theological connection of Spirit/Church/Risen Body, which will become one of the bases for subsequent interpretations of *communio sanctorum*. In the East, a major theological position was: "What is not assumed is not saved." There is a fundamental communion (*koinonia*) between God, the source of all holiness, and what is sanctified (saved). Eastern theologians, such as Cyril of Alexandria and Athanasius, make this a touchstone for christology and soteriology. The incarnate Logos is not only holy but holy-making (sanctifying). The presence of the incarnate and risen Logos in the church is the basis for communion with holiness. In Eastern thought this is accomplished through the Holy Spirit of Jesus. This theology of *ta agia* antedated the formula *communio sanctorum* and gave a basis for its subsequent interpretation. Since *communio sanctorum,* in the trinitarian creed structure, is associated with the Holy Spirit, it must be seen against the pneumatology of the early centuries.

In the West, Faustus of Riez interpreted *communio sanctorum* as a cult of the holy dead; a homily from the same

period connects it with the cult of relics. A Pseudo-Augustine sermon of the sixth century reads: "The communion of the saints signifies that we form a society with the saints who have died in this faith, and which we have received, and that we are with them in a communion of hope" (Ser. 242). *Ta agia,* although it has not lost totally its neuter meaning of holy things, begins to take on a personal meaning, "holy persons."

During the early Middle Ages most of the authors (e.g., Alcuin, Rhabanus Maurus, Walafrid Strabo) followed the Pseudo-Augustine approach, i.e., a personalizing of *sanctorum.* Ivo of Chartres nuanced this so that *communio sanctorum* referred to a communion in the sacraments, in which those saints who have departed from this life in the unity of faith also take part (Ser. 23). Jocelin of Soissons repeats Ivo. A few, however, continued to stress the neuter interpretation of *sanctorum* (Abelard, John Fecamp). Bernard of Clairvaux interpreted *communio sanctorum* as an interchange of merit with the saints in heaven. Peter Lombard concurs in this interpretation.

Alexander of Hales viewed *communio sanctorum* as both a sharing in the sacraments and a sharing in a relationship with all the members of the church, Albert the Great picked up the sharing in the sacraments, but also mentions a sharing of one believer in the holy elements of another believer, a combination of both person and things. Thomas Aquinas tended to a more neutral interpretation, namely, a sharing in the holy elements of the church, but he included at least indirectly a sharing between persons. For Thomas this communion is based on Jesus Christ.

In the counter-reformation period, a polemical aspect was given to *communio sanctorum,* namely a communion with the pope (Bellarmine). Stress was also placed on a sharing of good merits by the souls in purgatory (Canisius). This rather moral and apologetic approach was continued by others (Alexander, Sailer, Drey, Hirscher), but through J. A. Moehler and later Jungmann a mystical communion was emphasized.

Contemporary Interpretation

Communio sanctorum has not been a major focus, but in the wake of Vatican II some theologians, such as W. Breuning, attempted to relate it to the church as a basic sacrament, and even Jesus as the primordial sacrament. This has given it a strong christological and ecclesiological base. Already Pius XII had related *communio sanctorum* to the Mystical Body teaching on the church. One could say that fellowship with Jesus is the basis for fellowship in the church and in the kingdom. Such fellowship with Jesus is concomitantly fellowship with the Holy Spirit, for it is the Spirit of Jesus which founds the church. This theological interpretation helps to understand the reason for locating *communio sanctorum,* in the creed, in the section dealing with the Holy Spirit.

Nonetheless, one must say that for today's theology a clearer connection between *communio sanctorum* and the kingdom is needed. Up until now the stress, both in Catholic and Protestant interpretation, has been on the church, not on the kingdom. Vatican II teaches that the church and the kingdom are not coterminous, and therefore there must be a communion in the holy: (a) outside the Roman Catholic Church; (b) outside the christian church generally; (c) outside the Judaeo-Christian tradition, and therefore in the area of other world religions as well.

To do this, one must distinguish between the "core" meaning of *communio sanctorum,* which one can consider "defined" due to its incorporation in the creed, and the theological interpretation, which is not defined.

Like other articles of the creed, there is a certain indefiniteness about the statement of *communio sanctorum*; cf., e.g., the creedal statements on salvation, which are general: "Christ died for us." Over the years, many theological positions on the meaning of this phrase, none of which are creedally defined, have taken place. Ghellinck noted this when he wrote: *communio sanctorum* "is one of the most difficult passages to interpret in the whole Creed." Lamirande continues this line of thought: "Not history or contemporary theologians or the magisterium have succeeded in giving a precise definition to the article. Since its first appearance, there have been a number of interpretations; not one of them has proved able to oust the others." One thing is clear, however, unless *communio sanctorum* is rooted in a solid christological base, it will have little meaning within the ecclesiological spheres.

See **Church**

J.P. Kirsch, *Die Lehre von der Gemeinschaft der Heiligen im christlichen Altertum* (1900). P. Bernard, "Communion des Saints," *DTC*III (1908). H.B. Swete, *The Holy Catholic Church, the Communion of Saints* (1916). F.J. Babcock, "Sanctorum Communio as an Article of the Creed," *JTS,* 21 (1919). H. Seesemann, *Der Begriff der Koinonia im Neuen Testament,* (1933). J. de Ghellinck, *Patristique et moyen-age,* 1 (1949). J.N.D. Kelly, *Early Christian Creeds,* 1950. A. Piolanti, *Il Misterio della Communione dei Santi nella Rivelazione e nella Teologia* (1957). G. Morin, "Sanctorum communionem," *Revue d'histoire et de litterature religieuses,* 9 (1904). E. Lamerande, *The Communion of Saints,* trans. A. Manson (1963). P.A. Liege, *Catholicisme* (1949).

KENAN B. OSBORNE, OFM

COMMUNITY

According to Webster's Dictionary, a community is a body of people having common organization or interests or living in the same place under the same laws. The German philosopher Max Scheler would refine that definition by distinguishing a community from a family and from a corporation. A community is like a family in that relationships between members of the community are basically personal in character rather than impersonal; it is unlike a family in that the association between members of the community is based on free choice rather than common ancestry. Contrarily, a community is like a corporation (*Gesellschaft*) in that membership is based on free choice, but unlike a corporation in that it is person-oriented rather than task-oriented. The ideal community is, accordingly, a free association of individual persons who prize their interpersonal relationships more highly than any other goal or value which they might otherwise achieve in living and working together. As such, person and community are correlative concepts: to be a true person is to be a member of a genuine community.

What remains ambiguous, however, is the notion of the community itself as a specifically social reality. Scheler, for example, refers to it as a *Gesamtperson* (totality-person) which in its being and activity resembles an individual person. Implicitly, therefore, he is thinking of community in organismic terms. That is, like Plato and Hegel in their respective theories of the state, Scheler conceives the community as a supraindividual person with a mind and will of its own which is in some sense distinct from the minds and wills of its individual person-members. The community, accordingly, enjoys a theoretical priority over its members which in some cases might be used by unscrupulous individuals as a justification to exercise totalitarian control over the others in the name of the common good. The other classic approach to the ontological reality of the community, however, has equally grave limitations. Philosophers and sociologists who conceive the community to be nothing more than a functional unity created by the dynamic interplay of already existing individuals run the risk of so emptying the notion of the common good of any real significance and value that rugged individualism or a *laissez-faire* approach to community life is the inevitable result.

Clearly needed is a mediating third position which would make evident the ontological status of the community as a specifically social reality without compromising the independence and integrity of the person-members. Josiah Royce, teaching at Harvard at the beginning of this century, argues in *The Problem of Christianity* that a community is a social process (literally, a "time-process") which has a corporate identity in some sense distinct from the life histories of its members, taken singly. The history of the United States, for example, is not simply reducible to the sum total of the lives of all its individual citizens. More importantly, however, he specifies that this time-process is a communal process of interpretation which arises naturally out of the ongoing exchange of "signs" by the members of the community with one another. That is, each of the community members is continually engaged in the effort to establish their identity within the group. As such they are obliged to interpret whatever happens to themselves and formulate a response in terms of some appropriate word or deed. Others perceive these "signs" and, in turn, must respond with signs representing their interpretations of what is transpiring between them. Thus their efforts to communicate with one another through the exchange of signs or individual interpretations of various events spontaneously brings about the reality of the community as a communal process of interpretation. Out of this communal process, moreover, come by degrees all the trappings of civilized existence: language, culture,

political and social institutions, etc.

In the same book, Royce also makes clear that in his judgment Christianity is the world religion *par excellence* because of its doctrine of the Mystical Body of Christ. That is, Christians are thereby encouraged to believe that the forgiveness of sins and/or salvation is to be achieved not simply through a person's individual relationship with God but also and more significantly through an intensified life in community with other believers as members of Christ's Body: in the first place, the Church as the Beloved Community of Interpretation; but, in the end, all of humanity as the Universal Community of Interpretation. The familiar christian precept to love one's neighbor as oneself should then be understood as the mandate to remain in communication with others through the exchange of signs and thus to perpetuate the reality of church and civil society as interrelated communities of interpretation. Only thus will the Kingdom of God be revealed in its intended fullness, namely, as a Universal Community of Interpretation or, perhaps more precisely, as an overarching community of subcommunities, each of which is involved through its person-members in the task of articulating its corporate self-identity while remaining aware of its interdependent relationship with other communities at work on the same task.

Even if one has reservations about this speculative attempt to reinterpret christian charity, first, as loyalty to the communities of one's choice but ultimately as loyalty to the worldwide community of humankind, Royce's basic hypothesis that Christianity is a religion based on an ideal of life in community seems well grounded. Admittedly, some christian denominations give the impression of being more group-oriented than others. Roman Catholicism, for example, with its strong sacramental life and clearly defined moral code has traditionally placed heavy emphasis on disciplined group behavior, above all, regular participation at Sunday Mass. Yet Protestant denominations, on the contrary, might well claim that their own more loosely organized, democratic approach to church life actually fosters a stronger sense of community among its members. In any event, Royce's claim is that Christianity has a divine mission to foster worldwide community through the example of its own members' active participation in community life. Included in this mission, of course, must be the further mandate to establish communities based on justice and equality rather than on power and privilege. But the very willingness to remain in communication with those who interpret reality differently from oneself and to seek with them grounds for common action is the indispensable precondition for the establishment of true justice and genuine equality within any community.

Curiously missing in Royce's theory is any significant reference to the Trinity as a community of three divine persons. In *The Problem of Christianity,* to be sure, Royce calls attention to the lack of a fully developed theology of the Holy Spirit which he sees as essential to the understanding of the workings of the christian community, the idea that the worldwide Community of Interpretation might somehow participate in the primordial Community of Interpretation constituted by the divine persons presumably did not occur to him. Juan Luis Segundo in *Our Idea of God,* on the other hand, argues that the traditional notion of God as a single, self-sufficient personal being has contributed notably to the spirit of rugged individualism in Western culture. For, to be like God is thus to be self-sufficient, independent of others. The concept of God as a community of three divine persons who are sympathetically involved with men and women in their struggle to

form and maintain stable forms of community life, however, would set forth the opposite ideal of interdependence as the perfection of human existence. By implication, then, the mission of Christianity to promote worldwide community will not be satisfactorily carried out until Christians themselves internalize the notion of God as a community of divine persons who offer salvation to their rational creatures in the form of intensified life in community.

See **Church**

John MacMurray, *Persons in Relation,* London: Faber & Faber, 1961. Ernest Ranly, *Scheler's Phenomenology of Community,* The Hague: Nijhoff Press, 1966. Josiah Royce, *The Problem of Christianity,* 2nd ed., Chicago: University of Chicago Press, 1968. Juan Luis Segundo, S.J., *Our Idea of God* [*A Theology for Artisans of a New Humanity,* Vol. III] Maryknoll: Orbis, 1974. John P. Schanz, *A Theology of Community,* Washington, D.C.: University Press of America, 1977. Joseph A. Bracken, *The Triune Symbol: Persons, Process and Community,* Lanham, MD: University Press of America, 1985. Frank G. Kirkpatrick, *Community: A Trinity of Models,* Washington, D.C.: Georgetown University Press, 1986.

JOSEPH A. BRACKEN, SJ

CONCILIARISM

Conciliarism, or the conciliar theory, is the name given to the various forms of teaching which held the belief that a general council constitutes the supreme authority in the church. The origins of this teaching are found in medieval ecclesiology and canon law, though it was only at the time of the Western Schism (1378–1417) that conciliar thought came into prominence and won wide acceptance.

Antecedents of conciliar thought appear in the efforts of early thirteenth century canonists who, while holding that the pope was the divinely willed head of the church, explored ways to offset possible abuses in the growing power of the papacy. Discussions of the relationship between papal power and the church represented in a general council (or, in some early forms of this speculation, of the pope's relation to the local church or to the college of cardinals) were largely theoretical. Topics treated included such issues as the possibility of a pope's error in the faith, his violation of the canons of previous councils, or his persistence in notorious crime. In the discussions and writings of this period, it was generally agreed that the authority of pope and bishops acting in a general council was greater than the authority of the pope acting alone. More radical views held that bishops in council, in united agreement against a pope, had greater authority.

Discussions of conciliar theory became more practical in the late thirteenth and fourteenth centuries in the face of increasing centralization of ecclesiastical power in the papacy and Roman Curia and tensions between the papacy and state authority. The most important treatise which sought to describe the limits of papal power came in the works of the Dominican John Quidort (John of Paris) c. 1300. More radical expressions of conciliar thought came in the fourteenth century, in the writings of Marsilius of Padua and William of Ockham. An earlier view, however, that conciliarism was the creation of these last two writers has not been sustained in recent scholarship.

Conciliar teaching became a viable option in the wake of the Western Schism when there were two and, after 1409, three contenders to the papal chair. In the face of these events many moderate thinkers and church leaders turned to conciliar thought as a way out of the impasse of the current situation. We find such exponents of conciliar theory in Conrad of Gelnhausen and Dietrich of Nieheim of Germany, Peter of Ailly and Jean Gerson of France, and Francesco

Zabarella of Italy. The most thorough presentation of conciliar thought came in the work of the German cardinal and philosopher, Nicholas of Cusa. While these late fourteenth and fifteenth century writers used some of the arguments of Marsilius of Padua and William of Ockham, they did not espouse their more extreme positions, such as Marsilius' denial of the divine origin of the papacy.

It was the Council of Constance (1414-1418) which gave what are considered the classical formulations of conciliar thought, most especially in the decrees *Haec sancta* (Session 5) and *Frequens* (Session 39). The first decree called for people of every state and dignity in the church, including the pope, to submit to a general council in an effort to uproot the current schism and unite and reform the church in its head and members. The second decree looked to frequent general councils to promote the church's reform and growth. While the binding value of these decrees has been the subject of much discussion even in recent times, it is generally recognized that the decrees are best understood in the context of the need for reform and unity occasioned by the Western Schism.

Conciliar thought suffered a reversal in the quarrels that marked the Council of Basle (1431). Popes of the period prohibited appeals from the pope to a council. The Council of Florence (1438-1445) in its Decree for the Greeks (1439) made a strong affirmation of the primacy of the Roman Pontiff. Pius II in 1460 explicitly condemned an appeal from a pope's sentence to a universal council. Even so, conciliar teaching in moderate forms continued to find advocates among canonists and theologians in the later fifteenth and sixteenth centuries. Conciliar thought, sometimes in more radical forms, had an influence on the development of Gallicanism and Febronianism in the seventeenth and eighteenth centuries.

Conciliarism must be understood and evaluated in the light of its origins and the specific historical situation which led church leaders to turn to it as a means of ending an intolerable situation. In the light of the Western Schism one can understand how pope and council could be viewed as separate entities. But conciliar tenets that the council of bishops independently of the pope possesses supreme ecclesiastical authority or that the pope is but representative of the entire church or of its bishops are today incompatible with Catholic doctrine. Many of the positive values of conciliar thought survive in current church doctrine and theological teaching on collegiality. The teaching of Vatican II, in its Constitution on the Church, emphasizes the collegial unity between pope and bishops. United with the pope as head of the college and never apart from him the college of bishops has supreme and full authority over the universal church. This supreme authority which the college possesses is exercised in a solemn way in an ecumenical council.

See **Collegiality, Council, Pope**

V. Martin, "Comment s'est formée la doctrine de la supériorité du concile sur le pape," RSR 17 (1937), pp. 121-43, 261-89, 404-27. B. Tierney, *Foundations of the Conciliar Theory,* Cambridge, 1955. H. Jedin, A History of the Council of Trent, I, St. Louis, 1957, pp. 5-61.

FREDERICK J. CWIEKOWSKI

CONCUPISCENCE

The orientation or inclination of lower human faculties towards some created good without respect for or subordination to the higher faculties. In Catholic belief, man was created exempt from concupiscence, whose existence and power, therefore, are the result of original sin. Against the Reformers, the Council of Trent taught that concupiscence is not itself sinful, but results from and induces towards sin.

See **Anthropology, Christian; Grace; Sin**

CONFESSION

"Confession" has two meanings in connection with the sacrament. First, together with "penance" and "reconciliation," it is a name for the sacrament itself; second, along with contrition and satisfaction, it is one of the elements in the matter of the sacrament necessary for its validity, namely, the telling of sins by the penitent to the confessor.

The 1974 Rite of Penance prefers "penance" or "reconciliation" as a name for the sacrament; the 1983 Code of Canon Law uses "penance" and "confession." The code uses "confession" principally in its treatment of the faithful's obligation to confess serious sins and of the faculty necessary for priests validly to hear the confession of and absolve penitents.

The most important act of the penitent is contrition, but confession of sins to the priest and satisfaction for sins committed are also essential. Contrition comes from an inner examination of heart and confession is the exterior accusation requiring in penitents the will to open their hearts to the minister of God (Rite of Penance, no. 6).

Canon law states that all the faithful, after having attained the age of discretion, are bound to confess their serious sins at least once a year (canon 989). Ordinarily, it must be an individual and not a general confession of serious sins which one is conscious of having committed after baptism and which have not yet been confessed and absolved in individual confession. Moreover, it must be an integral confession, that is, telling of both the kind and number of serious sins (canon 988). The sacramental confession of *venial* sins is recommended but not required (988).

General confession and absolution is permitted only under restricted conditions (canon 961). For the validity of a general absolution, the penitents must be suitably disposed and intend to confess individually their serious sins which cannot be so confessed presently. The law also requires, but not for validity, that after receiving a general absolution the penitents in serious sin approach individual confession as soon as there is an opportunity to do so and before receiving another general absolution unless a just cause intervenes (canon 962).

Besides the annual precept to confess serious sins, canon law requires sacramental confession of persons who are conscious of a serious sin before they may celebrate Mass or receive Communion. However, if there is a grave reason and there is no opportunity for confessing, they may celebrate Mass or receive Communion if they elicit an act of perfect contrition, which includes the intention of confessing serious sins as soon as possible (canon 916). The requirement of sacramental confession before First Communion (canon 914) strictly obliges only those conscious of serious sin.

The faculty for priests to hear confessions can be granted by law or delegation. By law, the following have the faculty: the pope, cardinals, and bishops for anywhere in the world; local Ordinaries who are not bishops, canons penitentiary, and pastors within their jurisdictions; superiors of clerical religious institutes or clerical societies of apostolic life for their subjects and others staying in their house day and night; and any priest for a penitent in danger of death. The local Ordinary alone is competent to grant to presbyters the delegated faculty to hear confessions of all the faithful; the superior of a clerical religious house or a clerical society of apostolic life can delegate any presbyter the faculty to hear the confessions of his subjects and others staying in the house day and night. (See canons 965-976).

All the faithful are free to confess their sins to a lawfully approved confessor of their choice, even to one of another rite (canon 991). The proper place to celebrate individual penance is in a confessional room located in a church or oratory; it can take place outside of a confessional for a just cause (canon 964).

See **Conversion, Reconciliation, Sin**

M. Francis Mannion, "Penance and Reconciliation: A Systematic Analysis," *Worship* 60 (1986) 98-118. Ladislas Orsy, *The Evolving Church and the Sacrament of Penance,* Denville, N.J., 1978.

JOHN M. HUELS, OSM

CONFIRMATION

The sacrament of confirmation has had an extremely complex historical development. No other sacrament has changed so frequently through the centuries in its ritual and meaning. No other sacrament has so clearly shown such a variety of interpretations, especially in the Western church.

The development of confirmation cannot be separated from the development of all three initiation sacraments: baptism, confirmation, eucharist. Christian initiation in the NT focuses on two persons: Jesus the Christ and John the Baptizer. John's baptism, like his preaching, pointed beyond itself. His purpose was to prepare the way for Christ. His message was eschatological: "Repent, for the kingdom of heaven is at hand." (Mt 3:2) Jesus, too, began his preaching career in the same way (Mt 4:17) The close connection between Jesus and John was the fact that Jesus accepted baptism at the hands of John. Jesus' baptism by John serves as a revelation of the mystery of salvation in Jesus. Jesus is baptized, not for his own sins, but for the sins of others.

He is baptized in view of his death, which will cause the Spirit of forgiveness to be given to the church. Thus, after the death of Jesus, his followers continue to use the water-rite as the chief vehicle of expressing the forgiveness of sins and the imparting of the Holy Spirit. The Jordan event, Jesus' baptism by John, sets the tone for the way christian initiation is understood. Just as Jesus was anointed with the Spirit in the Jordan, so his followers are anointed with the same Spirit. The water-bath of conversion is primarily an event of the Holy Spirit.

In certain passages of the Acts of the Apostles, however, there seems to be a disjunction between water and the spirit. In one case (Acts 8) baptism in the name of Jesus is administered by Philip to the Samaritan, but is not accompanied by the gift of the Holy Spirit. This creates a problem for a Pauline understanding of baptism. In Paul's eyes the Spirit is the fundamental mark of belonging to Christ, and the gift of the Spirit is the result of baptism. For Paul, sacramental dying and rising with Christ is one reality, and it brings about union with the pneuma-Christ. In light of this many scholars argue that the writings of the NT offer no ground for a distinction between baptism and confirmation, and that the problem of confirmation as a separate sacrament seems to be a post-NT problem.

Nevertheless, from a very early date in the church's life, certain elements of the baptism complex began to receive varying degrees of attention with varying degrees of emphasis and meaning attached to them. As early as Tertullian we find in his *De Baptismo* (c. 200) the baptismal rite being divided into two parts: the water-bath with its anointing, and the imposition of hands, with the gift of the Spirit being attributed to the latter. The Roman pattern is seen in the *Apostolic Tradition* of Hippolytus (c. 215) where the presbyteral postbaptismal anointing is brought to completion by the action of the bishop when he lays on his hand, anoints, and seals the forehead of the candidate. Pope Innocent in a letter (c. 416) to the bishop of Gubbio sets the rule quite firmly: presbyters may anoint the baptized with chrism but they are not to sign the brow with the oil, "for that is reserved to bishops alone when they deliver the Spirit the Paraclete." This papal insistence on reserving to the bishop the "signing of the brow" was to mark the West for its excessive concern for the presence of a bishop for the administration of confirmation, while the East would be more concerned with the traditional order of the sacraments: baptism, chrismation, and eucharist. The Eastern churches would see the presence of the bishop in the chrism that had been consecrated by him.

Influential in the understanding of confirmation as a separate sacrament was a certain Faustus, who became the bishop of Riez in 458. He delivered a homily on Pentecost that would be frequently quoted and would play an important role in history. This homily is the first doctrinal explanation of a separated "confirmation ceremony" outside cases of rebaptism and reconciliation of heretics. Faustus states that baptism is complete as to innocence, but as to grace there is a question of its augmentation through confirmation. In baptism we are regenerated to life; after baptism we are confirmed for battle. In baptism we are washed; after baptism we are strengthened. Confirmation brings this "augmentation in grace" enabling one to take part in the struggle of human life. Baptism is what is passively received, while confirmation stresses human effort and involvement. This semi-Pelagian approach to the understanding of confirmation offered by bishop Faustus would have widespread bearing in the church of the West, and would be passed down right to modern times both in conciliar teaching and in popular understanding.

During the course of the Middle Ages confirmation gradually became separated not only from the paschal vigil but even from the context of christian initiation itself. Some authors call the historical development of confirmation the disintegration of the primitive rite of initiation. In the West the overall trend was to separate confirmation from baptism. Insisting that confirmation be done by a bishop would cause problems in large dioceses where frequent episcopal visits were impossible. Likewise the growing belief in water baptism as the sole means of salvation would result in infants being baptized shortly after birth.

In seventh- and eighth-century Gaul the liturgical books reflect only one postbaptismal anointing, since confirmation by the bishop was not yet insisted upon. However, with the Carolingian reform the mandatory presence of a bishop according to the Roman pattern was insisted upon. The addition of a second anointing by the bishop created a problem in Gallican understanding, and theologians of the day worked to find a theology for the new practice. Alcuin greatly influenced later thinking by his comment that the imposition of the hand of the bishop confers the Holy Spirit so that the person may be strengthened through the Holy Spirit to preach to others. This emphasis on one particular gift of the Spirit (fortitude) opposed the earlier emphasis on the reception of the gift of the Spirit as such. In addition, this interpretation was reinforced popularly by the gesture of the confirming bishop being changed from a welcoming kiss of peace into a symbol of spiritual combat, the bishop striking the candidate's cheek.

Likewise during this period confirmation was being separated from the eucharist. During the first millennium, even when newly baptized infants could not be confirmed due to the absence of a bishop, there was no question about their receiving first eucharist after their baptism. But gradually the practice died out. In 1215 the Fourth Council of the Lateran stated that communion was not obligatory until one reaches the "years of discretion." The final blow was dealt by the Council of Trent (1545-1563) which stated that baptized infants had no need of communion since they were incapable of losing their baptismal grace. This brought about the final dismemberment of the three sacraments of initiation: baptism, confirmation, and eucharist. Confirmation, in the West, stood on its own. All the while the Eastern church preserved the original unified rite of initiation, and viewed initiation as a whole as being imbedded in pneumatology. Furthermore, the Easter initiation theology included not only the Pauline concept of dying and rising with Christ, but also the Jordan event where Christ is born of water and the Spirit.

The scholastic theologians treated the sacrament of confirmation not in the older context of initiation, but more in the context of what effect the sacrament had upon a person already baptized. They took for granted the ideas presented by Faustus and others, seeing confirmation as an increase of grace and a strengthening for battle. In the framework of Thomas Aquinas' dominant analogy between bodily growth and spiritual growth, confirmation is seen as the sacrament of spiritual maturity. Thomas describes that maturity as preparation for a spiritual battle outside one's self against the enemies of the faith. Baptism, for him, pertains to salvation in so far as one lives for oneself. For Aquinas, confirmation, like baptism and holy order, imprints a character which is a "certain kind of participation in the priesthood of Christ."

Conciliar teaching followed very closely

the teaching of Aquinas. The Council of Florence (1438-1445) stated that in place of that imposition of hands of Acts 8, confirmation is given in the church. The text was not an attempt to see "confirmation" in the Acts of the Apostles, but an assertion that the sacramental reality today called confirmation accomplished that which the imposition of hands accomplished in apostolic times. The Council of Trent spoke in the cultural milieu of the Reformation. It defended the sacramental character of confirmation against the reformers who had denied it. The reformers had felt that the importance of baptism had been weakened by attributing too much to the subsidiary rites such as handlaying and anointing. The Council of Trent "defended" confirmation against such a teaching.

The 1917 Code of Canon Law prescribed that confirmation be conferred by the imposition of the hand with the anointing of the forehead. This was interpreted by canonists as referring principally neither to the imposition of the hand nor to the anointing but to one act by which the hand was imposed and the chrism was applied at one and the same time.

The Second Vatican Council said very little about the sacrament of confirmation. By far the most important thing it did state was: "The rite of confirmation is also to be revised in order that the intimate connection of this sacrament with the whole of christian initiation may stand out more clearly" (S.C. 71). Confirmation's connection with the total initiation process is the key for an understanding of the sacrament. This was stressed by Pope Paul VI in the opening words of his Apostolic Constitution, *Divinae Consortium Naturae,* which promulgated the new rite of confirmation in 1971: "The sharing in the divine nature which is granted to men through the grace of Christ has a certain likeness to the origin, development, and nourishing of natural life. The faithful are born anew by baptism, strengthened by the sacrament of confirmation, and finally are sustained by the food of eternal life in the eucharist."

Both the Apostolic Constitution and the *Rite of Confirmation* avoid the term "matter" and "form" of the sacrament. The rite includes two laying on of hands: the general or global imposition over all the candidates that the bishop performs before the anointing as he says the prayer for the sevenfold gifts of the Spirit, and the individual imposition on each candidate as the anointing takes place. Paul VI explained in the Apostolic Constitution that the former imposition, while pertaining to the integral perfection of the rite, does not belong to the essence of the sacrament. He stated: "The sacrament of confirmation is conferred through the anointing with chrism on the forehead, which is done by the laying on of the hands, and through the words: *Accipe Signaculum Doni Spiritus Sancti.* ("Be sealed with the Gift of the Holy Spirit.") The formula, the words of the rite, presents an adoption of a Byzantine formula that probably had been in use in the East since the fifth century. The formula combines two NT passages: Eph 1:13 where Paul writes that in Christ "you were sealed with the promised Holy Spirit," and Acts 2:38 where Peter in his Pentecost sermon urges his hearers to be baptized: "and you shall receive the gift of the Holy Spirit."

The rite states that the "original" minister of confirmation is the bishop. The switch from the previously used "ordinary" minister to "original" minister was due to a sensitivity to objections from the Oriental Catholic Church where priests are able to confer the sacrament, using chrism blessed by their patriarch or bishop. This ecumenical sensitivity has been abandoned by the 1983 Code of Canon Law where the bishop is once again called the ordinary minister (canon 882).

The age of confirmands is something that varies a great deal throughout the Western church. In 1774 the Congregation for the Propagation of the Faith issued an Instruction for priests on the missions who were allowed to confirm, and that Instruction was reproduced in all rituals down to that of 1925. A delay until the seventh year was spoken of, but the minister may and should confirm earlier if there is any danger to the child or chance of a valid minister not being available in the future, since the child would thus be deprived of a greater glory in heaven. In the late nineteenth century Pope Leo XIII approved the practice of conferring confirmation before first communion. He argued that all the faithful need the grace given in confirmation, even from their youth, because it better prepares them to receive the eucharist. In spite of his plea, the practice of placing confirmation after first eucharist rather than before continued in most dioceses throughout the world.

The 1917 Code of Canon Law stated: "Although the administration of the sacrament of confirmation should preferably be postponed in the Latin Church until the seventh year of age, nevertheless it can be conferred before that age if the infant is in danger of death or its administration seems to the minister justified for good and serious reasons." (canon 788). In 1932 the Sacred Congregation for the Sacraments stated that it was more in conformity with the nature of confirmation that children should not come to first communion until they had received confirmation. In summary it can be said that the Holy See frequently urged during the first half of the twentieth century that the age of confirmation be lowered in practice, and that the traditional order of

the initiation sacraments be maintained.

Both the *Rite of Confirmation* (1971) and the *Rite of Christian Initiation of Adults* (1972) show the ideal of giving to adults all three initiation sacraments together: baptism, confirmation, eucharist. With regard to children the *Rite of Confirmation* repeated the legislation of the 1917 code of postponing confirmation until the seventh year of age, but it added a new option: "For pastoral reasons, however, especially to strengthen in the life of the faithful complete obedience to Christ the Lord in loyal testimony to him, episcopal conferences may choose an age which appears more appropriate, so that the sacrament is conferred after appropriate formation at a more mature age" (no. 11). Interestingly, the 1983 Code of Canon Law makes no mention of conferring confirmation at a more mature age. Canon 891 stated: "The sacrament of confirmation is to be conferred on the faithful at about the age of discretion unless the conference of bishops determines another age or there is danger of death or in the judgment of the minister a grave cause urges otherwise." It would seem that an earlier as well as a later age could be chosen, and that episcopal conferences could even opt for the practice of infant confirmation, although certainly the thrust of the canon is for the conferral of confirmation at the age of discretion.

Underlying the diversity of practice as to the age of confirmation lies a diversity of the theological understanding as to the meaning of the sacrament of confirmation. Some sacramental theologians identify the initiation sacraments with distinct moments in the life cycle while others do not. This has given rise to two general schools of thought. Those who deny the identification tend to stress aspects of dogmatic and liturgical theology and argue for the unity of the initiation process and the traditional order of baptism, confirmation, and eucharist. Those who affirm the identification of the initiation sacraments with the moments in the life cycle tend to stress pastoral and anthropological aspects of theology and argue for the faith involvement of the subject, viewed from the psychological explanation of the development of personality. They would not insist on the traditional ordering of the sacraments and would argue for a later age of confirmation at the time of adolescence.

This great diversity in practice concerning confirmation also includes parishes that have opted to confirm children at the time of their first eucharist. Advocates of this approach argue that it respects the traditional order of the sacraments of initiation. They argue that this approach would not destroy programs of religious catechesis, rather it would base such programs upon personal development and ongoing needs, rather than coming to a stop after the reception of confirmation.

A final polarity in thinking would be reflected by the theological analysis given to the *de facto* separation of confirmation from baptism. While some would view this as a positive development under the influence of the Spirit in the church, others would view it as a regrettable disintegration of the primitive rite of initiation. This latter group of theologians would view the current state of the sacrament of confirmation as "a practice in search of a theory."

See **Baptism; Eucharist; Initiation, Christian**

Gerard Austin, *Anointing With the Spirit: The Rite of Confirmation, The Use of Oil and Chrism in Studies in the Reformed Rites of the Catholic Church,* Vol. 2, New York: Pueblo, 1985. Michael James Balhoff, (Unpublished doctoral dissertation.) "The Legal Interrelatedness of the Sacraments of Initiation: New Canonical Developments in the Latin Rite from Vatican II to the 1983 Code of Canon Law." The Catholic University of America,
1984. J.D.C. Fisher, *Christian Initiation: Baptism in the Medieval West.* London: S.P.C.K., 1965.

GERARD AUSTIN, OP

CONSCIENCE

The word "conscience" has had such a complex, ambiguous history and has been used with so many meanings that it is difficult to confine it to a simple definition, yet it is central to any discussion of morality. The phenomenon itself is a universal experience. In fact, no culture has yet been found in which conscience is not recognized as a fact. Ancient people spoke of "heart" and "loins" to describe the innermost nature of man with reference to responsibility and morality. Down through the centuries there have always been people who did not conform, who refused to accept or obey because they responded to a higher law, the law of conscience. Socrates, Joan of Arc, Thomas More, Martin Luther King, Alexander Solzhenitsyn are just a few of the prophetic figures who incarnate conscience in dramatic fashion.

History

The Greeks were the first to reflect philosophically on the nature of conscience and they described it as "self-consciousness in its role of making moral judgment." They did not restrict it to abstract knowledge of right and wrong but recognized the influence of feeling and will, so they spoke of good and bad conscience, operative not only after the deed, but before and during it. The OT uses the word conscience only once (Wis 17:11), but the reality of the internal voice as the voice of God continually calling for fidelity to the covenant runs all through. Genesis 3 is an excellent description of remorse of conscience. The term is not found in the gospels, but the teaching of Jesus moves the emphasis from external action to the heart, to interior disposition and the need for purity of intention. In the rest of the NT the word occurs thirty times. St. Paul took over the popular concept and even the technical term he found in Greek culture and developed it as a central part of the christian moral message. For the NT writers, conscience meant a consciousness of the true moral content of human life as seen by faith, the basic outlook on life governing all one's actions. But it involved also a prudent assessment of each human situation in the light of christian responsibility and love.

This was the basic approach handed down by the early christian writers to succeeding generations until it was constructed into a critically reflective science of moral theology by Thomas Aquinas. This traditional treatment of the subject was considerably affected by later developments: the Reformation, modern philosophy and the human sciences. Kant still thought of conscience as the "consciousness of an interior court of justice in man," but Darwin, Spencer, Durkheim, Nietzsche and Freud saw it in terms of evolution, sociology and a particular type of psychology. Newman and Kierkegaard restored the balance by bringing conscience back to its traditional roots as a unique phenomenon, not only as a functional guide for action or the capability of moral evaluation, but as the "basic form of primary value consciousness" (Hartmann), the "call of care" (Heidegger), or that voice speaking to man "which is man himself" (Jaspers).

Levels of Conscience

More and more christian writers are coming to see that it is a misleading metaphor to speak of a person "having a conscience." The reality is that one *is* a conscience. In this sense it is not a special faculty or power, or indeed a specific act, nor is it simply the unconscious superego or the effect of guilt-feelings. Indeed it is not a function of physiological,

psychological or sociological factors. It is rather the whole human person characterized by a drive towards and a demand for the realization of value. It is the dynamic thrust towards authenticity and self-transcendence at the core of a person's consciousness, the demand for responsible decision in accord with reasonable judgment (Lonergan).

There are several levels in which the word conscience can be used to describe aspects or levels of the experience itself. 1) One uses conscience to deliberate on a concrete moral action to discover what one "ought" to do. 2) Conscience is also used to mean the knowledge of moral principles, and is often extended to cover knowledge of a particular code or set of rules to help in applying the principles. 3) But most basically conscience is a special kind of personal consciousness. It is the awareness of oneself as a morally responsible being who can be called to account not only by one's fellow human beings, but by one's own inner self, and in religious terms, by God. In this sense conscience is basically *the person as morally conscious.*

The awakening and development of this kind of consciousness is a gradual process, beginning in childhood and continuing all through life. In the early years a child learns to control behavior on the basis of pleasure and pain, reward and punishment; this is not yet conscience. Parents lay down the law and the child is expected to obey. But from the ages of six to seven onwards, the child begins to interiorize the law, to see the reasons behind it and the values it promotes, so that gradually the young person obeys the law because it is the right thing to do. It is not merely a question of intellectual development, but a growth of the whole person which presupposes a continuing experience of emotional support and affirmation of self-worth from parents and others. Later again the person may progress to the stage where the morally right action is done because of personal conviction, irrespective of any law or outside authority. But not many people reach this level of moral maturity; it seems to be an ideal attained only by a minority.

Sacredness and Freedom of Conscience

The Second Vatican Council says that "conscience is man's most secret core, and his sanctuary" (G.S. 16). As a sanctuary it must be respected by others, but it must also be respected by the person as well. A central element in the moral consciousness we call conscience is not simply knowledge of right and wrong, moral good and evil, but an awareness of the element of *obligation,* of *ought.* "Deep within his conscience man discovers a law which he has not laid upon himself, but which he must obey" (G.S. 16). The obligation is not a burden or restraint imposed from without, but an awareness from deep within our beings that this is what we *must* do if we are to be true to our nature as responsible beings, if we are to become what we ought to be as people, if we are to respect in others the rights we claim for ourselves. Our conscience is at work in this kind of deliberation (what is traditionally called *antecedent conscience*), and if we actually do what we decided was the morally right thing, we experience the peace and joy of a good conscience, otherwise we feel remorse (both of these reflect what tradition calls *consequent conscience*).

This experience of *remorse* is a clear indication that the act of conscience was a *free* act. It would be irrational to feel remorse or guilt about an action in which one was not free, for which one was not responsible. Of course, human freedom is not absolute, but may be diminished in a variety of ways, and any lessening of freedom lessens the degree of guilt incurred in objective wrongdoing. Through ignorance or emotional up-

heaval, moral principles can become blurred, facts can be selfishly or mistakenly assessed and decisions made and acted upon which are commonly judged to be mistaken or morally wrong. This is the case of the *erroneous conscience.* But the sanctity of conscience is such that even in this case an individual is obliged to *follow his conscience.* In terms of conscience, people will be judged, not according to rules they learned by heart, or the views of parents, or ecclesiastical documents, or laws from the bible, or even some law in God's mind if it could be read, but according to their own personal conscience; not according to whether they did the objectively right thing, but basically according to whether they did *what they saw and understood* as the right thing.

In fact, others too must respect the sacredness of that conscience insofar as all individuals have a moral right not to be obliged to act contrary to their conscience *even if it is in error.* No outsider can intrude on the sanctuary of a person's conscience. However, it is one thing to claim freedom of conscience for one's conscientious beliefs and decisions, but it is a different matter when it comes to acting upon them. People cannot be forced to act against their conscience, but their right to live publicly by the convictions of their conscience is limited by the rights of others and the demands of the common good. Jehovah's Witnesses may refuse a blood transfusion on the grounds that it would violate their conscience, but most states deny them the right to prevent their underage child from having a transfusion needed to save its life.

Formation of Conscience

Emphasis on the freedom of conscience and the right and obligation to *follow it* should not blur the fact that there is an equal obligation *to form one's conscience.* As already mentioned, conscience is not something which a person simply *has* and uses, either as a list of right and wrong actions or as a special calculator for discovering the difference. On the day of judgment, whether before God or a court of justice, it is not sufficient to claim "I followed my conscience" in order to be exonerated from all blame, any more than the excuse of "obeying orders" dispenses one from the obligation of asking about the morality of the orders. The defendant may have followed his conscience faithfully, but he can be called to account for the *kind of person* he has become through the pattern of his repeated decisions. Serious decisions taken lightly, judgments made on the basis of insufficient information, failure to consult appropriate authorities in complex questions, can all lead to an erroneous conscience. Besides, repeated failure to listen to the call of conscience can blunt one's sensitivity to values and deaden one's conscience.

What this means is that the appeal to conscience as a moral authority for one's actions presupposes a "good conscience." It remains true that even in error one is obliged to follow one's conscience. But it is not enough to invoke "conscience" simply because one feels strongly about something or spontaneously judges that a certain action is the morally correct one. Sincerity alone is not sufficient. The conscience which most fully carries moral authority and to which one can appeal is the conscience which is continually self-critical, aware of the dangers of ignorance, bias, prejudice, selfishness, arrogance and self-sufficiency. Conscience is present in every normal person in so far as they have some moral sense or awareness, but it needs to be *formed and developed throughout life,* so that ideally it becomes the consciousness of a morally converted person, of a mature adult who has moved away from the levels of mere satisfaction, conformism and self-interest as criteria

of choice to the higher levels of authentic values and responsible, principled morality. It is in this context that Aristotle's famous dictum makes sense: a rounded moral judgment is ever the work of a virtuous man. When we wish to know what true virtue is, we must look to the virtuous person.

Objective Norms

It is sometimes said that the right and obligation to follow conscience applies only to an "informed conscience," but the impression is sometimes given that formation of conscience is largely a matter of obtaining the right information. Of course responsible choice requires that we seek all the relevant information, but correct conscience is not established merely by being *told* what to do. Rather it is gradually attained in so far as people move away from blind choices and are guided by objective standards or norms of moral conduct. This does not mean unthinking acceptance of some law laid down by authority. It means rather that the reasons for claiming that a particular action is the morally right one must be good reasons, not mere whim, that in one's search for the right thing to do one will be faithful to the laws of reason, be aware of one's obligations, of the possible consequences of one's action, and in complex questions seek expert advice. These are all *objective norms*, in the light of which one discovers the right thing to do in a concrete situation. A Christian will also be guided by the gospel and church teaching and helped by prayer and God's grace. The guidelines provided by laws are an important factor in the deliberation, and in most cases little reflection is needed to realize that obedience to the law is the responsible and morally right choice. But there are many situations where there is no specific law, and even where there is a law, there may be occasions when conscience will dictate that we disobey it in the name of a higher law, the law of conscience. It would be a mistake to imagine that this holds true only with regard to civil laws, that conscience could not clash with ecclesiastical authority. History proves the contrary, and the church has indeed benefited from this.

Conscience not Infallible

Insistence on the sacredness of conscience, however, should not allow us to forget that conscience is not infallible, that even good individuals can be guilty of self-deception. Humility and openness are necessary virtues in the development of true conscience. But the solution is not to abdicate one's moral responsibility and let someone else take the place of one's conscience. We who are perplexed or in conflict with authority should look to those around us for counsel, seek guidance from the Bible and church teaching, and turn to God in prayer. These may alert us to our own ignorance or self-deception, and we must always remain open to this possibility. They may also point us in a direction we did not expect. But should we find that, having done everything possible, we are still convinced that we cannot accept the ruling of authority, this is the conviction we are bound to follow. Individuals who break a law that conscience tells them is unjust and then willingly accept the consequences of their stand, are in reality expressing the highest respect for law and morality. Should this mean losing their reputation, their standing in the community or even their lives, their conscience is still the voice they must obey. No church, no authority, no superior can take its place. It is not the actual voice of God, but it is God's will that they obey it.

See **Law; Guilt; Moral Life, Christian**

Walter E. Conn, *Conscience: Development And Self-Transcendence,* Birmingham: Religious Education Press, 1981. C. Ellis Nelson (ed), *Conscience: Theological and Psychological Perspectives.* New York: Newman Press, 1973. William C. Bier, S.J., *Conscience, its Freedom and Limitations.* New York: Fordham, 1971. Philippe Delhaye: *The Christian Conscience.* New York: Desclee, 1968.

SEÁN FAGAN, SM

CONSCIENTIOUS OBJECTION

Conscientious objection, the refusal to participate in war or military training, has only recently won recognition as a legitimate and respected option for Catholics subject to conscription. This is not to say, however, that it is something new. Historians and theologians may differ as to the extent of the pacifist witness of the early church or the reasons why Christians of the first four centuries rejected military service and committed themselves to a nonviolent life-style, but there is no denying that the writings of the fathers and the behavior of the faithful in what we call "the Age of Martyrs" supported both.

The church's roster of honored saints includes names like Maximilian Martyr, beheaded in 295 A.D. for refusing military service, and Martin of Tours who, some forty years later withdrew from the armed forces to which he was already committed declaring, "I am the soldier of Christ. It is not lawful for me to fight." Francis of Assisi included a prohibition against bearing weapons or using them against anyone in the Rule he established for his Third Order. Jean Baptiste Vianney, the beloved Cure of Ars, deserted the French forces in the time of Napoleon.

In more recent times Catholics have been inclined to reject conscientious objection as a position associated only with the so-called "peace churches"—the Society of Friends (Quakers), the Mennonites, and the Church of the Brethren—and similar religious communities in the Pietist or Anabaptist traditions. The "just war" teachings, introduced by St. Augustine following the conversion of the Roman Empire under Constantine and developed over the succeeding centuries by St. Thomas Aquinas and the Later Scholastics, seemed to exclude conscientious objection as an option for the Catholic. This interpretation appeared to find authoritative support in the 1956 Christmas Message of Pope Pius XII in which he affirmed the right of a freely elected government to take "necessary" defensive measures "in a moment of danger" with "legitimate instruments of internal and external policy" and declared, "Therefore, a Catholic cannot invoke his own conscience in order to refuse to serve and fulfill those duties the law imposes."

Despite such changes in emphasis and direction, there has always been a minority Catholic witness against war and military service. In 1943 Franz Jaegerstaetter, a simple peasant, was beheaded in Berlin for refusing to report for duty in Hitler's army (Zahn, *In Solitary Witness*). Nor was he alone. Continuing research has found other inspiring examples of individual Catholics who—without the support and against the advice of priests, theologians and even bishops—paid the supreme price for being true to their conscience. In the United States, where the law included provision for conscientious objection, a handful of Catholics chose alternative service rather than serve in what so many still consider "the last good war" but which they felt obliged to reject in conscience as immoral. (Zahn, *Another Part of the War*.)

More recent and more authoritative statements, taking into account the nature of modern war with the threat it now poses to the future existence of the world and its inhabitants, represent something of a return to the earlier church tradition. Thus, the legitimacy of conscientious objection was formally acknowledged by the Second Vatican Council in its recommendation "that laws make humane provision for the case of those who for reasons of conscience refuse to bear arms, provided, however, that they accept some other form of service to the human community (G.S. 79). Still more recently, in his public address of February 12, 1984 to a group of young people in Rome, Pope John Paul II referred to conscientious objection as "a sign of maturity when people manage to accept another form of public service that is not military service." In its 1983 pastoral letter, *The Challenge of Peace: God's Promise and Our Response,* the U.S. hierarchy echoed several of its earlier statements in which conscientious objection was endorsed "as a valid moral position, derived from the Gospel and Catholic teaching" (nos. 231-33).

Conscientious objection, it is well to note, does not depend solely upon the pacifist commitment that characterized the first four centuries of church history. The "just war" tradition which, as the bishops put it, "has clearly been in possession for the past 1,500 years of Catholic thought" sets forth a set of conditions *all of which must be fulfilled* if a war is to be considered just. It follows, then, that where there is official disregard or violation of one or more of these conditions in the origin or conduct of a given war, that war becomes *unjust,* and Catholics should recognize a moral obligation not to support or participate in it.

Such *selective* conscientious objection presents a special problem. Our nation's present Selective Service law provides exemption from military service only to individuals who object to all war in any form and, in effect, discriminates against those who, following the traditional "just war" teaching, refuse to participate in a war which, they are convinced in conscience, does not meet the conditions set forth in that teaching. The U.S. bishops have recommended that the law be changed, but these recommendations have been ignored or dismissed as impractical. Since this obviously does not release the individual from the obligation to refuse to violate the higher law of christian morality (that is, "to obey God rather than man"), it means that a Catholic who is convinced in conscience of a war's injustice would have no alternative but to disobey orders and accept the penalty for doing so.

Finally, some consideration must be given to *situational* conscientious objection, the refusal to commit or participate in some specific act of war one considers immoral. In *The Challenge of Peace* the bishops declare, "No Christian can rightfully carry out orders or policies deliberately aimed at killing non-combatants" (no. 148). Although this appears in the context of their discussion of large-scale bombings of population centers, it logically applies as well to more localized battlefield actions as well. Direct disobedience of orders from military superiors carries with it the risk of severe punishment, so this is perhaps the most difficult of all forms of conscientious objection. Its justification is clear enough in situations like a My Lai atrocity during the Vietnam War or the killing of enemy prisoners; but other more "normal" military actions ("free-fire zones," "search and destroy" missions, etc.) could impose the same obligation to refuse. Indeed, given the repeated condemnations of the use of weapons and strategies which fail to discriminate between combatants and non-combatants, it may well be that the limits set by traditional "just war" teachings will require Catholics who volunteer for, or accept, military service to avoid or reject assignment to any services or units where the likelihood of receiving morally dubious or certainly immoral orders is greatest.

As Catholics become more aware of the implications of Vatican II's call for "an entirely new attitude" (G.S. 80) with regard to war, more of them will recognize their obligation to make a personal choice

between conscientious objection and what might be termed "conscientious participation." It can no longer be a simple matter of automatic response to the nation's call-to-arms; instead it must be the result of prayerful reflection and mature moral judgment. And if it is true that, as Pope John Paul II declared at Coventry May 30, 1982, "the scale and the horror of modern warfare—whether nuclear or not—makes it totally unacceptable as a means of settling differences between nations," there is reason to believe that many will find their answer in the example set by the Christians of the first few centuries of church history.

See **Moral Life, Christian; Peace; War**

Jean-Michel Hornus, *It Is Not Lawful For Me To Fight*, Scottdale. Pa: Herald Press, 1980. Gordon C. Zahn, *In Solitary Witness; The Life and Death of Franz Jaegerstetter*, Springfield: Templegate, 1986. Gordon C. Zahn, *Another Part of the War: The Camp Simon Story*, Amherst: University of Massachusetts Press, 1979. National Council of Catholic Bishops, *The Challenge of Peace:* God's Promise and Our Response, 1983.

GORDON C. ZAHN

CONSUBSTANTIAL

The term is taken from the Latin translation to the Greek term, *homoousios,* which was used at the Council of Nicaea to define that Christ was "of the same substance" as the Father. At the Council of Chalcedon, Christ was defined as "consubstantial to the Father" and "consubstantial to us" human beings.

See **Chalcedon, Council of; Homoousios; Jesus Christ; Nicaea, Council of**

STEPHEN FUNK

CONSUBSTANTIATION

The view, rejected by the church, that in the Eucharist the bread and wine remain present in their substance and thus coexist with the Body and Blood of

Christ. At the Reformation, this view was associated with Martin Luther, and it was against it that the Council of Trent defined the Catholic doctrine of transubstantiation.

See **Eucharist**

STEPHEN FUNK

CONTRITION

Heartfelt sorrow for and detestation of sin, with the resolve not to sin again. Contrition is "perfect" when it is motivated by the love of God; for "imperfect" contrition, see "Attrition."

See **Reconciliation**

STEPHEN FUNK

CONVERSION

The call to conversion is one of the most important religious and moral themes found in both the OT and NT. The term is historically rich in meaning, and evidence of a renewed interest in the concept can be found in contemporary Protestant and Roman Catholic theology. Though conversion can be defined in a variety of ways and applied to a diverse range of events in an individual's life, what seems characteristic of the experience is a radical change in the convert's existence.

According to the gospel accounts (Mt 4:17 and Mk 1:15), the first challenge spoken by Jesus in his public ministry was "Be converted!" Jesus' call to conversion and repentance, however, was not entirely new to his audience because the prophets of Israel had frequently issued this summons. The prophets used the Hebrew word *shub* to call Israel to turn away from idols (Jer 7:9), injustice and immorality (Isa 55:7), and to turn back to God for mercy and salvation. In Rabbinic writings, conversion and repentance are conditions for the coming of the Messiah, who himself will convert others to God.

In the NT, the Greek words for conversion or repentance are *metanoia* (largely in the Synoptics and in The Book of Revelation) and *epistrophe* (in Acts, the Pauline Epistles, and in 1 Peter). Though these Greek words are virtually synonymous and can both be translations of the Hebrew *shub*, there is one difference in emphasis. *Metanoia* tends to stress more the processes of thinking and willing that lie behind an action, whereas *epistrophe* emphasizes more the visible characteristics of an external act. In any case, both terms signify a radical turning around of the whole person and a return home. Thus, the call to conversion as it is used in both testaments always connotes an intense yearning for return to the Lord and divine friendship.

The biblical injunction to conversion reveals three important facts about the divine-human relationship. First, sinful humanity is alienated from God and is in need of reunion. Second, conversion is primarily God's work towards humanity, since it is God who first offers mercy and salvation. In fact, the call to conversion is itself a gospel, a message of good news. Finally, conversion requires a response on the part of humanity—a confession of sinfulness, an openness to receive God's mercy and forgiveness in faith, and a joyful desire to love God and neighbor in word and action.

The conversions of St. Paul and St. Augustine have probably stirred the most reflection in all the christian tradition. The biblical accounts of Paul's conversion (Acts 9:1-27, 22:1-21, 26:9-23; 1 Cor 9:1, 15:8-11; Gal 1:15-17) and Augustine's autobiography in his *Confessions* illustrate well the pattern of the conversion experience. Both men experienced (1) a disorientation, (2) a gathering together of elements from their past, (3) a forgiveness for failures and a sense of mercy, and (4) the intervention and call from some enabling Other. Though the dramatic fashion in which Paul and Augustine experienced their conversions does not always seem typical, the pattern does.

Theological reflection on the experience of and need for conversion in the christian life somewhat waned during the scholastic period but became a central theme again in Luther's reformation theology. From the sixteenth through the eighteenth centuries one finds many references to conversion in the writings of Ignatius of Loyola (*Spiritual Exercises*), the Pietists in Germany (e.g., Philipp Spener), John Wesley in England, and Jonathan Edwards in New England. In the early twentieth century William James authored his famous *The Varieties of Religious Experience* wherein he analyzed at some length the psychological dynamics of unifying the self that are commonplace in religious conversion. More recently, many scholars have returned to the biblical foundations of conversion in order to develop systematic treatises in theology.

Despite the fact that the term conversion has never had a univocal meaning in its long history, one finds an even greater proliferation of meanings particularly in the twentieth century. Conversion can refer to the fact that someone has become a member of a specific christian church, or it can refer to a Christian's deeply emotional experience of being "born again" in turning to Jesus as one's personal savior. Such widely diverse meanings have caused a certain confusion about the precise definition and essential characteristics of conversion.

Most theologians today, however, would agree that conversion entails a radical reorientation of one's desires, thought processes and actions. It involves not only an entire personal transformation but also, because of the effects of sin in the world, a transformation of the social structures in society. The effectuation of such fundamental reorientations can neither be accomplished in a single moment nor be attained by the self in isolation. Rather, conversion must be viewed developmentally, as a constant striving for holiness that is assisted and sustained by others within a larger faith community. From this perspective then, all conversion is the gradual, if not arduous, turning away and withdrawal from sin and selfishness and the turning towards God who is the source of all goodness. Because we are beings who come to authenticity and maturity over a long period of time within a community, it is only reasonable to expect that those who are engaged in the process of conversion will be at different stages in their commitment to the gospel. However, because the effects of personal sin and the sin which infects the world will continue with us until the *eschaton* or final coming of Jesus in glory, it would be impossible for converts to claim that they are totally and absolutely converted. As pilgrim people, we experience ourselves existentially as both sinful and converted.

Recently, several theologians have suggested that although the structure of all conversion is the same, that is, a fundamental turning towards God, it is probably best to think of conversion as occurring at different levels within the person. From this contemporary perspective, one might isolate, but not separate, various conversions which are ongoing in christian life and community. Each one of these conversions interacts with the others, and all are related structurally to one another.

In the moral life of individuals and the community we can speak of the gradual but fundamental withdrawal from serving our own needs first and the turning towards true value as the source or criterion of decisions and choices. Such a moral conversion is related to the conversion of our affects, whereby we withdraw from all selfishness and turn towards the love and service of others. Because our feelings are guided by the images that flood our imaginations, affective conversion requires a fundamental shift in the symbols and images that inform our decision-making. Thus, images that instill prejudice and hatred against groups in society based on race, sex or creed need to be eradicated and new images adopted. Being aware that our knowing processes are profoundly shaped and limited by our own personal and communal perspectives requires a shift in the ways in which we understand and judge reality. To know not just what we know but also how we know entails a fundamental withdrawal from a naive and absolute dependence on authority as the criterion of what is true and good and a turning towards the inner operations of human subjectivity as the criteria of knowing reality. Finally, there is religious conversion, which is the turning away from all worldly realities as the final object of our desires and commitment and a turning towards the divine. It is the joyful falling in love with God in response to the divine gift of grace.

See **Grace; Holiness; Mercy; Moral Life, Christian; Reconciliation; Sin**

The Confessions of St. Augustine, trans. Edward B. Pusey, New York: Random House, 1949. Walter Conn, *Christian Conversion: A Developmental Interpretation of Autonomy and Surrender,* New York: Paulist, 1986. Beverly Roberts Gaventa, *From Darkness to Light: Aspects of Conversion in the New Testament,* Philadelphia: Fortress, 1986. Stephen Happel and James J. Walter, *Conversion and Discipleship: A Christian Foundation for Ethics and Doctrine,* Philadelphia: Fortress, 1986. "Metanoia," in *Theological Dictionary of the New Testament,* Grand Rapids: Wm. B. Eerdmans, 1967, 4:975-1008.

JAMES J. WALTER

CO-REDEMPTION

One of the terms used by some to refer to the subordinate and cooperative role of the Blessed Virgin Mary in Christ's redemption of the human race, either by her assent to the incarnation or by her participation at the foot of the cross in Christ's sufferings. The nature of this cooperation has never been defined by the church, which has also never formally adopted the title "Co-redemptrix" for Mary.

See **Mary, Redemption**

COUNCIL

In the broad sense of the term, a council or synod is an occasional gathering of church representatives, and especially of official leaders, for consultation and decision-making. As the term is technically used in theology and canon law, a council is an occasional meeting of ecclesiastical persons having juridical power to make joint decisions of a doctrinal or disciplinary character that bind the constituencies represented. Councils in this sense are to be distinguised from consultative agencies, such as the Synod of Bishops, which in its present form is seen as advisory to the pope.

The concept and form of councils has varied considerably in the course of the centuries. Since the fourth century an important distinction has been made between ecumenical (or general) councils on the one hand and particular (or local) councils on the other. The standard Catholic enumeration recognized twenty-one ecumenical councils from Nicaea I (325) to Vatican II (1962-65).

1. Biblical Foundations

The saying of Jesus, "When two or three are gathered in my name, there am I in the midst of them" (Mt 18:20), has sometimes been applied to councils. The principal biblical precedent is the apostolic consultation at Jerusalem as described in Acts 15. This was an extraordinary meeting convened under apostolic authority to settle serious disputes about the obligation of Gentile converts to observe the precepts of the Mosaic law. After the views of Peter, Paul, and Barnabas had been heard, a decision was reached and expressed by James the "brother of the Lord." This decision, attributed to the inspiration of the Holy Spirit (15:28), won acceptance with the "apostles and elders" and was embodied in an apostolic letter carried to Antioch by the prophets Judas and Silas.

2. Patristic Developments

Even before the legal toleration of Christianity in the Roman Empire, the bishops of various regions, such as North Africa and Asia Minor, frequently met in councils. The councils that met at Antioch in the third and fourth centuries established the pattern that was taken over by the patristic ecumenical councils. Among the councils held before the end of the eighth century, seven have, by general agreement in the East and West, come to be recognized as ecumenical. These are: Nicaea (325), Constantinople I (381), Ephesus (431), Chalcedon (451), Constantinople II (553), Constantinople III (680-81), and Nicaea II (787). Many other councils, some of them called by the Emperor with the intention of defining the faith, have failed to win acceptance as ecumenical, because they were too local, or insufficiently free, or lacking in orthodoxy, or because they failed to arrive at the intended consensus.

The first four councils have been accorded a primacy of dignity and importance. Pope Gregory I (c. 540-604) compared them to the four gospels, and Isidore of Seville (c. 560-636) compared them to the four rivers of Paradise. Luther and Calvin regarded the doctrine of these councils as pure and binding, because wholly in accord with Holy Scripture. The Anglican formularies accept these four councils, while not excluding others.

The ecumenical councils of ancient times, unlike those of later centuries, were convoked by the Emperor, who presided in person or through delegates, but did not himself have a vote. The voting members were the metropolitans and other attending bishops, who seem to have been recognized as ecclesiastical counterparts of the Roman senators. The councils attempted to give final settlement to major doctrinal and disciplinary questions. They frequently attached anathemas, or solemn excommunications to the errors they condemned. No formal confirmation of the conciliar decrees by the pope was considered necessary, presumably because he had, through his legates, participated in the consensus. But in the case of the 28th canon of Chalcedon, which had been adopted without the concurrence of the papal delegates, Pope Leo I used his apostolic authority to declare it null. Confirmation by the Emperor gave the decrees civil authority within the Empire. Within the church, the doctrinal decisions of these councils have been considered universally and permanently binding, at least by Roman Catholic and Orthodox theologians.

In ancient times the authority of councils was justified on a variety of grounds, such as the agreement of their decisions with the teaching of Scripture and with apostolic tradition (Athanasius), their conformity with the constant and universal tradition of the church (Vincent of Lerins), the assistance of the Holy Spirit (Constantine, Celestine I, Cyril of Alexandria), and approval by the Petrine see (Leo I). In the first systematic discussion of the theology of councils the Melchite bishop, Theodore Abu Qurrah (c. 740-c. 820), maintained that councils were of divine institution and that their decisions, when received by the bishops of the patriarchal sees (Rome, Constantinople, Antioch, Jerusalem, and Alexandria) were divinely guaranteed and binding.

The ecumenicity of the eighth council, Constantinople IV (869-870), which deposed the Patriarch Photius, is a matter of dispute. Although reckoned as ecumenical by Pope Gregory VII (1073-1085) and regularly appearing on Catholic lists since Robert Bellarmine (1542-1621), it has little claim to ecumenical status, and has never been so accepted in the East. Some Catholic authorities have proposed that it be dropped from the list, and even that the council of 879-880, which reinstated Photius as patriarch and restored communion with Rome, should be substituted for it.

3. Middle Ages and Renaissance

In the Dark Ages synods of bishops in the West, and notably in Spain, were transformed into national assemblies presided over by kings. Secular princes and nobles as well as bishops attended. The eighteen Spanish synods of Toledo exemplify this development.

In the high Middle Ages the pope convoked and presided over a number of general councils of the West, which have found their way into Catholic lists of ecumenical councils. The first four Lateran councils (1123, 1139, 1179, and 1215) and the two councils of Lyons (1245, 1274) were papal and Western. Lateran IV, the greatest representative assembly of the medieval world, was convoked by Innocent III with the clear intent of continuing the tradition of the ancient ecumenical councils. This council drew up a notable summary of the Catholic faith, amounting practically to a new creed, and repudiated certain scholastic theories regarding the Trinity. Lyons II, though a purely Western and

papal council, remains important for the Decree of Union it imposed on the Eastern Emperor, Michael Paleologus, on disputed questions, including the procession of the Holy Spirit.

Many of the medieval councils were attended not only by popes, bishops, cardinals, and abbots, but also by envoys of emperors, representatives of the leading cities, noble laymen, and theologians. The Council of Vienne (1311-1312) was attended by only a relatively small number of specially invited bishops. Its decrees were promulgated by the pope only several years after the council, after consultation with theological faculties.

The Council of Constance (1414-1418) is in some ways unique because it was convened primarily to heal a schism between rival popes. It deposed the papal claimant who convened it along with two rival popes, and then elected Martin V. Meeting at the height of the conciliar movement, Constance claimed that it had its power from Christ himself and that the pope was obliged to obey it in matters of faith and discipline (Haec sancta, 1415). Constance also adopted the decree Frequens (1415) calling for future councils to be convened at regular intervals. This decree, if enforced, would have made ecumenical councils a regular, rather than an exceptional, feature of the church government. The force of the decrees Haec sancta and Frequens is still a matter of dispute among Catholic theologians. At Constance and Basel (1431-1437) the doctors of theology played a dominant role, far outnumbering the bishops. Basel was marked by discord and is not generally reckoned as ecumenical.

The Council of Florence (1439-1445), at which the pope regained control against the conciliarists, succeeded in effecting several unions, at least partial and in some cases ephemeral, between Rome and separated Eastern churches

(Greek, Armenian, Jacobite, etc.). The next ecumenical council, Lateran V (1512-1517) was a papal council concerned with a variety of issues, including internal church reform. But its measures fell far short of what would have been required to avert the Reformation.

4. The Modern Period

The contemporary understanding of ecumenical councils in the Catholic Church is shaped predominantly by the three modern councils: Trent was set by the drastic need for inner-Catholic reform and for meeting the doctrinal challenges of the Reformation. Presided over by papal legates, it was essentially a council of bishops of the Roman Catholic Church, with theologians playing an important advisory role. The decrees, both doctrinal and disciplinary, were backed up by anathemas and were considered obligatory on all Catholics under pain of excommunication.

Vatican I, in its Constitution on Divine Faith, dealt with a variety of doctrinal questions regarding faith and reason. In its constitution on the church it dealt with papal primacy and infallibility. In both Constitutions the canons were put forth as infallible teachings and backed up with anathemas. The decrees of Vatican II, like those of some earlier papal councils, were issued by the pope himself "with the approval of the sacred council."

Vatican II, although it met in a much different atmosphere, followed the organizational patterns of Vatican I. Aimed at modernization and ecumenism, it produced a massive restatement of the standard Catholic teaching, with particular emphasis on ecclesiology. Unlike Trent and Vatican I, Vatican II refrained from defining any new doctrines under anathema. The decrees were signed by the pope "together with the venerable Fathers."

5. Theological Aspects

Although councils are not of divine institution, they correspond to the basic structure of the church as a communion in which the faith is possessed in common by the hierarchy as teachers and by the faithful as believers. Since the gospel is entrusted to the church as a whole, the universal church, under the guidance of its pastors, is preserved from error. It is governed by the college of bishops in union with the pope as head of the college and successor of Peter. The college of bishops, as the successor to the apostolic college, possesses the fullness of ecclesiastical power and exercises this most solemnly when the college, or a representative number of members of the college from various regions, deliberate and decide together. Councils are the most practical way to determine the mind of the church by weighing the arguments of theologians and debating the merits of various formulations.

Because of the vast differences from one age to another, it is difficult to give a satisfactory definition of an ecumenical council. Some recent theologians distinguish various degrees of ecumenicity. Whatever the popes may have intended, the medieval councils of the West remained essentially Western. Thus Paul VI in 1974 could refer to Lyons II as "the sixth of the general councils celebrated in the Western world" (A.A.S. 66 [1974] 620). Vatican I was ecumenical in its inclusion of the bishops united with Rome, but it remained somewhat narrowly Western and European. Vatican II has greater claims to ecumenicity, thanks to the presence of Catholics from many continents and traditions, as well as observer delegates from other churches.

An important factor for the verification of ecumenicity is the process of reception, which can occur either at the official level, as ratification, or at the popular level, as consent. Constantinople I, though in itself a local council, won recognition as ecumenical when its creed was accepted by Chalcedon. Orthodox theologians commonly require reception by the five patriarchates (Rome, Constantinople, Alexandria, Antioch, and Jerusalem) as a prerequisite for ecumenicity. Roman Catholic theologians regard acceptance by the bishop of Rome as decisive.

6. Authority

The idea that ecumenical councils are infallible has only gradually gained currency. Vatican I evidently claimed infallibility for some of its doctrinal statements. Vatican II grounded the infallibility of ecumenical councils in that of the episcopal college—i.e., the whole body of bishops in hierarchical communion with the pope. Although the pope can teach infallibly by his own authority as head of the college, ecumenical councils have advantages for establishing the faith in greater depth, expressing it with greater amplitude, and renewing ecclesiastical discipline more effectively.

Ecumenical councils do not invoke their own infallibility except in favor of certain specific statements. Vatican I made it clear that its canons, each followed by an anathema, were irreformable definitions. The chapters of Vatican I's two dogmatic constitutions are regarded as irreformable only to the extent that they state in positive form the doctrine opposed to that condemned in the canons. At Vatican II the Theological Commission explained that the new teachings of that council were not to be regarded as infallibly defined unless the council clearly stated that they were—and in fact it made no such statement. Thus the teachings of Vatican II are irreformable only where that council repeats what had already been infallibly taught. To decide what is irreformable in the decrees of earlier councils, such as Trent, can be extremely

difficult, since no precise formula of words is decisive. In doubtful cases, infallibility is not to be presumed (C.I.C., canon 749, #3).

According to many contemporary theologians, who would seem to be correct, the authority of councils derives primarily from the Holy Spirit. Councils are regularly asserted to be "legitimately assembled in the Holy Spirit," who is prayerfully invoked. The unanimity required for an authentic conciliar teaching is considered to be a sign of the action of the Holy Spirit. One contemporary authority on councils (G. Alberigo) has called an ecumenical council an "epiphany of the Spirit."

Modern authors distinguish between inspiration in the strict sense, which was given to certain prophets and to the authors of Holy Scripture, and a more general assistance given to popes and councils when they issue definitions of a doctrinal character. The latter is a grace of a lesser order, sufficient to prevent error, but not necessarily giving new and creative insights or guaranteeing aptitude in the verbal expression. The distinction between these two types of assistance is legitimate, but it would be unwarranted to concluded that the Spirit assists the Fathers in council in a merely negative way, for error is not normally prevented except by the perception of truth. Even though the inspiration of councils is not to be put on a par with that of Holy Scripture, it may properly be seen as a positive assistance, and was so regarded by ancient authorities such as Cyprian, Constantine, Cyril of Alexandria, and Leo I.

The assistance given to the pastors in council should not be viewed in isolation from the gift of the Holy Spirit to the church as a whole. The church is by its very nature a communion established in the Spirit. Councils are meetings of pastors who engage in collegial interaction on the basis of their communion in the faith. When the collegiate action results in decisions that authentically express the faith of the church, ecumenicity is achieved. Reception in its various modes and degrees is the response whereby such ecumenicity is validated and made effective.

7. Canonical Aspects

According to the 1917 Code of Canon Law, which expresses the recent consensus of Catholic theologians, an ecumenical council has supreme power in the church, and thus there is no appeal from its decrees (canon 228). Every ecumenical council must be convoked by the pope, who presides over it either in person or through his legates, and who can draw up the agenda, suspend, transfer, and dissolve the council at his pleasure (canon 222). The council's decrees have no obligatory force unless confirmed and promulgated by the pope (canon 227). Among those who have the right to attend with deliberative vote are all cardinals, patriarchs, archbishops, residential bishops, supreme heads of exempt religious orders of clerics, and certain abbots (canon 223). Titular bishops may be invited and given a deliberative vote. Other theologians and experts may also be invited, but not given a deliberative vote.

The 1983 revised Code reflects the Vatican II doctrine that all bishops in communion with the pope constitute a college succeeding to that of the apostles. The councils are thus seen as corporate exercises of the episcopal ministry, with and under the pope, who succeeds to Peter in the primacy. In general the new Code reaffirms the provisions of 1917, but there are certain changes. Although the authority of the pope (canon 331) and that of the college of bishops in union with the pope as its head (canon 336) are both described as supreme, this adjective is no longer applied to councils, which are described as exercising the power of the college over the universal church in a solemn manner (canon 337, no. 1). With regard to membership, canon 339, no. 1, specifies that all bishops who are members of the college are entitled to take part in an ecumenical council with a deliberative vote. Thus all auxiliaries and retired bishops in union with Rome must be invited as full voting members. No one other than bishops has a legal right to attend. But the same canon goes on to say (no. 2) that non-bishops may be invited by the supreme authority of the church, which shall determine the degree of their participation. Thus popes and councils are not prohibited from inviting other clerics and lay persons and from giving them even a deliberative vote.

8. Particular Councils

From ancient times it was customary for the bishops of a given area to gather periodically under the direction of their metropolitan in provincial councils. The Council of Nicaea ruled that provincial councils should be held at least twice a year—a ruling that was repeatedly modified by later councils. The Council of Nicaea ruled that provincial councils should be held at least twice a year—a ruling that was repeatedly modified by later councils and popes until the Code of 1917, which required provincial councils only once in every twenty years. The 1983 Code states that such councils are to be held as often as seems opportune in the judgment of the majority of the bishops of the province (canon 440). Provincial councils are primarily meetings of bishops, but others may be invited to attend with a consultative (not a deliberative) vote. Since Sixtus V (1585-1590) it has been required that the decrees of provincial councils be reviewed by Rome before being promulgated—a requirement repeated in the present Code, canon 446.

In North Africa by the time of Augustine it was customary for the bishops of a region including several provinces to hold larger councils, generally called plenary. Medieval councils such as those of Toledo, mentioned above, and similar ones in other countries, fall into this category. In modern times plenary councils have normally been national. National councils proved particularly valuable in the nineteenth century, when the hierarchy was becoming established in several new areas, such as the United States, where plenary councils were held in Baltimore in 1829, 1866, 1884. Under present legislation plenary councils are called at the discretion of the conference of bishops, provided that the Holy See approves (canon 439).

Although in the past particular councils have played a major role in the development of doctrine, such councils are today considered to have pastoral and disciplinary, rather than strictly doctrinal, functions. Since Vatican II the episcopal conferences, which in some ways resemble councils, have taken on many of the functions of particular councils.

9. Ecumenical Aspects

As noted above, the first seven councils, and especially the first four, have been accepted as authoritative by Christians of many traditions, including Orthodox, Lutheran, Reformed, and Anglican. Protestants, however, tend to regard such councils as having authority because and insofar as their teaching is biblically warranted. Orthodox theologians do not recognize any councils that have taken place since the split between East and West in the eleventh century as truly ecumenical. The Orthodox are not in full agreement among themselves regarding the source of authority of councils. Some hold that councils, being legitimately convoked in the Holy Spirit, have authority in themselves; others hold that their decrees receive authority from reception on the part of the body of the faithful. In recent years the Orthodox

have been making preparations for a possible pan-Orthodox synod, but presumably such a synod, even if it comes to pass, would not have the status of an ecumenical council without the participation of Rome.

Organizations such as the World Council of Churches (founded in 1948) and the various national, state, and metropolitan councils of a multi-denominational character, being merely consultative agencies whose members owe allegiance to different churches that do not fully recognize one another, lack power to make binding decisions and for this reason cannot be considered councils within the framework of the present article. Indeed, the very meaning of the word "council" in the title of these organizations differs from its meaning in Catholic theology and canon law. (The difference is indicated in French, which calls a "council of churches" a *conseil* rather than a *concile;* and in German, which speaks in this connection of a *Rat* rather than a *Konzil.*)

Nevertheless, the World Council of Churches at its Uppsala Assembly (1968) spoke of itself as "a transitional opportunity" for eventually actualizing a truly universal, ecumenical conciliar form of common life and witness. It went on to urge its member churches to "work for a time when a genuinely universal council may once more speak for all Christians, and lead the way into the future" (*Uppsala Report*, p. 17). In response to this initiative Catholic theologians have taken very seriously the possibility of a representative gathering from churches that as yet enjoy only partial communion with one another. Whether such an assembly could be an ecumenical council as understood in the Catholic tradition remains problematical. What would be the role of the pope in convening the assembly and in influencing its agenda? What would be the status at this "council" of non-bishops, or bishops whose orders Rome does not recognize as valid? What binding force would attach to its decrees? Would it have authority to modify the teaching or discipline of a body such as the Catholic Church, or would its utterance have the force of mere recommendations? Because of unresolved questions such as these, it would seem impossible in the near future to hold on such a universal scale anything more than what some have called a "precouncil."

See **Anathema, Bishop, Church, Collegiality, Gallicanism, Infallibility, Inspiration, Pope, Synod of Bishops**

Bernard Botte, et al., *La Concile et les conciles,* Paris: Cerf, 1960. Peter Huizing, and Knut Walf, Eds., *The Ecumenical Council: Its Significance in the Constitution of the Church.* Concilium 167. New York: Seabury, 1983. Hans Küng, *Structures of the Church,* New York: Nelson, 1964, London: Sheed & Ward, 1965; rev. ed., New York: Crossroad, 1982. Vittorio Peri, *I Concili e le Chiese,* Rome: Studium, 1965. Hermann-Josef Sieben, *Die Konzilsidee der alten Kirche,* Paderborn: Schöningh, 1979. Hermann-Josef Sieben, *Die Konzilsidee der lateinischen Mittelalters, 847-1378,* Paderborn: Schöningh, 1984.

AVERY DULLES, SJ

COUNTER-REFORMATION

Counter-Reformation is a serious misnomer for a period in Roman Catholicism which began in the later fifteenth century and lasted well into the seventeenth and even eighteenth centuries. This article discusses the Catholic Reform, using the term counter-reformation only for endeavors to thwart the advance of Protestantism. Thus, the Catholic Reform was an era of purification, innovation, and consolidation in the spiritual life, discipline, doctrine, and administration of the Roman church. In the particular fields of spirituality, mission activity, and sacred art, it was an era of unparalleled innovative genius and heroic accomplishment.

The origins of Catholic Reform can be traced to the spiritual energies by which new religious communities were founded (e.g., Oratory of Divine Love, Theatines, Ursulines, and especially the Jesuits) or by which older orders developed reformed branches (e.g., Carmelites, Capuchins, Benedictines Cistercians). After the sixteenth-century foundations in Italy and Spain, there followed in the seventeenth century another wave of new congregations in France. The spiritual teachings underlying these foundations are customarily classified according to the Italian school (affective, devotional, actively apostolic), the Spanish school (mystical, speculative), the French school (theologically grounded, rigorist, sacerdotal), and the Jesuit school (voluntarist, pragmatic, actively apostolic).

Agitation against administrative abuses and the humanist advocacy of learning initiated further reform. Under Cardinal Ximenes de Cisneros (d. 1517), King Ferdinand (d. 1516), and Queen Isabella (d. 1504), successful reform of the hierarchy and education of the clergy were well advanced in Spain before Luther emerged. Elsewhere reform of some abuses dragged on into the seventeenth century. This is understandable, however, since the educational and spiritual norms newly established for the clergy required extensive economic and political support, as well as long, even painful institutional adjustments. To that end, the Catholic Reform fortified the authority of bishops in their sees by settling jurisdictional conflicts which had impeded diocesan administration. On the whole, absenteeism, pluralism of benefices, concubinage, fiscal abuse, and inadequate clerical education were eliminated. The reinvigorated pastorate attacked residual paganism among the faithful and it regularized catechesis of the laity. Indeed, both Protestant and Catholic Reforms institutionalized the catechism as chief means of religious instruction.

While attempts to win back Protestant territories were seldom successful on a large scale (except in Eastern Europe), the propagation of Roman Catholicism to new lands was an unqualified success. As the age of exploration had been initiated by Catholic powers, so had Catholic missions encircled the globe by 1550, a work in which Jesuits and Franciscans showed sanctity and genius for over 150 years. Outside of Europe, Protestant missions were few and weak until the early eighteenth century.

At first with austerity, then with increasing exuberance, the spiritual vitality of Catholic Reform and the largesse of clerical and noble patrons produced art which left an indelible mark on the Western religious imagination: painting, music, drama, poetry, and above all architecture expressed the purposeful confidence, moralism, emotional intensity, and joy in creation of the contemporary Catholic spirit. In theology, after the comprehensive accomplishment of the Council of Trent, the age tended to works of systematization and apologetics, although it saw sustained and bitter controversy on issues of grace and free will. Doctrinal vigilance made the Catholic Reform an age unsympathetic to the contemporary philosophical and scientific revolution underway.

To conclude, it is essential to dismiss certain misconceptions. First, the stereotype of the age as negative, authoritarian, repressive, and polemical, epitomized by the reinvigorated Inquisition and the trial of Galileo, exaggerates what was but one element of the period. Such elements were present in all christian religion (Catholic and Protestant) in that period: it was an age of unparalleled religious watchfulness. But that was only one feature of a much larger picture.

Second, the accomplishments of the Catholic Reform were by no means inspired or directed by the papacy. Apart

from three or four vigorous popes from 1540 to 1590 and a Roman Curia of generally more integrity thereafter, the papacy was politically and often spiritually insignificant from 1590 to 1800. Successful reform was due more to regional episcopates, saintly individuals, and the Catholic political rulers who controlled the life of the national or local church. Only very gradually after 1800 did the pope and Curia assume effective control of national episcopates and churches.

See **Trent, Council of Catholicism**

Erwin Iserloh, et. al., *Reformation and Counter-Reformation,* [History of the Church, Hubert Jedin et. al., eds., vol. 5] New York, 1980. A.G. Dickens, *The Counter Reformation,* New York, 1969. H. Outram Evenett, *The Spirit of the Counter-Reformation,* South Bend, 1970. Jean Delumeau, *Catholicism between Luther and Voltaire,* Philadelphia, 1977. John O'Malley, S.J., *Catholicism in Early Modern History,* St. Louis, 1987. John Bossy, *Christianity in the West 1400-1700,* New York, 1985.

JAMES MICHAEL WEISS

COVENANT

Definition

A covenant is a binding agreement or bond between two parties. The common OT term for covenant is *berith,* which probably derives from the root meaning "fetter." Covenants may be between equals or superior and inferior. A covenant may obligate both parties or only one.

Old Testament

The covenant history in the OT begins with Abraham. There are three narratives of the covenant-making between God and Abraham (Gen 12:1-9; 15:1-21; 17:1-27). The covenant binds God; Abraham is the free recipient. The only demands placed on him are to believe the covenant-maker (Gen 15:6), to walk before God and be perfect (Gen 17:1), and to preserve the sign of the covenant, i.e., circumcision, in order that the covenant bond not be forgotten (Gen 17:10-14). God, on the other hand, is bound to give Abraham land and descendants and to maintain a special relationship with him, i.e., election.

God renews the covenant with Abraham's descendants by a personal manifestation to Isaac (Gen 26:1-5) and Jacob (28:10-22). The covenant privilege is also passed from generation to generation by means of blessing (Gen 27:1-29; 28:1-4).

Since the covenant with Abraham binds only God, it is unconditional. It cannot be broken. Therefore it persists throughout the history of Abraham's descendants.

The story of the Sinai covenant begins as the covenant people suffer oppression in Egypt in the thirteenth century B.C. God hears their cry and moves to deliver them because "he remembers his covenant with Abraham, Isaac, and Jacob" (Exod 2:24). The exodus from Egypt creates for God a special people. The experience at Sinai solemnizes the bond created through the exodus.

The Sinai covenant is a conditional covenant, binding both God and the people. The covenant is made in the midst of a theophany on the mountain. Inserted in the midst of the narrative is Israel's charter, the Ten Commandments. Several chapters of law follow, most dating from a later time, signifying the fact that all Israelite law is incorporated into and dependent on the covenant bond at Sinai.

The Sinai covenant is sealed by a dual ceremony: a meal and a blood rite (Exod 24:1-11). Both rituals signify the sharing of life. Those who eat together share the nourishment that sustains their lives, and ancient custom understood that to share bread with someone was to become responsible for that person's life. The sprinkling of the blood on the altar, which signifies Yahweh, and on the people indicates that Yahweh and the people have become blood relatives, next-of-kin. Yahweh's deliverance of the people in the exodus, which is an exercise of the responsibility of the next-of-kin to ransom one who is enslaved, has already demonstrated this relationship.

The form of the Sinai covenant is often compared to the form of the Hittite suzerainty treaty (c. 1400-1200 B.C.), a treaty between a lord and a vassal. Parts of the treaty form include: preamble, historical prologue, stipulations, list of witnesses, blessings and curses. The complete form is not found in any one biblical narrative, although the Book of Deuteronomy and the renewal ceremony in Joshua 24 come closest.

The sealing of the covenant, however, indicates that the bond is understood as more intimate than that of a political treaty. This intimate bond is imaged most frequently by the two closest human relationships: father (mother)-son (Exod 4:22; Isa 49:14-15; Jer 3:19; 31:9, 20; Hos 11:1-11) and husband-wife (Isa 54:5-8; Jer 2:2; 3:20; Hos 2:4-25). The formula which signifies the covenant is modeled on the formula which seals a marriage: "I will be your God; you will be my people" (cf. Song of Songs 7:11; Tobit 7:11). The demands placed on the people and on God are essentially not obedience and service, but the much deeper virtues of love and fidelity (Ps 117:1-2).

In the priestly narrative of the Pentateuch the Sinai covenant is marked by a *sign* as are two other covenants. The Sinai covenant is marked by the sabbath (Exod 31:13, 17). The covenant with Abraham is marked by circumcision (Gen 15:11). The covenant with Noah is marked by the sign of the rainbow (Gen 9:12, 15).

The Sinai covenant, which is a conditional covenant, is broken before the people ever leave the mountain (Exod 32:1-29). The fashioning of the golden calf is an attempt to create a god whose presence they can control and see. Moses breaks the tablets of the law, symbolic of the broken covenant. God declares his intention of abandoning the broken covenant and forming a new covenant people from the descendants of Moses. The covenant with Abraham still stands, however; and after Moses reminds God of this bond, the Sinai covenant is renewed. Thus in the paradigmatic telling of the Sinai covenant the model of renewal is already given.

The breaking of the covenant continues throughout the history of the twelfth to the sixth centuries. The prophets declare that covenant breaking will result in the loss of covenant privilege, the loss of land and descendants and return to slavery in a foreign land. The fall of the northern kingdom of Israel (722 B.C.) with the subsequent Assyrian captivity and the fall of the southern kingdom of Judah (587 B.C.) with the Babylonian exile are directly attributed to covenant breaking.

The prophets, however, do not leave the people without hope. They promise a new covenant which will be written on the people's hearts (Jer 31:31-34; Ezek 36:23-28).

In addition to the Sinai covenant, another covenant shapes OT theology, the covenant with David. The covenant with David is modeled on the covenant with Abraham. It is unconditional; it binds only God. The covenant is revealed to David by the prophet Nathan (2 Samuel 7:1-17). David has wished to build a house for God, i.e., a temple. God reveals that instead he will build a house for David, i.e., descendants. His house and his throne will remain forever. A descendant of his will always reign. This covenant also gives hope during the exile, even when it seems irrevocably broken. The hope for a descendant of David, a king anointed (messiah), is the basis for the messianic hope.

New Testament

The NT (New Covenant) is built upon the whole web of covenant theology of the OT. The identification of Jesus as Christ (i.e., messiah), as Son of David, as fulfillment of the messianic prophecies, depends upon the theology of the unconditional covenant with David (and with Abraham [cf. Mt 1:1-17]). The narrative of the Last Supper, set at Passover which is a renewal of the exodus event, is told with covenant terminology. "This cup is the new covenant in my blood...." (1 Cor 11:25; Lk 22:20; cf. Mt 26:27; Mk 14:24). The new covenant is thus sealed in blood and with a meal.

In the Letter to the Romans Paul refers to the lasting covenant between God and Abraham and his descendants. He identifies the descendants of Abraham as those who follow his example of faith. Therefore Abraham is the father of the uncircumcised who believe as well as the circumcised (Rom 4:1-25). Paul contrasts the old covenant and the new, emphasizing the superiority of the new covenant, its openness to Gentiles, and its reliance on spirit rather than the letter of the law (2 Cor 3:1-18; Gal 4:21-28). He warns believing Gentiles, however, not to be proud, for the covenant with Abraham does not fail: "God's gifts and call are irrevocable" (Rom 11:1-36; cf. Rom 9-10). The author of the Letter to the Hebrews also emphasizes the perfecting of the old covenant by the new (Heb 7-10).

Throughout the NT the covenant imagery persists. The parent-child relationship is integral to the message of Jesus (Mt 6:9-15; 11:25-27; Jn 1:14-18; 5:19-30) and to the understanding of the early church regarding the relationship between the Christian and God (Rom 8:14-17; Gal 4:1-7). The bridegroom image is also important for the identification of Jesus (Mt 9:15; 25:1-13; Jn 3:19; cf. Eph 5:22-27) and to the hope for the kingdom which he preaches (Mt 22:1-14). The Book of Revelation brings the imagery to the final day. The wedding of the Lamb is celebrated (Rev 19:16-10). The new Jerusalem is portrayed as his bride (Rev 21:2). God proclaims: "I will be their God and they will be my people" (Rev 21:3).

See **Israel**

J. Behm, "*diathéké,*" TDNT 2. 106-34. W.J. Dumbrell, *Covenant and Creation: A Theology of Old Testament Covenants,* Nashville: Thomas Nelson, 1984. T.E. McComiskey, *The Covenants of Promise: A Theology of the Old Testament Covenants,* Grand Rapids, MI: Baker Book House, 1985. E.W. Nicholson, *God and His People: Covenant and Theology in the Old Testament,* Oxford: Clarendon, 1986. K.G. O'Connell, "Continuity and Change in Israel's Covenant with God," *Bible Review* 1 (4, 1985) 46-55. M. Weinfeld, "*bérîth,*" TDOT 2.253-279.

IRENE NOWELL, OSB

CREATION

A. Introductory

The Greek verb *krinein,* cognate to the English *to create,* means *to found* or *to make habitable.* In Latin, *creare* means *to beget.* The German *schöpfen* connotes the action of shaping or forming. The Irish *cruthaigh* or *cruthú* evinces the same idea: *rud do chruthú* means *to make, to shape, to create, to test* or *prove* something. Thus, behind the English *to create* there are several resonances: founding, begetting, shaping, making. Anterior to all these shades of meaning is the Hebrew *bárá*—reserved for the mighty and wondrous acts of God. *Bárá* denotes ". . . a work of God altogether *sui generis,* independent of any preexistent material and realized without effort on the part of him who wills it . . . ." (Leo Scheffczyk).

B. The Biblical Witness

1. Witness in Exile. Deutero-Isaiah, Ezechiel and certain others—perhaps another—are the chief source of the biblical doctrine of creation/origins. Deutero-Isaiah attempts to strengthen people whose faith was under strain. Exposed to the values of their captors

and solicited by the lurid pantheon of Babylon, the Hebrews' faith seemed threatened and about to falter. Was Yahweh really all-powerful? Was he all-good? The text holds out a promise. It promises the return to Jerusalem of the captive people—a return which took place from 537 under Cyrus. It looks to a new Exodus, a new covenant, a new creation. As Yahweh had once made possible an Exodus from Egypt, he would again effect an Exodus from Babylon. Deutero-Isaiah emphasizes not only God's willingness but also his ability to do what he has promised. Drawing upon an existing, although possibly latent, creation faith, Deutero-Isaiah shows that God's salvific power embraces not only this small Jewish people but the whole world. The God of the covenant is the God who created—and who therefore has power over—the universe. Over Babylon and its gods. Over Cyrus the liberal king. Over diviners, soothsayers and wise men. Over natural, human and preternatural force.

Of the forty-seven times the word *bárá* is used in the OT, twenty instances are in Deutero-Isaiah. *Bárá* is a technical word from the theological language of the priests. Used almost exclusively of divine actions, it denotes the independence and transcendence of God's creative work. It is not that Deutero-Isaiah initiates a faith in God the creator. Rather, his significance is to have aided the progression whereby creation and salvation are fused into one theme. Here the triple base upon which christian theology rests is first laid: creation, covenant, new exodus or universal salvation.

2. Creation, Origins in Genesis. Genesis is composed of protohistory and prehistory as well as of an extended narrative dealing with the patriarchs of Israel who lived in "historical" times. The "author" wished to encourage a people which had suffered grievously and, perhaps, were still demoralized as a result of captivity. An unknown "editor" of the same school as Deutero-Isaiah appears to have fused strands of tradition into the patchwork known as the book of Genesis. The strands which concern us are the Priestly and Jahwist texts. The latter had reached definitive form by the time of Solomon (ninth to eighth century B.C.). The Priestly text did not do so until the end of the fifth century B.C.

It is accepted that the Genesis narratives are not literal *rapportage*. These narratives bear the main features of myth. Insofar as Genesis 1 and 2 is a pictorial, dramatic, even symbolic treatment of something at the heart of reality, it *is* myth. Many writers describe it so. Others prefer to say that the minds behind Genesis adapt mythical elements to express a truth which transcends myth (Von Rad; Voegelin). In summary, although the accounts in the early chapters of Genesis are not to be read literally or taken as history in the strict sense, they are situated within a deeply historical faith. Here is a major difference from the cosmogonies of other peoples.

The Genesis account is unambiguously monotheistic. God is transcendent, pre-existent. His creative work needs no prior substratum. His *fiat* is creative: God said.... and it was so. Bodies which in other accounts of origins are divinized, here are treated as creatures of Yahweh.

The Priestly strand addresses the question: is Yahweh the mighty God we have worshipped? And, if he is, what does he ask of us now? The Yahwist text examines the origin of evil: does it come from a principle independent of God? Could it come from God himself? The combined texts present the benign sovereignty of God and a subtle account of the origin of suffering, wickedness and death. God is really God. He does care for his people. He is all powerful. He made all things

good. Evil and suffering are not to be blamed on him.

In summary, Genesis seems to say:

(a) The whole world, at once threatening and great, owes its being to the free, sovereign action of God.

(b) Whether one views its genre as world history or as aetiology, Genesis bears many characteristics of myth.

(c) Creation is basically good. The OT view of creation has a tranquillity and a warmth not found in comparable literature. For Genesis, creation is "the expression of God's goodness in action" (Desmond Wilson).

(c) The dark side of life, the cruel edge of things is not due to God's positive will. God made all things good. The harmony to which we aspire and which we experience as a grievous absence, was part of God's creative gift. "The distortion we experience is not a necessity but a perversion" (John Shea). The Genesis account strikingly presents the flawed human response to temptation. Questions still remain. Is evil only *moral* evil? Surely there are other considerations? There is the fractiousness of nature which can issue in ruined lives. There is the tragedy—surely an evil—when children and innocent suffer horribly. We are therefore still challenged to deepen our idea of evil beyond the idea of a single moral fault, occurring at the dawn of the race.

(e) The world exists for man and woman. The Priestly account reaches a climax in the creation of man and woman. There is an unforgettable beauty to the blessing pronounced over them and to the hymn of joy proclaiming their nobility (Gen 1:26-29). Man and woman are the image of God: they are to increase, multiply and care for the earth. Humankind is suffused of the breath of God, is a uniquely living spirit with an especial mission of stewardship. Here is the ground for the claim made by many theologians that the first theology of secularity is in the book of Genesis.

(f) The technical doctrine of *creation ex nihilo* is not explicitly contained in these chapters. The text emphasizes that everything is dependent upon God's creative presence. Yet, the first explicit reference to "creation out of nothing" does not occur until the second book of Maccabees.

3. Psalms and Wisdom Literature. Creation as an *article of faith* emerged with the spirituality of the synagogue. It is therefore, relatively late as an explicit teaching. Nevertheless, the Hebrews had long possessed oral traditions witnessing to a belief that we are God's creatures, living in God's world. Insofar as these traditions can be reconstructed, e.g., from certain psalms, they articulate an experience of "givenness." One finds striking examples of this in Psalms 8, 19 and 104.

With the Wisdom literature one encounters another perspective on creation thought. Job, Wisdom, Ben-Sirach, and Daniel are the product of the Jewish *diaspora*. Whereas the OT is spare on abstract concepts, Wisdom literature has a technical vocabulary for such ideas as world, cosmos and universe. Repeatedly one is struck by its subtlety of thought. The mystery of creation is considered for its own sake. The perfection of the world is extolled. Thus, Wisdom literature leads us to God by contemplation of nature as a witness to the divine (cf. Wis 13; Job 28:12).

4. Creation in the New Testament. There is little direct reference to creation/ origins in the gospels. They present the tradition about Jesus, not a theological system. Yet, one can find there a rich source of reflection on creation. The evangelists presuppose the OT doctrine of origins. The gospels show God as Father present to the world he called forth. The parables are redolent of God's creative presence, of his support of, and concern for, the least of things.

Acts 14 and Acts 17 presuppose the Hellenist-Jewish model of instruction for Gentiles wishing to become Jews. In Acts 14:15 and Acts 17:22-51 Paul uses a Christian version of that schema. In Acts 17 he proclaims a God (1) who has created the world and everything that is in it, who is Lord of heaven and earth, (2) who has appointed a day on which he will judge the world according to righteousness (3) through a man whom he has appointed for that purpose. In Acts 14, there is a similar approach. The pattern of creation, conversion and consummation is discernible in the missionary preaching of Paul at Lystra and Athens. Creation occupies a large part of this schema. Belief in God the creator was the ground from which grew belief in the God of Jesus Christ.

For NT christology, Jesus is the link between protology and eschatology, creation and salvation. The awareness of Jesus' significance for the world gives impetus to the belief in Jesus' mediation of creation. In 1 Cor 8:6, Paul speaks of "one Lord Jesus Christ through whom are all things and through whom we exist."

Several models are used in the NT to proclaim Christ's person and work. Some of these appeal to the role of Christ in creation. In the prologue of John's Gospel there is a studied parallel between the Genesis creation account and the new creation in Christ. One notices John's skillful adaptation of the Jewish tradition on the creative work of God. It is the Word made flesh in Jesus who created in the beginning. There is an equally striking use of the Word concept in Hebrews 1. God *spoke* in many ways through his prophets, but in the last days through a Son, the heir of all things, through whom this world was created. In this pericope, Word (*logos*), image (*eikon*) and stamp (*charakter*) coalesce. The author of

Hebrews transfers the splendid words of Psalm 102 to Jesus Christ: "You Lord, in the beginning created the earth and with your own hands you made the heavens. They will disappear, but you will remain" (Heb 1:10-11; Ps 102).

The unity of creation and redemption is clear in Ephesians and Colossians. Christ is the reconciliation of a multiple disorder; "He is our peace who made us both [Jew and Gentile] one .... and [reconciled] us both [Jew and Gentile] in one body through the Cross" (Eph 2:16). "Through Him are reconciled all things, whether on earth or in heaven, making peace by the blood of His Cross" (Col 1:20).

The limitation in Ephesians to Jewish/ gentile relations is superseded in the universal range of Colossians—"all things, whether on earth or in heaven." Together, these epistles review the effect of Christ's ministry on the cosmic, ecclesiological and ethical dimensions of life. The reconciliation is of sinners with God. People once again have access to God's favor. This reconciling lordship of Christ is exercised through the church. The reconciliation is cosmic—extending to thrones, dominions, principalities, powers and authorities. The harmony disrupted by the curse of sin has been restored in Jesus Christ. The Christian no longer has cause for cosmic anxieties, no longer need attend to taboos or horoscopes, no longer should fear the forces of destiny.

Ephesians 1:9-10 insists that creation is planned with Christ in mind. God's plan is to bring everything to unity in him. Ephesians also speaks of *anakephalaiósis,* meaning primacy, or principality, with the connotation of recapitulation or bringing together in one point. Christ is the summit, the *acme* of creation upon whom converge all else. In him the deepest reality of things is restored— their being for God. Creation is, as it were, Christoform.

For NT thought, creation is broader than origins. Creation transcends even that sense of the presence of God which the OT hymns. Creation in the NT is closely related to the project of reconciliation of people among themselves, as well as with nature and with God. The project laid in creation reached its high point in the ministry of Jesus Christ. In the work of discipleship the new creation is being built and the "new man" fashioned. Hence the NT forces our ideas on creation to embrace a cosmic christology (L. Boff), an eschatology, and an exciting perspective on discipleship. It points up the identity of the recreative Holy Spirit with the spirit which hovered over the aboriginal chaos.

C. The Patristic Witness

1. Early Post-Apostolic Works. The doctrine of creation appears in the earliest post-apostolic works. The Shepherd of Hermas insists that the first commandment is to believe that "God is one, who created and established all things, bringing them into existence out of non-existence." This is the first allusion in christian literature to *creatio ex nihilo.* Both the Didaché and the Epistle of Barnabas teach that God is the Lord who governs the whole universe. The first epistle of Clement carries anthems of praise to the creator: "The Father and creator of the entire cosmos," "creator and Father of ages," "creator and guardian of every spirit" (*1st Epistle of Clement* 19:2; 35:6; 59:3).

Nevertheless, the first major theological works on creation were in response to Gnosticism. Irenaeus of Lyons is the most consistent opponent of the *Gnosis.* In *Adversus Haereses* he attacks the dualism of the Gnostics, by proclaiming the unity of creation and redemption. Irenaeus establishes that God the Creator and God the Redeemer are one. God's plan for the world is of a piece. It was redemption in Christ which God had in mind at creation.

Since it is the same God who creates and redeems, there is nothing outside the scope of his creative and redeeming activity. Irenaeus highlights the absurdity of supposing that there is any being over whom God's power does not obtain. If there were such a being, it must be a second divinity. On this key idea rests Irenaeus' conviction of "creation out of nothing." Matter is not eternal. God needs no pre-existing material upon which to work. He did everything with "his own hands," not from need but from the motive of beneficent love.

2. Eastern Fathers: Clement and Origen. Both Clement and Origen had to take account of Gnosticism. It is a tribute to their unwavering christian sense that they used tenets of Platonism, Stoicism and neo-Pythagoreanism as a sub-structure for an orthodox theology. Clement moves away from a literal interpretation of Genesis. He believes that creation is a timeless act in which all things, were brought to be. Creation is a continuing reality, a *creatio continua* (*Stromata* 4:16, 5:16). Origen, too attempted to bring coherence to christian thought on creation. He speaks of a divine pedagogy guiding things back to an original unity in God. This is his schema of *exitus-reditus,* the creation goes out from God only to find an original unity in him. For this idea of a divine economy or pedagogy in creation we are indebted to the eastern fathers.

3. Western Patristic Thought on Creation. In the West there was a less mystical, more strictly rational, view of creation. Lactantius, Tertullian and, later, Hilary of Poitiers forsook the Platonic bent of the East, although they continued to use neo-Platonism as a crutch to reflection. In Jerome, there is an attempt to relate creation theology to a theology of the Trinity. Yet it was Augustine who gave western thought its fullest shape. Augus-

tine combined a leaning to scriptural exegesis with an outstanding ability to use diverse philosophic aids. His commentaries on the book of Genesis *De Genesi ad litteram, De genesi ad litteram imperfectus liber,* and *De Genesi contra Manichos* mirror Augustine's creation theology. He is very clear about a "creation out of nothing." Even matter - (*terra invisibilis et incognita*) - is a creature. Creation is neither a semi-divine emanation nor independent of the Savior God. Rather, everything has come from God, being called forth by him out its own nothingness.

Augustine's genius enabled him to contribute the original insight of the concreation of time and cosmos. The world is created with time rather than in it. Time is neither a space nor a receptacle. It is a function of change, a measurement of duration. Rejecting Aristotle and Plato, Augustine offers an analysis which is both metaphysical and psychological. Another achievement of Augustine was to relate creation to Trinity. Creation is a trinitarian act. It is from the Father through the Son. Its eventual perfection is guaranteed by the Holy Spirit. All things bear the mark of the Trinity—the term *vestigium Trinitatis* comes from Augustine and is applied in christian theology to the whole creation. Partly because of this link to trinitarian theology there is a basic optimism in Augustine's thought on creation. Unfortunately, his optimism does not mitigate the severity of his judgment on the body and on marriage.

D. An Emergent Tradition on Creation

1. Creation as Relation. St. Thomas Aquinas (1225-1274). St. Thomas' starting point is the experience of God mediated in the tradition of the church. His creation theology is best understood when related to the text at *Exod* 3:14. Aquinas' thinking on creation springs from a theology of the God of Abraham, Isaac and

Jacob, the Father of our Lord Jesus Christ. St. Thomas came to believe that creation can be rationally demonstrated. However, it is doubtful that he would attempt a proof of creation apart from religious experience or the tradition in which such experience is mediated.

For St. Thomas, creation is the reception of being from the giver of all existence. Creation is a relation to the creator as the fount of our being. God *is* being. He is the fullness and perfection of existence. All created beings *have* being. They have being as a participation in what God *is* fully and perfectly. This participation defines creaturehood.

Creation may be viewed in two aspects: *creatio activa* and *creatio passiva*. Active creation refers to the creative act of God. Passive creation focuses on the effect in the creature. In the first (active) sense, creation is defined by St. Thomas as the production of something from its own nothingness (*productio rei ex nihilo sui nec subiecti* S.Th., Ia, q.45, art. 2 ad 2). This highlights the radical nature of creation. It precludes any prior reality from which the new being is educed. In creation, something is called forth, is constituted, where previously there was a void. The statement of the French episcopate, *Je Crois en Toi,* puts it well: "... God does not *make* something by creating, rather he exists contagiously, he communicates of himself as do all good educators." Creation is not an artifact. It is a gift, not of improved or altered being, but of being pure and simple. At this point we are drawn from the mythological view of origins. We are drawn from origins to the metaphysical level of dependence upon God in all points of individual and universal existence.

There remains the second aspect— *creatio passiva*. Creation, in this second sense, answers the question of the ground of being. It is a relation which arises from the gift and reception of existence. St.

Thomas writes: "creation is none other than the relation of the creature to the creator as to the principle of its very being" (S.Th. Ia, q.45, art 3(c)). Such a relation subsists throughout reality without prejudice to the autonomy of nature and cosmos. In the Thomist perception, creation is a unilateral relation of dependence: the creature depends upon the Creator, but not the Creator upon the creation.

This, is the background to St. Thomas' systematic definition of creation as "the emanation of all being from a universal cause"(S.Th., Ia, q.45, art 1(c)). "Emanation" reminds us of the priority of God: from God all things come. Aquinas speaks of emanation without danger of pantheism since his concept of participation combines likeness and distance. "All being" implies that every scrap of reality is indebted to the Creator for its being and continuance. Another facet of this truth is the anti-Gnostic affirmation that there is no principle of being co-equal to God. "From a universal cause" reminds us of the level at which creation should be situated. There are many agents of change in human affairs and in the course of nature. Yet, the creative act belongs to God alone. It reaches to the core of being. It confers existence as such. Temporal categories are misleading—as if one could say "*before* being there was nothing." Creation is not about the before and after. It is rather about an order of being—of reception from a total source.

God's activity underlies, without interfering in, our powers and activities. God keeps us in being and enables our action— even our free action. There is a distinction between primary or transcendent causality, and secondary or predicamental causality. Secondary causality runs the gamut of activity from the gentleness of love to the working of the indomitable forces of nature. Yet, underlying all, enabling all is the primary causality which is God's alone. One can attribute causality totally to God and totally to creatures. A good action, a beautiful gesture, comes from God as well as from the doer. Indeed, we can say of an evil action that it is permitted by God for he does not subtract his conserving force from the evildoer.

2. *Creation as Process. Pierre Teilhard de Chardin.* (1881-1955). Teilhard de Chardin's lifelong search was for synthesis: of reason and authority, of matter and spirit, of science and faith. This shows itself in his exigence of continuity: between matter and spirit, between past, present and future, between body and soul. His range of vision is all-comprehensive and has a tincture of mythopoesis. Teilhard spoke of his system as "hyperphysics"—the perception of the structure of reality in its main lines, as they stand out from comparing the results of the experimental sciences with the main thrust of the Judaeo-christian tradition. Teilhard views the cosmos as a process which mirrors the inner life of God. Despite its pain, failure and apparent absurdities, creation is destined to share the life of the Trinity. For Teilhard the goal of the universe discloses its meaning. The question remains of how this goal and, hence, this meaning can be discerned. Teilhard believes that an anticipatory understanding can be achieved through attention to the overall pattern emergent on "an immense time graph." The experience of a palaeontologist of front rank dominates Teilhard's speculative imagination here. Dealing with the relics of millions of years, he can more easily attempt to draw the co-ordinates of such a time graph.

The confluence of his several interests—in particular, his theology, his philosophy and his science—leads Teilhard to speak of "evolutive creation" (*Creation evolutive*). All life, is developmental. It is process, Its direction is centripetal. It tends towards a creative center and moves by convergence upon that center. Teilhard argues: "evolution is not really creative as science at one time thought; rather, it is the expression, in terms of our own experience, of creation as it unfolds in space and time" (*Oeuvres,* vol 2, pp 80-81). If one accepts this idea of creation as development, under God, of the evolutionary process, one is speaking of a *creatio continua* much as did the early Fathers of the Church and the medieval schoolmen.

The Directedness of Creation. This minuscule *Credo* embraces *cosmogenesis*—i.e., the universe as a cosmos or whole is developing in a precise direction. The broad development from Alpha point to Omega point is yet another Teilhardian shorthand for evolving creation. *Evolving:* for the upward sweep of things, despite the pressures to dispersal and disintegration, is a thesis dear to Teilhard. *Creation:* for in his view such upward sweep is under the ever present *aegis* of God the creator and preserver.

The life thrust ranges from extreme dispersal or multiplicity towards God, the supreme unity. In the *Phenomenon of Man* Teilhard speaks of a "within" to all things, operative even at the atomic level. It is a force for convergence, cohesion and unity.

Teilhard's perspective on Omega point takes account of a personal, transcendent center to the creative-evolutionary process. This center is outside and above the process—or, to use more traditional language, is transcendent to it. Omega point influences the thrust of ascending life by attraction, drawing all things to itself. Its greatness is at once to support personal uniqueness even in the closest unity and collaboration. Such union is creative rather than assimilative. Far from swallowing up personality, union with Omega point causes personality to flower in full strength. Thus, Teilhard's oft-repeated adage is *l'union differencie* (union differentiates). Creative union cherishes diversity. Omega point, in this sense, is active in history not only through the provision of motive for action but principally through its own personal effectiveness. Teilhard names this active Center of centers, God.

3. *The First Vatican Council* (1870). At its third session, Vatican I expounded the constants of christian tradition on creation and providence. It reaffirmed the "otherness" and transcendence of God: the one, true God is "the creator and Lord of things visible and invisible." Canons 1-3 of the chapter *De Deo omnium rerum Creatore* disavow every affirmation that God and creation are one and the same. Pantheism or any confusion of creator with creation is ruled out. Similarly, Canon 4 disallows that God is a kind of world-spirit which "by evolution of itself becomes all things." The thrust of these four canons is to reaffirm the ancient faith in the personhood of God who can never be reduced to the measure of the universe. The fifth canon of the chapter emphasizes the gratuity of creation. Creation is a divine gift freely given. Furthermore, creation is *ex nihilo*—an aspect underlined by St. Thomas Aquinas. Its motive—*ratio propter quod fit*—is the glory of God. Lest this suggest some form of divine egoism, the chapter has it that creation is "not for the increase or acquirement of God's own happiness but to manifest God's perfection by the blessing which he bestows on creation."

In its opening chapter on Revelation, the Constitution *Dei Filius* retrieves St. Paul's assertion of a knowledge of God gleaned from his creative works. Canon 1 of the chapter *De Revelatione* states: "If anyone shall say that the one, true God, our creator and Lord, cannot be certainly known by the natural light of reason through created things, *anathema sit*."

Much has been written on the precise meaning of the Canon. Decades later, Karl Barth would oppose the Council for its natural theology. It should be noted that Vatican I affirms the possibility rather than the actuality of a natural knowledge of God. This possibility seems to be demanded by a biblical tradition from Wisdom 13 through Romans 1 to Acts 14 and 17. Likewise, a theological argument, well formulated by Gottlieb Söhngen, Henri Bouilbard and Hans Urs Von Balthasar, urges that for revealed knowledge of God to strike home the human spirit must have prior capacity to recognize such revealed knowledge—and this presupposes some inchoate "natural" knowledge.

4. *Twentieth-century Science: New Light on Creation.* For several centuries a foundational assumption of the empirical sciences was that the secrets of nature are in principle transparent to scientific rationality. The world was conceived of as a mechanism where freedom and contingency are at a minimum while necessity and predictability are at the maximum. Twentieth-century science has put severe strain on this assumption. With the new postulations of quantum theory, Heisenberg's "principle of uncertainty," and the theory of relativity, freedom, contingency and finality—once outlawed from the language of scientific dogma—are reconsidered if not espoused. The nineteenth-century assumption of the eternity, stability and imperishability of matter is less credible since the consolidation of the "big bang" theory of the origin of the universe we inhabit. The dominant perception is that the universe had a beginning and may well be limited in duration. And so the perception of a cosmos in the making, corroborated by the model of an expanding universe and by the hypothesis of evolution, challenges the rigidity of a mechanistic paradigm.

It is insufficient to halt at a description

of cosmic development while balking at the mystery of existence and the *sense* of that development. Both theology and philosophy should regain nerve. It has been said that "to the question: What existed before the 'big bang'?, most of modern science is mute." Many would reply that scientists *qua* scientists properly refuse to answer this extrascientific question. Nevertheless, here one is at a point of intersection. From the perspective of a creation theology the possible dialogue will be facilitated by attention to the "new cosmology" and to the recognition by many scientists of the mysteriousness of the physical manifold. Nor can a theology of creation afford to ignore works such as those of Fritjof Capra (*The Turning Point*) and of Rupert Sheldrake (*New Science of Life*). To this dialogue, the Judaeo-christian tradition has immense riches to bring.

5. *Creation and the Mystery of Evil.* At the close of this overview a caution is appropriate. An exclusively optimistic perspective on creation overlooks the massive "surd" of evil. The *mysterium iniquitatis* must be considered not simply in an individualistic manner but also in its social implications. "A creation in which life is ignored, threatened or crushed is a vitiated creation" (Jon Sobrino). Thus we are led to consider the related problems of the wasteful and unjust use of the goods of creation.

E. Contemporary Perspectives on Creation

Although ecology was already debated in the 1960's, the Second Vatican Council did not advert to it as a major problem. However, the issue was taken up in the subsequent years (cf. *Octogesima Adveniens,* para. 21 and *Justice in the World,* 1971).

It is imperative to develop a theology of nature. To acquiesce in the rape of nature derogates from our stewardship of the earth. Inattention here leaves the field open to the cruelest exercise of technological imperialism, on the one hand, and the kind of ecology which makes light of social justice, on the other hand. However, reflection on the ecological demand must be more than "the neurosis of members of the Club of Affluence because their hitherto protected domains are being threatened." A theology of the earth must reflect more than middle-class, first-world interests. The ecological imperative must include the call to justice.

The Problem Stated. There is always a cost to ecological irresponsibility. Thus, through the depletion of valuable resources, pollution, and the threat to people's health, the attack upon the ecosphere entails a punishment not simply on the guilty but also on the innocent. The paradox of technological advance is that the solution of one problem often leads to the creation of a new one. The disastrous thing is that the prevalent scientific world view regards the universe as a mechanism. To use Charles Birch's phrase: "It has led to a factory view of nature, with humanity pitted against nature." And if it is true that science reflects the society in which it is practiced, then in an unjust society these injustices will be reinforced through scientific expertise.

One must question the assumption that scientists are always disinterested, that they are always competent in risk management as well as honest about failure. An apparently value-free science and an unbridled technology lead to destruction rather than to genuine development.

Whereas technology makes a bad master it could become a good servant. Converted technological reason could help develop and use our resources for the benefit of all. The just, humane and sustainable society is not willed into existence by good intention or fair speech.

It has to be constructed. In such construction a properly directed technology can represent an opportunity for the poor of the earth.

Theology in a Nature-Sensitive Mode. The process theologians: Hartshorne, Cobb, Ogden and Whitehead—present the idea of a God compassionate and solidary with a striving cosmos. Rather than stand over against creation, God enters it, is part of it, draws it upward and forward. In such a model, nature is not viewed as something to be dominated, battled or exhausted. The systems within nature can be seen both as subjects and as objects. This is neither animism nor Romanticism. Process theology elucidates a hierarchy of values: from the vibrant earth to lesser creatures through mammals to human beings. Relative to humankind, the rest of nature has both an intrinsic value—for itself, as it were—and an instrumental value as the support of human life and well-being.

It is not an indulgence when people argue towards a new cosmological myth, a new story of the earth. A critically re-established story of creation is needed. The Judaeo-christian tradition has supplied us with materials for the purpose: the OT itself, the gospel's haunting memory of a Christ who loved people in the concreteness of their surroundings, Paul's relation of creation to God's redemptive purpose. The Eastern conception of Christ's universal rule—Christ the Pantocrator or Cosmocrator—has much to offer this reconstruction. So, too, has the Franciscan estimation of nature as a graced interlocutor of humankind. There is the relational concept of creation dear to medieval theology and devotion. And for those who search for an holistic view of life, of nature and of religious faith, the world-view offered by Teilhard de Chardin continues to exercise a fascination.

To walk lightly on the earth enjoins a respect for nature, stewardship of its resources, and co-operation with its systems. It means care to replenish renewable resources. It commands opposition to the consumerism which trivializes people's lives with implanted need and arid satisfaction. It challenges the tastes of the rich countries and the rich classes—tastes which are met at high cost to people, animals and nature. As if to show that the ethics of justice and sustainability raise socio-political issues, the question of limits to growth arises. Here one must tread carefully. Whose growth is to be limited? Is a moratorium to be placed on the growth of countries depressed by the injustices of the present economic order? What kind of growth is being discussed? Is it growth on the coat-tails of expansionist capitalism to the benefit of the multi-national corporations?

The World Council of Churches has given a lead in its application to the study of "faith and science in an unjust age." Particularly significant is its insistence on the mutual implication of social justice and ecological sustainability. Worthwhile guidelines have also come from Roman Catholic sources linking the work of justice to creation. The Catholic Church precisely in its long hostility to the changes wrought by the Enlightenment, has the opportunity to move around and beyond the unacceptable consequences of that *bourgeois* revolution. The critique of injustice to people and nature has been effectively articulated within Catholic theology in the last twenty years. For that critique we are particularly indebted to the several strands within the theology of liberation.

F. Creation and Just Use of the Goods of the Earth

A subversive memory has haunted the best of Jewish religious consciousness. The memory was of a time when Israel itself was subject to a harsh slavery, reversed by God's liberative gesture in the Exodus. The memory served as a criticism of domination emergent in Israel itself (cf Exod 22:21; Lev 19:33-4; Deut 10:19).

In the NT several parables criticize social injustice. The story of Dives and Lazarus highlights a distortion of right relationship. In the riches of one and the poverty of the other the relationship of equality which we accept every time we call God Father, is being denied.

The parable of the rich landowner extends the critique—the single minded pursuit of wealth is a deformation of right relation to God. There is a radical critique of wealth in the gospel paradox: "It is easier for a camel to go through the eye of a needle than for a rich man to enter the kingdom of God" (Mk 10:24). Perhaps the most striking glimpse we get of the early church's critique of inequality is the "communism of love" (Bloch) described in Acts 4:32.

St. Basil of Caesarea (fourth century) complained that people forgot that they were stewards, not owners, of God's creation. Thus they became unjust. St. John Chrysostom responded to a criticism of his preaching: "I am often reproached for continually attacking the rich. Yes, because the rich are continually attacking the poor ... those I attack are not the rich as such, only those who misuse their wealth ..." (Fall of Eutropius 2.3). In the third century, Clement of Alexandria emphasized that "all things are common and not for the rich to appropriate an undue share. God has given us ... the liberty of use, but only insofar as necessary; and He has determined that the use should be common. And it is monstrous for one to live in luxury, while many are in want" (Pedagogus 2, 119-120). Cyprian stressed that "whatever is of God is common to our use, nor is anyone excluded from His benefits and gifts." With customary vigor, Ambrose of Milan reminded his hearers: "God has ordained all things to be pro-

duced so that there shall be food in common for all and that earth should be the common possession of all. Nature has produced a common right for all but greed has made it a right for a few" (Duties of the Clergy, 1,132). One better understands Ambrose's denial that alms could ever be a sufficient excuse for inequity: "You are not making a gift of your possessions to the poor person. You are handing over to him what is his" (Naboth 55). Chrysostom is even sterner: "the rich, even those who have acquired their goods honestly, are in possession of the goods of the poor" (On Lazarus, Homily 2).

Under the surface of this tradition is the conviction that private property, with its attendant divisions and inequalities, is the result of the Fall. The most accurate reflection of the patristic teaching is that the earth and its fruits are intended by God for the enjoyment and sustenance of all. This finality has precedence over any individual property rights.

In St. Thomas' view, the common purpose of the earth's riches to meet human need over-rides all legal dispositions when it comes to urgent necessity. No title or property disposition can hinder the relief of human necessity. Two consequences ensue. First, there is a lien on wealth in regard to the need of the poor. Second, those in urgent need have the right to take what they need from the superfluity of others. In regard to the social lien on wealth St. Thomas appears to be more radical than his commentators. Whereas many commentators made much of an obligation in charity, Aquinas sees it as an obligation in justice. This is clear from his citation of Ambrose: "It is the bread of the poor you withhold, the clothing of the naked you retain."

Despite recurrent papal criticism of the harshest element of capitalism, the first clear subordination of private ownership to another principle is in Mater et

Magistra. Here, John XXIII, in affirming the right to private ownership, subordinates it to the common good. The keynote is private ownership with social responsibility. Towards the end of John's pontificate, *Pacem in Terris* (1963) describes private ownership as a *means* to an end, a suitable *means* for safeguarding the dignity of the person. In effect, this is a reversal of the earlier emphases—or, better, a recovery of a more ancient tradition. Thereafter, the universal purpose of created goods becomes the main principle while the right to private ownership is affirmed in a subsidiary way. Thus, one of the major documents of the Second Vatican Council, *Gaudium et Spes,* underlines that God intended the goods of the earth for the use of every human being. To this main purpose "all rights whatever, including those of private property and free commerce, are to be subordinated" (*Populorum Progressio*, 22).

A contemporary understanding of ownership must take account of the process of industrialization and the problems posed by advanced technology. In his encyclical *Laborem Exercens,* Pope John Paul II stresses the priority of labor over capital. He speaks of the revision both in theory and practice of the right to private ownership of the means of production. To this can be linked the "social mortgage" spoken of by the same pope at Puebla and taken up recurrently by the final document of that assembly.

G. Towards a Creation Spirituality

Creation spirituality affirms that between us and nothingness there is the supportive power of God. This is not a metaphysical proof. It is, rather, an acknowledgment built upon glimpses of meaning and anticipations of fulfilling value. It is a faith, a personal stance. In the experience of our own contingency we can be drawn, or driven, to affirm a ground of our being. At the root of all faith, forming part of its definition, is "the acknowledgment of a power that sustains our existence in all the concrete circumstances of human living." The sense of contingency, in whatever form it strikes home to us, is really a grace—"an invitation to see [our] world and [our] present history [as] grounded in a being [we] call God and relate to as such" (James P. Mackey).

A consistent theological emphasis is upon God's creative activity as trustworthy and faithful. It corresponds to the OT *emeth* (faithfulness) and the NT *aletheia* (loyal truth). It is an approach which, without minimizing the reality of evil, sin and apparently malign fate, affirms hope in God's purpose and the triumph of God's justice. It is only when one regards creation as a positive gift and a project entrusted to human action that one can assimilate the call of the Creator who is also the liberator. The God who gives us being is with us in every liberative impulse. The experiences of God as creator of the universe and as liberator of oppressed people nourish each other. A creation spirituality, therefore, thrusts towards a vibrant spirituality of liberation.

A recurrent witness of the Bible is that God gave us a *good* creation. The creation accounts emphasize this "God saw that it was good .... very good." The Book of Job, outstanding in its "wintry experience" of God, refuses to lay blame at God's feet for the woes that seem to constitute the human condition. In the threatening circumstances of today's scale of terror, we can better understand that many cultures see good and evil as warring powers, with the sway tilting now to one, now to the other, and with the ultimate outcome deeply uncertain. There is a tendency to dualism which seems almost innate to humankind. Historically dualism takes a number of forms. One form makes a distinction between two principles, one of good, one of evil, equal in power, independent, and manipulative of human endeavor. An attenuated form of this dualism affirms not so much an independent principle of evil as an evil endemic to creation itself. Matter and the body are considered evil while spirit and the soul are regarded as the only good. The hallmark of this perception is the identification of finitude with evil and sin. Salvation is achieved only by transcending one's creaturehood for higher reality outside the body.

The chief argument used by the Church Fathers against Gnosticism was the universal fatherhood of God, shown in the goodness of creation. The first article of the creeds dwells upon this fatherhood: One cannot reject the material, the bodily and the worldly, without impugning the God who created these dimensions of existence. Hence, the teaching of Marcion and of Tertullian was repudiated. There is, however, an acceptance of Tertullian's insistence: "we must not consider by whom things were *made* but by whom they have been perverted .... between the created and the corrupted state there is a vast difference." This distinction between the goodness of God's creation and its deterioration due to human malfeasance is important to maintain. Creatureliness and sinfulness are not mutually implicative. Nature is the presupposition of grace, not the contradiction of it. Only if creation is seen as God's good gift which has been disordered due to the misuse of freedom, can it also be regarded as in deep need of healing, and yet as the place where God's loving purposes can be effected.

Creation faith precludes flight from the world through an evasive spirituality. Such flight would be an abdication of responsibility. Hence, the readiness to cooperate in shaping a better future flows from the acceptance of creation and the service of the Kingdom of God. This,

however, must be accompanied by a realism—critical of oneself, one's society and of the structures established by sinful human beings. The appropriate critical analysis finds motivation in a search for justice and in a love of God's creation. Where such an analysis is attempted, the contemplative model of spirituality embraces a transformative dimension. Contemplation of the goodness of God's creation is then accompanied by a realistic assessment of evil and sin.

Robert Butterworth, *The Theology of Creation,* Theology Today (5), Cork: Mercier Press, 1969. J.G. Donders, *Creation and Human Dynamism,* Mystic, Conn: Twenty-Third Publications, 1985. Matthew Fox, *Original Blessing. A Primer in Creation Spirituality,* Santa Fe: Bear and Co., 1983. Jürgen Moltmann, *The Future of Creation,* Philadelphia: Fortress, 1979. Leo Scheffczyk, *Creation and Providence,* New York: Herder and Herder, 1970. Michael Schmaus, *Dogma 2, God and Creation,* New York: Sheed and Ward, 1969. Jürgen Moltmann, *God in Creation. An Ecological Doctrine of Creation,* [The Gifford Lectures, 1984-85], London: S.C.M. Press, 1985. Séan McDonagh, *To Care for the Earth: A Call to a New Theology,* London: Chapman, 1986.

DENIS CARROLL

CREATIONISM

In recent decades the United States has been the scene for a new controversy between teachers of evolutionary theory and proponents of creationism, or creation-science, which holds that a literal reading of the Bible provides a better account of the world's order than evolutionary theory does. The dispute has a peculiarly American character, reflecting a biblical fundamentalism deeply rooted in many segments of American society and also our public school system from which the formal advocacy of religious belief is constitutionally barred.

The principle antecedent for the current discussion was the "Scopes monkey trial" in which John T. Scopes, a high school biology teacher, was indicted for violating a 1925 Tennessee law which forbade the teaching in public schools of any theory that denied the biblical story of the creation of mankind and held that human beings are descended from a lower order of animals. William Jennings Bryan was the prosecutor, and Clarence W. Darrow the defense attorney. Scopes was convicted, but a state appellate court reversed the ruling on technical grounds, and no appeal to the Supreme Court ensued.

The Tennessee law was repealed in 1967, and a year later the Supreme Court struck down an Arkansas law against teaching evolution (Epperson v. Arkansas). In 1969 the California Board of Education agreed to the presentation of the Genesis creation story as an alternative to the evolutionary account but then reversed itself in 1974 after years of controversy. During these years, advocates of creationism adopted a new approach, seeking now to win equal time for teaching creationism as a science. The Institute for Creation Research was established in San Diego and the Creation Research Society in Ann Arbor, Michigan. Arkansas and Louisiana enacted "balanced treatment" statutes in 1981, requiring any public school teaching the theory of evolution to teach creationism as science, too. But a coalition of religious leaders, theologians and scientists challenged the Arkansas law and won their case in December 1981. Then, in June 1987, the Supreme Court declared the Louisiana law unconstitutional because "the pre-eminent purpose of the Louisiana Legislature was clearly to advance the religious viewpoint that a supernatural being created humankind" (Edwards v. Aguillard). Without giving a final ruling on the constitutionality of teaching scientific creationism, the Court thus disallowed it wherever it would be tantamount to promoting religious belief.

While the creationist controversy has important political consequences for the relations between church and State in the United States, its religious and cultural significance may be even greater. Defense of a biblical understanding of the human condition on scientific grounds ineluctably heightens the public sense that religion and science are mutually exclusive. If proponents of Genesis argue that it is correct in its literal sense and that science must accordingly be wrong, empirically minded students, when persuaded by the general theory of evolution, are very likely to conclude that the Bible must be correspondingly wrong. Instead of profiting from a dialogue between the perspectives of biblical faith and evolutionary science, and seeking a contemporary understanding of creation in an evolutionary universe, our culture would then witness their further estrangement. The interaction of the two concepts over the course of centuries has proven itself a more fruitful option.

See **Creation**, **Evolution**

Langdon Gilkey, *Creationism on Trial: Evolution and God at Little Rock,* Minneapolis, 1985.

LEO J. O'DONOVAN, SJ

CREEDS

Creeds, etymologically and historically, are in the first place confessions of faith. The classic christian creeds have their origins in the baptismal rites of the early church and in the course of time came to serve as rules of faith (*regulae fidei*) and in other roles. After briefly describing the origins of the word, this essay traces the development of the classic christian creeds, explores their structure and functions in the history of the church and, finally, discusses ecumenical efforts to reach a common confession of faith acceptable to Christians everywhere.

Etymology traces the word *creed* back through the Latin *credo* to the conjunction of two other Latin words: *cor* (heart) and do (a third conjugation verb meaning "I place" or "I put"). Thus *creed* implies a commitment, the giving of one's heart or self to someone or something. A creed is a statement that casts in verbal form the faith of an individual or a community. In this sense Christianity is a creedal religion; but there are political and social groups as well as individuals who declare their fundamental beliefs in the form of a credo.

The baptismal creed was known in the Latin West by the name of "symbol," as in *Symbolum Apostolicum* (Apostles' Creed), a designation that by the fifth century was in common use also in the Greek East (*to sumbolon*). The most common explanation of *symbolum* is the one found in Tyrannius Rufinus' *Commentarius in symbolum apostolorum* (A.D. 404). In the early church the creed or symbol functioned as a password, a sign or token whereby members of the christian community could recognize one another.

Although the creeds as we have come to know them had their origins in the baptismal ritual, creed-like affirmations appear in the earliest NT writings (1 Cor 8:6, 12:3, 15:3-7; 2 Cor 12:14; Mk 8:29 and parallels; and 1 Tim 3:16). The trinitarian formula, "Baptize them in the name of the Father, and of the Son and of the Holy Spirit" (Mt 28:19) ultimately shaped the tripartite structure of the classic creeds of Christianity, the Nicene and Apostles' Creeds.

From NT times onward a confession of faith, however expressed, was, for adults at least, a precondition of baptism. The most common creedal formulas in the second and third centuries were in the form of questions addressed to the candidate for baptism. St. Irenaeus witnesses to the fact that by A.D. 200 these "interrogatory creeds" had a trinitarian structure consisting of three questions regarding belief in the God the Father, Jesus Christ the Son of God, and the Holy Spirit of God (*Epideixis,* chs. 3, 6, 7 and 100). The person being baptized responded by a simple "I believe." The liturgies of the second and third centuries show no trace of any fixed formula whereby the baptized, speaking in the first person, declared his or her faith.

"Declaratory creeds," that is to say, short declarations couched in the first person affirming belief in the work of God the Father, Son and Spirit, began to appear in the third century and by the fourth century were common throughout the church. They were by-products of the church's catechetical system, representing efforts to recapitulate basic christian teaching in formulas structured to conform to the trinitarian framework of the baptismal interrogations. Thus the ancient creeds had a central part in the preparation for baptism, though not in the water rite itself.

It was in connection with the instruction of catechumens that the rites of handing over (the *traditio symboli*) and giving back (the *redditio symboli*) developed. In the later weeks of Lent, as the time of baptism approached, the bishop "handed over" the creed to the candidates in a formal ceremony and proceeded on subsequent days to explain it clause by clause. The catechumens in turn were expected to learn it by heart and "give it back" on the eve of their baptism.

Despite the fact that the wording of the creed varied from local church to local church, it was marked by a notable uniformity. By the beginning of the third century the general lines of the creed had begun to solidify. The interrogatory form of a Roman creed found in the *Apostolic Tradition* of St. Hippolytus, for example, has the characteristics of a fixed creedal formula. Although it is not clear whether Origen was drawing on an interrogatory or declaratory confession of faith, passages in his writings indicate that a triadic formula containing expressions similar to several found in Hippolytus' work existed also in the East. The exchange of correspondence between St. Cyprian of Carthage and Firmilian of Caesarea provide further evidence that the form of the baptismal interrogations had become fixed and had acquired official recognition in both North Africa and Asia Minor by the middle of the third century.

The Apostles' Creed

An early form of the baptismal creed of the Roman Church can be traced to the closing decades of the second century (*textus Romanus* = *R*). It had a marked influence on Eastern creeds and was the direct ancestor of all other local creeds in the West. The Apostle's Creed, which, in time, replaced the baptismal creeds in the Latin West and as we have it today (*textus receptus* = *T*), is the best known of R's descendants.

The primary source for the Latin text of R is Rufinus' Commentary, which attributes the Old Roman Creed to the apostles themselves; he described how each of the Twelve contributed a clause. Although Rufinus did not invent the story, his account of it became the basis for the medieval practice of singling out twelve articles in the creed. The birthplace of T, however, seems to have been somewhat north of the Alps, probably in southwest Gaul. In all likelihood the Carolingian liturgical reform caused it to be adopted as the common form throughout western Europe about the beginning of the ninth century. Charlemagne's policy of imposing uniformity on the baptismal rites and of emphasizing the place of the creed in catechesis gave the Apostles' Creed a practical monopoly in the liturgical life of the church. By the twelfth century T was regarded as the authoritative version of the creed in the West, including Rome.

Although R and related creeds grew up in the context of catechetical and baptismal rites, St. Ambrose and St. Augustine described the *symbolum fidei* as a talisman to be memorized and recited frequently. "Say your creed daily," said Augustine. "When you rise, when you compose yourself to sleep, repeat your creed, render it to the Lord, remind yourself of it, be not irked to say it over" (*Serm.* 58, 11). Similarly, the Apostles' Creed has always served mainly as a confession of faith linked to baptism; but early on it had a place in the daily worship of the church. Almost from the time of its final redaction T became a part of the divine office, first in compline and later in matins and prime.

The Ecumenical Creed

The Apostles' Creed was virtually unknown in the Eastern churches, where the dominant text came to be the creed of the First Council of Constantinople (A.D. 381), popularly, though inaccurately, known as the Nicene Creed. It is also called "the creed of the 150 fathers," a reference to the number of bishops in attendance at Constantinople I, and the Ecumenical Creed illustrates still another function that creeds came to exercise in the church, namely, that they serve as a norm for orthodoxy.

In the second century St. Irenaeus and Tertullian both speak of "a rule of faith" (*regula fidei*). They cite several examples of summary statements of the principal christian teachings which, they insist, have been handed down from "the apostles and their disciples" (*Adv. Haer.* I, 10, 1). The fact that the wording of these summaries resembles that of the baptismal creeds has prompted some authors to argue that the creed functioned as a rule of faith almost from the beginning. Most scholars, however, while acknowledging a close relationship, argue that the practice of using the baptismal creed as a rule of faith came into vogue in the fourth century with the Council of

Nicaea (A.D. 325).

With the intention of condemning Arius' teaching regarding the Logos, the Council of Nicaea promulgated a document that consisted of a creedal statement to which were attached several anathemas clearly directed against Arian doctrine. The Nicene Creed (= N) was based on the text of a local baptismal creed of Syro-Palestinian provenance that was edited to include certain key phrases contradicting Arius' teaching. The basic text does not seem to have been, despite the eyewitness account of Eusebius, the creed of Caesarea. The Nicene alterations consisted of (a) the clause "that is, from the substance of the Father" and (b) the passage "true God from True God, begotten not made, of one substance [*homoousion*] with the Father." (Kelly, p. 227, pp. 235-42). N is an early example, if not the first, in a long line of conciliar creeds that could be used as norms to certify the orthodoxy of church teachers and leaders. It was not intended for use by catechumens, nor did it supersede the baptismal creeds of local churches. In the course of time, however, phrases distinctive of Nicene orthodoxy were gradually interpolated into the existing baptismal formulas.

To avoid confusion it must be emphasized that the text that has come to be known popularly as the Nicene Creed is not that of the Council of Nicaea (= N) but the formula adopted by the Council of Constantinople in 381 (= C). The original framework of C was most probably a baptismal confession that belonged to a family of creeds used around either Antioch or Jerusalem and that had been modified in the spirit of Nicaea to include the *homoousion*. The distinctive clauses proper to C are those concerned with the doctrine of the Holy Spirit. The wording of the third article in particular was a carefully crafted statement contradicting the Pneumatomachian doctrine that denied the full deity and consubstantiality of the Holy Spirit with the Father and Son.

C, like N before it, functioned as a formal test of orthodox belief; but unlike N the Creed of Constantinople became incorporated into baptismal and eucharistic liturgies C came into general use as a baptismal creed in the Eastern Churches from the sixth century onwards. Even in Rome and in certain churches in the West where vestiges of Arianism lingered (e.g., Spain), the Creed of Constantinople seems to have taken the place of R in baptismal catechesis until ultimately displaced by the Apostles' Creed (= T) later in the middle ages. In an effort to proclaim their own orthodoxy and at the same time to disparage the Council of Chalcedon (451), monophysites introduced the practice of reciting the creed in the eucharistic liturgy. Though begun in dubious circumstances, the novel practice caught on in the East and was regularized by an ordinance of Emperor Justin II (568). In the West the practice grew more gradually. Introduced first in Spain by the third council of Toledo (589), it was soon adopted by Irish monks and later spread throughout the Frankish empire in the Carolingian period. Rome itself introduced the recitation of the creed in the eucharistic liturgy only in the eleventh century.

About the same time that the Creed of Constantinople was introduced into the eucharistic liturgy in the West, the *filioque* was introduced into the Latin text of the creed itself. The phrase affirmed St. Augustine's position regarding the double procession of the spirit, that is, the Holy Spirit "proceeds from the Father *and the Son*" and not simply from the Father, as taught in the East. In spite of acrimonious complaints of Eastern patriarchs and theologians, the phrase, first interpolated into the text in Spain, spread to France, Germany and Northern Italy. Despite pressure from Charlemagne, Rome resisted tampering with the authorized text probably until the time of Emperor Henry II at the beginning of the eleventh century.

The Athanasian Creed

Another creed, different in origin and style, that found a niche in the church's worship is the Athanasian Creed, known in Latin by its opening words *Quicunque vult* ("Whoever would be [saved]..."). It was for centuries attributed to St. Athanasius, the great defender of the Nicene faith, because it presented the most complete, formal statement of the trinitarian doctrine known in the early middle ages. The *Quicunque* was, in fact, composed in Latin about A.D. 500 by a student of St. Augustine in the South of France, probably St. Caesarius of Arles. The Latin text, a rhythmic paraphrase of St. Augustine's *De Trinitate* (I, iv, 7), seems to have been intended as a guide to orthodoxy for the clergy who were in danger of being misled by latter day Arians. The so-called Athanasian Creed was never used in baptism, but its stately cadence lent itself to public recitation in the Liturgy of the Hours at prime. Though it was dropped from the Liturgy of the Hours after Vatican II, *Quicunque* has been retained in the service books of a number of Protestant Churches, notably the Lutheran and Anglican.

A Common Confession of Faith

The Ecumenical Creed, the Apostles' Creed and the Athanasian Creed, ensconced in the liturgy, continue to be generally accepted in the West despite the doctrinal differences and divisions of the sixteenth century. Reformed (Zwinglians and Calvinists), Evangelical (Lutherans) and Anglican divines were as explicit as the Council of Trent in affirming their allegiance to the Nicene Faith and the Apostles' Creed. Although the schism between East and West endures, the Ecumenical Creed of Nicaea-Constantinople remains a bridge over an otherwise impassable chasm.

In recent years leaders in the ecumenical movement, recognizing the scandal of a divided Christendom, have affirmed that a common confession of faith is a compelling need. Pope John Paul II states, "Unity in the profession of faith is the fundamental element in the manifestation of ecclesial communion." The World Council of Churches' Commission on Faith and Order has initiated a project whose aim is "the common recognition of the apostolic faith as expressed in the Ecumenical Symbol of that faith, the Nicene Creed." Underlying the projects is the assumption that the churches will find it easier to confess their faith in an ancient formula representing continuity with the past than to find a new formula on which all can agree.

Although the Roman Catholic, the Orthodox, the Anglican and most churches of the Reformation assign the Ecumenical Creed a privileged status, the Faith and Order Commission has encountered several obstacles on the way to achieving its goal. There is first of all, the problem of language. Modern scientific awareness and shifts in philosophical outlook, it is said, have rendered the traditional creeds unintelligible. The meaning of the Ecumenical Creed is no longer accessible because of phrases that refer to the virgin birth, the ascension into heaven, and similar references that imply a mythological world view. On the other hand, Christians in the "young churches" of mission countries find difficulties with the language because it represents an alien culture. In addition, many American women complain that the traditional creed uses language and images that describe christian realities in patriarchal terms.

Some christian bodies, moreover, are suspicious of all creeds. Disciples of Christ and many Baptists, for example, fear that creedal formulas, when given privileged status, rival the authority of the Bible and emphasize the doctrinal aspects of faith at the expense of a personal confession of faith. Others like the Methodists, for example, who describe their churches as "creedless," accept the Ecumenical Creed in worship as a doxology but not as a rule of faith.

The Creed in Contemporary Catholicism

The traditional functions of the creed as rule of faith and baptismal formula received new prominence in the years after the Second Vatican Council. Pope Paul VI took the occasion of the nineteenth centenary of the martyrdom of Saints Peter and Paul in 1967 to promulgate the "Credo of the People of God." It was, in Pope Paul's own words, intended not as a dogmatic definition but as a creed that "repeats in substance, with some developments called for by the spiritual condition of our time, the Creed of Nicaea, the creed of the immortal tradition of the holy church of God." In form it is a paraphrase of the Ecumenical Creed, interpolated with phrases and theological explanations applicable to current issues; but it was clearly designed as a guideline for preaching and teaching the faith.

In the revised rite of Christian Initiation of Adults, the presentation of the creed—*traditio symboli* (RCIA, 183-187)—and rendering it back—*redditio symboli* (RCIA, 194-199) have been restored to their former prominence in the baptismal rites. Either the Ecumenical Creed of Nicaea-Constantinople or the Apostles' Creed may be used. Although a declaratory form of the creed is handed over and recited back in the final stages of preparation, in the tradition of the ancient church an interrogatory form of the creed is used in the water rite itself.

See **Faith, Revelation**

P. Schaff, *The Creeds of Christendom*, 3 vols., 6th ed., Grand Rapids: Baker Book House, 1983. J.N.D. Kelly, *Early Christian Creeds*, 3rd ed., Essex: Longman Group, 1972. J.N.D. Kelly, *The Athanasian Creed*, New York: Harper & Row, 1964. B.L. Marthaler, *The Creed.* Mystic, CT: Twenty-Third Publications, 1987. A.M. Ritter, *Das Konzil von Konstantinopel und sein Symbol*, Gottingen: Vandenhoeck & Ruprecht, 1965.

BERARD L. MARTHALER

CULTS

Cults generally refer to non-traditional religious groups that differ from sects, churches, and denominations. The term can be considered generic, however, and need not pertain exclusively to religious phenomena. Broad fields such as politics, popular culture, psychotherapy, and personal development have produced organizations with social characteristics associated with cults.

As is the case with the concept of sect, there has never been a clear consensus in the published literature as to which religious groups should appropriately be termed "cults" and which should not. There is general agreement, however, that sects and cults do not fit into the same typological continuum and that they are formed by different sociocultural factors.

Typologies in the human sciences associate cults with organizations that manifest some or all of the following characteristics: a focus on individual concerns and privatized and/or ecstatic religious experience; syncretistic doctrines of a mystical, esoteric, or psychic nature, or doctrines that draw inspiration from other than the religion of the tradition in which they exist; the presence of a charismatic leader; indifference to the world; lack of formal criteria for membership and/or weak organization structure; and the absence of ethical demands on members. Cults are also tolerant toward other religious groups and often have transitory and short-lived existence. Many of these correlates of cults hearken back to Ernst Troeltsch's less known mysticism type of religious organization characterized by an emphasis on inner personal experience, loose and provisional forms, voluntary adherence, inclusiveness, and indifference toward the demands of society. Cults in Troeltsch's view represented an expression of technical mysticism that broke with traditional religion and that understood itself to be nonhistorical, independent of religious principle, and timeless. In this vein, groups such as Spiritualism, Theosophy, New Thought, and some Asian religions have been identified as cults.

More recent initiatives distinguish cults on the basis of their organization, the source of their ideology, and in terms of their practical goals and objectives.

Audience cults generally lack formal organization. They give expression to parallelisms of spontaneities in which individuals with common interests, ideas, and experience gather informally for sharing and mutual support.

Client cults are more formally organized. They promulgate doctrines and services and resemble consultant/client relationships in their organizational structure. Cults of this nature tend to emphasize pragmatic considerations related to self-adjustment and self-mastery.

Cult movements are imbued with religious language and symbolism and are concerned with meeting the need for religious rewards and compensation. While sects are potentially schismatic groups seeking to purify or refurbish an established religious tradition, cult movements are a type of religious innovation that rearranges familiar cultural and symbolic patterns or imports new ones. By so doing, cult movements signal a break with the general patterns of established religious tradition and organization and give expression to the emergence of new religious movements.

Why cults form and what factors are conducive to their spread has been the subject of long-standing discussion and debate. Anthropological and psychoanalytic perspectives associate cult formation with the callings of charismatic leaders who experience some type of personal crisis or psychological trauma and who are believed to be in contact with a spiritual or supernatural order via religious visions or revelation. This psychopathology model of cult formation is popular where magic and religion are viewed as projections of neurotic wishfulfillment or psychotic delusions.

In anthropological literature, in addition, cults ("crisis," "cargo," "revitalization") have been identified with messianic, millenarian, or nativistic religious movements that arise in areas of culture contact where native social structures and tradition have broken down and where values, norms and myths from an alien culture have been introduced. Under these conditions, cult-like movements often arise that make it possible for native populations to reinterpret and communicate religious experience in unconventional terms and fresh symbols. From this perspective, cults are viewed as novel cultural responses to personal and social crisis. Cults arising under such circumstances have also been interpreted as disguised or latent manifestation of indigenous anti-colonialist political aspirations.

Sociological perspectives influenced by exchange theory have linked cult formation to the presence of entrepreneurial personalities who are adept at developing various spiritual, social, and psychological products—typically by assembling components of pre-existing religious systems into new configurations—for which there is a demand in the religious economy. Sociologists have also associated cult formation with urban areas undergoing rapid social and demographic change, where middle-class individuals experience anomie and alienation, where established institutional churches are weak, and where there are many individuals with religious problem-solving perspectives but who are adrift from conventional religious organizations.

Aside from the issues of how and why cults begin, and what sociocultural factors facilitate their growth, considerable attention has been focused on the dynamics by which cults institutionalize over time and enter the religious mainstream. The transformation of cults to more generalized forms of religion is marked by a change from emphasis on personal mystical or psychic experience as the basis of faith to emphasis on the acceptance of belief on the authority of others, or on a specific scripture or holy book. Further indicators are the formalization of doctrine, concern with maintaining the purity of teaching, the development of a bureacratized leadership structure, ritualization of prior spontaneous practices, and the ability of the cult to dominate the sociocultural milieu.

In the late 1960's and 1970's, the term "cults" came to be associated in the United States with a proliferation of new, non-conventional religions. Many of these movements were of Eastern derivation (International Society for Krishna Consciousness, Transcendental Meditation, the Divine Light Mission, Zen Buddhism, and various guru and yoga groups). Others were a variation on Christianity (Children of God, Way International, Christian World Liberation Front, Jews for Jesus, and the Unification Church of Sun Myung Moon). Others were quasi-therapeutic self-help groups (Church of Scientology, Erhard Seminars Training [est], Synanon). Psychic/occult/astral/satanic groups were also often identified as cults.

These non-conventional religious and self-help groups flourished in a cultural climate marked by dissent, crisis, and widespread social turbulence. They also spread at a time when liberal mainline churches were experiencing upheavals and declining membership.

The growth of such movements among the middle and upperclass, dramatic changes in their participants' values and life-styles, and controversies surrounding their proselytizing strategies and organizational characteristics gave rise to considerable opposition in the form of a loose coalition of anti-cult groups. Widespread revulsion over the 1978 tragedy in Guyana in which 900 followers of Rev. Jim Jones died also contributed to public hostility toward cults.

Anti-cult groups sought to confer deviant status on the new religious movements and to restore former social relations and structures of family, religion, and society, that had allegedly gone awry under the influence of such organizations. The anti-cult associations, composed primarily of former cultists and parents of members, and often supported by fundamentalist and conservative christian churches, labeled as "destructive cults" those groups characterized by authoritarianism, totalistic control, exclusivism, isolation, emotional dependency, deceptive soliciting, financial and sexual exploitation of membership, and adulatory preoccupation with the leader. Individual families and coalitions of anti-cult organizations undertook legal and legislative initiatives to restrict cult activity. Brainwashing and mind-control metaphors were employed to discredit cults. "De-programming" and forcible removals were also carried out in attempts to "save" youth from allegedly "counterfeit religions." For the most part, these initiatives were unsuccessful due to anxieties about the constitutional legitimacy of anti-cult measures and because there was little substantive evidence that cult participants were brainwashed or that they had been kept in such movements involuntarily through the use of mind control techniques.

Although the label "cults" is still widely used in the mass media and popular culture to refer to groups that are small, unorthodox, and culturally anomalous, the term is considered by many scholars to be obsolete, because of both its pejorative connotation and lack of empirical clarity. The academic treatment of marginalized or non-conventional religions has moved away from the traditional typological approach and has utilized, instead, theories and methodologies derived from resource mobilization and social movement perspectives. Within this framework, cults are treated as types of social movements concerned with transformations in religious meaning, symbolism, and innovation.

See **Religions**

Ernst Troeltsch, *The Social Teachings of the Christian Churches,* London: George Allen and Unwin, 1931. Bruce Campbell, "A Typology of Cults," *Sociological Analysis,* 29, 3 (1978): 228-240. Charles Glock and Robert Bellah, *The New Religious Consciousness,* Berkeley: Univ. of California Press, 1976. Anson D. Shupe, Jr. and David G. Bromley, *The New Vigilantes; Deprogrammers, Anti-Cultists, and the New Religions.* Beverly Hills: Sage, 1980. Rodney Stark and William Sims Bainbridge, *The Future of Religion: Secularization, Revival, and Cult Formation,* Berkeley: Univ. of California Press, 1985.

WILLIAM D. DINGES

D

DAMNATION
See **Hell**

DEACON

The earliest christian use of the word "deacon" (Gk., *diakonos*: servant, minister, helper) occurs in Phil 1:1, predating the account in Acts 6:1-6 of the choice of seven "assistants" to facilitate the mission and ministry of the Twelve. The qualities of a deacon are set forth in I Tim 3:8-13, following a passage in which the characteristics of a good bishop are described. This juxtaposition of texts reflects the close association between the two ministries as they developed throughout the period of christian antiquity.

Initially, this ministry was not required for ordination to the presbyterate. During the patristic age, it was understood to be a permanent, lifetime office. Admission to the diaconate was effected through a diversity of practices, each of which was proper to a given local church: ordination, consecration, institution or some form of mandate to a diaconal service. In the case of ordination, the ceremony included imposition of hands (cf. *Apostolic Constitutions,* VIII).

References to the role and function of the deacon can be found in early christian writings of the patristic period (c. 95–608 [West], 759 [East]). Clement of Rome (I Cor 40, c. 96) compares the deacon to the Jewish levite, one of the ministers in a tripartite hierarchy. Ignatius of Antioch (+110) frequently refers in his letters to the deacon as an assistant to the bishop and as one who is an imitator of Christ because deacons "are the servants of the bishop as Christ is the servant of the Father" (*Magnesians* 6:1; *Trallians* 3:1).

Deacons were entrusted with responsibilities that were charitable, liturgical and evangelical. In the realm of charity, they collected donations and alms which were to be distributed later to the sick and the needy. The deacon was the dispenser not only of these goods, but also of kindness, compassion and dedication to the poor and the afflicted. According to the *Didascalia* (2:44), the deacon is to be "the bishop's ear, and eye, and mouth, and heart, and soul" in his care for the church. Deacons were also responsible for the "service of the table," seeing that the hungry and homeless who came to the church for food or lodging were received with hospitality, given shelter and fed.

The liturgical responsibilities of the deacon were exercised in relation to the sacraments of christian initiation and the eucharistic celebration. St. Augustine's *First Catechetical Instruction* was written in response to the request of a deacon charged with the instruction of catechumens. Thus, catechesis in preparation of candidates for the baptismal rites was often entrusted by the bishop to a deacon.

During the actual rites of initiation, following the triple immersion of the candidate, the deacon performed services more properly exercised in private, including anointing of the neophyte's body, while the bishop remained with the community. It was not unusual for the deacon to assume the role of spiritual guide of the newly baptized, thus continuing the relationship of mentor begun during the catechumenate.

Deacons held an important place in the celebration of the eucharist, although they were never permitted to preside at the celebration in Catholic Christianity. They walked in the liturgical procession, were seated next to the bishop, carried to the altar the sacred elements and the offerings (*oblationes*) of the people. The deacon distributed the eucharist to the participants and carried it as Viaticum with a blessing of the sick to those confined at home through illness. Another aspect of the deacon's liturgical ministry was that of maintaining order in the eucharistic assembly and of leading the people in prayer.

The evangelical ministry of the deacon consisted in the proclamation of the word, either through catechetical instruction or, more properly, through preaching and teaching. Evidences of this aspect of the deacon's service can be found in the accounts of Stephen (Acts 7) and Philip (Acts 8:26-40) as well as in the histories of Athanasius, the "old lion of Nicaea," and Ephrem, "harp of the Holy Spirit," both of whom, as deacons, accompanied their bishops to the First Ecumenical Council in 325. Hilary, a deacon, was sent as papal legate to the Council of Ephesus (449) by Leo the Great, whom he succeeded.

The order of deacons flourished during the first three centuries of the christian era. The archdeacon, as principal administrative officer of the bishop, exercised great power in the local church. In the city of Rome, the practice of appointing seven deacons was maintained with ever greater power entrusted to them. In the middle of the third century, Pope Fabian placed each of the seven in charge of the administration of two of the fourteen regions of Rome. As this practice spread to other churches, the influence of deacons continued to increase and, even, to dominate the clergy. By the time of the Council of Nicaea (325), it seemed necessary to take steps to limit the powers of deacons (cf. canon 18), because of their attempts to usurp jurisdiction reserved for presbyters. The Council of Toledo (633) and the Trullan Synod (692) chose to affirm the superior role of priestly, over diaconal, ministry.

The decision made at Nicaea, the development of a clerical ministry, changing sacramental practice and the rise of monasticism were among the factors leading to a gradual diminishment of the role of the deacon, especially, in the West. In the East, this ministry continued with vigor until about the eleventh century. However, from the fifth century on, a number of monastic institutions founded for charitable purposes gave rise to centers known as "deaconries," where the poor and the sick were served. Toward the end of the eleventh century, the administrators of these deaconries came to be known as "cardinals." The institution of the cardinal deacons was completed under Urban II (1088-99). Although a "diaconal" rank continues to exist in the college of cardinals, members of that body must have received episcopal consecration.

Until the Second Vatican Council, the office of the diaconate, especially in the West, had been for many centuries a temporary ministry required for ordination to priesthood. In *Lumen gentium,* the Dogmatic Constitution on the Church, the diaconate was restored as a "proper and permanent rank of the hierarchy" (29). Married or celibate, the permanent deacon was to be "[d]edicated to works of charity and functions of administration" (29). The deacon's role between the "higher ranks of the church's hierarchy and the rest of the people of God" was to be a "sign or sacrament of the Lord Christ himself, who 'came not to be served but to serve'" (*Ad pascendum*).

The teaching of the Council of Trent implies that the diaconate is a divinely instituted order. Pius XII (*Sacramentum ordinis*) taught that deacons receive the sacraments of Holy Orders, as do priests and bishops, by the imposition of hands (D.S. 3859). Theologians continue to debate the nature of the character of the diaconate. As dialogue among christians addresses the implications of mutually recognized ministries, the question of the diaconate—permanent or transitional, married or celibate—may become a point for serious consideration.

See **Deaconess, Orders and Ordination**

J.M. Barnett, *The Diaconate: A Full and Equal Order*, Seabury, 1981. J. Colson, *Les fonctions ecclésiales aux deux premiers siècles*, Bruges, 1956. J.G., Davies, "Deacons, Deaconesses and the Minor Orders in the Patristic Period," *J.E.H.*, XIV, 1963, p. 1-15. E.P. Echlin, *The Deacon in the Church*, Alba House. K. Rahner and H. Vorgrimler, Eds., *Diaconia in Christo (Quaestiones disputatae* XV-XVI), 1962.

AGNES CUNNINGHAM, SSCM

DEACONESS

The discussion of deaconesses in Catholic Christianity is based on two scriptural texts. In Rom 16:1, Paul refers to Phoebe, "*diakonos* of the church at Cenchreae." In 1 Tim 3:8-13, where the qualities of a deacon are given, one phrase refers to "[t]he women" (3:11). The nature of Phoebe's "diaconate" and identification of "the women" continue to be matters of debate for exegetes, historians and theologians. What is certain is that "deacon-esses" did exist in the early church. A deaconess was a woman officially charged with certain ecclesial functions.

Pliny's *Letter to Trajan* (111-113) is frequently cited as a witness to the existence of deaconesses, because of his reference to two women who were called by the name. In the literature of the patristic era different titles are ascribed to women who seem to have exercised a specific service in the church: *diacona, vidua, virgo canonica*. By the fourth century, the Latin word, *diaconissa*, appears. Both the *Didascalia* and the *Apostolic Constitutions* are recognized as significant documents for determining the history of the deaconess in early Christianity.

It is possible to understand the word, "deaconess," in at least three different senses, although scholars remain divided in their opinion on this matter. One reason for this confusion is the lack of clarity in some texts concerning the distinction between widows and deaconesses.

The first meaning of the word suggests that the "deaconess" was, actually, a female deacon. In this light, all that can be attributed to the male deacon applies to her. Admission to the diaconate for a woman was the same as for a man, with the manner differing only (for both) according to the custom of the church to which they belonged. The woman deacon's responsibilities were equal to those of a male deacon. They encompassed the same areas: charity, liturgy and proclamation of the word through catechesis and post-baptismal spiritual guidance of the neophytes. A female deacon was as truly the assistant to a bishop as a male deacon. In the East, there are indications that she was invested with the stole.

Some restrictions did apply to the female deacon. The *Didascalia* (*Dida.*) requires that she be at least fifty years of age; the Council of Chalcedon adjusted this to forty. Further, the woman deacon exercised her ministry in the service of women, girls and young boys below the age of twelve. Baptismal practice and the *mores* of Roman society were largely the causes for this reservation, as the following texts indicate: "This is why, O bishop, you must take to yourself workers for justice, helpers who will cooperate with you in guiding others toward life. Those among the people who most please you in this respect should be chosen and instituted as deacons: on the one hand, a man for the administration of the many necessary tasks; on the other hand, a woman for ministry among the women. For there are houses where you may not send deacons, on account of the pagans, but to which you may send deaconesses (*Dida.* 16).

In the second place, "deaconess" is understood as a title given to any woman who fulfilled an assigned function in the church. This interpretation respects the complexity of the subject, as scholars have sought to study it, the ambiguity which results from the vocabulary associated with the question and the confusion, noted above, between widows and deaconesses in their roles of ecclesial service. This understanding of the term recognizes more extensive limitations to the woman's role and a greater difference between her ministry and that of a male deacon.

A final interpretation of "deaconess" (*diaconissa*) is that the woman so designated was the wife of a deacon, just as the *presbyterissa* was the wife of a presbyter and an *episcopissa,* the wife of a bishop, prior to the universal practice of celibacy of the clergy. The service of these women consisted in support of their husband's ministry and collaboration with him in ways appropriate and available to them. Recent studies have brought to light evidence of the importance of the role these faithful women exercised in the christian community.

The restrictions imposed by Nicaea on deacons, because of attempts to usurp powers beyond those within their jurisdiction, envisioned both women and men. As deaconesses in the Monophysite and Nestorian communities arrogated ministerial functions not entrusted to them, later councils (Epaon, 517 and Orleans, 533) abolished the office. In the East, the office of the female deacon perdured from the fifth to the eleventh century. In 1736, the Maronite Synod of Mount Lebanon empowered their bishops to ordain deaconesses in selected monasteries of women. The office of deaconess was revived in modified form in the nineteenth century (1836) through a Protestant foundation in Kaiserwerth, Germany. This venture became the model for later efforts along the same line. The Church of England followed in 1871 and the ministry of deacon for women was introduced into the Church of Scotland and the Methodist Church in 1888.

In the Roman Catholic Church, theologians, historians and scripture scholars have been challenged and motivated by the ecumenical movement and the feminist movement to study the question of the diaconate for women.

A renewed understanding of lateral ministries and a recognition of the role women are to fulfill in the church have contributed to an interest and discussion in this topic. Today, women engaged in pastoral services in parishes, hospitals and other church-related institutions engage in some activities associated historically with diaconal service.

See **Deacon, Order and Ordination**

J.G., Davies, "Deacons, Deaconesses and the Minor Orders in the Patristic Period," *J.E.H.,* XIV, 1963, p. 1-15. Roger Gryson, *The Ministry of Women in the Early Church,* The Liturgical Press, 1976. A.G., Martimort, *Deaconesses: An Historical Study,* Ignatius Press, 1986. C.R. Meyer, "Ordained Women in the Early Church," *Chicago Studies,* vol. 4, no. 3, 1965, p. 285-308.

AGNES CUNNINGHAM, SSCM

DEATH

From a theological perspective, death is the final point of the human person's individual history. As such, it cannot be simply identified with clinical definition of death nor with near-death experiences.

Scripture

The Bible offers no univocal teaching on death. In the genealogical material of Genesis 5 and other early levels of the tradition (Gen 25:7-11; 2 Sam 14:14) death seems to be a normal event to be expected after a long and full life. The fate of the deceased was expressed in the concept of *sheol* (see Hell). The idea that death is related to sin occurs in Gen 2:17 and Wis 1:12ff. Significant reflection on death is found in the Wisdom literature. The mood of Eccl 2:9-17 borders on the cynical. On the other hand, Job moves through the experience of apparently senseless destruction to the confession of God as a living redeemer (Job 20:25). Wis 3:1ff employs the Greek notion of an immortal soul to express the belief that the just who have died are in the hands of God. Reflection on the fate of the martyrs of faith in time of persecution led to hope for some form of meaningful survival after death, and eventually to the concept of resurrection as a form of divine vindication (Ps 16:10; Ps 73:23-28; Dan 12:2).

The NT assumes these traditions and employs them in its reflection on the redemptive meaning of the death of Jesus. As the true martyr for God's cause, Jesus is vindicated by the resurrection. Other traditions and metaphors are used to reflect further on the meaning of Jesus' death; e.g., sacrificial theology, vicarious suffering, the fate of prophets in Jewish history, etc. Through his death and resurrection, Jesus has overcome the power which death has held over human life (Heb 2:14; 2 Tim 1:10). Paul reflects the OT tradition by connecting death with sin in his attempt to contrast the fallen condition of humanity with the condition of grace and redemption (Rom 5:12-21; 6:23).

Teaching of Magisterium

Magisterial statements about death are relatively few in number. The magisterium has affirmed that death is a consequence of sin (D.S. 222, 372, 1511, 1521). The Second Vatican Council has reaffirmed this ancient teaching and has placed it in a more phenomenological description of death (G.S. 18). The most recent statement is that of the Sacred Congregation for the Doctrine of the Faith in its "Letter on Certain Questions concerning Eschatology" (May, 1979). In response to contemporary speculations about what happens between the death of the Christian and the general resurrection, the Congregation has affirmed that a spiritual element endowed with consciousness and will survives the death of the human person. The Congregation defends the use of the term "soul" to designate this spiritual element.

Theological Reflection

The principal concerns of theology are the relation of death as a universal human phenomenon to the mystery of sin on the one hand; and to the redemptive mystery of the death of Jesus on the other hand. In attempting to shed light on these relations, contemporary theology commonly is convinced that the handbook definition of death as the separation of body and soul says far too little. It is likewise convinced that, though Scripture and the magisterium teach that there is a connection between sin and death, it is far from adequate to see death merely as a punishment for sin.

It is widely accepted by theologians that death for human beings is not merely something that happens to a person from the outside, but is a distinctively human act related to the peculiar nature of human existence. As the final moment of a free, personal history, death is seen as the decisive act of human freedom in which the person can either accept or reject the mystery of God and thereby put the final seal on his or her personal history and destiny. K. Rahner has argued that it is not the mere fact of death that is caused by sin, but the present way in which we experience death as a mystery of darkness and threat. If sin distorts and darkens all our experience in life, it is consistent that it distorts and darkens our final experience in death. For both Rahner and Ratzinger, the free act by which we give ourselves over into the hands of God's love and mercy is the central mystery of the theology of death; it is the way in which believers enter fully into the dying of Christ. Seen in this way, the basic mystery of death is already anticipated throughout life in the "little dying" by which we give ourselves over to others and to God in charity. As an act of human freedom, the moment of death is also seen as the moment of purgation and judgment. Some theologians hold that purgation takes place fully in the moment of death; others hold that it may be thought of as extended in a process that gradually penetrates to all levels of our being.

See **Eschatology**

L. Boros, *The Mystery of Death,* Herder & Herder, 1965. M. Hellwig, *What Are They Saying about Death and Christian Hope?,* Paulist Press, 1978. R. Moody, *Life after Life,* Bantam, 1975. K. Rahner, *On the Theology of Death,* Herder & Herder, 1961.

ZACHARY HAYES, OFM

DEDICATION OF A CHURCH

The Rite of Dedication of a Church (1977) presents a comprehensive vision of God's relation to the church as it exists in society. The rite defines the building analogously. "Church" is primarily understood as the christian community. Even more specifically it is the community which has "gathered to hear the word of God, to offer intercessions and praise to him, and above all to celebrate the holy mysteries"(13). Thus it is the community in action, doing its greatest work which is the analogue for the building.

The central elements of the rite consists of the celebration of the eucharist and a special prayer of dedication. These two elements are part of the most ancient tradition in both the east and west. Secondary elements consist of anointing the altar and walls; incensation; and lighting the altar. Missing from this list is the ancient lustration or washing which was purificatory and applied to claiming secular spaces for worship.

The secondary elements, although they have special meaning in liturgical history, may be adapted and the texts changed with permission from the Holy See. This indicates a genuine openness for adaptation to regional understanding. The deepest meaning of dedication, therefore, comes from the way in which various cultures claim their spaces and designate their meaning. The celebration of the Eucharist and prayer of dedication remain the prime mark of the Roman ritual.

The theological image of God in the rite is clearly trinitarian. The preface proclaims a universal presence of God in which the whole world is God's temple shaped to resound to God's name. Such an affirmation of the goodness of creation erases the dichotomy between the sacred and profane. The Church is not a refuge for God's holiness against a world which is diametrically opposed to God. The world, like the church, is an icon of the sovereignty and creative goodness of God.

The christology of the rite understands Christ as the perfect temple (cf. Jn 2:21), who by his death and resurrection gathered a people to be his own. This paschal understanding combines with an incarnational one in which his body is proclaimed a temple consecrated to God's glory.

The Spirit is the agent of holiness who hallows the church and prepares the altar as a ready table of Christ's sacrifice.

Like Christ, the people are described as the temple of God, a holy people made one, the church built of living stones. This spiritual understanding is the premier designation from which the building takes its identity.

The church building, then, becomes a house for the church and a temple of worship. It is also a beacon to the world, the dwelling place of God on earth and a shelter for the victims of oppression. The prayer of dedication makes it quite clear that the church building is not a static reserve nor an escape from the world. It is a place where the church is most itself in proclaiming the reality of the kingdom of God and bringing that reality to birth by a life of conversion, justice and true freedom.

Structure of the Rite

The rite is inserted at various places in the eucharistic liturgy. It begins at the entrance to the church. Classically the portals had been the point of intersection between the profane and the sacred. Such a contrast does not appear in the current rite. The entry has become the occasion for the bishop to receive the building. The sprinkling rite follows.

The next part takes place immediately before the liturgy of the word when the bishop inaugurates the lectern as the place from which the mystery of Christ is proclaimed.

The central portion of the rite follows the profession of faith. It begins by the Litany of the Saints which unites the church of the living with the church at rest, thus representing the whole community. Following the litany the optional rite of depositing relics takes place. The relics are placed beneath the altar in the ancient custom rather than within the altar. Pieces which are not distinguishable as parts of bodies are not to be used. The optional character of this action indicates a significant change from the previous rite. Further the action is no longer listed among even the secondary elements of dedication.

The Prayer of Dedication follows; it is a berakoth which announces God's sovereignty, describes the meanings of the church and petitions that God will establish the building in the richness of its many images.

Next the altar and walls are anointed with chrism. No special prayer is said. The walls are then anointed in four or twelve places which represent the apostles upon whom the church is founded.

An incense brazier is brought forward and placed on the altar. The walls and the people are then incensed. The text associated with the action is an allegorical image in which the fragrance of the church is to fill the world.

The rite then focuses on preparation for the eucharistic liturgy as the altar is prepared and the church lighted. The final part of the rite takes place after communion as the eucharist is brought to the chapel of reservation.

The simplicity of the rite and its focus on the assembly makes the rite a profound occasion to reflect on the nature of the church. In the words of the rite, the building is to be ". . . a house of salvation and grace where Christians gathered in fellowship may worship you in spirit and truth and grow together in love."

See **Assembly; Architecture, Church; Liturgy**

JAMES NOTEBAART

DEIFICATION

The term used to refer to elevation of the redeemed to a participation in the life of God himself, a dimension of the life of grace powerfully stressed by the Greek Fathers.

See **Grace**

DEISM

A form of belief in God which affirms his personal being and his creation of this world and its intelligible order, but denies that he otherwise guides it or intervenes in it. Deism became a common view during the Enlightenment, when it was proposed as a "rational" alternative to traditional christian faith in God.

See **God, Providence, Rationalism**

DEMONS

In world religions, belief in evil spirits is virtually universal, whether ghosts of the dead, especially of the evil dead, demons, or other natural spirits, etc. Belief in a supreme spirit of evil is almost as universal. Demon-possession and the practice of exorcism are less universal but widespread.

In ancient Judaism, belief in the existence of evil spirits or demons was neither well-developed nor particularly important (Deut 32:17; Ps 109:6; Isa 13:21, 34:14; 1 Sam 16:14, etc.). By contrast, the notion of a master evil spirit appeared very late and largely as a result of Jewish contact with other Near-Eastern religions. Concepts of both demons and the devil subsequently entered christian belief from a late Judaism in which they had acquired central importance in reaction to conquest, persecution, and apocalyptic speculation.

Although early Hebrew belief centered on the demons' power to tempt, corrupt, and physically injure or kill human persons, under the influence of Canaanite, Babylonian, and other Mesopotamian religious beliefs and practices, interior or psychological possession came to be ac-cepted by the intertestamental period as an important manifestation of demonic power. Similarly, by the time of Christ, exorcism—the ritual expulsion of the demon or the liberation of the possessed person from its external control—had acquired a prominent place in Jewish religious practice.

OT belief originally admitted of a variety of demons, such as the *nephilim* of Gen 6:1-4, giants fathered by fallen angelic beings (later known as "Watchers" or "Fellers") of human females. Other strange creatures such as the *sedim, seirim,* and *lilit* haunted the wastelands or prowled the night (e.g., Ps 106:37; Isa 34:14).

By the beginning of the christian era, such demons had been spiritualized, organized under the headship of Satan ("Adversary"; see Ezek 28, Dan 8:10, 1 Chr 21:1, and Wis 2:24), and identified in their opposition to the Reign of God principally by possession, which caused seizures, frenzy, aggressive violence, obscenity, and sometimes paralysis in its victims. The chief of the evil spirits, Satan, the Devil (from the Greek *diabolos,* "Accuser"), was still interpreted primarily as the tempter.

The NT contains many references and allusions to the devil, demons, and unclean spirits, although far fewer than in apocryphal Jewish and christian writings of the same period. Some of these references are poetic metaphor and hyperbole. Nevertheless, it is clear that NT authors regarded the subject seriously. Demons were allied, if not identical, with Satan's fallen angels (cf. Mt 25:41; 2 Pet 2:4; Jude 6; Rev 12:4, 8). Heathen "gods" and divining spirits were also considered demonic (Acts 16 16; 1 Cor 10:20-21). Such deceiving spirits turned believers away from the gospel by means of wonders and false promises (1 Tm 4:1, Rev 16:14; etc).

Paul's mature doctrine interpreted demonic opposition to the gospel in terms of angelic Principalities, Authorities and Powers (Rom 8:38; 1 Cor 15:24; 2 Cor 11:14; Eph 1:21; 3:10; 6:12; Col 2:15), Thrones and Dominations (Col 1:16). These personal and cosmic forces had, however, been brought under subjection by God through the death and resurrection of Christ (1 Cor 6:3; 1 Pet 3:22; 2 Pet 2:10-11), a victory yet to be fully realized in the final revelation of God's glory at the end of the Age.

The synoptic gospels portrays Jesus as overturning the kingdom of Satan by expelling demons. The term *exhorkizo* ("to adjure," exorcize) was not used, however, either of Jesus or of his disciples (Acts 19:13). "Casting out" unclean spirits was signified by the word *ekballein* (Mt 8:16, Lk 11:14), which was often coupled with *therapeúō*, "to heal or cure" (Mk 1:34 and Lk 6:18; 8:12). In Acts 10:38, the word *iáomai,* which also means "to heal," is similarly employed.

Scriptural and postscriptural evidence points to the practice of ritual exorcism in the early church, however, as in, for instance, the sacramental observance of baptism. Here, however, "possession" was normally external, forensic, and collective. In the eucharistic liturgy, *energumenoi,* demented or spiritually agitated members of the community, were placed among penitents and catechumens under the care of minor clerics called "exorcists." Such disturbed persons were routinely prayed for by the whole community, but seem not to have been subjected to extended rituals of exorcism such as those developed in the Middle Ages and post-Reformation era.

Doctrinally, the existence of demons and the reality of possession have never been defined and are not so much articles of faith as presuppositions of biblical and traditional belief (see D.S. 800). In pastoral practice, the Church continues to offer Christians spiritual resources to resist the power of evil, including the practice of solemn exorcism when that is deemed appropriate. But that practice has also been to resist the effort to draw from such experiences anything about the existence, nature, or character of demons.

From a scriptural and theological perspective, the reality of the devil is similarly taken for granted as a spirit of malice, created good, but turned from God and hostile to humankind. *What* the devil is is not a part of the Church's defined teaching, nor is it of major concern except as an aspect of the theology of creation. Traditional teaching regarding the devil's activity focuses on temptations to sin and the need for Christians to be aware of the transcendent aspect of both temptation and sin, which they ought to resist in advance by prayer, spiritual discipline, and works of love and justice and in combating which they can always rely on the superior power of Christ and the Holy Spirit.

See **Angels**

RICHARD WOODS, OP

DEMYTHOLOGIZATION

This term refers to Rudolf Bultmann's program of interpreting the NT, first presented in his "New Testament and Mythology" (1941) and subsequently refined in writings like *Jesus Christ and Mythology* (1958). Bultmann's point of departure is his radical distinction between "myth" and "event." The historical event of Jesus Christ has been transmitted to us mostly in mythological form, yet our twentieth-century consciousness does not share the mythological worldview of the Graeco-Roman mind, and thus is unable fully to understand the biblical texts. Therefore, Bultmann suggests that we "demythologize," that is interpret these NT myths in order to retrieve for us the basic proclamation (*kerygma*) of what God had done in Jesus Christ. Existentialist philosophy (particularly the work of Martin Heidegger) provided Bultmann with the principal question for his interpretation of the NT: how does the text challenge the modern reader's self-understanding? The factual history of Jesus of Nazareth's life and death is only essential as the event of God's judgment of the world and not in its historical particularities. Important for us is *that* God calls us, through the kerygma of Jesus Christ, to accept that we live by God's grace and find our true human authenticity only in God's love. The *that* of God's call is more important than the how of its historical expression. Thus, we ought to appreciate the eschatological message contained in mythological formulations like Incarnation, Sacrificial Death, Victory over Demonic Forces etc., and the fact that already the NT itself suggests ways of interpreting such expressions. Unlike some of the nineteenth-century liberal theologians, Bultmann does not wish to ignore the myths in the Bible, but he wishes to interpret them. Therefore, the term demythologization is not an adequate description of his hermeneutical program.

In spite of Bultmann's hermeneutical initiative which led to a fruitful and sometimes heated debate in all christian churches and which showed the need for new ways of biblical interpretation, it must be said that his reduction of the gospel into a mere call for existential decision and the subsequent a-historical approach to Jesus Christ do not seem satisfactory today. Such a timeless kerygma will quickly loose its connection with an always changing consciousness. Bultmann's existential interpretation may be appreciated as an important effort to proclaim the gospel in a particular historical and philosophical context. While this context has changed already since

Bultmann's time, his hermeneutical insistence that the biblical texts do not just speak for themselves, but always call for interpretation, remains a challenge for all future generations of Christians.

See **Hermeneutics**

Rudolf Bultmann, "New Testament and Mythology," in H.-W. Bartsch, Ed., *Kerygma and Myth,* ET 1953, and *Jesus Christ and Mythology,* 1958. Paul Ricoeur, "Preface to Bultmann," in *The Conflict of Interpretations,* ET 1974.

WERNER G. JEANROND

DEPOSIT OF FAITH

The Catholic Church has always held that in Christ Jesus, God's revelation to humankind has been completed. Consequently, the church may expect no new revelation, nor may anything be deleted from that which the community has, from the time of the apostles, professed.

Additionally, from the very beginning, the church has understood these teachings of Jesus, received in faith by those who accepted Jesus as God's Christ, to be the treasure with which the church was entrusted. It was further believed that this treasury of teachings laid down within the community were articulated and taught by its acknowledged leaders, authentically and without error. This knowledge was accepted as salvific, to be of divine origin. It is this salvific knowledge which God communicated through Christ Jesus and which was received by his followers that has become known as the "deposit of faith."

Among the NT passages which are often appealed to as the basis for this understanding of the deposit of faith, those most frequently cited are 1 Tm 6:20 and 2 Tm 1:14. In these letters, the author appeals to Timothy, evidently an acknowledged church leader, to "take great care of all that has been entrusted to you" (1 Tm 6:20). And in 2 Timothy, the author exhorts Timothy in this fashion:

"You have been trusted to look after something precious: guard it with the help of the Holy Spirit who lives in us" (2 Tm 1:14). Further, those things which are to be passed on are not simply verbal teachings. In 1 Corinthians 11:23 we read that the Lord's Supper itself is to be celebrated and passed on: "For this is what I received from the Lord, and in turn passed on to you: that on the same night he was betrayed, the Lord Jesus took some bread, and thanked God for it and broke it, and he said, 'This is my body, which is for you, do this as a memorial of me . . . .'" Thus, the eucharistic liturgy, the enactment of the Mystery of Christ's death and resurrection is also to be understood as the repository of faith, indeed as the locus of faith par excellence.

Although such has always been the faith of the church, the term "deposit of faith" used in a technical sense was unknown until the Council of Trent and did not enjoy widespread usage until the pontificate of Pius IX (1846-78). Two documents promulgated by Vatican Council I secured its place in magisterial and theological language and subsequently it became part of the common terminology among all constituencies within the church: magisterial, clerical, theological and lay. In the Dogmatic Constitution on the Catholic Faith of Vatican Council I we read: "For the doctrine of faith which God revealed has not been handed down as a philosophic invention to the human mind to be perfected, but has been entrusted as a divine deposit to the Spouse of Christ, to be faithfully guarded and infallibly interpreted" (D. 1800). Likewise in the Dogmatic Constitution on the Church of Christ of the same Council we read, "For, the Holy Spirit was not promised to the successors of Peter that by His revelation they might disclose new doctrine, but that by his help they might guard sacredly

the revelation transmitted through the apostles and the deposit of faith, and might faithfully set it forth" (D. 1836).

To understand the connotation of "deposit of faith" as it was used in these documents, its historical context must be explored. The church of the nineteenth century understood itself as an embattled church. The revolutionary spirit spawned by the American and French Revolutions and which was sweeping Europe led to the democratization of governments and to the end of monarchical power in secular government. Further, liberal Protestantism, the offspring of the Enlightenment, brought into question all religious and dogmatic teachings accepted simply on authoritarian grounds. Advances in biblical scholarship resulted in the questioning of long-held assumptions such as the historical facticity of events narrated in some of the texts.

Gregory XVI (1831-1846) and especially Pius IX (1846-78) perceived in these movements grave threats to Roman Catholic orthodoxy and the accepted mode of institutional government. To add to papal dismay, even Roman Catholic theologians became involved in reassessing traditional church teaching.

It was in this climate, which to a great extent prevailed until after World War II and Vatican Council II, the term "deposit of faith" came into prominence. In such a milieu, the term came to connote a much narrower concept than it had in the NT texts. It was applied solely to dogmatic statements as these were enunciated propositionally by the magisterium. In a church which understood itself to be under attack, even from within, emphasis was put not on the passing on of the truth of Christ in teaching and liturgy that led to holiness of life, but in an exaggerated safeguarding of orthodoxy by a clerical elite which had not yet come to terms with the fact of doctrinal development and historical consciousness. The treasure, the living word of God, entrusted to the whole church, was, at least functionally, turned into an object dissociated from the religious experience of the ecclesia, an object to be safeguarded by a few, and accepted by all, not because of its intrinsic worth, but simply because it was proposed by the magisterium.

Immediately preceding, during and subsequent to Vatican Council II, the church, however, seeking to resource itself anew in Scripture and to take into account the historicity and development of truth, returned to a broader, more traditional understanding of the deposit of faith. In this broader context, it was perceived that the Christ event itself was the treasure, the living treasure of the church. Because the treasure was living, it could never be turned into an object existing outside of history, impervious to human questions posed by developments in philosophy and in the human and natural sciences. Thus, in the Dogmatic Constitution on the Church of Vatican Council II, in reference to the function of the bishops, we read: "By the light of the Holy Spirit, they make that faith clear, bringing forth from the treasury of revelation new things and old, making faith bear fruit and vigilantly warding off any errors which threaten their flock" (L.G. 25).

"Making faith clear and bringing forth new things and old," situates the term "deposit of faith" (treasury of revelation) in the wider context of tradition. The concept of tradition implies that new aspects of revelation emerge as the gospel is reflected upon in new circumstances. The NT itself gives evidence of this process. Thus, even though there is one revelation in Christ, there are, nevertheless, four gospels which reflect upon the meaning of Christ as understood by the various churches which emerged in apostolic times. The questions of Mark's church were not those of John's church.

So, while there is similarity between the two gospels, there is not uniformity.

Consequently, while it may be stated that revelation has been completed with the death of the last apostle, still it cannot be claimed that revelation had been completely understood and perfectly articulated for all time and for all people. This acknowledgement of the church's ongoing understanding of God's revelation in Christ is the basis of the church's belief in tradition and is the reason why magisterial statements, couched in non-biblical language and in philosophical concepts unknown to the biblical authors, has always been accepted within the Catholic Church as part of authentic revelation.

So, while the term "deposit of faith" is still current, it should not be understood in the positivistic sense of the preservation of merely verbal formulas as was the tendency in the church of the nineteenth century. This would not be an act of safeguarding the truth but of rendering it ineffective in promoting holiness of life. Instead, the term should be understood as commensurate with tradition, the handing on of God's revelation which is contained in Scripture, expounded in statements of the magisterium and in the church's liturgy.

Indeed, the eucharistic liturgy is the principal locus of the Living Word, the deposit of faith, the place in which the paschal mystery, the death-resurrection of Jesus Christ is embraced by the faithful and appropriated by the faithful as the living dynamic which informs their lives. The living fruit which is thus brought forth is evidence that the tradition, the deposit of faith, has been authentically retained and passed on.

See Doctrine, Faith, Revelation, Tradition

M.D. Chenu, O.P., *Faith and Theology; Tradition and Traditions. The New Catholic Encyclopedia.*

NANCY C. RING

DESCENT OF CHRIST INTO HELL

Like Jesus' ascension into heaven—with which it is inextricably linked and of which it is a necessary counterpart—his descent into hell is a metaphor, reflecting a cosmology, according to which under the earth there is a vast cavern into which all mankind—without exception—descend at their death. Thus the "hell" in question is not a place of punishment but the traditional resting place of all the dead (Isa 38:18; Ezek 31:14), a virtual prison from which they are destined never to escape (Ps 88:10; Job 7:9).

Viewed against the OT background of Sheol, the abode of the dead, Jesus' descent into this hell is, first and foremost, an affirmation of the reality of his death. Unlike Henoch and Elijah, he was not "taken up" living by God; he underwent the common lot of humanity and died, entering the underworld, the realm of the dead. Unlike all other mortals before him, however, Jesus descended into hell not to stay but, subsequently, to ascend from it and this not just for his own sake but also for that of the whole of humankind. If his descent into hell is a vivid expression of the reality of his death, his ascension from hell is a brilliant revelation of his real triumph over death. Although he died really, his presence in Sheol was an active one: he preached to those in prison (1 Pet 3:19-20; 4:6). And by his ascension from Sheol he broke open the "gates of hell" (Mt 16:18), thus inchoatively destroying humankind's last enemy: death (1 Cor 15:26), showing himself to be "the first fruits of those who have fallen asleep" (1 Cor 15:20), and "the first-born from the dead" (Col 1:18).

By descending into hell *and* ascending from it, therefore, Jesus has destroyed the kingdom of death and has opened up the way of life for humanity. But his descent into Sheol also has a cosmic significance. Sheol is, after all, part of creation—the antipodes of heaven. By passing, actively, from Sheol into heaven, Jesus has made his presence felt in the whole of the cosmos. Nowhere, no created thing, is outside the sphere of his all-embracing influence. His descent into the nether recesses of the cosmos, followed by his ascension "far above all the heavens" is part of the process by which he fills "all things" (Eph 4:10). Jesus' descent into hell—like his subsequent ascension into heaven—is, accordingly, an expression of his supremacy.

C.A. Bouman, "He descended into Hell," *Wor* 33 (1959): pp. 194-203. G.B. Caird, "The Descent of Christ in Ephesians 4:7-11," in: *Studia Evangelica* II (TU 87), Berlin 1964, pp. 535-545. W.J. Dalton, *Christ's Proclamation to the Spirits (1 Peter 3:18-4:6)*, Analecta Biblica 23, Rome 1965. H. De Lavalette, "The Descent into Hell," *Way* 7 (1967); pp. 106-116.

LIONEL SWAIN

DESPAIR

See Hope

DETERMINISM

See Freedom

DEVELOPMENT OF DOCTRINE

The development of doctrine needs to be understood both as a reality within the life of the church and as a theological idea. Both have been present in the church since the beginning, but it was only in the nineteenth century that theologians began to focus explicitly on the problem of doctrinal development and to develop various theories in attempt to explain it.

The history of theology provides many examples of doctrinal development. Some obvious examples within Roman Catholicism include the doctrine of the primacy and papal infallibility (1870) and the Marian dogmas of the Immaculate Conception (1854) and the Assumption (1950). Other christian doctrines which show clear signs of development include the Trinity, the perpetual virginity of Mary, original sin, the sacraments, the ordained ministry, and christology itself.

The study of scripture shows that doctrinal development is already taking place within the NT. An argument going on at the time of Jesus between the Pharisees and the Sadducees over the resurrection of the body (Mk 12:18-27) is at root an argument over doctrinal development. While the Sadducees reflected the common OT view that human existence ended with death, the more liberal Pharisees included in their teachings a number of ideas which had emerged in the post-exilic Jewish tradition, among them the belief that Yahweh would give life to the dead.

One can trace the church's christology developing through the various levels of the NT. The early communities of Palestine, influenced by the apocalyptic tradition, proclaimed a "parousia" or second coming christology; Jesus would soon return as Messiah (Acts 3:20) and Lord (1 Cor 16:22). As the gospel spread to the Diaspora the Hellenist-Jewish Christians developed an "exaltation" christology; Jesus was described as exalted to power at God's right hand (Acts 5:31) and made Lord, Messiah (Acts 2:32, 36) and Son of God (Rom 1:4) by (after) his resurrection from the dead. The gospels represent still later strata in this development. Mark (A.D. 68) presents Jesus as Son of God from the time of his baptism at the Jordan. Matthew and Luke (A.D. 85), both with accounts of the virginal conception, see Jesus as Son of God from the time of his conception by the Holy Spirit. The "pre-existence" christology of John's gospel (A.D. 90) represents the high water mark of this development.

The dogma of papal infallibility presents a more difficult case. The NT does not use the word infallibility, nor does it attribute an infallible teaching authority to either church authorities or to the church itself. But as early as Pope Siricius (A.D. 384-99) popes began appealing to Jesus' prayer to strengthen Peter's faith, that he might strengthen his brethren (Lk 22:32) as the basis of their own teaching authority. As the church of Rome gained the reputation of being the preeminent apostolic see, the corresponding belief that it had never deviated from the truth was transformed into the belief that the Roman church or its bishop could not err. It was not until the thirteenth century that the word infallibility was used of the papal teaching authority, in the context of a dispute within the Franciscan order over poverty. But infallibility did not become official Catholic doctrine until it was defined by Vatican I in 1870.

Some recognition of doctrinal development was present among theologians from the beginning. Early writers like Irenaeus, Tertullian, Basil, Jerome, and Vincent of Lerins spoke of development using organic images, the seed developing into a plant or a man growing from infancy to maturity. Theologians in both the patristic and the medieval period were aware that there was a progressive understanding of what was thought of as the unchanging deposit of faith. Yet at the same time they assumed that revelation had come to an end with the death of the last apostle and followed the norm of Vincent of Lerins for recognizing authentic doctrine: "what has been believed always, everywhere, and by all" (P.L. 50, 640). Innovations were to be rejected.

It was only in the nineteenth century that various theories attempting to explain doctrinal development began to appear. A number of currents of thought contributed to this. One was the development of the systematic study of history, and with it, the study of the history of christian doctrine. Another was the emergence of evolutionary thinking, particularly through the influence of the German philosopher G.W.F. Hegel. In Germany Johann Adam Möhler of the Catholic faculty at Tübingen described doctrinal development as an aspect of the total life of the church which continues to grow and develop under the guidance of the Holy Spirit. And in England, working independently of the continental philosophical tradition, John Henry Newman developed his famous theory in the process of the study of early church history which led him into the Roman Catholic Church; his classic *Essay on the Development of Christian Doctrine* appeared in 1845. In it he stressed how the divine reality grasped by faith gradually becomes clarified, expressed, and formulated in doctrines recognized as true when defined by the church's magisterium, all under the guidance of the Spirit.

In the latter half of the ninteenth century two dogmatic definitions, indirectly made possible by the work of Möhler and Newman, raised a new issue. In 1854 Pope Pius IX defined the Immaculate Conception of the Blessed Virgin. And in 1870 Vatican I defined papal infallibility. Now the problem was to show how the new definitions could be reconciled with the principle that the deposit of faith was complete from the time of the apostles.

In the following decades various theories of development were elaborated. Avery Dulles has described three different approaches. First, the "logical" approach followed a deductive method of syllogistic reasoning; from the original doctrines of revelation others could be deduced. The problem with this approach was that it presumed that revelation was initially given in propositions. Second, the "organic" approach, influenced by the work

of Möhler and Newman and refined in the 1950's by Karl Rahner and Edward Schillebeeckx, proposed an intuitive model of revelation; the church initially grasps divine revelation not in propositions but as an indistinct whole which unfolds gradually as the church guided by the Spirit continues to reflect on the mystery of faith. The logical approach could reason from the two natures of Christ to his having two wills. The organic approach could move over the centuries from a prayerful reflection on the relation between Jesus and his mother suggested by scripture to the doctrine of the Assumption. But according to Dulles both assumed that dogmas asserted truths contained implicitly in the deposit of revelation. Borrowing a term from George Lindbeck, Dulles calls the third, more recent, approach "historical situationism." Rather than seeing doctrinal development as the historical unfolding of an initially given revelation, this approach understands doctrines as human interpretations and historically conditioned responses to God's word which continues to address the church through scripture. In each age the message of the gospel must be restated and applied to new circumstances. Thus doctrine develops as a result of an ongoing dialogue in history between God and God's people.

At the beginning of the Second Vatican Council Pope John XXIII distinguished between the substance and form of doctrines: "The substance of the ancient doctrine of the deposit of faith is one thing, and the way in which it is presented is another." Today most theologians take for granted that doctrines are subject to development and reformulation. Raymond Brown insists that "a doctrinal trajectory should be traceable from the NT outlook to the later dogma, even if the connection between the two goes beyond pure logic." Some theologians prefer to see doctrines as symbols expressive of deep human experience rather than as propositional expressions of objective realities. Others take an intermediate position. Arguing that the symbolic theory does not sufficiently respect the traditional characteristics of doctrine, Lindbeck proposes that doctrines be understood as having a function similar to that of grammatical rules within a language; thus doctrines are seen as norms of belief and practice, subject to reformulation even if some of them may be necessary, permanent, and irreversible.

Any contemporary Catholic understanding of doctrinal development should include a recognition of the following: First, an understanding of doctrinal development always implies a particular understanding of revelation. Second, even if God's revelation implies a propositional element, revelation is not given in propositions but in God's self disclosure in Jesus Christ. Third, all doctrines are ecclesially authorized human expressions of that revelation, thus efforts to formulate in language the mystery of God grasped through faith. Finally, as the Vatican's Congregation for the Doctrine of the Faith stressed in its 1973 instruction *Mysterium Ecclesiae*, all expressions of revelation are culturally conditioned, that is limited by the knowledge available, the specific concerns addressed, the changeable conceptions or conceptual framework used, and the vocabulary current at the time they were formulated. Therefore new insights, whether from scholarly research, cultural developments, or the movement of the Spirit, may require that a particular doctrinal statement be reinterpreted or placed in a new context, with the caution that the doctrine defined cannot be directly contradicted.

See **Doctrine, Faith, Revelation, Tradition**

Raymond E. Brown, "Critical Biblical Exegesis and the Development of Doctrine," in *Biblical Exegesis & Church Doctrine*, New York: Paulist 1985, pp. 26-53. Avery Dulles, "Doctrinal Renewal: A Situa-

tionist View," in *The Resilient Church*, Garden City, New York: Doubleday, and Dublin: Gill and Macmillan, 1977, pp. 45-62; *Models of Revelation*, Garden City, New York: Doubleday, and Dublin: Gill and Macmillan, 1983. George A. Lindbeck, "Doctrinal Development and Protestant Theology," in Edward Schillebeeckx, Ed. *Man as Man and Believer*, Concilium vol. 21, New York: Paulist, 1967, pp. 133-49; *The Nature of Doctrine*, Philadelphia: Westminster, 1984, and London, S.P.C.K., 1985. *Mysterium Ecclesiae*, English translation: *Declaration in Defense of Catholic Doctrine on the Church Against Certain Errors of the Present Day*, Washington: USCC, 1973. John Henry Newman, *An Essay on the Development of Christian Doctrine*, Garden City, New York: Doubleday—Image Books, 1960. Jan Walgrave, *Unfolding Revelation*, Philadelphia: Westminster, 1972.

THOMAS P. RAUSCH, SJ

DEVIL
See **Demons**

DEVOTION AND DEVOTIONS

Devotion is the feeling side of christian faith. It consists of emotions and affections which are common and appropriate responses to commitment to Jesus Christ and belief in his gospel within the church. Some components of christian devotion are admiration at God's wonderful works, a feeling of familiarity with Jesus, abiding sorrow for sin, a sense of security because of God's providential care, the consequent habit of frequently praying about important events in one's life, and joy in companionship with other believers in the church.

Devotion links christian belief and christian action. Habits of feeling engendered by faith and christian experience are the actual personal environment in which believers are motivated and enabled to embody gospel principles in their lives. Thus devotion is classically defined as readiness for service in obedience to the divine will. Devotion is authentic when it prompts and sustains christian behavior, and religious feelings which do not eventuate in christian behavior are not true devotion but some form of religious sentimentality.

In allied meanings, the word "devotion" may also refer to the whole affective dimension of a particular person's religious life, or to the affective approach characteristic of a particular group or school of Christians (with a meaning roughly equivalent to "spirituality"), or to an individual's transient state of religious emotional engagement. (One might say, for example, "Distractions hindered my devotion.")

The common worship of Christians, among other things, inevitably expresses and formulates christian devotion, and in turn functions as a school of devotion. This expressive and educative function of common worship, at least until the liturgical reforms mandated by Vatican II, could be fulfilled only very imperfectly by the official Roman Catholic liturgy. The prayer texts and gestures of the Roman liturgy, especially in comparison with those of the other ancient churches, are characterized by sobriety and reticence. Classical Roman prayers speak about joy and sorrow and other religious emotions, but at a distance, as theological themes rather than as actual feelings. The Roman prayers do not express and cannot well foster the emotions they name. In addition, and much more importantly, throughout most of its history official Roman Catholic worship had been celebrated in a language unintelligible to the vast majority of the worshipers.

In part to compensate for the devotional deficit in the received Roman liturgy, other forms of Catholic worship have come into being to supplement or replace the official services. These are appropriately called "popular devotions" or simply "devotions." As contrasted with the official liturgy of the times in which they were composed, they express, cater to, and foster devotion—precisely the religious feelings and affections dis-enfranchised in the official services. The term "popular devotion" is used in two senses. (1) It means actual exercises of piety—worship services, prayers, church rituals—somehow other than those of the official Catholic liturgy. In content and theme a popular devotion and an official service might be closely related. Thus, for example, the Way of the Cross is a popular devotion, but the veneration of the cross on Good Friday is part of the official liturgy. (2) "Popular devotion" also designates themes and attitudes characteristic of the popular devotional exercises, even when these may have been accepted into the official liturgy. Thus, for example, the devotion to the Sacred Heart of Jesus.

Popular devotions are popular in several senses. (1) They often have origins outside the accepted liturgy-making establishment of the church, though they may soon attract official backing. (2) They were usually designed for and were in any case practiced primarily by ordinary people and not mainly by religious professionals. (3) At some periods of history, including the recent and remembered past, they have appealed to a large proportion of church members, whatever their religious status and function or their ethnic, educational, and socioeconomic background. (4) They were designed for communal celebration: they are worship for structured groups of Christians and not just for individuals.

Though there are phenomena analogous to popular devotions in some eastern and Reformation churches, the category applies mainly to Roman Catholic worship. The origins of many Roman Catholic popular devotions can be traced to the Middle Ages. Beginning in the eighth century, monastic reformers began to augment the received western monastic form of the liturgy of the hours with other prayers and offices, such as the gradual psalms, the Office of the Dead, the Office of All Saints, soon supplanted by the Office of the Blessed Virgin. In time these "accretions," as they are called, were universally celebrated intermingled with the older canonical hours of the monastic office. They were also separated from their monastic setting and gathered together to form the core of the collection called in English the Primer. This book of hours, first in Latin and then translated into the various vernaculars, and enriched over the centuries with other devotions, remained the prayer book of choice for the literate laity up through the eighteenth century. The Office of the Blessed Virgin, whether in Latin or in a vernacular, was the usual liturgy of the hours prayed by lay religious congregations until after Vatican II. The origins and subsequent history of these early devotions make it reasonable to suppose that the devotional accretions arose when the received monastic office was becoming inadequate as a means of worship for the monks, and that most of the real communal prayer of the medieval monasteries took place during the devotional offices rather than during the adjacent canonical hours.

The cultivation of the popular devotion as a specific and distinct category of worship is a feature of the Roman Catholic Counter-Reformation. As a result of the codification of the Roman liturgy following the Council of Trent, the limits and content of official and now uniform Roman Catholic worship were quite definitely set. The slow evolution of the received rites was almost halted, and the vigorous and creative response of the Counter-Reformation church to the needs of its worshipers had to take shape outside the official liturgy. In time explicit official authorization came to be considered a necessary constitutive element of the Catholic liturgy. Thus the popular devotions, even though they were often approved, fostered, and even imposed by church authority, fell into a kind of second-class, less-than-liturgical legal status. The popular devotions were considered good worship but not real liturgy, and were thus left to flourish freely, unhampered by liturgical legislation, with much room for development and local adaptation.

Most of the popular devotions could be shown to have at their origins some point of contact with the official liturgy. Thus the Marian rosary, with its 150 Hail Marys, is a kind of surrogate for the liturgical psalter. So too the already-mentioned devotional offices were at first intended to exist in the context of the canonical liturgy of the hours, and in contents and structure they were exactly like their official counterparts. They were composed of psalms, antiphons, readings, hymns, responsories, collects—all arranged in the traditional way. But the selection of elements was attractive: favorite psalms, beautiful antiphons, affecting themes. And there was only one office of each kind, almost the same each day, rather than a series of offices distributed throughout the days of the week. Other devotions, "little offices," were modeled on the commemorations that concluded the principal hours of the canonical office.

Some services, though long intrinsic to the annual paschal celebration of northern European churches, fell into the legal category of devotions because they had not been celebrated at Rome and thus did not find a place in the revised Roman liturgical books. At a time when the official and prescribed Easter Vigil had become a mere vestige, celebrated in nearly empty churches early on the morning of Easter Saturday, the actual paschal worship of the northern churches focused on the watch before the reserved eucharist in commemoration of the burial of the Lord, and on the subsequent triumphal eucharistic procession early Easter Sunday morning in remembrance of his resurrection.

Other devotions, more strictly products of the Counter-Reformation, were designed to mediate the official liturgy to the worshipers. In Catholic countries in which the vernacular tongue was not a Romance language, programs of metrical hymns were composed for congregational singing in the native language to popular melodies while the official mass liturgy was recited quietly in Latin by the priest and his servers. The hymns of these first "folk masses" paraphrase parts of the ordinary of the mass that would be sung in Latin at high mass, like the Gloria and Sanctus, direct translations of which were forbidden. Other hymns are catechetical interpretations to accompany moments in the mass liturgy, like the penitential prayers at the foot of the altar and the offering of the gifts.

Another kind of Counter-Reformation devotion provided a substitute for the popular celebration of the liturgy of the hours. Sometimes a vernacular reduction and simplification of the canonical hour of vespers was provided for use in parishes on Sundays and feastdays. More frequently, entirely new vernacular prayer services were composed, reminiscent in style and structure of the formal meditations that were being proposed for the use of individuals. These prayer services, on popular devotional themes and also for the principal seasons of the church year, were for Sunday and feastday afternoon worship, usually in connection with canonical vespers and benediction with the Blessed Sacrament.

Exposition of and benediction with the Blessed Sacrament became universally practiced and treasured by Roman Catholic worshipers during the Counter-Reformation period. Sometimes on special occasions the reserved sacrament was exposed in the monstrance to solemnize canonical vespers and especially its conclusion, which was then amplified with additional prayers and songs. The people were blessed with the sacrament before it was returned to the tabernacle. In time the benediction became a distinct devotional service, which might be celebrated alone or in conjunction with some other devotional exercise.

Throughout the Counter-Reformation period, because of their minority status and/or strictures imposed by civil authority, English-speaking Roman Catholics were not free to develop a distinctive pattern of popular devotions. They had to be satisfied with a minimum loyal observance of the offical rites. By the mid-nineteenth century, however, a more elaborate devotional life became possible. The attention of English-speaking Catholics was then focused on devotion to the Blessed Sacrament, which was regarded as central and essential. Prayers to the Mother of God and the saints and Sunday vespers, when this office was still celebrated with the people, inevitably concluded with eucharistic benediction. The rite of benediction, in a way highly ceremonious and yet easy to understand, acted out the benevolent and effective presence of Jesus in the midst of his church, and at the same time enabled believers to adore him clearly, directly, and graciously. It is probable that the eucharistic and ecclesial piety of Roman Catholics during this period and well into the present century was formed and expressed more by the experience of Blessed Sacrament devotions than by attendance at mass and reception of communion.

In the years immediately preceding and following Vatican II, the official attitude of church authority towards the popular devotions may be fairly described as reserved. The Vatican II Constitution on the Sacred Liturgy maintains the distinction between devotions and the official liturgy. Devotions that conform to church laws and norms are recommended; they form part of the actual though extraliturgical spiritual life of the church. The devotions should be oriented toward the official liturgy, which is by its very nature superior to any of them. Devotions should harmonize with the church year. They should lead people to the official liturgy.

The attitude of popular liturgical reformers toward the devotions both before and after Vatican II may be fairly described as grudging. The devotions are criticized as being out of accord with the seasons of the liturgical year and as being unchanging, sentimental, esthetically unpleasing, crude. Attempts to supplant them by various kinds of liturgy of the word have not been successful. Attempts to reform existing devotions or to create new ones have not met with wide acceptance. Potential reformers often appear deficient in sympathy for devotional structures and themes and lacking in empathy with the worshipers.

In fact, controversy about the relative value and propriety of the official liturgy and the devotions is now largely academic. The evolution of church life following Vatican II has blurred the distinction between the liturgy and the devotions. And for many reasons the devotions are no longer widely practiced. The nineteenth-century forms familiar in the United States were couched in a language and style and set to music that no longer appeal. The afternoon celebration of mass has taken over the time formerly reserved for afternoon devotions. Individual, private devotion to the Blessed Sacrament still flourishes. But the greater familiarity with the eucharistic species occasioned by placing the host into the hands of communicants and the widespread use of lay ministers of communion have rendered the ceremonious exposition of and benediction with the Blessed Sacrament somehow incongruous.

Much of the appeal of the devotions

lay in the use of the vernacular language, familiar expression, and light music; but now all of these have a place in the official liturgy itself. The warmth and directness in worship formerly associated almost exclusively with the devotions can now be found both in the liturgy proper and in the piety and styles of the charismatic movement. And though the typical worshiper probably has more leisure time to dispose of, less leisure time is available for worship.

Even though the distinction between the official liturgy and the popular devotions is fading, as are many of the devotions themselves, it is worthwhile to note some features of the popular devotions that might rightly continue to flourish in Roman Catholic worship in the future. The devotions catered to christian devotion. Though they undoubtedly served other political and social functions as well, they expressed and evoked the religious affections and habits of feeling that go with christian faith. Such enhancement of christian affectivity does not happen automatically. It is possible for a new liturgy to serve new orthodoxies and proprieties—to be exact in performance, contemporary in expression, up-to-date in theology, current in social awareness, and inclusive in language— and yet to be perceived by the worshipers more as a political statement or an educational moment than as a way of experiencing their relationship with God.

How then did the popular devotions embody and promote christian devotion? Three characteristics of the devotions can be mentioned: of attitude, of content, and of structure.

(1) With regard to attitude. In the devotions the worshiper is a privileged person rather than someone to be instructed. The devotional service is conceived of as enabling the worshiper to do something rather than as doing something to the worshiper. The educative function

of the devotion does not have to do with the transmission of data but with initiation of the believer into the experience of the christian mystery.

(2) With regard to content. The perennial devotions tirelessly repeat the central mysteries of the christian faith: the incarnation, the saving passion and resurrection of the Lord, the enduring presence of Jesus in the church. This constant repetition of the same themes is not boring precisely because its purpose is not to inform the mind but to nourish the spirit of the believers.

(3) With regard to structure. The devotional structure is circular or spiral rather than straight-line: like a prayer rather than a lecture, like conversation rather than formal discourse. Devotions usually consist of a number of similar small units frequently repeated (like decades of the rosary, Stations of the Cross). They are almost unvarying in form. The devotional predilection for sameness and repetition is a hint that the rhythm of prayer, both private and public, is one. Variety, whatever its value in other contexts, is not the spice of prayer.

See **Liturgy, Worship**

C. Dehne, "Roman Catholic Popular Devotions," *Worship* 49 (1975) 446-460. A. Taves, "Context and Meaning: Roman Catholic Devotion to the Blessed Sacrament in Mid-Nineteenth-Century America," *Church History* 54 (1985) 482-495. A. Taves, *The Household of Faith,* Notre Dame, 1986.

CARL DEHNE, SJ

DISCIPLINA ARCANI

A term that refers to the practice of early Christians of keeping the rituals and doctrines of the church secret from all but initiated members of the church.

DISSENT
See **Magisterium**

DIVORCE

In christian thought the issue of divorce is dialectically linked to the indissolubility of marriage they appear mutually exclusive. Behind the seeming simplicity of this opposition, however, there is a complex set of traditions.

Historical Background

The disciples of Jesus certainly understood that the new law meant a new attitude toward marriage: man and wife had the moral duty to remain faithful to each other for life (cf. Mt 5:31-32). From the earliest, the church has never ceased to proclaim this obligation and support it by various rulings and acts of legislation.

Problems, however, about the correct interpretation of Jesus' teaching arose fairly soon. Paul ruled that if one of a pagan couple converts and the other does not want to live in peace with the believer, the new Christian is entitled to separation (cf. 1 Cor 7:12-16). Whether or not he granted the right to remarry as well, we do not know; the text is ambivalent. But we know that from the fourth century, this text has been regularly invoked to justify in an identical situation the right of a convert to divorce and to a new marriage; the apostolic grant became known as the "Pauline privilege." Much later, mainly in the sixteenth century during the period of great missionary expansions this grant was extended by the popes to analogous situations; this new type of concession was called "privilege of faith." None of these grants, however, have ever been made applicable to marriages among Christians; the bond that tied them was considered as having a special firmness.

During the first millennium, while the church continued to proclaim, in East and West, the absolute duty of fidelity, the ecclesiastical authorities displayed some hesitations (perhaps more in the West than in the East) in concrete cases where two Christians were involved, especially when an innocent person had to suffer because of the other's infidelity.

From about the beginning of the second millennium (as far as one can ascertain) the Eastern church accepted fully that the clause in Mt 5:32 and 19:9 referring to "unchastity" constituted an exception to the rule and in the case of adultery divorce and remarriage was to be permitted. The Western church did not receive this interpretation as a practical norm of action; by the twelfth century, however, it developed the doctrine that the bond of a non-consummated marriage between two Christians can be dissolved through religious vows or through an intervention of the "power of the keys." Under the impact of Roman law and scholastic philosophy, the Westerners elaborated also a theory of institutional and legal indissolubility (as distinct from a moral duty): since the sacramental bond between baptized persons signified the union of Christ with his church, once consummated, it could not be broken ever.

The most important conciliar texts concerning divorce and indissolubility are found among the decrees of the Council of Trent (see Denzinger-Schön-metzer 1797-1816). The intention of the Fathers was to repel the attack of the Reformers who claimed that the church was in error when teaching indissolubility; it was not the Council's desire to condemn the Greeks who, although they went on their own way by permitting divorce and remarriage in the case of adultery, had not accused the Romans of having fallen into an error.

Modern Canon Law

From these historical traditions a complex set of beliefs and practical norms developed, which either inspired or are an integral part of our modern canon law of marriage.

The Code of Canon Law actually does not use the term "divorce"; it speaks of the "separation of the spouses," but uses this expression in two radically different senses; (1) separation with freedom to marry again; (2) separation with no freedom to marry. In the first case the bond is dissolved; in the second case the bond remains.

(1) *Divorce with the dissolution of the bond.* Such divorce is never granted or recognized by the Roman Catholic Church in the case of a sacramental (between two baptized persons) and consummated marriage. In the case of all other marriages, although theoretically held indissoluble, as a matter of pastoral practice, for reasons of faith and religion, the church is willing to declare the dissolution of the bond. Thus, divorce with freedom to marry can be granted in the following cases:

(a) if a sacramental marriage has not been sexually consummated, a dispensation that brings with it the cancellation of the bond can be obtained;

(b) if a marriage has taken place between two non-baptized persons, and one converts to Christianity and receives baptism, after which the unbeliever refuses to live with the believer "without insult to the Creator" (that is, without due respect for the other's conscience), the christian party is free to marry again; no dispensation is needed; the local ordinary, however, has the right and duty to ascertain the facts;

(c) if a non-baptized man, living with several wives simultaneously (polygamy), receives baptism, he is entitled to choose any one of his women to be his only wife; the same rule applies to a woman in similar situation with several husbands (polyandry); again no dispensation is required; the local parish priest or the ordinary has the right and duty to see that all is done according to the law; the new marriage, however, must be contracted in the canonical form;

(d) if man and wife, neither of them baptized, become forcibly separated and for no fault of theirs they cannot restore their common life, the reception of baptism even by one entitles both to marry again; no dispensation is needed but the local ordinary has the right to check the facts;

(e) if both of such forcibly separated persons receive baptism, theoretically a sacramental non-consummated marriage comes into existence; still if they are not able to restore their common life, the law grants them the freedom to marry; this amounts to a dispensation by the law from the bond of a non-consummated sacramental marriage; the ordinary must ascertain the facts;

(f) if a natural (non-sacramental) bond exists between two non-baptized, or one baptized and another who is not, dispensation from the bond can be requested through the competent ordinary from the Apostolic See; to obtain it an appropriate reason is required, e.g., the desire to marry a Catholic.

(2) *Divorce without the dissolution of the bond.* Canon law grants the right to an innocent spouse to terminate the common life if the other one is guilty of adultery or becomes a threat to the spiritual or bodily well-being of any member of the family. Although the innocent one may act on his or her own authority, ordinarily the case must be submitted within six months to a competent ecclesiastical authority for its judgment.

Questions and Problems

While it is true that the Roman Catholic Church never grants the dissolution of the bond of a consummated sacramental marriage; it remains a disputed question among theologians if this stance is rooted in an enduring prudential judgment or is the result of a perception that the church lacks the radical power to dissolve such a bond. In all likelihood, the resolution of this issue can come only through further developments in ecclesiology; that is, through a better understanding of the power that the church possesses. Presently, no satisfactory theological explanation exists why and how the consummation of a sacramental marriage can restrict the power of the church over the bond.

In the practical order one difficulty persists: whenever the law does not grant the "privilege of faith" in the case of a non-sacramental marriage, the diocesan bishop is not permitted to act on the petition but must send it to Rome. Such a prescription not only takes out of the hand of the bishop an issue that he is well qualified to handle but causes unnecessary expense and delays.

Ecumenical Aspects

The Orthodox Church, while continuing to uphold the right of an innocent spouse to divorce and remarriage in the case of adultery, gradually has come to grant the same freedom to those who are victims of other type of misbehavior by their spouse, such as cruelty, abandonment or serious neglect of duties toward the family. Other christian churches and communities mostly recognize a decree of divorce by the civil authorities.

Even from this brief exposition a solid conclusion emerges: while there has been a substantial continuity in Catholic beliefs and practices, there have been also changes in response to emerging needs. When this article describes the present state of the doctrine and practice, it shows how far the church has progressed in understanding and applying the new law of Jesus. The process is clearly not completed.

See **Annulment, Canon Law, Marriage**

The source book for the law is the *Code of Canon Law*, in particular its chapter on "The Separation of the Spouses," canons 1141-1155. Canonical commentaries, with indications of the historical roots and the theological background of the canons, are Thomas Doyle, "The Separation of the Spouses" in *The Code of Canon Law: A Text and Commentary,* New York: Paulist, 1984, pp. 811-822, and Ladislas Orsy, *Marriage in Canon Law,* Wilmington, DE: Glazier, 1985 (with extensive annotated bibliography covering the biblical and doctrinal aspects of divorce). An amply documented historical work with theological reflections is Theodore Mackin, *Marriage in the Catholic Church: Divorce and Remarriage,* New York: Paulist, 1984. For the practices of the Orthodox Church *see* John Meyendorff, *Marriage: An Orthodox Perspective,* Crestwood, N.Y.: St. Vladimir Seminary, 1975.

LADISLAS ORSY, SJ

DOCETISM

The view of some early Christians that Christ's human nature, life, and suffering were only apparent.
See **Jesus Christ**

DOCTRINE

The christian faith is founded upon the belief of the community, that "Christ died for our sins, in accordance with the scriptures; that he was buried; and that he was raised to life on the third day, in accordance with the scriptures (1 Cor 15:3-4); and "that God has made him both Lord and Christ, this Jesus whom you crucified" (Acts 2:36). Since the first generation of believers, this *kerygma* has been the basic doctrine or teaching of the christian church.

Consequently, for those who receive Jesus as God's Christ, the meaning of the words and deeds of Jesus have continued to be the focus of reflection, study and teaching. The primary source of Jesus' words and teachings upon which the community reflects is, of course, the inspired writings of the NT, preeminently the gospels. In addition to being sources for the understanding of the meaning of Jesus' life, however, these writings are also attempts to understand how the

meaning of the life, death, and resurrection of Jesus addresses the specific concerns which resulted from the life circumstances of the various christian communities. Thus, for example, the Gospel of Mark teaches that Christ is the crucified messiah. The doctrine of the Gospel of Matthew is that Jesus is the New Moses. The Gospel of Luke instructs us that Christ is our salvation, and the Gospel of John that Christ is the *logos* or the wisdom of God. These are all examples of the earliest elaborations of the *kerygma,* examples of the earliest strata of church doctrines.

These examples also show that church doctrines share these characteristics: they are rooted in the person of Christ; they are not merely repetitious either of the *kerygma* or of the words and deeds of Christ, but faithful interpretations of the meaning of these for particular times and circumstances. Further, doctrines enunciate the truth, but since they respond to the Mystery of God in Christ, none of them, nor even all of them taken together, exhaust the truth. They are shaped by the language, thought patterns, and concerns of the particular community or historical era in which they are formulated (See Mysterium Ecclesiae, 1972). Doctrines are, furthermore, primarily evocative and symbolic in that their primary purpose is to foster the community's relationship to Christ rather than to be juridical or legislative.

The NT is the primary, but not the only source of christian doctrine. The church expounds and teaches the meaning of Christ's life in a variety of ways: in its preaching, in its liturgies, in the writings throughout history of its theologians, in the lives of its holy and wise men and women, in specific decrees of ecumenical councils as well as in papal pronouncements and encyclicals. We are reminded by the Document on Revelation of Vatican II (D.V.10), however, that all of these manners of teaching, in order to be considered authentic, must be in the service of and under the authority of sacred scripture. It can be seen that the purpose of this whole complex of doctrinal expressions is to provide Christians with a worldview by means of which they may undersand themselves and their relations to the God of Jesus Christ, and to other men and women. From the earliest times the church has believed its self-understanding to be protected from error by the Holy Spirit. This protection from error is recognized in the reciprocity that exists between those who exercise the office of teachers and those who themselves living under the governance of the Holy Spirit recognize and receive such teaching. Thus, authentic teaching is not arbitrarily exercised. Doctrine is not extrinsic to the community, but an expression of the community's insight into the meaning of Christ's words and deeds.

By far, the vast majority of christian teaching is communicated and received within the self-authenticating christian tradition, without having been specifically defined by the teaching office. Examples of such doctrines are: the importance of personal prayer, the imperative to love one's neighbor as oneself, and special concern for the poor.

On the other hand, since the christian community is the locus not only of the Holy Spirit but also of historical development as well as ideologies resulting from various biases, there have been instances throughout history when the teaching office of the community has responded to particular crises of christian self-understanding by defining what is understood to be authentic and true. The pronouncements of the Ecumenical Councils of Nicaea (325), Constantinople (381), Ephesus (431) and Chalcedon (451), are examples of such teaching, which because of its importance to christian self-understanding is characterized as dogmatic teaching. Dogmatic teaching refers to those doctrines understood to be certainly revealed and which mark the parameters of orthodox faith. These councils responded to the christological and trinitarian disputes that marked the life of the early church, disputes initiated and perhaps exacerbated as the church moved from a Palestinian milieu into a Greco-Roman environment. In our own day, Vatican Council II (1962-65) performed a similar function by enabling the church to shift from a medieval to a contemporary mind-set. Thus, transition from one culture to another necessitates the reformulation in new thought forms of the revelation of God in Christ.

Besides defined dogmas, however, which are understood to be teachings of the greatest significance, there are teachings which speak authoritatively to specific situations, but which are considered neither revelatory nor unchangeable. Papal encyclicals, the pastoral letters of the episcopate and the teaching of clergy in union with their bishops are examples of this type of doctrinal teaching.

The doctrine or teaching contained in papal encyclicals and the pastoral letters of the episcopate perform an important service within the church, a service often underestimated by those whose understanding of doctrine is limited to "what must be believed or accepted." Such writings and exhortations draw upon the central components of the church's self-understanding, such as the goodness of creation and the incarnation, to respond to particular historical concerns. Thus, when western Europe was in the process of changing from an agrarian to an industrial economy, the rights and dignity of labor became a social concern. In *Rerum Novarum,* (1891), Pope Leo XIII responded to these concerns by promulgating the first of an impressive series of papal encyclicals which teach the christian position on social justice. A study of these encyclicals, written over a period of nearly one hundred years, demonstrates how church teaching develops. What was considered counter-cultural and revolutionary in the first encyclical is not denied but is, due to changing sociological and historical conditions, further developed in later encyclicals. Pope Paul VI's encyclical, *Populorum Progressio* (1967), addresses questions of justice resulting from the economic conditions engendered by the rise of multinational corporations. This was a question outside the experience of Pope Leo XIII. Similarly, some cultural developments give rise to questions, not of a worldwide scope, but of particular interest to a local church. Thus, the bishops of the Appalachian region wrote a pastoral "This Land is Home to Me" (1978), that spoke to the specific concerns of the Appalachian church.

For many, influenced by a social milieu that reduces reality to legalities, the question arises: Are such doctrines as those contained in encyclical and episcopal pastorals binding in conscience for the Catholic Christian? The answer is complex. Their authority is much less than that of formal definitions of revealed truth. But if one's christian self-understanding were to be limited to formally defined dogmas, the richness and vitality of one's christian life would be impoverished. The purpose of this other sort of teaching is not to define legal boundaries of church membership, but to teach and instruct church members in the appropriation of christian self-understanding as this is interpreted by the teachers of the church.

On the other hand, no Christian is expected to accept any mode of church teaching uncritically. A person receptive to church teaching may also question its adequacy in addressing certain circumstances. Only a person, though, who is genuinely and authentically engaged in appropriating the revelation of God in Christ has sufficient grounds to criticize the ordinary teachings of the church. Such persons, furthermore, have not only the right but the duty both to receive teaching and to question it. In such a manner doctrine develops, and the ecclesial community continues to bring the teachings of Jesus to bear on contemporary questions such as the economy and nuclear warfare.

Finally, and most importantly, the function of doctrine within the christian community is not primarily juridical or legalistic. The primary function of church teaching, or doctrine, in all the forms it takes, preaching, liturgy, church pronouncements, the work of theologians, the lives of holy men and women, is to enable each person to appropriate, to internalize, the meaning for the world that God has revealed in Christ. This meaning is dynamic and is understood in relation to the particular concrete circumstances of one's life. Such a task is never-ending. The final word has not been said nor will it be until the end of history.

See **Deposit of Faith, Faith, Revelation**

Walter Abbot, ed., *The Documents of Vatican II,* "Dogmatic Constitution on Divine Revelation." Yves Congar, S.J., *Faith and Theology.* Piet Fransen, S.J., *Intelligent Theology.* Walter Kasper, *An Introduction To Christian Faith.* Bernard Lonergan, S.J. *Method in Theology.*

NANCY C. RING

DOGMA

The term "dogma" refers to the church's belief that in scripture and tradition God's intention for humankind has been revealed to the ecclesial community and that the community's leadership can authoritatively interpret and promulgate this truth. To be adequately understood, therefore, dogma, should be situated within the context of revelation. Dogma, of course, is not coincident with revelation, but it is one manner in which revelation is explicated. Functionally then, dogma fulfills the same purpose as revelation: the engagement of one's entire person, mind, feelings, and body, in an existential encounter with truth. This understanding of dogma's sacramentality is an aspect of dogma which has been lost in modern times and which needs to be recovered lest the church fall into dogmatic positivism, merely repeating formulae.

Although the church has always considered itself the recipient of God's revelation and has understood its leaders to have the authority to proclaim God's truth, it has not always termed such pronouncements as "dogma." In the NT there is only one instance in which the word "dogma" is used to denote a decision rendered by authority. This occurs in Acts 16:4 and refers to the decisions of the Council of Jerusalem concerning the admission of Gentiles to the community. Concerning these decisions, Luke writes; "As they visited one town after another, they passed on the decisions [dogmas] reached by the apostles and elders in the community, with instructions to obey them" (Acts 16:4).

The scriptural context reveals that this was a decision based on how the apostles and elders had received God's revelation in Christ. In arriving at these decisions, various viewpoints had been discussed, but the faith of the community was revealed in the decisions (dogmas) which the leaders of the community enunciated. It is imperative to note that these decisions of the community are based on God's revelation in Christ, and although not inimical to reason, cannot be reduced to empirical verification.

This meaning of the term "dogma" was used in the apostolic period to denote christian belief as a whole as well as specific teaching of the church. It was also used to distinguish christian belief from non-christian belief. The term was little used by the scholastics, including Thomas Aquinas who preferred the term "article of faith" to refer to dogmatic reality.

The preoccupation with dogma and the understanding which is ascribed to it in modern ecclesial documents began in the late seventeenth and early eighteenth century. The Enlightenment called into question the teaching authority of the christian church, especially that of the Roman Catholic Church, as it had never been called into question throughout its history.

In this historical context, the meaning of dogma was modified. The meaning it had attained in its previous contexts was never denied, but its new connotation prevailed and remains so to this day. In its attempt to stem the tide of rationalism engendered by the Enlightenment, the church not only emphasized that revelation is a source of truth, that authoritative decisions flow from the church's reception of God's revelation, but did so in the currency of its time, the proposition. It was at this time that dogmatic statements became identified with syllogistic reasoning propositionally expressed. This understanding of dogma grew in direct proportion to the development of the theology of papal magisterium, a theology also conditioned by the Enlightenment. Thus, Karl Rahner defines the current understanding of dogma as: "A proposition which the Church explicitly propounds as revealed by God [D. 1792] in such a way that its denial is condemned by the Church as heresy and anathematized" (C.I.C. canon 751). It must be emphasized that to be considered dogmatic a proposition must be set forth explicitly, and must pertain to divine, public and official christian revelation, that is, sacred scripture and Tradition.

It should be noted that although

dogmatic propositions are expressions of revelatory truth, they are neither commensurate with the totality of truth, divine mystery, nor are they primarily juridical or legal statements. They are intended, as the early church knew so well, to communicate truth to the church in order that the church as a community and each person within the community could become existentially engaged with God's truth. When dogma is conceived primarily or solely as an appeal to the intellect, dogmatic statements tend to be understood and received juridically. Consequently, the importance of such statements for the life of the church is minimalized.

Many times dogmas, in the modern sense, are enunciated to eliminate error and to establish the parameters of revelation rather than to teach what is already commonly believed by the faith community. Consequently, some truths of revelation which are essential to christian self-understanding have never been expressed in dogmatic propositions because the christian community has never called them into question. Examples of such beliefs would be the Mystical Body of Christ, and the reality of grace.

Finally, the distinction between dogma and doctrine should receive attention. In ordinary conversation the two words are often used interchangeably. Technically, however, there is a difference. Dogmas relate the truth of revelation. Doctrines explain and teach how a particular dogma may be understood. There may be several acceptable explanations or doctrines surrounding a single dogma. For example, it is christian dogma that Mary is the Mother of God. Theological explanations of this dogma are doctrines. It is on the level of doctrine that the church admits of pluralism, not on the level of dogma.

See **Faith, Infallibility, Revelation**

Yves Congar, O.P., *Faith and Theology,* Bernard Lonergan, S.J., *Method In Theology,* Karl Rahner, S.J., Ed., *Sacramentum Mundi,* Edward Schillebeeckx, O.P., *Revelation and Theology.*

NANCY C. RING

DONATISM

Donatism was a long-standing schism which wracked the church of Latin North Africa in christian antiquity. It began following the Great Persecution of the emperor Diocletian at the beginning of the fourth century. Certain rigorists claimed that those Christians who had handed over the Sacred Scriptures and other church books to be burned at the demand of the persecutors, had forfeited all claim to be Christians, and if they were bishops or priests, all authority as church leaders. The dispute crystallized around the issue of the ordination of a new bishop of Carthage, in which city each party came to have its own bishop. Donatus soon emerged and long remained the effective and impressive leader of the dissident group.

During the fourth century the Donatists were probably the larger christian group. They were in fact a mass church with a bishop in almost every town and village; yet they maintained the rhetoric of the pre-Constantinian church, small, persecuted by the world. They saw themselves as the remnant, since the rest of the world church had apostatized by remaining in communion with the *traditores,* the descendants of those who had handed over the scriptures during the persecution.

Whether the Donatists should be classified as heretics as well as schismatics has long been debated. It is unclear whether the charge that they taught that the validity of the sacraments depended entirely on the moral and spiritual state of the minister is correct or is an overly systematized interpretation of their view that the ecclesial standing of their opponents was destroyed by their (alleged) status as christian apostates during the time of persecution.

During the fourth century there were occasional periods of government pressure against the Donatists. This usually did not last and stirred them to greater enmity against the Catholics. Donatist leadership proved superior to that of the Catholics until the entry of Augustine into the controversy at the end of the fourth century. Largely through his efforts, a great conference was held in Carthage in 411 in which the government decided decisively and definitely against the Donatist position. Sustained and persistent government coercion then forced most Donatists back into Catholic unity and destroyed the leadership although it seems that Donatist groups continued to survive here and there in North Africa until the Arab conquest.

ROBERT B. ENO. SS

DOUBT

The classical description of theology as "faith seeking understanding" seems to suggest that doubt is inescapable from time to time in the exercise of theology. A faith that seeks understanding will inevitably have to cope with the presence of doubt in the pursuit of understanding. Yet, for the most part, classical theology has had very little to say about the place of doubt in faith. One possible reason for this is that faith has been perceived more often than not in predominantly propositional terms; faith is all too often presented as an unqualified assent (i.e., without any traces of doubt) to a series of propositions.

In the twentieth century, especially since Vatican II, a more personalist emphasis of faith recognizes that possibility, and even at times the presence, of doubt alongside faith. Likewise, the pilgrim and developmental character of faith in this century as well as the existence of so much pluralism would seem to make faith more vulnerable to the presence of doubt.

The kind of doubt that can exist alongside faith is usually described as "existential doubt." This doubt needs to be distinguished from methodical/scientific doubt which refers primarily to matters of empirical enquiry or logical deduction. Existential doubt is equally different from skeptical doubt, which is more an attitude of underlying skepticism towards life than a formal assertion about this or that particular proposition. In contrast existential doubt is that particular doubt which precedes or accompanies the ultimate decisions and personal ventures of life. Existential doubt arises from the incompleteness of human evidence or the lack of personal security in the choices we make. For example, the decision to marry can often be preceded and/or be accompanied by an existential doubt. In a similar vein the personal act of faith in terms of love, trust and surrender addressed to the living mystery of God can be made in the context of existential doubt. Indeed the presence of existential doubt can often provoke a personal act of religious faith. When this happens we can say that something of a dialectical relationship exists between religious faith and existential doubt. For some this relationship between faith and doubt will be a temporary phenomenon and for others it may be a more permanent struggle, with faith sublating doubt. To this extent, doubt in some instances can play a positive role in promoting and sustaining the life of faith.

On the other hand, it must be admitted that doubt can play a negative part in the personal life of faith. Doubt, especially the methodical or skeptical variety, can become so dominant and permanent within the life of the individual that it crushes the personal act of faith.

Soren Kierkegaard in the last century, more than most, captures the ambiguous role that doubt can play in the life of the individual. Kierkegaard holds that the doubt which most people experience must sooner or later move in one direction or another. On the one hand it can give rise to faith, provoking what Kierkegaard characteristically calls "the risk to take the leap of faith." On the other hand, doubt, if not checked, can move in the opposite direction, ending in despair.

It is important here to strike a balance in understanding what Paul Tillich called "the dynamics of faith." The personal act of faith includes the positive and the negative, light and darkness, pain and celebration. The reduction of faith merely to golden sunsets is neither realistic nor properly christian. The christian story of faith embraces the crucified and risen Christ, the suffering of Calvary and the joy of Easter. Christian faith is ultimately about learning to live securely with questions and to walk with confidence in the darkness. Within the great questions of life and in the frightening moments of darkness there will be doubt. The existence of such doubt can coexist with the loving surrender and venture of religious faith. The removal of all doubt from the personal act of faith could come dangerously close to the extremes of either fideism or rationalism. A faith that can be proved by reason alone is no longer faith and a faith that is blind to the demands of critical inquiry is unworthy of the name of faith.

See **Faith, Theology, Rationalism**

P. Tillich, *The Dynamics of Faith,* London: G. Allen and Unwin Ltd., 1957; Chap I. M.P. Gallagher, *Help My Unbelief,* Dublin: Veritas Publications, revised edition, 1986.

DERMOT A. LANE

E

EASTER TRIDUUM

The Easter triduum (Latin: three days) is that period in the liturgical year which Christians consider to be the most sacred. It lasts from Holy Thursday evening to Easter Sunday evening. It is really one liturgical feast, the full celebration of Easter. It sets out the one liturgical mystery event of Christ who is alive in the world today. The triduum is not an historical walkthrough of the Jesus who lived once on this earth, so it is incorrect to treat the triduum as a recounting of the last week in Christ's earthly life. There can be no question of pretending that on Holy Thursday Christ institutes the sacrament of the Eucharist, that he dies on Good Friday so that he can rise again at the Easter vigil. The triduum is in theological, not chronological, time. It is the christian passover. While the triduum has its roots in past events, in the passion, death and resurrection of Jesus Christ, its reality is always a contemporary experience. As the Jewish people hold their passover festival in the belief that the exodus event is now present, so Christians hold their passover celebrations in the belief that Christ in his redemptive activity lives now in the liturgical assembly.

The controlling image of the Easter triduum is the vigil. The rhythm of the triduum is marked by a series of liturgical assemblies, beginning with the evening liturgy of the Lord's supper on Holy Thursday, climaxing in the Easter vigil, and then closing with evening prayer on Easter Sunday. In order to understand this paschal time and in order to plan intelligently for its celebration, it is necessary to appreciate how the vigil is at the heart of the triduum. The vigil was originally a night watch charged with salvation themes. It was a watch of praise because of the death/resurrection event. Later it was seen primarily in terms of christian initiation, the time when the church renews itself by bringing in new members. Both of these aspects are articulated in the restored vigil service of the Roman liturgy. The prayers and readings of the vigil are the recital of the most important stories of the christian tradition, all reaching a high point in the announcement of the resurrection. Having prayed in the communion of the saints, having undergone the paschal fast, and having invoked the Holy Spirit, the church now opens itself to new members. The baptismal candidates having completed their period of election during the time of Lent, now experience the Easter sacraments of baptism, confirmation, and eucharist.

The celebration of the Lord's Supper constitutes the opening movement of the Easter triduum. It is the first step of the celebration of Christ's passover. The liturgy of Holy Thursday is held in the evening in accordance with the custom of the ancient church. The focus of the liturgy is found in the antiphon of the entrance rite: "We should glory in the cross of our Lord Jesus Christ, for he is our salvation, our life, and our resurrection; through him we are saved and made free."

The Holy Thursday liturgy of the word narrates three stories: the passover meal in Egypt, Paul's story of the Lord's supper, and the story of Jesus washing his disciple's feet. The Roman sacramentary indicates several topics for the homily: the institution of the eucharist, the institution of the priesthood, and the commandment of Christ for brotherly and sisterly love. The service of footwashing concludes the liturgy of the word. This is called the *mandatum* after the Latin text of one of the antiphons sung during the washing (*mandatum novum,* "a new command"). The term, maundy, for Maundy Thursday also comes from this Latin word. The foot-washing service is not to be a mere reenactment of what Jesus did at the Last Supper. It is meant to be a sign that the church is the place where the members minister to each other through acts of loving service. It is significant that the gospel of Holy Thursday is that of the washing of the feet from John (13:1-15). The gospel does not speak explicitly about the institution of the sacrament of the eucharist; it presents a dramatic example of christian service. Thus the liturgy itself teaches that Holy Thursday's meaning is not found in the adoration of the blessed sacrament nor the institution of the cultic priesthood. The liturgy is a feast of footwashing which proclaims that in the eucharist is verified the acts of loving service of the worshippers. With it the Lenten reconciliation process is now completed. Christians are to prepare themselves to confront the glorified Christ at the personal cost of stripping themselves and washing the feet of marginal people.

The Roman sacramentary encourages that at the beginning of the liturgy of the eucharist there be a procession of the faithful with gifts for the poor. Accompanied by the song, *Ubi Caritas* (*Where Charity and Love are Found, There is God.*) At the end of the liturgy, the remaining bread is taken to the place of reservation with song and procession. It is kept for the sick and for the Good Friday liturgy, emphasizing the unity between the two liturgies.

Good Friday is also Easter. Thus, the mood this day is not of funereal sadness; it is characterized by the exhilaration of the suffering servant who sees the light of the fullness of days, of a people who have a high priest who has opened the way for others, and of a chosen race whose king reigns from a tree. A special fast is kept, different from Lenten fasting. *The Constitution of the Sacred Liturgy* of the Second Vatican Council states: "Let the paschal fast be kept sacred. It should be observed everywhere on Good Friday and, where possible, on Holy Saturday" (10). The whole church fasts this day, both those baptized as well as those who are to be baptized. The fast is the way the catechumens prepare for baptism and the way the baptized express their solidarity with them.

The one liturgy of Good Friday takes place at three o'clock in the afternoon or later. It is composed of three ritual actions: a liturgy of the word (with readings, responses, homily, and solemn intercessions), the veneration of the cross, and a communion service. The ancient tradition of Good Friday is the adoration of the cross, not the crucifix. It is the cross of victory which the church proclaims today. "We should glory in the cross of our Lord Jesus Christ..." is the theme song of the entire triduum.

The service of the word begins with Isaiah 52-53, the fourth servant song.

The suffering servant is seen in terms of Christ's own death and resurrection. Then Hebrews 4 is proclaimed, portraying Christ Jesus in his human dimension. Then follows the passion narrative of John, a deliberate choice. It stresses the kingship of Christ; the cross is a throne of glory; Christ reigns from the cross; he is buried as a king with the proper preparation of spices and ointment. After the passion, the congregation responds by praying the great prayers for the world, traditional in the Good Friday liturgy.

The dramatic action of the veneration of the cross follows the liturgy of the Word. Through this ritual the church expresses its belief in the cross as its means of salvation. The liturgy concludes with a simple communion service, it is the one day the Roman church fasts from a full eucharistic celebration. Good Friday, the pivotal point in the church's triduum, is a restrained but definitely joyful celebration of Christ's victorious death and leads the community toward the Easter vigil and its rites of initiation.

The Easter vigil is composed of four major liturgical components: the service of light, the liturgy of the word, the rites of initiation, and the liturgy of the eucharist. It is a liturgy replete with symbols such as fire, word, nakedness, water, oil, white garments, perfume, bread, wine, and gestures of peace. The movement from the lighting of the new fire to the final dismissal is the symbolic enactment of the passing over into the death and resurrection of Jesus Christ.

In the service of the light the Easter candle is lighted from a new fire and blessed. This light is then spread throughout the assembly as it sings "Christ our Light. Thanks be to God." The light service concludes with the *Exsultet,* the Easter proclamation of the risen Christ through a prayer of blessing and thanksgiving celebration, the Easter light.

The liturgy of the word comprises a series of readings (up to nine) from scripture recounting the whole sweep of salvation history from the world creation through the giving of a first covenant and the promise of a new one. The word service climaxes in the new life of the church as experienced in its new members.

The celebration of the sacraments of initiation during the Easter vigil brings to a ritual high point the journey of the catechumens, those who are entering the church. After the rites of initiation all the members of the assembly stand to renew their own baptismal promises.

The Easter vigil concludes with the eucharistic liturgy. The triduum itself concludes with Easter vespers, late Easter afternoon.

The Easter of three days sets the tone for the entire liturgical year. The triduum is the second stage of what can be called the church's retreat, and needs to be understood in this large context. The church enters into a special period of reflection on Ash Wednesday; the first period of its retreat is the Lenten time. The third stage of this more intense christian living is the period of Eastertime, the great fifty days, the time between the triduum and the feast of Pentecost. Each stage of this lengthy retreat has its own character. During Lent, for example, Christians are called to fast so as to be in solidarity with those who are in the final moments of their becoming Christians. Lent is also the time to engage in the practice of reconciliation, that life-giving forgiveness which ideally takes place in community, calling to mind the meaning and power of christian baptism, and leading to eucharistic sharing and which is so closely connected with the death and resurrection of the risen Lord.

The third and final stage of the retreat is spread over the fifty days of Eastertime and is highlighted by the celebrations of the feasts of Ascension and Pentecost. This breaking up of the Easter time is not an historical description of what actually happened chronologically in the life of the risen Jesus. Rather it is the richness of the paschal mystery which demands sufficient ritual time so that the various facets of this mystery can be incorporated into christian living. Thus, the church's retreat devotes ample time to deepening the festivity of its central celebration. To be in retreat during the fifty days means joyous thanksgiving with the new members of the community as well as a recovered sense of one's own happiness with being a Christian. The liturgy is clear that Easter time is a single period of rejoicing in Christ's passage from death to glory. Ascension and Pentecost are also Easter celebrations. Pentecost is not an isolated feast of the sending of the Holy Spirit; it is the crowning feast of the church's retreat.

Gabe Huck, *The Three Days: Parish Prayer in the Paschal Triduum,* Chicago: Liturgy Training Publications, 1981. Patrick Regan, "The Three Days and the Forty Days," *Worship* 54 (1980) 2-18. Patrick Regan, "The Fifty Days and the Fiftieth Day," *Worship* 55 (1981) 194-217.

JAMES L. EMPEREUR, S J

EASTERN CHURCHES

The designation "Eastern" (or "Oriental") churches has become a customary way of identifying that large number of christian churches whose distant origins are rooted in eastern regions of the ancient Roman Empire, as opposed to the western or Latin regions that included Italy, Spain, Gaul and Africa. It is a way of denoting churches associated with the ancient sees of Antioch, Alexandria, Jerusalem and the New Rome, Byzantium or Constantinople, although in modern times members of these Eastern churches are found throughout the world in the "diaspora."

In contemporary usage Eastern churches are classified in four groups: (a) the Oriental Orthodox Churches, (b) the Eastern Orthodox Church, (c) the Assyrian Church of the East, and (d) the Eastern Catholic Churches in full communion with the Church of Rome.

(a) The Oriental Orthodox Churches, to use the name they themselves prefer, have also been known in the past as the Ancient Oriental, the pre-Chalcedonian, the non-Chalcedonian Churches, or even the Lesser Eastern Churches. Frequently their members have been incorrectly labeled as "Monophysites." The Oriental Orthodox Churches are a communion of five ancient churches of the East: Armenian, Coptic (Egyptian), Ethiopian, Syrian ("Jacobite"), and Malankar (Indian). Although they share different liturgical traditions and widely divergent histories they have a common element differentiating them from the Eastern Orthodox and other christian churches including Roman Catholic in that they did not adopt the fourth ecumenical council held at Chalcedon (A.D. 451) which asserted that Jesus Christ is one person in two natures, undivided and unconfused. In their view the terminology "two natures" suggests a duality in Christ and compromises the unity within the person of Christ. Yet these Christians reject the classical "monophysite" position of Eutyches who held that the humanity of Christ was absorbed into his single divine nature. They prefer the formula of St. Cyril of Alexandria which speaks of "the one nature of the incarnate Word of God."

The number of members within the Oriental Orthodox Churches is estimated at some 40 million, most of whom reside nowadays in areas with an Islamic majority or under hostile Marxist governments. A sizable portion of their membership also live in the diaspora within Western countries. In recent times, they have been carrying on a fruitful dialogue with the Eastern Orthodox Church and Roman

Catholic Church. They continue to preserve precious ancient christian traditions especially in liturgy, spirituality, and church polity. Out of each of these churches has emerged a segment which entered into full communion with the Church of Rome (cf. below). From an Eastern Orthodox perspective the designation they use to describe themselves, "Oriental Orthodox," is somewhat misleading inasmuch as, for the former, a person must assent to all the first seven ecumenical councils to be "Orthodox."

(b) A very small group of Eastern Christians (perhaps fewer than 200,000) is called the Assyrian Church of the East, the East Syrian Church whose life originated in Palestine through Antioch and Edessa with minimal Greek influence and which eventually settled in the ancient Persian Empire. At a synod held in A.D. 484 this church officially adopted the christology of Nestorius which the rest of the churches opposed. The Assyrian Church of the East has always been a minority in Persia, but it carried on wide missionary activity even in Mongolia, Tibet and China.

The heavy concentration of these Eastern Christians living in Eastern Turkey were decimated during World War I by means of deportation and massacres. Some relocated in Iraq. Their spiritual leader, Mar Denkha IV, elected in 1976, resides in Teheran, Iran. Small groups of them live in Southern India and the United States. Although the Assyrians accept only the first two ecumenical councils and officially accept the Christological teaching of Nestorius, they do not wish to be referred to as the "Nestorian Church," a designation used in the past to denigrate them.

(c) The third and by far the most extensive group of Eastern Christians belong to the [Eastern] Orthodox Church, a vast and multi-cultural community of believers. Best known probably for the churches associated with the four ancient patriarchates of Constantinople, Alexandria, Antioch, and Jerusalem and to which more recently have been added Moscow and other churches, they are the largest part of Eastern Christianity. What unifies the Orthodox Church besides its adherence to scripture and ancient christian creeds and tradition is its acceptance of the teachings of the seven ecumenical councils of the first millennium. The Orthodox do not recognize as ecumenical any council held since Nicaea II (A.D. 787).

Although it is difficult to obtain statistics on the total number of Orthodox believers, the figure is estimated at about 105 million. The various churches among the Eastern Orthodox are commonly subdivided according to the following designations: the autocephalous (or autonomous) churches, associated with the patriarchates or churches of Constantinople, Alexandria, Antioch, Jerusalem, Russia, Romania, Greece, Serbia, Bulgaria, Georgia, Cyprus, Poland, Albania and Czechoslovakia; the autonomous churches of St. Catherine's Monastery on Mount Sinai and the churches of Finland, Japan and China; four canonical churches under the jurisdiction of Constantinople: the Carpatho-Russian Orthodox Church, the Ukrainian Orthodox Church of America, the Russian Orthodox Archdiocese in Western Europe, and the Albanian Orthodox Diocese of America; and finally six churches of "irregular" or "noncanonical" status: the Old Believers, the Russian Orthodox Church Outside Russia, the Ukrainian Orthodox Church, the Byelorussian Orthodox Church, the Macedonian Orthodox Church, the Old Calendar Greek Orthodox Church. The canonical status of the "Orthodox Church in America," (the OCA), which received a decree of autocephaly from the Patriarchate of Moscow in 1970 is disputed by the Ecumenical Patriarchate who claimed jurisdiction over them at that time. Because the OCA is not everywhere recognized as autocephalous it is not represented at international Orthodox synods although it has been given a sort of de facto canonical status in the Americas by membership in SCOBA (the Standing Conference of Canonical Orthodox Bishops in the Americas).

Orthodox Christians consider themselves to be one church in the sense that they share the common Orthodox faith and parallel Byzantine liturgical, canonical and spiritual tradition. They also share a similar tradition of religious art in the icon, which is closely integrated into its piety and liturgy. Insofar as church polity is concerned, Orthodoxy is a communion of sister churches which recognizes the Patriarch of Constantinople as Ecumenical Patriarch, the "first among equals."

The origin of the separation or "schism" between the Orthodox Church and the Church of Rome is commonly associated with the year 1054 in which there was a mutual excommunication between the bishops of Rome and Constantinople. In fact, because of theological, geographical, political factors, the churches in the eastern and western parts of the Roman Empire had long been estranged and had little sympathy for one another's distinctiveness. The separation existed especially between the Old Rome and the New Rome (Constantinople) but it also affected other churches. The involvement of the Western Christians in the Crusades, the sacking of the city of Constantinople by the Latins in 1204, the establishment of Latin Patriarchates in the West all further exacerbated existing tensions between East and West. The mutual anathemas of 1054 were jointly lifted by Pope Paul VI and Patriarch Athenagoras in 1965.

The Orthodox Church considers the Church of Rome to be in schism or possibly heresy because of its teachings on the primacy of jurisdiction of the Pope, the Bishop of Rome, and the teaching on papal infallibility especially as formulated at Vatican I (1869-70). Eastern Orthodoxy teaches that the Church of the West unjustifiably added the *filioque* to the Constantinopolitan-Nicene Creed, an addition which asserts that the Holy Spirit "proceeds" from the Father *and from the Son.* Orthodoxy, however, argues that the Holy Spirit has received far too little attention in western theology and liturgy. The Orthodox and Roman Catholic churches have over the centuries developed distinctive theological and ecclesiastical characteristics. In modern Orthodox theology there is a pre-eminence given to the hesychast theology inspired by St. Gregory Palamas (1296-1359) and a more recent "eucharistic ecclesiology." Especially since the 1960's, through official theological exchanges between the Orthodox and Roman Catholics underway both internationally and nationally, there has developed a mutual commitment to explore a "dialogue of charity" and to discover whether present differences are irreconcilable matters reflecting errors in dogma (and hence justify the term heresy) or are legitimate historical differences of theology and church polity which of themselves do not warrant the exclusion of full communion.

There has been considerable hostility and misunderstanding between the churches of Orthodoxy and Roman Catholicism, including tension over the existence of Eastern Catholic churches in full communion with Rome (the so-called "Uniate" churches) and proselytism, i.e., the attempt of Latins to "convert" Orthodox to Roman Catholicism especially in certain areas of the world.

The presiding Orthodox church is that of Constantinople, whose headquarters are located in a section of modern Istanbul, the Phanar. This patriarchal church also exercises jurisdiction over the Greek Orthodox Archdiocese of North and South America, and the Orthodox faithful in Australia and New Zealand. Because of the original size of this patriarchate, its early missionary activity in Kiev and other Slavic regions, Constantinople has exercised a kind of primatial leadership among the Orthodox although, in light of Orthodoxy's conviction about the conciliar nature of the church, this primacy is quite different from the kind of primatial jurisdiction exercised in the West by the pope over particular Catholic churches. Under the leadership of the late Ecumenical Patriarch Athenagoras a decision was reached in 1968 to begin plans for a Great and Holy Council of all the Orthodox Churches; preparations for the eventual convocation are still underway, although at a somewhat slow pace. In recent times church historians and theologians have focused also on the traditions and practices of other Orthodox churches, especially those of Antioch, Alexandria, Russia, and Romania, to name only several, to see how the distinctive character of Eastern Orthodoxy has been preserved in those cultures. Many Orthodox churches, as well as Oriental Orthodox churches, have suffered oppression and restrictions that have weakened its monastic and theological life and hindered free exchange with other christian communities.

(d) The fourth grouping of Eastern Churches are the Eastern Catholic Churches in full communion with the Church of Rome. Total membership in these churches is currently estimated at some 9 million. These have also been known by the pejorative term "Uniate" churches, a designation nowadays usually avoided. These churches have generally maintained their original traditions and practices, with some Latinizing influences.

Within the Roman Curia there is a Congregation for the Eastern Catholic Churches and at the present time experts are formulating a Code of Canon Law for the Eastern Catholic Churches.

These Eastern Catholic Churches usually have either a counterpart in the Oriental Orthodox, Eastern Orthodox, or even the Assyrian Church of the East. Among those related historically to the Oriental Orthodox are: the Armenian Catholic, the Coptic Catholic, the Ethiopian Catholic, the Syrian Catholic and the Malankar Catholic churches; those related to the Orthodox Churches of Byzantine traditions: the Melkite Catholic, the Ukrainian Catholic, the Ruthenian Catholic, the Romanian Catholic, the Greek Catholic, the Bulgarian Catholic, the Slovak Catholic, the Hungarian Catholic and several other communities of Byzantine practices. Corresponding to the Assyrian Church of the East are the Chaldean Catholic Church and the Malabar Catholic Church. Finally, there are two Eastern Catholic churches that claim to have entered into union with Rome at an early date and hence have no Orthodox counterpart: the Maronite Catholic (originating in the monastery of Beit-Marun in the territory of Antioch, now largely located in Lebanon and the diaspora) and the Italo-Albanian Catholic Church.

Two of these churches were notably affected by actions taken in recent history. The Ukrainian Catholic Church numbered some 3.5 million members in Ukraine during the mid-1940s. In 1946 a synod of Ukrainian Catholic priests held in Lvov voted to integrate this church with the Russian Orthodox Church. All Ukrainian Catholic bishops were imprisoned. The Moscow patriarchate described this merger as an exercise in legitimate freedom, but Ukrainian and other sources in the West argue that this was orchestrated by the Soviet government. Also within Romania in 1948, after the start of Communist rule, some 1.5 million Romanian Catholic were suppressed and required to become members of the Romanian Orthodox Church. Romanian Catholic bishops and priests were imprisoned. Both of these officially suppressed churches exist now only underground in their homelands or openly in the diaspora.

At Vatican II, because of the interventions of Eastern Catholics as well as the serious preparatory work of eastern and western historians and theologians, the Church of Rome was able to admit its past failure in not properly respecting the traditions of the Eastern Catholic Churches. One of its decrees was devoted to the Eastern Catholic Churches (*Orientalium ecclesiarum*) and made a number of significant assertions about Eastern Christianity. This decree needs to be read in conjunction with the lengthy section of the Council's decree on ecumenism (Unitatis redintegratio), which addresses the special distinctive role of the Eastern Churches not in communion with Rome (U.R. 13-19). In this latter decree, it is noted that: "... from their very origins the Churches of the East have had a treasury from which the Church of the West has drawn largely for its liturgy, spiritual tradition, and jurisprudence. Nor must we underestimate the fact that the basic dogmas of the Christian faith concerning the Trinity and the Word of God made flesh from the Virgin Mary were defined in Ecumenical Councils held in the East" (no. 14). Persons who labor for the restoration of full communion between the churches of the East and West are asked "to give due consideration to this special feature of the origin and growth of the Churches of the East, and to the character of the relations which obtained between them and the Roman See before the separation, and to form for themselves a correct evaluation of

these facts" (no. 14). The text praises the strong liturgical life of the East and states that "these churches, although separated from us, yet possess true sacraments, above all—by apostolic succession—the priesthood and the Eucharist, whereby they are still joined to us in closest intimacy" (no. 15). Furthermore, "the Churches of the East followed their own disciplines, sanctioned by the holy Fathers, by Synods, even by Ecumenical Councils. Far from being an obstacle to the Church's unity, such diversity of customs and observances only adds to her beauty and contributes greatly to carrying out her mission." The text continues by stating that these churches "have the power to govern themselves according to their own disciplines" (no. 16). It also stresses that there is a legitimate variety in theological expression of doctrine (no. 17), and finally prays for the removal of the wall dividing the Eastern and Western Church (no. 18).

Vatican II, in its decree on Eastern Catholic Churches, states that "History, tradition and very many ecclesiastical institutions give clear evidence of the great debt owed to the Eastern Churches by the Church Universal" (no. 5). The Council "not merely praises and appreciates as is due this ecclesiastical and spiritual heritage, but also insists on viewing it as the heritage of the whole Church of Christ" (no. 5). It states also that "The Eastern Churches in communion with the Apostolic See of Rome have the special duty of fostering the unity of all Christians, in particular of Eastern Christians, according to the principles laid down in the decree of this holy council 'On Ecumenism,' by prayer above all, by their example, by their scrupulous fidelity to the ancient traditions of the East, by better knowledge of each other, by working together, and by a brotherly attitude towards persons and things." (no. 24). Here it states that if separated

Eastern Christians should find themselves called to Catholic unity, no more should be required of such persons than a simple profession of the Catholic faith.

There are some difficulties in unifying these two separate documents of Vatican II. Both Orthodox and some Catholics think that is is inconsistent to regard the Eastern Catholic churches as "bridge churches" between the East and the West if the Orthodox Churches are elsewhere described as "sister churches." In the eventuality of official recognition of full communion between Orthodoxy and Roman Catholicism, what would be the "home" of the Eastern Catholics? Would they retain their autonomy or would they perhaps seek appropriate bonds of unity with their Orthodox Eastern counterpart? The sometimes troubled history of relationship between the Eastern and Western Churches is not brought to the fore in Vatican II's texts. The disedifying incidents regarding Rome's interference in the affairs of the Eastern churches are not mentioned specifically, although in the decree on ecumenism there is a brief reference following the citation of 1 Jn 1:10 ("If we say that we have not sinned...") which states: "This holds good for sins against unity. Thus, in humble prayer we beg pardon of God and of our separated brethren..." (no. 7).

Despite the recent progress in mutual understanding between the churches of the East and West there still remains much ignorance and prejudice that needs to be overcome by proper education and change of heart.

See **Orthodoxy**

Demetrios Constantelos, *Understanding the Greek Orthodox Church: Its Faith, History, and Practice,* New York: Paulist, 1982. *Does Chalcedon Divide or Unite? Towards Convergence in Orthodox Christology,* eds. P. Gregorios, W. Lazareth, N. Nissiotis, Geneva: World Council of Churches, 1981. Ronald G. Roberson, CSP, *The Eastern Christian Churches: A Brief Survey,* Rome: Gregorian University, 1986. Timothy Ware, *The Orthodox Church,* Harmondsworth: Penguin, 1976.

MICHAEL A. FAHEY, SJ

EASTERN AND ORIENTAL ORTHODOXY

"Orthodoxy" means "right belief." The term was initially applied to those Eastern Churches which retained the true faith notwithstanding heresies in the early centuries. According to usage established in recent ecumenical dialogue, the term "Eastern Orthodox Church" refers to the four ancient patriarchates (Constantinople, Alexandria, Antioch, Jerusalem), the more recent patriarchates (Russia, Rumania, Serbia, Bulgaria) and a number of autocephalous ("self-governing") churches like Cyprus and Greece, all in communion with Constantinople. "Oriental Orthodox" designates the five ancient autocephalous churches of Egypt, Syria, Armenia, India and Ethiopia which broke with Constantinople because of the council of Chalcedon (451).

Diversity and Division

At Pentecost, the Spirit Christ sent to his church appeared in the form of cloven tongues, a symbol of unity-in-diversity. But, as a result of doctrinal disputes, that unity was compromised. Thus, Arianism (not extant) taught that the Logos is not God by nature, but by grace. The oldest surviving separation originated with Nestorius (c. 451). Whether he taught the heresy for which he was condemned at Ephesus (431), namely, that there are two persons in Christ, still engages modern theologians. The Nestorians retired to Persia, whence they carried extensive missionary activities as far as India and even China, as Marco Polo (1324) discovered. Tracing their origin to the apostles, they prefer to call themselves the (Assyrian) church of the East. They recognize only the first two ecumenical councils, and revere Our Lady, but not as *Theotokos* ("Mother of God"), the title adopted at Ephesus. At first they abandoned compulsory celibacy, but re-introduced it soon aftwards for their bishops. The Assyrians are now a tiny church. A schism arose after the marriage (1973) of their former patriarch, Mar Shimoun.

In the wake of Chalcedon (451), which defined that Christ is one person in two natures, four churches broke off with Constantinople. Armenia (eastern Turkey, as well as bordering regions of Iran and the Soviet Union, outside the empire), was the first country where Christianity became the state religion. It was organized around the office of the *catholicos* ("primate"), as the patriarch is called. After Constantinople returned to Chalcedonian orthodoxy (518), Armenia seceded. Inside the Byzantine Empire, opposition to imperial politics led to the formation of the national churches in Syria and Egypt. On account of its organizer, Jacob Baradai (578), the Syrian Orthodox Church is sometimes referred to, inappropriately, as "Jacobite." In Egypt, the non-Chalcedonian Church became known as Coptic, the Arabic-Greek word for Egyptian. Egypt had sent missionaries to Ethiopia since Athanasius (373) was patriarch of Alexandria, and the Ethiopian mission followed suit in abjuring Chalcedon at a time difficult to make out exactly. At any rate, it remained dependent on the Coptic partriarchate until 1950, when Ethiopia became completely independent. A fifth church, claiming descent from the apostle Thomas, broke communion with Rome in protest against the Portuguese in India (1653); a part re-established communion, and, of the rest, one group became later known as the Malankar Orthodox Syrian Church.

These five churches have been accused of "monophysitism." According to this heresy, the divine nature absorbs the human, so that only one nature is left, a teaching traditionally attributed to Eutyches (454). Individual theologians apart, these churches do not hold this teaching, but follow Cyril of Alexandria (444), whose formula, "the one incarnate nature of the God-Logos," has been suggested as a possible basis for unification between Eastern and Oriental Orthodox. In four unofficial conversations between the two church communities (Aarhus, Denmark, 1964; Bristol, 1967; Geneva, 1970; Addis Ababa, 1971) the church representatives recognized in the two traditions the one orthodox faith of the church and emphasized full agreement especially in the Christological dogma. Differences dwindled to three main points; (1) the role of certain councils in church life; (2) the anathematization or acclamation as saints of controversial figures; (3) jurisdictional matters concerning church unity.

In trying to elaborate conciliar fellowship between these two traditions, there emerged a broad basis of agreement in worship, spirituality, ecclesiology and dogma. In what follows, the traits exposed as typical of Eastern Orthodoxy hold true to a large extent of Oriental Orthodoxy. The Catholic Eastern Churches (which do not fall within the compass of this article), while conforming with Rome on all points of doctrine, have a high measure of communality with Eastern and Oriental Orthodox regarding liturgy and spirituality.

Primacy of the Spiritual

Eastern Orthodoxy assigns the Spirit a central role. Created in God's image (Greek: ikon), man is called to become like God through the Spirit dwelling within him. This indwelling is called *uncreated grace,* since God himself is the gift, not created surrogates. The underlying anthropology in one word is called *deification:* every man ought to become by grace what God is by nature. Through deification, man really shares God's own life, but his communion is not to be confused with either the unity between the three persons of the Trinity or with the hypostatic union of Christ's two natures. While remaining entirely inaccessible in his *essence,* God becomes completely accessible in his *energies* (operations), chiefly in revelation and grace. Western theology, especially in the past, tended to see in the distinction between God's essence and energies something which impaired his simplicity. A less polemical approach takes the distinction to mean that the union between God and man in grace is real, and yet really distinct from either the essential unity of the three persons or the hypostatic union.

To the same distinction corresponds a twofold sort of theology. The first is *apophatic* or negative theology. It has as its object God's transcendence and shows the inadequacy of every human effort to achieve access to God as he is in himself. The second is *cataphatic* or positive theology, which, while recognizing that God always remains an ineffable mystery, nevertheless makes affirmative statements about God on the basis of his own initiative in revelation and grace.

The same double approach characterizes the spirituality Mount Athos monks propagated in the fourteenth century, *hesychasm* ("quiet"). Negatively, it unburdens the mind of its hyperactivity by integrating it into the heart, a purification which incessant prayer brings about. "Lord Jesus Christ, Son of God, have mercy on me (a sinner)" runs the constantly repeated prayer of the heart, or *Jesus prayer.* Breathing techniques often accompanying it remain accessory. Positively, hesychasm's scope is to gain an experiential, rather than a purely intellectual, insight into God: to see as in the Transfiguration the uncreated divine

light, a divine energy. G. Palamas (1359) gave hesychasm a doctrinal synthesis which Constantinopolitan councils (1341, 1351) endorsed. To avoid self-deceit, devotion is subordinated to the sacramental liturgy, as borne out in the Palamite humanist, Nicholas Cabasilas's (c. 1390) *Life in Christ* and *Commentary on the Liturgy.*

The "fool for Christ's sake," exemplifying a characteristic type of holiness, synthesizes the negative and positive approaches. Like the icon, he reverses people's usual perspectives to introduce them to God's own.

Icons and Orthodoxy

Far from being a flight from reality, Orthodox spirituality has a constant visual reference, since the whole man, the body included, has to be deified. Indeed, light symbolism plays an important role in Eastern Orthodoxy's "three theologians": John the Evangelist (cf. Jn 1, 39), Gregory of Nazianzus (c. 390) and Simeon the New Theologian (1022). The iconostasis, the icon-covered partition between sanctuary and nave, helps bring together, in the liturgy, heaven and earth under one roof. Icons are arranged along definite patterns so as to make the church itself one icon. Creativity manifests itself through faithfulness to time-hallowed models, and artists prepare themselves spiritually, e.g., by fasting, The underlying conviction is that beauty saves the world, since man has been fashioned after God's best icon, Christ.

The link between icons and orthodoxy becomes manifest if one remembers that "orthodoxy" means "right glory (worship)" too. Icons show the priority of worship over doctrine; they have been aptly called a "theology in color" because icons commit theology to quite specific views. These nuanced positions (dogmas) are amenable to be couched in the language of worship. Thus, the Spirit's divinity was upheld at Constantinople I (381) by ascribing him the same honor and glory which pertains to the Father and the Son. That Christ is one person in two natures was—apophatically—enshrined at Chalcedon in four negative terms, to safeguard the mystery. Eastern Orthodoxy is often apostrophized as the Church of the Seven Councils, and Nicaea II (787), the last of them, by recurring to the already formulated trinitarian and Christological dogma, forms a kind of mosaic of these seven ecumenical councils. Little wonder that Nicaea II, which acknowledged the orthodoxy of the image, should give rise, in 843, to the Feast of Orthodoxy itself. The *Synodicon* read for the occasion on every first Sunday in Lent forms a compendium of heroes and heretics, Palamas's feast the following Sunday being a kind of continuation.

Fullness of Tradition

Besides icons, the *pleroma* ("tradition" in its entirety) includes the Bible, never divorced from its church context, the councils, the Fathers, the canons and the service-books. The celebration of the liturgy guarantees the vitality of tradition. There is no higher authority than that of the local church, gathered around the bishop who celebrates the eucharist. The unity of the bishops among themselves ascertains the unity of the church. Infallibility accrues to the church as a whole, primarily when assembled in ecumenical councils. There is strong lay participation in synods, but bishops decide faith issues. A council qualifies as ecumenical if celebrated in the liturgy by all churches possessing full orthodoxy. From the councils, especially the ecumenical ones and the Quinisext (692), derive the canons. Noteworthy is the compilation *Nomocanon in Fifty Titles* (883). Canon law in general is thought of as dogma in practice and as guided by the spirit of

oikonomia, a supra-judiciary pastoral sense of balance.

East-West Estrangement

A turning-point for church organization as a whole proved to be Chalcedon. The *pentarchy* (the five ancient patriarchates taken collectively) became now complete: in order of precedence, Rome, Constantinople, Alexandria, Antioch and Jerusalem. Due to Constantinople's political importance, its patriarchate claimed a position befitting a "second Rome." This was guaranteed by canon 28 of Chalcedon, which Pope Leo never approved. The Semites' (Syrians,' Copts') revolt against Constantinople accelerated the emergence of independent local traditions. The minority among the Semites still loyal to the Byzantine emperor became known as "melchites" or "emperor's party" ("melek" meaning king), adopting in due course Constantinople's liturgy. This process of unifying local liturgical usages around the chief ecclesial centers gave gradual rise to the seven extant Eastern rites: Armenian, Byzantine, Coptic, East-Syrian, Ethiopian, Maronite and West-Syrian.

East and West, already a permanent political division since Theodosius's death (395), drifted apart culturally and theologically. Things came to a head with Charlemagne's coronation (800) by Pope Leo III. Still, the schism under Photius (863-867) could be healed, as both sides had enough in common. In 868, the apostles of the Slavs, Cyril and Methodius, Photius's friends, obtained in Rome support against harassment by Westerners. What consolidated the schism under Cerularius (1054) was the Fourth Crusade, which set up in Constantinople a Latin empire and partriarchate (1204-1261) and which, in Greek eyes, made the fall of Constantinople inevitable (1453). Since fear of another Latin empire dominated Lyons II (1274) and fear of the

Turks, Ferrara/Florence/Rome (1438-45), these councils could not attain a lasting union. After 1453, Moscow aspired to become "Third Rome" and in 1589 was made a patriarchate (abolished in 1721 by Peter the Great, re-established in 1917). Western influence after the Reformation enabled Eastern Orthodoxy to define its positions through councils and creeds.

Growing Consensus

Now, Orthodox and Catholics are drawing closer again. Symbolic gestures (e.g., Paul VI and Athenagoras I met in 1964 in Jerusalem and lifted the 1054 excommunication a year later) initiated a "dialogue of love." The "dialogue of truth," the official theological discussions between the two churches, started in 1980, the year John Paul II proclaimed Cyril and Methodius co-patrons of Europe. At times, the discussions seem to falter, but there is room for hope. Vatican II stressed the collegiality of bishops and the equality of rites East and West. The pope's jurisdictional primacy and the addition of the *Filioque* to the Creed are the main difficulties, the other points of discussion including the Immaculate Conception, original sin, purgatory, the exact moment of consecration and the status of the Catholic Eastern Churches. When John Paul II visited Constantinople (1979), Dimitrios I called Rome the "president of charity" (Ignatius of Antioch); besides, the council of Sardica (343) allows a certain right of appeal to the pope.

Consensus presupposes reciprocity: estrangement created separation, drawing close must precede reunion. Put somewhat simply, the West has developed more a theology of hearing the word of God, with iconoclasm as the peril to watch out for; whereas the East has created a theology of seeing God's glory in Christ, but has to be careful against

excessive anthropomorphization. Seeing and hearing need to be mediated so as to enrich both traditions, which have the first millennium in common. There is something innate to orthodoxy, with its emphasis on cosmic transfiguration and *philanthropia* (God's love for humanity and human beings' friendship among themselves), which make her aspire to union. In turn, Vatican II has warned not to add unnecessary burdens.

E. Benz, *The Eastern Orthodox Church,* New York: Anchor Books, 1963, P. Gregorios, et al., Eds., *Does Chalcedon Divide or Unite?* Geneva: World Council of Churches, 1981. J. Meyendorff, *The Orthodox Church,* New York: St. Vladimir's Press, 1981. J. Pelikan, *The Christian Tradition II: The Spirit of Eastern Christendom (600-1700),* Chicago: U. of Chicago Press, 1974. H.J. Schulz, *The Byzantine Liturgy,* New York: Pueblo Publishing Company, 1986. K. Ware, *The Orthodox Church,* New York: Penguin Books, 1984.

EDWARD G. FARRUGIA, SJ

ECCLESIOLOGY
See Church

ECONOMICS

Economics and theology stand in dialectical relation to one another. Economics, whether considered as that dimension of society concerned with the production, distribution and consumption of goods or as the science of that dimension, has been and continues to be influenced by theology. And theology is in turn influenced and conditioned by economics.

This has been the case since the beginning of the judaeo-christian tradition. According to the revolt model for explaining the origins of Israel (see Gottwald), the conquest of Canaan took place through the combined efforts of a group of outsiders who believed in Yahweh and those from the underclass in Canaan. They revolted against the stratified, hierarchical structure of Canaanite society with a feudal economy strongly oriented toward the benefit of the ruling class. In its place Israel developed an egalitarian, decentralized society based on a federation between various tribes. The primarily agricultural economy was marked by this same equality, with land ownership and enjoyment of the fruits of production widely shared.

Israel with its egalitarian, decentralized social structure was the symbol of Yahweh, the manifestation of who this God is. Thus, the marginalized situation of the poor in Israel was a countersign and a contradiction. The outcry of the prophets against the loss of egalitarianism grew as power was centralized during the monarchy and wealth became concentrated in the hands of a smaller number.

In the christian scriptures, especially in Luke's gospel, Jesus is presented as standing in continuity with the egalitarian thrust of the Hebrew scriptures. Jesus identifies himself with the poor who are declared blessed (Lk 6:20) and proclaims "the Lord's year of favor" (Lk 4:19), that is, the Jubilee year when all debts will be wiped out and possessions restored.

Although Jesus requires his first disciples to renounce their possessions (Lk 14:33), he does not demean the goods of the earth. He calls upon people to respond out of love to those in need. This response is not a program of social reform, but a preparation for the coming of the kingdom through direct assistance of those in need within a fellowship of love.

The early Christians accepted trade as a legitimate way to make a living (Acts 16:14). But charging interest on loans was unacceptable; for, in doing so, one offended against the commandment of love by taking advantage of those in need.

For the early christian community with its ethic of poverty, wealth presented a problem. Riches were a block to God's kingdom (Lk 18:24-27). Yet the wealthy became part of the community. The early church drew its converts primarily from the marginalized groups within society, and the wealthy were included among the marginalized. Birth and legal standing determined social status, not riches (see Gager).

The presence of the affluent forced the church to reconsider its stance on wealth. Gradually attention focused on the use made of wealth rather than its possession. Those with enough resources for themselves should help those in need out of a spirit of love. This was carried out not only within the local church (Acts 6:1) but also between churches (Acts 11:29). Such care became a sign by which this fellowship of love was recognized.

With the church thus gradually accommodating itself to the economic order of the day, monastic life developed in the fourth century as a reaction to secular society. Not only wealth but private property as well were rejected and a system of common property was developed. This was based now, however, on asceticism and not on the commandment of love as had formerly been the case.

With the breakdown of the Roman empire, society moved away from the urban centers and trade diminished. Agriculture was the primary occupation and feudal structures were the organizing principle for society, including the economy. In such a setting, monasteries became centers for learning and for economic life as well.

In the twelfth century, however, as urban life began to revive and with it manufacturing and commerce, new forms of economic and religious life appeared. A monetary, profit-oriented economy developed; and a middle-class was able to secure a degree of political and economic freedom in the midst of the feudal structures of the day. The Dominicans and the Franciscans got their start at this time. Rather than remain in monasteries, the friars lived through begging and were actively involved in the public, social life of the day.

The friars also taught at the universities, the new centers of learning. There theology adopted a dialectical method organized around *lectio* and *disputatio*. This method reflected and was influenced by the activity of the dominant members of the new society whose principal activity was neither praying nor fighting, but negotiation, discussion, and argument (see Little).

In the universities, theologians took up the issues raised by the new developments in society: private property, just price, profits, moneylending. While the traditional strictures against usury remained in place, arguments were put forward that would eventually allow for the taking of interest on money.

Theologians focused primarily on the city with its new economic and political structures. Yet through their specific teachings as well as the overall structure of their argumentation they continued to support the general feudal structure of society marked by hierarchical authority and class stratifications (see Levi).

In the 1500's, the reformers confronted this new social and economic order primarily in the context of their discussion of "calling." They emphasized that each person most faithfully responds to God and neighbor not through monastic or mendicant living but by responsibly carrying out the duties imposed by their place within the world.

Luther spoke of "calling," but in a way that challenged the new economic forces at work. He stressed the need to remain within one's social class and not question the social order. For Luther, according to Troeltsch, "It is against all law, both Natural and Divine, to wish to rise in the world, to break through existing institutions on one's own free initiative, to agitate and destroy Society by individual efforts, to improve one's manner of life, or to improve one's social position." (Troeltsch, II, p. 555)

Calvin, like Luther, emphasized the importance of work. But writing within the context of Geneva where a money economy and industrial production were in place, he accepted the new economic forces. He rejected the ban on taking interest on money and underlined the need to be frugal and save.

Thus capitalism found its first fundamental acceptance within Christianity.

"It was just because the economic conditions at Geneva were so bourgeois, and on such a small scale, that Capitalism was able to steal into the Calvinistic ethic, while it was rejected by the Catholic and Lutheran ethic." (Troeltsch, II, p. 643)

The Roman Catholic Church had as much difficulty coming to grips with the capitalist economic system as it did with democratic political structures. Social Catholicism arose in Europe in the 1820's as Catholics sought ways in which the church might respond to the destructive effects of the industrial revolution. Three different approaches developed. One group, which included le Play and Périn in France, called for personal moral conversion and greater charity and argued against any structural reform or governmental intervention. Another group, among whom were La Tour du Pin in France and Vogelsang in Germany, condemned capitalism and called for a corporatism in which workers and employers would be organized into associations like the medieval guilds with the employers exercising paternalistic authority, and in which the government would exercise restricted power over the semi-autonomous guilds. A third group, for whom Von Ketteler in Germany was the primary spokesman, accepted the capitalist economic system and sought ways to improve and reform it gradually and piecemeal.

It was Von Ketteler who strongly influenced Pope Leo XIII's 1891 encyclical, *Rerum Novarum*. Leo rejected socialism, primarily because of its proposal for a "community of goods" (para. 15). This was wrong, he argued, because "private ownership is according to nature's law" (para. 9). Thus, to protect people's rights, especially those of the family, Leo sought to insure that everyone was a property owner.

Leo likewise denied the validity of socialism's class warfare. Opposing social equality, he stated that social harmony would be achieved if workers accepted their station in life and carried out their work honestly, and if owners treated their workers justly and respectfully and met the duty for charity their wealth placed on them.

Forty years later (1931), in the depths of a worldwide economic depression, Pope Pius XI issued *Quadagesimo Anno*. Because of the terrible economic situation, social reform was no longer adequate; social reconstruction was required.

Pius set forth a program based on solidarism, a social theory emphasizing the social nature of humanity while at the same time upholding the right of private property. He proposed an economic order built around "functional 'groups'" which organized people "according to the diverse functions which they exercise in society" (para. 83). In this way, the division between workers and owners could be overcome. While according to Pius the state has a definite place in society, its interventions are to be governed by the principle of subsidiarity which encourages the formation of mediating organizations and calls for problems to be addressed at the most local level possible.

In Pius' proposed reconstruction, capitalism had a place; while it had become destructive because of too great a concentration of economic power, "it is not vicious of its very nature" (para. 101). But there was no room for socialism, even in its more mitigated form. Socialism subordinates the individual to society and blinds people to the demands of the spirit.

Beginning with Pope John XXIII, Roman Catholic thought on economics has deepened and broadened. Instead of looking just at the impact of capitalism on western nations, attention has turned to the international sphere, with special concern being expressed for third-world countries. Pope Paul VI, for example, calls for a program of "authentic development": one that addresses "the development of each person and the whole person" and that is not "restricted to economic growth" (*Progressio Populorum,* 1967, para. 14).

Recent popes have continued to enunciate the principle of subsidiarity. But because of the enormity of the problems confronting them, they have highlighted more the essential role government has in responding to them. Paul VI has pointed out the "radical limitation to economics" and has stated that "in the social and economic field, both national and international, the ultimate decision rests with political power" (*Octogesima Adveniens*, 1971, para. 46).

In *Pacem in Terris* (1963), John XXIII set forth the Roman Catholic stance on human rights, including among them economic rights such as "the inherent right not only to be given the opportunity to work, but also to be allowed the exercise of personal initiative in the work one does" (para. 18).

In that same document John XXIII took a stance toward socialism that was significantly different from that of his predecessors. Without naming socialism directly, he said that "...it is perfectly legitimate to make a clear distinction between a false philosophy of the nature, origin and purpose of people and the world, and economic, social, cultural, and political undertakings, even when such undertakings draw their origin from that philosophy .... Besides, who can deny the possible existence of good and commendable elements in these undertakings, elements which do indeed conform to the dictates of right reason, and are an expression of humanity's lawful aspirations" (para. 159).

Paul VI later quoted this statement and applied it specifically to socialism (*Octogesima Adveniens,* paras. 30-34). At the same time he challenged both socialist and capitalist ideologies, saying that they cannot "escape the materialism, egoism or constraint which inevitably go with them" (para. 37); and he called upon Christians to make use of a "forward-looking imagination both to perceive in the present the disregarded possibility hidden within it, and to direct itself towards a fresh future" (para. 37). And in *Laborem Exercens* (1981), John Paul II, arguing that the use of capital is a more important issue than its ownership, calls for a socialization that will ensure each person the right "to consider oneself a part owner of the great workbench at which one is working with everyone else" (para. 69). The pope sees many ways in which this might be accomplished, although he rules out a "rigid capitalism" (para. 68) or a collectivist system (para. 69).

There have also been shifts in the methodology by which economics is addressed. The Second Vatican Council, in its *Pastoral Constitution on the Church in the Modern World* (1965), accepted economics as a separate and autonomous discipline: "... economic activity is to be carried out according to its own methods and laws but within the limits of morality..." (para. 64). In using natural law to determine these "limits of morality," the appeal is to what is needed for the well-being of humanity rather than to a more

general and abstract moral law. This has introduced a dynamic, historical element into church social teaching. And John Paul II has placed primary emphasis on scripture in developing his moral criteria, basing his discussion of work in *Laborem Exercens* on the creation account of the first chapter of Genesis.

Finally, there is a growing appreciation in official Roman Catholic statements about the importance and centrality of concern about social justice for the mission of the church. In *Justice in the World,* the 1971 Synod of Bishops said that

"...action on behalf of justice and participation in the transformation of the world fully appear to us as a constitutive dimension of the preaching of the Gospel ..." (para.6)

In *Laborem Exercens* John Paul II stated:

"Let the Christian who listens to the word of the living God, uniting work with prayer, know the place that one's work has not only in earthly progress, but also in the development of the kingdom of God...." (para. 131)

In the United States, neither economics nor politics has been far removed from the religious realm. The social gospel movement, led by Walter Rauschenbusch (1861-1918), made economic issues central to the theological enterprise. For Rauschenbusch Christianity has transformed the family, the church, education, and the state. Now the economy had to be infused with christian values, a task he believed could be accomplished—and without the use of force.

The optimism of the social gospel movement, however, was eroded by the savagery of the First World War and then by the Great Depression. It gave way to the realism of Reinhold Niebuhr (1892-1971) who argued that the social gospel movement overlooked the egoism that is inevitably a part of the fallen human condition and the issues of power that raises. Niebuhr held that creative powers of self-interest should be utilized; but they must be kept within bounds through social and political structures that can maintain a balance of power. Christianity should assist by developing wider loyalties in people.

Within Roman Catholicism, Msgr. John A. Ryan (1869-1945) followed closely—but by no means totally—papal social teaching. He sought reform of the U.S. economy, accepting the basic tenets of capitalism but attempting to move it toward economic or industrial democracy by which workers are given the opportunity to share in ownership and management. He stressed distributive justice, seeing the problem as one of income rather than possession: thus his strong emphasis on a just wage.

Ryan, while underlining the need for subsidiarity, gave a strong role to the state since he sought to achieve his proposed reforms primarily through social legislation. To the church, however, Ryan assigned an otherworldly mission with a primary responsibility for saving souls, not society.

Ryan's stance was countered by that of the Central-Verein, a national German-American Catholic federation. This group supported corporatism and called for a reorganization of society along organic, hierarchical lines, with owners and workers organized into guilds, and industry kept as much as possible at a small scale.

The American Roman Catholic bishops in their "Program of Social Reconstruction" (1919), followed the direction charted by Ryan. While dismissing socialism, they criticized capitalism for its inefficiency and waste and for the great discrepancies between the income of the capitalists and that of the wage earners. They proposed a reform more than a reconstruction, calling for greater participation of workers in ownership and production and for an increase in wages.

Since 1919, the American bishops have spoken out many times in response to particular economic problems—always from a reformist perspective.

In 1980 the American bishops published their "Pastoral Letter on Marxist Communism" in which they pointed out the fundamental disagreements between the theory of Marx and Christianity, particularly "on such crucial issues as the nature of man, of his alienation in the present and his redemption in the future" (para. 13). Nevertheless, the bishops call for cooperation and common effort between Christians and Marxists on matters of "world peace and eradication of global poverty" (para. 60).

The pastoral on Marxism in turn prompted the bishops to write "Economic Justice for All: Catholic Social Teaching and the U.S. Economy." This pastoral considers the existing U.S. economy rather than the theory of capitalism. It argues that economics is an ethical issue, not just a technical matter for scientists. As such, these questions must be asked: "What does the economy do *for* people? What does it do *to* people? And how do people *participate* in it?" (para. 1)

In the pastoral, the bishops are addressing the Roman Catholic community; and so they draw upon "a long tradition of Catholic social thought, rooted in the Bible and developed over the past century by the popes and the Second Vatican Council in response to modern economic conditions" (para. 25).

The bishop's criterion for judging the U.S. economy is "the dignity of the human person, realized in community with others" (para. 28). To arrive at this criterion, the bishops look first to the Hebrew scriptures for a vision shaped by the theology of creation and covenant that underlines the dignity of the person and reciprocal responsibility. Justice in any society is measured by its treatment of the poor, that is, the powerless who are denied social participation. The christian scriptures place this vision in the context of the call to discipleship, the call to imitate "the pattern of Jesus' life by openness to God's will in the service of others" (para. 17).

Out of this scriptural vision an ethical norm is developed which sets forth duties of solidarity and justice (especially social justice) and rights to the "prerequisites for a dignified life in community" (para. 79) such as food, employment, and old age security.

Although the bishops call for an application of these criteria to the U.S. economic system as such (para. 132), they themselves take a pragmatic, reformist approach. They analyze, criticize and suggest solutions in the areas of employment, poverty, agriculture, and U.S. involvement in the world economy; but they never call the system itself into question.

In response to the bishops' pastoral, some U.S. Catholic theologians (e.g., Novak) influenced by neo-conservatism are arguing that the Roman Catholic tradition would best be served by reconsidering the hesitations and questions Roman Catholicism has had about democratic capitalism and by adopting its principles as the basis for Roman Catholic economic thought.

But one of the reasons the Roman Catholic Church falls so easily into a reformist stance is that it has not given serious attention to the Marxist tradition. Without that, the church lacks a basis for a serious challenge to the classical western liberal economic tradition.

Liberation theology is exploring ways of bringing Marxist concepts and analysis within the Roman Catholic tradition. Some Latin American liberation theologians (e.g., Miranda) and some North American liberation theologians (e.g., Reuther) are arguing for a socialism as the most appropriate christian response to the economic issues of the day.

See **Justice**

John G. Gager, *Kingdom and Community,* Englewood Cliffs, N.J.: Prentice-Hall, Inc., 1974. Norman K. Gottwald, *The Tribes of Israel,* Maryknoll: Orbis, 1979 and London: S.C.M., 1980. Albert William Levi, *Philosophy as Social Expression.* Lester K. Little, *Religious Poverty and the Profit Economy in Medieval Europe,* Ithaca: Cornell U.P., 1978. National Conference of Catholic Bishops, "Economic Justice for All: Catholic Social Teaching and the U.S. Economy," *Origins* 16/24 (November 27, 1986). Ernst Troeltsch, *The Social Teaching of the Christian Churches,* 2 vols. Translated by Olive Wyon. London: George Allen & Unwin Ltd., 1956.

THOMAS F. SCHINDLER, SS

ECONOMY

The theological term used to refer to God's activity in the world, particularly with reference to the two dispensations of the OT and NT. A second meaning of the term, more common among the Orthodox, uses it to refer to certain exceptional dispensations from church law.

ECUMENISM

The Roman Catholic Church comes to the ecumenical movement with its own set of commitments and principles. While open to the common biblical understanding of the ecumenical movement shared by Orthodox, Protestant and Anglican Christians, it stands on unique ground. In this essay we will cover three elements of Roman Catholic participation in the ecumenical movement: (1) the Roman Catholic understanding of ecumenism, (2) the modern ecumenical movement, and (3), the situation of Roman Catholic ecumenism today.

The Roman Catholic Understanding of Ecumenism

The Roman Catholic participation in

the ecumenical movement is based on its ecclesial self-understanding which sees the church as one, recognizing separated sisters and brothers as somehow participating in the reality of Christ's mystery on earth through their faith and sacramental life. The charter for modern Roman Catholic participation in the ecumenical movement is the decree *Unitatis Redintegratio* of the Second Vatican Council where ecumenism is defined: "The term 'ecumenical movement' indicates the initiatives and activities encouraged and organized, according to the various needs of the church and as opportunities offer, to promote Christian unity" (#4). Thus it is the unity of the church which is the primary focus of Roman Catholic participation in the ecumenical movement, while for many of the churches of the Reformation it is collaboration in mission. For the strongly confessional Protestant churches, the Orthodox and Roman Catholics, the doctrinal divisions among believers becomes a primary motivation.

Since the publication of the decree on ecumenism (November 21, 1964) there has been a full development of Roman Catholic ecumenical work. Yet the process of reception of the decree on ecumenism and the subsequent leadership of the Roman Catholic Church in the ecumenical movement only gradually penetrates the life and spirituality of Roman Catholic Christians. The Extraordinary Synod (November, 1985) reiterated the Roman Catholic commitment to take its proper place in the modern ecumenical movement. Following his four predecessors, Pope John Paul II has continually reinforced the priority of placing the ecumenical movement at the very center of modern Roman Catholic identity. The theology on which the Roman Catholic principles of ecumenism are based is the "real, but imperfect communion" which joins Catholics to all who confess Jesus Christ as Lord and Saviour according to the scriptures and share a common baptism.

In the decree on ecumenism and subsequent Roman Catholic developments there are three very clear elements to which the Catholic Church is committed in the ecumenical movement: spiritual renewal, theological dialogue towards restoration of full communion, and common mission and witness in the world.

The commitment to internal renewal takes two forms. The first is the theological, liturgical and biblical renewal which makes the evangelical reality of the church to shine through the contemporary Roman Catholic communion. The decree on the liturgy of the Second Vatican Council, returning to the common patristic sources shared with the Orthodox on the one hand, and receiving the insights of the biblical witness of worship in the Reformation churches on the other, urges the fullness of the gospel to be manifested in Catholic liturgical life. Such elements of renewal as the Rite of Christian Initiation for Adults, a more nuanced approach to the rites of reconciliation, and a eucharistic liturgy more in harmony with the great tradition of the church are all elements which bring us closer to the separated brothers and sisters in non-Catholic communions. The decree on revelation, *Dei Verbum,* renews Roman Catholic commitment to the primacy of scripture, within the context of the church's tradition. It makes clear that the word of God is the center of christian faith and worship. The decree on the Church and the Modern World, (*Gaudium et Spes),* and the decree on Religious Liberty, (*Dignitatis Humanae*), renew the Roman Catholic understanding of the relationship of church and society, and thus enhancing opportunities for ecumenical cooperation with both Orthodox and Reformation churches in the areas of social ethics and mission to the world.

The second element of renewal which is essential to the ecumenical movement is an enrichment of the theological, spiritual, historical, and prayer life of the diversity of traditions embodied in our still divided churches and ecclesial communities. Key in this personal spiritual renewal is the Week of Prayer for Christian Unity, founded by the Graymoor Friars. This kind of regular common worship and prayer with other Christians enriches personal and parish development. An essential element in this spiritual renewal is the renewal of the educational life of the church in order to help all Roman Catholic Christians place the ecumenical movement at the very center of their identity. The *Directory Concerning Ecumenical Matters: Part II, Ecumenism in Higher Education* (1969) points out some general principles in this element of the spiritual renewal of the church.

The second major element in Roman Catholic understanding of the ecumenical movement is theological dialogue toward restoration of full communion. The principle underlying these dialogues is that reunion is effected not by compromise but by common biblical and historical study to find a ground of truth which transcends the historic division, by the power of the Spirit working in the ecumenical movement. Roman Catholics take full responsibility for the errors of their forebears in history, and take up the task of dialogue to overcome the theological barriers.

The Catholic Church has been engaged in the Faith and Order dialogue of the World Council of Churches since 1963 and since 1968 has been a full member of that Commission. Specific bilateral dialogues were begun soon after Vatican II, with hopes of restoring full communion. These dialogues with Lutheran, Method-

ist, Presbyterian/Reformed, Eastern Orthodox, Oriental Orthodox, Disciples of Christ and Anglican theologians have been most fruitful. The Anglican-Roman Catholic International Commission *Final Report* (1981) is the most well known. The Eastern Orthodox dialogue has been very slow to begin, but remains an important commitment of the Catholic Church. A common declaration with the Oriental Orthodox patriarch of Antioch has opened the way to limited eucharistic sharing, the first such step taken by the Catholic Church in its commitment toward restoring full communion with these churches. In addition to the dialogues leading towards full union, there are other dialogues which involve building a common base of understanding and trying to alleviate historic prejudices. The Baptist, Pentecostal, and Evangelical Dialogues on Mission with the Roman Catholic Church are most notable among these.

The Vatican Secretariat for Promoting Christian Unity, founded in 1960 by Pope John XXIII, oversees these dialogues on a worldwide level. In the United States seven national dialogues are overseen by the Bishops' Committee on Ecumenical and Interreligious Affairs of the National Conference of Catholic Bishops.

The third major Catholic commitment to the ecumenical movement is through common mission and witness, with local initiatives in parishes for social service, evangelism, peace and justice at the very center of Roman Catholic developments. The Vatican has issued a statement on *Ecumenical Collaboration at the Regional, National and Local Levels* (1975) to support these collaborative ventures. At the present time, the Roman Catholic Church is a member of twenty-seven national councils of churches around the world. In the United States, with the exception of five states with heavy

Catholic populations, dioceses are members of half of the state councils or conferences of churches. The Vatican Secretariat and the World Council of Churches have a Joint Working Group that has been working since the Second Vatican Council to enhance their relationship. This Joint Working Group points to the fact that the Roman Catholic Church is as involved with the World Council, though not a formal member, as are some member churches. This relationship has been reinforced by the visits of both Pope Paul VI and Pope John Paul II to the World Council Headquarters in Geneva, Switzerland and their encouraging words about the work of the WCC.

In addition to the 1969 directory, there is a first part of the *Directory Concerning Ecumenical Matters* (1967) which governs Roman Catholic participation in the ecumenical movement. With the publication of the new *Code of Canon Law* (1983), and the inclusion in it of Catholic ecumenical priorities, the emphasis on the Bishops' role in fostering ecumenism, and guidelines for eucharistic sharing, a need was seen for a new directory of ecumenism for the church. The revision of the directory is in progress and should be completed in light of the new code, by 1990.

The Modern Ecumenical Movement

The ecumenical commitment of the church is a persistent ministry, dating from the life of Jesus himself. It is most apparent in the NT in the Acts of the Apostles, with the Council of Jerusalem (Acts 15), where the mission to the Gentiles had to be adjudicated by the meeting of Peter, Paul and James, with the other Apostles in Jerusalem. Furthermore, the NT attests, in I Corinthians, to Paul's reconciling ministry among the divisions in the early christian communities. Throughout history the ecumenical councils have provided for judgment and healing of tensions raised over doctrinal divisions within the Body of Christ.

Attempts at reconciliation with the churches of the East are attested to in the council of Lyons in 1274 and the Council of Florence (1438-1442), both of which were unsuccessful, and the Reformation Conference at Ratisbon (1541) with the Lutherans, which was likewise unsuccessful. While there have been attempts since the time of the schism between East and West in 1054, and the Reformation fissures in the church dating from 1530, it is only with the nineteenth century missionary movement that a new context is set in worldwide Christianity for what we call the modern ecumenical movement.

The groundwork for the modern ecumenical movement began with the nineteenth century missionary expansion by Protestants and the contacts, often tension, with Orthodoxy, produced by these missionary efforts. The scandal of a divided Protestant Christianity on the one hand and the dissension caused by "evangelism" in Orthodox territory on the other brought those confessing Jesus Christ to a new awareness of the need to reconcile the divisions among Christians. At the same time, Roman Catholic interest in ecclesiology stimulated by historical, liturgical and biblical studies in the late nineteenth and early twentieth century was another facet of this groundwork. The vision of the Roman Catholic Church's relationship to the world began to evolve with the collapse of papal rule in Rome in 1870, and was taken up by the renewal of social teachings in its new context by Leo XIII. The liturgical renewal, beginning to receive sanction under Pius X and by work begun in France and Germany on return to the sources in the Orthodox tradition, and biblical researches already under way in the Protestant world created a theological basis for a renewed doctrine of the church.

The specific history of the World Council of Churches is rooted in the missionary conference in Edinburgh (1910) and the resolution of the Protestant Episcopal Church in that same year to call for a world conference on Faith and Order. While there is a pre-history to this modern ecumenical movement, it was only after World War I with the encyclical of the ecumenical patriarch (1919) that the wheels were set in motion for on-going structured relationship between Protestant and Orthodox. In the 1920's the Roman Catholic Church was invited to participate in the ecumenical movement, but Pope Benedict XV, upon receiving the delegates of the Faith and Order movement, decided that the only ecclesiology under which ecumenism would be possible for the Roman Catholic Church was "return to Rome." Participation of Roman Catholics in conversations with non-Catholic Christians began after World War II in spite of the fact that the Vatican's public policy had not changed.

By the 1950's in Europe, relationships created during the struggles of World War II moved forward on a theological level, so that communications with the World Council of Churches (founded in 1948) and the major traditions of Orthodoxy and Protestantism were well in place. When Pope John XXIII announced the Second Vatican Council and the revision of the Code of Canon Law (1959), scholars were available for beginning the Roman Catholic entry into the modern ecumenical movement.

The Second Vatican Council, having as one of its goals bringing the Roman Catholic Church into the modern ecumenical movement, and with its decree on ecumenism, set the stage for beginning to create ecumenical relations. In preparation for the Council, Pope John opened the Secretariat for Promoting Christian Unity (1960), with Cardinal Bea at its head.

The Catholic Church was present as an observer for the first time at the 1961 Third Assembly of the World Council of Churches in New Delhi, India. Observers from the major christian world communions, eventually including Orthodox, were present at the Second Vatican Council. In 1963 at the World Conference on Faith and Order in Montreal, the presence of Catholic theologians began to influence the theological work through its statement on *Scripture, Tradition and the Traditions.* By 1968 the Roman Catholic Church became a full member of the Commission on Faith and Order of the World Council of Churches and many of the bilateral dialogues were begun.

As a result of the initiatives of Vatican II, relations were begun on many continental, national and more local levels with other christian communions on the spiritual, dialogical and pastoral level. As a result of the theological dialogues, there are before the churches statements on scripture, tradition, the papacy, the shape of a conciliar fellowship that would include Orthodox, Protestant and Catholic Christians, a multiplicity of ethical issues, the sacraments of baptism and eucharist, the ordained ministry and a wide range of other topics. The Roman Catholic community worldwide, in its years of engagement in the ecumenical movement, has hardly had time to assimilate the mass of material provided for it by these ecumenical relationships.

The Situation of Roman Catholicism in the Ecumenical Movement Today

The dialogues engaged in by the theologians in the Faith and Order Commission and the bilateral conversations have been an unprecedented success. The Catholic Church and its theologians are presently in discussion about the appropriate means of theological response to these statements of consensus, or of substantial agreement or convergence emanating from the dialogues. Responses have been made at the highest levels to the Anglican/Roman Catholic *Final Report,* and the World Council of Churches *Baptism, Eucharist and Ministry.* Other dialogues, like the Lutheran/Catholic Dialogue are presenting very concrete proposals for moving forward in new steps toward visible unity.

A considerable theology has developed around the question of "reception" in the new context of documents created outside of full communion with the Roman Catholic Church, but with full officially delegated Roman Catholic participation. How the issues of response, reception, and other steps forward in the ecumenical movement are finally decided are points for future development. Various suggestions have been made by bishop's conferences and by specific dialogues to aid these next steps. A much clearer theological understanding of "reception" will be necessary, but a good beginning has taken place with this statement by Cardinal Willebrands: "In *Catholic understanding* reception can be circumscribed as a process by means of which the People of God, in its differentiated structure and under the guidance of the Holy Spirit, recognize and accept new insights, new witnesses of truth and their forms of expression because they are deemed to be in the line of the apostolic tradition and in harmony with the *sensus fidelium*—the sense of faith living in the whole People of God—of the Church as a whole. Because such witnesses of new insights and experiences are recognized as authentic elements of apostolicity and catholicity, they basically aim at acceptance and inclusion in the living faith of the Church. The decree on Ecumenism of Vatican II says that divisions among Christians make it more difficult for the Church to express in actual life her full catholicity in all its aspects (U.R. 4). In its

full form reception embraces the official doctrine, its proclamation, the liturgy, the spiritual and ethical life of the faithful, as well as theology as systematic reflection about this complex reality" (Toronto, July, 1984). What is becoming clear is that certain stages short of full communion are necessary, like the arrangements between the patriarchate of Antioch (Oriental Orthodox) and John Paul II.

Further pastoral provisions will be necessary for dealing with the local situations, which are consistent with the level of faith the dialogues recognize. The role of the local church and bishops' conference in participating in the theological judgments on these ecumenical documents is gradually emerging.

Likewise, institutional creativity in various episcopal conferences and dioceses is contributing to the worldwide ecumenical understanding of the Roman Catholic Church. Parish covenants and covenants between dioceses and non-Catholic dioceses or presbyteries are showing institutional ways of moving forward, while keeping faith with the worldwide character of the Roman Catholic community. Changing attitudes in pastoral patterns on ministering to ecumenical marriages, cooperating in education and even worship practices are being researched by the National Association of Diocesan Ecumenical Officers (NADEO) in collaboration with the Commission on Regional and Local Ecumenism of the National Council of the Churches of Christ, USA, and the Episcopal Diocesan Ecumenical Officers Association (EDEO). As more progress is made in the dialogues, new problems and new challenges are surfacing.

One of the challenges to the ecumenical movement in the U.S. is the worldwide character of Roman Catholicism. In the United States, there is a network of diocesan ecumenical officers (NADEO) that provides pastoral and sometimes theological studies to be of service to the Bishops' Conference and the local bishops and to clarify developments on the local level in the ecumenical movement. The situation of the ecumenical movement in the Latin American world is complicated by the preponderance of evangelical and pentecostal Christians there who are more dominant and less ecumenical than the historic churches with whom the Church is in dialogue. For this reason, Latin American Catholics are often more suspicious of the ecumenical movement than are their North American coreligionists. The type of Protestantism they experience is quite different from that experienced by ecumenical Catholics in North America. Catholic communities in Asia, Africa, and behind the Iron Curtain likewise present very different situations.

The mass of dialogical material available as a result of the officially commissioned conversations becomes overwhelming. The educational task before the Catholic schools, parishes, seminaries and other institutions for forming pastoral agents requires consistent attention in order to assimilate the developments and their eventual implications. Furthermore, communities with whom there are no major dialogues, like the Pentecostals and conservative evangelicals, become an important priority even where there are no clear models for ecumenical progress. The few dialogues that have attended to ethical issues are very important in the U.S. context where the environment tends to be charged by social and personal ethical commitments in a way that can inhibit the ecumenical progress based on sacramental and doctrinal convergences.

The central element in Roman Catholic developments towards an ecclesiology appropriate to the ecumenical movement is a trinitarian, Christocentric spirituality in which the focus is on Jesus Christ and the action of the Holy Spirit, and which is open to God's direction of the pilgrim people in history. Recognizing the mystery of the risen Christ in the world as larger than Roman Catholic experience at this moment in history leaves Catholic Christians open to enhancing their own identity by ecumenical dialogue and by the evolution that will be necessary within the Catholic Church to remain faithful to its call to be the sacrament of Christ in the world for the sake of the human community.

See **Church, Vatican II**

Harding Meyer and Lukas Vischer, Eds., *Growth in Agreement: Reports and Agreed Statements of Ecumenical Conversations on a World Level,* New York: Paulist and Geneva: World Council of Churches, 1984. William Rusch, *Ecumenism: A Movement to Church Unity,* Philadelphia: Fortress, 1985. Thomas Stransky and John Sheerin, Eds., *Doing the Truth in Charity,* New York: Paulist, 1982. W.A. Visser't Hooft, *The Genesis and Formation of the World Council of Churches,* Geneva: World Council of Churches, 1982. Geoffrey Wainwright, *The Ecumenical Moment: Crisis and Opportunity for the Church,* Grand Rapids: Wm. B. Eerdmans, 1983.

JEFFREY GROS, FSC

ELDER

A literal translation of the Greek *presbyteros.*
See **Priest**

ELECTION

The term used to refer to the act by which God chooses a people (Israel in the OT, the church in the NT) as the objects of his special revelation, love, and care.
See **Grace, Israel, Predestination**

ENHYPOSTASIA

The term used in Christology to refer to the fact that the human nature of Christ does not have its own created subsistence or *hypostasis* but subsists in the *hypostasis* of the divine Word.
See **Hypostasis, Jesus Christ**

ENLIGHTENMENT

In response to his own question, "What is Enlightenment?", Immanuel Kant wrote in 1784 that it "is man's release from his self-incurred tutelage." For Kant, the guiding principle of Enlightenment was the use of individual critical reason without direction from any external authority and without deference to tradition. In his choice of the admonition, "have courage to employ individual reason," as the motto of Enlightenment, Kant captured the set of attitudes and ideas which inspired the most advanced thinkers in eighteenth century western societies. These cosmopolitan intellectuals and men of letters rebelled against their spiritual and cultural inheritance and saw themselves as the heralds of a modern age in which humanity would emerge from a prehistory of immaturity and servility. In the century of Enlightenment, then, autonomous secular reason subjected the theological, philosophical, moral and devotional components of the christian tradition to a radical critique. And while there were predictable variations in the range and depth of this critique, the enlightened thinkers generally repudiated theological and metaphysical inquiry in favor of an almost exclusive concentration on inner worldly horizons.

The profound cultural upheavals, which occurred in the preceding centuries, prepared the ground for the emergence of the distinctive mentality of the Enlightenment. In particular, the disruption caused by the Reformation, the recovery and exploitation of ancient skeptical arguments, and the increased awareness of civilizations which had not been touched by European influences poses new and disturbing questions in the religious, philosophical and moral domains. Again, various strands in the cultural ferment of the Renaissance emphasized human autonomy and self-sufficiency to such an extent that the traditional conception of man's contingent and created condition was eroded. The theoretical and practical repercussions of the scientific revolution also challenged traditional perspectives on man's place in nature and his status in the totality of being. Finally, the skeptical crisis of the sixteenth and seventeenth centuries, the provocative humanism of the Renaissance, and the new mechanistic cosmology weakened the theological and metaphysical foundations of christian ethics.

It was the vague and often ambivalent synthesis of the English philosopher, John Locke (1632-1704), which inaugurated the Enlightenment and established the contours of all subsequent developments. Locke's critical empiricism and naturalism, his antipathy to speculative theology and metaphysics, his vindication and extension of the new scientific method, his defense of individual rights, and his constant recourse to utilitarian and hedonistic criteria evoked a sympathetic response throughout the Enlightenment. Although Locke did not explicitly reject divine Revelation, his critical standpoint effectively emptied Christianity of its supernatural content and prepared the way for the attenuated deistic theology of his immediate successors and the anti-christian polemics of more uncompromising thinkers. Likewise, Locke's sensationalist psychology, and his characteristic indecision on the nature and identity of the person, laid the foundations for the reductionist and materialist systems of the later Enlightenment. Furthermore, whereas classical and christian ethics considered the order of human existence in the light of a final end or supreme good, Locke's moral philosophy almost excluded any orientation to a final end and concentrated instead on a psychology of passion according to which pleasure and utility were the criteria of value. More than any other thinker, Locke was the inspiration for the Enlightenment's break with traditional attitudes and ideas and for the confident assumption that critical and pragmatic reason could bring about a decisive change in the conditions of existence at both the individual and social levels. It is not surprising therefore, that the critical philosophy of Locke—and the equally prestigious physics of his compatriot, Isaac Newton—exercised a profound influence on the French *philosophes* who were the most adventurous thinkers of the Enlightenment. The radicalization of the Lockean program is evident in a characteristically succinct statement of one of the most prolific and influential of the *philosophes*. "What our eyes and mathematics demonstrate," Voltaire asserted, "we must take as true. In all the rest we can only say: we are ignorant." But it was in the materialist and determinist systems of such thinkers as d'Holbach and La Mettrie, and in the skeptical naturalism of the Scottish philosopher, David Hume, that the most extreme conclusions were drawn from Locke's premises. It was in this context too that the momentous project of extending the Newtonian scientific method to all levels of reality was conceived. From the beginning, therefore, the "human sciences" of psychology, sociology and political economy were marked, not only by a mechanist and naturalist outlook, but also by the enlightened assumption that the imperfections and inequalities of existence could be gradually eliminated.

Predictably, the critical, pragmatic, scientific mathematical and progressive currents, which formed the mainstream of the enlightened worldview, were themselves subjected to criticism in the volatile intellectual climate of the age. The often facile rhetoric and narrow rationalism of the anti-christian polemics were countered by numerous defenders of the religious and theological traditions. And although the leading intellectuals were united in their opposition to the christian tradition, they frequently disagreed among themselves on the strategy and tactics which would bring about the required changes. It is significant also that the seeds of the Romantic reaction against the enlightened mentality were sown in the period when this mentality was ascending and that Immanuel Kant, who was himself an enthusiastic exponent of the Enlightenment, reacted against what he saw as the superficial materialism and exaggerated optimism of the age. Despite the variations and disagreements which occurred in the Enlightenment, it nevertheless posed the most formidable challenge, not only to Christianity, but to the possibility of any religious or metaphysical interpretation of existence.

Ernst Cassirer, *The Philosophy of the Enlightenment*, Princeton U. Press, 1951. Lester G. Crocker, *An Age of Crisis: Man and World in Eighteenth Century French Thought*, Baltimore and London: The John Hopkins Press, 1959. Peter Gay, *The Enlightenment: An Interpretation*, 2 Vols., London: Wildwood House, 1973. Norman Hampson, *The Enlightenment*, Harmondsworth: Penguin Books, 1976. Paul Hazard, *European Thought in the Eighteenth Century*, trans. by J. Lewis May, Harmondsworth: Penguin Books, 1965. Basil Willey, *The Eighteenth Century Background*, Harmondsworth: Penguin Books, 1972.

GERALD HANRATTY

EPICLESIS

Introduction

The eucharistic epiclesis, to which this article limits itself, has received renewed attention in these days of ecumenical dialogue. For some, to focus on it is theologically myopic. For others, it is a microcosm of theological issues - the role of faith, of the praying assembly, of the ordained and universal priesthood and of the Holy Spirit in the realization of the Eucharist, as well as Eucharistic "real" presence.

Historically, the epiclesis has possible

forerunners in the NT and in the Jewish meal *berakoth* or blessings. In the *Apostolic Tradition* (c. 215) of Hippolytus, the epiclesis asks that the Holy Spirit be sent upon the church's offering that those partaking may be gathered together into one and that they be filled with the Holy Spirit for the strengthening of their faith in truth. The fully developed form, however, traditionally contained three elements: 1. an appeal for the Holy Spirit; 2. to transform or sanctify the bread and wine; 3. so that they may benefit those who partake of them worthily. This is the form which this article presupposes.

Theologically, the epiclesis is rich and many faceted. First of all it serves as a reminder of the vital role of the Holy Spirit in the realization of the eucharist. The same Spirit who penetrated Jesus of Nazareth — now the risen, Spirit-filled Lord — is in the process of bringing Christ's work to fulfillment. This Spirit makes the body and blood of Christ, in a sense, capable of achieving its saving effects in the faithful. The Spirit also works in the hearts of the faithful to open them to the action of the sacramental body and blood of the Lord. By making possible the presence of Christ offering himself *and* the acceptance of the assembled faithful, the Holy Spirit enables the full sacramental encounter to take place. It is thus Christ and the Spirit - "the two hands of the Father" - drawing us to new life.

In addition, the epiclesis can serve as a reminder that God realizes the eucharist *for* the assembly, and in particular for the partaking assembly. The ancient texts of the epiclesis almost invariably speak of a transformation of the gifts so that those partaking might receive such benefits as unity, forgiveness, and life in the present and/ or in the eschatological future. This underlines the unity between the transformation of the gifts ("consecration")

and the transformation of the communicating assembly ("communion"). Such a relationship reflects the thought of such classical writers as Thomas Aquinas and Nicholas Cabasilas, as well as modern personalistic thought which sees Christ's "bodily presence" in the eucharist as a means to fuller presence of Christ in his faithful and, in this sense, a transformation of the faithful.

The epiclesis also brings out the fact that God realizes the eucharist *through* the believing assembly. That it is God who takes the initiative, that God remains absolutely free and sovereign in realizing the eucharist, is undeniable. It is also undeniable that the church plays a role, however subordinate, in the realization of the sacrament. Without the church's faith there is no sacrament and no sacramental encounter. The epiclesis affirms that it is normally, ideally, the faith of the church here and now present, i.e., the local assembly, which shares in the realization. It does so, however, by *praying*. In the epiclesis the assembly, having recalled the events of saving history and having made thankful acknowledgment of these events, confesses its own helplessness. It appeals to God to act upon the bread and wine in view of those about to partake of them. The assembly appeals to God to transform both the gifts and the communicants so that this celebration of the eucharist may bring about a mutual eucharistic presence.

The epiclesis, and the theology implied therein, thus tends to broaden the context in which eucharistic or "real" presence is viewed. In the liturgical sphere this takes place by viewing, as patristic writers often did, the entire eucharistic prayer as "consecratory." Within this consecratory eucharistic prayer one would then see two high points or essential moments, viz., the institution narrative and the invocation of the Holy Spirit or the epiclesis. Within the Roman Catholic tradition, Odo Casel, for example, argued for this approach as early as the first quarter of the twentieth century as did the *Faith and Order Studies 1964-67* more recently.

In the theological or more speculative sphere, a number of theologians, while not denying an ontological change, are suggesting a more personalistic approach to "real presence," i.e., an approach which uses as the basic analogy the intersubjective relationship between two persons rather than the change of one physical substance into another. Such an approach stresses the ultimately reciprocal nature of "real presence" and thus makes it more difficult to pinpoint the exact moment in which this reciprocal or mutual presence takes place.

There is a clear tendency, then, in both liturgical and theological spheres to de-emphasize the "moment of consecration." This is helpful, since the "moment of consecration" has been a constant stumbling block to a satisfactory solution of some vital questions raised by the eucharistic epiclesis.

Pastorally, one might look at the need for an epiclesis, its position in the eucharistic prayer and some modern attempts at expressing this prayer. As to the need, there can be no doubt that the intervention of the Holy Spirit is absolutely necessary. Nor can there be any question that the assembly, while playing a necessary role in the realization of the sacramental encounter, must always approach the eucharist as a *praying* assembly, acknowledging its own helplessness, appealing for the realization here and now of God's promises, while believing firmly that God will answer its appeal. In other words, the "epiclesis attitude" is also an absolute necessity in the realization of the eucharist, even when it is not made explicit in an epiclesis proper. It belongs to the nature of human beings, however, to give some expression to their deepest beliefs and feelings or risk having them stagnate. It would seem, therefore, to be a *practical* necessity for the eucharistic assembly to express its awareness, for instance, of the need for the intervention of the Holy Spirit and its own need for a praying or epicletic attitude. Otherwise, it risks having this awareness stagnate or fall into the oblivion of forgetfulness. The epiclesis proper is not the only means of expressing these important aspects of the eucharistic celebration, but it is a preeminent one—historically and theologically. This is one reason modern eucharistic prayers have included an epiclesis proper.

Where should it be positioned? One cannot exclude the possibility of placing the epiclesis, or part of it, before the institution narrative. Nevertheless, the weight of evidence favors a position after the institution narrative. Two reasons seem particularly forceful. First, such a position would emphasize the basic helplessness of the assembly in the realization of the eucharist and thus help avoid a magical understanding of the words of institution. Positioning the appeal for the transformation of the gifts before the institution narrative, on the other hand, could allow the impression that the "magic" words of institution are alone responsible for the realization of the eucharist. Secondly, such an arrangement would avoid a split epiclesis, i.e., one in which the appeal for the transformation of the gifts is separated from the appeal for the benefits to those partaking in the gifts. The split epiclesis sacrifices one of the traditional advantages of the epiclesis proper, viz., its ability to underline the unity between "consecration" and communion.

Finally, a study of modern American attempts at expressing the epiclesis is revealing both liturgically and theologically. Our starting point is the epiclesis in the early christian eucharistic prayers.

While in no way being an inflexible norm, these texts can serve as a basis for comparison. In them some general characteristics are evident. One is the reference to some change in the bread and wine in the direction of Christ's body and blood. Another is the frequent appearance of the eschatological dimension and the rich variety of "other benefits." Finally, there is almost invariably a reference to partaking of the gifts.

The epiclesis in the *Book of Common Prayer* seem to exhibit no significant variances from this pattern. One might simply note that had the term "word" been left as Cranmer intended it, as a reference to the institution narrative rather than the incarnate Word, we might have a compromise form which would draw us closer to the early christian emphasis. This viewed the eucharistic prayer in its entirety as "consecratory," with two high-points—the institution narrative and the epiclesis.

The Lutheran epicleses reveal a significant variation. There is no reference to a change of the bread and wine into the body and blood of Christ. This element is characteristic of most early epicleses. Is its absence due to an emphasis on the institution narrative as "consecratory" or a desire to avoid the implications of certain terms—or both? On the other hand, the Lutheran prayers show a strong sense of the eschatological dimension.

The Methodist epicleses reveal an emphasis on calling down the Spirit upon the people. The eschatological note is missing in the first six Great Thanksgivings but is present in the next sixteen—mainly because they use number seven as a prototype. The text made official in May 1984 has a strong eschatological emphasis and is probably the most complete resumé of elements traditionally associated with the epiclesis. It also forcefully underlines the transformation of the gifts as well as the assembly.

The Presbyterian prayers also show a great awareness of the calling down of the Spirit upon the people as well as the gifts. The eschatological dimension is lacking in most of the epicleses. The option to say the institution narrative with the breaking of the bread—thus placing the epiclesis before the institution narrative—is a significant variant from the ancient pattern.

The Roman Catholic pattern is perhaps the most problematic when compared to the early christian epicleses. Here we find the stress on the unity of those partaking which is common to many of the modern epicleses and a good number of the ancient ones. The "split" epiclesis, however, is found only in the Alexandrian type of earlier prayers and is an isolated phenomenon among more modern ones. Most probably this is a vestige of the old (but *not* ancient) "moment of consecration" problem and the fear that mentioning a change in the gifts *after* the institution narrative would somehow rob the latter of its consecratory power.

Unfortunately, this pattern has several disadvantages. It neglects the stronger of the ancient traditions. It also interrupts the flow of the narration of the wonderful things God has accomplished in creation and in history. It fails to emphasize the basic helplessness or praying attitude of the assembly and thus fails to help avoid a "magical" notion of the institution narrative. Finally, as mentioned above, this pattern could rob the epiclesis of one of its greatest strengths, viz., the ability to underline the unity between "consecration" and communion. The fact that this pattern continues to be normative for Roman Catholic eucharistic prayers invites serious reconsideration.

The changing of the gifts into Christ's body and blood finds forceful emphasis in the Roman Catholic epicleses. There is, however, no trace of an eschatological dimension (which appears in the intercessions following the epiclesis) and, besides unity, other benefits to those partaking are extremely sparse.

Obviously, the epiclesis is only one element in the eucharistic prayers and to isolate it is to risk onesidedness. Nevertheless, a comparison of the epiclesis in different traditions is revealing. At times, it shows contrasting mentalities, if not theological biases. At other times, it reveals the fruit of ecumenical dialogue and scholarship. One can only hope that this latter will yield further enrichment for all traditions and lead us closer to that day when Christ's final victory and the unity for which the epiclesis so often prays will become a reality.

See **Anamnesis, Body and Blood, Eucharist**

J.J. Von Allmen, *Worship: Its Theology and Practice,* London: Lutterworth Press, 1965. A. Kavanagh, "Thoughts on the New Eucharistic Prayers," *Worship* 43 (1969): pp. 2-12. R. Ledogar, "Faith, Feeling, Music and the Spirit," *Worship* 43 (1969): pp. 13-23. J.H. McKenna, *Eucharist and Holy Spirit,* Alcuin Club Collections #57, Great Wakering: Maylow-McCrimmon, 1975. J.H. McKenna, "Eucharistic Epiclesis: Myopia or Microcosm?", *Theological Studies* 36 (1975): pp. 265-84. J.H. McKenna, "The Epiclesis Revisited," *Ephemerides Liturgicae* 99 (1985): pp. 314-336. D.C. Smolarski, *Eucharistia: A Study of the Eucharistic Prayer,* New York: Paulist Press, 1982.

JOHN H. MCKENNA, CM

EPIPHANY

The feast of the manifestation or appearing of Jesus Christ. The name derives from the Greek, *epiphania* (manifestation). Among Eastern Christians the feast is also called *theophaneia,* the appearing of God. The date for the feast is January 6.

The origins of Epiphany are obscure, but probably associated with a celebration of the Incarnation as a whole. Egyptian Gnostics may have celebrated a feast of the Baptism of Christ on this date in the second century. For the Egyptian tradition the baptism has been the main content of the feast. On the other hand,

Clement of Alexandria (early third century) regarded January 6 as the birth date of Jesus, perhaps calculating this date from April 6, taken as the date of Christ's death and also his conception. At one time most scholars considered January 6 to be the date of an old Egyptian winter solstice, much as December 25 had been in the West, but this theory has recently been overturned by Thomas J. Talley.

In other parts of the eastern Mediterranean Epiphany was the nativity feast of Christ. This was the practice of the fourth century Jerusalem (including Bethlehem) church according to the Old American Lectionary. The Jerusalem church did not adopt the December 25 nativity feast until the fifth century, and following its earlier practice the Armenian church has never done so. By the end of the fourth century most churches of the East had accepted the western Christmas and assigned January 6 as the feast of the Baptism of Christ. This date was an important day for baptism in the Byzantine church, which still has a blessing of water on this feast.

At the same time as the western Nativity feast of December 25 was being adopted in the East, Epiphany was accepted as a feast in the western churches. At first it seems to have been the feast of the three miracles (*tria miracula*): the visit of the Magi, the baptism of Christ, and the wedding feast at Cana. This original western content is still evident in the antiphon for the Gospel Canticle (*Benedictus*) at morning prayer in the Roman Catholic Liturgy of the Hours. Eventually, however, the Roman rite concentrated solely on the visit of the Magi as the content of the feast, assigning the baptism to January 13.

In the current Roman calendar January 6 has been retained as the date for the feast in countries where Epiphany is a holy day of obligation. In all other places Epiphany is celebrated on the Sunday following January 1. The liturgical readings assigned for this solemnity (Isa 60:1-6; Ps 72; Eph 3:2-3, 5-6; Mt 2:1-12) all point to the wider manifestation of Christ incarnate to the whole world.

See **Baptism, Jesus Christ**

Thomas J. Talley, *The Origins of the Liturgical Year,* New York: Pueblo, 1986.

JOHN F. BALDOVIN, SJ

EPISCOPACY

See **Bishop**

ESCHATOLOGY

Eschatology in the minds of many is understood to refer to the study of the last things (*Eschata*), namely death, judgment, heaven, hell and the second coming of Christ. Within this perception, eschatology appears as an appendix to the rest of theology. However, from a historical point of view this description of eschatology is derivative, coming from broader and more biblical understanding of eschatology which is founded on the Christ-Event: the announcement of the coming reign of God, the public ministry of Jesus, the death and resurrection of Jesus, and the outpouring of the Spirit. In the first century of Christianity the "end of time" was understood to have been anticipated in the death and resurrection of Jesus; the "last days" have been inaugurated by the outpouring of the Holy Spirit. This primary meaning of eschatology should be the basis of any particular understanding of death, judgment, heaven, hell and the second coming of Christ.

In the course of the history of theology these two aspects of eschatology have tended to become detached. As a result it is possible to detect the existence of at least two different strands of eschatology, the one focusing on the destiny of the individual with graphic accounts of the hereafter in terms of heaven, hell and purgatory, and the other attending to the collective destiny of the world—natural and human—in terms of the general resurrection of the dead and the dawning of a New Creation. These two eschatologies, individual and collective, must be kept together in any adequate theological treatment of the last things.

The twentieth century has witnessed something of an "eschatological renaissance in christian theology" (C. Braaten "The Kingdom of God and Life Everlasting," *Christian Theology: Introduction to its Traditions and Tasks,* ed. P. Hodgson and R. King, Philadelphia: Fortress Press, 1982, p. 275). A major factor influencing this rediscovery of eschatology has been the biblical renewal in christology. Karl Barth points out that "Christianity that is not entirely and altogether eschatology has entirely nothing to do with Christ" (K. Barth, *The Epistle to the Romans,* London: Oxford University Press, 1933, p. 314). This renewal in eschatology in turn is having an important influence on the rest of theology. J. Moltmann maintains: "The eschatological is not one element *of* christianity, but it is the medium of christian faith ... Hence eschatology can not really be only a part of christian doctrine. Rather, the eschatological outlook is characteristic of all christian proclamation, of every christian existence and of the whole church." (J. Moltmann, *The Theology of Hope,* London: S.C.M. Press, 1967, p. 16). As a result eschatology in this century is exercising an important critical function in regard to the whole of theology, especially in areas of christology, ecclesiology and liberation theology. However, before we can gather the fruits of this renewal in twentieth century eschatology we need to review the origins and development of eschatology. The first part of this article will concentrate on the biblical origins and the history of eschatology, and the second part will pull together some of the emerging insights of twentieth-century eschatology.

Biblical and Historical Background

Old Testament Eschatology. The OT is an appropriate point of departure for any overview of eschatology, not simply because it helps us to understand the NT better, which it certainly does, but also because it introduces us into a world of symbol, myth and metaphor which is the primary language of eschatology. Further, many of the concerns of OT eschatology as we shall presently discover, overlap with the concerns of twentieth-century eschatology.

In broad outline it is possible to detect the presence of different forms of eschatology in the OT. On the one hand there is a strongly prophetic eschatology. The future promised by the prophets is a future about life in this world: an end to poverty and injustice among the chosen people, the creation of peace on earth among nations, and the introduction of a new harmony between people and nature. On the other hand there is within late Judaism the gradual emergence of an apocalyptic eschatology, an eschatology that is primarily other-worldly in its concerns. Within apocalyptic eschatology there is an emphasis on the transformation of this world into a new reality.

From the eighth century onwards the prophets begin to point towards a time in the future when Yahweh will judge Israel and the rest of the world. This time is known as the "day of the Lord," a time of upheaval and destruction as well as a time of renewal and return to the ways of Yahweh. One way of describing this imminent future is to employ the ancient myth of a struggle between good and evil, between the God of life and the black monster from the deep. This myth is used in the biblical account of creation and in the eschatology of the prophets. In both instances God overcomes the forces of evil and darkness. One of the prophets in the Book of Isaiah predicts: "In that day the Lord with his hand and great and strong word will punish Leviathan, the fleeting serpent ... and he will slay the dragon that is in the sea" (Isa 27:1). At the same time: "On this mountain the Lord of hosts will make for all peoples a feast of fat things, a feast of wine ..." (Isa 25:6-8).

It is this victory of Yahweh over the forces of evil that is the basis of the promise of a new creation in this life. The theme of a new creation, developed after the Babylonian exile, is a statement of dissatisfaction about the world as it is and an expression of hope that this world will be changed by Yahweh: "For behold, I create new heavens and a new earth, I will rejoice in Jerusalem and be glad in my people; no more shall be heard in it the sound of weeping and the cry of distress" (Isa 65:19). Clearly, the eschatology of the prophets which is a major part of OT eschatology is *this-worldly*, with little or no reference to what we today would call the next life. Hope is centered in what will be done in this life by way of divine intervention on behalf of the people of Israel. This action of Yahweh will bring about the restoration of Israel to its former position of power and glory among the nations.

Within this vision length of days is interpreted as a blessing of Yahweh and short life as a curse to be overcome in the future. For the prophets, Yahweh is at the center of *this-worldly* eschatology; Yahweh is the one who will in the future change our world into a better place to live. It is Yahweh alone who can make good a world that has gone astray through the failure of people to be faithful. In addition, the prophets focus their eschatology on the future of the people as a whole rather than simply on the individual.

This prophetic eschatology of the OT is taken up in the second century B.C. and changed into a new movement called apocalypticism. The word apocalypse means a special kind of revelation, usually given in symbolic and dramatic language which requires the interpretation of an angel. The main example of apocalypse in the OT is given in the Book of Daniel which was written during the Maccabean crisis. During that time, the Jews were persecuted under the reign of Antiochus IV Epiphanes; Jewish laws and practices were suppressed; many were put to death as martyrs for practicing their religion. Within this context the author of the Book of Daniel raises the question of a reward for the righteous. For the first time in Judaism the possibility of life beyond death is explicitly affirmed: "And many of those who sleep in the dust of the earth shall awake, some shall live forever, others shall be an everlasting horror and disgrace. And those who are wise shall shine like the brightness of the firmament; and those who lead the many to justice shall be like the stars forever." (Dan 12:2-3).

What is significant here in the late emergence of apocalyptic thought within Judaism is the explicit hope for some form of existence beyond this world. This new dimension of Jewish faith points beyond life in this world, implicitly critiquing a purely prophetic, this-worldly form of hope. Once again the victory of Yahweh over the beast and the conquest of evil by the forces of good are affirmed—but now in a manner that goes beyond life in this world. This new faith and hope in some kind of life after death develops in subsequent centuries. By the time of Jesus there is an emerging faith and hope among different Jewish groups in some form of resurrection.

These hopes, both prophetic and apocalyptic, generate a keen expectation that the Lord will come and reign as King among his people: initiating an era of peace and justice, restoring the fortunes of Israel, and bringing about a new alliance between people and nature. The details of this expectation are extremely varied in late Judaism. Yet they coalesce into an expectation summed up in the powerful symbol of the coming Reign of God.

The New Testament Period. These eschatological hopes and expectations make up the atmosphere in which the mission and ministry of Jesus is played out. The over-riding horizon of the life of Jesus is the announcement of the Reign of God: "Now after John was arrested, Jesus came into Galilee, preaching the gospel of God, and saying 'the time is fulfilled, and the kingdom of God is at hand, repent and believe in the gospel'" (Mk 1:14; Lk 4:43). The parables and the miracles of Jesus are about the coming Reign of God into our world.

On the one hand the Reign of God is "at hand" (Mk 1:14-15) and "in the midst of you" (Lk 17:21) according to Jesus. The signs of this presence of the Reign of God are healings and exorcisms: the blind see, the lame walk, the deaf hear, the dead are raised up, and the poor have good news preached to them (see Mt 11:4-5 and Lk 4:18-19). On the other hand the Reign of God is also something straining to be fully realized in the future: Jesus prays "thy kingdom come" (Lk 12:2-4); Jesus intimates a future Reign of God in the parables of growth (Mt 13:18-33); Jesus looks to a time of final judgment and consummation (Mt 25:1-46). Throughout the preaching of Jesus there is a tension between the present and the future, between the visible and the invisible, between the prophetic and the apocalyptic elements of the Reign of God. Thus of all the categories used to sum up the life of Jesus, the one most acceptable and agreeable among commentators is that of Jesus as eschatological prophet

(R. Bultmann, K. Rahner, and E. Schillebeeckx). Jesus is the prophet pointing towards the end: proclaiming the imminence of the Reign of God and the dawning of God's salvation. Further, it is as eschatological prophet announcing the Reign of God that Jesus is put to death. This nearness of the Reign of God proclaimed in word and deed becomes a threat to the political and religious leaders of the day. It is this threat that provokes the death of Jesus on the cross. For the disciples of Jesus, his death on the cross is *the* moment of eschatological crisis. Everything that Jesus had said and done, especially in terms of the coming Reign of God, is called into question.

This crisis of the cross is not annulled by subsequent experiences. Instead, the eschatological crisis of the cross is interpreted apocalyptically as the turning point of history. This can be seen in Matthew's apocalyptic interpretation of the death of Jesus: "And behold, the curtain of the temple was torn in two, from top to bottom; the earth shook and rocks were split; the tombs were also opened and many bodies of the saints who had fallen asleep were raised, and coming out of the tombs after his resurrection they went into the holy city and appeared to many" (Mt 27:51-53). Equally, Mark's association of darkness with the cross and his reference to the tearing of the curtain in the temple from top to bottom also have apocalyptic connotations (Mk 15:33-39).

At the same time it must be acknowledged that it was the new experiences after the death of Jesus that brought out the full force of the eschatological significance of the life and destiny of Jesus. Something new, in terms of presence, peace, reconciliation, power, and the Spirit is now experienced by the disciples from the other side of the cross. This new and transforming experience is interpreted in a variety of different images: exaltation, glorification, living with God, resurrection, ascension, and Pentecost. Among these different interpretations of one and the same experience of the living Jesus in a new form after Calvary, the image of resurrection predominates. The image of resurrection takes over from the other images because of its eschatological and soteriological significance. Within Judaism, resurrection from the dead was one of the important signs of the end of time and the dawning of salvation.

It is Paul who spells out explicitly the eschatological significance of the death and resurrection of Jesus. Paul's eschatology is an explicitly Christ-centered eschatology, beginning with the historical Paul in First Thessalonians which emphasizes the resurrection of Christ and the second coming and then moving to the Deutero-Pauline writing of Colossians, Ephesians and the pastoral epistles. In broad terms Paul argues that the death and resurrection of Jesus inaugurates a new era in history. Something new has been set in motion through the resurrection and the outpouring of the Spirit. Humanity and the world have entered into the final stages and are now moving together towards the end. The general framework of Paul's eschatology is that of the difference between the first and second coming of Christ. The language of this framework is one of contrast between the the aeons. The horizon is the permanent tension that exists between what has already taken place historically in Christ and that which is not yet fully realized.

This eschatology of Paul is closely bound up with his christology and the one cannot be understood without the other. For Paul, Christ is "the fulness of time" (Gal 4:4 Eph 1:10), so that "if anyone is in Christ, he is a New Creation, the old has passed away and the new has come" (2 Cor 5:17). Further, Christ is "the revelation of the mystery which was kept a secret for long ages but is now disclosed" (Rom 16:25, 26; see also Col 1:26; Eph 1:9, 10; Eph 3:4,5; 1 Cor 2;7). Thus the appearance of our Savior Christ Jesus "abolished death, brought life and immortality to light" (2 Tim 1:10). In virtue of this we are now living in "the end of ages" (1 Cor 10:11) and in the "later times" (1 Tim 4:1) so that we are encouraged "to put away the old man, (and to) put on the new man" (Eph 4:22; Col 3:9). Above all, the glorified and risen Christ is "the first born among many" (Rom 8:29; Col 1:18), "the first fruits of those who have fallen asleep" (1 Cor 15:20). A new ontological unity and solidarity has been established between Christ and humanity in and through the resurrection. To highlight this Paul draws a parallel between Adam and Christ: "For as by a man came death, by a man has come also the resurrection of the dead. For as in Adam all die, so also in Christ all shall be made alive." (1 Cor 15:21-22).

It is impossible to develop a wholly consistent and systematic account of eschatology from the Pauline corpus of writings. The strength of Paul's eschatology is that it resists any easy categorization: moving as it does from dialectic (the already into the not yet) to paradox (dying and rising in Christ) to mysticism (being "in Christ"). Yet what is clear is that something new has been introduced into our world by the Christ-Event. This something new, effected through the resurrection and the Spirit of Christ, affects the direction of humanity, history and the cosmos which are now moving together towards the time of fulfillment. Sin and death have been overcome by the cross and replaced by grace and new life in Christ.

The Patristic Period

The concerns of the first few centuries of Christianity within the patristic era are closely connected to those of the first century even though the time between the first and second coming of Christ has been prolonged. They include a preoccupation with the Parousia, the resurrection, judgment and the transformation of the present world order (J.N.D. Kelly, *Early Christian Doctrines,* London: A. and C. Black, 1958/1960, p. 462). These concerns are symbolized in the emergence of two contested and controversial positions within the eschatology of the patristic period: Millenarianism and *Apokatastasis.*

Millenarianism arose out of discussions about the meaning of the second coming of Christ. For many, when Christ does return he will reign on earth with his redeemed followers for a period of one thousand years. Though no longer taken seriously, this particular view of the second coming can be found among a few of the early Fathers.

Another popular outlook among some of the Fathers in the early church was the claim that at some time in the future all things will be restored in Christ and that therefore even hell will come to an end. This outlook, known as *apokatastasis,* is associated with Origen and can be found in varying degrees in Gregory of Nazianzus and Gregory of Nyssa. Although *apokatastasis* was condemned under the influence of Augustine by an edict of Justinian in 543 A.D. and by the Council of Constantinople in 553 A.D., it continues to exercise a cautious fascination among some theologians.

By far the most intriguing and arresting development within patristic eschatology concerns the understanding of death and its relationship to the resurrection. Several Fathers of the early church grapple with the meaning and necessity of death. It is suggested that God invented death as a kind of remedy for sin. Without death, sin is in danger of becoming immortal, whereas with death sin can be removed once and for all. For many, the sinful individual is likened to a flawed piece of art that needs to be reduced to its raw state so that it may be restored to perfection. Theophilus writing about the Fall sometime in the year 180 A.D. gives the following example: "Take some sort of vessel that is discovered to have a particular defect after its completion. It is recast and refashioned so that it becomes new and perfect. A similar thing happens to man through death: he is, if I may put it that way, broken in pieces that he may be found whole and sound at the resurrection." (Theophilus of Antioch, *Ad Autolycum* No. 2, 26 [Sources Chrétiennes, 20, 162-164]). A similar perception of death can be found in Methodius, writing towards the end of the third century in a work on *The Resurrection*. God through death "dissolved man into his primeval matter, in order that, by a process of remodelling, everything blameworthy in him might melt away...for the melting down of the statue ... corresponds to the death...of the body, while the refashioning and restoration of the original material finds its parallel in the resurrection" (taken from W.J. Burghardt "The Eschaton and Resurrection: Patristic Insights," *The Eschaton: A Community of Love,* J. Papin, ed., Philadelphia: Villanova University Press, 197, pp. 203-229 at 211). Thus the breakdown of the individual in death becomes the basis of the breakthrough in resurrection. In this way, it begins to emerge that death is not simply the wages of sin but also the remedy of sin. As such, death is not only a part of the Fall but also an essential element in the story of salvation which terminates in the resurrection.

Eschatology During the Middle Ages. During the medieval period it is possible to detect a series of shifts that were to have a significant influence on the shape of subsequent eschatology. Though some of these shifts took place over centuries, they do add up to a particular theology of the last things during the Middle Ages. At the risk of oversimplification these shifts could be said to include at least the following developments: the particular demands of history begin to overshadow the faraway Parousia; the unified vision of present and future, of body and soul, is broken up into a variety of sharp dualisms, the general and individual resurrections of the dead give way to a strong emphasis on the doctrine of the immortality of the soul. All in all medieval eschatology became highly individualized and largely neglectful of the social dimension of eschatology. Some of these shifts in medieval eschatology can be seen in the developments that are distinctive of the medieval period.

One such development in the late twelfth century is the emphasis given to purgatory as a separate place and state existing somewhere between heaven and hell. While it is true that a sense of purgation and the forgiveness of sins can be found in the biblical tradition (2 Mac 12:43-46; Mt 12:32; 1 Cor 3:10-15) and in the early christian tradition (e.g. through the practice of praying for the dead which was established by the third century), it was only in the twelfth century that the existence of purgatory as a place came into prominence. The Second Council of Lyons (1274) refers explicitly to the doctrine of purgatory, though it carefully avoids any discussion of the question of fire out of deference to the Eastern Church. Less than a hundred years later purgatory was to become fixed in the western imagination through Dante's Divine Comedy. With the rise of interest in purgatory came the development also of an elaborate system of indulgences applicable to those in purgatory. This development was later to become the source of bitter division within the christian tradition.

Another development illustrative of the above shifts in medieval eschatology can be found in the teaching of Pope Benedict XII in the Constitution *Benedictus Deus* (1336). In that document the enjoyment of the Beatific Vision by the souls of the just immediately after death, and the existence of an intermediary state between death and bodily resurrection, are affirmed. The context of this document was a series of speculative sermons given by Pope John XXII as a theologian claiming that the blessed will enjoy the full vision of the triune God only after the general resurrection. Whatever way one adjudicates this not unimportant medieval controversy, it seems reasonable to hold in retrospect that the unified vision of biblical eschatology is diminished.

A third example of the shifts taking place in the medieval period can be found in the teaching of the church at the Fifth Council of the Lateran. That Council affirmed in 1513 the immortality of the soul as a dogma of the faith. The immortality was seen as something that could be proved by reason and found in the scriptures. The contemporary debate about the relationship of the philosophical doctrine of the immortality of the soul to the biblical doctrine of the resurrection of the body is an issue that the Fifth Council of the Lateran as such did not address and therefore should not be seen as settled by that Council. Once again the individualist concern, as distinct from the collectivist concern, of the medieval eschatology becomes quite evident.

These developments in the medieval period reappear to some extent at the time of the Reformation, especially in regard to the doctrine of purgatory. The reformers objected strongly to the possibility of obtaining merit after death through the sale of indulgences and the performance of good works on behalf of the dead. The Council of Trent at its twenty-fifth session reaffirmed the doctrine of purgatory and the value of prayers offered for the dead as something intrinsic to Catholic faith.

Post-Reformation Period. It is probably true to say that very little development occurred directly in the area of eschatology between the time of the Reformation and the twentieth century. What did take place, however, were certain developments in the world of natural and human sciences that were less and less sympathetic to the biblical and theological perspectives of eschatology. A review of these is not possible here, yet some passing account of them will help towards an understanding of the state of eschatology at the beginning of the twentieth century.

The seventeenth century saw the rise of science and the adoption of a mechanistic view of the world. Within this new scheme there took place in the eighteenth century what has become known as "the death of nature" (C. Merchant, *The Death of Nature: Women, Ecology and the Scientific Revolution,* New York, Harper & Row, 1980) and the emergence of a strongly supernaturalistic dualism. Both of these affected eschatology directly in later times. On the one hand the demise of nature placed the natural world outside the influence of eschatology. On the other hand the adoption of a supernatural dualism had the effect of playing down the significance of the element of "the already" and over-emphasizing the "not yet" within eschatology.

These effects are compounded in the Enlightenment of the eighteenth century and the early nineteenth century with its claim to be able to control the course of history and to dominate nature. A secularized form of eschatology moves to the center of the stage with progress, control and domination becoming the new "last things." In effect eschatology is reduced to a kind of naturalistic teleology. Whatever room is left for the eschatological creativity of God's presence is confined exclusively to the outside realm of the supernatural and the next life.

The late nineteenth and early twentieth century felt the impact of the social and industrial revolutions as well as the emergence of the evolutionary hypothesis. Christian faith did not adjust comfortably to these developments. If anything, the christian faith became defensive and introverted. The gap between the natural and the supernatural widened, the split between the sacred and the secular increased, the dualism of body and soul became more marked, and the separation of this life and the next world became more apparent. The possibility of an immanent eschatology was taken over by the myth of unlimited progress, social revolution (Marx) or evolution (Darwin). The potential for change in the world and the promise of unlimited progress become the object of a this-worldly hope. Thus Ernst Troeltsch could write at the beginning of the twentieth century: "The eschatological bureau is closed down" (quotation taken from K. Braaten, art. cit. p. 289). Insofar as eschatology did continue to exist, it operated at a private and individualistic level within theology.

Twentieth Century Eschatology

Vatican II and the 1979 Instruction. In terms of teaching by the Catholic Church we must turn to the documents of the Second Vatican Council and an instruction issued by the Congregation for the Doctrine of the Faith in 1979. Vatican II did not develop a formal eschatology as such. Yet it does deal with eschatological issues in its *Dogmatic Constitution on the Church* and its *Pastoral Constitution on the Church in the Modern World.* Both documents reflect some of the fruits of the renaissance in eschatology that have been taking place in the twentieth century.

The Constitution on the Church devotes a chapter to "The Eschatological Nature of the Pilgrim Church and her Union with the Heavenly Church" (48-51). This chapter begins with a description of the future in terms of the restoration and reestablishment of all things in Christ: "The final age of the world has already come upon us" through the work of the risen Christ .. and his life-giving Spirit. "The renovation of the world has been irrevocably decreed and in this age is already anticipated in some real way" (48). Article 49 goes on to affirm a close union between the living on earth and the saints in heaven. It points out that the saints in heaven help to build up the church and to make intercession with the Father on behalf of the living. Article 50 reminds us that the "Church from the very first ages of the christian religion has cultivated ... the memory of the dead" and always encouraged prayers for the dead. In particular the church venerated the saints and the blessed Virgin Mary in heaven: imploring their help and being inspired by their lives. Finally, article 51 notes the existence of a vital solidarity of the church on earth with those "who are in glory or who are still being purified after death." This section concludes by noting that in our worship here on earth "we are responding to the deepest vocation of the Church and partake in a foretaste of the liturgy of consummate glory."

In the *Pastoral Constitution on the Church in the Modern World* there are two articles on eschatology which are significant because they locate the importance of human efforts to build a better world and the struggle for justice within the overall eschatological plan of God. Article 38 begins by saying that Christ through his life, death and resurrection sums up the meaning of history. The same Christ is now at work in the world through the energy of his Spirit, enabling people to look to the future with hope and at the same time animating people to work in the here and now towards that future. Some are called to witness to the next life *and* some are called to "dedicate themselves to earthly service . . . and to make ready the material of the celestial realm." Article 39 states explicitly that "the expectation of a new earth must not weaken but rather stimulate our concern for cultivating this one." Why? Because human efforts to build a better world are "able to give some kind of foreshadowing of the new age." To be sure, the Council points out, there is a difference between earthly progress and the growth of the Kingdom of God. Yet, if this earthly progress "can contribute to a better ordering of society," then "it is of vital concern to the Kingdom of God" because one day we will find the values of the human enterprise "freed of stain, burnished and transfigured."

This teaching of Vatican II on eschatology is remarkable for the way it overcomes the separation of individual and social eschatology, links the present and the future, and establishes a unity between the earthly and the heavenly.

In 1979 the Congregation for the Doctrine of the Faith issued an instruction "On certain questions concerning eschatology." The context of this document would seem to be certain controversies, mostly in Germany, surrounding the anthropology and language of traditional eschatology. In general this document reaffirms the faith of the church in regard to eschatology: the resurrection of the whole person, the subsistence of the "human self" after death, the practice of praying for the dead, the second coming of Christ, the bodily assumption of Mary, eternal punishment for the sinner, and the possibility of the purification of the elect before they see God. In particular, the document warns against "arbitrary imaginative representations" which are "a major cause of the difficulties that christian faith often encounters." It also points out that a proper picture of life

after death must acknowledge the existence of a "fundamental continuity" as well as a "radical discontinuity" between the present life and the future. One curious feature about this document from the Congregation for the Doctrine of the Faith is the slight but significant difference between the official text in the *Acta Apostolicae Sedis* (1979, p. 939) and the text published in *Observatore Romano,* 23 July 1979, pp. 7-8. The official texts says that the human self subsists "though deprived for the present of the complement of its body." This statement reflects the traditional view that the general resurrection of the dead takes place only at the end of time. In contrast, the text in *Observatore Romano* omits the clause "though deprived . . .," leaving open the possibility of individual resurrection immediately after death.

Two Examples of Twentieth-Century Eschatology. The rise of eschatology in the twentieth century has been brought about by a number of factors. Triggering off this interest was the important work of Johannes Weiss, especially his book *Jesus's Proclamation of the Kingdom of God* (German Original, 1892). Weiss argued that eschatology was at the very center of first-century Christianity and that if we are to understand the gospel of Jesus we must come to grips with eschatology. This emphasis was taken up and continued by Albert Schweitzer. This biblical focus in turn was complemented by the many questions about the future of humanity arising out of the horrors of two world wars and the Jewish holocaust. Further, the sixties saw the development of different theologies of hope (J. Moltmann, W. Pannenberg), and the seventies the emergence of political theology in Europe and liberation theology in Latin America. In addition, eschatology has been given a new urgency through the result of the real possibility of a nuclear destruction of the human race and the world. A whole new cluster of questions has arisen for eschatology from the possibility of being able to think about what up to now was regarded as unthinkable: a man-made ending of our world and its future. Alongside these developments there has also been the emergence in this century of a new historical consciousness, a new ecological awareness, and a new sense of the solidarity of the human race. In response to these developments, a variety of different eschatologies has emerged. We will sample here two different but complementary examples.

Jürgen Moltmann has pioneered the rediscovery of eschatology in this century, especially through his work *The Theology of Hope* (1967) and numerous other publications (e.g., *The Future of Creation*). For Moltmann eschatology should permeate the whole of theology and should not be left as a single tract coming at the end. Moltmann sees the future as something which breaks in upon the present from above. The future is about advent (*adventus*). The major emphasis in Moltmann is on the future as something radically new and different from the present. The foundation of this particular approach is the God of the scriptures who is first and foremost a God of promises. God has broken into history from above in the past, in the Exodus experience and in the resurrection of Jesus, and God will break into history again in the future. The primary emphasis in Moltmann is upon the category of the future as advent; the future exercises an important and creative influence upon the present. For Moltmann there is a radical break between the present and the future as advent. "Present and future, experience and hope, stand in contradiction to each other in christian eschatology" (*The Theology of Hope,* p. 18; see also p. 143).

In contrast to Moltmann, Karl Rahner grounds eschatology in our experience of the present, especially our christian experience of the present. Eschatology is based on the dynamism of present experience (transcendental revelation) and the particular thrust this experience has received from the gift of the Spirit poured out upon the world through the death and resurrection of Christ (categorical revelation). "To extrapolate from the present into the future is eschatology" (*T.I.* Vol. 4, p. 337). The future is seen as that which brings to fruition what has already been set in motion by the self-bestowal of God's grace in creation (first grace) and the Christ-Event (second grace). For Rahner, the emphasis is placed on the element of "the already" brought about by the Christ-Event and the outpouring of the Spirit. It is only in virtue of God's gracious copresence to the creature in the first instance that we can begin to talk and to hope about the possibility of a consummation of that relationship in the future. Having established this point of departure in eschatology, Rahner is quite careful to acknowledge that there is a radical difference between the present and the future, between historical beginnings and transcendental endings in the *eschaton.*

These two approaches to eschatology should not be counterposed against each other. Instead they should be seen as mutually enriching and complementary. The strength of Rahner's position is the recognition that something new, dynamic and creative has been set in motion by the reality of the crucified and risen Christ. Without this new moment in history, it would be difficult to sustain the confidence and hope in the future that Christians have. Indeed one of the problems with Moltmann's emphasis on the future is that it could give the impression of deferring life's meaning to the future alone, whereas an important element in the christian message is that God is already present and active in our world.

This particular impression is less true of the later writings of Moltmann. On the other hand the strength of Moltmann's emphasis is that it properly locates the future as belonging primarily to the creative love and gracious mercy of God. In this way, Moltmann makes room for the important elements of newness, transformation and unexpectedness in regard to the future. He also brings out the prophetic conflict that can exist between the present and the future, and the consequent implications this has for the political role of the Christian in the world.

These theologies of Rahner and Moltmann have done much to rehabilitate the state of eschatology in the twentieth century. They have certainly brought eschatology to the center of theology. Yet this rehabilitation is itself in need of further refinement on at least two fronts. On the one hand eschatology requires a new and coherent conceptual framework. This framework will have to be in touch with our contemporary experience and understanding of the world. Further, this framework will have to have some compatibility with the inherited tradition of eschatology. On the other hand this new framework will have to be governed by basic principles of interpretation and theological understanding.

The Possibility of a New Framework. One of the basic problems with classical eschatology is that its particular frame of reference belongs to a social and cultural era quite different to the present one. As a result the conceptual mode of expression begins to lose contact with the underlying context of eschatological statements. The mode of signification (*modus significandi*) is no longer in touch with the reality signified (*res significata*). The dualism between heaven and earth, the separation of body and soul, the sharp contrast between this life and the next do not translate adequately our contemporary experience of existence, society and the world. Bernard Lonergan's observation that we have passed from a classical culture to a historical consciousness is particularly applicable to the world of traditional eschatology. Also noteworthy here is the influence of modern science upon the classical framework of eschatology. A further factor, already alluded to, is the impact of the nuclear threat upon eschatology (see G. Kaufmann, *Theology for a Nuclear Age,* Philadelphia: Westminster Press, 1985). Rahner sums up this shift in the following way: "The change in cosmology from ancient to modern times certainly presents a deep-seated problem for eschatological assertions" (*T.I.* Vol. 4, p. 324). Vatican II makes the point: "... the human race has passed from a rather static concept of reality to a more dynamic, evolutionary one. In consequence, there has arisen a new series of problems, a series as important as can be, calling for new efforts of analysis and synthesis" (G.S. 5). A new framework is needed as a first step to provide eschatological statements for theological interpretation. The purpose of such framework is not to provide new information about eschatology as such but rather to present a coherent system capable of mediating the appropriate symbolic meaning of eschatological statements. It would be important that such a framework be able to overcome the individualism and dualisms of much classical eschatology. Equally, it will be important that the framework be able to unify, or at least hold together in creative tension, what we have referred to as the prophetic and apocalyptic as well as the individual and social dimensions of eschatology. Thirdly, this framework should be able to take on board the broad findings of modern science that might inform a contemporary cosmology and anthropology. An exclusively antropocentric view of the cosmos runs the risk of ignoring the place of ecology within eschatology, while an overly ecological eschatology could forget about the unique place of the person within creation.

Such a framework is at present struggling to come to birth through the confluence of many impulses from different areas of life: feminism, ecology, the new physics and process philosophy. Feminism (A. Carr, R.R. Ruether) focuses on the interconnectedness of the whole of life; ecology (J. Cobb, C. Birch) encourages a new relationship between the individual and nature; the new physics (F. Capra, D. Bohm) points towards the dynamic character of all reality; process philosophy (A.N. Whitehead, C. Hartshorne) highlights the permanency of becoming within being. These emphases are beginning to add up to a new vision of life which is described, for want of a better name, as a Post-Modern view of the world (D. Griffin). Within this emerging vision, it is impossible to understand the part in isolation from the whole. An organic unity obtains between the one and the many. A fundamental line of continuity exists between the past, the present and the future. Above all, a strong emphasis is placed on "the obvious solidarity of the universe" (A.N. Whitehead) and the forgotten "roots of all togetherness" (W.H. Auden).

This Post-Modern vision of the world enables us to overcome many of the dualisms of classical eschatology in regard to matter and spirit, nature and humanity, humanity and history, historical process and the Kingdom of God. Because this view of reality is open-ended and unfinished, it is vulnerable to the unifying spirit of Christ presently at work in the world, and the creative love of God that will transform the whole of reality in the fulness of time. In this way a new series of critical correlations can begin to take place between this post-modern view of

our world and eschatology: the unity of the person and individual resurrection, ecology and the new creation, the struggle for justice and the second coming, the historical process and the Kingdom of God, the solidarity of the human race and the general resurrection of the dead. These critical correlations between this emerging post-modern view of the world and eschatology should be able to keep open the important dialogue between the world and Christianity called for by Vatican II (G.S. 4, 5, 36, 62). Within this dialogue eschatology has an important critical and constructive role to play.

By way of conclusion we must outline some principles that might guide the development of eschatology. These principles can be divided into two closely related categories: general principles governing the interpretation of eschatology and theological principles guiding the construction of eschatology.

Principles of Interpretation. The interpretation of eschatological statements needs to be guided by a few basic principles. In the first instance it must be pointed out that eschatological statements are not about the provision of information concerning the future, nor are they about the prediction of events to come, nor do they deal with a sphere of reality that is in any sense empirical. Instead, eschatological statements are a particular interpretation of the potential of human experience, especially human experience that has been shaped by the christian reality of grace and Christ. In the words of the early Rahner, our "knowledge of the future ... is an inner moment of the self-understanding of man in his present hour of existence—and grows out of it" (*T.I.* Vol. 4, p. 331), and more explicitly in the later Rahner "eschatology is man's view from the perspective of his experience of salvation" (*Foundations of Christian Faith*, p. 433). Eschatological statements, therefore, must be grounded and controlled by an appeal to christian experience. The kind of experience in question would include the human experience of being personally incomplete and unfinished, an experience that generates hope, discloses our orientation towards the future as promise, and ultimately reveals our dependence/relatedness/belongingness to the mystery of God as absolute future and fulfilment.

A second principle guiding the interpretation of eschatological statements concerns the language of eschatology. This language is both metaphorical and symbolic as well as dialectical and analogical. Like all theological language, eschatology is significantly limited in its final import. The little we do know about matters eschatological is given to us more by way of negation than by affirmation. The words of the Fourth Lateran Council in 1215 about the relationship between the creator and the creature are particularly applicable to the relationship that exists between human experience and eschatology: "No similitude can be expressed without implying a greater dissimilitude" (D.S. 806). What Aquinas had to say about the mystery of God is also equally valid to the mystery of the *eschaton:* "The ultimate of man's cognition of God is to know that he does not know God" (*De Potentia* q. 7, 5, ad. 14).

A third principle of interpretation for eschatological statements must take account of the critique leveled against eschatology by the modern masters of suspicion (Marx, Nietzsche, Freud), namely that eschatology is a distraction from the pressing problems of this life. In the light of this criticism it must be affirmed that authentic christian statements of eschatology commit us with a new energy and deeper zest for the cultivation of this life in virtue of the christian promises held out for the future. An eschatology that does not take seri-

ously our responsibility for this world is not a truly christian eschatology. Interpretations of eschatology that fall short of this requirement are in danger of becoming ideological and are also at the same time theologically defective. Thus we find the *Pastoral Constitution on the Church in the Modern World* stating: "They are mistaken who, knowing that we have no abiding city but seek one which is to come, think they can shirk their earthly responsibilities" (G.S. 43; see also 39).

Theological Principles of Eschatology

These principles of interpretation must be complemented by equally important theological principles that ought to guide the construction of eschatology. The first of these principles affirms that the person of Christ is the norm and foundation of eschatology. As one author puts it: "The future is an extrapolation of what has already been given in Christ and the Spirit" (H. Berkhoff as quoted by J. Moltmann in *The Future of Creation*, p. 41). It is the crucified and risen Christ who is the hope of the world and the shape of the future to come. The resurrection of Jesus from the dead gives us a preview of the end and an assurance that the world is on its way to a still outstanding future. The resurrection of Jesus is the acorn of the oak tree to come. The resurrection of Jesus is, therefore, the centerpiece of eschatology germinating personal, social, and ecological hope. To this extent eschatological constructions ought to be translatable into christological statements.

A second theological principle of eschatology would suggest that a "red thread" should be seen to run through the doctrines of creation, redemption and consummation. The God of creation is the God of consummation. What God has set in motion in creation, God brings to fulfilment in the *eschaton.* Within creation God calls all human beings to communion (L.G. 13; G.S. 19). This universal calling, this first grace, is the seed of eternal life that is made explicit in Christ, the second grace. This offer of eternal life must be freely acknowledged and cultivated in present existence. Eternal life, therefore, is something that is initiated in this life and not something simply coming at the end of this life, a point emphasized by Pauline (Gal 4:6-7; Col 3:3-4; 2 Cor 1:22; Eph 1:7, 14) and Johannine (Jn 5:24; 17:3) writings. What is all important here is the image of God adopted in our eschatology. The God of eschatology is a God who is personally copresent and coactive in creation and the christian community. The God of christian eschatology is the living God of Abraham, Isaac, Jacob and Jesus, a God of historical covenant and incarnation: Emmanuel. Once this God is allowed to become an outsider God, as has happened in the christian tradition from time to time, then eschatology is reduced to the level of being an appendix to theology.

At the same time the transcendent dimension of this creational and incarnational God within eschatology must also be acknowledged. This brings us to our third and final theological principle for eschatology. In emphasizing the unity between creation, salvation and consummation, the impression must not be given that historical beginnings and eschatological endings exist on the same level or that they coincide. Eschatology goes beyond the action of God in creation and salvation, explicitly affirming the introduction of something qualitatively different, new and transformative in the gift of eternal life. Our hope in the future is not simply about an optimistic development, or progress, or evolution of the present in an unending line. The logic of christian hope is not the logic of inference but rather the logic of imagination. Thus we find theologians cautioning against

understanding eternal life simply as the continuation of this life (K. Barth, *Dogmatics in Outline,* E.T. 1949; J. Moltmann, *The Crucified God,* p. 170) or merely a matter of going on "after a 'change of horses'" (K. Rahner, *T.I.,* Vol. XIII, p. 175). To give this impression would be to ignore the finality of death and to run the risk of playing down the uniqueness of historical existence. Instead, eternal life must be presented in terms of the completion of this life. A new and creative tension between the present and the future, between the already and the not yet, between the known and the unknown, between the present life and eternal life, must be maintained in eschatology. At most we can merely image the promise of new life in Christ to come because "no eye has seen nor ear heard, nor the heart of man conceived what God has prepared for those who love him" in this life (1 Cor 2:9).

See **Reign of God**

Z. Hayes, *What Are They Saying About the End of the World,* New York: Paulist Press, 1983. A. van der Walle, *From Darkness to Dawn,* London: S.C.M. Press, 1984. J. Moltmann, *Theology of Hope,* London: S.C.M. Press 1967. K. Rahner, *Foundations of Christian Faith,* London: D.L.T., 1978, Cht. IX. E. Fontinell, *Self, God, and Immortality,* Philadelphia: Temple University Press, 1986.

DERMOT A. LANE

ESSENCE
See **Nature**

ETHICS
See **Moral Life, Christian**

EUCHARIST

If the Mass is the principal celebration of the christian people, the liturgy of the eucharist is the principal part of the Mass, joined to the liturgy of the word to form one complex of celebration. The very word "eucharist" is one of the earliest names of this form of celebration, and it is itself an indication of the kind of rite it is. The dictionary will tell us that "eucharist" means "thanksgiving." In fact this is the term chosen by the early Christians to translate into Greek the Hebrew word for "blessing." For the Jews, blessing was the basic form of all prayer, but it was applied in a particular way to familiar prayers and rituals with which the pious Jew filled his day. Seen against this background the term "eucharist" is already telling us a lot about the nature and origin of our central christian ritual. From it we learn that the eucharist is essentially prayer and celebration. It is an act of praise and thanksgiving, a movement of worship by which the people respond to the great things the Lord has done for them.

One of the main occasions during the day when the Jew blessed the Creator was at the family meal together. Here the prayer of blessing took the form of a ritual, celebrated in bread as grace before meals, and in wine as grace after meals. In these rituals the prayer was led by the father of the family, with the others responding. In a gathering of a rabbi with his disciples the rabbi would preside in the father's place. These then were the rituals out of which the Lord formed his eucharist. It is striking that, when he came to give a form of worship to his community, he took the external form of that worship, not from the pomp of the temple, but from the familiar rituals of the Jewish home.

Scripture

As we turn to the early eucharistic texts it will be useful to state briefly what this sacrament is. The eucharist is a celebration of christian community as the people commemorate in the rituals of bread and cup the key events from which their community draws its life, namely the death and resurrection of the Lord. Many exegetes find this kind of gathering reflected already in the "breaking of bread" in Acts 2:42 and 46. But the clearest picture of the early eucharist emerges in the four versions of the Lord's institution of the eucharist at the Last Supper: Lk 22:19-20; 1 Cor 11:23-25; Mk 14:22-24; Mt 26:26-28.

It is important to understand the literary genre of these passages. It seems that in composing their gospels, when the evangelists came to their accounts of the Last Supper, they simply incorporated into their narratives pieces of early liturgy in which the origin of the eucharist was commemorated. Consequently these passages are not primarily intended as historical report but as liturgical recital. One might compare them with the way the events of the Exodus are recalled during the celebration of the Passover.

This liturgical approach to the texts helps us to explain the differences between them. These points of contrast reflect different emphases in the early church's theology of the eucharist, within, however, a common tradition and a common framework. In this way too we see that the biblical basis for a eucharistic theology today has to be the eucharistic faith of the early communities reflected in these texts rather than any appeal to the very words and deeds of Christ at the Last Supper. Our theology of the eucharist has to take its stand on the faith of the church, indwelt by the Holy Spirit, as we find it in these early texts, rather than in any historical reconstruction of the institution event, for about the latter little agreement is possible.

Not that nothing can be said historically about the course of the Last Supper. Scholars discuss whether or not the supper was a Passover. While many consider that it was, others concede simply that it was a festive celebration in a paschal context. The only statement attributed to Christ which is generally accepted as historical in its main lines is that in the eschatological saying in Mk 14:25 par. In trying to date the various traditions about the supper, scholars discern in our four versions two main traditions, that in Luke and Paul on the one hand, and that in Mark and Matthew on the other. Sometimes scholars go on to attempt to assign a certain priority in time to one or other of these traditions, but this discussion has not been conclusive. However, the agreement among the four versions of the Institution Narrative that the eucharist was founded at the Last Supper, and the versions' common structure of a celebration in bread and wine referring to Christ's death, do point to an historical nucleus in the ordinary belief of Christians concerning the origin of the eucharist. This is strengthened by Paul's account in particular, since it can be argued that this account goes back at least to the mid 30's. This gives us a date too close to the lifetime of Christ to allow for the emergence of the kind of cultic legend by which skeptics once tried to give an alternative explanation on the analogy of Hellenistic parallels.

For the meaning of Our Lord's words and actions at the Last Supper we come back to the four versions of the institution and to the two kinds of tradition they reflect. Many scholars approach these words and actions through the category of "prophetic gesture" associated with some of the great figures of the OT. These gestures were symbolic actions in which the prophet enacted beforehand some future event which was threatened or promised to Israel. The action of the prophet was understood, not simply to mime the event, but to bring it about. In this way Our Lord's giving of himself through the ritual of bread and cup at the Last Supper could be seen as a prophecy of his self-giving in his sacrifice.

Some of the implications of such a gesture by a prophet can be seen to be referred to by the words in the Lukan and Pauline versions, "Do this in memory of me." The key word here is "memory," which has a very special meaning in the Jewish liturgy of the time. The appreciation of the force of this word "memory" is one of the great discoveries of modern eucharistic theology. It is an insight shared by Catholic and Protestant scholars alike, though with different emphases, and so it represents a breakthrough for ecumenism as well.

The commemoration in liturgy of the great salvific events of their history meant more for the Jews than a mere calling to mind of the things of long ago. God was part of those original events, intervening in history, not only on behalf of the immediate beneficiaries, but in a sense for the whole people and each generation. Consequently, this grace and blessing, won for them in the past, was understood by the succeeding generations to become an actuality for them, particularly when they celebrated those events in prayer and liturgy. For example, the Passover is not only the calling to mind of the Exodus, but it is what we might call its "living memorial," that is to say, a memorial filled with the reality of that which it commemorates. Seen against that background, the words "Do this in memory of me" indicate that the ritual just established by Our Lord is to be understood as the living memorial of the events commemorated there, namely of his sacrificial death and resurrection, which one text describes as his "exodus" (Lk 9:31 in Greek). In this notion of Jewish ritual memorial we have discovered a dimension which lifts the whole biblical theology of the eucharist out from under the shadow of a purely subjective interpretation and gives Catholics and Protestants alike a new basis for approaching the actuality of eucharistic sacrifice and the reality of what we receive in the sacrament.

These sacrificial implications, which are glimpsed only fleetingly in the tradition of Luke and Paul, are brought out into the open in the tradition of Mark and Matthew. Where the former tradition was focused on the eucharist as the celebration of the New Covenant foretold by Jeremiah 31:31-34, Mark and Matthew center their versions on the covenant sacrifice in Exod 24:3-8. In both of these versions the word over the cup is closely patterned on that of Moses in Exod 24:8. In this we see how the Christians of these early communities, when faced with making sense of what they were doing in the eucharist, found help in the explicitly sacrificial categories of the Sinai event. The implication is clear: just as Moses there established the Old Covenant in the blood of ritual sacrifice, so Christ on the cross and in the eucharist seals the New Covenant in a similar way.

However in treating the eucharist and the events of Calvary in explicitly sacrificial terms we must allow for a special nuance of meaning in the minds of the early Christians. This is brought home to us in particular by the Epistle to the Hebrews, but it must have been realized in the community some time prior to that writing. In one way the application of sacrificial categories to the cross and so to the eucharist could only be a kind of metaphor for first-century Jews. Their idea of sacrifice, in the proper sense of the term, was linked too closely to ritual sacrifice in the temple. If the eucharist itself is ritual from the beginning, in Jewish terms it is not a sacrificial ritual. But as a growing christology led them to appreciate more clearly who and what Christ was as Son of God, they came to see that his death on the cross was really the point towards which the whole OT system of sacrifice was leading (Heb 10:10). Because of who and what Christ is in salvation history, his death on the cross belonged to the category of sacrifice

in a proper but unique sense, at once the point of convergence of the ancient sacrificial system and the watershed of all future worship in the christian community. Consequently, when the notions of sacrifice are applied to Calvary and to the eucharist, we must allow that these terms are being used in a unique sense, because grounded in a unique person. Christ's sacrifice is not just an additional instance within the genus "sacrifice." In the light of our christology it appears as really the prime analogate of all sacrifice, what Augustine called the "verissimum sacrificium" (R.J. 1655).

Before concluding the topic of Christ's sacrifice, it only remains to make clear how the resurrection enters in. Inevitably, mention of sacrifice highlights Christ's death on the cross, and this corresponds to the emphasis in each of the institution narratives; it is his love in dying which is offered. But the aspect of resurrection cannot be absent, since, as the Epistle to the Hebrews points out, this event is really equivalent to the second and most important stage in a Jewish sacrifice, when the immolated victim was brought into union with the altar. This then is reflected in the institution narratives in that his death is seen to bear fruit in a new covenant and in the forgiveness of sins. These are indirect testimonies to the victory of Christ, which in the light of the rest of the NT can be identified only with his resurrection. Then there is the mere fact that Our Lord's death is being celebrated at all; this too is an indirect testimony to his resurrection. Finally, if in Paul the eucharist is presented as the proclamation of his death, the horizon of resurrection is opened up by the perspective of the Lord's, that is the risen Lord's, second coming (1 Cor 11:26).

Having considered the eucharist as celebration and sacrifice, we can now turn to the meaning of Our Lord's words over the bread and wine when he identifies them with his body and blood. In the past, theological treatises on the eucharist usually began with this aspect. In taking it up only after the aspect of celebration, theologians are making the point that the context of celebration and worship helps to make the mystery of these words of Our Lord somewhat more understandable. While biblical theology can scarcely be expected to establish by itself the meaning of these words with the clarity and certainty which is found in subsequent teaching on the matter, it can certainly vindicate the claim of the church that its teaching on this mystery has indeed a scriptural basis.

In the history of the understanding of these words of the Lord, two main lines of interpretation may be identified. In one line the words are taken in a purely symbolic way: bread and cup are simply signs of Christ's body and blood. In the second line of approach the words are taken literally: bread and wine are not only symbolic of Christ's body and blood but are somehow identified with them. It simplifies matters if one grants that, taking words by themselves, they are capable of either interpretation. What points towards some kind of literal meaning is the context of cult and sacrifice within which they occur.

If the whole celebration is not only the sign of Christ's death and resurrection but its living memorial, in the sense described above, it fits in that these gifts are not only the signs of Christ's body and blood but that, in some mysterious way, they are indeed what Christ says they are, his very body and his very blood. The identification of Christ's person with the gifts seems an appropriate part of the identification of the whole ritual with the sacrifice of Christ's death and resurrection. In the New Law the offerings of bread, wine, incense, beasts, have all been replaced and fulfilled by the body and blood of Christ offered on the cross. If bread and cup are truly offered in the eucharist, as the words of Mark and Matthew imply, then they can only be in some way identical with that body and blood which are the sole offerings of the New Law. The middle term between bread and wine on the one hand and body and blood on the other is Christ as victim, offered on the cross, with his offering renewed and made available in the eucharist. A Jew enters into a sacrifice by consuming the victim, and so for the apostles the eucharistic gifts would have been a way of entering into communion with the sacrifice of Christ. That this was the way the words over bread and cup were understood in those early liturgies seems confirmed by passages such as 1 Cor 10:16-17; 11:27-32, and by the insistent realism of Jn 6:51-58. The bread and wine have become the body and blood of Christ. In what follows we refer to this mystery as "the eucharistic change."

The Fathers

When we move from the apostolic into the patristic period, we find that the process of developing understanding of the eucharist, already initiated in the NT, continues. This affects both the liturgical setting of the eucharist and the theology on which that liturgy was based. Gradually the familiar meal-character of the eucharist became less pronounced, particularly after the ritual was joined to a regular liturgy of the word (first witnessed in St. Justin, c. 150 A.D.) to form what we call the Mass. The eucharist now belongs to the solemn public worship of the christian community. In other ways, too, cultic aspects of the eucharist are brought out more and more. Cultic terms begin to occur more frequently, such as "sacrifice," "altar," "priest." A particularly significant stage is reached when the eucharist is seen as not only the sacrifice of the whole people (the NT sense) but as one answering the sacrificial needs of the individual. Tertullian's reference to offering the eucharist for the dead would be an early instance of this (*On the Crown* 3). Some have seen this whole cultic development as a deviation, but once one recognizes the acceptance of cultic categories for the eucharist in the institution narrative itself, especially in Mark and Matthew, then these later developments can only be seen as explicating what is implicit in the NT.

The understanding of the eucharistic change also underwent significant development at the hands of the Fathers. In the gospel this mystery had been expressed in what we might call the language of identity, "This is my body." Early on, other forms of language emerged side by side with that of the NT. Very soon there was the language of change: bread and wine *become* Christ's body and blood. This is just beginning in St. Justin (*Apology* I, 66). Later there emerged the language of symbolism.

To appreciate this last we have to set aside a common modern assumption that sign and reality are opposed. In the ancient world this is not necessarily so. Symbolism is realist or ontological. Signs not only signify what they symbolize but participate in the reality itself. As an example we might cite the fourth-century Anaphora of Serapion. In this prayer the bread becomes the "likeness" of Christ's body, the wine becomes the "likeness" of Christ's blood, and the whole eucharistic action is seen as the "likeness of his death." In the mentality of that time these expressions affirm the actuality of Christ's body and blood and sacrifice in the eucharist.

Generally the great eucharistic prayers of the church are a convenient place in which to study the understanding of the eucharist in the patristic period, since so many of the main prayers were composed at that time. From the Canon of Hippolytus at the beginning of the third century these prayers have spoken of the eucharist

as an offering. The sacrificial nature of the celebration is particularly clear in the Roman Canon. Finally the "epiclesis" section of the canons, namely that part which prays that bread and wine become the body and blood of Christ, is a very clear manifestation of belief in the fact of the eucharistic change.

The Middle Ages

In the history of the eucharist in the medieval period four major developments may be singled out. The first, and perhaps the most fundamental one, arose as a result of the passing of the culture of classical times. As that ancient world gave way before the rising influences of the Middle Ages, many of the thought-forms of that world passed away also, and in particular that sense of "ontological symbolism" which we have just described. Platonic thought-forms gradually gave way to Aristotelian ones, and with the loss of the ancient sense of symbolism medieval thinkers lost the key to the sacramental synthesis of the Fathers. Already in the ninth century, in Paschase Radbert (+860), we meet an exaggerated realism, which takes Christ's mode of existence in the sacrament in a crudely physical way. In the eleventh century, in Berengar (+1088) and his followers, we meet the opposite extreme, an exaggerated symbolism, according to which you may call the eucharistic gifts Christ's body and blood, but after the consecration they really remain bread and wine. Such extreme positions inevitably led to controversy in their own day, but they also gave rise to vigorous reflection on this mystery all through the medieval period in a way that would bear significant fruit.

The second significant development concerned the way the Mass was understood. One of the dominant characteristics of medieval piety was a focusing on the historical Christ on earth rather than on the heavenly Christ of the patristic church. In the eucharist this took the form of an emphasis on the passion of Christ. Indeed the Mass was commonly understood as a kind of allegory of the passion. Details of the rite were related to details of the passion in a way that had nothing to do with their objective meaning: for instance, the washing of the celebrant's hands recalled for them the similar action of Pilate. While this popular practice might be deplorable from a liturgical point of view, it made some pastoral sense at a time when the people knew no Latin and had been reduced to the status of silent spectators. It also kept alive some sense of the eucharist as the living memorial of the Christ-event, though it easily suggested to popular piety a notion that the best theology of the time would disown, namely that the Mass was a repetition of the cross.

The most distinctive innovation of medieval eucharistic piety was the development of devotion to the Blessed Sacrament. The reservation of the sacrament was ancient tradition, but originally its purpose was simply communion outside Mass, especially in the case of the sick. From the eleventh century on it began to take the form of exposition, processions, devotion to the tabernacle, and later of benediction. To some extent this development was a compensation for the decline in active participation in the liturgy itself, especially through increasing infrequency of holy communion and through the incomprehensibility of a liturgy in Latin. But this new form of devotion also corresponded to deeper movement in the spirituality of the times, to the new and profound devotion to the humanity of Christ as well as to certain aspects of medieval contemplation and mysticism. It was one of the main factors in giving rise to a new kind of language for speaking of the mystery of the eucharistic gifts, the language of presence.

The agenda for the medieval theology of the eucharist was largely determined by the developments just described. As both controversy and piety focused on the eucharistic gifts in themselves, these came to be treated theologically in isolation from their essential context and sacrifice. The theology of eucharistic sacrifice was not treated systematically to the same extent, and so a certain imbalance in the over-all theology of the sacrament came about.

The central achievement of the medieval theology of the eucharist was the development of a mean position between the two extremes of Paschase and Berengar. Theologians wished to identify a level of being on which one could maintain that a real change of the bread and wine had taken place without getting involved in a crude Paschasian physicalism, from which even the magisterium was not at first immune (D.S. 690). It is important to keep in mind how slowly progress came about, taking about two hundred years in all. It was in the course of this development that the term "transubstantiation" first began to be used, c.1130 A.D., as a way of underlining against the Berengarians the objectivity of the change in the eucharistic bread and wine. Though this general orientation of meaning is clear enough, a coherent, philosophical account of it took a further hundred years to reach formulation. Consequently the term in itself was applied to more than one approach before we find it in the classical sense of Aquinas (1225-1274). Again it was prior to Aquinas, and so in this looser dogmatic anti-Berengarian sense, that the term is first used in the documents of the magisterium (D.S. 782, 802; cf. 700).

For Aquinas the body of Christ was present in the host, not the way a body is ordinarily present in another material reality, namely through the contact of quantity with quantity ("per modum quantitatis"), but rather more like the way the soul is present in the body ("per modum substantiae"). As metaphysical rather than physical, this mode of presence avoids the crude materialism of Paschase. As ontological and objective, it avoids the threat of a pure symbolism.

Aquinas also took the view that the change of bread and wine was implicit in the words of consecration in the eucharist. Those who came after him, especially Scotus (+1308), and those under his influence, had a different notion of metaphysical reality and, as a result, were less sure of this last point. They believed that bread and wine were changed in the eucharist, but they conceded this only because they felt obliged to so so by the teaching of the church, especially that of the Fourth Lateran Council (D.S. 802). Given the way they understood reality, they placed more emphasis in their theology on the notion of presence, and it was from this time on that the expression "Real Presence" begins to predominate in eucharistic terminology.

The Sixteenth Century

In the sixteenth century the story of eucharistic theology reaches the dimensions of a tragedy. This sacrament of unity becomes the sign of conflict between the contending parties into which Christendom is now divided. The Reformer's view of the eucharist can be seen as a more radical development of tendencies already found in medieval theology both as regards eucharistic sacrifice and the eucharistic change. Following the lead of Luther, the Reformers deny the sacrificial nature of the eucharist. For them the Catholic Mass is the very epitome of the "works" which their notion of "faith alone" wishes to exclude. Building on the medieval devotion to the Mass as a memorial of the passion, they reduce the eucharist simply to a subjective commemoration of the cross, not in the sense

of "living memorial" which we found in the NT, but as a nostalgic calling to mind of an event of long ago.

As regards the eucharistic gifts, again building on tendencies in medieval theology, Luther distinguished the aspect of presence from that of change. The Reformers generally were united in denying any change of the bread and wine into Christ's body and blood, but, after that point was made, their paths diverged. Luther personally maintained that the force of the words of the institution narrative required some kind of literal presence of Christ's body and blood in the sacrament. The Lutheran confessions of faith expressed this as Christ's presence "in, with and under" the bread and wine (consubstantiation). At the other extreme, Zwingli held that the bread and wine are simply signs of the body and blood of Christ (pure symbolism). An intermediate view is that of Calvin. For him the bread and wine are effectual means of the grace which flows to us from Christ, who is "in heaven and not here," as the Book of Common Prayer put it. In this view the bread and wine are means of grace much like the water in the sacrament of Baptism, containing within them the power of the heavenly Christ (virtual presence).

The Council of Trent confronted the Reformers as regards both of the main aspects of the sacrament. They first dealt with the eucharistic gifts, condemning as heretical the denial of the change of bread and wine into Christ's body and blood (D.S. 1652), and referring to this change as "transubstantiation." Theologians have discussed the force of this teaching. Does it require of us the full philosophico-theological concept of one like Aquinas, whose language Trent itself employed, or does it simply require the looser, dogmatic sense, corresponding to what is in the Fathers and the great eucharistic prayers? Theologians today generally take it in the latter sense, alleging in support the history of the term "transubstantiation" to which we have referred above.

Only much later did the Council define their position on the question of eucharistic sacrifice. On this point theology was much less developed than on transubstantiation. They did not have a very clear notion of sacrifice; nor did they appreciate the technical meaning of "memory" in the institution narrative in Luke and Paul. They were clear, however, that the doctrine of the Reformers, as it was being presented, could not be reconciled with the tradition of the church, and so they defined that the Mass is a sacrifice in a true and proper sense and not just "a bare commemoration" (D.S. 1753). They also taught, without a formal definition of the point, that the Mass is the same sacrifice as that of the cross, though offered in a different manner (D.S. 1743).

Modern Times

With Trent and the Reformers the lines of division were drawn which have remained the main parameters of the theology of the eucharist until recently. In contemporary reflection two main developments have contributed to a renewal of eucharistic theology, the first coming out of theology itself, and the second arising within the ecumenical movement.

First, a deeper study of the history of doctrine and of the background to the Council of Trent has brought theology to be more aware of a distinction between the basic tradition on the eucharist on the one hand and the formulation of it in Aristotelian terms on the other. This development coincided with a renewed appreciation of the nature of symbolism. For the Fathers of the Church symbols were not seen as signs of the absent but rather as signs of what is present. In line with these developments theologians today are trying to express the mystery of the eucharistic change by invoking a more personalist philosophy and one more in keeping with the new notion of symbol. These attempts are often referred to as "transignification" or "transfinalization." It is important to realize however that these terms designate a style of approach rather than one determinate position. As the medievals with transubstantiation in the twelfth century, theologians today are still exploring this new approach. In his encyclical *Mysterium Fidei,* Paul VI warned that some of these theologians have spoken in a way which cannot be reconciled with points to which the church is committed. But at the same time Pope Paul did not close off this line of enquiry, and in the presentation of the matter to be outlined below an attempt is made to present the mystery in the manner of this new approach, while taking account of the points to which Pope Paul referred.

The second main development of significance in contemporary reflection on this sacrament is the number of Agreed Statements on the eucharist which have emerged within the ecumenical movement. Just as eucharistic theology was at the center of the divisions which occurred in the sixteenth century, so today it is in the vanguard of an ever-growing consensus on a whole range of questions, not only sacramental but also ecclesiological. Four principal documents may be mentioned. That between Catholics and Lutherans in the United States is noteworthy for the way it speaks of Christ's sacrifice in relation to the eucharist. Drawing on the appreciation of the NT meaning of "memory," which we have considered above, it speaks as follows: ". . . in this memorial we do not only recall past events; God makes them present through the Holy Spirit." In this way the NT notion of memory has become basic to all these agreements, and this particular statement of it was to be influential in the preparation of subsequent agreements.

If the Lutheran-Catholic statement made progress by a return to scripture, the agreement between Anglicans and Roman Catholics carried that progress further by turning also to the language of the Fathers and of the liturgy. As well as accepting the new notion of memory, this document is remarkable for accepting the language of the eucharistic prayers to express our faith as regards the eucharistic gifts: "The bread and wine become the body and blood of Christ by the action of the Holy Spirit, so that in communion we eat the flesh of Christ and drink his blood." An agreement between Catholics and Reformed Christians in France, as well as moving along the lines just referred to, is remarkable for accepting as legitimate the custom of reservation of the Blessed Sacrament. Finally, we might notice the influential document of the World Council of Churches, *Baptism, Eucharist, Ministry,* accepted at its conference in Lima, Peru, in 1982. Though the Catholic Church was not involved in this officially, individual Catholics worked on the commission which drew up the document. Of the eucharist as commemoration it says that "it is not only a calling to mind of what is past and of its significance. It is the Church's effective proclamation of God's mighty acts and promises." Concerning the eucharistic gifts we read: "Christ's mode of presence in the eucharist is unique. Jesus said over the bread and wine of the eucharist: 'This is my body . . . this is my blood . . . .' What Christ declared is true, and this truth is fulfilled every time the eucharist is celebrated."

In these statements we can see the churches reaching out to one another in an ever more remarkable consensus concerning truths which once seemed to divide them. As they stand, these statements represent simply the views of the various groups which drew them up. The ultimate judgment on them rests with the various churches to which they have recently been submitted for approval. In the meantime, as we await such acceptance by the churches, the documents have a beneficial effect on church life by making people realize that they are closer to one another than was once thought.

Theological Synthesis

As well as giving an account of the church's doctrine and of its basis in scripture and tradition, theology has as one of its primary tasks the development of an "*intellectus fidei.*" By this we mean a synthetic viewpoint which will both present the main aspects of the mystery in their basic unity and will open the way for spirituality and preaching.

In the case of the eucharist such a presentation could take as its starting-point the notion of sharing, *koinonia.* This word "sharing" not only suggests immediately the ritual setting of the eucharist in the celebration of the "breaking of bread," but it also brings together two basic aspects and movements of the entire mystery. The sharing implies the community which the eucharist strengthens and deepens; but in order to share bread and cup we must divide them, and so "sharing" points to that sacrificial dying to self through which alone true community is possible.

What we are talking about are the two basic movements of christian love: giving and receiving, or, as Our Lord put it, losing life to find life. Christian love means finding life and fulfilment with other people through being unselfish towards them and ever at their service. This was Our Lord's basic program of life (Mt 16:25). He not only preached it but practiced it, bringing it to its climax in the events which crowned his life. The death and resurrection of Jesus are the supreme instance of a person's losing life to find life, and as there is something of Our

Lord's dying and rising present in the dying and rising of daily christian love and service, so his dying and rising are present in a unique way in the church's liturgy.

But there is another level of sharing which we must also keep in mind. The church's liturgy signifies very clearly that the source of our love and community must be sought in Christ and in his redemptive acts. Ultimately their source has to be in the love which passes between Father and Son in the mystery of Trinitarian life. The sharing which is achieved here below is only the outflow of a deeper level of sharing by which God shares life with us, which in turn is an image of the sharing between Father, Son and Holy Spirit, the ultimate source of all sharing. Both as food and as sharing the symbolism of the eucharist is a symbolism about *life*, but the life it signifies is ultimately the life of God, Father, Son and Holy Spirit, shared with us. The traditional image for this is the banquet of the kingdom, for the kingdom and the banquet are really ways of speaking of heaven and of our eternal communion with Father, Son and Holy Spirit. Eternal life with God, and with one another in God, is the overflowing banquet which is the ultimate reality beneath the veil of our eucharistic signs.

Once we see how the eucharistic banquet comes to us from God's own life, we can understand more clearly how our celebration and the community life it expresses cannot be creations of human initiative but are primarily the work and gift of God to us. One of the great signs of that fact lies in the way that the eucharist comes to us only through the church and is totally dependent on the church. As we shall see in looking at the fruits of this sacrament, the eucharist makes and builds up the church, but this is true only if it is first the church which makes the eucharist.

These two mysteries belong intimately to each other, the eucharist and the church. The one is the manifestation of the other, and both of them express, not only our total dependence on God, but also our dependence on one another. We cannot go to God on our own, but only in community with other people, and so we find the eucharist only within the church. The celebrant of the eucharist is really the church. This comes out, firstly, in the way the eucharist presupposes faith and baptism in those who take part, something which has been required by the church from the beginning (*Didache* 9:5). It is in baptism that God's call comes to us to participate in the eucharistic community. Secondly, the eucharist presupposes the sacrament of Orders. Though in one way it is the whole community which celebrates the eucharist, and all present "offer to God the Father the divine victim" (P.O. 5), yet each does it in each one's own way and "in each one's own place" (cf. 1 Clement to the Corinthians, 40). The doctrine of the priesthood of the baptized does not rule out the special role of the ordained. To understand this special role we can follow the suggestion of Vatican II that the priest in the eucharist is the sign of Christ the head and acts in his person (P.O. 2). Without this sign, the congregation remains simply a local assembly, but priest and congregation together mean that the local assembly becomes a sign of the universal body of Christ; together they are an organic sign of the whole Christ, head and members, mediating divine life to the world.

Having seen the eucharist as banquet and manifestation of the church, we are in a better position to understand what we saw to be one of the main points about the eucharist on which the church has come to insist, namely that it is a sacrifice. The banquet and the church are signs to us of the kingdom of God, and that kingdom is the cause for which Christ gave himself in life and death. Sacrifice is first a truth about life before it is a truth about ritual. By his own manner of life and death, as well as by his words, Christ has asked us to understand our lives as a daily self-sacrifice for this same cause for which eventually he died. With this background it makes sense that the eucharist cannot be just banquet, resurrection and community. It must also incorporate the aspect of self-sacrifice, giving, dying, through which alone the kingdom and the community of the resurrection became possible.

How this sacrificial aspect comes about in the eucharist has been the subject of much theorizing in the history of theology. Perhaps the best theory today, and the one closest to the scriptural and patristic tradition, is that of sacramental sacrifice. Sacraments effect what they signify; and as the eucharist is the sacramental sign of Christ in his death and resurrection, so it brings about the actuality of that sacrifice in a sacramental way in the liturgy. Tradition has found this expressed in a particular way in the eucharistic prayer, which is to be seen as, above all, a prayer of offering. It seals the union of our offering of our lives with Christ's one great offering of his life, which we evoke in the central section of every eucharistic prayer. It is not a question of adding a new sacrifice to that of Christ, nor of asking for an historical repetition of the cross; but simply of the one great historical sacrifice of Christ becoming present now, not historically but sacramentally, so that we might make our own what was done once for all on our behalf. If it is true philosophically that action is the actual presence of the cause in the effect (cf. Aristotle's "action is in the patient"), then in the church's action of self-oblation in the Mass we have the actual presence of Christ's self-oblation on the cross, which is the ulti-

mate cause of the action of the church.

The consideration of the sacrificial aspect of the eucharist prepares us for the next aspect of this mystery, namely that which we have referred to as the eucharistic change. At this point it is not a question of "proving" the change of bread and wine into Christ's body and blood. Our reason for believing this mystery is really the fact that it is the church's faith from time immemorial. But once we believe this mystery, then we have some hope of seeing some appropriateness in its truth and in the way it fits in with other mysteries of the faith.

Nor can it be a question of taking these gifts as objects on their own, theorizing about their physical constitution, as though we were chemists or physicists. The starting point must be their symbolism as gifts in the ritual context to which they belong intrinsically. The question is, what do these gifts *mean*? At the outset they are simply signs of ourselves, of our self-giving and of the way we human beings give to one another and to God. When first brought to the altar, the bread and wine are very imperfect signs of very imperfect creatures, ourselves: ". . . what earth has given and human hands have made." The force of the eucharistic prayer and of the whole institution of the eucharist is that the meaning of our gifts is changed. They are taken over by Christ, and from being signs of ourselves and of our self-giving they become signs of Christ and of his self-giving. It is this change of meaning in our gifts which provides the key to what the gifts become in the eucharist. A change of meaning can require a change in what the gifts actually are. In the abstract, perhaps, it need not necessarily be so, but that it is so in this case is clear from the whole eucharistic tradition. The new meaning of the gifts is that they are signs of Christ's self-giving and of the way he gives. Now Christ is the perfect giver.

When he gives himself to the Father and to us, he gives himself totally. Consequently, when this is expressed in the prophetic gesture of the eucharist, he gives not just a sign of himself, nor a part of himself, nor an influence flowing from himself, but he gives his whole self, body, blood, soul and divinity. Total self-giving is the key to the meaning of the eucharist. Total self-giving on the stage of human history meant Christ's death on the cross. Total self-giving in the world of sacramental signs means the change of bread and wine into Christ's very self. Nothing else will do!

The final aspect of the eucharist which we will consider is that of its effects on us, or, to put it more biblically, the way it bears fruit in our lives. One of the problems in this matter is the richness and diversity of those fruits which tradition attributes to the eucharist. In this article my principal purpose is not to give an exhaustive account of them but to propose a framework which can hold these diverse effects together in some kind of unity. We might also note that in speaking of these effects we think primarily of those worshipers whose participation in the Mass includes reception of holy communion. The same effects of the eucharist apply to those who do not receive holy communion, but in this case most probably to a lesser degree, depending on their dispositions and on the reasons why they do not participate more fully.

As principal effect of the eucharist we can single out our ever deeper incorporation into the unity of the People of God. This effect can be described in various ways: love, community, the body of Christ, the unity of the church. Henri de Lubac summed up tradition on the point by saying that the eucharist makes the church. Karl Rahner described this aspect as the first effect of the eucharist and the instrumental cause of the other effects.

As we have seen, eucharist and church belong together, and indeed they do so in a mutual causality. It is not by chance that the expression "mystical body," which we apply to the church, originally referred to the body of Christ in the sacrament. The eucharistic body makes the ecclesial body. In this way the eucharist not only solidifies and deepens the unity which already exists in the church, but it holds before us all an ideal of unity still to be achieved, not only among Christians but in the human family generally. "The eucharist signifies what the world is to become" (WCC Statement at Lima, 1982), and one writer put it that the eucharist is the most political thing we do. It challenges Christians to respond to the cause of community and justice among all those for whom Christ died.

In virtue of this grace of unity the eucharist draws us ever more deeply into the life which circulates in the People of God and binds us more closely to God and to one another in the reality of that life. Being drawn in this way into the mystery of the People of God as it makes its way through history, we are also given an ever deeper share in the historical relations which constitute that people. Two of these relationships may be singled out, and in virtue of each of these relationships we can recognize two main kinds of further effects of the eucharist.

The people of God was born of the heart of Christ on the cross. That heart is "the source of sacramental life in the Church" (Preface of the Sacred Heart). Consequently, central in the life of this people is a grace coming from the cross, the grace of the forgiveness of sins. That the eucharist conveys the forgiveness of sins is part of our tradition from the words over the cup in the first gospel (Mt 26:28). The prayers of the liturgy often speak of the eucharist as a "remedy," a "medicine" for our sinfulness. For the Council of Trent the sacrament is "a remedy by which we are freed from our daily sins and preserved from mortal sins" (D.S. 1638). This point of doctrine is particularly important in dealing with the remnants of Jansenism, which presented the eucharist more as a reward for virtue than as "a remedy for human frailty" (St. Pius X, *Quam singulari*). A deeper appreciation of this truth will inevitably require a review of how we present the sacrament of Penance, particularly confessions of devotion; but a renewed understanding of both sacraments will discern more clearly the true identity of each of them. Karl Rahner once remarked that the proper purpose of the eucharist cannot be sinful man's appearance before the tribunal of divine grace. We must also bear in mind the norms of the Council of Trent about the confession of grave sin prior to holy communion (D.S. 1646-7).

Just as there is grace in the People of God in virtue of the relationship to our origins in the past, so there is grace in virtue of our goal in the future. For this point in particular the language of tradition is confusing by its very richness. It is what we referred to above as the banquet of heaven anticipated here below. The word for it in the fourth gospel is "eternal life," namely the life of the future, which the eucharistic worshiper "has" already (Jn 6:54). Another way of presenting it is to see the eucharist as giving us the presence of God in our lives, the Trinity dwelling within us. The presence of Christ in bread and cup is not the end of the story of eucharistic presence. This form of presence is but a means towards nourishing and deepening that presence of God which remains with us as long as we are in the state of grace. That life which the eucharist nourishes and deepens is the life of Father, Son and Holy Spirit, to share in which will be heaven itself; but this sharing, as the fourth gospel assures us, begins already in this world (Jn 6:54; 14:17,23). It is in the extraordinary depths of these words of the gospel that we find the special subject matter for thanksgiving after communion and the well-spring of eucharistic spirituality and mysticism.

The framework of present, past and future, through which we have considered the effects of the sacrament, is also a framework for summing up the basic nature of the eucharist. In virtue of its external form the eucharist is a Jewish table ritual of praise and thanksgiving. On this level it is neither sacrifice nor banquet, but because of the unique content which the Lord has given to this simple rite, the eucharist is much more than its external form might at first suggest. In virtue of its relationship to its origin, the eucharist is sacramentally a sacrifice and so really a sacrifice. In virtue of its relationship to its future, the eucharist is sacramentally a banquet and so really a banquet. This rite is the prophetic gesture of the Lord's presence within the celebrating community, proclaiming the marvel of his death until he comes again, summoning the people to experience in the present the riches of their origin and their goal.

E.J. Kilmartin, *The Eucharist in the Primitive Church*, Englewood Cliffs: Prentice-Hall 1965. L. Deiss, *It's the Lord's Supper: The Eucharist of Christians*, London: Collins, 1980. E. Schillebeeckx, *The Eucharist*, London: Sheed & Ward 1968. N. Mitchell, *Cult and Controversy: The Worship of the Eucharist Outside Mass*, New York: Pueblo 1982. R.A. Keifer, *Blessed and Broken: An Exploration of the Contemporary Experience of God in Eucharistic Celebration*, Wilmington: DE Michael Glazier, 1982. C. O'Neil, *New Approaches to the Eucharist*, Dublin: Gill and Macmillan 1967.

RAYMOND MOLONEY SJ

EVANGELICAL COUNSELS

The evangelical counsels must be understood in the context of "The Call of the Whole Church to Holiness"(L.G. chap. 5). In a particular way, this holiness is shown in "the practice of the counsels customarily called 'evangelical.'" By the influence of the Spirit, these counsels are followed by many Christians, privately or in some situation or state approved by the church. Such a way of life is to be a witness to holiness in the world. The new Code of Canon Law (canon 573) speaks of the "consecrated life," as the profession of the evangelical counsels, in a stable form of life in which the faithful, under the action of the Holy Spirit, follow Christ more closely.

There are three significant theological questions which call for attention: the notion of "perfection"; the relation between precept and counsel; and the ecclesial significance of the counsels.

A Greek conception of perfection as an ideal led to the notions of degrees of perfection, and a distinction between ordinary, "second class" Christians and a spiritual elite. However, in the gospel sense, to be called to be "perfect" is to be called to a radical faith, to a "perfection" found uniquely in the following of Jesus (Mt 5:48). Where wealth (Mt 19:21) or affective relationships (Mt 8:21-22) are a block to this, they must be abandoned. All followers of Jesus are called to perfection; some are called to specific renunciations as witnesses to all. Christian perfection consists above all in fulfilling the great commandment of love of God and neighbor.

If the christian life is conceived as conforming to an external law, then following the counsels appears as a striving for added perfection. The counsels, then, are presented as works of supererogation, in the sense of non-required, special performances. However, when understood from the perspective of the new law of grace and freedom, they are seen as calls to free

response to freely given grace. It would be more in keeping with the gospel to speak of "evangelical imperatives," to which all are called to respond, but in different ways. It is when the quality of freedom and love in the response is poor, that these imperatives are experienced merely as burdensome obligations. A life of minimum adherence to obligations is indeed "second class." But it is false to identify this kind of life with that of the generality of Christians and to reserve "perfection" for an elite.

Although there are many "counsels" in the gospel, the "evangelical counsels" are traditionally identified as poverty, chastity and obedience. These have been discerned through the experience of Christians as having a special symbolic function in and for the church and the world. Poverty, as renunciation of one's own possessions, does not deny the value of possessing the good things of creation, but radically challenges that possessiveness which stands in the way of equitable sharing. All Christians are called to share their goods, so that there may be no poor among them (cf. Acts 4:34). The real overcoming of poverty in the community is then to be a sign to the world that poverty can and must be challenged. Radical chastity as renunciation of genital, sexual relationships, witnesses to the deeper possibilities of personal communion latent in all human (sexual) relationships. It does not devalue the sexual, but challenges making the secondary element (genital embodiment) the primary constituent of human loving relationships. Radical chastity, to which some are freely called, thus witnesses to the authentic, chaste relationships to which all, whether married or unmarried, are called. Obedience, as renunciation of self-will, abandons the mechanisms of power and domination which persons erect in self protection. It neither denies legitimate human authority, nor makes of it an absolute. Symbolically, it drives a wedge between genuine authority and its distortions by self-assertive power; it demonstrates that true authority is not lording it over others, but serving them (Mk 10:42). The specific form of obedience to which some are called, points to possibilities of transforming all human social relationships.

The following of all or particular counsels is thus a kind of prophecy in action. It is a witnessing to possibilities of transformation in this world, made possible by the radical transformation wrought by God in his Kingdom.

Thaddée Matura, *Le radicalisme évangelique: aux sources de la vie chrétienne*, Paris: Éditions du Cerf, 1978. Francis J. Maloney, *A Life of Promise: Poverty, Chastity, Obedience,* Wilmington, DE; Michael Glazier, 1984.

BRIAN V. JOHNSTONE, CSSR

EVANGELIZATION

A few years ago a term such as "evangelization" would have been unusual in a conversation about the Catholic Church's sense of mission and purpose. Since Vatican II, however, the impetus of renewal has introduced the term into the very heart of the church's discussions of itself and its mission. Evangelization can be properly viewed as the entire work of the church to "proclaim the reign of God" (Mk 1:15). One can, in summary fashion, divide the responsibility of evangelization into three broad categories of ministry: 1) *evangelism*—proclamation of the gospel to the unchurched within our own society or culture: 2) *missionary activity*—cross-cultural proclamation of the gospel; 3) *pastoral activity*—nourishing and deepening the gospel among those already committed to it. The best working definition of the term is found in Paul VI's *Evangelii Nuntiandi* (E.N.)

(1975): "...if it had to be expressed in one sentence the best way of stating it would be to say that the Church evangelizes when she seeks to convert, solely through the Divine Power of the Message she proclaims, both the personal and collective consciences of people, the activities in which they engage, and the lives and the concrete milieux which are theirs" (18).

The U.S. Catholic bishops developed this theme in their own statement, "A Vision of Evangelization," (November, 1985). It underscores the point that to proclaim Jesus (E.N. 23) or the "Good News" (E.N. 18) is the "essence" of evangelization. The content of evangelization, the statement points out, is a proper grasp of the notion of salvation or liberation. Salvation is liberation from everything that oppresses human beings, and while the primary liberation needed is from personal sin, it includes all forms of human bondage, personal and social. The notion of sin itself should be broadly understood as every human disobedience to the will of God and not reduced simply to personal culpability.

The statement also stresses three other points regarding evangelization. (1) Since evangelization calls people to conversion, it must also "lead us to receive individuals into full communion with the Catholic Church." (2) It must be an effort, therefore, to "reach out" to those who are not Christian or who are unchurched. (3) Finally, evangelization should not be reduced to concern with personal sin or ecclesial membership. A truly effective proclamation of the Good News, calls for a thorough-going conversion, one which is attested in a complete effort to turn oneself around in an affective (experiential), an intellectual (understanding), a moral (judging) and religious (ecclesial, action) manner, i.e., holistically.

The Biblical Background

In the synoptic gospels "the preaching

of the Good News" is Jesus' self-definition of his mission or purpose. Thus, when the disciples of John the Baptist question him as to his mission, Jesus' response is "Go back to John and report what you hear and see: the blind recover their sight, cripples walk, lepers are cured, the deaf hear, dead people are raised to life, and the poor have the good news preached to them" (Mt 11:4-5; par. Lk 7:22). In Mt. 4:17 Jesus makes his appearance as a preacher of the Good News with this message: "Reform your lives! The kingdom of heaven is at hand." In Mark, the announcement is only slightly different: "This is the time of fulfillment. The reign of God is at hand. Reform your lives and believe in the gospel" (Mk 1:15). The proclamation of the "reign of God" is not, however, only verbal. It effects new reality which gives expression to its presence through the signs of the messianic time: glad tidings have been brought to the poor, liberty proclaimed to captives, sight given to the blind and freedom offered prisoners (Lk 4:18). Living under the rule of God effects, therefore, new possibilities or, better, makes it possible to see them become realities. "Preaching" or "speaking" of the kingdom is only, a partial understanding of the intention of the synoptic gospels. They also attest that Jesus' entire life is a proclamation or revelation of a new way of living and valuing which has broken into history (Mt 4:23; 9:35; Lk 9:6).

While the gospel writers often use the word "preach" when speaking of the Good News of the kingdom of God, they also use words which bespeak more than the verbal and refer to actions and events as well. The birth of Jesus itself (the incarnation) is, for example, a sign of the Good News (Lk 2:10). The non-verbal aspect of the proclamation is seen clearly in Paul's emphasis on the salvific nature of Jesus' death and resurrection (esp. Eph 2:13ff.).

When the Good News is preached, it is not only the word about the resurrection, but the event itself which releases the power of God into our lives and world. It is in this sense that evangelization is the announcement and unveiling of the "fact" that God's saving power is with (in) us.

The best summary of Jesus' own self-understanding is the passage in Lk 4:42-3 (par. Mk 1:38): "The next morning he left the town and set out into the open country. The crowds went in search of him, and when they found him they tried to keep him from leaving them. But he said to them, 'To other towns I must announce the good news of the reign of God, because that is why I was sent.'" The biblical texts indicate that Jesus' mission or purpose was passed on to his followers (Mt 28:19; Mk 16:15; Lk 24:47-48; Jn 17:17-20). All believers, therefore, are to proclaim the inbreaking of the kingdom of God, i.e., the presence of the grace to live and value as taught and revealed by Jesus.

Evangelization as Conversion

The proclamation made by Jesus is couched in terms of reformation and conversion (Mt 4:17; Mk 1:15). "Reform your lives" sets the theme of evangelization. The christian tradition has often struggled with the temptation to reduce the message and revelation of Jesus merely to knowledge. When this has occurred the christian proclamation has been reduced to "teaching" people information which it is supposed they do not already have. Yet, information of itself does not "save" or "liberate." Knowledge is, indeed, an important facet of the conversion process, but it is only that. It constitutes the desired intellectual (rational) conversion. But the gospels seem almost single-minded on this matter: the Good News is at hand. This is not so much information about place or time of arrival as it is an announcement and unveiling of the fact that God has drawn close to us and that the power of God is available to be drawn upon. It is a conversion in how we think, experience, act, and value.

The contemporary understanding of evangelization and conversion recognizes that the evangelizer must also be evangelized, a point forcefully made by the bishops in their statement of 1985. Evangelization and conversion are ongoing processes.

Evangelization and Church Affiliation

Evangelization, as the bishop's statement noted, must also "lead us to receive individuals into full communion with the Catholic Church." The church is the instrument of Jesus' proclamation extended to each succeeding generation. It is difficult to understand how faith can be nourished or sustained without the support of an ecclesial community. This does not mean, however, that the church proclaims itself any more than Jesus did (Jn 5:30; 1:46; 16:25). Rather it exists to proclaim its Lord and Savior. This all seems self-evident, but, in fact, has frequently been a source of difficulty. Our human propensities have often led us, whether as individuals or church, to speak more of traditions, structures, organizations and parish business than they have led us to proclaim the Kingdom.

A program of evangelization which has as its object merely the recruitment of new members for the parish, the planting of new churches or parishes, or the refurbishment of Catholic identity falls short of the vision of evangelization in Paul VI's *Evangelii Nuntiandi*. The Protestant theologian Wolfhart Pannenberg said that a church shrivels up and dies if it no longer sheds light on people's lives. Jesus' revelation is precisely that kind of evangel which sheds light onto our history as a people and as individuals. The stress in current thought about evangelization on the experiential and religious dimensions of conversion does not negate the importance of doctrine or the church. The aim is rather to place in better balance the importance of the doctrine and church with the experiential, moral/ethical and justice dimension that so often have been less fully explored in discussions of evangelization.

In a manner very similar, then, to the the problem of revelation when reduced to information, there also exists the danger that evangelization is reduced to questions of church membership. In each instance something, admittedly vital, is placed mistakenly in the prime position.

Evangelization and the Other Christian Bodies

A consensus appears to be emerging in much of the christian family today regarding the nature of evangelization. Both evangelical and mainline traditions within Protestantism have recently issued statements which reflect this rapprochement. These traditions had been divided along lines which seemed insuperable just a few years ago. On the one side were those who proclaimed Jesus as the exclusive source of salvation and, at the same time, seemed to deny any great significance to ecclesial involvement in social justice issues. On the other side were those who appeared uncertain of the evangelical and missiological importance of the church, since they felt that all sincerely religious people were or could be saved. The emphasis for these Christians centered, then, on involvement with issues of social justice inasmuch as this gave expression to a lived witness of christian faith for the world.

In the statement "Evangelism Today," the National Council of the Churches of Christ (USA, 1976) offered a corrective to "the recent dichotomy between 'personal' evangelism and 'social action.'" It further emphasized that "growth in church membership and calling people to discipleship [are] not necessarily the same thing." The statement went on to add a very significant sentence: "...the churches still seem strangely bound by a reluctance to name the name of Jesus as Lord and Savior."

From the evangelical tradition in 1980 came "The Thailand Statement," which, while stressing more strongly the urgency of Jesus' name and explicit adhesion to Jesus as the basis for salvation, nonetheless provided a bridge to the mainline tradition as well as Roman Catholicism. The statement reads, "Although evangelism and social action are not identical, we gladly affirm our commitment to both...." The statement goes on to address several issues of great importance to the mainline tradition. In each instance it suggests that the evangelical tradition can do well to renew itself. 1) "We have to repent of prejudice, disrespect, and even hostility towards the very people we want to reach for Christ." 2) "Our study has led us to confess that other people's resistance to the gospel has sometimes been our fault." 3) "Our witness loses credibility when we contradict it by our life or lifestyle." 4) "Strategy and organization are not enough; we need to pray earnestly for the power of the Holy Spirit."

The understanding of evangelization has renewed itself in recent years. It places importance, but not prime importance, on the role of the church, correct understanding (doctrine), proper moral behavior, and Jesus' himself. The primary interest, however, is Jesus' own self-understanding of his mission (especially since we understand ourselves to share in that mission): to proclaim the kingdom of God.

See **Basic Communities; Moral Life, Christian; Conversion; Jesus Christ; Mission; Preaching; Reign of God; Repentance; Revelation, Sin**

U.S. Catholic Bishops' Statement, "A Vision of Evangelization," Nov. 15, 1985, *Origins* 15, 1985, 24:407. Paul VI *Evangelii Nuntiandi, On Evangelization in the Modern World,* 1975, Washington, DC: U.S.C.C., 1976. Consultation on World Evangelization, " The Thailand Statement," August, 1980, in Alfred Krass, *Evangelizing Neo-Pagan North America,* Scottdale, PA: Herald Press, 1982, pp. 242-248. The Governing Board of the National Council of the Churches of Christ, "Evangelism Today," March, 1976, in Alfred Krass, ibid., pp. 230-233. Heinrich Friedrich, "Kerygma," in Gerhard Kittel, Ed., *Theological Dictionary of the New Testament,* III, Grand Rapids: Eerdmans, 1965, pp. 714-718. Bernard Lonergan, *Method in Theology,* NY: Herder & Herder and London: Darton, Longman & Todd, 1972. Johannes Verkuyl, *Contemporary Missiology,* Grand Rapids: Eerdmans, 1978.

LOUIS MCNEIL

EVIL, PROBLEM OF

The reality of evil raises important question for christian theology. In the eighteenth century, David Hume put the question much like this: Is God willing to prevent evil, but not able? Then God is impotent. Is God able to prevent evil, but not willing? Then God is malevolent. Is God both willing and able to prevent evil? Then why is there any evil in the world?

To answer these questions, many theologians construct theodicies, explanations of why God allows evil in the world. One group of theodicies is *retrospective,* explaining evil in terms of its causes. Dualist theories postulate two ultimate forces in the universe, one good and the other evil. This world is the battleground on which one or the other will win. For Christians, dualist theories are unacceptable: if the Evil One is independent of God, the christian belief that there is only one God of this world is breached; if the Evil One is dependent on God, then the problem evil presents is simply removed from this world to another level. Dualist theories won't do.

Privative theories, associated with St. Augustine, St. Thomas Aquinas and most Catholic thinkers, claim that evil is not something in itself, but the absence of good. Inspired by Genesis 3, they see evil enter into the world when humans and angels sin, that is, they turn away from the highest good, God, choose what is less, and fall away from the best. The original sin brings with it inevitably the wages of sin: the accelerating diminution of life by death, suffering, and more sin. Hence, evil is not willed by God, but willed (whether consciously or not) by those who will to do evil. God only permits people to choose evil and evil to happen to them. God may even permit people to choose evil ultimately, that is, to damn themselves.

This theodicy has been challenged. If all evil is due to an original sin, what caused that? Either God couldn't or wouldn't make it possible for the first sinner (human or angelic) not to be attracted by less than the best. So either the problem remains unsolved or the "first evil will" is said to be an impenetrable mystery, which undercuts the explanatory power of this theodicy. Further, why must God make all humanity pay the price for one sin? How can a God of love be justified in permitting all the suffering, including the suffering of innocent children, that is the "effect" of that sin? Many find such retrospective theodicies not solutions, but exacerbations, of the problem.

A second group of theodicies are *prospective,* explaining evil by showing what purposes it serves in this world. Irenaeus of Lyons and F.D.E. Schleiermacher are named as historical inspiration for the individual eschatological theodicies of contemporary theologians J. Hick and R. Swinburne. The realities of pain and suffering, temptation and sin, are necessary for humans to develop ultimately into people worthy to share life with God. If no evils challenged people to overcome them, no one would develop sufficient character strength to be with God. If no evils "veiled" the irresistible beauty of God's countenance, no one could freely choose to love God. Each person's life is a journey which should develop a height-ened capacity to know and love God and thus fully and freely to realize one's deepest desire.

A collective eschatological theodicy can be found in the works of P. Teilhard de Chardin, S.J. Inspired by the vision of the cosmic Christ in St. Paul's letters and the emergence of a global community, Teilhard saw humanity together progressing to the "Omega point," when the Christification of the universe will be complete and *all* will be united in Christ. Some evil is an inevitable part of the process, the pain of growth and development of the tragedy of loss. More evil is the danger we pose as we develop the ability to destroy the earth, a terrifyingly real temptation in a nuclear age. Instead, we must build the earth if we are not to perish.

Prospective theodicies also have problems. They explain the obscure in this world (evil) by what is more obscure (an ultimate good in another world). It is hard to see that there is any appreciable difference between such a God so thoroughly obscured by evil and no God at all. Moreover, they image God as a harsh schoolmaster, "educating" humans in a school of very hard knocks: could God not have found a better pedagogy than the Holocaust to educate people? For individuals, suffering does not always make a person better. All too often, suffering does not ennoble but diminishes and destroys a person. For humanity, can we believe that we progress forward toward a parousia? The horror of World War I destroyed the theories of general human progress popular in the nineteenth century. Is that lesson forgotten today? The prospective theodicies must claim that all the evil in the world is either "good for you" or a necessary condition of life. Since sin is an evil, it must either be good for us (which is incoherent) or a necessary condition for life, so that no human being could have avoided sin (a damning indictment of God's goodness in creating humans so inevitably flawed). Hence, many find prospective theodicies not solutions, but exacerbations of the problem.

A third group of theodicies redefines key terms to eliminate the question. Process theologians, such as J. Cobb and L. Ford, redefine divine power to be only the power of persuasion or attraction, not of coercion. God is omni-persuasive. Evil enters the world as a price one pays for evolutionary progress or when actual entities willfully resist the divine lure to the best. Many find process theodicy a problem because it implies God's goodness could be overcome by evil and ascribes very little power to God, who must not be very attractive or persuasive, given all the evil in this world. Other theologians tacitly redefine all evil as hidden good or limit God's love to only a few, implying that God turns a wrathful vengeance on all others. But word games about evil or imaging God as schizophrenic also won't do.

Hence, some have given up trying to develop theodicies which explain God's reasons for permitting evil in the world, and have instead constructed defenses of the compatibility of believing both in the existence of God and in the reality of worldly evil. Such defenses, such as A. Plantinga's "Free Will Defense," do not provide solutions to the problem, and so evil remains a mystery. But they do show that Christians are not irrational to believe in God in the face of evil even though they can't solve the mystery. It is not irrational to have faith that God has the answers. Of course, one might then ask why one *should* have faith in God or how one might help nurture a nascent faith or sustain a wearying faith. Defenses cannot provide any help for those problems.

The problem of evil is often treated as an invitation to theological debate. But when the endlessness of philosophers' debates reveals the hollowness of human explanations, something more remains. In solidarity, people can enable each other to face evil of every kind without denying its reality.

In the face of the genuine evil of suffering, Christians must learn how to ease suffering by performing corporal and spiritual works of mercy. To acquire merciful skills helps both the suffering and the merciful. To lose such skills means all suffer more. Suffering is not abolished or explained, but faced.

In the face of each individual's sinfulness, Christians must enable each other to own their sins. It is all too easy to create cover stories which exonerate us from any guilt or responsibility. The destruction of sin is worst when we disown the acts which we have committed or omitted. When we disown our sin, we disown divine forgiveness as well. To "own up," to confess, to admit one is a sinner, is terrifying, for to request and accept divine forgiveness means to accept a deep change in one's life, "to go and sin no more," and to walk the way of the Crucifield One, "to pay the high price of reconciliation."

In the face of social evils, those structures of domination and repression which do twist and can destroy people's minds and hearts, Christians must admit their complicity in constructing and perpetuating them. Structures of racial, sexual, social and economic prejudice and exploitation cause people to suffer. They are also conditions which lead people to sin and inflict more suffering on each other. As with individual sins, the destruction of evil structures is worst when we disown them, when we say they are not our fault or when we deny that we profit from them. When we disown our complicity, we disown divine forgiveness as well. To overcome social evil begins with our "owning up," admitting that we have chosen our own gain through exploiting others. But this is terrifying, for to request and accept divine forgiveness means we must change our shared life, perhaps deconstruct the comfortable but evil structures that we know, and work for radical change in our society. Overcoming social evil also requires us to "pay the high price of reconciliation" and to "go and create no more evil structures."

Evil is not a problem, finally, that can be solved by theories, by the explanations of theodicies or by defenses of the coherence of christian beliefs. To see evils as part of the divine mystery rather than as compelling evidence for atheism requires a perspective such as one a Christian can develop by being part of a community that imitates Christ in recognizing sin, suffering, and exploitation and in overcoming evil by incarnating the patient power of a harsh and dreadful love that reconciles.

See **God, Providence**

J. Hick, *Evil and the God of Love,* San Francisco, 1978. D. Griffin, *God, Power and Evil,* Philadelphia, 1975. A. Plantinga, *God, Freedom and Evil,* New York, 1974. K. Surin, *Theology and the Problem of Evil,* Oxford, 1986.

T.W. TILLEY

EVOLUTION

Greek natural philosophy discussed in a rudimentary way the origin of diversity in the world, with a clear contrast drawn by Aristotle between his own teleological view and the earlier affirmation of random process by Democritus and Empedocles. Plato's *Timaeus* offered a myth of the world's making which religious thinkers have often interpreted as favorable to the biblical perspective of creation, but which more likely represents a dramatic vision of the permanent dialectic between reason and necessity. With the Stoics the cyclical cosmogonies of earlier thinkers reappeared. Among christian philosopher-theologians Augustine offers the first extended discussion of the world's development in his commentary on Genesis, in which he argues that all natural kinds of things were created by God in the first moment of time but that they made their appearance only gradually (from their *rationes seminales*).

In the high Middles Ages Aquinas distinguished between the primary cause of the world's being and secondary causes of its course in time; significantly, he also maintained that only revelation gives reliable knowledge that the universe had a beginning in time. Early in the modern period Descartes held that the nature of things is best explained by considering how they have come to be mechanically (a genetic account). For Isaac Newton, however, the mechanics of his *Principia* was insufficient to explain the planetary system; an Author of the system must be invoked. Another argument from design was developed by the proponents of physico-theology like John Ray, William Paley, and Robert Boyle, who thought that the adaptation of means to ends among living organisms implied a supreme, intelligent agent.

At the beginning of the eighteenth century, important elements toward a theory of evolution were established. It was agreed that the earth had changed since creation. Fossils were recognized as organic remains, laid in strata over long periods. Newton's "matter in motion" had been accepted as the context for explaining natural events. The idea then developed that species might change into other species. The French naturalist Georges Buffon raised the question whether all animals could be considered related. Linnaeus, founder of the modern system of biological classification, came by 1760 to believe that species could vary. Erasmus Darwin, grandfather of Charles, concluded that evolution had occurred and proposed in his *Zoonomia* (1794) that the Great First Cause had endowed living matter with power to improve itself.

Lamarck, who coined the term biology, in 1809 proposed a system of evolution and drew up an evolutionary tree. Supposing a tendency to complexity and perfection and an "interior sentiment" that led to new organs which satisfied animals' needs, Lamarck's theory also depended on the inheritance of acquired characteristics. On the other hand, Georges Cuvier, the founder of modern vertebrate paleontology, rejected evolution, relying on divine creation to account ultimately for the fossil forms that were then known and on "catastrophes" to explain their absence in later strata of the geological record. In England, Sir Charles Lyell's three-volume *Principles of Geology* advanced a theory of uniformitarianism (the regular determination of events by natural geological causes) which, in his view, excluded evolution.

It was during the voyage of HMS "Beagle" that Charles Darwin abandoned the orthodox notion of the fixity of species and committed himself to the evolutionary hypothesis. Darwin observed related but different species near each other on the same continent; similarities between fossils and living forms in the same areas; resemblances between species on distant islands and those on the nearest continent; and differences between species on neighboring islands of the Galapagos Archipelago. These data could best be explained, he concluded, if species were not the result of divine intervention but were descended with modification from common ancestors. In 1838, while reading Thomas Malthus, he developed his pivotal explanatory notion of natural selection, according to which inherited variations, advantageous in relation to a particular environment, enable the fittest organisms in a species to survive in the struggle for life and thus to be "naturally selected" for reproduction. Only when Alfred Russel Wallace came independently to a remarkably similar position did Darwin decide to publish *The Origin of Species* (1859). In *The Descent of Man* (1871) he extended his theory to include humanity.

Darwin's evidence for evolution was indirect. His argument provided an explanation for facts that otherwise remained inexplicable. With it he offered a unifying general principle for the study of all living beings and introduced time itself into the science of organisms living through time. Subsequent developments challenged but then strengthened his position, though not without important variations. With the recovery in 1900 of Gregor Mendel's work in genetics, a reliable basis for evolutionary inheritance became available. More direct evidence than Darwin's was gathered by comparative anatomy, embryology, ethology, biochemistry, parasitology, biogeography, and, especially, paleontology. In 1930 Sir Ronald Fisher showed how genetic mutations function in the process of natural selection and thus opened the way for neo-Darwinism or the synthetic theory of evolution ("a synthesis," in Ernst Mayr's phrase, "of mutationism and environmentalism"). The relative importance of natural selection has been and is still debated, however, from R. B. Goldschmidt's argument for macroevolution (contrasted with the microevolution of gradually accumulated mutations) to Stephen Jay Gould's proposal of "punctuated equilibrium," according to which morphological change most often occurs suddenly and in association with speciation events (rather than gradually, during the lifetime of a species).

Evolutionary science has been at once a challenge and an invitation to the authenticity of religious thought over the last century. For many, Darwin's revolution called in question the authority of the Bible, the centrality and spirituality of humankind in the created order, the meaning of suffering, and the reality of evil. Above all, it seemed to exclude final purpose and transcendent reference from a self-contained world. Indeed, early supporters of Darwin such as T. H. Huxley or Herbert Spencer in England and Ernst Haeckel in Germany were militant materialists, atheists, or agnostics (Huxley's coinage). Karl Marx likewise greeted Darwin's work as confirming his own.

But other thinkers sought a reconciliation between the evolutionary view of the world and a sense of transcendent purpose. In France, Henri Bergson's *Creative Evolution* (1907) developed a teleological and spiritual evolutionism dependent on the creative power of God. A similar vision appeared in the writing of Pierre Lecomte du Noüy and, with still more influence, the Jesuit paleontologist Pierre Teilhard de Chardin. In America, the great Harvard botanist Asa Gray had represented a rational, supernaturalistic orthodoxy that read an innate sense of design in evolution. For the romantic liberalism of John Fiske, similarly, "evolution is God's way of doing things." Fiske's views were echoed by popular churchmen such as Henry Ward Beecher and Lyman Abbott. Among his contemporaries at Harvard, C.S. Peirce, Chauncey Wright and William James were other influential figures in the rise of American evolutionism, though with varying positions on the question of religion. Both British and American evolutionism found expression in the process thought of Alfred North Whitehead.

For Roman Catholics, no official statement came from Rome in response to Darwin. In 1860 a provincial council of Cologne did reject as contrary to scripture and faith the theory of transformism whereby a lower form evolved

into the human body. Vatican I argued from the origin of both revelation and reason from the same divine source to the formal impossibility of their contradicting one another (D.S. 3017). A number of Catholic authors such as J.A. Zahm, Henry de Dorlodot and E.C. Messenger appealed to Augustine's authority for accommodating an evolutionary view of the world. But biblical scholarship eventually became crucial in recognizing the different purpose and forms of thought represented by the new theory and the Bible. The charter document for such studies was finally presented by Pope Pius XII's encyclical *Divino afflante Spiritu* (1943).

With Pius XII's Allocution to the Papal Academy of Science in 1941 and his encyclical *Humani generis* in 1950, the way was further opened for a "moderate evolutionism" in Catholic thought. According to the encyclical: "The teaching of the Church does not forbid that the doctrine of evolutionism, insofar as it inquires into the origin of the human body from already existing and living matter, be, according to the present state of human disciplines and sacred theology, treated in research and discussion by experts on both sides" (D.S. 3896). The encyclical insisted, however, on the immediate creation of human souls by God and expressed stronger caution still about polygenism, since "it is not at all apparent how such a view can be reconciled with the data which the sources of revealed truth and the doctrines of the church propose concerning original sin (D.S. 3897).

With the *aggiornamento* of Vatican II, still another phase of discussion between evolutionary thought and Catholic faith has begun. In "The Pastoral Constitution on the Church in the Modern World" especially, the Council adopted a historical-evolutionary perspective in its descriptive analysis of the contemporary world. It should be noted, however, that evolutionary terminology is used in these texts in an extremely general and undefined sense (cf. G.S. 5, 54). No distinctions are drawn between cosmic, organic, and sociocultural forms of evolution. One may nevertheless date from the Council a new freedom and fruitfulness in theology concerning the unitary character of human beings in their multiple relations with the natural world; the compatibility of teachings on original sin and redemption with either a monogenistic or a polygenistic account of human origins; and the far more impressive view of the world and its history within the framework of evolutionary time.

We must not assume that the dialogue between theology and evolutionary theory was concluded by the Council, nor that a rapprochement between evolutionary theory and the theology of creation has been simply supplanted by the recent, and indispensable, emphasis on Christianity's social responsibility. It is accepted scientific practice to refer to both organic and psychogenetic development as being aspects of one evolution. This may remind political and liberation theologians, when considering our responsibilities for the future, that no discipline dealing with humankind can afford to forget the natural basis for our historical development—least of all theology, which understands God's redemptive purposes as directed to a world continually created in goodness.

See **Creation, Creationism**

T.C. Dobzhansky, *Mankind Evolving: The Evolution of the Human Species,* New Haven, 1962. Ernan McMullin, ed., *Evolution and Creation,* Notre Dame, Ind., 1985. L.J. O'Donovan, "Was Vatican II Evolutionary?", *Theological Studies* 36 (1975) 493-502. Walter Ong, ed., *Darwin's Vision and Christian Perspectives,* New York, 1960. Karl Rahner, *Hominisation: The Evolutionary Origin of Man as a Theological Problem,* tr. W.T. O'Hara, New York, 1965. Pierre Teilhard de Chardin, S.J., *The Phenomenon of Man,* tr. B. Wall, New York, 1959.

LEO J. O'DONOVAN, SJ

EX OPERE OPERANTIS

A term used in the theology of the sacraments to refer to the actions or merits of the minister or recipients of the sacrament as distinct from the action of God in and through the sacrament.

See **Ex opere operato, Sacrament**

EX OPERE OPERATO

A term used in the theology of the sacraments to refer to the fact that in a sacrament it is God or Christ who is the chief agent infallibly at work if the required conditions are present in the minister or recipient.

See **Sacrament**

EXISTENTIALISM

Philosophical existentialism.

Although existentialism is very influential in western philosophy, it remains difficult to define or even to describe. E. Friedman calls it a "mood" which embraces a number of diverse philosophies. The unifying factor is "the reaction against the static, the abstract, the purely rational, the merely irrational, in favor of the dynamic and the concrete, personal involvement and engagement, action, choice, commitment" (p. 3). Not only is existentialism opposed to rationalism and idealism, but it is also opposed to romanticism and psychologism. Although one finds strong roots for existentialism throughout western philosophy, from the Greeks onward, it is primarily with Soren Kierkegaard that contemporary existentialism begins. It was Kierkegaard who reacted strongly against the essentialism of Hegel and made existentialism a self-conscious part of western thought. After an initial period of notoriety, Kierkegaard's position underwent a time of disfavor, only to be reevaluated at the beginning of the twentieth century.

Berdyaev, Buber, Jaspers, Camus, Sartre, Dostoyevski, Heidegger were among the many notables who revitalized existentialism. S.E. Stumpf also sees existentialism as a "mode of philosophy" rather than a true philosophy, with a focus on existing individual persons rather than on distant universal concepts. Existentialism emerged strongly after World War II, influencing literature, art, theology as well as philosophy. "In sheer scope of its influence, existentialism has achieved a far wider response than any other mode of philosophy in modern times and does not seem to be waning" (p. 478).

H. Krings distinguishes existentialism and *Existenzphilosophie*. The first is more literary, and finds rootage in Rilke and Kafka; the latter more philosophical and rooted in Kierkegaard, Nietzsche, Schelling and to some degree Fichte. Such a division is at times difficult to maintain, unless one focuses exclusively on literary figures, such as S. Beckett, J. Osborne, E. Ionesco, on the one hand, and Heidegger and Jaspers on the other.

Of vital importance to existentialism is temporality, and this stress fits in well with a wider phenomenon in western thought, namely, the rise of historical consciousness, which began towards the end of the eighteenth century. All life processes, including evolution (Darwin, etc.), economic history (Marx, etc.) and thought (Husserl, Heidegger, etc.) are subject to the historical process. This relativizes many "eternal verities," and "ultimate causes." Contemporary science and technology (e.g., Einstein, Whitehead) concur in this process of relativization. Existentialism offers the kind of relative truth and relative meaning that seems compatible with this contemporary movement.

One finds, further, that authors such as Sartre, Camus, Heidegger, Merleau-Ponty, Ricoeur, tend to separate on the issue of interpersonal relationship. For some there is an atomistic or privatized relativity (the early Camus, Sartre) and the *Mit-Sein* or *In-der-Welt-Sein* of Heidegger. This will have repercussions in the area of philosophical ethics, which can either be relativized on an individual basis or relativized on a communitarian basis.

Theological existentialism.

No christian theologian relativizes the Word of God, but christian theologians have indeed been influenced by existentialism in their interpretations of the Word of God. German Protestant theologians, such as Barth, Brunner, and Tillich, were, early in the twentieth century, caught up with Kierkegaard, but it was R. Bultmann, influenced by Heidegger, who has done the most to bring existential thought into the biblical, and therefore theological world. Bultmann utilized categories of existentialism to interpret John's gospel, and went on to the synoptics and Paul as well. The Word of God in the NT confronts the reader with a personal or existential challenge, which one must respond to *now*, i.e., at the moment of hearing this Word. In other words, the *Wort Gottes* requires an immediate *Antwort* on the part of the hearer. It is this confrontation of the Word beneath the words of the NT, at any given moment, which is the proclamation-event. Such a view lies at the heart of Bultmann's program. Past historical data, even that found in the NT referring to Jesus, is relativized, and the details of Jesus' life are left to the historically-minded scholars to pursue. Such historical details might not have occurred, but this is secondary to the challenge of the Word of God made to the reader now as he or she reads the word of God. The response to such a personal challenge can only be yes/no, whereas the response to the historicity of the NT narratives might be a perhaps.

Post-Bultmannians did not disagree with the basic existential thrust of Bultmann, but they emphasized more than the master the need to establish an historical basis for the NT. In all of this Bultmann remains, today, one of the most influential scholars on contemporary Protestant and Catholic exegetical endeavors. Since existentialism is not a philosophy *per se,* Catholic scholars have been able to incorporate many principles of Bultmann's thought and not have to claim an espousal of a philosophical system. The development of the critical methods, e.g., *Formgeschichte, Traditionsgeschichte, Redaktionsgeschichte,* confronts the literal interpretation of the fundamentalist position and its absolutizing of NT passages. These various critical methods in many ways relativize the human words which in a way incarnate the Divine Word. Existential biblical scholars in no way deny the inerrancy of scripture; but they do deny an unscholarly and rather blind disclaimer of the theological pluralism inherent in the NT itself. A fundamentalistic absolutizing approach to the Bible is, in their view, basically anti-historical and anti-human.

To some degree Barth's neo-orthodoxy called into question this existentialism of biblical thought, but the major opponent of existentialism in theology has not been neo-orthodoxy but biblical fundamentalism. The perduring dispute over evolution and creationism is more indicative of this division than the Schleiermacher-Barth confrontation at the heart of contemporary German Protestant theology.

A second area which contributed to existentialism and theology is the contemporary interest in historical theology. The publishing of H.C. Lea's *A History of Auricular Confession and Indulgences in the Latin Church* in 1896 produced not only a Catholic response to the history of the sacrament of Penance, but opened the way to a historical study of each of the christian sacraments. This history likewise had a relativizing effect, since many so-called dogmatic positions in sacramental theology had to be nuanced and modified the more the history of the sacraments came to light. A theology based heavily on scholastic philosophy was seen to be in some degree untenable when confronted with the pluralistic and relativistic approaches of prior histories.

In Roman Catholic thought it has been K. Rahner who has had the most influence in bringing existentialism into theology. His early studies were strongly influenced by Heidegger, and although Rahner maintained his Thomistic stance throughout his career, one can only understand his writings if one understands Heidegger. Since Rahner was a major theological architect of Vatican II, the council itself reflects to some degree Rahner's foundation idea of the "supernatural existential" which has a strong Heideggerian rootage, and this "supernatural existential" lies in a central way along every step of his theologizing: revelation, grace, sacraments, church.

Many Catholic theologians of the *nouvelle theologie,* though rooted more in historical theology than in existentialism, were aided by existentialist categories to make their positions meaningful. E. Schillebeeckx, again a Thomist, utilized existential and phenomenological approaches to present his views on transignification. Congar's stress on the lay person in the church came out of his historical studies and found value in the utilization of existential thought processes.

Liturgical theology was advanced primarily by historical studies of liturgical practices in the east and west. Liturgical pluralism has been helped by existentialism, since every liturgy is geared to the *now* and to the personal. Liturgy is not an externally, essentialistic repeatable event; rather it is a personal, existential experience of the risen Lord. Liturgy can only be focused on the liturgical action of the concrete, space-time moment in which it takes place.

Perhaps the most delicate area of theology in which existentialism plays a role is moral theology. Situation ethics caused an enormous stir in both Protestant and Catholic thought, and Rahner's article, "On the Question of a Formal Existential Ethics," (*Theological Investigations,* vol .2) attempted to bring perduring truths of right and wrong into the concrete historical situation. *Humanae vitae* created an aftermath which still today remains indicative of this struggle over moral absolutes. In this area of moral theology, existentialism has been seen by many as inimical; by others as a helpful ally.

The effect of existentialism in all areas of theology is not over and this applies to Catholic, Protestant and Jewish theology alike. Existentialism has raised serious question to age-old answers and in many ways this very questioning by existentialism of many presumed "eternal verities" has enriched rather than impoverished contemporary theology.

R.M. Zaner, *The Way of Phenomenology,* 1970. R. Zaner and D. Ihde, *Phenomenology and Existentialism,* 1973. M. Friedman, *The Worlds of Existentialism,* 1964. A. Dondeyne, *Contemporary European Thought and Christian Faith,* 1958. W. Luijpen, *Existential Phenomenology,* 1960. John Wild, *Challenge of Existentialism,* 1963. S.E. Stumpf, *Socrates to Sartre,* 1983.

KENAN B. OSBORNE, OFM

EXPERIENCE, RELIGIOUS

To speak of religious experience is to speak of those encounters with the sacred, the transcendent, which are available to human beings in their concrete, historical existence. The nature of religious experience is to be understood within the context of a consideration of the characteristics of human experience in general. Authentic human experience requires that a conscious human subject encounter reality in a way that leads the subject to respond to that reality and to critically appropriate that encounter as an event in his or her personal history (Smith). All authentic experience is interpreted experience and more than simply a subjective feeling or passive reception of sense-data. Experience is related to previous experience and influenced by it. Formed by their experience and tutored by human communities, individuals create frameworks for understanding and naming their experiences. These frameworks or horizons of understanding are initially employed in a pre-critical and pre-reflective fashion, but with continued experience they are used critically and reflectively (Lane). The community's wisdom and its corporate experience serve as a standard against which an individual can check out his or her interpretation of experience and correct distortions or biases in interpretation (Denis Edwards, *Human Experience of God,* 1983).

Many experiences are of the ordinary type and comprise the daily subject-object encounters that are on the surface of life. Other experiences are of the depth or extraordinary type and lead the experiencer to perceive something not immediately apparent. Religious experience is a depth experience which brings the subject into a relationship with the sustaining ground of life. In fact, it is legitimate and more accurate to speak of the religious dimension of human experience inasmuch as various experiences hold the possibility of opening the subject to a new world of meaning and a new way of understanding self and reality in relation to the sacred. Such experience transcends senses and intellect even though the experience may involve senses and intellect. Interpretation seeks to grasp the experience, and yet seems inadequate for capturing the "something else" disclosed in the experience. The individual is in touch with the "really real" which escapes neat concepts and categories (Edward Schillebeeckx, *Christ: The Experience of Jesus as Lord,* 1980). Images and concepts enable a person to talk about the experience, and yet the experience is pre-conceptual and beyond words.

The religious dimension in human experience puts people in touch with limits even as it points to the limitless against which all that is limited is recognized as such. Limitless mystery grounds the concrete experiencing of human beings and is the atmosphere which makes knowing and loving possible. This mystery is the ground against which all figures are discerned, even though it may not be explicit to the human subject (Karl Rahner, *The Spirit in the Church,* 1979). Religious experience makes explicit this mysterious presence and attends to it. Through the medium of human experience, human persons have opened themselves to that which is immediate and present in all religious experience although known only indirectly. For the Christian, religious experience comes as a gift in which an individual is enabled to see within and beyond the world to that sustaining and prior reality. In the graced event of mystical experience an individual may be led to experience the presence of God and union with the divine Other without attending momentarily to any medium, as it were, in an illuminating darkness or blinding light.

The religious wisdom of the community, expressed in doctrines and beliefs and ritually enacted, guides the religious experiencing of the individual and supplies language and norms for understanding and interpreting it. Symbols and sacred narratives handed on by the community are appropriated by individ-uals and used to make sense of their religious experiences (Lonergan, pp. 115-128). Theology which is informed by and builds on religious experience points out how such experience leads to fuller religious knowledge. Yet theological formulations and interpretations, dependent on varying modes and patterns of understanding, pale before the original experience even though there is and should be a basic unity between doctrine and experience.

Because religious experience is a human experience which impacts on a person's psyche, psychologists, philosophers, and social scientists have attempted descriptions of the human side of religious experience and noted the psychic processes involved. William James (1902) drew attention to the varieties of religious experience and, on the basis of the information he had available to him, offered a limited typology. The outstanding feature of religious experience for James was its richness. He repeatedly underscored the "more" to be found in such experience. "The further limits of our being plunged...into an altogether other dimension of existence from the sensible and merely 'understandable' world" (p. 399). He theorized that the subliminal consciousness or the subconscious is a possible means of contact with an all-encompassing reality. In fact, James wondered if the subliminal, what is today called the unconscious, might not be the "hither side" of the something more which people call the holy. Whereas Freud, in his negative critique of religion ("Obsessive Actions and Religious Practices," in *The Standard Edition of the Complete Psychological Works of Sigmund Freud,* Vol. 9, 1959) focused on the psychic origins of religious ideas, James was concerned with the "fruits," the good resulting from religious experience. When James considered mystical experience, he noted the union with something larger than the self which occurs and the great peace which results from that union. For him mystical religious experience was a sudden extension of the boundaries of consciousness so that "it appears rather as if the whole of reality were uncovered at once" ("A Suggestion about Mysticism," in *Collected Essays and Reviews,* 1959, pp. 505).

Rudolf Otto, in his classic *The Idea of the Holy* (1923), wrote of a faculty of divination, a talent for discerning the presence of the holy. The holy was for him a fascinating and terrifying mystery (*mysterium tremendum et fascinans*) which dynamically poses itself and elicits certain feeling responses in the religious experience of the human subject. It both reveals and conceals, both brings bliss and evokes awe. Religious imagery is a protective covering or veil over this mystery. Erwin Goodenough amplified this notion of a covering and spoke of people as throwing curtains between themselves and this tremendous mystery (*The Psychology of Religious Experiences,* 1965). On these curtains Goodenough saw humanity projecting or painting myths and symbols which give meaning to the mystery and take away its terror. Paul Pruyser (*A Dynamic Psychology of Religions,* 1968) also developed this metaphor of curtains or a covering but reformulated it in terms of a screen on which people project images out of their own experience and on which God is actively revealing and concealing the divine mystery. What matters in Pruyser's formulation is the goodness of fit between God's revelation and people's experience. Distortions in the interpretation of one's religious experience would be instances of an improper fit between the two sides.

Understanding distortions in religious experience as well as locating religious experience psychically is facilitated by recent developments in a branch of contemporary psychoanalysis called object relations theory. This theory gives central place to early relationships with primary figures (parents, close relatives, others who live in the same house, etc.) in the constitution of one's personality and the establishment of one's relationship to the world. It claims that mental representations of others are gradually built up in the mind by a process of internalization. Memories of interactions with others in the past and present consolidate in the mind so as to form these mental representations which are not carbon copies but subjective, sometimes quite distorted, renderings of others. Out of the affective experiences with people in the external world each person fashions an internal world, a "theater" of the mind, where "actors" (mental representations) from the past continue to impact in varying degrees on how a person relates to others, including God in the present. Object relations theory provides a helpful perspective for understanding the various components of religious experience.

The most fruitful concept of object relations theory in understanding religious experience is D.W. Winnicott's notion of a transitional realm of experience. Rather than the usual two worlds of standard Freudian psychoanalysis, the inner world of fantasy (pure subjectivity) and the outer world of hard facts (clear objectivity), three worlds are postulated: inner, outer, and transitional. The latter world is the result of a creative blend of materials from the outer and inner worlds. Winnicott had noted the attachment which older infants develop to some special object which seems to provide them with solace and which he designated a transitional object. This special object is a result of the creative activity of the infant who is able to fuse material from the inner world, remembered experience of good mothering, with some object such as a teddy bear from the outer world which can then serve as a mother-substitute and whose meaning to the child is typically shared by the rest of the family. Winnicott saw the broader ramifications of his formulation and stated that he was staking a claim for a way of experiencing that was present in culture, religion, art, and creative living. In effect, Winnicott rehabilitated the notion of illusion to which Freud had reduced all religious ideas and experience. Illusion, like the transitional object, can be a vision of the "more" of reality which provides needed solace and has a place in the lifelong development of persons. It is a way of creatively approaching life by seeing reality and oneself as charged with surplus and shared meaning.

In prayer or other religious experiences the believer enters the realm of illusion, the transitional arena, to encounter there various illusionistic products (Paul W. Pruyser, "Forms and Functions of the Imagination in Religion," *Bulletin of the Menninger Clinic,* 1985, pp. 353-370). Winnicott spoke of a "potential space" between mother and baby, a space made safe because of mother's dependability and the baby's continuing feeling of union with her, which allows for creative play and a movement toward the use of symbols for absent reality. Believers likewise enter potential space, a space free of the usual internal and external pressures, in religious experience to meet their God. The God they meet is actually a psychic representation, a special transitional object, which they have fashioned on the basis of their experience with significant others and what their community and family have told them about God (Anna-Maria Rizzuto, *The Birth of the Living God,* 1979, and Meissner). Of course, because of its idiosyncratic nature resulting from the unique life experience of each person, it may or may not look like the God of their particular religious tradition.

When the notion of God is first introduced to a child, usually in response to his or her questions about the cause of things, the child images this superior being as similar to his or her parents, only of greater power and size. The child fleshes out this notion of God on the basis of various interpersonal experiences. Opportunities for revising the psychic representation of God to fit more with one's current sense of self and the perspective of a religious tradition present themselves at various points in life but are not always taken. Consequently, religious experience will range from the immature and possibly pathological to the very mature and healthy which approximates the best descriptions of such experience in the theological and psychological literature. In addition to the adequacy of the God-representation, variation will also be found in the mental representation of the self and the way the self is loved as well as the nature of faith, the trusting relationship to some transcendent power (Meissner).

In the religious experience of the mature believer, elements from early life experience are carried forward but hopefully refined and specified in an age-appropriate manner. Erikson noted how an experience of the sacred is rooted in early infancy when a person develops a basic trust toward reality and at the hands of a loving caretaker senses a hallowed presence which confirms his or her distinctiveness even as it overcomes any sense of separateness. Such basic trust continues to be a core element in the mature faith of an adult believer even though faith has also now a more complex cognitive dimension. Faith develops then from a rather unnuanced basic trust to a gradual literal appropriation, in early childhood, of images and stories for understanding the transcendent. With the advent of adolescence faith has the possibility of becoming more group-bound and inter-personal. Young adulthood typically leads to a more intellectual faith in which symbols and stories are demystified and reduced to their intellectual content. Midlife often pushes people to return to symbol and myth as pointers to a depth dimension in reality and in themselves. Mature age can witness the development of a faith which perceives the transcendent as a unifying presence in all reality, the ultimate trustworthy object in life (James W. Fowler, *Becoming Adult, Becoming Christian,* 1984).

Religious experience provides the believer with a basic sense of relatedness which is essential for a healthy self. Here religious experience also recapitulates and then goes beyond early life experi-ence. Crucial to the development of a healthy, cohesive self is the "mirroring" which parents and other caretakers provide to the growing child. In a sense the child discovers the self as beautiful and good in the face of its mother, and thus a human foundation is laid for the discovery of the self as of infinite worth in the face of God. Parents' continued mirroring of their pleasure at the child's pleasure in discovering emerging talents and skills allows him or her to go forward in life with adequate goals and ideals (Heinz Kohut, *The Analysis of the Self,* 1971). Self-pathology results from in-adequate mirroring and can manifest itself in a religious experience in which there is an inauthentic experience of the sense of no-self. Psychology provides as a criterion for authentic religious experience the possession of a basically healthy self (John McDargh, "The Life of the Self in Christian Spirituality and Contemporary Psychoanalysis," *Horizons,* 11, 1984, 355-360). However, granted the posses-sion of a self, spiritual theology describes a movement beyond images of self and images of God through a negation that is ultimately transformative and grace-inspired. These upper reaches of religious experience imply metaphorically a dis-covery of the Face which gives the pro-foundest sense of affirmation (James E. Loder, *The Transforming Moment,* 1981). Self-love is transformed and exhibits itself in a new-found wisdom, creativity, empathy, and sense of humor.

Verification of the authenticity of relig-ious experience at all developmental levels requires consideration of its adequacy and its appropriateness. Evaluation of the adequacy of religious experience entails exploring its roots and meaning-fulness in terms of common human expe-rience. This evaluation is facilitated by the contributions of psychology and other sciences which continue to probe human experiencing. Adequate religious experi-ence reaffirms the value of human life even in the face of negative experiences. Determination of the appropriateness of religious experience centers on whether the experience has truly put a person in touch with the ultimate and effected a conversion in his or her life. From the christian perspective, appropriate relig-ious experience must meet the demands of a christian understanding of existence which sees the transcendent as ultimately trinitarian and is guided by gospel values. Such religious experience will bring the individual into a fuller experience of the paschal mystery of dying and rising with Christ. It will be continuous with the experiences of the christian community and its tradition and be coherent with the contents of the community's faith. Finally, the experience will point in the direction of the final fulfillment. For "now we see indistinctly, as in a mirror: then we shall see face to face" (1 Cor 13:12).

See Faith

William James, (1902) *The Varieties of Religious Experience: A Study in Human Nature,* New York: Collier, 1961, London: Fontana, 1971. Dermot A. Lane, *The Experience of God: An Invitation to Do Theology,* New York: Paulist, Dublin: Veritas,

1981. B.J. Lonergan, "First Lecture: Religious Experience," In *A Third Collection,* Mahwah, N.J.: Paulist, 1985. W.W. Meissner, *Psychoanalysis and Religious Experience,* New Haven and London: Yale U.P., 1984. John E. Smith, *Experience and God,* New York: Oxford U.P. 1968.

RAYMOND STUDZINSKI, OSB

F

FAITH

Anthropological Starting Point

The Second Vatican Council's decree *The Church in the Modern World* (no. 22), affirms that Christ, the new man, reveals the mystery of man to himself. Presupposed in this affirmation is that the human person is a riddle to himself, that being who precisely puts his own being and existence in question, searches for the ultimate sense of his life and longs for a fulfillment which human sickness and death, injustice and war, cannot destroy. For the twentieth century as well as for that of St. Augustine, it remains true that human existence is characterized by the restlessness of the heart.

Philosophically one could say that this restlessness is rooted in human finitude. This finitude manifests itself in every act of knowing and willing. But it becomes especially manifest in certain human experiences which have been described as limit-situations. The primary among these is no doubt death. But among other such situations one could mention a moral decision in which I risk my being in an absolute way in some finite choice or a resolute hope even when humanly speaking I can find no grounds for hope. A contemporary theologian such as Karl Rahner analyzes the human finitude of knowing and loving and argues that it is precisely the awareness of finitude which reveals the human person's dependence upon the Infinite. In every act of knowing and loving I am restless, striving beyond my present situation toward an horizon which I can never reach but which is inescapably present to me. In this situation the religious question inevitably arises. Can I content myself with limited areas of knowledge (such as the empirical sciences) and of choice, or do I allow myself to be open to Mystery, which is always present to me but which I can never manipulate and control? Rahner argues that this Mystery is God and that it is only God who can fulfill my restless longing, and in fact it is only God who allows my life to appear as a totality. Without this ultimate Mystery, my life is merely a bagatelle of fragmented experiences.

Although the human person is referred to Mystery in every experience, philosophical reflection upon Mystery leaves him with an unresolved but still burning question: does the Holy Mystery remain merely silent and distant or does this Mystery wish to speak, to communicate himself to me, to enter into dialogue with me? At the end of philosophical reflection, every man and woman is left listening either to the silence of God or to a possible Word of God. Hence philosophical reflection opens up space for biblical, historical revelation. Such an historical revelation is critical to the human person for a number of reasons.

First of all, human beings are not only questioners. They are also dialogical. The deepest level of my being can only be opened up by being addressed by another. Secondly, since the human person is not in the first instance a knower but a source of ineffable freedom, the resolution of his or her questioning can only be met by the free response of another. Hence the human person's search leads him or her to history to find if God, the infinite source of freedom, has chosen to enter into dialogue with humanity. As the catechism of the German episcopal conference has put it, "When we ask: who is God, we do not have to engage in complicated speculation...Rather faith in God is a response to God's history with humanity. Therefore we can only answer the question of God insofar as we narrate the history of God with human beings and say: Look, there is our God! the God who guided Abraham, liberated Israel, raised Jesus from the dead, called us into fellowship, and the God who comes to save us (see Lk 21:28). Faith in God lives from the memory and re-presentation of this history, which has happened once for all (see Rom 6:10)" (*Katholischer Erwachsenen Katechismus,* 1985, p. 39).

Biblical Understandings of Faith

When one looks at the OT understanding of faith, one sees that faith has to do with that which is reliable, that which gives security, that which can be trusted. Faith presupposes a correspondence between that which is promised and that which is realized. Something is worthy of faith which does not disappoint. Naturally, in the perspective of Israel's covenant relationship, only God is worthy of faith in this sense. Israel is summoned to believe in God's word which is a word of promise. This word will not disappoint because it has God himself for its guarantee. God has bound himself to his word and his fidelity to his word is equivalent to his fidelity to himself. Therefore God summons his people to obey absolutely, to listen to his word, to surrender to it totally. The OT understanding of faith is thus far from intellectualistic; rather it involves an existential surrender of the whole person in obedience. It has to do with the totality of a person's life. Faith is consequently not belief in something but belief in someone. Only God is the person worthy of faith. The paradigm of faith for the OT is Abraham who according to Gen 15:6 believed the Lord, i.e., he accepted God's promise that in spite of all human obstacles he would become the father of a great nation and later was willing to sacrifice his son, trusting in God to fulfill his promise in his own unpredictable manner. The faith of Abraham remains a model even in the NT where he is praised by St. Paul in the Letter to the Romans (chapter 4) and again in the Letter to the Hebrews (11:8). Like Abraham, Israel was called to let go of its own security and to risk all on God. Without this rock of faith, one is left only with counterfeit securities. As Isaiah so beautifully puts it, "If you will not believe, you shall not be established" (7:9). Faith in the God of the covenant, on the other hand, gives one a new and unshakeable foundation.

When we come to the NT, the center of our attention must naturally be focused on Jesus. Here we can consider three points. The first is whether Jesus himself lived by faith. The great medieval tradition represented, for example, by St. Thomas Aquinas, rejected this possibility on the grounds that Jesus always enjoyed the beatific vision. For Aquinas, such a vision is incompatible with faith. Today many theologians reject this approach and argue that it is part of the kenosis of the Incarnation for Jesus to accept our human condition of ignorance and darkness. This is not necessarily to say that Jesus was ignorant of his divinity. One could argue, for example, with Rahner that such knowledge was implicit and became explicit in the same way as our knowledge of ourselves becomes explicit. The moment of full vision would then be the resurrection. Such an approach does greater justice to Jesus's humanity and to the testimony of scripture which speaks of ignorance, growth and even radical darkness on the part of Jesus in the agony in the garden and on the cross. Indeed a number of theologians speak of a growth in faith during the life of Jesus. One could say that the first part of Jesus's ministry was characterized by a certain success and thus the hope that God's kingdom would come shortly. But as his people rejected him, Jesus had to rely ever more on faith in God alone. He was thus subjected to the trials of faith, not in the sense of intellectual doubts, but rather in the sense of the apparent failure of his mission and finally the seeming abandonment by God himself. But whereas Israel, when tested, turned to other gods, Jesus remained absolutely faithful to the end . His life was obedience and his one desire was to do the will of his Father. In this sense, Hans Urs von Balthasar ("Fides Christi," pp. 45-79) argues that Jesus is the perfect fulfillment of the OT understanding of faith: through his obedience, his surrender to his Father, his perseverance in times of trial, he fulfills the OT covenant, and as the Letter to the Hebrews (12:2) says, becomes the pioneer and perfecter of our faith.

There is, however, a second point of importance, namely, that Jesus is not only the embodiment of faith but is also faith's catalyst. When we look at the ministry of Jesus, we see that it was precisely his role to arouse faith in others. When, for example, the father of the epileptic boy comes to Jesus and asks in desperation, "If you can do anything, have pity on us and help us" (Mk 9:23), it is Jesus' rebuke that stirs up faith in the man, so that he cries out, "I do believe; help my unbelief!" (v. 24). In that moment, the father's act of faith enabled him to share in the power of Jesus and his son was healed. Such episodes are typical in the gospels where it is precisely Jesus' mission to summon people to faith.

However, the analysis of Jesus' faith cannot stop there. More important is the third dimension of the NT testimony, namely, that on the basis of the resurrection, Jesus who was the witness of faith has become the ground of faith. We not only believe in Jesus as object of faith but we believe because of him. It is the risen Lord who makes our faith possible. It is striking that Paul can characterize the whole event of Christianity as the coming of faith (Gal 3:23). Christianity and faith are almost synonomous expressions.

We have been speaking about Jesus's faith, that which the NT often describes as *pistis christou*. We could ask ourselves whether the genitive here (of Christ) is a subjective or an objective genitive, that is, is Christ the subject or the object of faith? As is so often the case, we are probably required to say both and indeed to go beyond both. Balthasar suggests that we could call this a mystical genitive, that is, the Christian is called to live within the reality of Christ and his faith. What Christ lived, he now makes possible for us. We are called to be incorporated into his innermost attitude.

Perhaps we could sum up these biblical reflections upon faith by looking briefly at St. Paul, for it is this apostle who for the first time develops so beautifully the theology of faith for the Christian community. Paul carefully balances the objective and the subjective dimensions of faith, the *fides quae* and the *fides qua*. The *fides quae* is nothing less than Christ himself. As Paul puts it in Gal 2:20, "I live by faith in the Son of God who loved me and gave himself for me." This faith is presented to the believer through the preaching of the kerygma. According to a central text of the Letter to the Romans, "Faith comes from what is heard and what is heard comes by the preaching of Christ" (10:17). At the same time, hearing the gospel demands a response from the subject, which is nothing less than a total abandonment and surrender to the grace of God. Such a surrender Paul calls the obedience of faith (Rom 1:5; 16:26). As one lets oneself be totally grounded in the gospel which is the gift of God, one is justified. One's situation before God is made right, not by any human effort or by the works of the law, but solely by the gift of grace in Christ. Hence faith as an act of obedience implies the total renouncing of every form of self-glorification in favor of the foolishness of the cross (1 Cor 18:25). In place of boasting on the basis of human righteousness or works, Paul knows only the humble admission of his weakness in which the power of God's grace shines forth (2 Cor 4:7; 12:5, 8-10).

In this perspective, Ugo Vanni defines the Pauline understanding of faith as "a radical and total opening of the self to the content and message of the gospel, i.e., Christ himself: a process begun at a precise moment, drawn out and developed, and shared by the community of believers." Faith begins at the moment of conversion in which there is an initial adhesion to Christ. This is followed by a progressive assimilation to Christ. We are gradually purified of sin and our lives become ever more Christocentric. The culmination of this process is the replacement of our egoism with the person of Christ. As Paul expresses it, "I live now, not I, but Christ lives in me" (Gal 2:20). Finally, it is important to note that this Christification of our lives is not something which happens individualistically, but it is a process which is sustained by the community; supported by the diverse charisms and responsibilities of the

community and nurtured by the celebration of the Lord's eucharist, the believer's faith grows and matures.

Historical Perspectives

Naturally, in an article of this length, it would be impossible to trace the history of the theology of faith. However, it is essential to look at least at two theologians of the christian tradition who significantly influenced the interpretation of faith and whose theologies are still of great importance for an ecumenical dialogue between the Catholic and Protestant understandings of faith today. I am thinking of Aquinas and Luther.

The first thing which strikes one when one studies Aquinas's theology of faith, especially after one has looked at biblical perspectives on faith, is the markedly intellectualist account of faith in Thomas' interpretation. Although faith is for Aquinas a virtue, it is primarily an act of the intellect and Aquinas stresses its cognitive character. Interestingly, whereas Aquinas' predecessors, including St. Albert the Great, had situated the act of faith in the affective intellect, Thomas situated it in the speculative intellect. Faith, then, is an act of the judgment which is directed to the First Truth, God himself. All other articles of faith can be reduced to this primary act of faith. In the *Summa Theologica,* Aquinas offers the following definition of faith: "To believe is an act of mind assenting to divine truth by virtue of the command of the will as this is moved by God through grace; in this way the act stands under the control of the free will and is directed towards God" (S.Th. I-II, q. 2, art. 9).

A number of points call for comment. First, as we have seen, Aquinas stresses more the intellectual character of faith than the existential surrender, although the latter is not missing, as we shall see. Secondly, Aquinas notes that the motive for faith is the authority of God. This objective authority, however, becomes credible because of the interior inspiration by which God invites the believer to make the act of faith. Hence we see a very close interplay between the intellect and the will. Without God's grace moving the will, the intellect could never make the necessary assent of faith. As Aquinas puts it in *De Veritate,* "The virtue of faith does not have the function to move the intellect directly to assent to the revealed truths, but disposes it to follow docilely the motion of the will. Faith is, in fact, rooted in the intelligence, considered formally, however, insofar as it is subjected to the command of the will" (q. 14, art. 4). According to scholastic theology, therefore, faith is *formaliter in intellectu* but *causaliter in voluntate.*

The other interesting aspect of Aquinas's treatment of faith is the relation between faith and charity, a point which is critical for the reformation debates about faith. Naturally, St. Thomas sees a close link between faith and charity, since God is not only the First Truth but also the Supreme Good, and Aquinas recognizes that it does the believer little good to know the supreme truth and not to adhere to it as his ultimate need. Thus Thomas recognizes that faith comes to its full fruition when it is accompanied by charity. This type of faith Thomas calls formed faith, *fides formata caritate.* But given his intellectualist understanding of faith, he recognizes another type of faith, which he calls *fides informis,* i.e., faith without love, which is of no avail to our salvation.

For many today, Thomas's intellectualist approach seems seriously deficient, since it seems to offer little to contemporary man's questions, doubts and existential concerns. Nonetheless, it is important not to divorce Thomas's theology of faith from its fuller context within the *Summa Theologica.* For Thomas, as well as for Luther, faith is only possible within the *ambiance* of God's offer of himself in grace and is ordered to human participation in the divine life. As Otto Hermann Pesch puts it (*Theologie der Rechtfertigung bei Martin Luther und Thomas von Aquin,* 1967, p. 723), even for St. Thomas, faith is ultimately an act of turning toward the justifying God, who makes this act possible and sustains it by the converting power of his grace. For all the complexity of its derivative parts, in its roots faith is simple, for it is man's conversion to God.

When we turn to Luther's doctrine of faith, we note a polemical rejection of the intellectual tradition of Aquinas and a reappropriation of the biblical tradition with its emphasis on surrender to God. This aspect is so central in Luther's thought that faith becomes almost synonymous with *fiducia* and trust.

Luther stresses that the primacy in faith belongs to God. It is God who takes the initiative in regard to the sinner, summoning him to the new life of grace. Faith is thus in the first instance that which God works in us, not something which we do. In this sense, faith is anything but a human work.

Faith comes about concretely when the believer hears the Word of God addressed to him and recognizes its promise. When the Word of God, by the power of the Holy Spirit, works on the heart of the believer, it moves him to surrender to God in trust. Here we find in Luther's thought a paradox. On the one hand faith is a passivity, not something which the human being does but that which is done in him. On the other hand, Luther exhorts his hearers to lay hold of the gift, which is offered to them, in faith. Such texts make it clear that there is an active dimension to this passivity. A logical mind would perhaps find Luther's thought contradictory. But it is important to realize that Luther is not working with logical categories but with existential ones.

Another dimension of Luther's teaching on faith is that it is intensely personal and soteriological. To believe in Christ is not to accept an objective set of truths; it is to accept Christ as my personal saviour, that is, to see that Christ was born and died for me. Typically Luther writes in his *Commentary on Galatians* (1535), "He did not give a sheep or an ox or gold or silver for me. But he who was completely God gave everything he was, gave himself for me—for me, I say, a miserable and accursed sinner. I am revived by this giving of the Son of God unto death and I apply it to myself. This applying is the true power of faith" (*Luther's Works*, Vol. 26, p. 177).

Since faith is for Luther such an intensely existential experience, it carries with it its own certainty. To doubt the certitude of faith and consequently to doubt one's salvation is not possible within faith, for faith is precisely the recognition of and the surrender to the God who is for me. In the act of faith I am delivered from sin, death and hell and find the God who is on my side. Luther writes, "This grace truly produces peace of heart until finally one is healed from corruption and feels he has a gracious God. It is this work which fattens the bones and gives joy, security, and fearlessness to the conscience so that one dares all, can do all, and in this trust in the grace of God, laughs even at death" (Ibid, Vol. 32, p. 227).

For all the certainty of faith, Luther's own struggles, experiences of depression and spiritual assaults, made him realistic enough to see that faith also has to do combat. Faith is never a once for all possession but a continuous battle. In this sense Luther took up again the biblical tradition of the perseverance of faith amid life's temptations. Faith thus has an essentially eschatological character and is linked to hope. Faith enables one to wage the battle to the end.

Finally, we might mention Luther's understanding of the relation between faith and charity. Given Luther's existential understand of faith, he could never accept the scholastic idea of *fides informis*. According to Luther, the salvation-event for the sinner takes place not through charity but through faith. Luther rigorously excluded all ideas of meritorious acts as deciding a person's salvation. Nevertheless, Luther taught that there is a deep bond between faith and charity, since charity flows inevitably from faith. A faith which does not overflow in charity is for Luther a contradiction in terms. In this sense, he appropriated the Pauline dictum of Gal 5:6 where the apostle speaks of "faith working through love."

From Vatican I to Vatican II

To understand the contemporary Catholic approach to faith, one must see the striking development of magisterial teaching on faith in the last two ecumenical councils. First, we must look at the teaching on revelation and faith as it is presented in Vatican I. The context of the council is very important, for the council was addressing concrete problems of its time and was trying to steer a middle course between fideism and rationalism.

The first point to note is that revelation is considered to be a series of supernatural truths which God makes known to the human being. There are divine mysteries which the human intellect cannot know on its own but which God reveals because God has freely chosen to give men and women a supernatural end, and the knowledge of these supernatural truths is necessary, if they are to achieve their end. In this context, faith is understood to be the submission of the intellect and will to God when he makes a revelation. Faith is accordingly defined as "a supernatural virtue by which with the inspiration and help of God's grace, we believe that what he has revealed is true—not because its intrinsic truth is seen with the natural light of reason—but because of the authority of the God who reveals it" (D.S. 3008).

A number of points call for comment. First, the council is working with what is called a propositional view of revelation. God reveals certain truths about himself and about the final end of human beings which they must believe. Secondly, the council's thinking is dualistic. The council thinks in terms of two orders of reality—the natural and the supernatural, and of two orders of knowledge, natural knowledge derived from reason and supernatural knowledge derived from revelation. These two orders can never be in conflict, for they have the same God as their author. Finally, the motive for believing is a strictly extrinsic one. One doesn't believe because one sees the inner harmony between God's revelation and the human search for salvation. One believes on the authority of the God who reveals.

When we evaluate the teaching of the First Vatican Council on faith, we note a permanent achievement in the council's rejection of fideism and rationalism. Within the turbulent historical situation in which the council found itself, it correctly steered a middle course. Against the fideists and the agnostics, it defended the capacity of the human intellect. The truths of faith as such cannot be demonstrated by human reason nor can one be coerced into believing by rational arguments. Nevertheless, as we shall see, the dualistic and extrinsicist framework within which the Council developed its teaching on faith has been largely superseded by the doctrine of the Second Vatican Council.

When we compare the development between the two Vatican councils, we see that the principal contribution of Vatican II is its effort to overcome the two-storied view of reality and knowledge inherited from Vatican I. If in Vatican I, the problematic was faith and reason, in Vatican II it is faith and history. Revelation is considered within the framework of salvation history. God made himself known in his saving deeds in the OT, and in the fullness of time he has perfectly revealed himself in Jesus Christ. Hence revelation is identical with the person of Christ, and to discover God's revelation of himself one is referred precisely to Jesus Christ. The council fathers write, "For this reason Jesus perfected revelation by fulfilling it through his whole work of making himself present and manifesting himself: through his words and deeds, his signs and wonders, but especially through his death and glorious resurrection from the dead and final sending of the Spirit of truth" (D.V. 4).

Although Vatican II does not deny the theory of propositional revelation and repeats the assertions of Vatican I, it is in fact offering a new and profounder interpretation of faith. Number 5 of *Dei Verbum* appeals to the biblical concept of the "obedience of faith," whereby a person entrusts his whole self freely to God. Gregory Baum comments that faith is here understood as "the surrender to the revealing God, surrender engaging the entire personality of man" (Baum, p. 62).

The other significant development is the attempt of the council to overcome the dualism between the natural and the supernatural. In *Dei Verbum,* the council fathers speak of God's revealing the hidden purpose of his will and affirm that in Jesus Christ "the deepest truth about God and the salvation of man is made clear" (no. 2). Here there is no longer a dominant extrinsicist perspective in which one believes solely on the authority of the God who reveals. Rather, in God's revelation, the truth of God and the truth of my humanity are revealed together. There is a certain connaturality between the two, so that *Gaudium et Spes* can say, as we noted at the beginning of this article, that Christ reveals the truth of every man to himself (no. 22).

Finally, we might advert to the integration of the historical and intrinsicist approach in the document *Gaudium et Spes*. According to the vision of this document, it is too simplistic to see the human being as a citizen of two worlds or of two cities (in Augustinian language) that have nothing to do with one another, or that at best are so related that the earthly city is merely a preparation for the heavenly one. Rather the council tries to think of the two as intrinsically linked together. Although each person and indeed history itself has a transcendental goal, this goal is not detached from present history. God does not want to bring about his kingdom without reference to what happens in history through our human efforts. Building a genuinely human kingdom of justice and peace is already the first step toward the kingdom of God. In what has become a classic text, the council tried to express the relation between the two cities in this way: "While we are warned that it profits a man nothing if he gain the whole world and lose himself, the expectation of a new earth must not weaken but rather stimulate our concern for cultivating this one. For here grows the body of a new human family, a body which even now is able to give some kind of foreshadowing of the new age. Earthly progress must be carefully distinguished from the growth of Christ's kingdom. Nevertheless, to the extent that the former can contribute to the better ordering of human society, it is of vital concern to the Kingdom of God" (no. 39). This text is significant for the theology of faith, because it clearly affirms that it is mistaken to believe that one's faith in God can bypass this world and its history. Just as faith is rooted in God's historical events culminating in Jesus Christ, so faith is challenged to discover God's presence amid the vicissitudes of the historical realities of everyday life.

Faith and Dogma

In this article we have stressed faith as a personal relationship with God based on trust. Nonetheless it is important to recognize, as St. Thomas stressed, that faith does have a cognitive dimension. This dimension comes to expression in the so-called dogmas of the faith. Since the First Vatican Council, the Catholic Church has understood three elements to be constitutive of a dogma: a divinely revealed truth, proclaimed by the infallible magisterium, binding on the faithful now and forever. Historians of theology have shown that such a restricted use of the term dogma only emerged in the eighteenth century. Nonetheless in earlier centuries there were certain analogous notions such as "articulus fidei" of which St. Thomas Aquinas speaks.

That faith comes to expression in defined truths has its roots in the eschatological nature of the Christ-event. Because Christ is God's definitive Word to the world and because he has won a victory which will last until the end of time, it is necessary for his church to be able to proclaim that victory faithfully in every age. Otherwise Christ's eschatological grace would be lost. This context helps us to see the value and the limits of dogmas. First, it is important to note that dogmatic definitions are not to be identified with the Word of God as such. In the primordial sense, only Jesus Christ is the Word of God, and because of the Holy Spirit this Word is preached in every succeeding generation. The primary movement in the church is therefore the freedom of the Spirit to interpret the Christ-event to each generation. Nonetheless, as Rahner says, there is no listening to the Word of God without its theological moment. Dogmatic statements are the result of the church's becoming conscious of its faith and of its being able to give an account of itself. Hence there is always a tension between fidelity to the past (the non-transcendable Christ-event) and openness to the future. Every dogmatic decision not only delimits the truth but also opens up the future. A dogmatic definition has the task of pointing to the absolute future when God's saving work will be completed. Kasper suggests that in this perspective, we must see dogmas as thoroughly historical and dynamic (Kasper, p. 108). They grow out of a given situation and point to God's future. As historical, they share the properties of other human assertions, for example, they are limited and perspectival. They are also influenced by the human situation of sinfulness. A dogma as defined by the church is true but this does not necessarily mean that it is apt or perfectly expressed. In "What is a Dogmatic Statement?" (pp. 45-46), Rahner argues that even a true dogma can be hasty, ambiguous, dangerous and seductive. Hence the church has the obligation to seek to formulate her beliefs, so as to bear the most adequate witness possible to the gospel. This mission is most faithfully carried out, according to Rahner, when a dogma is mystagogic, i.e., when it truly points beyond itself to the Absolute Mystery who is God himself. In Kasper's words, there is always more unsaid in a dogma than is said and it is the task of hermeneutics to discover this unsaid mystagogic dimension.

The Mysteries of Faith

If faith is ultimately the radical surrender of the totality of the person to God, what is the believer to make of the fact that he is asked to believe so many dogmas of the church? Does not the multiplicity of dogmas obscure the unity of faith, so that Christianity appears as a collection of strange propositions that one must believe? In a creative early essay, "The Concept of Mystery in Catholic Theology" (pp. 36-73), Karl Rahner addressed this problem. First, Rahner unswervingly affirms that there is only one mystery of faith and that is Mystery itself. The truth of each man and woman is that he or she is called to surrender to the nameless Mystery who is beyond all our finite, this-worldly experience and who is yet the ground of our existence. However, as Rahner points out, Christianity wants to say something more and indeed more astonishing: this God, the ultimate Mystery, wants to give himself away and draw so close to us that he becomes, in Rahner's words, a co-constitutive dimension of our very subjectivity (*Foundations of Christian Faith*, pp. 116-137). God comes to dwell at the center of each human being. In theological language, this indwelling is the work of God's uncreated grace, i.e., the work of the Holy Spirit. However, the human person would not be fully redeemed if God touched only his interiority. Human life is radically historical and unfolds in the world. Christianity claims that God has so loved this world that he chose to become incarnate in it. God has perfectly expressed himself in space and time in the person of Jesus Christ. But when we consider these two mysteries more closely, we see that the one God, the Absolute Mystery, has given himself to the world in the two missions of the Son and the Holy Spirit. Hence we experience God, the origin of our salvation (Father) through the Son in the Holy Spirit. Such an experience of God is what is technically called the experience of the economic Trinity, i.e., God as he is known in the economy of salvation. But if God has really revealed *himself* (and not merely something about himself), then it must follow that God, in his own life, is as he reveals himself. Hence, Rahner proposes the thesis that the Trinity of the economy of salvation is the immanent Trinity and vice versa. In this way Rahner shows that at its root Christianity consists of three mysteries: Trinity, incarnation and grace. All the other truths of the faith can be reduced to these and these three are really three different aspects of God's one communication of himself to the world.

The Credibility of Faith

We have already seen that according to Vatican I faith cannot be demonstrated by reason nor can the act of faith be coerced. How then does one come to believe? Here a number of considerations can help us to understand the credibility of faith. First, there is Newman's idea of the illative sense, that is, a series of convergent probabilities which lead one to an absolute assurance, which is greater than any of the components which led to it. This type of illative sense is seen most clearly in personal relations. My trust in another person is based on a love which allows me to see more in the person than I can rationally demonstrate. Nevertheless, such a trust is not irrational, even if it cannot be logically proved.

A second idea which helps us to understand the credibility of faith is Rahner's distinction between the object of faith and the ground of faith. According to Rahner every ground of faith is an object of faith, but not every object of faith is the ground of faith (Ibid., pp. 238-240). A typical instance would be the belief in the empty tomb. The important point, however, is that the object of faith is perceived within faith itself, i.e., the object of faith is not perceptible outside the realm of faith. Ultimately this is not a vicious circle, for as Rahner argues, the subject who believes is not just an objective knower but a graced subjectivity. God's grace (ground of faith) is already operating in me, allowing me to perceive the truth.

Hans Urs von Balthasar has powerfully developed the epistemology of faith according to his aesthetic model of revelation. According to Balthasar, it is aesthetic categories above all which help us to overcome the dichotomy between the objective and the subjective in the act of faith. According to Balthasar's aesthetics, perceiving the beautiful requires two dimensions. The first is the perception of the form, the second is the act of being enraptured (*The Glory of the Lord, A Theological Aesthetics,* Vol. 1, 1982). But these two elements always work harmoniously together. First, there really is something to be perceived. The beautiful manifests itself in the form. However, what is objectively there to be seen can only be perceived by the person who is enraptured. What is required is the yes of faith. Being enraptured happens when God's grace transports the believer into God's world. Even in purely human experience, one can verify this process. Mozart's *Magic Flute,* for example, is a work of supreme beauty. In this sense it is self-authenticating. However, it is possible that some persons cannot perceive its beauty. This says nothing about Mozart, but rather reveals a lack in the perceiver.

In this approach to the credibility of faith, Jesus Christ is perceived as the form of divine beauty. In him we see the glory of God made manifest. However, the biblical revelation of God's beauty requires a conversion, literally a metanoia or turning-around on the part of the human subject. Why? Because God's glory, God's form, is manifested in the formlessness of the cross. In Isaiah's words, "He had no form or comeliness that we should look at him, and no beauty that we should desire him" (53:2). That such a revelation is a paradox and not a contradiction becomes evident when one sees that the beauty revealed here in the formlessness of the cross is the revelation of love. Love is the form of revelation and in the cross, we see the supreme manifestation of love, the love of Christ, who loved his own to the end (Jn 13:1). In this sense, Balthasar would argue that only love is credible (*Love Alone: The Way of Revelation,* 1970).

Faith and Hope

Precisely because the object of faith is unseen, discussions about the credibility of faith often center on the relation between faith and reason. Nevertheless in order to preserve a more integrated anthropology, it is also important to see the inter-connection between faith and hope. The First Letter of St. Peter adverts us to this truth when the apostle writes, "Always be prepared to make a defense to any one who calls you to account for the hope that is in you" (3:15). This exhortation reminds us again that it is the nature of human beings to be historical, and that as such they are propelled to the future and long for a future which will satisfy their hunger for the fullness of life. This anthropological perspective is essential, if one is going to appropriate Jesus's message of the Kingdom of God and the church's gospel about the risen Christ. For this gospel is a message about human hopes, the hope for a kingdom of justice and peace, the hope for the fullness of life without end which only God can give. Hence the credibility of faith is proportionate to the human being's capacity to hope. Gerald O'Collins has stressed this point in his book *Fundamental Theology* (1981, pp. 150-152). O'Collins refers to Kant's famous three questions: what can I know; what must I do; what can I hope for? Christian faith provides its own response to each of these questions. In faith I know the Mystery of God revealed in Christ. But, as we saw above in the section on St. Paul, such knowledge implies an orthopraxis, a progressive assimilation to him, the Christification of our lives. But this faith also provides a response to our human hopes—I can hope for the kingdom of God and life everlasting.

The hope of faith, however, always involves the element of "in spite of." Here in this life we are confronted daily with the reality of suffering and death, war and injustice, the brutality of human beings to one another. A faith, however, which is rooted in the resurrection of the crucified Christ, is able to hope in spite of these appearances. Here one can appropriate again the OT dimension of the endurance of trials, perseverance amid tribulation, which Christ himself knew and through which he held out in faith to the end (Heb 12:2). With Christ as our model of faith, we can say with the author of the Letter to the Hebrews, "Faith is the assurance of things hoped for, the conviction of things not seen" (11:1).

The Spirituality of Faith

The whole thrust of this article has been that faith is anything but a dry assent to intellectual propositions. Rather faith is the letting-go by which I surrender my own securities and take Christ alone as my rock. In St. Paul's great hymn in the second chapter of Philippians, he sings of Christ, who did not consider his equality with God a thing to be clung to, but emptied himself taking the form of a slave (Phil 2:6-7). The Christian is invited in faith to relive this self-emptying of Christ. The more one is assimilated to Christ, the more one abandons one's self-boasting and lets Christ become the center of one's personality. Again St. Paul says, "I live now, not I, but Christ lives in me" (Gal 2:20).

A fitting word to sum up this spiritual truth is poverty. It is the testimony of the saints that the more one comes to know Christ, the more one is aware of one's own poverty. Such poverty, however, is not paralyzing, because one's trust is not located in oneself but wholly in him. This is the testimony of Paul in his Second Letter to the Corinthians, and it is the continual testimony of the saints. The difficulty is that so often we cloak over our refusal to accept our spiritual poverty with a spurious idea of holiness, which is a subtle form of pride. Ruth Burrows writes, "Striving for perfection is the most disastrous of the mistakes good people fall into. It feeds the very vice it intends to destroy. Most fervent souls are prepared to give God any mortal thing, work themselves to death, anything except the one thing he wants, total trust: anything but surrender into his loving hands. 'You must become as little children' whose one virtue is that they know they are unimportant"(*Guidelines for Mystical Prayer,* 1980, pp. 83-84). For Burrows, St. Thérèse is a striking model of this type of spiritual childhood, for she refused to take herself seriously and was unwilling to play the saint. Asked to say a few pious words to the doctor on her deathbed, she refused, letting him think what he wanted. Although she had many neurotic qualities, she reached true sanctity, for she had the courage to accept herself as she was, since her center of gravity was not in herself but in Christ. If the spirituality of faith is childlike surrender, its polar opposite is a pride which manifests itself in self-trust. The faith to which Christ invites us is an insecurity which drives us (in Burrows's words) to throw ourselves upon him like a starving man throws himself upon food. As Burrows puts it, the attitude of faith "consists fundamentally in a total acceptance of the bitter experience of our poverty and an obstinate refusal to evade it; to accept to stand, in very deed not just in pious imagination, stripped before the living God, our leprosy laid bare, crippled in limb, blind, deaf, dumb—a living need" (Ibid., p. 89). When we face this poverty radically, we are in a position for the first time to live the meaning of faith: "In you alone, have I hoped; let me never

be put to shame" (Ps 71:1).

See **Anthropology, Christian; Dogma; Hope; Revelation**

Hans Urs von Balthasar, "Fides Christi," in *Sponsa Verbi Skizzen zur Theologie* II (Einsiedeln: Johannes, 1961), pp. 45-79. Hans Urs von Balthasar, *Love Alone: The Way of Revelation,* London: Sheed and Ward, 1970. Gregory Baum, "Vatican II's Constitution on Revelation: History and Interpretation," *Theological Studies* 28, 1, 1967, pp. 51-75. William Dych , "The Dualism in the Faith of the Church," in *The Faith that Does Justice,* New York: Paulist Press, 1972, pp. 47-66. Gerhard Ebeling, *The Nature of Faith,* London: Collins, 1966. Walter Kasper, *Dogma unter dem Wort Gottes,* Mainz: Matthias-Grünewald, 1965. Karl Rahner, *Foundations of Christian Faith,* London: Darton, Longmann and Todd, 1978. Karl Rahner, "The Concept of Mystery in Catholic Theology," *Theological Investigations,* IV, London: Darton, Longmann and Todd, 1974, pp. 36-73. Karl Rahner, "What is a Dogmatic Statement?" *Theological Investigations* V London: Darton, Longmann and Todd, 1966, pp. 42-66. St. Thomas Aquinas, *Summa Theologica* II-II, qq. 1-7.

JOHN O'DONNELL, SJ

FALL, THE
See **Original Sin**

FATHERS OF THE CHURCH

"Father of the Church" is the traditional title given to the christian preachers, writers and theologians of the post-canonical period. Unlike that of "doctor," which denotes a particularly outstanding teacher, it is a popular title and not one bestowed officially by the church. Thus also, Father and doctor are not synonymous terms, although some Fathers are in fact doctors as well.

Inasmuch as the Fathers came immediately after the age of the NT, contributed decisively to the shape of christian belief, and by and large enjoyed a reputation for sanctity (although some of the most famous of them have never been referred to as saints), their opinions have always carried considerable weight in the church. The documents of the

Second Vatican Council, to mention a significant example from recent times, cite them very frequently. But the Fathers' influence is by no means limited to Roman Catholicism. The Orthodox are probably more devoted to them than Catholics are, while Anglicans and those in the Protestant tradition have also traditionally made extensive use of them.

The Fathers for the most part were bishops, and some fewer held other clerical rank. As such they exercised a degree of pastoral responsibility, and their writings often reflect this. But laymen are also to be found in their ranks. Clement of Alexandria (c. 150-c. 215) and Tertullian (c. 160-c.220) are perhaps the two most important lay Fathers, and at least part of Origen's (c. 185-c. 254) prodigious literary career occurred when he was a layman. The Desert Fathers, i.e., the monks of the Egyptian Desert who flourished in the fourth and fifth centuries and who are known primarily from stories told about them and from pithy sayings attributed to them, were generally laymen as well. Finally, a few women can be numbered among early christian writers, the most notable being the Spanish (?) nun and pilgrim Egeria (fl. before 448).

The writings of the Fathers take numerous forms—sermons, letters, treatises on various subjects, biographies and hagiographies, autobiographies, histories and chronicles, apologies, scriptural exegesis, accounts of martyrdom, texts of liturgies, apophthegms and maxims, songs and poems, journals, apocryphal literature and inscriptions. In some cases a writing is anonymous, like the *Epistle to Diognetus,* written toward the beginning of the second century. In others the ascribed author is certainly not the correct one, as with the apocryphal literature purporting to have been composed by some NT figure. And there are still other cases in which we possess a writing only

in fragments, or no longer possess it at all but know of its having existed and its author from some other source.

The patristic age (patristic is the relevant adjective, while patrology and patristics denote the study of the Fathers) runs from near the end of the first century of the christian era until roughly the middle of the eighth. In this lengthy period several smaller periods are occasionally distinguished by scholars. The first is that of the Apostolic Fathers, so called because of these men's nearness in time to the apostles; it extends from the earliest writer to around the middle of the second century. The second half of the second century is another such distinct period, characterized by numerous apologies or defenses of the faith, and the Fathers here are known as apologists. Finally, what is sometimes known as the Golden Age runs from approximately the '60's of the fourth century until about the death of Cyril of Alexandria in 444; it is referred to as such because so many of the greatest Fathers lived then and worked out enduring solutions to perennial christian problems, particularly in trinitarian theology and christology.

The earliest surely datable patristic work is the so-called *First Letter of Clement,* which was composed c.96. The mysterious work known as *The Didache,* however, may date even earlier, although this is a matter of some dispute. In the Greek East the patristic age is said to come to a close with the synthesizing theologian John Damascene, who died c. 750. In the Latin West the age ends with one of three Fathers—either Gregory the Great, who died in 604, or Isidore of Seville, who died in 636, or Bede the Venerable, who died in 735. The uncertain terminal point in the West only serves to illustrate what is true of the East as well, namely that such cut-off dates are rather arbitrary. Indeed, the patristic spirit continued in the East for many centuries after the death of John Damascene, and Orthodox Christians often argue that it continues undimmed in Orthodoxy today. In the West this spirit was fostered especially by monastic theologians until the thirteenth century, when it began to be eclipsed by the new approach of scholasticism. Yet even in the scholastic and post-scholastic West the teachings of the Fathers have never been utterly neglected, and one of the characteristic marks of a great theologian has always been his or her familiarity with patristic thought.

Although for the sake of convenience a distinction is often made—as just now in this article—between the Latin West and the Greek East, both part of the immediate Mediterranean world or at least including the world directly influenced by Greece and Rome, in fact the geographical and linguistic scope of the Fathers is much broader. It also includes peoples who lived on the fringes of or outside that world and who spoke and wrote in Syriac, Coptic, Armenian, Arabic and several other languages. The Latin and Greek Fathers attained the importance that they enjoy in the European and American sphere because Europeans and Americans are in large part the heirs of the Greco-Roman civilization from which those Fathers came. Yet the body of patristic literature in Syriac, dominated by the brilliant and prolific Ephrem of Nisibis (c. 306-373), is beginning to be more widely known, thanks to translations, and much of it is equal in depth and beauty, in its own way, to anything written in Greek or Latin.

The nearly seven centuries of the patristic era and the diversity of culture implied in the regional and linguistic differences among the Fathers guarantee a corresponding diversity of thought and concerns. R.M. Grant cites G. Bardy in this regard: "The writers of Rome are distinguished from the others by their practical spirit, by their sense of responsibility, by the firmness of their moral concern. The Egyptians, more idealistic, attempt vast syntheses; they try to explain the world, or at least to give general pictures of christian teaching. The Asiatics hold above all to the transmission of the tradition they have received from the apostles, and struggle with an invincible firmness against heresies. Finally the Syrians and Palestinians usually become chroniclers or historians, unless they draw up codes of liturgy or morals" (R.M. Grant, *Second-Century Christianity*, London, 1957, pp. 10-11).

While agreeing with Grant (p. 11) that Bardy's distinctions do not hold in every case, we can nonetheless say that his brief description of the era is an evocative one. To it might be added, however, a few words on the theological ferment of the age. Early Christianity was not only menaced by such non-christian and seductive rivals as Judaism, Gnosticism and Manichaeism, and threatened by powerful heresies from within, like Arianism, Nestorianism and Monophysitism. It also had to endure sometimes bitter controversy among the orthodox themselves. In this respect we can mention such events as the crisis over the rebaptism of heretics that broke between Stephen of Rome and Cyprian of Carthage in the mid-250's; the question of the exact standing of the see of Constantinople vis-à-vis the sees of Rome and Alexandria, which arose in the final quarter of the fourth century; and the dispute surrounding the acceptability of Origen's theology, which emerged at the very end of that same century. There were, moreover, different schools of theology, which held jealously to their different views; the most notable of these were Antioch and Alexandria in the fifth century. Finally, two Fathers in particular stand out as having occupied highly ambiguous positions, namely Tertullian and Origen. The former, an incisive thinker and the first theologian to use Latin, seems to have fallen into schism in his lifetime, while the latter espoused so many daring ideas, subsequently judged heterodox, that his writings were condemned and burned in the sixth century in the East, and many of them were lost as a result. The fifth-century author Vincent of Lérins speaks of both as having been a great trial to the church of their day precisely because of their brilliance and influence (cf. *Commonitorium* 17.42-18.46). Still, thanks to their positive contributions and to their gigantic intellectual stature, the two of them enjoy the status of Fathers.

It is perhaps all the more amazing, then, that in the midst of such unsettled conditions—with not only diversity but actual conflict and well-founded suspicions of heresy—there should nonetheless have emerged a consensus of opinion on the part of the Fathers regarding the essential elements of the faith. This consensus consisted at least in the following points: 1) belief in a three-personed God, each person being equally divine; 2) belief in the creation of the world by God out of nothing, and hence belief in its goodness and its utter dependence on him; 3) belief in the perfect divinity and humanity of Christ, his human nature having been taken from the Virgin Mary and assumed for the salvation of a sinful humankind; 4) belief in the institutional church, with its hierarchy and its sacraments, as the means whereby one would obtain participation in the salvation achieved by Christ, with the corollary that salvation was unattainable apart from the church; 5) belief in a heaven and a hell, and in the resurrection of the body; 6) adherence to a rigorous moral code; 7) the conviction that certain ascetical practices, chief among them almsgiving and fasting, as well as prayer, were indispensable helps to the acquiring of salvation; 8) belief in an invisible world, inhabited by angels and demons, who exercised some influence on human affairs; and 9) belief in a twofold level of scripture, i.e., literal and spiritual, the spiritual offering the deeper understanding of the sacred text.

It should be remarked, however, that not all the Fathers succeeded in expressing each of these truths with equal clarity; nor did all give the same attention to them (indeed, many of them went unmentioned by many Fathers); nor were all the truths in question even understood to be as indisputable in the earliest stages of the patristic era as they were taken to be in its later stages. Something like the constitution of the Trinity, for example, had to be puzzled out until well into the fourth century, and we should not be surprised to find a second-century Father like Justin Martyr (c. 100-165) or a third-century one like Origen seeming to suggest that the divine persons were not absolutely equal to one another. By the middle of the fourth century, though, when a broad agreement had been arrived at, such an opinion would have been clearly a deviation. On the other hand, things like belief in an afterlife and in an invisible world were never controversial issues.

This gradual acquiring of a consensus, the transition from doctrinal confusion to doctrinal clarity, is commonly known as the development of dogma. Yet this development does not necessarily imply the eradication of certain different emphases that went unreconciled and that, far from being heretical, represent legitimate variations within a single orthodox stance. Perhaps the most striking instance of this is the two views of the human condition in East and West—more optimistic and less explicit about the absolute necessity of grace in the East, while, especially from the time of Augustine on, more pessimistic in the West.

The key to understanding almost any patristic view is seeing how it fits into the scheme of salvation. Christology dominates patristic thought—with some exceptions, as when during much of the fourth-century trinitarian theology came to the fore—because the exact make-up of Christ was determinative of how, and if, human beings would be saved. Any imbalance in Christ's constitution, an overemphasis on either his humanity or his divinity, would have profound and tragic consequences for the believer. Hence the patristic concern for an exact theological vocabulary, one which would most closely express the truth of the mystery, was entirely justifiable and was not merely a case of nit-picking.

But the Fathers did not come together only on the important doctrinal matters noted above. Also characteristic of them is a unanimity, usually unexpressed, in a number of other areas: 1) a passionate rather than an abstract approach to truth, with, in general, a corresponding intolerance for opposing points of view (hence, for example, the embarrassing anti-semitism in so much patristic literature); 2) an extensive use of rhetoric in the presentation of a topic; 3) a tendency to overdevelop a point and to digress at length; 4) a love of imagery and, in particular, of the scriptural image; 5) a popular appeal, and the use of popular language; 6) a synthetic thrust, resulting in the treatment of the christian mystery as an ensemble rather than as composed of discrete parts; 7) a reverence for antiquity, tradition and the established order, not only in the realm of the sacred but even in that of the profane, and a corresponding suspicion of novelty; and 8) a sense of the mystery of reality, and especially of the mystery of God, which resisted probing and intrusion. The doctrinal points that have been enumerated, placed in the context of this "atmosphere," constitute the patristic spirit that was spoken of at the beginning of this article.

As would be the case with any other grouping as large as this, the Fathers are not all equally profound and expressive. If we were to name the very greatest of them, the list would certainly include Irenaeus (c. 130-c. 200), the most important theologian of the second century, who developed extensively the idea of the recapitulation of all things in Christ, known as the *anakephalaiosis;* Tertullian and Origen, about whom something has already been said; Cyprian of Carthage (?-258), less important for his doctrine, perhaps, than for his moral leadership; Athanasius (c. 298-373), the champion of orthodoxy against the Arians who denied Christ's divinity; Ephrem, who has been previously mentioned; Basil of Caesarea (c. 330-379), Gregory Nazianzen (329-389) and Gregory of Nyssa (c. 330-c. 395), all three seminal theologians of the Trinity and known together as the Cappadocian Fathers from their birthplace; John Chrysostom (c. 329-407), courageous bishop of Constantinople and reputed to be the greatest preacher in Greek; Jerome (331-420), the renowned student of scripture; Ambrose (c. 339-397), who more than anyone else influenced the course of church-state relations in the West; Augustine (354-430), preceptor of the West; Cyril of Alexandria (?-444), the subtle and polemical christologist; Leo the Great (c. 400-461), perhaps the first pope in the medieval sense of the term; Gregory the Great (c. 540-604), second only to Augustine in molding Western thought; and Maximus the Confessor (c. 580-662), whose brilliance has only recently been rediscovered.

Among these, in turn, Origen and Augustine stand out as having exercised, and as continuing to exercise, a particularly significant influence, the former in the East (albeit sometimes surreptitiously, due to his spotty reputation) and the latter in the West.

It is harder to name the most important

patristic works, although the best known Father in the West is certainly Augustine, whose *Confessions* enjoy unparalleled popularity and whose *City of God* is, if not actually read, at least universally acknowledged as a classic of Western literature. For the East one could mention Origen's great speculative treatise *On First Principles,* with its synthetic view of the whole of reality; Athanasius' *Life of Saint Antony,* the first hagiography and in some respects the blueprint for monasticism, both Eastern and Western; and John Climacus' *Ladder of Paradise,* a collection of ascetical maxims composed sometime in the seventh century. The Fathers' influence, however, stems not so much from individual writings as it does from the whole of the approach of all of them to reality—from their "spirit."

See **Theology, History of**

Library of the Fathers of the Holy Catholic Church, Oxford, 1838ff. *A Select Library of Nicene and Post-Nicene Fathers of the Christian Church,* Buffalo, New York, 1886ff; New York, 1890ff. *The Ante-Nicene Fathers,* New York, 1926. *Ancient Christian Writers,* Westminster, Md., 1946ff. *The Fathers of the Church* Washington, 1947ff.

BONIFACE RAMSEY, OP

FEMINIST THEOLOGY

Feminist theology is a recently recognized type of theological reflection. Indeed, many schools of theology throughout the world either regard its legitimacy as in question or do not comprehend its necessity. So in order to define feminist theology one must spend time on the historical and social conditions of its genesis. Feminist theology is not primarily a reflection on special "feminine" themes in theology and does not intend to create a special subcategory of theology relevant primarily to women. Rather, feminist theology arises from a recognition that traditional theology in Christianity (as well as in other major religious traditions)

has been done primarily by males. Women until recently have been excluded from the study of theology at the advanced level in seminaries and universities and also excluded from the professions that flow from advanced theological studies; namely, the ordained ministry, public preaching and teaching at the advanced level.

The result of this historic exclusion of women from the shaping of the public tradition of theology is that theology has suffered from an androcentric and misogynist bias. This means that males, and indeed males of the dominant class and race, have unconsciously been assumed to be the normative human persons. The experience of this class of males has been taken to be normative for humanity as a whole. In addition to this pervasive androcentrism, theology has also been distorted by explicit misogyny. For example, women have been defined as possessing an inferior and non-normative humanity, to be more responsible for the origins of evil than males, to be more prone to sin than males, to be in a state of subjugation, both as an expression of their lesser nature and as punishment for their role in original sin, to lack the image of God and to be unable to represent Christ and to be unordainable. The misogynist teachings have arisen as a way of reenforcing women's exclusion from study, teaching and ministry. They have been received by the tradition as normative and thus bias the fundamental structure of christian theology.

Feminist theology arises as a critical response to the recognition of this androcentric and misogynist bias in the tradition. This bias is perceived to be pervasive and systematic, conditioning the whole tradition through much of its main lines of history from scripture to the present. It is not simply occasional nor the expression of idiosyncratic patterns of thought of particular individuals. This bias is also seen to be illegitimate, as a falsification of the authentic religious message, not a genuine expression of the nature of women in relation to men or as an authentic expression of the will of God. This implies alternative norms of theological anthropology by which these misogynist traditions can be challenged.

Thus feminist theology implies a three-part development. First, there is a convincing demonstration that the androcentric and misogynist bias of the tradition is serious and constitutes a major flaw. Secondly, one needs to establish alternative norms and sources of tradition to challenge these biases. And, thirdly, one seeks a reconstruction or reenvisioning of the theological themes that will free them from these biases against women.

Since this kind of criticism and reconstruction could not take place until women have some public presence in the theological academy, the development of feminist theology has begun to take shape only in recent years, since women have begun to be admitted to seminaries and to the ordained ministry. In other words, only when there is already a sufficient cultural change to throw the traditional arguments for excluding women from public ministry and teaching in doubt, and to cause some denominations to admit women to public leadership, has it been possible for women to gain access to the academic tools and public forum of teaching and research where a more systematic inquiry and critique of this tradition of exclusion of women could be carried out. Thus feminist theology arises as a "second wave," following the actual admission of women to theological study and ministry in some churches and as a part of extending and consolidating this change in practice. Women now become present in sufficient numbers as students, and also as professors, that it becomes possible, not merely to include them *de*

facto, but to critically examine the content of the christian culture so that it confirms rather than negates their presence.

This does not mean that the last twenty years has been the first time that women have reflected critically on theology. In the christian tradition one can find expressions of women's affirmation of their equality and leadership from the beginning. But these are very early (by the end of the first century) marginalized from the dominant tradition. Something like a major movement in which many women criticize misogynist use of biblical texts and affirm their right to leadership in church and society can be found during the seventeenth century in England. This is the first period of popular access to printing and publishing and many women wrote tracts that can be called "feminist" at that time.

There were women preachers among many of the left-wing Civil War sects. The Society of Friends particularly developed a systematic hermeneutic of scripture to affirm women's equality in Christ and their inclusion in preaching, evangelization and church administration. One expression of Quaker feminist theology is the tract by Margaret Fell, co-founder of the Society of Friends with George Fox, "Women's Speaking Justified, Approved and Allowed of by the Scripture" (1667).

Nineteenth-century American feminism can be said to be based on a liberal feminist theology. Many of the American feminist leaders had Quaker roots and brought together Enlightenment and radical christian traditions. In 1837 Sara Grimke, a Quaker, abolitionist and feminist leader, wrote a series of letters against the Massachusetts Congregational clergy in which she argued the theological and scriptural basis of women's rights. She used the text of Genesis 1:27 to argue that God has given equality to men and women as co-sharers in the image of

God. Both men and women therefore shared in dominion over non-human nature, but no dominion was given to man over woman in the original creation. The subordination of women therefore is an unjust and sinful perversion of women's original equality in creation. Reform of society to give women equality both in society and in the church, therefore, is not contrary to the divine will, as the clergy had declared, but indeed is a restoration of God's original plan of creation.

Toward the end of the nineteenth century, leading feminist Elizabeth Cady Stanton gathered a group of educated women into the Women's Revising Committee to do a systematic critique of patriarchy in the Bible (*The Women's Bible*, 1896-98). Other nineteenth-century American feminists like Matilda Joselyn Gage were not sure that the christian tradition could be reformed. They felt that it was inherently patriarchal and needed to be replaced by a new spirituality that would affirm women's original equality before the rise of patriarchal religions such as Judaism and Christianity. This more radical view was continued by other feminist leaders in the early twentieth century, such as Charlotte Perkins Gilman, in her book, *His Religion and Hers: A Study of the Faith of our Fathers and the Work of our Mothers*, 1923.

The fact that these expressions of feminist critique of Christianity are mostly unknown to students of christian thought, and have been rediscovered and studied in the last decade or two, illustrates the basic problem of women *vis-à-vis* christian "tradition." Basically what is regarded as the "tradition" has been defined by male control of teaching. Feminist critique, even when it has managed to attain written form and some public discussion in its own day, has not been incorporated into the tradition of what is taught and

studied and thus disappears. Thus even if women today rediscover these feminists of the past and add considerably to a body of new criticism, this will not reshape the tradition until those who control what is taught as christian history and thought are willing to incorporate this material into the curriculum and reshape the teaching of theology to reflect feminist critique. Needless to say, this can only happen when feminist theology becomes not merely a marginal and occasional item in the theological curriculum, but is regarded as a major perspective through which to teach the foundational tradition.

Although the new wave of feminist theology is only twenty years old, it has already developed a broad base of critical scriptural studies, revisionist church history, historical systematic theology, as well as work in ethics and pastoral psychology, upon which to base a comprehensive rethinking of tradition. Some of the first work on feminist theology took the form of a critique of the masculinist bias of classical theology. In 1968 Kari Børresen, a Norwegian Catholic feminist, wrote a comprehensive study of the role of gender in the theological anthropology of St. Augustine and Thomas Aquinas. The same year saw the first book by Mary Daly, a Catholic trained in the theological faculty of Fribourg, on the sexist bias of the whole christian tradition from earliest times to the present: *The Church and the Second Sex*, 1968. Other studies since that time have provided similar analysis of the sexist distortion of particular authors and theological periods.

Having established the basic reality of sexist distortion of the theological tradition, feminist theology has been concerned to find alternative sources of tradition. The work of recovery of women's history and theological reflection in the christian tradition mentioned above has flowed out of this desire to find new foremothers for a feminist theology. This may take the form of discounting the lines between what the dominant tradition has declared "orthodox" or "heretical." Reexamination of marginalized early christian groups, such as gnostics and Montanists, or new study of popular christian texts, such as the apocryphal gospels, may expand the reading of the christian tradition to include traditions more affirmative of women's participation (Pagels; Davies).

Reevaluation of medieval sectarians, such as Waldensians, Joachimites and Beguines, left-wing Reformation sectarians, and American utopian and sectarian groups, such as Shakers and Christian Scientists, can throw light on the types of traditions that have affirmed both women's theological equality and their participation in leadership. But new study from a feminist perspective, of women accepted both in their own day and in the tradition, such as Teresa of Avila, can also shed new light on a women's reading of christian faith and experience. Neglected writers are rediscovered and taken with new seriousness as theologians, such as the twelfth-century mystic, Hildegard of Bingen.

Of particular importance for both Christians and Jews is the patriarchal bias of Scripture. It is one thing to critique the tradition as flawed, but on what basis can one speak of scripture as distorted by sexist bias and still regard it as an authoritative source of revelation? This question has given rise to a major project of feminist biblical hermeneutics of both Hebrew Scripture and the NT. The participation of Jewish women has also shown the very different way that Jews use the Bible as authoritative and has given a forum for Jewish feminists to critique the way christian feminists may continue to take for granted an anti-Jewish bias in their thought (Russell).

In NT studies, Elisabeth Schüssler Fiorenza has emerged as the leading feminist critic. In her book, *In Memory of Her: A Feminist Theological Reconstruction of Christian Origins,* 1982, Fiorenza argues that early Christianity was a counter-cultural religious movement subversive of traditional hierarchical religious and social patterns. This radical vision was gradually submerged and erased as institutional Christianity reintegrated itself into patriarchal and slave-holding social systems. Patriarchal Christians rewrote the tradition to justify these household patterns, not only for the organization of the christian church and society but also as a metaphor for the relationship of Christians to God and Christ. Fiorenza has continued to lay the basis of her hermeneutic in *Bread Not Stone: The Challenge of Feminist Biblical Interpretation,* 1984.

Feminist theology has not seen itself only as dependent on finding new insights from the past. It sees women's experience as a contemporary category by which sexist theology can be reevaluated. By "women's experience" it has generally meant, not simply gender-specific biological experiences, such as childbirth, since in patriarchal society these too are socially appropriated into a system of subordination of women. Rather 'women's experience" means primarily women's critical experience of the devaluation of her person under patriarchal domination and her own journey of liberation. These stories of women's experience can serve as critical paradigms for critique of sexist ideologies and also for new symbols affirmative of women's full humanity. Story-telling thus becomes an important source for feminist theology (Christ).

Feminist songs, poetry and dance also can become sources for a new feminist spirituality which, in turn, can become material for theological reflection. Since women lack major bodies of tradition which spring from their own experience and point of view, they are in effect, probing the primary basis of theology in direct religious experience as a major foundation for new theological symbol-making. This has also led to major work on feminist liturgy as a way of expressing women's spirituality and journey of liberation in communal worship. Christian, and especially Roman Catholic women, have been active in the development of women's liturgical communities and the publication of handbooks of resources for feminist worship (Ruether and Heschel). Jewish women also have been active in the development of feminist rituals, such as rites of entrance of a daughter into the covenant, women's *minyan* and feminist Seders.

These new sources of theological reflection, both from the past and from contemporary experience, may lead to tentative efforts to restate basic symbols of theology in systematic form. These may focus on the critique and reconstruction of a particular theme in theology, such as the nature of sin, the nature of God, anthropology, christology or eschatology. Since all christian symbols interconnect, all have been biased by the sexist distortion of theological symbols. Examples of works rethinking doctrine, such as God-human relations and sin and grace, are Carter Heyward, *The Redemption of God,* 1981 and Judith Plaskow, *Sex, Sin and Grace, Women's Experience and the Theologies of Reinhold Niebuhr and Paul Tillich,* 1980. An example of a beginning effort to rethink the christian symbols systematically is Rosemary Ruether, *Sexism and God-talk: Towards a Feminist Theology,* 1983.

There are some feminists of Jewish or christian background who have become convinced that these religious traditions cannot be reformed to admit women fully in leadership or to rethink their theology sufficiently to be freed of their sexist bias. They believe the Jewish and christian religious have been patriarchal from their inception in such a way as to make the sacralization of male domination fundamental to their purpose. These women have opted to leave the Jewish or christian traditions and to seek a religion or spirituality that authentically affirms women's humanity as image and expression of the divine. Some of these women believe that there was once an egalitarian society that existed before the rise of patriarchy and that ancient religions centered in the Goddess reflect this pre-patriarchal society. Remnants of these mother-centered religions survived, they believe, in groups persecuted by Christianity, such as medieval witches, which christian inquisitors falsely described as "devil worshippers." Thus these women, with Starhawk the most prominent voice among them, see themselves as reviving an ancient feminist religion.

Other counter-cultural feminists would concede that no feminist religion that is fully satisfactory existed in the past, but women can create new spiritualities out of their experience today (Goldenberg). Mary Daly has become the spokeswomen for those women who have repudiated the possibility of reform of the christian tradition and are seeking a radically new spirituality: *Beyond God the Father,* 1973; *Gynecology: The Metaethics of Radical Feminism,* 1979; *Pure Lust: Feminist Elemental Philosophy,* 1984.

Feminist reflection is not confined to Christians and post-Christians. Increasingly Jewish women are defining their own independent position, not only in matters of ritual, but also in scriptural interpretation. Muslim women and Buddhist women also have begun to do theological critique and reenvisioning of their tradition (Falk and Gross). The contextualization of feminist reflection in many kinds of women's experience, such as black women or lesbian women, is also developing (Grant and Heyward).

Although the development of feminist theology has been associated, in the last two decades, primarily with North America, it is increasingly being internationalized. The Women in Theology Network has been meeting on a monthly basis in Britain since 1984. Feminist theology networks have also been organized in Scandinavia and in Germany and Holland. Writers such as Elisabeth Moltmann-Wendell in Germany and Catharina Halkes in Holland are recognized leaders of European feminist theology. Feminist theology networks are also beginning in Latin America, Africa and Asia, representing a christian feminist perspective in these areas. Thus one can look forward to increasing contextualization of feminist theology in a global framework.

Although much of feminist theology remains christian in inspiration, a new ecumenism is developing that seeks genuine dialogue among women across religious as well as cultural lines. In the United States this has taken the form of beginning efforts at dialogue between christian, Jewish and counter-cultural or "Goddess" feminists (Kalven and Buckley). Dialogues of Jewish and Muslim feminists and Buddhist and christian feminists are also developing. Whether feminist theology will remain primarily as a reform and renewal movement within existing historical religions, such as Christianity, or whether it may give rise to a significant new movement of religious expression is unclear. But there is an important tendency in feminist reflection to overcome the closed lines of religious demarcation and to seek a new vision of wholistic spirituality that transcends such divisions.

See **Anthropology, Christian; Theology**

Carol Christ, *Diving Deep and Surfacing, Women Writers on Spiritual Quest, 1980.* Steven Davies, *The Revolt of Widows: The Social World of the Apocryphal Acts,* 1980. Nancy Falk and Rita Gross, *Unspoken Worlds, Women's Religious Lives in Non-Western Culture,* 1980. Kari Elizabeth Bϕressen, *Subordination and Equivalence: The Nature and Role of Women in Augustine and Aquinas, Eng. tr. 1981.* Judith Goldenberg, *The Changing of the Gods,* 1979. Jacquelyn Grant, "Black Theology and the Black Woman," in Gayraud Wilmore and James Cone, *Black Theology: A Documentary History, 1966-79,* 1979. Susannah Heschel, *On Being a Jewish Feminist,* 1983. Carter Heyward, *Our Passion for Justice: Power, Sexuality and Liberation,* 1984. Elaine Pagels, *The Gnostic Gospels,* 1979. Rosemary Ruether, *Religion and Sexism, Images of Women in the Jewish and Christian Traditions,* 1974; *Women-Church: Theology and Practice of Feminist Liturgical Communities,* 1986; Letty Russell, *Feminist Interpretation of the Bible,* 1985. Starhawk, *The Spiral Dance, The Rebirth of the Ancient Religion of the Goddess,* 1982; *Dreaming in the Dark: Magic, Sex and Politics,* 1984. *Women's Spirit Bonding,* Janet Kalven and Mary Buckley, Eds., 1984.

ROSEMARY RADFORD RUETHER

FIDEISM

Fideist was the name attached to the nineteenth-century philosophers and theologians who claimed that some sort of revelation was absolutely required for the human mind to know anything about God's existence or nature with certainty, to have assurance of personal immortality, or to justify the moral demands of personal or social life.

Vatican I's *Dogmatic Constitution on Faith* endeavored to steer a safe middle path between two extreme positions concerning the relation between faith and reason. Fideism denied that human reason, through its own unaided power, could acquire any certain knowledge about the world's transcendent creator. Rationalism, on the contrary, refused to concede that the knowledge of God transmitted through christian revelation exceeded its range. Fideists conceded too little to natural reason; rationalists demanded too much for it. Fideism would make philosophical knowledge of God impossible; rationalism would submit revealed knowledge of God to the criticism of philosophy.

In the early nineteenth century empiricist and Kantian epistemology had caused great distrust of the abstractive discursive reason on which Aristotle and the scholastics had relied. Aristotelianism was dismissed as a discredited rationalism, and the metaphysics associated with it was considered to be without foundation. Reacting against the rationalism of the enlightenment, the Catholic thinkers called traditionalists claimed that a primitive divine revelation, received through faith and transmitted through language and tradition, was required for the mind's grasp of the first principles on which speculative philosophy and ethics depended. And so, without the prior help of divine revelation received through an implicit act of faith, no philosopher could establish God's existence or ground the demands of ethics. In their various forms, theologies in the traditionalist current became quite widespread in the nineteenth century.

Theologians attached to the older scholastic tradition in philosophy and apologetics found them disturbing. First, they denied the validity of the scholastic arguments for God's existence. Second, they questioned the validity of scholastic apologetic arguments for the reasonableness of faith based on prophecies and miracles. Lastly, if the "faith" which these traditionalist theologies required for the mind's intuitive grasp of philosophy's first principles was supernatural faith, theologians in the older traditions were afraid that the necessary distinction between faith and reason was being overlooked.

As a result, a number of theologians were censured on the grounds of fideism in the second third of the century. Bautain was forced to sign two sets of propositions repudiating fideism in 1835 and 1844. Ventura was obliged to do the same

in 1855. Vatican I's *Dogmatic Constitution on Faith* outlawed fideism by declaring that, absolutely speaking, unaided natural reason could acquire certain knowledge of God's existence and nature. The Council, however, did not declare that any of the arguments which individual philosophers had proposed to prove God's existence were, in fact, valid. Neither did it deny that faith and revelation could be morally necessary for an individual mind to know with certainty God's existence and the fundamental truths of ethics.

See **Faith, Proof for Existence of God, Revelation**

Roger Aubert, *Le Problème de l'Acte de Foi,* Louvain: Warny, 1950. Gerald A. McCool, SJ, *Catholic Theology in the Nineteenth Century: The Quest for a Unitary Method,* New York: Seabury Press, 1977. Hermann-Josef Pottmeyer, *Der Glaube vor dem Anspruch der Wissenschaft,* Freiburg: Herder, 1968. Paul Poupard, *L'Abbé Louis Bautain,* Paris: Desclée, 1961.

GERALD A. MCCOOL, SJ

FILIOQUE

A Latin term meaning "and from the Son," introduced into the Nicene-Constantinopolitan Creed in the West to assert that the Holy Spirit proceeds from both the Father and the Son as from one principle. The Eastern Church never accepted this addition to the Creed and its introduction was one of the causes of the tensions between East and West which resulted in the schism of the eleventh century.

See **Holy Spirit, Trinity,**

FOREKNOWLEDGE

See **Predestination, Providence**

FORGIVENESS

See **Conversion, Grace, Reconciliation**

FORM CRITISICM
See **Biblical Criticism**

FORM AND MATTER
Philosophical Meaning

These two terms which are usually correlated in some way, have a wide range of uses in our everyday, scientific, and philosophical languages. Thus the term "matter" has a long and complicated history of use in science, from the earliest Greek philosopher-scientists down to the latest search of physicists into the ultimate "structure of matter." Thus understood, it simply means material things, the physical world as such. This article will not enter into the scientific history of these terms where matter is spoken of more often than form, at least in modern science. We shall restrict ourselves to the philosophical use of the terms, with some application to theology.

In their philosophical usage, form and matter are correlative terms, combining to explain the underlying structure of the changing material beings of our experience, although form can also be extended to independent uses (as in the ideal Forms of Plato existing independently in the Platonic World of Ideas, or the "pure forms" of angels in St. Thomas). In their widest general sense, form and matter are two of the most basic and indispensable terms for speaking about our everyday experience of the world. *Form* signifies the shapes, patterns, structures, or designs of things, whether natural or artificial, i.e., in general that which *determines* something to be *such and such,* to be *this kind* of thing. *Matter* signifies the "material," that *out of which* something is made, that which is capable of receiving a form or pattern, i.e., in general that which is *determinable* by form. Thus we say of a piece of clothing, "*What* is that? It is a sweater," and again, "What is it made *out of?* It is made out of wool, or cotton, etc." We recognize the irreducible distinction between the two when we discover that the *same form or pattern* can be reproduced in many different materials, (e.g., a cup made of glass, clay, or metal) or the *same material* may be successively worked into many different forms (a child molds a piece of clay now into this form, now into that). It is clear that the form and matter of something cannot be identical, although neither can exist by itself alone: a form is always the form *of* something, a form in some material, and a piece of matter is never found without some form or structure to it. Were it totally formless, totally indeterminate, it would be nothing at all.

Plato and Aristotle, building on the work of their pre-Socratic predecessors, introduced the first systematic analysis of form and matter. Projecting them by analogy from the external, visible dimension of human artifacts, where they got their start, into the deep inner natures of natural beings, including man himself, they saw the latter as composites of an *essential form,* defining the nature or kind of the thing, and an ultimate formless *material "stuff"* which received the form and was molded by it. Plato's principal interest was in the form as the source of the intelligibility of the thing and hence the ground of its truth. Since the important truths about reality (such as the truths about mathematics and ethics) had to be stable and unchangeable—not true just today or yesterday, but always and everywhere, if we are not to fall into the relativism of the Sophists—and since intelligible forms were realized so imperfectly and transiently in the ever changing material world of the senses, he postulated a world of ideal, perfect, unchanging Forms, existing "apart" from the world of change in a heavenly "World of Ideas, or Ideal Forms." (Later Platonists and Neoplatonists soon located these ideal Forms in the mind of God.) Genuine philosophical knowledge, therefore, was of this eternal, unchanging World of Ideal Forms, the realm of the "really real," as the only sufficient ground for unchanging truth. The world of matter, on the other hand, conceived as a primordial chaos of matter in motion (the primeval "receptacle" or place—*chora*), participated in the Ideal Forms only imperfectly, as transient, unstable images or "'shadows" in a half-real world; such a world could not be the sufficient ground of unchanging truth but only of opinion and "likely stories."

Aristotle, after a telling criticism of the Platonic separate Forms as being of no help to understand our world of change as long as they remained apart and inactive, brought the intelligible forms of natural things right down into matter as their primary mode of existing and their natural habitat and energized them to become the core of active natures. His philosophy of nature posits an ultimate composition, in all the changing beings of our natural world, of *essential or substantial form* and *primary,* of itself formless, *matter;* both were real, though not equally intelligible, since he agreed with Plato that all intelligibility was reached through form. Neither the form nor the matter of a material thing can exist by themselves: the form abstracted from its individuating matter would become an abstract universal idea in a mind; the matter by itself would be purely indeterminate, pure potency with no act at all, and so could not exist in the real world.

This form/matter composition was used to explain two main facts in the natural world of our experience: (1) How is it that there can be many different individuals in a given *species* or kind of being, all possessing the same *specific* intelligible essence or nature, yet *numerically* distinct from each other as individuals (this man is not that man, though both possess the same human nature)? Aristotle's answer was that they all possess the same essential or substantial form, but this form or formal structure is individuated and hence multiplied by being received in different parts of quantitatively extended matter, of which one part was here and another there. This multiplication of form, by itself formless matter, leaves the intelligibility of the form intact and essentially unchanged in each member of the species defined by this form.

This form/matter composition also serves as ground for explaining our human mode of knowing by abstracting the essential form from the individuating matter to form universal concepts applicable to all the members of the same species. This is the basis for all scientific knowledge, which, as unchanging, can deal only with the universal and not with the particular material individual as such.

(2) The second fact about the world of nature needing explanation is that of *substantial change,* i.e., a change so deep that the very essence or substance of the changing being is broken down to become a new and different individual being. Since all change involves some continuity between the two poles of the change, something passing over as well as something passing away, Aristotle postulated a composition of essential or *substantial form* and *primary matter* as the necessary condition of possibility of any substantial change: what passes away in such a change is the substantial form, the old one giving way to a new one; what passes over as the bond of continuity between the old and the new form is a non-formal principle which he called primary matter. What passes over cannot have its own fully actual substantial form: since substantial form is what determines a being to be this kind of being, having two such forms at once in one essence would destroy the unity of the essence, making

it two different kinds of thing at once. Since the principle of continuity is thus potential in the essential and not merely the accidental order, i.e., a potency to be determined by the one substantial form to become this one essence, it is appropriately called matter, or substantial potency, as the complementary opposite of substantial form.

In both the above cases of the form/matter composition, especially that of substantial change, the general Aristotelian theorem of act/potency is applied: the form functions as the *act* or actual perfection now present in the being; the matter functions as the *potency*, i.e., the capacity to be informed by this form now and by an indefinite series of other substantial forms later in the unceasing world process of the "generation and corruption" of individual material things. And as we noted above, the form and matter, though irreducible and hence really distinct from each other, cannot exist separately by themselves. Each is a complementary co-principle making up the one unified essence of every being in nature. Aristotle also admits, of course, that every change in this world of nature must be ultimately traced back to some unmoved Prime Mover that is beyond this material world of change, and hence is pure Form.

Form and matter can also be applied analogously to the accidental order. Thus an entity which already has its own substantial form and primary matter can become the subject of further accidental modifications, called *accidental forms,* and the entity thus further determined is called *secondary matter.*

Medieval Philosophy. This basic form/matter doctrine, at least in its role as explanation for substantial change, was taken over widely by medieval thinkers of all schools, christian, Moslem, and Jewish. *St. Thomas Aquinas,* as principal spokesman for the orthodox Aristotelian school, was primarily responsible for its more careful and precise technical formulation and application. While St. Thomas defended the full Aristotelian doctrine of form/matter as explanation both for substantial change and also individuation in a species, other christian thinkers of the Augustinian-Franciscan school, such as St. Bonaventure, refused to go along with the theory of individuation by matter, since they were unwilling to accept the consequence, drawn by St. Thomas, that each angel, as pure form without matter, must be unique in its own species.

Two central controversial points remained in this Aristotelian doctrine as interpreted by St. Thomas, points which were the focus of intense dispute in thirteenth century medieval thought, flowing over into the modern period:

A. Unity or Plurality of Substantial Forms? In the complex higher beings of our experience, such as plants, animals, man, there are clearly levels of being: inanimate body, vegetative life, sense life, intellectual life, all operating at the same time, in man, for example. And it seems clear enough that the lower elements and lower levels continue to endure and operate in some way when taken up into higher compounds. (This has become even clearer today from what we know of atoms and molecules from modern science and their reappearance when the higher unities break down.) One philosophical tradition, represented by the Augustinian-Franciscan school (St. Bonaventure, etc.), with strong injections of the Arabic philosopher Avicebron (*Fons Vitae*), held that there must be a distinct substantial form operating on each of these levels: e.g., in man there is a form of the body as such, a vegetative soul for vegetative life, a sensitive or animal soul for sense life, and an intellectual soul for intellectual life. All are subordinated to the highest form, the intellectual soul, but they are all still actually present and operating in the whole we call man. Thus in substantial change the higher form would pass away, but what passed over to the new state need not be pure primary matter but could be matter informed by one or more of the lower substantial forms already present in the previous whole. This was the *Plurality of Forms School.*

St. Thomas, with St. Albert the Great, was the principal spokesman for the *Unicity of Form School.* His point was that to posit several different substantial forms actually present and operating as such in one essence at one time would be to destroy its unity and make it several different kinds of being at once. What we call a man would be at one and the same time a mineral, a plant, an animal, and a man. Unity is an absolutely primary attribute of every real being, and to say truly of a being that it is one nature, e.g., a human being, it must have only one fully actual and autonomously operating substantial form at one time, that which makes it to be this essence, this nature, as a natural unit with one center of operation. Unity has priority as a metaphysical requirement for any real nature.

St. Thomas was willing to admit, however, that the forms of the lower elements in the composite were not simply wiped out all the way down to totally indeterminate primary matter when taken over by a higher form in a substantial change, but remained in what he called a "virtual presence," stronger than merely potential, weaker than fully actual. In a word, they were present but had lost their full autonomy of existence and action; they were subordinated and controlled by the higher form not merely by accident but in a way extending deep into the essences of these lower elements, so that they were in potency to be integrated by the higher form into the unity of a single active nature. Hence it could be truly said that there was only one fully actual,

autonomously operating, substantial form in the one nature at one time. All the lower elements were in potency to its unifying control, functioning therefore as matter to form. Matter would here be understood in an analogous manner, sometimes signifying pure primary matter with no determinations at all (when the change is between particles at the lowest level), sometimes the lower elements as potential in the substantial—not merely accidental—order to be integrated by a higher form into the new ontological unity of a single essence.

Thus in fact, despite their differences in terminology, the two schools ended up not too far apart, each conceding something to the other. But their priorities and stresses remain distinctive, one school stressing the unity of one dominant form, the other the real presence of the subordinated forms. The position of St. Thomas, if interpreted in a nuanced and sophisticated way to take into account the data of modern science, seems to many to have the edge in metaphysical strength and consistency. But feelings ran so high at the time, especially because of theological implications regarding the body of Christ in the tomb, that John Peckham, Archbishop of Canterbury and strong defender of the Plurality of Forms doctrine, condemned the Unicity of Form position as heretical in 1286 and banned its teaching in his jurisdiction. The ban was not long effective.

In applying this theory to our world today it should be noted that current scientific data are revealing more and more as a fact what St. Thomas held to be necessary for metaphysical reasons: namely, that lower elements (cells, molecules, atoms, electrons, etc.) do not operate in exactly the same way outside a compound on their own as they do inside the compound, where they are integrated into a higher unity with a new center or subject of characteristic actions. Thus we now know that the electron inside the atom is not a locally concentrated little particle circling the nucleus like a planet circling the sun, but rather a pulsing wave of energy spread all around the atom at once; only when we perform a certain experiment on it to detach it from the whole does the energy wave packet collapse and show up as a determinate tiny particle with a strictly localized size, location, weight, etc. So too atoms bonded into a molecule do not form merely a juxtaposed aggregate, but share a common electron between them, thus opening up each atom to internal energy exchanges with the other allowing new types of operation as a unity. So too with the cells of a living body when they have reached a certain complexity.

Modern Period

When the new mathematically oriented science came in with Galileo, Descartes, and Newton in the seventeenth century, the old Aristotelian-Thomistic explanation of natural things in terms of form and matter was widely rejected. The main reason was that neither form as a qualitative principle nor matter as indeterminate and potential, and unable to exist on its own, were susceptible of being studied by the new mathematical method based on empirical measurement reduced to mathematical laws. Thus Descartes introduced a new metaphysics of the world as divided into pure thinking substances (minds) on the one side, and on the other one single vast material substance consisting of nothing but quantitatively extended matter plus motion, all governed by purely mathematical laws.

As a result, the whole Aristotelian world of distinct *qualitative natures,* based on different qualitative substantial forms embodied in matter, was swept away, to be replaced by a material world seen as a great lifeless machine, whose only properties were purely quantitative extension and motion. The matter which for Aristotle and St. Thomas was merely a co-principle to be determined by form now became a thing in itself, knowable by itself without form (save the abstract relational forms of mathematics). Man himself now became split into a mind that is purely spiritual, inhabiting a machine that is purely quantitative, operating by its own independent laws, with the ontological unity of the human being seriously if not irreparably compromised. The only link between these radically disparate worlds of mind and matter was mathematical law. Since matter was (in principle, at least) reducible entirely to mathematical laws, and the most characteristic activity of mind (including the mind of God) was mathematical thinking, it did follow that the world of matter was in this sense an image both of mind and of God. But there was clearly no place in such a completely mathematized science, and in the world it claimed to represent, for irreducible, qualitatively different forms in nature, for *levels of being* within material nature itself.

Once matter had been turned into an independently existing, purely quantitative thing or substance on its own, and science had been reorganized in terms of measurement and mathematical laws, there was little further attention to, or use for, Aristotelian *hylomorphism*—the technical name for the form/matter doctrine (*hyle*=matter; *morphe*=form)— in modern science or philosophy, outside of the small number who still carried on the Aristotelian, Thomistic, or other scholastic traditions.

For *John Locke,* the empiricist, the objective qualitative essences of things are unknown to us. What material things reveal objectively to us by their action is only their "primary qualities," extension, figure, number, motion (or rest); the "secondary qualities" reported to us by our five senses, such as color, sound, taste, smell, etc., are all subjective transformations by our sense organs of the primary qualities in the real world. For *David Hume,* anything like the form/matter composition of real things has dissolved into the flow of atomic sense impressions, bound together only by relations of contiguity and regular repetition.

Immanuel Kant does indeed restore the traditional form/matter distinction, but radically transforms it from a structure of the real world to a structure of our human thought about the world. Man imposes his own built-in *a priori* forms of sense and understanding onto the sense-manifold or "matter" of our sensations, resulting in the world as human beings cannot help but affirm it. *Hegel* and *Whitehead* do signal a return to qualitative dynamic forms in nature, but not to the primary matter as originally understood in the Aristotelian tradition. For Whitehead, as for most contemporary thinkers, matter is now fundamentally and irreducibly atomic and discrete in character.

In the contemporary world of physics, however, a return to something like the old Aristotelian distinction of form and matter may be discerned, according to some interpreters. For matter, as Einstein showed, is now convertible into or reducible to energy—in his famous formula, $E=mc^2$, which made possible nuclear fission and the atomic bomb. Thus the whole of nature can now be seen as a vast, ongoing process of *transformations of energy,* where the primordial material energy of the universe remains constant in amount, has no fixed form of its own (though it always appears under some form), and like a vast reservoir or ultimate substratum of potential energy moves restlessly from this form to that, sometimes held by one form for a considerable time, sometimes shifting at high speed from one to the other as we descend into the subatomic world of evanescent particles. This radical material or quantitative energy, formless in itself, but potential to innumerable forms, would seem to be a highly relevant adaptation of the ancient Aristotelian primary matter, without the connotation of pure passivity unduly taken for granted by Aristotle and St. Thomas.

In any case, something like the form/matter distinction, understood in a broadly analogous sense, would seem to be indispensable for a reflective understanding even today, not only of our ordinary experience of human artifacts and technology, but of the world of nature itself understood non-reductionistically as composed of levels of being where lower elements are integrated into higher unities or *natures,* which become new centers or subjects of characteristic new properties and actions.

Application to Theology

The form/matter distinction, understood in a broadly analogous way, is useful in many areas of theology. Thus the virtue of charity is spoken of as the "form of all the virtues," since it determines all the other virtues by integrating them into a new higher meaning and motivation. Probably the most important application, with a long tradition behind it, is to the seven sacraments. The nature of each sacrament is explained in terms of its distinctive form and matter. Thus the "matter" of baptism is the pouring of the water, which of itself has no religious meaning. The "form" is the saying of the accompanying words, "I baptize you in the name of the Father and of the Son and of the Holy Spirit." This gives religious meaning to the material gesture and makes the composite act an efficacious supernatural sign of grace. The matter of the sacrament of reconciliation is the confession of one's sins; the form is the absolution pronounced by the priest. And so on for the other sacraments. Although this form/matter analysis is not the only or the exhaustive explanation of the full meaning and reality of the sacraments, it is a very illuminating one as far as it goes, and it would be difficult indeed to dispense with it entirely.

The positive goodness and value of matter as a principle of material things is also an important consequence of the Judaeo-Christian revelation. Many of the old Manichaean and Gnostic sects at the beginning of Christianity scorned the body and matter as evil, a prison for the soul, either uncreated or created by an evil principle. The Book of Genesis affirms clearly that God made all kinds of material things in creation and "saw that they were very good." The incarnation of the eternal Son of God, taking on human nature for our salvation, and raising it up again in his resurrection in a glorified form to be with him forever, is a strong confirmation of the positive goodness of matter and material things. The condemning of matter as evil would thus become a christian heresy.

See **Metaphysics**

"Form" and "Matter," in *The Great Ideas: A Synopticon of the Great Books of the Western World,* Encyclopedia Brittanica, 1952. D.A. Callus, "Forms, Unicity and Plurality of," *New Catholic Encyclopedia,* V: pp. 1024-27. L. De Raeymaeker, *Philosophy of Being,* St. Louis: Herder, 1962. E. McMullin, Ed., *The Concept of Matter,* U. of Notre Dame, 1963. J.A. Peters, "Matter and Form in Metaphysics," *New Scholasticism,* 31 (1957), pp. 447-83. M. Sachs, *Ideas of Matter from Ancient Times to Bohr and Einstein,* Washington: U. Press of America, 1981. E. Schlossberger, "Aristotelian Matter, Potentiality, and Quarks," *Southern J. of Phil.,* 17 (1979): pp. 507-21; U. Thobe, "Hylomorphism Revisited," *New Schol.,* 42 (1968): pp. 226-53. D. Callus, "The Problem of the Plurality of Forms in the 13th century: The Thomistic Innovation," in *L'homme et son destin d'après les penseures du moyen-âge,* Louvain, 1960.

W. NORRIS CLARKE, SJ

FREEDOM

In the basic sense of the word, freedom is a property of one's deliberate choices and actions. But precisely what type of a property is it? And, as thus understood, does it ever actually occur? In assaying the various answers offered to these two questions, we may distinguish at least five different kinds of stances: hard determinism, indeterminism, soft determinism, voluntarist self-constitutionism, and intellectualist self-constitutionism.

Hard Determinism

For the hard determinist, freedom is characterized through simple contrast with all factual necessity. A choice or action is free exactly if it is not related as effect to cause, not under the sway of some exceptionless and irresistible law, not individually predictable even in principle. But any such breach in the fabric of universal factual necessity is just what the hard determinist rejects. The grounds for this rejection vary. Some persons, for example, argue that such necessity is a logical requirement for the truth of statements about the future. Others see it as an inevitable conclusion of sound metaphysics; others as the inescapable consequence of a religious belief in the omnipotence of God. For still others, it is an essential presupposition of scientific inquiry or at least a highly probable scientific conclusion. But whatever the precise bases, thinkers so diverse as Democritus of Abdera, Chrysippus, Pierre Laplace, John Dewey, B.F. Skinner, and John Hospers, for example, agree that every choice and action, like every other thing and event, is factually necessitated. Therefore, any appearances to the contrary notwithstanding, no choice or action is free. Properly understood, "freedom" is nothing other than the label for a certain kind of logical contradiction, or for one's ignorance of the necessitating factors that in principle can be disclosed through metaphysics or religion or science.

Indeterminism

Like the hard determinist, indeterminists conceive freedom as precisely the absence of factual necessity. Unlike the hard determinist, however, they maintain that such necessity is not universal in its scope. Appealing to a metaphysical theory like that of Epicurus, for example, or to a religious belief that diminishes the omnipotence of God, or to the Heisenberg interpretation of quantum theory in modern physics, or to personal moral experience, such persons as Charles Peirce, William James, and Charles Hartshorne argue that there is a certain radical spontaneity, contingency, indeterminacy, in nature itself. It is not the case that every individual event is factually necessitated, related to all other events according to some universal logical or causal law, and thus predictable at least in principle. On the contrary, some events, including at least some of one's choices and actions, just happen. They are purely random, quite simply uncaused, matters of sheer chance. And in just this sense, therefore, at least some of one's choices and actions are indeed free.

Soft Determinism

The soft determinist stands with the hard determinist and over against the indeterminist in maintaining that every thing and event falls entirely within the sweep of factual necessity. Whatever exists or occurs does so because, whether for logical or metaphysical or religious or scientific reasons, it cannot not exist or occur. But the soft determinist disagrees with both of the foregoing in regard to the notion of freedom itself. Freedom is not the absence of *all* factual necessity; rather, it is the absence of *involuntary* factual necessity. Or, positively, freedom is identical with voluntariness. Now, all of one's actions, like everything else in the universe, are factually necessitated. But psychology manifests that while some of those actions are necessitated by such factors as external force, fear, passion, and habit, others are necessitated solely by one's choic-

es: I do X simply because I choose to do X. The former actions are involuntary and thus unfree; the latter, voluntary and thus free. On this view, maintained by Augustine of Hippo, Thomas Hobbes, David Hume, John Stuart Mill, and Bertrand Russell, among others, for an action to be factually necessitated is not necessarily incompatible with that action's being free. Thus the view is often labelled "compatibilism."

Voluntarist Self-Constitutionism

The first three stance-takers have this in common, that the most basic explicit structure in terms of which they pose their questions about freedom and proffer their answers is an object-structure. The hard determinist, the indeterminist, and the soft determinist, whatever their differences, all presuppose that the primary ground of any claim's meaning and the fundamental criterion of its truth stand entirely within the network of the various objects that they do or could know. And thus the most basic kinds of assertions are logical, metaphysical, creedal, or scientific—assertions about various types of objects (some of which may be other subjects) and their relations. For the next two stance-takers, on the other hand, the most basic explicit structure in terms of which they pose their questions about freedom and proffer their answers is at least largely the concrete operational structure of themselves as conscious subjects doing the posing and proffering. Both voluntarist and intellectualist self-constitutionists maintain that the primary ground of any claim's meaning and the fundamental criterion of its truth reside in the normative pattern of their own concrete conscious operations, a pattern so inescapable that even in the attempt to deny it they must follow it in order to make the denial. And thus the most basic kinds of assertions are concretely phenomenological—assertions about the operationally incontrovertible features of one's own concrete subjectivity.

For the voluntarist self-constitutionist, freedom has three distinguishing features. First, there is the absence of *factual* necessity, the absence of any logical or metaphysical or religious or scientific factor such that one's choice and actions in a given circumstance could not have been other than what they actually are. Second, there is the presence of spiritual spontaneity, the ability creatively to determine or constitute one's own choice and actions and thereby to determine or constitute oneself. Third, there is the absence of *moral* necessity, the absence of any ethical factor external to one's choices and actions themselves such that those choices and actions in a given circumstance either should be or should not have been what they actually are. In addition, such thinkers as Johann Fichte and Jean-Paul Sartre maintain that these three features do indeed distinguish at least some of one's choices and actions. More amply, they argue that a concrete phenomenological investigation of one's own conscious performance makes clear that the three features characterize certain of one's choices and actions precisely because they characterize the very structure of one's subjectivity, a structure that those choices and actions reflect. Consequently, any effort to deny either the occurrence or the absolutely basic character of the three features is operationally self-defeating. And thus one cannot but admit that, in exactly the specified sense, at least some of one's choices and actions are free.

Intellectualist Self-Constitutionism

The intellectualist self-constitutionist endorses much of what the voluntarist self-constitutionist says, but also disagrees in two important respects. First, freedom is indeed characterized by the absence of factual necessity, of irresistible governance, and by the presence of spiritual spontaneity, of the propensity for creative self-constitution. But the absence of moral necessity is not a distinguishing feature of freedom. For moral necessity, correctly understood, is nothing other than the body of ethical requirements that follow from one's intellectual grasp of the true order of reality, conclusions about how one ought to choose and act that follow from knowing one's own place in the universe. One is morally bound to observe these requirements but factually at liberty to ignore them. Hence the absence of accordance with moral necessity is the distinguishing feature of an abuse of freedom, the mark of choices and actions that, though free, are morally evil. Similarly, accordance with moral necessity is the distinguishing feature of the proper use of freedom, the mark of choices and actions that are free and, in addition, morally good. Second, the intellectualist self-constitutionist maintains that this notion of freedom, together with the associated notions of knowledge, moral goodness, and moral evil, is just the notion that is verified in fact. According to such thinkers as C.A. Campbell, Karl Rahner, and Bernard Lonergan, concrete phenomenological investigation of one's own conscious performance manifests that some of one's choices and actions are free in just the sense indicated, that their freedom expresses something of the essential freedom of one's subjectivity as such, and that any attempt to deny or relativize this claim inevitably involves one in a performative self-contradiction.

See **Conversion, Sin**

Joseph M. Boyle, et al., *Free Choice* Notre Dame: U. of Notre Dame, 1976. Bernard Lonergan, *Grace and Freedom,* New York: Herder & Herder, 1971. Bernard Lonergan, *Insight: A Study of Human Understanding,* New York: Philosophical Library and London: Longmans Greene, 1957, pp. 596-633. Bernard Lonergan, *Method in Theology,* New York: Herder & Herder and London: Darton, Longman & Todd, 1972, pp. 47-52, 120-22, 237-44, 309-310.

MICHAEL VERTIN

FUNDAMENTAL OPTION

The theory of the fundamental option was developed in Roman Catholic thinking in the context of a personalist moral theology. It appears in at least three types. The personalist-existentialist type draws on the Thomistic concept of person, and certain currents of existentialist, personalistic philosophy. The transcendental type adopts the basic features of transcendental anthropology, as developed especially by Karl Rahner. The biblical type is based on the notions of *metanoia* as first conversion, and continual conversion as the development which follows upon it. Concepts drawn from depth psychology are often used to mediate between the theological theory and experience, to provide an account of development in the moral life and to conceptualize the different levels in the self.

As a corrective to a legalistic, act-centered image of the moral life, punctuated by frequently alternating choices for and against God, the idea of fundamental orientation presents that life as a unified, dynamic process. It points to an enduring stance, beneath more peripheral choices. However, all would agree that the fundamental option is not a once and for all choice; it can be changed, deepened or reversed.

The theory makes a distinction of levels in the moral subject, for example between "core" freedom and "peripheral" freedom, or between "transcendental" freedom and "categorical" freedom. To the former correspond the fundamental option and orientation; to the latter particular, concrete, choices. A fundamental option for God, or away from God, constitutes the person's basic orientation. Those who support the theory generally insist that core freedom is exercised in and through particular, concrete, free choices. However, this distinction of levels has given rise to

criticism. Some have argued that it sets up an unexplained gap between the self and history. Others have challenged what they see to be the implication of the theory, namely, that true responsibility lies at the inner, core level, but not on the level of concrete, specific choices. This is said to lead to the evacuation of moral importance from particular choices, and to a weakening of the sense of sin.

The debate comes to a head in the question as to whether a fundamental option against God can take place in a particular, historical act of choice. An answer, based on the main tenets of the theory, would include several points. (1) The fundamental option can be exercised only within particular, concrete choices, but not all particular choices involve fundamental options. (2) The fundamental orientation, constituted by the option, cannot be simply identified with particular choices. But it may be changed in particular choices. (3) A definitive change of orientation, for example turning away from God, may be made in a particular choice, where this is a culminating event, prepared for in a process or story formed by other choices. This suggests that the notion of narrative might be useful in the further development, and perhaps modification, of the theory.

The notion has been taken up in official church documents. The *Declaration on Certain Questions Concerning Sexual Ethics* (1975) acknowledged that the fundamental option ultimately defines a person's moral disposition, but insisted that it can be completely changed by particular acts. The *Apostolic Exhortation on Reconciliation and Penance* of Pope John Paul II (1984) stated that mortal sin should not be reduced to an act of fundamental option, where this is taken to mean an explicit and formal act of contempt for God or one's neighbor. The document corrects an inadequate interpretation, but does not reject the idea itself. It emphasizes again that the fundamental orientation can be radically altered by particular acts.

See **Conversion, Freedom, Person, Repentance, Sin**

John Paul II, Apostolic Exhortation on Reconciliation and Penance, *Reconciliatio et Paenitentia,* Dec. 2, 1984, *Origins* 14 (1984): pp. 432-458. Eugene J. Cooper, "The Notion of Sin in Light of the Fundamental Option: The Fundamental Option Revisited," *Louvain Studies* 9 (1983): pp. 363-382. Bernard Häring, *Free and Faithful in Christ,* Vol. 1, *General Moral Theology,* New York: Seabury, Crossroad Book and London: St. Paul Publications, 1978, pp. 164-222.

BRIAN V. JOHNSTONE, CSSR

FUNDAMENTAL THEOLOGY

The words fundamental and foundational translate the Latin word *fundamentalis*. They are often used interchangeably, but some authors distinguish them. Fundamental theology then would refer to the mainstream neo-scholastic tradition. It connotes the independence of fundamental theology from systematic theology and its use of neutral philosophical and historical arguments. Foundational theology, however, would refer to those new approaches, opposed to the sharp distinction between fundamental and systematic theology, that emphasize the theological nature and method of the discipline.

The term "fundamental" can have diverse meanings. Fundamental can mean "basic" or "essential." Fundamental theology then deals with the basics or essentials of theology. Or "fundamental" can mean "ground," "support" or "basis" as the foundations of a building provide the support for the whole edifice. Fundamental theology then deals with the foundational basis or ground of theology.

Two different images of foundations exist. Foundations can be imagined as the foundations that an archaeologist discovers in searching for the base of a city. Or they can be imagined as that which an architect consciously constructs to provide support. The difference between these images displays contrasting conceptions of the task and nature of fundamental theology.

Origin and History

The historical emergence of the discipline of fundamental theology took place in three stages:

Pre-History. The Council of Trent decreed that seminaries should offer a basic course of studies concentrating on the central truths of the christian faith. Under the influence of the Renaissance, one sought to return to sources and origins. The discipline of "positive theology" developed to study the truths of faith as contained in the scriptures and in the early christian writers. This discipline as a basic course was also called fundamental theology in some places.

The Renaissance also generated an interest in the nature of religion. Marsilio Ficino's *De christiana religione* expressed this interest and sought to demonstrate Christianity as the true religion. The structure and argument of his treatise influenced the apologetical works of Vives, Duplessis-Mornay, Charon, Grotius and others and represents an important beginning of what was to become the discipline of fundamental theology.

Enlightenment. The deism and rationalism of the Enlightenment criticized the historical and positive religions along with the notion of a supernatural religion and miracles and prophecies as proofs of revealed religion. This critique led to a defense of supernatural revelation in a treatise on religion. This treatise consisted of three sections (revealed religion, christian religion, Catholic religion) and came to form the basic structure of fundamental theology. Its method was extrinsic insofar as it sought to base its demonstrations on external signs of credibility such as miracles and prophecies. This extrinsic method endured for the next two centuries in neo-scholastic fundamental theology.

Nineteenth Century. The increasing location of theology within universities in the nineteenth century sparked justifications of theology as an academic discipline. Thus it received an additional foundational task. In addition to providing the foundation for the christian faith, it now took on the task of establishing the foundation of theology's scientific or academic nature as a university discipline.

As a result of the influence of Descartes and Kant, transcendental philosophy provided as the standard an account of scientific rationality. Moreover, the starting point from human subjectivity allowed one to relate faith intrinsically to free human subjectivity. During this period Johann Nepomunk Ehrlich, a student of Anton Günther, held the first chair and published in 1859 in Prague the first book so entitled, *Fundamentaltheologie.* He correlates faith and reason by showing the relation between revelation and human subjectivity. By taking into account modern transcendental philosophy, he sought to show the foundations not only of christian faith but also of christian theology. The neo-scholastic revival toward the turn of the century halted the influence of this approach. In the twentieth century Blondel and later *la nouvelle théologie* and transcendental fundamental theology revived it with modification. Theologians also developed further the function of fundamental theology to discuss the "scientific" or disciplinary nature of theology (Söhngen, Lonergan, Tracy, and Peukert).

Content

The traditional content of the discipline was divided into three treatises. The first treatise, revealed religion, explicated a critique of deism by demonstrating the possibility and facticity of a revealed religion. The second treatise, christian religion, consisted of historical arguments that the OT prophecies, Jesus' miracles, especially his resurrection, proved that he was God's legitimate legate. The third treatise, Catholic religion, argued that Jesus established a church with Peter as the first pope. The argumentation was primarily philosophical and historical. A difference emerged between Roman handbooks of fundamental theology and German texts. Faith and the Sources of Dogma were normally included within the treatises of fundamental theology, but not the German texts. The focus in fundamental theology on this content was radically challenged by historical criticism and new philosophical currents.

Relation to Apologetics

Fundamental theology and apologetics are closely related but not identical disciplines. To some extent apologetics was a part of traditional fundamental theology, for example, the section of fundamental theology seeking to demonstrate the divine mission of Jesus and the church. To the extent that traditional fundamental theology sought to show the credibility of the church's revelation and to provide a rational defense of the Catholic faith, it undertook apologetical tasks. Each discipline dealt with the sources of doctrine, not a theme of apologetics. Apologetics, however, included questions that did not belong to fundamental theology, for example, proofs for the existence of God, immortality of the soul, possibility of objective knowledge of truth. In short, the medieval preambles of faith were considered to be the object more of apologetics than of fundamental theology. Moreover, apologetics gave certain themes a more extensive treatment than did fundamental theology. For example, the analysis of the cultural situation, the history and comparison of religion, the unicity of

Christianity, etc.

Current Directions

Current directions in fundamental theology tend to emphasize its theological task and to expand the methodological issues. There are three distinctive current approaches.

Existential Transcendental. Influenced by Heidegger and Kant, Karl Rahner appropriates existential and transcendental categories to present a "formal-fundamental theology" that should complement the traditional approach. Rahner distinguishes a first and second level of reflection. On the first level there is a reflective justification that embraces into a unity fundamental and dogmatic theology. This level is distinguished from faith's second level where the individual theological disciplines use their specific methods. Rahner's conception advocates a basic course of theology that promotes confidence from the very content of christian belief insofar as it relates this content to the human question as radical question.

Hermeneutical. Fundamental theology is developed with reference to contemporary hermeneutical theory to illustrate that christian beliefs relate to experience not simply as the explicit to the implicit. These beliefs are expressed in narratives and metaphors which display a world of meaning that opens experience to new horizons expanding, overturning, or criticizing that experience. Therefore, fundamental theology takes as it starting point christian beliefs and seeks through hermeneutical reconstruction to disclose their paradigmatic and ideal potential for human life and to relate them to background theories of current science.

Political-Practical. Johann Baptist Metz's argues that the challenge of the Enlightenment is not simply a theoretical challenge, but also a practical and a political challenge. This challenge requires political theology as a practical fundamental theology. Practice does not simply mean action but relates to the identity of the human subjects. Whereas the belief in historical progress as the subject of history overlooks the victims, oppressed, and dead within history, the idea of God constitutes these human subjects in their identity.

Whereas the fundamental theology of political theology is rather formal and general, liberation theologies elucidate fundamental theological reflections from concrete experiences of oppression. They propose that theology must be done out of personal and societal experience. The traditions should be examined in their potential to be ideological or to be liberative. The credibility of faith faces human suffering and therefore requires a fundamental theology as a critical theology of liberation.

Current Issues

Content. The relation between fundamental theology and faith raises the issue of content. In the neo-scholastic conception of fundamental theology, it served as a distinct discipline from systematic theology. Its subject matter was concerned prior to faith with the credibility and signs of credibility of revelation. This limitation is challenged from diverse directions.

Henri Bouillard argues that fundamental theology took shape in the period of deism, which rejected the existence of revelation but not God. Today the existence of God is controverted. Consequently, fundamental theology should not focus on revelation but rather on God. Rahner's conception of a "formal-fundamental theology" seeks to explicate all themes of systematic theology. The content of all christian belief is related to the human quest for ultimate meaning. A political-theological conception of fundamental theology brings the thematic of religion, society, and human subjecthood into the center of fundamental theology and deals with issues of ideology criticism.

Relation to Faith. A task of fundamental theology is to provide a grounding of religious belief. Some argue that this grounding is best provided by appeals to common human experience, to a natural philosophy, to historical demonstration, or a universal transcendental reason. Others argue that these overlook the extent to which human experience is historically and linguistically conditioned. Therefore they propose that fundamental theology should begin with initial faith-commitments and should seek to justify them hermeneutically and retrospectively. Its grounding of faith does not need to exclude faith from the starting point.

Relation to Theology. Fundamental theology explicates foundations not only of faith, but also of theology. Fundamental theology does not simply defend the christian faith, but it also seeks to clarify the nature of theology, its goal, sources, and criteria. As a theoretical discipline theology is more than faith, for it entails research programs, methodologies, and epistemic paradigms. One of fundamental theology's tasks is to reflect critically on these.

Method. Currently several distinct proposals exist. Some advocate a predominantely philosophical method insofar as the philosophical dimension of various individual sciences, e.g., history, sociology, psychology, is the arena in which the religious question can be raised and correlated with theological responses. Or a transcendental fundamental theology can seek to be a more immediate first level of reflection where faith gives an account of itself. Or fundamental theology should start out with experiences of oppression and suffering from which one brings a hermeneutics of suspicion to the tradition before one retrieves the tradition. Or a hermeneutical-pragmatic conception of fundamental theology should seek a broad reflective equilibrium

among diverse elements: hermeneutical reconstruction, retroductive warrants, and background theories. Thereby, it grounds faith not by constructing a foundation but through interpretation and retrospective argument.

Francis Schüssler Fiorenza, *Foundational Theology. Jesus and the Church,* New York: Crossroad, 1984. Johann Baptist Metz, *Faith in History and Society, Toward a Practical Fundamental Theology,* New York: Crossroad, 1980. Gerald O'Collins, and Rene Latourelle, *Problems and Perspectives of Fundamental Theology,* New Jersey: Paulist Press, 1980. Helmut Peukert, *Science, Action, and Fundamental Theology,* Cambridge, MIT Press, 1984. Karl Rahner, *Foundations of the Christian Faith,* New York: Crossroad, 1978.

FRANCIS SCHÜSSLER FIORENZA

FUNDAMENTALISM

Fundamentalism is a cognitive style, a cultural-theological world-view, and a religious social movement.

As a cognitive style, fundamentalism has been associated with a closed and dogmatic personality type, with exclusivism, particularism, literalism, and moral rigorism.

As a cultural-theological framework, fundamentalism stands in opposition to religious and cultural liberalism and in defense of orthodoxy and tradition.

As a social movement, fundamentalism is organizationally and ideologically distinct from other types of religious movements.

Although fundamentalism is usually treated as a provenance of American Protestantism, the term is generic and should not be thought of as culture or religion specific. Fundamentalism is, however, more likely to be prevalent in religious traditions in which high emphasis is placed on correct belief and where the forces of modernization have penetrated.

Historically, fundamentalism first emerged among American Protestant evangelicals in the latter part of the nineteenth century in response to the spread of theological modernism in northern churches, especially the Baptist and Presbyterian denominations. Fundamentalism was not, initially, a distinct movement, but part of a broad wave of conservative Protestant discontent with liberal theology. The movement first became prominent in late nineteenth century premillennial prophetic and biblical conferences that stressed the literal interpretation of scripture. In 1910, the Presbyterian General Assembly, responding to questions raised about the orthodoxy of graduates of Union Theological Seminary, adopted a five-point declaration of "essential" doctrines: (1) the inerrancy of scripture, (2) the Virgin Birth of Christ, (3) his substitutionary atonement, (4) his bodily resurrection, and (5) the authenticity of the miracles. Because of their parallels with other fundamentalist short creeds, these articles became the basis of the "five points of fundamentalism." They were also promoted in a series of small volumes entitled *The Fundamentals: A Testimony to the Truth* published between 1905 and 1915. These booklets, financed and promoted by two southern California oil millionaires, Milton and Lyman Stewart, were written by various authors in defense of the inerrancy of scripture against higher criticism, Darwinism, the Social Gospel, and other thought patterns associated with modernism. Over three million copies of *The Fundamentals* were eventually distributed. In 1919, William B. Riley founded the World's Christian Fundamentals Association. This initiative brought heightened visibility and organizational coherency to fundamentalism and marked a new, more active political phase of the movement.

Throughout the 1920's, Presbyterian, Methodist, Baptist, and Disciples of Christ congregations struggled with polarization along fundamentalist/modernist lines. Like their kindred Holiness and Pentecostal co-religionists, fundamentalists stressed the authority of scripture and the necessity of righteous living. Unlike these movements, however, fundamentalism also placed great emphasis on right doctrine and the necessity of organized warfare against the forces of modernism.

Although fundamentalism was often characterized as a naive and simplistic type of religion, there is little evidence that fundamentalist apologists were inherently anti-intellectual or unthinking. Many were committed, instead, to a pattern of thought structure and logic (esp. Scottish Common Sense Realism) that had dominated nineteenth century American theology only to lose credibility by the twentieth century. Distinguished scholars such as John Gresham Machen and Benjamin B. Warfield, both of Princeton University, wrote articulate and spirited defenses of fundamentalist theology.

The sociocultural causes of fundamentalism have long been disputed. Fundamentalism has been associated with the decline of the role of religion as an element of social cohesion, with the social nihilism and attendant revolution in manners and morals during the Jazz Age, with mass urbanization and the loss of Protestant hegemony, with the declining vitality of the Social Gospel movement, with the rise of hyper-patriotism and xenophobia in the 1920's, and with the pessimism surrounding World War I and its aftermath. The hardening of fundamentalist lines has also been attributed to the welding of the movement to a crusade to save American culture from the dangers of "evolutionism."

Largely through fundamentalist pressures, several state legislatures barred the teaching of evolution in public schools. John T. Scopes, a high school biology teacher in Dayton, Tennessee, was brought to trial in 1925 for violating an anti-Darwinism law. After a court room debacle in which Clarence Darrow, a witty and agnostic attorney, humiliated William Jennings Bryan, a Presbyterian layman and political leader who defended the fundamentalist cause, the movement became indelibly stamped with derision as an example of rural and small-town Protestant bigotry and irrational resistance to change.

Although fundamentalism has often been tied to the anti-evolution crusade, the Darwinistic challenge to evangelical Christianity would not, in itself, have been as critical in fermenting opposition had it not been for the fact that Darwin's theories coincided with other intellectual developments of a critical nature in European biblical scholarship. The importance of the evolution issue lay in the symbolic manner in which it marked the inroads of modernism into the christian religion and threatened Protestant hopes for a "christian America."

Throughout the 1930's and 1940's, fundamentalism remained somewhat peripheral to the American religious landscape, although the movement grew steadily through a network of transdenominational agencies, schools, publications, and through the employment of radio technology. The movement split in the 1940's over the issue of consorting with apostasy. The strict separatist American Council of Christian Churches was founded in 1941; the more accommodating National Association of Evangelicals in 1942.

In the 1950's, fundamentalism became identified with a militant "radical right" anti-communist crusade. Its main organizations at this time were the Christian Crusade (Billy James Hargis), the Church League of America (Edgar Bundy), the Christian Anti-Communist-Crusade (Fred Schwartz), and the American Council of Christian Churches (Carl McIntyre).

By the mid-1970's, a conservative evangelical Protestantism with clear linkage to the fundamentalist movement began to reawaken. The culture crisis and uncertainties of the preceding decade, the ascendancy of political conservatism, a growing anti-abortion campaign, the rise of the "electronic church," the proliferation of conservative Protestant educational institutions and publishing activities, and the decline in prestige of the liberal-secular-scientific establishment worked to stimulate the rise of a "New Religious Right" (the Moral Majority, Christian Roundtable, Christian Voice, and others). This new fundamentalism was avowedly political and more concerned with life-style issues (abortion, homosexuality, feminism, "secular humanism") than anti-communism and the defense of literal inerrancy and "Wasp" supremacy that had been the focal point of the old religious right.

While certain anti-modernist trends in Catholic theology paralleled Protestant fundamentalist patterns—especially opposition to evolution and the scientific study of scripture by ultraconservative Catholics—Catholicism's institutionalized conservatism, hierarchical centralization, early suppression of "modernism," and insular posture vis-a-vis the modern world precluded the development of a full-blown fundamentalist movement. This situation changed dramatically, however, after Vatican II. The embrace of theological concepts associated with modernism and the turmoil and polarization in the church in the wake of the Council proved highly conducive to the rise of a "Roman Catholic Traditionalist" movement—a clear analogue to Protestant fundamentalism. The Traditionalist cause, led primarily by French Archbishop Marcel Lefebvre and his priestly Society of St. Pius X, is literalistic and dogmatic in its approach to church doctrine and teaching, preoccupied with the "subversion" of the faith, in high tension with the modern cultural milieu, and exemplifies a reified conceptualization of liturgical practice. The symbol around which Traditionalist discontent has galvanized is the campaign to save the Latin Tridentine rite of the Mass.

S.G. Cole, *The History of Fundamentalism*, New York: N.F. Furniss. *The Fundamentalist Contro-versy, 1918-1931*, New Haven: 1954. E. Sandeen, *The Roots cf Fundamentalism: British and American Millenarianism 1800-1930*, Chicago: 1970. G.M. Marsden, *Fundamentalism and American Culture: The Shaping of Twentieth-Century Evangelicalism, 1870-1925*, New York: 1980. W.D. Dinges, "Catholic Traditionalist Movement," in J. Fichter, Ed. *Alternative to American Mainline Churches*, New York: 1983, pp. 137-159.

WILLIAM DINGES

G

GALLICANISM

The term Gallicanism describes the various theories and practices which sought to curtail the authority of the papacy vis-à-vis the rights of the government or of the episcopacy and the local church. Though the phenomenon was most prominently associated with the Church in France and found its most developed expression in French writings, similar tendencies were present in other countries as well. Political Gallicanism was concerned with relations between the papacy and the king or parliament; episocopal Gallicanism focused on the rights of the papacy and of the episcopacy; theological Gallicanism reflected on the relationship between the pope and a general council or between the pope and the local church.

Political or royal Gallicanism had its origins in the notion that the king of France had a privileged role in church affairs and an independence from papal authority in temporal affairs. Tensions over competing claims by the two powers came to the fore in the struggles between Boniface VIII and Philip IV the Fair, and between Louis XIV and Innocent XI. They were present also in the first of the Gallican Articles of 1682 and in the Organic Articles added to the 1801 concordat between Napoleon and the pope. Political Gallicanism came to an end with the overthrow of the ancient mon-archy and Pius VII's resistance to Napoleon.

Theological Gallicanism was based on claims of ancient privileges and customs granted to the French Church. It was influenced as well by fifteenth-century efforts to overcome the impasse of the Great Schism, most especially in the teaching of P. D'Ailly and J. Gerson who themselves drew upon the teaching of the Sorbonne. The classical expression of theological Gallicanism is found in the work of J.B. Bossuet, bishop of Meaux. It was he who led the Assembly of the Clergy in 1681-82 to publish the famous Four Gallican Articles of 1682. The first article recognized the authority of the pope in spiritual matters but asserted the independence of the king in temporal and civil affairs. The second upheld the decrees of the Council of Constance (1414-18) concerning the authority of the pope and of the general council. The third maintained the inviolability of the laws and customs of the Gallican Church. The fourth held that although the pope had the ultimate teaching authority in the church, his judgments were not irreformable without the consent of the universal church. Though the articles were condemned by the pope in 1690 and solemnly withdrawn by the king and the clergy in 1693, the teaching of the articles was widely taught in France during the eighteenth century.

Support for theological Gallicanism weakened in the nineteenth century, especially with the development of ultramontane thought. Excesses of the latter, however, gave impetus to a revival of theological Gallicanism, most significantly in the two volumes written on the eve of Vatican I by bishop H. Maret, dean of the faculty of theology at the Sorbonne. The definitions of papal primacy and infallibility at Vatican I (1870) were a direct repudiation of Gallican teaching.

Vatican II, in its teaching on the relations between church and state, on collegiality, and on the local church, may be said to preserve, though in a very different form, some of the concerns of the Gallican tradition.

See **Bishop, Church, Collegiality, Pope**

V. Martin, *Les origines du Gallicanisme,* 2 vols., Paris, 1939. A.G. Martimort, *Le Gallicanisme,* Paris, 1973.

FREDERICK J. CWIEKOWSKI, SS

GENERATION

The term used in the theology of the Trinity to refer to the origin of the Son or Word from the Father.

GIFTS OF THE HOLY SPIRIT
Scriptural Basis

The traditional listing of "the seven gifts of the Holy Spirit" derives from the opening verses of Isaiah 11 in the translation of the Greek Septuagint: "There shall come forth a shoot from the stump of Jesus, and a branch shall grow out of his roots. And the Spirit of the Lord shall rest upon him, the spirit of wisdom and understanding, the spirit of counsel and fortitude, the spirit of knowledge and piety, and he shall be filled with the spirit of the fear of the Lord." This passage represents one of the OT's best-known descriptions of the ideal king of the future. Although these seven "spirits" are not listed as such in the NT, it is clear that Jesus is there seen as the fulfillment of the messianic text. This is above all the case in the gospel descriptions of his baptism in the Jordan, when the Spirit descended from the heavens and "came to rest on him" (Jn 1:32). Numerous passages in the NT likewise speak of the Holy Spirit as being given to the followers of Jesus (e.g., Jn 14:16-17; Acts 2; Rom 5:5). It was primarily in the light of such texts, in which God's primary gift is said to be the Holy Spirit as such, that the sevenfold listing in Isaiah could readily be given a christian interpretation.

Development in Christian Thought

Already in the First Letter of Clement of Rome, written about 96 C.E., there are references to the Holy Spirit's being poured out on christian believers, but only in the following century were the seven Isaian "spirits" first called "gifts of the Holy Spirit." This terminology is found in Justin Martyr's *Dialogue with Trypho* (chap. 87), where Justin writes that whereas some OT figures enjoyed one or two of these gifts (Solomon the spirit of wisdom; Daniel, the spirits of understanding and counsel, etc.), Christ alone received them all and so can distribute them "to all his believers according to their merits."

Of later patristic writers, it was mainly the Latin Fathers who speculated about the precise interrelationship among these seven gifts. Hilary of Poitiers and Ambrose of Milan, both commenting on Psalm 118 (119): 38, put the gifts in ascending order, beginning with the fear of the Lord as the lowest or most fundamental for us. Augustine followed them in this, holding, for example, that "when the prophet Isaiah speaks of the seven spiritual gifts which are so well-known, he begins with wisdom and concludes with the fear of the Lord, as if he were descending toward us from on high in order to teach us how to ascend" (Sermon 347).

During the early Middle Ages there was little theological elaboration on this subject. Those theologians who did treat of the gifts regularly identified them with the virtues (e.g., Hugh of St. Victor and Peter Lombard), but around the year 1235 Philip the Chancellor, in his *De septem donis Spiritus Sancti,* argued that the gifts and the virtues are distinct from one another. In this he was followed by Thomas Aquinas, whose theological reflection on the gifts (S.Th. Ia IIae, q. 68) was to become the most influential treatment of this theme in the history of christian theology. What Thomas wrote deserves to be quoted in part: "In distinguishing the Gifts from the virtues, we ought to follow Scripture's own way of speaking. There they are spoken of as *spirits* rather than *gifts* .... From this way of speaking, we are obviously given to understand that these seven are enumerated there as in us by divine inspiration. Inspiration, however, denotes a motion coming from the outside. For there are two principles of movement in man: one which is intrinsic to him, namely, reason; the other extrinsic, namely, God.... Now it is evident that the human virtues perfect man insofar as it is his nature to be moved by reason in the things he does, both interiorly and exteriorly. There must, therefore, be still higher perfections in man to dispose him to be moved by God. These perfections are called Gifts, not only because they are infused by God, but also because they dispose him to become readily mobile to divine inspiration, as is said in Isaiah: *The Lord opened my ear; I do not contradict him, I did not pull back* (S.Th. Ia, IIa, q. 68, a. 1).

This passage helps explain why the theologoumenon of the Gifts of the Holy Spirit became particularly important in mystical theology, since it is there that the note of docile receptivity to divine inspiration is especially pronounced. Spiritual writers who treated the gifts at considerable length were Jan van Ruusbroec in the fourteenth century and Denys the Carthusian in the fifteenth, while among Thomistic theologians John of St. Thomas (d. 1664) wrote extensively and lucidly on the subject in his *Cursus theologicus.*

Contemporary State of the Question

In our own day it is perhaps largely the new hermeneutical approaches to scripture which have caused most theologians and spiritual writers to refrain from seeing in the seven "spirits" of Isa 11:2 any kind of exhaustive listing of the gifts of God's Spirit to humankind. In fact, the only mention of the gifts of the Holy Spirit in the Second Vatican Council's Dogmatic Constitution on the Church does not even refer to the Isaian passage but rather to St. Paul's discusson of spiritual gifts in I Corinthians 12 and 14 (L.G. n. 7). There is, however, every reason to think that the traditional treatment of the seven gifts will retain a privileged place in Christian thought, being as it is a time-honored way of articulating the christian belief that only those who are "led by the Spirit of God are children of God" (Rom 8:14).

See **Grace, Holy Spirit**

Gustave Bardy, et. al., "Dons du Saint-Esprit," *Dictionnaire de spiritualité* 3:1579-1641. Yves M.J. Congar, *I Believe in the Holy Spirit,* trans. David Smith, 3 vols., New York and London, 1983. See 2:134-141. Ambroise Gardeil, "Dons du Saint-Esprit," *Dictionnaire de théologie catholique* 4:1728-1781. John of St. Thomas, *The Gifts of the Holy Ghost,* trans. Dominic Hughes, OP, New York, 1951.

JAMES A. WISEMAN, OSB

GLORY

1. Old Testament

If we turn to the scriptures in order to discover what is meant by God's glory, we quickly find a variety of terms, images and events, not a single, well-defined concept. In fact, it is probably best to treat the word as something of a cipher, a heuristic term used to point to the "godliness of God" as it has appeared rather than as a notion with a meaning already defined which is then applied to God. In the OT, *kabod* is perhaps the most important of many related words and refers in its root meaning to what is weighty, important or impressive. It is the concrete, sensible impact and power of the transcendent God's appearance in the world. It would be utterly foreign to the OT to conceive of a direct experience of God but God's glory is God's self-revelation insofar as human beings are given to experience it.

Thus we find glory associated with God's name. It refers basically to the power, holiness, majesty and splendor of this Lord. According to the OT, these can be recognized in a variety of ways. Central, of course, are the ways in which God reveals God's glory in Israel's history. God's appearance on the scene is frequently associated with natural phenomena such as the dark cloud, a devouring fire, thunder and lightening, earthquake and storm. Such occurrences are meant to signal the presence of the transcendent Lord who acts in power for Israel's salvation. The manifestation on Mount Sinai, which may be viewed as the climax of the Exodus, is foundational. Here God's glory is seen in God's absolute lordship. God's power overcomes all other gods and nations in order to liberate Israel and graciously enter into covenant with them. Throughout the OT the glory of the Lord is associated with all the places connected with God's earthly appearances: Sinai, the Tent of Meeting, Solomon's Temple. Especially in the Psalms we find the further reflection that the glory revealed by the Lord in Israel's liberation is the very glory and power of the creator of all. And so, in speaking of God's glory, the Psalms refer to the creative, sustaining and ordering power of God evident in the awesome beauty and majesty of the cosmos. Finally, in the Prophets and Psalms, the glory of God refers in a special way to the kingdom of covenant peace and justice which God will establish in its fullness at the end of time. All of the different perspectives find a central unity in the recognition that God's glory is what humans are graciously given to experience of God and God's saving action in the world.

In the OT we also find that glory is something which men and women are expected to give God. In view of what we have said above, this can only mean giving acknowledgement to the glory which belongs to and is revealed and established by God. Thus, giving God the glory refers to the obedient response of faith to God's saving action in history.

2. New Testament

The notion of God's glory (*doxa*) in the NT also refers to the power, majesty, honor and radiance which belongs to God alone. What is new is the confession that the glory of the Lord which has appeared in so many ways has in these last days appeared in Jesus Christ. The glory which had always been associated with the saving, self-revelation of God refers now in a unique way to the person of Christ. This is the reason why the traditional association with meteorological phenomena, although still present, no longer plays a significant role. Jesus reflects the glory of God; in him we see just what the godliness of God is. Through an astounding diversity of voices, the NT proclaims in unison that central to the experience of God's glory is the paschal mystery: the suffering, death and resurrection of Jesus. The essential paradox of the figure of Jesus reaches its climax in the utter poverty and powerlessness of the one who claimed to speak with unheard of authority, who was conscious of a relationship with God (*abba*) so intimate that it could only be thought of as madness or blasphemy. Both Paul and John, from different perspectives, saw the cross of Jesus as the place where the true glory of God is revealed. The cross of Jesus as the end and fullness of a life lived completely from God for others is the revelation of God's majesty and power as self-emptying love. That such apparently powerless love is, in reality, the absolute power of God, becomes visible, of course, only in the light of the resurrection. Seen in their essential unity, however, the cross and resurrection of Jesus Christ are the revelation of the glory and majesty of a love stronger than all powers of sin and death, a love greater than which it is impossible to conceive. It is precisely God's glory that God, while remaining God and Lord of all, is powerful enough to enter into the sin and death which has disfigured God's creation and from within, in loving solidarity, to save God's beloved world. Thus God's glory is revealed as the mystery of trinitarian love which empties itself in order to become one with the world, and so to establish the salvation which was always God's eternal design as a sharing in God's own life and freedom. In this context the eschatological perspective of God's glory in the NT can be appreciated. The glory of the divine love revealed once and for all in the life, death and resurrection of Jesus Christ will be established fully at the end of time when the Son comes in glory, and God will be all in all.

Like the OT, we find that the NT thinks of God's glory primarily as God's own initiative and action. God's glory reveals and establishes itself as the salvation of the world. This can be experienced, even now, in a concrete, sensible way in the church as the community of believers who, in the obedience of faith, allow the glory of God's kingdom to appear in their lives. Thus, for the NT, giving God glory is the response of faith to the self-communication of God in Jesus Christ. Since God's glory is seen for the first time to be real self-communication, and not only self-manifestation, the acceptance of this gracious gift is itself an integral part of the establishment of God's glory. Thus history as a whole, seen as the transforming entrance of the world into the reality of God's own divine life, is the glorification of God by believers in the power of the Spirit. The glorification of God is the salvation of the world: doxology is soteriology.

3. Theological Implications

Inasmuch as the biblical notion of God's glory refers to the appearance of God in human history as the one who saves, we can conclude that it is a central category of *revelation theology* and *soteriology*. It is closely tied with the concepts of God's holiness, lordship, power and might, a fact echoed in the *Sanctus* of the eucharistic liturgy. To speak in such a way of God's glory in today's world might seem impossible or undesirable. And yet, at its center, christian faith proclaims a God who has drawn near to us in self-emptying love and has shown the power of such love to transform us and our world. The message of God's power in us to overcome the powers of sin and death can be a source of hope and courage for christian life. A theology of God's glory, and the proclamation flowing from it, would have to be centered upon the cross and resurrection of Jesus as the eschatological establishment of God's kingdom and then develop an understanding of the Spirit poured out into the hearts of believers as the one who enables men and women to give God glory by working for the justice of God's kingdom. The glorification of God does not mean the rejection of this world or the denigration of humanity. It consists in the salvation of this world and the divinization of humanity.

Two contemporary theologians who have made glory a central concept in their work are Karl Barth and Hans Urs von Balthasar.

See **Beauty, God, Revelation, Salvation**

Hans Urs von Balthasar, *The Glory of the Lord: A Theological Aesthetics,* 6 vols., San Francisco and New York, 1982-   and Edinburgh, 1983. Karl Barth, *Church Dogmatics II/1: The Doctrine of God,* Edinburgh, 1957, 608-77. Walter Kasper, *The God of Jesus Christ,* London and New York, 1984.

JOHN R. SACHS, SJ

GLOSSOLALIA

In his instructions to the Corinthians about the charismatics Paul lists glossolalia or speaking in tongues among the gifts of the Spirit (1 Cor 12:10; 14:5). Yet he warns against practicing it in community assemblies unless there is an interpreter present. It cannot edify others unless an interpreter explains it (14:28). Paul is grateful that he speaks in tongues himself, a gift he claims to possess in greater measure than all of them (14:18). He values this gift, which he possibly refers to as "tongues of angels" (13:1), because it provides edification for those who enjoy it.

Glossolalia is a concrete manifestation of controlled ecstatic prayer. It results from a concrete encounter with the indwelling Holy Spirit, a blessing that Paul wants all the Corinthians to experience (14:5). His warning is only against making this gift the essential sign of one's sharing in the Holy Spirit.

Paul knows also of a preconceptual manifestation of the Spirit that enables believers to make intercessory prayer (Rom 8:26). That too is a gift but different from glossolalia, which does not illumine the mind (1 Cor 14:14). Paul urges believers to foster every such type of gift when he advises, "Do not quench the Spirit" (1 Thess 5:19).

The teaching of Paul on speaking in tongues seems to contradict the description of the experience that occurred on the first Pentecost. Those who received the Spirit are described as speaking "in different tongues" (Acts 2:4). As a result of this special presence of the Holy Spirit, the assembled group was able to speak "the wonderful works of God" in the languages of the pilgrims in Jerusalem (2:6-11).

Yet commentators identify the two prayer experiences. They attribute the difference in description to Luke's desire to present Pentecost as the new Sinai. The Holy Spirit is the new covenant which empowers all nations to join their voices in the worship of God, and his presence enables the apostles to convert all nations. The other two accounts of glossolalia in Acts 10:46 and 19:6 describe overwhelming prayer experiences of the Holy Spirit, similar to those of the Corinthians.

Among the Fathers of the Church, St. John Chrysostom identified glossolalia as a characteristic of the apostolic church, a gift no longer needed nor enjoyed once the faith was solidly established. Yet speaking in tongues has been attested time and again within the mystical tradition of the church.

The contemporary church is experiencing a widespread practice of glossolalia, which is often linked to "baptism in the Spirit." It is a special prayer gift that remains in those who experience it so that they can activate it at will. This upsurge has led psychologists to investigate the phenomenon. Research, still in its early stages, is seeking to determine whether any link can be established between psychological conditions and glossolalia.

JAMES M. REESE, OSFS

GNOSTICISM

Gnosticism, derived from the Greek for "knowledge" (*gnosis*), refers to a religious movement which claimed that salvation was based on secret knowledge conveyed to the elect by a heavenly revealer. This knowledge set the "gnostics" apart from others whose faith was placed in such "public" scriptures as the Jewish Law, the canonical christian gospels or the well-known teachings of Greek philosophers. Gnosticism flourished between the second and fourth centuries C.E. when it was embodied in many different sects. Gnostic teachings posed a strong challenge to the emerging orthodoxy in the christian church, since its teachers claimed that they, not the orthodox bishops, possessed the secret revelations which Jesus had transmitted to individual disciples after his resurrection. Only gnostics would attain salvation by incorporation into the heavenly "church." Only they would regain the primordial male-female unity lost at Adam's fall when their souls were reunited with their heavenly counterpart. Other Christians might at best receive some lower form of salvation in the heavens, or their souls might be subject to reincarnation until they attained enlightenment. Some humans are even incapable of that destiny, since their souls do not possess any affinity for the divine world. Such persons are simply "material beings" ruled by the passions and the evil demonic god who dominates the world of matter.

Christian forms of gnosticism identify Christ as the heavenly redeemer, whose call the gnostic answers in awakening to the knowledge of the true heavenly home which frees the soul from its ignorance and bondage in this world. However, many gnostic writings show a deeper concern with Judaism. The god of the OT is a demonic, vengeful creator, who came into being as the result of a fall by the heavenly Wisdom (Sophia). This god, frequently called "Ialdabaoth," has created an earthly, demon-ruled world as a prison to keep humanity from discovering the true divine world above this one. The story of Adam and Eve is treated as one in which the first couple is "enlightened" until the lower god causes them to forget their true being. Sometimes this punishment is represented by division of humanity into male and female governed by sexual and other passions to remain in the realm of death. Enlightenment comes to humanity through the mediation of angelic figures or even a heavenly form of the material Wisdom herself. The pervasiveness of Jewish elements in gnostic mythologizing leads scholars to suggest that gnostic origins lie in some form of heterodox Judaism which had rebelled against its own tradition. The biography of the third-century founder of the gnostic religious movement known as Manichaeism, Mani, provides additional evidence for this suggestion. Before his enlightenment by his heavenly twin, Mani had belonged to a sectarian Jewish baptismal group.

Preoccupation with the ascent of the soul to a divine realm beyond the confines of the changing material world, the world of death, can also be found outside Jewish and christian circles. Religious forms of Platonic philosophy stressed the need for the soul to turn inward, away from the world of the senses and matter, in order to find the divine. Some gnostic groups combine their cosmology and mythology with such Platonic philosophy. The third century C.E. Neoplatonic philosopher, Plotinus, wrote a sharp attack against the influence of such gnostics among his disciples. He castigated the gnostics for their hostility toward the material world, whose beauty Plato had insisted could guide the soul on its upward ascent. But that same hostility toward the material world and rejection of bodily passions led many gnostic sects in an ascetic direction that sometimes made them difficult to distinguish from their monastic counterparts in fourth century Syria and Egypt. A small gnostic religious group, the Mandeans, has survived from pre-christian times until the present in modern Iraq and the Khuzistan province in Iran. They are known among Muslims as "Subba," "baptizers," since as is the case in many gnostic sects, purification is associated with a baptismal rite, followed by special "sealing" of the initiate and a sacred meal of bread and water. Among the Mandeans, as among many other ancient gnostic groups, baptismal rites might be repeated and special rituals accompany death to ensure that the soul reaches its destiny in the light world.

Gnosticism and Christianity

Gnostic sects were clearly most prolific in their Christian forms. Famous gnostic teachers like Valentinus, Ptolemy, Heracleon, Theodore and Basilides were able to gather groups of disicples in the christian communities of Rome and Alexandria in the middle of the second century C.E. Their teaching was carried on by disciples. Other gnostic groups are only known by names such as "Sethians," "Ophites," "Naasenes," given them in the Church Fathers, Justin Martyr, Irenaeus, Hippolytus, Clement of Alexandria, Origen, Tertullian and Ephiphanius, who wrote extensively against the gnostics. In addition to the reports and citations of gnostic teaching preserved in the writings of their opponents, a considerable number of gnostic writings were translated from Greek into Coptic, the language of Roman Egypt. The most famous collection of such Coptic texts was found ca. 1945 near Nag Hammadi in Egypt. The collection originally comprised 13 codices and over 50 treatises. The copies appear to have been made in the mid-fourth

century C.E. The bindings of the codices contained "waste paper" from the christian monasteries of Pachomius that were in the region. Some scholars speculate that the monks might have preserved such writings because of the ascetic emphasis but later buried them when the bishop of Alexandria began to insist on controlling the orthodoxy of the monks.

Gnostic teachers and orthodox Christians differed sharply on fundamental theological points. The gnostic claim that creation is the instrument of a malicious god was sharply rejected. So were gnostic claims about what represented "authoritative revelation." The OT was retained in the christian canon. Orthodox teachers also insisted that there were no "secret meanings" buried in the NT writings which had to be revealed by the secret knowledge of a gnostic teacher. The various gospels and revelations put forward by gnostics as true tradition handed down in secret from such persons as John, Peter, Paul, James the brother of the Lord, Mary Magdalene, and Thomas, were all rejected. Only the "four gospels" contain apostolic tradition.

Since the gnostics emphasized the fact that Christ had descended as a heavenly revealer, they challenged the common Christian emphasis on "Jesus" and the crucifixion as the means of salvation. They insisted, often by affirming the virginity of Mary, that the heavenly Christ had merely assumed bodily form in order to communicate with his "brothers and sisters," the gnostics, trapped in this world. However, it is irrational, they insisted, to think that the spiritual Christ could actually have died on a cross. The crucifixion was simply a deception put over on the demonic powers and their associates in this world. They nailed an empty body. "Jesus," to the cross. The spiritual Christ had already left the body and in some gnostic accounts stands by laughing. This docetic picture of Christ also meant that the heavenly Christ was never corrupted by any of the passions of the material body. Gnostics consider the orthodox doctrine of Christ's atoning death and emphasis on bodily resurrection to be a foolish way of clinging to a material reality which cannot ever become part of the divine, heavenly world. Salvation, they insist, only comes through the revealed knowledge which unites the soul with its heavenly counterpart and makes it possible to follow the redeemer out of this world. Without such "enlightenment" rituals like baptism, anointing and eucharist, are powerless.

Responding to gnostic challenges led christian writers to insist upon the humanity of Jesus, the effectiveness of his death as atonement, the resurrection of the body, the adequacy of the canonical writings as revelation, the effectiveness of sacraments, and the possibility of salvation for all believers rather than of the elite who possessed "knowledge." Rejection of gnostic theologizing, also meant insisting upon an "orthodox" interpretation of NT passages such as the imagery of Christ as a divine figure "sent from God" in John or the treatment of the cosmic powers in such Pauline passages as 1 Cor 2:6ff and Eph 6:12 or the "spiritual body" of resurrection in 1 Cor 15:42-54 or the "heavenly dwelling" in 2 Cor 5:1-5. Gnostic writers often pointed to passages like these to support their claims that a gnostic understanding of salvation represents the true message of Christianity. Though it is sometimes argued that the Johannine and Pauline traditions were shaped by a gnostic environment, they lack many of the characteristic features of the gnostic syntheses known to us from the second century C.E. onward. It seems more appropriate to understand the "gnosticizing" imagery found in the NT as derived from the same milieu of heterdox Judaism in which the building blocks for the great gnostic syntheses of myth, biblical interpretation and religio-philosophic speculation, were being cut. Christianity itself provided a significant communal base for the emergence of gnostic sectarianism in the second century C.E.

The most comprehensive general account of gnosticism is Kurt Rudolph, *Gnosis. The Nature and History of Gnosticism*, San Francisco: Harper & Row, 1983. A classic attempt to capture the intellectual mood of gnosticism remains Hans Jonas', *The Gnostic Religion*, Boston: Beacon, 1970. Selections from the patristic, Coptic and Mandean literature can be found in Werner Foerster, *Gnosis*, 2 vols, Oxford: Oxford, 1972/1974. An English translation of the Nag Hammadi collection can be found in James Robinson, ed., *The Nag Hammadi Library in English*, New York: Harper and Row, 1977. Recent studies of the relationship between Gnosticism and Christianity can be found in Charles W. Hedrick and Robert Hodgson eds., *Nag Hammadi, Gnosticism and Early Christianity*. Peabody, MA: Hendrickson, 1986.

PHEME PERKINS

GOD

The etymology of the English word "God," as well as of the equivalent words in Latin, Greek and Hebrew, is much disputed. The English word seems to come by way of Old Teutonic from an Aryan root *gheu*—meaning either "to invoke" or "to pour out in sacrifice." Thus "God" means "the object of worship." The Latin word *deus* appears to come from a Sanskrit root *di*, meaning "to gleam," whence *dyaus* "heaven," and *devas* "God." The Latin seems thus to mean "the bright god of the sky." Though it is much disputed, the Greek word *theos* probably has a like origin and meaning. Hebrew has three common words for "God": *el*, *elohim* and *eloah*. They seem to be all somehow related to one another and to refer to "power" or "strength." The ordinary dictionary definition of the word "God" is "the one Supreme Being, the creator and ruler of the universe."

I. Knowledge and Language about God
Meaning of God Language. The word
"God," of course, like all words derives
its actual meaning from its use in human
speech and communication. For example,
people in saying "God" may refer to the
cause of the being and unity of all that is,
or to the actual object of worship, the one
to whom unconditional loyalty and obedience is due, or to one who is providentially active in history, and so on.

However, in the last two decades,
beginning with Radical Theology or the
Death of God movement, not only has
the validity of the word "God" been
denied, but its actual meaning has been
called into question. That is, not only is it
maintained that the word has no objective
referent in reality, but that it has no real
meaning for human intelligence; it is said
to be defined by a series of words and
images that are not ultimately grounded
in human experience, and is therefore
finally meaningless. One cannot talk
meaningfully about a maker of the world
if one does not experience any such
claim. One cannot speak intelligibly about
the one who guides history unless one
experiences that history is in fact guided.
Thus all the conventional ways of understanding the word "God" are said to be
groundless.

A closer examination of common
human experiences, however, does manifest a ground of meaning for the word
"God," inasmuch as there are common
experiences that point to a transcendent
reality beyond the knowing subject and
beyond all that is immediately given.
Such meaningfulness does not directly
guarantee the validity of the language,
the actual existence of what the word
means, but the first step toward validity
is taken here.

The experience of questioning illustrates this dimension of transcendent
ultimacy in human experience. To question anything, to ask what it is and why it
is and where it came from, is already to
go beyond it, to look for something that
is not immediately evident which may
ground it. But the questioning power of
the human mind does not naturally stop
at anything until it reaches something or
someone that is in itself an unquestionable
final answer, that exists of itself, by
reason of what it is, and grounds whatever
else may exist. The word "God" means
just this, and hence its meaning is present
in the very process of asking questions,
even on the supposition that no objective
reality corresponds to this meaning.

The experience of moral obligation
(not just of taboos) also points to a
transcendent ground of value. For the
experience of obligation is the experience
of a value that lays an unconditional
claim upon me, for example, the claim of
truth, or of justice, or of human dignity.
In these cases the human dignity comes
to me from beyond myself and from
beyond the particular concrete things or
persons that embody these values. This
"beyond" is precisely a transcendent
ground of value signified by the word
"God."

Similar reflections could be made about
many other common human experiences
like spontaneous gratitude for life, or
wonder, or recognizing the permanence
of truth amid change, or making positive
affirmations of existence, or hoping into
the indefinite future. They all imply a
dimension of transcendent ultimacy, and
hence ground the meaning of the word
"God."

Validity of God Language. If we ask how
human experience not only gives meaning
to the word "God" but enables us to
affirm that meaning validly and certainly
in referring to a reality existing independently of our experience, the key
insight is convergence: these common
human experiences, as well as other more
specifically religious experiences, converge upon a single transcendent referent,

the origin and ground of being, purpose, truth, beauty, value, love, order, etc. Just as the convergent testimony of witnesses enables an historian to discover what happened, or as the convergence of clues enables a detective to establish the identity of one responsible for a crime, or as the convergence of experimental data enables a scientist to affirm the existence of a particular cause, so the convergence of the transcendental dimension of human experience enables us to affirm the existence and the reality of God.

In the affirmation of God we can distinguish (but not separate) the activities of reason and of faith. Reason can establish a more or less necessary connection between a particular existential fact and the transcendent reality of God. We can have arguments from motion to the Unmoved Mover, from contingent beings to the Necessary Being, from purposeful activity in unreasoning beings to the Wise Governor of the world, and so on. But, though these conclusions of reason are valid, by themselves they frequently leave the mind restless and without firm certainty. It is faith that perceives the pattern of convergence in all these arguments and affirms with assurance the reality of the One they point to.

Faith, as it is used here, is not just a religious activity, but a universal human activity by which we reach certitude even when the evidence is not rationally compelling. It is faith, for example, that makes us sure of our friends, or enables us to accept the testimony of others, or gives us confidence about the worthwhileness of life. It is in fact a kind of faith that leads a scientist to certitude about a particular theory. These various certitudes are necessary for living a human life, but they do not flow with absolute necessity from the evidence, either inductively or deductively.

Faith becomes a religious activity when the ground of the affirmation is, or tends to be, the sum total of all our experience (granted the special influence of certain "peak experiences"), and the reality we affirm calls for total acceptance or worship on our part. In the perspective of biblical faith we also recognize the attractive power or invitation of God leading us to make this affirmation. We recognize that the knowledge we may have of God is much more the result of divine self-disclosure than of human inquiry. God makes himself known both in the transcendent dimension of our many experiences and in the inclination to accept and affirm him. Faith as gift is both light and attraction, as God is supreme truth and supreme goodness.

The scriptures indicate four areas of divine disclosure, where the light and the attraction of God are particularly evident: the world of nature, the events of history, the life of the community, and individual personal experience. The psalms of praise and gratitude summarize these indications; for psalms of praise celebrate the action of God in nature and in history (e.g., Ps 33); psalms of gratitude thank God for his goodness to the community and to the individual (e.g., Pss 116, 67).

St. Paul points to the world of nature when he writes: "Ever since the creation of the world his invisible nature namely, his eternal power and deity, has been clearly perceived in the things that have been made" (Rom 1:20). The prophets in a particular way allude to the revelation of God in history; for example, Ezekiel writes: "I will execute judgments upon Moab. Then they will know that I am the Lord" (Ezek 25:11). The disclosure of God's presence in the life of the community appears especially in covenant formulas reflecting the union of the people with God: "I will put my law within them, and I will write it upon their hearts; and I will be their God, and they shall be my people. And no longer shall each man teach his neighbor and each his brother, saying, 'Know the Lord,' for they shall all know me, from the least of them to the greatest, says the Lord; for I will forgive their iniquity, and I will remember their sin no more" (Jer 31:33-34). Finally, St. John has a special instance of the disclosure of God in the personal experience of *agape* or unselfish love: "One who loves is born of God and knows God. One who does not love does not know God; for God is love" (1 Jn 4:7-8).

Limitations of God Language. It should be noted that ideas of God that are formed on the basis of such experiences merely point to the reality of God; they do not grasp or comprehend it, as human ideas generally do to some degree. The world of our experience reveals aspects or qualities that are directly verified in what we immediately perceive, but which point to something beyond, to something that exceeds the limitations that mark these as creaturely. Being, power, value, goodness, intelligence and so on are all found in the world in a recognizable and limited mode of reality, but they point to a transcendent realization which is beyond any limit and mode we conceive.

Human beings have always used an abundance of metaphorical language to speak of God. The experience of God is of one who is unique and transcendent; but all of our language was created to structure and express our experience of what is multiple and various in the world around us. We can apply this language to God only in a metaphorical or analogous way. The qualities or relations expressed in these words describe to some degree what God is like. If he is called "potter" it is because he shapes his people somewhat the way a potter shapes clay. If he is called "shepherd" it is because he looks after his people the way a shepherd looks after his flock. If God is described as "mother," it is because in her love and tenderness she cares for her people as a mother looks after her child. There are impersonal metaphors as well: God is a rock of refuge, a light, a tower of safety, a consuming fire, etc.

But the metaphors that are drawn from human personality are the commonest and the most illuminating: king, husband, mother, father, lord, etc. Given the cultural background in which most religions developed (including the biblical), it is not strange that the vast majority of these metaphors are masculine rather than feminine; but the divine transcendence is compromised if male figures predominate to such an extent that God somehow appears to be more appropriately represented as male rather than female. The image of God, we are told in Genesis, is found in the human being, male and female together (Gen 1:27).

All of this raises a special problem about the pronouns one uses of God. Should we say only "he" and "him"? Or should we also say "she" and "her"? Or should we write "she/he" and "him/her"? There is at present no easy and graceful solution to this limitation of language. It seems confusing to say sometimes "he" and sometimes "she" with no reason coming from the context. It seems even more confusing to say "he/she." Without claiming to solve this linguistic problem, or maintaining that the course adopted here is the best one, this article will continue to use masculine pronouns, except where context suggests otherwise, simply because this is consistent and traditional. However, this is not meant to say either that God is more male than female, or that men are more like God than women are.

II. Human Understanding of God

The Biblical Understanding of God. The sacred writings of the OT and NT express the religious experiences and faith convictions of a people through many centuries. In the Hebrew scriptures we may discern a development in the understanding of God from one that is more concerned with divine immanence to one that emphasizes divine transcendence. Their understanding begins with an appreciation of God who is at work in their history and moves to an ever greater awareness of God as beyond all history, though not in any way removed from history.

The ancestors of the Hebrew people, like all other people of the ancient Near East, were polytheists (Josh 24:2, 14). Some traces of polytheism can be found in ancient patriarchal narratives, as when God manifested himself to Abraham as three visitors (Gen 18:1-3). God in these early days was regarded as a clan or tribal deity, chosen in turn by successive patriarchs in response to a personal revelation (Gen 28:21). But almost from the beginning they recognized that if God was to function as their protector and guide he must be more than a tribal deity; he must indeed be "Maker of Heaven and Earth" (Gen 14:19, 22). It is this insight into God as the Creator and Lord of Heaven and Earth that distinguishes the living and true God of Israel from the dead and false gods of those around them (Isa 45:18; Jer 10:10-12), and at the same time provides the ground for a deeper appreciation of both the divine immanence and the divine transcendence.

It is because God is the creator of the world that he can guide the events that take place within it, that he can be immanent in world history; Jeremiah begins an account of God's activity in the history of Israel by exclaiming, "Ah Lord God! It is you who have made the heavens and the earth by your great power and by your outstretched arm! Nothing is too hard for you who show steadfast love to thousands, but requite the guilt of parents to their children after them" (Jer 32:17-24). It is the Creator God who chose the Hebrew people as his own (Gen 12:1-3), made a covenant with them after freeing them from the slavery of Egypt (Exod 19:5-6), gave them the land of Canaan (Jos 1:11), established the Davidic monarchy (2 Sam 7:8-16), sent them prophets (2 Kgs 17:13), delivered them into captivity in Babylon for their rebellion and brought them back again (Isa 40:1-2). God's concern for Israel, however, looked beyond them to the salvation of the world (Isa 2:2-4; 45:22; Jer 16:19; Jonah; Ps 116).

God aroused and sustained in his people Israel the hope for a messiah, thus preparing them for a future, definitive saving intervention. This hope became more focused in response to an increasingly clearer word of promise: first to Abraham (Gen 12:1-3), then to David (2 Sam 7:7-17), then in the promise of a new covenant (Jer 31:31-34), and later in the prediction about a mysterious Servant of Yahweh, whose sufferings would remove sin (Isa 52:13-53:12), and finally in the vision of a "Son of Man" who would inaugurate in history the universal kingdom of God (Dan 7:14).

But, always there was a concomitant growing awareness of the transcendence of God: he could act everywhere in the world of time and space because he was not confined or limited by it. Their God is the unique God, there is no other (Isa 35:18; Jer 10:10-12). In his creative power he transcends creaturely weakness (Jer 32:17; Ps 135:5-7; Isa 55:8-11). In his eternity he is beyond the perishable world of time (Lam 5:17-20); Isa 40:28; Pss 90:1-4; 102:25-27). In his immensity he transcends all limitations of place (1 Kgs 8:27; Jer 23:23-24; Ps 139:8-10). His Spirit contains all things (Wis 1:7) and his Wisdom orders all things (Wis 8:1). God is beyond our ability to comprehend (Ps 139:6; Job 42:3) or to praise as he deserves (Sir 43:28).

Thus, according to the OT, the living and true God is the Maker and Lord of heaven and earth, one, almighty, eternal, immense and unspeakably exalted, who for the salvation of the whole world chose a people as his own, and prepared them in many ways for the coming of a savior, the messiah or anointed one.

In the NT the word "God" (Gk. *ho theos*) regularly signifies the living and true God of the OT (Mt 4:10; Mk 7:8; Jn 8:54; Rom 3:2), who is the Father of Our Lord Jesus Christ (Jn 2:16; 5:18; Rom 15:6; Heb 1:1-2; 1 Pet 1:3). This God sent his Son into the world (Rom 8:3; Gal 4:4; Jn 8:42), worked in him and through him his prophetic and saving mission (Jn 14:10; 2 Cor 5:19), raised him from the dead (Eph 1:20), glorified him and gave him the Holy Spirit to be given to all believers (Acts 2:33; Jn 7:39).

The NT also teaches that God is our Father (Mt 6:9; Rom 1:7), for he made us his sons and daughters in and through his Son Jesus Christ (Mt 12:50; Eph 1:5-6). This lays upon us the obligation to live as children of God (Mt 5:48), especially through forgiveness (Mt 6:14-15), mercy (Lk 6:36) and mutual love (1 Jn 4:7). It also inspires us with confidence and trust for everything we need (Mt 6:31-33), and in all that happens to us, even suffering and death (Mt 6:25; 10:29-31). The NT revelation of God is most fittingly summed up in St. John's expression "God is Love" (1 Jn 4:7-21).

This NT teaching about God reflects Jesus' own profound religious experience manifested in his consistent address of God as "Abba!" (Mk 14:36), a heretofore unheard of way of speaking to God. For the word means not simply "father," but expresses a degree of intimate familiarity that no one previously had ventured to presume. "Abba!" is the way a child addresses his or her father, like "Daddy!" or something similar. Jesus saw himself entrusted by his Father with a saving mission and endowed with the Holy Spirit to accomplish that mission (Lk 3:22; 4:1, 14, 18; 10:21; Acts 10:38). In his teaching he proclaims his Father's will (Mt 7:21-27), and asserts that one who does that will is his brother, sister and mother (Mt 12:50).

The first generation of Christians experienced the power and the presence of God in the freedom, forgiveness, unity, peace and love that generally characterized their communities (Gal 5:22; Eph 4:3). They recognized here the gift of the Holy Spirit, given by the Risen Lord to those who believe in him (Jn 7:39; Acts 2:38), in fulfillment of the promise of the Father (Lk 24:49; Acts 1:4). In this Spirit they experienced and acknowledged Jesus as Lord (1 Cor 12:3) and addressed God in the same way Jesus had "Abba! (Daddy!)" (Gal 4:6; Rom 8:15). In these experiences of Father, Son and Holy Spirit, and in their verbal articulation, the foundations for the doctrine of the Holy Trinity were laid.

Understanding of God in Christian Tradition. The major development of the christian understanding of God was the unfolding of the doctrine of the Trinity. But in doing this and in meeting heresies within and pagan culture without, the christian community clarified and elaborated its own understanding of the reality of the divine.

The most frequent designation of God in christian professions of faith is *pantokrator,* "almighty" or "omnipotent." This word was used frequently in the LXX translation of the OT (e.g., 2 Mac 8:18) and occurs in the NT in 2 Cor 6:18 and eight times in the book of Revelation (e.g., 1:8, 4:8). The sense of "almighty" is not that God alone has power, but that he has power over all things, that he rules all things. This power over all things is shown first of all in creation, a work attributed in a special way to the Father, the ultimate origin of all reality. God's power is further shown in the saving mystery of his Son Jesus Christ, in his life, death, resurrection and ascension. It is finally shown in the sanctifying works of the Holy Spirit, in the church, the forgiveness of sin and the future resurrection of the dead. Thus, the power of God is manifested and confessed in works of divine love: creation, redemption, sanctification and eternal life.

Christian faith had to insist upon the unity or uniqueness of God for two reasons in particular: to combat the prevailing polytheism among pagans and to counter the charge of tritheism in professing the doctrine of the Trinity. Thus, many professions of faith began, "We believe in one God..." (D.S. 40, 41, 42, 44, etc.).

One of the major problems in proposing a doctrine of three persons in God was that of subordinationism, making one person supreme and the others somehow inferior. It became common, therefore, to state that what is properly divine belongs fully to all three. It was this concern that led the christian church to state what are divine attributes, so that these could be affirmed fully of the Son and the Holy Spirit as well as of the Father. Thus eternity belongs to all three persons, the Son and the Spirit not coming into being at some later time (D.S. 75, 126, 147, etc.). Likewise, *"pantokrator,"* "omnipotent" belongs to the Son and the Spirit as well as the Father (D.S. 75, 173, 325, 415, 441). All three are involved in the works of creation (D.S. 171, 325, 546). They are also all knowing (D.S. 164) and omnipresent (D.S. 169). They give life to all things, and save all things (D.S. 173). The divinity itself is invisible (D.S. 21) and incapable of suffering (D.S. 166, 196).

Christian faith was concerned also to make clear the distinction between God and creatures, so that no creature, not even the human soul, has truly divine attributes. Thus, in 447 Leo I teaches that only the Trinity is truth, justice and wisdom, eternal and immutable. In explanation of immutability he writes; "To the immutable nothing is added, nothing taken away: because to be belongs always to what is eternal. Hence, remaining in himself [God] renews all things, and receives nothing which he has not given" (D S. 285).

The all-embracing mercy of God, which lies behind the missions of the divine persons, was reaffirmed in the way dying sinners were to be treated. Leo I directed that they should be reconciled, even though they would have no time to do works of penance; "We cannot place limits or times to the mercy of God, who does not allow true conversion to suffer any delay in receiving forgiveness" (D.S. 309). Celestine I had said much the same thing before him (D.S. 236).

When Eunomius in the fourth century claimed to have complete comprehension of the divine nature, orthodox teachers insisted on the incomprehensible mystery of God. This appears then in various professions of faith (D.S. 294, 501).

The First Vatican Council in 1870 summarized not merely the conclusions of scholastic theology but the constant tradition of nearly eighteen centuries when it wrote: "The Holy Catholic apostolic Roman Church believes and confesses that there is one living and true God, creator and Lord of heaven and earth, almighty, eternal, immense, incomprehensible, infinite in intellect and will and every perfection; who, since he is one unique and altogether simple and immutable spiritual substance, must be proclaimed to be really and essentially distinct from the world, in and of himself most blessed, and unspeakably exalted above all things which exist and can be conceived outside him." (D.S. 3001).

Against the evolutionary pantheism of its day Vatican I also reaffirmed the freedom and graciousness of God in creation: "This only true God by his goodness and omnipotent power, not to increase his blessedness, and not to acquire, but to manifest his perfection through the goods granted to creatures, by a most free determination 'at the very beginning of time made from nothing a twofold creation, the spiritual and bodily, namely the angelic and worldly, and then the human, constituted as it were in common from spirit and body'" (D.S. 3002).

And finally against various forms of deism this council taught the ever present protection of God's providence: "God by his providence guards and rules all things which he has made, 'reaching from end to end mightily and disposing all things gently' (see Wis 8:1). 'For all things are naked and open to his eyes' (Heb 5:13), even those things which by the free actions of creatures are future." (D.S. 3003).

Misunderstandings about God. Against the biblical view of God as both transcendent and immanent, there stand three common failures in conceptualizing God. One is a denial of divine immanence and conceives God as distant, remote, unrelated and indifferent; deism is the classic expression of this. But this failure is also present to some degree in philosophical and theological expositions which describe the divine essence as absolute in such a way as to be utterly unaffected by anything that happens in the world. This is clearly in conflict with God's involvement with the world as seen in scripture.

The other two misconceptions effectively deny divine transcendence. One of these conceives God as just another being among beings, more powerful in his influence, more universal in his concern, more comprehensive in his knowing, but finally operating under the same conditions of time and space as any finite agent. This misunderstanding appears in the so-called "god of the gaps" who operates in nature doing the things that we are so far unable to explain by ordinary created causality. In earlier times this meant keeping the planets from wandering too erratically, preventing universal gravitation from causing the fixed stars to fall together, etc. More recently, it has meant explaining the emergence of life from non-living matter. In all these cases God is thought of as making up for the deficiencies in the way the material universe operates, but not as doing anything that is in principle beyond a created cause.

"Process-relational" modes of thought, associated with the work of Alfred North Whitehead, also effectively deny the divine transcendence (though an effort is made to avoid this denial by speaking of the "primordial nature" of God). For God is regarded as the "primordial creature," the first embodiment of the creative process rather than its origin (*Process and Reality,* New York, The Free Press, 1978, p. 31). He interacts with all things within the creative process so as to achieve his own perfection or "phase of satisfaction." More than anything else he resembles the demiurge of Plato's *Timaeus.* Modern attempts to make Whitehead's God the origin or cause of the creative process should lead to a denial that God himself is "in process," but so far this conclusion has not generally been drawn.

The second way of denying divine transcendence is through some form of pantheism, which identifies the whole of reality with God: whatever is, is in some sense divine. This may be an evolutionary pantheism, according to which God is coming to be and developing in all things, or a simple affirmation that all things taken together as they now are, are God.

But the biblical view, as we have seen, is expressed in the phrase "creation from nothing" (2 Macc 2:28), and sees all that is not God as completely dependent upon his free choice to create them. This means that God is utterly different, wholly "other"; for he is uncreated and completely independent, and in this sense transcendent. But as the entire universe depends totally on God, he is intimately present to it, supporting it in existence and activity, and is in this sense immanent. The three basic misconceptions mentioned above simply fail to take adequate account of this radical affirmation of God as Creator, one who makes the world without dependence on any pre-existing material, i.e., from nothing.

III. The Mystery of God and the World

Once we think of God as uncreated and completely independent, existing simply by reason of what he is, we are confronted with the reality of God as infinite being, life and activity, a mystery utterly exceeding our powers of comprehension, one whose positive perfection must be acknowledged as limitless. For since this perfection is derived from no other, it exists without limitation from without. And since it is only what it is, without admixture of anything that might be thought of as limiting it, it exists without limitation from within. This understanding of God as pure and infinite being poses profound problems when we begin to consider the divine activity concerning the world.

Divine Activity. First of all, if we are speaking of a transcendent agent, we must recognize that his activity cannot be thought of as the operation of some particular force like gravity or electricity or magnetism. All these forces operate to link things together from their "without," at particular locations in time and space. The activity of the transcendent agent is all-pervasive, as Paul observes, referring to the activity of God: "All things are from him and through him, and unto him" (Rom 11:36). That is, God through his activity is the creative source of all things (from him), the sustaining ground

of all things (through him), and the final goal or end of all things (unto him). This divine activity does not touch merely the "without" of things, their external structures, and their relations to other finite things, but their deepest "within," their essential identity as what they are, the center and root of their dynamism and existence. God as the source of the most intimate reality of a thing makes it stand forth in existence, upholds it, draws it into the future. The divine activity undergirds the whole network of created causes, forms them into the unity of one universe, and guides all within them to the goal of the divine goodness as the end in which all things participate. The transcendence of God is thus the ground of his immanence.

But the affirmation of God as both transcendent and immanent, as wholly other yet intimately present, does not entirely answer the question of how we are to conceive God at work in the world. God's activity with respect to the world is spoken of in terms of power, wisdom and love. As powerful, God calls the world into being, sustains and moves it to achievement of his purpose. As wise, God fully comprehends the reality of the world and the ways in which it can move toward his goal. As loving, God intends the communication of his life and goodness to created things. Power, wisdom and love are inextricably united and intertwined in all that God does. But which of these is the most fundamental in the sense of providing the basis for understanding the other two? This question, as we will see, is not merely a matter of theological curiosity, but of profound importance for our understanding of the kind of dominion God exercises over the world.

God's activity means God's sharing or communicating the divine goodness and reality. From revelation and faith we acknowledge first of all the intra-Trinitarian divine self-communications or activities. Besides this there is the creative activity of God, sharing the divine goodness with finite beings. Here God perceives all the ways in which the communication of reality to created beings can take place, then chooses to realize some of these, and then executes his choice. In this perspective, wisdom as the perception of all possibilities is first; then love of the divine goodness as gift to be given, expressed in the choice to create, is next; and finally divine power, in the actual execution of the choice, is last. Thus power can be understood only in function of love; and love is understood as guided by divine wisdom. But the actual guidance of wisdom which is manifested in the world is that which divine love has chosen. And hence love finally forms the ultimate context for understanding divine activity: love that is guided by wisdom and executed by power. Power, in fact, can be understood only as the union of wisdom and love; what God perceives in wisdom as the good to be shared and actually intends in love to share is *eo ipso* what he is in power effectively sharing.

This exercise of divine power is, furthermore, the way in which God knows the actually existing world; for God knows whatever else is by actually extending his power to it, by communicating truth and reality to it. As an artist knows his works in the moment of creating them, so God knows all things in the act of making them exist. God does not receive truth and knowledge from the world, but comprehensively grasps all finite reality in giving it existence.

The immediate creaturely experience of God is the "feeling" of absolute dependence, a contact with his sovereign power causing the creature to be; such an experience generates awe, and hence "The fear of the Lord is the beginning of wisdom" (Prov 9:10). But if the power of God is not further resolved into his love and his wisdom then the all-powerful God can seem capricious, arbitrary and uncaring about some or all of his creation. This appears in some approaches to predestination, where emphasis rests only on the power of God to do whatever he pleases. For this reason it is important to recognize that love and not power is the ultimate context for understanding God's wisdom, power and love.

Divine Power and Creaturely Freedom. But having said that God's causality or the exercise of his power is the basis of God's knowledge of all created reality, we are confronted with a central problem concerning human freedom. If God has infallible knowledge of our free human acts by causing them to exist, how is it possible for us to be free in doing them?

In Catholic theology there have been two main attempts to reconcile the divine causality with created freedom, one associated with the Jesuit Luis Molina (1533-1600), the other with the Dominican Domenigo Banez (1528-1604). Neither of these today commands many adherents. Molinists maintained that God has a special kind of knowledge: *scientia media* or "middle knowledge" in virtue of which he knows what every possible free creature would freely choose to do in every conceivable set of circumstances, even before any divine decision to create them. By deciding to create them and put them in particular situations, God knows and causes their free acts. Banezians maintained that God moved created free wills to particular and definite choices with a "physical premotion" that not only brought about the act itself, but the mode of the act: freedom. The controversy surrounding these two positions raged for centuries, with no mutually acceptable solution emerging.

But the problem is a real one, and to maintain God as omniscient and omnipotent on the one hand, and the human being as truly free and responsible on the other calls for some effort at synthesis. The following attempt deals first with the divine causality in general and then applies it to the case of free creatures.

Divine Causality in General. When one considers the union of wisdom and love in the originating act of creation, then no other being is involved in the production of God's effects. For every other being depends precisely upon this union. But when one considers this union of wisdom and love in God's sustaining activity, then the creature itself becomes a kind of intentional medium for the union of wisdom and love; for God's love intends the creature as something already existing and ordered to the reception of the divine goodness which he knowingly wills to share. The loving intention of God to conserve this creature in being is thus actually joined to the wisdom of God contemplating his goodness, through the creature he wills to conserve. This is indeed the first aspect of the divine immanence, of God's presence to creatures.

But there is a further depth to the divine immanence when we consider not only the conservation of created reality, but the way in which God endows creatures with the capacity to cooperate in communicating the divine goodness, and activates that capacity. Creatures not only exist, but they act: they actively share within themselves and with one another the goodness or reality which they receive from God. Here God and the creature are both involved in the production of created effects or activities. In this case also God communicates reality to these effects by the power which is a union of wisdom and love, but the acting creature is an intentional medium for this union, as in the case of conservation. The acting creature, sustained in being by the union of wisdom and love which it mediates, acts within that union to share

in some way the goodness and reality which it receives. This means that the creature acting according to its own nature and abilities is an instrument of the power of God, of the union of wisdom and love, in the production of creaturely acts and effects.

Divine Causality of Free Created Acts. All this applies to the free creature, exercising the power of choice God has endowed it with. A free creature is one that has an active power that can be extended to many different possibilities and is not simply determined to one effect. Knowing the possibilities that lie within its power, it freely intends the extension of that power to one or another of these possibilities. This intention adds nothing positive to the perfection or reality it has and intends to communicate, but simply orders that perfection to communication. Sustained thus within the wisdom and love of God, moved and inclined by this power of God to act, the free creature chooses by freely intending the extension of its power of acting to one of the several possibilities perceived lying within its power. This free intention becomes a medium of intentional union between the divine wisdom and the divine love, so constituting the divine power as producing the existence of this activity through the free creature choosing to act in this way.

From this it is clear that the divine immanence means that God is in some sense affected by what creatures do. It does not mean that God is in any real sense *passive* to creaturely activity, as if the creature brought to realization in God some reality or perfection which was his only potentially. It means rather that God's activity is conditioned in its effects by creaturely activity and dispositions. What the active power of God actually brings about in the world is dependent on conditions found in creatures, conditions for which they are to some degree responsible through their powers of acting.

Pattern of Divine and Human Interaction. Throughout the scriptures and in common christian faith we may discern a three-step pattern characterizing the divine and human interaction. In the first step God takes the absolute initiative. Out of pure love and sheer gratuity God acts to communicate his goodness. This is the divine initiative of grace, which always goes before anything that a creature may do. The second step is the creature's response to God's initiative. It may be faith and acceptance, or wilful blindness and refusal, or some combination of these. Any activity of a creature always has about it an aspect of some kind of response to God. In the third step God responds to the creature's response to the divine initiative. This, in its most general sense, is the divine judgment.

The first step, that of the absolute divine initiative, is found in creation and in redemption from sin. "He has first loved us," (1 Jn 4:19) summarizes this step. This initiative continues throughout God's dealings with us, opening up new and unmerited possibilities of growth and divine union. This first step contains the antecedent divine plan with all the possibilities of the future, the divine intention for the salvation of every human being with the superabundantly sufficient means to bring this about. It embodies the divine invitation to advance toward fuller participation in the divine goodness. It is an offer that bears within it the divine power ready to execute the plan of God's love and wisdom. This is what Paul means by the "call" of God (Rom 8:30; 1 Cor 1:2; Gal 1:6).

The second step, that of the human response to God's gracious initiative, is found in every free choice in some way. "We love because he has first loved us" is the full message of 1 Jn 4:19, cited in part at the beginning of the previous paragraph. In every free act the human will is either aligning itself freely with the divine purpose or is more or less departing from it. It is either accepting the divine love, allowing this love to work in it and through it, or is to some extent refusing and obstructing it.

The third step, God's response to the human response, is where we observe God's activity being affected by created activity. Here what God actually accomplishes in the world is conditioned by the dispositions of the creature. This is the activity of divine judgment, where God achieves his gracious purpose to the extent and in the way that created wills are willing. This judgment is the effective expression of the consequent plan of God, that portion of the antecedent plan actually put into execution through the free acceptance of the creature. It is what we see actually happening in the course of history.

It would, of course, be a mistake to conceive these steps in terms of chronological succession, though they do have a reference to time. The future does set before us the initiative of God's love and the past embodies the divine judgment, but at all times in the present, God is here in gracious love, inclining and illuminating the created agent, and the free creature is more or less accepting the gracious love of God (or refusing it), and God is responding in effective judgment. In this way God is profoundly immanent in our lives and in the whole course of human and cosmic history, guiding events and accomplishing his gracious purpose.

The Positive Function of Unbelief. Atheism is almost always the denial of some particular conception of God. It rejects the existence of God as conceived and affirmed by someone else. This rejection of God can bring about a purification of believers' own understanding and belief in God, by leading them to reexamine their own belief and to reject false and distorted conceptions of God.

The problem of evil probably leads more people to reject God than any other single consideration. Faced with the misery and wickedness of the world, people reject a God who is supposed to be in total control of all that happens. This conception of God is usually more strongly influenced by Stoic philosophy than by biblical faith. The Bible, no doubt, has its own "problem of evil," but its answer always involves a God who has compassion on our sufferings and leads us to life even through sin and its effects. This is not the God rejected by those who become atheists because of evil in the world.

Others reject the "god of the gaps," one who is the answer to our inability to explain the activity in the world. When Laplace presented Napoleon with his work on the motion of the planets, Napoleon asked him what place God had in his system. The scientist replied, "I have no need of that hypothesis." This God is after all only an overgrown creature, an idol constructed to offset our ignorance.

Marxists reject a god who looks at the injustice of the world and then merely counsels generosity to the rich and resignation to the poor. Belief in such a god is, indeed, the opiate of the masses, lulling them to accept the unjust deprivation of their rights while giving divine legitimation to the status quo. This god too is an idol, constructed by greed and hardness of heart.

Existentialists reject a god who deprives human beings of freedom by his total monopoly of all power and action. This is the god who plans everything in complete detail and executes it by his omnipotence, leaving no room for creaturely freedom or initiative. Again, this god is an idol, constructed by a well-meaning but deficient metaphysic, or by a theology that seeks to praise the Creator by annihilating

all that is truly worthwhile in his creation.

God and Prayer. An area where faith in God is finally tested and where theology about God achieves some kind of coherent understanding or fails in its essential task, is prayer. For prayer is the expression of what one believes about God and about one's relationship to God. If you think that God listens to prayer and responds to it, if you believe that prayer really makes any difference in the way God acts in the world, your faith is consonant with biblical faith and you believe in a God who is personally concerned with creation, and answers its cries for help. If you think that prayer is simply a way of changing yourself, or an expression of despair, or just a response to some kind of psychological urging, your faith is at odds with biblical faith and you believe that God is unconcerned and unresponsive to human need.

Prayer of all kinds fits the pattern of divine and human interaction outlined above. Prayer is always a human response to divine initiative. Prayers and thanksgiving are forms of the prayer of faith responding to what God has graciously done and continues to do in the world and human history, acknowledging and accepting this in oneself, recognizing thereby the greatness and goodness of God in himself. God's response to this prayer is to deepen within us the relationship that his love seeks to have with us through what he does.

The prayer of petition likewise acknowledges one's relationship to God, a relationship of dependence and trust toward him as our loving and powerful Father. Whatever else the prayer of petition asks for, one fundamental request underlies all others: that we may grow in our relationship as sons and daughters of God and as brothers and sisters of one another and of Jesus Christ. God responds by deepening this relationship, and by granting what will serve to advance it, either what we have asked or something that in the end is more effective.

Prayer is thus a form of effective symbolic activity. As symbolic, it brings a relationship to expression and, as effective, it thereby establishes, deepens and intensifies it. Symbolic activity between human beings also expresses and establishes relationships. As they buy and sell, marry and rear children, converse and write letters, make friends and choose leaders, etc., they are in all of these activities expressing symbolically different human relationships, and thereby establishing and intensifying them. The same is true of our relationship with God, a relationship he initiates in grace and we accept in the symbolic activity of our prayer.

See **Grace, Providence, Trinity**

Langdon B. Gilkey, *Naming the Whirlwind: the Renewal of God-Language,* Indianapolis: Bobbs-Merrill, 1969. John Macquarrie, *In Search of Deity: An Essay in Dialectical Theism,* The Gifford Lectures, 1983. N.Y.: Crossroad, 1985. John Courtney Murray, S.J., *The Problem of God, Yesterday and Today,* New Haven: Yale U.P., 1964. John H. Wright, S.J., *A Theology of Christian Prayer,* N.Y.: Pueblo, 1979. John H. Wright, "Divine Knowledge and Human Freedom: the God Who Dialogues," *Theological Studies* 38:3 (1977): pp. 450-477.

JOHN H. WRIGHT, SJ

GOOD WORKS

For followers of Jesus Christ discipleship involves a life in which good works are practiced with his grace. In Mt 25:31-46 the final judgment depends on what each of those being judged has done or left undone. The Epistles of Paul in which justification comes by faith have God judge according to works (Gal 6:7-8; Rom 2:6). The Epistle of James (2:17)—perhaps written as a corrective against a caricature of Paul's teaching—says that faith without works is dead. But one of the most striking presentations of the role of good works in christian life is found in the gospel according to John. There such works appear in a way that should elicit assent from Christians who disagree among themselves about merit.

This is particularly true of the discourse connected with the final meal Jesus celebrated with those closest to him before he suffered and died. He speaks of a union of vine and branches that are pruned to produce much fruit (Jn 15:2). Through this image the gospel has Jesus convey a message about discipleship and good works.

Jesus is the true vine and his followers are the branches. His Father is the gardener who both cuts off every branch that does not bear fruit and prunes those which do so that they may be more fruitful yet (Jn 15:1-3). The branches must remain on the vine and receive their life from it. Earlier in this same gospel (6:48-51), Jesus spoke of himself as nourishment coming to human beings from above or without. Now life comes to disciples from within and this in the closest of unions.

That union involves prayer that is effective if and when the memory of Jesus and his words abides in the disciples (Jn 15:7). But it is as well a union leading to productivity on the part of the branches which bear much fruit. Indeed in the bearing of *abundant* fruit by the branches united to the vine, God is glorified (Jn 15:8). Finally that union means that disciples abide in the love of Jesus with a readiness to obey. They are to keep his commandments as he kept those of the Father and abided in the Father's love (Jn 15:9-10).

In the sixteenth century Christians on both sides of the Reformation drew important insights from Christ's words "Without me you can do nothing" (Jn 15:5). The *Augsburg Confession* (20:35-39) rejected the charge that Lutheran teaching denied the need for good works. To indicate what it meant by the latter it spoke, among other things, of patience in suffering and love of one's neighbor. But works such as these, it says, cannot be performed without faith in Christ, who bears witness to this while saying: "Apart from me you can do nothing" (Jn 15:5). As for the Council of Trent, it taught that Christ Jesus exerts a continuous influence on those who have been justified as the vine on the branches. That influence never fails to precede, accompany, and follow every good work performed by disciples. Without it there is no way that such works can be pleasing to God (D.S. 1546). Despite misunderstandings the imperative of performing good works and therefore the need of Christ appear to have been non-negotiables for both sides.

As for good works in relation to faith, Luther could not have been clearer than when he wrote in the *Smalcald Articles:* "To this we must add that if good works do not follow, our faith is false and not true"(III, 13, 3). Despite differences, that may not be incompatible with what the Council of Trent taught when it said: "Without hope and charity, faith does not unite one perfectly with Christ or make one a living member of His body" (D.S. 1531).

Is every good work defective or somehow sinful because of the presence of concupiscence even in those justified by faith? Can good works performed freely but as a result of grace by disciples following Christ merit life everlasting? These are issues where even today ecumenical dialogue between Roman Catholics and the spiritual descendants of the Reformation has not yet resulted in consensus.

See **Justification, Merit, Sanctification.**

CARL J. PETER

GRACE

History up to Second Vatican Council

The theology of grace reflects the general range of uses of the word, grace. "God's grace" in some contexts refers to God's own loving kindness and favor toward human beings; in others, God's gifts themselves are called "graces"; and the thanks that fills the hearts of those who appreciate God's love and God's gifts is expressed, for instance in "grace (formerly graces) at table." These same three meanings of the Latin word *gratia* are singled out in the thirteenth century by Thomas Aquinas as most important for theology.

But the term "grace" occurs in a still wider range of expressions in common use, among them "the grace of office," "your Grace" (as a form of address), "have the grace to," or "show me the grace." There is a further variety of nuances in related forms like "gracious," "graceful," "graced." Also in common parlance, though originally derived from theology, are "the state of grace," "full of grace," "there but for the grace of God," "grace builds on nature," "free grace," "*sola gratia,*" and "cheap grace." To these may be added the scholastic distinctions of various graces, listed below.

The basic notion underlying both the secular and the religious uses is the notion of favor. The theological concept of grace tries to sum up God's relations with the human race with special attention to the fact that these relations are loving, generous, free and totally unexpected and undeserved. The real object of the treatise is no specific event, person, thing or act of God, but the very gratuity of God's acting and of God's gifts. That this came to be looked on as a mystery worthy of special, concentrated, profound investigation is in itself somewhat surprising. The reason lies in the history.

The NT expresses frequently and in many ways the amazement, the deep appreciation and the gratitude which the early Christians felt for God's salvation in Christ. One of these expressions is the term "grace," applied to God's loving concern, to the gifts God gives, as well as to humanity's thankful response. But in these NT occurrences, "grace" is not yet a technical term. The biblical writers are not trying to reserve one special word to denote a sharply conceived, distinctly christian phenomenon. The Christians use the words they have in the traditions they know in order to record what has happened to them and to express their reactions to it.

They express themselves grateful for God's choice of Israel, for God's giving the Gentiles a share in Israel's election, for the forgiveness of sins, for the newness of life in Christ and in the Spirit, for the presence of the indwelling Spirit, for the joy and peace that is theirs, for the new world of love now opened to all, for the anticipated transformation of the world and the return of Christ in glory to consummate God's gifts in a final fulfilment of all promises. But there is little evidence that they ever consciously tried to sum these things up in a single concept. NT writings on these themes shows awareness of being in continuity with the hymns of praise which Israel had long been singing to God for their election, for the promises, for the gift of the Law, for the security of God's embracing love.

Our English translations show the NT writers using the word, grace, and variations thereof, as when they speak of their gifts as graces, or give glory and thanks to God's grace, or say they live in the grace of God or have been saved by grace. Behind the translated word, grace, lie different Greek words (with their own histories and relations to still other sets of Hebrew words and expressions). But in every place where an English NT now says "grace," some other term or terms, such as "favor" or "kindness" or "gift" or "thanks" or "for the sake of" could plausibly be substituted, even in the letters of Paul.

Some of the controversies which will later generate reflection and eventually systematization do begin to appear already in the NT. Clearly Paul is concerned to rebut any notion that anyone can earn salvation by performing the works of the Law. Occasionally he reflects on the mysteries of divine choice. He affirms both divine initiative and human freedom. These eventually become classic problems of the treatise on grace. But Paul's vocabulary continues to be basically the normal language of Greek discourse.

This situation prevails throughout the earliest centuries. Inner-church controversies occur, forcing the kinds of reflection which will result in a future theology of grace: controversies on sin and forgiveness, on the need for infant baptism, on predestination and foreknowledge. But for the most part, the focus of attention in these controversies remains practical, sometimes merely juridical.

That situation began to change seriously only with Augustine's writings against Pelagius. Pelagius was a spiritual writer who uncovered a major tension within the traditional christian conviction of amazed gratitude. For, to be strictly logical, unbounded rejoicing in the generosity God showed in saving us seemed to imply that we could not have saved ourselves. But, on the other hand, if we really could not live a good, transformed moral life without God's help, then an intelligent, reasonable God could hardly hold us responsible and threaten to punish us when we failed. Pelagius stressed the latter point, and based his exhortations on the principle that both logically and morally we must be able, even without God's help, to keep God's law and attain salvation. Augustine stressed the opposite implications of the tradition: without Christ we can do nothing. His enormous powers of persuasion carried the day.

Later Augustine's disciples and some followers of Pelagius reenacted the whole controversy on a slightly lower level in a dispute over the remote beginnings of grace. Was there not some reason in the individual which explained why God showed favor to this person? The decisions of the Council of Orange (529) said no. Technically not an ecumenical council, its decisions in favor of a moderate Augustinianism nevertheless feature in the teaching of most christian churches down to the present.

In the course of those controversies and the subsequent wide circulation of Augustine's writings, "grace" did begin to become a technical term and a center of attention in its own right. The frequency with which "*gratia*" occurred in a wide variety of constructions and contexts set the stage for an effort to define this "grace" and to specify its causes, properties, efforts and rules of operation. That attempt would be made when the growing influence of Aristotle stimulated a general interest first in logic and then in metaphysics.

In refuting Pelagius, Augustine had focused his emphasis on the universality of human sinfulness as a way of explaining the absolute necessity of God's loving benefits. Taking up Paul's metaphor in Romans 5 and pushing it as far as it would go, Augustine insisted that humanity had fallen in Adam and Eve's sin from the state God had planned, where all of human powers would have been subject to reasonable control and used for the service of God. After the fall, some human powers stood in rebellion to reason and in insubordination towards God. The incarnate Son of God healed this state, so those who followed him and believed in him could, by the gift of God's

Spirit, be restored to lives of virtue, though they would always feel the rebellion of the flesh within themselves as a mark of their true sinfulness. This analysis will be at the root of further controversies in the sixteenth century.

The focus of theological reflection in the Eastern churches continued to be trinitarian and christological. The basic christian conviction of gratitude led the Eastern Fathers to emphasize the transformation of human nature through Christ and the Spirit, which they called "divinization" or "goddening"—*theosis*.

In ninth-century Western Europe, Gottschalk noted that God's freedom in gracing humanity implied the "eternal plan" of Ephesians and other NT letters. He concluded that salvation of those who were saved was simply predestined, and the loss of those who were damned as well. His doctrine was resisted because it threatened the tradition from NT times that God's gifts had to be accepted and lived freely. The local council of Rheims, condemned a series of Gottschalk's propositions.

Up through the twelfth century, the basic questions continued to be psychological: How are human beings free and responsible if they need God's help to live the good life? But in the thirteenth century explicitly metaphysical considerations were added. In Aristotelian philosophy the end or goal of something's existence and actions settled the question of what kind of thing it was. Now the christian life described in the NT had for its end and goal the eternal possession of God in face-to-face beatifying vision. "Human nature" was not enough to explain a life like that. The Bible itself suggested a new technical term. "We shall be like him, for we shall see him as he is" (1 John), "sharers of the divine nature...." (1 Peter 1:4). A new concept was formalized: the absolutely supernatural. Like the Incarnation, like the Beatific Vision itself, the life of the religiously converted believer had to be considered "supernatural" in the technical sense of "exceeding the proportions of any created nature." Each of these was an instance of God's sharing with human beings God's very self.

In the synthesis of Thomas Aquinas, a life freely directed toward God is the only way to fulfilment for the infinite hungers of the human spirit. By God's free gift, that fulfilment is given in the unexpected reality of an end exceeding the proportions of any created nature; namely, in divine friendship and personal union in Beatific Vision. Sin, turning away from God by freely orienting oneself to other objects as ends, is the antithesis of human fulfilment. But, since the free sinful choice of the first woman and man, human beings are born into a world dominated by sin.

Justification, God's act of turning the sinner into a just person, is God's greatest work, greater even than the original creation. It is simultaneously conversion, forgiveness of sin and the infusion of grace. Grace in the sense of God's favor, benevolence and love is God's own self, eternal and unchangeable. Conversion is the opening of a human person to God's love. Insofar as that opening is a real change in the person, grace is the way of being of the one who receives God's favor. As white, hot, wet are qualities, so are wise, kind, happy and "graced." Grace in this sense is a new habitual orientation of the entire person toward God as personal goal and life. In this it is like a new nature and so comes appropriately provided with new powers, new principles of operation, which heal and elevate and make the person able to be sweetly and promptly moved by God toward eternal shared divine life.

These new powers are the infused supernatural virtues of faith, hope and love, which express themselves through all other virtues and lead to still further

perfection in the gifts of the Holy Spirit. By all these, graced persons are enabled and inclined to perform operations tending toward ultimate perfect union with God. All such operations depend on the light of faith as natural virtues do on the light of reason. All such operations, moreover, are ultimately good and excellent insofar as they are performed in love. And "the love of God is poured forth in our hearts by the Holy Spirit who is given to us" (Rom 5:5).

Just as this habitual orientation to God as friend, lover, personal fulfilment and consummation, is a gift beyond the proportions of human nature, so is every human act corresponding to this orientation. This includes the act of conversion, as well as all the acts which prepare it, implement it or preserve it. Such acts then are grace in act and themselves deserve the name of grace. Is God then asking the impossible in commanding the good human life? Thomas regularly responds: What one cannot do of oneself may be possible with the help of a friend. God always offers the divine friendship which does make these acts possible.

Certain theses which never met much success after Thomas' time were necessary in order to make this synthesis work. Among them is Thomas' teaching that it is never right to act in contradiction to what one believes to be true. For instance, if a person's mind had always been filled with the idea that belief in Christ was something evil, that person would be guilty of choosing evil in converting to Christianity (S.Th. I-II, 19, 5).

Another is Thomas' insistence that when a young unbaptized person comes to the full use of reason and makes his or her first fully deliberate act, that first human act can never be a venial sin. Choosing between a good and an evil possibility in one's first human act, one is setting one's course either for or against God as one's true final goal, the perfect

Good. If one rejects good (and implicitly, the Good), one's first human act is a mortal sin and one begins one's human (adult, self-determining) life in a state of serious sin. If one chooses good (and, implicitly, the Good), one receives the entire panoply of supernatural life (I-II, 89, 6).

A third is Thomas' theory of operations. The problems of freedom under divine motion is not a problem special to grace, arising from data of faith. It is only one instance of a general philosophical problem. It can be resolved without appeal to mystery, and without the elaborate paraphernalia proposed in the sixteenth to eighteenth century intra-Catholic disputes on actual grace. (The pattern of texts in which Thomas expounds this theory is assembled and explained in Lonergan, *Grace and Freedom*, Chapters 4 and 5).

A fourth is the natural desire for the vision of God. The human intellect wants to understand—that is, to know the essence—of all that is. As soon as it knows or believes that God exists, it wants to know God by his essence. But that is impossible without the direct vision of God.

These theses disappeared from most theology after the thirteenth century, though they are essential to Thomas' integrated doctrine of grace. Thomas' synthesis failed to have its full effect, partly because it was never understood, partly because the voluntarism of Scotus, elaborated to do greater honor to God, in fact opened the door to the later debasement of nominalism. In place of appreciative attention to the gifts of divine intimacy, theology occupied itself with testing the limits of divine power in improbable limit-cases. Under full-blown nominalism, grace was finally debased to a mere name for the completely extrinsic reality of God's arbitrary will and absolute power.

Pastoral practice followed the easier path of simple exhortation to fulfill the commands of the law, combined with sermons on faith and humility. Whatever the theoretical explanation, God's gifts were made available to believers in Christ, acting within a community of believers. Grace came through baptism and the other sacraments, and through prayers, of which the greatest were the official liturgical prayers of the church. Forgiveness was available through the church. An extreme extension of this principle was the offering of indulgences, allotted measurements of divine favor and privilege, as determined by church authorities in return for specific good deeds.

In the sixteenth century, Luther led the protest against a doctrine and practice which seemed to put God's grace under human control, making salvation dependent on human achievement, leaving God only the role of the dread Enforcer. Having no first-hand acquaintance with Aquinas' synthesis, Luther rejected the debased scholasticism he did know. From his study of scripture, he came to his personal realization that all of the christian life is a gift; that God's graciousness is responsible for the first call and for every move on the way to salvation. God stands ready to give all to anyone who believes in Christ crucified and risen, the embodiment of human powerlessness transformed by God's goodness into supreme power, honor and glory. Faith in God's call, not achievement, is all that is asked of the Christian. He concluded that there is no room for human merit, and no assured means of receiving grace except pure trust in God's promise.

Luther's call seemed to respond to a deep need of many Christians. It prompted considerable rethinking among Catholics, though many were so horrified at his rebellious language and manner, and at Rome's immediate strong reaction that they never seriously attended to the theological content of what he was saying.

Others, notably Calvin, accepted Luther's criticisms enthusiastically and pushed the positions to their logical conclusions; e.g., if everything was God's work, then an absolute and formal predestination was clearly a fact, and human free will played no part in one's being saved or lost. Others, still more extreme, drew antinomian conclusions and acted on them.

The church's formal response came in the Council of Trent, which undertook to state the full Catholic synthesis in a way that would correct the imbalance of Luther's summary, yet heed the objections he legitimately raised. Trent formally incorporated into its binding teaching the doctrine of the ancient Council of Orange affirming both free will and the gratuity of the beginnings of grace, while denying predestination to damnation. But Trent added, following the exhortation of the Bible and of common sense, the necessity of doing good works. It also clearly affirmed that good works done in Christ merit a reward, not of themselves, but because of Christ. Trent finally insisted that the christian sacraments were efficacious instruments through which God acted to confer grace. This did not suffice to heal the divisions in the church. Moreover, no matter how carefully balanced the teaching of the Council might have tried to be, it was inevitably interpreted in the heated polemical atmosphere of the times. It became the basis for exaggerated emphases and reactions which brought recurrent charges of semi-Pelagianism against Catholics and antinomianism against Protestants in the generations to follow.

Since Trent wanted to answer the Protestants without taking sides in questions still disputed among Catholics, it drafted its teaching in language which avoided scholastic technical precision.

But the very event of the Council brought new vigor to some ancient disputes and in succeeding generations Rome did sometimes intervene with censures against various Catholic positions. These censures inevitably had an effect on subsequent teaching about grace. Most of these disputes had to do with actual grace, which theologians during this period were commonly convinced they found expounded in St. Thomas and in Trent.

For instance, forty propositions of Baius of Louvain, reflective of an extreme Augustinianism, were censured in 1567. Then the Jesuits, following Molina, and the Dominicans, supporting Banez, clashed repeatedly over how God helped the performance of good acts ("De Auxiliis" controversy). Though Rome stopped their mutual name-calling, the shape of their dispute put the issue of human freedom versus divine foreknowledge and control at the center of the treatise on grace. Continued efforts were made to solve the issue by subtle distinctions concerning the mysterious nature of actual grace. Between 1653 and 1713 teachings of Bishop Cornelius Jansen and his followers were repeatedly censured for apparently denying the universality and the sufficiency of grace.

Out of this history and these materials was forged in the late eighteenth century a standard textbook treatise "De Gratia" which prevailed until Vatican II. Like other major treatises in theology at that time, this treatise consisted largely of the collected results of the series of historical disputes, arranged after the fact into some appearance of systematic order. The outline of the treatise was usually: Actual grace—its existence, gratuity, necessity, division, compatibility with human freedom, the possibility of merit; Sanctifying or habitual grace—its existence, necessity, appended considerations of the infused virtues and divinization/

inhabitation; and the supernatural quality and metaphysical status of grace.

Different kinds of actual grace were distinguished as needed to explain traditional expressions or to respond to classical difficulties. For instance, grace was elevating, insofar as it lifted a person to the divine level; it was healing, insofar as it remedied the sinful tendencies which kept one from functioning well even on the human level. Grace was operating insofar as God gave us new life in Christ; it was cooperating insofar as living that life required that we too do our parts. Grace was sufficient in answer to the question whether God had given even to the damned enough grace to be saved; but grace was efficacious in those who were ultimately saved.

The focus of the course was to learn the many errors which had been made, how those errors were categorized in official declarations of the church, and how to refute those errors from the Scriptures and the Fathers as well as from the traditional arguments of theologians.

The substance of the treatise is reflected in some basic answers of the Baltimore Catechism. According to that staple of American Catholic pre-conciliar education, a chief effect of Christ's redemption was "the gaining of grace for men"; grace was "a supernatural gift of God bestowed on us, through the merits of Jesus Christ, for our salvation." "There are two kinds of grace, sanctifying grace and actual grace." Sanctifying grace, or "habitual grace," "is that grace which makes the soul holy and pleasing to God." Actual grace "is that help of God which enlightens our mind and moves our will to shun evil and do good." "Grace is necessary to salvation, because without grace we can do nothing to merit heaven." "We can and unfortunately often do, resist the grace of God." "Mortal sin deprives us of spiritual life, which is sanctifying grace, and brings everlasting death and damnation on the soul." "Grace of perseverance is a particular gift of God which enables us to continue in the state of grace till death." "The sacraments have the power of giving grace from the merits of Jesus Christ." "Another means of obtaining grace ... is prayer."

As is clear from those answers, the standard treatise fostered the image of grace as an entity intermediate between the soul and God, given in measured quantities according to merit. Its relation to salvation seems arbitrary in the catechism, but in the treatise itself is explained in terms of the two ends: a natural end, proper to human beings as such, which could be attained by human efforts; and a supernatural end, attainable only by actions which elevating grace has raised to the supernatural order.

Grace also played an important role in other theological treatises. The treatise on the sacraments covered sacramental grace, its nature, effects, causes. Another distinct treatise, the Incarnation and the Redemption, discussed how all grace came to the human race through the suffering, death and resurrection of Christ. Finally, original sin, the doctrine that human beings are born into the world without sanctifying grace and in need of redemption, the relation of that fact to an original righteousness which was God's plan, spoiled in the sin of the first parents, the conceivable characteristics of a human race to which God would never have extended or intended the gifts of grace—all these related questions made up part of still another separate treatise, that on "God creating and elevating."

Dissatisfaction with the narrowness of this approach was among the motives behind such nineteenth century protests as those of de Lammenais, Frohschammer, Guenther, Hermes. These however were maneuvered into becoming authority-crises and, one at a time, condemned. Scheeben and a few others made some effort to restore attention to divinization and inhabitation as important themes. Some interest in the Mystical Body of Christ as an integrating image for the study of grace also developed. At the beginning of the twentieth century, the Modernist crisis blocked any further positive developments. Efforts to link dogma with religious experience, to connect the promises of religion with natural human aspirations, tended to be denounced as Modernist in inspiration and were generally avoided.

Current State of Theological Discussion

Discussion in Catholic theology since Vatican II has abandoned the track of the old seminary course. The biblical movement, the patristic revival, the ecumenical movement, and the modern philosophical rejection of neo-Scholasticism all were major influences in Vatican II, begun well before its time. Confirmed by the Council itself as valid trends in Catholic theology, their influence has continued and dominated post-conciliar work.

The Council's first-session controversy over contemporary scripture studies was closely related to certain themes of the theology of grace. The 1950 encyclical *Humani Generis* had said that the church rejected polygenism because "it in no way appears how it can be reconciled with the Church's traditional doctrine on original sin." Most theologians, even for a time Karl Rahner, accepted that as closing the question. René Dubarle, taking those words rather as an invitation to further research, devoted the years before the Council to biblical and patristic studies on original sin, demonstrating that it did not have to be understood as a single act of a single human couple.

The biblical texts used classically for original sin and redemption had been studied by Stanislaus Lyonnet of the Pontifical Biblical Institute. A preparatory schema for the Council rejected his reinterpretations and the methods of modern scriptural research which had led to them, but the Council finally rejected this schema.

Many twentieth-century theologians who had been trained in the neo-scholastic manual tradition surpassed that tradition in their thinking and writing in the decades before the Council, even while being forced to meet the criteria of that tradition in their public writings. Three such important for the theology of grace were Henri deLubac, Karl Rahner and Bernard Lonergan.

DeLubac circumvented anti-modernist neo-scholasticism by concentrating on patristic and medieval historical studies. He established two points: 1. The common seminary manual teaching, that human nature has an end of its own apart from the supernatural end of the vision of God, not only has no foundation in patristic and medieval literature through the thirteenth century, but is in flat contradiction to it. 2. The theology of St. Thomas does not hold together if one denies what he clearly and repeatedly taught: that there is a natural human desire for the vision of God. Within the same movement of "la nouvelle théologie," Henri Bouillard showed that the actual grace of the sixteenth to eighteenth centuries' intra-Catholic disputes did not correspond to anything in Thomas Aquinas' synthesis. When Thomas used the word "grace" for a divine motion or help over and above the habitual gift (I-II, 110, 2 is the classic text), the reference is not to anything created. God's action is identical with God, and Thomas' reference accordingly is only to God acting graciously. The encyclical "*Humani Generis*" warned that all these notions might threaten the gratuity of grace and the supernatural. But in fact the research has come to be generally accepted as accurate.

The understanding of why those notions do not threaten the gratuity of grace is best presented by Bernard Lonergan, who adds to historical research in the text of Thomas a concern to satisfy the systematic exigency which Thomas considered the *raison d'etre* of theology. Lonergan's systematic treatise, "*De Ente Supernaturali*" is available only in Latin, and his text-study, *Grace and Freedom* is largely in the technical language of the schools. But the basic doctrine of both these treatises may be found in *Insight,* especially Chapter 20, in non-technical, non-theological language.

Lonergan assigns the systematic theologian the task of trying to understand the doctrine which the theologian's own community professes and out of which it tries to live. For the Catholic theologian, that means primarily the dogmas of the church, once having specified which are the dogmas and what precisely they are affirming. In the area of grace, the dogmas are: 1. the goal of human life is personal union with God in beatific vision; 2. to attain or even to make serious progress toward the beatitude God has promised is possible only with God's help; 3. God gives that help in a way out of proportion to all created nature, granting human beings a share in God's own nature, God's knowledge, God's love. As dogmas, propositions expressive of mystery, these are known only by faith. The mission of the systematic theologian is not to demonstrate, verify, falsify or improve upon the dogmas, but only to try to make them intelligible in every living context.

The mystery implied in Rom 5:5 ("for the love of God is poured forth in our hearts by the Holy Spirit who is given to us") is the central mystery of grace. The rightly ordered life in love is the gift of the Spirit. But human life is effort, growth, development, through use of human faculties of intelligence, judgment and

reasonable choice. They too are God's gift and form the basic context in which the mystery must be understood.

Lonergan shows how the confusing differences in Aquinas' many statements on grace can be integrated and understood by reading Aquinas historically, as a thinker gradually broadening his synthesis of the philosophical and scientific insights of his own time. Only gradually does Thomas succeed in bringing those new insights to bear on the traditional psychological questions about grace.

Lonergan also provides the structure for a reformed, truly systematic treatise on grace. Its core and key would be the reality of conversion described in Rom 5:5.

Justification is the state of being linked to God in the love of friendship. It is new in each individual when the individual, responding to God's invitation, begins to open to that love. But God's love for every individual is not new or old, but always simply there. It is a call to intimate and eternal friendship, and, like all invitations to friendship and intimacy, is a completely gratuitous offer. But the offer is made to every human person.

That love of friendship is identifiable only by faith. But it can have significant experiential effects in the lives of saints and martyrs, seeking God as end in all their deliberate choices. Ordinary believers may be less frequently or keenly conscious of their own ultimate value, but manage to appeal to it successfully every time they resist temptation to serious sin. Any normal person experiences it at least in the form of a certain restless hunger, an ultimate dissatisfaction with any concrete possession or achievement.

Recognizing that "actual grace" is post-medieval tradition, Lonergan nevertheless tries to give a coherent account of what systematic reality that term might be trying to express. He shows that, as with habitual grace, it is not enough to talk about grace as God's own benevolent disposition. If God's love is real, then some created being is really loved by God, and that makes a difference. So with the divine motion or help. God's action is God's self. But there must be in the created world some reality corresponding to and resulting from God's action. This is the reality of the human actions themselves—the personal, subjective acts of sorrow, faith and love. These acts proceed from the one being converted, but they proceed by God's motion and as a result of God's gracious will, for only God can make human acts center on God's self. The very acts of faith, hope, love, sorrow which the human being performs deliberately, consciously, as steps to the supernatural goal of God to be possessed, known, eternally loved, are the graces. The acts which make up the good life, the acts exhorted to in the gospel, are the acts which please God and to which an eternal reward is promised. They are the "actual graces" or the instances of "grace in act."

This analysis stands in contrast to the ones behind the sixteenth to eighteenth century disputes which presupposed that actual grace must be something between God and the soul, preceding or accompanying the actions, and through which God moves or elevates. The mystery of grace is the mystery of God's self-gift and of God's moving human beings to be open to it and faithful to it. It is not a mystery of the inner constitution of an otherwise undetectable entity not mentioned in scripture or classical tradition.

Karl Rahner too is interested in recovering all of the christian tradition and expressing it in a way which is alive and meaningful with the help of contemporary philosophic categories. He defines grace as the free, unmerited and forgiving self-communication of God. He considers the doctrine of grace as that which is most distinctive of the christian message.

The human being is, by intellect and will, open to transcendence and conscious of operating against a background of infinity. In anxiety, in the subject's absolute concern, in love's unshrinking acceptance of responsibility in freedom, in joy, the ordinary person can experience transcendence. At the term of such transcendence, one can intuit the presence of the infinite, the indefinable and the ineffable, something not at our disposal, "the holy mystery," which is somehow the explanation of all, upholding all and which can be approached, but only asymptotically.

The essence of the christian message is that that holy mystery, God, communicates God's self to every human being in a free, absolute, unmerited, forgiving self-communication, which is for every human being an existential reality. God has already communicated God's self as an innermost constitutive element of every human being. Every human being has already, here and now in his or her own personal life, accepted or rejected the invitation to intimacy extended by the living God. Those who have accepted the invitation have already experienced the mystery not only as an infinitely distant horizon, a remote judgment on themselves and their world, but also as a hidden closeness, a forgiving intimacy, their real home, as a love which shares itself, something familiar which they can approach and turn to from the estrangement of their own perilous and empty life.

The frequency and depth of such experience varies of course with individuals. In any individual it knows its more intense moments—in experiences of death, of radical authenticity, of love. But it is real enough that those who hear the christian explanation can recognize that the explanation makes sense. That explanation claims that such experience implies God's love, acceptance, forgiveness, God's strength for all of life, God's pledge of an eternal embrace. Receiving from the believing community an explicit formulation of what such experience means, one becomes more sensitive to the experiences themselves and learns to recognize them with the message they bear.

"Man is the event of the absolute, free and forgiving self-communication of God." Such self-communication by God is plausible only because the human being is created from the beginning as an orientation to transcendent mystery. Still, nothing necessitates God's offering himself in this way, as the analogy of human invitations to friendship, to intimate knowledge and love make clear. Only with another person, another created infinite, can one really be friends, and a person always remains free to give or withhold friendship. Conversely, a person can be a friend only by approaching another human being and opening oneself up to him or her. The opening up must be free. So is it in our relation with God as well.

Secondly, the intrinsic freedom of this offer of friendship is not diminished in the slightest by the fact that God actually offers friendship to each and every human being. As a personal self-communication, it is always a free communication. The number of times the personal self-communication is actuated has nothing to do with its intrinsic, real freedom.

Thirdly, the invitation to divine friendship *could* not be accepted unless the divine friendship were already granted. God must be present as divinizing in order to make acceptance possible. But, since the invitation is sincere, acceptance is always possible. Therefore God is always present as friend, unless formally rejected.

This is the meaning of Rahner's famous "supernatural existential." Every human being exists already in a supernatural context. The offer has been made. There is no more pure nature, anywhere. As a matter of fact, there never was. Every human being ultimately either accepts or rejects God's offer of God's self. There is no neutral position.

Finally, a human being remains free to say "no" to God. This will normally be done not explicitly, but implicitly in rejecting concrete good choices, decisions and objects. But since every decision is really a constitutive decision of the subject, these rejections of the built-in good order of things mean a rejection of the horizon against which they are perceived to exist. True human freedom includes the freedom to opt for radical loneliness, self-abandonment, in saying "no" to God. This is sin and hell.

With a few exceptions (Otto Pesch is another outstanding example) most theologians working since the Council do not feel the old constraint to answer the classic question on grace. They are more inclined simply to describe the mystery, show its roots in scripture and tradition, and relate it to the needs of human beings today. Their analysis places other needs above the human drive to understand and integrate, to make sense of the whole. Contemporary writings often touch the questions only indirectly, by means of a review of the history. After surveying past answers, they tend to leave the impression that satisfactory answers are not really available, but that that is no tragedy. It is doubtful that future generations will be satisfied with this.

Place in the Life of the Church, Particularly in the Light of Vatican II

The work of deLubac, Lonergan, Rahner and others bore significant fruit in Vatican II, even though the Council did not devote any one of its documents to the subject of grace. The Council wanted to be ecumenical, pastoral and scriptural. All three of these had enormous implications for the way Catholics would henceforth think of and experience grace.

Because the Council wanted to be ecumenical, it avoided concentration on long-standing disputes among Christians. It tried to incorporate all that was positive in the Protestant and Orthodox viewpoints. It laid a strong emphasis on God's universal salvific will that has endured in all Catholic writing since the Council. The presumption generally seems to be that every human being is on the way to salvation unless he or she has deliberately rejected it; that grace is the normal state of the human being, and *a fortiori* of all Christians.

Because the Council wanted to be pastoral, it tried to set the truths of faith into a context which would make clear their importance for the life of the Christian in today's world. The Council made a deliberate effort to avoid scholastic abstractions and technicalities. Where the word "grace" occurs in the Council documents, it occurs most frequently in an active sense, the grace to do something: the grace of the apostolate, the grace of vocation, the grace of conversion, the grace of the martyr, etc. Without denying classical Catholic emphasis on the hierarchical gifts, the importance of ordination and explicit church commissioning, the Council gave a new and moving recognition to the charismatic gifts of the Spirit which are distributed quite independently of public assigned roles in the church. The Council's emphasis on "the people of God" and its chapter on "the universal call to holiness" have been the motivation for many new movements in Catholic spirituality.

At every turn, the Council's emphasis was on the experiential, trying to tie the theory in to life. "Grace" provokes to thankfulness, as in the hymn, "Amazing Grace," not to metaphysical reflections.

Grace is a gift to be appreciated and used, not merely the measure of the reward to be received in the future. Holiness is described experientially in terms of perfect charity, not abstractly, in terms of quantity of grace. The faithful are exhorted not in terms of increasing their merits but concretely to bring forth fruits of grace in deeds of sacrificial love.

Because the Council wanted to be scriptural, its reforms in liturgy and in christian education put Catholics into closer contact with the NT period, when those phenomena were occurring which the theory of grace would have to try to explain. The NT writings clearly were produced in a community convinced that something wonderful and special was happening to it. First- and second-century writers do not hesitate to appeal to manifestations of God's action in their midst. They appeal to the transformation of life demonstrated in christian converts. They list the fruits of the Spirit: "love, joy, peace, patience, kindness, goodness, faithfulness, gentleness, self-control" (Gal 5:22). "To one is given through the Spirit the utterance of wisdom and to another the utterance of knowledge according to the same Spirit, to another faith by the same Spirit, to another gifts of healing by the one Spirit, to another the working of miracles, to another prophecy, to another the ability to distinguish between spirits, to another various kinds of tongues, to another the interpretation of tongues. All these are inspired by one and the same Spirit, who apportions to each one individually as he will" (1 Cor 12:8-11).

But the greatest of these gifts and expressions of the Spirit, it came to be agreed, was love (1 Cor 13). That love was "poured forth in our hearts by the Holy Spirit who is given to us" (Rom 5:5) and would become recognized as the fulfilment of the law and the sign by which "all shall know that you are my disciples" (Jn 13:55). The post-Vatican II

Catholic expects to see some of this.

The supreme manifestation of grace is in the lives of the saints. That is where the new orientation to God in Christ shows itself, and where one can see how that orientation is at once beyond ordinary human nature and at the same time the perfection and fulfilment, the healing and wholeness, of what human nature can be. Catholics today, asked to name examples of saints, would turn to outstanding instances of self-sacrificing charity, even beyond the formal membership in the church. John XXIII, Gandhi, Martin Luther King, Mother Teresa, Dorothy Day, certain leaders and martyrs of the peace movement might be lumped together.

As a result of taking seriously the teaching of the Council, many changes have occurred among Catholics. In the sacraments, one has moved away from anything which could suggest automatism, even in the baptism of infants. One continues to believe that the sacrament rightly administered means God's grace conferred, but in practice one makes every effort, through preaching of the word, reading of Scripture, gathering of a community in loving celebration, to do all one can to promote conversion by setting the mood for conversion. but one does it in an atmosphere of trust and gratitude, which affirms implicitly that ultimately it all depends on God and must come from God.

Works which formerly were preached chiefly as valuable in order to increase one's store of grace and potential merit are either restructured in a more meaningful way or little practiced. For instance, purely devotional confession, once recommended largely for this reason, has declined severely except where a good counselor or spiritual guide can make such a confession meaningful in itself, not just because one can gain grace thereby. The same thing has occurred with regard to indulgences.

In general, the post-conciliar focus has been on seeking to live a christian life by doing christian deeds, above all those which clearly bear the mark of the Easter mystery of life out of death by self-sacrificing love. The spiritual and corporal works of mercy therefore appear much more prominently in sermons and devotional literature, where before the explicit focus might have been on ritual practices, devotions and prayers.

Vocations are now judged by how much they enable one to serve God in one's fellow human beings, and how vividly they embody not just isolated verses but the whole picture of life in the gospels. The simple justification of obedience and assured reward no longer suffices. Experiments abound in efforts to find new ways of dedicated life embodying the gospel counsels—not only the traditional three of poverty, celibacy and obedience. but the many other equally explicit challenges in various gospel texts, especially in the Great Sermon of Matthew 5 and Luke 6 and the Last Discourse of John 13-17.

Mysticism has had a new birth, partly under the new opening to world religions, partly in a retrieval of elements from the historical christian heritage which had been left comparatively neglected. Spirituality, meditation, contemplation are good words in general use, without distinction of cleric, religious and lay person.

In the practice of prayer it becomes clear to the individual believer that virtue is not a self-help program. Prayer is the supreme recognition that one lives in God's presence, dependent on God and hoping in God for everything. The christian belief in perpetual prayer, in prayer before and during all works, in asking forgiveness in the Lord's prayer, all are the living embodiment of what the treatise on grace attempts to account for in concept and word.

The reformed post-conciliar liturgy keeps this spirit alive. It implements the Council's emphasis on the importance of understanding and personal active participation through the new emphasis on preaching, the wide selection of readings from scripture. At the same time, the post-conciliar emphasis on the eucharistic celebration, where all the church comes together in joyful thanksgiving, drives home in practice the basic message of grace. The ancient central theme of the mass brings contemporary Catholics once again to grips with the original global feel for "grace," out of which the later theology grew, and is, if well lived, the best hope for a long term renewal of that theology.

Bernard Lonergan, *Grace and Freedom: Operative Grace in the Thought of St. Thomas Aquinas,* ed. Patout Burns, New York: Herder and Herder, 1970. Otto Pesch, *Einfuhrung in die Lehre von Gnade und Rechtfertigung,* Darmstadt: Wissenschafliche Buchgesellschaft, 1981. Henri de Lubac, *Surnaturel: Etudes Historiques,* Paris, 1946. Henri Rondet, *Gratia Christi: Essai d'histoire du dogme et de theologie dogmatique,* Paris, 1948. Henri Bouillard, *Conversion et grace chez saint Thomas d'Aquin,* Paris, 1944. Hans Küng, *Rechtfertigung: Die Lehre Karl Barths und eine katholische Besinnung,* Einsiedeln, 1957.

QUENTIN QUESNELL

GUILT

The phenomenon of guilt is a universal human experience and seems to be one of the ultimate basic traits of human nature. No culture has yet been found in which it is not recognized, together with its correlative term conscience, as a central fact of life. It presupposes an ordered world of norms and laws, the fact of human freedom and responsibility, and the possibility of people acting against the accepted order. In general, guilt means the awareness that he has done wrong, sinned, disrupted the general order. It also refers to the objective condition of the person who has acted in this way, judged by himself or the community, and in this sense it may be legal ground for punishment. In religious terms, the rebellion is against God, so guilt is a transgression of divine law and the transgressor bears his burden of guilt until he is reconciled and receives God's forgiveness.

History

In primitive societies guilt was recognized as the condition of one who had disturbed the social or religious order, and it was believed that such disturbance brought misery and misfortune for the individual or the community until expiation had been made to restore the original order. This expiation was carried out through symbolic practices like the expulsion of the scapegoat, carrying away the load of sin to be lost in the desert, or through specific sacrifices, including blood sacrifices.

In the Bible the words sin and guilt are often used indiscriminately and even the early Christians did not make much distinction between the two. Sin in the sense of guilt was often described as a burden, a punishment too heavy to bear. But the OT concept of guilt frequently referred to infractions of ritual law involving little or no personal responsibility. Through simple mistake or inadvertence one could become ritually unclean, therefore guilty, and bound to voluntary atonement. But most often sin was understood as a personal offense against the goodness of God who had committed himself to his people in a sacred alliance. Sin incurred the wrath of God and this was not always appeased nor did it end with the death of the sinner. It endured for generations, implying collective guilt. Israel had a very strong sense of this collective guilt because of its experience of the covenant with Yahweh: solidarity in blessings led to solidarity in guilt.

The prophets developed a more spiritual sense of guilt as a personal offense against a loving God, which brought sorrow and shame on the sinner and became an unbearable burden for him. He could pray for forgiveness, but to receive it he needed to confess his sin and make atonement. The Septuagint translators introduced the notion of debt, which only God could remit, and in the NT this was extended to mean not just an external debt, but an interior state of sinfulness, the guilt of sin which could be overcome only by turning to God in sorrow and repentance. In the teaching of Jesus there was no end to God's forgiveness, but one needed to forgive others in order to experience God's forgiveness oneself.

The OT's interchanging of sin and guilt is a useful reminder that moral evil, or in religious terms sin, is more than a simple external action for which one can be blamed. Jewish symbolism presents sin as missing the mark, taking a twisted path, rebelling, being stiff-necked, unfaithful, deaf, unheeding, lost, inconstant, empty and hollow. It includes the notion of defilement or stain. It contaminates the heart, poisons the interior life. It is the wounding or severing of a relationship between man and God, between man and neighbor, between man and himself, resulting in alienation at the deepest level of one's being.

Objective and Subjective

The state of sin as the kind of person one has become through wrongdoing, the objective condition one is in as a result of sinful action, can be called *objective guilt*. It can be recognized and declared by the person concerned or by others, particularly by the community through a judge or court of law. But a court of civil law does not enter into the realm of conscience, though it tries to assess the degree of responsibility involved. Thus civil guilt may or may not be related to morality; Jews condemned to prison or death for violating Nazi law were objectively guilty of law-breaking, but they were not thereby guilty of moral fault.

Subjective or psychological guilt refers to the subject's awareness of a burden of guilt. It involves both the intellectual recognition of a personal fault having been committed and the feelings of uneasiness, of remorse that so often accompany this recognition. Subjective guilt is the moral consciousness which puts oneself before an invisible, internal tribunal or court of justice which accuses, judges, condemns and inflicts punishment. There is no need to decide on an appropriate punishment, because it is automatic, a natural consequence of conscience itself. The punishment is simply the pain, remorse (biting), dissatisfaction, alienation one feels through having failed, and therefore not being at-one with the moral order and with one's better self.

In psychological guilt it is important to distinguish between the personal recognition of real fault or sin, namely the awareness of one's state of objective guilt and, on the other hand, the *guilt-feelings* that are sometimes confused with "conscience" but may in fact bear no relationship to either real personal guilt or civil objective guilt. Guilt *feelings* are a normal part of the experience of a guilty conscience, but one can have a genuine guilty conscience without very much feeling. Subjective guilt is normal, healthy, rational, based on the knowledge of real wrongdoing for which one was responsible, and it may be accompanied by equally natural, healthy *feelings* of guilt. But this is quite different from that morbid, neurotic state of emotional disturbance unrelated to any wrongdoing or out of all proportion to the wrong done.

Normal and Abnormal

The distinction between healthy and morbid, normal and abnormal guilt is clear in principle but may be confusing in practice. One reason for this may be that not many people reach a high degree of moral maturity, and even when they do, they still carry within themselves the infant and adolescent they once were, and can be troubled by ghosts from the past. Another reason may be the emphasis on fear and punishment in preaching and moral training, causing anxiety, which is fertile ground for guilt feelings. Likewise, the emphasis on law and precise measurement aggravated the tendency to scrupulosity, a further source of exaggerated guilt-feelings. All of these can reinforce the notion of a taskmaster God easily vexed and quick to punish, so there is a spiraling vicious circle of fear and guilt.

The "super-ego" described by Freud is often blamed for excessive guilt feelings. Freud noticed that psychotic patients often had the delusion of being watched and judged, and from this he formed the idea of a *super-ego* above the normal self, judging the self as an object. In early life this super-ego is formed by internalizing the attitudes and rules of parents, and as time goes on the young person accepts these personally, along with the conventions of society, and gradually the super-ego takes on all the function of early authority figures: observing, accusing, punishing or rewarding.

The super-ego is quite normal and natural in the child. Indeed, it is the basis on which conscience will later develop. The mature conscience outgrows it, but many people never leave it fully behind. It begins with the child's first experience of the basic human need to be loved, accepted, approved, and this is accompanied by fear of rejection, which causes terror, felt almost as a threat to life itself. The child quickly learns what actions bring approval, acceptance and love and which ones bring disapproval and cause feelings of rejection. This "learning"

extends all the way from toilet training to table manners and the moral principles of right and wrong. When disobeying, the child experiences *guilt feelings,* not because of any appreciation of the wrongfulness of the action, but because of the fear of rejection. The disobedience brings on feelings of not being loved or lovable, a feeling of badness which is hard to bear. The mature conscience can cope with these feelings and to a large extent outgrows them, but many people remain blocked at this stage and will continue to experience neurotic guilt feelings that have little to do with conscience. This is more likely among introverts than extroverts, and especially in people who experience an insecure childhood, who lacked a sense of basic trust, or whose parents were themselves insecure, rigid, overbearing or perfectionist.

Repentance

True guilt does not simply say "I feel guilty" but acknowledges "I am guilty." It is the experience of conscience making its judgment in the light of rationally evaluated circumstances and recognizing that it has done wrong. We feel guilt and remorse, realizing that we needn't have done so, and accept responsibility for the wrongdoing or sin. Our feelings are of inner alienation, a lack of oneness with our better selves, and a general disharmony within us. But the healthy reaction is not to inordinately punish or torment ourselves with irrational fears. The guilty person knows he can repent, be forgiven, repair the damage, make restitution where necessary, regain his peace of mind, and continue to grow. As Christians we know that we are still loved by God, that we don't have to *earn* that love, but *respond* to it, and that the appropriate response in sin is repentance and the acceptance of God's gift of forgiveness.

See **Conscience; Moral Life, Christian; Sin**

Robert Imperato, "Thomas Merton on Compunction and on Nothing," *Cistercian Studies* (1986) vol 21, no. 3: 259-71. Geraldine Thompson, "Hierarchies of Guilt," *The Canadian Catholic Review* (July-August 1985) 3: 3-4. Arnold Uleyn, *Is it I Lord? Pastoral Psychology and the Recognition of Guilt.* New York: Holt, Rinehart and Winston, 1969.

SEÁN FAGAN, SM

H

HABIT

A term borrowed from Aristotle and elaborated by St. Thomas to refer to the regular disposition of a faculty or potency to perform acts of a particular kind. Habits may be acquired by repeated acts. In Thomist theology, sanctifying grace is considered a habit infused into the soul by God.

See **Grace, Virtue**

HAGIOGRAPHY

See **Saints**

HEAVEN

In cosmology, the term "heaven" refers to the sky or the vault that appears to arch over the earth. In religion and theology, the term designates the dwelling place of God, the angels and the blessed; or the condition of final and perfect bliss itself.

Scripture

1) *OT.* In the OT there is no clear evidence of belief in a place of eternal bliss for those who die in the state of grace. The term *heaven* is, however, used in a variety of ways. As a physical part of the created order, heaven is the vault of the sky (Gen 1:1; Isa 40:22; Ps 104:2). It is also thought of as resting on pillars (Job 26:11). In the events that will usher in the end of history, the heavens will collapse (Isa 13:13; 34:4; 51:6). As a place reserved for God, it is called a sanctuary (Ps 11:4; Mic 1:2; Hab 2:20) and the place of the divine throne (Ps 11:4; Isa 66:1). As God's dwelling place, it is called the house or city of God (Gen 11:5; Ps 18:10; Dan 7:7.13). Yet, heaven and earth cannot contain God (1 Kgs 8:27; Jer 23:24). The physical heavens serve as a symbol of the divine transcendence and sovereignty over the world and its history. As the first creation involved the creation of the heavens and the earth (Gen 1:1), the eschatological renewal at the end of history will involve the creation of a new heaven and new earth (Isa 65:17; 66:22).

The imagery of heaven is developed elaborately in the inter-Testamental literature. There in particular we find the concept of many levels in heaven (3, 7, or 10) which would leave its impress on later christian literature.

2) *NT.* The imagery of the OT and inter-Testamental period is taken up into the language of the NT. To this is added the conviction that heaven is a place of eternal bliss where God's faithful ones will find their reward. A special christian element is the association of heaven with Jesus Christ. The Son of Man comes from heaven to become incarnate in Jesus (Jn 3:13), and after the resurrection, Jesus ascends to heaven to sit at the right hand of God (Mt 26:64; Mk 14:62; Lk 22:69; Acts 7:55). In heaven, the eternal high priest offers his true sacrifice (Heb

8:1ff). From there he will appear again as judge at the end of time (Mk 8:38; 14:62; 1 Thess 4:16; Heb 9:28).

In as far as heaven becomes the place of the final reward for the faithful, it is called the Kingdom of God (Mt 25:34); eternal life (Mt 18:8ff; Jn 3:15ff; 4:14; 5:24); an eternal wedding feast (Mt 25:10; Lk 14:15ff); and vision of God (Mt 5:8).

Paul is taken up to the "third heaven" (2 Cor 12:2). Paul calls the faithful "citizens of heaven" (Phil 3:20). He sees the heavenly life as conformity with Christ (Phil 3:21; Rom 8:29), and speaks of sharing in the resurrection and the reign of Christ (2 Tim 17:24; Eph 4:12). In Pauline eschatology, one hopes to "be with the Lord always" (1 Thess 4:17; 2 Thess 2:1; Rom 2:23; Phil 4:19; Col 13:2ff).

The relation of heavenly life to Christ is reflected also in John. The believer is united with Christ already in this life, but what lies in the future as the fulfillment of this relationship has not yet been revealed (1 Jn 3:2). For the believer, Christ is the way, the truth, and the life (Jn 14:6). Heaven is simply being with Christ (Jn 14:3).

The rich imagery of the NT indicates heaven more as the quality of human life in its full maturity and perfection in the presence of God than as a place that could be located somewhere. This fullness of life is connected with the believer's relation with Jesus. The characteristic mark of the NT is the transformation of the OT hopes into the notion of the vision of God and the reunion of the faithful around Jesus who is the unique Son of God, and the Son of Man leading his brothers and sisters to the Father (Mt 11:27).

Teaching of the Magisterium

Creeds of the ancient church often include an explicit article affirming belief in eternal life (D.S. 3-5; 15; 19; 21; 22). The most important texts of the hier-archical magisterium pertaining to heaven are: the fourteenth century papal consti-tution *Benedictus Deus* of Benedict XII (D.S. 1000-1002) and the *Decretum pro Graecis* from the Council of Florence in 1439 (D.S. 1304-1306). The text of Benedict XII affirms the existence of the beatific vision and its essence as an intuitive vision of the divine essence without the need of creaturely mediation. But the direct concern of the constitution was to affirm that for those who need no further purification the beatific vision follows immediately upon death and endures continuously and forever. This was affirmed in reaction to the teaching of John XXII who had held that the joys of heaven would be experienced only after the resurrection of the body. The Council of Florence affirms the inequality of the vision which will be experienced in accord with the diversity of merit. The "Letter on Certain Questions Concerning Eschatology" issued by the Sacred Con-gregation for the Doctrine of the Faith (1979) is very reserved concerning details of doctrine on heaven. It reaffirms belief in the resurrection of the body, the survival of the "human self" after death, and the belief "in the happinesss of the just who will one day be with Christ." For the rest, it warns against arbitrary imag-inative representations since "neither Scripture nor theology provides sufficient light for a proper picture of life after death."

Theological Reflection

Christian tradition uses the word *heaven* to express the final fulfillment of human existence which is hoped for as the definitive actualization of the love to which Jesus summons his followers. It has understood that fulfillment to be related to the present experience of grace and yet to transcend any present, his-torical experience. In as far as the eschat-ological fulfillment is precisely the ful-fillment of grace, it is possible for theology to reflect on the present experience of grace so as to come to some sense of that fulfillment which remains always a mystery as long as we are in history.

Scholastic and neo-scholastic reflection on heaven have been centered almost exclusively on the analysis of the notion of beatific vision. This style took no explicit account of the Christological aspects of heaven as intimated in the NT. Since the christian experience of grace is centered on the experience of God mediated to us by Christ, contemporary theology attempts to make this Christological dimension explicit both in the theology of grace and in the doctrine of heaven. In its primary, christian sense, heaven is that mode of being that is realized when Christ is taken, in his full humanity, into the presence of God (resurrection, ascension). At this level, heaven means: (1) the final and decisive self-communication of God to creation; and (2) the full acceptance of this gift and the transformation of the creature in the divine presence. In as far as the glorified Christ is the anticipation of the universal destiny of creation, the reality of heaven will reach its fullest dimensions only with the realization of the entire Body of Christ in union with its Head.

From this Christological basis, it becomes clear that heaven is not primarily a place but a personal relationship. The believer is "in heaven" to the degree that he or she is with Christ; for it is in Christ that one finds an authentic relationship with God (Ratzinger 190). Personal union with Christ means being taken into Christ's eternal self-giving to the Father. In this sense, heaven has the character of adoration. Since cult, in its heavenly form, takes place in the immediate contact between God and human creatures, it is appropriately clarified in terms of the traditional notion of beatific vision. In essence what is involved is the fulfillment of the openness of humanity by the pure self-gift of God.

The Christological orientation alleviates the excessive individualism of the Scholastic notion of beatific vision by situating the individual in the context of the Body of Christ. Thus, the social nature of humanity is taken into account as well as the dignity of the individual. The christian doctrine on heaven cannot be simply identified with the notion of the immortality of the soul nor with the idea of merely personal salvation. In its corporate dimension, heaven means the fulfillment of all human relationships in the depth of the final relation with God.

Since the glorification of Christ means that a representative "piece" of creation has entered into the divine life, the Christological orientation includes a cosmic dimension. Salvation is not an escape from the world but the salvation precisely of the world of God's creation. This salvific process has begun in the glorification of Christ and is to be brought to completion in the transformation of the Body of Christ and the realizaton of God's rule throughout the cosmos. Until material creation is brought to participate fully in the perfection of the spirit, God's victory in Christ is not complete. The fulfillment symbolized by the word *heaven* does not mean the disappearance of the material world but its radical transformation. "Heaven ... is nothing other than the future of glorified humanity on a glorified earth, or the glorified creation" (Schmaus 273). The whole of created reality will be the instrument through which the glory of God will be expressed in the end.

See **Beatific Vision, Eschatology**

J. Ratzinger, *Eschatologie,* Regensburg, 1977. M. Schmaus, *Dogma 6,* London, 1977.

ZACHARY HAYES, OFM

HELL

"Hell" is a common name for the dwelling place of the devils and the damned. Since, in early times, it was located under the ground, it is also known as the underworld. Related but not identical are Hades in non-biblical literature and Gehenna and Sheol in scripture.

Scripture

1) *OT.* There is no clear and consistent teaching in the early Hebrew writings concerning the fate of the dead. Similar to the views of surrounding cultures, the pre-prophetic writings reflect the notion of an underworld (Sheol) which should not be identified with the later christian concept of hell. It is a place of a shadowy existence involving neither joy nor punishment. The dead neither thank nor praise God, for there is no communion with God in the underworld (Isa 38:18; Ps 6:6). No human being can escape the underworld.

Writers of the inter-Testamental period develop a distinction between the fate of the good and that of the wicked. The pious enter into the rest of God while the wicked live on in pain (Wis 4:19). The underworld is no longer thought of as neutral but takes on the nature of a punishment for the wicked. No doubt this development is related to reflection on the problem of retribution and the attempt to gain some insight into the disparity between the moral quality of human life and the good and bad fortune by people on earth.

The notion of punishment is graphically presented in the idea of *Gehenna.* Originally the name of a place which had been the site of cultic human sacrifices (2 Kgs 23:10), the term is used later to designate a place of unquenchable fire and undying worms where the corpses of those who have rebelled against God are viewed by the pilgrims from Jerusalem (Isa 66:24). In 2 Macc 6:26 ff, the prospect of eternal punishment serves as motivation to strengthen people in their earthly suffering. Wisdom 4:19 states that the godless will be an endless mockery among the dead.

The notion of a place of punishment is found frequently in the apocalyptic literature of the inter-Testamental period where it is frequently enhanced with many imaginative details. It is seen as a place of darkness, eternal fire, chains, and a wide range of fitting punishments.

2) *NT.* Christian writers presuppose and utilize the earlier Jewish traditions. The term *Gehenna* appears eleven times in the Synoptic Gospels. There it is typically accompanied by the traditional imagery of fire, darkness, worms, howling and gnashing of teeth, etc. (Mt 3:12; 5:22; 5:29ff; 10:28; 13:42, 50; 18:9; 23:15, 33; Mk 9:43ff; Lk 13:28).

Paul expresses the idea of eternal punishment but without the concrete images found elsewhere in the NT. He speaks of eternal destruction and banishment from the face of God (2 Thess 1:9; Rom 9:22; Phil 3:19). Romans 2:9 speaks of the tribulation and distress that will be the lot of those who do evil.

While the gospel of John does not use the term *Gehenna,* it does speak of punishment in terms of judgment and darkness. But above all, punishment is exclusion from the fullness of life communicated by the Son (Jn 2:19; 8:24; 10:28).

Elsewhere in the NT, apocalyptic imagery is used. Revelation 21:8 describes the place of punishment as a lake that burns with fire and sulphur. It is equivalent to a second death. In 2 Peter 2:17, the nether gloom of darkness is reserved for the wicked. Jude 6-7 uses the images of eternal chains, nether gloom, and eternal fire.

Teaching of the Magisterium

The concept of eternal punishment is expressed in a number of ancient creeds such as the Athanasian Creed from the late fifth century (D.S. 75-76) and the *Fides Damasi* dating from the same period (D.S. 71-72). Councils that have spoken on the question of eternal punishment are: IV Lateran in 1215 (D.S. 801); II Lyons in 1274 (D.S. 856-58); Florence in 1439 (D.S. 1306); and Trent in 1547 (D.S. 1539, 1543, 1575). From these we can conclude that the official teaching of the church afirms a punishment after death for those who die in the state of mortal sin. This punishment, which begins immediately after death, will be in conformity with the evil works of the persons involved.

The Synod of Constantinople in 543 condemned the views of the followers of Origen concerning the final restoration and reintegration (apocatastasis) of the demons and evil persons (D.S. 411).

A decree of Innocent III in 1201 distinguishes between the loss of the vision of God and pain of hell (D.S. 780).

The papal constitution *Benedictus Deus* issued by Pope Benedict XII in 1336 is an important medieval document (D.S. 1000ff). In it the pope corrects the erroneous teaching of his predecessor, John XXII, who had preached that the souls of the elect would enjoy beatific vision only after the final judgment and resurrection. Between death and final judgment, they were said to enjoy only an imperfect happiness. A similar interim condition was held in the case of the damned. *Benedictus Deus* affirms that for those who have no need of purgation, beatific vision follows immediately upon death. A parallel teaching regarding the fate of the damned is contained in this document.

In 1979, the Sacred Congregation for the Doctrine of the Faith published a "Letter on Certain Questions Concerning Eschatology." In paragraph 7, this document reaffirms the traditional teaching of an eternal punishment for sinners, "who

will be deprived of the sight of God." It is further maintained that "this punishment will have a repercussion on the whole being of the sinner."

In summary, the official teaching recognizes punishment of the lost following immediately after death. Such punishment is everlasting. Some distinction is made between the loss of the vision of God (the essence of hell) and punishment of sense (caused by created things and known as the positive punishment of hell). Beyond this, the official magisterium offers no details of the condition of hell and its punishments, nor does it affirm that any individual human person has been condemned to hell.

Theological Reflection

For the most part, the development of the doctrine of hell is based on the principle of retributive justice. As criminals are tried, judged and subjected to punishment, so, it was believed, the damned are tried, judged and punished by God. In this way, the inequity of historical existence could be balanced out by God's justice. Another principle that supported the development of the doctrine was that of deterrence; the fear of eternal punishment in hell would serve as motivation for not sinning and for not upsetting the harmony of society by crime. Popular preaching in the Middle Ages and down to very recent times used the message of hell to provide motivation for upright behavior.

Since Patristic times, many theologians such as Origen, Gregory of Nyssa, Ambrose and Jerome, have interpreted the fire of hell in a symbolic sense as referring to spiritual torments. This view has never been condemned by the church, but the main line of Western theology (Augustine, Aquinas) has held that the fire is real and physical. Some, following the lead of Origen, held that there would be an end to the punishment of hell when history ended with a universal restoration of all things. Even though this view has been condemned, it finds adherents in various theories of universal salvation. The most detailed account of hell in Western thought can be found in Dante's *Divine Comedy* where hell consists of nine circles or layers. The deeper one descends into hell, the greater the degree of wickedness and the more intense the punishment. Most accounts of hell's geography are simpler, and the punishments are generally limited to fire and heat.

In contemporary theology, the physical style of interpretation has given way to a more anthropological style. The need to distinguish between symbolic discourse and religious message is seen as basic. The message of hell has to do with the seriousness with which we view human life and with the possibility of total failure in working out the project of human life. If the positive outcome of life is a union of love with God, such union presupposes freedom. But freedom in turn involves the possibility of refusing the gift of God's self-communication. Therefore, the very conditions for the possibility of the christian view of positive fulfillment are simultaneously the reasons why theology holds that hell is a possibility. The possibility of hell cannot be denied without denying human freedom itself. But if freedom itself is incalculable, then it is impossible to say definitely whether salvation will be universal. Christians can appropriately hope for the salvation of the entire human race. They cannot know definitely whether, in fact, that will be the outcome of history. The traditional language of hell and punishment holds before us the negative possibility of human freedom. Thus, contemporary theology is inclined to interpret the teaching of the church as referring to the *possibility* of hell. There is no official church statement about the actual damnation of any individual human being. The possibility of hell stands in sharp

contrast with the affirmation of the *reality* of heaven as the fulfillment of human history that has already been accomplished in the person of Jesus.

See **Eschatology**

Z. Hayes, "Visions of a Future: Symbols of Heaven and Hell," *Chicago Studies* (August 1985), p. 145-165. M. Himmelfarb, *Tours of Hell,* Fortress, 1983. J. Michl, "Hell," *Sacramentum Verbi, I,* Herder & Herder, 1970.

ZACHARY HAYES, OFM

HERESY

In the NT, *hairesis,* translated as "faction" and used in a pejorative sense implying culpability, is found in three instances: 1 Cor 11:19, Gal 5:20; and 2 Pet 2:1. In each of these instances, the context reveals that the evil associated with heresy results from behavior that shatters the community. The result of "heresy" is that the bond of charity that unites the hearts and minds of the community of believers is broken.

In the Corinthian passage, the factionalism results from the social elitism of some members who, gathering to share the Lord's Supper, engage in pretentious and disorderly behavior that marginalizes other more impoverished members. In the passage from Galatians, "factions" is listed along with other immoral conduct such as idolatry, gross indecency and drunkenness as the consequences of a self-indulgence that violates the command, "Love your neighbor," and which destroys the community. In 2 Peter, the warning is against false teachers who, by leading others astray, will bring the Way of Truth into disrepute.

In an age of extreme individualism such as the one from which we are just beginning to emerge, it is difficult to grasp the insight of the church of the NT which guided the theology of the first centuries of Christianity stating that the

Holy Spirit, the Spirit of Truth, dwells within the community; thus, damage to the bonds of community results in an impairment or distortion of the truth that is being revealed through the community. Vatican II (especially L.G. 9 and 12), as well as the theologians who reflected on the documents of Vatican II, reiterate for contemporary society this communitarian nature of the church as well as the fact that the church is the locus of revelation in that it reveals, in its scripture, symbols, rituals and doctrines, God's meaning for humankind. That is why the sin of heresy, the violation of the revelatory purpose of the church by actions and teachings leading to disunity, has always been understood to be a sin of such dire consequence, one which canon law defines as: "the obstinate post-baptismal denial of some truth which must be believed with divine and catholic faith, or it is likewise and obstinate doubt concerning the same" (canon 751). By qualifying such doubt or denial as obstinate, however, the canon is narrowly limiting the category of those to whom heresy can be ascribed. Those who are honestly seeking to understand their faith and who encounter difficulty accepting some prevailing understanding of faith are not included in the sanction of this canon.

Consequently, an understanding of heresy involves at least a minimal understanding of the interrelation of truth and doctrine, for if the heart and mind of the community is unified by adherence to a common teaching or symbol system, then heresy results from a departure by one person or a group from this common self-understanding.

The foundational truth of all christian self-understanding is that God's meaning is revealed in Jesus the Christ. This truth is intrinsically tied to the community's original and subsequent expe-rience of God in Christ which it expressed in scripture, sacrament and doctrine. Therefore, the subjective experience of the community and its objective understanding expressed in dogmatic truth are reciprocally and inextricably linked. Philosopher-theologians such as Bernard Lonergan, S.J., express this concept by stating that subjectivity and objectivity are intrinsically related. To deny one aspect is to deny the other.

Further, to appreciate what dogmatic truth means, the historicity of truth must be understood. Even though dogmatic truth is revealed by God, it is known and received by human knowers and believers and the dynamics of human knowing remain intact. All human knowing is modified by the historical circumstances in which the knowing occurs. Thus, the philosophical, cultural and historical milieu in which dogma is enunciated conditions every dogmatic statement. What is proclaimed may be absolutely true in its context, but it can never embrace or comprehend the totality of truth. Only divine consciousness embraces the absolutely unconditioned. As Aquinas observed, "Everything is received according to the mode of the receiver" (S.Th. I, q. 84, a 1).

A second characteristic of truth is that it is dialectical. This means that no statement of truth is an identity, but that every statement of truth contains within itself a remainder, or even its opposite, which, when developed, gives rise to a new insight into reality. Unless this is acknowledged, those persons and those communities who first glimpse a new facet of divine truth and seek to bring it to expression may be accused of heresy, violating the bonds of community, when, in fact, they are working to move the community forward and to mediate faith to contemporary society.

History is replete with instances in which those who were enunciating new insights were suspected of heresy and later vindicated by the wisdom of the community. Their position was much like that of original and creative artists who in actualizing a new vision went beyond the artistic canons commonly accepted. Their work, often initially rejected because it revealed reality in a new way, many times became the standard of another generation.

The implication of the fact that truth is both historical and dialectical is that the communion of believers is not threatened by the diversity of doctrinal expression or by pluralism as long as continuity with the meaning and truth of God's revelation in Christ is maintained. In fact, such diversity is a natural result of the kerygma's having been truly appropriated and incorporated into the mindset of people living in diverse cultures and in various historical periods.

Rather, the lack of a variety of doctrinal and liturgical expressions would seem to indicate that doctrine and liturgy had devolved into mere verbalism or formalism, a situation in which lived experience and its doctrinal and liturgical expression had become detached. Conformity in expression is not to be confused with unity of heart and mind.

Who, then, are those who contribute to the conditions which lead to heresy? First, they may be either the majority within the ecclesia who historically endorse the status quo or the minority who historically express new dimensions or insights into the christian message. In either case, there are those who lack continuity with the dogmatic tradition either because they divorce dogmatic truth from religious experience which results in objectivism or dogmatism, or because they divorce religious experience from dogmatic truth which results in historical relativity or subjectivism.

Secondly, there are those who prematurely terminate dialogue and thereby truncate the works of the Holy Spirit by refusing to consider and understand the many historical factors such as language, culture and philosophical mindsets that condition diverse expressions of the meaning of christian revelation. In such a case, ideology may become more important than the charity which binds the community.

Finally there are those who forget that any humanly acquired truth is always tenuous and imperfect, or as T.S. Eliot writes: "There are only hints and guesses. Hints followed by guesses, and the rest is prayer, observance, discipline, thought and action. The hint half guessed, the gift half understood is Incarnation. "The Dry Salvages," vv. 29-32. It is, of course, christian belief that the gift of Incarnation has, in fact, been given. Christ has definitively entered into human history. Still, the gift is so magnanimous, its source being Mystery itself, that it is only "half understood" by those who accept the gift. The reception of the gift includes the responsibility of assimilating, personally and communally, its significance ever more fully.

Thus, people or groups who speak, write and act as if their or their community's expression of the truth is final and absolute for all times and all places, pre-empt the position of God. Scripture and tradition reveal a God who enters lovingly, patiently, and graciously into the human undertaking of coming to know and express ever more fully the infinite love of God in Christ. The presence of Christ's love is signified by a community working together in purposeful conversation and dialogue to incarnate God's meaning for humankind, emulating the Jesus of Luke's gospel who "increased in wisdom and in stature, and in favor with God and humankind" (Lk 2:52).

See **Faith, Revelation**

————

Yves Congar, OP, *Faith and Theology.* Bernard Lonergan, SJ *Method In Theology,* "The Transition from a World View to Historical Mindedness," in *Second Collection.* Karl Rahner, SJ, Ed. *Sacramentum Mundi.*

NANCY C. RING

HERMENEUTICS

This term refers to the theory of interpreting verbal and aesthetic expressions. In a theological context hermeneutics refers usually to the theory of text-interpretation. Not to be confused with the act of interpretation itself, hermeneutics is concerned with the development of criteria for text-interpretation. The need for such criteria is, of course, as old as the human will to understand texts, especially texts with a normative status in a community (e.g., religious and legal texts). The term hermeneutics points back to the Greek word *"hermeneuein"* (= to interpret) which contains a reference to the Greek god Hermes, the messenger of the gods. His task was to explain the decisions of the gods to the humans. Thus, the etymology of the term hermeneutics leads us to appreciate the continuing question of all interpreters: how can we today understand the sense of texts, especially of ancient texts whose world view we no longer share? This basic question of hermeneutics is connected with the ultimate epistemological question: how can we understand at all?

Long before christian theologians addressed the hermeneutical problem of understanding the biblical texts in a critical way, some hermeneutical criteria had already been developed by Greek and Jewish thinkers. Greek philosophers attempted to understand the actual meaning of linguistic components of a text (grammatical method) and to appropriate this meaning within the wider spiritual framework of the time (allegorical method). Similarly, Jewish scholars were concerned with the adequate interpretation of the directly legal parts of the Torah (Halacha), yet they also provided a more liberal explanation of the more narrative sections (Haggada). Philo of Alexandria united the Jewish and Greek hermeneutical traditions and developed the thesis that an interpretation should disclose the text's spiritual sense on the basis of an explanation of the text's literal sense.

This hermeneutical program influenced also the christian interpreters. Their particular theological interests which directed their understanding of the spiritual sense were their witness to the ultimate event of salvation in Jesus Christ and their belief that in Jesus Christ God's promises to Israel had been fulfilled. The first major christian hermeneut, Origen, emphasized the need for both ways of text-interpretation; the historical-grammatical (literal) sense and the spiritual sense (further distinguished in moral application and allegorical-mystical assessment) need to be understood by every interpreter of Sacred Scripture. Augustine, then, through his philosophy of language (the *signum* points to the *res*) provided the necessary philosophical support to the now refined hermeneutics of the two senses. This model remained the authoritative way of biblical interpretation until well into the Middle Ages. The allegorical interpretation, however, remained controlled by the norms of the church (*regula fidei*), i.e., what church authorities considered to be the orthodox understanding of the scriptures. With Thomas Aquinas and his contemporaries the literal sense became more important again as the bearer of theological truth. According to Aquinas, appropriate interpretation is the task of dogmatic theology while exegesis concentrates on the purely philological task of preparing the text for theological understanding. Since the Council of Trent (1545-63), the ultimate decision on the criteria and the validity of results of biblical interpretation remained the prerogative of the Teaching Office (Magisterium) of the Roman Catholic Church.

While the new importance given to the scriptures in the Protestant Reformation did not alter the basic scholastic concern for an adequate theological understanding of the literal sense of the biblical texts, it freed this understanding from the formal authority of the Magisterium and emphasized—at least in principle—the need for all individual believers to read and understand the scriptures. However, certain theological reading perspectives dominated more and more the actual reading of the biblical texts.

In the aftermath of the Enlightenment and especially through the work of Friedrich Schleiermacher (1768-1834), hermeneutics received a new philosophical foundation. Schleiermacher rejected all formal, i.e., extra-textual authorities as illegitimate impositions on the individual act of understanding, and therefore ruled out all special hermeneutics, such as a special "theological" or a special "legal" hermeneutics. Rather, *every* written text must be understood both in terms of its individual sense (psychological understanding) and in terms of the linguistic procedures through which this sense is achieved (grammatical understanding). Hermeneutics is now understood as the art of understanding the sense of the text. Allegorical interpretation is ruled out, the text must be allowed to speak for itself.

The increasing awareness of the historical conditions of human existence since the nineteenth century and the influence of philosophers such as Hegel and Heidegger led to a more cautious view of the art of understanding: no interpreters approach the text neutrally, rather they move within a *hermeneutical circle,* and therefore must reflect upon the historical conditions of their interpretations. We understand the parts of a text first in view of our preunderstanding of the whole which is challenged in the act of understanding itself. Hans-Georg Gadamer emphasized the productive role of these preunderstandings for the process of interpretation. Without perspectives we do not see at all, yet through perspectives we see only as far as they allow us. Gadamer calls the condition and the perspectives of interpreters their "horizons" and the act of understanding a text's sense "the fusion of horizons." Through this fusion of horizons the interpreter enters the tradition of the text, and thus shares in the text's particular representation of truth. Gadamer's hermeneutics has been criticized mainly for his refusal to allow for methodological controls of the act of interpretation. Paul Ricoeur demanded that our first understanding of a text's sense must be validated or corrected through various explanatory procedures (formalist and structuralist methods) in order to lead to a responsible disclosure of the text's modes of being in the world, i.e., its sense. Jürgen Habermas insisted that only a critical and self-critical attitude towards interpretation could reveal possible systematic distortions in human communication and their impact on our interpretive activity. In view of these suggestions it seems imperative to distinguish three necessary and related dimensions in every act of text-interpretation: understanding, explanation and critical assessment.

The insight into the impossibility of purely "objective" interpretation on the one hand and the concern for an appropriate analysis of the textuality of the text on the other hand helped hermeneuts to appreciate the fact that every complex text necessarily demands a pluralism of interpretations which is limited only by the text itself. Readers are conditioned by their horizons and therefore in need of the support of the entire community of interpreters for the critical assessment of their particular interpretations. Such a communal assessment might also help to unmask ideological distortions especially of normative (or "classic") texts.

Theologians found it difficult often to respond constructively to these hermeneutical insights. Seeing the pluralism of interpretations more as a threat than as a productive challenge, they either preferred to assert anew the doctrine of verbal inspiration of scripture which provided them with a formal, extra-textual criterion, or they accepted uncritically the pseudo-security provided by an often very rigid church authority.

A positive theological response to the insights of modern hermeneutics would want to appreciate the basic hermeneutical dimensions of all theological thinking: christian theology is concerned with adequate interpretations of the texts of the Jewish-christian tradition as well as with appropriate efforts to interpret the different manifestations of other human experiences in this world.

The results of the interpretations of both realms could then be assessed in a mutually critical correlation (Tracy). The advantages of this model are obvious: first, this theological method would be open for a dialogue with all other hermeneutically interested sciences and could learn how to use critically all suitable methods of text-interpretation (from the historical-critical method of exegesis to post-modern literary criticism) in order to interpret most adequately the biblical, traditional and contemporary expressions of christian faith. Second, this method would be well equipped to detect and correct possible ideological distortions in traditional and modern presentations of christian faith. Third,

this method would call for an appropriate organization of christian community so that all members could contribute their interpretive experiences, and thus enrich the faith-praxis of the entire christian church.

See **Bible, Theology**

Gerhard Ebeling, "Hermeneutik," in *RGG* III (1959). Hans-Georg Gadamer, *Truth and Method,* (EVT 1975). Paul Ricoeur, *Hermeneutics and the Human Sciences,* 1981. David Tracy, *The Analogical Imagination,* 1981. Werner G. Jeanrond, *Text und Interpretation als Kategorien theologischen Denkens,* 1986.

WERNER G. JEANROND

HIERARCHY

Literally, "sacred order" or "principle," the term used to refer to the divinely willed distribution of orders and ministries in the church. It is often used generically, to refer to the pope and bishops.

See **Authority in the Church, Church, Ministry, Orders and Ordination**

HIERARCHY OF TRUTHS

This phrase refers to the following teaching from Vatican II's Decree on Ecumenism of November 21, 1964: "When comparing doctrines with one another, they [Catholic theologians] should remember that in Catholic doctrine there exists an order or 'hierarchy' of truths, since they vary in their relation to the foundation of the Christian faith" (U.R. 11). The immediate context of this teaching is chapter two of the decree— "The Practice of Ecumenism"—and in particular a description of ecumenical dialogue aiming not so much at mutual understanding as at "a deeper realization and a clearer expression of the unfathomable riches of Christ." The motive for including this sentence in the decree was clear both from the speech which first mentioned the concept as well as from

Modus 49 which introduced it into the text of *Unitatis redintegratio:* the unity already existing between Christians may be more accurately assessed when truths are weighed and not merely enumerated. Archbishop Pangrazio, in his speech of November 25, 1963, distinguished between truths pertaining to the ends of salvation and others pertaining to the means. For the most part, doctrinal divisions among Christians concern the means to salvation. However, Pangrazio added, "when this journey comes to an end, so too do these means." Echoing Pius XI's condemnation of the distinction between fundamental and non-fundamental articles of faith (*Moralium animos,* 1927), both Pangrazio and Modus 49 affirm that all truths must be believed "with the same faith," but this should not obscure the fact that all truths are not of the same importance.

Theologians representing a wide range of traditions responded enthusiastically to the hierarchy of truths, many calling it a very important step for advancing christian unity. However, the notion required much further elaboration. In the twenty years following the Council, some thirty-five writings were devoted precisely to a further clarification of the hierarchy of truths. Results ranged from the historical to the systematic.

Historically, the scriptures support the notion that the gospel has a center. Kerygmatic expressions of the paschal mystery (1 Cor 15:3-5), statements regarding the foundation of the faith (1 Cor 3:10-11; Heb 6:1), hymns concerning the christian mystery (Eph 1:3-10; Phil 2:5-11; Col 1:12-20), trinitarian formulae, the Johannine focus on acceptance of the person of Jesus through use of the various "I am" passages (Jn 8:24 among others) and the accent upon the principal virtues of faith, hope and love (Mk 12:28-44; Gal 5:5-6; 1 Cor 13) all point to a certain ordering among christian truths and

values. In post-biblical times, the development of creeds tended to focus the faith upon those elements which were to be professed upon entrance into the christian community at baptism and during celebrations of the eucharist. During the early centuries of Christianity, the Fathers of the Church repeatedly displayed the knack for always considering particular aspects of the faith in light of the central christological and trinitarian mysteries, a tendency also reflected in the development of the liturgy. Later, scholastic theologians (St. Thomas Aquinas in particular) were fond of underlining the order within theology by showing how all christian truths were reducible to the twelve articles of the creed. The Reformation was characterized in part by a zeal to return to certain central aspects of salvation in christian faith. Later, Reformation theologians attempted to provide a doctrinal basis for unity among Christians by introducing the notion of fundamental articles. In Roman Catholic thought, the emergence of the idea of development of doctrine included an organic understanding of christian truth. M.J. Scheeben tried to show how all christian mysteries grouped themselves around several central mysteries. Finally, Vatican I's exhortation about the profit obtained from considering the relationships of christian mysteries among themselves and with the final end of humankind (D.S. 3016) has been seen by some as a prefigurement of Vatican II's hierarchy of truths. Thus many historical precedents support the idea that there exists an order or "hierarchy" of truths.

Systematically, authors have made a distinction between the hierarchy obtaining among christian truths considered as an objective body of doctrine and the various existential hierarchies of truths posited by individuals and groups of believers. The subjective act of faith responds to the objectively ordered body of truths in such a way that one would expect more central truths to exercise a stronger existential attraction upon believers. For this reason some have suggested that the teaching that all truths must be believed "with the same faith" should be nuanced to reflect the fact that not all truths are of the same importance.

The hierarchy of truths promises to have an important impact on several areas of church life. From the standpoint of church mission, it provides an opening into the question of reformulating the core of christian faith in a way that can be effective for evangelization. In this regard, the hierarchy of truths touches upon the question of formulating short creeds and of doctrinal inculturation. From the standpoint of ecumenism, the hierarchy of truths offers a framework for doctrinal unity which does not eliminate legitimate diversity. From the standpoint of an historically sensitive theology, the hierarchy of truths is a principle of doctrinal hermeneutics. It brings perspective to the tradition, which is ever to be received and ever to be handed on anew.

See **Creeds, Determinism, Faith, Revelation**

D. Carroll, "'Hierarchia veritatum': A Theological and Pastoral Insight of the Second Vatican Council," *Irish Theological Quarterly* 44, 1977, pp. 125-33. William Henn, *The Hierarchy of Truths according to Yves Congar, O.P.*. Rome: Gregorian U. Press, 1987. George Tavard, "'Hierarchia veritatum': A Preliminary Investigation," *TS* 32, 1971, pp. 278-89.

WILLIAM HENN, OFM CAP.

HINDUISM

Hinduism at times seems to embrace as many religious responses as there are human needs. It is not a coherent body of cult, belief, or community; no single founder, prophet, saint, or deity holds exclusive position. The word Hinduism is derivative from the geographical identification, made by Muslins, identifying the land and peoples of the Indus river valley and the subcontinent as Hindustan. It refers to a diversity of cults and communities within the common social matrix of a broad caste system. Social scientists sort out such diversity by speaking of the great and little traditions. The great tradition embodies the classical literary heritage in the Sanskrit language which gives to India, and especially the higher castes, its initial cultural unity; the little tradition of lower caste and tribal India exhibits an exuberance of customs and cultures geographically contained. The little tradition includes rituals and beliefs of local village life, while the great tradition is circumscribed by both religious and secular Sanskrit literature. The distinction, however, is not discrete, for both traditions frequently impact on the same local community or caste.

The ancient seers, mostly nameless, who composed the first sacred literature, called the Vedas, are viewed as the source of India's religious history. The four Vedas, received as revealed literature (*sruti*), consist of hymns, prayers, creation myths, ritual texts, meditational reflections, and early attempts at philosophical speculation Although ancient civilizations existed a millennium prior to the Vedas, the composition of this vast body of sacred literature took place approximately between 1500-400 B.C.E. Considering it profane to put the Vedas into written form, they were fully committed to memory by the learned community who orally transmitted the sacred texts from father to son and teacher to student. From the earliest moment secular literature and other forms of religious literature entered written form, but this was not true of the Vedas until well after the eighth century C.E.

The Vedas speak about "the absolute as one but the wise calling it by many names." When the sacred is named, a plethora of gods emerge: high sky gods (Surya, Mitra, Varuna, Visnu); mediator gods (Indra, Rudra, warrior gods); and earth gods (Agni, Soma, nature spirits, the goddess). Creation mythology is extremely rich in offering a variety of sources and reasons for the creative act: time (*kala*), sacrifice, desire, divine dismemberment, That One (*tad ekam*). The sacrificial ritual was the unifying factor in early Indian religion; ritual was creator, preserver, and restorer of the cosmic order. Although not an exclusive summary, the great axioms of the *Upanisads* (the end of the Vedas) have traditionally been put forth as the highest wisdom in identifying the absolute (Brahman) with the most radically subjective aspect of the self (*atman*): "That Thou Art," "I am Brahman," "The Self is Brahman," and "All is Brahman."

Hindu orthodoxy stemming from the Vedas had its limitation since revealed literature was only open to the upper classes (twice-born) and not to the lowest caste (*sudras*) or those outside caste. Another body of Sanskrit religious literature emerged which was equally formative and revered (*smrti*) by all Hindus. Of importance are the Puranas, a massive corpus of myth and legend, and the Sastras which contained laws and customs governing family life, social classes, temple and home rituals. Two monumental epics appear with the range and depth of the Greek epics: the *Mahabharata* and the *Ramayana*. In the former is found the popular and revered *Bhagavad Gita* (The Song of the Lord,), depicting the teaching and the self-revelation of Lord Krsna. The classical tradition is, conceptually, fairly well formalized during the historical period (400 B.C.E.–600 C.E.) of these literary compositions.

A group of concepts, developing from both revealed (*sruti*) and revered (*smrti*) literature distinguished the Indian world of experience: rebirth, *karma,* and liberation (*moksa*). Rebirth or reincarnation is foundational to the Indian worldview. The idea is closely linked to *karma,* that is, the law by which personal deeds determine one's present and future status in this life and future lives. Liberation (*moksa*) involves the cessation of the endless round of births in which transcendence of the world results in eternal life with Brahman.

The most central and practical concepts underlying the Indian worldview are sacrifice (*yajna*) and renunciation (*vairagya*). In the early Vedas sacrifice is ritual in its most material and extrinsic sense, with the sacrificial fire, oblations, chants and hymns as constitutive; by the time of the *Upanisads* sacrifice is interiorized and ritual is transformed into meditation and self-reflection; with later literature, especially the *Bhagavad Gita,* sacrifice evolves into selfless action and devotional love for the deity. Nothing is lost or put aside in this historical development of concept and practice as all forms of renunciation have parallel histories from this point forward. In this light the great yogas or spiritual disciplines can be understood as inclusive: *karmayoga*—sacrifice as ritual or selfless action; *bhaktiyoga*—sacrifice as devotion and love of a deity; *jnana-yoga*—sacrifice as self-knowledge and wisdom; *rajayoga*—sacrifice as meditation. These spiritual paths (*margas*) raise orthopraxis far beyond orthodoxy as the primary focus of Indian religious life.

No single concept of sacred reality pervades in any single form the entire tradition. Brahman is recognized as ultimate reality: one without second, without qualities, the ground of life, unnamed, neither as an object of worship nor devotion. When the sacred is worshipped and named, a vast godhead is revealed, in classical Hinduism, superseding the gods of the early Vedas: Brahma (the creator), Siva (the cosmic energizer), Visnu (the preserver), Devi (the goddess). A number of *avatars* (divine descents into time and history in order to restore cosmic order) appear, with Lord Krsna and his consort Radha, or Rama and his consort Sita as popular figures. Each temple, pilgrimage site, and even village may possess a variation of this classical godhead or name the sacred in another completely idiosyncratic or provincial manner. A village or caste resolves the diversity according to geography, language, or custom; an individual or a family, in its devotion, singles out one form of the godhead for worship as their chosen deity (*ista devata*). The major sects of the Saivas, Vaisnavas, and Shaktas in their respective worship of Siva, Visnu or one of his *avatars,* or the goddess, give to such a personal deity the qualities of the entire godhead.

During the medieval period the devotional poets and religious philosophers carry the tradition to its fullest expression. The regional poets were the first to create a vernacular religious literature, bringing religious inspiration and sentiment to the masses in their own language for the first time. Schools of Tamil, Marathi, and Hindi-speaking poet-saints captured the imagination and esteem of religious India. Much as the teacher-saints (*gurus*) of the past, these were men and women who experienced the divine and now sang in verse about their highest spiritual experiences as they moved throughout the villages of India. Some of the poet-saints stood within the Sanskritic tradition and their theology reflects this, while others were more representative of the little tradition which was more indigenous to a locale.

By the end of the fourth century C.E., six orthodox philosophical systems had taken form: Nyaya, a school of logic and epistemology, clarified the means for obtaining knowledge; Vaisheskika analyzed nature and concluded to the atomic structure of reality; Mimamsa, a school of scriptural exegesis, emphasized duty and ritual; Samkhya, a system based on the eternal play of pure spirit and primal matter, offered a classical structure for the involution and evolution of the entire cosmic process; Vedanta, drawing upon the *Upanisads,* produced the most comprehensive basis for articulating religious experience. The philosophical systems had as objective the spiritual liberation of the human person. The schools of thought developing from the Vedanta could be viewed as theological, for they alone not only discussed the means of liberating the human person but also the nature of the absolute and its relationship to the self (*atman*) in both its liberated and non-liberated state.

The classical period of the Vedanta began with Sankara (eighth-ninth century C.E.), considered the greatest thinker of the school of nondualism (*advaita*), who argued for the pure identity between the self (*atman*) and the absolute (Brahman). Ramanuja (eleventh century, C.E.) established a school of qualified nondualism in which the self is dependent upon yet distinct from Brahman, even in a liberated state, but such a state is one of profound communion of these two fundamental realities. Madhva (thirteenth century, C.E.), founder of the dualist position, maintains a consistent distinction between the self, Brahman, and the world, and completes the comprehensive range of Indian theological speculation. Other thinkers work within this spectrum. Hindu sectarianism is articulated within one or another of these positions. The spiritual disciplines, whether the path of ritual, selfless action, devotion, meditation, or knowledge, along with the special emphasis a particular thinker gives to each, are the means for achieving the quality of union with the divine suggested above.

The major form of worship and devotion, superseding the early Vedic sacrifices, is *puja* which may be performed in both home and temple before a distinct image of a deity. *Puja* as ritual action includes invocation of the deity, ablutions, bathing the image of the deity, clothing the deity with the sacred thread and a new garment, offerings of food, flowers, and incense, and finally obeisances of praise, circumambulation and prostration. Home *puja,* temple visits, pilgrimages to sacred sites, vow-taking, chanting sacred syllables and prayers (*mantra*), communal singing of the devotional songs, celebrating seasonal public festivals, meditation, and rituals consecrating the passage through stages of life (birth, puberty, marriage, and death) make up the world of religious practice.

Hinduism did not have a missionary thrust in the past because it was tightly structured by caste and the Indian experience of pollution and purification. Even so, it did influence the Middle East, the Mediterranean world, and especially Southeast Asia. In modern times Indian culture has gone through a renaissance, from the early nineteenth century to the present, due in part to British colonialism and the independence movement from British rule. Charismatic figures such as Ram Mohan Roy, Dayananda Sarasvati, Keshab Chandra Sen, and Swami Vivekananda brought about socio-religious reform; saintly and prophetic personalities like Ramakrishna, Sri Aurobindo Ghose, and Rabindranath Tagore contributed to both a spiritual and intellectual rebirth; religio-political leaders emerged with Mahatma Gandhi and Pandit Nehru who created a new socio-political order; traditional philosophers such as S. Radhadrishnan and T.M.P. Mahadevan tried to revitalize the old Vedanta. The prominence of saints and gurus had been as prevalent in this century as in the past. But only in this century do religious figures leave India to teach Hinduism throughout the world. In the past India's influence on the rest of the world had been through literary and scholarly interaction, such as India's influence on American Transcendentalism, but now Indian gurus establish themselves and teaching centers throughout the world.

Although Christians have acculturated themselves to Indian life since the time of the St. Thomas Christians, the encounter between Christianity and Hinduism has advanced in recent times. Christian ascetics and monastics in India are adapting themselves to Indian customs and paths of salvation while entering into profound spiritual dialogue with their counterparts from Hinduism. The theological encounter between groups of Hindus and Christians may well be the most vibrant example of inter-religious dialogue existing today. The works of Raimundo Panikkar are but one special example. A score of Indian Christians, trained in the best theological schools of Europe and North America, along with advanced degrees in Indian thought from Indian universities, are forging an indigenous theology for the Christian community. As this century comes to an end, Hinduism exhibits more vibrancy today than in the last several hundred years and, for the first time in its history, it is emerging as a world religion as Indians establish communities throughout the world with their teachers, temples, and traditions.

Thomas Hopkins, *The Hindu Religious Tradition,* Belmont, CA: Wadsworth Pub. Co., 1971. William Theodore de Bary, Ed., *Sources of Indian Tradition,* New York: Columbia U.P., 1958. Cornelia Dimmitt & J.A.B. van Buitenen, *Classical Hindu Mythology,* Philadelphia: Temple U.P., 1978. S. Radhakrishnan, *Indian Philosophy,* 2 vol., London: George Allen & Unwin, 1962. John M. Koller, *The Indian Way,* New York: Macmillan, 1982.

WILLIAM CENKNER

HISTORY

The word "history" has several meanings. It refers to past actuality, to events which have in fact occurred. It is also used of the processes of discovering, interpreting and recording past actuality and of the finished product of those processes. History presupposes change. Without change there can be no history. The stuff of the historian's discipline is change. History is out of place in a fixed universe operating according to immutable laws. From this comes a basic uneasiness between history and at least some interpretations of theology, the one dealing with becoming, the other with being. History's relationship to theology is further affected by the fact that it is conventionally restricted to the study of human beings and events and more particularly to events of significant social interaction among human beings, to their impact on society and its impact on them. History's object is the ongoing story of the continuing human community, including the church community, and its mutable affairs.

The historian strives for objectivity, to recreate in words and with the help of visual aids, statistics, graphs, charts and the like, the human past as it actually was. Scholastic philosophers developed the notion of "historical certitude," and laid down conditions for its attainment, but it is "objectivity" that has rather been the historian's admittedly elusive goal. Nineteenth-century German historian Leopold von Ranke set the historian's task as that of recording the past as it actually happened, but subjective factors inevitably affect each stage in the historical process from the initial choice of topic down to the final presentation. While careful attention to received scientific method can produce a measure of scholarly agreement, conclusions reached by individual historians are influenced by their differing preoccupations and prejudices, their competence, personal degree of involvement with the subject-matter, and other factors. The line separating subjective interpretation from objective research is thin and porous. This reality often discomfited theologians, particularly in eras like that of the mid-nineteenth century when preoccupation with certitude seemed to outdistance concern for truth.

There are other reasons why the study of the history of the church finds an uneasy home among the theological disciplines. Several take the form of replies to the question, "What is the 'church' in church history?" The whole christian church down the centuries and across the world? A specific tradition—Catholic, Orthodox, one of the Reformation groupings—within that totality? One specific denomination? What meaning is intended by terms such as "Roman" or "Catholic?" What importance is given to factors arising from Christianity's geographical spread (or concentration) and its presence within various cultures? A second line of questions follows. Some historians focus on church leaders, and much church history, both of Roman Catholicism and of other christian bodies, has been written in those terms. But the late twentieth-century vogue for statistically fortified social history has combined with the image of the church as "people of God" popularized by the Second Vatican Council to generate a new "people's history" approach which, in addition to the inevitable statistical tables, pays closer attention to popular piety and belief, to devotional life and to artistic, architectural and musical manifestations of the religion of Christians.

A further conflict is between acceptance that the church is mystery—and thus beyond historical consideration—and the fact that it is also a human institution, manifested in radically contingent fashion and subject to the actions and passions of the men and women who make it up. Should the church historian use the same historico-critical methods as does the secular historian? The question, answered affirmatively by many contemporary church historians of all denominations, has been answered negatively by others, for whom the church's past must be seen as that of a pilgrim people with a christian world-view, conscious of a particular origin, mission and destiny, achieving its goal through the action of God in history.

There are echoes here of the "substantialist" or "classicist" approach prevalent throughout most of the christian era. It allows for only accidental external changes in the church's passage through history. In the case of Roman Catholicism, this concept produced an image of the church which emphasized order and unchangeableness. In terms of teaching, Vincent of Lérins canonized this mindset when he set the norm of what has been believed everywhere, always and by everyone. A new charter came for the church historian with Vatican II's movement away from an exclusively conceptual approach to theology to an emphasis on the biblical-historical. The contemporary Catholic historian focuses on the being and faith of the church, a tradition understood as dynamic, which comes from the apostles [and] develops in the church with the help of the Holy Spirit.

Many early church histories were mere chronicles, a style which lasted into the middle ages and still recurs. Other writers, more properly theologians of history than historians, interpreted the human story as a sacred one of progressive stages toward the fulfillment of all things in Christ at the *parousia*. Augustine of Hippo and imitators in subsequent ages elaborated schemes demonstrating the working out of the divine plan in time, studying humanity specifically as God's creation with the Incarnation at the center of its earthly pilgrimage. History for them was made intelligible precisely because guided by a transcendent Providence, with God as origin and goal.

History itself was the tale not only of human deeds, but preeminently of the actions of God whose will directed every event.

The orientation of a given historian's theological anthropology weighed heavily in historical interpretation. Those unduly influenced by Augustinian pessimism sometimes slipped over into the approach called "primitivism" or "decline-history," picturing the world in conflict between light and darkness, with the latter prevailing. The assumption made was of a decline from an earlier golden age. In more extreme forms which saw the historical process as one of continuous decay, decline-history was characteristic of medieval Cathar heretics. The more general christian approach was marked by cautious optimism, seeing in human history the slow but sure advance of Christ's kingdom.

Since the Renaissance, emphasis on the individuality and particularity of human persons and events, and on free will and its consequences in the understanding of historical reality, have all contributed to the theologians' uneasiness with historical study. Historians for their part found increasing significance in their awareness of the constant change taking place in church government, structure, thought and religious expression, as well as in the fact that a western Christianity for so many centuries a European religion, had become indigenous to all the inhabited continents. This set ill with those for whom church history was valued for its entertainment potential or as a source of "exempla" or "proof texts" to dress up already arrived-at conclusions.

More positive challenges came from several quarters. The canonists were old adversaries whose twelfth-century triumph in western Christianity was a profoundly anti-historical event. Revival in the late nineteenth century of an essentialist-leaning scholasticism struck no less a blow at history's place in the theological spectrum. Despite theories of the organic growth of the church proposed by theologians at Tübingen, and of development of doctrine advanced by John Henry Newman, mainline Roman Catholic theology rejected the dynamism offered by history, which was seen as leading to "historicism," the relativization of all reality. The issue was a major component of the turn-of-the-century "modernist" crisis and of later attacks on the "new theology" of post-World War II France, which had as a major element emphasis on return to christian sources.

The Second Vatican Council's Constitution on Divine Revelation (c. II, n. 8) provided a charter which drew the church historian as never before into the heart of the Catholic theological enterprise. "Tradition," it became clear, was no arcane treasure trove of propositional statements of revelation waiting enunciation, but an understanding arising from and discerned in the life, thought and worship of God's people down the ages and around the world. The council also declared that "this tradition which comes from the apostles develops in the church with the help of the Holy Spirit." Teaching, life, worship as they change and develop over time and place, these are the proper object of church historical study. Revelation, in the thought of Vatican II, is not seen, as a scholastic concatenation of a series of propositional truths. A sense of history has been recovered. God makes himself known by both deeds and words. It is in contemplation of the life and the worship, as well as the thought, of the christian community down the centuries and in its global extent, that God is known. The historian does not claim to discern the tradition, only to aid in its discernment. Historians are aware that there is a distinction between "the tradition" and the plural traditions, which may be distorting as well as legitimate. In helping to discern the difference the historian makes his/her chief contribution to the overall theological enterprise.

R.G. Collingwood, *The Idea of History,* New York: Oxford University Press, 1956. Jaroslav Pelikan, *Historical Theology: Continuity and Change in Christian Doctrine,* New York/Philadelphia/London: Corpus/Westminister/Hutchinson, 1971.

JAMES HENNESEY, SJ

HOLINESS OF THE CHURCH

As with the unity of the church, so also is it true of the church's holiness that what is realized in Christ is communicated to us by the Holy Spirit initially in baptism. By its relationship to Christ and the Holy Spirit, the People of God is a holy Temple (Acts 1:5), a holy priesthood (1 Pet 2:5) and offers spiritual sacrifices in the Holy Spirit (Rom 15:16). Just as Israel by reason of its election by God and the covenant, so also do the People of God of the New Covenant form "a holy nation" (1 Pet 2:9). By the grace of election and covenant, the People of God are called "saints" (Col 1:12). The holiness of the church is realized between baptism through which the Spirit initiates it and its eschatological fulfillment in the kingdom (Eph 5:25-27). Thus holiness characterizes the church because of its election by God, its vocation from God, its covenant with God in Christ and the very indwelling of the Spirit of Christ. As spouse of Christ and Temple of the Holy Spirit, the church offers authentic worship to God and in this act is perfectly itself (Eph 1:10, 13). Holiness also pertains to Christians who are called to live a holy life; "Rather, become holy yourselves in every aspect of your conduct, after the likeness of the Holy One who called you; remember, Scripture says, 'Be holy as I am holy'" (1 Pet 1:15-16).

To the degree that it is of God, the

church is holy. But a certain dialectic between what God has given to the church and what is received and realized by Christians. This is the dialectic of the already-given but not-yet-fully-realized condition of the church in its earthly pilgrimage. This condition represents a tension in the church to be adequate to the gifts bestowed on it by God. Thus, in affirming the holiness of the church, one is really affirming the fidelity of God to the covenant in Jesus Christ. But this is not to deny the fact of sin in the church.

The church is holy in its formal principles or in that which it has received from God as the universal sacrament of salvation. These formal principles include the deposit of faith, the sacraments of faith and the corresponding ministries. These realities are holy in that they proceed from God and seek God as their goal. They are instruments through which God sanctifies his people.

The Holy Spirit dwells within and animates the church as its principle of operation. By the power of the Spirit the sanctifying actions of Christ takes place in the church, such as the witness of preaching, the faith of believers, pastoral activity, the life of christian communities and sanctification through sacraments. Thus, holiness assured to the church as spouse and to the means whereby it constitutes itself enables the church to produce saints and the fruits of holiness. The transcendent cause of this holiness is the Holy Spirit. As the church of saints, the church does not cease through its proper operations to raise up, educate and nourish innumerable saints. But it is also a church of sinners.

Inasmuch as the church is established in union with God and is given the means of union with God, as the *ecclesia congregans,* it is without sin. Sin belongs to the members of the church, the *ecclesia congregata,* in the sense that they can be unfaithful to their identity as members of the church and are committed to that which is alien to the church's holiness. Strictly speaking, one cannot attribute sin to the church because the subject of sin can only be a personal subject and because the church is totally pure in its formal, constitutive elements. Sinfulness cannot be regarded as a manifestation of the essential being of the church.

Yet the church is an historical reality composed of human beings who are sinful. Sinners belong to the church but with an imperfect holiness: they are in the church as sinners bound by faith to the communion of grace for penitence and sanctification. So while the church is holy in its formal principles, it is led by its members to imperfect, historical manifestations of what it is and aspires to be. As a concrete historical reality the church as spouse of Christ will only be perfectly holy in the eschaton and in the "time-between" must be penitent and ceaselessly purify itself (L.G. 8).

Yves Congar writes: "Whoever speaks of eschatology also speaks of historicity. Whoever speaks of historicity necessarily speaks of imperfection." Imperfection involves the necessity for renewal, ongoing reform and continual change of heart within the church. Christian reform represents a judgment brought to a certain state of things in the name of a return to the principles and sources of life of the church. Such authentic reform questions and researches tradition, the scriptures, the Fathers, expressions of faith and prayer in worship, the authentic research of theologians and spiritual leaders, the development of piety and doctrine and finally the thought and movement within the church in its contemporary historical reality. The normative elements are scripture and the dogmatic definitions which are unanimously held in the universal church. This process always takes place within the communion of faith.

Authentic reform respects acquired forms from the past and upholds fidelity, rootedness and continuity. But it also permits movement, growth and adaptation. The task of reform is to attend to all aspects of tradition and not get locked into an exclusive condition of immobility and inertia. There are many human structures in the church, and even essential elements which have taken on certain forms in the course of history which are contingent, historical and subject to change. Christianity is eternal but the forms, such as the concrete forms of the apostolate, the administration of the church and the celebration of worship are bound to history and conditioned by a given state of development. Hence to assimilate them into a condition of permanence is to absolutize the relative. The living principle of tradition must be helped to create new forms of existence which can be efficaciously applied to the contemporary situation.

In its dialectic of gift and task the messianic people of God must respond to the signs of the times and from Christ, its fullness, seek to renew itself. In this process, the Holy Spirit as source of holiness promotes those initiatives which renew the church, inspirations for reform and hence a more faithful living of the gospel.

See **Church**

Hans Küng, *The Church*, New York: Sheed and Ward, 1967.

TIMOTHY MACDONALD

HOLY SEE

A term used to refer to the See of Rome presided over by the pope. It is often used generically to refer to all the offices of the Roman Curia.

HOLY SPIRIT

1. Experience and Doctrine

"We believe in the Holy Spirit, the Lord and Giver of Life, who proceeds from the Father and the Son, who with the Father and the Son is adored and glorified, who has spoken through the prophets." This affirmation of the creed, professed each week by millions of Christians as their common faith, serves as initial orientation for reflection upon the meaning of christian faith in the Holy Spirit. It also serves to remind us that faith in the triune God, Father, Son and Holy Spirit, is rooted in liturgical celebration and experience. God is encountered, experienced, confessed, before God is reflected upon in more systematic concepts. Such systematic thinking is an indispensable task of theology; but its purpose lies in assisting and promoting the life of faith. Dogma, however necessary, is ever the discernment of christian experience. It is, as Karl Rahner suggests, "mystagogic": clarifying and leading more deeply into the encounter of the mystery who is man and woman with the Mystery who is God.

Therefore, the church's teaching about the Holy Spirit should always refer to the privileged liturgical context in which that teaching touches Christians most personally and directly: the context of the rites of initiation. Here the new disciple of Christ, having renounced the death-dealing spirits of evil and sin, confesses the gracious power of the triune God, is baptized into the death and new life of Jesus Christ, and is anointed with God's life-giving Spirit. This radical turning to God through Christ in the Spirit, this conversion of life, remains the experiential point of reference for christian doctrine. In its fullest liturgical expression at the Easter Vigil, the liturgy of initiation provides the classic text, upon which all our doctrinal treatises are dependent and for which they provide commentary.

2. The Spirit in the Old Testament

Within the framework of the rites of initiation, the OT readings bear witness to Israel's experience of the Spirit who is Lord and Giver of life ... who spoke through the prophets. By incorporating the OT's witness into its liturgical celebration and scriptural canon, the church recognizes that Israel's wrestling with God and willingness to be led in God's way is intrinsic to the church's own faith and self-understanding. Israel's experience of God's Spirit certainly undergoes a rich and complex development in the course of the centuries. Yet the original associations of "Spirit" with life and power—the Hebrew word *ruach* has as its root meaning "breath" or "wind"—perdure, even within the variety which historical challenge and communal experience produce.

Clearly, not every OT reference to "spirit" concerns the Spirit of God. Many passages refer to "natural" phenomena: the mighty desert wind or the indispensable breath of life. But, in Israel's experience, even these are not removed from God's creative purpose. Hence, in the account of creation penned by the priestly writer (Gen 1:2), the wind blowing over the abyss passes imperceptibly into an image of the Spirit of God hovering over the waters. So too the vital breath of life, which distinguishes the living human being, is a mysterious gift of God, not to be taken for granted, but held in trust (cf. Gen 2:7). Indeed, one of the loveliest of Israel's psalms generalizes this perception and applies it to all living creatures: "When you hide your face, your creatures are dismayed; when you take away their breath, they die and return to their dust. When you send forth your Spirit, they are created; and you renew the face of the earth. (Ps 104:29-30).

The impression given by these and other texts is that all must be seen in relation to God and pondered in terms of God's creative purpose. God acts in the Spirit to bring forth and sustain life; but the specific goal of God's creative action is not yet fully revealed. Within Israel's historical experience the revelation of Spirit proceeds slowly, respectful and mindful that the human is still untutored in the ways of God.

Thus, in a number of early texts, extraordinary achievements are attributed to the action of God's Spirit. These include heroic feats of courage and strength (cf. Judg 6:34; 1 Sam 11:6), ecstatic speech (1 Sam 10:10 and 19:23), and even artistic skill (cf. Exod 35:31). At this stage of Israel's experience and reflection there does not yet appear an explicit ethical dimension to the working of the Spirit. Instead, the unpredictable, non-manipulable otherness of the Spirit's inspiration stands to the fore. Here the Spirit often overpowers, but does not necessarily transform.

A second sphere of the Spirit's activity concerns prophecy, as this develops in Israel both before and after the Exile. In the former period, the need to discern *what* was being said in God's name became more and more urgent. Thus the classical prophets begin to stress the "Word" of God, the content of God's will and plan. They are more reticent about appeals to "the Spirit," perhaps because these have been abused at the hands of the professional prophets serving the king. In light of this overriding concern to discern God's will, Spirit-language, when it appears, assumes a new moral quality, contrasting the divine order of holiness with the human order, frail and prone to sin. "The Egyptians are men and not God," cries the prophet Isaiah; "their horses are flesh and not spirit" (Isa 31:3).

The one who first associates the Spirit of the Lord with an ethical judgment upon God's people is the prophet Micah. In opposition to the lying prophets who lead Israel astray, Micah presents the basis for his own radical critique: "But, as for me, I am filled with power, with the Spirit of the Lord, and with justice and might, to declare to Jacob his transgression and to Israel his sin" (Mic 3:8). Thus the theme of the purifying judgment of the Spirit begins to be sounded; it will reach a climax in the preaching of John the Baptist at the dawn of the NT (cf. Mt. 3:11-12).

Even as the prophet's message more and more turns to a denunciation of Israel's present, it also announces the hope of a new and redeemed future. Isaiah personalizes the hope of redemption in the figure of a messianic king who shall be anointed with the Spirit of the Lord: "a spirit of wisdom and understanding, a spirit of counsel and might, a spirit of knowledge and the fear of the Lord" (Isa 11:2). Ezekiel, in the wake of Israel's loss of nationhood and exile, foresees, in his poignant vision of the dry bones, the reconstitution of an entire people indwelt by God's Spirit (cf. Ezek 37:1-14), in effect accomplishing a new creation.

During Israel's long exile and return to the land, the great prophetic voices of hope and consolation (known rather unimaginatively by scholars as Second and Third Isaiah) offer a deepening sense of the activity of God's Spirit and bring us, theologically, to the threshold of the new covenant. In the first of the so-called "Servant Songs," the prophet proclaims: "Behold my servant, whom I uphold; my chosen, in whom my soul delights. I have put my Spirit upon him, he will bring forth justice to the nations" (Isa 42:1).

The mysterious figure of the Servant is introduced as one (whether individual or nation) upon whom God's Spirit rests and who will be the instrument through whom God's justice will come, not only to Israel, but to the nations: a mission universal in scope.

From Third Isaiah comes a passage that will be quoted by Jesus at the inauguration of his public ministry in the gospel of Luke (cf. Lk 4:18-19). The passage is particularly noteworthy in that the anointing usually reserved to kings is here claimed for the prophet sent by the Lord: "The Spirit of the Lord is upon me, because the Lord has anointed me to bring good tidings to the afflicted. He has sent me to bind up the brokenhearted, to proclaim liberty to the captives, and the opening of the prison to those who are bound; to proclaim the year of the Lord's favor" (Isa 61:1-2). The Spirit, working through God's anointed, here opens a space, as it were, which is to be filled by a people freed and made whole for the Lord.

In Israel's vision and experience, therefore, the Spirit symbolizes God's saving power in creating and re-creating a world and a people. It signifies both God's graciousness and God's might, and finds concrete embodiment in the one especially anointed to God's service: whether charismatic leader, messianic king, eschatological prophet, or the restored and redeemed people.

As we turn to consider the experience of the Spirit in the NT, two aspects of the OT experience should be underscored, for they will continue to characterize the distinctive biblical use of Spirit-language. First, Spirit in the bible ought not be placed in opposition to the material or the corporeal as such. It connotes not the denial of the bodily, but its enhancement and transformation. Second, there is a pronounced future-thrust to Spirit-language: it points toward the fulfillment of God's plan and purpose for humankind. This fulfillment will be marked by an outpouring of God's Holy Spirit, effecting an unheard of intimacy between God and the people called to manifest God's glory in the world. Thus has the Lord promised: "And it shall come to pass on that day that I will pour out my Spirit on all flesh.

Your sons and your daughters shall prophesy; your old men shall dream dreams, and your young men shall see visions. Even upon the menservants and maidservants in those days, I will pour out my Spirit" (Joel 2:28-29).

3. The Spirit in the New Testament

As important as is the reality of the Spirit in the experience of the OT, it almost pales before the Spirit's presence and action in the NT. In the NT there abounds the conviction that the time of fulfillment has dawned, that the Spirit of God has indeed been poured out upon all flesh (cf. Acts 2:14-39 for Peter's discourse on the day of Pentecost in which the fulfillment of Joel's prophecy is proclaimed). The one through whom this has been accomplished is Jesus the Christ, *the* anointed one. Consequently, at the heart of the rites of christian initiation stands the proclamation of the gospel of Jesus Christ: whether in the form of an explicit reading from one of the four gospels, or in the pouring of water and the invocation of the triune name according to the charge of the risen Lord at the close of Matthew's gospel (Mt 28:19), or in the eucharistic memorial of Christ's self-gift and the epiclesis or invocation of the Spirit which brings the rites of initiation to completion.

A prime way in which the uniqueness and centrality of Jesus Christ is proclaimed in the NT is in terms of Jesus' unique relation to the Spirit of God. Thus, at the very beginning of Paul's Letter to the Romans, we read: "Paul, a servant of Jesus Christ, called to be an apostle, set apart for the gospel of God which he promised beforehand through his prophets in the holy scriptures, the gospel concerning his Son, who was descended from David according to the flesh and designated Son of God in power according to the Spirit of holiness by his resurrection from the dead, Jesus Christ our Lord" (Rom 1:1-4).

Many NT scholars suggest that Paul here is quoting an early christian hymn which celebrated Jesus Christ as the one "descended from David according to the flesh, designated Son of God in power according to the Spirit of holiness by his resurrection from the dead." The context of this affirmation of faith in Jesus Christ would then be a liturgical one: praise of God through Jesus Christ serves as the setting for the proclamation of the unique identity of Jesus. That identity is specified as being God's Son, a dignity revealed in the resurrection and attributed to the power of the Holy Spirit.

This appeal to the Spirit to specify the identity and role of Jesus is also apparent in the narratives of Jesus' baptism, recounted in each of the Synoptic gospels, and also referred to in the gospel of John (cf. Mt 3:13-17, Mk 1:9-11, Lk 3:21-22; also Jn 1:25-34). Though there are interesting variations in the accounts, what clearly emerges from them is a double confession of faith. On the one hand, Jesus' unique relation to God is placed prominently to the fore: Jesus is the "beloved Son" in whom God is "well pleased." This relationship to God, the "Abba" of Jesus' prayer and revelation, is constitutive for his own identity. On the other hand, that identity also finds clarification through Jesus' relation to the Spirit. He is the one who, in contrast to John the Baptist, will "baptize with the Holy Spirit" (an affirmation contained in each of the gospels). This "baptism with the Spirit" defines Jesus' mission. Moreover, Jesus is not merely the bearer of the Spirit, in the line of one of the prophets of old; he is the one through whose ministry the Spirit will be definitively bestowed. Thus, like the dove after the flood, the Spirit heralds a new creation, a new and redeemed people of God.

Significantly, it is the same Spirit who "drives" (Mark) or "leads" (Matthew, Luke) Jesus into the wilderness, the place of testing, the proverbial dwelling-place of evil spirits. During forty days, symbolic of Israel's journey through the desert, Jesus' vocation is put to the test; and here his sonship, his total filial dependence upon God is first vindicated. In the power of the Spirit, then, he returns to pursue his ministry which entails the continuing combat against all those forces which hinder the human from realizing its true relation to God and its own proper dignity. Jesus emerges from the desert to inaugurate in the Spirit the redeemed people of God. Hence a fitting commentary upon the whole of Jesus' ministry is given in the gospel of Luke when Jesus enters the synagogue at Nazareth and announces the fulfillment, in his person, of Isaiah's prophecy: "The Spirit of the Lord is upon me, because he has anointed me to preach good news to the poor" (Lk 4:18).

The accounts of the baptism, testing, and ministry of Jesus are not purely historical. They are theological and pastoral affirmations as well. They concern not only the identity and mission of Jesus, but also the identity and mission of the disciple who follows the way of the Lord. Thus, in moving through the gospel narratives, the reader is confronted with a two-fold issue of identity: who is Jesus? who is the disciple? The two questions are intimately related and interwined. The followers of Christ are led through a catechumenate of progressive discovery, until they are willingly plunged into the baptism of Jesus and accept it as their own. Only then will they begin to grasp what Jesus' baptism with the Spirit signifies and to what mission it impels.

It has become commonplace in NT studies to insist that the heart of Jesus' proclamation concerns the "kingdom" or "reign" of God; and that Jesus himself does not seem to refer to the Spirit with any great frequency. Yet the whole thrust of the gospels suggest that Jesus' entire ministry might best be understood as the exorcising of the unclean spirits which mar human communion with God and the establishing of a renewed people in the power of the Holy Spirit. For the kingdom of the Spirit, proclaimed and inaugurated by Jesus, is locked in combat with the kingdom of Satan; and with Jesus has appeared that "stronger one" who will unbind those whom Satan has held in bondage (cf. Lk 11:22).

The dual mission of exorcising evil and founding on solid rock God's redeemed people culminates in the death and resurrection of Jesus. Here is completed the baptism of the Lord; and from here the baptism of the disciple derives and receives its definition. The kingdom of the Spirit becomes fully manifest in the crucifixion and resurrection of the Son. The power of evil is absorbed and transformed in the very body of Jesus and every barrier to God is decisively broken down. If, in the early hymn cited by Paul, Jesus is designated "Son of God" at the resurrection, in the earliest of the Synoptics, Mark, the crucifixion itself becomes the setting for the confession of Jesus as "Son of God" (Mk 15:39). In George Montague's striking phrase: "Martyrdom, not miracles, is the ultimate testing of the Spirit" (Montague, p. 252).

What the Synoptics suggest, the gospel of John makes theologically explicit. An important assertion which John shares with the Synoptics is that Jesus, in contrast to the Baptist, will baptize with the Holy Spirit (Jn 1:33). This theme receives further development in the gospel of John in the course of Jesus' conversation with Nicodemus. There Jesus asserts: "Unless one is born of water and the Spirit, one cannot enter the kingdom of God. That which is born of the flesh is flesh, and that which is born of the Spirit is spirit" (Jn 3:5-6). Only through such birth in the Spirit can true life be attained. This acknowledgement, already present in the most insightful of the OT prophets, obtains in the NT a Christological focus. Jesus Christ is the way to true life, the giver of God's Spirit. He, who "comes from above," "gives the Spirit without measure" (Jn 3:34).

John's presentation of the Spirit as mediated through the person of Jesus Christ is further clarified in the great account of Jesus' appearance in Jerusalem on the Feast of Tabernacles. The evangelist recounts: "On the last day of the feast, the great day, Jesus stood up and proclaimed, 'If any one thirst, let that one come to me, and let the one who believes in me drink. As scripture has said, "Out of his heart shall flow rivers of living water"'" (Jn 7:37-38).

Then the evangelist himself supplies the interpretation: "Now this he said about the Spirit, which those who believed in him were to receive; for as yet the Spirit had not been given, because Jesus was not yet glorified" (Jn 7:39).

The giving of the Spirit, which several times in the gospel is foretold, is reserved to that hour in which Jesus is exalted, raised up. In John's profound vision Jesus' hour of glory is his elevation upon the throne of the cross, from which Jesus reigns as king. And from the cross, at the moment of the consummation of Jesus' mission, the Spirit is bestowed: "Jesus bowed his head and handed over the Spirit"(Jn 19:30).

Jesus' own baptism in the Spirit is followed immediately by the baptism of his disciples. For at the foot of the cross stand the mother of Jesus and the disciple whom Jesus loved, representative of those who will believe in his name. It is they who are the initial recipients of the Spirit's bestowal; they who, when Jesus' side is pierced, witness the outpouring of blood and water (cf. Jn 19:34). Thus what Jesus had promised at the Feast of Tabernacles comes to fulfillment: Jesus' hour of glory is also the hour of the Spirit.

What was accomplished in principle upon the cross finds further explication on the evening of the day the Lord rose from the dead. When the dispirited disciples are huddled together in fear and hopelessness, the risen Jesus appears in their midst and, breathing upon them, bestows the very breath and power of new life. The appearance of the risen one and his giving of the Spirit entails a commissioning of the disciples: "'As the Father has sent me, even so I send you.' And when he had said this, he breathed on them, and said to them, 'Receive the Holy Spirit. If you forgive the sins of any they are forgiven; if you retain the sins of any, they are retained'" (Jn 20:21-23).

The centrality of Jesus' death and resurrection as the saving act par excellence is the common witness and kerygma of the NT. Both implicitly and explicitly the NT links the bestowal of the Spirit to Christ's paschal mystery, the transformation of death itself into new life, the harrowing of the power of evil whose threat and surrogate is death. What was hinted at and anticipated in Jesus' baptism and testing here attains its full import and victory.

Now the one who has consummated God's definitive at-one-ment of humankind must owe his entire being and existence to the initiative of God. Luke attributes Jesus' very conception to God's Holy Spirit: "The Holy Spirit will come upon you, and the power of the Most High will overshadow you; therefore the child to be born will be called holy, the Son of God" (Lk 1:35). And Matthew concurs: "Joseph, son of David, do not fear to take Mary your wife, for that which is conceived in her is of the Holy Spirit. She will bear a son, and you shall call his name Jesus, for he will save his people from their sins." Thus the whole of the existence of Jesus transpires in the Holy Spirit: from conception through baptism to ministry and salvific death, culminating in resurrected life in the Spirit.

The outcome of Jesus' ministry and paschal mystery is the new community, already foreshadowed in the calling of disciples and the choosing of the twelve; but definitively founded in the death and resurrection of the Lord: the eschatological baptism into which believers are henceforth immersed. The church appears, then, not as a mere aftermath of Jesus' life in the Spirit; it is that life's organic outflow. We have already seen indications of this in the close connection which John's gospel postulates between the glorification of Jesus, the giving of the Spirit, and the new life of believers. The same organic interrelationship lies at the heart of Luke's vision in his unique two-part history: the history of Jesus and that of the new community of Jews and Greeks, which issues in the Spirit from the crucified and risen Savior.

The conclusion of the gospel of Luke takes place in Jerusalem, the holy city to which the way of Jesus has led. But it is apparent that the whole story has not yet been told. For the last words of the risen Lord to the disciples in Luke's gospel are an instruction and a promise: "Behold, I send the promise of my Father upon you; but stay in the city, until you are clothed with power from on high" (Lk 24:49). The reader of the gospel might well be unsure of the reference intended. Who or what is the "promise" of the Father, and what will be the effect of being clothed "with power from on high"? In the Acts of the Apostles Luke provides the response.

Reiterating his injunction to await in Jerusalem "the promise of the Father," Jesus continues: "before many days you shall be baptized with the Holy Spirit" (Acts 1:5). Then, in reply to the apostles' inquiry about when the kingdom would be restored to Israel, Jesus further speci-fies both the promise made and the scope of the mission it would enable: "you shall receive power when the Holy Spirit has come upon you; and you shall be my witnesses in Jerusalem and in all Judea and Samaria and to the end of the earth" (Acts 1:8). From the very beginning of Acts, then, the entire narrative is put under the sign of the Holy Spirit, who will guide the way of the church from Jerusalem even to Rome itself.

One of the highlights of that narrative is Luke's account, in the second chapter of Acts, of the pentecostal outpouring of the Spirit upon the small community of believers, moving them spontaneously to proclamation and praise. A crowd gathers, composed of Jews from all corners of the earth assembled in Jerusalem for the celebration of the feast.

With astonishment all understand the paean of praise in their own tongue. Then Peter arises and in the first of the great apostolic discourses in Acts proclaims the fulfillment of Joel's prophecy, confesses the Lordship of Jesus, and promises that the same Spirit will come upon all who repent and are baptized in Jesus' name (cf. Acts 2:14-39).

Striking and unique as the occurrence is, one also notes that the way of the christian community is marked by a number of other "pentecostal" outpourings of the Spirit. Each enlarges the boundaries of the redeemed people and further overcomes the dispersal and division which the babel of tongues and nations has introduced into God's plan of salvation. Thus, through Peter and John, the Holy Spirit is received by the Samaritans who had been baptized in the name of Jesus (Acts 8:14-17). Through the Spirit's descent upon Cornelius and his household, in the course of Peter's preaching to them, the body of believers for the first time welcomes gentile converts (Acts 10:44-48). Finally, the missionary journey of Paul and Barnabas is initiated and guided by the Spirit (Acts 13:2-4), as is the confirmation of their enterprise at the so-called Council of Jerusalem (Acts 15:28).

Throughout Acts, then, the Holy Spirit is shown extending the salvation accomplished through Jesus Christ by inspiring bold witness to Jesus, joyful praise of God, ongoing discernment of God's will, steadfast courage in adversity. The Spirit acts in a manner that is sovereign and free; and the community must learn the ways of the Spirit and be prepared for new beginnings and new journeys. Yet Jesus ever provides the point of reference and criterion. The "name of Jesus" and the "power of the Spirit" are the constants of the christian way.

The organic unity in the Spirit between Christ and church, which structures Luke's two-part composition, is also a key theological affirmation of the Apostle Paul. In Paul this takes the form of an understanding of the church as the very body of Christ. "You are the body of Christ," he reminds the Corinthians, "and individually members of it" (1 Cor 12:27). Membership and unity in the body of Christ is the fruit of the one Spirit which all have received. "For by one Spirit we were all baptized into one body—Jews or Greeks, slaves or free—and all were made to drink of one Spirit" (1 Cor 12:13). This Pauline vision accords a primacy to the whole body as the outcome of the paschal mystery and the goal of all God's action in the world. From this vision derives Paul's practical instruction. Thus, for example, the criterion for discerning authentic gifts or charisms of the Spirit is precisely whether they contribute to the building up of the church (cf. 1 Cor 14:12). Each individual may, indeed, be given and even legitimately seek a particular charism of the Spirit; but it must always be used "for the common good" (1 Cor 12:7).

This essentially "corporate vision" of the Apostle (based, perhaps, upon his own privileged experience of the risen Lord) finds distinctive expression in Paul's teaching about Christ as the "new" (the definitive or eschatological) Adam. In contrast to the first Adam, whom Paul characterizes as "a living soul"; the new Adam, Christ, has become "a life-giving Spirit" (1 Cor 15:45), whose resurrected body is a "spiritual body," a body transformed in the Spirit of God (1 Cor 15:44). Believers, who have been baptized into Christ, have been baptized into that body crucified in the flesh, but now alive in the Spirit. They too, through Christ, participate in that "spiritual body." The full radicality of the perception needs to be stressed again and again: "Do you not know that your body is a temple of the Holy Spirit within you, which you have from God?" (1 Cor 6:19). The pronouns here and elsewhere are plural, corporate.

There is ever, in Paul, a close reciprocity between being "in Christ" and being "in the Spirit." Both terms are corporate in connotation; both define the new people which God is creating in these last days. While Christ gives concrete form and content to the Spirit, the Spirit makes present and extends the reality of Christ. The whole of God's age-old plan of salvation is fulfilled in the "new covenant" (2 Cor 3:6), which is conjointly the work of Christ and the Spirit. Hence Paul can give this almost elliptical summary of his teaching: "the Lord is the Spirit, and where the Spirit of the Lord is, there is freedom" (2 Cor 3:17).

The NT discloses the intimacy and depth of God's plan to be nothing less than that of making believers sons and daughters after the image of God's beloved Son. Jesus Christ, as the new Adam, is the beginning and end of all God's ways with humankind, the alpha and the omega (Rev 1:8). Christ is "the first-born of all creation" and also "the first-born from the dead" (Col 1:15, 18).

But, for this very reason, Christ is not alone. Others are required to "fill up" the body, the new people of God's sons and daughters through Jesus Christ. The Holy Spirit who evokes this new creation is thus most personally revealed as "the Spirit of Christ" (Rom 8:9) and inseparably, "the Spirit of God who raised Jesus from the dead" (Rom 8:11). It follows that the Spirit we receive through Christ does more than merely inspire certain distinctive actions. It transforms our very being, thereby establishing us in a new relationship with God. "For all who are led by the Spirit of God are sons and daughters of God. For you did not receive the spirit of slavery to fall back into fear, but you have received the spirit of adoption. When we cry, 'Abba! Father!' it is the Spirit bearing witness with our spirit that we are children of God" (Rom 8:14-16).

Here we attain the height and depth of NT meditation upon the mystery of salvation, accomplished through Christ and realized ever anew by the Spirit. Here Paul and John concur. All has been accomplished with the revelation of Christ, God's unique offspring and image. All remains to be accomplished as the Spirit gathers into one God's scattered sons and daughters. This at-one-ment, already accomplished and still to be accomplished is not only corporate of its very nature; it also bears cosmic resonances. For "all creation waits with eager longing for the revealing of the children of God . . . and not only the creation, but we ourselves who have the first fruits of the Spirit, groan inwardly as we wait for adoption, the redemption of our body" (Rom 8:19, 23).

The Spirit-guided process, in realizing humanity's true vocation and dignity, will effect authentic liberation. The Spirit of adoption is the Spirit of true freedom. Personal weakness, hostile powers, persecution, and even death no longer stand as barriers to the Spirit's sway. Through Christ the Spirit has penetrated and permeated all.

A special NT tradition concerning the Holy Spirit is found in the Gospel of John in those chapters which recount Jesus'"discourse at the last supper." This rich and theologically subtle narrative contains within it Jesus' words and promise concerning the "Paraclete," who is identified in a distinctive way as the "Spirit of truth" (Jn 14:17, 15:26, 16:13) and the "Holy Spirit" (Jn 14:26). This Paraclete (Greek: advocate or counselor) plays a decisive role in the gospel's cosmic drama between Jesus and the "world," between those who are people of the truth and those who, by rejecting the truth, show themselves to be people of the lie. In this drama and trial the Paraclete's role is to "bear witness" on behalf of Jesus (Jn 15:26) and on behalf of the truth who is Jesus. In doing so, the Paraclete both "convicts the world of sin, of justice, and of judgment" (Jn 16:8), and leads the disciples of Jesus "into all truth" (Jn 16:13). Vis á vis the world, therefore, the Paraclete appears as prosecutor; while, vis á vis the disciples, the Paraclete appears as defender.

In the gospel of John the NT understanding of the God of christian faith has attained its most nuanced elaboration in trinitarian terms. Though we do not yet find a formal doctrine of the Trinity, we perceive the basis for the doctrine which will be explicitly articulated in the early councils of the church. In this regard the Johannine teaching about the Paraclete makes an important contribution. For, as Paraclete, the Holy Spirit assumes its most personal mode, such that the gospel repeatedly speaks of the Paraclete using the personal pronoun (Jn 14:26, 15:26, 16:8, 13). Moreover, by being designated "another Paraclete" by Jesus (Jn 14:16), the Paraclete assumes the personal characteristics which the gospel attributes to

Jesus himself. One discerns, therefore, a clear trinitarian pattern in the theme of "witnessing" which pervades John's gospel: Jesus bears witness to the Father; the Paraclete bears witness to Jesus in and through the disciples.

What must be reiterated in concluding this sketch of the NT's experience of the Spirit is the decisive originality of the revelation realized through Jesus Christ. Through Christ, especially his death and resurrection, a new sense of God impresses itself upon christian believers: a God whose richness and generosity, majesty and intimacy, height and depth can only be thankfully acknowledged in terms which embrace Father, Christ and Spirit. Concomitant with and inseparable from this sense of God is a new appreciation of human vocation and dignity: of its "predestination" in Christ (Rom 8:29) and its destiny in the Spirit to be the very "dwelling place of God" (Eph 2:22).

The entire NT groans and rejoices in hope, aware that this destiny, though inaugurated, has not yet been fully attained. Hence the tension of "already" and "not yet" governs the whole of christian experience in the world. Nor does life in the Spirit dissolve the tension; paradoxically, it heightens the tension. For the Spirit as "first fruits" (Rom 8:23), as the "down payment" which serves as "guarantee" of the glory still to be revealed (2 Cor 1:22; Eph 1:14), urges the disciples toward the full realization of God's plan of salvation. On this transforming journey of discipleship, which baptism initiates, the guiding star for the community of believers ever remains the trinitarian faith summed up in the great benediction at the close of Paul's Second Letter to the Corinthians: "the grace of the Lord Jesus Christ, the love of God, and the communion of the Holy Spirit" (2 Cor. 13:14).

4. Tradition and the Spirit

The new covenant in the Spirit, which the Christian enters through baptism, is a sharing in the very filial relation of Jesus to the God he calls "Abba," "gracious Father"; a relation ratified on the cross and renewed beyond death in the inexhaustible life of resurrection. Hence the Spirit is both the Spirit of Jesus and of the Father: the Spirit of the One who raises Jesus to life; the Spirit of Jesus who receives life in full. Indeed, what the Spirit-language of the NT points to is just this relational giving and receiving, wedding believers to God and to one another in a vast network of praise and joyful service in the Spirit.

The relational sensitivity, this passion for communion, distinguishes the christian understanding of the identity of God and of the disciple. God is the triune God, the God of relationality, of overflowing goodness and graciousness; the disciple is member of the body of Christ, incorporated into a cosmic communion whose animating principle is God's Holy Spirit. Christian existence manifests, therefore, a trinitarian structure: it moves in the Spirit through Christ to the God who will be "everything to every one" (1 Cor 15:28). In this movement a new self and a new community are called forth: recreated in the image of Christ who is "all and in all" (Col 3:11).

The trinitarian structure of christian experience, though clearly discernible in the NT, receives further clarification and more technical articulation in the course of the ensuing centuries. The richness of christian experience requires time and effort to disclose its full import; and "tradition" represents just this unfolding of revelation given through Christ and continually appropriated in the Holy Spirit. This appropriation occurs both in Spirit-inspired living and Spirit-guided reflection, as Vatican II's *Constitution on Divine Revelation* makes clear (cf. D.V. 8).

Theological attention in the first centuries of christian history focused most explicitly upon the identity and person of Jesus Christ; with a decisive breakthrough taking place at the Council of Nicaea (325 A.D.), which defined that Jesus Christ is "of the same being or substance as God the Father" (the famous *"homoousios"* doctrine). The great champion of the Council of Nicaea was Athanasius of Alexandria, a figure of monumental importance in christian tradition. The guiding sensitivity of his arduous pastoral and theological labors concerned the issue of human salvation. For Athanasius nothing less than God could establish and assure human wholeness and re-creation. If Christ is not God, we have no sure access to transformation.

The coherence of Athanasius' vision compelled him to extend his line of reflection to include the Holy Spirit. Thus, whereas the creed of the Council of Nicaea had merely concluded tersely with the confession: "we believe ... in the Holy Spirit" (D.S. 125), Athanasius himself recognized, in his later writings, the need also to speak of the Holy Spirit as "of the same substance" as God. Once more, concern for human salvation guided the advance. The Holy Spirit who works the sanctification and transformation of the human cannot be other than God, who is the blessed source and goal of all things. The God of christian faith, therefore, is irreducibly triune: Father, Son, and Holy Spirit. Those who deny the divinity of the Holy Spirit destroy, thereby, the Trinity.

The so-called Cappadocians (Basil of Caesarea, Gregory of Nazianzus, and Gregory of Nyssa) mediated a further theological advance during the second half of the fourth century by confronting and wrestling with further questions. If the Spirit is not only the sanctifying gift bestowed by God upon the creature called to share the divine life, but is itself intrinsic to the Giver, then should not the

Spirit be confessed as God, thus explicating yet more clearly the God of christian faith and experience as fully trinitarian?

Basil, in effect, responded affirmatively in his treatise, *On the Holy Spirit,* by stressing that the Spirit, together with the Father and the Son, is to be worshipped and glorified. He insisted that christians' prayer of praise to the Trinity need not only take the classic form: "glory to the Father, through the Son, in the Spirit"; but might legitimately give glory "to the Father, to the Son, and to the Holy Spirit." Nonetheless, Basil still refrained from explicitly calling the Holy Spirit "God."

Basil's friend and fellow-bishop, Gregory of Nazianzus, draws out ineluctably the logic of faith. If the Spirit is truly worshipped in the liturgy, if the Spirit initiates the process of human transformation in baptism and sustains it through the outpouring of grace upon grace, then the Spirit cannot be other than God, proceeding from the Father's bounty.

Finally, Gregory of Nyssa, Basil's brother, who combined in a unique way speculative brilliance and spiritual depth, helped provide the terminological clarification that unmistakably affirmed the consubstantial unity, yet distinct modes of existence of Father, Son, and Spirit. They were one in being or substance (*ousia*), but three in subsistence (*hypostasis,* which, in the Latin tradition, would be translated as *persona*). This decisive linguistic advance, this elucidation of the grammar of faith in the God of christian experience, never resulted, at the hands of the Cappadocians, in a rationalistic reduction of God's Mystery. The words were necessary, but ever inadequate pointers to the living God, revealed in Jesus and realized in the Spirit, who remains ever beyond human categories and capacities.

The Cappadocian achievement received formal recognition in the Council held in Constantinople in 381 A.D., whose amplification of the creed of Nicaea remains normative for christian faith. Whereas, as we have seen, the Nicene Creed had merely confessed: "we believe . . . in the Holy Spirit"; the expanded version, known as the Nicene-Constantinopolitan Creed, contains the familiar confession of the Holy Spirit as "the Lord and Giver of life, who proceeds from the Father, who together with the Father and Son is adored and glorified, who spoke through the prophets" (D.S. 150).

In tracing thus briefly the development of the church's dogma concerning the Holy Spirit in the crucial formative centuries of its history, two features should be brought into greater relief. On the one hand, the development is rooted in the church's liturgical and spiritual experience and seeks to illuminate more fully that experience. Because the Spirit is experienced as the One who endows humankind with new and divine life, because the Spirit is worshipped, the Spirit cannot be other than the divine Source of blessings. On the other hand, with the raising of and response to the questions posed by faith and given form in determinate cultural settings, dogma contributes a genuine illumination and enrichment of experience. There ensues what Bernard Lonergan has termed a "differentiation of consciousness," an advance in appreciation for what is at stake in an issue and a genuine insight into its resolution. From this perspective, dogma is an authentic attainment in the Spirit, from which there can be no turning back to a less differentiated stage without risking experiential and not merely intellectual loss.

One of the fruits of this intellectual advance is manifest in the person who is, arguably, the Latin Church's most influential theologian: Augustine of Hippo.

Starting from the common dogmatic tradition of both East and West, Augustine's passionately probing mind sought a fuller understanding of the faith which had transformed his life. Perhaps the richest fruit of his speculative-spiritual synthesis is his work, *On the Trinity,* which he labored over for twenty years.

In meditating upon the Holy Spirit and what is proper to the Spirit within the very life of God, Augustine associates the Spirit in a special way with love: with the mutual love of Father and Son. This inner-trinitarian property of the Spirit is the foundation for the Spirit's salvific function as the bond of love which constitutes the life of the christian community. Deeply embedded in Augustine's experience and thought are a yearning for and an insistence upon unity: the unity of God, the unity of the church, the unity of the person whom sin has fragmented. The Spirit, as the mutual love of the persons within God, is also the unifying bond of love amongst human persons, called into communion with the triune God. In the Spirit the city of God grows to reflect the glory of the One who is its never-ending life.

This perspective, so congenial to Augustine, decisively influenced the development of the entire theological tradition of the Western Church for well over one thousand years, setting its particular sensitivities and even supplying much of the language it would employ. It led to one outcome which, though justifiable as a theological position, contributed to the deplorable division between Eastern and Western Christianity: the *filioque* controversy.

The Nicene-Constantinopolitan Creed confessed that the Holy Spirit "proceeds from the Father." In the centuries following Augustine, under the sway of this theological and pastoral genius, the theology of the Latin West developed the creed's confession further by the addition of the words: "and from the Son." In doing so it reflected Augustine's perspective upon the Mystery of the Trinity and sealed the intimate relation between the work of Christ and of the Spirit. By contrast, the Greek Eastern Church saw in this development not only a slighting of the Father's originative function within the Trinity, but also an undue subordination of the Spirit to Christ.

Theological differences were exacerbated by cultural misunderstandings and political considerations, all of which conspired to bring about that schism which has rent the church of Christ. Different perspectives upon the inexhaustible Mystery of God, deriving from different sensitivities and legitimate theological insights, hardened into uncompromising stances. What might have remained complementary and reciprocally enriching became conflictual and mutually condemnatory. In light of this sad history, one rejoices in the moving symbolism of the encounter in Jerusalem, during the Second Vatican Council, of Pope Paul VI and the Orthodox Patriarch Athenagoras I, and the later exchange of visits between them both in Istanbul and in Rome. This parabolic action, one can only prayerfully hope, presages a new age of the Spirit who has spoken and continues to speak through the prophets.

5. Vatican II under the Sign of the Spirit

The danger of an excessively polemical theology lies in the narrowing of vision which follows in its wake. This occurred not only as a consequence of the schism with the East, but, in an even more pronounced fashion, in the centuries following the Protestant Reformation in the West. In many ways the experience and theology of the Holy Spirit was a prime casualty of these conflicts, not surprising if the Spirit is one of peace and communion, not of discord and division. Within Roman Catholicism the "forget-

fulness" of the Holy Spirit was abetted by two other trends, each intelligible and even defensible in itself, but which assumed a somewhat isolated and disproportionate development.

The first of these, already beginning in the late Middle Ages, saw a gradual breakdown of the speculative-spiritual synthesis, so characteristic of the age of the Cappadocians and Augustine, and still flourishing in the great medieval syntheses of Thomas and Bonaventure. In its place there arose a division into dogmatic theology on the one hand and spiritual theology on the other. The former concentrated upon the Church's past dogmatic formulations; the latter concerned itself with the individual's personal relation to God. Whatever the merits of either enterprise, both represented an impoverishment of the rich experience of life in the Spirit, whose matrix must be the whole christian community and whose goal is the transformation not of individuals, but of persons in relation.

The second trend consisted in the increasing institutionalization of the church, with prerogatives claimed for its institutional office-holders and a consequent reduction of active involvement on the part of the laity. One lamentable outcome of this was that the legitimate distinction between church and world hardened into a dichotomy. There followed the one-sided and still prevalent association of the Spirit with things ecclesiastical, while things secular were relegated to the merely "temporal" sphere. Lost to sight in this process was the full biblical vision of the Spirit working the transformation of all creation in Christ and effecting that communion of which the church is prototype and sacrament.

In so many respects, then, the Second Vatican Council represents an inspired effort to repair divisions of centuries-long duration, to recapture a deeper sense of tradition, rooted in biblical experience and in the early centuries of the undivided church, rather than in the narrowly construed positions of a more recent and polemical past. This Council, aptly celebrated by the Extraordinary Synod of 1985 as "a grace of God and a gift of the Holy Spirit," was convoked by Pope John XXIII and immediately placed under the aegis of the Holy Spirit in the prayer composed by the Pope to be offered in preparation for the Council.

This sign of the Spirit continued to leaven the labors of the Council and influenced most notably the Council's renewed vision of the church as set forth in its *Dogmatic Constitution on the Church (Lumen Gentium),* and its consideration of the Church's mission, discussed in the *Pastoral Constitution on the Church in the Modern World (Gaudium et Spes).*

In *Lumen Gentium* institutional concerns, though present and significant, are clearly subordinate. The primacy rests upon the gracious action of the triune God whose life, communicated through Christ in the Spirit, establishes that trinitarian communion which is the very essence of church (L.G. c. 1: "The Mystery of Church"). The whole church participates in that mystery of life which begins with baptism. This life takes concrete shape through the particular gifts or charisms of the Spirit with which the whole people of God is richly endowed (L.G., c. 2: "The People of God"). Within this people, indispensable offices of pastoral service and authority in the Spirit are exercised by the bishops who, in communion with the pope, the bishop of Rome, constitute a truly collegial body (L.G., c. 3: "The Hierarchical Structure of the Church"). However, despite these different ministerial roles within the one people of God, the entire people is called to holiness through a responsible nourishing of the gift of the Spirit each has

received (L.G., c. 5: "The Call of the Whole Church to Holiness"). Finally, this people of God constitutes an eschatological reality in a two-fold sense. It bears the gift of the Spirit of the new creation, poured out by Christ, the risen Lord; but it also is charged with responsibility to allow the sanctifying Spirit to permeate ever more fully its action and to direct its way (L.G., c. 7: "The Eschatological Nature of the Pilgrim Church").

The way of the church transpires, of course, in history. And in *Gaudium et Spes* it is evident that the church cannot be insulated from history, but is immersed in history. Moreover, that history, authored by the diverse peoples and cultures of the world, though always ambiguous because of sin, is not intrinsically hostile to the church and its mission.

Indeed, there is a firm basis for hope and dialogue, since the Spirit is also at work beyond the church, preparing for and pointing to Christ. As *Gaudium et Spes* declares: "Since Christ died for all, and since the ultimate vocation of humankind is in fact one, and divine, we must believe that the Holy Spirit, in a manner known only to God, offers to every person the possibility of being associated with this paschal mystery of Christ" (G.S. 22). Consequently, the Council can confidently affirm: "Christ is now at work in the hearts of men and women through the energy of his Spirit. He not only arouses a desire for the age to come, but also vivifies, purifies, and strengthens those generous impulses by which the human family strives to render its life more human and to submit the whole earth to this goal" (G.S. 38).

Under the sign of the Spirit, then, the Second Vatican Council has begun to integrate once more what centuries of one-sided dogmatism and clericalism had sundered: experience and doctrine, church and world, clergy and laity.

So many of the developments in theology and pastoral practice brought into being since the Council have explicitly or implicitly been placed under the same sign of the Spirit. The Council's teaching that the local church, called and gathered in the Spirit, is the concrete actualization of the church of Christ (cf. L.G. 26), and that communion of these local churches constitutes the universal people of God, sharing the diverse gifts of the Spirit (cf. L.G. 23), has led to a new appreciation of collegiality on all levels of the Church's existence. The liturgical renewal, mandated by the Council, has made available to ecclesial assemblies new eucharistic prayers, a prominent feature of which is the restoration of the epiclesis: the prayer invoking the Holy Spirit upon the gifts offered by the community that they might indeed be transformed into the body and blood of the Lord.

The extremely significant post-conciliar publication of the Rite of Christian Initiation of Adults (RCIA) restores the early church's practice of the catechumenate as not merely an instruction in the doctrines of the faith, but an introduction into the life of the Spirit. This formation in the Spirit finds its proper setting within the community of believers and draws upon the Spirit-bestowed gifts of numerous members of the community. The recognition, promoted by the Council, that many are endowed with such gifts of the Spirit, has led to the formal commissioning of many to act in the name of the church, using their gifts for the church's public good and order. Hence the Council itself restored the diaconate as a permanent order in the church and opened the way for the rich profusion of lay ministries which followed.

Finally, the remarkable series of papal and synodal documents on issues of peace and justice, which drew inspiration from the Council's teaching in *Gaudium et Spes,* often refers explicitly to the Holy Spirit as the ultimate theological justification for the church's engagement in social ministry. To all of these developments one might fittingly apply Paul's sage observation to the Corinthians: "All these are inspired by one and the same Spirit, who apportions to each one individually as he wills" (1 Cor 12:11).

All of the Vatican II and post-Vatican II developments we have traced combine, in newly integrated fashion, experience and doctrine, each illuminating and supporting the other. In this regard, a remarkable phenomenon within post-Vatican II Catholicism is the "charismatic movement," which uniquely joins experience of the Holy Spirit and teaching about the Spirit. For many the charismatic movement has mediated a new experience of the presence and power of the Spirit in the christian community and in individual lives. It has also led to a new and deeper appreciation for the implications and responsibilities to life in the Spirit as that which makes for the true specificity of christian existence. The charismatic movement has played a major role in renewing in our time the NT's promise of the Spirit and the NT's insistence that discernment of spirits remains an ongoing necessity for the whole community.

Reflecting in 1973 on what the Council had achieved, Pope Paul VI presciently remarked: "The Christology and particularly the ecclesiology of the Council must be succeeded by a new study of and devotion to the Holy Spirit, precisely as the indispensable complement to the teaching of the Council." Paul VI's desire has been realized, in part, by the growing number of studies devoted to the theology of the Holy Spirit, to "pneumatology"; and by the increasing awareness that authentic reform in the church must move beyond the merely institutional or intellectual to the depths of transformation which only the Spirit can reveal and empower. Significant in this regard is the issuance by Pope John Paul II, on Pentecost Sunday 1986, of an encyclical dedicated to the Holy Spirit and entitled, "The Lord and Giver of Life" (*Dominum et Vivificantem*).

In this encyclical John Paul II dwells meditatively upon the coming close of the second millennium after Christ and the approach of the third; and is prompted to place the journey of the church through history under the explicit sign of the Holy Spirit, who is the gift of the new creation. This Spirit draws men and women into the fullness of God's life of personal giving and receiving. Because the Spirit is the Spirit of God's truth, all that is wayward in the human stands convicted, so that the heart of stone may be truly transformed into a heart of flesh.

The encyclical starkly contrasts those signs of slavery and death in contemporary society with the sign of the Spirit who gives life; and urges that, as we journey toward the year two thousand, humankind place itself under the liberating lordship of the Spirit. Christians, in particular, are called to consider anew, in light of the signs of our times, that baptismal renunciation and conversion, into which they have been initiated by the Spirit. For, by an ongoing surrender to this Holy Spirit, creation is christened and the whole Christ comes to birth, the communion of God's sons and daughters in the Spirit.

See Initiation, Christian; Vatican II

Yves Congar, *I Believe in the Holy Spirit,* 3 vols, New York: Seabury and London: Geoffrey Chapman, 1983. James D.G. Dunn, *Jesus and the Spirit,* Philadelphia: Westminster, 1975 and London, S.C.M., 1978. Alasdair I.C. Heron, *The Holy Spirit,* Philadelphia: Westminster, Basingstoke: Marshall, Morgan & Scott, 1983. George T. Montague, *The Holy Spirit: Growth of a Biblical Tradition,* New York: Paulist, 1976. John V. Taylor, *The Go-Between God: The Holy Spirit and the Christian Mission,* Philadelphia: Fortress, 1973, and London: S.C.M., 1975.

ROBERT P. IMBELLI

HOMILY
See Preaching

HOMOEANS
One of the parties of Arians who maintained that Christ was similar (*homoios*) to the Father.
See Arianism, Homoousios

HOMOIOUSIANS
The party of the Arians who maintained that Christ was of like substance (*homoiousios*) with the Father.
See Arianism, Homoousios

HOMOOUSIOS
A Greek term meaning "of the same substance," adopted by the Council of Nicaea to state the orthodox faith against Arian denials of the divinity of Christ. In St. Athanasius' interpretation of the term, it means that all divine predicates made of the Father can also be made of the Son, except the name "Father." At the Council of Chalcedon, *homoousios* was also used to state that the one Christ was of the same substance as the Father in his divinity and of the same substance as we humans in his humanity.
See Chalcedon, Council of; Jesus Christ; Nicaea, Council of

HOMOSEXUALITY
Homosexuality is a predominant and persistent psychosexual attraction toward and preference for persons of the same gender. Homosexuality goes beyond genitality, encompassing the totality of the person's affective response to others. A distinction is made in contemporary science and ethical literature between homosexual tendencies of an occasional or temporary nature which might exist in an otherwise heterosexual person and the

deeply ingrained and substantially irreversible orientation of a homosexual person. Same-gender sexual acts which might occur during certain stages of human growth or under certain circumstances are not necessarily indicative of a homosexual orientation. Psychosocial sexual research in this century has ascertained the importance of there being a balance between the hetero- and the homo-sexual components present in every human person in order to achieve healthy interpersonal relationships with persons of the same or the other gender. Reacting against the pejorative connotations associated with the label "homosexual" in western culture, many same-sex oriented persons prefer to be called "gay" (male) or "lesbian" (female).

The etiology of sexual orientation, whether homosexual or heterosexual, remains a matter of speculation and continuing scientific research. Theories range from genetic and biological causality to learned behavior resulting from parental influences or early childhood experiences. Basic sexual orientation is considered to be relatively fixed by age five or six. It is estimated that approximately ten percent of human society cross-culturally is homosexually oriented. Not all will act out genitally and some will develop heterosexual lifestlye patterns in conformity with general societal expectations. Attempts to change sexual orientation may alter some overt sexual behavior but seldom effects change in feelings, desires, or sexual fantasy. Because homosexuality is so little understood by a predominantly heterosexual society, homophobic attitudes and unfounded stereotyping coalesce to create an often oppressive social environment of the homosexual. Resulting psychological and behavioral problems led some to believe that homosexuality itself was a pathology or mental illness. This contention is less prevalent today, but the homophobia has not lessened appreciably.

Evidence of homosexual behavior is recorded among peoples of all cultures and religious beliefs. Societal reactions toward the homosexual vary from acceptance to active persecution. Within those two poles one encounters civilizations where homosexuality took on institutionalized cultic significance or was simply ignored as a social phenomenon. Among Judeo-christian cultures the influence of certain scriptural references has produced a strongly negative attitude toward homosexuality and the homosexual person.

Homosexual activity when encountered or referred to in the OT and NT is condemned. Modern biblical scholarship, however, suggests that the condemnation in the OT is often directed against homosexual acts by heterosexual persons, especially when the situation suggests rape (Gen 19, Sodom and Gomorrah), or against acts in a context with idolatrous connotations (Lev 18:22; 20:13, the Leviticus Holiness Code), or which are seen as violations of social justice demands for hospitality (Isa 1:9; Ezek 16:46-51; Jer 23:14). Both male and female homosexual relationships are condemned in a NT citation as an expression of idolatry (Rom 1:25-27) and same-sex genital acts are mentioned among those which violate God's law and exclude the perpetrator from the Kingdom of heaven (Rom 1:25-27; 1 Cor 69:10; 1 Tm 1:9-10). Most modern exegetes acknowledge the difficulty of determining the precise meaning of these texts and the consequent problem of applying them ethically to condemn homosexuals or their genital acts. Cultural and religious attitudes in the Judeo-Christian world relative to homosexual rape, idolatrous fertility practices, rejection of Greco-Roman pederasty, the non-procreative waste of male semen, violation of a guest's rights, and promiscuity all color attempts to interpret and apply these texts accurately and ethically. That the scriptural texts cited do not address and could not have addressed in those ages the question of homosexual *orientation* is clear. The contemporary question of homosexual acts between consenting adults in loving relationships was neither the question nor the context addressed in the scriptural passages traditionally noted in discussions about the morality of homosexual behavior. Despite these acknowledged academic difficulties, the scriptural passages have contributed to and reinforced strong negative attitudes toward homosexual persons and actions.

Early christian church moral theology took a somewhat tolerant, though not approving, stance toward homosexuality, judging those acts in much the same fashion as it did heterosexual acts. Natural law arguments were brought against same-sex acts in the Middle Ages (S.Th. I-II, Q. 154) on the ground that such genital expression could not conform to the procreative ordering of the natural finality of genitality. Thus, Aquinas, in his moral evaluation of homosexual acts writes: ". . . a sin against nature in which the natural order itself is violated is a sin against God who is the creator of that order." Hostility toward homosexuals became largely the rule in western society into our present century.

Moral theological positions on homosexual orientation and genital expression fall within several schools of thought.

(1) The traditional and official Roman Catholic teaching judges homosexual acts to be "intrinsically evil," that is, of their very nature disordered acts. Responding to the findings of other human sciences in regard to the genesis of sexual orientation, the church insists that despite homosexually oriented persons' being not responsible for their essentially flawed condition, as "Christians who are homosexual [they] are called, as all of us, to a chaste life." Concretely, this means total abstinence from genital expression even in those relationships which are otherwise potentially life and love giving. This is the position taken by official Roman Catholic magisterial documents which argue that, since in God's creative plan genital sexual expressions must be open to their life (procreative) and love (unitive) giving potentials, homosexual acts will always be "'intrinsically disordered' and able in no case to be approved of" (cf. No. 3, *The Pastoral Care of Homosexual Persons,* Oct. 1, 1986). Reacting to an "overly benign interpretation" accorded the homosexual condition itself by some Catholic moral theologians and pastoral ministers, current church documents insist that "although the particular inclination of the homosexual person is not a sin, it is a more or less strong tendency ordered toward an intrinsic moral evil and thus the inclination itself must be seen as an objective disorder" (*The Pastoral Care*). Pastoral ministers are directed to advise the homosexual person that the living out of this orientation in homosexual activity is not a morally acceptable option.

(2) Some more fundamentalist christian traditions have rejected as immoral both the "unnatural acts" and the homosexual orientation, viewing the latter as a chosen condition in violation of what are judged to be clear and literal condemnations of homosexuality by God in the scriptures. Frequently, proponents of this position have harassed and persecuted gays and lesbians.

(3) Another school of thought, while viewing homosexual acts as "essentially imperfect," accords homosexual persons a more qualified acceptance. Heterosexuality is still accepted as God's intention revealed in nature. Persons who find themselves, however, through no conscious choice of their own, homosexually oriented should, first, seek a corrective to their condition and, that failing, they, like heterosexuals, should order their

genital relations in as responsible a manner as possible, emulating the monogamous commitment of heterosexual marriage. Those holding this position still view homosexual orientation as a departure from the normative and consider genital expression as a lesser evil, lesser than the disvalues associated with being unable to affect and express deep and humanizing love relationships.

(4) Some ethical positions in this matter are formulated around the proposition that the primary finality or end of marriage and sexuality is a unitive one. The purpose of sexuality is to assist persons in achieving unity in interpersonal relationships and to sacramentally signify that unity in and through the genital act. In some sense this theory stands as a reaction against the procreational bias which marked much of traditional christian sexual ethics, especially in the Roman Catholic moral theology where procreation was termed the primary end; love and unity, the secondary ends of sexual intercourse (*Casti Connubii,* 1930, No. 43, 84). The emphasis on the unitive purpose for sexual expression allows for a shift from a biophysical calculation to one which is more relational and interpersonal for assessing the appropriateness (morality) of a genital act. Whether the act is heterosexual or homosexual is essentially inconsequential. What is of consequence is whether or not the act is an honest expression and summation of a genuine and committed love relationship. Homosexual relationships and acts are judged to have the same potential as heterosexual ones for reflecting the central quality of God's love for humankind, a love which is unitive rather than creative.

(5) The move away from an essentially procreationally purposed sexuality has spawned a revisionist school of moral analysis which regards homosexual acts as either neutral or good. Almost the sole criterion for assessing the morality of same-sex acts is a determination of their potential to enhance or to destroy the self or the other. The self-expression captured in the act and the motivation which directs it will infuse what is an otherwise neutral act with positive and justifying ethical meaning. In this school of thought essentialist arguments are replaced totally by a relational ethic.

When seeking to develop or to discover directions in christian theology for understanding and appraising homosexuality and homosexual acts, it becomes clear that there exists a plurality of positions relative to the meaning of human sexuality, the interpretation of primary texts, e.g., the scriptures, the use of data from the human sciences, and the methodologies for doing christian ethics. The task becomes more complex with the recognition of certain homophobic social, cultural and denominational attitudinal factors which inhibit a more reasoned study of this phenomenon. However, even a strong moral policy stance against homosexual behavior does not provide grounds for denying civil or ecclesiastical rights, or for perpetrating other acts of discrimination and violence against homosexual persons.

E. Batchelor, Jr., Ed., *Homosexuality and Ethics,* 1980. *Declaration on Certain Questions Concerning Sexual Ethics,* S. Cong. for the Doc. of the Faith, 1976. J. Boswell, *Christianity, Social Tolerance, and Homosexuality,* 1980. A. Guindon, *The Sexual Language,* chap. 8, 1976. *The Pastoral Care of Homosexual Persons,* Cong. for the Doc. of the Faith, 1986. R. Scroggs, *The New Testament and Homosexuality,* 1983.

ROBERT M. FRIDAY

HOPE

"In hope we were saved" (Rom 8:24). As one of the three "theological virtues," the "three things that last" (1 Cor 13:13), hope has traditionally been understood together with faith and love as *the* modalities which describe christian existence. As such, these virtues, grounded in the grace of the Spirit, express what never changes in christian anthropology. "Where the Spirit is, there is freedom" (2 Cor 3:17). This freedom *is* christian discipleship as actualized in faith, hope, and love.

While christian hope is a *spes docta* ("learned hope"), hope itself is a fundamental human affect. Hope is the presupposition behind the human "will to live." In this basic sense hope is the wager that there is some correspondence between this human will to live and the world which supports and sustains life. Without this hope the human will would be paralyzed, because the will to live presupposes that life is somehow worthwhile despite all evidence to the contrary. Against every invitation to despair, "for any among the living there is hope" (Eccl 9:4). Hope is the name of the human spirit as conative openness to reality, as outreach in search of the meaning and value of life. And where there is hope, there is religion (Ernst Bloch). Hope is at once the source and the product of religion. As "pre-thematic" or "transcendental" hope is the *a priori* ground of religion, and religion is the language of hope.

In scholastic theology hope was understood as a part of the supernatural organism of the state of grace. As the natural powers (or "faculties") of intellect and will emanate from the essence of the soul, so the three theological virtues are the operative elevation of these powers, emanating from the entitative elevation of the soul which is habitual grace. In the state of glory love remains, but faith gives way to vision and hope cedes to possession. Once God, the highest good and "most difficult to attain" (St. Thomas), is possessed securely in eternal bliss, there is nothing more to hope for.

The recent "theology of hope," however, insists with Paul that hope "lasts" (1 Cor:13:13). In his reflections on hope Karl Rahner understands this "middle virtue" as the medium between the other two—both faith and love are *spe formata* ("formed by hope"). This is an interesting variation on the traditional Catholic teaching that faith and hope are *caritate formata* ("formed by love"). In light of the trinitarian formulation of the foundational christian mystery of God's self-communication to humanity through Christ and in the Spirit, hope becomes human hospitality for the divine guest. Hope is the human spirit as receptive to the divine indwelling, while faith and love are correlated with Christ and the Spirit as the two ways the one God comes to us. Thus is hope the grace-enabled surrender of self to the self-giving God. Hope remains forever as our capacity for God to be our salvation. In this perspective hope is a person's fundamental self-interpretation in relation to God. From this basic acceptance of the "exocentric" character of authentic humanity, from the truth of this radical humility, issues that freedom which describes life as self-enactment in a world of grace.

Christian hope as such is a *spes docta*. Christians hope in a particular way because they have been formed by the linguistic efficacy of the christian tradition. This language of hope which is Christianity has educated the anticipatory consciousness of all who have come within its sphere of influence. Constant throughout the history of the christian tradition has been a general concurrence regarding the ultimate object of hope which is life eternal in "the age to come." But diverse answers have been given to what might be called the penultimate range of christian expectation. The source of this diversity has been the problem of the relationship between time and eternity. In the recent theology of hope a consensus among theologians on this problem has begun to emerge. But this consensus cannot be appreciated without an overview of the history of theological reflection on the connection between hope for eternity and the understanding of historical existence. The following questions will guide our historical overview. Does hope for the future of history encompass hope for some form of proleptic progress within history? What have Christians learned to hope for from that witness to the God of hope which is living tradition? If "faith is confident assurance concerning what we hope for, and conviction about things we do not see" (Heb 11:1), how has faith formulated "what we hope for?"

Theological concentration on christian hope in this century is a consequence of the rediscovery of the centrality of eschatology in the scriptures. In the OT eschatology emerged in the prophetic tradition through its displacement of the memory of Yahweh's past salvific acts with the expectation of a future divine action on behalf of the people of the promise. Eschatological symbolism— *New* Exodus, *New* Covenant, *New* David—became the special language of hope. For this language, which both engenders and sustains hope, the future becomes the most important of the three tenses. Through the prophets Israel found the future as the fulfillment of that hope which describes the fundamental attitude of the people who discovered a God whose very name is a promise: "I will be for you who I will be for you" (Exod 3:14).

Prophetic hope was hope for history as the place of God's future action. When history continued, and the fortunes of the people went from bad to worse, the prophetic form of hope gave way to what might be called a religious despair regarding the possibilities of "this age." In late Judaism this religious despair was expressed in a new language of hope in God—apocalypticism. The apocalyptic symbolism radicalized and universalized hope by interpreting all of history in terms of a temporal dualism between "this age" and "the age to come." The fulfillment of the divine promise was no longer expected within history. Beyond and transcending history, hope anticipated eschatological salvation in the symbols of the Kingdom of God and the resurrection of the dead. Replacing the mediational role of the messianic leader (the prophetic "New David") was the strange figure of the "Son of Man" coming in judgment.

For christian faith Jesus is the eschatological Son of Man, the definitive apocalypse of hope. In his words, deeds, and destiny the Kingdom of God is revealed as God's irrevocable commitment to humanity. In his crucifixion hope is defined as total self-surrender in trust to the God whose self-surrender to us is our salvation. In his resurrection the fulfillment of hope is anticipated for all humanity. Jesus, the Christ, is the *prolepsis* ("anticipation") in history of the destiny of history. Through his bestowal of the eschatological Spirit we are saved now as we await in hope "the redemption of our bodies" (Rom 8:23).

The subsequent story of christian discipleship in the history of the church has remained a story of hope with trust in God expressed in patience. At times this patience (itself a "fruit of the Spirit") seemed to be a passive endurance of a world passing away. At other times this patience became passion for further historical anticipations of the Kingdom yet to come. Both attitudes were evoked by the concrete unfolding of events. In the early church hope meant patience in the face of persecution. But in the fourth century the official persecution of Christians came to an end with the grand surprise of the Constantinian recognition of the church. This event quenched eschatological urgency and evoked new understandings of the christian mission in the world. Pilgrims became politicians! Christian eschatology was politicized for the first time as "imperial theology" with its optimistic notion of the *tempora christiana* ("the Christian times"). For some it seemed evident that the OT "history of salvation" was to be rehearsed in NT times. Just as Exodus-Sinai led to the conquest of Canaan and the Davidic monarchy, so now the cross and resurrection of Jesus had led to the conquest of the Roman Empire in the person of a christian emperor. In the eastern church imperial theology, illustrated by Eusebius of Caesarea, legitimated caesaropapism, while the peculiar twist of imperial theology in the west, illustrated by Ambrose of Milan, promoted papocaesarism. Church and empire became one since both were constituted by one people, the christian people of God. In the early fifth century, however, this imperial theology was rendered implausible by the collapse of the christian empire. The connection made by the imperial theologians between eschatological hope and historical events was too uncritical. Christianity had to be extricated from the fortunes and misfortunes of political arrangements. This was the task and the accomplishment of Augustine of Hippo.

To protect christian hope from the vicissitudes of historical progress and decline, Augustine both individualized and de-historicized its meaning. Hope is personal hope for heaven after death. This Augustinian eschatology has been identical with doctrinal orthodoxy until its recent modification by a new understanding of the relation between time and eternity. Rejecting the theological core of imperial theology (the notion of the *tempora christiana*), Augustine averred that history after Christ is theologically homogeneous because Christ is the definitive (eschatological) *novum*. Nothing really new could happen after the

bestowal of the gift of the Spirit on the church through the crucified and risen Lord. Christians remember the "once and for all" salvific event of Jesus Christ in order to anticipate in hope the final consummation of that event in the City of God at the end of history. Christian hope is the grace-engendered expectation of life eternal in "the age to come." As long as the fundamentally hopeless reality of "this age" lasts the Christian is a restless pilgrim.

In Augustine the temporal dualism of apocalyptic symbolism became doctrinal otherworldliness. The political order as such was radically desacralized, and the church became the only manifestation of the Kingdom of God in history. Regarding the "earthly city," symbolized by the state, Augustine recommended a purely pragmatic attitude open to cooperation where necessary to maintain the necessities of life. This pessimistic assessment of the prospects of historical existence was coupled with the pessimistic doctrine of predestination. After Augustine eschatological language would no longer be simply the education of hope. In resonance with Tertullian's prayer for "the delay of the end" Augustinian eschatology would often become the language of fear and dread.

The Augustinian doctrine reminds Christians that patience is an essential feature of hope. But there is a tension between patience as faithful expectation and that dynamic anticipatory consciousness inspired by remembrance of the Christ event. For christian hope to await is to anticipate, to make progress toward the still outstanding goal. Here is the place of the christian doctrine of interior sanctification or growth in the grace of the Spirit. In the meantime, i.e., in history after Christ, genuine progress is possible, but this progress is identical with the interior development of the soul through an ever more perfect following of Christ in the power of the Spirit. This Augustinian understanding of the spiritual life as the process of sanctification was further clarified by the Thomistic identification of grace and glory—the life of grace now is inchoate future glory. Given this understanding of grace as "realized eschatology," there can in principle be no fuller gift of the Holy Spirit short of its ultimate consummation (cf. S.Th. Ia IIae, 106, 4). Hope during history is hope *for* eternity, a higher plane of perfection above and beyond history. Such hope begets patience on earth as it focuses on heaven as its ultimate satisfaction. For many people this religious vision continues to define the meaning of christian hope.

But the patience of hope is a gift of the Holy Spirit who "renews the face of the earth" (Ps 104:30), and whose activity cannot be limited to human interiority. A revolutionary chapter in the history of christian reflection on the range of hope opens rather abruptly in the late twelfth century with the Calabrian monk, Joachim of Fiore. Joachim was a visionary whose style of thought was contrary both to the scholastic sobriety and the hierarchical order of the thirteenth century. He began what can be called the historicization of christian hope as a result of linking history with the doctrine of the Trinity. For Joachim the trinitarian hermeneutic revealed history as a progression of periods in which the succeeding era supersedes its predecessor. Thus, the "age of the Son" constituted an advance upon the previous "age of the Father," and the "age of the Spirit" will advance upon the "age of the Son." Herein, of course, lay the danger, for any portrayal of a "third age" of the Spirit superseding the age of the Son is a denial of the finality of Christ. Augustine had already domesticated such millenarian hopes by identifying the millennium of Revelation 20 with the period of the

church. And in his trinitarian teaching on the *Filioque* Augustine had intensified the Pauline connection between Christ and the Spirit. As the Spirit *of Christ*, the Holy Spirit is the divine power whereby God's redeeming work in Christ is appropriated by the Christian—the Spirit is not the principle of unmediated freedom granting direct access to God in a new age transcending Christ. Despite his intentions Joachim relativized both Christ and the institutional church. In fidelity to Augustinian and Thomistic Christocentrism on this issue the church rejected the Joachimite pneumatology of hope.

Although it was driven underground, the historicized hope of the Joachimite vision became a potent, if indirect, force in the subsequent history of revolutionary thought in the west. It was an important factor in the religious self-understanding of the mendicant movement in the thirteenth century, especially for the "Spiritual Franciscans" who embraced it in its radical form. It formed and energized the hopes of the leaders of the Peasants' Revolt in the sixteenth century. For the this-worldly humanism of the Renaissance it conveyed the sense of a meaningful history filled with promise. For "the modern history of freedom" (the tradition of thought on the philosophy of history from Kant to Marx) it mediated the understanding (ultimately biblical) of reality *as history*. Because historicized, the Joachimite vision of hope was readily secularized in ideologies of immanent progress in history. For the twentieth century revisionist Marxist philosopher, Ernst Bloch, Joachimitism symbolized the authentic interpretation of the Judeo-Christian tradition as a powerfully evocative vision of utopia. Joachimite Christianity states the religious dream for a better tomorrow—Joachimitism demystified is authentic Marxism. Bloch indeed has become a catalyst for the retrieval of interest in Joachim. Publications on

Joachimitism have significantly multiplied in recent years.

One way, and perhaps a most fruitful way, of understanding the new image of the church that has emerged in Catholicism since Vatican II is to see contemporary Christianity as revitalized by the spirit of Joachim. The centripetal ecclesiology of Augustine wherein the church is a vessel of salvation for its members has given way to the centrifugal ecclesiology congenial to Joachim wherein the church is "the universal sacrament of salvation" (L.G. art. 48). Something momentous has happened here. Traditional hope for heaven has become hope for the earth. Other-worldly dualism has yielded to an historicization of the christian tradition. From biblical eschatology, the religious language of hope, has emerged political theology, liberation theology feminist theology, black theology, etc.—all of them in concurrence on the central thesis that human history must become the *locus* for the provisional realization of christian hope for salvation. The traditional primacy of theory over *praxis* has been reversed. Christian "idealism" has become christian "materialism" as the disciples of Jesus appropriate for themselves Marx's eleventh thesis on Feuerbach! The new line of division among Christians is revealed in the answer to the question, "What can we hope for?" For "traditional" Christians the answer remains: eternal life after death for the purified soul. For "progressive" Christians the answer is partially in agreement: yes, ultimately eternal life, but penultimately a more just, more peaceful world order. For the latter hope has become both communal and historical. They have appropriated the new image of the church as the hopeful servant of the world.

This current historicization of hope, however, must never reduce Christianity to another form of secular humanism.

"Ockham's razor" is pertinent here! What must be done is to show the intrinsic connection between hope for eternity and hope for history. This connection is grasped by theological reflection on what is called "historical consciousness." For several centuries a new understanding of time has emerged in philosophical thought, an understanding that defines time as the raw material of human freedom. History is the cumulative result of human action, and as such it is constituted by human meaning. This historical consciousness leads to the conviction that there is only one world while there are different hermeneutical perspectives upon the one world. The transcendent meanings and values discovered by and mediated through the religious traditions of the world do not constitute another world. They name the ultimate meaning and value of this world— again from different perspectives. For the Judeo-Christian tradition the great eschatological symbols express hope for the future of this world in terms of the continuing experience of the divine promise. Eternity is not over and above time. There is no "infinite qualitative distance" between time and eternity. The incarnation has removed that distance as the focal revelation of God's action in and for this world through Jesus and through those empowered by the Spirit. Eternity is the future of time. Eternity is the fruit, the issue of history. Eternity is the ultimate value of all the penultimate values realized in the history of the world.

From this consensus on the problem of the relation between time and eternity it can be seen that there is no real contradiction between Augustinian "transcendentalism" and Joachimite "historicism." Both Augustinian otherworldly dualism and Joachimite visionary idealism are overcome by the turn to the primacy of *praxis* as a result of historical consciousness. Hope is our hospitality for the God of the promise who has come and who will come. To live in hope is to reject every pretentious utopianism that would identify the Kingdom of God with any intrahistorical realm of freedom. To hope for oneself is to hope for all, and the resurrection of the dead entails a "new heaven and a new earth" (Rev 21:1). Hope opens us to the future of God. Sustained by the Spirit of God, hope remembers Jesus Christ as the *prolepsis* of God's future. Hope demands patience, but this patience is not supine escapism from responsibility in and for the world. Hope opens us to an open future to be filled by the *praxis* of liberation which is the creation of provisional anticipations of that ultimate realm of freedom which is the Kingdom of God.

See **Eschatology, Reign of God**

Ernst Bloch, *The Principle of Hope*, 3 vols., Cambridge: MIT Press, 1986. Langdon Gilkey, *Reaping the Whirlwind*, New York: The Seabury Press, 1976. Nicholas Lash, *A Matter of Hope*, Notre Dame: U. of Notre Dame Press, 1982. John Macquarrie, *Christian Hope*, New York: The Seabury Press, 1978.

MICHAEL J. SCANLON, OSA

HUMANISM

Humanism (also called the "New Learning") refers to those efforts, begun in the middle of the fourteenth century, to recover the learning of the ancient Greek and Roman world through the discovery, editing, and careful study of ancient texts. The movement is associated with such names as Petrarch in the fourteenth century, Lorenzo Valla, Marsiglio Ficino, and Pico della Mirandola in fifteenth century Italy, and, across the Alps, with such sixteenth century figures as Erasmus of Rotterdam, Thomas More, Lefevre D'Etaples, Johannes Reuchlin, and a host of others.

The older view, often associated with the work of Jacob Burckhardt in the last century, that humanism was "pagan" in its spirit and anti-Christian, requires major modification. The Humanists, especially those in the north, were anti-scholastic, anti-monastic, and sympathetic to an interiorized piety (like that of the *devotio moderna*) but their efforts were largely oriented to church reform. They played a major role in the rise of critical biblical studies and the careful study of patristic literature. The role of the New Learning in both the Protestant and Catholic Reformation is both complex and profound. One sees their legacy in everything from bible translations (both Luther's translation and that of the King James Version would have been unthinkable without their pioneering labors) to education (both the Ignatian *ratio studiorum* and the English public school curriculum are in its debt). Finally, the fecundity of classical humanism can be seen in the large body of enduring literature that it produced from Erasmus's *Praise of Folly* and More's *Utopia* to Machiavelli's *The Prince*, Castiglione's *The Courtier*, Montaigne's *Essays*, and Rabelais's *Gargantua and Pantagruel*.

As P.O. Kristeller has shown, Renaissance humanism was more a profession than a philosophy of life. The idea of a humanistic philosophy as "man centered" may be seen germinally in Pico's famous "Oration on the Dignity of Man" (1492) but its full articulation would come in the nineteenth century. Ludwig Feuerbach's *The Essence of Christianity* (1841) argued that religion was nothing more than the projection of the noblest aspirations of humans; thus, the proper study of the theologian is not what transcends man but man himself: *homo homini deus est*. Karl Marx attempted to spell out the implications of Feuerbach's theory in terms of his own philosophy of dialectical materialism in order to create what today is called a "Marxist humanism." The classic source for this approach to humanism is the third part of Marx's *Economic and Philosophical Manuscripts of 1844* under the title "Communism as humanism."

One other strain of humanistic philosophy, traceable to Frederick Nietzsche's proclamation of the death of God in modern culture, is the existential situation of humans as beings-in-the-world. Jean Paul Sartre's *Existentialism is a Humanism* (1946) argued, in a famous formulation, that "existence precedes essence" and, as a consequence, there is no human nature. Man is what he makes of himself; man is how he acts. Partially in response to Sartre, Martin Heidegger's *Letter on Humanism* (1947) emphasizes the unique position of man as existing in the thick world of being but hesitates to embrace Sartre's subjectivity as too Cartesian and his emphatic atheism as too hasty.

The secular humanism of today is most often identified with a movement which had its origins in the 1930s, whose credo can be found in a series of manifestos. The Humanist Movement denies any supernatural realm, looks to empirical science as the ultimate arbiter of truth. and professes the Enlightenment values of freedom, social equality, and the values of secular society. Secular Humanists, as an organized group, constitute a tiny elitist minority but their influence is perceived as pervasive by many conservative religious people in this country.

The christian response to humanism has been varied. Karl Barth spoke for many Christians in his insistence that there is no true humanism outside the imperatives of the gospel. Jacques Maritain's notion of an integral humanism, rooted in the values of the Incarnation and the transcendent reality of God was an influential formulation for Catholics in the immediate post-war period. Neither Barthian Neo-Orthodoxy nor Maritain's Neo-Thomism holds the

imagination of most religious thinkers today. Pope John Paul's attempt to reconstruct a humanism from his own sense of philosophical personalism and Catholic orthodoxy has met with mixed reactions; praised by some as a new and serious synthesis of classical thought while criticized by others as betraying a classicist mentality without sufficient attention to the historical character of thought. Teilhard de Chardin's controversial theories about the place of the human in the evolutionary scheme of things and the "hominisation" of the planet has found some acceptance by those attracted to process thought but his "weak" theory of human evil has caused hesitations among others.

The paradigmatic shift brought about through the work of the Second Vatican Council with its emphasis on incarnational thinking, its ecumenical outlook, and its genuine concern for human problems outside the household of the faith makes the possibility of a newly articulated christian humanism a desideratum. Such a humanism would have to take account of both the inherited wisdom of the Catholic tradition and the newer insights derived from the humane and social sciences as well as the various impulses of those who attempt to give voice to those whose voices have not had a full hearing in the church. It does seem clear that any new approach to articulating a christian humanism will have to modify (or even transcend) the narrower biases of Western intellectual history to account for the insights of what Karl Rahner has called the "world church." Whether the times are ripe for such a synthesis now is an open question, but the materials for such a synthesis are surely there.

See **Atheism; Anthropology, Christian**

Giorgio Bof, "Umanesimo," in *Nuovo dizionario di teologia*, G. Barbaglio, Ed., Rome, 1982, s.v. Louis Bouyer, *Christian Humanism*, Westminster: MD,

1959. Paul O. Kristeller, *Renaissance Thought,* New York, 1961. *Renaissance Thought II,* New York, 1965. Jacques Maritain, *True Humanism,* New York, 1938.

LAWRENCE S. CUNNINGHAM

HYLEMORPHISM
See **Form and Matter**

HYPOSTASIS

The Greek *hypostasis* literally means a thing that "stands under" (like the Latin *substantia,* substance). Hypostasis can stand under passively as simply underlying (like sediment or a river bed), or actively as a support, substructure, basis, a military or architectural plan. It occurs some twenty times in the Greek OT, denoting property (the basis of daily life), foundation, power-base, purpose, guarantee, and being (Ps 89:47). In the NT it is found five times, confined to 2 Corinthians and Hebrews. In Heb 1:3 it means the divine nature, reality or being. In Heb 3:14 and 11:1 it signifies that same reality present in Jesus and in faith. For Stoicism hypostasis conveyed an actual material being bodying forth the divine in the cosmos. Neo-Platonism (important for the trinitarian debates) applied it to an emanation of the One, true being. It was of a lower order, yet the hypostasis had ultimate being. A note common to the foregoing is that of an objective reality meeting the mind, in contrast to an abstraction or an illusion. This accords with the cognate verb *hyphistanai,* to root in being.

The Christian Trajectory of Hypostasis

Originally hypostasis (Stoic) was taken as synonymous with *ousia* (Platonic), the essential being or nature which defined something as belonging to a class, for example, by Origen and Nicaea I in 325. Its tendency was not to refer to being in general, a species (Aristotle's secondary substance), but to an individual existing entity with specific characteristics (Aristotle's primary substance). However, the often platorizing Fathers rarely use this Aristotelian classification, although they follow the common-sense distinction of universal and particular beings. If *ousia* answered the question, "What is it?," hypostasis in its intermediate stage answered, "Which is it?"

Increasingly hypostasis was distinguished from *ousia*. From the third century the christian God could be described as three hypostases in one *ousia* or nature. The Latins noted the exact etymological correspondence between their substance and the Greek hypostasis, each meaning the reality underlying a set of properties, a nature or essence. Therefore in the West the eastern formula of three hypostases in God seemed tritheistic to Dionysius of Rome, Jerome and others. Conversely the East was suspicious of the term used for hypostasis in the West, *persona*. For them it suggested a mere stage personage, a role. It lacked the ontological density of hypostasis that made it appropriate for the divine Father, Son and Spirit. However, Gregory of Nazianzen and Basil the Great (Letters 210, 5; 214, 4) accepted the terms as synonyms. Towards the end of its christian trajectory, therefore, hypostasis answered the question, "Who is it?" Yet it preserved its earlier ontological independence (What?), and its individual character (Which?). It belonged to beings, and not to a nature, and still less to any qualities making up a nature. A hypostasis constitutes an entity as a particular being. Hypostasis, so to speak, possesses and integrates the essential reality (*ousia*) of a specific being—whether a house, a horse, or a human. In consequence the hypostasis enables this being to be observed and classified, and to act and relate to other beings. Hypostasis is the personal dynamic source of human or divine life;

but it is not that life, that nature, itself.

The trinitarian settlement of the late fourth century did not end confusion over hypostasis in christology. Nestorians claimed two hypostases in Christ, divinity and humanity. Cyril insisted that the union of the two natures was hypostatic, real; so that he was not a coordinated Son of Man and Son of God, but a single concrete individual. It was Chalcedon in 451 which clearly stated these natures were joined in the unique hypostasis or person (*prosopon*) of the Christ, Son and Lord.

The Fathers of Chalcedon used a term like hypostasis in an intuitive and not a speculatively refined way. They could not have defined their abstract concepts (A. Grillmeier). It is consequently hardly surprising that further elucidation was needed. Leontius of Byzantium and Leontius of Jerusalem in the sixth century clarified that the hypostasis of Christ was the pre-existent Logos and Son, and that a perfect human nature was "enhypostasized" in the one divine person of the Son. No nature can exist without a hypostasis to bear and project it. But a nature need not exhaust a hypostasis. Therefore the Logos hypostasis, while remaining fully divine and impassible could be limited in knowledge, develop humanly, and suffer in an integral humanity.

Maximos the Confessor (about 580-622) further coordinated christology and triadology (trinitarian theology). He taught that the divine hypostasis of the Son does not constitute a third reality in

Jesus Christ along with the two natures. The hypostasis *is* his godhead and manhood. This agrees with there being no distinction between the three eternal hypostases and the divine nature in God, but only between the persons (hypostases). The divine hypostasis of Christ incarnate, moreover, mediates between the Father and all human beings (created hypostases), whom he reconciles to God the Father through the Spirit (Letter 15). (Western and later development of hypostasis is found under "Person.")

Exegetically hypostasis refers to the personification of a divine attribute such as wisdom in the intertestamental period. It sheds light on such intermediary beings as angels, Philo's Logos, and the targumic Memra. These concepts in turn fed into primitive christology.

See **Nature, Person, Trinity**

Gerald Bray. *Creeds, Councils and Christ,* (Downers Grove: Inter-Varsity, 1984. John C. Dwyer, *Son of God and Son of Man,* New York: Paulist, 1983. Aloys Grillmeier, *Christ in Christian Tradition* 1, 2nd ed., Atlanta; Knox, 1975. Jaroslav Pelikan, *The Christian Tradition* 1 and 2, Chicago: U. of Chicago, 1971 and 1974. Frances M. Young, *From Nicaea to Chalcedon,* Philadelphia: Fortress, 1983.

BRIAN M. NOLAN

HYPOSTATIC UNION

The term used to refer to the union of divine and human natures in the one person, or *hypostasis,* of Jesus Christ. It is classically expressed in the dogmatic definition of the Council of Chalcedon.

See **Chalcedon, Council of; Hypostasis; Jesus Christ.**

I

ICONOCLASM

Taken from the Greek word for image-breaking, iconoclasm refers to a controversy that occurred in two stages and that disrupted the Eastern Church for more than a century. In 726, Emperor Leo III forbade the use of religious images and ordered them destroyed. The Empress Irene undid this policy in the early 780's, and the Second Council of Nicea (787) defined images as worthy of veneration and ordered them restored. In 814 iconoclasm broke out again under Emperor Leo V, but the movement finally ceased in 843 under the regency of Theodora. The precise origins of iconoclasm are somewhat obscure, but the struggle that it evoked aroused high passions. The theological justification for iconoclasm was basically that images were idols and that any representation of Christ in particular divided his humanity from his divinity. The fundamental theological justification for the veneration of images, on the other hand, which was well expressed, for instance, in John Damascene's *First Apology Against Those who Attack the Divine Images* 16, was that all matter—and hence images—had been ennobled by the Incarnation and was worthy of bearing representation of the holy and even of the divine.

See **Art, Jesus Christ**

BONIFACE RAMSEY, OP

IMAGINATION, RELIGIOUS

Religious imagining is an intentional operation in which symbolic images, gestures, sounds, words, or actions disclose the ultimate horizon of God in human experience. Though there have been many advocates of the creative power of imagination in human history, few secular or religious thinkers would support Anatole France's claim that "to know is nothing at all; to imagine is everything." Imagination has a highly controverted history in philosophy and theology. In what follows, we shall (1) discuss the primary diverging interpretations of the process of imagination; (2) outline christian attitudes toward imagination in religion; (3) point to the recovery of imagination in twentieth-century theology; and (4) look at contemporary consequences and questions.

The Process of Imagining.

Imaging operates in all facets of our knowing process. What we call the artistic imagination intensifies, encapsulates, and condenses the ordinary procedures of perception. In dance, normal gestures are stylized into patterned movement; in music, random sounds are schematized to convey meaning; in poetry, ordinary words are juxtaposed into metaphors and narratives. Yet what human beings are doing when they engage in these activities and what such processes reveal are much discussed topics. Moreover, it is impossible to discuss the performance of imagination without elaborating the theories about it and its products.

Pre-enlightenment reflections about these topics do not ignore the process of imagining, but they grant it only reproductive ability. They focus upon the making of art and upon its harmony with the canons of beauty or truth. Plato insists that artists must internalize the principle of measure while at the same time being taken by the enthusiasm that relates poets to the gods. He distrusts the imitative quality of poetry, since it seems to remove the viewer another step from contemplation of the pure forms of reality. Aristotle, on the other hand, specifies the mimetic characteristics of poetic metaphors and describes the powerful cathartic effect of tragedy upon the audience. Plotinus developed a metaphysics of beauty in which natural things, in successively higher levels, symbolize the divine harmony. Physical beauty gives way to intellectual beauty which in its turn cedes to an ecstatic formless and boundless unity with the One.

Does the mimetic quality of art simply copy what it sees or hears? Does art pervert what it produces, since it can only be at second-hand? Or does art create something new? Does art lead its participants toward the divine? The fundamental questions of post-Enlightenment thought with regard to the nature and function of imagination are already present within the classic philosophies of western civilization.

Yet it must be said that the eighteenth century invented the imagination as a creative act. Without the poetry and philosophy of Akenside and Tetens, the philosophical investigations of Priestley and Stewart, the inquiries into aesthetics and morals of Shaftesbury and Hutcheson, and the cognitional theories of Locke, Leibniz, Hume, and Kant, there

would have been no "faculty" of imagination. In Aristotle, knowing certainly involved "becoming" what one knew through a "conversion to phantasm." But when eighteenth-century thinkers focused upon how we know what we know, they promoted imagination to a faculty alongside the intellect and the will.

One fundamental issue for eighteenth-century cognitional theory was whether imagination repeated only what it received from the senses or whether it produced something new. Followers of Locke and Hume maintained that images were simply faint copies of sense impressions. Hence poetry and art were the rearrangement of what one already knew in another form. The work of art, therefore, could entertain and even teach through the pleasure it gave; but it was decorative, secondary to the works of science, politics, and economy.

Kant, however, gave imagination a more active role in human knowing through his distinction between the productive and reproductive imagination and his analysis of teleological and artistic judgments. The productive imagination makes a unity of our sense experiences. The reproductive imagination, dependent upon prior unified manifolds of sense, completes the work of sense by "imagining" what is unavailable (e.g., the nonvisible sides of a six-sided cube). In the Critique of Judgment, Kant's analysis of judgments of taste and of the sublime give imagination a mediating role between speculative and practical reason.

Kant's analyses electrified Coleridge, who found support for his own experience of the innovative energy of imaginative poetry. Coleridge contrasted fancy, which dealt with already established images, and imagination which was the source of poetry and the creation of new images. He distinguished between the primary imagination that operates in all perception and the secondary imagination that dissolves, diffuses, dissipates in order to recreate. For Coleridge, imagination was a participation in the creative act of God. If imagination was so all pervasive, thinkers were convinced that the faculty of imagining could unify the dualisms that seemed to exist between nature and humanity, body and soul, mind and heart, subject and object, ideal and real.

Nineteenth-century thinkers in general blessed this mediating role of imagination. Its symbolic products became prime data for an understanding of literature, history, philosophy and religion. The early Schelling practically identified religion and art. Hegel himself granted that the content of christian images (*Bild*) could not be surpassed, though they required transformation (*aufgehoben*) into philosophical concepts (*Begriff*). Catholic scholars at Tübingen (Drey and Moehler) developed notions of historical process, church, creed and the sacraments influenced by Schelling's understanding of the creative imagination. Arnold described the work of the NT as symbolic like that of literature. Newman postulated an illative sense that mediated between thought and action; he originally entitled it an imaginative sense.

These optimistic notions of how imagination worked and what it could produce encountered both cultural and religious objections. At the beginning of the twentieth century, when Catholic thinkers, called modernists, attempted to use the notion of imagination and its correlative symbol to explain the sacraments, the nature of the church, and the scriptures, they were condemned in papal encyclicals (*Lamentabili, Pascendi,* 1907) for reducing the supernatural action of God to a purely human process.

This condemnation, however doctrinally and politically motivated, paralleled radical criticisms of imagination made by Freud and Sartre. Freud was convinced that art has its origins in the libidinous instincts. Cultural artifacts are only achieved by the artists' denying themselves immediate gratification and sublimating the energy available for the production of art. Artists seem to substitute art for their unresolved phantasies. In this sense, art is like dreams, an example of displaced wish fulfillment. For Sartre, imagination is negative consciousness, the necessary distancing of human beings within the world of things. In one sense, it is the characteristic human mode of existence, even if it is not privileged. What the artist creates does not exist. Imagination enacts consciousness as creative, but what it makes is revealed as not being. For Freud, imagination is illusion; for Sartre, it is nothing.

The manifold vicissitudes of the act of imagining in the history of philosophy are described here in the most typological terms. In what follows, we will argue for a position in which imagination discloses both what is the case about the world and what it is not yet. As an act of consciousness, it defines the self, the world, and the symbol that mediates or discloses both.

If we reflect upon the process of imagining, we can see that artistic imagination is in fact a displacement from the world of ordinary activities. In imagining oneself as president of the United States, one is giving speeches, making treaties, and receiving diplomats. But one is also the prime spectator at one's own play. Imagining requires a readjustment of one's holding of oneself. Though I am sitting in a chair, I am also in the White House making decisions. There is a similar doubling of self when I view a painting, listen to a symphony, hear a play, and go to the ballet. Caught up in the new aesthetic pattern projected by the artist, we become (for the moment) what we imagine. We are not intellectually comparing the imagined world with the "real" world, but rather the envisioned world becomes a particular kind of reality governing our other worlds.

The act of imagining is an intentional arc; it has as its object a symbol. Symbols reveal to us not only a world which we can inhabit, but subjects who can dwell in those worlds. Images are not postulated mental acts, nor are they "things" like shoes and tables. Imagining does not faintly copy our senses, realigning already established meanings into different configurations; rather imagination discloses a realm unavailable to us otherwise. Through works of art, we are invited and persuaded by their pleasures, their prodding questions, and their tensive juxtapositions of line, color, words, and sounds to participate in the world disclosed. Even if the artwork is utopian, an absent social system judging the present polity, we experience the work as present, as part of our imagined present. It is not "unreal," but a specific, alternate mode of reality that requires our continued participation to permit it to occur. Imagining requires our self-involvement and commitment. If the musicians cease playing and the audience goes home, there is symphonic music only as memory or as an anticipation of another performance.

The shock of recognition when the music clicks, the play works, or the poem sings is what we mean when we have successfully imagined a work of art. Such successful enactment of a work of art is a new interpretation, a further implementation of the world of the art work in the wider world. Gradually, incrementally, we and society at large are transformed into the world disclosed by an artwork. We "rest in" a great work of art at successive times to re-enter our ordinary world where the artwork is not yet completely embodied. Art is never neutral. It either leads us toward the self-transcendence of what is just, loving and true or it guides us toward absurd self-destruction.

Christian Attitudes Toward Imagination

We do not cease imagining when we become religious. Because of the power of imagination, it matters how we image God, the stories of the NT, holy men and women, and ecclesiastical governments. Christian attitudes toward imagination have reflected a wary respect for its force.

Throughout the history of the eastern and western churches, there have appeared campaigns against luxurious artistic display. Image-breaking or iconoclastic controversies agitated the eastern churches from c. 725 to 842. The opponents of religious paintings of Christ or of the saints (icons) alleged that such images could only present the humanity of Christ and not his divinity; hence, they were idols if they were venerated. Patriarchs and emperors ordered all icons to be destroyed. After persecution and martyrdom of icon supporters, the seventh general council of Nicaea (787) declared that icons should be venerated, but not adored, and ordered their restoration throughout the eastern empire.

The eastern controversies about icons were paradigmatic of the successive ascetic "purifications" of image in the churches. Cistercians criticized Benedictine liturgical and architectural ornament in the twelfth century; early Franciscans rejected luxury and espoused poverty; Catharist heretics angrily refused the delights of the senses; late medieval mystics and the *devotio moderna* argued for artistic simplicity; Zwingli and the English Puritans smashed windows and whitewashed churches—all these reforming movements have their origins in the same ascetic impulse that motivated desert monks, like Antony of the Desert, to flee the pleasures of the city and to seek out a quiet, unadorned life. The gospel commanded it: "If you would be perfect, go, sell what you possess and give to the poor, and you will have treasure in heaven; and come, follow me." (Mt 19:21) As Bernard of Clairvaux said: "Interior beauty is more comely than external ornament, more even than the pomp of kings" (*Sermones in Cantica* XXV, 6).

This emphasis upon interior piety has its literary origins in Augustine. On the one hand, the author of the *Confessions* mistrusted the sensible as seductive and illusory, able to tie us down to earthly things, preventing our minds from contemplating the eternal and unchanging. As a result, music was a purer art and surer guide for the soul's return to God than painting. But better than music were the words of the scriptures, as long as readers transcended the literal, material image for the true inner meaning. On the other hand, Augustine developed a theology of beauty derived from Plato and neo-Platonist thought that saw human making (art) as able to participate in divinity when it shared in the appropriate measure. Proper measure meant proportion, rhythm, the appropriate relationship of parts to the whole, and finally the harmony bestowed by God. Simultaneously, Augustine bequeathed to the Middle Ages a theology of the sacraments that emphasized their objective effectiveness as signs, whether the minister of the sacraments was schismatic or not (against the Donatists), and their ability to convey believers to true inward faith.

Christian attitudes toward imagination, therefore, were mixed from the beginning. True beauty could lead one to God—as long as what was beautiful was intellectual and not sensible. Sacramental signs, however, could in some way put us in the presence of God. Art could mislead us, but religious icons, stained-glass windows, frescoes, statuary, and architecture could teach us doctrine and point the way toward heaven.

At the center of christian discussions was the status of the incarnation of Christ. On the one hand, the very human Jesus of Nazareth was flesh and blood; on the other, that limited human nature was the presence of a God who was infinite. Sensuous images were therefore seen as both an access to God (in Christ, the church and the sacraments) and as a temptation away from God (by attention to the senses). Since philosophically imagination constructed what did not exist and made it sensuous, it was a lure, a seduction away from God, a distraction in prayer or the fantasies that might lead to sin. Theologically, imagination could not penetrate the divine darkness. The author of the *Cloud of Unknowing* tells his readers to put all sensible reality below them in a cloud of forgetting. God is able to be truly contacted in imageless and wordless wonder.

Twentieth-Century Theological Recovery of Imagination

This traditional ambivalence towards the imagination has not much affected contemporary Catholic attempts to understand the role of imagination in christian life. Archaeological discoveries concerning early christian and Jewish art (Dura-Europos), comparative religious history, and the biblical, patristic, and liturgical revivals made a discussion of the status, nature and role of the imagining process necessary.

At the same time, thinkers were recovering neo-scholastic faculty psychology and its ability to include the affective, moral, and cognitive dimensions of the imagination. Maréchal studied the psychology of the mystics, emphasizing the imageless and wordless aspects of religious consciousness. Rahner studied the role of the material phantasm in human knowing and later argued for the intrinsic role of symbol in theological investigation. Maritain established the notion of radiance at the heart of the scholastic notion of beauty. Von Balthasar developed from biblical typologies, patristic sources, and doctrinal principles an extended theological aesthetics that overarches nature and history, unites secular and religious literature, and correlates interior movements of grace and the exterior products of the imagination. Schillebeeckx included the phenomenological dimensions of encounter, language, and image in his studies of the sacraments.

Building upon neo-scholastic theology, contemporary philosophy and literary criticism, Lynch analyzed classic literature and developed an integrated understanding of imagination with its theological and christian dimensions. Tracy describes a systematic, confessional theology based upon an analogical imagination that is seized by the classics of literature and history. Theologians, using narrative and literary themes as primary categories (Shea, Navone, McFague), analyze the imaginative dimensions of ethics (Hauerwas), liturgy (Searle), and scripture (Crossan, Via, Alter).

Consequences and Questions

Imagination and related aesthetic categories have clearly established themselves as a crucial factor in Catholic theology. Parallel to the ongoing investigations of philosophy, psychology, and the natural sciences, theology has studied the ways in which metaphor, symbol, and the language of the imagination have been operative in christian life. Research into the role of imagination has permitted the exploration of all aspects of how we learn, whether affective, conative, or cognitive, By studying imagining and its products in an interdisciplinary fashion, theology has learned to engage with conversation partners other than philosophy, and thus has extended its disciplinary reach. Articulation of the power and range of images has assisted contemporary christianity in its attempts to inhabit a new cultural world.

Yet appeal to the imagination process also has created difficulites. Since the nineteenth century, art and the language of imagination have been marginalized, relegated to an odd social fringe whose primary task is to act as gadfly. The overpowering rapidity with which images change in our culture, the pervasive presence of images and non-verbal communication, and the way in which such images are manipulated by governments, advertising agencies, and corporate boards make appeal to imagination as a process and symbols as their product somewhat difficult. Are religious images to be classed with the socially marginal, however creative, fringe? Should religious images be disposable like built-for-obsolescence business products? Should the religious imagination be packaged like an advertising spot on television?

Much of the philosophical language that has appeared since the Enlightenment has attempted to argue that there is a presence that can be disclosed to human beings that is not manipulable. The natural sciences had as one of their primary objectives to control natural processes and to extend human dominion over uncontrollable catastrophes. Investigation into moral behavior produced the discovery of a certain relativity to normative action, dependent upon psychological circumstances, history, and culture. The sole area in which it seemed plausible to maintain that human beings, despite their obvious role in making art, were measured by the radiance of the other was in the products of the imagination.

Nineteenth- and twentieth-century religious thinkers capitalized upon this new currency to disclose the surplus of grace, the reality of an other that originates, a place where humanity is a listener rather than a speaker. This discovery will yield new benefits if imagination is seen, investigated, and understood as a prime operator, not only in art or religion narrowly defined, but also in scientific experiment and the various modes of ordinary discourse. The ultimate horizon that is disclosed in the process of imagining will not be relegated to one area of human life.

The more fundamental problem that abides, however, relates to the problematic of an incarnate divinity. The "visible invisible" that is at the center of christian discourse always risks splitting in two— into an unimaginable deity and into an eminently visible human being. The ability of the religious imagination to risk constructing images of divinity without idolizing its own products is a tenuous one, dependent upon recognizing that even its most august symbols are incomplete, not yet the presence of the reign of God. "For us, there is only the trying. The rest is not our business." (T.S. Eliot, "East Coker," *Four Quartets*)

See **Art, Symbol**

E.S. Casey, *Imagining: A Phenomenological Study,* Bloomington, In., 1976. U. Eco, *Art and Beauty in the Middle Ages,* New Haven, Ct., 1986. Engell, *The Creative Imagination: Enlightenment to Romanticism,* Cambridge, Mass., 1981. N. Goodman, *Languages of Art: An Approach to a Theory of Symbols,* Indianapolis, In., 1976. W. Lynch, *Christ and Apollo: The Dimensions of the Literary Imagination,* New York, 1960. J. Maritain, *Creative Intuition in Art and Poetry,* New York, 1953. W.J.T. Mitchell, *Iconology: Image, Text, Ideology,* Chicago, 1986. L. Roberts, *The Theological Aesthetics of Hans Urs von Balthasar,* Washington, D.C., 1987. R. Rubenstein, *The Religious Imagination: A Study in Psychoanalysis and Jewish Theology,* Indianapolis, In., 1968. M. Warnock, *Imagination,* Berkeley, Ca., 1976.

STEPHEN HAPPEL

IMMACULATE CONCEPTION

Dogmatic Content

On December 8, 1854, Pope Pius IX solemnly defined as a dogma of Catholic faith that Mary is the Immaculate Conception in the following words of the apostolic constitution, *Ineffabilis Deus:* "We declare, pronounce, and define that the doctrine which holds that the most Blessed Virgin Mary, in the first instant of her conception, by a singular grace and privilege granted by almighty God in view of the merits of Jesus Christ, the Savior of the human race, was preserved free from all stain of original sin, is a doctrine revealed by God and therefore to be believed firmly and constantly by all the faithful" (D.S. 2803). This dogmatic definition contains a number of truths. First, Mary is preserved from original sin at the very beginning of her existence as a human person within her mother's womb, but precisely when that takes place in embryonic development is not determined. The phrase "by a singular grace and privilege" indicates that Mary is the only *human person* in salvation history who has been immaculately conceived (her Son is a divine person). The phrase "in view of the merits of Jesus Christ" is of paramount Christological and soteriological importance since this unique privilege does not exempt Mary from the need to be redeemed by her Son through an "anticipatory" or "preservative" redemption which has kept her free from all sin and such consequences of sin as concupiscence.

The primary theological reason for Mary's Immaculate Conception given in *Ineffabilis Deus* is that she was predestined to be the *Theotokos* (God-Bearer) by the Persons of the Trinity (cf. D.S. 2801). It was for the sake of her divine Son's dignity that she received this unique grace. Other reasons for the dogma found in *Ineffabilis* will be discussed in the context of its development. The doctrine has been reaffirmed several times by the magisterium since 1854. Pope St. Pius X recalled it in his encyclical *Ad Diem Illum* on the occasion of the fiftieth anniversary of *Ineffabilis Deus.* Pius XII issued an encyclical, *Fulgens Corona,* to commemorate the centenary of the definition in 1954, which he declared a Marian Year. In it he related this dogma to that of Mary's bodily Assumption which had been solemnly defined by him in 1950. And references to the Immaculate Conception in the mariological teaching of Vatican II are: "Enriched from the first instant of her conception with the splendor of an entirely unique holiness..." (L.G. 56); and, "...the Immaculate Virgin preserved free from all stain of original sin..." (L.G. 59).

Dogmatic Development

The main scriptural texts that have been used to support the dogma are: "I will put enmity between you and the woman, and between your seed and her seed; he shall bruise your head, and you shall bruise his heel" (Gen 3:15); "...and she [Elizabeth] exclaimed with a loud cry, 'Blessed are you among women, and blessed is the fruit of your womb!'" (Lk 1:42); and, "And he [Gabriel] came to her and said 'Hail, full of grace, the Lord is with you.'" (Lk 1:28). Vatican II, when referring to the dogma, did so in the context of the angelic salutation at the Annunciation (cf. L.G. 56). In *Ineffabilis Deus* Pius IX uses the three texts in giving reasons for defining the Immaculate Conception as a "doctrine revealed by God." As in the case of the Assumption, it is the task of a theological theory of the development of dogma to propose just how the Immaculate Conception may have gradually become explicit in the Catholic tradition on the basis of such biblical insinuations or suggestions in the inspired word of God. Likewise, their implications seem to have contributed toward the earliest image of Mary after the NT, namely, the New Eve. Principally developed by St. Irenaeus, it portrays Mary as intimately associated with Christ, the New Adam, in his total victory over sin and death symbolized by the "serpent" of Genesis 3:15. If Mary had been infected by original sin, even for an instant, it would have detracted from the perfection of her Son's redemptive act, since his own mother would have come under the dominion of Satan.

Among the Fathers of the West, St. Augustine taught that Mary was free from all personal or actual sin, but he could not theologically exempt her from original sin. According to his doctrine, Mary unlike her Son, was not conceived virginally and so must have incurred original sin because of the concupiscence inherent in sexual intercourse. Augustine's incomparable authority in the West was a deterrent in the development of the dogma. Several of the Eastern Fathers, particularly St. Andrew of Crete, St. Germanus of Constantinople, and St. John Damascene, at the conclusion of the patristic period in the seventh-eighth centuries, seem to speak of Mary in ways that she was free from all sin, even original. They do not, however, discuss the mystery of original sin in the precise terms of the Western Fathers.

As in the case of the Assumption, the most significant factor in the development of the dogma was the *sensus fidelium*, i.e., the beliefs of the faithful, especially as reflected in their liturgical devotion. Towards the end of the seventh century, a feast of Mary's Conception arose, probably originating in the monasteries of Syria, which spread throughout the Byzantine world. It reached England c. 1050, and, after a period of suppression during the reign of William the Conqueror (1066-1087), was revived c. 1125 and spread from England to Normandy, France, Spain, Belgium, and Germany. For the first time, a critical debate emerged about the precise theological meaning of the feast. Eadmer, an English monk and close associate of St. Anselm of Canterbury, wrote a treatise, "On the Conception of the Blessed Virgin Mary" (P.L. 159, 301-318), in which he defended the feast and its doctrinal foundation. He considered the devotion of the faithful a better guide than the learned who opposed the feast, and argued that the holiness of Jesus required that his mother have a holy beginning, and, that God, who kept the good angels sinless, could do no less for his own mother. St. Bernard opposed the feast mostly on Augustinian grounds. The great scholastics of the thirteenth century were unable to reconcile Mary's Immaculate Conception with the universal need for salvation by Christ. Finally, John Duns Scotus (1266-1308) was chiefly responsible for introducing the notion of "preservative" redemption into the explicit consciousness of the church, which was a breakthrough in helping pave the way for its definition in 1854. On February 2, 1849, Pope Pius IX issued an encyclical, *Ubi Primum,* asking the bishops to inform him about the devotion of the faithful as well as of the clergy concerning the Immaculate Conception and their desire for a papal definition along with the thoughts of the bishops themselves in the matter. An overwhelmingly affirmative response was a clear sign of the *sensus fidelium,* leading to the decision for the definition.

F.M. Jelly, *Madonna - Mary in the Catholic Tradition,* Wilmington, Del., 1986. M. O'Carroll, "The Immaculate Conception," and "Ineffabilis Deus," in *Theotokos: A Theological Encyclopedia of the Blessed Virgin Mary,* Wilmington, Del., 1983. E.D. O'Connor, Ed., *The Dogma of the Immaculate Conception - History and Significance,* Notre Dame, Ind., 1958.

FREDERICK M. JELLY, OP

IMMORTALITY
See **Eschatology**

IMMUTABILITY

A term used to refer to the unchangeable nature of God. It should not connote passivity, but the utter fullness of active and infinite knowledge, love, and being.
See **God**

IMPASSIBILITY

Another term used to refer to God's unchangeable nature, but accentuating that God is always and only active and never receptive, passive, or acted upon by another.
See **God.**

INCARNATION
See **Jesus Christ**

INCULTURATION

Inculturation, a new term used in theology, refers to the central and dynamic principle governing the christian missionary outreach to peoples not yet evangelized, or among whom the church is not yet rooted firmly and indigenously. More commonly, this is known as the principle of catholicity, or accommodation, or adaptation, or indigenization, or contextualization; more radically, the principle of incarnation. All these terms indicate the dominant method to be followed by those engaged directly in the church's primordial and perennial mission of evangelizing all peoples, and thereby calling the church into historically tangible and culturally integrated existence throughout the inhabited earth. It is through obedience to the principle of inculturation, with its acceptance of humankind's changing historical condition and invincible cultural pluralism, that the church is supposed to become culturally catholic, and thus a universally intelligible "sign raised up among the nations inviting all who have not yet believed" (Vatican I, D.S. 1794).

Although frequently ignored in missionary practice throughout the ages, the principle of inculturation may be traced back to its earliest articulation in St. Paul's great debate with the Jewish Christians. These first believers, in whose narrowly circumscribed Judaic world the original historico-cultural enfleshment of Christianity occurred, had erroneously confused their new faith with their own ethnic conventions, cultural practices and local laws which they wished to impose upon all non-Jewish converts to Christianity (Acts 15:1-30; 17:22-28; Gal 2:1-4). Thanks to the broader vision of the missionary to the gentiles, who even "withstood Cephas to his face" on this account (Gal 2:11), the Judaizing Christians failed. Vindicated by St. Paul, the principle subsequently yielded the second epochal enfleshment of the church in ephemeral cultural forms and social structures; this time in Hellenic and Roman terms with Teutonic, Gallic, Ethiopian, Iberian, Celtic, Slavic, Scandinavian and Anglo-Saxon variations.

The same theological debate was later renewed when the seventeenth-century Jesuit missionaries, following the initiatives of Matteo Ricci in China and Roberto DeNobili in India, tried to prepare the way for a third epochal incarnation of Christianity in very different cultural worlds. Had they succeeded, the church would then have begun to be a World Church, historically and culturally catholic. But this effort to inculturate the faith in non-Western symbol systems and social structures was authoritatively terminated by order of Pope Benedict XIV in the middle of the eighteenth century. Since then, although the principle has always been given official lip service, the customs, laws, myths, symbols, practices, styles, gestures, conceptualizations and formulations of European Christians have been treated as normative for all the other christian communities in the much larger world

outside of Europe. Where the Judaizers failed the Westernizers triumphed.

This ecclesiastical ethnocentrism may be attributed to what Bernard Lonergan called the "classicist mentality" which took Western culture to be essentially superior to all others, and thus universally normative. This imperial attitude is expressed succinctly in these words of Hilaire Belloc: "Europe is the Faith, the Faith is Europe." This cultural arrogance, still perverting the missionary enterprises and stifling new christian communities, was excoriated by Karl Rahner in his eloquent call for a new Pauline boldness in our time: "The actual concrete activity of the Church in its relation to the world outside of Europe was in fact (if you will pardon the expression) the activity of an export firm which exported a European religion as a commodity it did not really want to change but sent throughout the world together with the rest of the culture and civilization it considered superior" (*Theological Studies,* 1979, p. 717).

Vatican II vigorously reaffirmed the validity and urgency of the church's incarnational approach to all peoples (cf. A.G. 9, 10, 11, 21, 22; G.S. 44, 58; L.G. 13, 17, 23; N.A. 2; S.C. 37). The church, in spite of all appearances to the contrary, "is not tied exclusively or indissolubly to any race or nation, to any one particular way of life, ancient or modern"; it is supposed instead to grow in catholicity by entering "into communion with different forms of culture, thereby enriching both itself and the cultures themselves" (G.S. 58). Through this "wonderful exchange, in keeping with the economy of the incarnation, all the riches of the nations which belong to Christ as an inheritance," are to be assumed by the new christian communities in their respective socio-cultural regions (A.G. 22). In this way the good news of christian revelation is able to function as a leaven within each culture.

The church, therefore, if it is to become a universally visible and intelligible sign of humankind's unity and salvation (cf. L.G. 1), must learn to experience and express itself through the cultural riches not only of Western peoples but of all peoples (cf., A.G. 6-9). These are "the tribes and tongues and peoples and nations," mentioned frequently in the Bible, to whom the church is divinely sent, for whom the church exists, and from whom the church is called into historically tangible existence. They are "the large and distinct groups united by enduring ties, ancient religious traditions and strong social relationships" (A.G. 10). This is why the church "*must* implant itself among all these groups *in the same way* that Christ by his *incarnation* committed himself to the *particular social and cultural circumstances* of the people among whom he lives" (ibid., italics added).

The principle of inculturation is thus rooted in the mystery of the incarnation; it is to be understood and applied in this radical sense, because the action of God in history is paradigmatic for the church's mission. Against a recurring monophysite tendency to "divinize" the church by regarding it in an overly spiritualized and ahistorical manner that minimizes or even denies the ephemeral nature of the historically conditioned and culturally limited elements in its life, the incarnational approach takes seriously the implications of human finitude, flesh, history, creativity, temporality, vulnerability and fallibility. God so loves the world that he sent his Son to assume human nature from the inside, thus giving himself over to a mode of existence that was not his previously. The church must not pretend to be less human or more divine than the Lord of history himself.

The incarnational self-donation, through which humanity is embraced from within, involves an incomprehensible self-emptying (Phil 2-6). Giving himself to us in this intrinsic manner, the divine Word discounted his divinity and humbled himself that he might become truly one of us in everything except sin (Heb 2:14; 4:15): thinking, acting and loving with a human mind, will and heart during a brief participation in the human sojourn circumscribed by the particularity of time, place, ethnicity, culture, folly and sin. Jesus of Nazareth is not a disguise used by God, not a human outer garment covering the divinity, not something foreign or extrinsic to the Jewish people of his time.

What God has done in Jesus Christ "once and for all" (Heb 7:27; 9:26-28) in the historico-cultural terms of one particular people, the church must do among all the peoples who, with their varied historical experiences, myriad cultures and social constructs, constitute the whole of humanity in its spacio-temporal reality. After the manner of the divine Logos, the church must go out of herself, emptying herself of power, foreign riches and alien accretions, thus opening herself to modes of human existence, experience, expression and celebration that were not hers previously. The Church, in other words, is to make herself completely at home among each people in the same authentically human way that Jesus was at home in Nazareth. To ignore the missionary implications of the incarnation is to foreclose the church's real growth in genuine catholicity.

The word inculturation—sometimes mistakenly confused with the social science terms "acculturation" and "enculturation"—gained prominence only after its use during the 1977 Synod in Rome, notably by Cardinal Jaime Sin of Manila and by Jesuit superior general, Pedro Arrupe who argued convincingly for greater pluralism in the life of the church. In Arrupe's words, "real pluralism is the most profound unity" and "the present crisis of unity, in many cases, is due to insufficient pluralism which fails to provide the satisfaction of expressing and living one's faith in conformity with one's culture" (*Teaching All Nations* 1978, p. 21). Father Arrupe gave further currency to the term when he used it in his 1978 letter to Jesuits throughout the world.

The idea behind the word had been strongly reaffirmed by Pope Paul VI in his 1975 apostolic exhortation *Evangelii nuntiandi,* urging the evangelization of peoples not as though they were merely aggregates of individuals without particular historical contexts and cultural matrices, but together with their cultures in their respective spacio-temporal situations. Far from ignoring indigenous cultures, much less trying to replace them with foreign ways of being human and religious, the cultures themselves were to be evangelized "not in a purely decorative way as it were by applying a thin veneer, but in a vital way and right to their very roots" (20, 63). The word inculturation finally appeared in an official papal document in 1979: *Catechesi tradendae* by Pope John Paul II.

It is assumed that the reason for using a new term for an ancient principle was to focus attention on the broader implications of the incarnational theme which Vatican II had emphasized particularly in reference to the strictly missionary evangelization of peoples and their cultures, while many of the older christian communities of the non-Western world still retained the appearance of Western spiritual colonies. Inculturation is a relevant and indispensable principle always and everywhere because the human condition is ever changing and always pluriform. The Holy Spirit does not speak more efficaciously in Western cultural terms than in the more numerous and varied symbol systems of the vast majority of redeemed human beings living in other parts of our planetary village.

See **Church, Church and Culture, Evangelization, Mission**

M. ce C. Azevedo, *Inculturation and the Challenges of Modernity,* Rome, 1982. P. Beauchamp, *et. al., Bible and Inculturation,* Rome, 1983. L. Boff, *Ecclesiogenesis: The Base Communities Reinvent the Church,* London, 1986. A.J. Chupungco, *Cultural Adaptation of the Liturgy,* New York, 1982. J.B. Metz, *Faith, History and Society,* London, 1980.

EUGENE HILLMAN, CSSP

INDULGENCES

According to the 1983 Code of Canon Law an indulgence is a divinely recognized remission or removal of temporal punishment for sins whose guilt has already been forgiven. It is received when specified conditions (e.g. prayer together with the reception of the Sacraments of Reconciliation and Eucharist) are fulfilled by a baptized person who is not excommunicated and who is in the state of grace at least at the completion of the required process. It comes through the assistance of the church, which ". . . as a minister of redemption authoritatively dispenses and applies the treasure of satisfactions of Christ and the Saints" (canon 992).

This description repeats one that Paul VI gave when as a result of discussions during the Second Vatican Council he reformulated the teaching and discipline of the Roman Catholic Church regarding indulgences (A.A.S. 59 [1967] 5-24). Almost all the elements incorporated into his description of indulgences derive from earlier papal teaching and date in their interconnectedness at least to Clement VI in 1343 (D.S. 1025). A notable exception is the phrase *treasure of satisfactions* instead of *treasure of merits.* The latter had been used by Leo X in 1518 even though Luther had objected to it in his *Ninety-Five Theses* of 1517 and Cajetan in reply had—as would Paul VI and the 1983 Code later—proposed *satisfactions* rather than *merits* as the *treasure* dispensed in indulgences. Throughout their history indulgences have frequently been the occasion of misunderstanding (e.g., forgiveness of sin itself was confused with an indulgence remitting only the temporal punishment due to *already-forgiven* sin) and abuses (Pius V was the first pope to forbid offerings made to acquire indulgences—this in 1567). Today they are in special need of explanation not least of all because of a lack of familiarity on the part of many educated Roman Catholics with regard to their church's form of piety prior to the mid-sixties.

To understand the origins of indulgences it helps to recall that very early the church distinguished between the forgiveness of sins committed *before* and *after* baptism. The ritual cleansing with water in baptism was believed to signify and effect (by the power of Christ's death and resurrection) a rebirth involving the forgiveness of *all* past *guilt* as well as *all* *punishment* due to it. For neither was there need to do penance *after* baptism. Not to be repeated, baptism was supposed to be followed by a life in which future sin was avoided. But even the NT (e.g., 1 Cor 5:1-6) attests to the fact that this ideal was not realized. For its part, the *Epistle of Polycarp* to the Philippians (110-30 cc.) shows that a church community which Paul himself had evangelized had to cope with sin affecting even its leaders—as in the case of Valens the presbyter (XI:1-4). In that same *Epistle* Christians in general and presbyters in particular are urged to call back those who wander (VI:1).

A triple conviction grew with regard to those who sin after baptism: a) they are brought to forgiveness by God's grace but not without personal engagement in a process of prayer and self-denial; b) other Christians can help them because of the solidarity existing between the disciples of Jesus; and c) through the ministry of the church such repentance

after baptism leads to divine forgiveness of guilt as well as pardon with regard to the eternal punishment deserved for serious offenses or "mortal" sins, but with the possibility or even likelihood that penance must yet be done (earthly or "purgatorial") before the forgiven sinner can be united with the Trinity in heaven. Indulgences arose as *a* way in which the church helped its members who needed to do that kind of penance (known as *temporal punishment*).

An early precedent is provided by those who survived in the persecutions after having confessed and suffered for the faith. These "martyrs" had credentials which called for respect from church authority—especially in their pleas for clemency with regard to the works of penance expected of less heroic brothers and sisters who had compromised in the persecutions and needed forgiveness from the church and God. Having by Christ's grace more than satisfied or made up for any wrong they themselves had done in sinning, these "martyrs" asked that their sufferings be taken into account so as to mitigate the rigors of penitential discipline for others. This implies the idea of one's satisfaction being available to help others because of Christ and the church. Later the popes would make explicit appeal to the merits of Christ and the saints in promising to those who went on the crusades the remission of temporal punishment for their sins. This practice grew when e.g. those who went on pilgrimages were made eligible to receive indulgences.

Luther objected to any association of alleged merits of saints with those of Christ in indulgences. For him indulgences were acts in which the church excuses from penalties it (rather than God) imposes. He thought indulgences were neither useful nor necessary and regarded them as being connected in practice with the worst kind of abuses (e.g. avarice) and with errant faith.

Belatedly, indeed in its final hour, the Council of Trent reaffirmed papal teaching on indulgences while mandating stringent efforts to correct abuses (D.S. 1835).

During the Second Vatican Council Cardinal Döpfner called for an *aggiornamento* of the church's teaching and discipline regarding indulgences. As noted above, Paul VI responded. He presented the church's teaching in a manner calculated to allay suspicions that indulgences involve a quasi-commercial exchange in which the saints in heaven help people on earth when the latter call on them for intercession. He limited the availability of indulgences so that they can scarcely be at the center of piety even for those who might be inclined to seek and acquire them as often as possible. As for plenary indulgences (those remitting *all* temporal punishment) he stipulated that the disposition required to receive them excludes even the slightest affection for what is even venially sinful. Finally after commending indulgences as part of the church's heritage, he says it belongs to the christian liberty of the church's members whether they wish to acquire same or not (A.A.S. 59 [1967] 11-2, 20, 22).

Indulgences remained a burning issue with the Reformation's descendants, who saw in them a striking example of works-righteousness rather than justification by faith alone in Christ alone through grace alone. Whether or not Paul VI's reformulation of teaching and discipline as well as the virtual disappearance of interest in indulgences on the part of vast numbers of Roman Catholics suffice from the perspective of Protestant Christianity is at this moment not clear. In the summer of 1986 the General Convention of the Lutheran Church in America adopted a report listing indulgences among the issues to which the doctrine of justification by faith as a criterion of churchly discourse and practice must be applied before concluding that the Lutheran-Roman Catholic Dialogue in the United States is right in saying it has achieved "... a fundamental consensus on the Gospel."

See **Good Works, Merit, Justification, Sanctification**

C.J. Peter, "The Church's Treasures (*Thesauri Ecclesiae*) Then and Now" in *Theological Studies* 47 (1986), 251-72.

CARL J. PETER

INERRANCY

The term "inerrancy" designates, negatively, the Bible's quality of being free from error; the positive correlative expression is the "truthfulness" of the Bible. Belief in the Bible's inerrancy is rooted in the conviction that it has been inspired by God, the preeminently truthful one, who is incapable of falsehood. Theologians of the patristic and medieval periods were not unaware that many passages of Scripture, in various respects, pose difficulties regarding biblical inerrancy. It was, however, only from the Renaissance on that the question became the object of intense intra- and extra-ecclesial controversy. This shift was stimulated, e.g., by advances in the natural sciences, recovery of ancient extra-biblical documentation and the emergence of a more critical "demythologizing" reading of the Bible itself. All these developments relentlessly pressed home challenges to the reliability of the Bible's description of natural phenomena (e.g., its "triple-decker" world picture), chronological and historical data (e.g., the sequence of kings in Daniel), the morality of the OT (e.g., with regard to polygamy, divorce, the "holy war") and internal consistency (e.g., the discrepancies as to the number of animals Noah takes into the ark and the duration of the flood in Genesis 7-8). This many-pronged assault on the traditional understanding of biblical inerrancy culminated in the late nineteenth and the first half of the twentieth century. Accordingly, it is not surprising to find inerrancy receiving a previously unprecedented degree of attention in a whole series of magisterial pronouncements of this era, beginning with Leo XIII's *Providentissimus* (1893), continuing through Benedict XV's *Spiritus Paraclitus* (1920), Pius XII's *Divino Afflante Spiritu* (1943), the various drafts of what became Vatican II's constitution *Dei Verbum,* and climaxing in Article II of that document as finally promulgated on November 18, 1965 which states: "the books of Scripture firmly, faithfully and without error teach that truth which God, for the sake of our salvation, wished to see confided to the sacred Scriptures." In reading the relevant portions of this set of texts, one readily discerns a progressing awareness on the part of the magisterium of the necessity of nuancing its own earlier "absolutist" claims concerning the immunity from error of the Bible in all its parts and in every respect. At the end-point of this process of rethinking stands the modest and sober formulation of *Dei Verbum* which, in the decades since 1965, has served as the point of departure for theological reflection concerning inerrancy and which likewise informs the following considerations.

In trying to specify in what sense and to what degree the Bible can be called inerrant/truthful, several points should be kept in mind. First of all, as *Dei Verbum's* phrase "truth. . . for the sake of our salvation" suggests, the Bible's inerrancy has to do primarily with what it says to us on matters of salvific import, i.e., the nature of God and the exigencies of the God-human relationship. Where (and to the extent that) the Bible speaks of points without such salvific significance (e.g., the life-spans attributed to the first humans in Genesis or the figures given

for the forces of Israel and its enemies in various OT books), the same degree of protection from error/reliability is not to be expected. Secondly, it is the "salvific relevance" of the Bible as a whole, rather than of its individual passages or books, which has the primary claim to inerrancy/truth. This affirmation derives from the fact that the church gives us a particular biblical book (and its component elements), not as an isolated fragment, but as part of a canon, containing both an OT and a NT, whose constituent documents mutually condition and complement each other's affirmations about God and humans. Thus, e.g., when considered against the witness of the Bible as a whole, the practice regarding divorce enjoined in Deut 24:1-4 clearly appears as a time-conditioned misreading of God's intentions concerning the man-woman relationship (see e.g., Mal 2:16; Mk 10:6). In this connection it should be borne in mind that while it is usually the NT which functions as a "corrective" for particular portions of the OT, the process is not completely unilateral; e.g., the OT's so-pointed statements on social justice and its application of feminine imagery to God represent important and necessary complements to the NT treatment of these questions. Similarly, the detached skepticism of the book of Qoheleth which places it outside the mainstream of OT-NT theology and anthropology does not simply invalidate that book's message. Rather, Qoheleth functions in the canon as a salutary caution vis-á-vis the over-confidence in our ability to penetrate the secrets of God and the human situation to which much biblical material is prone (just as, in turn Qoheleth's own agnosticism is relativized by the affirmations of the rest of the canon).

Regarding finally the inerrancy/truthfulness of the individual biblical books and passages themselves, it should be kept in view that the truth about reality can be articulated in many other ways than simply the accurate recording of empirically ascertainable "facts" about nature or the human past. In other words, the first question to be asked about a given portion of the Bible is not "is this true or false?", but "how has the author chosen to convey truth here?"; "what is the literary form of this passage?" E.g., the Bible, like ordinary language ("it's raining cats and dogs") is full of overstatements, exaggerated ways of putting things (camels passing through needles' eyes; Jesus' words about self-mutilation in the face of temptation) which, nevertheless, make a valid point about reality, and make it far more effectively than could any flat, literal formulation. The studied parody of the book of Jonah is another such mode of articulating the truth of things which needs to be recognized and appreciated for what it is. It has further to be remembered that the inerrancy/truth-fulness of a particular biblical passage, as of the Bible as a whole, always primarily concerns its underlying religious intention as opposed to its more surface chrono-logical, historical or cosmological asser-tions. Thus while the author of the Book of Daniel is certainly in error in his detailed account of the course of ancient Near Eastern history, his fundamental theological point about the providential purposefulness of all history remains both true and of far greater significance, salvifically speaking, than any mistakes about the names and sequences of rulers.

In summary, belief in the inerrancy of the Bible comes down to the affirmation that, taken as a whole, the Bible, in its dominant theological and anthropolog-ical thrusts, does not deceive us, but offers a reliable, trustworthy guide for our spiritual pilgrimage. This conviction pre-supposed, one may approach the question of the degree of religious, scientific, historical truth (or error) of the Bible's individual portions with a calm and open mind that carefully weighs the balance of probabilities of the particular case, always with the awareness that, so often, the available data will not permit a definitive judgment.

See **Bible, Inspiration**

N. Lohfink, *The Christian Meaning of the Old Testament*, Milwaukee: Bruce, 1968, 24-51. R.F. Smith, "Inspiration and Inerrancy," *JBC*, Engle-wood Cliffs: N.J.: Prentice-Hall, 1968, 499-514. B. Vawter, *Biblical Inspiration*, Philadelphia: West-minster, 1972, 132-155. J. Jensen, *God's Word to Israel*, Wilmington: Glazier, 1986, 267-270.

CHRISTOPHER BEGG

INFALLIBILITY

Infallibility in its literal sense implies not only the absence of actual error, but also the fundamental inability of erring. Consequently, in the strict sense of the term, infallibility is attributable to God alone. In all other instances, infallibility must be understood as a divine gift that is operative only under restricted conditions.

Infallibility differs from both revelation and scriptural inspiration. Revelation is God's communication of truth; scriptural inspiration is a charism enabling biblical writers authentically to record what God has revealed; infallibility is a charism with a two-fold aspect: it enables its recipients authoritatively both to believe and to proclaim God's revelation. Insofar as God wills that the revelation given by Christ to his church must be immune from error in teaching and distortion in believing, infallibility is that gift of the Holy Spirit which preserves the church in its teaching, as well as its members in believing, from error in regard to what is divinely revealed. Infallibility, however, does not prevent the church from making mistakes in teaching, nor its members from error in believing, matters other than those concerning revelation.

What today is called "infallibility" has

been expressed in various ways at different times in the church's history. Although the divine guidance of the church in both its belief and its teaching is evident in the NT and early christian doctrine, the term "infallibility" was first used by medieval theologians and canonists. From medieval times, there have been disagreements about the nature, the recipients, the exercise, and the applicability of the charism of infallibility; such controversy could be anticipated, insofar as the working of divine grace in the life of the church always remains a mystery that surpasses human comprehension and expression.

Roman Catholics generally understand infallibility as a divinely given assistance, implied in Christ's promise to send the Holy Spirit to his apostles and their successors to enable them to believe and to teach without error those truths that are necessary for salvation. Thus, acceptance of the church's infallibility is basically a faith-commitment that presupposes that God provides the church with effective means both for faithfully believing and authoritatively proclaiming the authentic message of the Gospel.

This understanding of infallibility is not shared by most other Christians. For example, some Christians believe that it is impossible for God's revelation to be subject to human control and so reject the claim that the church can ever be the recipient of infallibility either in its belief or in its teaching. Others acknowledge that the church as a whole is infallible in its belief, but deny any exercise of infallibility in the teaching of the pope or the college of bishops. Still others believe in the church's infallibility, but insist that it is manifest only when the teaching of an ecumenical council is subsequently accepted by the whole church.

The principal Roman Catholic teaching on infallibility has been given by Vatican I and Vatican II. In the fourth chapter of

Pastor Aeternus, Vatican I described "the infallible magisterium of the Roman Pontiff" as follows: "The Roman Pontiff, when he speaks *ex cathedra,* that is, when he discharges his office as pastor and teacher of all Christians, and, in virtue of his supreme apostolic authority, defines a doctrine concerning faith or morals that is to be held by the universal church, through the divine assistance promised him in St. Peter, exercises that infallibility with which the divine Redeemer willed to endow his church" (D.S. 3074).

This compact, yet complex, description has been the subject of quite different interpretations and the source of considerable debate. The Council did not teach that "the pope is infallible," but stated that the pope exercises "that infallibility with which the divine Redeemer willed to endow his church," without explaining the nature of infallibility and without restricting the exercise of infallibility to the pope. Also, the Council did not speak of "papal infallibility," but of the "infallible magisterium of the Roman Pontiff," apparently in order to indicate that infallibility is not a permanent personal attribute of the pope, but a temporary assistance divinely bestowed on him precisely in his capacity as universal pastor and authoritative teacher.

For any exercise of infallibility, Vatican I presupposed that the pope can act freely and reasonably, with the necessary mental competence, and without fear or coercion. The Council also insisted that the pope, prior to issuing any definition, is morally obliged to consult the church to determine the belief of its members; by implication, as a prerequisite for infallibility in teaching, the pope must ascertain the presence of an infallibility in believing. And while the Council did not require any specific type of consultation, it did specify that the pope must speak, not as a private theologian, but *ex cathedra,* "as pastor and teacher of all Christians;" thus, the pope must employ "his supreme apostolic authority" with the intention of definitively teaching in a way that is universally obligatory.

In regard to what can be defined, Vatican I was deliberately ambiguous about the "subject-matter," which it described as "doctrine concerning faith or morals that is to be held." While any definition pronounced with the charism of infallibility is obligatory, the type of obligation varies: a definition concerning revelation must be believed with an assent of faith; however, matters that are not revealed (e.g., teachings about the natural law) require acceptance, yet not, strictly speaking, an assent of faith. Another ambiguity concerning "subject-matter" is the interpretation of "morals"; since there is no clear-cut instance where infallibility has been exercised about a matter of "morals," theologians disagree whether the Council intended "morals" to mean: a person's fundamental moral option, or basic principles of morality, or universal precepts of the natural law, or specific commandments.

The Council's statement that these "definitions of the Roman Pontiff are irreformable of themselves, not by the consent of the church," implicitly rejected the position advocated by the Gallican Articles of 1682, which asserted that papal definitions are binding only if they are subsequently ratified by the churches; in response, Vatican I taught that definitions enunciated under infallibility are "irreformable" in the juridical sense that they are not subject to further appeal. However, from an ecclesiological viewpoint, infallibility in teaching (in docendo) must always be accompanied by an infallibility in believing (in credendo); thus, the actual acceptance of an irreformable papal decision by the church's members confirms that a definition really has been made under infallibility; if such accep-

tance or "reception" were not given, it would suggest that a particular papal pronouncement lacked some condition essential for it really to be a genuine exercise of infallibility.

It should also be noted that Vatican I spoke of "irreformable definitions," not "infallible propositions"; this distinction is theoretically important insofar as "irreformable definitions," understood as definitive responses to specific questions, would still allow for additional amplification and future revision in the light of new questions; in contrast, "infallible propositions" would seemingly preclude any further development of doctrine. However, insofar as the only generally acknowledged exercise of infallibility since Vatican I is the papal proclamation of the Assumption of Mary (1950), the actual use of infallibility seems a rarity in the life of the church.

The teaching of Vatican I on infallibility was amplified by Vatican II in *Lumen Gentium,* (No. 25). After noting that bishops "individually do not enjoy the privilege of infallibility," the Council taught that bishops can exercise infallibility in two ways: first, "when, even though dispersed throughout the world but preserving for all that amongst themselves and with Peter's successor the bond of communion, in their authoritative teaching concerning matters of faith and morals, they are in agreement that a particular teaching is to be held definitively and absolutely"; and secondly, "when, assembled in ecumenical council, they are, for the universal Church, teachers of and judges in matters of faith and morals." While it is usually evident when bishops assembled in council intend (or do not intend, as was the case at Vatican II) to teach infallibly, it is extremely difficult to verify an exercise of infallibility when the bishops are dispersed throughout the world.

Vatican II partially clarified the question of "subject-matter" by stating that infallibility "is co-extensive with the deposit of revelation, which must be religiously guarded and loyally and courageously expounded;" thus, "when the Roman Pontiff, or the body of bishops together with him, define a doctrine, they make the definition in conformity with revelation itself." By identifying the "subject-matter" of infallibility with matters of revelation, Vatican II seemingly disowned the position of those theologians who maximalized the scope of infallibility to include practically any type of official papal pronouncement. Other questions about the "subject-matter" of infallibility, for example, the meaning of "morals," still need clarification.

The Council also underlined the moral responsibility of the pope and the bishops, when defining matters of revelation, to "apply themselves with zeal to the work of enquiring by every suitable means into this revelation and of giving expression to its contents." The exercise of infallibility in teaching requires a certain reciprocity insofar as the same charism is given to both the pope and to the bishops: the pope would seemingly always join the bishops in their unanimous infallible teaching of revelation, just as the bishops would presumably never fail to assent to a papal teaching under infallibility. This papal/episcopal exercise of infallibility in teaching presupposes a reciprocal infallibility in believing: insofar as the pope/bishops are given a charism to teach infallibly, the members of the church are given a charism to believe infallibly.

In spite of the progress at Vatican II, infallibility still remains a problematic issue. For example, on the centennial of *Pastor Aeternus* in 1970, Hans Küng's *Infallible? An Inquiry,* attacked the doctrine of infallibility, as being unreconcilable with the factual errors which popes have made in the past, as lacking any historical-critical basis in scripture, and as failing to consider the historically conditioned nature of all doctrinal statements. As a solution, Küng suggested replacing "infallibility" with some other term, such as "indefectibility," or "indeceivability," or "perpetuity in truth," that would indicate that the church, in spite of any mistakes that it has made or might make, is continually guided by the Holy Spirit, who will ultimately lead the church to truth. Though Küng's proposal has been both applauded and attacked, the ensuing discussion has helped highlight numerous philosophical, theological, ecclesiastical, and ecumenical questions about infallibility.

While infallibility remains one of the most controversial issues separating Roman Catholics and other Christians, some consensus has been achieved in the ecumenical discussions that have taken place since Vatican II. For example, the Lutheran/Roman Catholic Dialogue in the United States, while acknowledging the continuing differences between the two ecclesial traditions, has jointly affirmed that they "share the certainty of Christian hope that the Church, established by Christ and led by his Spirit, will always remain in the truth fulfilling its mission to humanity for the sake of the gospel." This emphasis on the belief of the church leads one to wonder whether future discussions of infallibility might well focus more on "infallibility in believing" as a way of resolving the long-standing problems about "infallibility in teaching." In any event, given both the unresolved theological issues and their crucial ecumenical implications, discussion on infallibility will likely continue for the foreseeable future.

See **Church, Magisterium**

Teaching Authority and Infallibility in the Church, Lutherans and Catholics in Dialogue VI, Paul C. Empie, T. Austin Murphy, Joseph A. Burgess,

Eds., Minneapolis: Augsburg, 1978. Francis A. Sullivan, *Magisterium: Teaching Authority in the Catholic Church;* New York/Ramsey: Paulist, and Dublin: Gill and Macmillan, 1983. Hans Küng, *Infallible? An Inquiry,* Garden City, New York: Doubleday, and London: Collins, 1971. *The Infallibility Debate,* Ed. John J. Kirvan, New York/ Paramus/ Toronto: Paulist, 1971. John T. Ford, "Infallibility: Recent Studies," *Theological Studies* 40 (1979) 273-305.

JOHN T. FORD

INITIATION, CHRISTIAN

This refers to the process by which an individual comes to full membership in the christian community. Those seeking membership are known as catechumens. They become members of the catechumenate—a community of those learning the way of Christianity. The *Rite of Christian Initiation of Adults* (1986) outlines the stages and rituals which form the process.

Stages of Initiation

Within the structure of the *RCIA*, there are four distinct periods in the course of the catechumenate:

a. The *pre-catechumenate* refers to the initial period of evangelization, suited to the individual needs of the person. Its structure is therefore flexible and its length indeterminate. It is characterized by informal exchange during which initial conversion crystallizes. Beginning with the first preaching of the gospel, this time of inquiry reaches its culmination in the individual's educated decision to pursue the catechetical and ritual process further.

b. The *catechumenate* is generally the longest of these periods, encompassing the entire span of catechetical preparation, often of several years' duration. Through formal catechesis, the catechumens become acquainted with the doctrinal, practical, liturgical, and evangelical dimensions of the local community and the universal church. Guided by priests, deacons, catechists, and other individuals, the catechumens are led to understand the principal dogmas and precepts of the church. An appreciation of the mystery of salvation is fostered through celebrations of the word during the liturgical cycle.

c. The *period of purification and enlightenment* usually corresponding to the season of Lent, is the time set aside for more profound spiritual preparation for reception of the sacraments of Initiation (Baptism, Confirmation and Eucharist).

d. *Mystagogy* lasts throughout the Easter season, and is intended to provide the newly baptized (neophyte) with the time and opportunity to develop a deeper understanding and appreciation of the mysteries of the faith after having participated in the sacraments.

Rituals of Initiation

The *Rite of Entry into the Catechumenate* is the first liturgical celebration in the process of initiation. Solemnly marking the candidates entrance into the catechumenate, this rite is often celebrated in the presence of the assembled community on the first Sunday of Advent. Before entering the church building, each candidate asks God's church for that faith which leads to eternal life, and promises to follow the path of faith under the leadership of Jesus Christ. The community similarly promises to help the candidate know and follow Jesus.

Each candidate is presented to the community by a sponsor, whose responsibility it is to assess the catechumen's disposition and moral character. More importantly, however, the sponsor serves as a prototype of christian living and a companion on the journey of faith.

While special celebrations of the word, minor exorcisms, and anointings may be held during the course of the catechumenate, the next major liturgical celebration is the *Rite of Election* which is usually celebrated on the first Sunday of the Lent preceding baptism.

After the homily, the catechumens are called forward, and they ask to be admitted to the ranks of the "elect." After the godparents testify to the purity of the catechumens' intentions and the faithfulness with which they received the word of God, the catechumens are examined and questioned individually concerning their intention to receive the sacraments of initiation. They are then officially admitted to the ranks of the elect, and reminded of their duty to continue to strive toward their goal.

During the period of purification and enlightenment, several special celebrations may take place. The *Scrutinies* take place on the third, fourth, and fifth Sundays of Lent. They are meant to heal all that is weak or sinful in the hearts of the elect, and to strengthen all that is strong and good. The elect and their godparents are called forward after the homily on each of these Sundays, and the elect are asked to demonstrate their spirit of repentance (by kneeling, bowing their heads, or by some other means). During the community prayer for the elect which follows, the godparents place their right hands on the shoulder of the one they are sponsoring. This concludes with a prayer of exorcism over the elect and their dismissal.

On the weekdays of Lent, there may be *presentations* of the Our Father and the Creed, although these rituals might also be celebrated during the catechumenate.

The apex of the initiation process is the celebration of the sacraments of initiation, ideally during the Easter Vigil service. As the elect and their godparents approach the baptismal font, the celebrant asks the community to join in the litany of the saints, praying that the elect will be given the new life of the Holy Spirit. The blessing of the water is followed by the renunciation, anointing with the oil of catechumens, and the profession of faith.

Baptism may be by immersion of the whole body or the head only, or by infusion. The adult is either immersed three times by the celebrant or deacon, or the water is poured three times as the individual is baptized "in the name of the Father, and of the Son, and of the Holy Spirit." One or both godparents place their right hands on the neophyte's shoulder while the community joins in a short acclamation. Each neophyte is then clothed with a white garment, receives a candle lit from the paschal candle, and is confirmed by the celebrant. After this rite the neophytes participate fully in the general intercessions of the faithful and the celebration of the eucharist for the first time.

There are no specific liturgical rites either during mystagogy or to mark the end of it, but it remains an important element of the process of initiation, providing time for a denouement after the intensity of the celebrations.

See **Baptism, Catechumen, Confirmation, Eucharist**

Robert Duggan, ed. *Conversion and the Catechumenate,* New York: Paulist, 1984. Michel Dujarier, *A History of the Catechumenate: The First Six Centuries,* Translated by Edward J. Haasl, New York: Sadlier, 1979. Michel Dujarier, *The Rites of Christian Initiation: Historical and Pastoral Reflections,* Trans. and ed. by Kevin Hart, New York: Sadlier, 1979. Robert Hovda, ed., *Made, Not Born: New Perspectives on Christian Initiation and the Catechumenate,* Notre Dame: Univ. of Notre Dame Press, 1976. William J. Reedy, ed., *Becoming a Catholic Christian: A Symposium on Christian Initiation,* New York Sadlier, 1978.

JULIA UPTON, RSM

INSPIRATION
Church Teaching

The most recent statement of the church's teaching on biblical inspiration is found in the Apostolic Constitution on Divine Revelation of Vatican II (D.V. 11): "The divinely revealed realities, which are contained and presented in the text of

Sacred Scripture, have been written down under the inspiration of the Holy Spirit. For Holy Mother Church relying on the faith of the apostolic age accepts as sacred and canonical the books of the OT and NT, whole and entire, with all their parts, on the grounds that, written under the inspiration of the Holy Spirit (cf. Jn 20:31; 2 Tim 3:16; 2 Pet 1:19-21; 3:15-16), they have God as their author, and have been handed on as such to the church herself. To compose the sacred books, God chose certain men who, all the while he employed them in this task, made full use of their powers and faculties so that, though he acted in them and by them, it was as true authors that they consigned to writing whatever he wanted written and no more."

For the first two sentences of this statement the Council refers to Vatican I (D.S. 1787), the Biblical Commission Decree of 1915 (D.S. 2180 [3629]) and to the Holy Office Letter of 1923 (Enc Bib 499). For the final sentence reference is rightly made to the Encyclical *Providentissimus Deus* of Leo XIII (18 Nov. 1893; D.S. 1952 [3293]) which reads as follows: "He (the Holy Spirit) so stirred and moved them to write by a supernatural power, he so stood by them while they were writing, that they correctly understood, willed to write down faithfully and expressed aptly and with infallible truth all that and that only which he ordered them to write. Otherwise he would not be the author of the whole of Sacred Scripture." The teaching of Leo XIII was taken up by the Encyclical of Benedict XV (15 Sept 1920; D.S. 3650).

The first real attempt by church authority to give a description of biblical inspiration, in fact, was that made by Leo XIII, and this was motivated by the desire to clarify issues that had been raised in discussions on the matter within the church during the preceding decades. It was only in the course of the nineteenth

century, in fact, that the nature of biblical inspiration became an issue and that a theology of biblical inspiration became an issue and that a theology of inspiration was put together. During the preceding centuries the truth of the inspiration of the Bible was taken for granted without any keen need being felt of entering into the implications of this belief, especially in the face of the emerging new biblical criticism. In the document *Dei Verbum* the church has indicated the NT basis for this her belief (cf. Jn 20:31; 2 Tim 3:16; 2 Pet 1:19-21; 3:15-16). The NT in its turn took the belief in the inspiration of the Hebrew Scriptures from Judaism, a belief common in Judaism for some centuries before Christ and shared by Christ with his fellow Jews.

Inspiration and the Word of God

The constant tradition of the church speaks of the Bible as the word of God, or as the written word of God. *Dei Verbum* (no. 9) speaks of Sacred Scripture as the speech (*locutio*) of God in as much as (*quatenus*) it is consigned to writing under the inspiration of the Holy Spirit. God is present in his word (*verbo suo*) since it is he himself who speaks when the Holy Scriptures are read in the church (S.C. 7). In keeping with this belief, the liturgical biblical readings end with the profession of faith: *"Verbum Domini,"* "The word of the Lord." This belief in the scriptures as the word of God was also inherited from Judaism by the christian community.

Bible as Word of God and Inerrancy

There is no small polyvalence in the simple expression "the word of God." It can easily be taken to mean that the Bible is the expression, even the infallible or unerring expression, of the divine mind, and as such guaranteeing in the Bible freedom from every shade of error and of statements not corresponding with objective reality. History shows that in fact it has only been too often taken in this manner.

Biblical inerrancy, an inerrancy often wrongly construed, has been the cause of much acrimonious discussion between believers. While the problem of the Bible and the natural sciences is an old one (faced by Augustine in his day), it became all the more acute in the context of modern science. Because of the problems involved, non-Catholic scholars tend to speak of the authority, rather than of the inerrancy of the Bible. Catholic scholars prefer to retain the older terminology, but give it a more refined interpretation. The discussions have led to the following formulation in the Constitution (D.V. 11): "Since, therefore, all that the inspired authors, or sacred writers, affirm should be regarded as affirmed by the Holy Spirit, we must acknowledge that the books of scripture, firmly, faithfully and without error, teach that truth which God, for the sake of our salvation, wished to see confided to the Sacred Scriptures" (with references to St. Augustine, St. Thomas, Council of Trent, Leo XIII and Pius XII). The concept of the word of God should be distinguished from that of revelation. In the context of the inspiration of the Bible, "word of God" is more probably to be understood in the tradition of the prophetic word (cf. Jer 1:9, 12; Isa 55:10-11; Hab 2:2-3) and of the meaning of word in the NT writings (cf. 2 Thess 3:1; 2:13; Heb 4:12-13), that is, as a dialogue between God and man, and at the same time a divine power within man and history to make the message it contains become a reality. This concept of God's word, whether by the prophets or in the scriptures, as spoken to establish a dialogue is more in keeping with the biblical evidence than one regarding it as the revelation of abstract propositions or truths, valid for all time, and necessarily true and valid, since the word of truth itself cannot be conceived as even possibly erroneous. Viewing the word primarily as dialogue leads to a certain ambiguity in the terminology, but an ambiguity inherent in the biblical evidence itself.

In one sense God's word stands forever, and the Bible says so (cf. Isa 40:8). It is also true that the concrete expression of the divine mind can change with time and circumstances. The manner of the expression of God's mind is often determined by pedagogical considerations, not from concern with revealing abstract, immutable, truths. What is spoken as divine word in one text can be modified or even annulled in another word by that same God or by his messenger (cp. Exod 20:3; 34:7 with Jer 31:29; Ezek 14:10-20; Deut 24:16). God can utter unqualified prophecies, with threats or promises, only to change his mind ("repent") should those addressed change their ways (see Jer 18:5-11 for the principle). These are principles to be borne in mind when considering the truth of the scriptures. In the reformulated Catholic expression of the doctrine, ". . .the books of Scripture, firmly, faithfully and without error, teach that truth which God, for the sake of our salvation, wished to see confided to the Sacred Scriptures" (D.V. 11).

Biblical Inspiration and the Structures of the Church

Inspiration, canonicity and the church are linked together in a manner that is currently a matter of investigation by some scholars. Exploration of these inner connections bears promise both for ecumenism and the understanding of the role of scripture in the life of the church. The scriptures, because inspired, have God for their author, and have been handed on as such to the church herself (*Deum habent auctorem atque ut tales ipsi Ecclesiae traditi sunt*) (D.V. 11, repeating teaching of Vatican I, D.S. 3006 [1787]). More thought could very profitably be given to the final end of inspiration, the reason why God willed to inspire, i.e., be the author of, the scriptures. Divine dialogue with his chosen people and humanity will figure prominently in the answer. Since they are inspired by God, the scriptures make the voice of the Holy Spirit sound again and again in the words of the prophets and the apostles. In the sacred books the Father who is in heaven comes lovingly to meet his children (D.V. 21). Sacred Scripture is the speech, the actual speaking (*locutio*) of God (D.V. 9).

Both the biblical and church teaching on inspiration has to do with the biblical books in their final form, as received into the canon of scripture. It is these that are put before us in traditional teaching as inspired. We must, however, go beyond this and inquire whether there was a divine, and as such a biblical, inspiration at work before this and in the process that led to the book's final and canonical state. Scholars differ as to whether the sources used by the final editors or authors were also inspired. I believe that a distinction is in order in this regard. Not every and any source should be regarded as possibly inspired, but only those which originated within the covenant community (whether OT or NT), which were originally intended by God as part of his dialogue with his people, and were also intended by him to remain (even if in modified form) as part of the heritage that would be passed on within the covenant community and in due time become canonical. As such sources one would naturally instance first and foremost the sources of the Pentateuch, e.g. the Yahwist, the various recensions of the Deuteronomist; the original Priestly Codex or the Holiness Code, the exilic and post-exilic recension of the Pentateuch. We could include such early written collections of oracles as those of Isaiah (cf. Isa 8:16-20; 30:8-11), the first and

second scroll written at Jeremiah's dictation (cf. Jer 36), a text such as Hab 2:2-3 and larger editions of the prophetic corpus. All these would have played a formative role in the self-definition of the community, and in turn shaped later self-definitions. To these we could add, and for the same reasons, the prolonged editorial work on the corpus of wisdom writings, evidence of the questioning inherent in Israel's self-definition, in all its catholicity. Similarly with regard to the NT, at least with regard to the gospels. Earlier forms of our present canonical gospels, if they served a community function, may well have been inspired.

Inspiration, the Interpretation and Application of Scripture

The historical interpretation of scripture needs no apologia. It is that now generally practiced by biblical scholars, and has been so for over a hundred years. Christian tradition, at least in theory, admitted the priority of the historical sense, even though only too often in practice it was relegated to a secondary position, in favor of the allegorizing method.

Fidelity to the truth of scripture must always ensure concern for what the original writers intended by their words, which means attention to the literal sense of the Bible. However, it is becoming more and more recognized that there is more to the Bible than just this. The Bible itself bears witness to an interpretation of the earlier inspired writings within the scriptures themselves, and within the communities that produced them, that was not an historical or literal interpretation as we understand the terms. There is a growing awareness of the need to so interpret the inspired writings as to make them relevant and inspirational to the men and women of our own generation. This updating interpretation has been a feature of Jewish tradition down through the centuries, and is evidenced by the Qumran pesharim and Rabbinic midrash. Renewed study of this religious phenomenon has tended to restore respect for the motives behind traditional allegorical interpretation. The more widespread use of the scriptures in the Roman Catholic liturgy is indicating the need for a form of biblical interpretation somewhat different from the purely historical. The introductions to the new Mass lectionary and the new Liturgy of the Hours have opened up the pastoral problems involved. The broader approach to inspiration, canonicity, and the history of interpretation in both the Jewish and christian traditions have prepared the ground for a fuller examination of how the scriptures should be interpreted within the believing community. It remains for our own generation to take up the challenge set by the changed circumstances so that "the Word of God may speed on and triumph" (2 Thess 3:1; cited in D.V., end).

Bruce Vawter, *Biblical Inspiration* (Theological Resources), London: Hutchinson; Philadelphia: Westminster, 1972. Wilfrid Harrington, *Record of Revelation: The Bible,* Dublin: Helicon, 1966. Wilfrid Harrington, Liam Walsh, *Vatican II on Revelation,* Dublin and Chicago: Scepter Books, 1967; James A. Sanders, *Canon and Community. A Guide to Canonical Criticism,* Philadelphia: Fortress Press, 1984. James A. Sanders, *Torah and Canon,* Philadelphia: Fortress Press, 1972. James A. Sanders, "Hermeneutics," in *The Interpreter's Dictionary of the Bible.* Supplementary Volume, Nashville: Abingdon, 1976, pp. 402-07.

MARTIN MCNAMARA, MSC

INVINCIBLE IGNORANCE

Ignorance is lack of knowledge in a subject naturally capable of it. It is different from error, in which knowledge is present but is inadequate and so leads to false judgment. In the context of morality and responsibility, ignorance is the lack of knowledge a person *ought* to have with regard to the nature or moral quality of an act being performed or intended to be performed. It may be ignorance *of law* (that there is a law covering the action in question, or that the law applies in this case), or ignorance *of fact* (i.e. of some circumstance that would bring the action under a law already known in general).

One is not accountable for an action performed in total ignorance, since in this case it is involuntary from the objective moral point of view. But at times one can be blamed for not knowing, hence the importance of the distinction between *vincible* and *invincible* ignorance. The former is that which could be dispelled with reasonable effort, and to the extent that the effort was not made, it is voluntary and therefore imputable. When no effort whatever is made, especially in an area where the subject ought to know what is involved, it is said to be crass or supine ignorance. Affected or studied ignorance is that of the person who studiously avoids getting information in order to feel free of obligation. Since it is deliberately willed and is vincible, any action done in this kind of ignorance remains entirely voluntary.

Invincible ignorance, on the other hand, is that which cannot be dispelled by the reasonable efforts a prudent person would make in a particular situation. What is unknown cannot be directly willed, so there is no moral fault in this case. A person who injures others in a car accident caused by road conditions he could not foresee or by mechanical defects in the car he rented or borrowed in good faith is not morally to blame, though he may make restitution for the damage he caused. When it is a matter of ordinary morality, however, the invincibility is usually suspect. When it is a question of knowledge which a person ought to have as a normal part of professional competence (doctor, lawyer, etc.), the invincibility is even more suspect. But to the extent that the ignorance is truly invincible it involves no moral fault. Indeed a person in this situation has as much obligation to follow his erroneous conscience as he would have to follow a true conscience.

See Conscience; Moral Life, Christian

SEÁN FAGAN, SM

ISLAM

Islam, with more than 900 million adherents, is the second largest of the world's religions. While the Islamic world includes some forty-five Muslim countries extending from Morocco to Indonesia, significant Muslim populations may be found in such diverse environments as the Soviet Union, India, China, England, and the United States.

Historically, Islam is often viewed as a religion which originated in the seventh century with the Prophet Muhammad (570-632 C.E.) and the revelation of the Quran. However, Muslims do not regard Islam as a new religion. They believe that Allah ("the God") is the same God who revealed his will to Abraham, Moses, Jesus, and Muhammad and therefore that Islam constitutes the last stage in the history of revelation. Jews, Christians and Muslims are followers of the same living God, an extended family with a common ancestor, Abraham.

The word *islam* means "submission"; a Muslim is one who submits or surrenders to God. Submission to the Divine Will is not simply a passive act; the Quran teaches that a Muslim has a duty as God's agent *(khilafa)* to spread the rule of God throughout the universe. This universal mission is communal as well as individual. All Muslims constitute a community *(ummah)* of believers, based upon a shared faith which should transcend all other loyalties. The Islamic community or state provides the context for Muslim life and is to be an example to the rest of humanity.

The Quran

Muslims believe that the Quran is the final and complete revelation. Islam teaches that God's revelation has occurred in two forms: in nature and in scripture. God revealed his will for humankind by sending his message to a series of messengers or prophets: "Indeed We sent forth among every nation a messenger, saying: 'Serve your God and eschew idols'. . . . " (16:36).

The scriptures of Judaism (Torah) and of Christianity (the Evangel) are regarded by Muslims as having been corrupted. The current texts are viewed as a composite of human fabrication mixed with divine revelation. The Quran does not abrogate or nullify, but rather corrects and completes Hebrew scripture and the NT. As "People of the Book," Jews and Christians under Muslim rule were regarded as protected people *(dhimmi)*. In exchange for payment of a poll tax, they were free to practice their religion without religious compulsion and, in general contribute to and benefit from the development of the Islamic empire and civilization.

The Quran, "The Recitation," consists of 114 chapters *(surahs)* revealed to the prophet verbatim over a period of twenty-two years and codified after his death. It is God's book, the word of God *(kalam* Allah). The text of the Quran, like its author, is regarded as perfect, eternal and unchangeable. Islam's doctrine of revelation *(wahy)* contrasts with that of modern biblical criticism. Both the form and the content, the words and the message, of revelation are attributed to God alone. The Quran is viewed as the *literal* word of God; Muhammad is merely a conduit or messenger.

Muhammad

The Prophet Muhammad serves as a living model for the community, the embodiment of Islamic practice and values. Muhammad's words and deeds (*sunnah,* practice or example) were collected in narrative reports (traditions, *hadith*) attributed to the Prophet. God's revelation and the example of the Prophet are the primary textual sources of Islam, the foundation stones of Islamic law. They reflect the comprehensiveness of the Islamic worldview. The content of the Quran is concerned not only with belief in and worship of the one, true God but also with socioeconomic reforms regarding marriage, divorce, business practice, criminal punishments, the conduct of war. Similarly, Muhammad was the religio-political leader of the Muslim community/state in which religion was integral to all aspects of life.

Islamic Law

The comprehensiveness of Islam was elaborated in Islamic law, the ideal blueprint for Muslim life. Islamic law (the *shariah,* the path) was developed from the eighth to tenth centuries by jurists who sought to clearly delineate the Islamic way of life. It provides guidelines for the individual and the community, for private and public life. Classical jurisprudence recognized four sources of law, (*usul al-fiqh,* the roots of interpretation): (1) the Quran; (2) the Sunnah of the Prophet; (3) analogical reasoning *(giyas)* or deductions derived from the Quran and Sunnah, and (4) the consensus *(ijma)* of the community. Islamic law is as much a system of ethics as it is of law. To violate the law is not only to risk legal sanctions on earth but also to face divine judgment in the hereafter.

Law is traditionally divided into two parts: duties to God, (*ibadat,* worship) and duties to society (*muamalat,* social transactions). Thus, law covered all aspects of life: prayer, dress, hygiene, marriage, crime and commerce. At the heart of the law are the five fundamental

duties or obligations which constitute the "Five Pillars of Islam".

(1) The Profession of Faith: A Muslim is one who confesses (*shahadah,* witness) "There is no God but The God and Muhammad is the messenger of God." Islam affirms a radical monotheism in which the doctrine of the oneness of God (*tawhid*) is dominant. God is the creator, ruler, and judge of the world. He is merciful and compassionate, but he is also a just judge. On the last day, he will judge all of us according to our Book of Deeds.

The second part of the confession of faith is the affirmation of Muhammad as the messenger of God, the last and final prophet, who serves as a model for the Muslim community.

(2) Prayer: Muslims are called to prayer five times each day. On Friday, the noon prayer is a communal prayer and should be said preferably at a mosque with a congregation. Since there is neither a priesthood nor sacraments in Islam, any Muslim may lead the prayer and may officiate at weddings, burials, etc. Though there is no clergy, a clerical class did develop consisting of religious scholars *(ulama)* and local religious leaders *(mullahs).*

(3) The Poor Tithe: Alms-giving or the sharing of wealth institutionalizes a sense of social responsibility by establishing a fixed proportionate (2 1/2%) wealth tax.

(4) Fasting: Once every year, Islam prescribes a rigorous fast (abstention from food, drink, and sex from sunrise to sunset) throughout the month of Ramadan, the ninth month of the Islamic calendar.

(5) Pilgrimage: All adult Muslims, physically and financially able, are expected to perform the duty of the pilgrimage (*hajj* to Mecca) at least once in their lifetime.

Given the importance of law, the scholars (*ulama,* "learned"), who had developed Islamic law, became a religious establishment with special status and power in Muslim society. They functioned as the guardians of religious orthodoxy, the conscience of Islamic society. The *ulama* interpreted the law, ran the state's school *(madrasa)* system and controlled religious endowments *(waqf),* i.e., property whose income was used to subsidize religious and social services such as mosques, schools, hospitals, hostels. The *ulama* served as advisers and, at times, as critics of Muslim rulers.

Sufism

Alongside the "path" of law (shariah) was the "way" *(tarigah)* of sufism, mysticism. Reacting to the excesses of conquest and wealth and driven by a desire to approach God more directly, sufism combined asceticism with devotional love. Although often regarded by the *ulama* as blasphemous, since only God's will (shariah) and not the transcendent one can be known in this life, sufism became an integral part of popular Islam. Sufi orders and centers developed in the twelfth century, organized under the guidance of a director (shaykh/pir) and engaged in ritual activities to remember *(dhikr),* experience, the presence of God.

Sunni and Shii Islam

The Muslim community divided into two major groups, Sunni (85%) and Shii (15%). While sharing a common faith, each group differs somewhat in its vision of history, practice and politics. The split occurred over the question of succession to Muhammad. The Sunni majority in the Muslim community believed that Muhammad had not designated an heir. They therefore adopted a process of selection of a caliph (*khalifa,* "successor") as the political, though not religious, authority or head of state. The Shii, or "Party of Ali," believed that Muhammad

had designated Ali, his cousin and son-in-law, as his successor and that leadership of the community was restricted to the family of the prophet. The descendants of Muhammad and Ali, according to the Shii, were to be the religio-political leaders (Imams) of the Islamic community/state.

Shii Islam divided into several communities based upon differences in succession. The majority of Shii, the Twelvers (Ithna Ashari), recognize twelve Imams down to the ninth century when the twelfth ("Hidden Imam") Imam is believed to have gone into concealment ("occultation") to return at the end of time. During the interim, Shii are to follow the example and leadership of their religious leaders, *ulama* or *mujtahids,* i.e., those who interpret the faith for the community.

Today, Muslims struggle with the integration of their Islamic heritage in modern society. Throughout much of the Muslim world, a spirit of religious revival has embraced individual and public life. Many have emphasized greater attention to personal religious observances and behavior. Others have reasserted the primary role of Islam in public life, calling for the implementation of Islam in state and society. The process has raised many questions about the relationship of past Islamic teachings and laws to the process of contemporary reform.

Fazlur Rahman, *Islam,* 2nd ed., Univ. of Chicago Press, 1979; and *Major Themes of the Quran,* Bibliotheca Islamica, 1980. Annemarie Schimmel, *Mystical Dimensions of Islam,* Univ. of North Carolina Press, 1975. Malise Ruthzen, *Islam in the World,* Oxford Univ. Press, 1984. Yvonne Haddad, *The Islamic Impact,* Syracuse Univ. Press, 1984. W. Montgomery Watt, *The Formative Period of Islamic Thought,* Univ. of Edinburgh Press, 1973. John Obert Voll, *Islam: Continuity and Change in the Modern World,* Westview Press, 1982. John L. Esposito, *Voices of Resurgent Islam,* Oxford Univ. Press, 1983; and Islam and Politics, 2nd ed., Syracuse Univ. Press, 1987.

JOHN L. ESPOSITO

ISRAEL

Israel. (Heb. (*yiśrā'ēl*, etymology uncertain), proper name which carries several meanings in scripture: (1) the eponymous ancestor of the people Israel, the grandson of Abraham, identified with Jacob; (2) the people Israel, the descendants of the patriarch Israel taken collectively, at any period in their history; (3) the nation Israel, which at various periods, beginning with the time of the settlement, would be identified with (a) the Tribal League, (b) the united kingdom under Saul, David, and Solomon, (c) the Northern Kingdom, the Kingdom of Israel, during the time of the divided monarchy, and (d) the restored Israel after exile; (4) Judah after the destruction of the Northern Kingdom; (5) the geographical territory occupied by Israel (usually used with (*'adāmā* or *'ereṣ*); (6) in the NT, the "new Israel" of faith.

1. The great ancestor of Israel is more commonly called Jacob, but according to Gen 32:23-32 his name is changed to Israel (v 29) after he has wrestled with God. This account also proposes to give a derivation of the name from *śārâ*, to contend, and *'ēl*, God, because "you have contended with divine and human beings and have prevailed"(cf. also Hos 12:4-5, where the same import of the name seems to be supposed). Israel is surely a personal name, but the accuracy of this popular etymology is doubted by scholars ("God" in such names would regularly be the subject, not the object, of the verb). More likely is "let God contend" or "God rules," but none of the derivations proposed has gained a consensus. The identification of Jacob with Israel, it is suggested by some, results from the fusion of originally distinct cycles of tribal and ancestral traditions, possibly when separate tribal groups merged.

2. "Israel" most frequently designates the people. a usage that is found through all periods of the OT, referring back (sometimes anachronistically) to periods as early as patriarchal times (Gen 34:7; 47:27; 49:7) and the sojourn in Egypt (Exod 4:22; 5:2). In this usage the reference is often to "the children of Israel"(*běnê yiśrā'ēl*—Gen 32:33; 36:31; etc.) or to "the house of Israel" (*bêt yiśrā'ēl*)—Exod 40:38; Lev 10:6; etc.), though the latter phrase occasionally refers to the nation rather than to the people (1 Kgs 12:21; 20:31). Although the nation can be said to have existed from the moment Israel possessed its own land and acknowledged a political organization of sorts (i.e., from the period of the Tribal League and the covenant at Shechem [Joshua 24], at least), as a people their traditions claimed an earlier origin in the deliverance from Egypt under Moses, with a family history that stretched back to patriarchs who ranged through Canaan before the descent into Egypt. While the schema of twelve sons descended from Jacob/Israel is a retrojection of the later historical situation into the patriarchal period, John Bright and other historians argue that there was indeed a prehistory to the Israel that emerged on Palestinian soil. The earliest non-biblical reference to Israel is on a stele of Pharaoh Marniptah's fifth year (c. 1220 B.C.), where he claims to have destroyed Israel (with the determinative for people rather than nation). It is Israel the people that is the bearer of the most important theological traditions, especially the promises from Yahweh, election, and covenant; even outside their own land and without any national organization, these things could and did exist in Israel the people, giving it identity and the ability to survive and prosper even in exile and in the diaspora. Israel the people is God's first-born (Exod 4:22), his chosen servant (Isa 44:1), his bride

(Hos 2; Jer 2:1-2; 3:6-15; Isa 54:4-8) whose mission is to be his witness (Isa 43:9-10; 44:6-8).

3. Israel's earliest attested organization is as a confederation of twelve tribes (Tribal League); the number is constant (though the Canticle of Deborah, Judges 5, names only ten) but arrived at in different ways. Levi is not among the tribes with territories, but Joseph is split into the tribes of Ephraim and Manasseh. Israel as a political entity is not easily separable from the people during the period of the Tribal League and the united monarchy, but the distinction can be seen especially in those texts in which Israel is distinguished from Judah, as when David's acceptance as king over Israel (i.e., the northern tribes) comes several years after acceptance by Judah (2 Sam 2:1-4 5:1-5), or where the two are simply listed as distinct entities (i.e., 1 Sam 11:8; 2 Sam 12:8; 1 Kgs 1:35; 4:20). After the rejection of Rehoboam, Solomon's son and successor, by the northern tribes (c. 922 B.C.) "Israel" usually designates the Kingdom of Israel as distinct from the Kingdom of Judah, and this continues until its destruction by Assyria in 721 B.C. The division of north from south was considered a supreme disaster (Isa 7:17), whose healing prophets continued to look for, even long after the destruction of the northern kingdom (Ezk 37:16-22). By metonymy, especially in poetic texts, "Israel" may be replaced by or be used in parallel with terms such as Joseph, Ephraim, Jacob, or (less frequently) Isaac (Hos 5:3, 5, 9, 13-14; 12:1; Amos 6:6; 7:2, 5, 9).

4. With the destruction of the northern kingdom, Judah, as sole survivor, inherited the name, though at this point the reference is to people rather than to nation. In some cases use of Israel for Judah occurred even before the fall. Israel's favorite title for the Lord is "the Holy One of Israel" (Isa 1:4; 5:19; 30:11, 12) and, while Israel still stands, he can refer to Judah and Israel as "both houses of Israel" (8:14); see Jer 18:6, 13. Ezekiel regularly uses "Israel" to refer to Judah, even while Jerusalem and the Kingdom of Judah still stand (Ezek 2:3; 3:1, 4, 7, 17; etc.). Deutero-Isaiah, addressing the exiles of Judah in Babylon, hardly uses the term Judah, but speaks almost exclusively of Israel (frequently in parallel with Jacob).

5. Presumably when Ezekiel addresses "the mountains of Israel," "Israel" refers to the land (Ezek 6:2, 3), though this is rare; the normal usage is to refer to the land of Israel ('admat yiśrā'ēl or, more rarely, 'ereṣ yiśrā'ēl) or to the territory of Israel (gĕbûl yiśrā'ēl).

6. In the NT "Israel" functions in a number of different ways. It can refer to the Israel of old (Lk 4:25, 27; Acts 7:23), but most frequently it refers to contemporary Judaism (Mt 8:10; Lk 1:16; 2:34; John 1:31; 3:10), sometimes in combination with "house of," "people of," or "men of" (Mt 10:6; Acts 2:36; 4:10; 13:16). Sometimes Israel both old and new is intended, as when it is said that Jesus comes as the consolation, glory, or redemption of Israel (Lk 2:25-26, 32; 24:21); likewise, when Paul says that Israel pursued righteousness based on the Law, through works, he means Israel both of old and contemporary to him (Rom 9:31). Paul's reference to Israel "according to the flesh" (1 Cor 10:18) suggests there is also an Israel "according to the spirit." This term does not occur, but in a passage that asserts that neither circumcision nor its absence counts for anything, Paul speaks of "the Israel of God" (Gal 6:16). So also in Rev 7:4-8 the sealing of 144,000 out of the twelve tribes of Israel is a symbolic representation of all the redeemed rather than of Israel as such. Jesus' naming of twelve apostles suggests a new Israel (cf. Mt 19:28 and

Rev 21:12-14), a concept surely reflected in the address to "the twelve tribes of the dispersion" of Jas 1:1 (cf. 1 Pet 2:9).

D.I. Block, "Israel's House: Reflections on the Use of *Byt Ysr'l* in the Old Testament in the Light of its Ancient Near Eastern Environment," *Journal of the Evangelical Theological Society* 28 (1985): pp. 257-75; " 'Israel'—'sons of Israel': A Study in Hebrew Eponymic Usage," *Studies in Religion* 13 (1984): pp. 301-326. J. Bright, *A History of Israel,* 3rd ed., Philadelphia: Westminster, 1981. G.A. Danell, *Studies in the Name Israel in the Old Testament,* Uppsala: Appelbergs Boktryckeriaktiebolag, 1946. N. Lohfink, "Warum wir weiter nach Israels Anfängen fragen müssen," *Die Zeichen der Zeit* 39 (1985): pp. 173-79. M. Noth, *The History of Israel,* New York: Harper & Row, 1960, pp. 53-138. R. de Vaux, *The Early History of Israel,* Philadelphia: Westminster, 1978.

JOSEPH JENSEN, OSB

J

JESUS CHRIST

Christ has come to function as a surname for Jesus of Nazareth. First, however, it was a title employed by Christians to express Jesus' religious significance. The word derives from the Greek translation of the Hebrew word Messiah, or anointed one. What distinguished early Christians from their fellow Jews was their recognition of Jesus as the Messiah, or Christ. Jesus' proper name comes from the Greek rendering of the Hebrew name, Yeshua, or "Yahweh saves."

Biblical scholarship points to Easter as the initial impulse of the process, still ongoing, whereby Christians bestow names on Jesus and seek to express his religious significance. At Easter, Jesus' disciples encountered the crucified one as alive with God and present to them in a new way. In following this transformed Jesus and in carrying forward the mission begun in his lifetime they discovered what God intended for human beings as well as the solution God had provided to the problem of evil. In order to grasp for themselves and communicate to others this experience of God's salvation in Jesus, they needed to articulate who it was whom they followed.

This was a task for the religious imagination. It was not, however, a task to be performed from whole cloth. Both Jesus and his first disciples were Jews; in the tradition of their people, especially the Hebrew Scriptures, and in the religious milieu of the day a wealth of symbolic material lay ready at hand. Very early, for example, an apocalyptic framework was taken up to picture Jesus as presently with God but about to return in victory and judgment. At his return he would exercise the functions of the one like a son of man in Daniel 7 and only then, with the Reign of God established, would he be Messiah. In the meanwhile this community prayed in Aramaic, *Maranatha*, Come, Lord Jesus.

But even as the Judaism of the day was diverse, so were the first christian communities. If some shared an apocalyptic mindset, others turned to the wisdom tradition of Israel. Forging hymns subsequently preserved in the Pauline literature, they took up the feminine image of the one who personified God's own wisdom, the one who existed before the foundation of the world and through whom God had created the universe. Applying this imagery to Jesus, they were enabled to express their conviction that in him they had encountered nothing less than the divine wisdom which had established the universe and set its goal.

If these examples illustrate the diversity at the origins of the early christian movement, scholars also seek to reconstruct the developing oral tradition out of which the writings of the NT emerged.

The title, Lord, provides a case in point. *Mar* in Aramaic, it was an expression of respect like "sir" or "mister" and as such might well have been addressed to Jesus in his lifetime. In the apocalyptic context mentioned above, however, it has acquired the connotation of eschatological judge and messiah-designate. In a Greek-speaking context, the term is *Kyrios,* and the title becomes weightier still. The Bible of the Greek-speaking Jewish Christians was the Septuagint, and in their Bible *Kyrios* referred regularly to God. These Christians used the same title for both God and Jesus, and as the hymn cited in Phil 2:6-11 indicates, they knew full well what they were doing. Drawing on the enthronement psalms, they pictured the risen Jesus as exalted to the Father's right hand, ruling from heaven, pouring forth God's Spirit, and endowed with the title Lord, God's own name.

Development and diversity continued to mark the christian tradition even as written documents began to emerge. If form criticism probes the prehistory of the NT documents, redaction criticism explores the distinctive theology shaping and unifying each document. No longer can the gospels be read as straightforward biographies of Jesus. Rather, each draws communal memories of his words, deeds, and fate into a symbolic narrative expressing the religious significance of Jesus and its ramifications as grasped by a particular author seeking to meet the needs of a particular community.

The earliest gospel, Mark, weaves an apocalyptic tale of the wonderworking Son of God. In its NT usage this title is innocent of metaphysical connotations of strict divinity. In the Hebrew Scriptures it had imaged Israel's sense of divine election as a people and designated as well specially commissioned individuals like kings and prophets. In Rom 1:3-4 Paul could confess that Jesus had been established Son of God at the resurrection, insofar as it was then, by pouring out the Spirit of holiness, that like the kings of old Jesus formed his disciples into a new people, a new Israel. Thus titles like Son of God or Messiah that first referred to Jesus in his risen state or at the second coming came in the gospels to be retrojected onto his earthly career.

Matthew, though literarily dependent on Mark, tells quite a different story. If none in Israel surpassed Moses in authority and closeness to God, Matthew presents Jesus as the new Moses who on a mountain proclaims the new Law and who, again on a mountain, commissions a new and universal Israel with which he will abide until the end of time.

Unlike Matthew, Luke sets Jesus' great sermon on a plain, not on a mountain, for in his symbolism the mountain is the place of withdrawal for prayer in Jesus' story. And unlike Matthew, whose audience is steeped in Jewish tradition, Luke needs to remind his community of their Jewish roots, and so he can plot his gospel as a steady progress up to Jerusalem, sacred city of the Jews, in which the church is founded and from which, in the Acts of the Apostles, salvation spreads to the ends of the earth.

Mark, Matthew, and Luke provide variants on the synoptic tradition. John, the last of the gospels, emerges from a complicated composition process representing an independent tradition, and again it composes a unique figure of Jesus. Taking the wisdom tradition a decisive step forward, John presents a Jesus in whom the divine Word, with God in the beginning, has become incarnate, a Jesus whose "I am" sayings echo Yahweh's self-expression in the Hebrew Scriptures, a Jesus whose self-manifestation in his risen state evokes Thomas' "My Lord and my God."

In time the twenty-seven documents eventually canonized as the NT took shape. Scattered among them were the elements of a symbolic narrative extending from God's eternity with the Word before creation to the second coming of the Christ and the eternal kingdom it would inaugurate. In liturgical ritual Christians raised their hearts to God and to the central figure of the story of God's creative and redemptive activity, Jesus. This Jesus, memories of whose earthly ministry they shared, they found themselves imaging as sharing God's royal prerogatives, exercising God's functions, bearing God's name. If they followed their Jewish heritage in drawing a sharp line between the transcendent God and all that God created, they found themselves imaginatively locating the man Jesus, now raised from the dead, on the other side of that line.

The NT provides evidence that in their liturgical practice and its symbolic narrative Christians were broadening their notion of God to include not only the one to whom Jesus had prayed but also Jesus himself. The task of thinking coherently the confession of Jesus' divinity set in motion the interplay of theological creativity and authoritative doctrinal judgment leading to the Council of Nicaea (325). Christian practice raised a specific question: How could the Father be one, the Son another, both be divine, and yet there be only one God? In some Jewish-christian circles a cultural anachronism prevented the question from arising with its full force. Content to acknowledge Jesus as Messiah and Son of God by election, they escaped the tension generated by confessing his divinity and remained with an adoptionist position. To others it occurred that if God were one, Father and Son cannot be really different; instead, these names must designate no more than modes of God's existence or successive phases of God's self-manifestation. These positions came to be known as types of monarchianism. The Hellenistic bias against matter and

human corporeality also challenged elements of the christian story. Ignatius of Antioch encountered docetic conceptions of Jesus which denied his human bodiliness, and the same issue was among those at stake between Irenaeus and christian versions of Gnosticism.

The image of the divine *Logos* or Word provided by the Fourth Gospel proved an especially apt vehicle of christological reflection as the christian movement advanced into the Hellenistic world of the Roman Empire. In the Hebrew Scriptures the Word of God designated the medium of God's creative and redemptive involvement with the universe, while in the Stoicism which permeated the popular philosophy of the day *Logos* was the principle holding the universe together as an ordered cosmos rather than mere chaos. Justin Martyr was able to seize upon this image in order to transpose Christianity to the culture of Rome. If the Hellenistic world honored philosophy as the highest human endeavor, Justin could present Christianity, based on the direct teaching of the Word Incarnate, as the true philosophy that summed up, corrected, and completed the partial manifestations of the Word found in both the Hebrew Scriptures and Greek philosophers.

The cultural plausibility gained by the development of such a *Logos* christology came at a price. Tertullian, for instance, could affirm that God remained one because the Father, to whom divine power belonged, conferred its exercise on the Son in a manner which in no way diminished or divided that power, and that the Son was divine because he was made of the same *Spiritus,* or divine stuff, as the Father, even though he only came into existence when the Father decided to create the universe. Origen represents an advance upon Tertullian in affirming the eternal existence of the Son as divine, yet for him the Son is inferior to the Father in knowledge and divine only by participation. In each case Hellenistic culture has introduced unexamined philosophic assumptions resulting in a conception of the *Logos* or Son as divine, but subordinate and inferior in divinity to the Father.

Against this background Arius, a presbyter from Alexandria in Egypt, rejected the notion of degrees of divinity. It followed for him that only the Father is divine, while the *Logos* represents God's first creature, the cosmological principle through which all else was created. Hence Arius can be seen to have exposed and sought to resolve the ambiguity introduced into christian thought with the development of *Logos* christology.

The Council of Nicaea rejected Arius' solution, interpolating into a baptismal creed such phrases as "true God of true God." Arius' position was neither impious nor incoherent, but it undercut the structure of christian experience whereby, in encountering Jesus, one encounters not the embodiment of some cosmological principle but the reality of the one true God. The Council's reception was anything but immediate, taking some forty years. It had introduced into its creed a non-biblical term, *homoousios* or consubstantial, and the ambiguity of this term, suggesting as it did to some a material conception of the divine, led many to resist its acceptance until Athanasius' clarification prevailed.

Among the staunchest defenders of Nicaea was Apollinarius; yet his articulation of the Alexandrian Word-flesh christology, with its emphasis on the unity of the divine with the human in Jesus, led him to postulate that in Jesus the divine *Logos* replaced a human, rational soul. This denial of Jesus' full humanity, taking to its extreme the tendency of Alexandrian thought, was condemned at I Constantinople (381). It also evoked a reaction in the formation of the Antiochene school of thought associated with Theodore of Mopsuestia, which stressed the completeness of Jesus' humanity and its distinctness from his divinity. This school, in turn, found difficulty in articulating the unity of Jesus. The tension between the two schools, heightened by ecclesiastical rivalries and political intrigue, set doctrinal development on the path towards the Council of Chalcedon (451).

Nestorius, Patriarch of Constantinople, addressed his Christmas sermons in 428 to the question of an appropriate title for Mary. Alexandrians were honoring her as Mother of God, while Antiochenes resisted the title: strictly speaking, Mary was the mother only of the humanity which the Word assumed. Nestorius proposed Mother of Christ as a compromise, but at the same time he severely criticized the Alexandrian position. Informed of these sermons, Cyril, Patriarch of Alexandria, seized the opportunity to extend the prestige of his see. Having delated Nestorius to Rome on charges that he divided Christ into two persons and that he entertained a Pelagian view of the merit by which the human Jesus earned his preeminent grace, Cyril was empowered to call Nestorius to order. After Nestorius ignored several letters from Cyril, one of which contained twelve anathemas aimed at the whole of Antiochene theology, Cyril prevailed upon emperor and pope to convene a council. This was held at Ephesus on June 22, 431. On that day, under Cyril's presidency, his second letter to Nestorius was canonized as an authoritative exposition of the faith of Nicaea, while Nestorius was found heretical and deposed.

Only in the present century have scholars rehabilitated Nestorius: in the philosophical system he employed, he was unable to distinguish adequately between *prosopon* or person and nature, and in order to affirm the completeness of two natures in Christ, he had to speak of two *prosopa* as well, while attempting to articulate Christ's unity in terms of a third *prosopon* of the union. Thus his difficulties turn out to be semantic and philosophical, not doctrinal. But the charged atmosphere of the day precluded such fine considerations. When, on June 27, 431, John, Patriarch of Antioch, and his party of bishops arrived at Ephesus, they found its decisions already taken. In protest they excommunicated Cyril, leaving the East torn by schism. This state of affairs lasted until, under imperial pressure, Cyril gave up his ambition to impose the Alexandrian theology throughout the East, and the Antiochenes accepted the deposition of Nestorius. In his letter marking the end of the schism, Cyril incorporated in full a formula composed by the Antiochenes, and in 433 peace was restored.

Events picked up again when, in the course of a local synod at Constantinople, heresy charges were raised against the monk Eutyches, Alexandrian in his theology and a favorite of the imperial household. In this awkward situation the patriarch, Flavian, was unable to avoid holding a trial, and under the prodding of the imperial commissioner Eutyches refused to accept the Formula of Reunion which Cyril had approved; instead, he took his stand on the phrase "after the union, one incarnate nature," which Cyril had used in an orthodox sense though its origin lay, unknown to him, with Apollinarius. Flavian reported Eutyches' condemnation to the pope, Leo I, who responded approvingly with a *Tome* affirming the completeness of Christ's two natures.

Meanwhile Eutyches had taken refuge with Dioscorus, Patriarch of Alexandria, who, it turns out, had been manipulating the trial through the imperial commissioner. With Eutyches condemned, Dio-

scorus persuaded the emperor, Theodosius, that a council was necessary, and in 449 he presided over what has become known as the Robber Synod of Ephesus. Refusing the papal legates' request to have Leo's *Tome* read, he saw to it that Eutyches was rehabilitated, Flavian condemned on a technicality, and other major Antiochene bishops deposed from their sees. The Alexandrian dream of complete hegemony in the East seemed fulfilled.

Leo's protests and efforts to convene a new council went unheeded until in 450 the emperor died suddenly. The accession of his sister, Pulcheria, to the throne with her husband, Marcian, saw a reversal of imperial favor and the restoration of the Antiochene bishops. This satisfied Leo, who stopped pressing for a council, but now it was the Emperor Marcian's turn to press for one in hopes of obtaining religious uniformity in his realm. With Leo's reluctant consent the Fourth Ecumenical Council met in October 451, first at Nicaea and then nearer the capital at Chalcedon. The definition of faith at which it eventually arrived marks a climax to the development of christological doctrine in the ancient church. Reiterating the creeds of both Nicaea and I Constantinople, it confesses Christ as one and the same, complete in divinity and complete in humanity. Balancing Nicaea's *homoousios* with the Father, it affirms that the Son is likewise *homoousios* with us, like us in all things except sin. Summing up the two sets of attributes, divine and human, which it has been predicating of the Son, it adds a technical term: he exists in two natures. Reaffirming his unity, it states that these come together in one *prosopon* and one *hypostasis* or person. Chalcedon thus articulated the dogma of the hypostatic union, and this dogma, with its terms of substance, person, and nature, came to provide subsequent christological reflection with its starting point, terms and framework until the present century.

The upshot of the Council was not however, what the emperor had hoped. Alexandrians rejected it as a victory for Nestorius, and the eventual Monophysite schism proved permanent. Chalcedon's defenders sought to win over their opponents by appealing to the conciliar definition's compatibility with Cyril's thought, and this line of defense led, at II Constantinople, to a condemnation of the writings of Theodore of Mopsuestia and two other Antiochenes, Ibas of Edessa and Theodoret of Cyr. III Constantinople, however, rejected an Alexandrian view of Christ as operating with a single energy ("Monenergism") and drew out the implication of Chalcedon's two natures by affirming in Christ the existence of two natural operations and two wills.

With the exception of a brief flare-up of adoptionism in eighth-century Spain, this body of patristic conciliar doctrine proved a stable possession throughout the Middle Ages and beyond. Scholastic theology systematized it in a metaphysical christology, though it is noteworthy that theologians like Thomas Aquinas found room in their treatises for consideration of the major events in the biblical narrative of the life of Christ. Thomists debated Franciscans on such particular questions as the primary motive of the Incarnation, and increasingly subtle responses were devised to questions regarding the mode of union of Christ's two natures, but none of this disturbed the plausibility of the major christological doctrines.

Nor was this situation changed by the Reformation. Luther emphasized that saving knowledge of Christ involves more than doctrinal correctness, but neither he, Calvin, nor the Protestant scholastics who followed in their wake thought to question the Chalcedonian framework.

With the Enlightenment, however, matters changed drastically. Kant's reduction of religion to morality produced a corresponding image of Jesus, while Schleiermacher, in attempting to vindicate the irreducible originality of religious consciousness, read in the fourth gospel a portrait of Jesus as archetypal religious genius.

Meanwhile rationalistic British deism filtered into Germany in the person of H.S. Reimarus. Refusing to take the gospels at face value, Reimarus sought to determine what Jesus' goal had been by setting Jesus' message of the approaching Kingdom of God in the context of first century Judaism. By this route Reimarus arrived at a picture of Jesus as a failed political Messiah, while Christianity originated from the fraud whereby Jesus' disciples spiritualized his teaching, overcame the scandal of his execution by attributing redemptive significance to it, and invented the story of the resurrection. The posthumous publication of fragments of Reimarus' writings in the years 1774-1778 is generally credited as the opening of the "Old Quest for the Historical Jesus."

The traditional self-understanding of christian faith had taken shape in an age which accepted the Bible unproblematically as the true story of the origin and destiny of the human race. In the encounter with modernity, founded on historical consciousness and the newly emergent empirical natural sciences, the cultural plausibility of the Bible was shaken. The encounter of traditional belief with modernity took the form of a cultural clash, and this provided the dynamic of the Old Quest.

Through the first third of the nineteenth-century debate focused on the scriptural miracle stories, with traditionalists defending the historical veracity of the biblical accounts as they stood, while rationalists brought forth plausible natural explanations of the same events. The real miracle behind the tale of the multiplication of loaves and fishes, for example, lay in the generosity to which Jesus' example inspired his audience, so that provisions were shared and all were fed. But if both parties to the debate equally assumed the basic historicity of the scriptural narratives, that assumption was challenged when D.F. Strauss argued that the gospels belonged to the genre of myth in which the values inspired by Jesus were projected onto an ideal figure, the God-man, whose story was intended to reveal those values to others. At about the same time the chronological priority of Mark over the other gospels began to be established, and on the assumption that the earliest must be closest to the historical facts, liberal Protestants began mining Mark and the other synoptics to produce lives of Jesus complete with a chronology of major events and an account of his psychological development. The upshot, epitomized in the work of A. von Harnack, was a Jesus who preached that God's Kingdom was being gradually established in the hearts of human beings as people acknowledged God as a loving Father and related lovingly to everyone else, since everyone was valued by God. Towards the end of the century, however, such liberal lives of Jesus were challenged from two directions. W. Wrede set out to demonstrate that Mark, the earliest gospel, was constructed around the idea of the messianic secret, and that that idea was a literary device invented by the author to meet the apologetic needs of his community. In that case Mark provided ample material on the beliefs of the early church, but very little on the career of Jesus. From another direction J. Weiss and A. Schweitzer sought to understand Jesus from the context of first-century Judaism; the result was an apocalyptic-minded Jesus who anticipated the imminent end

of the world and who, when it failed to materialize, sought to force its coming by his death.

At the close of the Old Quest four options were available. If traditional belief seemed inextricable from the supernatural dualism of an earlier world-view, biblical fundamentalism sought to preserve that world-view from the threat posed by modernity. Liberals, however, espoused modernity and portrayed a desupernaturalized Jesus whose message both mirrored and legitimated their own cultural values. Wrede, in turn, questioned whether the scriptural sources employed by liberals yielded access to the life of Jesus; on his position, Jesus' earthly career lay buried beneath an impenetrable overlay of first-century christian belief. Weiss and Schweitzer, to the contrary, found in those same sources ready access to Jesus' life, but the Jesus whom they discovered was an apocalyptic-minded failure firmly rooted in first century Judaism and quite irrelevant to modernity. None of these options adequately resolved the issue of the relationship between what can be known of Jesus by historical methods and Christian expressions of his religious significance; the Old Quest left behind a gap between the "historical Jesus" and the "Christ of faith."

Subsequent developments in Protestant theology made a virtue of necessity. Christian faith was rendered immune to the results of historical critical research, and such research was deemed irrelevant to christian faith. For Karl Barth, for example, those who would require historical knowledge of Jesus were like Adam, hiding in the garden and seeking to evade the decision demanded by God's proclaimed Word. Rudolph Bultmann insisted that research into the historical Jesus was not only practically fruitless, because of the nature of the sources, but theologically illegitimate as an effort at self-salvation through human intellectual works.

This state of affairs lasted until 1953, when former students of Bultmann launched a "New Quest for the Historical Jesus." E. Käsemann argued that unless the question of the continuity between historically-ascertained data on Jesus and the Christ figure of scripture were resolved, Christians had no answer to the charge that their beliefs were mere myth with no connection to the one whom they claimed as founder of their religion. Form-critical research, he suggested, provided access to the historical data required, and, ironically, those data could even be gleaned from Bultmann's own research findings. Very shortly thereafter G. Bornkamm presented the initial results of the New Quest: eschewing any attempt at a full-blown biography as impossible in view of the character of the NT writings, he sketched the characteristic traits of Jesus' activity and message. Though similar to a rabbi or prophet, Jesus was unique in the authority, greater than Moses, with which he spoke and acted, and implicit in this authoritative manner was a claim to be, in his person, decisive for how people stood with God. It was this implicit claim which, in light of Easter, Jesus' disciples acknowledged and expressed by the various titles they conferred upon him.

If the Enlightenment set Protestant theology on a course of learning through trial and error, Catholicism, in reaction to both Reformation and Enlightenment, took a different path. The initial result was impoverishment as theology became dogmatic, shifting in form from the question of Thomas' *Summa* to the thesis of the manuals and in goal from understanding what the tradition proposed for belief to demonstrating the truth of those beliefs with a certitude gleaned largely from an appeal to authority. In this shift Catholic theology mirrored the rational-

ism of the Enlightenment against which it sought to defend itself. One result was a narrowing of the christological treatise. Consideration of the gospel narratives was relegated to devotional literature, while the miracle stories, and chief among these the resurrection of Jesus, were claimed by an apologetic form of fundamental theology as warrants for recognizing in the founder of the Roman Catholic Church God's legate.

The drive toward centralization in ecclesiastical polity that culminated at Vatican I entailed as well a concern for uniformity in theology. That concern led, in the latter part of the nineteenth century, to the official legitimation of Thomistic neo-scholasticism, and in this context the christological treatise of the Jesuit Cardinal Franzelin served as an oft-imitated model. The neo-scholastic treatise, the dominant genre of christology until well into the present century, focused on a series of three topics. Occurring in a set curriculum in which it was preceded by tracts on the One and Triune God, it presented first the manner in which the Second Person of the Trinity became incarnate, working out the metaphysics of the hypostatic union. The treatise proceeded next to consider the consequences for the human nature of being thus assumed by the divine person, laying out the special gifts of knowledge, sinlessness, and grace with which, one could deduce, Christ's humanity must have been endowed. There followed finally a soteriological reflection in which it was shown that the divine-human agent thus equipped with special gifts effected salvation by offering satisfaction for the sins of humankind.

The year 1951 marked the fifteen-hundredth anniversary of the Council of Chalcedon, and the scholarship generated by that occasion marked a turning point in Catholic christology. What became clear was first of all a gap between the dogma of Chalcedon and the neo-scholastic systematization of that dogma. Where Chalcedon unambiguously affirmed the full humanity of Jesus, the theological manuals exhibited a "neo-chalcedonianism" in which Alexandrian emphases in interpreting the dogma prevailed at the expense of that full humanity. Various critiques of the neo-scholastic manuals began to emerge. On the level of method, the question was raised whether the treatise's "high, descending" approach whereby it simply took for granted the divinity of Christ was not inappropriate to a cultural situation in which the very existence of God was problematic. With regard to content, it was found odd that christology could content itself with dealing with the humanity of Jesus under the abstract metaphysical rubric of nature, finding no room for his life's story or for the resurrection. Finally, with regard to terminology, it emerged that simple repetition of the language of "one divine person" in an age which constructed the notion of person psychologically rather than metaphysically engendered, on the popular level, what Karl Rahner called a "crypto-monophysitism"; people tended to imagine Jesus as an historical figure whose consciousness was simply divine, so that he could read minds, foretell the future, and employ miraculous divine powers over nature. Such a figure was hardly, as Chalcedon had affirmed, "like us in all things except sin."

Precisely out of fidelity to Chalcedon Roman Catholic christology set about recovering the full humanity of Jesus. In the nineteen fifties and sixties this movement operated on two fronts, one philosophical and the other biblical. Karl Rahner drew upon a contemporary development of Thomism to dispel a crudely mythological understanding of the incarnation. On his view, far from representing an alien intrusion into an otherwise indifferent world, the hypostatic union effected the supreme fulfillment of the universal call to self-transcendence into the holy mystery of God which constitutes humanity as such. Similar resources allowed Bernard Lonergan to meet the difficulties attending the traditional language of a single divine, and hence not human, "person" in Jesus. Transposing the Chalcedonian terms into the realm of human interiority, he was able to show how the Chalcedonian formula calls for a full human subjectivity in Jesus coherent with the contemporary, psychologically informed understanding of what it means to be human. Meanwhile, on the biblical front, exegetes who had long operated in the shadow of dogmatic theologians began to highlight in the gospel portraits of the Christ precisely those human features—ignorance, anger, sorrow, weariness, and the like—which the dogmatic textbooks had tended to explain away.

The 1964 *Instruction* of the Pontifical Biblical Commission marked the full emancipation of Roman Catholic biblical scholars, and within a short time they had joined the forefront of their discipline. Their practice of form and redaction criticism rendered available the prehistory and variety of biblical christologies, while newer sociological and literary methods of analysis and interpretation are facilitating the appropriation of those christologies in the contemporary church.

Catholic exegetes have also joined in the pursuit of historical data on the figure to whom the biblical christologies bear witness. Among the historical facts upon which a consensus has emerged are the following: Jesus originally participated in the movement initiated by John the Baptizer; he took as the central theme of his own ministry the nearness of the Reign of God and communicated this theme in a variety of manners, notably through parables; he directed his ministry to all sectors of the population of Israel, including women, tax-collectors, and the poor; he performed healing and exorcisms; he gathered about him a circle of twelve; he encountered hostility from the Jewish leadership and was executed by the Romans.

Facts such as these provide the data for a wide range of theological interpretations of the historical Jesus, a diversity explained by the fact that contemporary authors, as did the original Evangelists, bring their own faith commitment and historical situations to bear in rendering the significance of the data with which they work. Thus, for example, in a context of massive political and economic oppression enforced through systemic violence, Latin American theologians focus upon Jesus' identification with the poor and downtrodden, discovering the liberating potential of his earthly ministry. Feminist theologians similarly find in Jesus' prophetic activity resources for challenging the evils of patriarchal culture within and outside the church, and some have articulated a methodology for reconstructing the early Jesus movement as itself an egalitarian community.

The developments set in motion by the 1951 anniversary of Chalcedon have shattered the framework of the neo-scholastic manual and issued in a christology with a wholly different shape. Contemporary christologies typically open with the question of the historical Jesus, offering an interpretation of the historical data obtained by exegetical research. In a second move they commonly take a position on the nature, knowability, and significance of the resurrection of Jesus. Having thus secured the factors accounting for the genesis of christian faith, they survey the diverse christologies of the NT and proceed to reconstruct the development of the classical christological dogmas of the patristic era and to reformulate these in a manner appropriate to the present day situation.

Extending the christological process into that situation, they articulate the significance of Jesus for those who seek to follow him as disciples today, thus reintegrating soteriology with christology. In a final move, they frequently attend to the newly emergent question of the relationship of Christ to the world religions.

In all of this the movement of recovering the full humanity of Jesus begun under Chalcedon's tutelage some three decades ago has outstripped its mentor. From providing the starting point, terms, and framework for christology, the Chalcedonian dogma has been relativized, acknowledged as but one moment, albeit privileged, in the ongoing christological process. Nor is the precise significance of Chalcedon a secure possession in contemporary theology; given the pluralism of philosophical foundations and methods which inform the new christologies. one not uncommonly finds the formulae of both Nicaea and Chalcedon interpreted as confessions of the unique presence of God in the man Jesus, a line of interpretation which others would regard as regressive to a pre-Nicene stage of christology. Such debate becomes inevitable, however, as christology takes on the historical consciousness of modernity, a consciousness which bestows on it the hermeneutical task of rendering available the full span of tradition for the sake of the praxis of discipleship in which alone the tradition finds its life.

E. Schillebeeckx, *Jesus. An Experiment in Christology,* New York: Seabury, and London: S.C.M., 1979 and *Christ. The Experience of Jesus as Lord,* New York: Seabury, and London: S.C.M., 1980. B. Lonergan, *The Way to Nicea,* Philadelphia: Westminster, 1976. R.V. Sellers, *The Council of Chalcedon,* London: S.P.C.K., 1953. K. Rahner, *Foundations of Christian Faith,* New York: Seabury, and London: Darton, Longman & Todd, 1978, pp. 178-322. R. Ruether, *To Change the World,* New York: Crossroad, 1981. J. Sobrino, *Christology at the Crossroads,* Maryknoll: Orbis, 1978. Schüssler

Fiorenza, *In Memory of Her,* New York: Crossroad, 1981.

WILLIAM P. LOEWE

JUDAISM

The history of Judaism could fill volumes. Even during the biblical period which Jews consider the time from the first gathering of the disparate tribes into a peoplehood entrusted with a covenantal mission by God until the end of the Maccabean Wars (c. 150 B.C.E.) the practice and interpretation of religion underwent many developments. A major reformulation of the meaning of the Sinai covenant, for example, is found in Deuteronomy and the prophetic books represent a significant rethinking of the relationship between cultic worship and the practice of justice as covenantal obligations. And in the post-biblical period (from the Jewish perspective) the Wisdom literature followed by the Pharisaic-rabbinic movement transformed Judaism in some fundamental ways, enabling the Jewish community to survive, and at times even to thrive, in a totally diaspora situation without the Jerusalem Temple or priesthood which had been the centerpiece of its faith for centuries.

The medieval period brought new problems for Jews because of frequent persecution in christian nations, but also saw new attempts to relate its tradition to christian and Islamic philosophy. With the dawn of the modern age, especially the Enlightenment, which resulted in the political emancipation of Jews in Europe and North America, Judaism became far more varied in its religious expression with the rise of totally new movements—the Reform, the Conservative, and the reconstructionist. Finally, our own century has witnessed two principal events that have profoundly affected the soul and spirit of Judaism: the annihilation of six million Jews by the Nazis (called Shoah or Holocaust) and the rebuilding of a Jewish national homeland soon afterwards with the creation of the State of Israel by the United Nations in 1948. Though Jews today are by no means agreed on the ultimate significance of these events, they have become central in some way to nearly all of them. And while no one wishes to see Israel merely as a recompense to the Jewish People for the sufferings inflicted upon them during the Shoah, many Jews themselves posit a close connection between the two realities, even a theological link in which death-resurrection language imported from Christianity is sometimes utilized to describe the relationship between the two.

Yet, despite the many sweeping changes that have transformed the practice and organizational structure of Judaism over the years, there remain a few central ideas that have persisted as the cornerstone of Jewish existence these many years: peoplehood/covenant; torah; and land. We shall briefly examine each of these.

Covenant/Peoplehood

Covenants between the Creator God and human beings are a core component of the theologies found in the Hebrew Scriptures. After the great flood, God addressed Noah and his sons with these words: "As for me, behold, I established my covenant with you and with your seed after you and with every living creature that is with you ... And I will establish my covenant with you; neither shall all flesh be cut off anymore by the waters of the flood, neither shall there anymore be a flood to destroy the earth" (Gen. 9:9-11). The Genesis author then goes on to describe God setting the rainbow in the sky as an eternal sign of this pact with humanity.

The universal covenant with Noah and his sons is followed in the Genesis narrative by the one with Abraham. Here the divine promise is given to the great patriarch that he would be the father of a great and numerous nation, and that the land of Canaan would remain its perpetual possession: "I will maintain my covenant between me and you and your offspring to come as an everlasting covenant throughout the ages, to be God to you and to your offspring to come. I give the land you sojourn in to you and your offspring to come, all the land of Canaan, as an everlasting possession; and I will be their God" (Gen 17:7-8). God subsequently reaffirmed this covenant with Isaac and Jacob (Gen 22:15-18).

Finally, at Mount Sinai, God seals a special covenantal relationship with the entire people of Israel. This covenant does not invalidate the original Noahic covenant, but rather places upon Israel special responsibilities in the spheres of ethics and worship. It also provides the Jewish People with a unique mission—to bring the knowledge of the one loving God to all of humankind. In return God promised that Israel would enjoy divine blessings and protection. But God also warned of dire consequences for the people if they should renege on their covenantal obligations. Nonetheless God promises never to totally abandon the Jewish People. In the final analysis the covenant remains in force forever. After enumerating various punishments likely to befall the Jewish People for non-compliance with the Sinai covenant God still pledges to remain faithful to the bond that has been established despite the nation's sinfulness: "I will remember my covenant with Jacob, and my covenant with Isaac, and also my covenant with Abraham will I remember; and I will remember the land .... When they are in the land of their enemies, I will not reject them, neither will I abhor them, to destroy them utterly, and to break my covenant with them; for I am the Lord their God. but I will for their sakes remember the covenant of their ancestors whom I brought forth out of the land of Egypt in the sight of the nations that I might be their God: I am the Lord" (Lev 26:42, 44-45).

The twenty-fourth chapter of Exodus describes the actual covenant-making ceremony which included a sacrifice. First, an altar was erected and the sacrificial offering prepared. Then the terms of the agreement were read out. The people in turn responded, "We will do everything that the Lord has told us" (Exod 24:3) The sacrificial offering was then killed. Moses took half its blood and sprinkled it on the altar, the symbol of God's presence. The other half he poured on the twelve stone pillars which stood for the twelve tribes of Israel, adding the words "This is the blood of the covenant which the Lord has made with you in accordance with all these words of his" (Exod 24:8). Blood was a symbol of life for the Hebrew people, as it was for many others ancient peoples. Moses' action thus affirmed that the life of Israel was joined to the life of Yahweh. This bond would henceforth be expressed by the people's observance of the laws spelled out in the covenantal treaty.

The meaning and symbolization of the Sinai covenant underwent many transformations in the course of time. The prophets stressed its fulfillment through acts of justice, mercy and loving kindness though it would be wrong to view them as totally opposing cultic commemoration of the covenantal agreement. And in the later prophets, from the time of Hosea onwards, the covenant began to be described in less legal terms through the use of an analogy to the marriage relationship. In this imagery, Yahweh became the patient and loving husband while Israel was viewed as the frequently unfaithful wife. Deuteronomy and Ecclesiasticus offered new theological reflections on the enduring covenant bond between God and Israel. And the very nature of the God who was the Jewish People's covenantal partner was beginning to change. There was a growing sense of intimacy between this God and Israel reflected in the emergence of new divine names such as "Father."

As we come to the post-biblical period in Judaism (after the Maccabean Wars—150 B.C.E), the challenge to the Temple-priestly based model of Jewish faith expression by the Pharisaic revolution led to new cultic ways to remember the covenant. The meal in the home on the Sabbath, and the special family meal on the occasion of Passover ("the Seder meal") in which the covenant and God's enduring faithfulness to it were recalled in a solemn, but still festive, manner, became the primary liturgical context for covenantal renewal. Except for the great day of communal and personal repentance—Yom Kippur, which is based exclusively in the synagogue—the liturgies for Sabbath and for the great Jewish covenantal festivals begin in the home.

Torah faithfulness in worship and in deed served as the keystone of preserving Jewish covenantal existence during the centuries of exclusively diaspora-existence of Jews in Europe, the Middle East, North Africa and the Americas. Some Jews, especially in Poland, did develop a new covenantal piety for a time based far more directly on mystical encounter with the divine. The performance of the "mitzvoth," the deeds of mercy and righteousness mandated by the covenant, became a source as well of immediate, personal union between the believing Jew who performed them and the Creator God.

The Enlightenment produced new possibilities for Jewish life outside a strictly ghetto setting. This led some Jews virtually to abandon any notion of a special relationship between the People Israel and God. Jews shared a generalized ethical commitment with people of other faith traditions. These early classical Reform Jews were quite universalistic in their interpretation of covenantal religion. In keeping with the Enlightenment accent on the individual person they also struggled with the issue of human autonomy and the covenant. This still remains the central theological problem for some contemporary Jewish scholars such as Rabbi Eugene Borowitz.

In recent years Judaism has seen several new attempts to refocus the understanding of covenantal peoplehood. Reconstructionist Judaism, which emerged out of Conservative Judaism, has tried to return the peoplehood concept to a central place in Jewish identity, but in a considerably redefined manner. The various strains of Zionism, some of which are deeply religious, have moved the biblical land tradition back to center stage after its virtual abandonment as a covenantal priority by many Reform Jews. And the experience of the Holocaust has elicited a growing theological debate between those Jewish scholars such as Irving Greenberg, Arthur Cohen, Emil Fackenheim and Richard Rubenstein who insist the covenantal relationship must be totally rethought after the Shoah and those such as David Hartman, Eliezer Berkovits and Michael Wyschogrod who feel the Sinai covenant remains more than ever the basic building block for Jewish identity.

Torah

The term Torah has a variety of meanings in Judaism. It is a far richer and more expansive term than the usual English translation of it by "law" tends to convey. In its widest sense "Torah" signifies a mark of approval on a human deed—it is one performed in conformity with the obligations of the covenant as defined by leading Jewish teachers. More narrowly, it includes all Jewish religious writings, including the Hebrew Scriptures, the Talmud, the Responsa literature, rabbinic commentaries and so forth.

Frequently, however, it will be used in a yet more restricted sense—the books of the Hebrew Bible, especially the Pentateuch.

Traditional Judaism regards the Torah as God's revelatory gift to the Jewish People. It represents the very embodiment of God's word and God's presence. Hence Torah scrolls are kept in the ark (or tabernacle) and are carried in procession, much as Catholics have traditionally done with the eucharist. Within the Torah the faith community can find the totality of the divine will, not only for the Jews but for all humankind. Although transmitted to the People Israel at a particular historical moment the teachings of the Torah are eternally valid in the eyes of the Orthodox Jew. Every word and letter, even the designs or "crowns" on top of the letters as they appear in the parchment scrolls, are considered by the traditional Jew to be revealed by God. By immersing themselves in the sacred act of Torah study, Jews believe that they come to understand better the content as well as the source of God's word. As a result Jewish education, and particularly what is known as *Talmud Torah,* or "study of the Torah," constitutes one of the most vital religious duties in Judaism.

Traditional Judaism has always maintained that everything within the Torah is from God, especially the teachings found in the Pentateuch. But its notion of biblical inerrancy, even within traditional circles, has never been quite as rigid as that found among some Christians. Certain portions of the scriptures were frequently treated in an allegorical fashion by the rabbinic commentators.

Notice should also be taken of Judaism's "collective" sense of revelation. While the Jewish tradition has considered Moses to be the person who wrote down the words of God, nonetheless the Sinai theophany in which the basic revelation occurred was experienced by the Jewish People as a whole (cf. Exod 20:19). The concluding words of the Torah here, "in the eyes of all Israel," makes clear the centrality of the revelation's communal dimension.

During the Second Temple period the Pharisaic movement in Judaism pushed to the forefront a method of continual reinterpretation of the written Torah in light of new experiences and social situations facing the covenantal community. This process eventually came to be known as "oral Torah." In the second century C.E., Rabbi Judah the Prince organized the various interpretations of the written Torah which had emerged up till then through the oral Torah process. This new codified version of oral Torah was called the Mishnah. Henceforth rabbinic authorities no longer derived laws by wrestling with the scripture texts directly. Rather they discussed the formulations found in the Mishnah. These subsequent discussions were also collected into what is termed the Gemara. The Mishnah and the Gemara form the Talmud which exists in two editions, the Palestinian and the Babylonian.

In the modern period non-Orthodox Jews have moved away in varying degrees from the classical understandings of Torah and Talmud. Many would question, if not outrightly deny, the divinity of the written and oral Torah. Reform Judaism by and large discarded the Talmudic teachings as a binding guide for Jewish life, although there has been some modest return to halakic practice among a growing number of Reform Jews the past several years. Classical Reform Judaism left it up to the individual to decide which traditional practices should be maintained. Conservative Judaism always retained a group commitment to Talmudic observance, but offered legal decisions and interpretations which attempted to mold Jewish law to the conditions of modern society.

Orthodoxy continued to hold to strict observance, although a few "modern" Orthodox Jews have found leeway for modest adaptation within the traditional structures.

The authority of Torah and Talmud remains a source of deep division within Jewry today, both in the diaspora and in Israel. No imminent resolution appears to be in sight. If anything, the respective positions appear to be polarizing even further. Where a particular Jew comes down on this question affects their *raison d'etre*. It defines their basic Jewish identity.

Land

The third major component of Jewish existence—land—once again has deep roots in the Hebrew Scriptures. It is very much a part of the covenantal tradition. While Jews may see themselves as an eternal people, they also have understood themselves as a "landed" people. The Abrahamic covenantal experience involved the granting of the land to the patriarch and his seed through Isaac (Gen 17:7-8). And in Deuteronomy we find the promise of the land to the people as a whole (Deut 30:3-5). And Psalm 147 speaks of the Lord rebuilding Jerusalem where the dispersed of Israel will be healed and the wounds of the suffering will receive attention. Finally, the land tradition is buttressed by the biblical accounts of territorial conquest by Joshua and King David and the resettlement of the land under Ezra after the first Exile.

For many Jews the land takes on within the covenantal framework a theological significance equal in importance to peoplehood and Torah and just as binding and eternal. It is integral to the concreteness of the Jewish understanding of religious existence. One of the giants of contemporary Jewish theology, Rabbi Abraham Joshua Heschel, in his volume *Israel: An Echo of Eternity* (Farrar, Straus and Giroux, 1969) understands

Israel, and its heart the city of Jerusalem, as holding an almost mystical meaning for Jews. "Jerusalem," he says, "is a prelude, an anticipation of the days to come .... She is the city where waiting for God was born."

The dream of returning to the land of Israel gave hope to the Jewish people during their nineteen hundred years of enforced exile. This longing for the land was repeated each year at the closing of the Passover Seder meal when the people prayed, "Next year in Jerusalem." Classical Reform Judaism did perceive this land tradition as contrary to its universalistic spirit for the time and removed this prayer from the Passover liturgy. But that situation has now basically changed and the prayer has been restored in the recent editions.

When an actual return to the land became thinkable at the end of the nineteenth century with the foundation of the Zionist Congress, a variety of viewpoints surfaced as to how this land tradition should be interpreted in a modern context. Some gave a highly philosophical or theological interpretation, including some like Israel's first Chief Rabbi Rav Kook who offered a mystical approach. Others preferred a more conventional political/cultural analysis, while still others linked the return to the ideas of socialism that were beginning to generate steam at that point of history. The meaning of the State of Israel in terms of the land tradition has remained a vigorous point of discussion among Jews since that time. But few today deny the basic centrality of the land tradition in some way. The once significant opposition to Zionism within sectors of Reform Judaism has all but vanished.

Recently christian authors such as W.D. Davies and Walter Brueggemann have begun to highlight this biblical land tradition in a new way. They stress its importance for Christians not only in terms of understanding the Jewish People but also in terms of authentic christian faith expression.

Judaism and the Christian Covenant

The enhanced, positive understanding of Judaism that has developed over recent decades has led to major rethinking of Christianity's theological relationship with the Jewish People. This process started in Western Europe right after World War II with christian scholars such as Jacques Maritain, Augustine Cardinal Bea and Karl Barth. They looked anew at Romans 9-11 where Paul speaks of the eternal validity of the Jewish covenant and concluded that the church's traditional theologies of this relationship which focused on the displacement and fulfillment of Judaism could no longer be maintained, especially in light of the christian collaboration with the Nazi Holocaust. So they began to rethink the relationship. Pope John XXIII and the Vatican Council II gave this process official sanction in the 1965 conciliar declaration *Nostra Aetate* on non-christian religions. The section on the Jews repudiates the historic deicide charge and begins to speak of the enduring, positive bonds between Judaism and Christianity. This direction has been enhanced by two further Vatican statements (1975 Guidelines for the Implementation of *Nostra Aetate* and the 1985 *Notes for the Correct Presentation of Jews and Judaism in Catholic Preaching and Catechetics*) and by the statements of various Protestant bodies, as well as the growing number of writings by individual christian theologians such as Paul Van Buren, Johannes Metz, Franz Mussner and Clemens Thoma.

No real consensus has yet emerged regarding this new theology of the Jewish-christian relationship. But there is growing recognition of (1) a deep, pervasive bonding between Judaism and Christianity that makes the church's relationship to Israel part of its core existence and unlike any relationship it has with other world religions. This point has especially been stressed by Pope John Paul II; (2) that the Sinai covenant remains valid and ongoing in its own right. It was not invalidated by the Christ Event nor did the church replace Israel in the covenantal relationship after Easter. Rather the original covenantal relationship was now expanded to include the gentiles; and (3) Christianity needs to reincorporate dimensions of its original Jewish context (both the Hebrew Scriptures and Second Temple Judaism) into its contemporary faith expression. This is especially so with respect to Pharisaic Judaism, so maligned over the centuries in christian preaching and teaching, but which, as the 1985 Vatican *Notes* have insisted, was the form of Judaism that most positively impacted on the teachings and spirituality of Jesus.

See Covenant

John T. Pawlikowski, *What Are They Saying about Christian-Jewish Relations,* Paulist Press. Eugene J. Fisher, A James Rudin and Marc H. Tanenbaum (eds.), *Twenty Years of Jewish-Catholic Relations,* Paulist Press. Frederick M. Schwietzer, *A History of the Jews since the First Century A.D.,* Macmillan. Leon Klenicki and Geoffrey Wigoder (eds.), *A Dictionary of the Jewish-Christian Dialogue,* Paulist Press. Yechiel Eckstein, *What Christians Should Know about Jews and Judaism,* Word Books. Emil Bernhard Cohn with a revision by Hayim Perelmuter, *This Immortal People,* Paulist Press.

JOHN T. PAWLIKOWSKI

JUST WAR
See Peace, War

JUSTICE
A Biblical Call

"Let justice roll like a river" (Amos 5:24-27). Prior to Vatican II no Roman Catholic treatise on justice would have begun with scripture. It would have taken its start from the definition of justice—*Suum cuique tradere*—to render to each one's due and proceeded then to analyze in the light of reason the various relations this involves. With Vatican II but especially with the 1971 Synod, Justice in the World, justice becomes a call to the Christian from the God of the two Testaments.

The idea of justice being a vocation was not, of course, foreign to an earlier Catholic tradition, as will be evident below, from popes beginning with Leo XIII's *Rerum Novarum*. But the 1971 Synod, preceded by the Latin American Bishops' Medellin Conference of 1968, moved more decisively from concern for rational definition to call to commitment to the doing of justice. Connected with this call to commitment is stronger emphasis on love as the form of justice, providing new interior force and motivation. Justice is now being proposed as the first requirement of love. Christian love radicalizes the doing of justice.

Justice in the World begins with the proclamation of the call. "Action on behalf of justice . . . fully appears to us as a constitutive dimension of preaching the gospel"(*The Gospel of Peace and Justice: Catholic Social Teaching Since Pope John*, Presented by Joseph Gremillion, Orbis Books, Maryknoll, 1976, No. 6). "The Church," the document continues, "has the right, indeed the duty, of proclaiming justice on the social, national and international levels" (*Ibid*, 36). This identifies "with her mission of giving witness . . . of the need for love and justice contained in the Gospel message" (*Ibid*, 36). This language is reinforced in many church documents, e.g. Paul VI's 1975 *Evangelization in the Contemporary World*, in Latin America's Third Episcopal Conference held in Puebla, Mexico in 1978, and in several statements of the U.S. Catholic Bishops.

On justice in the OT the 1971 Synod states: "In the OT God reveals himself as liberator of the oppressed and defender of the poor, demanding from man faith in him and justice toward man's neighbor. It is only in the observance of duties of justice that God is truly recognized as liberator of the oppressed" (*Ibid*, 30). This paragraph sums up the wealth of verification of this definition of God that runs through Exodus, Deuteronomy, prophets like Amos, Deutero-Isaiah, the Psalms. The Covenant God, in a word, is a God of Justice. God's own righteousness demands in response to the Covenant our justice toward all in need.

Turning to the NT the Synod avers that "In his preaching he [Jesus] proclaimed . . . the intervention of God's justice on behalf of the needy and oppressed" (*Ibid*, 31). Further, Jesus identified himself with his least brethren. "Insofar as you did this to my least brethren (giving a cup of water, visiting the imprisoned, etc.) you did this to me" (Mt 25:40). Hence, says the Synod, "For a Christian, love of neighbor and justice cannot be separated. For love implies the absolute demand for justice, recognition of dignity and the rights of one's neighbor." And it is "because everyone is the visible image of the invisible God and brothers and sisters of Christ that the Christian finds in everyone God himself and God's absolute demand for justice and love." The final consequence is "Whoever loves must commit oneself to liberating from injustice, economic, social, political, national and international."

Justice and Justification

Formal theological reflection affirms these biblical considerations. For the justification that makes us just is the justice of God. According to the Council of Trent, "The formal, intrinsic cause of our justification is the justice of God. Not that justice by which God is just but that by which God makes us just" (Session 6, ch 7). Our God has an order of justice that ought to exist among the peoples of this earth and indeed all other creation. Accordingly, the justice by which we are made just ought to be in some measure the realizable form of society. Far, then, from giving justification a purely personal and subjective interpretation, it is seen to require conversion of men and women to bringing that justice of God to some measure of realization in our fallen world. This presence of the reign of God's justice also in our time is a theme eminently present in Vatican II's decree on *The Church in the Contemporary World* (*Gaudium et Spes*).

It is obvious how far the language of Scripture and Synod is from that minimalizing of justice which derives from treating the Beatitudes as an ideal or an optional work for those seeking perfection, while assigning to the main body of believers a minimal ethic of justice, the bare bones of justice in free exchange between individuals. Everything said above affirms a claim in solidarity on behalf of all victims of injustice. Biblical justice embodies the principle "To each according to need." It calls for a very large degree of equality of opportunity and of life style.

Natural Law and Justice

Turning to Catholic social teaching's more traditional natural law approach to justice it would be a mistake to suppose this totally superseded by a more biblical understanding. For the natural law approach, rightly conceived, has a powerful dynamism that complements the biblical. This is akin to the notion of justification discussed above. Where the latter sought the ordering of justice willed by God, the natural law expresses the justice that resides in God's knowing, so that natural law is the human expression of eternal law.

The notion of law that results from discussions of natural law has often been static. But this need not be. The ordered set of relations resulting from considerations of natural law can set significant bounds of rights and duties for agents of social life seeking to give each other their due: *Cuique suum.*

As a force moving us to give what is owed another, justice is a virtue, indeed one of the four cardinal virtues along with prudence, fortitude and temperance. The Catholic tradition adopted Aristotle's three forms of justice, legal, commutative and distributive (Nichomachean Ethics) via Thomas Aquinas who elaborated them in his *Secunda Secundae.*

For Aquinas and the tradition influenced by him there is a general justice called legal and two particular justices—commutative and distributive. General or legal justice is that which sets out the overall ordering or norms which ought to govern social behavior. Pius XI called them the "norms of right order" in his Encyclical Letter, *Quadragesimo Anno,* 1931. Because the word *legal* narrows for many this justice to positive law—what is on the books—the term was gradually abandoned in favor of social justice, to be treated below.

The two particular justices are named for the objects to which general justice impels us. First is commutative justice which is the justice that lies between individuals or groups. Since this is characteristically the relation of market exchanges it got the name *commutative.* Two notes must here be made. First, it is generally said that commutative justice is strict justice, implying mathematical equality. But Catholic social teaching has always insisted that commutative justice, as all justice, is personal as well, and must be a loving respect extended to the other. The second note is that commutative justice is not that of individuals simply as individuals. It is always the justice of *parts* of a social whole, hence always exercised within the embrace of the common good of that social whole and under the ordering of the virtue of general justice.

Distributive justice is the justice of the whole to the parts (individuals, groups, classes.) Those who hold authority have a prominent role in achieving the common good, including peace and a productive economy, and distributing burdens involved in producing that good, and then distributing benefits therefrom. Aristotle considered proportionality to be the guiding norm of this justice. That may be translated to say that the lawgiver in judging the *suum*—what is *yours*—looks to other factors than just merit. The law-maker will look also to need as well as ability to contribute. A social sense of justice is offended where too great a disparity exists in income (*Quadragesimo Anno.* 58).

Social Justice

In the latter part of the nineteenth century dissatisfaction with the term *legal* grew widespread. It had all too widely been interpreted to mean that justice was enshrined in legal codes. The term no longer conveyed the idea of a general virtue ordering relationships in society toward the common good. Hence a new name was sought.

The term social justice became enshrined in papal teaching, especially that of Pius XI in his 1931 *Quadragesimo Anno* (*Q.A.*) and his 1937 *Divini Redemptoris* (*D.R.*). The question that entered debate was whether this was a new name for general or legal justice, or whether it was some new *specific* justice as well. Students of the question do well to read the two encyclicals of Pius XI as well as the continuing tradition. Here we confine ourselves to certain key texts. "... there is also social justice with its own set of obligations ..." (*D.R.* 51) "... the distribution of created goods ... must be effectively brought into conformity with the ... common good, i.e. social justice" (*Q.A.* 57, 8). "Produc-

tive effort cannot yield its fruits unless a truly organic body exists, unless a social and juridical order watches over the exercise of work ...." (*Q.A.* 69). "Institutions ... of all social life ought to be penetrated with this justice (*Q.A.* 88; cf. 110, 70).

Several characteristics of social justice emerge: 1. It is the equivalent of the earlier general or legal justice, for its object is the common good. 2. In the name of that common good it commands all specific acts of justice—at a minimum, commutative and distributive justice acts. 3. It is given some central thrust toward *organizing* the institutions of a social and juridical order. It is from this organized and productive society that benefits will be distributed. 4. Social justice commands individuals, organizations and the state.

One other piece of this somewhat fluid tradition needs to be entered before trying to say a final word on social justice. Scholars are aware that the first draft of what was to become John XXIII's *Mater et Magistra* (1961) attempted to resolve the debate over social justice. But the final draft uses the term just twice and without any elaboration or definition. It turns with seeming indifference to such equivalents as *justice and equity,* or *justice and love.*

Accordingly, something like the following consensus might be framed over the term in the Catholic tradition: 1. Doing justice, not naming it, is what is important. 2. Nothing in recent times has so commanded the Catholic conscience as the Synod of 1971 with its reliance on the unmodified word *justice.* 3. Worked out from the social nature of the person and the common good, the concept of social justice has established itself as at least a replacement for legal (general) justice. 4. This social justice commands acts of justice in the individual and hence in some way becomes also a particular justice of the part to the whole. 5. In this latter function, social justice commands especially acts of organizing of such institutions as may be called for in the name of the common good. 6. Social justice, as all justice, must be informed by love.

The concepts remain fluid; where scriptural influence is strong, as in *Justice in the World,* the unmodified *justice* will be used most commonly. Those attracted to the power of the symbol of *social* justice may make distinctions: some confining its use to substitution for legal justice; others, using the term—however ambiguously—also to describe the call to all to organize toward a just society.

Libertarian Tradition and Justice

Social theory in the U.S. has throughout its history thrown exclusive emphasis on freedom of the individual and on the right to one's own good(s) on the basis of meritocracy. For extreme individualists, society is not innate to human beings. There is no positive duty toward others, other than not to invade their claim. Where society exists it is the fruit solely of individual choices freely made to enter society. Society thus results from purely contractual relationships.

From this perspective, taking from one individual in favor of another less fortunate is an abuse, for the more fortunate bears no responsibility toward the less fortunate. Individuals possess the absolute freedom to do as they desire with what is theirs, so long as no injury is done others. The poor and unfortunate are to rest content that they possess the same freedom to enter the market and to gain satisfactions through their own effort and merit. Many assert that the economic energies thus unleashed will effect a productivity which will eventually benefit the poor.

Some libertarians, disturbed by the foreseeable consequences of this policy, have sought to modify this untrammeled freedom—even while they assert that freedom of the individual retains undisputed priority. John Rawls has made a philosophical attempt to bring concern for the unfortunate into some balance with individual freedom, though this freedom remains for him also the primary value.

Rawls declares that each has equal rights to all possible liberties, provided possession of these is compatible with the liberty of others. Rawls desires some significant level of social cooperation—basic goods should be equally distributed. But social cooperation must be compatible with the right to free and equal liberty and opportunity, with each pursuing a life plan as that individual sees fit. The fact that there can be, so they believe, no agreement on life plans is for most libertarians the best proof that unfettered freedom must be prioritized. For Rawls himself free and equal people could conceivably come, at least hypothetically, to some agreement over their fundamental institutions. This could lead to planning the attenuation of privilege through some basic equality. The efforts of philosophers like Rawls should be compared with theoretical efforts to integrate both individual and social wholeness in the Catholic conception of social justice.

Justice and Love

A time-honored distinction among the virtues assigns primacy to love. Love *informs* all other virtues, lives in them, is their soul force. Love transforms justice from within. More fundamentally, the doing of justice stems from the fundamental option for God who loves me and wants me to love others as God loves them, and out of this love to give them full due in the community of social living. Still another sense of the priority of love over justice is the christian conviction that owing to human sinfulness the motive force of justice may not be adequate to the job of getting justice done: on occasion the power of love may have to reinforce a sense of justice.

If one shifts perspective from motive-force to acts, love finds expression in acts of charity. It is recognized that there can well be charitable acts congenial to, if not absolutely required by, social living that go beyond the call of justice. That creates no problem. What is problematic for christian faith is the equating of charitable works to works of counsel or supererogation. This device serves to narrow the field of obligation. Thus, what is of obligation is only what results from what is contracted. All else is charitable work and not of obligation. If one pays a worker the contracted wage in a free market, one's obligations to the worker are dissolved. Yet pope after pope has warned that, the charitable works undertaken to cover need not met by the market wage must be considered no more than provisional. Social justice calls upon the employer and others to create the institutions that will provide the worker with a socially just wage/income. The Catholic tradition will never say that deeds of free giving are nobler than giving what is owed in justice.

It is sometimes said that justice is the objective norm of the christian social morality called for by love. Two remarks: love is also normative; justice is also a virtue of command.

See **Economics**

Jean-Yves Calvez, and Jacques Perrin, *The Church and Social Justice: The Social Teaching of the Popes from Leo XIII to Pius XII (1878-1967).* Leiden: E.J. Brill, 1969. Donal Dorr, *Option For the Poor: A Hundred Years of Vatican Social Teaching.* Maryknoll: Orbis and Dublin: Gill and Macmillan, 1983. David Hollenbach, S.J., *Claims in Conflict: Retrieving and Renewing the Catholic Human Rights Tradition,* New York: Paulist, 1979. Daniel Maguire, *A New American Justice,* New York: Winston, 1980. John Rawls, *Theory of Justice,* Cambridge: Harvard U.P., 1971.

PHILIP LAND, SJ

JUSTIFICATION

Justification is a theological term referring to (*a*) an act on the part of God, (*b*) the results that follow therefrom and (*c*) the centrality of Jesus Christ in both. As to (*a*), in this act God *renders a verdict of acquittal* like a judge and *brings it about* that human beings who are guilty of sin receive the forgiveness they can in no way achieve for themselves. With regard to (*b*), sinners are forgiven precisely because they are thus declared and made to be *just;* i.e. to be *righteous* or to stand in the *right* relation to God because of faith. Finally, (*c*) means that in both what God does and in what happens as a result of this, Jesus Christ is crucially important. To be more specific, because of the latter's life, death, and resurrection God does not wait for sinners to make themselves acceptable (that could never happen!) only then to accept them. On the contrary, because of Jesus Christ and in the Holy Spirit, God accepts those who have no claim to be accepted; promises to make sense out of each individual's existence no matter how senseless it may seem; and values every human life however valueless others may regard it. Revealing who God is, justification stands at the heart of the gospel and enters into the definition of christian hope. Understood as described above, it is the common heritage of those who accept the NT.

The Bible is the source of these shared christian convictions, which draw heavily on the OT. There the Hebrew root *ṣdq* in its various forms came to mean, among other things, God's gracious and saving action shown in a judgment that is just (Isa 46:3; 51:5-8; 56:1). Divine justice or righteousness is understood not as rendering to each what is his or her due but rather as steadfast love or compassion. Humans too are righteous when they are ethically upright; when they obey the Torah; when they manifest fidelity to the covenantal promises. At times divine justice or righteousness and that of humans are related as when God chooses Abraham to observe the Lord's way by doing righteousness and justice (Gen 18:19).

As for the NT, historical-critical method leads to the conclusion that the heart of Jesus' message was the Kingdom of God and not justification as such. But Mt 6:33 (as distinct from its parallel Lk 12:31) does attribute to Jesus the imperative: "Seek first God's kingdom and *righteousness.*" And it is the publican throwing himself on God's mercy who goes home *justified* (Lk 18:14). As for his conduct, table fellowship with sinners is interpreted as showing on the part of Jesus a willingness to accept persons deemed otherwise unacceptable. His urging "Do not fear but *only* believe" has also been presented as worthy of consideration by those asking about antecedents for Paul's teaching (Mk 5:36).

But whether or not it figured prominently in the preaching of Jesus, justification was a theme to which Christians had recourse very early as they reflected on his death and resurrection. In this context justification was understood, in dependence on the OT, as God's vindication of the one who is tested through unjust oppression and persecution. Justification-language had therefore already been used to describe what God had done for human beings in Jesus Christ by the time Paul wrote his Epistles to the Romans and Galatians. His was nevertheless a unique contribution: he related that language more precisely to the faith through which one is justified. For him the phrase *justice of God* seems to have stood for both a gift that comes from God as well as the divine saving power present in that gift to sinful humanity. This inclusive sense was later missed: Catholic scholars argued at times for the first of these meanings and Protestants for the second. But what made inter-

pretation of his thought even more difficult was this: in the same Epistles where he speaks of justification by faith, Paul describes God's final judgment of human beings as based on their works. In this sense the Epistle of James (esp. 2:14-26) may have been written in opposition to a caricature of Paul's position, one presenting as living and salvific a faith with no relation to good works.

The NT nowhere makes justification more important than e.g. salvation or redemption for describing what God has done for sinful human beings in Jesus Christ. What is more, for long centuries in the church's history, justification was subsumed under a developing doctrine and theology of grace rather than treated as a subject in its own right.

Things changed in this regard in the sixteenth century. Martin Luther was convinced people were being encouraged to expect to become acceptable to God by: fasting or performing other works of mortification; going on pilgrimages; entering religious orders and taking vows; becoming priests; confessing all their sins and receiving absolution; having the sacrifice of the Mass offered for themselves or others; as well as gaining indulgences. Luther thought this would lead to spiritual disaster. He was equally sure that the way in which human life comes to be meaningful, valuable, and acceptable in God's eyes is by grace *alone* through faith *alone* because of Jesus Christ *alone.* And this truth, he insisted, comes not through human traditions under whatever disguise they masquerade but rather through the gospel, which is attested to by scripture *alone.* In the *Smalkald Articles* (2, 1) Luther stated his conviction with great clarity: "...faith alone justifies us.... Nothing in this article can be given up or compromised.... On this article rests all that we teach and practice against the pope, the devil, and the world." The importance of justification is vindicated!

Painfully slow in coming, the Catholic response to Luther and the other Reformers took two forms at the Council of Trent, which met at various times between 1545-63. The first was a series of decrees aimed at reforming Catholic life and worship in order to bring out more clearly the centrality of Christ in believers' relations to God. But the Council also dealt with justification directly. In so doing, it taught, among other things, that when God justifies: a) what is accomplished results from Christ's grace and utterly surpasses the powers of human nature; b) adults who had no role to play in their own birth freely cooperate with that grace in their rebirth; c) sinners are declared to be and are in fact just and holy with nothing odious in God's sight remaining in them (concupiscence included); d) faith is the root and foundation of humans' acceptance by God; e) to be united perfectly with Christ, faith does not suffice without hope and charity; and f) the renovation of the human being is such that eternal life in heaven may be proposed not only as a grace but also as a reward promised for grace-sustained works (D.S. 1520 -83).

These two presentations of justification competed with each other for centuries and were generally viewed as being mutually exclusive. Today they are coming to be assessed differently. Biblical studies conducted on the basis of historical-critical method have had a role to play in this change as has historical research aimed at discovering the questions that e.g. the Lutheran Confessions and decrees of Trent were intended to answer. But ecumenical dialogue has also helped, not least of all that conducted by the Luther-

an-Roman Catholic Bilateral Consultation in the United States. In 1983 this dialogue group concluded that the doctrine of justification need no longer divide the two communions. This did not mean that all important differences on the matter had been resolved to the mutual satisfaction of the parties involved. The Lutheran approach to God's dealings with sinful human beings may still be generally speaking more existential and the Catholic way more sapiential. Many Lutherans may still wish to make justification by faith not only a doctrine but *the* critical principle used to test all churchly discourse and practice so as to ascertain whether it does or does not lead people to place their reliance, trust, and hope in God alone because of Jesus Christ. Catholics in turn may reply, as this one has, that another critical principle may be needed as well: to preserve and avoid losing important parts of the Catholic substance, e.g., means of grace inherited from the apostolic age. But the two approaches, however dialectically related, are being seen today more and more as different expressions of the one christian faith with regard to God's acceptance of sinful human beings because of Jesus Christ.

See Grace, Salvation

Justification by Faith: Lutherans and Catholics in Dialogue VII, eds. H.G. Anderson, T.A. Murphy, and J.A. Burgess: Minneapolis: Augsburg, 1985. J. Reumann, J.A. Fitzmyer, and J.D. Quinn, *Righteousness in the New Testament,* Philadelphia: Fortress, 1982. O.H. Pesch, "Rechtfertigung," in *Neues Handbuch theologischer Grundbegriffe,* 3, Ed. P. Eicher: Munich: Kösel Verlag, 1985: pp. 452-70. C.J. Peter, "Justification by Faith and the Need of Another Critical Principle," in *Justification by Faith . . . op. cit.,* 304-15, 376-8.

CARL J. PETER

K

KENOSIS

A Greek word meaning "emptying," derived from St. Paul's description of Christ as having "emptied himself, taking on the form of a man, born in the likeness of man" (Ph 2:7). A "kenotic theory" of the Incarnation has argued that the Son of God laid aside certain attributes of the divinity in becoming man. The Catholic view is that Christ was fully divine and fully human, but emptied himself of the glory that is his by nature.

See **Hypostatic Union, Jesus Christ.**

KERYGMA

Kerygma has the general sense of proclamation. The cognate verb, *kēryssein*, in the Septuagint usually denotes a prophetic or priestly proclamation (Isa 61:1; Exod 32:5). Such preaching and proclamation usually involves the declaration of an event. In the NT kerygma includes the following: (1) the content of christian proclamation (Rom 16:25; 1 Cor 1:21); (2) the activity of proclamation (1 Cor 2:4; 15:14); and (3) the task given to a preacher or herald (Tit 1:3). The christian kerygma is the proclamation of the crucified and risen Jesus as God's final and definitive act of salvation (1 Cor 15:3-5). Jesus, who was the herald of God's message, became the very content of that message. In the classical expression of R. Bultmann the proclaimer became the proclaimed.

For C.H. Dodd the kerygma is the public proclamation of Christianity to the non-christian world. He maintained that the proclamation of the Christ Event was by no means the same as moral instruction or exhortation (*didachē*). However, Dodd's views did not escape criticism. While 1 Cor 15:3-5 limits the kerygma to the salvific message of the death and resurrection of Jesus, Peter's speech in Acts 10:34-43 includes the account of the historical Jesus. The summaries of the discourses of Peter and Paul in Acts envision the conversion of both Jews and pagans to the Good News. While the kerygma focuses on the redemptive death and exaltation of Christ, it includes Jesus' public ministry, introduced by the proclaiming of the Baptist (Mk 1:4, 7).

An examination of Luke-Acts shows that Dodd's use of kerygma was much too restrictive. For Luke the kerygma of Jesus includes the training of the disciples to carry on his message (Lk 10:16). At the end of the gospel Jesus charges the disciples to preach (*kēryssein*) repentance for the forgiveness of sins (Lk 24:47). In Acts the disciples proclaim the word with boldness (Acts 4:13, 29, 31). The character of their proclamation is well expressed in this passage: "'you and all the people of Israel must realize that it [the cure of a cripple] was done in the name of Jesus Christ the Nazorean whom you crucified and whom God raised from the dead. . . . There is no salvation in anyone else, for there is no other name in the whole world given to men by which we are to be saved'" (Acts 4:10, 12). Concerning the content of the kerygma, Luke notes that the person of Jesus and his proclamation constitute the fulfillment of God's plan announced in the OT (Lk 4:18-21; 7:22).

Kerygma is linked to the literary genre of gospel. The very form of the gospels reflects the concern of the evangelists to teach believers the very heart of the kerygma. Mark does this by presenting the words and works of Jesus against the background of the mystery of the cross and its implications for discipleship. Matthew arranges his gospel by carefully constructing five great discourses that accentuate the meaning of Jesus' message for his community. Luke uses the journey motif to draw out the significance of Jesus' death and resurrection. Finally John offers believers the gradual revelation of Jesus' glory—from the wedding feast of Cana to the consummation of Good Friday and Easter Sunday. Kerygma, therefore, lies at the very core of the fourfold message of the Good News.

See **Preaching**

JOHN F. CRAGHAN

KINGDOM OF GOD
See **Reign of God**

KOINONIA

A Greek word meaning "communion" or "fellowship," and used to refer both to Christians' participation in the life of God and to the communal life it creates. *See* **Church, Community, Communion of Saints.**

L

LAITY

A. The Term and its History

As Vatican II's *Dogmatic Constitution on the Church* reminds us, the NT writers use the term *laos* ("people") to refer to all the members of the church (L.G. 9); it designates those who constitute the spiritual Israel, the new "People of God" (*laos theou*). Since in this context the term continues to bear the OT sense of consecration/election, the first Christians are routinely referred to as the elect (*kleī os*), the saints (*hagioi*) of God. While differences among this "people" do exist, Paul explains that these are primarily a matter of function and stem from the different gifts (*charismata*) given by the Spirit for the purpose of building and strengthening the community. Thus while every Christian must serve the gospel (Eph 4:12), this service (*diakonia*) can and does take many forms. Paul's delineation of the different charisms (Rom 12:4-8; I Cor 12:4-11) underscores his belief that everyone has some specific contribution to the community and its mission that they must make; by this means too, the apostle indicates the various ways in which the Spirit's gifts are exercised to the benefit of all.

The derivative term *laikos* first appears in Clement of Rome's *Epistle to the Corinthians* (40, 6) c. 96; it is used here to denote the larger body of Christians governed "by regulations affecting the laity" which the author contrasts with the smaller group of individuals to whom special ecclesial tasks have been assigned. In his classic study, de la Potterie argues that while *laikos* derives from *laos*, the adjective never takes on the rich meaning traditionally associated with the noun. Rather, *laikos* maintains its classical sense of "the people" in contrast to their leaders; furthermore, the term acquires from Hellenistic Judaism the additional nuance, "that not consecrated for service in divine worship." In a christian context therefore *laikos* (later the Latin *plebius* and transliteration *laicus*) refers (1) to those who are not leaders of the community, and (2) those who exercise no cultic function, i.e., those who are neither priest, deacon nor cleric. And while *laikos* is rarely used prior to the third century, already in the writings of Clement of Alexandria (*Strom.* V, 6, 33, 3; *Paed.* III, 10, 83, 2) it has acquired a pejorative sense.

If originally *laikos* was merely a way of designating one segment of the christian population, it was but a short time until this term of distinction came to connote subordination, inequality. For the lay Christian, this subordination and inequality were experienced both politically and spiritually. In the first instance, all power and authority in the church came to be vested in the body of clerics. While at the outset personal charism had proved a sufficient authentication for ministerial service, such was later sacrificed in favor of the charism of office. And if before all Christians were presumed to have a responsibility for the corporate mission and some share in church governance, in time, this type of lay activity was also circumscribed. If initially as the NT reports, all the baptized were active participants in every aspect of christian life and mission, subsequent church history shows that involvement to have been greatly curtailed.

The clergy/lay distinction affected the development of christian spirituality as well. Once the clergy became identified with the realm of the sacred, it was natural to link the laity with the profane, the temporal. From the beginning, christian theologians tended to be ambivalent about the world. On the one hand, because of its divine source, they fully accepted the fact of creation's essential goodness. On the other, since it proves to be a source of evil and distracts the Christian from spiritual things, the early church fathers also regarded the world with suspicion, even contempt. Since it was the clergy who were in a position to articulate the christian world view, they were prone to define holiness in terms of a flight from the world, thus repudiating the very structures and values natural to the lay estate. In time it was simply accepted that if one wished to take seriously his or her christian calling, this could be successfully done only within the framework of monasticism. "The way of the counsels" thus became the preferred means of christian discipleship, while because of a presumption of their inherent weakness and the inferiority of their state, the laity had to be content with a minimalist ethic, "the way of the commandments." On the basis of this type of thinking Gratian in the eleventh century could truthfully declare: *"Duo sunt genera Christianorum."*

The propensity to identify the church with its hierarchical element culminated in the ecclesiology of Vatican I. Here the essence of the church is equated with the three-fold powers of teaching, sanctifying and governing; in this "perfect society" of "unequals" the laity are presented as being the passive, subordinate recipients of the things necessary for salvation available only through the ministrations of the clergy.

But in the nineteenth century, as its temporal power waned and as it grew ideologically isolated from what was fast becoming the modern world, the official church began to rediscover the laity. Practically, the church awakened to the fact that it possessed a valuable resource in an educated and politically aware membership, one well able to promote and defend christian interests in a secular society. At the same time, the hierarchy began to recognize that the laity also represented a formidable moral force in an increasingly pluralistic world. Taking the initiative, laymen in France, Germany and England regularly sought to bring a Catholic influence to bear on the important social issues of the day. An eventual outcome of this grass-roots lay movement was the papacy's (Pius XI and Pius XII) official acceptance and promotion of Catholic Action, i.e., a definite mandate enabling the laity to cooperate with or even participate in the hierarchy's own apostolate.

The same period saw theologians taking new interest in ecclesiology; thus they too began to view the laity in a very different light. The Tübingen school's retrieval of the patristic vision of the church as an organic fellowship of believers with Christ at its head served to underscore the fundamental unity and equality of all the baptized. Continuing reflection on "the Body of Christ" imagery led to new appreciation of the supernatural character of the ecclesial fellowship based on the presence of the Spirit that constitutes and vivifies the corporate life. The same themes were later taken up in Pius XII's encyclical *Mystici Corporis;* here it is frankly acknowledged that no less than the hierarchy, the laity has an obligation to the church's total mission. Finally, biblical scholars' rediscovery of the early church's view of itself as the new "People of God" also helped to confirm the dignity and importance of laity, themselves by baptism full members of the royal priesthood.

In this century but prior to Vatican II, most writing on the subject of laity had the apostolate as its main focus; out of this effort did come new appreciation of the richness and variety of lay life itself. More importantly, this work helped set the agenda for the council's own deliberations; above all, issues fundamental to a theological understanding of the laity had been thematized. Three critical matters with which the council fathers saw a need to deal were: (1) formulation of a definition of the laity that surpassed the purely negative one found in canon law; (2) determination of how the lay person's secular status relates to membership in the church; (3) the basis and extent to which the laity share in the church's mission.

B. Vatican II on the Laity

The ecclesiology of Vatican II marks an official shift away from identifying the church's essence with its hierarchical element to its relocation in the collective socio-historical experience of the community (L.G. 7). As a result, laicity is no longer to be thought of as constituting a separate rank or class; indeed, from the council's standpoint, to be laity *is* to be church. In attempting a definition of the church, the council began by highlighting the original unity that exists among the members of the Body of Christ. "The chosen People of God is one: 'one Lord, one faith, one baptism' "(Eph 4:4); more impressively, it states that members of the church "share a common dignity from their rebirth in Christ ... they possess in common one salvation, one hope and one undivided charity" (L.G. 32). Such assertions were later made the basis for the revised Code of Canon Law (1983).

The emphasis placed on the essential oneness of the People of God also affected the council's understanding of the nature of the lay/cleric relation. Whereas these two terms were previously used to identify two classes within the church, they are here used in a functional way. Reiterating the Pauline statement that there is in the church a unity of purpose but a diversity of service (A.A. 2), the council spelled out the necessary but distinct contribution lay and cleric must make to the successful achievement of the community's twofold mission. For example, the clergy does its part in the work of evangelization by proclaiming the gospel on behalf of the whole church (L.G. 19); the laity evangelize unofficially by the witness of their lives (L.G. 12). In the task of directing the world towards its salvation in Christ, the laity involve themselves directly in the conduct of secular affairs; the clergy, in the main, serve this cause magisterially and pastorally. To further overcome past efforts to negate the laity and their role, the council fathers also reassert that while it is to be achieved by different means, the same call to holiness is addressed to all (L.G. 32). Finally, if it can be said that there is a definite vocation to orders, the council's teaching on the *charismata* makes clear that to be lay is itself a special calling, that this condition is equally a result of the Spirit's gift (L.G. 12, 31).

The Dogmatic Constitution on the Church (chap. 4) begins with a positive definition: the laity are those faithful who by virtue of baptism are "made one body with Christ and are established among the People of God" (L.G. 31). No less than the clergy, they too share in the priestly, prophetic, and kingly functions of Christ; as such, they have a responsibility for "the mission of the whole Christian people with respect to the Church and the world." Yet it is emphasized that the laity carry out this responsibility in a manner entirely appropriate to them—they do so as non-office bearers.

By way of clarification, the council fathers add that "a secular quality is proper and special to laymen" (L.G. 31). This is so because laity exist at the intersection of church and world, in that dimension of reality that has yet to be brought under the Kingdom's dominion. And so, on the one hand, by their very presence, the laity permeate the secular with the spirit of Christ. There by virtue of their education and competence, temporal affairs are ordered according to the plan of God; by their efforts, the world is sanctified (L.G. 31). Yet at the same time, the council fathers acknowledge that the laity bring the secular to the church. They not only present to the community the world's longings and questions in order that these might be illumined in the gospel's light (A.A. 10); the laity's every endeavor on behalf of the Kingdom becomes a spiritual sacrifice and thus "as worshipers whose every deed is holy, the laity consecrate the world itself to God (L.G. 34)."

What was perhaps most revolutionary was the council's admission that the laity have a definite charge in the church's work of evangelization and sanctification. Authentication for service comes with one's baptismal union with Christ and one's participation in the life of grace (L.G. 11). As indicated, this missionary responsibility encompasses both church and world. As regards the former, the laity participate in the ministry of the word as parent educators, as catechists—both parochially and as missioners (A.A.

9). They also contribute time and money to every type of apostolic endeavor sponsored by their local, diocesan, national communities. Lay men and women offer support and advise pastors, bishops; they serve on councils where among other things, they bring to attention contemporary problems that are in need of a christian interpretation and resolution (A.A. 10). The laity may also be given a direct mandate "by the hierarchy to exercise church functions for a spiritual purpose" (L.G. 33).

It is, however, primarily within a secular context that lay men and women achieve their own sanctification (A.A. 7). They do this implicitly by preparing the world for the seed of the gospel by means of the example of their own lives. By their labors to construct a more just society, by imbuing the temporal order with christian values individuals are "a leaven" (L.G. 31). The laity make the church present in an explicit way by bringing the good news of the gospel to unbelievers, by explaining and defending christian principles to society at large (A.A. 13).

But this is not all. The laity have the critical task of renewing the temporal order. On the one hand, they are obliged to exercise proper stewardship of the created world. This means that lay talent and expertise must be put to use developing created realities and bringing their potentialities to their rightful completion; this work is an essential means of preparing for the Kingdom (G.S. 43). More importantly, care for the temporal involves thorough renewal of the human social order that has been permeated by sin. Christians consequently are obliged to reform social institutions and reconstruct them in such a way that they operate more effectively for the advancement of all (G.S. 37). *The Pastoral Constitution on the Church in the Modern World* makes particular mention of the need to eradicate all forms of discrimination, especially sexism, racism; it cites the need for Christians to see to it that every person has access to at least a minimum of culture's benefits, i.e., to a job, a living wage, an education (G.S. 60, 67). This same document treats at some length other important aspects of social existence—marriage and family, economics, and politics—other areas also calling for the laity's attention and concern.

C. Developments since Vatican II

In the post-conciliar period, two factors have effectively controlled thinking about the laity. First of all, the council documents spurred such creativity in the local churches that many of these innovations have simply outpaced sustained systematic reflection. Even now as new communities are established in diverse cultural settings and as old ones try to adapt to a post-christian world, bishops and theologians are pressed to assess these outcomes in the light of the council's teaching. Especially demanding questions present themselves in the area of ministry and it is here that discussion of the laity has tended to center.

In the council's aftermath, new opportunities for lay ministry in the church have opened up. Lay people, men and women alike, have assumed many of those functions formerly reserved to the clergy, e.g., those of reader, acolyte, extraordinary minister of the eucharist. Because of a growing shortage of priests in many places, laity have found it necessary to take primary ministerial responsibility for their communities. But as such things occur, the boundaries demarcating lay and clerical responsibility become blurred and difficult questions arise concerning the relationship of ordained and non-ordained ministries. At the same time, some express fear that excessive attention to ministry within the church will lead to a devaluation of critical ad extra tasks and bring about the clericalization of the laity. Another important issue concerns the participation and role of women. While at the local level Catholic women perform all sorts of ecclesial tasks, some have begun to question the limits for service the official church continues to impose on them.

Other serious questions present themselves in terms of the laity's ministry to the world. According to the first section of *Gaudium et Spes* (1-45), the church not only helps the world in its self-understanding by positioning both creation and human history in an indispensable framework of meaning; it also goes on to make explicit mention of the practical responsibilities Christians have for human society. To the challenge of *Gaudium et Spes,* individuals and communities alike have made a most effective response: there has been a determined effort to look to the humanizing of institutions, to a caring for the world and its resources.

But at the same time, it has become evident that a dualistic approach to the church/world relation no longer suffices. First, the idea that the church can or does exist independently of the world is an inaccurate one. The truth is, at the same time the church attempts to alter society, this is invariably a reciprocal process. Secondly, the opposition created between church and world overlooks the council's affirmation of the fundamental reciprocity of this relation. Not only is a secular quality proper to the laity, but also the specific and typical lay experience of the world is supposed to have an impact within the church. And of course, the long-standing tendency to perceive the world in a negative way ignores the council's presumption of its innate goodness and the episcopal claim that there is much of value the church must learn from the secular.

In addition, there are competing views as to how best the church can serve the world. Should the church play the prophet or the activist? Some of the ambiguity here has deep roots in the theology of redemption; it has to do with the unresolved issue of the church's relation to the Kingdom of God—does the former actively assist the Kingdom's coming or is this something that God alone can do? One contemporary solution seems to be a division of labor, the clergy taking a prophetic role in respect to the world, the laity for their part becoming political activists. But in this instance too, questions about the proper roles of lay and cleric come to the fore. Many priests and religious question the assumption that ordination effectively bars them from full participation in the church's outreach to the world and that their efforts here can never be more than subsidiary to those of the laity.

And even if all were agreed that the world belongs principally to the laity, there is considerable question about the degree to which the hierarchy is willing to respect the former's right to discern what in effect constitutes the Catholic way. The council clearly states that because of their familiarity and expertise the laity are best suited to mind the world and its affairs (L.G. 31, 36). Yet at the same time, several texts caution that pastors alone have the right to judge the authenticity and proper use of lay charisms (A.A. 3); furthermore, clergy are obliged to "clearly state the principles concerning the purpose of creation and the use of temporal things" (A.A.7). This last suggests that in the final analysis, the council fathers could not bring themselves to grant lay persons full autonomy in their dealings with the world. The council's ambiguity at this point proves to be a source of continuing tension today: the conflict between lay "expertise" and clerical "discernment" reveals itself in the disputed areas of sexuality, attitudes towards the arms race and American economic poli-

cies, and the Catholic responsibilities of elected officials.

A second important factor affecting progress towards a theology of the laity relates to developments in ecclesiology. Since the Council, a "models" ecclesiology has been prominent. This effort to formulate a theology of the church on the basis of a series of images which present the christian community in a variety of perspectives is inadequate for underwriting "a sound and sufficient theology of the laity" such as that recommended by Congar. Besides the fact that there has been almost no interest in thematizing the lay element of the individual models, this fragmented approach seems incapable of providing that "total ecclesiology" necessary to support a comprehensive lay theology. And, just as there is an incipient tendency to deal with the church by breaking down its reality into a series of discrete sub-categories, so too as a subject "laity" tends to be treated piecemeal under the individual headings of lay spirituality, lay/clergy relations, lay ministry (further sub-divided into its church and world aspects). To meet Congar's requirement, what has yet to appear is an ecclesiology whose conceptual framework is capable of highlighting and exploring the dynamic, dialectical relationship that exists between a community and its members. Here will be provided an understanding of the church that attends to the ways in which the activity of the membership is intrinsic to the community's very self-actualization. Only when this more systematic view is taken will a satisfactory understanding of the church as laity finally emerge.

See **Church, Ministry**

Yves M.-J. Congar, "My Path-findings in the Theology of Laity and Ministries,' *The Jurist* 32 (1972): pp. 169-188. Leonard Doohan, *The Lay-Centered Church: Theology and Spirituality,* Minneapolis: Winston. 1984. Jacques Fontaine, "The Practice of Christian Life: The Birth of the

Laity," in *Christian Spirituality: Origins to the Twelfth Century*, New York: Crossroad, 1986. pp. 453-491. Rosemary Goldie, "Laity: A Bibliographical Survey of Three Decades," *The Laity Today* 26 (1979): pp. 107-143. Ferdinand Klostermann, "Decree of the Apostolate of the Laity," in *Commentary on the Documents of Vatican II*, vol. 3, 586-635. Eds., Franz Xaver Arnold, et al. Freiburg: Herder, 1968. David N. Power, *Gifts that Differ. Lay Ministries Established and Unestablished*, New York: Pueblo, 1980 Edward Schillebeeckx, "The Typological Definition of the Christian Layman according to Vatican II," in *The Mission of the Church*, New York: Seabury, 1973. pp. 90-117.

GEORGIA M. KEIGHTLEY

LANGUAGE, RELIGIOUS

Like all other forms of language, religious language operates in a system of interacting networks: grammatical, semantic, pragmatic; that is, networks of words, of meanings, and of usage. It is related to and yet distinct from theology, which is the speculative study of God and the universe in relation to God. Both have God as their referent, but theology is an apologetic and systematic science. Religious language, arising out of personal experiences of God, accepts divine existence as a given and seeks existential appropriation of the transcendental world available to devotees of a tradition.

Every religious tradition has its authentic language forms. For Judeo-Christians the Bible is the source and prototype of religious discourse. The self-manifestation of God in creation was followed by a series of divine revelations to humans, beginning with Abraham. Through the call of Moses and the setting up of a cult directed by Aaron and his descendants, the Israelite religious tradition evolved. When members faltered, the prophets were moved by the divine Spirit to remind Israelites that they were a people formed to be God's special possession. After rescuing them from exile, the God of Israel finally sent his Son Jesus Christ, the Word made flesh, to be the second Adam, savior and head of the new humanity.

This long series of divine interventions generated a special language with special literary types that include: cultic myths, religious narratives, laws to guide community worship and conduct, songs for public worship, prophetic oracles, pieces of didactic wisdom, and apocalyptic visions. Christians adopted this sacred literature as their own, and added other forms: narratives of the Christ event, apostolic letters of instruction and exhortation, and accounts of apostolic mission activity.

Fundamental qualities of biblical religious language are: (1) its referent is God, not in the sense that it treats God as object but that it is directed toward God as dynamic horizon who offers ultimate meaning to believers; (2) it predicates a transcendent "universe of discourse" that originates in divine revelation and directs back to God as creator of the universe and savior of the human race and all reality; (3) it is self-involving, that is, it commits users to the glory of God as their ultimate good and goal. This involvement best expresses itself in literary forms like prayers, oracles, blessings, creeds, parables, and exhortations.

These three qualities are linked to the double origin of biblical faith, namely, that it was evoked by divine revelation, and that it cultivated personal experiences of God as ultimate goal of human existence. These three qualities also account for its two distinct expressions: primary and secondary.

Primary Religious Language. Those who were the active participants in God's self-revelation within history created its primary forms. Primary biblical religious language is paradoxical, figurative, imaginative—seeing more than it said. Stretching words beyond normal usage, it enlarged the God-ward horizon of believers. No attempt was made at consistency. The writings of the NT captured the emotion and power felt in encountering God in Jesus and in being possessed by the Holy Spirit. Its language invites readers to become part of a unique community of faith, a group that trusts completely in the God who shapes humanity under the lordship of Jesus. It warns against rejecting or misusing God's saving gifts lest one lose the reward of eternal salvation.

Secondary Religious Language. Once the actual participants of the Christ event died, the saving community was challenged to preserve this traditional faith without possessing many of the ecstatic experiences of the first witnesses. The original paradoxical expressions became familiar, and a technical vocabulary arose to insure correct belief. Secondary or derivative christian religious language for example, in theology and catechesis, tends to be defensive, systematic, repetitive and stereotyped. It often stresses formulas, codes, rules for conduct to clarify responsibilities. A lessening of personal commitment can evoke more explanations and justifications that may obscure the original personal experience.

As christian theology developed, it sometimes narrowed the scope of revelatory language and adopted a way of discoursing about God that is technical and repetitious. On the other hand, spiritual revivals have infused new life and color into christian tradition time and again. Since the eighteenth century, the Enlightenment, scientific discoveries, secular ideologies, and the rise of the social sciences have challenged the "universe of discourse" of christian religious language and culture. By way of response, imaginative believers have sought help from the linguistic revolution to develop a pluralistic discipline known as theolinguistics to investigate, encourage and enlarge religious language.

After a period of defensive linguistic analysis to affirm the significance of religious statements, theolinguistics matured to produce a variety of positive contributions that nourish religious language. These developments provide a variety of methods to show how divine revelation and its transcendent presence can be meaningful in modern society. Religious language promises to reduce alienation resulting from pressures of modern life. It encourages universal human rights, urges protection for the environment, and fosters the peace that Jesus promised through the gift of the Holy Spirit.

An imaginative literary thrust within the discipline of theolinguistics to purify christian religious language is called theopoetics. It seeks to retranslate the profound vision of Jesus' obedience to the Father into images capable of having an impact on secular culture. Theopoetics offers the faith community a way to repossess the power of Christ's saving death and resurrection in images that appeal to contemporary aspirations. Then believers will have the resources to communicate their hope that the cross can free humanity from enslavement to sin and death.

James M. Reese, *Experiencing the Good News: The New Testament as Communication*, Wilmington, Delaware: Michael Glazier, 1984. J.P. van Noppen, Ed., *Theolinguistics*, Brussels: Vrije Universteit, 1981. Amos N. Wilder, *Theopoetics: Theology and the Religious Imagination*, Philadelphia: Fortress, 1976.

JAMES M. REESE, OSFS

LAST JUDGMENT

As an eschatological theme, this is related to the symbol of the parousia and the question of the end of history.

The ancient Jewish prophets had proclaimed a future Day of the Lord when the sinful would not be able to avoid meeting God and rendering an account of their actions (Jer 25:30-31). In a similar way, the psalms frequently appeal to God as judge, asking that God would hasten the Day of Judgment. The early christian community associated the Day of the Lord with the parousia of Christ and saw it as the day of salvation which was eagerly awaited. On the other hand, the NT offers warnings of punishment (Mt 25:14-30) and speaks of the possibility of condemnation (Mt 13:38-42; 25:31-46; Heb 10:26, 31).

In medieval theology and piety, the emphasis moved from a positive expectation of the day of salvation to reflection on the coming of Christ as the final Judge. Metaphors used to express this were drawn largely from the courtroom, and the arrival of the Judge was awaited with fear and terror.

Contemporary theology has difficulty with the idea of the vindictive anger of God communicated by the late medieval metaphors and has attempted to view the question of judgment in terms of a more dialectical understanding of the relation between divine love and divine justice. Both of these attributes pertain to the biblical image of God, and both are necessary to attain a more nuanced understanding of the meaning of judgment. This together with a shift from descriptions in the Synoptic Gospels to the language of the Gospel of John accounts for the tendency to think of judgment as a moment of self-understanding in which one sees one's own reality in relation to what could have or should have been. This moment of enlightenment is seen to arise out of the personal confrontation with God's truth.

The central theological concern is the conviction that humanity, both individually and collectively, is responsible for what is done in history. As the truth of individual history is manifested to the individual in the experience of death, so the truth of the collective history of humanity will be manifested universally in the light of the truth of God when the history of the human race is brought to completion.

See **Eschatology, Reign of God**

ZACHARY HAYES, OFM

LAST THINGS

A term used to refer to death, judgment, purgatory, heaven, and hell.
See **all these terms and Eschatology**

LAW

Law plays an essential role in Christianity. As an instrument of God's self-communication, it guides graced natures to a share in divine life through love. The role of law is summed up in the triple command to love God above all, to love oneself for the sake of God, and one's neighbor as oneself (Mt 22:34-40). Here are the major aspects of law: its definition, method, kinds, knowability, and fulfillment.

1. The Definition of Law

In simplest terms, law is an action about actions. A lawmaker acts to establish how others should act. Thus the Code of Canon Law is not a mere historical or exhortatory document; it is a continuing action of church authority: commanding, forbidding, or permitting conduct by the faithful. Two definitions given by Aquinas reflect, when taken together, this notion. From the viewpoint of the lawmaker, he wrote: "Law is an ordinance of reason for the common good made by the one who has care of the community and promulgated" (S.Th., I-II, q. 90, a. 4c); from the viewpoint of the subject: "Law is a rule and measure of acts" (S.Th., a. 1c). The action of regulator and regulated complement one another in seeking a common goal.

A more modern way to define law is in

terms of power or, in Kant's term, "heteronomous decision," whereby one person governs the conduct of another (*heteros*) by establishing a norm (*nomos*). A lawmaker does not merely advise or convince, he compels by communicating a policy (a choice of values) coupled with a sanction (a deprivation consequent on disobedience). Good law, however, puts heteronomy at the service of automony by fostering a mutual responsibility.

Though force underpins power, and power underpins law, law is more than sheer power. Law is power rooted in authority. By authority is meant the right to decide for another in order to increase the subject's good; this right comes ultimately from God, though it may be mediated, for example, through the church, the state or the family. Ideally, law is an instrumentality of love moving toward the common good in such a way that its sanctions also prove to be, in Luther's words, "the strange work of love."

2. The Method of Law

Since law deals with decisions about human actions, conscious intentionality with its focus on the subject is more immediately relevant and helpful than abstract metaphysics. Law operates in the realm of common sense rather than theory; it is concerned with orthopraxis, doing practical things rightly and successfully.

What is needed is the self-appropriation of the mental operations involved in law: the experience of the data of sense and consciousness; the understanding of the data; the verifying of that understanding or insight through a factual judgment; and consistent with that judgment, the deliberating, evaluating, deciding, and acting, which constitute the level of consciousness where law is found. This generalized empirical method, as detailed by Bernard Lonergan, establishes the central principle upon which all moral and legal integrity is based, namely, consistency between knowing and doing. Underlying this practical principle is the cognitional one, that objectivity is the fruit of authentic subjectivity. Proper use of mental operations, through differentiated consciousness, gives the surest knowledge of law.

3. The Kinds of Law

The traditional division of law is still helpful: eternal law, natural law, divine positive law, and human positive law, civil and canon.

The *eternal law* rests on the fact that God knows individually and generically all the beings that he has created and how they must act to fulfill their destiny. His willing of that order of beings and its operation is eternal, the dictate of practical reason by which God rules the universe. God alone knows his law directly, yet through reason and revelation, humans are able to participate in his eternal law and thus fulfill their destiny.

The *natural law* is human participation in the eternal law through the light of reason—the ability to ask and answer questions—seeking norms of human conduct. From the perspective of subjectivity, the empirical discovery of the natural law entails gathering data about human inclinations, verifying the resulting insight, and deciding about the values discerned in terms of the first principle of the natural law: good should be done and pursued; evil should be avoided. Natural law norms are neither innate nor external but are personally enunciated by the individual. Incidentally, one must distinguish natural law, which governs the free choice of rational human beings, from the law of nature, which reflects the emergent probability of schemes of recurrence in the non-human universe.

Positive law finds its necessity in the inadequacy of natural law, which, owing to its generality, does not provide specifically for the particular situations that human beings face. *Divine positive law* is most important; by the Mosaic law and the law of the gospel, God has revealed further aspects of his eternal law in order not only to direct humans to their supernatural destiny in ways transcending the competence of natural law, but also to assist them in matters that are essentially natural but which, without an added light, may be fraught with uncertainty and error.

Taking natural law and divine positive law as authoritative, *human positive law* continues asking and answering questions about reality in order to bring these higher norms to bear on practical life through a prudential determination. Note that for the church, the combination of revealed law and natural law does not suffice in governing the *congregatio fidelium;* positive ecclesiastical law, canon law, is a needed supplement. All the more evident, then, is the need of a positive law for the civil community. Both types, canon and civil, rely on practical wisdom (*phronesis, prudentia*) in making concrete, common sense decisions.

4. The Knowability of Law

Law to be a rule and measure of acts must be known. For unless it is communicated or promulgated in some way, it cannot bind human beings. Our grasp of various laws, however, is not uniform but goes from probability to certainty.

Only God knows the *eternal law* directly, but humans can know it indirectly. They participate in this indirect knowledge of the eternal law in two ways: through self-generated knowledge (verified understanding of data) and through belief (acceptance of facts on reliable testimony).

The sphere of *natural law* is characterized essentially by self-generated knowledge as it emerges from a rational investigation by the human subject of his nature and his historicity, in an attempt to discover the universal norms governing human conduct.

But knowledge of the natural law also relies heavily on belief: for example, in the textual accuracy and precise interpretations of past formulations; in the historical circumstances of these earlier formulations; and in relevant matters learned subsequently from philosophy and theology, science and the humanities.

Natural law discoveries are neither made nor transmitted in an intellectual vacuum; nor is the body of natural law born full-bodied; rather it has been a communal project of emergent probability. Belief helps hold the system together, preserving the accumulation of true insights and their accurate formulation through the process of juridic dialectics, as, for example, in the current controversy over whether there are any absolute norms and intrinsically evil actions or whether an exception to any law owing to an unforeseen change in circumstances can ever be ruled out.

Positive law gives rise to even more hermeneutic issues. Divine positive law is based on belief rather than self-generated knowledge; human positive law is based on both. So questions arise: What did God actually reveal about the human actions? What norms did civil legislators or ecclesiastical authorities promulgate? How can changes in circumstances be adapted to the immutable divine will or in civil and canon law to an original legislative intention? What is the role here, and in natural law, of dispensation by an authority or of epikeia by one subject to authority?

5. The Fulfillment of Law

The OT and NT aim at fulfilling the law of God through conformity to his will, thus uniting human beings with him in love. Major derailments may occur: legalism, from emphasizing the letter at the expense of the spirit; antinomianism, from emphasizing the spirit to the exclusion of the letter. But faith and good work must complement one another (Jas 2:19f). Christian freedom implies work as an objectification of faith.

In fulfilling the law through the gospel, the true center becomes the person: the Father in the OT and, in the NT, his self-revelation in the Son through the Spirit as well. This personal focus subordinates law to love in a dynamic complementarity. Law and love together, by fostering integrity, justice, community, and transcendence, bring human beings through authentic self-appropriation to that union which is the restoration of all things in Christ.

See **Canon Law, Natural Law**

Thomas Aquinas, "On Law." *Summa Theologiae.* I-II, Questions 90-97. David Granfield, *The Inner Experience of Law: A Jurisprudence of Subjectivity.* Washington: The Catholic University of America Press, 1988. Gerhard Kittel, ed., Nomos. *Theological Dictionary of the New Testament.* Trans. G. W. Bromley, Grand Rapids: Eerdmans, 1967. Vol. IV: 1022-1091. John T. Noonan, Jr., *Persons and Masks of the Law.* New York: Farrar, Straus and Giroux, 1976. Karl Rahner, ed., "Law." *Sacramentum Mundi: An Encyclopedia of Theology.* New York: Herder and Herder, 1968. Vol. II: 276-297. Reprinted in *The Concise Sacramentum Mundi.* New York: Seabury, 1975. Pp. 822-836. D.M. Walker, *The Oxford Companion to Law.* Oxford: Clarendon, 1980.

DAVID GRANFIELD, OSB

LECTERN

The lectern (ambo) is the reading stand where the liturgical proclamation of the word takes place.

The Architectural Setting

The christian architectural setting for the lectern derives from two uses of the secular basilica form, those of Syria and of Africa. The Syrian christian church in the fourth century adopted the floor plan already used by the synagogue. The Syrian synagogue had rearranged the basilican space axially, with the empty apse representing the holy of holies in the Temple. In the center of the nave stood a raised platform for the presiding ministers and the proclamation of the word (bema). Between the nave and the apse there was a chest containing the biblical scrolls (the ark). Prayers faced the empty apse.

When the christian church adopted this floor plan, the apse became the place of the altar, while the presiding platform with its place of reading remained in the nave. The ark for the scriptures disappeared at an early date, possibly because of spatial conflict with the altar. There is mosaic evidence, however, that during the early Byzantine period some churches had an ark.

The African (or Roman) plan uses the arrangement of the civil basilica without adapting it. In the African plan the presiding platform is divided into a place for presiding ministers and a place for the proclamation of the word. The presider and assistants take the seats in the apse which had been designated for the civil magistrate. The two legal stands on either side of the apse where lawyers presented their cases became the lectern as well as the place for the music schola. The altar (often portable as Augustine indicates) was located in the center of the nave.

The ancient architectural settings suggest three things: the location of the lectern related to the assembly as well as the presiding ministers; the lectern was liturgically central and distinct from the altar, which had its own centrality; the focus of the word was its proclamation rather than a static sense of abiding presence as with the synagogue's ark.

Gradually the spatial relationship between the presiding platform, the lectern and the altar was condensed until all three focuses withdrew into the apse. By the sixteenth century the altar was at the back of the apse, the word was read on either side of the altar and below it, although without a lectern; the chair was located on one side of the apse. This arrangement effectively eliminated an architectural setting for the proclamation of the word. The pulpit which previously had been the place of proclamation became the preaching place. Often it could still be found within the nave.

The sixteenth-century setting suggests a deteriorating sense of the liturgical word of God in the Roman Catholic Church. The opposite remains true among most sixteenth century reformers. Their churches deepened the assembly's experience of the proclaimed and preached word. In extreme cases the altars disappeared, while the place of proclamation grew in singular architectural importance.

Current Liturgical Practice

The current pre-eminence accorded the lectern is due to a renewed interest in sacred scripture and an emphasis on the word's place within worship. Emphasis on biblical research began in the ninteenth century. About the same time the liturgical movement, which was inspired by men like Gueranger, Casal, Beauduin, enlivened and deepened appreciation for the liturgical word. Pope Pius XII's *Divino Afflante Spiritu* was official support for Roman Catholic scripture scholarship. The equivalent liturgical support came with *Sacrosanctum Concilium* which speaks of a distinct presence of Christ when the scriptures are read in church (S.C. 7).

The conciliar teaching states that the proclaimed word has a double effect: it is evangelical, calling the whole world to faith and conversion; and it is nourishment and challenge for the faithful (S.C. 9). Further, the liturgy of the word is considered one of two equal parts which comprise the eucharistic liturgy: the word and the eucharist. Therefore, the lectern shares a prime focus with the altar.

It is clear in the Council's text that the word is not primarily understood as instruction nor even doctrine but, like the eucharist itself, it is a revelation of the mystery of redemption and salvation (Introduction to the Lectionary 25 May 1969, No 1; General Instruction on the Roman Missal (G.I.R.M. No. 33).

It is evident from the direction set by the Second Vatican Council that the lectern is a place of action, a central focus in the midst of the assembled people, a dynamic place of the presence of God as the word is proclaimed.

The church, therefore, established the primary use of the lectern as the actual proclamation of the readings, response psalm (unless chanted), and the singing of the Exsultet. Secondarily it may also be used for the homily and general intercessions, which may be done elsewhere. The lectern is an inappropriate place for commenting, the cantor's singing, and choir direction (G.I.R.M. 272).

Physically, the lectern should function as a standing desk for reading. Two criteria apply to the design: "It should not be made in such a way that it is far removed from the print of the human hand and craft, and all furnishings taken together should possess a unity and harmony with each other and the architecture of the place." (Environment and Art, 67).

The specific design is left to competent territorial authority which can take into consideration local and cultural values (S.C. 22, 128).

See **Architecture, Church; Liturgy**

JAMES NOTEBAART

LIBERATION THEOLOGY

Liberation theology represents both a social and a theological movement that emerged principally in Latin America in the late 1960's. The social movement responds to the massive poverty of the continent which is due to the active subjugation and oppression of the indigenous population during the colonial period and their continued neglect and socio-economic repression in modern times. Since Vatican II many Christians explicitly motivated by christian values have aligned themselves with this social movement. Liberation theology in a narrower sense is a disciplined understanding of christian faith, and an interpretation of reality as mediated through the symbols of christian tradition, that has grown out of this commitment to the social movement of the poor and in behalf of the oppressed.

This account of liberation theology focuses on its specifically theological dimensions rather than the social movement that lies behind it or its implicit strategies for social reconstruction. It will treat the origin, the method, and the major themes of this theology and conclude with an interpretation of its universal significance beyond Latin America.

Origins

The causal factors leading to development of liberation theology are multiple and can be understood at a variety of different levels. The most fundamental explanation of liberation theology lies in the historical social situation of the people in Latin America. The gross statistics of poverty, malnutrition, lack of housing, unemployment and non-existing health services inadequately reflect the social human suffering across the many different cultures, nations and societies of the south. The "people," that is, the majority of the population of Latin America, live in destitution, so that poverty and oppression are the deepest causes of the growth of this theology. Liberation theology is analogous to the movement and theology of the social gospel at the turn of the twentieth century in North America in the wake of the unemployment and poverty left by rapid industrialization; it springs from the same conviction that the vision and moral resources of christian faith must have

something to say about massive social human suffering. In liberation theology, then, a religious response to the actual social condition of "the poor" is the ultimate rationale behind liberation theology.

Institutional landmarks and symbolic events helped to give external impetus to the inner development of liberation theology. The Second Vatican Council, in particular its "Pastoral Constitution on the Church in the Modern World," *Gaudium et Spes,* opened the way for what would become liberation theology. *Gaudium et Spes* described and to a certain extent defined the church in its relation to the world; it defined human existence socially and referred to the social dimension of sin; it recognized the enormous social problems of humanity and pledged the church's commitment to them; it recognized the inadequacy of an individualist morality to deal with these issues; it urged local churches to use the social sciences to understand their specific conditions, encouraged theologians to inculturate christian teaching in their particular situations, and guaranteed them freedom in their efforts (G.S. 25, 30, 44, 62).

In 1968, the Second General Conference of Latin American Bishops met at Medellin in Columbia and took up the mandate of Vatican II. It described poverty and injustice that prevailed on the continent, "those realities that constitute a sinful situation," and in one dramatic event committed the whole church to the integral development and liberation of the people of that continent ("Peace," no. 1, in *The Church in the Present-Day Transformation of Latin America...* USCC, Washington, D.C., 1973, p. 54).

Liberation Theologians

After the Bishops Conference at Medellin, the development of what came to be called liberation theology moved forward rapidly on a variety of levels: it included grass-roots reflection on specific issues, pamphleteering, popular and more technical articles, papers, mimeographed essays and published books. Although a vast number of people and authors have shared in the construction of liberation theology, the work of four theologians has been especially influential even beyond Latin America.

In the early 1960's the Uruguayan Jesuit Juan Luis Segundo was already addressing the need of the church to respond to the particular cultural, political and social situation of his own region. At the end of the decade he wrote a five volume work that treated some of the traditional doctrines of theology in a liberationist mode. His more recent work deals with method in liberation theology and a five volume treatise in christology.

After the synod at Medellin, the Peruvian Gustavo Gutiérrez published his *A Theology of Liberation*. This book canonized the label of "liberation theology" and won world-wide attention as one of the most influential books of the decade of the 1970's. By virtue of this book Gutiérrez became the acknowledged leader of the liberation theology movement.

Leonardo Boff, a Brazilian Franciscan, is another prolific liberation theologian who has dealt with the method of liberation theology, christology, the church, grace and spirituality.

Finally, since the late 1970's, the work of Jon Sobrino, a Basque Jesuit working in El Salvador, has gained international prominence. His writing in christology and on the church represents accurately the method and content of liberation theology.

These and other liberation theologians do not agree at every point; liberation theology is not a tightly knit fabric. Yet there is enough homogeneity to characterize generally its method and some of its major theological themes.

Methodology

Several characteristics coming together may serve to define the method of liberation theology. In the first place, liberation theology generally follows the procedure of *Gaudium et Spes* of presenting its doctrine in two steps: the first describes the human situation being addressed; the second presents theological teaching in response to these human dilemmas. In liberation theology this is more than a pedagogical mode of presentation; it is a deep structure that interprets traditional christian doctrine by allowing the concrete situation of poverty and oppression to pose questions to the tradition and in turn elicit responses that are inculturated to the specific situation of Latin America.

This fundamental procedure requires the use of social sciences, which has become another characteristic of liberation theology's method. Not only sociology, but also economics, history and political theory enter into liberation theology in a variety of ways. On an obvious empirical level, social analysis is required simply to understand the social world in which people live; it also governs the moral consequences of a faith that seeks to respond to social oppression. On a much deeper level the social sciences have mediated a social anthropology and theory of knowledge that enters intrinsically into the theological imagination. For example, some liberation theologians, realizing that all human language and conception, including theology, are influenced by the dominating forces of society, allow social analyses of oppression to break open and call into question previous theological understandings and thus open the way to reinterpretation (Segundo, *The Liberation of Theology*, pp. 7-9). Other liberation theologians interpret those christian doctrines that refer to human existence, such as sin, the effects of grace and salvation, in social terms. In other words, sin and salvation refer not only to individual personal realities but also to social structures (Gutiérrez, *A Theology of Liberation,* pp. 36-37). In each of these last two cases social analysis enters intrinsically into the discipline of theology itself insofar as it is hermeneutical and begins with human questions addressed to traditional christian symbols and doctrines.

A third characteristic of the method of this theology lies in the stress it puts on what it calls the option for the poor and praxis, two distinct terms that are closely related. The commitment of the whole church to an option for the poor enters into theology as a foundational and intentional bias. It is recognized today that all knowing and conceptualizing unfold from a particular point of view and implicit socially conditioned interests. An explicit commitment to the amelioration of the victims of society controls the dynamics of liberationist theological thinking. When this initial commitment is already mature and played out in action, it becomes praxis, that is, participation in social action for the liberation of the poor and oppressed. This corporate action as a way of christian faith life thus becomes the ground work out of which arises thought and theological reflection; in this sense praxis precedes and is the groundwork for the theory generated in theology.

Finally, liberation theology has often been linked with Marxism even though this connection is ambiguous and reference to it often misleading. On the one hand, some liberation theologians know very little of Marx or Marxism and have merited the connection simply because they describe the situation of the poor and respond to it. On the other hand, others have studied Marxist thought and use it as a vehicle to analyze society in much the same way as in any depart-

ment of social science in European and North American universities. Encouraged by Vatican II to dialogue with Marxists (G.S. 3, 21, 43, 92), some liberation theologians use Marxist language; but no liberation theologian has incorporated an integral Marxist vision of reality, which would be incompatible with christian faith. (The Council never explicitly names Marxists, but refers to all people, and at certain points the context shows that it implicitly intends Marxists.) The connection between liberation theology and Marxism is not necessary or intrinsic; it stems from the Latin American situation of poverty and oppression which first Marxism and now the church are both addressing.

Major Themes

With a method that allows the specific features of Latin American social life to enter into the theological imagination, liberation theology has developed some distinctive interpretations of classical christian doctrines. Five themes seem to be particularly important and characteristic.

Liberation theology has internalized the doctrine of Vatican II of the universality of the offer of God's grace, and in particular Karl Rahner's explanation of that doctrine and its implications. If God's saving grace is conceived as actually being effective in all human lives, and if much and in many cases all of human life transpires outside of any formal religious sphere, then God's grace must be seen as being effective most fundamentally, but not exclusively nor perhaps even explicitly, in the personal and secular social spheres of moral response. While it treats the social, political and economic realms as autonomous and secular on an historical level of conscious behavior, in effect liberation theology attributes religious and salvific value to these areas of life. Following Vatican II, liberation theology overcomes in its basic conception of the unity and integrity of christian life the quasi-reflex tendency to split and separate christian faith from human response in the social secular order (G.S. 43). In liberation theology human life in its entirety is an encounter with God's salvific grace.

Although it was not the area to which attention was first given, the central christian doctrine of liberation theology concerns Jesus Christ. Since christian faith is a response to an historical revelation, and not merely a philosophically mediated way of life, liberation theology turns to Christ for its doctrine of God. And since Christ is the name for Jesus of Nazareth, liberation theology attends carefully to what can be said of the historical Jesus from the NT documents. In the "praxis" of Jesus, liberation theology finds revealed the nature of God and what God's will is for human existence. As portrayed by the NT, Jesus lived out a commitment to the will of the one whom he called Father, and this involved a particular concern and "option" for those beyond the margins of social acceptance. Jesus thus becomes the focal point for the constructive theological imagination behind all liberation theology.

Another preoccupation in liberation theology concerns a spirituality that is integrally christian. Spirituality is defined generally as identical with the christian way of life: "A spirituality is a concrete manner, inspired by the Spirit, of living the Gospel; it is a definite way of living 'before the Lord,' in solidarity with all human beings, 'with the Lord,' and before humanity" (Gutiérrez, *A Theology of Liberation*, p. 204). Systematically this spirituality is determined by the revelation of God's will in Jesus and by the empowerment of the Spirit or grace of God; it is a following of Jesus as a disciple by the power of the Spirit of love that militates against sin. The integrality of liberation spirituality flows from its social

anthropology of human solidarity; its premise is that the fundamental issue at stake in all spirituality is ultimately union with God. Since all personal human existence is socially constituted, so that all are our neighbors, the evangelical maxim that one is united to God through love of neighbor takes on social dimensions. Social action on behalf of the neighbor, especially the ones most in need, thus becomes spiritual activity which forges our union with God. The integrality of this spirituality lies in the fact that the individual, personal and transcendent dimensions of spirituality are preserved by being subsumed into this wider framework for a wholistic view of the christian life.

The earliest doctrinal emphasis of liberation theology fell on the church. Taking the lead from *Gaudium et Spes*, liberation theology views the church primarily in terms of its function in relation to the "world," even though a functional view presumes a definable church substance. In answer to the fundamental question of why the church exists at all, (Segundo, *The Community Called Church*, trans. by John Drury, Maryknoll: Orbis, 1979, pp. 240-259), liberation theology finds its response in the mission from God for the world beginning in and extending forward from Jesus. Thus liberation theology avoids ecclesiocentrism by resolutely reinterpreting all aspects of the church including its sacraments in terms of its having a mission for all aspects of human life in history. Ministry and spirituality are conceived less in terms of minimum legal requirements for being a member and more in terms of responsibility for helping to make the church a sign before the world of God's values as revealed in Jesus. In Latin America this highly intentional view of the church is nurtured by the movement of basic ecclesial communities which are small groups of Christians, often from the lower strata of society, and often organized around prayer, reflective reading of scripture and common social concerns.

Finally, eschatology is a major issue in liberation theology, and it finds its focus in one of Christianity's central symbols, the kingdom of God. The kingdom of God was the subject matter of Jesus' preaching, and thus a concern for this symbol naturally arises out of liberation theology's attention to the historical Jesus. Liberation theology is quite free in using such language as "building the kingdom of God." This optimistic phrase should not be construed as minimizing the power of sin in the world, even though the rhetoric of liberation theology in its early phases appeared too sanguine. Rather two reasons make this language essential to this theology. First, liberation theology argues negatively that if human action does not in some way contribute to the ultimate end of things, then creative human freedom and even human existence itself *in this world* is ultimately meaningless. It does not make any ultimate difference. Second and positively, liberation theology takes seriously the implied intention of God in the creating of freedom, the empowerment of it by cooperative grace, and the continuity between Jesus' exercise of his freedom and his resurrection, all of which point to a continuity between the values human freedom is able to create in this world and the end-time. As opposed to a totally discontinuous eschatology, liberation theology holds a partly discontinuous and partly continuous eschatology. (Cf. Juan Luis Segundo, "Socialism versus Capitalism: Crux Theologica, " *Frontiers of Theology in Latin America,* ed., by Rosino Gibellini and trans. by John Drury, Maryknoll: Orbis, 1979, pp. 240-259).

The Significance of Liberation Theology

Although the most pervasive development of liberation theology has occurred in Latin America, it is more than a merely local theology, and its significance reaches far beyond that continent. Some indications that this is the case are the following: liberation theology is now being developed all over the world. At first other regions such as Asia, Southeast Asia and Africa were influenced by the Latin Americans, but they have begun to appropriate liberationist themes in idioms more inculturated to their own situation. Secondly, a number of kinds of theology which are independent of liberation theology bear close structural and thematic resemblance to it and share its deepest concerns. Black theology, political theology and feminist theology are among them. And thirdly, in the Roman Catholic Church the magisterium has been deeply influenced by liberation theology and has begun to incorporate its language into its teaching. This is true not only of papal discourses but also in the teachings of episcopal conferences. For example, in 1979 the Latin American Episcopal Conference at Puebla confirmed what it had begun at Medellin (Eagleson and Scharper). In 1984 the Vatican's Congregation for the Doctrine of the Faith, in a document wrongly construed as a censure of liberation theology, actually confirmed the movement while warning abstractly against possible doctrinal deviations (*Instruction on Certain Aspects of the "Theology of Liberation, "*Vatican City: 1984). And in 1986 the same congregation's *Instruction on Christian Freedom and Liberation* (Vatican City: 1986) reasserted the social teaching of the church within the context of liberation theology and language. (The importance of this document lies both in its content and the development it represents. It is not about liberation theology, but a teaching about christian freedom and liberation that completely appropriates the perspective and the content of liberation theology. Thus it represents the completion of the cycle of the mandate of Vatican II, that is, for the inculturation of its teachings at the periphery in the local churches and, twenty years later, the reappropriation of what was learned there at the center, i.e., by the Vatican. Liberation theology is now the universal theology of the Roman Catholic Church).

Several reasons account for this gradual spread and appropriation of the themes of liberation theology. Liberation theology is a continuous development of the spirit and the teachings of Vatican II. It is an attempt to interpret christian doctrine in a way that is responsible to the universal problem of human suffering, which is especially manifest in the social oppression of today's world. It draws together in a new way theology and the social teachings of the church by providing the social ethics with theology and doctrinal grounding. And by uniting theology, ethics and spirituality, it provides answers to fundamental questions of why one chooses to be a Christian in the modern world.

See **Eschatology, Praxis, Spirituality**

Leonardo Boff, *Jesus Christ Liberator: A Critical Christology for Our Time*, trans. by Patrick Hughes, Maryknoll: Orbis, 1979; *The Way of the Cross: Way of Justice*, trans. by John Drury, Maryknoll: Orbis, 1980; *Saint Francis: A Model for Human Liberation*, New York: Crossroad, 1982; *Church, Charisma, Power: Liberation Theology and the Institutional Church*, trans. by John Dierksmeyer, New York: Crossroad, 1985. Gustavo Gutiérrez, *A Theology of Liberation: History, Politics and Salvation*, trans. by Caridad Inda and John Eagleson, Maryknoll: Orbis, 1973; *The Power of the Poor in History*, trans. by Robert R. Barr, Maryknoll: Orbis, 1983. Juan Luis Segundo, *A Theology for Artisans of a New Humanity*, 5 Vols., trans. by John Drury, Maryknoll: Orbis, 1973-5; *The Hidden Motives of Pastoral Action*, trans. by John Drury, Maryknoll: Orbis, 1977; *The Liberation of Theology*, trans. by John Drury, Maryknoll: Orbis, 1976; *Jesus of Nazareth Yesterday and Today*, 5 vols., trans. by John Drury, Maryknoll: Orbis, 1984-7. Jon Sobrino, *Christology at the Crossroads: A Latin American Approach*, trans. by John Drury, Maryknoll: Orbis, 1978; *The True Church and the Poor*, trans. by Matthew J. O'Connell, Maryknoll: Orbis, 1984. John Eagleson and Philip Scharper, eds., *Puebla and Beyond: Documentation and Commentary*, Maryknoll: Orbis, 1979. Phillip Berryman, *Liberation Theology: Essential Facts about the Revolutionary Movement in Latin America and Beyond*, NY: Pantheon, 1986. Rebecca S. Chopp, *The Praxis of Suffering: An Interpretation of Liberation and Political Theologies*, Maryknoll, Orbis, 1986. Roger Haight, *An Alternative Vision: An Interpretation of Liberation Theology*, Ramsey, NJ: Paulist Press, 1985. Ricardo Plannas, *Liberation Theology: The Political Expression of Religion*, Kansas City: Sheed and Ward, 1986.

ROGER HAIGHT, SJ

LIBERTY, RELIGIOUS (TOLERANCE)

Terminology

The terms religious liberty and tolerance (or toleration) are often used synonymously. However, there are differences in meaning that should be kept in mind.

Toleration in its verb form was used in the Middle Ages to describe the act of permitting or conceding the practice of a religion one considers false (Aquinas, S.Th., IIa IIae, q.10, art. 11). Tolerance begins to be frequently used in the latter half of the century to describe concessions concerning religious freedom (Lecler, p.x). Toleration or tolerance generally describes a negative approach to issues arising from religious diversity. Toleration is a concession allowing something to exist that in an ideal situation ought not to exist.

Religious liberty is a more modern way of addressing the issue of a plurality of faiths or religions in one community. Its use becomes frequent in the nineteenth century, and it has largely supplanted both the terminology and the concept of toleration. Religious liberty denotes not a concession but a right. The language of religious liberty addresses something inherent in the dignity of the human person as well as something inherent in the very nature of religion itself.

For most of the church's history only rarely were Christians able even so much as to tolerate other religions, and they were almost never able to tolerate other forms of their own religion (heresies). This fundamental and consistent intolerance seems to have been generated by three articles of faith: belief that the unity of all believers in one church was willed by Christ, the belief that the gospel of Jesus was addressed to all peoples, and the belief that there was no salvation outside the one church of Christ. The church's conceptions of its unity, catholicity, and its exclusiveness as source of salvation made it difficult for Christians to see how heresy could be tolerated and how those who refused to accept the gospel could be allowed to practice any other religion. Only as notions of the human person and human community changed, and the primacy of conscience was more clearly defined, did it become possible for Christians to tolerate religious diversity and even envision the possibility of religious liberty.

History

a. Primitive Christianity and the Patristic Age (Lecler, 11-64). The early church, before the Edict of Milan (313 A.D.), was guided by the example of its Master, the counsels of the gospel, and the need to justify its right to freedom of worship in a world and culture hostile to this new religion. The early church argued that Christians could be and were loyal subjects of the Emperor even if they did refuse to participate in the Roman imperial cult. It likewise argued for freedom of conscience and religious liberty. Tertullian puts the argument in these terms: "By both human and natural law each one is free to adore whom he wants; the religion of an individual neither harms nor profits anybody else. It is against the nature of religion to force religion; it must be accepted spontaneously and not by force; the offerings

demanded, indeed, must be made willingly. That is why if you force us to sacrifice, you give, in fact, nothing to your gods: they have no need of unwilling sacrifices" (*Ad Scapulam,* c.2).

The right to religious liberty is already seen as rooted in the nature of the human person and in the nature of religion itself. Freedom is of the essence.

The early church was also quite clear that it had no right to use physical force or violence to discipline its own members. The only punishments it could inflict on sinners and heretics were spiritual punishments. Physical violence was contrary to a gospel which insisted on patience, leniency, and mercy.

However, after the church gained its own liberty in 313, it very easily fell in with imperial policies which aimed at religious unity in the empire. By the end of the fourth century paganism was an illicit religion and even its practice in private was subject to punishment by death. Heretical factions were treated in like manner. The harsh legislation of the emperors of the fourth and fifth centuries, even if never uniformly enforced, would later establish precedents for even harsher legislation against heretics in the Middle Ages. It seems that once the church secured its own privileged place in society, it all too easily accepted the use of force and violence to deprive others of their right to religious liberty. Some voices within the church were raised in protest against imperial persecutions of pagans and heretics, but they were few, and ultimately ineffectual.

Finally, it is sad to note that with some few exceptions (Justin, Origen, Clement, Augustine) the writings of the Fathers are filled with invective against the Jews. In some places, Christians incited riots which led to the destruction of synagogues.

b. The Middle Ages (Lecler, 65-101). In principle, there was some toleration of

Jews and unbelievers in the Middle Ages; they were not to be forced to enter the church. In practice they suffered many forms of discrimination and periodic acts of violence. They were in fact not truly members of society, of Christendom. They were utterly dependent on the good will of the christian majority. In justifying this tolerance, medieval theologians reaffirmed the principle that the act of faith must be made in freedom. They also clarified the notion of conscience as the proximate norm of morality, such that even the erronous conscience must be obeyed. Finally, they gave expression to what was to become the thesis/hypothesis approach to toleration: in itself it is not good that a worship should continue that is based on erroneous belief (thesis), but it can nevertheless be tolerated either to obtain a greater good or to avoid a greater evil (hypothesis).

If there was at least some tolerance in principle for Jews and unbelievers, there was absolutely none either in principle or in practice for heretics. It was universally believed that while the act of faith was to be made freely without any coercion, once made the Christian was not free to abandon the faith. Heresy was punished by death. Many factors influenced this extreme intolerance of heresy: the punishments of the OT, the imperial legislation of christian antiquity, the custom itself of burning heretics, and the conception of Christendom as a society based on unity of faith.

Towards the end of the Middle Ages in the fifteenth century, some few voices, proponents of humanism, cautiously called for greater toleration and understanding. These include Nicholas of Cusa, Marsilio Ficino, and Pico della Mirandola. All aimed at conciliating religious differences by recognizing what was fundamental to each position. Thomas More and Erasmus would carry on this humanist tradition of toleration in the next century.

c. The Reformation to the Nineteenth Century. The Reformation raised the question of toleration in a most acute fashion. Efforts were made to lay the intellectual foundation for the development of greater toleration of religious diversity. The erroneous conscience had to be respected, particularly if one was born into an heretical faith and therefore had no responsibility for one's error. In France, serious attempts were made to distinguish political unity from religious unity, the needs of the state from the needs of the church. In Poland, Bohemia, Brandenburg toleration of religious differences within one national community was partially successful. Ultimately, however, the conception of one nation, one religion prevailed. Europe was divided into Catholic and Protestant states. Within the latter, the divisions within Protestantism required a measure of tolerance of religious diversity, but such toleration never included Catholics. In Catholic states, Protestants suffered severe disabilities and in general Protestant churches were not allowed to function as a public cult.

The Enlightenment, the end of the *ancien régime,* and modern conceptions of human dignity and freedom all contributed to creating an era of greater toleration of religious differences. Protestant states enlarged conceptions of tolerance to include Catholics. In Roman Catholicism, the thesis/hypothesis view of toleration prevailed. Notions of genuine religious freedom as a human right were soundly rejected by Popes Gregory XVI, Pius IX, and Leo XIII, because in their view these notions were inextricably bound up with indifferentism and rationalism. Nevertheless, in practice, if not in theory Catholics took a far more tolerant view of Protestants.

d. The Twentieth Century. In this century the rise of totalitarian regimes of both the right and the left, the destruction of two world wars, and growing global consciousness helped religious leaders to focus on human dignity, the inviolable rights of the human person, the nature of the human community and its relation to the state, and other issues affecting human solidarity. It was in this context, too, that Popes Pius XI, Pius XII and John XXIII moved toward the acceptance of ideals of human dignity and freedom consonant with the teachings of the church. These papal initiatives together with research of scholars in the period immediately following the Second World War laid the groundwork for the declaration on religious liberty of Vatican Council II.

Teaching of Vatican Council II
   a. *History of the Declaration on Religious Liberty, "Dignitatis Humanae," December 7, 1965.* John Courtney Murray, *peritus* at the Council, and perhaps the strongest theological proponent of religious freedom in the Church, wrote: "It can hardly be maintained that the Declaration is a milestone in human history—moral, political, or intellectual. The principle of religious freedom has long been recognized in constitutional law, to the point where even Marxist-Leninist political ideology is obliged to pay lip-service to it. In all honesty, it must be admitted that the Church is late in acknowledging the validity of the principle."

The document's significance lies first and foremost in the fact that at long last the church did solemnly recognize that "the dignity of the human person consists in his responsible use of freedom." Secondly, at another level entirely, the declaration not only raised the issue of doctrinal development, but was in itself an exercise in this development authenticated by the Council itself. In this sense it has theological impact which goes far beyond the subject matter of the decree.

This declaration began its life in 1962 as Chapter IX of the schema of the *Constitution on the Church.* The chapter was entitled "On the Relation between Church and State, or on Religious Tolerance." Its teaching was that which had been considered "traditional" for a millennium. In principle all must embrace the true faith, and the civil society through its authorities must promote that faith alone, and publicly participate in its cult. However, on the hypothesis that there are those who do not accept the true faith, while they do not enjoy *the right* to profess another religion, the State may, for the sake of the common good and public peace, tolerate their profession of a false religion. This is the "thesis/hypothesis" teaching on the relationship between church and state. There was such dissatisfaction with this approach that the section was later removed from the Constitution on the Church.

At the same time, the Secretariat for the Promotion of Christian Unity was also preparing a text on the relations between church and state. The competence of the Secretariat to deal with this matter was first denied. In October, 1962 Pope John XXIII recognized the Secretariat's competence to submit drafts to the Council.

The first draft of the declaration was submitted to the Council as Chapter V of the Decree on Ecumenism in November, 1963. It was discussed briefly, but detailed discussion was left to the second and third sessions. Suggestions and emendations amounted to 280 pages. But the major change was the decision in April, 1963, to propose a separate declaration on religious liberty.

A second draft of the declaration was presented in April, 1964, and a third draft was presented in November of the same year. No vote was taken. The decree was perhaps the most controversial document presented to the Council. The fourth draft was presented in May, 1965 and was discussed by the Council in September of the same year. The arguments surrounding it were heated. The first vote to approve the direction was approved by ninety percent of the Council. A fifth amended text was approved article by article on October 26 and 27. While receiving overall approval, a significant number of fathers continued to vote negatively, and close to a quarter voted positively but with reservations. It was on December 7, 1965 that the final text (a sixth draft) was approved by 2,308 votes. Seventy voted against the declaration.

The opposition to the declaration was strong and vocal, though perhaps not as numerous as opponents suggested. Major objections centered around the following six issues: 1) abandonment of the "traditional" thesis/hypothesis doctrine; 2) the question of development in doctrine; 3) fear that the church would lose status; 4) the lack of clear evidence that the declaration was supported in scripture; 5) fear that the declaration promoted religious indifferentism; 6) concern that it would enhance the power of the state *vis-à-vis* the church.

b. The Teaching of the Declaration on Religious Liberty The Declaration is composed of a prefatory article; two chapters: *The General Principle of Religious Freedom* (Arts. 2-8) and *Religious Freedom in the Light of Revelation* (Arts. 9-14); and a final article on religious freedom in the current situation (1965).

In a very real sense the first article of the declaration is a solemn pronouncement which asserts four things: 1) that the right to freedom in religious matters, freedom from psychological and external coercion, and freedom to seek truth, embrace it, adhere to it, and act on it, inheres in each man and woman by reason of his/her dignity as a person endowed with reason and free will and therefore endowed with conscience and

personal responsibility; 2) that all men and women are impelled by nature and morally obligated to seek the truth and adhere to it; 3) that while Catholics believe that in Jesus and his church God has made known the true religion, this truth, like all others, can impose itself on the human mind only in virtue of its own truthfulness; and 4) that the Council in making this declaration intends to develop the teaching of the recent popes on the inviolable rights of the human person and on the constitutional order of society.

Theological Argument. Chapter I contains a closely argued presentation of this right to religious freedom, its ground in the nature of the human person, and the obligation of the human person to seek truth and to adhere to it once it is discovered. In this chapter the Council also insists that since the human person is inherently social, this right has a necessary social dimension which must be preserved and protected by the civil authority; and when necessary, regulated by that same authority.

The Council describes persons, as "beings endowed with reason and free will and therefore bearing personal responsibility" (2). It argues that the right to religious freedom is grounded in the two-fold obligation of all human beings, given their nature as rational and free, to seek the truth and to seek to do that which is in accord with the truth. Human beings are "both impelled by their nature and bound by moral obligation to seek the truth, especially religious truth" (2). But as the Council declares, human beings "cannot satisfy this obligation in a way that is in keeping with their own nature, unless they enjoy both psychological freedom and immunity from external coercion" (2).

Truth, considered from the perspective of "the highest norm of human life," is the divine law "eternal, objective and universal, by which God orders, directs and governs the whole world and the way of human community ... " (3). It is by means of conscience that the human being recognizes truth as a norm of human behavior. And just as persons "must adhere to the truth they have discovered" in order to respond faithfully to their nature, so too the human being "is bound to follow his conscience faithfully in all his activity so that he may come to God, who is his last end" (3). Consequently no one can be forced to act contrary to conscience nor prevented from acting according to conscience. "The reason is because the practice of religions of its very nature consists primarily of those voluntary and free internal acts by which a man directs himself to God."

But the Council is not content merely to protect the internal acts of the individual person. The Council insists that the human person is inherently social (3). In the very process by which a person seeks the truth the human being is social. Likewise, the social nature of the human person demands the free expression of internal commitment. "But his own social nature requires that man give external expression to these internal acts of religion, that he communicate with others on religious matters, and profess his religion in community. Consequently to deny man the free exercise of religion in society, when the just requirements of public order are observed, is to do an injustice to the human person and to the very order established by God for men" (3).

And because private and public acts of religion are acts by which people direct themselves to God they transcend the temporal order. "Therefore the civil authority, the purpose of which is the care of the common good in the temporal order, must recognize and look with favor on the religious life of the citizens. But if it presumes to control or restrict

religious activity it must be said to have exceeded the limits of its power" (3).

In Articles 4 and 5, the Council next affirms that the subject of the right to religious freedom is not only the individual person, but religious communities and families. In discussing how this right applies to communities and families, it goes into some detail concerning the practical content of this right.

Article 6 of the Declaration is a succinct primer on the obligations of civil authority with respect to human rights. It asserts as a general principle that: "the common good of society consists in the sum total of those conditions of social life which enable men to achieve a fuller measure of perfection with greater ease. It consists especially in safeguarding the rights and duties of the human person" (6).

While it is the duty of all individuals, groups, religious communities, and the church to protect the rights of all, it is especially an obligation of the civil authority. "The protection and promotion of the inviolable rights of man is an essential duty of every civil authority" (6). However, in any human society rights may be in conflict. The Council therefore considers the need to recognize that the exercise of rights is subject to regulation.

The Council insists that in regulating the exercise of human rights, the civil authority be guided by the principles of public peace, morality, and good order which are requisites of the common good. However, civil authority should respect "the principle of the integrity of freedom in society" and consequently, human freedom "should be given the fullest possible recognition and should not be curtailed except when and insofar as it is necessary" (7).

The final section in this chapter is an exhortation on the part of the Council urging education for responsible freedom in the name of religious freedom itself. "Religious liberty therefore should have this further purpose and aim in enabling men to act with greater responsibility in fulfilling their own obligations in society" (8).

Revelation. In Chapter II (Article 9-14), the Council considers this right to religious freedom from the perspective of divine revelation. The Council points out that the right to religious freedom as known from reason (Chapter I) and as known from revelation (Chapter II) does not differ with respect to origin of the knowledge of the right.

Articles 9-11 argue that while revelation does not state in so many words the right of the human person to be free of coercion in religious matters, it does affirm the almost god-like dignity of the human person in grace, and the necessity that the human response to God be genuinely free. "Man, redeemed by Christ the Saviour and called through Jesus Christ to be an adopted son of God, cannot give his adherence to God when he reveals himself unless, drawn by the Father, he submits to God with a faith that is reasonable and free. It is therefore fully in accordance with the nature of faith that in religious matters every form of coercion by men should be excluded" (10).

The Council also cites the example of Jesus, his free response to the Father and the graciousness of the invitation to believe that Christ addresses to the freedom of his disciples. From this example, the Council concludes: "For he bore witness to the truth but refused to use force to impose it on those who spoke out against it. His kingdom does not make its claims by blows, but is established by bearing witness to and hearing the truth and grows by the love with which Christ, lifted up on the cross, draws men to himself" (11).

Finally, the Council refers to the example of the preaching of the apostles:

"From the very beginnings of the Church the disciples of Christ strove to convert men to confess Christ as Lord, not however by applying coercion or with the use of techniques unworthy of the Gospel, but above all, by the power of the word of God" (11).

In the twelfth article of the Declaration the Council solemnly apologizes on behalf of the church for past failures to be faithful to the revealed truth in the matter of religious freedom: "Although in the life of the people of God in its pilgrimage through the vicissitudes of human history there has at times appeared a form of behavior which was hardly in keeping with the spirit of the Gospel and was even opposed to it, it has always reminded the teaching of the Church that no one is to be coerced into believing" (12).

Perhaps to quiet the fears of those who are concerned that full freedom may indeed harm the church , the Council insists that it is only in a truly free society that the church can fulfill her divine mission (13). It also reminds all who are members of the church, that freedom of religion does not absolve them from the obligation to Christ, "to grow daily in . . . knowledge of truth . . . received from him, to be faithful in announcing it, and vigorous in defending it without having recourse to methods which are contrary to the spirit of the Gospel" (14).

In the concluding article (Article 15) of the Declaration, the Council treats of the current situation (1965) and affirms that people want to be able to profess freely their religion in private and public. This desire is a sign of the times. The Council deplores the fact that there are civil societies where freedom of religion is not possible or is unduly hindered. The Council concludes its declaration on this note: ". . . to establish and strengthen peaceful relations and harmony in the human race, religious freedom must be given effective constitutional protection everywhere and that highest of a human being's rights and duties—to lead a religious life with freedom in society—must be respected" (15).

c. *The Significance of the Declaration.* The primary value of the *Declaration* is that it lays down the theoretical foundations for a new charter governing relations between religious and civil authority in general, and specifically, the relations between church and State. In this brief *Declaration,* the church returns to a healthier, more realistic, and more evangelical vision of its relationship to the civil society. Furthermore it affirms that the principles which govern church-state relationships are accessible to human reason but are also to be found in the revelation God makes in Jesus, the Christ. Finally, this charter recognizes that what is prior to both church and state is the dignity of the human person, which neither institution can infringe on, and which both are called into existence to foster and serve.

More specifically, the *Declaration* represents a number of important advances in the understanding on the part of the church in the area of rights, religion, and civil authority.

First, the *Declaration* represents a significant development over the official teaching of the church since the Middle Ages. Not only is there real doctrinal development here, but there is also frank acknowledgement of that development as such, and an honest confession of error in the past. Such honesty is not frequently encountered when the church evaluates her teaching, and all the more salutary for its infrequency.

A second advance is the clear teaching that rights inhere in persons, not in values, and that they are rooted in human dignity, not in the subjective attitudes of persons. Once and for all the church abandons the notion that truth alone has the right to exist; error, no right at all.

The right to freedom in religious matters is not lost by abuse; it is validated not by beliefs and judgments accounted to be correct, but by the very nature of the human person as endowed with reason and freewill and the personal responsibility consequent on these. The thesis/hypothesis approach to religious freedom was finally put to rest.

Thirdly, of great importance is the Council's effort to define the responsibilities of the state: the promotion of the common good and the protection and fostering of human rights, limiting the free exercise of these rights when, and only insofar as necessary to preserve a just public peace, where people live together in good order and true justice.

Fourthly, the serious endeavor of the Council to root its teaching on religious liberty in divine revelation is very important. For the believing Christian it adds the sanction of God's Word to this teaching. No more can one say that natural rights can be superseded by divine revelation, as if the God of nature and the God of Jesus were not one and the same.

Fifthly, implicit in this Declaration is the notion that God may indeed have larger purposes in the divine plan than the prosperity of either church or state as human beings may conceive of either at any given point in history. Human institutions are relativized in favor of the dignity of human persons.

And last but not least, the ecclesial experience of the church in the United States, and the theology it derived from that experience were vindicated by the universal church in a variety of ways. The Council recognized and called for the constitutional recognition and legal implementation of those fundamental human rights which validate all democratic governments. The Council recognized implicitly the inherent rightness of that church-state relationship which the American church had long experienced and vehemently argued for during its almost two centuries of existence in the U.S. The great proponent of this American Catholic theology was John Courtney Murray, S.J., but his teaching was rooted in the insights of Martin Spalding, John Ireland, James Gibbons, John Carroll and many others.

Continuing Questions

The *Declaration on Religious Liberty* has worn well. It still speaks clearly of the inviolability of the rights of human beings in the face of institutions, be they religious or civil. Today totalitarianism, religious fanaticism, national security, the elitism of left and right, and terrorism, all threaten to overwhelm the basic message of this *Declaration*. So the *Declaration* as it stands bears repeating.

What more might be needed? Six things suggest themselves.

1) The *Declaration's* understanding of truth seems too static. There is need for a clearer recognition of the inherently dynamic nature of truth. We are dealing here with a human category. The phrases, "to seek the truth, embrace it and adhere to it," suggest a quantitative, once and for all, character to truth. What is missing here is the awareness of the dynamism of truth, its historicity, in a word, its elusiveness, always just beyond one's comprehension.

2) Advances in biblical scholarship since the Council would suggest that a much better understanding of human freedom in the light of revelation could be developed.

3) There is embedded in this declaration a theology of institutions, specifically civil and ecclesial institutions. This theology needs to be made more explicit to enunciate more clearly the role and value of these institutions for the development of human potential. Needed, too, is a political theology which clearly delineates the limits of institutions with respect to human dignity, and specifies the relationship of human freedom to the common good.

4) The vision implicit in this declaration of the world as a community of nations needs to be developed, specifically how this community relativizes nation states and religious institutions.

5) The principles which require freedom from psychological intimidation and external coercion in religious matters need to be applied to life within an ecclesial community. If believing is not just an act but a process of conversion stretching over a lifetime, not only must the act initiating this conversion be free, but the freedom of the person throughout this process must be assured. Even ecclesial authority is human authority, which by definition cannot infringe on the freedom of the person to seek truth through free exchange and dialogue, except when the common good of the church requires it.

6) Finally, a closer look at what this *Declaration* says about the nature of religion, its relationship to civil society, and the obligation of civil society to enable a human freedom that envisages even freedom *from* religion might put an end to the anachronism of diplomatic relations between the Roman Catholic Church and civil governments.

See **Anthropology, Christian; Vatican Council II**

A.F. Carrillo de Albornoy, *Religious Liberty,* New York: Sheed & Ward, 1967; *The Basis of Religious Liberty,* London: SCM Press, 1963; *Roman Catholic and Religious Liberty,* Geneva: World Council of Churches, 1959. René Coste, *Theologie de la Liberté Religieuse,* Glemblaux: Duculot, 1969. N. Edelby, & T. Jimenez-Urresti, (eds.) *Religious Freedom,* Concilium, vol. 18, New York: Paulist Press, 1966. Joseph Lecler, *Toleration and the Reformation,* 2 vols., London: Longmans, 1960. Gustav Mensching, *Tolerance and Truth in Religion,* University, Ala: Univ. of Alabama Press, 1971. John Courtney Murray, *The Problem of Religious Freedom,* Westminster, Md.: Newman, 1965; *Religious Liberty: An End and a Beginning,* New York: Macmillan, 1966.

JOHN LINNAN, CSV

LIMBO

From the Latin *Limbus*, which means a border or hem of a garment. As a technical theological term, it designates the place or condition of those who have died without the conditions necessary for entrance into heaven but also without the personal, mortal guilt necessary for condemnation to hell. Traditional theology distinguishes the *limbo of the Fathers* and the *limbo of infants*. The first designates the presumed state of the just who have preceded Christ in the history of salvation, both the great figures of the OT and the holy pagans of non-Jewish origin. The second refers to the state of children who have died without baptism but also without having committed any personal, mortal sin.

The concept of the *limbo of the Fathers* is no doubt a christian adaptation of the Jewish notion of *sheol* (Lk 16:22ff) (cfr. Hell). In Patristic theology and art, it is the place to which Christ descends after death (1 Pt 3:18-20). For christian theology, it provided a means for conceptualizing the possibility of salvation for those who preceded Christ in history while at the same time seeing that salvation as dependent on the salvific act of God in Christ.

The *limbo of infants* is an attempt to deal with the fate of children who have died without baptism in the time of the explicit christian dispensation during which faith in Christ and the reception of baptism are understood to be the necessary conditions for entrance into heaven. Pelagians, in harmony with their idea of original sin, postulated a place or state of natural happiness between heaven and hell for the unbaptized. Since the Pelagian theology of original sin envisioned no guilt in unbaptized children, they could not be consigned to hell. If one thought of baptism as necessary for entrance into heaven, then neither could such children be placed in a state of perfect heavenly bliss. Hence, the postulation of a place of natural happiness in harmony with the personal innocence of such children was consistent with the Pelagian theology of original sin. In his rejection of the Pelagian position on sin, Augustine was led to reject their notion of an intermediary place as well. Consistently, he had to consign such children to eternal punishment, even though he tried to mitigate the harshness of this conclusion by arguing that their punishment would be the mildest (*Enchiridion* 93).

The magisterium of the church has taken no official position on the question of limbo. Two Councils (II Lyons in 1274 and Florence in 1439) have stated that those who die "only with original sin" go to hell but that their condition would be different from that of those who die in mortal sin (D.S. 858, 1306). But the magisterium has not stated that, in fact, there are people who die "only with original sin."

Western theologians of the medieval period represent a wide range of variations on the thesis of Augustine. In general, the mildest punishment indicated by Augustine becomes even milder. For Peter Abelard, such souls are deprived of the beatific vision; for Thomas Aquinas, they lack both grace and beatific vision. Thus, one attributes to them a natural happiness in harmony with their natural spiritual faculties, but not the supernatural happiness of beatific vision (Aquinas, *De Malo* 5,4, ad 4).

Post-Reformation and modern theology has suggested a number of ways of supplying for sacramental baptism in an extra-sacramental way. Thus, a baptism of blood was envisioned in the case of the infants of Bethlehem (Mt 2:16). The prayer and desire of the child's parents might be seen as a vicarious baptism of desire (Cajetan). In the nineteenth century, H. Klee suggested that the child might attain the use of reason at the moment of death and thus decide for or against God. H. Schell argued that the suffering of death itself might be seen as an extra-sacramental means of attaining to heaven. The latter two positions would make the postulation of limbo unnecessary.

Contemporary theology generally tends to treat the question in the context of the theology of death. When death is seen as the moment of final choice (P. Glorieux, K. Rahner, L. Boros, G. Lohfink. G. Greshake), the concept of limbo becomes unnecessary. Others have suggested that salvation for such children is found not in death but after death (M. Laurenge, V. Wilkins). Here also a decision on the part of the child is necessary. This decision may take place either soon after death or at the time of the Last Judgment. In the latter case, it is necessary to affirm the existence of limbo until the end of history at which time it will cease to exist.

See **Baptism**

ZACHARY HAYES, OFM

LITURGICAL MOVEMENT, THE

"The Liturgical Movement" is the name commonly ascribed to the work of many scholars and pastors, especially in this century, who influenced the reform of liturgical practice based on renewed attitudes toward worship and its relationship to christian life. Although the movement first got under way in the Roman church, it has not been restricted to it. Roman fermentation influenced the reform of worship in most christian communions. The pivotal juncture for the transformation of Roman Catholic liturgical practice is located in the Constitution on the Sacred Liturgy *Sacrosanctum Concilium* promulgated on 4 December 1963 by Paul VI at the Second Vatican Council. This first of the council's documents marked the beginning of a new phase in

the church's liturgical life; it also served as the watershed for years of historical research, pastoral experimentation, and theological reflection on the church's experience of life and worship. An exposition of the origins of the movement, its fundamental purpose and theological foundations will draw out pastoral implications for the ongoing post-conciliar movement through liturgical reform toward authentic christian renewal.

The seeds for the Liturgical Movement were planted in nineteenth-century France. Dom Prosper Guéranger reestablished the Order of Saint Benedict in France by refounding the Abbey of Solesmes in 1833. He dedicated the monastery to the study of the church's liturgical traditions in general and to the restoration of Gregorian chant in particular. Under Guéranger's leadership the traditional Benedictine concern for the liturgy was revived and Solesmes gained a reputation as a center for both liturgical research and the proper performance of chant. The abbey consequently influenced other Benedictine foundations throughout western Europe. Eventually several monks came to be identified as pioneers who laid the foundations for liturgiological research. Solesmes' publication, *L'Année liturgique*, first issued in 1841, provided an organ for the communication of ideas and thus extended liturgical awareness. This phase of the movement, largely restorative in nature, has met with criticisms of being excessively medieval, hopelessly romantic, pastorally limited, and exclusively archaeological. Such judgments in hindsight must necessarily be accompanied by compassion conditioned by an historically-minded consciousness. Guéranger's world was in the midst of rediscovering the medieval era and valuing it as the ideal age, a time of goodness and right. That tendency along with the neo-gothic revival and romanticism in art and literature dominated the scene. Unwittingly blinded by that restrictive context, Guéranger nonetheless sparked a renewed interest in the liturgy as prayer and not performance. Although his scholarship remains questionable from our contemporary perspective, it has rightfully distinguished him as the precursor of the Liturgical Movement.

At the beginning of the twentieth century, the fundamental purpose of the incipient Liturgical Movement matured to the point where it showed itself as the church's reclaiming of its worship as central to its life and mission. The date of Pius X's Motu proprio, *Tra le sollecitudini*, 22 November 1903, is often cited as the dawn of the official Liturgical Movement in the Roman church. The pope's remarks were not limited to musical concerns; a call was made for a return to the liturgy as the indispensable source of christian life. The use of the phrase "active participation" first showed itself in this early document. Pius X considered the active participation of the worshiping assembly as the center of christian life and the chief source of renewal. On 22 December 1905 the same pope issued a decree *Sacra Tridentina Synodus* which encouraged a more frequent reception of communion. A few years later in 1909, those who participated in the Catholic Congress at Malines, Belgium, perceived the pastoral implications of those official statements and drew them out. The liturgy was valued as the fundamental means of christian instruction; active participation in the liturgy was considered the most effective way to nourish and deepen christian faith and life. Therefore, the congress called for a translation of the Roman Missal into the vernacular, for a recentering of the christian life in the church's liturgy, and for retreats based on the liturgy to be held in liturgical centers in order to relocate the liturgy at the heart of christian spirituality.

The most influential leader in the early liturgical reform emerged at the Malines congress as the spokesperson for the escalating Liturgical Movement. Dom Lambert Beauduin, a monk of Mont César, Louvain, Belgium, had been a priest of the Belgian diocese of Liége. After eight years of pastoral experience and involvement as a "chaplain of workers" appointed to assist in the implementation of Leo XIII's encyclical, *Rerum novarum*, Beauduin entered the monastery of Mont César and was assigned to teach the young monks who benefited from his pastoral insights. His address at the Malines congress proposed an intensely practical program for liturgical renewal and thus launched what came to be known as the pastoral Liturgical Movement. The liturgy was meant not only for an elite group but for all the baptized. The movement's primary aim was not to reach theologians and intellectuals but ordinary Sunday churchgoers. It did not plan for revolution; it sought to retrieve authentic tradition and move toward christian renewal. Beauduin's book, *La piété de l'église* (1914), set out fundamental principles for the Liturgical Movement. His christology and ecclesiology shaped those principles: an understanding of the meaning of the incarnation will trigger insight into the dignity of human life; an understanding of the meaning of the church as the body of Christ will lead to the need for unity and community both in life and in worship; an understanding of the meaning of Jesus's sacrifice will enable those who remember it to live their lives like him, for the sake of others. Before these principles could be applied on a pastoral level, Beauduin knew well that the first step was to convince priests of the urgent need for liturgical reform. In the years following the Malines congress, Mont César became an important center for the liturgical formation of clergy and laity.

the monks extended their ideas through two organs: *Les questions liturgiques*, later entitled *Les questions liturgiques et paroissiales*, and the conferences of the *Semaines liturgiques*. Since the movement sometimes rubbed against the established practices of the church, e.g., use of the vernacular, the altar facing the people, etc., it was often a source of friction and unrest. Despite considerable opposition on various fronts, the Liturgical Movement gained momentum.

The Belgian movement developed during and after the First World War, while significant fermentation was going on in German monasteries, especially the Rhineland Abbey of Maria Laach. Apparently novel ideas about the nature of worship which the Liturgical Movement actively endorsed and preached were held in suspicion by some as a departure from Roman tradition while others indiscriminately hurled accusations of modernism. At this juncture in the movement's evolution, pastoral necessity often overshadowed theological precision; the movement lacked a clearly articulated theological foundation. In response to that need, the historical and theological insights of the Abbot of Maria Laach, Ildephonse Herwegen, and one of his monks, Dom Odo Casel, set out an historical and theological framework to legitimate the necessity for liturgical reform and renewal. The *Ecclesia orans* series was initiated in 1918 from Maria Laach with its first publication, *The Spirit of the Liturgy*, by Msgr. Romano Guardini. The monastery also established the *Verein zur Pflege der Liturgiewissenschaft* for the publication of scientific studies on the liturgy. In 1921, Odo Casel, Anton Baumstark, and Romano Guardini founded the *Jahrbuch für Liturgiewissenschaft*, the organ through which Casel developed his controversial theory of the *Kultmysterium*.

While the work of Maria Laach pri-marily addressed the interests of liturgical experts, the Augustinian canons of Klosterneuberg in Austria complemented and balanced those theological contributions by combining speculative investigation with pastoral application. Under the direction of Pius Parsch they emphasized the place of scripture in the liturgy. Parsch's *Das Jahr des Heiles (The Church's Year of Grace)* (1923) encouraged a knowledge of scripture to enrich liturgical prayer throughout the church's year. A periodical, *Bibel und Liturgie*, first issued in 1926, disseminated similar ideas. Religious and parish priests in Austria and Germany, such as Johannes Pinsk in Berlin and Josef Jungmann in Innsbruck, extended the work of the apostolate. The turmoil of the war years unfortunately delayed an English translation of Beauduin's foundational work which finally appeared in 1926 under the title *Liturgy the Life of the Church*.

During the period between the two world wars and during the early years of the Second World War, the Liturgical Movement grew consistently in Europe and abroad. In 1929 an English Benedictine of Ampleforth Abbey, Dom Bernard McElligott, founded the Society of St. Gregory in England and initiated its quarterly magazine, *Music and Liturgy*. Shifting liturgical priorities later caused the editor, Fr. J.D. Crichton, a priest of the archdiocese of Birmingham, to change the journal's name to *Liturgy* and then to *Life and Worship*. As editor of Britain's sole liturgical journal, he capably ushered the clergy and laity of his country through the conciliar reform and into the post-conciliar renewal. The membership of the Society of St. Gregory sponsored annual liturgical weeks and various conferences thus raising the liturgical consciousness of the Roman church in Great Britain. The itinerant preaching of the English Jesuit, Fr. Clifford Howell, also served to extend the liturgical apostolate throughout the United States and Canada, Australia and Ireland.

A similar escalation was experienced in the United States. In 1926, Dom Virgil Michel, a monk of St. John's Abbey, Collegeville, Minnesota, first issued *Orate Fratres* later called *Worship*, a periodical directed especially to parish priests and interested laity. He also established the Liturgical Press which distributed books and pamphlets to churches and homes. By 1940 a series of annual liturgical weeks stimulated enthusiasm throughout the country and led to the formation of the North American Liturgical Conference. The American movement has consistently shied away from the academic and has moved more toward the grassroots experience of worship and its reformation. Although the intellectual component has never been ignored, the Liturgical Movement in the United States has regularly been associated with the reappropriation of lay liturgical ministries. In Paris the Centre de Pastorale Liturgique was established in 1943 under the direction of the French Dominicans. Two years later the Centre issued the first volume of *La Maison-Dieu* which sought to combine the efforts of Maria Laach and Klosterneuberg. It remains one of the most important and influential liturgical journals.

By the end of the Second World War the continental Liturgical Movement had spread to all the major countries of the world. Population scattered during the war years and parish life was disorganized; young people were absorbed into the armed forces. Because of rigidly enforced blackouts and fierce bombings of many European cities, liturgical activity was literally driven underground. One would suspect that wartime preoccupations would have detracted from liturgical concerns and thus cause a breakdown in the momentum already gained. But the opposite was true. The crisis established a milieu which fanned the fires of the continental Liturgical Movement. A wartorn people needed to find some means of expressing their religious identity and of reinforcing a much needed sense of solidarity. That was achieved by a communal celebration of the eucharist usually in the form of a dialogue Latin mass. When the war was over, both the priest-chaplains and the former military personnel could not possibly return to what they had known before.

In 1943, Pius XII published his encyclical, *Mystici Corporis*. Although the encyclical was not explicitly focused on the liturgy, its ecclesiology had pastoral implications for the Liturgical Movement. Practical principles of the movement led to sober experimentation. Some bishops tried to give leadership and encouragement while others were stuck in a rigid legalism. The unpleasant combination of enthusiasm and ignorance often ran ahead of prudence and discretion. In 1947, Pius XII promulgated another pastoral letter, *Mediator Dei*, the first encyclical entirely focused on the liturgy. Papal approbation was of the utmost importance for those who remained cautious or skeptical. Therefore, this encyclical served as the charter of the Liturgical Movement in the years before Vatican II. Soon after its publication, Pius XII instituted a pontifical commission for general liturgical restoration. Frs. Ferdinand Antonelli, O.F.M., Joseph Loew, C.Ss.R., and Annibale Bugnini, C.M., were among its leadership. The commission cautiously and slowly made efforts to implement the encyclical and to initiate a project for general liturgical reform. In 1951 the Sacred Congregation of Rites issued its decree *De Solemni Vigilia Paschali instauranda* which restored the paschal vigil. The decree *Cum nostra hac aetate* of 1955 provided a simplification of rubrics. That same year the decree *Maxima redemp-*

tionis nostrae brought about extensive changes in the Holy Week liturgies. The 1958 instruction *De musica sacra* dealt not only with the place of music in liturgical celebration but also set out important norms regulating the laity's active participation in the liturgy.

From the time after the Second World War and before the Second Vatican Council, the Liturgical Movement was in intense fermentation. The catalyst for the reforms in the 1950's came from national and international liturgical congresses throughout western Europe. Each congress progressively considered the nature of the liturgy, identified pastoral concerns emerging in churches throughout Europe and the entire globe, and gradually came to a clearer discernment of the need for liturgical reform. In September 1956 the fifth international liturgical congress gathered first in Assisi and then in Rome. Inconceivable only ten years before, the Assisi-Rome congress with its semi-official status marked the immense progress made by the Liturgical Movement throughout the world as well as the high priority placed on it by the church on its way to reform.

The work of scholars and pastors who aligned themselves with the Liturgical Movement came to full fruition in December 1963 with the promulgation of the Constitution on the Sacred Liturgy. The document concisely distilled the Liturgical Movement's principles and objectives. It clearly articulated a theology of liturgy built on firm biblical and patristic foundations with a distinctively pastoral thrust. Early in 1964, Paul VI took steps to implement the constitution by forming an international commission of experts to revise the liturgical books. The Council (Consilium) for the Implementation of the Constitution on the Liturgy embarked on its task of textual renovation, then conceived as the primary means of mobilizing the reform. In

1965 *Notitiae* was issued as its monthly journal. The International Commission on English in the Liturgy (ICEL), established in 1963, applied itself to the weighty task of offering an effective English translation of Latin texts that would satisfy all English-speaking Catholics throughout the world. In the United States the National Conference of Catholic Bishops monitored and mobilized the liturgical reform and renewal through the Bishops' Committee on the Liturgy (BCL). In 1965 that committee first issued a monthly *Newsletter* largely containing translations from the Latin *Notitiae*. Diocesan liturgical commissions were established to implement reform on the local level. Their primary task of informing and motivating parish renewal remains vital to effective liturgical formation. The Federation of Diocesan Liturgical Commissions (FDLC) oversees and supervises these diocesan commissions.

In 1969 the Congregation for Divine Worship absorbed the Consilium and by 1978 brought to completion the general reforms mandated by the liturgical constitution. Since that time, the illusion has grown in the final years of the twentieth century that the primary goals of the Liturgical Movement have been reached. Some maintain that the renovation of liturgical books has brought to fulfillment the dreams of early liturgical scholars and reformers; therefore, there is ample reason to bring the momentum of the liturgical reform to a halt. Yet there are others who know that the two decades following the council have only opened doors to further possibilities. For example, questions remain regarding the extent and quality of the entire assembly's active participation in the liturgical act; ideological stances often affect the way in which liturgical ministries are defined and enacted; various language groups seek to engage writers and poets of their own culture to compose prayer forms that emerge directly from the soul of the people; cultural adaptation and indigenization to a great extent remain open and unattended. The claim has been made that the liturgy is no longer a movement but has become an integral part of the church's pastoral ministry. That claim bears some truth; however, the recent institutionalization of the movement's original charism has reduced its initial fire to a smoldering glow. The illusion that the reform is in place has immobilized the movement toward renewal.

An apparent sense of unrest and urgency in the post-conciliar renewal stems from the conviction that the theoretical and the practical, the theological and the pastoral, mutually influence and transform one another. This reciprocal relationship between what is thought about sacrament and what is actually done in the rite is the core from which the agenda for the post-conciliar Liturgical Movement is being shaped. Liturgical praxis is currently the focus of several liturgists, liturgiologists, and liturgical theologians, especially those in western Europe and the U.S.A. who value the necessary interplay between the human and social sciences and sacramental theology. The emerging discipline of pastoral liturgical studies attempts to examine the human experience of symbol, ritual and their meanings which will then provide new data for ongoing theological reflection and renewed pastoral practice.

English-speaking countries have taken a lead in responding to the demands of liturgical renewal. The Irish Institute of Pastoral Liturgy founded in 1974 in Carlow serves those involved in liturgical renewal at diocesan and parish levels. The Liturgical Conference established in 1940 has extended the liturgical apostolate in the United states and Canada through its earlier sponsorship of an annual liturgical week and more recently in its ecumenical liturgical publications. Workshops and practical publications have aided both liturgical ministers and parish liturgical committees. The National Association of Pastoral Musicians founded in 1976 continues to promote good music in liturgy and has effectively drawn out new talent from its membership. The North American Academy of Liturgy established in 1973 has provided a place for the exchange of theological and pastoral insights among North America's most capable liturgists. Universities such as The Catholic University of America, St. John's University, Collegeville, and the University of Notre Dame continue to gather theological faculties with liturgical expertise who educate women and men for leadership within the ongoing liturgical renewal as the church moves into the twenty-first century.

See Liturgy

J.D. Crichton, H.E. Winstone, J.R. Ainslie, eds., *English Catholic Worship: Liturgical Renewal in England Since 1900*, London: Geoffrey Chapman, 1979. R.W. Franklin, "Guéranger and Pastoral Liturgy: A Nineteenth Century Context," *Worship* 50 (1976): 146-162. Jeremy Hall, "The American Liturgical Movement: The Early Years," *Worship* 50 (1976) : 472-489. Carl Last, ed., *Remembering the Future: Vatican II and Tomorrow's Liturgical Agenda*, New York: Paulist Press, 1983. Olivier Rousseau, *The Progress of the Liturgy: An Historical Sketch from the Beginning of the Nineteenth Century to the Pontificate of Pius X*, trans., Benedictines of Westminster Abbey, Vancouver, British Columbia, Canada, Westminster, Md.: Newman Press, 1951. Mark Searle, "New Methods: The Emergence of Pastoral Liturgical Studies," *Worship* 57 (1983) : 291-308. R. Kevin Seasoltz, *The New Liturgy: A Documentation, 1903-1965*, New York: Herder and Herder, 1966, and *New Liturgy, New Laws*, Collegeville, Minn.: Liturgical Press, 1980.

DANIEL P. GRIGASSY, OFM

LITURGY

Within the Roman Catholic tradition, liturgy designates the official public worship of the church. To call it official is to say that it is authorized by and takes place in communion with the local bishop according to the norms approved by the Roman See. To call it public is to say that liturgy is the activity of an assembly of believers visibly gathered. To call it worship is to say that it is prayer.

The word liturgy derives from the Greek *leitourgia,* a word in turn compounded from two other Greek words— *laos* (=people, cf. laity) and *ergon* (=work, cf. metallurgy). In its ordinary pre-Christian use it referred to whatever public works were judged necessary to promote the public well being. Not only public prayer but also road-building might have been termed *leitourgia* in pagan society. Christian use gradually narrowed the word's meaning to designate the public worship of the church. In the eastern tradition, it became customary to use the term liturgy even more narrowly as an equivalent for its eucharistic action.

Vatican II's Constitution on the Sacred Liturgy, *Sacrosanctum Concilium,* calls the liturgy "the outstanding means whereby the faithful may express in their lives and manifest to others the mystery of Christ and the real nature of the true Church" (S.C. 2). Acknowledging that the "liturgy does not exhaust the entire activity of the church," the bishops gathered in Council nevertheless asserted that "the liturgy is the summit toward which the activity of the church is directed; at the same time it is the fount from which all the Church's power flows" (S.C. 9, 10).

Scope of the Liturgy

Liturgy, like everything in the church, has been subject to historical development. The present scope of the Roman liturgy is identifiable by the contents of the officially promulgated liturgical books. The books themselves and the rites they present, newly revised since the Second Vatican Council, embody a vision of christian salvation that is centered in the eucharistic mystery. In that vision all other liturgical assemblies are either an anticipation or an extension of the eucharistic assembly. The church's eucharist is its memorial of Jesus Christ, because the church believes that in the life, death, and resurrection of Jesus lies the power of salvation for all peoples seeking communion with God. From early times, the church has named this mystery of salvation through Jesus the paschal mystery. It has proclaimed and celebrated the mystery in public worship and taught it as the pattern for christian living.

The baptismal liturgy (including not only infant baptism but all the rites of christian initiation of adults and children, which constitute the early phases of incorporation into the mystery of Christ and his church) comes to its completion in the eucharistic assembly. It is normally at the eucharist which culminates the Easter vigil that the newly baptized express and experience their present communion with Christ and the church and anticipate the full communion of all creation with God through Christ. The order of christian initiation, anticipating this moment, includes rites for enrolling catechumens, exorcism and blessing, the election of candidates for baptism, scrutinies, pre-baptismal anointings, the handing on of the creed and the Lord's prayer, and confirmation.

The liturgy of penance and reconciliation and the rites for the pastoral care of the sick both concern themselves with restoration to eucharistic communion of those who are separated from the eucharistic assembly. In the first case, the liturgy intends to overcome the ruptures in the church caused by the serious sin of its members. In the second case, it is debilitating or life-threatening illness which has resulted in the isolation of the believer from the church's assemblies and perhaps jeopardized the sick person's confidence in God's loving presence. The order for reconciliation includes rites for the reconciliation of individual penitents, for a gathering of penitents making individual confessions, and for the general absolution of a gathering without individual confession. The liturgical rites for the sick involve pastoral visits for prayer, for eucharistic communion, and for the anointing with oil and the laying on of hands for the comfort and healing of the sick person.

The liturgical celebration of christian marriage affirms, expresses, and deepens the loving communion of a baptized christian woman and man with Christ through their intimate communion with one another. The eucharistic mystery of Christ's gift of his life in order to bring abundant life for others takes on social visibility in the reality of a christian marriage. The marriage rites includes forms for celebration within the eucharistic liturgy and also in non-eucharistic assemblies.

The church's liturgy also includes rites of ordination and installation directed to official service within the church itself. Ordination to the episcopacy, the presbyterate, and the diaconate establish christian churchmen in permanent relationships of leadership within the church and so in its public assemblies for prayer. Accordingly, distinct roles within the liturgical assembly are designated for the ordained. Newly created Roman rites of installation to the liturgical ministries of acolyte and reader, also limited to churchmen, intend to give stability to these liturgical functions; the perceived need for these official installations rose after the 1972 suppression of the minor clerical orders and during the transition from exclusively clerical to lay ministries within the Roman liturgy. The reception and the future of rites of installation within the local churches is uncertain, since women, who serve widely as readers and ministers of communion in the English-speaking world, are excluded from formal instal-lation through these official rites.

Two rites for the dying, viaticum and the commendation of the dying, comprise another part of the church's public worship. Viaticum is the final eucharistic communion of the dying person, who is anticipating the fullness of eschatological communion with God in Christ. The prayer of commendation is prayed by the christian people assembled to accompany the dying person in the movement to the fullness of life. Laity as well as ordained Christians may preside at these official liturgies. After the death of a believer, the church celebrates the rites of christian burial. These guide the prayer of the mourners from the time of physical death to the moment of interment, cremation, or other reverent disposal of the body. Normally the center of these rites is the funeral Mass.

The church's daily prayer, the liturgy of the hours presumes regular gatherings of the christian people in households, monasteries, and local churches morning and evening for public praise, thanksgiving, lament, and intercession in Christ's name and in communion with him.

Additional occasional liturgies also anticipate or derive from the eucharistic center of christian worship. The liturgy for the dedication of a church consecrates a place and its furnishings for the regular eucharistic worship of the christian people. Rites of religious profession and the consecration of virgins publicly dedicate persons to divine service. The newly revised Roman liturgical Book of Blessings provides a wide variety of rites for gatherings of the christian people seeking to bring the various aspects of their domestic, social, cultural, economic, and devotional lives into clearer relationship with the paschal character of their life in Christ. National hierarchies are expected to adapt and to supplement the Roman book according to the cultural realities of their local churches.

While all christian liturgical assemblies focus on the paschal mystery of Christ as the way of salvation, the richness and complexity of the mystery have given rise to the development of a liturgical cycle of feasts and seasons commonly referred to as the liturgical year. In the movement of this annual cycle successive aspects of the mystery of salvation in Christ are celebrated. The principal festal seasons of the liturgical year are Easter and Christmas. The Easter season encompasses the time from Ash Wednesday through Pentecost. It has three periods: the forty days of Lent, the Paschal Triduum, and the fifty days of Easter. The Christmas season encompasses the four weeks of Advent plus the Christmas-Epiphany period proper, culminating in the feast of the Baptism of the Lord. The remaining weeks of the year are simply designated Ordinary Time.

The principal christian feast in every season is the weekly Sunday, when the church regularly assembles for its eucharistic memorial of the risen and glorified Lord Jesus. Other solemnities and feasts of the Lord Jesus and his mother Mary occurring in each season give expression to distinct aspects of the life, death, and glorification of Jesus. In addition, from the first christian centuries the church's public liturgy has taken note of days commemorating martyrs and saints, because the church recognized in their dying or their living an exemplary expression of profound communion with the risen Christ. This practice gave rise to the sanctoral cycle within the liturgical year. Its observances are ranked as solemnities, feasts, memorials, and optional memorials.

Characteristics of Liturgical Prayer

All liturgical assemblies have certain characteristic features. The liturgy is a trinitarian, paschal, ecclesial, sacramental, ethically oriented, and eschatological way of christian prayer.

Trinitarian and Paschal. Liturgy is the ritual prayer of the church. Ritual activity is always about relationships. Christian liturgy expresses the church's understanding of the relationships which save, as these have been revealed in the event of Jesus Christ. While christian liturgy is Christ-centered, because the baptized believe that salvation comes through Christ, it is always trinitarian, not narrowly directed to an idealized intimate relationship with the historical or the glorified Jesus. Christian salvation is experienced as a share in the Holy Spirit of love which eternally binds Christ Jesus to "Abba" and flows out to gather and reconcile the whole world.

That trinitarian understanding of salvation makes christian liturgical worship paschal. Liturgical prayer announces and celebrates as good news the truth that salvation involves letting go of control of one's own life, even dying, for the sake of love. This path of life is possible only for those who continually remember Jesus, enter into communion with him, and take heart from his promise that God will glorify like Jesus all those who trust and walk his path.

Ecclesial. The liturgical assembly is a visible gathering of the church as an ordered communion of the baptized. A local gathering of the baptized is the starting point of all christian worship; solitary liturgical prayer is an anomaly. Within the liturgical assembly roles are differentiated and ordered for the service of the church at prayer. Major liturgical ministers currently include the presider, the reader, the cantor and other ministers of music, ministers of communion, and the deacon. Other liturgical ministries are exercised by acolytes and ushers. Liturgical presidency is normally exercised by the ordained: a bishop, a presbyter, or a deacon. In special circumstances, as when an ordained minister is not available or pastoral circumstances dictate otherwise, liturgical presidency may sometimes be delegated to and exercised by a lay person. The norms for liturgical ministry are specified in the introductions to the various liturgical books.

When christian ministry is ritualized within the liturgical assembly it gives symbolic expression to the church's realization that all the baptized share in the one same Spirit of love even as they affirm there are many different spiritual gifts given for the good of all. In this way christian liturgy also celebrates the mystery that the power for salvation is mediated through relationships within the church.

The ordering of the liturgical assembly is traditionally called hierarchical. The term is misleading insofar as it is commonly understood to designate the ranking of ordained clergy, while the ordering of the liturgical assembly involves the ordering of the whole community of the baptized, a priestly people some of whom are also ordained, for mutual ministry at prayer.

Sacramental. Liturgical events are sacramental. Sacramental liturgy is the symbolic, ritual form of the church's prayer. To identify liturgy as ritual activity is to say that the prayer involves gathered believers in a series of patterned transactions and interactions which express their faith in Christ and their desire to deepen it. Characterizing liturgy as sacramental symbolic activity is to say that the people participating in the ritual acts are in their very activity also participating in the ultimate reality they signify, namely salvation through forgiveness and communion with the risen and glorified Jesus.

A limited number of symbols are central to the liturgical work of the christian people. The preeminent christian symbol is the assembly itself, the gathering of diverse peoples into one body in Christ's name. In the liturgical assembly, the baptized people of God understand themselves sacramentally as a people called to become the Body of Christ and to actually be so transformed in some measure by the power of God at work among them. Within the different liturgical rites of the church the christian people assembled make use of water, wine, oil, bread, light and darkness, laying on of hands, and the reading and interpretation of the scripture as a living and life-giving Word, and the sign of the cross to express and to become present to the mystery of salvation in Christ because the memory and the meaning of Jesus' saving work are embodied in these earthly realities. The church believes that their continued use in its liturgical memorial of Christ Jesus mediates to believers the power of salvation.

Ethically Oriented. The liturgical assembly is a temporary gathering of the baptized to make memorial of the Lord Jesus Christ. At the close of each liturgical assembly the local church is dispersed, members returning to their ordinary social milieu newly confirmed in faith, strengthened in hope, and renewed in the power of love. The people of God becoming the Body of Christ understand themselves to have a mission to be light to the world and leaven in the mass (S.C. 9).

The dismissal of the liturgical assembly contains a mandate to participants to live out in ordinary life the mystery of salvation in Christ which they have celebrated sacramentally. The specific demands of christian life become clearer as the local church reflects on the contrast between its social milieu and the vision of divine justice and mercy its liturgy celebrates. Family conflict, racial prejudice, economic injustice, sexism, civil disorder and violent international aggression are all challenges to the effective faith of those who gather for public prayer in Jesus' name. When *Sacrosanctum Con-*

cilium teaches that the liturgy does not exhaust the activity of the church, it acknowledges that the liturgy, constitutive of and central to the life of the church, intends to empower the people of God to lives of christian discipleship (S.C. 9-11).

Eschatological. The liturgical worship of the church proclaims and affirms the presence to the assembly of the saving mystery first revealed in the Christ-event. But liturgical prayer also involves believers in corporate invocation of the Spirit of Jesus to bring to completion the salvation already begun but not yet fully established. The ethical imperative of christian worship is complemented by the church's conviction that every manifestation of God's reign on earth as in heaven is always grace.

History of Christian Liturgy

The origins of the forms and even the calendar for christian liturgy can be found in large part in the pre-christian religious environment of the first disciples of Jesus who had gathered in Jewish synagogue, temple, and household. Connections are evident even when early christian communities went to great lengths consciously to distance themselves from the public worship of Judaism (Heb 4:14-10:39 1 Pet 2:1-10; Gal 3:26-28; Mt 6:5-13 and parallels; Mt 26:17-29 and parallels; Lk 4:16-22). The christian cycle of feasts and seasons, for example, is tied to the Jewish Passover-Pentecost and Sabbath observances. The christian eucharist draws for its forms and meaning from aspects of domestic and temple religious meals, even as it transforms all aspects of this heritage in the light of faith in the risen Christ Jesus. The christian reading and interpretation of the ancient scriptures in liturgical assembly derived from synagogue practice, even as the christian practice of reading the OT in the light of Jesus itself gave shape to the canon of the NT.

The origin of the spiritual power and the religious meaning of christian liturgy are found in the event of the life, death, and resurrection of Jesus Christ and in the apostolic interpretation of that Christ-event in the light of continuing post-resurrection experiences of Jesus' saving presence. Christian worship is always a memorial and invocation (*anamnesis* and *epiclesis*) of the risen Lord. It is public proclamation and celebration of the present power of his death and glorification and a call for the completion of this world's redemption.

The power of this new faith in cosmic salvation through Christ stimulated a rapid expansion of the Jesus movement throughout the Roman empire in the first christian generation. It prompted people of biblical faith to rethink their beliefs about the nature of God's decisive action on the long-awaited day of salvation. Among pagans it promoted an interest in the good news of the way of salvation revealed in Christ Jesus. It spurred re-evaluation of the deeds for which God was to be praised in public assembly and refocused believers' prayers concerning the completion of salvation, for which they were waiting.

Significant cultural forces beyond Judaism also influenced the development of the structures and the content of christian liturgy. During the second to fourth centuries, major urban centers in the Mediterranean world which became home to christian communities also became home to distinctive liturgical traditions, that is to variant patterns of interaction within the liturgical assembly and variant emphases in content within the common focus of a memorial of the suffering, dead, buried, and risen Christ. In the eastern Mediterranean area the cities of Antioch in Syria and Alexandria in Egypt were important cultural hubs that gave rise to distinctive liturgical rites. Antiochene Christianity itself reflected two cultural strains. The continuation of a predominantly Jewish ethos within the christian church generated the East Syrian liturgical tradition, with further local variations in content and form among the Nestorian Chaldeans and the Malabar Christians of South India whose faith derived from the Antiochene center. A West Syrian liturgical tradition, shaped more by a Hellenistic cultural ethos, also gave rise to further variants identifiable today as the Melkite, Maronite, and Byzantine rites. The Egyptian tradition of christian worship had an equally complex development. An Alexandrian rite took shape under Greek cultural dynamics; the Coptic liturgy of Ethiopia reflected greater Syrian influence.

Two pivots of liturgical development existed also in the western Mediterranean in these early centuries: Rome/North Africa and the western or Gallican provinces of imperial Rome. Beyond these major western centers for the development of christian liturgy, distinctive liturgical rites took shape also in the city of Milan, among the Celtic peoples beyond the frontiers of the Roman empire, and in Spain. In the early medieval period reciprocal borrowings among the distinctive rites east and west led to the gradual modification of the early liturgy of the city of Rome. It was this expanded and modified Roman rite which the emperor Charlemagne imposed on the whole territory of the Holy Roman Empire in the ninth century in an act of centralization which was decisive for the future of the western liturgical tradition.

The western liturgical tradition underwent another major development in its ritual structures and its religious content at the time of the sixteenth-century Reformation. Protestant reformers posed challenges to a Roman liturgy they found to be maladapted to the cultural, political, and religious ferment of western Europe in the fourteenth and fifteenth centuries. In response to the challenge and in consideration of matters treated during the Council of Trent (1545-1563), the Roman See promulgated uniform revised liturgical books to be used by all churches in communion with the Roman See, with a limited number of exceptions, for ancient local usage. The reformers own concerns with the renewal of public worship gave rise to the distinctive Lutheran, Anglican, Reformed, and Anabaptist rites.

Each of these distinctive liturgical rites has its own history of internal development, reflecting the spiritual, cultural, and political currents alive at different times within the local churches as they gathered generation after generation to pray publicly according to their own rites. Accordingly, the study of the complex history of christian worship is a central concern within the field of liturgical studies. Especially since the nineteenth century the scientific study of liturgical history has concerned itself with identifying and publishing manuscripts, establishing critical editions of extant liturgical texts, determining relationships among them, and identifying their social and ecclesial contexts in order to interpret them reliably. Classic early twentieth-century works in liturgical history include the monumental *Dictionnaire d'archeologie chrétienne et de liturgie* (1907-1953), a product of the collaborative work of Henri LeClercq and Ferdinand Cabrol; Josef Jungmann's *Missarum Solemnia* (1948); Gregory Dix's *The Shape of the Liturgy* (1945); and numerous volumes published in the Alcuin Club Series. Under the influence of the Vatican II liturgical reform, new impetus has been given to the study of liturgical history and to the pastoral significance of historical research into a living tradition.

Structural Elements

Within each one of the Roman church's

various liturgical rites, certain constant structural elements are evident. These include a physical assembly; the ordering of ritual space and its furnishings; the public reading of scripture; the proclamation of designated ritual texts; the handling of symbolic objects, and performative postures, gestures, sounds and movements.

However large or small the membership of any particular liturgical gathering, liturgy presupposes the physical coming together of believers. Even in the case of the rite for the reconciliation of individual penitents, an assembly of only two members, the church is visibly assembled for prayer and in that assembly a ritual action unfolds.

A ritual ordering of space within the place of assembly is another structural constant integral to the proper celebration of Roman liturgical rites. Appropriate liturgical architecture arrays the assembly and its ministers before God as church, one body with many members in relationship to one another and to the baptismal font, altar, and lectern. Good design of liturgical space facilitates the movements of people called for within the rite. Poor spatial configurations, by contrast, can distort ecclesial relationships and impede effective ritual interaction. Suitable furnishings for the place of ritual assembly are also structurally integral to effective liturgical action. Their design must attend both to their functional use within the rites and to their cultural and aesthetic suitability for the local church. The U.S. Bishops' Committee on the Liturgy, in its 1978 document *Environment and Art in Catholic Worship,* provides a detailed treatment of the physical environment required for the effective celebration of the Roman rite.

Proclamation of the scriptures is another structural constant of all liturgical rites. In its most expansive form, at the Easter Vigil, the Roman liturgy proposes nine readings for proclamation in the assembly. In other gatherings, for example, the rites for communion for the sick in institutions or in their homes, a single text or even a single verse may comprise this element. In most liturgical rites, two or three biblical texts are read from a ritual lectionary and an interpretation of their meanings for the assembly proposed in a homily. The renewed emphasis on biblical proclamation as one of the structural constants of the liturgical assembly is one of the fruits of the Vatican II renewal of the Liturgy (S.C. 24; 51-52).

Official nonscripture texts constitute a fourth structural constant within every Roman liturgical rite. Among these are formal orations to be prayed aloud by the presiding minister, the formal acclamations of the assembly, creedal formulae, and words of intercession, commendation, blessing, memorial, and invocation appropriate to the purpose of each distinctive liturgical event. The most ancient of these formulas, the acclamations *Amen!* and *Alleluia!,* recall the Semitic origins of christian liturgy even in an era of restoration of vernacular languages. In addition to the set liturgical texts, the reformed Roman liturgy provides for flexibility in the local assembly's liturgical speech. Where ritual structures specify greetings, admonitions, instructions, and exhortations, invitations, and intercessions, they propose model texts and instruct ritual leaders to use "these or other words." So also, structural provision for the singing of chants and hymns taken from the scripture or congruent with the biblical and liturgical traditions encourages flexibility in the assembly's linguistic expression.

Liturgical song itself is not considered optional but integral to the reformed Roman liturgy, the vocalization of transformed human spirits united in prayer. Liturgical structures provide for the solo song of the cantor and the presiding minister, for the song of the choir, and for that of the assembly, according to varying degrees of solemnity, dependent upon the size and the skill of the assembly and the nature of the liturgical event being celebrated. Instrumental music to accompany and to enhance liturgical action is another form of ritual sound structurally integral to liturgical celebration. In recent centuries, the organ was the instrument of preference for accompaniment in Roman liturgy; since the Vatican II renewal, the range of instruments used liturgically has expanded to reflect the historical and cultural reality of local assemblies (S.C. 120).

Ritual handling of symbolic objects is another structural constant of Roman liturgy. Oils for anointings are integral to the rites of initiation, ordination, the healing of the sick, and the dedication of churches. Water is used for baptismal immersion or sprinkling and for lustrations associated with baptismal renewal. Bread and wine are essential for eucharistic action. The physical laying on of hands is integral to some rites in the initiatory process, to ordinations, the healing of the sick, the reconciliation of penitents, and some blessings of persons and things. The liturgical lectionary or the book of the gospels is handled ritually to focus the believers' attention on the scripture as a Word of life. The Easter candle, celebrated as the Christ light shattering the world's darkness, is essential not only to the liturgy of the Easter Vigil but also to baptismal liturgy and to funeral rites. The liturgical renewal has called for authenticity and dignity in the materials and forms themselves and the use of these in liturgical action (cf. General Instruction on the Roman Missal, ch 6).

Patterned movements and gestures and distinctive ritual postures within the liturgical assembly are further structural constants of each liturgical rite, whatever its specific purpose. The ancient Roman eucharistic liturgy gave emphasis not only to processions of ministers entering and leaving the place of assembly but also to the people's processions for the presentation of their gifts and their communion. The latter two major processions have been restored with the recent reform of the Roman eucharistic liturgy. Processions or other formal movements within the liturgical space of persons who are special subjects of liturgical action are called for in the rites of marriage, funerals, christian initiation, ordinations, religious profession, dedication of churches, and some occasional blessings. Often these persons as well as the liturgical ministers wear distinctive ritual garb. The vesture of the ordained is prescribed; the ritual dress of others is customary. Processions accompanying the movement of the Book of the Gospels and the Easter candle are also provided for, as are formal ritual movements for the sprinkling of holy water and for the incensation of the altar table, ministers, and members of the assembly.

The orans-posture, arms extended and upraised in prayer, is customarily although not necessarily reserved in the Roman liturgy for the presiding minister praying in the name of the whole assembly. Kneeling as a posture of humility or repentance has been retained; sitting to listen to readings and their interpretation and standing at prayer to signify attention or identification with the risen Christ are other constant structural elements of the Roman liturgy. So also are prostration and immersion structurally designated posture of mystical identification with the Lord Jesus' dying or obedient submission to God's will.

Vatican II Reform
and Its Implementation

The Second Vatican Council affirmed the centrality of liturgical celebration for the existence, the renewal, and the vitality of the church, a theme that had been anticipated by participants in the pre-conciliar liturgical movement dating from the nineteenth century. The council took the concept a step further when it mandated a liturgical reform which would enable the church to renew itself and its public prayer not through a uniform Roman rite but one adaptable to the realities of the local churches (S.C. 37-40). Accordingly, the council characterized the bishop as the principal liturgist of his diocese (L.G. 26) and called for collaboration of regional and national episcopal conferences in the work of promulgating and adapting the liturgical books prepared by the Roman See. One organ of episcopal collaboration familiar to English-speaking Catholics is the International Commission on English in the Liturgy (I.C.E.L.), an episcopal commission established in 1964 to prepare English translations of the official Roman liturgical books and to take other initiatives for the adaptation of these books such as are called for jointly by the bishops' conferences of the English-speaking world.

Because Roman Catholic liturgical renewal has coincided with liturgical renewal and the promulgation of new liturgical books among Anglican/Episcopal, Lutheran, and Reformed churches, ecumenical collaboration has also been a factor in the implementation of the Vatican II reform of the liturgy. Among English-speaking people, official ecumenical collaboration has focused on the preparation of standard English translations of liturgical texts, like the Lord's Prayer and the Gloria, common to all these churches. It has also led to the exploration of the possibility of a common English-language lectionary.

Collaboration among academics engaged in liturgical studies has assisted in the clarification of the similarities and the distinctive emphases in the form and content of the Roman rite vis-à-vis the other western liturgical traditions. Two major academic organizations involved in ecumenical liturgical study are the North American Academy of Liturgy and the Societas Liturgica. Popular liturgical collaboration has taken two forms. Local ecumenical gatherings for public worship have helped to correct long-standing mutual misperceptions and distortions concerning the liturgy and the faith of Roman Catholic and Protestant Christians. And more frequent mutual participation of Protestant and Catholic laity in the various liturgical events of each others' churches has also created a pastoral foundation for future ecumenical collaboration in the renewal of worship and the reunion of the churches.

One other post-conciliar development which promises to affect the future of liturgical reform and church renewal is the decline in the number of ordained Roman Catholic clergy in the last quarter of the twentieth century. Pastoral necessity has given new prominence to a heretofore minor liturgy in the Roman rite, the rite for eucharistic communion outside Mass, at which a lay minister presides. The development, neither foreseen nor endorsed by the bishops in council in the 1960's, is at cross purposes with the liturgical theology, eucharistic focus, and ecclesial self-understanding of the Vatican II reform. Continuing pastoral and theological reflection on this development will constitute one of the major challenges to continuing liturgical renewal in the post-conciliar church.

See **Assembly; Church; Eschatology; Liturgical Movement; Ritual; Sacrament; Symbol; Vatican Council II**

Documents on the Liturgy 1963-1979. Conciliar, Papal, and Curial Texts, Tr. Thomas O'Brien, International Commission on English in the Liturgy. Collegeville, MN: The Liturgical Press, 1982. *The Rites of the Catholic Church,* Two volumes, New York: Pueblo Publishing Co., 1976, rev. 1984.

1980. Cyril Vogel, *Medieval Liturgy: An Introduction to Sources,* Tr. and rev. William Storey and Niels Rasmussen, Washington D.C.: Pastoral Press, 1986. Herman Wegman, *Christian Worship in East and West: A Story Guide to Liturgical History,* Tr. Gordon Lathrop, New York: Pueblo Publishing Co, 1985.

MARY COLLINS, OSB

LOGOS

Logos (Hb. *dabar,* Lat. *verbum, sermo*) as it occurs in biblical and in Christian theology has the general meaning of "word" with a family of connotations such as "speech," "meaning," "reason," "account," and so forth. For Christian theology and its later Catholic developments, the classic text is the Prologue to John's Gospel (1,1-18). Here the Word "was in the beginning," was "with God" and "was God" (v. 1). Everything is made through this personal Word, in whom "was life" which is "the light of men" (v. 3). The meaning of the Word culminates when "the Word was made flesh and dwelt amongst us . . . " (v. 14) Though "no one has ever seen God," this Word as divine Son makes God known (v. 18). St. Augustine indicates the emphasis of christian thinking on the Word when, in his *Confessions* (VII, 9), he noted that though he had found the equivalents of most christian doctrines in the pagan authors, what he had never found in such writings was that the Word became flesh.

Since it is a term in the most intense and exclusive understanding of christian faith, "Word" occurs in a rich and complex history of meaning. This has both occasioned intense scholarly debate, and suggested developments of christian theology itself. On the level of scholarly debate, because the philosophical term, *Logos,* is such a pervasive category in Greek philosophy, scholars have asked to what degree the Johannine writings have been influenced by philosophical thought on this issue. Heraclitus of Ephesus, where perhaps John wrote his gospel, introduced this category into Greek thought in the sixth century B.C. In later Stoic philosophy it figured with the meaning of universal quasi-divine reason inherent in the cosmos. The great Jewish philosopher, Philo, in his efforts to bring together Jewish and Greek understanding of the Word of God, used this term over a thousand times. For him, the *Logos* was the created intermediary between God and the world. It gave coherence to the universe, being at once the image of God and the exemplar of the human soul. In gnostic literature, usually later than the composition of John's gospel, e.g., *The Gospel of Truth,* the *Logos* comes from the fullness of the Father's mind and thought, and is to be understood as the savior.

Notwithstanding these affinities of vocabulary and meaning with the Johannine prologue, biblical scholarship tends to find it unnecessary to look to philosophical literature as the source of John's usage of this term. It is far more obviously related to the OT rhetoric and imagery of God's Word. The Hebrew *dabhar* is much less abstract, and far more active in its meaning compared to *Logos* in the philosophical tradition. In Genesis 1, it is situated "in the beginning;" it is creative; overcomes darkness with light, and gives life. Other Johannine themes are present in the theophany of Sinai with its images of divine presence in the "glory" of God and in the tabernacle, and in the divine covenant-love (Ex 19-29). These qualities and functions of the Word of God can, of course, be abundantly documented in the Prophetic and Sapiential writings, and in many of the psalms (Pss 19:8; 107:20; 119:105, 130, etc.). More important still for the Johannine Word are the descriptive passages referring to "wisdom" in the Sapiential literature. Indeed, the personified Wisdom passages in Prov 1:22-33; 8-9; Sir 24; Wis 7:22f are in poetic and hymnic form, genres closely allied to John's prologue. All in all, such parallels are far more impressive than those suggested with Philonic writings.

A purely Jewish and biblical provenance seems, then, to have provided the terms for the Johannine prologue with its culmination in the Word made flesh. On the other hand, the early christian Apologists (Justin), and later theologians (Clement of Alexandria, Origen, Tertullian, Augustine) were not slow to exploit analogical meanings of the Word of faith, thus to relate the meaning of the Word made flesh to the larger world of Greek thought. This more philosophical turn in christian theology had many advantages. The first was that it enabled Christian theology to repel the charge of mythological regression (e.g., Celsus) in speaking of the generation of the divine Son, by linking this to the utterance of the spiritual Word in the divine mind. Secondly, developing the analogy of the word as an inner and outer event, conceived in the mind, and then externally uttered, secured a way of speaking of the eternal Son and his historical appearance in the *economia*. Thirdly, it suggested a dialogical notion of the Word well-adapted to the requirements of christian mission: the eternal, creative Word now incarnate had enlightened, as the "seminal *Logos*," not only the prophets but all the revered truth-seekers of antiquity in the history preceding Christianity.

This kind of thinking gradually permeated the history of Catholic theology. It is exemplified in different ways in Aquinas' use of the psychological analogy in trinitarian theology, as in the more cosmic and processive vision of Teilhard de Chardin with Christ as "Omega point" of evolution, and in modern theologies of interfaith dialogue. In short, the original connotation of "Word" provoked a theology of dialogue. The christian Word is spoken into a conversation of other meanings of the Word, above all that of the Word of God of Israel and the *Logos* of philosophical and scientific speculation.

See **Jesus Christ**

R. Brown, "Appendix II: The 'Word,'" in *The Anchor Bible. The Gospel according to John (i-xii). Introduction, translation, notes,* Garden City, NY: Doubleday and Co., 1966, 519-524. "Logos," articles by D. M. Crossan and C. J. Peter, *The New Catholic Encyclopedia 8,* New York: McGraw-Hill, 1967, 967-972. Jaroslav Pelikan, *The Christian Tradition I: The Emergence of the Catholic Tradition (100-600),* Chicago: Univ. of Chicago Press, 1971, pg. 186-260.

ANTHONY J. KELLY

LOVE

Foundations

Theological Roles. Although Christians have always insisted on the centrality of *agape*/charity/love in the life and teaching of Jesus and of his followers, serious theological attention to this central feature has been intermittent. Most major theologians such as Augustine and Aquinas have treated the topic but none have given it the central, architectonic place one might expect. With the divisions of theology in the post-medieval period, doctrinal theology in the Catholic tradition practically ignored charity. In moral theology it received a very skimpy treatment concerned mainly with the "sin against" of scandal and cooperation. To spiritual and ascetical theology, ancillary and subordinate, was assigned the task of commenting, in limited fashion, on the love whereby we were created and liberated. The Protestant tradition from Luther on maintained more of the Augustinian emphasis although it issued in a sharp correction of Augustine with the publication of Anders Nygren's *Agape and Eros* in 1932. This may be said to have initiated much of the contemporary discussion, thrusting, for a short time, *agape*/charity/love into the heart of theological reflection. Major contemporary figures such as Barth, Tillich and Rahner wrestled with this crucial topic. Scripture scholars like Spicq and Warnach provided fresh views of the biblical material. Moralists, programmatically as in the case of Gerard Gillemann, and casuistically as in the case of Joseph Fletcher, sought to structure moral theology about "the primacy of charity." By the seventies much of this scriptural, doctrinal and moral discussion had given way to other concerns, even other fashions. *Agape*/charity/love has reverted to its former limited role in theological discussion.

Words. Word-usage makes theological discussion of *agape/caritas*/love particularly difficult apart altogether from substantive debate about the precise meaning of agape in the NT, for example. As the Greek word most used in the NT in a theological context and also used in similar contexts in the Septuagint, agape enjoys a special place of honor in all theological discussions. Related Greek words such as *philia* and particularly *eros* are defined in relation or contrast to it. The Latin *caritas* does not enjoy such a privileged position and may be readily replaced by *amor* or *dilectio*. (This may be debated in regard to Augustine, cf. Nygren). In English, charity has enjoyed a long tradition as translation for agape/caritas but has acquired its own peculiarities. It can sound anemic as in "charitable" works which are regarded as extra rather than central to christian living. The Anglo-Saxon word "love" enjoys the advantage of its origins but has the elusiveness and multivalence of all great words in any language. These very characteristics may turn out to be sources of enrichment if handled properly. At any rate for linguistic origins, modern accessibility and range of meanings "love" is the preferred word here.

Meanings. Within and without theological contexts the word "love" signals both common experience and incomprehensible mystery. These meanings are not always mutually exclusive as they seek to mediate a reality which many share (as common experience) but which few, if any, can comprehend (mystery). The human and common experience of love can be readily recognized between, for example, husband and wife, between parents and children, between friends and between various other partners and associates. (Recently a member of the Dáil [Irish Parliament] declared quite convincingly, "I love the people I represent.") That experience and its recognition are much less easy to comprehend and explain. One can easily enough distinguish such personal loves from love of objects such as ice cream, or money, although less easily from love of places. "I love New York" has a strong personal dimension to its object which applies to a range of loves involving countries and causes. It remains difficult to know what exact and personal meaning should be attributed to talk of love of justice, love of truth, love of country, love of the poor or love of neighbor. They clearly differ from love of purely physical objects, even of objects of such high cultural value as the Venus de Milo, and from love of personal activities whether walking or acting, and from love of social events such as elections or prayer-meetings or discos. Immediate self-enrichment plays a role in distinguishing love of objects, activities and events from such clearly other-directed meanings as are involved in love of justice and love of neighbor. However, there is a possible continuity of meaning more evident perhaps in love of social events, where self-enrichment depends precisely (frequently) on surrender to the event of the prayer-meeting or disco. Yet the questions about love's meaning abound.

A really difficult question for Christians concerns the distinction and relationship between self-love and neighbor-love. The love commandment as formulated in the synoptic gospels (Matthew 22, Mark 12, Luke 10) makes this question unavoidable. No less difficult and inevitable is the distinction and relationship in meaning between human love for neighbor and human love for God. The very range of "neighbor" from spouse to someone hitherto unknown fallen among robbers multiplies the potential meanings of neighbor-love enormously. And all this before one attempts to relate these "cool" meanings to the passionate temperature of that most common usage of the word, which for so many provides the standard meaning, sexual love, and its correlative, being in love.

To be in love and to make love, with their strongly sexual connotations, so heavily influence contemporary (and historical) usage that it is extremely difficult to use love in a theological context independently of this history. However, there are many biblical precedents for relating as well as distinguishing sexual love and love for neighbor/love for God and even God's love for humans.

Contemporary usage of the word love, then, with its distinctions and nuances, its continuities, discontinuities and confusions, is not greatly different from the biblical and theological tradition. At least there are sufficient parallels to justify giving priority to this elusive word in seeking to reveal the rich and resonant reference of the *ahabah/agape* motif (Nygren) outlined in the Hebrew scriptures and critically formed in the teaching, ministry, and death of Jesus Christ.

Biblical Foundations. In contrast to the theological neglect, biblical studies of love have been quite significant in this century. These have covered most comprehensively word-usage in both OT and NT. The *ahabah-agape* distinctiveness discussed above has been subject to massive and detailed study by Spicq and

others. There is a prevailing consensus about continuity between Hebrew scriptures, Septuagint, and christian scriptures on a common term and concept covering God's love for human beings, human love for God and human love for one other. In this context the contrasting of an OT God of fear with a NT God of love is seen to be unfounded. Continuity emerges in other ways also. Divine love is embedded in the narrative of divine activity, in creation, covenant and election for the people of Israel, in the mission and ministry, life, death and resurrection of Jesus for his disciples. The display in action and narrative of divine love calls for a similar display in action to God and neighbor by human beings. Covenanted to love Israel, the disciples and all humanity are summoned and empowered to love God and neighbor. In face of human failure to love God and neighbor this divine love becomes judgment, promise, forgiveness, and renewal. The overcoming of failure involves a level of acceptance of humanity by God that is paternal/maternal (Is 49:15), intimate and compassionate to the point where God becomes one with humanity in its suffering and sinfulness ("even a curse" Gal 3:13). The NT registers the continuity of God's creating and forgiving love but there is also a critical break as God takes on the human condition out of love and then goes to the extreme of that humanity by laying down his life for all. The depth and range of divine love for humanity and of human response to God and neighbor is manifest in Jesus, where the Word, the narrative of God's love, takes flesh. That is where the deepest character of Godself is revealed as love (1 Jn 4:16). Biblical foundations provide the inexhaustible source of God's own self as the appropriate object of a theology of love.

Synthetic Theology of Love

Despite the failure to place love (*agape*)

consistently at the center of the exploration and exposition of Christianity as vision of God/way of human life, it has influenced significantly major figures and movements in christian history from the Johannine community to the two great twentieth-century Karls, Barth and Rahner. A detailed historical account would need to chart complex highways and byways of christian thought and living. Such charting leads people in very different directions to very different conclusions as the twentieth-century studies of Nygren, Burnaby, de Rougemont and D'Arcy reveal. In this context it would not be helpful to attempt a summary of these and other historical works, and it is always history from a particular perspective at least in the sense that the questions asked and the arguments accepted as finally valid reflect the author's tradition (Lutheran, Anglican, Roman Catholic, etc.) and personal concerns (e.g., literature and philosophy for D'Arcy). It may be more useful to integrate these traditions and concerns with some synthetic survey of the basic elements and arguments in the theological discussion of love.

The Hebrew and christian scriptures speak of love and loving in terms of God's love for human beings and human beings' love for God and for one another, with a concentration on the words ahabah/agape to the near exclusive use of *agape* in the NT for love by God and by the followers of Jesus Christ. All this provides the basis for subsequent historical discussion and for any attempt at contemporary synthesis. However, there may be many different approaches to the task of synthesizing which keep faith with the biblical foundations and historical developments. The approach adopted here, if it does survive the fidelity test, is certainly not the only possible approach.

Creation or Recognition/Response? The sharpest debate on the nature of christian love focused with Nygren on the distinction between the spontaneous unmerited creative love of *agape* and the responsive, desiring love of *eros* based on recognition of the good or value of the person or object loved and desired. In Nygren's version such love of desire turns the beloved into a means of satisfaction for the lover. Even God becomes, in however spiritualized a way, a means to human happiness and fulfilment. The cry of Augustine, "Our hearts will never rest until they rest in thee, (Conf. 1.1) epitomizes the central tenet of this understanding of love as it distorted and dominated the christian-Catholic tradition down to the time of Luther. It derived from a misguided effort to combine NT and neo-Platonic elements. Only by Luther's return to the pure teaching of the NT could its stranglehold be broken, although subsequent Reform theologians repeated some of the mistakes of their Catholic forebears and contemporaries.

In emphasizing anew the purely gracious and creative character of the biblical tradition of *agape,* Nygren has usefully challenged the easy assumptions of some Catholic and other christian theology and spirituality that human desire for happiness and fulfilment is a simply valid basis for the biblical love for God. The elaborate and thoughtful work of such fine Catholic thinkers as Martin D'Arcy does not seem to have faced fully the challenge renewed by Nygren. Further discussion of the creative (value-bestowing) and responsive (value-recognizing) dimensions of love is required.

Divine Loving. Love by God for human beings and by human beings for God are described by the same word (*agape*) and very closely related, almost to the point of identity in the NT. Clearly the love by God is first of all creative, bestowing value rather than recognizing or responding to it. God's very act of creation is his primary act of loving, of freely expressing his own value and goodness in the created world (*diffusivum boni sui*). That free expression reached its climax in the creation of humanity: "In the image of God he created them" (Gen 1 and 2). Through the creation stories God is responding and recognizing as well as creating. He saw that what he created was good, in the case of human beings, very good (Gen 1:31). This response took a personal, dialogical turn in the conversation and covenant with the man and the woman. Responsive love was also of God as he established partners to love in the divine image. It was not that the divine creative activity was replaced by a simply responsive activity. The creator's love must remain creative and spontaneous, issuing freely from the divine graciousness, bringing into existence and sustaining in existence the creatures of his choosing. Yet that very graciousness had resulted in total creation of value and in particular creatures who could themselves respond freely to the divinely gracious love, and were to be treated as loving partners in a covenant that broke free of the simple relations of power. The all-powerful creator and the totally dependent human creature were involved in a partnership that included divine recognition of and response to the creature (value-recognition) as well as creation or value-bestowal. The bible itself charts the checkered history of this divine-human relationship but always in the context of the primacy of the creative-responsive love of God.

The creativity and responsiveness of the divine love finds particular expression in face of human failure. The just judgment of this failure is the first appropriate response to such failure by Adam and Israel. Divine justice, parallel to and closely related to divine love, is a powerful check on and challenge to human failure to love God as God loves. But that justice moves readily into the loving transformation of human failure by divine for-giveness, a fresh exercise of the inexhaustibly creative love of God. New creation is a Pauline phrase for the finally triumphant achievement of the divine love in life, death and resurrection of Jesus the Christ and Son of God. New creation is also restoration in New Adam and implies recognition as well as bestowal of value, although this particular argument for the responsive dimension of the love of God might raise for Nygren the whole debate about justification once again.

Human Loving. If there are serious difficulties about characterizing divine love as responsive, the difficulties about characterizing human love as creative are perhaps greater. Yet the intrinsic connection between divine and human loving in the sense of agape required by the biblical evidence at least poses the question. The love which is poured forth in our hearts by the Holy Spirit which is given to us (Rom 5:5), christian human loving, is clearly divine in origin and empowerment. The dominantly creative character of divine love seeks expression in the graced love of human beings for their God and their co-humans. And it may be here that the risk of distorting human love of God to self-satisfaction, which Nygren discerns, may be confronted.

The responsive character of human love for God is undeniable. In biblical and christian teaching the initiative of God is plain. That divine initiative calls for a human response. The dialogical-covenant character of all human history, of the history of Israel and of Jesus, rests on the divinely gracious initiatives of creation and election, of redemption, forgiveness and new creation. The embodiment of that divine graciousness in the person of Jesus of Nazareth brings divine initiative and human response together in climactic form. The loving response to God to which humans are summoned and empowered by the gracious love of God finds its model in the man from Nazareth.

Jesus, beloved of the Father (Mk 1:11), responded in love to the God he addressed as Abba (loving Father) and whose will had to be embodied in his living and dying. This loving response to the Abba God issued at the same time in love of those to whom he had been sent. For Jesus the summary of the law and the prophets was love of God and love of neighbor, love of those whom he chose as his own and called to be his friends (Jn 15:14, 15) and of those to whom he responded in their need (Good Samaritan, Good Shepherd, all who labor and are burdened). The responsive love of Jesus, the man for others, the Divine Other and the human others, became the standard and source for the responsive love of all those who would follow him.

Jesus' responsive love issued in New Creation (Gal 6:15). It had creative, liberating effects in overcoming the destructive, enslaving effects of the law, sin and death. The new Adam initiated the new, recreated humanity (1 Cor 15:45ff). He enabled human beings to become what they were called to be by God, beyond the hunger, sickness, blindness, oppression and poverty which was so often their lot. He enabled the blind to see, the lame to walk, the dead to rise again and the poor to hear the good news of salvation/liberation (Luke 4:1-13). Jesus' love enabled people to be their true and flourishing selves. He loved them into fulfillment. And he shared this enabling, creative love with his disciples, with human beings who were open to his word and power. The love poured forth by the Spirit of Jesus in human hearts (Rom 5:5) is not only responsive, it is also creative. It enables other people to be. Such loving lets people be in these fuller senses of allowing them, giving them space to be themselves, encouraging and stimulating them to be themselves and so

finally supporting and empowering them beyond their external privations and internal inhibitions to flower in their own true being. The true creativity of christian love of neighbor in personal and social form may thus be revealed. The Creator-God who is our ultimate enabler, who in the fullest sense lets us all be (Macquarrie), shares that creative loving with human creatures. This God, the great letter-be, is at once creative and responsive in relation to human beings as he sustains the originating creative act in letting/enabling human beings develop to their fullness.

God's creative-responsive love is matched then by humanity's responsive-creative love in regard to human beings. Can it still make any sense to speak of a creative dimension in regard to human love of God? If not, must not the purely responsive human love to God finally reduce to the desire/need for self-satisfaction which Nygren saw as distorting the Catholic tradition?

The supremely creative power of God which enables human beings to be as partners in dialogue and in loving, lets human beings be as free sources of response to God. Their responsive-creative relationships with one another are called to express this deeper relationship with God. God seeks expression in the human community's own internal relations. The stories of Israel and of Jesus are accounts of God's attempts to pitch his tent and to build his temple in a human historical context. So he seeks to form his people, sons and daughters of God. Finally he seeks acceptance into the human community by becoming human, emptying God's self, taking the form of a servant. All these divine attempts to find a place within the historical human community (and to transform it), frustrated in so many ways, express God's self-entrusting to humanity and the human freedom to let God enter into and transform in love the human community. This human freedom and obligation to let God become the saving, transforming God of humanity reveals the creative character of humanity's loving response. In love human beings let God be the God he would be for humanity. Their loving response to God is in that sense creative, letting God be God. All this of course is gift from God, gift to the point where the human creative response of love to God is for God's own sake and not simply as a way of human satisfaction. Letting God be God is true christian worship, authentic glorifying of God. *Amor benevolentiae* (Aquinas), gift-love (C.S. Lewis), agape as creative are valid descriptions of human love for God which is creative as well as responsive.

Nygren's criticism of the Catholic tradition of human love for God as fundamentally a form of love of desire or eros (*amor concupiscentiae* in Aquinas's terms, and need-love in those of C.S. Lewis) or as at least fatally infected by Eros, may still retain a certain specious attraction. It does challenge defenders of the tradition to spell out the creative dimensions of christian loving for God and neighbor. It also requires some further elaboration of the debate connecting links between movements marked dominantly by other-recognition, regard, concern, (G. Outka) and those marked dominantly by other-desiring and self-regarding. Two elements are of critical importance here. The first is the concrete and inviolable value of the divine other and of the human other. It is this which provokes desire, recognition and response whether for its own sake or to satisfy the desires of the recognizer. And it is this "independent," inviolable value of the other which exposes the movement of simple desire as finally inadequate. The ambiguous early character of the movement to the other may clarify into an authentic recognition and regard for the other as genuinely other,

thus to be valued, loved and let be for its own sake. It may, on the other hand, seek to use or possess the other in a utilitarian or at any rate self-regarding way, treating the other primarily as an object for self-satisfaction, as a possession, rather than as a subject in its own right. A self-destroying desire for absorption by the other, to become its possession is the further possibility. The human material condition with its history of sin provides the basis for this ambiguity which is never finally resolved in history. Selfish possessiveness, the final goal of eros-infected love according to Nygren, is, as D'Arcy hints, finally as self-destructive, shattering on the inviolability of the other, as the self-destructive passion which de Rougemont attributes to the medieval troubadours. Only in the reciprocity of communion, discussed below, is the other-regarding, self-giving of authentic loving able to provide the mutual letting-be and shared flourishing which is the thrust of the divine love for and in human beings. So creative-responsive loving by God issues in responsive-creative loving by human beings. The Word is made flesh and agape becomes human.

Care and Compassion. The relational reality of love (agape) with its creative and responsive dimensions has immediate practical implications. Letting be, enabling to be after the divine model and by divine power is active rather than passive. In the NT the Johannine writings stress the verbal form (*agapan*) at the expense of the substantive (*agape*) in a ratio of more than two to one (70-30). The love by God as well as the human love for God and neighbor underlined in the Mosaic Covenant and central to the New are practical, caring loves. The centrality and primacy of love imply a centrality and primacy of praxis in the current jargon. Doing the truth in love is as significant for Amos and Isaiah as for John. Worship, the loving response to God, is empty and unacceptable to God unless it really does express loving care for the deprived neighbor, the widow, the orphan and the stranger (cf. Amos 5). Just recognition of and response to Jesus is finally tested by practical attention to the hungry, the prisoner and the stranger (Matthew 25). The answer to who is my neighbor in love becomes the Good Samaritan (Luke 10) parallel to the forgiving father (Luke 15) and the Good Shepherd in search of the lost sheep. The more specific caring love of the God of Israel and of Jesus requires similar response from people and followers (Mt 5:48). And it is a specification in time and place, by election and covenant of the caring, loving Creator God who recognized the goodness of all creation (Genesis 1 and 2) and would not let a sparrow fall unheeded (Mt 10:29). The further thrust of creation in love is a caring providence. There is no hint of the detached God of Deism in the accounts of divine concern and involvement in the Hebrew or christian scriptures.

That divine concern and involvement must grapple with human failure to respond, with human weakness, indifference and rejection, not just in relation to God but in relation to one another. Into the history of human failure and suffering is drawn the God of creative power and transcendent majesty. Loving care involves solidarity with the marginalized Israelites in their Egyptian captivity, a solidarity into exodus and liberation. At their weakest and apparently most deserted in further defeat and exile, born at least in part of their own failure to live out the gift of their election in love, the people of Israel experience this forgiving and liberating compassion of God. Their God shares their destiny and their suffering and so it will be that through this suffering with and finally for that fresh hope is kindled. The paradox of the suffering servant as liberating Messiah (Is 52-53) remains a puzzle until the disciples of Jesus begin to understand his peculiar Jewish destiny and his ultimate divine significance. With Jesus, divine surrender to the suffering condition of humanity in liberating solidarity reveals the extent of and meaning of divine and human love. The healing of the sick, the feeding of the hungry, the fellowship with the excluded, and forgiveness of sinners are all indicators of Jesus' and his Father's commitment to acceptance of the identity with the least, the most deprived, the truly suffering. Only in Calvary did that divine compassion, co-suffering with humanity emerge in all its fullness. The God who suffered and the God who died for love of friend and enemy provides the standard and empowerment for human loving, not in resignation to evil but as challenge, and as final overcoming of it. The victim of Calvary pronounces the death of victimization by the power of loving which death does not only not destroy but opens up to new life in resurrection. Practical loving reaches this far. It demands vulnerability even in God. That vulnerability offers a way through, beyond the self-enclosure of a simply detached, self-sufficient and transcendent God and beyond the search for self-fulfillment of simply perfectible human beings. *Vulnerabilis et vulneratus* remain the critical christian criteria of the genuinely loving being, divine or human.

The compassionate co-suffering character of christian love incorporates love of enemies. Forgiveness of enemies after the manner and by the power of God in Jesus is one obvious and distinctive feature of this love. It has its own difficulties and ambiguities if it conflicts, for example, with the solidarity in suffering and resistance to which one may be called in face of enemy destructiveness. Jesus' own forgiveness from the Cross must be placed in the context of his sometimes harsh criticism of his opponents in their binding insupportable burdens for the poor and marginalized. And yet his blood was shed for all. His vulnerability opened him up to the sufferings of exploiters like the tax collectors as well as their victims. He could recognize the privations of the Pharisees in their blindness. He could weep over a Jerusalem rejecting him. He recognized the enslavement of the exploiters and masters as well as that of the exploited and slaves. He was inhabited by the suffering of all and sought its removal in the mutual emancipation of master and slave. Salvation, redemption, liberation, are of all and for all. Love would set both sides free for one another in Christ, a powerful theme of Paul in his letters to the Romans and the Galatians.

Compassion, co-suffering, being inhabited by the sufferings of others, including one's enemies, these are the marks of God's surrender to the human condition. These divine and inexhaustible resources of solidarity, forgiveness and liberation are available to human beings in and through Christ. They constitute the spirit of that love given in the Spirit (Rom 5:5) and destined to abide forever (1 Corinthians 13). This is the love by which human beings were first loved (1 John 4:19) and which sustains them in the face of rejection, with the hope that love finally prevails even beyond crucified rejection. Only such love, divine love in human form, can triumph over the inevitable malice and evil of history.

Reciprocity and Communion. In the Johannine and wider NT visions only by first being loved can human beings love (1 Jn 4:10ff). Intrinsic to this view is the reciprocity of loving. Whoever is first of all loved is called and empowered to love in return. The return of love provokes in turn further and deeper love from the original subject. In a sin-free, unambiguous world the dialectic of lover and beloved would constitute a dynamic spiral of intimacy and mutual growth, mutual letting be within ever-deeper unity. In a one-to-one model, this would involve fuller development and deeper differentiation of each in ever-richer communion as the growth of each provided more possibilities for interaction and connection, complementarity and community-making. In such an "ideal" world the risks of selfish use and possession, as suggested by the *Eros* of Nygren, or of self-destructive submission and absorption in the passion of de Rougemont would not exist, whether one was dealing with divine to human loving or human to human loving. In the broader context of human beings intrinsically social and not just individual, there would operate a more complex model of community and communion, with reciprocity of loving and letting be and unity between individual and group, group and group as well as between individuals. In the actual sin-laden world of humanity, threats of use and possession, submission and extinction cannot be precluded. In a world marked by death the most sin-free reciprocity encounters the difficulty of the disappearing pole of the reciprocating subject who is no longer there to respond. Death of human lover-beloved leaves the partner-in-love with a vacancy which threatens to render all human love-relationships finally absurd. This might be, in terms of Nygren's rejections of the arguments for immortality, the final demonstration of the pure disinterestedness and spontaneity of agape-love. Return is finally rendered impossible and its hope should never be included in authentic christian loving.

The thrust of the divine initiative in creation of and dialogue with human beings has, however, been covenant community. The agapeic divine love has been directed in spite of human weakness and rejection at establishing community: "I shall be your God and you shall be my people." The further reaches of this love of God for humanity in sending his own Son, in God's becoming human, manifest the flourishing together in communion to which the providential and salvific love of God has been moving. And the new relationships between human beings of freedom, equality and solidarity in Jesus Christ (Gal 3:28, etc.) underline how communion with God is expressed in the community of humanity, indeed how the communion of God, as Father, Son and Spirit, emerges in the history of human communion.

Letting be and enabling to be between God and human beings, as well as between human beings themselves require reciprocity for continuance and fulfilment. To continue to give oneself in true regard for the other requires the development of the self also, so that there is more to give. It is part of the rich paradox of divine creation and giving that human beings develop through giving, in the end through unconditional giving. Laying down one's life for one's friends (and enemies) is the final testimony to that christian way of love. In christian dispensation it opens the way to new life, relationship and communion. Falling into the ground and dying is the seed's way to new life. The raising of Jesus to new community with God and humanity completes for a material and destructive world the circle of life-giving love. Even death is overcome in the saving communion established by Jesus. Even when historical reciprocity fails through sin or death, communion may still flower.

Agape, Philia, and Eros. Although there is no absolutely consistent use of these terms in the biblical or later literature, it is worth considering again their usage and meaning in the light of the previous discussion. The dominant trend regards *agape* as distinctively christian love which originates from God, but is also truly expressed in human love for God and neighbor. Its creative character reflects above all this divine origin and empowerment. *Philia* or love of friendship is also used to express the new relationships of God, Jesus and the disciples. In its biblical context ("not servants but friends") as well as in more general usage it emphasizes a partnership of some equality as well as a responsive, caring attitude. It remains a word and concept of rich theological and spiritual possibilities for Christians, as very effectively demonstrated by Burnaby in *Amor Dei.* Apart even from its recent and highly complicating usage by Freud and successive psychoanalysts, *eros* remains the problematic concept in christian discussion of love. The movements of desire for the good, essential to a material historical being, can be distinguished in their ambiguity as they open the way to concern for the good in itself or simply to the good for the self. Grace and power of agape may develop and transform the movement to the good in itself. *Eros* in that positive sense provides the substrate for human agapeic regard with its responsive recognizing of value and its creative letting-be of the other. Of course, no human movement entirely sheds its ambiguity, so that elements of self-centered *eros* persist. It was perhaps the distinction within the ambiguity and the inevitable persistence of selfish elements which misled Nygren and others.

Christian Love and Systematic Theology

The attempt at synthesis of a theology of love suggests the need for integrating love with the elaboration of a general systematic theology. Only fitful efforts at this have surfaced in the history of theology. In recent theologizing they have been mainly in moral theology for Roman Catholics (e.g., Gerard Gillemann's *The Primacy of Charity in Moral Theology*), or christian ethics for other Christians (e.g., Joseph Fletcher's *Situation Ethics*). Neither of these and none of the earlier historical treatments pursued the discussion of love in regard to the central doctrines of Christianity which are integral to its way of life. Love for Christians must be as much a matter of truth as of life, of believing as of doing. Indeed the separation of truth and life, and so of doctrinal or dogmatic and moral theology, has been one of the more significant weaknesses of Catholic theology, certainly in recent centuries. The separation has undoubtedly contributed to the neglect of love as central to christian understanding, that is, theory and praxis. This brief survey of the relation between love and some of the canonized themes of christian theology can only adumbrate some lines of possible and necessary developments.

Object, Subject and Methods of Theology. Although definitions of theology vary with the theologian, culture and other context, the persistent influence of Anselm's "faith seeking understanding" is noteworthy. In this still widely-influential view, faith as personal-communal activity and as body of belief constitutes the object of theological investigation. The current attention to the engagement of believing persons and community, to commitment and praxis has shifted the emphasis away from belief to activity, and from the existential concerns of individual believers in response to God to believing community in response to neighbor, particularly neighbor in need, the poor, the oppressed, the marginalized. Interestingly the two virtues which have benefited from this shift are hope (Moltmann et.al.) and justice (liberation theologians). There are clearly positive reasons supporting these developments and emphases. The eschatological hope which Christianity mediates in history is to sustain the oppressed in their reaching for justice. Negatively, charity understood as almsgiving, as voluntary sharing of superflua, has obscured the divine intention that the resources of the world are intended equally for all in the building of an inclusive and just human community. The neglect of such charity in favor of hope and justice was inevitable. Faith seen primarily as belief or theoria had to give place in the development of theologies of hope and liberation, political theologies concerned with justice for all.

A more substantial and authentic theology of love with its creative-responsive, caring and compassionate promotion of communion could clearly be integrated with concern for hope and faith. Indeed, if the Pauline and continuing christian triad of faith, hope and charity were taken together as they should be, then Anselm's definition might be adapted to good purpose in our present context. Theology might then maintain its theory-praxis integration, its one study of Christianity as truth and way and life by defining or describing itself as "faith-hope-love" in search of understanding. The object would be more clearly unified, making for example the separation between doctrinal and moral theology untenable. And the subject would be more properly communal as the community struggled to understand its shared "faith-hope-love." The role of the greatest of these would be clearly crucial.

With hope and love integrated in this way the dangers of a purely intellectual or academic theology would be greatly reduced. Praxis would be already part of the object and subject. Method would be necessarily shaped by hopeful and loving engagement, and not just by the detached paradigms of observer scientists (a paradigm no longer simply available even to physical scientists). Love as a means to truth will have to enter more explicitly into discussion of theological method if this central feature of all that is Christian is to assume its due place in christian reflection.

Love and Some Classical Themes of Theology. The central classical theme of theology is naturally God, primarily God in relation to cosmos and humanity and then, however indirectly and still more inadequately, God's self. The history and nature of love as *agape* enters immediately into God's relations with cosmos and humanity as creator and redeemer. The biblical foundations outlined above and the synthetic theology of love, particularly in its creative and compassionate dimensions, must for reasons of space suffice as a discussion of love and the classical theological themes of creation and redemption. Some further discussion of love and Godself, although clearly in the relational language and context of revelation through Israel and Jesus, may be more appropriate at the close of this section.

Church and Kingdom

The subject and object of christian theology come together neatly in discussion of the classical theme of church and kingdom. The believing-hoping-loving community of disciples of Jesus is also the theologizing subject which must recognize, reflect on and promote the object of their faith-hope-love, the reign or kingdom of God, God's loving presence and transforming power in cosmos and history. Witnesses to the kingdom by their love for one another ("By this shall all know that you are my disciples" Jn 13:35), they are called to discern and promote the loving initiatives of God in the world. *Ubi amor, ibi Deus* becomes the test of their own internal fidelity and of their mission to humankind as a whole. Church members called and empowered to be a visible embodiment of divine and human love seek in the creative and responsive ways of *agape* to discern cosmic traces and human images of God and to let be, enable to be in their fullness all human beings, but especially the suffering and deprived. The bias to the poor is a sign of authentic love and kingdom fidelity. The church does not

exist for itself but for the kingdom, to let God and humanity be in their fullness. Prayer and community development as loving response to God and neighbor combine to let the kingdom come, to let God be God, be at home among those he has created and called as they move towards that fulfillment for which he created and called them. The final community of love is the fullness of the kingdom of which the church is now to be the sacrament or effective sign.

Historical Structures and Kingdom Values

Church and kingdom are primary symbols of the loving transformation of the world which God seeks and enables through human response. The range and complexity of this transforming process must correspond to the range and complexity of cosmos and humanity. Systematic theological attempts to explore this range and complexity take divergent and sometimes disorganized forms. All of them must mediate between human historical structures and kingdom resources. In relating love to some further theological themes the terms historical structures and kingdom values can be useful.

In one sense the primary kingdom resources available to human beings are faith, hope and love. As God-given powers and standards or ideals they might in contemporary discussion be described as values as well as virtues, and in an older idiom as supernatural values and virtues. Their primary structural expression is in the church. For the wider structural world what have been called, traditionally, moral virtues and values mediate the more basic kingdom resources and realities of faith, hope and love.

Critical among these mediating values as they emerge in biblical and christian history as well as in the broader moral history of humanity are freedom (cf. Exodus and Paul), justice (cf. the prophets and James) and peace or forgiveness with unity or solidarity (OT and NT passim). The much later secular triad of liberty, equality and fraternity emphasize both the human and historical or secular nature of these values and, for Christians, the confirmation of creation in the history of redemption through Israel and Jesus. The God who created out of love, and continued his commitment to humanity in love to the point of becoming incarnate and dying on a cross, made it clear how the goodness of creation was recognized and deepened so that secular values, values of the *saeculum,* of human history, could be bearers of the creative-responsive love of God and of human beings. Tensions undoubtedly may exist in history between these different values, as Christians strive to be both justice-seekers and peace-makers, for example (Mt 5:6, 9). These may be resolved by reference back to the originating creator whereby they are one, as, for example, the parallels of divine love (*ahabah*), loving-kindness (*hesed*), and justice (*sedaqah*) frequently emphasize in the OT. They may also be resolved eschatologically by reference to the final coming of the kingdom when God shall be all in all for all humanity and the cosmos. The primacy of praxis emphasized in liberation theology and the primacy of charity proposed by Gillemann for moral theology, might well become the primacy of love mediating between historical structures and kingdom values, and underlying kingdom values themselves.

Particular Historical Structures: Marriage, Politics and Eucharist. In the biblical and later christian tradition, the almost exclusively personal (and private character) of *ahabah/agape* love made marital and sexual loving an inevitable connecting point. The celebration of sexual-marital love in the Songs of Songs was frequently interpreted as an allegory of the divine-human relationship. This was all the more probable in the light of explicit parallels between the marriage and the Yahweh-Israel relationship in the prophets, particularly Hosea and Isaiah. The Genesis celebration of sexual and marital love, renewed in the NT by Jesus and developed in the Pauline image of the love of Christ and the church, contributed to an acceptance of the possibility that such human, secular loving could be the realization and manifestation of genuine *agape* and not be simply regarded as an inferior brand of *eros* or the love of desire.

However, it is only in recent decades that Catholic teaching and theology has taken this seriously into account, although there is still a tendency to swing between a negative, critical view of sexual love as the limited loving of desire and self-satisfaction (the *Eros* of Nygren) and a romantic view moving to the passionate self-surrender into absorption of de Rougemont's thesis.

The responsive-creative character of christian love of neighbor together with its compassionate and communion dimensions could find appropriate and admirable expression in the sexual love which moves into marriage. *Philia* and *Eros,* in their ambiguity, could help to unmask the rich complexity of a sexual and marital relationship which christian tradition has pronounced sacramental, an effective sign and realization of the love of the creating and redeeming God.

The personal character of loving in the christian and wider human traditions has tended to privatize it (Metz), concentrating on the personal I-Thou characteristics (Buber). More recent concern with the social and political dimensions of faith and of hope have alerted believers and theologians to the political and social dimensions of loving: "social love," "civilization of love" (John Paul II). The communal thrust of christian loving is already apparent in its demand for communion, once it is clear that such a communion cannot be confined to some *égoisme à deux* but must incorporate each in all her or his ramifying relationships. Adopting a different perspective, that of the field rather than the particle, as the physicists might put it, one images God-given love as a field of force within which human beings seek to orientate themselves. The community or communion enjoys equi-primacy with the individual person, who can only love and be fulfilled by recognizing and responding to this given and emerging field of force, another symbol for the kingdom and reign of God, the symbol of the kingdom and reign of love.

Communion with one another and with the God of Jesus Christ, the heart of christian aspiration and achievement in marriage and politics, receives its most powerful symbolic expression in the communion called eucharist. The social and personal dimensions of this sacrament of love make clear how far *agape* is from any enclosing the I-Thou phenomenon while still enabling the person to flourish in communion in community. Eucharistic theology could provide a center-point for a love-shaped systematic theology. Eucharistic theology would in turn be greatly enriched with its political as well as its liturgical aspects more fully revealed.

The Love which is God. Classical and controlling remains the discussion about God. OT limitations, in part at least permanent human limitations of human language and thought about God, did not obscure the close connection between God and loving acts in history, between God and the power or force called Love. NT history moved on with Jesus as the locus of God's saving-loving activity, sent out of love and expressing that love unto death. Incarnation, God-made-flesh was love, ultimate divine love in human form, for God was love. All the rich theology of the synoptics as well as of John and of Paul confront the believer-reader with some sense of God as primarily love, with some sense of the love which is operative in the histories of Israel and of Jesus as finally God. John puts it in just these words: "God is love," not as a sudden insight but as the climax of a careful argument in his own writings and those of his predecessors.

The simplicity of the description and of the reality must be balanced against the complexity of expression which that love finds in NT and earlier activity. Loving Father and beloved Son interact by the power and medium of the Spirit, of God, of Christ, of love, to invoke some of the descriptions available. As later theology grappled with this complexity, the love which is God emerged more clearly as the trinity of Father, Son and Spirit engaged in perchoresis, a permanent dance of love into which human beings are invited and empowered to join. The love which is God has been made available to all willing to join the dance, willing to draw others into the dance, willing to make place for others in the dance. The loving communion to which all human beings are destined is that dynamic movement from which one is only excluded for seeking to exclude others, for failing to open in love to the neighbor in need. In the end God means in the end love, means that ends must be sought in beginnings. The originator and the eschator, like the end and beginning, like the fire and rose, are one (T.S. Eliot, *Four Quartets*).

See **Moral Life, Christian**

J. Burnaby, *Amor Dei*, 1938. M.C. D'Arcy, *The Mind and Heart of Love*, 1945. M.C. D'Arcy, *The Meeting of Love and Knowledge*. Gerard Gillemann, *The Primacy of Charity in Moral Theology*, ET 1959. Aelred Graham, *The Love of God*, 1959. Jean Guitton, *Essay on Human Love*, 1948. C.S. Lewis, *The Four Loves*, 1960. Herbert McCabe, *Law, Love and Language*, 1968. McIntyre, *On the Love of God*, 1962. Enda McDonagh, "The Primacy of Charity," "Penance and Charity" in *Invitation* and Response, 1972. Enda McDonagh, "Love, Power and Justice" in *The Making of Disciples, 1982. Enda McDonagh, "Love"* in Richardson & Powden (eds.) *A New Dictionary of Christian Theology,* 1983. John McIntyre, *On the Love of God.* 1962. Karl Rahner, *Theological Investigations V,* 1966. Karl Rahner, *The Love of Jesus and the Love of Neighbor,* 1983. Anders Nygren, *Agape and Eros,* ET 1957. Gene Outka, *Agape,* 1972.

Denis de Rougemont, *Passion and Society,* 1956 (ET). Denis de Rougemont, *The Myths of Love,* 1963 (ET). G. Quell and E. Stauffer, *Love,* 1949 (ET). C. Spicq, *Agape in the New Testament* 1963 (ET). L. Schottroff, and R.H. Fuller, *Essays on The Love Commandment,* 1978. Paul Tillich, *Love, Power and Justice,* 1954. Warnach, *Agape,* 1951.

ENDA MCDONAGH

M

MAGISTERIUM

Magister in classical Latin meant "master," not only in the sense of "schoolmaster" or teacher, but in the many senses in which a person can be a "master," e.g., of a ship, of servants, of an art or trade, etc. Hence the word *magisterium* in classical Latin meant the role and authority of one who was a master in the various applications of the term. In the vocabulary of the medieval schoolmen magisterium generally meant the role and authority of the teacher. The traditional symbol of teaching authority was the chair, and St. Thomas speaks of two kinds of magisterium: that of the pastoral chair of the bishop, and that of the academic chair of the university professor (*Quodl.* III, 9, ad 3).

However, in modern Catholic usage, the term "magisterium" has come to be associated almost exclusively with the teaching role and authority of the hierarchy. An even more recent development is that the term "magisterium" is often used to refer not to the teaching office as such, but to the body of men who exercise this office in the church: namely, the pope and bishops. The Second Vatican Council several times describes their role as "authentic magisterium." It is important to realize that the term "authentic" as used here does not mean "genuine," but rather "authoritative," and indeed, "endowed with pastoral authority,

ultimately derived from Christ." If one did not keep this in mind, one would misunderstand the statement of the council (D. V. 10) that "the task of authentically interpreting the word of God has been entrusted exclusively to the living magisterium, whose authority is exercised in the name of Jesus Christ." The council did not intend to deny that theologians and exegetes can interpret the word of God with such authority as their learning confers on them. But it asserts that only the pastors of the church are endowed with authority to teach and interpret the gospel message in the name of Jesus Christ.

The Notion of Pastoral Teaching Authority

Where revealed religion is concerned, the ultimate authority is God the revealer, and the absolute truth of his word. The role of any human mediator is to help others to know what God has said, and what his word means here and now. Once the hearers recognize the message to be a word of God (and in this recognition the interior witness of the Spirit has its part to play), their act of faith is directed not to the human bearer of the message, but to the word itself, and to God who has spoken it. The motive of the act of faith is not the reliability of the human messenger, but the truth of the word itself as word of God.

However, for the act of faith to be a

reasonable decision, the hearers of the message need to be certain that what is proposed to them as revealed truth is actually God's word. They have to be convinced of the reliability of the one who tells them that this is what God has said. It is at this point that the notion of "authorized witnesses" enters the picture. All Christians agree that the apostles, and the "apostolic men" who were the authors of the NT, were chosen by God as authorized witnesses of the Christ-event. The teaching of the apostles was recognized as normative for the faith of the christian community, for they were the authoritative witnesses to what God had revealed in Jesus Christ.

The apostles entrusted their message to the church, and the faith of the church is normative for the faith of the individual who wishes to belong to it. Since the church is a community united in the profession of the same faith, it has to have a common creed and a common understanding of the basic truth of its faith. The pastors who are responsible for the well-being of the community have a special responsibility regarding its common profession of faith. When conflicts arise as to the terms of its creed, or to its interpretation, those with pastoral responsibility must have the authority to judge which of the conflicting opinions is in accord with the faith of the church. According to the Catholic understanding of the matter, it is part of God's design that in every age of the church there should be successors of the apostles, not as immediate recipients of revelation, but as authorized witnesses, with authority from Christ to preach and teach his word and to settle questions that arise concerning the normative faith of the community. It is in this sense that Vatican II speaks of bishops as "judges of faith" (L.G. 25). This of course does not mean that they are superior to the word of God. The council expressly denies this, in the following passage of *Dei Verbum:* "Now this magisterium is not above the word of God, but serves it, teaching only what has been handed on, listening to it devoutly, guarding it conscientiously, and explaining it faithfully, by divine commission and with the help of the Holy Spirit. From this one deposit of faith it draws everything which it presents for belief as divinely revealed" (D.V. 10).

There are several considerations which help to explain the legitimate role of authority where assent to revealed truth is concerned. The first is that the truth of most of what God has revealed to us is not intrinsically evident to us; we have to "take it on faith." When we give intellectual assent to an article of faith whose truth is not evident to our mind, our act of faith is a free assent, which means that our free will is involved, choosing to believe. Furthermore, we have to rely on the testimony of witnesses to know what God has revealed. Here again we do not have the kind of evidence that forces our minds to assent; so again our free will has a part to play in our choice to accept their testimony.

It is this role of our free will in the decision to believe which leaves room for the legitimate exercise of teaching authority. This has to be an authority which commends itself to us as reasonable to accept. As far as most Christians are concerned, it is reasonable to accept the authority of the apostles, since they were commissioned by Christ himself to bear witness to what he had revealed to them. As far as Catholics are concerned, it is also reasonable to accept the authority of the bishops, when they declare something to be obligatory for our faith, because we believe that they share in the mandate which Christ gave to his apostles. Furthermore, we believe that along with this mandate the bishops share in the promise of a special assistance of the Holy Spirit, which, while it provides an absolute guarantee of the truth of their teaching only in certain rather rare cases, gives reason for confidence in their guidance of the faith of the church, and thus makes it reasonable for us to be disposed to accept their teaching authority even when it is not infallible.

Source of the Teaching Authority of Bishops

Catholic belief that the bishops have inherited the teaching mandate which Christ gave to his apostles, is expressed in the following statements of Vatican II: "By divine institution bishops have succeeded to the place of the apostles as shepherds of the Church" (L.G. 20); "The order of bishops is the successor to the college of the apostles in teaching authority and pastoral rule" (L.G. 22); "As successors of the apostles, bishops receive from Christ the mission to teach all nations and to preach the gospel to every creature" (L.G. 24).

Admittedly, it is not possible to prove these assertions from the NT alone, because the development by which each local church came to have a single bishop as its pastor, assisted by a group of presbyters and deacons, is a development that took place in the post-NT period. Neither is it possible to show in detail just how this development took place, since there are so few written records from that period that could throw light on it.

However, what is certain and well documented is that by the end of the second century, each christian church was being led by a single bishop, and that these bishops were universally recognized by the faithful as legitimate successors to the apostles in their pastoral role. It is also a matter of historical fact that the whole christian church accepted these bishops as the authoritative witnesses to apostolic tradition, who had the authority to judge whether a particular doctrine was in conformity with this tradition or

not, and consequently the authority to define the terms in which the community should profess its faith. In other words, the whole church accepted the teaching of bishops as *normative* for its faith.

But it is fundamental for christian faith to believe that the church which Christ founded and to which he promised the abiding assistance of the Holy Spirit, will be forever maintained in the true faith by the Spirit of truth. On this basis, one must conclude that the second century church could not have been mistaken when it determined the very norms of its faith. During the same period when the church came to recognize certain writings as normative for its faith, it also recognized the bishops as authoritative teachers whose decisions about matters of christian doctrine would be normative for the interpretation of the gospel message. A church that is maintained in the true faith by the Holy Spirit must have been guided by that same Holy Spirit when it determined the norms of its faith. On this basis we can be confident that it was not mistaken either when it decided which writings belonged in the canon of the NT, or when it recognized the bishops as the successors to the apostles in their pastoral teaching role.

Various Forms of the Exercise of Magisterium

Each bishop who is the pastor of a diocese has responsibility and authority regarding the teaching of christian doctrine in his diocese. He exercises this responsibility by his own teaching, whether orally or in pastoral letters, and by his promotion of sound teaching in the catechetical and educational institutions of his diocese. When particularly difficult problems arise, the bishops of a nation or region may choose to exercise their teaching function collectively in their episcopal conference. Of the various doctrinal positions taken by an episcopal conference, only those are binding on the Catholic faithful of the region which were unanimously approved by the bishops of the conference. Sometimes their document itself will distinguish between principles on which all Catholics are expected to be in agreement, and concrete proposals on which there may be legitimate difference of opinion in the church. In any case, neither individual bishops nor episcopal conferences teach with the gift of infallibility.

This, however, is attributed by Vatican II to the whole episcopal college, when all the bishops, including the bishop of Rome, in their teaching on matters of faith and morals, propose the same doctrine as definitively to be held by all the faithful (L.G. 25). Apart from some doctrines which, while they have never been explicitly defined, are nonetheless certainly dogmas of faith, it is not easy to verify the conditions laid down for the infallibility of this "ordinary universal magisterium," namely, that a point of doctrine has been and is being universally taught as "definitively to be held."

Besides this "ordinary" exercise of their teaching function by the bishops in their dioceses or episcopal conferences, there is also the "extraordinary" magisterium which the whole college of bishops (necessarily including the pope) exercises when, gathered in ecumenical council, it solemnly defines a dogma of faith. It should be noted that the Second Vatican Council, while an extraordinary historical event, did not exercise such "extraordinary magisterium," because in fact it did not choose to proclaim any new dogmas of faith. Apart from the instances when this council reiterated already defined dogmas, its teaching has the binding force of "ordinary" magisterium; it calls on the faithful to give their assent, but does not proclaim any doctrine so definitively that culpable dissent from it would amount to heresy. When an ecumenical council does define a doctrine, thus settling a question definitively and strictly binding the faithful to adhere to it, it enjoys the charism of infallibility (L.G. 25). The First Vatican Council defined, as a dogma of Catholic faith, that the Roman Pontiff, acting as supreme teacher of all the faithful, can also settle questions of faith and morals definitively, and that his solemn definitions enjoy the same infallibility as do those of an ecumenical council (D.S. 3074).

Infallibility

Vatican II speaks of infallibility as a "charism of the church" (L.G. 25), and attributes it in the first place to the universal consensus of the body of the faithful as a whole, when "from the bishops down to the last member of the laity, it shows universal agreement in matters of faith and morals" (L.G. 12). Belief that the whole church cannot be led into serious error in its faith depends on belief in the abiding assistance of the Holy Spirit, promised by Christ to his church. Catholic doctrine about the infallibility of certain acts of the magisterium is based on two premises: that all the faithful are obliged to give their unconditioned assent of faith to dogmas which are proclaimed as such by the magisterium, and that in doing so they will not be led into error in their faith. From this it follows that such dogmas cannot be erroneous. And since no merely human teacher is immune from making errors, one rightly speaks of a "charism of infallibility," that is, a gift of grace, a work of the Holy Spirit, who alone can guarantee that such definitive teaching will necessarily be true. Solemn definitions of faith are said to be "irreformable": not in the sense that their formulation is so perfect or unchangeable that it could never be improved, but in the sense that their authentic meaning will always be true.

When the First Vatican Council declared that dogmatic definitions pronounced by the pope were "irreformable of themselves and not by virtue of the consent of the church" (D.S. 3074), its intention was to exclude the error of "Gallicanism"(D.S. 2284), which claimed that papal definitions would not be irreformable unless they were confirmed by the episcopate. It did not, and could not, rule out a real dependence of papal definitions on the faith of the church. For the pope can define as a dogma of faith only what is contained in the deposit of revelation, which "has been entrusted to the church" (D.V. 10) and is "handed on in her teaching, life and worship" (D.V. 8). Since the pope has no independent source of revelation, he cannot define a dogma of faith without having in some real way consulted the faith of the church. However, one cannot lay down the consensus of all the bishops or the faithful as a condition absolutely to be fulfilled prior to a papal definition, because this would eliminate the possibility of a decisive act of the papal magisterium that might be needed to overcome a threat to the church's unity in the faith, and bring about a consensus, or restore one that had been lost.

Limits of Magisterial Authority and Infallibility

The question here concerns the matter about which the bishops and pope can teach with authority, and, under certain conditions, with infallibility. Both Vatican Councils have described this object as "matters of faith and morals." Vatican II also describes the role of bishops as "preaching to the faithful committed to them the faith they must believe and put into practice" (L.G. 25). They cannot claim to speak authoritatively, much less infallibly, unless the matter about which they speak pertains to christian belief or to the practice of the christian way of life.

Now there are two ways in which something can pertain to this object: either directly, as formally contained in the gospel message, or indirectly, as something in itself not revealed, but necessary for the defense or explanation of gospel truth. Matters of christian belief and practice which are formally revealed constitute what is called the "deposit of faith"; this is the primary object of magisterium. It embraces everything that God has revealed to us "for the sake of our salvation" (D.V. 11). Other things which are not in themselves formally revealed, but still pertain to christian faith and practice insofar as they are required for the defense and explanation of the gospel, constitute the secondary object of the magisterium. Only what is in the primary object can be defined as a "dogma of faith"; matters in the secondary object can be defined as true, but not as to be believed with "divine faith," that is, faith directed to God as revealer. It is important to note that the infallibility of the magisterium with regard to "secondary objects" is itself not a dogma of Catholic faith, but a doctrine commonly held by Catholic theologians and confirmed by the "ordinary magisterium."

A question that is much discussed today is whether the particular and concrete norms of the natural moral law fall within the object of infallible magisterium. It is generally agreed that some of the basic principles of such law are also divinely revealed, and as pertaining to the primary object, could be infallibly taught. It is also generally agreed that the magisterium can speak with authority on particular and concrete applications of natural law principles. However, many reputable Catholic theologians question whether statements of this kind can ever be said to be irreversibly true. They argue that it is difficult to exclude the possibility that future experience, hitherto unimagined, might put a concrete moral problem into a new frame of reference which would call for a revision of a norm that, when formulated, could not have taken such new experience into account. And since the infallible exercise of magisterium issues in irreformable judgments, it seems inappropriate to speak of infallibility in this context.

Ordinary Papal Magisterium

By "ordinary papal magisterium" one means the teaching authority which the popes exercise in a non-definitive way, either by the publication of their encyclical letters, apostolic constitutions, etc., or by their explicit approval of doctrinal statements made by the Congregation for the Doctrine of the Faith. When the pope solemnly defines a dogma he is said to speak *ex cathedra*; Vatican II declares that "religious submission of will and mind must be given to the teaching authority of the pope even when he is not speaking *ex cathedra*, in such a way that his supreme magisterium is acknowledged with reverence, the judgments made by him are sincerely adhered to, according to his manifest mind and will" (L.G. 25). The fact that "religious submission of mind" and "sincere adherence" are called for, means that the response required is not mere obedience of the will (as it would be in the case of papal legislation) but rather obedience of the judgment. In other words, if I have already formed my opinion on a question, and the contrary view is authoritatively taught by the pope, I am obliged to renounce any attitude of obstinacy in my own opinion, and to adopt an attitude of docility toward the papal teaching. Docility calls for an open attitude toward the official teaching, giving it a fair hearing, doing one's best to appreciate the reasons in its favor, so as to convince oneself of its truth, and thus facilitate one's intellectual assent to it.

To give the required "religious submission" to such ordinary papal teaching means to make an honest and sustained effort to overcome any contrary opinion we may have, and to achieve a sincere assent of our mind to this teaching. It is possible that people who have made such an effort, still find that doubts about its truth remain so strong in their minds that they cannot actually give their sincere intellectual assent to it. Since such people have done all that they were capable of doing towards achieving assent, one cannot judge such non-assent or internal dissent, to involve any lack of obedience to the magisterium.

It is also possible that such dissent may be not only subjectively blameless, but objectively justified, since, as the German bishops stated in their pastoral letter of 22 September, 1967, the ordinary, non-definitive teaching of the church "can, and on occasion actually does, fall into errors." The bishops went on to say: "In order to maintain the true and ultimate substance of faith the Church must, even at the risk of error in points of detail, give expression to doctrinal directives which have a certain degree of binding force, and yet, since they are not *de fide* definitions, involve a certain element of the provisional even to the point of being capable of including error. Otherwise it would be quite impossible for her to preach or interpret her faith as a decisive force in real life or to apply it to each new situation in human life as it arises" (Quoted by Rahner, *Th. Inv.* 14, 85-87).

While, in its treatment of the ordinary papal magisterium, Vatican II spoke only of its obligatory force and said nothing about the possibility of its needing to be corrected, on several important issues the council clearly departed from previous papal teaching. There are very real differences between the Decree on Ecumenism and such an encyclical as *Mortalium animos* of Pope Pius XI, and between the Declaration on Religious Freedom and the teaching of Pope Leo XIII. It is difficult to see how the Second Vatican Council could have arrived at a number of its innovative decisions if it had not been for the preparatory work done by the theologians who, prior to the council, had been taking a critical stance toward elements of papal teaching which they judged were in need of correction. On this basis, one cannot exclude the legitimacy of the expression of responsible dissent on the part of those who are particularly competent to judge the issue and to contribute to the process by which the church would arrive at a better grasp of the truth.

See **Bishops, Church, Infallibility, Pope, Revelation**

P. Chirico, *Infallibility. The Crossroads of Doctrine,* Kansas City, 1977. C.E. Curran and R.A. McCormick, Eds., *Readings in Moral Theology no. 3, The Magisterium and Morality,* New York, 1982. R.C. Empie, et. al., Eds., *Teaching Authority and Infallibility in the Church,* Minneapolis, 1978. F.A. Sullivan, *Magisterium. Teaching Authority in the Catholic Church,* New York, Ramsey/Dublin, 1983.

FRANCIS A. SULLIVAN, SJ

MAN
See **Anthropology, Christian**

MANICHAEISM

Mani, a native of Persia (c. 216-c.276), taught a religion at whose core was an absolute dualism, a conflict between good and evil, light and darkness. As such, his views were related to various aspects of Judaism, Christianity, Gnosticism, and the traditional religion of Persia, Zoroastrianism. At one point he was exiled to India, but, returning, was executed by the Persian government.

Once the convert had come to accept the basic view of the cosmos in which particles of light were imprisoned in matter, the life-task was to liberate the light. The principal means to accomplish this for the individual was strict asceticism. The difficulty of the challenge was lessened considerably by the fact that only the small number of the "elect" were expected to carry out this struggle totally while the much larger number of "hearers" was not held to it. The movement had considerable success within the Roman empire, Augustine himself becoming a hearer for a while. Manichaeism is a variation on a basic religious theme of dualism as a means of explaining the existence and relationships of good and evil in the universe. Medieval Albigensianism was another version of the same tendency.

ROBERT B. ENO, SS

MARCIONISM

Marcion (d.c. 160) was one of the leading heresiarchs of the primitive church. Not much is known about his life and the traditional stories may be legendary or even symbolic. He was reputedly born in Sinope in Asia Minor on the southern shores of the Black Sea and some part of his later life was connected with the church in Rome. His writings no longer exist but judging from the quantity of material against him by authors such as Irenaeus and Tertullian, his views must have been considered very dangerous. His reputed views show affinities to Gnosticism but unlike the various contradictory Gnostic teachers, Marcion concentrated more effort on church organization and this alone may have rendered him more of a threat.

Marcion's most notorious tenet was his complete rejection of the Hebrew Scriptures or the OT. In addition, his heavily edited version of the NT emphasized the teaching of Paul. He kept a revised version of the Gospel of Luke but rejected other parts of the NT as vitiated by Jewish influence. The creator God whom the Jews worshipped was a God of the law, of harshness and cruelty. He was actually a lesser God who was responsible for the creation of the world and therefore of the evil of matter. He was most definitely not the Father of Jesus Christ. Jesus was the Son and messenger of the unknown, transcendent, supreme God. The true God, the Father of Jesus, is a God of love. Marcion's Christology is docetic; the Incarnation was not real. His moral teaching was rigorist and ascetic.

ROBERT B. ENO, SS

MARIOLOGY
See **Mary**

MARRIAGE
Introduction

The Second Vatican Council called for a renewal of understanding, approach and practice within the total life of the church. No other area of church life was more affected by this focus on renewal than those parts of ecclesial life associated with sacramental life. In its contemporary description of christian marriage, Vatican II blended insights about marriage drawn from scripture and from current social science to form a new theological framework for reflection and pastoral practice.

Stimulated by this reframing of the meaning of christian marriage found primarily in the *Pastoral Constitution on the Church in the Modern World,* (Sections 47-52), the theology of marriage has experienced steady growth in recent years. What occurred at Vatican II was the development of the new basic paradigm or model for describing christian marriage. This shift can be summarized as one which moved from viewing marriage primarily as a biological and juridical union to one which is more interpersonal, spiritual and existential.

This analysis of the theology of christian marriage will be based on an exploration of these three new emphases. These three spheres, the interpersonal, the spiritual and the existential, each contribute to the overall sacramentality of marriage and meaningfully position the married within the community of the church. This new theology provides a more integrated description of the faith life of married Christians. It serves in providing meaning to each and every part of their personal, relational and spiritual life. While the process of gaining an understanding in faith is progressive throughout life, the task of theology is to provide faith with a comprehensive depiction of the total landscape based on the accumulated testimony of the scriptures, the teachings of the church, the analyses of theologians and the experiential reflection of good Christians. Distilling a single product from these various sources is no easy task. Yet this challenge provides the theology of marriage with a vitality and applicability urgently required. The past, often quite narrow, theology of marriage offers an example of the results gained when a restricted search for understanding happens. Thus, an introductory comment on an appropriate method of inquiry is not without value.

Interpersonal Life

The first aspect of marriage, *the interpersonal life between the wife and husband,* is primary and merits more extensive comment than the other emphases. The most obvious feature of contemporary marriage is that it is a living together, the sharing of life-supporting tasks between a woman and a man who are married to each other in the eyes of the church and the community.

Their marriage is the result of a decision, freely made by both, to honor, respect and love each other until death.

Earlier views of marriage concentrated almost exclusively on the common task of producing offspring, along with providing those things necessary to insure the development of their children. The Code of Canon Law of 1917 described the primary purpose of marriage as the procreation and education of children. While the goals of achieving a high degree of emotional closeness, friendship and a sense of a shared life were not prohibited, they were not stressed. Social scientists add that the development of interpersonal intimacy (not simply biological intimacy) is a relatively recent phenomenon, stemming from improved social conditions and, in no small measure, from an understanding of woman as an equal to man in dignity and purpose.

With the possibility of creating a genuine community of intimacy and love in marriage, the whole weight of the christian tradition about the interpersonal life within the ecclesial community could come to bear on marriage. Interesting is the fact that only rarely before the twentieth century will one find christian love valued as a major component of marriage. The couple's biological sexual union was considered the most essential ingredient of marriage. Its value was not based on its power to deepen their interpersonal union, but rather on its biological outcome—the procreation of a child. Without any desire to minimize the importance of procreation, noteworthy is the fact that the christian significance of sexuality was based on its effect extrinsic to the couple, and not from its goodness as an expression of christian marital love.

Current theology and church teaching affirms the value of marital sexuality because it is part of each spouse's identity as a sexual person, and from their shared life, as sexual persons, in the marriage. Symbolized in their sexual union is the intimate nature of their relationship and that creative generosity required by christian marriage. This ordinarily indicates an openness to the procreation of new life. The present pattern reveals love giving forth life. Resultant new life can be understood as both life developed between them, and life offered to a new person. When new life occurs, it is always the result of a cooperative act of God as creator and humans as co-operators. What's important to note is that the language of this theological description of marriage is personal, and not simply biological. It is their personal union which is procreative, not merely their physical joining.

"Love generating life" is a fundamental description of God's own life. As much as we can grasp this essential life as Trinity, the pattern of God's love creating life in all its abundant forms is primary. Creation is the result of God's mysterious love, a love manifest in the Incarnation and Redemption. It is a love radically expressed "for us and for our salvation." The mystery of God's love for us is embodied in a special way in marriage. This is the insight in Ephesians 5 where marriage is related to and included in the life available due to Christ's redemptive death and resurrection.

Redeeming grace penetrates the love between wife and husband and builds the foundation for identifying and celebrating christian marriage as a sacrament. Yet right away it must be noted that the establishment of the sacramentality of marriage requires that the marriage possess qualities consonant with its divine-originated purpose. Founded on the account of the origin of marriage in Genesis and in Jesus' discussion of divorce, where he refers to the Genesis text (Mt 19:4-6), it can be argued that it was God's intent that marriage reflect in part

God's faithful and lifelong love for humanity.

God establishes a covenant of faithful and forgiving love. The interpersonal qualities of fidelity (being with) and forgiveness (being for) are the hallmarks of christian marriage and the divine covenant.

Marital fidelity establishes an interpersonal structure where one's spouse holds a place of exclusive preeminence among all others, even parents. The spouse's claim on one's life, its time, energy and talents, establishes the moral claims of marriage as an interpersonal community. While the spouse is first or primary, a fully adequate set of moral claims would include one's children, along with a wider circle of social commitments which extends ultimately to all of humankind. Fidelity, as is evidenced in the nuptial promises, includes a lifelong intent to be of service to one's marital partner. This responsibility addresses both spouses in equal measure. Where a person is psychically or physically incapable of this type of self-gift, no genuine christian marriage can occur. Fidelity is developmental as it responds to the self-revelation of each spouse as the marriage itself unfolds.

Marital forgiveness is that special virtue of marriage where one forgives the hurts inflicted upon oneself by one's spouse either intended or unintended. Given the nature of interpersonal development, it inevitably happens that each will experience the other's sinful nature and the narrowness which comes with human limitation. Acceptance and forgiveness are demanded to support an on-going relationship. Where possible, any evil within the relationship should be corrected as it is part of God's redemptive plan to convert evil to good. Totally passive acceptance of evil is inappropriate christian behavior.

Given the general lack of external support for preserving marriage provided by society, it is necessary that marriage be held together by values within. Thus, part of the moral responsibility facing the married is to do whatever is necessary to maintain vitality in their marriage. It is also clear that the well-being of the family is directly related to and caused by the health of the marriage.

The interpersonal dimension of marriage is not only valued through expansion in time, but also its development in depth. Marital love aims at comprehensiveness; it encompasses by intent the totality of what constitutes each person. Marital love is unconditional; it includes love's regard for the total bodily spirit and the spiritual body of one's spouse. The language chosen to describe this dimension of the marital union attempts to overcome one of the most insidious problems which has plagued the theology of marriage from earliest times: the use of an anthropological dualism which divided the human person into a material and a spiritual component. While one can discuss dimensions of the human person (and therefore, of human relationships) which are more or less material, at no time should one sever the corporeal from the spiritual. Such separation disregards the Incarnation of God in Jesus, and the unified redemptive purpose underlying Creation itself.

Marital Spirituality

A second focus of the theology of marriage is how the spirituality of marriage unfolds from this comprehensive, interpersonal description of marriage. A description of marital spirituality seeks to determine where the presence and power of God are situated in conjugal life. If, as a starting point, this identification of the holy points to wherever essential goodness is found, then it is clear that there is no purely secular dimension in marriage. It is all holy and sanctified. Nevertheless, it is possible to point out degrees of the holy based on a determination of those features of married life which most coincide with the dynamics of God's activity in the world.

In the church and through the church, God is saving the world. The process of salvation is basically one of creating and nourishing communal life, first that of God with humanity and then, humans with each other. The fundamental task of the church is to create and form the community of disciples to be sent forth in mission to do the work of God. Establishing and building communal life in both its divine and human dimensions occur simultaneously. Within christian marriage in its most basic form, there is joined in faithful love a man and a woman, two individuals who represent that which is most different and distinct within human creation, the difference between the sexes.

The movement from juridical categories to personal categories in the theology of marriage creates a new framework for discussion, and the need for considering spiritual development as central to marriage itself. The spirituality proper to marriage is a relational spirituality. It emphasizes love of neighbor where the role of proximate neighbor is taken by the spouse. It encourages not just the shared management of the home and family, but also the inviting of one's spouse to accompany one on the journey to God. This is done not in the spirit of surrendering what is individually good, but out of the value of enhancing one's own gifts by relating them to another's uniqueness. In microcosm, christian marriage is a life-cell of the church as it develops a life and spirituality genuinely communal. This is why christian marriage can be called a building block of the church itself and why recent conciliar and papal teaching refer to the christian family as the domestic church.

Special features of marriage which

contribute to church life are the prophetic way the married work through individual differences and speak to the real possibility of community in diversity. The married themselves worship God through their generosity in serving each other and serving the value of life itself, first within the family, and second through the hospitality offered by the christian family to "outsiders" in need.

Existential Focus

A final feature of the new emphases in the theology of marriage is its existential dimension. Because marriage as a human relationship is necessarily developmental, christian marriage exists first as intention, and moves toward accomplishment. The actualization of the marriage is dependent upon interpersonal revelation and the events of life which constitute the life of the married. It is difficult to reduce christian marriage to fixed categories of analysis because the relationship is always in process or continually becoming.

Earlier theologies focused on the wedding itself, the initial public exchange of vows in the presence of the community along with the first act of sexual intercourse as essential for establishing the validity of the marriage. It was believed that the sacrament of Matrimony was received at that time. Now Christian marriage is thought of as existing when there is established an adequate consciousness and awareness of the full range of relational requirements in marriage along with a serious willingness and the actual capacity to create a relationship of faithful love. Further, it is necessary to affirm the disposition of openness to the reception of new life within the marriage. All these features are qualities of a relationship which are not easily reduced to simple categories or to a single event in time.

Christian marriage is both a sacrament of the church, and a sacrament of creation.

With marriage being so tied to creation itself, in an age where the spiritual significance of matter is far from obvious, the religious meaning of marriage is easily overlooked. Because of its secular appearance, the importance that marriage be approached in faith is worth special emphasis. Theologians have described marriage as "a human reality" which is at the same time "a saving mystery."

Among the traditional seven sacraments of the church, marriage was the last one formally identified as such. Theologians discussed its sacramental nature as early as the twelfth century, but it was not until the Council of Trent in the sixteenth century that official status was given to marriage as a sacrament. The implication of this delay may partly be due to a certain resistance on the part of the church to include a relationship with its sexual emphasis as something essentially holy and sanctifying.

Certain questions relating to marriage still challenge theologians and the church. Among these are the determination of the nature of christian marriage where christian faith is present in only one of the spouses. Another is the need to describe more clearly the value of the marital relationship itself in relation to the procreative goal of marriage. Also, given the widespread presence of divorce, the question of whether christian marriage as such can die deserves discussion. And finally, the relationship of marriage customs of non-Western cultures to the theology of marriage which developed primarily in a European context calls for extended consideration. The theology of marriage has undergone significant development throughout history and will continue to do so, but now with an ever-widening body of discussants. It is not without significance that many contributors are married, some are women and a growing number come from non-Western cultures. Their contributions will insure that the theology of marriage remains a vital part of the church's theological endowment.

See **Annulment; Anthropology, Christian; Covenant; Divorce; Sacrament; Sexuality**

Denise Lardner Carmody, *Caring for Marriage: Feminist and Biblical Reflections,* Mahwah, New Jersey: Paulist Press, 1985. Walter Kasper, *Theology of Christian Marriage,* New York: Seabury, 1980. Theodore Mackin, *What is Marriage?,* New York: Paulist Press, 1982. Richard Malone and John R. Connery, Eds., *Contemporary Perspectives on Christian Marriage,* Chicago: Loyola U Press, 1984. Eileen Zieget Silbermann, *The Savage Sacrament: A Theology of Marriage after American Feminism,* West Mystic: Twenty-third Publications, 1983. David M. Thomas, *Christian Marriage: A Journey Together,* Wilmington: Michael Glazier, Inc. 1983.

DAVID M. THOMAS

MARTYR

The word, martyr (Gk., *martyr:* witness, hence, *martyros,* was originally used in early christianity in reference to the Apostles (cf. Acts 1:8, 22). In Acts (cf. 22:20) and the Apocalypse (e.g., 2:13; 11:3; 17:6), this meaning was extended to embrace all those whose suffering and death bore striking testimony to their faith in Jesus Christ, Son of God and risen Savior. Christians like Ignatius of Antioch and Polycarp of Smyrna (cf. Phil 9:1) looked to Christ as the first martyr.

The classic age of the martyrs occurred in the pre-Constantinian church under the emperors Septimus Severus (202-203), Decius (249-250) and Valerian (257-258). The persecution launched by Diocletian and Galerius in 303 was particularly fierce. Church goods were destroyed or confiscated, assembly and worship were forbidden, laity and clergy were tortured and condemned to prison or death. Relief came in the West under Maxentius and Constantine; the first Edict of Toleration was signed by a dying Galerius in 311.

Initially, converts to Christianity were persecuted, as Jesus had foretold, by their own people. The story of Stephen (Acts 6:8–7:60) reflects the reaction of the Jews to the followers of Jesus Christ whose teaching threatened that of the law and the prophets. As Christianity spread throughout the Roman empire, it was perceived by the pagans as a Jewish sect and suffered the oppression and discrimination directed against the Jews. Gradually, it became clear to Roman authorities that there was a religious movement other than Judaism attracting converts and undermining worship of the empire's deities.

Records of persecutions directed against Christians can be found in extant texts and in archaeological remains. The *Letters* of Ignatius of Antioch, the *Martyrdom of Polycarp* and the *Letter to the Churches of Lyons* and *Vienne* are significant, authenticated documents. Certain *Acts* of the martyrs are also instructive, even when their contents bear marks of the exaggerations of early hagiographical characteristics. Fragments, monuments and inscriptions continue to yield to scholars new insights into an era when to become a Christian meant almost certainly to take a first step toward martyrdom.

Early in the history of Christianity, martyrs became the object of veneration and a cult of the martyrs developed in the church. This cult consisted in several "moments." First of all, the physical remains of the women and men who had been put to death were gathered up as so many sacred fragments, "more valuable than precious stones and finer than gold" (*Martyrdom of Polycarp*, 18). Next, these remains were sealed in a container that was assigned to a "proper place" in the christian catacombs. Finally, friends and relatives gathered every year on the feast of the martyr's "birthday" (*natalis*) into heaven for a liturgical celebration in the presence of the relics. Much later, churches were sometimes built on the site of a martyr's tomb.

Veneration was accorded those who were seen to be truly martyrs, that is, who had fulfilled the "conditions" for martyrdom. In the first place, one had to lay down one's physical life and really experience death. Second, death had to be the result of hatred of the life and truth proclaimed by christian teaching. Last, such a death had to be voluntarily accepted in witness to and defense of christian values.

Some exceptions to these conditions can be found. Origen (+253) was condemned to death, imprisoned, tortured and later released. He died, subsequently, from the effects of his sufferings and was looked to as a martyr. During the years in which Cyprian was bishop of Carthage (250-258). Christians released from prison prior to death were considered martyrs. If catechumens, they were considered baptized; if Christians, they were permitted to exercise priestly functions. The abuse that developed from these practices had to be curtailed by the bishops of North Africa.

Catechumens who actually suffered death were considered to have been inititated into the christian community by a "baptism of blood." This was the same "blood" that Tertullian proclaimed "seed" of the church: "The oftener we are mown down by you, the more in number we grow" (*Apologeticum*, 50).

Insights such as these gave rise to a spirituality of martyrdom which marked the early church in a significant way.

The spirituality of martyrdom was rooted in the christian experience of initiation into the church through sharing in the dying and rising of Jesus Christ. The Christian's entire life was to be lived in consequence of participation in the death and resurrection of the Lord. Belief in the living truth of the Christ-Event inspired and motivated the women and men of christian antiquity to courageous witness. The yearly celebration at a martyr's tomb became a means of praising God for the witness of those who had gone on before to victory; it was also the occasion to draw courage from a heroic example and to pray for one's own fidelity in time of trial. Death, for the martyr, was the door to that domain where one became, in truth, fully a Christian, and where one was, finally, with Christ. After the inauguration of the Constantinian era, this passage was no longer assured to the followers of Jesus. In its dismay, the christian community sought a "substitute" for martyrdom in ascetical sects, in the eremetical life in the desert and, finally, in monasticism. In a very real sense, the development of religious life in the church can be traced back to the age of the martyrs: "From the first centuries, the Holy Spirit has stirred up, side by side with the heroic confession of the martyrs. The wonderful strength of disciples and virgins, of hermits and anchorites" (Pope Paul VI, *Evangelica testificatio,* 3).

The large numbers of martyrs who suffered and died in early Christianity gave rise to a concern that the memory of "so great a cloud of witnesses" (Heb 12:1) not be lost to the church. A series of documents known as "martyrologies" began to be compiled, listing the names of martyrs in the order in which their feast days were observed. One of the earliest (A.D. 354) of many such records was an almanac attributed to Furius Dionysius Filocalus. This became the basis for later works.

It must not be supposed that martyrdom is an event of the past, with no contemporary significance for the church. Persecution is still the lot of many christian women and men today. At times, it is expressed in outright violence that leads to torture, imprisonment and death in witness to faith in Jesus Christ and his gospel. Again, it is exercised through the more subtle forms of discrimination which inflict suffering on believers because of ideological, ethical or political values that are in conflict with a right conscience and a christian lifestyle. The Second Vatican Council clearly affirmed: "Martyrdom makes the disciple like his master .... Therefore, the Church considers it the highest gift and supreme test of love" (L.G. 42) The presence of martyrs in the church in every age assures the fidelity of the body of Christ to Christ, the head.

See **Paschal Mystery**

W.H.C., Frend, *Martyrdom and Persecution in the Early Church,* New York: Anchor Books, 1967. J.B. Metz and E. Schillebeeckx, Eds., *Martyrdom Today,* New York: Seabury Press, 1983; *Concilium* 163. A. Salignac, *"Martyre,"* DS 10, p. 718-730.

AGNES CUNNINGHAM, SSCM

MARXISM

Marxism and Christianity

It is not unsurprising that christian responses to Marxism, not least Roman Catholic, have generally been hostile. "The criticism of religion," Marx wrote in 1844, "is the premise of all criticism" (*Contribution to the Critique of Hegel's Philosophy of Right, Introduction*). In the same work he coined the famous *obiter* "(religion) is the opium of the people," and in his last work, *Capital,* his attitude remained substantially unchanged: "the religious world is but the reflex of the real world."

Marx's hostility to Christianity was general, applying to all its various denominations and its differing political alliances. It is sometimes supposed that Marx's criticism of Christianity was limited in its focus upon the German Lutheranism in which his father, a convert of convenience from Judaism, brought him up. This is not true. Certainly he identified early Lutheranism, with its individualistic emphasis on the "authority of faith" as against the Roman Catholic feudal emphasis on "faith in authority," as the natural ally of emergent sixteenth-century capitalism. But this was only because he regarded Roman Catholicism, to which he admittedly paid scant attention, as still less capable of taking up the concerns of revolutionary socialism, since it stood even further back along the line of reactionary doctrines, a hopelessly stranded medieval survival from a world which pre-dated even capitalism.

Nor did Marx limit his critique of Christianity to those forms of it which explicitly allied themselves with a reactionary politics. In *The Peasant War in Germany* his colleague, Friedrich Engels, analyzed the peasant revolt in the early Reformation period in Germany, paying attention not only to the increasingly reactionary stance of Luther, but also to the increasingly radical communism of the neo-Anabaptist leader, Thomas Münzer—the latter, on paper at least, a prototypical communist. But a "communist by fantasy" is how Engels describes Münzer, for, in Engel's view, the radical political program which Münzer proposed was inspired by utopian Christianity and as such "went beyond the directly prevailing social and political conditions" (F. Engels, p. 98). Being a theologically inspired idealism unrooted in real history, it could, therefore, hope to succeed only by virtue of violent imposition and so inevitably degenerated into the tyranny in which all utopianisms must end. Thus, commented Marx himself, "the Peasant War, the most radical event in Germany history, came to grief because of theology" (*Contribution to the Critique...*).

Marx's hostility to Christianity, therefore, allows no exceptions. Theism itself, wedded to no matter which politics, whether of left or right, is alienating, for to some degree it must always place the destiny of the human species under the control of forces other than the purely human. And Marxist "humanism" (a much disputed matter) at the very least sees humanity and its future to be made by human beings or not at all.

Not surprisingly, therefore, the christian response has usually been in kind. Frequently condemned in the last one hundred years by church authorities as atheistic. Marxism has often been regarded simultaneously as a rival religion or quasi-religion of secular humanism. Moreover, this is a view often shared by christian theologians of a more liberal persuasion than might be expected of ecclesiastical authorities. In one of the most perceptive and sensitive of recent studies of Christianity and Marxism, Nicholas Lash describes Marxism as a "secularized doctrine of providence" (Lash, p. 65), considering Marxism to be an invented expression in exclusively humanist terms of central christian doctrines.

It is within some such view of Marxism that the Catholic Church's most recent official response is couched. In the first of two commentaries on liberation theology, *Libertatis Nuntius* (August, 1984), the Vatican's Sacred Congregation for the Doctrine of the Faith criticizes attempts to work through a christian "option for the poor" via a marxist analysis of the political, economic and social conditions which generate and sustain Latin American poverty. A marxist social analysis, it argues, cannot be separated from an atheistic and humanist ideology. To attempt to harness that analysis in the service of a christian response to poverty leads to what it calls "immanentism," a re-reading of christian values of belief, worship and practice in purely secularist, humanist terms.

This, *Libertatis Nuntius* argues, is the inevitable fate of any alliance between christian theology and marxist theory, Marxism and Christianity are opposed irreconcilably. Consequently, where the attempt is made to situate both on the same territory, as within the theologies of liberation in Latin America, they must either exclude one another from it or else the one will cannibalize the other. The result will be either a "secularized messianism" or, conversely, a humanism given a merely verbal dress of the sacred.

The force of christian hostility to Marxism has therefore arisen out of the instinct that Marxism appears not merely to differ from Christianity but to be its rival. Not that either Marx or Engels thought of Marxism as an alternative religion, but certainly they saw socialist humanism as the alternative *to* religion. Socialism displaces religion because "the religious reflex" does in some way emerge, inarticulately and in distorted form, from that "cry of the oppressed people" of which socialism is the articulate expression. Since, therefore, Marxism and Christianity compete over the same territory, are rival claimants to the same constituency, Marxism has the character of a heresy. And heresies notoriously provoke the more bitter enmity in Christians than do doctrines they regard as merely false.

However, among theologians generally today, the spectrum of reactions has been more diverse than at any previous time. Pope John XXIII's encyclical letter, *Mater et Magistra,* was a watershed. By and large eschewing doctrinal and ideological differences with Marxism (which Pope John simply took for granted), he expressed scepticism of the value in regarding Marxism as nothing but a worldwide atheistic conspiracy. He chose rather to look upon Marxism as a *phenomenon,* a global movement of real men and women, a "sign of the times" to be scrutinized and interrogated for the indications it embodied of genuine aspir-

ations for justice in an unjust world. He saw Marxism as embodying aspirations (and in part fulfilling them) which scarcely figured on the agenda of christian pastoral and social action at all. Nor was his summons to a christian scrutiny of this "sign of the times" a call to a detached analysis of Marxism from the outside, but to an active, sympathetic if principled dialogue with Marxists themselves.

Characteristically the response to this call in the northern world (primarily in Europe) took the form of high-level, scholarly interchange between western European theologians and eastern European Marxists, looking for theoretical common ground. A flurry of seminars, learned papers and books was the result, but the process in Europe was brought to an abrupt halt by the Soviet invasion of Czechoslovakia in 1968.

By the late sixties the momentum for dialogue between Christianity and Marxism had shifted to the Third World, where it is now associated with the movement in Latin America called "liberation theology." Best known outside Latin America by the seminal work of the Peruvian Jesuit, Gustavo Gutiérrez, *A Theology of Liberation,* liberation theology is not properly to be regarded as a movement within classical academic theology. It is in the first instance a low-level "grass roots" movement of Christians who signal their commitment to the gospel by means of a primary option of solidarity with the poor and oppressed people of their land. Gutiérrez adopts at the methodological level the Marxist principle of the "priority of practice over theory" with a unity of both. Theology, therefore, is a moment of reflection in the light of the Gospel upon and within that initial "option for the poor."

For Gutiérrez theory and practice interact, involving a double articulation: on the one hand of the meaning of liberation from poverty and oppression in terms of the message of the Bible; and on the other, of the christian message in terms of the political, economic and personal practices of human liberation.

At the core of the christian commitment Gutiérrez places the demand for political, economic and social liberation, though he and fellow theologians of th s school refuse to separate the political and economic from the personal and spiritua, seeing them as interacting elements in a single, fused practice. Inevitably this practice of liberation from poverty and oppression in turn calls for an appropriate analysis of Latin American poverty and it is at this level that many liberation theologians have looked to Marxism as the analytical bedrock in which to anchor their theological and practical commitments.

For some, as for Gutiérrez himself and probably for the Brazilian, Leonardo Boff, the value of Marxism consists mainly in its socio-economic analysis of poverty and oppression. They both believe that this analytical use of Marxism can be separated from its ideological atheism and materialism. At the opposite extreme, the Mexican theologian J-P. Miranda sees Marxism as being essentially not an atheism at all, but as openly theistic. In between, many positions are occupied, and it is not safe to say that there is any one attitude to the place of marxism within the construction of an adequate theology of liberation which all its proponents share in common.

Nonetheless, even the minimalist account of this relationship, as found in Gutiérrez's writings, cannot be regarded as unproblematic. In the first place, the Vatican's conviction that the social analysis of Marxism cannot be separated from its ideological atheism is widely shared by scholars within both the christian and Marxist camps. Secondly, Marxists themselves are reluctant to concede that the social and economic analysis of oppression can be detached from the overall "materalist conception of history" according to which "the history of all hitherto existing society is the history of class struggles" (K. Marx and F. Engels, *The Manifesto* ... p. 35), and this seems hard to reconcile with a traditional christian view of the workings of divine providence within history. Thirdly, and following from this second difficulty, Marxism has resolutely insisted upon the "ideological" character of all religion, a character whereby men and women live out, within religion, a false and alienated relationship with each other, with nature and with society.

Marxist Theory

Materialism. Nearly all Marxists have been atheists. There is no denying that Marx and Engels were, and Miranda's claims to the contrary are generally regarded as an eccentricity. What can be and is disputed is the exact nature of Marx's atheism and what its implications are for religious belief.

Marx's atheism arises out of his materialism. But it is necessary to distinguish what Marx meant by "materialism" from that "ontological" materialism which Marx identified with the French *philosophes* of the eighteenth century. "Ontological" materialism simply denies the existence of anything other than brute physical matter. Almost certainly Marx himself was not a materialist in this sense, though just as certainly Engels was and later the Russian revolutionary leader Lenin indubitably was. Whatever the uncertainties are about Marx's metaphysical opinions, it is at least clear that Marx's atheism arose not out of a materialism of this sort, but out of a more characteristic *social* materialism. According to this materialism all is indeed matter. But what is meant by "matter" is *social relationship*.

Historical Materialism. For Marx,

human beings are as they relate with one another socially. To be human is to exist in social relationships, and what it is to be human is determined by the particular form of relationship which characterizes a particular historical form of society. There is no "absolute" human nature, but only the form of human living which men and women have inherited from their history. Indeed, as Marx put it, "men make their history, but they do not make it just as they please; they do not make it under circumstances chosen by themselves, but under circumstances directly encountered, given and transmitted from the past" (K. Marx, *The Eighteenth Brumaire, Louis Bonaparte*, p. 97).

In turn, all the products of human consciousness—art, philosophy, morality, law, politics and religion—get their life, their own particular form and shape, from the specific character of the society of which they are the "ideology." "Life is not determined by consciousness" he asserted, "but consciousness by life" (K. Marx and F. Engels, *The German Ideology*, p.47).

According to Marx, however, it does not follow that all human reflection *upon* social life is merely a reflection *of* it. The precise nature of Marx's "determinism" is much disputed, particularly among marxists themselves. Nonetheless Marx clearly did believe that, within whatever limitations imposed by "circumstances," "men make their history." And in making that history, "ideas" play a decisive role. Marxism itself, after all, is both the product of a particular phase of historical development, namely capitalism, and a powerful agency of revolutionary development towards a new phase, communism.

Ideology. Nonetheless, for Marx, "the ruling ideas of each age have ever been the ideas of its ruling class" (K. Marx and F. Engels, *The Manifesto*, p. 51) and within the social world of capitalism this meant the "bourgeois" class. The "bourgeoisie" in its narrowest sense was the class of capitalists, those who owned or possessed direct power over the means of production and distribution of wealth in a capitalist society.

On the whole, Marx did not believe that the ideas of the bourgeois class "ruled" in a capitalist society by virtue of any conspiracy to impose them by force or by propaganda. In a bourgeois society bourgeois ideas rule because they are, for that society, "its spontaneous and natural mode of thought"—in short, they are that society's "ideology." In capitalist society, social, economic and political transactions are dominated by market forces, by the buying and selling not merely of commodities and goods produced but also of the means of production themselves, that is, above all, labor. In such a society it is quite "natural and spontaneous" for capitalist and worker alike to see themselves primarily as individual buyers and sellers. The worker will see himself or herself as the seller of a "commodity," labor-power, and the capitalist as the buyer of it. And both will naturally see the price received or paid, wages, as determined principally by the forces of the market, supply and demand.

With corresponding "naturalness and spontaneity," therefore, both worker and capitalist will see the relationship between them as being, in the main, a "free and equal exchange" between independent individuals within a market relationship, for the market exchange is by its nature the exchange of equivalents.

Marx thought of this fundamental conception of capitalist society in terms of a structure of market "forces" as underpinning the ethical commitments of the bourgeoisie to the moral values of "freedom and equality" generally. Spiraling away from this basic economic perception are even "higher" perceptions of individual freedom and equality—equality before the law, equality of opportunity, the rights of man, the freedoms of the press, public opinion, the vote, the freedoms of a property-owning democracy and on from there into the "transcendent" realms of metaphysics and religion where these ethical commitments are endorsed and given "absolute," supra-historical value. All these values, "the ruling ideas" of the age, are but the projection beyond the conditions of historical particularity and class interest of the values of a particular form of society constructed in the image of its ruling class, the bourgeoisie.

But this complex layering of legal, political, moral and religious ideas are the "ideas of the ruling class" not in the sense that the bourgeoisie invented them as its propaganda but in the sense that they are its *lingua franca,* the "common sense" of an age, shared in common by all in that form of society in which the bourgeoisie are the ruling class. This "ideology" serves the interest of that class by being the mirror in which the bourgeoisie can contemplate its own moral, metaphysical and religious image and likeness.

Exploitation. In that mirror of ideology bourgeois society therefore honors and endorses its commitments to the values embedded in the market mechanism; and in that mechanism is found the most basic relationship of a capitalist society (indeed for the bourgeoisie, believing its values to be transcendent, of *all* society). "Society," for the bourgeoisie, is the free relationship of autonomous individuals in the equal exchanges it transacts. But on the score of each of these three central market values, "individualism," "freedom" and "equality," Marx saw bourgeois ideology as fundamentally misrepresenting the very social world from which it arises.

Most decisively, the exchange of labor-power for wages is, for Marx, a relationship of radical *in*equality. Certainly, the surface social routines represent that relationship as one of simple equality, for the worker at the factory gate receiving his wage-packet "naturally" seems to be receiving a value equivalent to what he has produced during the previous week. But, in Marx's view, this appearance of equality rests upon the false assumption that what the capitalist buys from the worker *is* the value which he or she has produced in the previous week—and it is not, nor could it be. What the capitalist buys is the use for a given period of time of the worker's *capacity to produce* value, his or her "labor-power." Moreover, the capitalist buys this labor-power at a price necessarily lower than the value which he can extract from its use, so that the value received from the worker is necessarily higher than the value of the wages given in return.

Without this unequal exchange there can be no surplus-value; without surplus-value, no profit; without profit, no capitalism. Appearing "naturally and spontaneously" as an exchange of equivalents, the most elementary relationship of capitalism is in fact a relationship of exploitation, a dehumanization forced upon the worker by virtue of his only alternative, unemployment. The worker must either impoverish himself by labor for wages, or live in poverty without them.

Thus, the capitalist mechanism of wealth production is inherently alienating for the worker. The more the worker produces, the more the worker produces his or her own alienation from self, his own powers, from other men and women. The atomic-individualist conceptions of self which form such a powerful element in the moral ideology of capitalism is but a symptom of the worker's own alienation, and a reinforcement of it.

Thus it is that capitalists and workers stand opposed to one another as classes in a conflict which is unresolvable within the framework of a capitalist society. Class warfare is not, for Marx, the chosen tool of a revolutionary group, for it is built into the very structure of capitalism itself. As Marx saw it, it is useless for Christians and other moralists to oppose class warfare on moral grounds within the assumptions of capitalism, for capitalism can exist only on the basis of a relationship between human beings divided by class antagonism. Moralizing idealisms are therefore futile gestures. Only the revolutionary overthrow of capitalism could make possible the conditions under which the human race can live united in true brotherhood and sisterhood.

The Marxist Challenge to Christianity. It is against this background that Marx throws down the challenge to Christianity. For the Marxist atheist, Christianity is not so much a body of doctrines which are false as a social practice which is ideologically committed to an anti-revolutionary strategy. Theism, for Marx, is both symptom and reinforcement of that strategy. For so long as men and women continue to worship alien powers they will be alienated from their own. For as long as men and women project the eschatological resolution of human conflicts on to a final "kingdom" beyond human history, for so long will they fail to take up the burdens of revolutionary action within history. And for so long as a christian ideology of "the individual" continues to reconcile men and women in the market principle of an atomic individualism, they must necessarily be in collusion with the principles of a capitalist society.

In the end Marx followed Feuerbach in seeing Christianity as having placed before human beings the need to choose; between the claims of God and the claims of the human; between an indifference to history and its tasks in the name of an individualistic "transcendence" and an immanentist, God-denying, historicist humanism; between an other-worldly salvation and a this-worldly socialism.

It is a matter of dispute among both Marxists and Christians whether Marx himself accepted that these were the real and only choices to be made and in each case chose the latter option as did Feuerbach; or whether on the contrary he saw these alternatives as false choices and refused to accept them in the name of what he saw as a *post*-theological socialism. It is certain that, for Marx, Christianity imposes these choices. Hence, the challenge which Marx throws down before Christians can be and has been met in one or other of two ways: one response, to insist that God can be affirmed only through the denial of the human; that the transcend-ence of God can be affirmed only through the negation of history; that religion itself can be defined only by contrast with the political, the social, the material. The alternative response is, in the name of a post-atheistic incarnational Christianity, to reject the need to make these choices at all. It is this latter way which the theologians of liberation are seeking to explore. Whether it is possible to do so in alliance with Marxism is a question on which the christian world remains for the time being divided.

See **Economics, Liberation Theology, Political Theology, Work**

Contribution to the Critique of Hegel's Philosophy of Right, Introduction, ed. and trans. by T.B. Bottomore, in *Karl Marx: Early Writings,* London, 1963. *Capital,* I, Part I, 1, i, iv, trans. by S. Moore and E. Aveling, London, 1970. F. Engels, *The Peasant War in Germany,* in *Marx and Engels on Religion,* Moscow, 1972. Nicholas Lash, *A Matter of Hope,* London, 1981. K. Marx and F. Engels, *The Manifesto of the Communist Party,* and K. Marx, *The Eighteenth Brumaire of Louis Bonaparte,* in Marx and Engels, *Selected Works in One Volume,* London, 1968. K. Marx and F. Engels, *The German Ideology,* Part I, ed. and trans. by C.J. Arthur, London, 1970.

DENYS TURNER

MARY, MOTHER OF GOD

Methodology in the study of Marian theology has changed from formal presentation of theses in successive chapters to research into the phases of theological development. The French Society of Marian Studies, founded some years before the Second World War, ordered the papers read at its annual session, which commanded universal respect, on this pattern. The work of one member, similarly planned, R. Laurentin's *Court Traité de théologie mariale* (later entitled *Court Traité sur la Sainte Vierge*) was to prove seminal. This was the approach of those who drafted the Marian text of Vatican II; they abandoned an earlier draft otherwise conceived.

Sacred Scripture

OT texts traditionally considered Marian in content have been scrutinized and sifted in the light of present-day biblical scholarship. These are the oracles in Gen 3:15 and Is 7:14 and the prophecy in Mic 5:2-4.

Gen 3:15 in the original reads: "I will put enmity between you and the woman, and between your seed and her seed; he shall bruise your head, and you shall bruise his heel." Interpretation of the text has been influenced by the Vulgate translation: "he shall bruise" read "she shall crush (*ipsa conteret*); "you shall bruise" read "you shall lie in wait" (*tu insidiaberis*). The text, on a minimal interpretation, strikes a note of optimism and ultimate victory. B. Rigaux, however, with competent use of modern techniques, justifies a Marian sense. "Seed" in early times was often understood collectively, though Christ would still be singled out; Irenaeus and others who admitted a messianic sense would see Mary in association with Christ.

The oracle in Is 7:14 raises likewise a translation problem, as it has been interpreted under the influence of Mt 1:23:

"Therefore the Lord himself will give you a sign. Behold, a young woman shall conceive and bear a son, and shall call his name Emmanuel." The word *Almah* (a young woman) was translated by *parthenos* (virgin) by LXX. The patristic support for a Marian sense is massive. Vatican II was reserved, as it was on Mic 5:2-4, composed about the same time: "But you, O Bethlehem Ephrathah, who are little to be among the clans of Judah, from you shall come forth for me one who is to be ruler in Israel, whose origin is from of old, from ancient days. Therefore he shall give them up until the time when she who is in travail has brought forth..."

In dealing with these texts and with Mary's place among the select minority, the *Anawim,* the Poor of the Lord, as with the title which sums up so much OT hope, Daughter of Zion, the Council sought to satisfy both exegesis and the perennial sense of the church: "The earliest documents, as they are read in the Church and are understood in the light of a further and full revelation, bring the figure of a woman, Mother of the Redeemer, into a gradually clearer light. Considered in this light, she is already prophetically foreshadowed in the promise of victory over the serpent which was given to our first parents after their fall into sin (cf. Gen 3:15). Likewise she is the virgin who shall conceive and bear a son, whose name shall be called Emmanuel (cf. Is 8:14; Mic 5:2-3; Mt 1:22-23). She stands out among the poor and humble of the Lord, who confidently hope for and receive salvation from him. After a long period of waiting the times are fulfilled in her, the exalted Daughter of Zion, and the new plan of salvation is established, when the Son of God has taken human nature from her, that he might in the mysteries of his flesh free man from sin." (L.G. 55)

H. Cazelles showed, in a seminal study,

the preeminence in OT royal history of the king's mother; an explanation too of the title Mother of Jesus in the new messianic kingdom. In Acts Mary has the title alongside her name (1:14); by the time of John's writings her own name is dropped (Jn 2:1; 19:25). She is the Mother of the King with all that this implies.

Very recently the Marian texts in the NT have been subjected to rigorous research: the Matthaean and Lucan infancy narratives; the two Johannine passages, telling of Mary at the wedding feast of Cana and on Calvary; the Woman in the Apocalypse; and Paul's significant phrase in Gal 4:4-5.

First in the chronology, however, come the sparse, apparently difficult texts in Mark. Of 3:35 Vatican II wisely says that Jesus "extolled a kingdom beyond the concerns and ties of flesh and blood." The interpretation of Luke's annunciation narrative with the aid of OT parallels (Zeph 3:14-17—Lk 1:28-33; 2 Sam 7:12-16—Lk 1:32-33; Exod 40:35—Lk 1:35; 2 Sam 6:9-11—Lk 1:43, 56; Jdt 13:18, 19—Lk 1:42), though less favored now than in the fifties, is stimulating

Different attempts have been made to explain why so little quantitatively refers to Mary in NT books. If nothing else but the annunciation story existed, her unique greatness would be truly seen. The theme of the woman associated with the Messiah reaches here a totally unexpected fulfillment. The *ruah* (Spirit) of the OT is immeasurably surpassed when, for the first time, he descends on a woman, and the descent is preceded by her consent, sought and given.

There is a vast field of research open on Mary in the NT. A theme renewed, Mary and the Spirit, raises the value of the Lucan infancy narrative, as it calls for exegesis of Acts 1:14, Mary among the disciples awaiting the coming of the Spirit. Apocalypse 12 was not always interpreted in reference to Mary but to the church. But the Mary—church parallel and typology allows a deep harmony between the two interpretations. And finally A. Serra has with consummate scholarship, revealed the deep roots of the Lucan "pondering them in her heart" (2:19, 51), citing texts in Jewish tradition whether recorded in the OT or elsewhere; he has similarly enriched study of the Johannine Cana and Calvary passages.

The Fathers

What Newman called "the great rudimental teaching of antiquity from its earliest date concerning Mary" is the intuition that she was the new or second Eve. The idea was to become locked within the permanent core of ideas about Mary from the second century to Vatican II. The link with apostolic times is a matter for research. But Irenaeus (d. after 193), Justin Martyr (d.c. 165) and Tertullian (d. after 220), a trio representing a wide area, are explicit on the basic concept. Irenaeus excels to this day. It was an integral element to his doctrine of *recirculatio,* a reversal of the original evil along the same path as it had come, which he expressed in an interesting metaphor: "The knot of Eve's disobedience was untied by Mary's obedience; for what Eve bound by her unbelief, Mary loosed by her faith" (*Adv. Haer.* XXII, 4). His essential passage is classic, frequently quoted: "Consequently, the Virgin Mary is found obedient, saying 'Behold your handmaid, Lord. Lord, let it be done to me according to your word.' But Eve was disobedient; though still a virgin she did not obey. For as she, though wedded to Adam, was still a virgin ... being disobedient, she became a cause of death to herself and to all mankind. So Mary, having a predestined husband, but none the less a virgin, was obedient and became to herself and to the whole human race a cause of salvation." (*Ibid.*)

That Mary was near the centerpiece of

the new creation was established. Had she a higher dignity? Thus arose the debate on the divine maternity, the validity of Mary's title, prestigious in so many ways, *Theotokos*. The key figure here was Cyril of Alexandria (d. 444) and the official pronouncement, due almost entirely to him, was made by the Council of Ephesus (431). The same Cyril in the aftermath of the Council delivered one of the great Marian sermons of all time. Therein he pointed to a role which Mary fulfills in regard to men, which was expressed by use of the Pauline word *Mesites* (Mediator) in its feminine form. Cyril's approach was to use the phrase "Through you" with reference to one benefit after another which man receives from God. *Mesites* appears in fourth century eastern writings and occurs regularly thereafter, appearing some centuries later in the west. The doctrine was to persist in the east after the eleventh-century break with Rome; it is more powerfully expressed by the fourteenth-century Theophanes of Nicaea (d. 1381) than any other writer in christian history.

Linked with this role is the growth of prayer to Mary and the emergence of liturgical feasts. Archaeological research will probably show very early petitions addressed to Mary. The firm evidence presently is in the Papyrus 470, in the John Rylands Library in Manchester, England, which gives a Greek verson of the popular prayer, "We fly to thy patronage"; it is probably from the third, not later than from the fourth century. The prayer was brought from the east to the west, as were the great Marian feasts.

The Privileges

From early times interest centered on the last moments of Mary's life; such thinking would be dictated by the mentality formed by meditation on the death and resurrection of Christ, drawn too by the example of the martyrs. Apocryphal narratives about the death and Assump-

tion of Mary were known to exist but dating was uncertain; theologians generally disregarded these documents. Important manuscript finds in recent years have changed things considerably. There is now the possibility of a third, even second century date. Noteworthy is the fact that the earliest affirm clearly the bodily Assumption.

Theologians and church authority prefer still to deal with past theologians. Until recently they were apparently restricted to a trio of eastern giants, Germanus of Constantinople, Andrew of Crete and John of Damascus, all of the eighth century. In 1955 the French Byzantine scholar, A. Wenger, A.A., published a sixth-century homily by Theoteknos of Livias, in which the Assumption is explicitly taught.

The doctrine was accepted in the east, chiefly through the influence of John of Damascus. Things moved more slowly in the west, largely through the effect of a homily improperly attributed to Jerome, which gained currency from the ninth century. It opposed the bodily Assumption. It was countered by another spurious text issued over the name of Augustine.

The feast of the Assumption was celebrated in the west but it was not the bodily Assumption. Pseudo-Augustine gradually eclipsed Pseudo-Jerome as an authority. From the tenth century eastern homilies were in circulation in the west and helped establish the idea more fully. By late medieval times belief in Mary's bodily Assumption was practically universal. It affected liturgical and popular devotion, was expressed in homiletics, hymnography and iconography. Yet the dogmatic definition did not come until the twentieth century. After the dogma of the Immaculate Conception in 1854, a movement of opinion within the church in favor of the other dogma appeared and in the twentieth century gathered force.

Pius XII (d. 1958), a Marian Pope in his teaching and official acts of piety—he consecrated the world to the Immaculate Heart of Mary in 1942—followed the example of Pius IX, the Pope of the Immaculate Conception. He consulted the church's hierarchy and set up an advisory commission of theologians. All converged on the possibility and, with minimal disagreement, on the opportuneness of a papal dogma. There was a last-minute reservation by a great Orientalist and Marian theologian, Martin Jugie, A.A. (d. 1954); he advised the pope that he could not define dogmatically that Our Lady had died. Accordingly the formula read: "We pronounce, declare, and define that the dogma was revealed by God, that the Immaculate Mother of God, the ever Virgin Mary, after completing the course of her life on earth, was assumed to the glory of heaven both in body and soul."

Though the dogma of the Immaculate Conception came earlier, the way to it was much more rocky. From the earliest times her immunity from all sin was seen as a necessary consequence. Did this mean from the very first moment of her existence? Again, certain of the eastern Fathers and sacred orators thought so, but in the west one great Latin Doctor after another demurred or openly disagreed. Augustine (d. 430) left a saying which seems to have embarrassed him as much as it has puzzled his commentators. Ambrose (d. 397) was against the idea, as were Anselm (d. 1109), Bernard, (d. 1153) Bonaventure (d.1274)—with some hesitancy—and Thomas Aquinas (d. 1274).

Whatever Augustine really thought, he expressed a theory on the mode of transmission of original sin, through concupiscence, which for centuries blocked development of doctrine. In addition, a major objection halted many: how could Mary be redeemed by Christ,

the sole author of salvation, if she were conceived immaculate? Eadmer (d. 1141), friend and biographer of Anselm, saw a way out. But it was Duns Scotus who breached the opposition wall: Mary could be redeemed by preservation, still due to Christ, as all others are by liberation.

An astonishing polarization of theological opinion was to take place in the following centuries between the Dominicans—in control of the Roman Holy Office—and the Franciscans. Strange repressive measures were used. In the seventeenth century when the debate was at the point of frenzy, Ippolyto Marracci (d. 1675), a defender of the dogma and the most prolific writer on Our Lady, was practically under "house-arrest"— and he never wrote better!

He had plenty of support. Writings proliferated: between 1600 and 1800 the Jesuits alone brought out 300 works in defense of the doctrine. The kings of Spain sent delegations to Rome to request a definition; one of them was led by an Irishman, the Franciscan Luke Wadding (d. 1657). The Popes, trying to keep the warring theologians apart, moved step by step towards a dogmatic solution. The temperature fell during the religious apathy of the eighteenth century. Devotion, an expression of the *sensus fidelium* (sentiment of the faithful), had an effect. It was never mentioned in official church documents but the Miraculous Medal (1830), widely distributed, was a factor in this devotion.

The Pope who made the decision took the proper steps: world-wide consultation of the hierarchy, advice from theologians. Of the 603 bishops consulted, 543 favored definition; theologians worked on eight successive draft texts. The final one was issued solemnly by Pius IX (d. 1878) on 8 December, 1854. The essential words were: "We declare, pronounce, and define that the doctrine which holds that the most Blessed Virgin Mary, in the first instant of her Conception, by a singular grace and privilege granted by Almighty God, in view of the merits of Jesus Christ, the Savior of the human race, was preserved free from all stain of original sin, is a doctrine revealed by God and therefore to be believed firmly and constantly by all the faithful."

The other privilege of Our Lady, her virginity before, during and after childbirth, was theologically expanded and accepted as early as the fourth century: her virginal conception had been taught in the gospels.

Great Ages of Marian Theology

An immense concentration of scholarship over the last sixty years, prompted by a charismatic figure, who was not a professional theologian, Desiré Cardinal Mercier (d. 1926), proponent of a dogma on Mary's universal mediation of grace, has given us certainty on themes of Marian interest as ancient and continuous. But there has been ebb and flow.

The fourth century, east and west, was an age of giants in the field, in Greek, Syriac and Latin. The eighth century, a peak in Byzantine civilization, has been mentioned; the impulse had not faded by the fourteenth century, which saw remarkable enrichment with, to offset theology, the most beautiful of all liturgies in honor of Mary, *Theotokos*.

The fine flowering of the high Middle Ages in the west, the twelfth and thirteenth centuries, was marked by amazing intellectual, liturgical, artistic and devotional products under the sign of the Blessed Virgin Mary. It was the age of supreme Gothic which in cathedrals honored her directly: Chartres represents a whole assembly of miracles in stone.

In theology more and more attention was given to Mary's role in salvation. In the Benedictine and Cistercian monasteries and in the Franciscan schools interest grew in such speculation: St.

Thomas had cleared the way by fixing in a rigorously argued synthesis the inherited themes: the imprint of scholasticism.

Both theory and practice waned in the fifteenth century, and ill-informed doctrine with piety nourished in places by superstition and spurious extravagant practices led to the radical reaction of the Reformers. The remedy was forthcoming in the works of the Doctors of the Counter-Reformation, Peter Canisius (d. 1597), Robert Bellarmine (d. 1619) and Francis de Sales (d. 1622). Canisius labored for years on a massive tome; Francis and Bellarmine used mostly the homiletic method.

Within a short time we are in a great age, the seventeenth century, especially in Spain and France. Now indeed Mary was seen as the associate of the Redeemer, as the universal Mediatress not only in the inspiring spiritual works of Louis Marie Grignon de Montfort (d. 1716), but in theological treatises from the pen of a singularly learned, hard-headed Spanish Jesuit, Quirino de Salazar (d. 1646). The theme of Mary as Co-redemptress would come to the fore again in the next great age of Marian theology, one coinciding broadly with the pontificate of Pius XII. This was an age of Marian movements or associations of many different kinds: apostolic like the Militia of Mary Immaculate, or the Legion of Mary, popular as seen in the expanding pilgrimages to the old and new shrines, theological in so many societies for scientific study, national and international. Congresses of different kinds increased in number, the most remarkable the joint Mariological and Marian congresses organized by the International (soon the Pontifical) Marian Academy.

The initiative of Mercier seemed about to attain its end. But instead of defining Mary's universal mediation, a question put by Pius XI to three different commissions, Roman, Spanish and Belgian, Pius

XII turned his attention to the Assumption. He seemed to disregard an immense literature, in which every aspect of Mary's cooperation with Christ, every possible argument, scriptural, patristic, historical was painstakingly examined.

A distinction was expounded between the objective redemption, that is, the essential saving work of Christ accomplished on Calvary and its sequel the Resurrection, and the subjective redemption, the application of the fruits of Christ's work completed once for all, to individual souls. Was the sufficiency of Christ's achievement and its essential unicity compromised by the title "Co-redemptress"?

Since co-redemption is comprised within the larger concept of mediation, the obvious difficulty arising out of Paul's text had to be faced: "For there is one God, and there is one mediator between God and men, the man Christ Jesus, who gave himself as a ransom for all, the testimony to which was borne at the proper time" (1 Tm 2:5-6). This text has been explained from its context, and from the fact that Paul himself elsewhere uses the term mediator of Moses. Vatican II which was, under the pressure to be presently considered, circumspect in its use of the word about Mary, had no hesitation in saying that priests of the new law "shared the unique office of Christ the Mediator" (L.G. 28).

Vatican II, Ecumenism, Apparitions

In the pre-conciliar worldwide consultation of the episcopate, 570 future Council Fathers requested a statement on Our Lady; 382 wanted a pronouncement on Mary's mediation, the largest group agreeing on one specific item in the entire agenda which was proposed. Instead of the smooth culmination of the movement growing in the pontificate of Pius XII, what took place was contentious debate, confrontation, *apparent* minimal-ist assertion, disappointment. There was a *feeling* reflected in Catholic opinion polls that the recession in Marian devotion, which was regretted, was caused and therefore willed by the Council: "apparent" and "feeling" are given emphasis to indicate the need for serious reflection.

This reflection will note that in chapter VIII of the Constitution on the Church there is an admirable summary of Marian theology and in ten other documents suggestive passages or mentions. The principal Marian text was newly drafted during the conciliar sessions; a preparatory draft had been rejected, or dropped after a capital moment in conciliar history, 29 October, 1963. By a majority of less than two percent of the voters, the assembly had ended a phase of tension and rivalry: it was decided to take the Marian text as part of the Constitution on the Church, not as a separate conciliar document.

It was made clear *within* the assembly that there was no question of lessening Marian doctrine or devotion. *Outside* the Council the impression was of division, fifty-fifty, about the Mother of God; some journalists worked to deepen this impression. Later when the new text came up for discussion the feeling was again of disunity, as speeches against this or that idea were reported. Bishops fighting about Our Lady!

There was ecumenical concern, urged upon the Council by John XXIII, recalled continuously by the presence of the Observers from the other communions. At issue were the titles Mediatress and Mother of the Church. The latter is implicit in the phrasing of article 53. The former was admitted but only along with other titles "Advocate, Helper, Aid-giver" which were meant to attenuate its meaning, but in fact imply it; a further reduction of the title was in the phrase "The Blessed Virgin is invoked in the Church" under these titles (L.G. 62). A scholarly submission to the drafting committee on the importance of the idea of mediation in the eastern tradition drew the uninformed reply that the easterns do not build a system on the idea—the author had apparently never heard of Theophanes of Nicaea! At the ceremony of promulgation, 21 November, 1964, Paul VI proclaimed Mary Mother of the Church, as Pius XII had proclaimed her universal Queen in the encyclical *Ad caeli Reginam,* 11 October, 1954.

The theme of Mary and ecumenism has been frequently discussed and explored since the Council. People have learned things they should have known: that the Orthodox have doctrinal and devotional traditions about the *Theotokos,* beautiful liturgies and a theologically inspired iconography, which they do not think negotiable; that the "founding fathers" of Protestantism were not as extreme as some of their followers have become; that among Protestants attitudes are changing and that in many areas, especially in biblical studies, representatives of the different communions can meet and conduct dialogue. The Ecumenical Society of the Blessed Virgin Mary founded in 1967 goes from strength to strength.

What of popular piety? It suffered a setback immediately after the Council, then recovered on its own. One sign of the revival is the constant increase in the numbers of pilgrims to the great shrines of Mary; 25 million some years ago to Aparecida, Guadalupe, Lourdes, Fatima and Czestochowa. Another is the attention given the numerous alleged Marian apparitions reported from so many places. The way local church authority has dealt with these phenomena, with those directly involved, is not uniformly edifying. To ignore them is the policy of the ostrich.

M. O'Carroll, CSSp *Theotokos,* 5th printing, Encyclopedia, bibliographies to each article, Wilmington, 1985. R. Laurentin, *La Vierge au Concile,* Paris. 1965; M.J. Nicolas, OP *Theotokos, Le Mystere de Marie.* Tournai, 1965. R. Brown,, *The Birth of the Messiah,* New York, 1977. John Paul II, *Mother of the Redeemer,* 1987.

MICHAEL O'CARROLL, CSSp

MEDIATOR

A term used in 1 Tim 2:5 to refer to Jesus Christ, "the one mediator between God and man," that is, the one in whom the full union between God and man is achieved in himself and, through his redemptive work, between God and the sinful human race.

See **Redemption**

MEDIATRIX

A term applied to the Blessed Virgin Mary to indicate her role in the distribution of graces to the human race. No dogmatic definition of the church applies this title to Mary, and those who favor its use insist on its subordinate and secondary role as compared to the unique mediatorial role of Christ.

See **Mary**

MEMORIAL

A sense of remembering pervades the church's worship. From one point of view the entire liturgy is a memorial, its celebration focused on the saving work of Christ in order to bring us back to that person and life from which we derive our christian identity. The scriptures, integral to all liturgy, recall God and God's deeds to the church's mind; the psalms, at the heart of the liturgy of the Hours, draw on a similar memory. The sacraments too have an essential dimension of memorial, as does the liturgical year in its celebration of the mysteries of Christ and its commemoration of the faithful departed.

However, here we shall concentrate on the eucharist, principally because the Church understands it as its memorial *par excellence,* celebrated in obedience to Jesus' command: "Do this as my memorial."

The Biblical Memorial

Since the 1950's scholars have been investigating more deeply the meaning of memory for the Jews, and, though there is still argument regarding interpretation and application, the extent of the terminology and the importance of the reality to which it refers have been established. The OT contains a rich usage of memory words in a religious context: both God and Israel remember and are reminded, and the range of people, events, things, qualities, etc., called to memory is great. The use of this vocabulary is of interest to us in connection with cult and, in particular, the Passover.

God's remembering in the cultic memorial implies action, knowing and being concerned for the people and turning towards them with help. Of this remembering, writers use such words as "efficacious," "creative," and "actualizing." Human remembering too is to lead to involvement and action. In the case of the Passover, scholars tend to conclude that in this memorial God acts in a salvific way to somehow join past event and present situation so that the saving deed is made actual or effective for participants today. For their part, those who celebrate the memorial are to commit themselves to what God has done and is doing. Authors differ in the ways they interpret this "efficacity' or this "actualization," but they find in the Passover a force and an effect that are not simply the power of human remembering, however strong, but can derive only from God. Thus it emerges as the common view that the biblical memorial has greater depth and density than recent use (christian and

more general) would suggest.

It is predominantly this OT tradition that forms the background to the Lukan and Pauline command of Christ: "Do this as my *anamnesis.*" In the interpretation of "*anamnesis*" all the virtualities of the Jewish memorial should be retained: God's remembering and reminding, human remembering and reminding, with all that is implied on both sides. The word "my" is taken in the objective sense ("as a memorial of me"), but, while this is retained, perhaps the subjective overtones should not be suppressed completely.

Historical Interpretations

"Do This": The Shape of the Eucharistic Memorial. The church gave its shape to the eucharist by adapting the actions and words of Jesus at the Last Supper, when he took the bread and the cup, said a blessing or gave thanks, broke the bread, and gave the bread and the cup to his disciples, with the words: "Take, eat: This is my body. Take, drink: This is the cup of my blood. Do this as my memorial." Thus the structure and the essential acts are themselves a memorial of Christ. To this the church joined a service of the word, with all the memorial elements that this was intended to bring. Within the eucharistic prayer—developed from Jesus' act of thanksgiving—the church recalled in thanksgiving and praise God's saving deeds in Christ and prayed that this salvation would be realized for it in the present and the future.

Memorial and Sacrifice. The sense of the eucharist as memorial continued to be important in the christian tradition—it could not have been otherwise, given the scriptural command of Christ—but the interpretation of memorial did not remain constant. It was weakened as the experience of the Jewish cult generally and of the Passover receded, but from the third century and before, a strong sense of sacrifice was developed. While this tended to displace the notion of memorial from the central position that it had been holding, at the same time it was able to maintain within the eucharist some of the aspects that memorial was in danger of losing. Thus the Godward movement of the Jewish memorial (God's being reminded) was now expressed by the church's offering of the sacrifice. Similarly, the moral demand, the commitment that the memorial required of the participants, would now be developed more particularly with reference to the sacrifice.

This close association of memorial and sacrifice came to be expressed strikingly in the eucharistic prayer (in the section technically called the *anamnesis*) in many parts of East and West. Two examples must suffice. The early third-century eucharistic prayer of Hippolytus has: "Remembering, therefore, his death and resurrection, we offer you the bread and cup." The primitive, fourth-century, version of the Roman Canon states "Remembering, then, his most glorious passion and resurrection from the underworld and ascension into heaven, we offer you this unspotted victim, spiritual victim, unbloody victim, this holy bread and the chalice of eternal life." It was as though in these places it was thought necessary or desirable to interpret the meaning of the memorial, to draw out what it involves for the church: this memorial implies an offering.

Perhaps St. John Chrysostom was thinking of texts like these when he formed his answer to the question: if we offer sacrifice every day, how is it that our sacrifice is one and not many? "We do offer sacrifice [every day] but in making memorial (*anamnesis*) of his death..." Our act takes place as a memorial of the act that took place then, for he says: "Do this as my memorial." We do not offer a different sacrifice, as the high priest did in the past, but we always offer the same one. Or rather, we celebrate a memorial of a sacrifice"(*Hom.*

in Heb. 17,3). This expresses the view that will long be commonly held in East and West: the eucharist is a memorial sacrifice, the memorial of Christ's sacrifice.

Thus both liturgical and theological traditions bear witness to the close link that was perceived between memorial and sacrifice. Medieval theologians in the West continued to relate these, though they were not of one mind as to the precise connection between them. An allegorical approach (see below) was found to be inadequate, and it was principally by concentrating on the aspect of sacrifice and on the relationship between the Mass and the sacrifice of Christ that theology advanced. The theme of memorial was retained—the eucharist is a memorial sacrifice—but now it was rather the sacrifical theme that grounded the efficacy and the objective character of the Mass.

Allegory. In speaking of the eucharist as a memorial, the mainline tradition understood that it was a rite in which Christ's saving mystery was represented and made effective in the present. But, first in the East and later, particularly with Amalar of Metz (d. 850) in the West, an allegorical approach to the memorial emerged. This found in the different rites of the Mass reminders of events in the economy of salvation and especially the passion, death and resurrection of Christ. No single system of allegorical interpretation was devised: variety abounded. But overall the Mass could be seen as a dramatic enactment through its various ceremonies of the events of our redemption, and it was in this figurative way that Christ's command—often invoked—to do this in his memory was thought to be fulfilled. This rememorative aspect was frequently accompanied by a moral concern to involve the people through the offering of themselves and their lives. Though opposed right from the time of

Amalar, the allegorical approach had a pervasive and enduring influence, and, in the scholastics and even for centuries later, it continued alongside the older tradition. In comparison with the sacramental understanding it is arbitrary, extrinsic and eclectic. However, it served to keep vividly alive the sense of the eucharist as memorial of Christ's saving mysteries and it reminded participants of the demands that the eucharist made of them.

The Sixteenth Century. At the Reformation the question of the sacrificial character of the eucharist was in dispute, so that the parties were deprived of that element that had strengthened the idea of memorial current before. The potentialities of the biblical memorial had long been lost, and the word was not regarded as having the capacity to reconcile the conflicting positions. The Council of Trent (Session XXII) taught that the sacrifice of the Mass was a propitiatory sacrifice and not a mere commemoration of the sacrifice consummated on the cross (canon 3) and also that by the words: "Do this as my memorial," Christ instituted the apostles as priests and ordained them so that they and other priests should offer his body and blood (canon 2). While these declarations link memorial and sacrifice, they show the latter as the dominant and determining element.

Recent Influences

For the Roman Catholic tradition, the convergence of liturgical, theological, scriptural and ecumenical influences can be discerned in the rediscovery of the virtualities of the Jewish and christian memorial and in the reemergence of the word in a central place in contemporary theological terminology.

The mystery theology of Odo Casel, and the fruitful controversy that it stimulated, focused attention on the nature and meaning of the liturgical mystery and the sense in which it makes present now Christ's saving activity of the past. This was accompanied by some investigation of the tradition of the liturgical memorial, which also confirmed that there were forgotten areas there to be explored.

Theologians too found that in their discussion of the relationship between the Mass and Christ's sacrifice the idea of sacrament was offering new possibilities. Discarding the excessively sharp textbook distinction of sacrifice and sacrament and the reservation of the latter term to the eucharistic species, authors understood the eucharist as the sacrament of Christ's sacrifice, and so as a sacramental sacrifice. This, they maintained, was the doctrine of St. Thomas and the authentic faith of the Catholic tradition. The "sacrament" of the dogmatic theologians and the "memorial" of the liturgical scholars thus found themselves converging.

The scriptural impact was made later, through the study of the biblical sense of memorial, particularly with reference to the Passover, and through the attempts to reconsider the eucharist in the light of the biblical discoveries. Aspects of this have been seen above and it will arise again later.

It is unnecessary to dwell on the ecumenical element here and the growing *rapprochement* among scholars from different traditions in the areas just mentioned. The significance of this for inter-church dialogue on the eucharist will be treated below.

Though interest in memorial emerged particularly because of questions in liturgy or sacramental theology, more recently this has been linked to the broader consideration of the role of memory in human affairs generally. Memory, remembering, and making memorial are recognized as essential in establishing a sense of identity for groups and for individuals. Through these we maintain a sense of continuity that helps us to grasp our present and move purposefully into the future. Solidarity in the present and with the past is strengthened through the various exercises of memory, as is the demand for fidelity in present and future to what we perceive to be our true personal or collective selfhood. Story telling is important here, and the significance of memory in the formation of history and in questions of hermeneutics and understanding is also relevant. The tendency to develop and to extend *"anamnesis"* as a technical term suggests interesting possibilities for this and other areas of theology.

Celebrating the Memorial of Christ

The liturgical memorial is a commemorative ritual act celebrating an event of salvation with the aim of making those celebrating it participants in the event of salvation itself. The memorial is not adequately understood as the subjective presence of a person or an event in the consciousness of the participants through the human act of remembering. Nor is it enough to appeal to the more objective power of a human rite. The power of this memorial is ultimately God's and its purpose is to make the participant's and God's saving works objectively and effectively present the one to the other. Thus—to keep to the language of memory—in this memorial God and the church, inseparably, remember the work of salvation and remind each other of it.

This recognition of the divine and the human sides is expressed in the interplay of *anamnesis* and *epiclesis*. In the eucharistic prayer the church proclaims in joyful thanksgiving and praise what God has done for the world and for God's people, and specifically in every eucharist it recalls Christ's deeds and words at the Last Supper and the paschal mystery of his death and resurrection. This memorial of God's deeds and promises engenders

confidence for the present and the future. The God made known through saving action in the past is the God who gathers the church for each celebration of the eucharist. But the church must not develop an attitude that would take God's intervention for granted. If the history just recalled is to become salvific for us, if the great redemptive deeds are to touch us in the present, if our memorial is not to rely on human power alone, God must act, and so the prayer turns to petition. The church is aware that all is God's gift: the gift of the past is acknowledged with grateful praise, the gift for the present and the future is sought with confident and humble petition. And so the *epiclesis* prays that the Father may send the Holy Spirit, and this or an equivalent petition is made in *each* celebration of the eucharist, for *this* community gathered *here today*.

God Remembers. Although the liturgy does not generally use the language of God's "remembering" in the immediate context of the *epiclesis*, the collocation of this prayer with our rehearsal of past saving events suggests that the same reality is at issue: God is reminded of this salvation and is asked to make it actual for us here and now. By the power of God our commemorative ritual imitation of the Last Supper transcends all its natural and human potential.

The western theological tradition from the Middle Ages expressed this objectivity by its teaching that at the heart of the eucharist the priest acted *in persona christi* or, to state the relationship in another way, that Christ was acting there *in persona ministri*. More recently Catholic theologians and liturgists, learning from the East and reverting to older elements in their own tradition, have given this a broader—trinitarian—expression.

The liturgical texts, following the classical pattern, ask the Father to send the Holy Spirit, and this prayer is made through Christ our Lord. The sacramental action has its source in the Father. At its center is the incarnate Son, Jesus Christ, the great highpriest ever living to intercede for us, the head who unites the church to himself as his body, the principal minister, through his church, of the entire eucharistic act. The Holy Spirit, the first gift to us from Christ's paschal mystery, realizes in the church the mystery first realized in the humanity of Jesus and consummated in his death and resurrection. The Spirit is the living power that gives life to the historical words of Jesus to make them active and effective in the present; the Spirit transforms the bread and wine into the living and life-giving body and blood of Christ for us (i.e., for our salvation) and transforms us too as we receive them, to make of us body, one spirit in Christ, filled with every grace and blessing.

The Church Remembers. If God remembers, it is *for us,* and this means that there must be a human reality and activity to respond to this divine initiative. The core of this memorial is located in the words and deeds of the ritual, but inseparable from this are the hearts and minds and lives of the participants.

The memorial celebrates the mystery of the death and resurrection of Jesus Christ, but this as the center of the whole economy of salvation. This is the evidence of many eastern anaphoras and of the Roman Eucharistic Prayer IV. In the present the christian people appropriates its past, a past that stretches back beyond Christ to those who prepared the way for him and beyond those again to the dawn of humanity and to the creation of the world: a past too that reaches from the incarnate life of Christ through the generations of those who have believed in him to this present gathering of the church. In this way the christian people is brought into touch with deep layers of its

own nature, so that it may understand what it is in the present and the movement of which it is part and which is part of it, with all that this implies for the future. Thus the eucharistic prayer embraces humankind as a whole with whom God again and again made covenant; it mentions Abel the just, Abraham our father in faith, and God's priest Melchisedech; it uses the history and the writings of Jesus' own people; it rejoices in the memory of the christian saints; it recalls in petition the faithful departed and all who have died in God's friendship—and all of these lines meet in the mystery of Christ. The memorial evokes a sense of solidarity with past generations and it reminds us of dimensions of the church sometimes undervalued.

The divine economy is not so transcendent or the church of all the ages so abstract that the concrete human collaboration can be forgotten, that collaboration which is made possible by God and which must be forthcoming if God's will is actually to have effect. This refers to the human involvement of Jesus in the first place, which must be taken with full seriousness to respect the realism with which he undertook the human condition and its history. It refers also in the light of Jesus to the imperfect though real work of those who went before him, faithful in their way to the covenants or to the lights that were theirs, and of those since him who through their lives have given the church its present existence under the Spirit of God.

Thus the memorial of the eucharist gathers together what God has done in the hard reality of human fidelity in order that the christian people may celebrate it as a gift. There the church of the present can appropriate the hidden depths of its own being, and it does so in a prayer and an action of thanksgiving (eucharist) that acknowledges God as its source. In the eucharistic action and most concretely in the body and blood of Christ the church recognizes and celebrates the gift that both symbolizes itself and gives it life.

This memorial commits the christian people in their turn to their own task in solidarity with their past and with their fellow humans throughout the world. The memorial concerns a mystery that transcends time and space and the human, but it will not allow those who celebrate it to lose their own particular location in time and space or to disregard the claims of the human. They must make their own the history that it recalls, the identity that it discloses, as their history, their identity; they must appropriate the salvation that it actualizes and dedicate themselves to the works that it implies. This has an important moral dimension, making demands on the way they live their lives, their ideals, their motivation.

Memorial properly understood—as the OT stressed with revelation to the covenant—permits no retreat into a closed world of the past or of ritual.

The Future. It is clear from what has been said that while the memorial recalls the past and is celebrated in the present, it looks also to the future. God's remembering has the effect of moving history forward, of advancing the work of salvation, still incomplete in the world, towards its final accomplishment in the parousia. Human remembering of the past can be creative for present and future, renewing and releasing energies for what lies ahead and stimulating hope for a future that Christians believe to be announced and indeed in some sense present in the Lord's resurrection. This future, as still to be realized and as already present, is celebrated in the church's memorial. Some implications of this have already been noted. The more recent Roman eucharistic prayers include this dimension explicitly: "Father, we now celebrate this memorial of our redemption. We recall Christ's death, his descent among the

dead, his resurrection, and his ascension to your right hand; and, looking forward to his coming in glory, we offer you. . ." To celebrate the memorial requires action in the present and commitment to the future.

Ecumenical Possibilities

The rediscovery of the biblical memorial has proved of great ecumenical import for the opportunities it offers to interpret afresh this earliest and most traditional of words in the eucharistic vocabulary of all the churches. Frequent reference is made to memorial in contemporary dialogue on the disputed question of the relationship between Christ's sacrifice and the eucharist and the issue of the sacrificial character of the eucharist. The Anglican/Roman Catholic International Commission in its *Eucharistic Doctrine: Statement* (1971) and *Elucidation* (1979), the Roman Catholic/Evangelical Lutheran Commission in its Document on the Eucharist (1979), the Faith and Order Commission of the World Council of Churches in its Lima text (1982)—to name just three important consultations—all appeal to the biblical idea of memorial and apply it to the eucharist in their efforts to transcend the older controversy, avoiding the extremes of empty symbolism and exaggerated realism, and reach convergence or agreement.

See **Epiclesis, Eucharist, Sacrifice, Trinity**

Shawn Madigan, "A Future of Liturgical Memory: Christian, American, Familial," *Worship* (July 1986) 60: 369-83. Patrick J. Foley, "Remembering, Imagining and Anticipation in the Judaeo-Christian Tradition," *Studies in Formative Spirituality* (Feb 1985) 6: 39-51 John Navone, "Love: Remembering to Share our Story of God," *Studies in Formative Spirituality* (Feb 1985) 6: 73-86. David Stanley, "Do This in Memory of Me (1 Cor 11:24, 25)," *Studies in Formative Spirituality* (Feb 1985) 6: 103-15. Louis Bouyer, *Eucharist* (Notre Dame, Ind: University of Notre Dame Press, 1968), pp. 50-135.

PATRICK MCGOLDRICK

MERCY

Mercy is the quality of care for another, willingness to make an effort, even at great sacrifice, to ease another's pain, readiness to forgive, eagerness to help. The English word "mercy" is weaker than the biblical concept. The words which convey the concept must be considered in the context of OT and NT to understand fully their power.

There are three Hebrew roots which are frequently translated "mercy." The first of these, *ḥesed*, carries a broad range of meaning. It refers to the kind of love which is mutual and dependable. This mercy is found between husband and wife, e.g., Abraham and Sarah (Gen 20:13), Orpah and Mahlon, Ruth and Chilion (Ruth 1:18); it exists as the bond in a deep friendship, e.g., between David and Jonathan (1 Sam 20:8, 14-15). It both initiates and characterizes the covenant bond: between Yahweh and the people (Exod 20:6; Deut 7:9, 12); between Yahweh and David (2 Sam 7:15; Ps 89). Thus it becomes a way of defining the covenant God (Exod 34:6-7) and the covenant people (Mic 6:8). This *ḥesed* always implies action, both on God's part (Gen 2:12, 14; 2 Sam 22:51) and the part of humans (Josh 2:12, 14; 2 Sam 2:5). It is mutual and it is enduring (Ps 136; Hos 2:20-22; Isa 54:8).

The second Hebrew word, *rāhamîm* (with the verb *rā ḥam*), is related to the word for "womb" (*reḥem*). It designates "womb-love," the love of mother (and father) for a child (1 Kgs 3:26; cf. Hos 2:6), the love of brothers and sisters who have shared the same womb for each other (cf. Amos 1:11). It implies a physical response; the compassion for another is felt in the center of one's body. This mercy also results in action. It is a word frequently predicated of Yahweh who has mother-love (Isa 49:15; Jer 31:20) or father-love (Ps 103:13; Isa 63:15-16) for Israel. The "womb-love" of Yahweh leads to forgiveness for the wayward children.

The third important Hebrew word which is translated "mercy" is *ḥēn/ḥānan* with its derivatives. This word originally has an aesthetic sense and means "grace" or "favor." It is a free gift; no mutuality is implied or expected. The quality is not necessarily lasting; it is dependent solely on the good will of the giver. It often occurs between unequals: Joseph finds favor in the sight of Potiphar (Gen 39:4), and David in the sight of Saul (1 Sam 16:22). It is sought from and granted by Yahweh: Noah finds favor with God (Gen 6:8). Moses and David seek God's favor (Exod 33:12-17; 34:9; 2 Sam 12:22; 15:25). The psalmist frequently pleads for God's favor (Pss 4:2; 6:3; 9:14; 51:3). God's favor is granted even to foreign nations (Jonah 4:2). The favor of God is a common component in blessings (Num 6:25; Ps 62:2).

These three roots, along with a few other words, describe an essential truth of OT theology. The God who is covenanted to Israel is defined as merciful: "The Lord, the Lord, a merciful (*raḥûm*) and gracious (*ḥannûn*) God, slow to anger and rich in kindness (*ḥesed*) and fidelity" (Exod 34:6; cf. Pss 103:8; 145:8; Joel 2:13; Jonah 4:2). The worshipper can continue to repeat the psalm refrain: "His mercy (*ḥesed*) endures forever" (Pss 100: 106; 107; 118; 136). The mercy of God, however, even while it is a gracious gift, implies mutuality. Israel is commanded to exercise mercy in response (Mic 6:8). The failure to do so will bring judgment (Hos 4:1; 6:4-6). Even in the midst of punishment Israel can hope for the faithful mercy of God to forgive, but this hope must always respect the inviolable freedom of God: "*Perhaps* he will have mercy" (Amos 5:15, cf. Exod 33:19; Tob 13:6). Thus the pervasive quality which characterizes both parties in the covenant is that of mercy, active and mutual, enduring yet free.

The NT builds on the concept of mercy developed in the OT. NT Greek also has three basic word groups which, however, do not correspond exactly to the three in the OT. The most frequent term for mercy in the NT is *eleos* with its related words. It is most closely related to *ḥeśed* in the OT. Luke uses the word five times in the canticles of the infancy narrative in phrases which are clearly dependent upon the OT (1:50, 54, 58, 72, 78). Matthew also uses the term in a citation from Hosea: "I will have mercy and not sacrifice" (Mt 9:13; 12:7; cf. Hos 6:6). The verb occurs frequently in the pleas of the sick to Jesus for healing (Mt 9:27; 15:22; 17:15; 20:30, 31; Mk 10:47, 48; Luke 17:13; 18:38, 39). The quality of mutuality, found in the OT concept, is also characteristic of the NT description. The mutuality is dependent initially on God's mercy. The wicked servant who benefited from mercy is judged for not showing it in return (Mt 18:33). Those who do show mercy are assured of receiving mercy in return (Mt 5:7). God's mercy demonstrates his fidelity to the covenant (cf. the Lukan canticles) but also his freedom. Mercy is offered even to the Gentiles (cf Rom 9:15-18; 11:30-32; 1 Pet 2:10). God's mercy is always embodied in action. The ultimate expression of this mercy is the salvation offered in Jesus (Rom 15:9; Eph 2:4-5; Tit 3:5; 1 Pet 1:3). One significant derivative of *eleos*, *eleēmosynē*, which originally meant simply "mercy," comes to denote specifically "almsgiving," a characteristic both of the Jewish and Christian believer (Mt 6:1-4; Lk 11:41; 12:33).

The second NT term, which is much less frequent, is *oiktirmos* with its related words. It refers primarily to sympathy and grief. Its basic OT referent is *rāḥam/rāḥamîm*. The connection to parental love and to bodily response is maintained. God is named the father of mercies (2 Cor 1:3). Through the mercy of God believers are urged to offer their own bodies as a living sacrifice to God (Rom 12:1). Twice the term is used with *splanchna*, which implies physicality (see below), to designate the mercy expected from the Christian (Phil 2:1; Col 3:12). This mercy is demanded from the Christian as an expression of mutuality, in response to the mercy of God. Luke interprets the OT command, "Be holy as I am holy" (Lev 19:2) as "Be merciful as your Father also is merciful" (Lk 6:36).

The third NT term carries the major weight of the physical feeling of mercy. The word *splanchna* with its derivatives connotes originally inner organs, especially heart, liver, kidneys (cf. Acts 1:18). From this origin it comes to mean the organs for sacrifice and thus the sacrifice itself. In a parallel development it also comes to mean the emotions which the ancients considered to be seated in the lower organs. This word also, therefore, is associated with Hebrew *rāḥam/rāḥamîm*. In the Synoptic gospels the verb is applied only to Jesus or to the main characters in his parables. Jesus feels compassion for the crowd hungry for bread (Mk 6:34 par.; 8:2 par.), the world hungry for the good news (Mt 9:36), the sick (Mk 1:41; 9:22; Mt 20:34), the grieving (Lk 7:13). In the parables this quality is exercised by the master who forgives the wicked servant his debt (Mt 18:27), by the father of the prodigal (Lk 15:20), and by the good Samaritan on his way to Jericho (Lk 10:33). The noun is used to describe the love between Christians in the rest of the NT. Philemon is strongly urged by Paul not only to forgive his runaway slave but to love him as a brother, even as Paul's own heart (Phlm 12, 20). Thus Paul loves the Philippians (Phil 1:8; cf. Titus in 2 Cor 7:15), and requests the same love from the Corinthians (2 Cor 6:12-13). This love results in action (1 Jn 3:17), and is possible only in imitation of the love of

Christ (Phil 2:1).

Thus the biblical concept of mercy is applied first of all to God and to Jesus, the incarnation of God's mercy. God's mercy is active and lasting, free and greater than any human expectation. The believer, made in the image of God, is required in turn to exercise mercy. Just as the relationship between God and the believer is characterized by mercy, so too the relationship between believers should manifest this same mercy. The mercy demanded of the believer must also result in action; the believer too must give flesh to the virtue. On the active expression of this quality the Christian will be judged (Mt 25:31-46). The mercy of the believer must be enduring and generous beyond ordinary expectation. This virtue is possible only through the power of God and in imitation of God, especially the manifestation of God in Christ.

The biblical notion of mercy continues to be developed in the early church. Clement exhorts the Corinthians to beg for God's mercy and kindness which he longs to give them (1 Clem 9.1; 23.1). This mercy is expressed and received most especially in Christ (1 Clem 20.11-12). The action flowing from this mercy is demanded of the Christian (Did 5.6; 15.4); those who have no mercy on the poor are condemned (Did 5.2). Thomas Aquinas includes mercy as a special quality of charity (*Summa Theologia* I, qu. 21, a. 3). Tradition has listed fourteen specific manifestations of mercy, seven corporal works (feed the hungry, give drink to the thirsty, clothe the naked, shelter the stranger, visit the sick, minister to prisoners, bury the dead) and seven spiritual works (convert the sinner, instruct the ignorant, counsel the doubtful, comfort the sorrowful, bear wrongs patiently, forgive injuries, pray for the living and the dead). All further development rests on the biblical foundation: "The mercy of God endures forever. Be merciful, therefore, as your Father is merciful."

See **Grace, Love.**

R. Bultmann, *"eleos, ktl.,"* TDNT 2. 477-84. R. Bultmann, *"oiktirō, ktl.,"* TDNT 5.159-61. D.N. Freedman, Lundbom, J.R.; and Fabry, H. -J. *"hanan,"* TDOT 5.22-36. H. Koester, *"splanchnon, ktl.,"* TDNT 7.548059. Pheme Perkins, *Love Commands in the New Testament,* New York: Paulist, 1982. Katherine Doob Sakenfeld, *Faithfulness in Action: Loyalty in Biblical Perspective,* (a study of *ḥesed*), Overtures to Biblical Theology 16; Philadelphia: Fortress, 1985. H.-J. Zobel, *"ḥesed,"* TDOT 5.44-64.

IRENE NOWELL, OSB

MERIT

In christian theology this term came gradually to refer to a quality of human conduct; namely, its worthiness of divine recompense by way of reward (*meritum* as over against *demeritum*). Intended to express this aspect of biblical teaching about good works, merit was destined to become a source of serious doctrinal disagreement among Western Christians, who gave different answers to the questions: "What value or worth can human achievement or works have before God?"

As for the Bible, the Vulgate uses *meritum,* from which *merit* derives in English, only three times (all in Sirach). Nevertheless the Hebrew and Greek scriptures speak often of divine retribution for human works; e.g.: "Behold, I am coming soon and my retribution (*ho misthos mou*) is with me, to repay each according to her/his works" (Rev 22:12). In the patristic period (especially with Tertullian and Cyprian) merit came to designate works as commending human beings to God; namely as having a seriousness that God both gives and yet judges to be worthy of reward.

But the theological notion of merit had its origin in other sources as well; namely, in a variety of human experiences such as when one person acknowledges either in justice (*meritum de condigno*) or in some other sort of appropriateness (*meritum de congruo*) services rendered by another. Given such referents, merit could easily lead to serious misunderstandings when stretched and applied analogously to the relation holding between human beings and God when the former carry out the latter's bidding. Consequently Augustine stressed that all good comes from God, who in rewarding our merits crowns his own works (Ep 194:5; C.S.E.L. 57:190). Because, however, he expressed the sovereignty of divine grace in a way that seemed to lead logically to double predestination (with some going to heaven and others to hell), the questions understandably arose: "How does one get out of the *massa damnata* all are in because of Original Sin?" Augustine's answer was that God's grace alone accounts for this—grace owed to (i.e., merited by) neither those who escape hell through grace nor those who do not. Then, of course, another question suggested itself: "And why does God give this saving grace to some rather than to all; to these rather than to others?" Augustine answered by pointing with Paul to the unfathomable mystery of God's will. This left many theologians unsatisfied in subsequent centuries, especially since it involved the eternal damnation of infants dying without baptism.

In the Middle Ages other answers were given after Aristotle's notion of nature was introduced into christian anthropology. One of these was: "God gives grace to those sinners who by nature do not raise obstacles to their conversion" (e.g. Thomas Aquinas in *Summa contra Gentiles* III, 159). Another was: "God gives grace to those sinners who do what lies within their natural powers." In Gabriel Biel this developed to the point that historical human beings were said to be able to love God above all else and detest sin above all other evils—both

with purely natural powers. To those who did this, God fittingly gives grace (*meritum de congruo*). Luther and other Reformers protested that this unwarrantedly exalts fallen human nature's ability to merit and minimizes its need of Christ's merit. To right matters, they maintained, one should confess that sinners are justified and saved without merits on their own part and because of Christ alone through grace alone by faith alone. For its part the Council of Trent taught that the grace of justification cannot be merited in the strict sense (*meritum de condigno*: D.S. 1532) and that the same is true of final perseverance, which is a pure grace or gift. Nevertheless for those who persevere to the end and place their hopes in God, eternal life (Heaven) is both a grace and a reward that God, faithful to the divine promises, will grant for good works and merits (D.S. 1545).

The Second Vatican Council spoke of the merits that the saints now in heaven won while on earth—this through the one Mediator, Jesus Christ. It connected those merits with the fact that the saints served God and filled up what was lacking in Christ's sufferings for his body, the church (L.G. 49). It also asserted a positive nexus between works done in the present by human beings with divine grace and God's coming kingdom (G.S. 39).

In the United States the Lutheran-Roman Catholic Dialogue has acknowledged unresolved differences about merit while at the same time asking whether this need divide the two churches as long as both are agreed that" ... our entire hope of justification and salvation rests on Christ Jesus and on the gospel whereby the good news of God's merciful action in Christ is made known; we do not place our ultimate trust in anything other than God's promise and saving work in Christ" (*Lutherans and Catholics in Dialogue*

VII, 72).

Today concerns for peace and justice are widespread. In this context Roman Catholic theology might make a positive contribution by seeking to retrieve the intent that lay behind merit-talk in the past. That would involve giving more stress to the conduciveness of graced human endeavors in the present to God's promised future. That would have the decided advantage of locating the realities to which merit-talk referred where they belong—in the realm of eschatology.

See **Justification, Good Works, Grace, Sanctification**

H. A. Oberman, "The Tridentine Decree on Justification in the Light of Late Medieval Theology," in *Journal for Theology and the Church* 3, *Distinctive Protestant and Catholic Themes Revisited,* Ed. R. W. Funk, New York: Harper and Row, 1967, pp. 28-54.

CARL J. PETER

MESSIAH

"Messiah" comes from Hebrew and means "anointed one." It is translated into Greek as *christos,* hence English "Christ." It is a title designating an anointed agent sent by God for the benefit or welfare of his people. The OT applies the title to the historical kings of the Davidic dynasty (Pss 2:2; 18:51; 89:39, 52; 132:10, 17). As a result, the title acquires political implications. In the prophetic literature it is often linked to the ideal Davidic ruler whom the God of Israel would send to occupy the throne of David (Jer 33:15; Ezek 37:23-24). When the Davidic dynasty died out during the exilic and postexilic period, the title was employed of the high priest, (Lev 4:3, 5). Even a non-Israelite could function as God's anointed agent, e.g., Cyrus according to Isa 45:1.

In the second century B.C.E. there is mention of a coming anointed one who is associated with the renewal of Jerusalem (Dan 9:25). However, the author of this apocalyptic passage does not supply any further information. About the same time the Qumran community speaks of two messiahs: an anointed king ("messiah of Israel") and an anointed priest ("messiah of Aaron"). The Qumran literature does not develop the identities of these anointed ones as if they were "savior figures."

In the Palestinian Judaism of the first century C.E. one should not anticipate *the* messiah. Thus there is no set figure that can be simply extrapolated and applied to Jesus of Nazareth. Instead there is the hope that God will radically alter the present age by means of heavenly and/or angelic agents. In addition to the two messiahs of Qumran there is the political son of David who will vanquish Israel's enemies and lead God's people to righteousness. In the controversies over the proper interpretation of the Mosaic Law there is the expectation of a prophet like Moses (Deut 18:18-19; see Jn 6:14; 7:40). Such a figure would provide the true interpretation, thus ushering in an age where everyone would follow the Law. There is also the leader of the eschatological war, often an angelic figure, who conquers the forces of evil in the great cosmic conflict. In addition there is the judge who presides over the final judgment, thus vindicating the righteous.

In this very fluid period of messiahs as well as other human and/or angelic agents of God, Jesus of Nazareth conducted his ministry. In the sayings of Jesus preserved in the "Q" document the title "messiah" is not found. In the Gospel of Mark the title appears in three passages (Mk 9:41; 13:21; 15:32) that are probably due to the post-resurrectional concerns of the early christian church and do not reflect the historical Jesus. In Mk 8:30 Peter identifies Jesus as the messiah (see, however, Jn 6:67-69). However, Jesus immediately corrects Peter's identification by interpreting it in terms of the suffering Son of Man (Mk 8:31) and subsequently rebukes Peter for the political implications of the title (Mk 8:32-33). Although Jesus answers the high priest that he is the messiah (Mk 14:62), the Synoptic parallels (Mt 26:64; Lk 22:67-70) raise some doubt. In the episode of the messiah being the son of David (Mk 12:35-37) Jesus perhaps intimates his messianic identity but gives no explicit answer. It is at least likely that the historical Jesus never used this title of himself.

In Paul (see Rom 1:4) "Christ" usually serves as a second proper name. This Pauline usage is primitive and is probably related to the inscription on the cross: "The King of the Jews" (Mk 15:26). This may have been the springboard for understanding messiah as the anointed agent of God who was crucified. The early confession of Acts reflects this early post-resurrectional interpretation: "Therefore let the whole house of Israel know beyond any doubt that God has made both Lord and Messiah this Jesus whom you crucified" (Acts 2:36).

See **Jesus Christ**

JOHN F. CRAGHAN

METAPHYSICS

Although the word itself was not used until later, metaphysics began in ancient Greece when philosophers first distinguished between the way reality appears in our ordinary experience and what we know it to be when we truly understand it. According to Parmenides and Plato, what appears to ordinary experience shifts and changes, presents itself in one form and also presents itself as the opposite, so that we do not know what to make of it. But true knowledge recognizes that no reality is possible unless a being persists in being whatever it is and does not cancel itself out by being or becoming

the opposite. Plato identifies the unstable and inconsistent objects of ordinary experience with the world physically experienced in sensation. He claimed, therefore, that reality depends on what stands above the changes and inconsistencies of physically experienced things. Physical realities persist in being what they are because they imitate and are governed by realities not subject to change and opposition. Thus, the need to know what accounts for the reality or being of what we know became associated with the need to know the "meta-physical," i.e., what is "beyond the physical" and separate from it. Aristotle, Plato's student, continues this association of concerns in his two descriptions of first philosophy: it seeks to understand being not as a special kind of reality but as being, i.e, what makes any being real; it seeks to understand unchangeable, immaterial beings that are separate from the physical world. The word "metaphysics" was first used by an editor of Aristotle's works to designate the collection of texts that deal with first philosophy.

Metaphysics became an important factor in the history of christian thought when the christian thinkers of medieval Europe, especially those who taught theology in the thirteenth-and fourteenth-century universities, used Platonic and Aristotelian philosophy to articulate and explain certain doctrines of christian faith. Plato's transcendent realities became for them the "ideas" or knowledge according to which God creates the world. The two objects of Aristotle's first philosophy became the unchangeable immaterial being of God and that aspect of creatures (being as being) which makes them completely dependent for their reality on God's creative act. Under the influence of Avicenna (Ibn Sina), a medieval Arabian theologian, they distinguished two principles of being as being. The being of essence is what a being is, it's being consistent in definition, not being opposed or contradictory in what it is, and hence its being what can exist and can be understood. Since what is possible does not necessarily exist, that which accounts for the possibility and intelligibility of a being is not the same as its actual existence. Thomas Aquinas distinguished between "what a being is" (plant, animal, human being) and the act by which "what it is" exists. He insisted, however, that "what a being is " has no other reality than that derived from its existing as what it is. Its possibility is the existence of a cause with the power to cause it. Creation is the act by which God, whose being is complete and necessary existence, gives to all things a certain way of existing; on this their whole reality depends. According to John Duns Scotus, "what a being is" accounts for its being the kind of thing that can be caused; a cause cannot cause what cannot be. A being is possible because it has a consistent nature, because it is not opposed or contradictory in what identifies it. Existence is just the fact that what is really possible actually exists. Scientific arguments for the existence of God, those based not on contingent facts but on what is necessarily true, begin with possible being, a certain kind of being can be produced, and show how this possibility necessarily depends on the existence of God. Under the influence of Scotistic thought, christian theologians began to define metaphysics as the science of possible being. This line of thinking, sometimes opposed to and sometimes merged with the influence of Thomas Aquinas, continued in christian theological circles until well into the modern age.

Meanwhile, in the early modern period (seventeenth to nineteenth century), secular philosophy challenged the traditional assumption that the consistency and order necessary for making sense of what we experience is also what reality itself requires. According to Descartes, Locke, Hume, and Kant, we must determine what questions human knowing is fit to answer before we trust its account of what reality is. Kant concludes that thought has access only to reality as it appears in the knower's physical experience of things. The consistency and order which makes this experience understandable are not conditions derived from an independent reality which governs thought; rather they are conditions imposed by thought itself. What reality is in itself we cannot know. But according to Hegel, who follows Kant in the nineteenth century, we can show from within the conditions of thought itself what reality truly is. The way we experience reality and the way we judge how true the experience is depends on what we expect the truth to be; and this is different for different kinds of experience. But the various ways of interpreting or representing the truth necessarily connect themselves to each other so that the complete and absolute truth is the all-encompassing thought that knows them as necessary differences within its unity. Thus, even the shiftiness and conflict of ordinary experience belong to and manifest what being necessarily and unchangingly is. In the twentieth century, Heidegger also demonstrated that being is what it is only within the interpretive framework of human experience. He insisted,however, that this experience is not a finished whole. It is an open project thrown into a world of beings to work out its endless possibilities. This never finished project represents things in a certain light, e.g., as being for a certain purpose, and thus reveals not only what they are, but also their not being the endless possibilities that they might be.

In 1879, Pope Leo XIII published an encyclical letter, *Aeterni Patris,* in which he called Thomas Aquinas the Common

Doctor of the Church and gave Aquinas' philosophical thought the name "Christian philosophy." Consequently, many leading Catholic thinkers began to study Aquinas in the light of contemporary metaphysical issues. All the most important and influential of these thinkers attack Kant's problem by showing that thought necessarily has access to being as being in which the being of God is in some way present. Etienne Gilson and Jacques Maritain, following Aquinas' own approach, have concentrated on what the object of thought is, i.e., a being which is what it is by existing as what it is and which therefore reveals itself in virtue of the existence it has from its creator. Pierre Rousselot, Joseph Maréchal, and Bernard Lonergan have focused on what knowing is, and have shown that in every judgment we make about the sensible world we measure what we know by the complete understanding we seek. Being as being, even the complete being of God, is present in all our knowing as the object of desire, the desire to know all there is to be known. Karl Rahner, influenced by Heidegger, has interpreted this desire as the openness of human being to its own endless possibilities which it must work out in the sensible world and which reveals this world as being for a never finished project.

See **Philosophy, Theology**

ARDIS B. COLLINS

MINISTRY

Today ministry in the christian church exists in a new situation. Change in ministry—diversification, decline, expansion—have followed upon the ecclesial event of Vatican II and the social upheavals of the last half of the twentieth century. They were not planned in advance but are the result of the meeting of the church and the world. The expansion of ministry, the questions concerning new or older church structures, a new evangelical vitality, are part of a cultural upheaval whose roots lie in freedom, ministerial efficacy, maturity and participation within the church.

"Ministry" comes from the ordinary Greek word for serving and attending upon someone. It has not fared well in translation: the abstract Latin, *ministerium,* can easily become an office, even a rather servile one, and was in fact replaced in Latin Christianity by *officium.* The Reformation wanted to rediscover the serving style in the word "minister," but centuries of too close contact with state churches or middle class ethos have obscured the active and servant-like nature of the word. The contemporary rediscovery of the word "ministry" highlights the sharp etymological challenge of service, while the new dynamic of a diversified ministry includes the theological reappreciation of every church office as an activity serving grace, serving people, and serving the spirit in people.

Until recently "ministry" was a Protestant word, but now it also describes a new situation in the Roman Catholic Church where more and more people want to be ministers and where priesthood and vowed life have been complemented by a variety of ministries. Other christian churches are experiencing similar alterations in their ecclesiastical structures as women enter the pastorate and as men and women find other ministries than the pastoral. Programs for training in varied ministries proliferate as parishes and dioceses expand their staffs.

Explosion of Ministry

What we call an "explosion" of ministry is a worldwide phenomenon, affecting countries and churches differently. It occurred because the renewal of the local church, priesthood, episcopacy and life in vows initiated by Vatican II led to the practical consequence of many men and women shifting from one ministry to another. New ministries, e.g., health care, penal institutions, adult religious education, become new paths (along with those of pastor, priest, sister) to ministry. As a result of these developments within and outside the churches, thousands of Christians have entered the ministry. Outside of Europe and North America, factors such as the emphasis upon the local church, decline of large numbers of expatriate priests and sisters necessitate numerous theological and pastoral openings for baptized men and women, modifying the ecclesiology of missionary countries.

What caused this explosion of ministry? Both society and church in our times led the ministry to seek out new activities and therein a new theology. The world is growing. The number of people living on this planet expands rapidly. At the same time, people are not content merely to subsist in a changeless life punctuated with rare moments of contentment, but they search for a fuller life. Quality in christian life, as well as increase in population and a search for freedom, are forces which have led Christians to expect wider ministry in their churches. The church is caught between a flood of numbers and an individual quest for spiritual maturity.

The Source of Ministry

The kingdom of God is the source, the milieu, the goal of ministry. From God's kingdom come the power and the inspiration to serve the reign of God. The church lives from and supports ministry within the kingdom of God. For people with diverse gifts, ministry has a variety of calls.

Paul welcomed all ministerial actions expanding the church. He saw them grounded in and expressive of what he called "charisms" or "spiritual gifts" given to all Christians with baptism. Minimalizing sensational gifts and accenting those which were public services to the gospel, he kept charisms within the life of the church and emphasized the building up of the temple of the Spirit (1 Cor 3:16), the growth of the body of Christ (Rom 12:4). Harmony is brought to a diversity of important ministries and necessary community services by the goal of "a unity in the work of service (*diakonia*), building up the body of Christ" (Eph 4:13). Far from charism being opposed to ministry, ministry is mediated from the Spirit to individual personality by charism. Ministries are diaconal charisms.

The word *diakonia,* ministry, in the NT sometimes means a particular kind of church action (Rom 12:7), and sometimes it means the general term which includes all the serving and evangelistic roles in the community (Eph 4:12). A service of services, it flows forth from christian life and community and then is channeled into various christian presentations of the word and power of God's new covenant. There is a contrast between the past religious "ministry of death" with the new "ministry of the Spirit" (2 Cor 3:7, 9). Every ministry is grounded in charism; some charisms in each Christian lead to ministry. Diaconal charisms come to baptized men and women in various modalities during their lives.

Variety of Ministries

A further characteristic of the fundamental ecclesial structure of the early church is the diverse arrangement of ministers in the early church: men and women whose work is so wondrous that they are called co-workers with God (Col 4:11).

First, there was the ministry of Jesus (c. 27 to 30 A.D.); second, in the first communities in Jerusalem, Antioch and Damascus, Jewish forms, presbyteral and prophetic, would be prominent (30-45); third, the wider foundations of gentile churches by the Twelve and by other apostles gave an internal prominence to teacher, prophet and apostle (45 to 70); fourth, bishop, presbyter and deacon (as a specific ministry of care, assisting leadership) more and more arranged, and in some ways replaced, the earlier stages (70 to 110). This gives us two triads in the first century; the first is apostle-prophet-teacher; the second is bishop-presbyter-deacon. How the christian churches throughout the Roman Empire moved from the first triad to the second and how they coexisted is uncertain.

We find women in the ministry, not first in a movement after 1970, but in names recorded in the NT. Full membership in the christian community for women was a revolution for the first century. The rivals of Christianity—mysteries, cults and philosophical schools—did not always admit women to full initiation. As an ecclesiological principle we must ponder the proclamation of Paul in *Galatians:* "There is neither Jew nor Greek, there is neither slave nor free, there is no male or female" in Christ (3:28). Women were among the followers of Jesus from the beginning just as they were faithful to the end where the gospels enhanced their role on Good Friday and Easter. Since ministry at the level of belief and theology derives not from human social arrangement (although this influences the realization of ministry in a culture), after the coming of the Spirit to all we would expect ministry in the Christian churches to be open to all the baptized.

The words for ministries in the first communities are words of action and service, not of power and honor. In the first century, ministry came not only from the Spirit and the Twelve but from the community itself. The ministry of coordination and leadership was not the whole ministry but one important ministry among others, with responsibilities and limits. We have no evidence for a christian church which did not contain a ministry of leadership (although we cannot give that ministry just one title) nor do we have an example of an *ekklesia* which had only a ministry of leadership. The three terms—overseer, elder, servant—are in history and etymology the source for the three ministries given special emphasis from the second century on by Christianity: bishop, priest, deacon.

The forms of the ministry can change as the structures of the christian community legitimately assume aspects of the forms of different cultures. As the church becomes more public in the Roman Empire, the bishop assumes greater stature; as the numbers within christian churches grow rapidly, the universality and diversity of ministry decline. In the Middle Ages, the priest is less of a civic leader and more of a mediator of grace, while the other ministries, including that of diaconate, have been absorbed by the religious orders. In the Baroque era, ministry is concerned either with the evangelization of new worlds or with the interior world of grace, while in the nineteenth century, embattled by the new secular states, the ministry is marginalized, removed utterly from the political sphere, ministering to sparks of interior grace in a world too fallen. The triumphs and the limitations of ministry—evangelist, bishop, priest, monk, *Herr Pastor, curé*—all these are partly the products of culture. Religious orders are ways the spirit and church emerge in service. The number of public ordained ministers is not fixed.

Characteristics of Ministry

Six characteristics stand out in the formation of each ministry and all ministry. Ministry is: (1) doing something; (2) for the advent of the kingdom; (3) in public; (4) on behalf of a christian community; (5) which is a gift received in faith, baptism and ordination; and (6) which is an activity with its own limits and identity within a diversity of ministerial actions. These six characteristics constitute the fundamental identity of ministry. They are not narrow laws; indeed, richer than ministry as it now exists, they lead us to consider calmly the new possibilities which our own times suggest. These characteristics cannot be easily set aside, although no single region or era may perfectly realize them. We can define ministry in the following way: christian ministry is the public activity of a baptized follower of Jesus Christ flowing from the Spirit's charism and an individual personality on behalf of a christian community to witness to, serve and realize the kingdom of God.

Pastoral Expansion of Ministry.

The ministry has expanded in a number of ways. Vatican II began the movement by its teaching on the common responsibility of all Christians. There have been quasi-formal expansions of ministry in several modes: in the staffs of parishes with ministries in education, youth, sick and aging, social action, and liturgy; in diocesan offices with a variety of facilitators and coordinators of ministries; in the appointment of religious women to formal roles in parishes or chanceries. When the ministries of acolyte and reader were re-structured, Pope Paul VI suggested that countries expand these two with other ministries needed by them, but this has not been encouraged recently. In some countries, pastoral assistants as substitute pastors have been developed while other areas have commissioned Christians other than presbyters or deacons to serve as educated and qualified preachers. The dynamic of the expansion of the ministry is hindered by the lack in the church of a theology of a wider ministry which will expand and modify but not compromise the position of bishop, pastor and presbyter.

Ministry: Paradoxes and Models

The English "laity," has generally been thought to be simply a form of the *laos*— a lay person who participated in the greatness of the new people of God. Critical studies have found that this is not the case. In secular literature and in translations of the OT after the Septuagint, the meaning of the word is much like our contemporary meaning: ordinary, not consecrated, even profane. To be a layperson is to have a modality of being, or, better, of non-being; not-being ordained a priest, bishop or deacon (married deacons are often contradictorily referred to as "lay deacons"). The phenomenologically pejorative or at least passive meaning of laity implies the exclusion of a baptized person from acting publicly on behalf of the community; that life is one of private virtue in an alien world. Today, as baptized Christians assume in large numbers ministry to the sick, teaching and preaching in communities where no ordained ministers are available, we should not be preoccupied with how they are *not* in the ministry. Decisions about the new situation in ministry are often made on the basis of fear or uncertainty concerning a priesthood now closed to those who are not male, celibate clerics.

How is the ordained secretary of the chancery in the ministry while the educated, full-time Christian employed in the team ministry in the urban hospital only in the lay state? We could cite dozens of such paradoxes. Their solution can only come from a coherent theology of the ministry which replaces the clergy-laity structure with a group of concentric circles. Yves Congar, the foremost ecclesiologist of the century and a major theological inspiration of Vatican II, described how this shift took place in his thinking after 1970: "I have come to see that the pastoral reality described by the New Testament imposes a view much richer (than a clerical church and laicized world). It is God, it is Christ who in his Spirit does not cease building the church .... The Church is not built up merely by the acts of the official ministers of the presbytery but by many kinds of services, more or less stable or occasional, more or less spontaneous or recognized, some even consecrated by sacramental ordination. These services exist ... they exist even if they are not called by their real name, ministries, nor have their true place and status in ecclesiology. Eventually one sees that the decisive pair is not 'priesthood-laity' as I used in my book on the laity but much more that of 'ministries or services and community.'"

A critique of the distinction between clergy and laity will not lead to a church without diversity or without ecclesiastical competence. Just the opposite is true: the clergy-laity distinction suppresses diversity and standards of competency in the ministry. Church administrators fear that a pietistic universalism will appear where anyone can perform any service in the church. In fact, distinction through education for every ministry will increase in depth and rigor as the general christian population grows in education. Taking ministry seriously according to the criteria of the NT includes a distinction of ministries. The identity of and difference between bishop, presbyter and deacon, and also of teacher and counselor in a parish is greater now than it was twenty years ago. Clear ministerial identity brings not monoformity but distinction and demand for competence.

Conclusion

The context of a theology of ministry for today is not decline but expansion: the expansion of the christian population, the expansion of their precise needs, the expansion of the number of Christians interested in various levels of ministry. Ministry is not a rare vocation or a privileged office but belongs to the nature of the new covenant and comes with baptism.

The context of ministry is grace: that multifaceted, active presence of God which Jesus calls God's "kingdom." In a time of rapid change, theology must be rooted in realities or it becomes absorbed in conflicts over past and present words. Grace brings a certain reality to ecclesial issues, for ultimately grace is the source and the goal, and the judge of all that the church is and does.

The diversity within the church (and there is considerable diversity) comes not through states of membership or biological modes of human life but through the choice of levels of ministerial activity. Christians are invited to degrees of ministry according to their particular charism. That charism looks both to the Spirit's plan for each Christian and to the needs, structures, leadership and discernment of the community.

The ministry of leadership in parish and diocese exists to serve ministry as catalyst and coordinator, and as sacrament and focus of other ministries. This leading ministerial role grounds the responsibility of presiding at eucharist and of focusing and maintaining union with the church's tradition and universality.

See **Church, Laity, Orders**

B. Cooke, *Ministry to Word and Sacrament*, Philadelphia, 1976. Y. Congar, *Power and Poverty in the Church*, London, 1964. A. Lemaire, *Les ministères aux origines de l'église*, Paris, 1971. R. McBrien. *Ministry: A Pastoral-Theological Handbook*, San Francisco, 1987. T. O'Meara, *Theology of Ministry*. New York. 1983. See biblio. E. Schillebeeckx. *Ministry*, New York, 1981; *The Church with a Human Face*, (bibliography), New York, 1985.

THOMAS F. O'MEARA, OP

MIRACLE

A miracle is an astounding event,

astounding because it is extraordinary, and extraordinary because what has occurred is or involves a breach of the usual natural order. Nature "on its own" does not bring forth miracles; if they occur, the laws of nature must, by way of exception, have been suspended or overridden; and such a suspension can only be ascribed, directly or indirectly, to God.

Such is the conception of miracle supported not only by common usage but by a long tradition of christian theology as well. According to Thomas Aquinas, for example, "those happenings are properly called miraculous which are done by divine agency outside the commonly observed order of things." Among contemporary theologians, however, there is a certain shyness about discussing miracle in this sense, and a tendency to shift the emphasis towards a personal and existential dimension which the received view omits but which clearly belongs to the miracles narrated in the NT. If these are taken as being in some sense definitive, miracle is more than an extraordinary event; it is a vehicle of meaning, a sign, which invites (though it does not compel) the personal response of commitment, conversion, and faith. In this regard miracle is intimately bound up with *kerygma*, the message or announcement whose validity is confirmed and accredited by the "mighty deeds" of the one who pronounces it. In the gospels, not everyone who listens to Jesus' parables takes them to heart, but only those who "have ears to hear"; likewise, not everyone who watches his miraculous deeds occurring can "see" what they signify—the glory of God disclosed in him—and those who "demand a sign," obstinately laying down their own conditions for believing in Jesus, are consistently refused. Hence the fact that these episodes were recorded, not by detached and "neutral" observers, but by interested parties,

Christians for whom faith in Jesus as the Christ made all the difference, cannot be dismissed as mere bias. On the contrary, their personal involvement was, in part, a result and so a continuation of the very events they narrate.

For contemporary biblical scholarship, then, the first question to be asked about miracle stories is not "What really happened?" but rather, "What is the meaning conveyed by this narrative?" In a somewhat similar vein, current theological discussion has been less interested in philosophical debate about the bare possibility of miracles than in restoring them to a religious and historical context which is intrinsically constituted by human meaning and value, human decision and discernment, in ways that natural science is not. But while this newer approach does subordinate the question whether miracles occur in fact, it does not render such a question meaningless. Although the NT provides ample proof that the earliest Christians believed certain events had occurred, some of which were miraculous, it is a further question whether Christians today should or can agree. Perhaps the NT authors wrote as they did because they were deceived or deceitful; that has always been a possible argument, and some have thought it the most likely one. "No testimony," David Hume wrote in 1748, "is sufficient to establish a miracle, unless the testimony be of such a kind that its falsehood would be more miraculous than the fact which it endeavors to establish." This famous sentence does not rest on what is, in the last resort, the only final argument against miracles: the dogma that they are impossible. To that dogma no theist, let alone Christian, could consistently subscribe. "It is not against the principle of craftsmanship," to quote Thomas again, "if a craftsman brings about a change in what he makes, even after giving it its first form." Yet even a reasoned and articulate belief in God as Creator implies only that miracles *can* happen, not that they do. The basic difficulty is removed, but all manner of lesser ones remain. For it remains that anyone who has not personally witnessed a miracle must weigh the testimony of others; and one of the criteria—not, certainly, the only one—will be whether the event in question fits into the real world as the questioner understands it. Hume's argument comes down to this: nobody can deal intelligently with any past event, miraculous or, for that matter, mundane, if it is unintelligible, no matter how impressive or unimpeachable the testimony to it may be.

To Hume himself, living as he did in the enthusiastic days of modern science's youth, miracles were thoroughly unintelligible: he could make no sense of anything that supposedly violated the uniform regularity of the universe that science was disclosing. And much the same logic as his came to dominate the explicit and implicit methodology of historical investigation, including "higher criticism" of the Bible, throughout the nineteenth century and well into the twentieth. Typical of its influence are the "biographies" of Jesus in which miracles are explained by explaining them away, either as commonplace occurrences misunderstood at the time, or else as later and more or less deliberate fabrications. More recent historians and historiographers have largely abandoned the rigidly rationalistic and *a priori* approach of their predecessors; yet it is still true that the credibility of reports about the past depends largely on the credibility of what they report, and that for many people the world view with which any reported event must be consonant in order to be credible is a world view colored by the same presuppositions about the law of nature that were accepted in the eighteenth century.

There is reason to think, however, that the longstanding "scientific" case against miracles, deeply ingrained though it is, has not long to last. The mechanistic determinism that was once thought inseparable from scientific knowledge as such has begun to be dismantled by science itself. The classical laws of physics, once construed as expressing what cannot possibly be otherwise, are coming to be recognized instead as expressing possibilities that are regularly verified; statistical laws, once denigrated as mere cloaks for ignorance of "real" laws, are increasingly being accepted as referring to actual randomness, and hence the possibility of genuine novelty, in the universe as it really is.

If these and other implications of twentieth-century physics succeed in making their way not only into the thinking of historians, philosophers, and theologians, but also into the ways in which intelligent Christians understand their faith, one major difficulty in respect of miracles will be palliated. Not the only one, however, for even if the intelligible universe is such that miracles can have an intelligible place in it, they can still be objected to on moral grounds as inappropriate or improper. Miracles may *fit,* but are they *fitting*? George Bernard Shaw, for one, considered that anyone "who is not Christian enough to feel that conjuror's tricks are, on the part of a god, just what cheating at cards is on the part of a man, and that the whole value of the Incarnation ... depends on whether, when the Word became flesh, it played the game instead of cheating, is no Christian at all." Rhetoric aside, the objection has its force. An assertion that some occurrences more than others reveal a divine plan can seem to mean, in effect, that God is whimsical, arbitrary, even tyrannical. But in comparing history with a game that ought to proceed uniformly, in accordance with agreed rules, Shaw ignored the possibility that it is precisely through particular events, and above all, for Christians, through the incarnation, that the "rules"—what the Creator wills for the persons he is creating—become known. On that hypothesis, the supreme miracle, Christ's resurrection, was no conjuror's trick; it was God's affirmation of a life and a death that show once and for all what the game, as it were, is all about and how it is to be won.

Morally as well as intellectually, then, the difficulties that cluster about miracles can be regarded as specific instances of a general theological problem: how best to interpret, in the present cultural milieu, the affirmation that grace perfects nature without abolishing it. And it is within that larger theological context that testimony to any particular miracle is best received and assessed.

See **Science and Religion**

David Hume, *An Enquiry Concerning Human Understanding* (1748), §10, "Of Miracles." Robert A.H. Larmer, *Water Into Wine? An Investigation of the Concept of Miracle,* Toronto: McGill-Queen's Univ. Press, 1987. C.S. Lewis, *Miracles,* New York: Macmillan, 1947. S. Vernon McCasland, "Miracle," *The Interpreter's Dictionary of the Bible,* volume 3, pp. 392-402.

CHARLES C. HEFLING, JR.

MISSION

This article has a narrower focus than its title would first suggest. In its broadest sense, "mission" is everything that the church does in service of the kingdom of God. In a more restricted sense, however, mission refers to "missionary activity," the preaching of the gospel among peoples and cultures where it is not known. In more recent discussion the topic is closely connected with that of "evangelization." In fact, a distinction between the two is often seen to be formal or arbitrary. Thus, it is appropriate that this article and that on "evangelization" should be read conjointly.

Pre-Vatican II Mission Theology

The theology of mission which developed at Vatican II can only be understood against the backdrop of twentieth century papal teaching on the mission and related theological discussions.

There are four significant encyclicals on the missions: Benedict XV's *Maximum Illud* (1919), Pius XI's *Rerum Ecclesiae* (1926), Pius XII's *Evangelii Praecones* (1951), and John XXIII's *Princeps Pastorum* (1959). Benedict's message is particularly poignant when read in the wake of World War I. His position is clear: there are still a billion people who are dwelling in darkness and in the shadow of death. There can be no lessening of energy in the church's missionary task. This task must be done in such a way that there is no confusion between the message of the gospel and nationalism, or no danger that the gospel become confused with the religion of a colonial power. The church must become indigenous. Pius XI reiterates the urgency of the missionary task and continues to stress the growth of indigenous churches. He is especially insistent on the need for a local clergy "equal in knowledge and powers" with the foreign missionaries. These themes are orchestrated further by Pius XII. Special emphasis must be given to raising up a native clergy and a local hierarchy. Particular attention is to be given to the laity, who are the source of the renewal of the social order. Pius also speaks to the need to preserve the natural culture of the pagans. His image is that of grafting an orchid (the gospel) onto a wild tree (native cultures) so that "fruits of a more tasty and richer quality may issue forth and mature" (par. 87). John XXIII repeats the themes of his predecessors, but in an interesting departure mentions the name of the controversial Jesuit Matteo Ricci as a missionary to be imitated.

In addition to the papal teaching, theologians were also attending to the theology of mission. Generally two schools of missiology are distinguished. The first is known as the Muenster school and is identified with the work of J. Schmidlin. Its approach is christocentric and personal, emphasizing proclamation of the gospel, conversion, and the salvation of souls. An alternate model, associated with Louvain and missiologists P. Charles and A. Seumois, has been characterized as "curial-canonical." It gives priority to the implantation of the church. The establishment of the hierarchy and indigenous churches is stressed. Although its emphasis is ecclesiocentric and territorial, the Louvain school tends to be less "European-centered" and more sensitive to cultural differences.

The Teaching of Vatican II

The missionary vocation of the church is the particular focus of the conciliar decree *Ad Gentes*. Yet it is a theme which runs through all the conciliar documents. Particular attention must be given to *Lumen Gentium* which provides the broadest theological context. There the church is described as a sacrament, a sacrament of both unity and salvation. Precisely as the *universal* sacrament of salvation the church is to offer its saving message to all peoples and all cultures. This sacramental nature thus carries with it the demand of a universal mission. This mission has been entrusted to the entire people of God. Driven by the Holy Spirit, "each disciple of Christ has the obligation of spreading the faith to the best of his abilities" (L.G. 17). In addition *Lumen Gentium* laid the foundation for a retrieval of the theology of local or particular church. Thus, the church of Christ is truly present in all legitimately organized local groups of the faithful, no matter how small or poor. Such a perspective would have profound implications for the renewal of mission within the Catholic Church. Thus the universal sacramentality of the church, its self-understanding as the messianic people of God, and the recovery of the theology of local church provide the background for the most specific attention to its missionary dimension in *Ad Gentes*.

The church is by its very nature "missionary" (A.G. 2), since it has its origin in the mission or sending of the Son and the Holy Spirit. The Son is sent as God in human flesh to effect peace and communion with God and genuine union among men and women. The church continues this mission. The Holy Spirit, always active in the world, is the source of charisms and gifts in the church, gathers the body of believers into communion, and at the same time inspires the hearts of the faithful with that "same spirit of mission which impelled Christ himself" (A.G. 4). In its missionary activity the church is the manifestation of God's saving mystery in the world. Its purpose, of course, is to make participation in the saving mystery of Christ available to all men and women.

A narrower use of the term "mission" in the sense of "missions" describes the preaching of the gospel and the implanting of the church among peoples who have not yet heard the word of God (A.G. 6). The result of the word of God effectively preached and freely accepted is the growth of indigenous particular churches. As these churches mature the obligation to preach the gospel devolves on them, not only within their own boundaries but in the larger world as well. For, "it would greatly help if the young churches took part in the universal mission of the church as soon as possible and sent missionaries to preach the Gospel throughout the whole world, even though they are themselves short of clergy" (A.G. 20). This is a concrete embodiment of the fact that missionary activity flows from the very nature of the church.

Ad Gentes addresses themes which will be especially significant in the post-conciliar development of the theory and practice of mission. The first of these is "inculturation." Christ and his church transcend every race and nation, "and so cannot be considered as strangers to anyone or in any place" (A.G. 8). Yet this non-exclusive gospel must become incarnate in particular places and cultures. While not succumbing to syncretism, local churches must become the locus of the adaptation of the gospel. They must borrow from the best of their respective cultures, adapt the christian life to local mentalities and traditions, and thus enhance the richness of Catholic unity (A.G. 22).

A second theme—that of the relationship between missionary activity and human progress or development—is also treated in *Ad Gentes*. The gospel is to function as a leaven "in the interest of liberty and progress ... brotherhood, unity, and peace" (A.G. 8). The sign of a maturing church is that its laity engage themselves, in collaboration with others (even non-Christians), in the ordering of social and economic affairs. In this the decree on missionary activity echoes the themes of *Gaudium et Spes* on the relationship between church and world (cf. G.S. 42).

Post-Conciliar Developments

The council provided the horizon in which missionary activity and mission theology would experience renewal. The ten years after the close of the council witnessed major developments. The Synod of Bishops, called by Paul VI in 1971, addressed the relationship of mission and justice. In its report the Synod reaffirmed that "the mission of the people of God [is] to further justice in the world" (par. 1). In fact, the synod would affirm that action on behalf of justice and participation in the transformation of the world are "constitutive" of the preaching of the gospel. This would further intensify the relationship between the commitment to mission and the commitment to human liberation. This has continued to be one of the persistent themes in the post-conciliar mission theology, especially in Latin America.

In 1975, ten years after the close of the council, Paul VI issued "Evangelization in the Modern World," a meditation on the result of the 1974 Synod of Bishops which had addressed this theme. Paul VI draws on *Ad Gentes* and deepens it. He names the essential mission of the church "evangelization." In its evangelizing mission, the church, empowered by the Spirit, is charged with proclaiming the gospel, but proclaiming it in such a way that the gospel penetrates societies and cultures. Those who have not heard the gospel have a first claim on evangelization. But the church must also turn its attention to cultures already evangelized, especially where non-belief has become pervasive. (This is suggestive of the notion of "mission on six continents.") This proclamation and penetration demands a linkage between evangelization and human liberation. While the gospel offers a salvation that is transcendent and eschatological, evangelization would be incomplete if it is not linked to the political and social orders. Those links can be justified in a variety of ways, e.g., the relationship between creation and redemption, or between justice and charity (par. 31). The letter gives cautious approval to "base communities." It concludes with a reminder: while indeed God can save men and women in a variety of ways, Jesus has given us the "ordinary paths for salvation." The judgment will be on those who received the gospel and neglected to preach it.

While magisterial teaching on mission was being articulated in *Ad Gentes* and

Evangelii Nuntiandi, the concrete shape of the church dramatically changed. Mission is being carried out in a church quite different from that which existed in the first half of this century. What Walbert Buehlmann has called "the coming of the Third Church" is very much in evidence. By the year 2000 roughly seventy percent of Catholics will live below the equator, with more than the half the world's Catholics living in Latin America. In the year 1980 the *Annuarium Statisticum Ecclesiae* reported that there are 2,452 particular churches (dioceses or their equivalents) in the Roman Communion. Of these only 948 are in Europe or North America. The majority of particular churches are in the so-called Third World. Karl Rahner has called this ecclesial configuration the emergence of the "world-Church."

This changed situation has important implications for the mission of the church. The traditionally "mission-receiving" churches have now become autonomous, co-responsible, and equal members of the world wide ecclesial communion. As such, while remaining poor and needy, they are challenged to share their often limited resources with other local churches. A further implication of the conciliar ecclesiology is that evangelization be done within the context of building up the particular church. The relationship among particular churches is to be one of respectful mutuality and reciprocity, not control or domination.

Another result of this changed ecclesial situation is the clearer sense that the particular churches be the loci of the inculturation of the gospel. The concrete cultural context in which the gospel is preached must be the object of more careful analysis. Traditional categories such as "translation" or "adaptation" do not do justice to the deep demand for integral incarnation in areas such as theology, spirituality, and liturgy. Such a demand respects both the integrity of the gospel tradition as well as the diverse ways in which that tradition can manifest itself. Paul VI gave a ringing endorsement to this task in his 1969 address in Uganda: "You may, and you must, have an African Christianity." The challenge of avoiding syncretism or an isolating parochialism remains.

The post-conciliar conversation has also raised the question as to the relationship of the mission of the church to soteriology. The documents of the council offered a decidedly more optimistic view of non-christian religions and non-believers within the context of a Christocentric world. The saving grace of God is available in the great religious traditions as well as in the human struggle for moral existence (L.G. 16). God's saving will is understood to be universal. Such a perspective engendered a crisis in the missionary consciousness of the church. If such is our understanding of God, why evangelize? One response emphasizes a shift away from a narrowly ecclesiocentric approach to salvation to one which gives due weight to the sacramental dimension of the church in the history of salvation. The church is to signify the reality of God's salvation operative throughout the world. As Walter Kasper has put it: "The Church's mission, which is rooted in the absolute claim of Christianity, is not so much to save the individual—who in principle can be saved outside the visible communion—as to represent and proclaim the love of God, to give testimony to hope, and so to be a sign among the nations." The church in mission responds to the presence, not the absence, of the saving gift of God. In its preaching of the Gospel, its celebration of the eucharist, its witness of evangelical life, and in its commitment to social and political transformation, the church is both the sacrament and servant of the kingdom of God. Because of the preciousness of this gift and the enduring reality of sin, there is an urgency to build up the community of faith throughout the world. For in it salvation is experienced in a reflective and conscious way. The recognition of God's gift demands a response from those who have received it. What you have received as a gift, give as a gift. Paul's words are haunting in this regard: "Woe to me if I do not preach the Gospel" (1 Cor 9:16).

See **Church, Evangelization, Inculturation, Justice, Redemption, Reign of God, Religions**

Walbert Buehlmann, *The Coming of the Third Church,* Maryknoll, 1977. Thomas Burke, Ed., *Catholic Missions: Four Great Missionary Encyclicals,* New York, 1957. Arthur Glasser and Donald McGavran, *Contemporary Theologies of Mission,* Grand Rapids, 1983. Robert Schreiter, *Constructing Local Theologies,* Maryknoll and London, 1985. Donald Senior and Carroll Stuhlmueller, *The Biblical Foundations of Mission,* Maryknoll and London, 1983.

WILLIAM MCCONVILLE, OFM

MODALISM

The trinitarian view that maintains that God is three only with respect to the modes of his action in the world, in distinction from the Catholic view that God is three in his very being.

See **Trinity**

MODERNISM

Coined in or around 1905, the term "Modernism" was intended as a pejorative description of certain scholarly trends which had been developing in the Catholic Church during the last decade of Leo XIII's pontificate. These trends arose out of the conviction that Catholicism was not incompatible with modernity. Critically-minded Protestantism had long since entered on a process of dialogue with post-Enlightenment thought, while Catholicism under Pius IX had decided on a policy of retrenchment and hostility.

The pontificate of Leo XIII (1878-1903) appeared to offer some hope to Catholic scholars intent upon effecting a bridgehead between their church and the modern world. Although one of the first of Leo's acts had been to impose Thomism on the universal church (*Aeterni Patris,* 1879), the pope did not discourage attempts made in the University of Louvain under the leadership of Désiré Mercier (1851-1926) to present Thomism historically and with some sensitivity to the demands of modern critical thought.

There were, however, Catholic scholars who felt that a more radical approach was called for, especially in the fields of history and philosophy. Protestant biblical scholarship had made notable progress throughout the nineteenth century, but this progress had had little general impact on Catholic biblical studies. In addition, neo-Thomistic philosophy remained stubbornly opposed to any dialogue with post-Kantian thought. Fundamental theology—at that time more or less identified with apologetics—was the area most vulnerable to modern historical and philosophical criticism, and its traditional structure was defended tenaciously by neo-Thomists in France and later in Italy. Their defense of the status quo, which came to be called "Integralism" because it was based on the conviction that no part of the Neo-scholastic theological structure could be touched without endangering the whole, marks the beginning of the anti-Modernist campaign which reached its climax between 1910 and 1914.

The French philosopher, Maurice Blondel (1861-1949), may be said to have inaugurated the Modernist period when he published his doctoral thesis, *L'Action,* in 1893. *L'Action* broke with the intellectualist and positivist pattern of Neo-scholastic apologetics by arguing transcendentally to the existence of revelation through analysis of the dynamic of willing. Blondel argued against the "extrinsicism" of Neo-scholastic fundamental theology and in favor of what came to be called "the method of immanence" which claimed to bring the would-be believer to the threshold of revelation by a means which respected the autonomy of the human subject. This Blondelian initiative was fiercely resisted by both French and Roman neo-Thomists, partly because it claimed to discover in human subjectivity an "exigence" for the supernatural and partly because it accorded little probative value to miracles, which at that time lay at the heart of Catholic apologetics. Although Blondel was never formally condemned, his principal collaborator, the Oratorian priest Lucien Laberthonnière (1860-1932) was, in 1913, forbidden to publish. Laberthonnière's theory of "moral dogmatism" incorporated Blondel's concern with the need for an immanent, and consequently moral, dimension in the whole revelatory process.

A far more serious threat to the prevailing Neo-scholastic orthodoxy was posed by the publication in 1902 of Alfred Loisy's L'Evangile et L'Eglise. Loisy (1857-1940) was a biblical scholar and as such he put forward the claims of scientific historical investigation to be the main instrument for determining the origins and character of Christianity. His well-known remark, "Jesus proclaimed the kingdom and it was the Church that came," encapsulated the thesis which he propounded against the liberal Protestantism of Adolf von Harnack who had claimed that the essence of Christianity had been obscured by the early church's creeds and laws. The church, according to Loisy, was the necessary and living medium for expressing the gospel in the post-apostolic era. It was, however, the corollary of this position which alarmed Cardinal Richard, Archbishop of Paris, as it was shortly to alarm the Roman Curia: church dogmas, Loisy claimed, are not absolute and timeless truths but must be seen as relative to the age which produced them. Although Loisy disclaimed philosophical intent and competence, he in fact maintained a contextual view of truth which was radically relativistic.

The Anglo-Irish Jesuit, George Tyrrell (1861-1909), devoted much energy to detaching the concept of revelation from its virtual identification with the propositions of contemporary scholastic theology. Tyrrell characterized revelation as belonging to the realm of experience, and he treated the dogmas which expressed it as symbolic utterances. Edouard Le Roy (1870-1954), a disciple of Henri Bergson, called for a refurbished idea, not of this or that dogma, but of dogma itself. The great christian dogmas are, for Le Roy, related to conduct rather than to speculative knowledge. They regulate attitudes rather than formulate absolute truths and have to be lived in order to be understood.

Friedrich von Hügel (1852-1925), an Austro-Scot of immense learning in a variety of fields, acted as an unofficial coordinator between scholars who might otherwise never have been aware of each other's work. In fact von Hügel's role among the Modernists reminds us that Modernism never possessed the unity and cohesion of purpose attributed to it by its Roman opponents. It was less a movement or school of thought than an adventitiously shared liberal and antischolastic attitude to philosophy, theology, and church government.

The movement (if such we choose to call it) flourished in France and Italy and was present in England by reason of the fact that Tyrrell and von Hügel lived there. In Italy it expressed itself politically in the north through the writings of Romolo Murri (1870-1944), the activities of the National Democratic League, and the publication of the short-lived journal, Il Rinnovamento (1907-9). Among those who wrote for *Il Rinnovamento* were Ernesto Buonaiuti (1881-1946), who did much to popularize the ideas of Loisy, and Tyrrell, whose writings (not always well translated) it made known to Italian readers and therefore to the Vatican.

Whether or not one wishes to speak of German Modernism depends upon how one chooses to define Modernism itself. That there were German Catholic scholars who shared many of the ideas of Loisy, Tyrrell and Le Roy is undeniable, but, unlike their predecessors in the 1860's, they were not at the center of the stage during the Modernist crisis.

Modernism was condemned first by the decree, *Lamentabili sane exitu* (3 July, 1907) and then, comprehensively, by the papal encyclical, *Pascendi dominici gregis* (September 8, 1907). *Pascendi* presents the historically sensitive theologian with insuperable problems today. Its view of Modernism as a coherent, organized movement with the intentionally concealed purpose of overthrowing Catholic orthodoxy from the inside is historically unsustainable. The encyclical constructed an elaborate system of thought which it condemned as the "meeting place of all the heresies." Historians of the period can show without difficulty that no individual Modernist, not even Loisy, subscribed to the system as delineated in the encyclical, which not merely alleged the existence of a conspiracy but also postulated a coherence of view among the Modernists which was not in fact the case. It singled out "agnosticism" and the doctrine of "vital immanence" as the governing principles of the movement which it condemned with unparalleled ferocity. Both principles were, however, to a large extent understood in a manner relative to the Neoscholasticism which provided the then prevailing orthodoxy with its conceptual tools.

Together with the *motu proprio,*

Sacrorum Antistitum (September 1, 1910), *Pascendi* prescribed draconian measures for removing Modernism from the church. Vigilance committees were to be set up in every diocese; censorship was to be extensive and intensive; delation was encouraged and assured of anonymity; an oath against Modernism was to be taken by office holders in the church. Benedict XV put an end to the worst excesses of anti-Modernism, but the sobriquet "Modernist" remained available for the next fifty years as a convenient label for any theological initiatives which attempted to reckon with the intellectual challenges of the modern world. The Second Vatican Council marked the end of the anti-modernist period.

See **Faith, History, Neo-Scholasticism, Revelation**

G. Daly, *Transcendence and Immanence: A Study in Catholic Modernism and Integralism,* Oxford U.P., 1980. R. Haight, "The Unfolding of Modernism in France: Blondel, Laberthonnière, Le Roy" *Theological Studies,* 35 (1974), pp. 632-66. E. Poulat, *Histoire, dogme et critique dans la crise moderniste,* Paris, Casterman, 1962. B.M.G. Reardon, "Roman Catholic Modernism," in N. Smart et al. Eds., *Nineteenth Century Religious Thought in the West,* Vol. 2, Cambridge U.P., 1985, pp. 141-177. J. Rivière, *Le Modernisme dans l'Eglise,* Paris, Letouzey et Ané, 1929. A.R. Vidler, *A Variety of Catholic Modernists,* Cambridge U.P., 1970.

GABRIEL DALY, OSA

MONARCHIANISM

An early christian view which denied the Trinity, insisting instead that there was a single divine principle.

See **Adoptionism, Trinity**

MONASTICISM

When Arsenius, the tutor of the sons of Emperor Theodosius I of Byzantium, fled into the Egyptian desert in 394 A.D. to pursue a way of salvation, he was certainly not the first. Many centuries before Christ his master walked the earth, men and women were pursuing the monastic way of life in the remote vastness of the Himalayas, in the caves of Arunchala, and in many other places. At the edge of almost every great religion—the inner edge rather than the outer—there have been monastics. Geographical apartness, however relative it might be, is of the essence of monastic life, an apartness for which the monk and nun have always had to struggle. The world wants to keep its own. The world has ever pursued the monk. If the world no longer comes clamoring after the monk, he must still struggle with the world he brings with him into solitude, the worldliness within his own heart. It tries to fill his solitude with its pleasure and cares or to impel him to go out from his solitude to involve himself in many activities. St. John Cassian defines the scope of monasticism as the attainment of purity of heart, emptying the heart of earthly attachments so that it can be free, be silent, hear God, and pray always.

Christians have ample witness from their divine Master of the importance of going apart, at least periodically. He initiated his ministry with forty days in the wilderness. In the midst of his busy public life, with all its pressing demands, he repeatedly withdrew into the mountains or some other solitary place to be alone with his Father to open his heart in prayer.

In the first years after Christ's ascension, the choice to follow the way of Jesus was enough to set one apart. Persecutions increased that apartness. Prison, exile, and death were apt to be the lot of a despised and hunted people. But within a couple of centuries Christianity conquered and in the conquest it was itself conquered. In overcoming the so-called civilized world and the masters of that world, it became worldly. It was then that courtiers like Arsenius heard the voice to "flee."

When Arsenius arrived in Scetis he found that many had lived there before him. Abba Anthony, father of monks, at age eighteen heard the Lord speak to him through the proclamation of the gospel during the liturgy: "Go, sell all that you have and give to the poor and come..." In 251 Anthony divested himself and took up a simple ascetical life on the edge of the village under the guidance of a recluse. Sixteen years later Anthony withdrew into the desert seeking greater solitude, and disciples pursued him. In 310 he retired to a place of even greater remoteness. though his solitude was never withdrawal from the church. Twice before he died at the age of 105 he journeyed to Alexandria, once to be with the martyrs in a time of persecution, and again to support the bishop, Saint Athanasius, in his sufferings at the hands of heretics.

The fourth and fifth century in the Mediterranean world, the era when Christian monasticism burgeoned. had many similarities to our own time. There was unprecedented unity and communication among people. The increasing affluence of the few weighed ever more heavily on enslaved peoples and nations. More and more young (and not so young) men and women decided that a cultural system based on materialistic progress was not worth the investment of their lives. They left the lecture halls of Rome and Athens, government positions and successful enterprises, prosperous families and great estates, and headed east in search of true wisdom. In Syria, Palestine, Arabia, and the deserts of Egypt, they sought out spiritual fathers or mothers and asked for a "word of life." They lived with them and followed their example. They formed communities of like-minded disciples.

Besides the hermits who were led by the Holy Spirit (or sometimes other spirits) to live completely on their own, the early monks and nuns formed two different kinds of communities. Some gathered around an abba or amma; their coming together was wholly because of a holy man or woman. They were like so many spokes centered on a hub. Their relation with each other was almost accidental. These semi-eremitical communities flourished in the deserts of Egypt and elsewhere. John Cassian brought their spirit to the West in his *Conferences* and *Institutes.*

At the same time other fathers, inspired by the early church of the Acts of the Apostles, stressed much more the communal life. Pachomius was said to be guided by an angel to form a community of this sort in Egypt. Other communities developed in Palestine. After a tour of these outposts, Basil of Caesarea founded such a community in Pontus in Asia Minor and wrote a rule for it which has become basic among eastern christian monasticism. The community came together as the Body of Christ, and the superior served as the eye. This tradition came to Europe as Greek monks settled in Italy.

Benedict of Nursia (480-547) gathered together the differing currents of the monastic tradition. It is the richness of his synthesis that makes his *Rule for Monasteries* so adaptable.

Benedict knew the tradition well. He knew of *sarabites,* monks "still loyal to the world by their action. They lie to God by their tonsure. Two or three together, or even alone, without a shepherd, they pen themselves up in their own sheepfolds, not the Lord's. Their law is what they like to do, whatever strikes their fancy." Against such as these Benedict prescribed a promise of obedience to an abbot. He knew the *gyrovagues* "who spend their entire lives drifting from region to region, staying as guests for three or four days in different monasteries. Always on the move, they never settle down, and are slaves to their own wills and gross appetites." Against these he prescribed a promise of stability to a particular community. He was cautious about anchorites and hermits. They "must come through the test of living in a monastery for a long time." For this he prescribed a promise of fidelity to the monastic way of life which calls for constant conversion. Benedict was enthusiastic about cenobites, "those who belong to a monastery where they serve under a rule and an abbot." These were the "strongest kind," for whom he wrote his *Rule.*

Reformers like St. Romuald (c. 950-1027) drew on earlier traditions to orient their communities toward a more eremitic existence. Other reforms, such as that of Cluny in the tenth century, emphasized liturgical prayer and expanded it till little time was left for the sacred reading necessary to nourish such prayer or for the labor necessary to support the monastic life and give it balance. The influence of the *Rule* came to its fullest flowering among the Cistercians. They worked for the goal that Benedict had set: "We shall run on the path of God's commandments, our hearts overflowing with the inexpressible delight of love." Thus the *Rule* became for the Cistercians a "school of love." There flourished among them some of the greatest mystical writers of the monastic tradition: Bernard of Clairvaux, William of Saint Thierry, Isaac of Stella, Lutgard, and Mechtilde. These writers centered everything on love and were practical contemplatives who rooted mystical love in everyday monastic life. Monastic life was a contemplative life. And precisely as such, through the great contemplative spirits it produced, it had an immense social, economic, and political impact on society. However, the more the monks attended to social, economic and political affairs to the detriment of their contemplative life, the more their impact diminished.

A man or a woman goes apart to embrace the monastic life because he or she wants to find the freedom and the support to enter into a very complete union with God. By God's grace they have somehow come to see that this is what they are made for. They may or may not immediately perceive the fact that it is by such a union with God that they can make the greatest contribution to the well-being of all, that they can be most fully an instrument of God's creative and redeeming love, the source of all good.

The whole of creation is his masterpiece, the work of God. Its meaning lies in his glory. The lover of God, the one who truly seeks God, is eager that the whole of creation, in accord with the divine will, ascends to him in glory. Through obedience, the monk seeks to be in constant harmony with this movement. Through his prayer services the monk seeks to give voice to this movement. When the monk stands in choir, using the divinely inspired texts and listening to the shared faith of the fathers, he best expresses and constantly increases his zeal for the work of God, the longing that all that takes place in his life and in the whole creation be to the glory of the God who loves us. In his hours of solitary prayer he responds to that love being profoundly a part of that movement of all to the glory of God.

See Asceticism, Mysticism

Anon., The Rule of the Master, trans. Luke Eberle, Cistercian Studies Series, 6, Kalamazoo, MI: Cistercian Publications, 1977. St. Athanasius, Life of Anthony, trans. Robert T. Meyer, Ancient Christian Writers, 10, Washington, DC: The Catholic U.P., 1950. St. Benedict of Nursia, Rule of Monasteries, Collegeville, MN: Liturgical Press, 1980. Chrysostomos Dahn, Athos. Mountain of Light, Ottenburg: Burga, 1959. Charles Fracchia, Living Together Alone. The New American Monasticism, San Francisco: Harper and Row, 1978. David Knowles, Christian Monasticism, New York: McGraw-Hill, 1961. Jean Leclercq, The Love of Learning and the Desire for God. A Study of Monastic Culture, New York: Fordham, 1961.

Louis Lekai, The Cistercians. Ideals and Reality, Kent, OH: State University, 1977. Thomas Merton, The Waters of Siloe, New York: Harcourt Brace, 1969, London: Sheldon Press, 1976. Basil M. Pennington, Ed. One Yet Two. Monastic Tradition East and West, Kalamazoo, MI: Cistercian Publications, 1976.

BASIL M. PENNINGTON, OCSO

MONENERGISM

See Monothelitism, Monophysitism

MONOGENISM

The doctrine that all human beings are descended from a single couple, the "Adam and Eve" of Gen 2-3. In the Encyclical, Humani generis (1950), Pius XII taught that it was not at all apparent that any view which denied this common origin of all members of the human race could be reconciled with the church's teaching on original sin.

See Original Sin

MONOPHYSITISM

The view that, after the Incarnation, Christ has only one nature. While Cyril of Alexandria had espoused an orthodox version of the formula, "the one nature of the Incarnate Word," Eutyches interpreted it in a sense which the Council of Chalcedon refused when it spoke of one person (hypostasis) in two natures, thus distinguishing two terms which earlier had been used almost interchangeably. The monophysite version continued to be held by those who rejected Chalcedon's formula, and the Second Council of Constantinople attempted to resolve the issue by offering an obligatory orthodox interpretation of "one nature" language. In a broader sense, monophysitism is used to refer to those who so stress the divinity of Christ as to overlook or deny his integral humanity.

See Chalcedon, Council of; Jesus Christ

MONOTHEISM

The belief that there is only one God, a supreme being who is transcendent, omniscient, omnipotent, all good, and creator of all that exists. It is opposed to atheism (belief in no God), polytheism (belief in many gods), and pantheism (belief that God is inseparable from the world). This article will discuss monotheism primarily as found in the Bible. Various other systems of belief are sometimes defended as being monotheistic, such as the cult of the solar disk Aten promoted by Pharaoh Akhenaten (Amenophis IV, 1364-1347 B.C.), Zorastrianism, and certain types of Buddhism, though some of these claims are open to question. Akhenaten's system was monotheistic, but it was so contrary to traditional Egyptian religion that it was considered a heresy, attracted few followers, and disappeared shortly after his death. It is unlikely that Moses was influenced by this movement, as is sometimes suggested. Zoroastrianism holds to the eventual triumph of the God of good, but it is basically dualistic in conception in allowing a divine force of evil which is equally primal. Hinduism, although proclaiming one God, also permits lesser divinities. Buddhism, in some of its forms, looks upon Gautama Buddha as a supreme deity, but generally he is considered a man who attained enlightenment and salvation. The three great monotheistic world religions are Judaism, Christianity, and Islam. Mohammed drew his monotheism from the Judeo-christian tradition, and Christianity's monotheism derives from Israel's Yahwistic faith.

Allegiance to one God, Yahweh, is basic to the ancient faith of Israel, though some development was involved. In the patriarchal period, the time of Israel's earliest ancestors, the deity worshiped is often designated "the God of (personal name)" (e.g., "the God of Abraham"— Gen 24:12) and then, in the next generation, "the God of my (or your) father" (Gen 26:3, 24; 28:13; 31:5, 29; 32:10; 46:3). This sort of terminology designates the deity of the clan, who is tied to no particular place but to a group. This designation alone would leave the god nameless, though he may be identified with a god known by a proper name in other contexts. This is a form of monolatry rather than monotheism. The patriarchal deity was frequently identified with El, the high god of the Canaanite pantheon, under one of his various titles, such as El Shaddai (Gen 17:1; 28:3; 35:11; 43:14; 48:3; 49:25), El Olam (Gen 21:33), and El Bethel (Gen 31:13). The striking fact that the God of the patriarchs is never identified with Baal probably attests to the antiquity of the patriarchal traditions (i.e., they date from a time before Baal supplanted El in this area), but also to the fact that the God worshiped by the patriarchs was of a different character than the nature god Baal. When, in the days of Moses, the divine name Yahweh was revealed to Israel, this God who delivers them from Egyptian slavery is identified with the god who was worshiped by the Fathers, who had covenanted with them, and who had promised them the land (Exod 3:4-17; 6:2-8). When the liberation from Egypt has been accomplished and Israel comes, under Moses' guidance, to Mt. Sinai, allegiance to Yahweh alone is the basic condition of the covenant entered into there, as expressed in the first commandment of the Decalogue (Exod 20:3; Deut 5:7). While not all agree that this faith dates as far back as the time of Moses, that position can easily be defended, whether the whole Decalogue in its present form stems from Moses or not.

The monotheism formulated in the Decalogue, and throughout much of Israel's history, might be conceived of as a practical or functional monotheism in the sense that the formulation "you shall not have other gods besides me" does not explicitly rule out the existence of other gods. However, a god that is not to be worshiped, who cannot vindicate any claim to reverence and awe, who is not to be feared, is hardly to be considered a god in any meaningful sense. Formulations are not infrequently found that seem to concede the existence of other gods. For example, Jephthah charges the Ammonites to possess the land their god has given them and to leave Israel to possess the land Yahweh has given them (Judg 11:23-24), and Elijah challenges the Israelites to choose whether Yahweh or Baal is God (1 Kgs 18:21). In fact, Jephthah is merely arguing that the Ammonites should not encroach on Israel's domain, and Elijah has no doubt as to who is God; the latter narrative includes a biting satire on Baal worship—especially vv 26-29.

Early formulations suggest Yahweh's association with particular geographical locations, especially mountains, as when he is said to come from Sinai, Paran, or Seir (Deut 33:2; Judg 5:4-5; Hab 3:3; Ps 68:18). Later this could be transferred to an association with Palestine (Exod 15:17) and, especially, with Jerusalem and the Temple. Yet Yahweh's ability to force the release of his people from Egypt, in spite of opposition from Egypt's occult forces (Exod 7:8-8:15; 12:12; cf. Deut 4:34-35) refutes any geographical limitations on his power and activity (and cf. 1 Kgs 20:22-29). Israel's conception of Yahweh overcame all geographical limitations; she knew him as a God whose power and majesty fills the earth (Isa 6:3). Although early OT formulations might not exclude the existence of other gods, a prophet such as Amos could attribute to Yahweh judgment upon nations other than Israel (Amos 1:3-2:3) and see him as the active force in the history of other nations (9:7-8), just as Isaiah saw the nations simply as instruments of his policy (Isa 5:26-29;

7:18-20; 10:5-15); many of the prophetic collections have lengthy sections of "oracles against the nations" (Isa 13-23; Jer 46-51; Ezek 25-32). But with Deutero-Isaiah comes the explicit or theoretical monotheism that simply rejects other gods as non-existent (41:21-24; 44:6 45:20-24). Monotheism logically implies universalism (cf. Rom 3:29), and, although the conviction of election never wavers, Israel recognizes that Yahweh's saving will extends also to the nations and that all are called to become one people under Yahweh (Isa 2:2-4; 19:24-25; 45:22-23; Jer 3:17; Zech 2:14-15; 8:20-22; 9:9-10; Pss 47:8-10; 96:7-10, 13; 99:1-3; 102:16, 22-23).

The aniconic aspect of Israel's cult accords well with the transcendent and ineffable nature of Yahweh (Deut 4:15-24), but he is proclaimed also as a God who is near (Deut 4:7), the sole creator (Gen 1:1-2:4), a just and jealous God (Exod 20:5; Deut 4:24; 6:15), holy (Isa 6:3; Lev 11:44, 45; 19:2; 20:26), defender of the widow and orphan (Deut 10:18; Ps 68:6; 146:9), and compassionate toward all his creatures (Ps 145:9).

The NT accepts as unquestioned Israel's strict monotheism. Jesus, when asked to name the greatest commandment, replies by citing Deut 6:4-5 (the opening words of the Shema). Assertions about the divine nature of the Son (e.g., John 20:28) and binary and trinitary formulas which closely link the Son and the Spirit with the Father (Mt 28:19; Rom 1:1-4; 16:27) are not perceived as undermining this strict monotheism in any way. Whatever tension might arise is eased, at least in part, by the dispensational schema in which the Son is presented as the revealer of the Father (John 14:7-11), as the one sent by him (5:36-37), and as the way to him (14:5-6). They are one in the operations they perform (5:19-30). It was the Father's will to bring redemption through the Son (6:37-40). As the Son departs from the world he leaves the Spirit, who is both the Spirit of the Father and closely identified with the Son (1 Cor 2:10-16; 2 Cor 3:17-18), as "another Paraclete" to supply for his presence and the carrying on of his mission among the community he formed (John 14:22-26; 15:26-27; 16:4-15). The doctrine of the Trinity as such, which requires philosophical distinctions such as that between nature and person, is not enunciated, but the foundations are laid on which the later formulations of Nicaea and Chalcedon would be built.

See **God, Trinity**

Robert J. Christen and Harold E. Hazelton, Eds., *Monotheism and Moses,* Lexington, MA: Heath, 1969. Frank M. Cross, *Canaanite Myth and Hebrew Epic,* Cambridge: Harvard U. Press, 1973, pp. 3-75. Bernhard Lang, *Monotheism and the Prophetic Minority,* Sheffield, England: Almond, 1983. Donald B. Redford, "The Monotheism of the Heretic Pharaoh: Precursor of Mosaic Monotheism or Egyptian Anomaly?" *Biblical Archaeology Review* 13 (1987), pp. 16-32. Roland de Vaux, "The Religion of the Patriarchs," *The Early History of Israel,* Philadelphia: Westminster, 1978, pp. 267-87. Michael F. Walsh, C.M., "Shema Yisrael: Reflections on Deuteronomy 6:4-9," *The Bible Today* 90 (Apr. 1977), pp. 1220-25.

JOSEPH JENSEN, OSB

MONOTHELITISM

A variant of Monophysitism which holds that in Christ there was only one will and one activity (monenergism). The idea, which was first proposed as a means of reconciling Monophysites to the doctrine of Chalcedon, was condemned at the Second Council of Constantinople (553), which taught that in Christ there are two natural wills and two natural operations.

See **Jesus Christ**

MONTANISM

Montanism was an apocalyptic movement which first emerged in the second half of the second century in the province of Phrygia in Asia Minor. Montanus, a former pagan priest, began to preach and prophesy (c. 156-7), proclaiming a new outpouring of the Holy Spirit, the Paraclete, upon the church. In particular, Montanists expected the descent of the heavenly Jerusalem on the Phrygian village of Pepuza. Noteworthy also was the prominence of the female prophets, Priscilla and Maximilla, some of whose oracles have been preserved.

Initially the movement does not seem to have had any doctrinal peculiarities; it emphasized a renewal of the spirit of the earlier decades of the church, especially the charism of prophecy, now viewed as fading from its former prominence. It also reasserted a moral and ascetical rigorism, e.g., condemning the remarriage of widows, putting special emphasis on fasting, especially dry meals called xerophagies. Montanism was fiercely attacked and condemned by local councils in Asia Minor.

Some have seen in Montanism an attempt of the charismatic, lay element in the church to reassert itself against the growing power of the institutional hierarchy and what sociologists would term the routinization of charisms. It may also be viewed as an early example of the apocalyptic sects or groups which arise throughout church history, predicting the early return of Christ and the end of the world.

ROBERT B. ENO, SS

MORAL LIFE, CHRISTIAN

There is a problem even in posing the question about christian moral life/ morality. It is the problem of determining what the expression means. It might be taken to refer to the actual morality of Christians as a distinguishable group in society. Or to refer to the official teaching of christian churches. The Catholic Church, for example, has strong official positions about abortion, sterilization and contraception. But there is a question about how it arrives at or where it finds its teaching. Generally speaking, the Catholic Church purports to argue to its positions from natural law. That means by definition that such positions are available to non-christians: indeed, the claim of the teaching is that anyone who argues correctly will arrive at the same conclusion. When we speak of christian morality have we in mind such moral positions arrived at even through philosophical argument or have we something else in mind? I think we do have something else in mind. Behind the expression "christian morality" lies the assumption that there is a morality that arises out of and that is necessarily bound up with Christianity, that is, as some have put it, specific to it.

There is another problem however. We might ask ourselves what would count as a christian morality. It is not uncommon to hear it said that Christians act morally out of love of God, that christian morality is a covenant morality. an invitation-response morality, an obedience to God, a bringing about of the purposes of God. Does that mean a christian morality? The contrast here is with the issue of content. All these expressions say something about a christian perspective on morality but none of them necessarily implies a christian content to morality: they are concerned with the context and motivation of morality. A Christian might well see morality as a matter of doing the same things as non-believers but from a different perspective.

Let us leave aside for the moment the central question of content and look at context and motivation. Certainly Christians see their morality in a particular context. In the christian religious tradition, as in the Jewish, morality is markedly religious. That is, it is immediately related to God and its significance is seen in the God-context. It must be so because the Christians view the whole of creation as God's creation and themselves as part of that creation. God is seen as the author and end of it. Everything—morality included—is contextualized and this must in some way be expressed if the Christian's total view of things is to find expression. Morality cannot be regarded as freestanding: in some way it must be described as part of God's purpose or plan. The preferred way for Jew and Christian of expressing this was to refer to morality as the law of God. This term, however, can mask different conceptions of morality and of revelation. One may use it because one believes that God did actually give or hand down morality in some historical event in the past—somewhat in the manner of the decalogue stories. Or, on much the same lines, that God has revealed moral precepts through the people, the prophets or Jesus Christ. Or contrariwise, one may use the term "law of God" to describe how one sees all reality, morality included,—as a way of describing the context of our morality—without any suggestion that God revealed moral precepts. One way or another, moral life has a very high significance for the Christian. It is the place where one meets God. It is a form of discipleship. It expresses one's faith, hope and love. It has, as some have put it, a theological significance.

It is also true that Christianity surrounds morality with a cluster of beliefs and stories that support and undergird the whole enterprise. The religious perception of Christians—the way in which they interpret the deity, the world and themselves—creates for morality a climate that is favorable to it. To believe in a God who is moral, who has an intelligent purpose for the universe, who is supreme and not threatened by other gods, who has power to bring good out of evil, who has given us hope for the future of the world, is to have a powerful support for morality. To believe in a Savior who is the perfect moral one and whose mission it is to overcome sin and its effects is to live a story that is shot through with moral concern. To believe that God sends his spirit into the world to spread abroad his love and that the outcome of the Spirit's action is charity, peace, patience is to have found a fusion of religious and moral ideas.

Christianity not only gives a climate of support to the moral enterprise, it also provides powerful stimulus and motivation. It has been a commonplace to refer to the indicative-imperative motif in Judaeo-Christianity. We find it in abundant variety. God is good, merciful, forgiving: so should we be. Christ has emptied himself, has washed the feet of his disciples, has laid down his life for us: we are to take up this challenge. We are in Christ; we should live as such. We have received the Spirit: we should walk in the Spirit. We are a community of his body: we should live in unity. This highlights the relationships between the religious and moral dimension. It is difficult to go on accepting and reciting the christian story without experiencing its thrust towards moral rectitude and the dissonance between it and moral carelessness.

This context, motivation, support, significance all pertain to christian morality. It would be a mistake to underplay any of it. All of it is important to the christian consciousness, because our problems with morality are not only with knowing what to do but in being able to do it, being faithful to the moral call and enduring in the face of difficulties. This motivational and supportive power of Christianity has been an inspiration to countless Christians through the ages in their efforts to love and forgive, in the struggle for justice and liberation, in the courage to undertake unselfish enterprise. And yet this is not

what has concerned christian thinkers when the question of a christian morality has been raised. That question has focused rather on the methodology of how Christians arrive at good judgment, how they justify it, what are their sources. And in the end on what is the result of such discernment and whether it yields a specific morality. It is to that question that we now turn.

On the issue of content Catholic theology has had a centuries-old-conflict. It centers around the question whether there is for the Christian a distinctive source of moral knowledge which gives a *Christian* moral life and a distinguishable science of moral *theology*. The conflict goes back at least to the sixteenth-seventeenth centuries when theology, abandoning the great synthesis of Aquinas, began to fragment into different specialties. The pressure for such fragmentation and particularly for the development of the practical aspect of christian theology came especially from the decrees of Trent regarding the administration of the sacrament of Penance. The pastoral mission to help the faithful understand the demands of right living and to wean them from sin became the main works of the priest. There was need for manuals which would deal not only with morality properly speaking but with the growing body of practical canon law. These manuals assumed an almost invariable pattern. They began with general principles which were followed in order by the commandments of God and the church, the sacraments, censures, indulgences and the particular obligations of the various states of life. This Latin manual reached its most complete form in neo-Scholasticism. It was in use in the church's seminaries until the time of Vatican II and had a profound effect on the understanding of christian moral life.

The manuals of moral theology set their sights low. They were concerned mainly to determine the exact limits between mortal and venial sin so that the faithful might be instructed how far they could go without incurring eternal punishment. It would be difficult to find any reference in their general principles to Christ, and they adverted to the moral teaching of the Bible only as corroborative texts for positions that had already been assumed. Their sources were philosophical ethics—a form of natural law—and canon law. This did not mean that the totality of christian life was ignored however. But christian life came to be divided into morality and spirituality: the latter was treated in ascetical, mystical and devotional works. Parallel to this division went a form of thinking which suggested that the basic commandments were the rule of life for the faithful while the further reaches of christian life were the preserve of priests and religious.

This was not the total picture of Roman Catholic moral theology. There had been in nineteenth century Germany a development of moral theology which was quite different in spirit from neo-Scholasticism. Its interest was to develop a christian theology along the lines of the great biblical themes. It concerned itself not with minimum demands but sought to set out the fullness and attractiveness of christian life. So it proposed a theology organized about the themes of grace, the kingdom, the Mystical Body. But because of the dominance of Latin as the language of theology the influence of the movement was limited to German-speaking areas and it declined towards the end of the century. At the beginning of the twentieth century and well into mid-century the Latin neo-Scholastic manual was the dominant influence in the world of Catholic theology.

In the 1940's and 1950's there emerged a strong current of dissatisfaction with the morality of the manual and an urgent call for a renewal of moral theology (e.g.,

Thils, Tillmann, Mausbach, Gilleman, Häring, etc.). The central criticism was that what had been proposed as moral theology was merely a mixture of philosophy, psychology and jurisprudence and failed to present the distinctive character of the christian vocation. It was negative and minimalist, so the criticism went, and concerned with what some called the science of sin rather than with the riches of Christianity. It lacked the dynamism and inspiration that one would expect from Christianity. Its basic error, it was said, was that it sought its inspiration and method in the wrong sources—in philosophy and natural law ethics. The assumption was that religion should make a difference to morality, that it should give it a different content from ethics.

It was a primary tenet of the renewal movement that morality, if it was to be christian, must be dependent on or derived from revelation. Above all, it was claimed that it must become biblical through and through. It must concentrate on the key themes of the Bible and not be satisfied with random quotations to bolster positions arrived at philosophically. It was a point of view that was canonized in the recommendations of Vatican II about the study of theology in general and of moral theology in particular: "Sacred theology rests on the written word of God, together with sacred tradition as its primary and perpetual foundation ... the study of the sacred page is, as it were, the soul of sacred theology" (D.V. 24). And: "Dogmatic theology should be so arranged that biblical themes are presented first ... Special attention needs to be given to the development of moral theology. Its scientific exposition should be more thoroughly nourished by scriptural teaching. It should show the nobility of the christian vocation of the faithful and their obligation to bring forth fruit in charity for the life of the world" (O.T. 16).

Much of the discussion of the 1940's

and 1950's was about the possibility of finding one basic christian principle on which a whole structure of christian morality could be built. Several candidates were advanced. (a) Christian morality, it was proposed, would be based on the new life of grace. This view depended on the accepted interpretation of grace as an entitative elevation of the soul and its faculties which was seen as giving the human being a new *esse*. It was argued that we should bring about in our actions the moral demands of the new being which constitutes our state as Christians, that there is a *vie morale christique* which corresponds to our supernatural status, that we must act like Christ because we are ontologically identified with him. Ethics and moral theology, it was said, are different in essence: christian moral life goes far beyond any merely natural thought and cannot be understood by it. (b) Christian morality should be primarily a morality of charity. In the soul which it has divinized sanctifying grace has given birth to a new reality of charity which makes the Christian capable of supernatural acts of charity-love. Charity is the root, form and foundation of all moral life by which we direct all our activity to our supernatural last end, God. The task of morality is to render the exercise of charity in us always more explicit: the activity of which charity is the form is not that which corresponds to natural law but something higher; the end or objects of the supernatural virtues of the Christian are different from the ends or objects of the natural virtues. (c) Moral theology is to be understood as the scientific presentation of the following of Christ in individual and social life. What contributes to the growth of the personality measured against Christ as model is good, what limits or destroys it is bad. Christ is the norm of morality and there is a specific morality based on the new life in Christ which is foreign to every other kind of morality.

All these approaches and others—moralities of the Mystical Body, of the kingdom, of sacramental life, of the new law as outlined by Aquinas—insist that there is a specific content to christian life that is different from and higher than the morality of natural law which had been favored by the manual. They all take the Bible as their starting point and are heavily dependent on reference to it. In spite of their claims, however, they did not in fact adduce any significantly different content. They often confused content with motivation or with the general context and spirit of morality. Their use of the Bible was uncritical: it sometimes consisted merely in gathering together the scriptural texts and themes relevant to their subject, so that the bearing of scripture on the moral argument was not clear.

The result was that there appeared in the late 1960's and early 1970's a reaction to this attempt to "christianize" morality. This was in part due to a dissatisfaction with what was seen as a lack of rigor in the writings of the previous two decades especially in the use of the biblical material. The criticism noted that it is one thing to elaborate the moral teaching of OT and NT—that had been done successfully and inspiringly by several biblical scholars (e.g., Schnackenberg, Spicq)—but another to delineate what bearing this was to have on moral argument. On this methodological issue the renewal movement had been less than successful, so that the whole project of elaborating a morality "from the middle of the revelation" (Böckle) was put in doubt. An equally important factor in the reaction was the feeling that the attempt to "christianize" morality gave the impression that Christians are a ghetto and christian morality something esoteric. This went counter to the mood of the time in continental Europe where the talk was of dialogue and solidarity. There was also anxiety to counter the suggestion that christian morality is a childish and unthinking acceptance of the morality of the Bible: revelation morality was stigmatized as a "morality from beyond," a biblical or revelational positivism which is destructive of human autonomy and responsibility.

An influential group of authors (Fuchs, Auer, Schüller, Mieth) began to propose that there is no christian content to morality. They agreed that there is a christian motivation, a specific christian context and a new significance and meaning given to the whole moral enterprise. But they argued that, as far as material norms are concerned, there is no difference from what they called human morality: this presumably was taken to mean morality as understood by non-Christians. They bolstered their claim by the contention that there is nothing in the morality of the Bible that could not be attained by non-Christians—including specifically the command of *agape* and of the forgiveness of enemies. The Christ-event, they said, is not ethically normative.

The battle was now joined about whether there is such a thing as specifically christian morality. At least it was ostensibly about that but in reality the debate went deeper and was about methodology, about the source and justification of christian moral positions. The point of view mentioned in the last paragraph was viewed with alarm by others (e.g., Ratzinger, von Balthasar, Stoeckle, Delhaye) who insist that it is a diminution of revelation, a denial of the church's teaching authority and even an undermining of Christianity itself. Their stance in particular stresses that the Bible is an indispensable moral source for Christians, that there are in the Bible material norms which are valid for all time—or at least christian values and a christian moral core. Christians, in this view, have had a

special moral revelation which is authoritative for them and which is authentically interpreted by the church. This is also the thrust of the Vatican II statement previously quoted and of official church statements on morality: recent statements refer to a revealed positive law (*Persona Humana*) or to the revealed word of God (*Laborem Exercens*) or state at least that the teaching is derived from reason "illuminated and enriched by divine revelation" (*Humanae Vitae*) or by "the light of faith" (Document on Procured Abortion). This has considerable practical implications. There is involved the question of the extent to which christian moral positions can or should be defended at the bar of reason: it is no coincidence that it was dissatisfaction with *Humanae Vitae* which occasioned some of the early articles of the autonomy school.

Why do we need a revelation of morality? Some of the earlier exponents of renewal appealed to the Bible because in their view the morality of Christians is altogether foreign to reason since it is the morality appropriate to one's new supernatural life. But even with regard to natural law the Catholic tradition has been that while revelation is not absolutely necessary it is morally necessary in order that the truths of natural law be known easily, with firm certitude and with no admixture of error (Vatican I). That means that in practice one cannot trust reason. The net result is that a Catholic may be asked to accept a moral position by appeal to revelation even though the position cannot be satisfactorily demonstrated by moral argument although held to be a matter of natural law. Such positions arrived at by appeal to revelation are of course also held to be the correct moral judgment for all people.

There are different degrees of appeal to the Bible. To say that one's position is illuminated by revelation (*Humanae Vitae*) is a weaker claim than to say that one's position is a revealed moral precept. There are different ways in which the Bible is regarded as authoritative. (a) There are revealed moral precepts which remain permanently valid in their precise biblical form. (b) There are values/dispositions/intentions/attitudes which the Bible declares to be appropriate to Christians and which they should foster. (c) There is a permanently valid core to biblical morality although the precise biblical statement of it is not permanently valid: what we have in the Bible are paradigms. All these positions hold that God is telling us in the Bible what to do but all regard the Bible as authoritative in different ways. When one appeals to the Bible—and it is done not only in official documents and in works of theology but very commonly by Christians generally—it is important to know exactly what claim is being made for it. It is also important to have a considered view on the manner or process of revelation, on how the community came to possess a revealed morality. By "revealed morality" do we mean some kind of direct communication from God to the sacred author; or do we attach authority to the apostolic community's attempts to discern how it should live its life in the light of its experience of Jesus Christ?

Some advocates of a biblical ethic are unhappy with suggestions that what we can point to are authoritative values and paradigms—both of these being open-textured concepts. They insist on the precise validity of material norms. The difficulties of this position have been well-documented. One faces questions about the dependence of the biblical writers on the philosophy of the time, about the cultural limitations of their horizons, about the distinction between normative and paranetic material, about exegetical and hermeneutical questions. In particular it has been suggested that in discriminating between still valid precepts (e.g., regarding adultery) and directives that the community has jettisoned (e.g., regarding slaves or the position of women), one has to step outside the Bible and subject it to the criterion of common sense or of common moral experience.

In spite of such objections it has been stoutly maintained that we have in the Bible inerrant moral teaching, not simply ideals or values but propositions which are normative for conscience (Grisez), not an appendage to Christianity, the contents of which could be changed, but the concrete assignation of what faith is, something guaranteed by the Lord (Ratzinger). *Persona Humana* rejects any suggestion that the precepts of the Bible are merely the expression of a particular culture at a certain moment of history. This seems to ignore the very human process of revelation which was received or perceived by a people with a very particular world-view and horizon. It takes the process right outside human personality and involvement. It may well be that the questions which the apostolic community was asking and the conceptions which it had of some of our problems and institutions were quite culturally limited and that it was impossible for it to transcend this cultural horizon. One cannot simply claim its moral directives as the necessary expression of faith. Indeed one has to face the uncomfortable fact that in the Bible we find faith-considerations adduced in support of moral positions that we no longer consider tenable, e.g., the position of slaves and of women.

To say that the Bible gives us values or dispositions that are permanently valid, while a weaker claim because such values and dispositions can be differently realized in different ages and circumstances, is not decisive either. Some of the Bible's general aims and purposes remain valid, e.g., injunctions to live in love, trust, detachment, thankfulness and joy. But there are attitudes that are based on the expectation of an imminent parousia: "The time we live in will not last long. While it lasts, married men should be as if they had no wives; mourners should be as if they had nothing to grieve them, the joyful as if they did not rejoice ... For the whole frame of this world is passing away" (1 Cor 7:29).

Nor does it give us easy access to the Bible to say that we find in it models or paradigms which contain a permanent core of truth. The implication is that the cultural form can be simply stripped' away from the core which remains undisturbed through the ages. This will hardly do: the interplay of subject, event and circumstances is more subtle and elusive than that.

However the opposite point of view which is favored by the autonomy school and which dismisses the need or the possibility of appeal to the Bible is not satisfactory either. Such appeal is not necessarily destructive of moral responsibility and is not to be conceived of as simply submission to a "morality from beyond," a biblical positivism. It is rather a matter of engaging with the faith and vision of an earlier age. It may not be possible to accept the biblical texts as they stand as a precise directive for today. But neither is one to reject them. What is required is genuine discernment. It is a discernment that is undertaken by a Christian, not by one who stands outside the faith of Christians but one who is shaped and formed by it. What we have in the Bible is not something given from without, "from beyond," but the attempt of the Judaeo-Christian community to allow its faith to bear on living. What we have there is a dialectic of ethos and ethic and it is into this that the Christian of today tries to enter. What is being suggested is a more indirect approach to the biblical material which is not limited to its explicit moral exhortations but

which focuses on the subject of moral discernment and on the dialogue between discernment today and the discernment of our ancestors in the faith.

What is intended is that we consider what it means to do morality as a Christian, that we take seriously the effects of our religious commitment on moral discernment. Such commitment goes deep. It gives basic meaning to life. Because religious faith has something to say about the major factors which shape personality: it has views about the nature of the human person, about origins and destiny, about salvation, beatitude, wholeness, perfection; it suggests attitudes to world and matter, to body and spirit, to success and failure. It determines to some extent one's meaning, what for the faith-adherent are the facts of life and what among them are the most prominent and relevant facts. It does this in a most complex and subtle way because it is communicated and received not just in abstract formulation of belief but in stories and symbols which subtly pervade a person's consciousness. It seems odd to say that this religious element would have no bearing on our perception of patterns of living and never impinge on moral judgments.

Attention needs to be directed to the total background out of which judgments and choices are made. Judgments are not made in a vacuum. They are made by people who see the world in a particular way because they are particular sorts of people. One's evaluative description of the field of action and the responsibility which is experienced in a situation depend on the sort of person one is. That in turn depends on the beliefs, loyalties, myths and symbols that shape consciousness. Religious faith might be seen then as forming or having the potential to form a particular kind of character and therefore to communicate values, to evoke certain kinds of awareness and sensibility which affect moral judgment. One might think of a living vital christian communty as a community that has its own character, formed by stories of what God has done for it in Christ—stories of creation, deliverance, covenant, incarnation, death and resurrection.

This is faith issuing in action, the perspective of faith leading to perspectives about living. The Christian lives in a tradition: what one tries to do today is what the apostolic community tried to do in its time. What the Bible gives is a statement of the apostolic community's experience of transcendence, of finite living intersecting with infinite boundaries. It is a statement of the imagination of those who were influenced by the divine irruption into history in Jesus Christ, woven most elaborately, colorfully, imaginatively. It is our classic statement of religious experience. It has much to tell about action—about living, loving and dying, about world, flesh and devil, about wholeness and flourishing, about success and failure, about weakness and sin, about honesty and hyprocrisy. It does not give it straightforwardly: it is textualized in a great variety of forms and genres—saying, aphorism, parable, narrative, proclamation, apocalypse—in a particular time and place, by people of a particular culture, language and religious tradition, with particular concerns and presuppositions. All of that must be appreciated and respected. In and through it one is confronted with the integrated ethico-mystical kernel, the moral and imaginative kernel which embodies the rooted experience of the apostolic community. What is important is that one be able to enter into this world of religious and imaginative meaning, that one allow the text to challenge and change through opening up a new and wider world of meaning and action than one might otherwise have.

It seems artificial then to make a sharp distinction between the religious and moral message of the Bible. Some moralists have done this to such an extent that they suggest that one accepts the one and may ignore the other. But the biblical imagination is inseparably religious and moral. There is an interplay, an intermingling of the two, a forming of an integrated christian imagination that expresses itself in saying and story. They are stories about how one experiences oneself in Christ and about the implications of this for living, about the effects of the "making new" that was the message. They tell us today that a life lived in fidelity to the final power of God is a life like the life of freedom, suffering and love confessed as lived by Jesus. Our own expectations of life, precisely the expectations that form the currency of the moralist—happiness, welfare, flourishing, fairness, justice—are jolted when placed against the preaching and the defamiliarizing life of Jesus Christ. This experience becomes the climate of and prepares the way for a discernment of what God is asking and enabling us to do in Christ. It is this nexus of ethos and ethic that is revelatory and authoritative.

The Christian's dialogue with the Bible in the search for a moral way is a subtle and complex matter—much more than has been suggested by some moralists. The one who tests the biblical ethic and present-day experience against one another approaches the text with a preunderstanding that is already inwardly Christian. There is a hermeneutical awareness required of us in the widest sense, i.e., an awareness not only of the text but of the referent of the text, of the world which opens out before the text and of the cultural presuppositions of that world, as well as a sensitivity to the variety of literary genres with their contrast and complementarity, and to the theological presuppositions that influenced the authors. There is equally required a critical awareness of oneself, of one's own place and time and one's own questions—one's cultural, linguistic, social, economic, political and sexual biases. A suspicion of ourselves and of what might unconsciously rule us, a suspicion in particular of the assumption that we know what the text is saying to us. Perhaps not just a neutrality but an advocacy stance in certain directions—in favor of the poor, of blacks, of women, of the marginalized. Only then can we be disciples of the text, free of our own ego with a new capacity for knowing ourselves. Only then can there be genuine conversation back and forward with the text, with the text throwing light on our lives and our present day experience and praxis illuminating the meaning of the message. Is this what Vatican II meant when it suggested what seems a second approach to moral discernment—that one should consider problems of living "in the light of the Gospel and of human experience" (G.S. 46)?

The challenge for the Christian is to discern in the light of or in the atmosphere of this total vision, to shape a character and life that are consonant with it, that pursue the ends and ideals that arise out of it. This will incorporate most of the great inter-personal values that are the heritage of the race as a whole—justice, respect, benevolence, equality, impartiality. But Christianity has its own perspective too which it will take into account. For Christians as a class there is an enlarged reality in which there are values and meanings that may not exist for the non-Christian and which, for example, relativize secular notions of welfare, success and failure. This applies to judgment both about what Christians should seek for themselves and what they should seek for others: the most urgent need of the neighbor, Barth said, is God himself. Knowledge of God, awareness of him, friendship with him is for the

Christian the supreme good; attention to it may well modify one's attitude to goods which a non-believer regards as important. The justification of the Christian's life is supra-historical and what appears to others as limitations on welfare or development may be regarded by the Christian as creative self-development.

One follows this line of thought into christian traditions about detachment and poverty. While there is in general Judaeo-Christian tradition a belief that God's world is good and a suggestion of a pro-attitude to it—in contrast with dualist or apocalyptic views—there are attitudes that derive from faith and that are summed up in the biblical injunction to be in the world but not of it and not to be anxious for tomorrow. It is true that one finds God in and through the human but one should so conduct oneself in human affairs as not to forget divine things. One should if need be sacrifice human development to progress in the divine. One may even renounce the normal human goods, e.g., marriage, family, friendship, society, as virgins and hermits have done, for the sake of the divine.

Likewise poverty of life and spirit is part of the christian tradition. While much of secular moral literature is based on concepts of interest and desires, on one's right to a fair share of the available goods, Christians understand the spirit of the gospels as saying that concern for the total meaning of one's life implies a certain kind of poverty in the pursuit of one's interests and that the way of radical poverty—of leaving all for the sake of the Kingdom so as to accentuate the religious dimension and one's wider sense of blessedness—may be an intelligible choice. Not pressing one's claim is related both to personal creativity and to one's response to others. We are to seek the interests of others and not our own, we are to give to everyone who asks, wash one another's feet, forgive enemies, be prepared to lay down our lives for the neighbor. This curious asymmetry in relationships seems to be the logic of a faith that has stories about the forgiving love of God for us, about a Savior who died for us when we were yet sinners, about the final and total meaning of our lives.

There is talk in Christianity too about bearing the cross. It is not a matter of opting out, of cowardice or weakness. It is that the experience of Jesus, and especially his death-resurrection, has something to say to every human being. Moral literature generally seems to envisage situations of logic and clarity in which we are dealing with perfectly reasonable people. But we live in a world in which justice will not be done, in which rights will not be allowed, in which goodness will not be rewarded, in which evil prospers. A fair slice of life is about injustice and about situations which have injustice written into them. In such situations there must be a christian response: it cannot be a response that is divorced from the stories and symbols that are the very stuff of Christianity. It is interesting that there is a strong tradition of non-violence in Christianity.

Hanging over the Christian discernment in the broadest sense is the central belief in an intelligent and loving God who is creator and last end. In the most general sense this shapes one's attitudes to oneself, to others and even to the inanimate world. It determines the perspective from which one sees reality: it gives a certain kind of metaphysic. We do not live solely for ourselves. "If we live we live for the Lord" (Rom 14:8). No one is a favorite before God: those who do the will of the Father are brothers and sisters of the Lord; there must be no room for personal rivalry or vanity. Whatever we have we have in stewardship: all is under the creative plan and purposes of God. Such considerations suggest a certain style of life—a respect for all, a modesty and humility of mien and behavior.

These are some of the general thrusts of the biblical world-view. It is not that one regards the Bible as a moral text. No. Rather one seeks to enter into the mind-set that was shaped by the experience of the inbreak of the Kingdom in Christ Jesus and that issued in the general contours of biblical morality. Much will depend, of course, on how one envisages morality. Some discuss moral life in terms of commands or rules. It may be important for the christian community to determine rules. This means that it chooses a point on the scale of good or bad which it regards as the minimum of community tolerance. But morality or moral life cannot be circumscribed in this way. Our moral lives are not about ten commandments but about the uniqueness of our possibilities and problems. One might think of it more satisfactorily in terms of character, as a perfection to be realized, and as the ability to choose and live in accordance with a settled vision and disposition. Christian vision will bear on the variety of our opportunities and temptations—temptations to be bitter or envious, to be enclosed in one's ambitions or those of one's family, to harbor resentment, temptations to self-aggrandizement of a political, sexual or intellectual kind, temptations to cheat and hoard, to take advantage, to insist on one's own share at all costs, to be seduced by riches, to ignore one's poor relations. About such one cannot elaborate rules. But one can in the light of biblical faith try to plot the portrait of the Christian and suggest the aims, aspirations, intentions and desires that are consonant with christian character.

It is true that the philosophical tradition made much of the distinction between duty and supererogation and that some elements of it did not even admit supererogation under the rubric of morality. It is also true that Catholic moral theology had a sharp division of command and counsel. But it is worth noting that even the philosophical tradition is now much more open to the notion of character and that Catholicism can be said to have abandoned the distinction of command and counsel (McDonagh). It is more satisfactory to envisage morality on a scalar model and certainly it is hard to see that the NT community was ready to recommend anything less than life in the likeness of Jesus Christ who loved to the end.

At the same time there must be no blurring of the discipline of the moralist. Christian morality must not collapse in a fog of pious sentiments. There is required an awareness of the different kinds of relationship between faith and ethics— the difference of the genesis and justification of moral positions, of normative ethics and parenesis, of reason, motive, content and context. There cannot be easy recourse to some esoteric discernment: Christians should be able to give an account not only of the faith that is in them but also of their moral judgments. Some have spoken of a "faith instinct" (Rahner) in moral matters. This is fair enough but it does not absolve the individual or the community from indicating at least in general terms the faith considerations which go into their judgment and the manner of their inference. However delicate the process of judgment it should be possible for the Christian to indicate the factors (the stories, symbols, loyalties, commitments) that seem to enter into it.

Is there a specifically christian morality? This is hardly a matter of primary importance. Christians should not feel any compulsion to prove a special morality. On the other hand there is no need to apologize for doing morality in fidelity to one's world-view. Everybody does so: there is no position of pure rationality that is uncontaminated by metaphysical presuppositions: the atheist or agnostic position is not "pure." What is needed is that Christians do their morality in line with their story. Whether and to what extent this gives them a morality that is specific, i.e., peculiar to Christianity and different from all other moralities, depends on a number of considerations. It depends, first, on the term of comparison. There are, obviously, some world-views that are more sympathetic to and more in harmony with the christian world-view than others. It also depends on what one regards as the domain of the moral: Are acts directed to God, acts of worship for example, part of morality as Catholicism has traditionally regarded them? Are vocational choices of poverty, chastity and obedience part of it? Is the judgment made in faith that one is called and enabled to give one's life for another part of it? Certainly this is. Again, how easily can one delimit what has been called the content of morality? Can one separate content from what some Catholic authors have called motive, e.g., the motive that enters into choices of celibacy, poverty or detachment? Does the motive not determine the description of the act, of what is being chosen, of the content of the act? Does the manner of performing actions enter into morality—one's intention, disposition, attachments, innermost desires, sentiments? In fact they do. The more attention given to such considerations the more likely is the claim that there is a specific christian morality— since morality will include not only what is done but why and how. The more morality is understood in terms of character and virtue, therefore, the more one can speak of something specific.

However, one wonders if Christians should spend much energy in proving specificity. There will be considerable areas of agreement between Christian and non-Christian—between all who have a concern for the person, for rights, justice, fairness and benevolence. Perhaps one can say that at the level of material norms there will be considerable coincidence. But it needs to be pointed out that one cannot catch much of morality in norms, especially negative norms. The moral vocation is dynamic and open-ended. It is highly personal. What is required is that one respond to individual situations with responsibility and imagination. The task of christian morality is to delineate the vision and the thrusts that are consonant with its faith. The task of christian moral education is to encourage the emergence of character that in the variety of human situations will know how to allow faith to bear on choice in continuity with the great tradition which we have inherited.

See **Anthropology, Christian; Biblical Criticism; Human Rights; Justice; Mysticism**

Vincent McNamara, *Faith and Ethics: Recent Roman Catholicism,* Dublin: Gill and Macmillan, and Washington: Georgetown Univ. Press., 1985. Joseph Fuchs, *Christian Ethics in the Secular Arena,* Dublin: Gill and Macmillan, and Washington: Georgetown Univ. Press, 1984. C. Curren and R. McCormick, *The Distinctiveness of Christian Ethics,* (Readings in Moral Theology #2) Mahwah: Paulist Press, 1980. Enda McDonagh, *The Making of Disciples,* Dublin: Gill and Macmillan, and Wilmington: Michael Glazier Inc., 1982. Bruno Schuller, *Wholly Human: Essays on the Theory and Language of Morality,* Dublin: Gill and Macmillan, and Washington: Georgetown Univ. Press., 1986.

VINCENT MCNAMARA

MORTAL SIN

See **Sin**

MYSTERY

The word "mystery" (Greek *mustèrion,* Latin *mysterium*) has many nuances of meaning. Central to the various meanings is the idea of something hidden which has been revealed, something unapproachable which invites entry, something unknowable which offers true understanding.

The Mystery Is Christ

While the NT uses the word in many different ways, it usually has some connection with the Jewish idea of the plan which God has in mind for the world. This plan is glimpsed by seers, but it continues to remain obscure, defying complete explanation. In Mk 4:10-12 we see something of this usage.

Two NT texts, Col 1:1-2:6 and Eph chaps. 1-3, have played a very significant role in determining the use of the word in christian circles.

The passage in Colossians tells us that the mystery is "Christ in you, the hope of glory" (1:27). Christ, the image of the unseen God, the beginning, the head of the body, the reconciler who makes peace through his death on the cross, is the revelation of the mystery which was hidden for ages but is now made manifest.

The first three chapters of Ephesians put forward a similar teaching. The mystery is God's plan to unite all things in Christ, to gather together those who were far off, to reconcile Jew and Gentile through the cross. This is the mystery which has now been revealed to the apostles and prophets through the Spirit. The unsearchable riches of Christ are to be preached to the Gentiles, so that they may come to know the love of Christ which surpasses all knowledge. Further on in the letter we read that the loving union between Christ and his church is like a marriage, and is indeed a great mystery (Eph 5:32).

This teaching animates the way in which ancient christian writers use the word. It may be noted that in contexts where Greek writers use the word *mustèrion,* Latin writers use either *mysterium* or *sacramentum,* and that much of what is said about mystery can be applied to sacrament. Of course individual authors use the word in different ways. This article gives some good examples of how the word is used.

In a devotional homily, which the Roman Rite uses for the Office of Readings on Easter Monday, Melito of Sardis, who lived in the second century, speaks about the mystery of the Pasch or Passover. He contrasts the figure which has passed away and the reality which is Christ, who contains all things, who calls all nations to receive forgiveness, and who promises to bring them to the heights of heaven and show them the Father who is from all eternity.

Origen, in speaking of mystery, seems to have allowed himself to draw a distinction between ordinary Christians who understand scripture in an ordinary way, and advanced people who have some understanding of the mysteries hidden in the apparently ordinary words of scripture. That is, he seems to have held that there is an elite in the church, people who understand the mysteries which remain hidden from the general run of Christians. This tendency is partly due to the influence of Platonism, which spoke about mystery with reference to the philosophical quest for wisdom.

The Celebration of the Mystery

During the fourth century, the rituals of the church are referred to as mysteries. We find this in, for example, the *Mystagogical Catecheses* of Cyril (or perhaps John) of Jerusalem. These catecheses were lectures delivered to the newly baptized during Easter week. They are an explanation of the great celebration which took place during the Easter vigil. The bishop has been longing to speak to the newly baptized about the "spiritual and heavenly mysteries." Both baptism and eucharist are called "divine mysteries." In the eucharist, the faithful are invited to communion in the "holy mysteries." They are advised not to judge things by their bodily appearances, but to put their trust in the tradition which Paul received from the Lord. They are urged to keep themselves free from sin so as not to be deprived of the mysteries.

Etheria (or Egeria), in her account of the pilgrimage she made to the holy places sometime around the year 400, helps us to see the customs of Jerusalem through the eyes of a Spanish visitor. Before the Easter vigil, at the ceremony in which the catechumens "gave back the Creed," the bishop promised to tell them about a deeper mystery, that of baptism. During Easter week, after the dismissal from church, the bishop and the newly baptized go in procession to the church of the Resurrection. There the bishop explains everything that the neophytes experienced during their baptism. Etheria emphasizes that no catechumen is allowed to enter, but only the newly baptized and other baptized people who may wish to be present. She relates that the bishop is so good at unveiling the mysteries that shouts of approval can be heard even outside the church.

The fact that the rites of the Easter vigil are called mysteries is an indication of the attitude which Christians in those days had to liturgy. It indicates that they saw the liturgy of the church as in some way the bearer of the great mystery about which we read in Colossians and Ephesians. It shows they believed that the salvation brought by Christ is in some way communicated to the believer during the rites of baptism and eucharist.

In the practices of Jerusalem, we see an example of how at least some Christians in the fourth century employed the deliberate technique of keeping the catechumens in suspense, impressing them with a very dramatic celebration of the Easter vigil, and only afterwards speaking clearly and in detail about baptism and eucharist.

There has been much discussion about the connection, if any, between the christian idea of mystery and the various meanings which the word had before and outside Christianity. In particular, there is the questions of the mystery religions which were popular in the Mediterranean region. There were quite a number of such cults. The cult of Demeter and her daughter Kore, practiced at Eleusis, is one of the most famous. The cult of Mithras had peculiarities of its own, and was especially popular among soldiers. In general, the mystery religions promised some share in the immortal death-conquering life of a god. This sharing in the life of the god was obtained through rites, "mysteries," which had to be kept hidden from the uninitiated. In these mysteries, the initiate relived the fate of the god.

The German monk, Dom Odo Casel, caused great discussion in the first half of this century. Historians of religion were suggesting that Christianity should be seen as one more mystery religion, and saying that Paul used the word "mystery" to make it easier for the pagans to accept the gospel. Rather than struggle against these suggestions, Casel thought it was best to say that while the essential message of the gospel comes through Jesus Christ, some christian forms of expression were borrowed from the mystery religions. He even said that Judaism was not a suitable soil for the seed of the gospel, but that God had provided a suitable soil among the Aryan peoples and in particular in the mystery religions. His theories have been expounded and criticized many times, and there seems to be fairly general agreement that he exaggerated the influence of the mystery religions on Christianity. For example, some of the words which he thought were direct borrowings had in fact passed into everyday use before being used to refer to christian liturgy; there also seem to have been instances where the mystery religions borrowed from christianity as they saw it growing in popularity. Probably the most important thing to keep in mind is that religious ideas and longings which are in some way similar tend to be expressed in similar ways. The fact that two rites resemble each other does not necessarily mean that one borrowed from the other. Still, it seems true that the mystery religions contributed something to the atmosphere in which the liturgy was celebrated in the fourth century.

Casel also caused discussion by putting forward a theory about the way in which, in the celebration of the mysteries, the original events are made present. In doing this, he injected fresh life into sacramental theology. Even authors who seriously disagreed with him tried to show that their traditional theology was just as wonderful and exciting as the theories of Casel. His work itself, though dated in many ways, remains a classical protest against the trivialization and the intellectualization of the liturgy. It is also a protest against the temptation to reduce liturgy to moral exhortation. He must be given much of the credit for the fact that we now speak readily of the liturgy as the celebration of the paschal mystery of Christ.

In connection with Casel, it is noteworthy that nowadays there is great interest in the Jewish roots of many christian customs. In particular, there is the work which is being done to show the links between Jewish and christian prayer and ritual. Added to this there is the use of the idea of "memorial," which in a less shocking way makes many of the points which Casel made in terms of mystery cults.

Vatican II, in the Constitution on the Liturgy (6, 2), incorporates the idea of liturgy as a celebration of the paschal mystery, an expression of the mystery of Christ and of the true nature of the church. The rituals which have been published since Vatican II present the liturgy as the celebration of the mystery of God's saving love which is communicated to us in Christ and in his body the church. For example, the Rite of Christian Initiation of Adults mentions mystery quite often, and presents christian initiation as a journey which takes the catechumen through various stages. However, there is no exaggerated atmosphere of secrecy. The mystery is one which cries out to be made known to all, not jealously guarded by the initiated. Likewise, while the RCIA obviously wants the ceremonies to be done with due appreciation of the power of symbolism to move our hearts, there is no suggestion that the catechumens should be manipulated by techniques designed to overawe them. It is much more a question of welcoming a new member into a loving community while maintaining an openness of spirit to all people.

The Mystery Is Above Reason

So far, the uses we have been looking at tend to emphasize that the mystery is God's plan which has been revealed, into which we are inserted through baptism and eucharist. Another use of the word tends to emphasize the unknowability of the mystery rather than its revelation. The rationalism of the nineteenth century caused Vatican I to define that there are mysteries which cannot be known unless they are divinely revealed, and that even when they are revealed and received in faith, they remain obscure in some way. Vatican I also reacted against fideism and said that the believer can gain some understanding of the mysteries; reason, illuminated by faith, can and should apply itself to gain some understanding of them. Mystery invites us to think more deeply rather than abandon all thinking.

The emphasis on this aspect of mystery was a significant shift. In the ancient writers and even in the Middle Ages, the Incarnation, in which the aspect of manifestation is so important, was the great mystery. In the nineteenth century, the Trinity, taken somewhat in isolation, came to be regarded as the great mystery. There was even a tendency to deal with mystery as if it were a statement which cannot be understood fully. In other words, mystery, like many other things, was affected by the "propositional model" of revelation.

The Mystery Is the God of All Things and All Peoples

In the twentieth century, many things have conspired to revitalize the use of the word "mystery." There was the study of ancient christian writers. There was the enthusiasm of Odo Casel. There was also Rudolf Otto's description of the sacred as *mysterium tremendum et fascinans,* the awe-inspiring mystery which fascinates us, which makes us hesitate between turning away in fear and gazing in wonder. The studies done by Mircea Eliade in the field of comparative religions have helped to flesh out our understanding of rituals and symbols.

One of the concerns of modern theology has been to try to assimilate some of these ideas. To mention one example, there is Paul Tillich's teaching on revelation, in which he correlates mystery, ecstasy, and miracle. For Tillich, reason encounters mystery when it is driven beyond itself to its "ground and abyss." The mystery is our ultimate concern, the ground of our being. A miracle is an astonishing event, which points to the mystery of being, and is received in an "ecstatic" experience in which the mind transcends its ordinary state. In Tillich's theology there is a broadening out, an openness to the possibility of encountering mystery not only in the rites of the church or the Bible, but in nature, in the events of history, and in the expressive power of language.

For Karl Rahner, mystery is the link between many of his key ideas. To be human is to be exposed to the mystery which pervades the whole of reality; the "transcendental experience" which plays such an important role in the theology of Rahner is an experience of the mystery which is at the heart of all being. It is an orientation to the infinite, and, for Rahner, it is the condition without which human knowledge and freedom are not possible. To be human is to be a questioner, not just by moving from one question to another, but by moving towards the mystery which is without limit. The answer to such questioning is God, who freely communicates himself to us.

For Karl Rahner, one and the same mystery is found in the mystery of grace and the beatific vision, in the mystery of the Incarnation, and in the mystery of the Trinity. It is the mystery of God's self-communication to us. Rahner's treatment of the Trinity has become a classic in this respect. As Rahner never tired of repeating, the economic Trinity is the immanent Trinity, that is, the God who comes to us as Spirit, Word and inexhaustible source is God's own self. In saying this, Rahner wished to restore the notion of manifestation to the theology of the Trinity, or, to put it another way, to restore the link between Trinity and Incarnation.

In saying that God is mystery, we are saying that no words can ever adequately express his reality, and that he remains greater than our best ideas about him. According to Rahner, among others, even the beatific vision does not put an end to mystery. God remains always "incomprehensible," in the sense of being beyond all definition and limitation, greater than the knowledge which any creature can have of him. This was taken for granted by most of the ancient writers of the church and by the great scholastics. Mystery is far more than a knotty problem which will be unraveled in heaven.

Of course the details of Rahner's theology are open to discussion. But any real theology needs to be aware of mystery, the mystery of God, and the mystery of human beings who are made in God's image.

Vatican II, in the Constitution on the Church in the Modern World (41, 22, 93), says that the mystery of Christ sheds light on the mystery of what it is to be human. The mystery of God is the ultimate answer to the human search for meaning. And the best way to share with others the mystery of God's love is to recognize, to love and to serve Christ in every person.

Conclusion

"Mystery" is a word which warns us against placing false limits and boundaries. The mystery we celebrate in the liturgy is the mystery which is at the heart of all being. It is the mystery which is in all our brothers and sisters. It is Christ, who reveals God to us, and reveals us to ourselves.

See **Paschal Mystery, Sacrament**

R.E. Brown, "Mystery (in the Bible)," *New Catholic Encyclopedia,* Vol. 10, pp. 148-151. O. Casel, *The Mystery of Christian Worship and Other Writings.* A. Dulles, "Mystery (in Theology)," *New Catholic Encyclopedia,* Vol. 10, pp. 151-153. H. Rahner *Greek Myths and Christian Mystery* (1963). K. Rahner, "Mystery," *Sacramentum Mundi,* pp. 133-36.

PHILIP GLEESON, OP

MYSTICAL THEOLOGY

If mysticism may be defined as the experience of a loving knowledge of God, then mystical theology is systematic reflection on that experience.

In the recent past, the mystical experience and its theoretical interpretation were relegated to a small corner of the field of spirituality, which itself had lost contact with the renewal taking place in the wider arena of theology. Spirituality as a lived faith, and its more intense mystical or supraconceptual knowledge of God, was not always so far removed from the heart of theology. The Eastern church has never maintained a sharp distinction between the experience and its theory. Experience and doctrine mutually condition one another so that the Eastern theological tradition is essentially a mystical theology. A dogma is to be lived in such a way that an inner transformation of spirit occurs as God is met.

The Fathers of the church and early christian writers did not identify "spirituality" as a discipline distinct from their normal theological endeavors. In the medieval period Thomas Aquinas held a balanced view of theology as both a science and a wisdom which comes from the love uniting God and humanity. Later, in the sixteenth century, John of the Cross continued to identify the experience of God with its articulation: "contemplation is the mystical theology which theologians call secret wisdom and which St. Thomas says is communicated and infused into the soul through love" (*The Dark Night* 2, 17, 2).

However, beginning about the fourteenth century, theology was increasingly viewed as a strictly rational endeavor. Consequently, spirituality and its mystical dimensions grew isolated from the mainstream of theology. And within the field of spirituality certain nineteenth and early twentieth century theologians attempted to articulate a discipline of mystical theology.

A. Poulain defined mystical theology as the science of mystical states which the person is powerless to produce. Ascetical theology treated ordinary ways of prayer which were understood as dependent upon human effort.

Adolphe Tanquerey described ascetical theology as the study of "Christian perfection" up to the passive or contemplative states of prayer. Mystical theology, then, was the theory and practice of the contemplative life of prayer, such as described by John of the Cross beginning with the night of the senses, and by Teresa of Avila beginning with the prayer of quiet.

In the effort to develop a mystical theology writers often neglected to provide a solid biblical foundation for their reflections. And the individualistic, subjective dimension of mysticism was emphasized with little regard for the social context and corporate nature of religious development.

This mystical theology of the recent past discussed issues such as the relationship between acquired and infused contemplation. What was the mix of human endeavor and divine activity that furthered the life of prayer? Also at issue was the possibility of a universal call to mysticism. Or is mystical experience a rare phenomenon given to very few people? And theologians discussed the subtle nuances of the life of union with God, and the accompanying extraordinary phenomena. Consequently, mystical literature appeared intimidating to ordinary Christians; the rarefied experiences and esoteric issues, often confused by deficient theological categories, guaranteed that the mystical writings would remain virtually inaccessible.

Contemporary theology, through the urging of Karl Rahner among others, is attempting to integrate once again the experience of God and reflection on that experience. The experience of Mystery is seen as the indispensable core of the theological task. And the mystics are viewed as persons who illumine the deepest realities present in all Christians. All are mystical people, that is, fundamentally God-targeted and God-touched. "Where have you hidden, beloved, and left me moaning? You fled like the stag after wounding me," writes John of the Cross as he describes the soul's profound experience of deep desire for God (*Spiritual Canticle,* stanza 1).

The theological task is to make intelligible this orientation to God as it is experienced, and often known only implicitly, in the guise of ordinary daily living. Even the very development of human consciousness, as Bernard Lonergan explains, is ultimately the result of God's love driving the human to awareness and responsible living in an ever transformative relationship.

The renewal of mystical theology includes a biblical orientation, beginning with a recognition of the mystical element in the life and teaching of Jesus. Jesus spoke from a powerful, intimate experience of Mystery which he referred to as "Abba, Father." The evangelist John in his "spiritual gospel" and the apostle Paul in his missionary journeys give evidence of a lived, mystical faith, a faith found throughout the pages of the NT.

A mystical theology will attempt to differentiate the primordial experience from its interpretation. The two cannot be divorced, but the mediation of consciousness in its symbolic expression of the experience of transcendence will have to be acknowledged.

The mystical dynamism within humanity may be examined as a transcultural core which all major religions are attempting to express. And the power of a religious tradition to open a person to the experience of God, through its images and doctrines, is another side of the issue.

These issues and many others, such as the relationship of mysticism with ordinary life, with prophecy, and with societal experience, begin to suggest tasks for a mystical theology.

The basic myth of humanity, as told by the christian mystics, is essentially a love story. The soul in the *Spiritual Canticle* of John of the Cross begins the adventure having been wounded by God's love, a love experienced in a world made beautiful with God's glance. And so the human search for final and complete fulfillment, a union of love, is initiated by God in the heart of every man and woman.

The mystery upon which the human rests, the center toward which the soul journeys, is in love with us and desires for us what we most deeply desire ourselves. The claim of the mystic is that this profound truth is the basic structure of reality. God's relationship and communication with us, in love, propels human consciousness into reflection and understanding and so makes necessary the task of a renewed mystical theology.

See **Mysticism**

Keith J. Egan, "The Prospects of the Contemporary Mystical Movement: A Critique of Mystical Theology," *Review for Religious*, 34 (1975), 901-910. Harvey Egan, *What Are They Saying About Mysticism?* Mahwah, NJ: Paulist Press, 1982. John of the Cross, *Spiritual Canticle. The Collected Works of St. John of the Cross*, Kieran Kavanaugh, O.C.D. and Otilio Rodriguez, O.C.D., trans. Washington, D.C.: Institute of Carmelite Studies, 1979. Bernard Lonergan, *Method In Theology*, New York: Seabury Press, 1979. Vladimir Lossky, *The Mystical Theology of the Eastern Church*, London: James Clarke and Co., Ltd., 1957.

JOHN WELCH, O CARM

MYSTICISM

Mysticism may be understood as referring to an experience of God, a process resulting from that experience, and to issues involving both.

As an experience, mysticism is traditionally described as a loving knowledge of God which is born in a personal encounter with the divine. Included in the encounter is an awareness of the presence of God, but not always in the initial stages, and an experience of being drawn into union with God.

As a process, mysticism refers to a way of life which is built upon one's direct experience of God and which proceeds in an organic manner as one is led ever more deeply into the reality of life and into a loving union with the Mystery revealed at its core.

Today mysticism, or contemplation as

it is often called, is viewed as a common and normal activity, although often implicit, in the lives of all Christians. Karl Rahner emphasized this development when he wrote, ". . . the devout Christian of the future will either be a 'mystic,' one who has 'experienced' something, or [the person] will cease to be anything at all" (Th.I. 7, p. 15).

Mystical experience is recognized as prevalent in the Bible. A direct encounter with God often characterizes the lives of the patriarchs, the prophets, and women of faith in the OT. These representatives of the Jewish faith experienced a God who was intimately present to, and involved in, their lives.

And Jesus knew the Father with a loving knowledge that is the epitome of mysticism. A striking feature of his life is his easy familiarity with God whom he experienced in a direct and unique way. Jesus' mystical life unfolded as he surrendered himself to his "Abba" and he experienced the Father's oneness with him. Jesus Christ is the model for the christian mystic.

The word "mysticism" is not used in the Bible. Its christian meanings find their source in the Bible, but etymologically its roots are traced to Greek Hellenism. The Greek mystery religions involved the disclosure of secret rites or ritual objects (*ta mystika*) to the initiated (*hoi mystai* or *hoi mystikoi*). These "secrets" which were revealed to the "mystics" were about aspects of the rites themselves and never referred to a particular experience.

The christian meaning of mysticism is found in the Greek Fathers of the Church who spoke of a mystical interpretation of scripture. Clement and Origen wrote about the mystical, or hidden and spiritual, meaning of scripture. The meaning is disclosed to one who approaches the scriptures with a prayerful and loving reading. By the fourth century A.D. the word "mystical" was used to refer to Christ's hidden presence not only in the scriptures but also in the liturgy and the sacraments.

Pseudo-Dionysius, a fifth-century Syrian Monk, is credited with gathering-up the patristic mystical heritage and definitively introducing the word "mystical" into the christian tradition. Following Gregory of Nyssa in particular, he used the word to refer to the deeper meaning of scripture and the sacraments, in which God's love is revealed and through which the Christian participates in this mystery.

In particular, Pseudo-Dionysius, a man of Neoplatonic thought, influenced the christian spiritual tradition through his treatise *Mystica Theologia*. In this work he spoke of a mystical contemplation that was a movement toward God beyond concepts and symbols. It was a knowledge of God by a way of unknowing. Concepts and symbols lead one into a darkness which is an experience of God's love and the soul is grasped by that love and transfigured.

Translated into Latin by John Scotus Erigena in the ninth century, Pseudo-Dionysius' *Mystica Theologia* greatly influenced the Christian mystical tradition from the twelfth century onward. Prior to the late Middle Ages, the Latin Church, exemplified in writers such as Augustine, Gregory, and Bernard, more commonly used the word "contemplation" instead of "mysticism."

The twelfth and thirteenth centuries saw the rise of schools of mysticism connected with centers of spirituality. Among them were the Cistercian and Franciscan schools, as well as the Victorines, a group of theologians associated with the Abbey of St. Victor in Paris.

In the fourteenth century the Dominican mystics of the Rhineland made notable contributions. Meister Eckhart stressed the radical otherness of God, who is approached through a "letting-be" of this passing world. This letting-go of sinful compulsions as well as noble activity is a serene, mature, and ordinary way which frees the spirit. Eckhart's influence continued in the Dominicans Henry Suso and John Tauler. It was Tauler whom Martin Luther admired and through whom Luther was influenced by Eckhart.

The fourteenth and fifteenth centuries produced a school of Flemish mystics, exemplified in Jan Van Ruysbroeck, a canon regular of St. Augustine. And English mystics became prominent, especially the Augustinian Walter Hilton, the anchoress Julian of Norwich, and the anonymous Englishman who wrote *The Cloud of Unknowing* and translated Pseudo-Dionysius' *Mystica Theologia* into English.

The Spanish mystics of the sixteenth century made major contributions to the christian spiritual tradition. The Carmelite mystic, poet, and theologian John of the Cross provided beautifully symbolic and subtly analytical accounts of the human experience of God. The way to God was through the "dark night," a journey of faith and love beyond images and thought. Echoing Pseudo-Dionysius John calls God a "ray of darkness." The total being of the Christian is transformed and integrated as the experience of God's love deepens into the union of the mystical marriage. John's way of knowing God by an unknowing is a prime example of apophatic mysticism which emphasizes the difference between God and creatures. God is no-thing (*nada*) and yet everything (*todo*).

This apophatic mysticism found contemporary expression in the writings of the Trappist monk, Thomas Merton. And while emphasizing silent contemplative prayer, Merton brought to spirituality a sensitivity to the need for social action and social transformation.

Ignatius of Loyola's experience of God led him to espouse a kataphatic mysticism which has as a premise the similarity between God and creatures. Consequently, images, symbols, and concepts form a major part of the Ignatian *Spiritual Exercises*. Especially, the events of the life, death, and resurrection of Jesus provide a sure oasis for prayer and reflection.

Ignatius' "service mysticism" stressed engagement with the world. This mysticism in action finds contemporary development in the cosmic consciousness of the Jesuit paleontologist Teilhard de Chardin, for whom the world is a divine milieu revealing God's presence.

The engaging Spanish Carmelite mystic and reformer Teresa of Avila provided a balanced exposition of the mystical life. Writing in the vernacular, Teresa was an incipient psychologist who created categories and images to communicate her subjective, interior responses to the experience of God, an experience which was basically ineffable.

Teresa observed that our greatest problem was the lack of self-knowledge. God is at the center of one's existence and as God is approached the individual increases in self-knowledge and enters more fully into the reality of existence. God is met and the self is born on this journey. The individual does not collapse into an Absolute but is differentiated and stands forth as union with God deepens.

Teresa experienced profound silent contemplative prayer but she stressed that this type of prayer will always need balancing with normal reflection and meditation. Life is long, she observed, and we should return from wordless, imageless attentiveness to God to meditation on the humanity of Christ. The events of his life provide the ground for prayer, especially the events of the passion.

Integral to Teresa's mysticism was the experience of locutions, visions, and ecstasies. But she herself said that such extraordinary events were not of the essence of mysticism. Conformity with God's will, opening one'e life to the activity of God, is the purpose of prayer. Extraordinary phenomena may indicate nothing about a person's sanctity, or they may be the reverberations of a sensitive mystic to the experience of God's love.

Teresa's "bridal mysticism" related her to the triune God and led to the mystical marriage with Christ. But always the intense experiences of interiority were to manifest themselves in virtuous living. The purpose of the mystical marriage, she wrote, is service, service of those for whom we are responsible and service in the work of the church.

The mystical tradition has been identified as a rich, largely untapped resource for theology and the church. Karl Rahner spoke of the necessity to do theology rooted in the experience of the Mystery which we find addressing us. And he believed that the mystical experience is found in the lives of all faithful Christians. And while our discussion has focused on specifically christian mysticism, the direct experience of God is certainly an element in other religions as well. Everyone has the experience of being addressed by God, no matter how implicitly.

This experience is not necessarily identical for everyone and across all religions. Experience is a product arising from the interaction of a person with reality. Consequently, the person's history, community context, conceptual framework, and images will all condition the experience. Mystical experiences will have similarities and differences.

We are mystical people whose destiny is to be in the presence of God. The mystical experience is an experience of the basic orientation to God. It is an experience which is often disguised and hidden deep within our human activities. But Christians can attend to this invitation and raise it to awareness and explicit articulation.

The classical mystics are consciously aware of the divine love story taking place within the themes and subplots of their lives. And, at times, whatever has mediated that awareness of God fades in part, or totally, and all that is left is a silent, loving attentiveness to Mystery.

God is being heard in a new way today in the voices of the laity and especially in the experience of women. And the cries of the immense numbers of the world's impoverished and marginated peoples are forcing an attentiveness to a presence of God in the world which is deeply upsetting and which challenges Christians to authentic conversion to the poor and solidarity in their suffering. This powerful experience of God in a people is calling for deepening christian commitment which leads to activities of social transformation; it calls as well for profound contemplative prayer in which God reveals one's basic poverty in common with all who suffer and wait in hope. Read through the eyes of the poor the mystical tradition is seen in a new light and offers resources for those struggling for justice and freedom.

See **Mystical Theology**

Harvey Egan, S.J., *Christian Mysticism,* New York, Pueblo Publishing Company, 1984. Segundo Galilea, *The Future of Our Past,* Notre Dame, Indiana: Ave Maria Press, 1985. William Johnston, S.J. *The Inner Eye of Love,* New York: Harper and Row, Publishers, Inc. 1978. St. Teresa of Avila, *The Interior Castle. The Collected Works of St. Teresa of Avila,* vol. 2, Kieran Kavanaugh, O.C.D. and Otilio Rodriguez, O.C.D., trans., Washington, D.C.: Institute of Carmelite Studies, 1980.

JOHN WELCH, O. CARM.

MYTH

The Definition of Myth

There are as many definitions of myth as there are theories concerning its nature and function (e.g., traditional, anthropological, psychological, phenomenological, structuralist). For the most part these may be regarded as complementary rather than competing definitions which point up the complexity of myth and its functions. The older form-critical definition of myth as "stories about the gods" popularized by the brothers Grimm (1812) is today generally rejected as inadequate, as is the view of those who regarded myth as the product of an early ("primitive") stage in the intellectual development of humankind whereby events and natural phenomena incomprehensible to the uncritical, pre-scientific mind were attributed to the direct intervention of gods. In so far as one may speak of an emerging consensus, myth may be broadly defined as *a narrative (story) concerning fundamental symbols which are constitutive of or paradigmatic for human existence.* Myth is a universal human phenomenon. It attempts to express through symbol ultimate reality, which ultimate reality transcends both the capacity of discursive reasoning and expression in ordinary human language. Myth points to a reality beyond itself which cannot be directly symbolized; P. Ricoeur refers to this as a "surplus of meaning." Every society and tradition, whether ancient or modern, has its myths and is given to myth-making. In nonliterate or archaic societies participation in myth is immediate and largely uncritical. In modern Western society participation and perception is non-immediate and critical, sometimes referred to as "broken" myth. Among the operative myths in a given society, usually one myth is dominant and gives order and coherence to the others. Myths die or are abandoned when they cease to function in the community as a carrier of the community's values or when they cease to signify for an individual the inner and outer realities which he discovers in the course of life. In such a situation new myths more congruent with the perceived reality may be created to take their place.

Formally, myths are narratives (tales) about symbols; functionally they are vehicles of ultimate meaning. The narrative form is basic to myth and distinguishes it, on the one hand, from other symbolic expressions of reality (e.g., poetry and art) and, on the other hand, from discursive reasoning about ultimates (e.g., science, philosophy and theology). The principal function of myth is cosmicization, i.e., making the world livable. Myth "establishes" the cosmos and the fundamental symbols by which a society orders its existence. Its story is "timeless" and paradigmatic for the present; for this reason the story is often placed either in primordial time ("in the beginning") or in eschatological time after the present world has come to an end. By its very nature myth contains an implicit truth claim; it states what is really real, true and good, even in face of seeming inconsistency with sensible experience. Accordingly, a myth demands of those for whom it is operative a conformity to the reality which it proclaims.

Myths are not necessarily connected with religion or ritual, as the Nazi myth in our own century demonstrates. Likewise, they need not be about divine activity or divine intervention in the world. The protagonist(s) may be human (e.g., the first humans, culture heroes such as Gilgamesh, Oedipus, Alexander the Great or George Washington) or even abstract symbols (e.g., death, kingship, democracy, justice). Many aspects of myth remain unclear. Whether myth originates in the imagination or in the unconscious mind, or is the product of the fundamental structure of human thought processes remains moot.

History Of The Study Of Myth

The original Greek term *mythos* in its widest sense meant a tale or something spoken aloud; included within its semantic range were: a public speech, a story, the plot of a play. Plato applied the term to the legends of early Greek tradition in which human and divine activity are often intertwined. The Sophists introduced an opposition between *mythos* and *logos* ("word"); the latter was identified with factual truth and the former with the unhistorical. Accordingly, *mythos* acquired a connotation of fictitious story (like Latin *fabula* "fable"). Echoing this usage, NT writers considered *mythos* as antithetical to authentic christian doctrine (1 Tim 1:4, 2 Tim 4:4; Tit 1:14; 2 Pet 1:16) and admonished Christians to "have nothing to do with profane myths or old-wives' tales" (1 Tim 4:7). The derogation of myth as pagan superstition and therefore false and incompatible with christian dogma remained the characteristic christian attitude until the modern period—and is still prevalent in some circles.

Although the Renaissance brought a renewed interest in classical antiquity, including Greek and Roman mythology, the modern study of myth began in earnest with the Enlightenment, when new myths from various parts of the world became known in Europe. From a comparative study of the religions of such far-flung lands as Persia, India, China, Africa and the New World, many Enlightenment philosophers posited an evolutionary development of religion. Rationalists such as Fontenelle, Bayle, Voltaire and Hume held that religion and myth developed as the awed but mistaken response of ignorant savages to natural phenomena which were beyond their comprehension and control. A more positive evaluation of myth was inaugurated by the early eighteenth century Italian philosopher Vico. With great insight Vico posited that myth came from within man's own deepest inner nature; using the imagination rather than reason the first men gave true—even if non-rational and pre-scientific—answers to the original human dilemmas. Vico's views would have considerable influence

in the following century upon the romantics like Herder and Schelling, who enthusiastically affirmed myth as primal wisdom in poetic form. With Freud the study of myth entered a new period, as the source for the mythic impulse was now sought within the interior workings of the human mind or psyche rather than in external conditions. The Freudians attempted to explain myth out of psychological rather than cultural development. They interpreted myth as the collective dream of a people, an infantile manifestation of group unconscious. Jung further developed the theory of the "collective unconscious" to include archetypes (i.e., inborn tendencies possessed by all humans to form certain general symbols) as an explanation of why certain symbols or images seem to be universally shared. Levy-Buhl maintained that myth is the product of a prelogical "primitive mentality." Perhaps most promising of all is the structuralist theory of Levi-Strauss. Myth, he says, is a fundamental mode of human communication which derives, apparently, from the basic structure of the human mind. The meaning of individual myths is determined by an underlying bipolar structure common to all myth, analogous to the manner in which the meaning of language is determined by its underlying structure. The analogy of language is apt, further, in that the underlying structure of myth, like speech, is normally accomplished without conscious reflection on the part of the participants. The phenomenological approach to the history of religions, popularized through the writings of van der Leeuw and Eliade especially, seeks to provide an objective description of religion through a comparative study of the actual religious experiences of humankind. Phenomenologists have tended to link myth and ritual as complementary aspects of religious experience.

Myth in the Bible

So long as myth was defined as erroneous, polytheistic beliefs or as the distorted imaginations of a primitive mentality, orthodox Christians were reluctant to admit the presence of myth in the Bible. Furthermore, most of the study of myth during the modern period was conducted apart from Catholic involvment and at times, e.g., during the Enlightenment, by those openly hostile to the Catholic Church. It is no wonder, therefore, that Roman Catholic magisterial teaching enunciated in the *Syllabus Errorum,* Vatican I, the encyclical *Providentissimus Deus* and the early decrees of the Biblical Commission universally excluded the possibility of myth. Pius XII's encyclical *Divino Afflante Spiritu* (1943) marked a turning point in Catholic teaching, therefore, in calling for renewed study of the historically conditioned literary forms in which the word of God is actually expressed, a position reaffirmed by Vatican II in *Dei Verbum.* The last four decades have witnessed a significant reevaluation of myth in the Bible by Catholic exegetes.

With the comparison of biblical texts to other ancient near eastern literature has come the conclusion that in ancient Israel, no less than in the ancient Near East generally, mythopoeism (myth-making) constituted one of the basic modes of speculation about the origin of the world and the place of humankind. The primeval history in Genesis 1-11 is generally acknowledged to be mythopoeic in character. Out of mythic elements common to their culture the biblical writers created a new myth of origins which more closely conformed to their religious tradition of Yahwism. In poetic texts some mythic references are little more than artistic license; in others they may be expressions of authentic myth (e.g., Ps 18:5-29; 99:1; Isa 51:9-11; Job 40:15-41:34). Increasingly the presence of myth is being recognized in "historical"

texts also. Thus, the Exodus is presented largely in mythic terms: a contest with the antigod Pharaoh, the splitting of the sea (chaos) and the creation of a new people; the establishment of Israel's religious institution according to a heavenly pattern revealed on the sacred mountain; the near divinization of Moses by the horns and veil for his face—all this in the foundational period which "established" the world by which Israel lived.

NT writers, too, employ mythopoeic speculations to express their religious insights. The portrayal of Jesus walking on the sea (Mt 14:22-33 & //s), for example, is deliberately reminiscent of Yahweh's powers in the OT (e.g., Job 9:8) in order to suggest Jesus' divine power. Understood in the positive way that myth is defined here, i.e., as the profound symbolization of realities which transcend human capacity to comprehend and express them in ordinary language but which are profoundly true and paradigmatic for authentic life, even the central christian mysteries of incarnation, resurrection and the second coming of Jesus may be understood as myth.

Some scholars make a distinction between historicized myth and mythicized history, i.e., between something which is really a mythic "event" but which is portrayed as if it actually occurred in time (e.g., creation, the flood), on the one hand, and an actual historical event but which is portrayed in language borrowed from myth (e.g., the Exodus, Jesus' birth), on the other hand. While useful for some purpose, it should be recognized that such a distinction is rooted in the Enlightenment heritage which regarded history as true and myth as false. The corollary, also frequently encountered, is that history is the principal medium of revelation. Without denying the essentially historical character of the biblical tradition, it would appear that biblical authors employed mythopoeism precisely so as to reveal the *extra*-ordinary, *super*-natural dimensions of the events which they record. It would seem out of keeping with the biblical tradition, therefore, to posit a dichotomy between myth and history.

Myth, Christian Dogma and Theology

Christian dogma may be regarded as "broken myth." Dogma, like myth, is an indispensable symbol (or symbol-set) which interprets and makes livable ultimate reality with its logically non-demonstrable truth claim. Theology attempts to make intelligible through discursive reason the mystery of God and the relationship of humankind and creation to God. Theology is similar to myth in that it attempts to symbolize that which transcends the human capacity for direct comprehension. The path of myth is through the imagination, resulting in an intuitive, immediate identification through symbol. The path of theology, by contrast, is through reason, resulting in an indirect, analytic understanding mediated by logic or syllogistic symbolization. Myth as a universal, non-mediated intuition of ultimate reality is logically prior to the theological analysis. Theology, like philosophy and science, is a critical, logically secondary formulation of ultimate reality. Theology, because of its greater capacity for logical precision in meaning, has naturally been the preferred mode for expressing christian dogma among the learned leaders of the church. It is a moot question, however, whether myth or theology is the more adequate for apprehending the "surplus of meaning" of christian faith.

See **Demythologization**

Mircea Eliade, *Myth and Reality*, New York: Harper & Row, 1963. Lee W. Gibbs, and W. Taylor Stevenson. eds., *Myth and the Crisis of Historical Consciousness*, Missoula: Scholars Press/ American Academy of Religion, 1975. G.S. Kirk, *Myth: Its Meaning and Functions in Ancient and Other Cultures*, Berkeley/ Los Angeles: University of California, 1970. Claude Levi-Strauss, "Structuralism and Myth" *Kenyon Review* N.S. III 2 (Spring 1981), 64-88. Paul Ricoeur, *The Symbolism of Evil*, Boston: Beacon, 1969; and *Essays on Biblical Interpretation*, Edited by L.S. Mudge, Philadelphia: Fortress, 1980. Percy S. Cohen, "Theories of Myth," *Man*, N.S. 4 (1969), 337-353. J.W. Rogerson, *Myth in Old Testament Interpretation*, Berlin/ New York: Walter de Gruyter, 1974.

B. BATTO

N

NARRATIVE THEOLOGY

Narrative theology is a contemporary North American movement rooted in some insights of theologian Karl Rahner, Karl Barth, H. Richard Niebuhr, and in new secular, academic and practical appreciation of the central role of narrative, story-telling, and story-enacting in handing on traditions and teaching virtue.

Narrative theologies are exercises in understanding, assessing, and proclaiming a religious tradition which take stories as conceptually and practically prior to doctrinal formulations or theological systematization, for these could not make sense without a narrative context. Thus, to understand the life and faith of the communities in the biblical traditions, one must retrieve the myths, legends, fairy tales, anecdotes, allegories, histories, and parables which constitute these ongoing sagas. To assess new ways of life and faith, one must evaluate practices and proposals for their appropriateness for carrying on the saga in new contexts. To proclaim Christianity is to retell, ritually reenact, and live stories of faithful discipleship to Jesus. Christian traditions differ among themselves as the range of stories differ: all accept the NT and OT narratives, but receive them and shape the rest of the story in different ways.

In contrast, traditional theological approaches see theological doctrines as primary and the stories as derivative. Doctrines were timely statements of Eternal Truths which were given their meaning by their reference to those Truths. Theology amplified, explicated, and grounded these doctrines. Stories were for identification or pedagogy, mere illustrations of moral or theological truths, or were histories, narratives irrelevant to the truth of theological statements. This picture, however, cannot account for the essential historicity of the human. For example, even if God directly revealed eternal truths, God would have to do so in a historically conditioned language, for humans understand no other kind. If God's revelation is God's ongoing presence to the community, that presence must be a presence in time. Hence, even divine revelation, however pictured, must be understood as an event or events in historical time. But understanding historical events requires understanding them contextually, that is, placing them in a narrative. Hence, narrative theology claims to have a more fundamental way to understand embodied christian truth and life.

The chief weakness of narrative theology is a tendency toward fideism, asserting the claims of a traditional way of faith while refusing to confront not only the problems of truth and credibility created by the multiplicity of narrative traditions within and without Christianity, but also the need to adapt the way of faith to varying social and political conditions. Protestants also tend toward biblicism, exalting the Bible (or parts of it) as the only source of knowledge of God and sole norm of christian faith and practice. Catholics tend toward allegorization, constructing stories to conform to a preconceived doctrinal scheme rather than allowing the doctrines to emerge from understanding narratives.

The chief strengths of narrative theologies are the connections they show between theologies and communities of faith, between the practice of faith in everyday life and the expression of faith in ritual, and between the past and the present ways of believing and living Christianity. Analyses by literary critics, reconstructions by historians, and the investigations by philosophers also enable some narrative theologians to discern important nuances often neglected by more traditional approaches. Although narrative theology will continue to contribute to theological development, it remains to be seen whether the change in perspective implied by the primacy of narrative over doctrine will become a predominant mode of theological reflection.

T.W. Tilley, *Story Theology,* Wilmington, DE, 1985. M. Goldberg, *Jews and Christians: Getting Their Stories Straight,* Nashville, 1985. J. Shea, *Stories of God: An Unauthorized Biography,* Chicago, 1978. R. Thiemann, *Revelation and Theology,* Notre Dame, 1985.

T.W. TILLEY

NATURAL LAW

The expression "natural law" is a familiar one in several normative contexts. Within the discipline of jurisprudence, for example, it names the most common alternative to legal positivism. In political philosophy it is frequently used to refer to theories of political obligation distinct from the prevailing social contract and natural rights views. In moral philosophy and theology, "natural law" refers to a distinctive conception of the foundations of moral responsibility. It cannot be assumed that "natural law" in these different contexts of inquiry always means even approximately the same thing. Thus, for example, when Jeremy Bentham referred to natural law as "nonsense on stilts" it would not be safe to suppose he had anything like Aquinas' moral theory in mind, or what popes mean by that expression when they appeal to it in the social encyclicals of the last one hundred years.

For purposes of theological inquiry, however, the task of understanding natural law is not simply an effort to uncover and disentangle its diverse meanings as used within some special context of inquiry, or by one or another thinker. For the most common context within which the language of natural law is used is that of Roman Catholic tradition of moral reflection and teaching. Within this tradition natural law has a special if not privileged place, and here it is reasonable to suppose that there is some continuity in its meaning even when used in different contexts and by different thinkers.

This supposition is reasonable partly for historical reasons. Since the time of Aquinas Catholic moralists have used the language of natural law which he established, and have made use of some of his key concepts, even when disagreeing with him more or less radically. This language has not remained isolated within the scholarly community of Catholic theologians but has become part of the ordinary moral teaching of the church and the everyday moral reflection of Catholics. But, since teachers within the church self-consciously link their use of natural law with the theological tradition, and with Aquinas' work in particular, and since the everyday moral reflection of Catholics is shaped by this teaching, the extensive usage of natural law within the Catholic community should not be assumed to lack a definite reference or clear meaning.

To determine this meaning it is useful to begin by clarifying what natural law is taken to mean within the teaching of the church. For this is a sense of natural law which theologians must take seriously even as they reevaluate and reappropriate the theological tradition.

The Core Conception of Natural Law in Catholic Teaching

The popes and bishops who make use of the language of natural law in their moral and social teaching not only affirm that certain moral norms are justified by the natural law and provide some suggestions of the relevant natural law considerations, they also teach about the character of natural law and its general place in christian moral life. Perhaps the most important teachings on these latter issues are those of Vatican Council II.

Several of the most fundamental components of the idea of natural law are delineated in the Council's discussion of conscience: "Deep within his conscience man discovers a law which he has not laid upon himself but which he must obey ... For man has in his heart a law inscribed by God. His dignity lies in observing this law and by it he will be judged [footnote to Rom 2:15-16]" (G.S. 16).

Although the Council does not explicitly call this law the natural law, there can be little doubt about the reference. For the text from Romans which the Council cites is perhaps the most important theological source for natural law. Aquinas, for example, used this text to settle the question of whether there is a natural law (S. Th. I-II, q. 91, a. 2, sed contra).

There Paul emphasized that all men will be judged for what they do; the good

will be rewarded, the evil punished. Jews will be judged by the Law of Moses, but what is the standard for judging those who do not have the Law? Paul answered: "When Gentiles who do not have the law keep it as by instinct, these men although without the law serve as a law for themselves. They show that the demands of the law are written in their hearts. Their conscience bears witness together with that law, and their thoughts will accuse or defend them ... " (Rom 2:14-15).

Revelation, Paul suggests, is not necessary for moral knowledge adequate for divine judgment. This knowledge is properly understood to be natural in the sense that it does not require supernatural revelation. It is written in the human heart and accessible to the human conscience. The emphasis of Vatican II, though compatible, is different: the law discovered within conscience is not self-imposed, it is somehow a given. The contrast with "natural" as applied here would, therefore, be "conventional," or "manmade."

This conviction of Vatican II expresses the core of natural law as understood within Catholicism—namely, that within the foundations of the consciences of all human beings there are nonconventional, nonarbitrary moral standards which make possible genuine moral self-criticism, and so true moral knowledge even for those who have not received the moral instruction of divine revelation. This core idea of natural law is neither sectarian nor uniquely christian. John Calvin, for example, held that what was taught in the decalogue is also dictated in some way by an interior law written in the hearts of all. And among at least some of the rabbis, a basis for discriminating between righteous and impious gentiles was found in the moral requirements of the covenants with Adam and Noah reported in Genesis. The moral knowledge given to these common ancestors of all humankind was widely taken by Jewish authority to be accessible to all insofar as it is inherently reasonable.

This core conception of natural law, in a way the common property of the entire Hebrew-christian tradition, does not contain all that the church teaches about natural law. But it does contain the basis for avoiding one common misconception.

This core conception supposes that human beings can discover within themselves an objective moral standard. The reality of this standard is a ground for rejecting all forms of ethical skepticism according to which moral standards are simply the results of personal preference or choice or of social convention. All such preferences and conventions are subject to evaluation by this standard.

The relevant objectivity, however, is not like that which is realized in the study of natural or social phenomena in the world outside the person. For the natural law is found within the human person, deep within conscience, written on the human heart. And it provides a norm, a standard for action. Knowledge of natural law, therefore, is a part of a person's self-knowledge, and so the objectivity of this knowledge must be the objectivity appropriate to honest reflection and critical self-awareness. Knowing the natural law, therefore has little similarity with knowing the laws of nature in scientific inquiry. It is a mistake, therefore, to suppose that the moral standards which comprise the natural law are identical with or established by the regularities known through the empirical study of human nature. The undeniable moral significance of this kind of knowledge is no reason to confuse it with knowledge of a law which is not a regularity but a standard, and which is natural in the sense explained above—a sense plainly distinct from that in which the regularities studied in biology are called "natural."

Natural Law and God's Plan for the Universe

Vatican II not only provides an expression of the core conception of natural law but also an important amplification of it. In defending the right of every person to religious liberty, the Council affirms that the exercise of this right should not be interfered with as long as the just requirements of public order are observed. To support this judgment a reflection upon the most fundamental basis of morality is offered: "This becomes even clearer if one considers that the highest norm of human life is the divine law itself—eternal, objective and universal, by which God orders, directs and governs the whole world and the ways of the human community according to a plan conceived in his wisdom and love. God has enabled man to participate in this law of his so that, under the gentle disposition of divine providence, many may be able to arrive at a deeper and deeper knowledge of unchangeable truth [footnote to St. Thomas, S. Th., I-II, q. 91, a. 1; q. 93, a. 1-2]" (D.H.3).

The divine law is the plan whereby God providentially directs all creation, and the human person is capable of participation in this plan. This participation is reasonably understood to be the natural law. For St. Thomas, in the article immediately following the first of his texts cited here, said that this participation of the rational creature in God's eternal law is just what "natural law" means. He made this identification in explaining why it is appropriate for human persons to participate in a special way in God's providence. Human beings are not simply governed by God's providence in the manner of nonrational creatures: unlike them, human beings can understand in some measure the plan of providence and in light of that understanding provide for themselves and others (S. Th. I-II, q. 91, a. 2). Citing Psalm 4, Aquinas continued: "'The light of your face, Lord, is written upon us,' as the light of natural reason, by which we discern what is good and what is evil, and this is nothing but the impression of the divine light upon us."

Many, among both defenders and critics of natural law alike, have supposed that, since natural law is a participation by human beings in God's providential plan, the moral force of natural law principles presupposes that they be understood within this ultimate, ontological and theological context. This supposition is mistaken.

Vatican II's teaching about human participation in the divine law is introduced as a justification of the obligation of all persons to seek the truth about religious matters; surely it does not suppose that people must know one of the significant conclusions of that effort of inquiry prior to recognizing the obligation to undertake it. Indeed, just prior to the text in question, the Council emphasizes that this obligation is based on human nature itself (see D.H. 2, 14). The special point of the teaching in its context seems to be that people's knowledge of moral truth can develop and deepen, and that consequently they have a duty, and so a right, to undertake to deepen it for the sake of forming prudent and sincere judgments of conscience. Thus, the special emphasis on the transcendent ground in God's providential plan of all moral knowledge serves the purpose of underlining the objectivity and universality of the immanent principles of conscience.

Aquinas' discussion is again helpful. The light of natural reason, which is the imprint of the divine light within us, does not immediately reveal something transcendent to human nature, but something within human nature which participates in the eternal law, and that is the natural inclination of human beings to their appropriate actions and end. As he explained more fully a few questions later, the principles of natural law are the goods of human nature—those basic aspects of human perfection towards which persons have natural inclinations (S. Th. I-II, q. 94, a. 2). The appreciation of these goods of human nature by practical reason appears, on Aquinas' conception, sufficient to generate moral obligation antecedent to the full, theological account of their ultimate significance.

In other words, it is a special kind of knowledge about human beings, their possibilities and perfection, not about God, which grounds natural moral obligation. It is in this sense that natural law must be said to be based on human nature. Morality is part of creation. Perhaps it is a part which points more obviously to its creator than do other parts, but knowing moral truth is primarily knowing something about the created order. Thus, for Aquinas, the light of natural reason is the source not only of the content of natural moral obligation but of natural moral obligation itself.

The meaning of natural reason in this context is clarified further by the conception of law as a plan—most fundamentally the providential plan of God. Human beings participate in this plan by understanding that part of it is necessary for them to direct their lives reasonably. So what natural reason understands is neither an arbitrary rule or command nor a sentiment or emotion, but something which provides guidance to a reasonable end. Natural law is concerned with the rational direction of human life towards ends human beings can understand as worthwhile. And these ends themselves are not arbitrary, but are part of the overall end of things to which God lovingly and wisely directs the entire universe.

It is misleading, therefore, to describe natural law as a divine command theory. For the obligatory force of moral norms can be appreciated by natural reason without the recognition of those norms as divine commands. And even when moral norms are fully recognized for what they ultimately are, they are seen as expressions of God's will that humans should live in accord with his wise and loving plan.

Misunderstandings and Controversies about Natural Law

The explanation of natural law provided by Vatican II provides a useful reference point for understanding the meaning of natural law within the Catholic tradition. This explanation by itself, however, provides little more than a basic framework for understanding the style of moral argumentation or the moral claims which are commonly associated with natural law morality. This framework can be briefly developed, however, and some common misunderstandings of natural law forestalled, by further considering Aquinas' classic exposition of natural law.

The natural law is reasonably taken to include all the moral truths which exist prior to human decision or independent of revelation, but the natural law tradition has never maintained that everyone has a complete knowledge of these truths, or that this knowledge can be easily acquired.

Aquinas' account of this matter is as follows: people can be ignorant of even relatively elementary moral truths. A person might be ignorant, for example, of one or another of the commandments of the decalogue, perhaps because of the bad customs of the person's society (see S. Th I-II, q. 94, a. 4). This possibility explains the necessity for divine revelation of the decalogue, the bulk of which Aquinas thought to be a matter of natural law (see S. Th. I-II, q. 100, aa. 1, 2, 3). He

was also aware that the application of general moral norms to the complex questions of casuistry was difficult and beyond the capacity of most people.

But he believed that everyone able to form the concepts necessary for moral judgment knows the most basic principles of moral life. No one can fail to know such things as the Golden Rule, the prohibition of harming persons, or the principles formulated in scripture as the Love Commandments. Aquinas regarded these moral truths as self-evident, propositions known to be true as soon as the meanings of their terms are grasped. Such knowing, for Aquinas, is "natural."

He regarded these naturally known moral truths as principles in the strict sense—the foundations for all other moral truths, including the precepts of the decalogue. Knowledge of these principles appears to be a prerequisite for criticizing mistaken moral judgments, and for determining how to correctly apply general moral standards in difficult cases.

In a word, natural law thinking takes full account of the complexity of moral experience, of the fact that people in different times and places differ in their level of moral awareness, of the fact that people make mistakes in moral thinking and must develop in their ability to think correctly about moral issues.

Even when misunderstandings are removed, however, the central claims of natural law as outlined above have long been disputed among academic moralists. Since Vatican II, disputes about many aspects of natural law have become an important part of Catholic controversies over moral issues like contraception, and the more general, theoretical issues which these controversies have raised among moral theologians.

One locus of controversy involving natural law has been the debate concerning the received teaching on particular moral issues, particularly in sexual morality. In this context there has been extensive criticism of particular arguments, for example, perverted faculty arguments, for conclusions the Magisterium proposes as part of natural law. These criticisms do not themselves question the basic convictions of natural law, and, indeed, are sometimes advanced and accepted by those committed to natural law approaches.

These criticisms, however, together with growing dissatisfaction with the moral theology of recent centuries, have raised a host of serious questions about the fundamental conception of natural law, its content, and its role in christian life and Catholic moral teaching. Among these questions are such important and discussed matters as: the competency of the Magisterium to teach in moral matters, the specificity of christian ethics, the role of proportionalism in moral reasoning, and the reality of moral absolutes. The discussion of these questions is beyond the scope of this entry.

See **Anthropology, Christian; Moral Life, Christian; Law**

Alan Donagan, *The Theory of Morality,* Chicago and London: U of Chicago Press, 1977. John Finnis, *Natural Law and Natural Rights,* Oxford: Oxford U Press, 1980. Germain Grisez, *The Way of the Lord Jesus: Volume I: Christian Moral Principles,* Chicago: Franciscan Herald Press, 1983. Josef Fuchs, S.J., *Natural Law: A Theological Investigation,* New York: Sheed and Ward, 1965. Josef Fuchs, S.J., "The Absoluteness of Behavioral Moral Norms," in *Personal Responsibility and Christian Morality,* Washington D.C. and Dublin: Georgetown U Press and Gill and Macmillan, 1983, pp. 115-152. Germain Grisez, "Moral Absolutes: A Critique of the View of Josef Fuchs, S.J." *Anthropos* 1 (1985), pp. 155-201.

JOSEPH BOYLE

NATURAL THEOLOGY

The term came into frequent use during the Enlightenment as a reaction against the inconclusive appeal of Protestants and Catholics to scripture. To escape devastating, yet indecisive, religious wars men looked for some norm of truth and concord besides supernatural revelation. Tolerance on the basis of reason became an ideal fostered in academic circles. This turn from scripture was greatly supported by the success of the new, mechanistic science which relied on reason, could be tested and certified by all reasonable men, and promised to subdue nature to human control. Whereas natural reason was originally seen as providing a common ground for union in questions about God, a least common denominator that might permit supernatural religions with conflicting claims to tolerate each other's existence in civic life, some began to assert reason's claim to judge the supernatural. Then what was accessible to reason was considered natural theology; beliefs and practices exceeding natural theology were deemed tradition, historical baggage, and even superstition. Many attempts were made to demonstrate the reasonableness of Christianity, but the result was usually a reduction of revelation to reason and of religion to morality. Few were the philosophers or anthropologists who could agree on the actual content of natural religion.

Despite the illuminating efforts of W. Schmidt and his disciples to gather evidence of a primordial monotheistic belief and corresponding revelation, the diversity among actual religions has discouraged attempts at identifying a natural kernel common to all religions and accessible to all men through reason or "religious experience." Rather natural theology now primarily refers to the manner in which knowledge of God can be attained as a presupposition for the perception of revelation by God. Although Luther and Calvin admitted a certain knowledge of God mediated by creation and much liberal Protestant thought relied heavily on reason, many recent Protestant thinkers strongly reject natural theology.

Vatican I defined the possibility of a sure knowledge of God "by the natural light of human reason from created realities" (D.S. 3004, 3026). Even though the same Council proclaimed the need of faith beyond reason for man's salvation (D.S. 3004f., 3008, 3012, 3015-3017, 3027, 3029, 3035, 3041) and acknowledged the weakness of man's present state which requires revelation to attain a knowledge of natural truths "with firm certitude and unadulterated by any error" (D.S. 3005), Protestants focus their objection to Catholicism on its position regarding natural theology. For them Catholic theology attempts to submit God to human reason as it employs a philosophically elaborated understanding to serve as the measure of truth, distinguishing proper from metaphorical use of language, in the interpretation of scripture. Thus God's freedom is subordinated to man's reason, as finite man presumptuously lays down the law for the infinite God.

For their part Protestants highlight the fundamental inability of finite men to grasp the infinite, which is interpreted as the manifestation of man's inherent sinfulness. If there is to be any communication bridging the abyss between finite and infinite, the initiative must lie entirely with God. Abandoned to itself, incapable of finding an absolute, all human thought is relativized and reveals its abysmal absurdity. But precisely because finite man cannot raise himself to the infinite, he can set no limits to God's power. The miracle of christian revelation consists in the fact that the infinite God has revealed himself in his word in the finite, indeed in the sinful finite, to call sinners to himself. This revelation of God *sub contrario* corresponds to the unmerited justification of the sinner and is confessed in God-given faith when the word of God is proclaimed.

However successfully this view maintains the need of revelation for meaning, its utter relativization of human reason leads to disastrous consequences. What does one believe? Fundamentalists take God's word, the Bible, literally and whatever objections science may raise are immediately discounted since human reason is in principle flawed and cannot stand against God. Many liberals, on the contrary, stress that since the Bible as a book is composed of human words, which are incapable of capturing God's infinity, it need not be taken literally. Decisive is the interior conversion effected by grace when scripture is proclaimed; the content of faith consists in a personal relationship, or something analogous to it, and cannot be reduced to objective categories. In a way somewhat disconcerting to the uninitiated, "word of God" refers fluidly to God's self-expression in his Logos, the Incarnate Word, Jesus' words, scripture, the event of the word's proclamation, and its presence, or effect, in human hearts. Speculatively brilliant as may be the transition from one referent to another and the systems developed out of God's word, they exhibit a basic flaw. Since human words do not suffice to grasp reality or God, no debate employing them can dissolve disagreement; having rejected reason as a valid means of knowing God, theologians are thrown back upon their own subjectivity or the absolutization of written words.

To avoid such intellectual chaos Catholic theology has rightly insisted upon natural theology. Once God can be known through reason, an absolute has been attained that prevents reason's total relativization, preserves the natural-supernatural distinction, and ensures that men will have some understanding of God's word when it is announced to them for their free acceptance. In recent decades Catholics have differed in grounding natural theology. The conceptualists, who maintain that being can be grasped in a concept, an abstraction that liberates its intelligible content from the unintelligibility of matter, tended to find many "absolutes," i.e., invariant concepts of natures that remain substantially the same through time, and based their knowledge of God primarily on Aristotle's proof from motion. It has been questioned whether such an argument really goes beyond the pure, finite form, that is Aristotle's Prime Mover. Others have stressed man's spiritual dynamism transcending all finite reality and concepts in its quest for the final ground of intelligibility. Only the infinite God can satisfy man's quest. This "natural desire to see God," however, involves a paradox, if not a contradiction. Since no concept of God can satisfy the desire, man desires to see God as he is. But God is Trinity, and the direct, beatifying vision of God has always been considered the flowering of grace, the greatest of supernatural gifts. If a supernatural fulfillment is required for man's fundamental natural desire, "nature" does not make sense of itself and there is danger of losing a natural basis for thought. Some point to the impossibility of adequately distinguishing nature from grace in the present order and note that Vatican I spoke only of the *possibility* of knowing God by natural reason. But a possibility, never actualized, enjoys no reality and contradicts the scholastic dictum, *ab posse ad esse non valet illatio.* If no proof of God's existence can be developed to anchor the natural order, the distinction of natural and supernatural becomes nebulous, if not vapid.

Catholic theology must retain the balance between natural and supernatural orders through a proper doctrine on analogy. Neither must God be submitted to conceptual laws nor must concepts be so relativized by the infinite reality of God that they lose all permanent meaning. The vivifying tension between finite and infinite must be so preserved that a field of activity remains open to human freedom which is both intelligent and uncompelled. Into that arena, wounded by sin, the new creation effected by Christ may enter. Ultimately a philosophy of freedom must be developed to supplant the Thomistic philosophy of natures so that many current *aporiai* may be surpassed.

H.J. Pottmeyer, *Der Glaube vor dem Anspruch der Wissenschaft,* Freiburg: Herder, 1968. R Aubert, *Le Problème de l'acte de foi,* 3rd ed., Louvain: Warny, 1958, pp. 131-222. E. Przywara, S.J., *Analogia Entis,* München: Kösel, 1932.

JOHN M. MCDERMOTT, SJ

NATURE

Nature is a wide-ranging term which has never achieved an agreed technical meaning in philosophy or theology. The Greek term for nature, *physis,* is rare in the scriptures. It shares a root association with birth and growth with its Latin counterpart *natura.* In general, nature denotes the elements that constitute the internal unity of an entity and govern its activity. In reference to humans' nature it is their essential qualities, capacities and condition. The common usage of the term is varied. A nature is something that exists and follows its own inner principles, e.g., any mineral, plant or animal. Again, it is the essence of a being without which it would not be what it is, and which enables particular instances of that being to be recognized, for example, the divine, human or angelic nature. Third, it is the complex of extra-human reality, the cosmos as distinct from history and culture. Last, it may even designate a predominant trait of a person or thing, such as an optimistic or an unstable or a brittle nature. The first two meanings are relevant here.

Nature is significant for such areas of christian theology as the doctrine of God, of Christ, of grace and (original) sin; of natural theology (revelation) and natural law; of creation, ecology and work; and of mission (inculturation). Nature will be briefly treated below in relation to God, Christ and grace.

The Triune God

In deference to strict monotheism, the nature of God has almost universally been considered (at least from the fourth century in the West) as abstract and utterly simple, and as shared equally by the three divine persons: infinite power, wisdom, love, and stability. Nature could be synonymous with the divine essence, substance, or even being. More recently the divine nature is being recast in dynamic terms as the infinite exchange of boundless love between the Father, Son and Holy Spirit. Following Gregory of Nyssa, Robert W. Jenson depicts God's nature as action. He uses "being" (*ousia*) in the sense of nature: "The divine *ousia* is the infinity. . . of the work done between Jesus and his Father in their Spirit . . . what these three do is *God*" (164). From the stance of A.N. Whitehead and J. Royce, Joseph A. Bracken proposes "that the nature or essence of God is to be an interpersonal process, i.e., a community of three divine persons who are constantly growing in knowledge and love of one another and who are thus themselves in process even as they constitute the divine community as a specifically social process" (7). This provocative hypothesis goes further than the many who today speak of God as sacrificial love, by nature freely giving of self and compassionate: see the different emphases of Jürgen Moltmann, Eberhard Jüngel, Walter Kasper and Edward Schillebeeckx. The paschal mystery thereby becomes the key to the nature of the christian God. The metaphysical divine nature is filtered and communicated through the historical, through the incarnate Son, giving a fresh twist to the Thomist assertion that only in God is essence or nature identical with existence.

Jesus Christ

A particularly complicated area of the meanings of nature is that referring to the identity of Jesus the Christ, the Son of God become a human. For the Antiochenes of the late fourth and fifth centuries nature meant an actual combination of characteristics. But the contemporary Alexandrines viewed nature as an independent, self-determining being. This latter notion betrayed an inadequate distinction between person and nature which gave rise to considerable misunderstanding. Leo the Great and Chalcedon (451) followed the Antiochene understanding of nature as what an entity is like and can do (a capacity or medium, *principium quo*), and not the Alexandrian view of nature as what an acting entity is (an agent, *principium quod*). This allowed the great church to proclaim two natures in the single person or hypostasis of Jesus the Christ, the divine and the human natures. Nevertheless, Chalcedon was not an assembly of philosophers, and the term nature is employed in a general, non-technical sense to indicate the complete humanity and undiminished divinity interacting in total harmony in this man Jesus. Nature is applied analogously by Chalcedon, and is not used in the same sense of the divine and human dimensions of Christ.

Grace

In reference to God and Christ nature has partly been considered in an abstract, even metaphysical, manner. But in the sphere of the freely offered love-relationship between the triune God and humans—grace—the shared story of the parties must be recalled. Augustine popularized the pastoral exegesis of Genesis 1-3 and Romans 5-8 as the sequence of creation, fall, and divine grace enlarging the human desire for good and the freedom to pursue it. He presents human nature as created for divine intimacy, but rejecting this grace, and turning in on itself (*The City of God* 14.13) until offered the possibility of renewed friendship with God through the healing grace of the Spirit of the saving Christ. Flawed nature (concupiscence) is at odds with the yearning core of personhood, which can be transformed by grace into the liberty to love without horizons (charity). Here human nature is not a fixed datum. It grows and shrivels through the quality of its relationships to the triune God and fellow humans. Augustine did not use the term "supernatural," which emerged briefly in the ninth century, became significant for the scholastics, and was vividly contrasted to the natural order in the sixteenth and later centuries. Augustine believed that creatures in their native state neither had a right to sharing the life of God nor earned it by their good living. But he did not oppose nature to the supernatural, a sphere of grace separate from it.

The scholastics acknowledged that human creatures have an intrinsic capacity for intimacy with God, and a corresponding desire for it. Grace presupposes and builds on nature. (See S.Th I 1.8 ad 2; 6.1 ad 2; I-II 99.2 ad 1). Later many sheerly hypothetical states of nature were described by theologians in order to highlight the graciousness of God in welcoming humans, and the creaturely incapacity to achieve such intimacy by unaided effort. In practice, as Aquinas averred, only a graced human nature, free and prone to sin, has ever existed. The contours and capabilities of their nature, and its interaction with subhuman, angelic, and divine natures, remain fields for faith-prompted exploration. The precise relationship of person and nature also requires elucidation. (The substance or nature of God is identical with the person of the Father for the East). But enough has been said to show that human nature or being is responsive to God's free invitation to friendship, and thrives on experiencing, willing and acting.

Whether it is a question of the nature of the triune God, of the Son made flesh, or of other humans, contemporary theologians no longer present such a nature in static, atemporal or essentialist dress. Each of them is depicted as dynamic and open to relationships, and is shot through with the befriending graciousness of our God. The triune *God* is an infinitely free and loving giving, receiving and sharing, sheer, sheer gratuity, generosity and joy. Chalcedon may have analyzed the inner constitution of the *incarnate Son* as two natures acknowledged as coming together in the unique divine person of the Logos. But modern Christology views the divine and human natures of Jesus Christ as openness to the lifegiving Father-Son bond in the power of the filiating Holy Spirit. The interpenetrating divine and human natures are programs rather than fixed coordinated parts of a whole. This integral and divinized human nature of Christ fosters an incarnational, world-cherishing spirituality, and an affinity with the nourishing symbolic life of the church sacraments, with the realist eucharistic presence of the risen Christ, and with the contemplation of icons as redeemed creation. Human nature in its radical openness is in the image of God and in solidarity with all other humans. The influences exercised on it by differences of sex, culture, color, economic status and political organization have scarcely begun to be plumbed and integrated theologically. *Grace* is the divine calling of this nature to achieve its highest vitality under the dynamism of the responding person living through it. Besides the customary separation of person and nature, it is profitable to view them as interacting dimensions of human being, which is the capacity for God.

Such a being is necessarily a being-in-relation, a self-achievement through the graciousness of others and the Other.

See **Anthropology, Christian; Creation; God; Grace; Hypostasis; Jesus Christ; Natural Law; Natural Theology; Person; Substance; Trinity**

J.A. Bracken, *The Triune Symbol: Persons, Process and Community,* CTS Studies in Religion, 1, Lanham, MD: U. Press of America, 1985. R. Haight, *The Experience and Language of Grace,* New York: Paulist, and Dublin: Gill and Macmillan, 1979. R.W. Jenson, *The Triune Identity,* Philadelphia: Fortress, 1982. W. Kasper, *The God of Jesus Christ,* New York: Crossroad, 1984. G.C. Stead, *Divine Substance,* New York: Oxford U. Press, 1977. J.D. Zizioulas, *Being as Communion,* Crestwood, NY: St. Vladimir's Seminary, 1985

BRIAN M. NOLAN

NEO-ORTHODOXY

In a theological context this term usually refers to the method and contributions of those twentieth century theologians, such as Karl Barth, Emil Brunner and the Niebuhrs, who tried to ground christian theology firmly on the principles of the protestant reformers in order to correct the damage to christian theology which they saw done by liberal theologians of the nineteenth and twentieth centuries (Harnack, Herrmann, etc.). The experience of the two World Wars, of the Holocaust and of the ambiguity of modern technological progress led the neo-orthodox theologians to conclude that the evolutionary optimism of liberal theologies was unjustified and misrepresented the Gospel. They demanded a dialectical theology which radically distinguished between God and the world. Thus, neo-orthodox theologians strongly emphasized the transcendent nature of God and the brokenness of all human beings. In the light of this radical distinction they retrieved the classical logos-christology according to which they saw the word of God hitting this broken world unexpectedly and confronting it with God's

judgment: the individual person is called to make a radical decision of accepting God's word.

More recently, the term neo-orthodoxy has also been applied to Roman Catholic theologians, such as Karl Rahner, who attempted to reinterpret classical Catholic doctrine in the light of our contemporary human experience and language, and thus helped to prepare the way for the Second Vatican Council. Although it is clearly a merit of neo-orthodox theologians to have emphasized the ambiguity of all human action and the mysterious nature of God and God's revelation in our world, they were unwilling to engage in a radically critical investigation of the biblical, philosophical, linguistic and cultural dimensions of christian faith, and therefore remained more or less hostile to the recognition of the pluralist character of these dimensions and its implications for the christian church in the modern world.

The neo-orthodox model continues to dominate much of contemporary christian theology.

See **Theology**

Karl Barth, *The Epistle to the Romans,* 1922, ET 1975, and *Church Dogmatics,* 1932 ff. Karl Rahner, *Foundations of Christian Faith,* 1976, ET 1978. David Tracy, *Blessed Rage for Order,* 1975.

WERNER G. JEANROND

NEO-PLATONISM
See **Platonism, Theology**

NEO-SCHOLASTICISM

Scholasticism had been the dominant theology in the church during the Counter-Reformation. At the beginning of the nineteenth century, however, it had all but disappeared. Except for a few scattered faculties in Germany and Italy, Catholic schools practically ignored it.

As Catholic theology began its revival after the French Revolution, its representatives were often ecclectics. If they were not, they either leaned toward the nineteenth century form of Augustinianism called ontologism or favored the new German theologies inspired by Post-Kantian idealism. Scholasticism was generally ignored as a discredited form of the rationalism whose foundations had been undermined by empiricist and Kantian epistemology.

About 1830, however, Taparelli, rector of the Jesuit Roman college, began a campaign to restore scholasticism. Unsuccessful at first, the campaign picked up momentum during the pontificate of Pius IX. Two other Jesuits, Liberatore and Kleutgen, were among its most active partisans. Their publications and their personal influence with the pope and the powerful Roman Congregations helped the movement's progress. Gioacchino Pecci, the future Leo XIII, was one of Taparelli's former students. When Pecci became bishop of Perugia he made his diocese an active center of the scholastic revival, and, once he was pope, he used the full power of the pontificate to extend scholasticism to the universal church. Leo's encyclical, *Aeterni Patris,* recommending that scholasticism be the only philosophy and theology used in Catholic seminaries, was considered the *magna carta* of neo-scholasticism.

Leo's neo-scholasticism was, in essence, a christian Aristotelianism. Aristotle's direct realism in which concepts were abstracted from sense experience, was contrasted favorably to the subjectivism and innatism of Cartesian and idealist epistemology. The unity of man, which Aristotle's metaphysics of matter and form made possible, was seen as a sign of its superiority to the Post-Cartesian metaphysics which had led to a split between matter and spirit in the human being. A return to the Aristotelian method, which the scholastic doctors had used in their "old" theology, would clear up the confusion between faith and reason, nature and grace which the "newer" methods, inspired by Cartesian or idealist philosophy, had introduced into Catholic theology.

Leo XIII drew on scholastic social ethics to structure his great encyclical, *Rerum Novarum,* on the condition of the working classes, and he urged scholastic philosophers and theologians to develop their system through intense historical research and dialogue with contemporary philosophy and science. As a result, scholasticism flourished in the first half of the twentieth century. Distinguished scholastics appeared in the religious orders, such as Garrigou-Lagrange, Sertillanges and Chenu among the Dominicans, or Rousselot and Maréchal among the Jesuits. Centers of scholastic philosophy and theology could be found in Italy, France, Belgium, Canada and the United States. Maritain's neo-scholastic treatises on the integration of knowledge and Gilson's works on the history of medieval philosophy won them international fame.

The ecclesiology, the theology of grace and nature, the hypostatic union and the moral theology taught in Catholic seminaries between the wars were scholastic in their origin and orientation.

Success, however, brought problems. Gilson and Chenu showed that there had been no common scholasticism shared by St. Thomas and the other scholastic doctors. St. Thomas' philosophy and theology were distinctively his own. They could be identified neither with the systems of the other medieval doctors nor with those of the Post-Tridentine scholastics with which they had been associated. Bouillard and de Lubac established that the Post-Tridentine theology of grace and nature which the neo-scholastics had attributed to St. Thomas had never been taught by him. Rousselot questioned whether the Aristotelian scientific method, which the neo-scholastics prized so highly, was even compatible with St. Thomas' own epistemology.

At the same time, neo-scholasticism, or Neo-Thomism as it had become, had developed into a plurality of competing systems. The epistemologies of Gilson, Maritain and Maréchal, for example, could not be reconciled with one another. Biblical and historical studies, which had also been encouraged by Leo XIII and his successors, were also flourishing in the church. The results of their research could not be integrated into theology by an Aristotelian method modeled on Greek logic and mathematics. Tension between scholastics on one side and exegetes, historians and patrologists on the other had become severe.

By Vatican II, neo-scholasticism could no longer maintain its dominant position in Catholic theology and the movement inaugurated by Leo XIII had run its course. Through the results of its historical research and through its rediscovery of St. Thomas' own philosophy and theology, it still has an influence on Catholic theology. Theologians, such as Rahner and Lonergan, for example, who received their early training as scholastics, continued to be influenced by the epistemology and metaphysics of St. Thomas in their own contemporary theology.

See **Thomism**

Roger Aubert, *Aspects Divers du Néo-Thomisme sous le Pontificat de Léon XIII.* Rome: Edizioni 5 Lune, 1961. Victor B. Brezik, CSB [ed.] *One Hundred Years of Thomism.* Houston: University of St. Thomas, 1981. Gerald A. McCool, SJ, *Catholic Theology in the Nineteenth Century: The Quest for a Unitary Method.* New York: Seabury Press, 1977. *From Unity to Pluralism: The Internal Evolution of Thomism.* New York: Fordham University Press, 1987. Laurence K. Shook, CSB, *Etienne Gilson.* Toronto: Pontifical Institute of Mediaeval Studies, 1984.

GERALD A. MCCOOL, SJ

NESTORIANISM

The views associated with Nestorius, Patriarch of Constantinople (d. ca. 451), have traditionally been identified as a denial of the real hypostatic union of divinity and humanity in Jesus Christ and the assertion of a merely "moral" union between the divine person and a human person. This position was considered to be implied in Nestorius's refusal to attribute the title "Mother of God" to the Blessed Virgin Mary. Nestorius was condemned by the Council of Ephesus (431). Recent scholarship question whether Nestorius was himself a "Nestorian" and maintains that his position was orthodox and that his differences with his great rival, Cyril of Alexandria, are to be explained more by the confusion of terminology from which both suffered, particularly the failure to distinguish clearly between "person" and "nature," rather than from any departure from the church's faith on Nestorius's part.

NICAEA, FIRST COUNCIL OF

According to tradition, the Council of Nicaea was the first in the series of ecumenical councils, held in 325. It was called by the Emperor Constantine I soon after his conquest of the eastern provinces of the Roman Empire (324). Not long after he had become the western emperor in 312, he convoked the Western Council of Arles in 314 to try to settle the Donatist question. Thus when he became ruler of the eastern provinces and found the Arian controversy threatening the unity of the Eastern Church, he immediately thought of a large council as the hoped for solution. The episcopal membership of the council was, as with most of the early ecumenical councils, overwhelmingly eastern. The answer to the question of who presided over the council is not clear although the Spanish bishop Hosius of Cordoba,

Constantine's long-standing ecclesiastical adviser, probably did.

After discussions, the teaching of the Alexandrian priest, Arius, that the Logos was ontologically subordinate to the Father and that, therefore, the Logos was divine only in an attenuated sense, was rejected. The famous and controversial term "homoousios" was adopted. Thus the basic teaching of the council was the modest, albeit essential, one that the Logos and the Father were ontologically equal. Since it specified no more than this, controversies on the trinitarian question continued at least until the Second Ecumenical Council in 381.

ROBERT B. ENO, SS

NIHILISM

Nihilism is usually thought of as the denial that life, morality, God, or truth has any meaning. It has often been a foil for christian theologians. Nihilism is portrayed in nineteenth-century Russian anarchist literature, in F. Nietzsche's, *Will to Power,* and in A. Camus', *The Myth of Sisyphus* and *The Stranger.* The term has come to have two basic meanings, often conflated.

On a more theoretical level, theologians sometimes call those who claim that there is no transcendent standard by which to measure moral claims nihilists. Dostoevsky's Ivan Karamazov presents their position: "If God does not exist, everything is permitted." Some contemporary theologians (e.g., S. Ogden, H. Küng) imply that those who claim that there is no Ultimate Meaning for the Universe must also be nihilists. Their position can be characterized as: "If the Whole is ultimately meaningless, then no part of it can be meaningful." Most philosophers skeptical of transcendent or universal foundations for morality, e.g.,

emotivists or prescriptivists, and most philosophical atheists, e.g., B. Russell, J.-P. Sartre, would deny that their theories are equivalent to nihilism. They would argue that the absence of ultimate meaning leaves it incumbent on humans to reject any meaning imposed upon the world by religious or traditional authorities, to construct a liveable morality and to make their own lives meaningful. Such theoretical disputes over the link of nihilism with moral skepticism or relativism and with intellectual atheism are probably irresolvable, at least in part because the opponents cannot agree on what would constitute "meaning" or "morals."

On a more practical level, nihilism can be seen as similar to one of the seven deadly sins, acedia, inability to care (often called sloth). Like persons trapped in acedia, practical nihilists value nothing—nothing has meaning for them. Hence, such persons may feel no moral obligation to others, because they have no value. They may be identified as moral anarchists, egoists, or psychopaths. Practical nihilists may also find no meaning in their own lives, since they find no real value in them. They often engage in feverish quests for meaning, self-hate, which, if successful, overcome nihilism. If unsuccessful, suicide may provide a viable option.

While the outcomes of practical nihilism may appear similar to the conclusions of theoretical nihilism, it is not clear that they are necessarily linked conceptually, nor that arguments theologians make against the latter constitute therapy for the former. The tragic contemporary epidemic of practical nihilism is not necessarily evidence for an increase in the acceptance of theoretical nihilism.

G. McCarthy, "Meaning, Morals and the Existence of God," *Horizons,* 1981. R. Olson, "Nihilism," *Encyclopedia of Philosophy,* Ed., P. Edwards, New York, 1967.

T.W. TILLEY

NOMINALISM

The philosophical theory that maintains that universal concepts have no essential validity but are merely names (*nomina*) which we use to put order into reality by grouping together realities which are irreducibly distinct and individual. This view arose in the late Middle Ages as a reaction to scholastic metaphysics and found its chief spokesman in William of Occam (d. 1349).

See **Metaphysics, Nature**

NOTES OF THE CHURCH

Origin and History

Ever since the Council of Constantinople in 381 the church has professed the article from the Creed of Nicaea-Constantinople (D.S. 150), reaffirmed at Ephesus and Chalcedon, that "We believe ... [in] the one, holy, catholic and apostolic church." The Fathers and the theologians of the Middle Ages saw the reality of church as intimately bound to and presupposed in the proclamation of the gospel and intimately linked to christology and pneumatology as its existential basis. In a comprehensive way the church was perceived within the movement of the economy of salvation from the Father, through Christ and the Holy Spirit. Within this perspective the fathers explained and interpreted the notes of the church and combatted heresy and schism by means of them.

In this struggle against heresy and schism, the fathers pointed to important ecclesiastical themes related to the creedal attributes of the church. Irenaeus stressed the unity of the christian teaching of faith and the teaching tradition of the apostles against a variety of gnostic views. This teaching was guaranteed by the apostolic church and the apostolic succession of bishops as expressed by Cyprian. Impelled by the secessions from the church of Carthage and of Rome, Cyprian wrote a treatise on the unity of the church. He taught that unity was preserved by the bond of the bishops who are closely linked to one another. He also stressed the significance of the primacy for the preservation of unity. Against the Donatists, Augustine emphasized the worldwide universality of the church in addition to its sanctity. He upheld the idea of the church as a worldwide communion as opposed to the local expression of the Donatists in North Africa.

In the fifteenth century the denial of the absolute character of the institutional aspect of the church in the spiritualistic teaching of Hus and Wycliffe, based on a distorted interpretation of the Augustinian themes of the church of the predestined, of the elect or of the saints and his teaching on grace, weakened the significance of belonging to the historical body of the church and showed the necessity for a better understanding of the church as mystery and as visible reality. The development of conciliarist ideas, interpreting the definition of the church as *congregatio fidelium* from individualistic and representative theories prompted John of Ragusa (*Tractatus de Ecclesia,* 1431) and John of Torquemada (*Summa de Ecclesia,* 1436) to compose their works apologetically based on the four notes.

The reformers questioned the whole system of ecclesiastical mediation (the primacy of the pope, the powers of the bishops and priests, the authority of tradition). This led theologians to concentrate in the definition of church on its juridical and visible reality and to give less prominence to the reality of grace. The external and socially organized aspect of the church was predominant in their teaching on the mystical body. Within the context of the Reformation considerable discussion among Roman Catholic and Protestant polemicists focused on how to identify the true church. Melancthon and Luther identified two: the pure teaching of the gospel and the proper administration of the sacraments. While Luther listed others in his treatise *On the Councils and the Churches,* these two seem to be the primary ones for the reformers. On the Catholic side Cardinal Hosius in 1553 maintained that the true church could be recognized by the four marks of the creed. Robert Bellarmine offered fifteen notes but saw them as an expansion of the four notes of the Creed. The Catechism of the Council of Trent also used the four creedal attributes which became standard in Catholic apologetics.

In Roman Catholic apologetics from the fifteenth century to the mid-twentieth century, the notes were often interpreted to uphold a highly institutional concept of the church. The church was understood primarily in its societal aspect with attributes definitively given by Christ. The four creedal attributes were used by Catholic apologists to support the view that the true church was identified with the Roman Catholic Church and the notes could distinguish the authentic from the inauthentic churches. With Vatican II, Roman Catholic ecclesiology undertook an important shift in which the notes were perceived as attributes of the church of Christ which subsists in the Roman Catholic Church. *Lumen Gentium* states: "This is the sole Church of Christ which in the Creed we profess to be one, holy, catholic and apostolic ... This Church, constituted and organized as a society in the present world, subsists in the Catholic Church, which is governed by the successor of Peter and the bishops in communion with him. Nevertheless many elements of sanctification and of truth are found outside its visible confines. Since these are gifts belonging to the Church of Christ, they are forces impelling towards catholic unity (8)."

The key shift in this ecclesiology of Vatican II is centered in the use of the word "subsists" for it represents a shift from the former apologetics which identified the church of Christ with the Roman Catholic Church. The use of this word implies a distinction between the two while maintaining a relationship between them. At the same time Vatican II teaches that the church of Christ is present in its essential completeness in the Roman Catholic Church but they are not identical. The creedal attributes are gifts bestowed on the church but still to be perfectly realized and actualized. The notes, then, can be understood as dimensions (Küng) of the church against which the churches should examine their fidelity to the gospel. In the words of Yves Congar, they are gifts to the church whose task it is to incarnate them as fully as possible in its life.

See **Apologetics, Church**

Yves Congar, *L'eglise, une, sainte, catholique et apostolique,* vol. 15 of *Mysterium Salutis,* Paris: Les Editions du Cerf, 1970. Congar, *I Believe in the Holy Spirit,* vol. II, New York: Seabury, 1983. Avery Dulles, *Models of the Church,* Garden City, N.Y.: Doubleday, 1974. *A Church to Believe In,* New York, Crossroads, 1982. Hans Küng, *The Church,* New York: Sheed and Ward, 1967. Karl Rahner *et al, Sacramentum Mundi,* vol. I, New York: Herder and Herder, 1968, the section on the church, pp. 313-357.

TIMOTHY MACDONALD, SA

NOVATIANISM

Novatian was a leading member of the Roman clergy in the mid-third century and the first Roman theologian to write in Latin. His treatise on the Trinity is noteworthy. After the Decian persecution, as after many persecutions, there arose a dispute as to the disposition of Christians who had apostatized. Novatian led the rigorist party which sought to exclude apostates and serious sinners from the church. After the persecution when it was once again possible to assemble to elect a new bishop, Cornelius, not Novatian, was elected bishop of Rome in 251. Novatian then had himself ordained a bishop illicitly and began to form a schismatic community in Rome. He himself eventually died a martyr in the persecution of Valerian in 257-8.

While rigorism as a tendency among a minority has been a consistent phenom-enon in church history, groups directly connected with the original Roman Novatianists appeared in the ancient church, even in the Greek-speaking areas. Novatianist groups in Constantinople are discussed by the church historian, Socrates (5th c.).

ROBERT B. ENO, SS

O

OBEDIENCE

Contemporary Western culture, with its dominant stress on individualism and personal freedom, often considers obedience a necessary evil. At best, obedience is a functional necessity in a complex rationalized society. Yet, concurrently, an opposite trend shows people looking for authority, even a dictatorial one, as a bulwark and solace in a threatening world. Christian obedience, as developed in the Catholic tradition, differs from both of these emphases.

The word obedience itself comes from *ob-audire* which means "to hear." It denotes a willingness to hear others and to do their will. For the believer, obedience refers to hearing God and obeying the divine will which may manifest itself in the will of other persons. The virtue of obedience is a freely chosen and stable disposition to submit our wills to others. The motivation for this submission is love for God.

Obedience is deeply rooted in scripture. The morality of both the OT and NT is a morality of obedience. In the OT the Israelite seeks to obey God's will (see Deut 1-4) in the context of the covenant, "You shall be my people and I will be your God" (Jer 11:4). The covenant Law governed all of the life of Israel and was to be obeyed. This included obedience to civil officials whose authority comes from God.

NT obedience focuses on Jesus. Jesus not only called for a deeper adherence to the spirit of the Law but exemplified obedience in his own life. His life was dedicated to doing his Father's will (Lk 2:49). He withstood the temptation to do his own will (Mt 4:1-11), gave an example of selfless service (Jn 13:1-17) and suffered unto death in fidelity to that will (Phil 2:8). The Christian is baptized into a community (1 Cor 12:13) and is animated by the Holy Spirit, the Spirit of Jesus. Filled with faith and love, he or she is able to obey even in suffering. This obedience includes obedience to human authorities (Mt 22:21) but is ultimately directed to God, "Better for us to obey God than men" (Acts 5:29).

Christian theology sees the human person not as an isolated individual but as a member of a community and thus in relationship with others. Both by nature and through grace, we are made to grow in and through relationships. In the context of the community of believers, a person seeks to understand and to do God's will. At times this will can be obscure and the members help one another to discern the Spirit's call, to understand its meaning and to will its accomplishment. Calls to obedience can come through the humblest of the members of the community, as well as through its leaders.

Obedience as a virtue is not robot-like

but a consciously willed and free choice. It forms the character of the believer to a sensitivity and docility to God's call in a variety of circumstances (though this can be a slow process). An attitude of obedience can come to penetrate one's whole life. Such obedience is ultimately a manifestation of christian charity. Through loving obedience, a person is opened up to the fullness of self-realization. Such realization is not in freedom from others but in free choices exercised with and for others. Obedience in its fullest sense involves self-fulfillment and self-sacrifice. Paradoxically, we are most free when we are most in compliance with God's will. This can involve asceticism and crucifixion, as with Jesus himself.

The virtue of obedience is not only a matter of discerning God's will in obscurity but also of following it in its clarity. Thus the obedient person follows the commandments, the beatitudes, and the other specific teachings of the scriptures as showing God's will for daily living. Believers also follow the just teachings and regulations of civil and religious authorities as these dutifully exercise their role in the community. In particular, as members of the Catholic hierarchy exercise a special ministry of sanctifying and teaching in the church, the Second Vatican Council declares that "... the faithful, for their part, are obliged to submit to their bishops' decision, made in the name of Christ, in matters of faith and morals, and to adhere to it with a ready and respectful allegiance of mind" (L.G. 25). Such allegiance does not destroy the ultimate authority of conscience but argues that a personal spirit of faith and love seeks to accept the commands of spiritual authority as indicating God's will. This allegiance is part of a person's overall commitment to seek God's will in all the circumstances of life.

As their life of faith develops, some believers experience a special call to obedience in imitation of Christ. Such a call is solemnized in particular by those who follow the three vows of poverty, chastity, and obedience in Catholic religious communities. Here the members submit themselves to discern God's will in a religious community under the guidance of religious superiors. By so seeking to do God's will, these believers hope to become more like Christ and to be of greater service in building the community.

See **Conscience, Freedom, Jesus Christ, Religious Life**

Austin Flannery, O P, Ed., *Vatican Council II: The Conciliar and Post Conciliar Documents,* Wilmington, DE: Scholarly Resources Inc., Dublin: Dominican Publications, 1975. Herbert McCabe, "Obedience." *New Blackfriars* 65 (1984): 280-87.

JOHN W. CROSSIN, OSFS

OCCASIONALISM

A view that denies the existence of created causes which are regarded instead as simply the occasions in which God, the sole cause of all, effects changes. A theological version of it, for example, denies that the sacraments are true secondary or instrumental causes and sees them as mere occasions on which God alone acts.

ONTOLOGICAL ARGUMENT

Anselm of Canterbury (1033—1109), a Benedictine monk, wrote in the broadly Augustinian tradition of faith seeking understanding. He believed God exists, and in the *Monologion* and *Proslogion* sought to give reasons for this belief.

He gives a number of arguments in the *Monologion,* but in the *Proslogion* he gives one argument that has provoked controversy for almost nine hundred years. Recently philosophers and theologians have paid increasing attention to it. The argument(s) from *Proslogion* cc.

2–4 can be formulated as follows:

Chapter 2:

(i) God is correctly called "that being than which a greater cannot be conceived."

(ii) When we hear the words, "that being than which a greater cannot be conceived," we understand what we hear. [Call that being the Supreme Nature = SN.]

(iii) What we understand exists in our understanding.

(iv) Therefore, the SN exists in our understanding.

(v) Suppose the SN exists only in our understanding.

(vi) We can conceive the SN to exist not only in our understanding, but also in extra-mental reality—which is greater.

(vii) Therefore if (v), the SN (a being than which...) would not be a being than which a greater cannot be conceived—a contradiction.

(vii) "Hence, without doubt, something than which a greater cannot be conceived exists both in the understanding and in reality."

Chapter 3

(i) God is correctly described as "that being than which a greater cannot be conceived."

(ii) God exists. (from chapter 2)

(iii) God exists either necessarily or contingently.

(iv) A being which exists necessarily is greater than a being which exists contingently.

(v) If God exists contingently. He (that being than which...) would not be that being than which a greater cannot be conceived—a contradiction.

(vi) Therefore, God exists necessarily.

On a first hearing, this strikes many as involving some logical trick or slight of hand: Anselm is involved in an attempt to pull real rabbits out of conceptual hats. The difficulty is in establishing precisely where the argument does go wrong. It is not difficult, however, to point out where it could go wrong, for many controversial philosophical issues are involved. What is meant by "exist in the understanding." i.e., what is the nature of intentional existence? Does it make sense to talk of objects that do not actually exist? Do they have properties? (Is Willy Loman washed up as a salesman?) How are these objects related to objects that do actually exist? Is necessity a property of propositions or of things? What is meant by "greatness and "conceive" in the argument? In what sense is it "greater" to exist extra-mentally than only "in the understanding?" Given such questionable origins, it is not surprising that instead of one pure "ontological argument," a whole family of arguments of various stripes has been spawned in the history of Western philosophy. Leibniz's version, criticized by Kant who thought it was Descartes', is not Anselm's.

One way of understanding the intuition behind Anselm's original version is the following. Many traditional christian thinkers have understood the data of scripture to imply that God is the supreme being: it is logically impossible that any thing exist and be greater than God. Hence, Anselm's description is not simply arbitrary: God is rightly described as "that being than which a greater cannot be conceived." Even the fool of psalm 13:1 who says in his heart "There is no God" can agree that this is part of what many theists mean by God. And this is what he means by God when he asserts "There is no God." By this, he claims it is conceivable that God exist only in the mind and not in reality. But, Anselm counters, this is not conceivable; it involves a contradiction. For if God is described as the greatest being, it is contradictory that He exist only in the understanding and not in reality. For what exists both in the understanding and in reality is greater than that which exists only in the understanding. So, if He does exist in the understanding, He must also exist in reality. But even the fool says He exists in the understanding; so He must exist in reality also.

The logical structure of the argument has been much disputed. Norman Malcolm and Charles Hartshorne claim to find not one but two arguments, the first dealing with existence, and the second with necessary existence. Only the latter is held to be a strong proof. Others claim to find only one argument; another finds an ontological proof for the existence of the devil.

What was Anselm's own intention? It is absurd to suggest that if Anselm's search for a proof failed, he would have given up his belief. He was not engaged in evidentialist apologetics, i.e., bringing his belief in God before "the bar of reason" and testing its credentials. This is a later project stemming from the "Enlightenment." Rather Anselm himself tells us his intention. He first entitled his work "Faith Seeking Understanding." As a believer, he wants to see the coherence, the necessary connections and implications of what he already believes. Further, in the context of the whole *Proslogion*, the argument functions as part of an exercise in mystical theology in the Augustinian/ neoplatonic tradition. One is asked to go with Anselm from an intellectually unappreciated faith to one that is appreciated (cc. 1-13), and finally to a mystical experience that cannot be grasped in concepts (cc. 14–26).

See **God**

MARK G. HENNINGER, SJ

ONTOLOGISM

The view, associated with Malebranche, Gioberti, and Rosmini, that all human knowledge is mediated through a direct, immediate, and implicit knowledge of God. This position, which maintains that the essences of all beings can only be known through knowledge of Being itself, was condemned by Pope Pius IX in 1861.

ONTOLOGY
See **Metaphysics**

OPERA AD EXTRA

A phrase referring to God's activity toward the world of creation, that is, "outside" the Trinity itself.
See **Appropriation, Trinity**

ORDERS AND ORDINATION

In Western Christianity, "orders" as a collective noun can mean the totality of public, recognized, fulltime, permanent ministries within the christian church. A particular "order" is one such individual ministry with certain rights, powers, responsibilities, ministerial area and identity. At present, modifying the medieval and Tridentine arrangement, the Western Catholic Church enumerates as orders bishop, presbyter/priest, and deacon (permanent and transitional). Their etymological sources represent different languages and different ages. Venerable christian churches, while agreeing upon bishop, presbyter and deacon, have had other orders, e.g. deaconess and exorcist. Ecclesiastical titles and duties, roles such as "archbishop," "cardinal," "canon," "monsignor," are honors although they may sometimes contain a proper duty in the church; they may be a modification of a particular order but are of more recent origin and are not included in the central public fulltime ministries of the church.

Order can be used for the arrangement and collectivity of orders and for the individual order, while its verbal form introduces the act of constituting someone in a public church ministry, "to ordain." Finally, the same Latin root can stand for the general determination by Jesus of the existence of a taxonomy of services within the church (The Council of Trent, canon 5; D.S. 1776) or for the liturgical structure of a ceremony.

In its English form the ecclesiastical term for church service, "orders," mirroring its Roman origins, bears political and theological overtones, as it connotes levels of membership and power, authority, hierarchy, the giving and receiving of commands. The German "office" (*Amt*) brings less of a feudal and more of an administrative tone. In the Greek christian world, "orders" and "ordination" are frequently expressed by *cheirothesia,* "laying-on of hands" which retains something of traditional commissioning and mission as contrasted to organization and office. Such words and linguistic theologies of church position and role modify the terminology of Jesus and the early Christians: "diakonia," concrete service.

A theology of orders begins with its underlying reality as church service as well as with its development in the Roman and medieval worlds. The early church did not lack for concrete roles. Jesus' position, that of the Twelve, those of charisms and services listed in the Pauline and Deutero-Pauline letters point not only to universal ministry of the baptized and its diversification but also to structure and authority in the church. Vital movements can live only through structure, and increased explicitness in structure is not (contrary to the expectancy of ecclesial movements such as the Spiritual Franciscans or the Quakers and the modern theological tradition reaching from A. Harnack to H.F. von Campenhausen) necessarily a devolution from a golden age of democratic equality before an enlightened spirit. Organic structure is

a condition of life: we would expect it in the church. As the Pauline letters reiterate, church role actively mediates salvation through word and service.

It is not the constitution and diversification of church order during the first two centuries which is puzzling, but rather the marked decline of diversity and broad ministerial involvement within the churches. Paul's Corinthian communities took for granted activities for most of the baptized in ministry, but this has been markedly altered by the turn of the second century as is indicated by the Ignatian letters with the emergence of the threefold ministry of bishop, presbyter and deacon (including in some churches deaconess as fully ordained). The reduction of church life during the second and third centuries—necessary perhaps at that time of expansion—prepared for the unfortunate separation of the christian community into a large, passive laity directed in word and sacrament by a very small separate group who alone were publicly constituted in fulltime service, i.e. ordained. While the early christian communities rejected titles and privileges, these now enter, even some borrowed from the pagan sacral world. The limited number of *"ordines"* led to a severe delineation of clergy and laity. Perhaps these developments reflect a general social move towards organization stimulated by the reforms of Trajan in the second century, so that the size of the church and the tendencies of cultural organization explain why ordained diversity in the church becomes fixed, sparse and prominent. Later, of course, the Constantinian appropriation of the higher clergy intensified this development.

The Roman world was marked by organization and arrangement of effective offices, flowing into clear arrangement of rights, duties and services ordered by law. The church could not help but be modified in its self-understanding by the powerful and useful thought-forms and political institutions of the Roman world bestowing fixed positions and subordinate arrangement. This Roman, social appropriation of order into church polity was intensified by the influence of Pseudo-Dionysius in the Middle Ages. There a neo-platonic canonization of a taxonomy of higher and lower orders took place. As the divine and angelic world were arranged in a hierarchy of metaphysical levels, so the church and society mirrored such a construction. The traditional, often only liturgical, orders of the church (the Middle Ages had no way of pursuing a biblical-historical critique of ministries) were glorious in their bestowal of social status and inner character as much as in their commissioning to evangelical service. For both society and church they represented a divine arrangement of levels in a pyramid, exercising influence only in a downward pattern. While this theology served well a time prior to the middle of the fourteenth century, it could give rise to problems: it confused the activity of public ministry with the constitution of the person in office; it removed most communication from within the church; it isolated each office in an unreal identity of ecclesiastical administration; it diluted the ministerial ordination of baptism; it was trapped in a polity which, after the Roman Empire and the Middle Ages, was outdated and injurious.

Despite the fact that Thomas Aquinas considered the social arrangements of offices in a society to be alterable and the diversification and naming of ministries to be the material for practical, changeable canon law, Trent and the Baroque era retained the Dionysian hierarchy, intensifying it with a new all-powerful focal point: not the divine world or being, not the eucharist or local bishop, but the Bishop of Rome. Moreover, the flow of power in this structure moved not socially, liturgically or mystically but mechani-

cally. A hierarchy of orders operated upon lower levels and, i.e., upon a passive laity (the Aristotelian "matter" of the entity of the church) through the forces of actual graces impressing their proper but usually too transient forms upon the faithful.

Just as the political forces of the contemporary world are not neo-Platonic or Roman, so the entry at Vatican II of modern aspects of freedom, education, individuality, professional mobility, participation and human rights into the life of the church could not help but critique and modify past theologies and forms of orders. This has come not through a hasty rejection of church structure, authority or ordination but first and foremost through an expansion of public ministry. Vatican II's documents alter the position of the ordained from a priestly caste to groups bound to each other and to other ministries and to all the baptized by a network of relationships. Grounded in the life of Christ, the ordained—those publicly and liturgically commissioned by community and authority—are witnesses to the Paschal mystery present in the world of our own times. Accepting the changes wrought by education, science and technology, yet drawing upon biblical writings and insights of other christian churches, the Council stressed not a solitary sacral function but a role both liturgical and evangelistic within and on behalf of the local community. These new emphases, far from weakening the role of the ordained place greater demands for ministerial efficacy and spiritual depth upon public representatives of the church.

The Roman administration of the church has furthered this movement by re-establishing in its distinction and fullness the orders of bishop and of deacon, by revising the ordination rites of all orders and by ending the outdated sub-diaconate and the minor orders. Thus the Vatican furthers in praxis ordination and orders seeking a deeper and clearer, more honest validity even while acknowledging the deeper reality of every order and its potential modifications in history.

In our necessarily historical meditation upon the shifts and developments of the church's ministries, we should observe the perduring presence of certain fundamentals for orders drawn from christian faith. They give the historical modifications a guidance and stability of tradition as well as a critique of the exaggerations in any theology and praxis of orders. As a sacrament, the ministries of the church mirror the two dimensions of the human and the divine. Their paradigm is, of course, bestowed by the incarnation of the divine Logos in Jesus of Nazareth. The public services of the church are empowered by the presence of grace in their ministers and are destined to serve the presence of grace in preaching, evangelization, care of the poor, liturgical leadership, etc. Ministry exists not as secular polity or as displayed power but as service to the on-going incarnation, the continuing presence of Jesus' Spirit in people and their church communities. Church orders are circumscribed by an incarnational theology: (1) they have true mediating roles in the community; (2) this mediation occurs with a modest, servant-like stance towards grace; (3) the goal of ministry is to make grace culturally concrete and existentially powerful (not to escape from these characteristics through a mechanical theology of mere validity).

Mindful of history and culture theologians have seen that the way in which Jesus established a diversity of roles in the church could not have been through identifying the names and definitions of a precise number. By calling men and women to levels of ministry, by calling them not slaves but friends, by extending the new presence of the Spirit and the gospel, Jesus (who calls himself "deacon") performed the dynamic core and ensemble of ministry which political influences and evangelical needs would modify, expand, diminish.

The move of Roman Catholicism from being a European church to being an international communion of churches, the move of theology from being the esoteric reading of clerics to the education of numerous Christians have increasingly rendered the model of the parish as pastor, curates and sisters educating children inadequate. In its place has come a wider staff of ministers, part-time and full-time, ordained and non-ordained. Thus one must now relate ordination to a wider community of active members, guaranteeing the rights and services of all but insuring the identity of those ordained.

All orders of service build upon the life-giving commissioning of baptism and confirmation. Far from debilitating the baptized, other services in the church find them as their *raison d'etre*. An order is not a reward or honor but a responsibility of service to other Christians; where diaconal zeal is absent, the point of ordination is unclear. At the same time, part of the demand and critique of orders from the community is the right of the community, particularly represented through its leaders, to determine the needs and qualifications of its ministers. The universality of the ministry of the baptized cannot be an excuse for weakening the authority of the local church (or the ministerial competency of those involved in the major ministries of diocese and parish).

The new Code of Canon Law reflects something of the direction of ecclesiology after Vatican II. Hierarchy is balanced by community; ministry is rooted in Christ; the church is a sacrament drawn from baptism. Orders are placed within the section on sanctifying the People of God. New movement comes from the restoration of the orders of bishop and deacon as well as from the permission for laity to preach. The identification of the ordained with sanctification (particularly liturgy), a separate section on the teaching office, as well as earlier canons on ecclesiastical offices (unfortunate in their earlier, separate position but positive in that such are open to laity) indicate ambiguities in present canonical thought frequently grounded in the medieval separation of orders and jurisdiction and the identification of orders with sacramental power.

Today the challenge to the theology, practice, canonical discipline and reality of orders in the church is threefold. First, the church must understand the historical development of different ministries. Then it should recognize and direct the expansion of the ministry even as it defends the identity of individual services such as bishop or presbyter. Second, the church must ponder some diversity of orders throughout the world for different cultures. Third, the church must be clear about the requirements in both theological and professional education, and in the christian life, for any who would publicly represent the kingdom of God. Finally the teaching and example of Christ should exercise constantly a critique on unproductive clericalism and upon tendencies to a "lay" secularization of church, order and liturgy.

Humane and legitimate facets of the modern world explain the metamorphosis of the terminology and political structure of Roman and feudal *ordo* into a community of ministries. The christian life is the indispensable ground and source of orders of ministry just as it is their goal. The diversity of peoples drawn today to Christ and the expansion of population motivate the diversification of the ministry which in turn is the reality ecclesiastically incarnate in every church order.

See **Baptism, Bishop, Church, Confirmation, Deacon, Deaconess, Laity, Ministry, Paschal Mystery, Priest**

The Sacrament of Holy Orders, Collegeville, 1962. Y. Congar, *Ministeres et communion ecclesiale,* Paris, 1971. J. Coriden, et al, *The Code of Canon Law: A Text and Commentary,* New York, 1985. Piet Fransen, "Orders and Ordination," *Sacramentum Mundi,* 4 p. 305ff. C. Journet, "The Power of Order," *The Church of the Word Incarnate,* Vol. I, *The Apostolic Hierarchy,* New York, 1955, pp. 50-120. A. Lemaire, *Les ministeres aux origines de l'Eglise,* Paris, 1971; *Les ministeres dans l'Eglise,* Paris, 1974. T. O'Meara, *Theology of Ministry,* New York, 1983. D. Power, *Gifts That Differ,* New York, 1978. E. Schillebeeckx, "The Catholic Understanding of Office," *T.St.* 30 (1969), 569ff.

THOMAS O'MEARA, OP

ORIGINAL JUSTICE

A phrase used to refer to the graced state in which God created man and woman and from which they fell in the original sin. The state has traditionally been thought to include supernatural grace and the preternatural gifts of exemption from concupiscence and from the necessity of death.
See **Original Sin**

ORIGINAL SIN

The doctrine of original sin received its classical formulation from St. Augustine, who set about countering the Pelagian belief that free will, supported by ascetic practices, was sufficient for the living of a full christian life and the securing of eternal salvation. This circumstance is the hermeneutical key to many of the problems which face modern Catholic theologians as they work out their position in relation to church doctrine, on the one hand, and scientific and critical developments since the Enlightenment, on the other. Such interpretation seeks to avoid the anachronistic tendency to read Augustine's position back into the biblical texts (principally Genesis 3 and Romans 5). It also adverts to the fifth century provenance of the terms "generation" and "imitation," when they are employed in later church teaching, notably in the Decree on Original Sin of the Council of Trent, which is the most authoritative conciliar source for the traditional understanding of the subject.

The principal aim of the Council of Trent was to correct the teaching of the Reformers on the radical corruption of human nature by Adam's sin. The Council therefore affirmed (1) that baptism removes, as distinct from merely covering over, the guilt of original sin, and (2) that concupiscence (the disordered condition of human appetites) is not to be identified with original sin in those who have been baptized. A strong statement like this in favor of the essential if regenerate goodness of human nature called for a redress of balance on the anti-Pelagian side. Trent therefore reproduced the basically Augustinian teaching of the Council of Carthage (A.D. 418) and the Second Council of Orange A.D. 529), when it parenthetically proclaimed that the sin of Adam "is one in origin and is passed on by propagation not by imitation." The term "imitation," as Pelagius had employed it, conveyed the impression of an environmental, purely extrinsic, conception of the origin of sin. In order to counteract the Pelagian view that original sin in the descendants of Adam amounts to no more than exposure to bad example, the Council of Carthage borrowed Augustine's term "generation" and proclaimed that young children who can not as yet commit personal sin should nevertheless be baptized "so that they may have cleansed in them by regeneration that [sin] which they have contracted by generation."

In traditional theology a variety of ingenious theories attempted to explain how the sin of an original pair could affect the fate of their descendants. Common to all these theories was the assumption that the early chapters of Genesis contain a factual account of the origins of the universe and that the third chapter narrates a literally true story of how the two progenitors of the human race (1) sinned against God *(peccatum originale originantis)*, and (2) were punished in a way which would affect all their descendants *(peccatum originale originatum)*. It is important to distinguish between these two phases of the doctrinal narrative. Scientific advances have rendered a literal and factual understanding of the book of Genesis critically impossible; but these advances have emphatically not explained away the phenomenon of evil and suffering so evident in the world. Augustine's question "Whence evil?" is as apposite today as it ever was.

The most fruitful theological response to scientific and philosophical developments as they bear upon questions of creation and redemption has been to interpret the stories in Genesis 1-11 as aetiological myths, that is, as narratives which give a symbolic account of how the world began and of what happened then to bring about the situation which we today experience. This mode of interpretation enables the modern theologian to make creative use of a part of scripture which might otherwise be dismissed as literally incredible. Thus, for example, to interpret the Adam and Eve of Genesis as the whole human race from its beginning to its end opens up a host of promising insights.

From the time of Robert Bellarmine onwards original sin was interpreted mainly in terms of the loss and continued privation of sanctifying grace. As a result of Teilhard de Chardin's attempt to bring contemporary scientific thinking about human origins into fruitful relationship with christian faith, attention shifted from the classical issues of guilt, fallen nature, grace, supernature, and the transmission of sin to the "Sin of the World" and the human experience of division within the individual and society. This was the approach taken by the

Second Vatican Council's Pastoral Constitution *Gaudium et Spes*. In its all too brief treatment of the matter, *Gaudium et Spes* took its inspiration from Romans 7, where St. Paul dwells on the theme of "man divided within himself," rather than from the more traditionally invoked Romans 5, in the old Latin translation of which had occurred the reference to Adam "in whom all have sinned."

It must be noted that the Roman magisterium has not been generally comfortable with attempts made by twentieth century Catholic theologians to respond positively and creatively to the challenge of modern consciousness and scholarship. In 1909 the Biblical Commission ruled out all but a literal interpretation of the first three chapters of Genesis. In 1943, Pius XII's Encyclical Letter, *Divino afflante Spiritu,* allowed a much more scientifically-based type of interpretation; but in 1950 the same Pope's Encyclical, *Humani Generis,* in condemning polygenism (the theory of human descent from more than one original pair) and, in general, in discouraging a Teilhardian evolutionary approach, placed a temporary brake upon further developments in this direction.

With Vatican II there came a fresh charter for theologians, resulting in renewed thinking about the doctrine of original sin, which was now given an existential interpretation by some and a more personal psychological interpretation by others. Fresh theological insights were incorporated into a refurbished catechetical movement. The *Dutch Catechism* (1966), following the lead of *Gaudium et Spes,* concentrated on the human condition as it is experienced by men and women today. A Commission of Cardinals, however, was set up to examine the *Catechism* (1967) and it threw attention back to an historical fall, reaffirmed the transmission of a real state of sin "by propagation," and warned

against the use of language which would suggest that original sin is contracted only by exposure to a sin-infected environment. Thus there appears to exist in the Catholic Church—in this as in other theological matters—two different and opposed methodologies which, however much they agree on the substance of what has to be believed, differ considerably in the way they formulate the question and seek to answer it.

The traditional formulation of the doctrine is inescapably tied in with a static and essentialist view of humankind. Contemporary anthropology deals with the dynamic and changing relationship between human beings and their culture down the ages. It sees men and women as constantly developing beings who, for good or ill, shape their own destiny by the way in which they interrelate with each other, individually and socially, and with their natural environment. For the last quarter century Catholic theologians have attempted to reconsider the doctrine of original sin while taking account of modern anthropology, paleontology, and scientific biblical criticism.

These attempts mostly agree in concentrating upon the grace-resistant dimension of the human condition rather than upon a calamitous sin committed by a specific couple from whom the human race is descended. In this way of treating the matter it is sufficient to indicate that men and women have sinned since the dawn of history. Biological, especially genetic, models are neither necessary nor helpful. Contemporary theories therefore tend to reflect the anthropological concerns of each theologian. Certain problems are common to all schools of thought and have to be faced by any theologians aware of their responsibilities towards both tradition and contemporary authenticity and relevance. Some of these are: (1) Whether the word "sin" is to be defined univocally or analogically; (2)

how to avoid treating sin as a necessary feature in the process of becoming human; (3) how to avoid Pelagian environmentalism while (4) giving weight to the notion of a sinful history; (5) how to affirm the essential goodness of creation, including *homo sapiens,* while not playing down the dark or shadow side of human nature and human history; (6) in short, how to relate creation to redemption, nature to culture, and both to Christ.

G. Vandervelde has classified the large recent literature on original sin into two major trends: the situationist and the personalist. Situationist theologians like P. Schoonenberg and K. Rahner treat men and women as historical beings who relate in personal freedom to their environment. This view of sin draws extensively on existentialism for its language. To be human is to be "situated in the world"; but this situatedness is sinful in that it is the product of a sinful history. Situationist theories thus focus attention upon historical and environmental evil (sometimes identifying it with the Johannine "Sin of the World"). Their strength lies in the fact that they take with due seriousness the social and historical dimension of sin. They are, however, open to the charge of denying an antecedent predisposition to sin inherent in human nature itself. Their proponents answer this charge by claiming that sin and grace are not to be related to each other in temporal sequence: they coexist existentially in social and individual experience.

The personalist view, as exemplified by A. Vanneste, reduces original sin to the factual universality of actual sins. Vanneste is not interested in origins, biological or metaphysical. Enough for him that every human being *de facto* sins. Personalist theories do not need to distinguish analogically between personal and original sin. Every man and woman needs redemption by Christ because every man and woman is in point of fact an actual sinner. It is not easy to reconcile this radically contingent view of sin with either human freedom or that depth dimension of human experience commonly described as the prepersonal disposition towards sin.

Both situationist and personalist theories avoid the crude essentialism of the traditional concept of a sinful nature inherited by generation from a sinful ancestor and meriting eternal sanction; but they do not find it easy to demonstrate the intrinsic universality of the need for redemption by Christ. They affirm that need as an *actual* historical, personal, social, and existential characteristic of humanity, but they do not always show convincingly how to be human is by definition to be in need of salvation. Their work witnesses to the continuing need for further critical study if the concept of original sin is not to be handed over by default to the biblical and doctrinal fundamentalists who are content with verbal repetition of inherited formulas.

The context of the debate over original sin is no longer that of classical Pelagianism (which presupposed moral earnestness, the practice of asceticism, and an elitist approach to christian life) but rather that of a complacent acceptance of the world as it is, coupled with a post-Freudian and post-Darwinian tendency to reduce phenomena which were formerly described as sin to the physical and psychological determinism of human nature.

A significant contribution to any theologian's understanding of sin will be his or her predominant models for treating of it. Characteristically Western models have been: the criminal, the courtroom, the judge, the sentence, the punishment, and/or the acquittal. Characteristically Eastern models have been: the immature child, the sick person, the disease, the doctor, the medical treatment, and the cure.

If privation of grace (a controlling feature in the Catholic theology of original sin since the late sixteenth century) is given juridical reference, it becomes difficult to avoid speculations which belong more properly to scientific anthropology than to theology. If, on the other hand, one's models, images, and language reflect the healing process which is built into human development as a free gift from God, but which calls for active cooperation from the patient, it becomes easier to relate the doctrine of original sin to the experience and preoccupations of post-Freudian and post-Darwinian men and women. The radical separation of the doctrine of creation from the doctrine of grace has resulted in many of the gratuitously insoluble problems posed for itself since the time of Augustine by the Western theology of sin and grace, which has not infrequently appeared to suggest with gloomy relish that sin is actually more prevalent than grace. Sound theology must show that the scope and power of sin are always abundantly exceeded by the scope and power of grace and the salvific will of God.

If Christ, in Augustine's splendid phrase, is "our physician," then the human condition is one of sickness which is terminal only if the patient forsakes the doctor and turns instead to homemade nostrums. Faith in Christ, made possible by grace, offers a "comfort against sin" (Julian of Norwich) and a passage from sickness to that state of health known to traditional christian spirituality as holiness. It is the process of healing which is primarily revealed: we know of the disease partly from human experience but mainly, and salvifically, from what Jesus Christ has done for us by his life, teaching, death and resurrection.

G. Vandervelde, *Original Sin: Two Major Trends in Contemporary Roman Catholic Reinterpreta-tion,* Amsterdam: Rodopi, 1975. E. Yarnold, *The Theology of Original Sin,* Cork: Mercier, 1971. A. Vanneste, *The Dogma of Original Sin,* Brussels: Vander, 1975. J.L. Segundo, *Evolution and Guilt,* New York: Orbis, Dublin: Gill and Macmillan, 1974. N.P. Williams, *The Ideas of the Fall and of Original Sin,* London: Longmans, Green and Co., 1927. P. Ricoeur, *The Symbolism of Evil,* New York, Harper & Row, 1976.

GABRIEL DALY, OSA

ORTHODOXY

The word orthodoxy comes from the joining of two Greek words: *orthe,* meaning right or correct, and *doxa,* meaning opinion or glory. While classical Greek authors sometimes placed these two words side by side (Plato, *Philebus.* 11 b) or employed the verb *orthodoxeo*— to have a correct opinion (Aristotle, *Nichomachean Ethics,* 1151²19), the substantive "orthodoxy" and the adjective "orthodox" only come into common usage during the Greek patristic period. Orthodoxy means correct or sound doctrine. Eventually, its use extended beyond a theological context and took on a generic meaning connoting the accepted or established doctrine in any given field.

The word "orthodoxy" does not appear in christian scriptures, although several biblical themes are congenial to the idea. St. Paul speaks of the teaching which he has received and has carefully handed on (1 Cor 11:2, 28; 15:1-3; Rom 16:17). He likewise speaks of preaching "the faith" (Gal 1:23) with the connotation that the faith is a doctrine to be handed on. Such a connotation also appears in Jude 3, which mentions "the faith delivered once for all to the saints." The Pastoral Letters, showing a marked interest in soundness of doctrine, use the word teaching (*didaskalia*) fifteen times and differentiate healthy teaching (1 Tim 1:10; 2 Tim 4:3; Titus 1:9; 2:1) or good teaching (1 Tim 4:6) from heterodox (literally "of another opinion") teaching (1 Tim 1:3; 6:3). These points are complemented by the additional biblical theme of warning against apostasy, an apostasy which clearly carries doctrinal overtones (Gal 1:6-9; 2 Tim 4:3-4; Heb 6:4-8).

In the post-biblical period, one finds reference to heterodox teachers and doctrines as early as Ignatius of Antioch (d. 108; see Mag 8, 1 and Smyr 6, 2). The word orthodoxy finally catches on in the writings of Eusebius of Caesarea (d. 339), Julius I (d. 359), Athanasius (d. 373) and Basil (d. 379) and was used by the Councils of Ephesus (431) and Chalcedon (451). Thus gradually orthodoxy came to mean not simply right doctrine but the traditional and universal doctrine of the church as defined in opposition to heterodoxy or heresy. In this context it was seen as the pure tradition, handed down in unbroken line from the authentic Gospel of Jesus and his apostles. Churches were said to be orthodox insofar as they adhered to the faith proclaimed at Ephesus and Chalcedon in opposition to Nestorius, Eutyches and others. After the defeat of iconoclasm in the ninth century, a liturgical feast day of orthodoxy was introduced in the Eastern Church, to be celebrated each year on the first Sunday of Lent. During this feast, a litany of orthodox and heterodox teachers was chanted, to which the congregation responded by praying for the honoring or for the anathematization of the particular teacher whose name had just been mentioned. From the fourth to the ninth centuries, Greek authors applied the adjective "orthodox" to interpretations of scripture, the faith of the church, the church's liturgical worship, various decrees and opinions, writings, churches and individuals. The term appears much less frequently in Latin literature; it seems even to have been deliberately avoided in the writings of the Popes. It appeared at times in the history of the Reformation Churches, as when some seventeenth

century writers spoke of a Lutheran orthodoxy, that is, a Lutheranism which remained close to the writings and original inspiration of Martin Luther. In the twentieth century, Barth's critical reaction to liberalism ushered in a period of neo-orthodoxy which resisted attempts to water down traditional christian beliefs. The Second Vatican Council uses the adjective "orthodox" only once, in a comment about Marian devotion falling within the bounds "of sound and orthodox doctrine" (L.G. 66).

Insofar as Christianity proposes some distinguishable truth pertaining to faith and morals, it may always be said to have a body of doctrine which might be called its "orthodoxy." Just what criteria are used to determine the extent of that doctrine are manifold: inclusion in scripture, proposal by the church's teaching office, belief by the faithful (*sensus fidelium*) and so forth. Orthodoxy has never eliminated a legitimate diversity of interpretations among believers. It does not amount to a strict uniformity in faith.

Societies sensitive to historicity and to the rights and duties of individuals in pursuing the truth may, on the other hand, adopt a prejudice against orthodoxy, equating it with intolerance and closed-mindedness. Actually, however, orthodoxy simply refers to that sound doctrine which the church has been commissioned from its inception to proclaim.

Frequently today, orthodoxy is recognized as being only one aspect of the life of the church, an aspect concerned with the cognitive side of being a Christian. Orthodoxy invites reflection upon the complement to right doctrine—that is, upon right or correct action, which is called orthopraxis.

See **Doctrine, Orthopraxis**

Walter Bauer, *Orthodoxy and Heresy in Earliest Christianity*, Philadelphia: Fortress, 1971. William A. Curtis, "Orthodoxy," *Encyclopedia of Religion and Ethics*, J. Hastings, Ed. vol. IX, Edinburgh: T. & T. Clark, 1917, pp. 570-72. H. Rengstorf, "didasko, didaskalia, heterodidaskaleo," *Theological Dictionary of the New Testament*, G. Kittel, Ed. vol. II, Grand Rapids: Wm. B. Eerdmans 1964, pp. 135-65.

WILLIAM HENN, OFM CAP

ORTHOPRAXIS

Immediate Context

Orthopraxis (*orthos:* straight, right, correct; *praxis:* human action, conduct) is a term that achieved theological currency with the rise of political theology in Europe and liberation theology in Latin America in the 1960's and 1970's. It expresses a deeply felt lack or defect perceived in hitherto prevalent theologies' exclusive focus upon the profession of the true contents of christian belief or orthodoxy (*doxa:* established belief or teaching, closely associated with the cognate terms, *dogma*: rule of belief or faith; and *doctrina*: more or less authoritative teaching). Academic or seminary theology can be and has been infected by a conceptualist misunderstanding of faith that erroneously severs the intimate link between faith and action, especially activity in the social and cultural spheres of technology, economy, and politics. In principle and in fact this split contradicts both the biblical understanding of "faith working through love" (Gal 5:6); and the intellectualist ideal of a love of truth that entails a love of all human beings. Hence, the assertion of the primacy of orthopraxis over orthodoxy may be understood as an attempt to reintegrate faith and action and to take seriously the NT affirmation that "not everyone who says to me, 'Lord, Lord,' shall enter the kingdom of heaven, but he who does the will of my Father who is in heaven" (Mt 7:21).

Approaches to Christian Identity

Both the recent stress on orthopraxis and the traditional concern with ortho-doxy are ways of facing the issue of christian identity as constituted by distinctive meanings and values. Properly understood, orthopraxis deals with the constitution of christian meanings and values by concentrating on the communicative (e.g., base communities) and effective (e.g., social justice) functions of meaning. In contrast, orthodoxy takes the constitution of christian meanings and values seriously by focusing upon the cognitive function of meaning, i.e., on the truth and intelligibility of Christian beliefs. From an adequately differentiated viewpoint orthopraxis and orthodoxy represent distinct yet complementary concerns, both of them integral to Christian living. But from less differentiated perspectives the two concerns tend to diverge into differing sets of attitudes or overall approaches to the grave and complex identity problems facing christian communities of worship and witness today. When such divergences arise out of opposed foundations, polemical characterizations of the two approaches abound.

Within a polemical context, defenders of orthodoxy are portrayed as stultifying reactionaries so insistent on doctrinal conformity as almost to suggest that nothing counts so much as (even merely verbal and nominal!) adherence to the unchanging truths contained in the deposit of faith. Similarly, prophets of orthopraxis are depicted polemically as relativistic and opportunistic activists who so absolutize sheer historical process as to relegate christian revelation and redemption to oblivion. It has to be conceded that inasmuch as adequate theological foundations are missing, various approximations to these polemical grotesques can actually occur in theological and ecclesial communities, and their numbers increase as the christian identity-crisis oscillates between accommodating and restorative trends.

However, in the measure that serious foundational discussion takes place among theological proponents of the priority of orthopraxis/orthodoxy, common ground comes to light. Serious theologians realize that we cannot just take hold of a confession of faith, which had in fact resolved some past identity-crisis within the christian community, and use it as if true meaning and values can get along without concrete, historical human minds and hearts. To submit confession of faith to "doctrinization" is to try to gain religious conformity at the price of a kind of derailment that hinders rather than aids a genuine union of minds and hearts. Dead orthodoxy is no answer to the existential issue of christian and religious identity.

But thoughtful theologians also sense the superficiality of reducing the dangerous memory of the praxis of Jesus into a merely exemplary tale of emancipation by turning practical effectiveness and relevance into the sole standard for the validity of christian faith. To let an undifferentiated concern for practicality collapse the truth of faith into a merely this-worldly effectualness would render us insensible to the supernatural gift of God's redemptive and transformative love. The antidote to dead orthodoxy cannot be a well-meaning practice that defers to nothing higher than human doing and making, because then the christian community would be cut off from the sources of its redemptive power and lose its radically critical potential.

Problem of Method

Disagreements between theologians favoring the primacy of orthopraxis and those promoting the priority of orthodoxy are traceable to different views regarding the touchstone for specifically christian existence. Yet surely it is not enough for those in favor of orthopraxis to cite texts such as Mt 25:31-45 about the last judgment's being based on effec-tive love of those in need or the Epistle of James on the insufficiency of faith without good works; or for those favoring the primacy of orthodoxy to insist with Rom 10:9f that "if you confess with your lips that Jesus is Lord and believe in your heart that God raised him from the dead, you will be saved." The radical underlying question in the debate about the relative priority of orthopraxis or orthodoxy is one of theological method.

The best exponents of the priority of orthopraxis want to keep constantly in view the *concrete conditions* of human being and knowing. Thus, their insistence that a conversion of heart and life is the condition for true knowledge of God and that following Jesus is the presupposition for knowing him is both typical of their approach and quite orthodox. Their theological method does, it is true, reflect the eleventh of Karl Marx's *Theses on Feuerbach:* "The philosophers have only interpreted the world in various ways; the point, however, is to change it." But it might as rightly be associated with the procedures of *prudentia* as set forth by St. Thomas Aquinas. It starts with the daily practice of christian believers, analyzes the models and mindsets motivating that practice, and then evaluates this practice critically in the light of gospel demands. To be sure, Marx-inspired social theory may often inform their analyses and evaluations of everyday christian practice. But the point of the procedure is to lead not just to changed practice, but to a transformed and deepened appreciation of the christian message as time goes on.

Far from eliminating orthodoxy in the sense of "holding certain judgments of fact and value as true," the intention of this method is to allow God's grace to interrupt the patterns of life-as-usual and to promote concrete discipleship both personally and in relation to suprapersonal institutional frameworks.

Ambiguities of the Term "Praxis"

The coining of the word "orthopraxis" as a counter to the word "orthodoxy" is connected with the theological revival of Marx's notion of praxis. The word "praxis," therefore, has a specifically dialectical thrust. It is meant to overcome the opposition of theoretic and practical life (which was never asserted as such by Greek philosophy) which had become commonplace in christian theology. It is also used to counter both the rationalism of late medieval scholasticism and the rationalism of the Enlightenment—each of which praxis-oriented theologians tend to label "idealist."

In fact Greek philosophy originated as a resistance to the corruption of public order, and it was grounded in the tension between the pure, disinterested, and unrestricted desire to know embodied by the philosopher and the more or less biased and undifferentiated self-understandings of the city. Hence, although Plato and Aristotle argued the superiority of the theoretic or contemplative life over political life, they never separated them artificially (Consider the paradigm of the citizen-philosopher, Socrates). Even so, in terms of the object-oriented cast of Aristotle's *Posterior Analytics, theoria* in the strict sense was to be directed toward objects that are immutable, necessary, and eternal. This separation from changeable, contingent, and temporal objects was solidified by medieval faculty-psychology. Speculative reason (as a faculty) and speculative science (as a habit) were split off from practical reason and science in a manner quite alien to Greek philosophy.

What praxis-oriented theologians oppose in late medieval speculative reason as well as in the Enlightenment's calculating reason (e.g., Hobbes, Descartes) or pure reason (Kant) is the supposition that reason operates in isolation from the limited and biased processes of sociali-

zation, acculturation, and education. Contemporary exponents of the primacy of orthopraxis take seriously Marx's and Nietzsche's critique of rationalism by thoroughly acknowledging the end of innocence for all theory.

Nevertheless, praxis-oriented theologians generally have joined themselves to the tradition of social theory from Rousseau to Marx which justly criticized the exploitively commercial and philistine notions of "bourgeois" practicality and reason by taking up Marx's notion of praxis. That notion, rooted as it is in Romantic and Hegelian conceptions of human activity as self-expression, usually entails the idea that all properly human action is production. But this idea not only blurs the classic distinction between *praxis* (human activity of all kinds as resulting from one's own free choice of ends) and *poiesis* (making as subordinated to ends already chosen by others); but it subverts the hoped-for critique of instrumental reason. Marx himself tried not to succumb to the limits of instrumental reason by pointing to a "realm of freedom" in which specifically human labor would be emancipated both by the technological overcoming of scarcity and the revolution of the proletariat so that it could match the full scope of the "wealth of human needs." However, since he never adequately faced the question about what would be choiceworthy once humanity had reached the "realm of freedom," the reductionist strain in Marx's notion of praxis remains ineradicable.

Consequently, those tacitly assuming Marx's notion of praxis (instead of the classic one) may also be tempted to bend all theoretical activity and truth to fit the contours of what Machiavelli called "effectual truth." To this temptation an intellectualist (vs. conceptualist) and nondoctrinaire stress on orthodoxy can supply a salutary antidote. Moreover, the wider range of human flourishing as self-transcendence inculcated by the classic teaching of the supremacy of contemplation can help to keep vivid and unforgotten the transpolitical, trans-historical, and utterly gratuitous moment of God's saving love. Such a dangerous memory, it seems, would need to be integral to theology as a praxis that mediates critically between unconverted and biased patterns of practical living and the praxis of the kingdom paradigmatically manifested in Jesus who suffered, died, and was raised again from the dead in complete solidarity with all of history's victims.

See **Orthodoxy, Praxis**

FREDERICK G. LAWRENCE

P

PACIFISM

Pacifism generally signifies a renunciation of any recourse to arms and a refusal to participate in warfare. It has usually been religiously motivated, although new developments have made room for secular proponents as well. Christian pacifism appeals to the example of Christ as well as to the writings of the NT. While it is recognized that pacifist interpretations are not uncontroverted, and while there exist exegetical and hermeneutical problems, nevertheless, the religious pacifist believes that the overall depiction of Christ's forgiveness, his mercy, his refusal to defend himself by violence, the total tenor of his life and especially of his dying, all of these warrant some ethical claim that the shedding of blood is incompatible with discipleship.

Pacifists also appeal to the witness of the early church. Historians generally agree that until the Constantinian era Christians did not generally participate in warfare, and, in fact, before 170 A.D. they seem to have been almost totally absent from the ranks of the military. Recall the famous complaint of Celsus against the Christians, that their failure to defend the empire would leave it fall into the hands of barbarians. Origen's response is illustrative in that he argues that their prayers and disciplined lives are of greater service than that of soldiers. Various factors are adduced to explain the christian absence from the army, such as their minority status, or the idolatrous practices common to the Roman military. Yet others hold that there is sufficient evidence to show that it was the Christians' distaste for any violent shedding of blood that primarily motivated the early church pacifism.

After Ambrose and Augustine, the church's posture toward violence became encapsulated in what is now known as the just-war teaching. While this teaching carried a presumption against killing and attempted to restrain violence, it nevertheless allowed for war under certain conditions. Even after the Reformation, this teaching is said to have been in "possession" among Catholics and Protestants. Yet, throughout the Middle Ages, reformers such as the Waldenses and Franciscans called for a return to the pre-Constantinian abstention from any killing. Similar calls for reform occurred in the seventeenth and eighteenth centuries with sectors of the Anabaptist movement as well as with George Fox' Society of Friends. From these movements have emerged what are known today as the Historic Peace Churches which include Mennonites, Quakers, the Brethren, and other groups, all of whom for the most part have eschewed any cooperation whatsoever with the wars of the nations.

In recent years something of a new

respect for pacifism and pacifists has developed within all the churches. On the one hand there has occurred a fresh appraisal of the horrors of modern weaponry, especially nuclear weaponry. On the other hand the churches themselves are undergoing forms of spiritual renewal nurtured, for example, by the return to scripture and the revitalization of patristic studies. Certainly the lay-clerical stratification, which for centuries has stood behind too easy a distinction between evangelical counsels and obligation, now yields to an inevitable question: if the clergy are called to a level of holiness that is incompatible with killing, why not laypersons as well?

In fact, in North America it is the lay movement of Dorothy Day and the Catholic Worker which has been extremely influential among activists of all faiths in providing a model of social spirituality. Of special significance in the past several decades have been the writings of Thomas Merton. They have allowed many to find in western spiritual tradition a contemplative basis for nonviolent action. And, of course, the teacher par excellence of a special form of nonviolent pacifist practice in North America is the Baptist preacher, Martin Luther King. One cannot mention King, without moving beyond North America to evoke the memory of this century's first teacher of nonviolence, Mahatma Gandhi. Gandhi's teaching on nonviolent tactics and on the power of a truth spoken compassionately (*satyagraha*) stands today as the cornerstone for all that has followed and all that will follow in the various transformations of pacifism that are occurring throughout the world.

It is true that pacifism is not always seen as synonymous with the term nonviolence in today's usage. While the nonviolence of Mahatma Gandhi and Martin Luther King drew their inspiration from faith sources, the practice of non-violence is not limited to religious pacifists. Yet today's religious pacifist owes to the nonviolence movement a greater emphasis on strategy, on organization and a greater historical involvement in social justice. One contemporary expert in the history of nonviolence describes 198 modes of action for correcting human rights abuses (Gene Sharp).

The Church too has not been immune from the influence of this activist form of nonviolence. Indeed, some suspect that we are in the midst of a very significant evolution of consciousness. While the Second Vatican Council continued to utilize just-war teaching, it also recognized and praised those who renounce the use of violence (G.S. 78). And the 1983 Peace Pastoral of the U.S. Catholic Bishops saw pacifism as one of two distinct moral options open to individual Christians, the other, of course, being that of just-war teaching. They even suggested that work to develop non-violent means of resolving conflict "best reflects the call of Jesus both to love and to justice" (para. 73-78). And they go so far as to recommend what is today called "popular defense," that is, an entire people's organized effort to nonviolently defend their rights (para. 224-27). Statements of other denominations are amazingly similar not only in seeing pacifism as a legitimate church tradition but also in manifesting a transformation of its meaning through the impact of this century's practice of nonviolence.

It is important to mention that contemporaneous with this development in christian teaching on pacifism, one finds a similar movement regarding the respect due the conscientious objector. This constitutes a shift from the position of the moral manuals and from the thought of Pius XII. In her articulation of just-war teaching, the church no longer grants the state's warmaking a presumption of justice. It is rather the individual who is summoned to make a personal discernment.

One must mention in this context today's use of the term *nuclear pacifist*. It refers to one who opposes any use of nuclear weapons. This nuclear pacifism is not to be confused with pacifism as such, since its conclusions are argued in the terms of just-war teaching, especially those criteria of just-war teaching which forbid improportionate and indiscriminate destruction. Nevertheless, it can be said that the very dread of nuclear devastation can be seen as a "sign of the times" impelling the church "to evaluate war with an entirely new attitude" (G.S. 80). And in the formation of this new attitude the lines between just-war teaching and pacifism are sometimes less sharply drawn. Indeed, the U.S. Catholic bishops already have blunted the usual dichotomous mode of opposing pacifism with just-war teaching by declaring a "complementary relationship" between them, in that both seek to protect the common good (para 74).

Because of this intertwining of religious pacifism with contemporary theory of nonviolent action, today's pacifism is less vulnerable to the charge of neglecting the values of human justice in history. Thus a pacifism, now transformed by nonviolent techniques and increasingly targeted at the accomplishments of justice within world history, is seen by ethicians as more teleologic in character (i.e., consequentialist), differing therefore, from the more deontologic mode of pacifism. As a result pacifism today is less easily accused of being sectarian, and unites under its umbrella peoples of wider motivation and inspiration. (Perhaps a more careful hermeneutic would reveal some earlier forms of pacifism to be less doctrinaire and other-worldly than first meets the eye.) One can now, at least, envision how a development of doctrine could take place in which both Catholic and Protestant churches in view of the threat of nuclear devastation could find themselves effectively joining the historic peace churches without repudiating the justice values which just-war teaching had traditionally sought to protect, and without the church's retreating from its necessary and influential dialogue with the sociopolitical world.

See **Peace, War**

Roland Bainton, *Christian Attitudes Toward Peace and War* Nashville, Tenn.: Abingdon, 1960. Cecil J Cadoux, *The Early Church and the World,* Edinburgh: Clark Pub. Co., 1925. James Childress, "Moral Discourse About War in the Early Church," *Journal of Religious Ethics* 12, no. 1, Spring 1984. Dorothy Day, *The Long Loneliness: An Autobiography,* New York: Harper and Row, 1952 (1982). Mohandas Gandhi, *An Autobiography: The Story of My Experiments with Truth,* Boston: Beacon Press, 1962. Thomas Merton, *Gandhi on Non-Violence* New York: New Directions Press, 1955. National Conference of Catholic Bishops, *The Challenge of Peace: God's Promise and Our Response,* Washington, D.C.: The United States Catholic Conference, 1983. Gene Sharp, *The Politics of Nonviolent Action,* 3 vols., Boston: Porter Sargent Press, 1973. John Howard Yoder, *Nevertheless: The Varieties and Shortcomings of Religious Pacifism* 2nd ed., Scottdale, Pa.: Herald Press, 1976. Gordon Zahn, *War, Conscience and Dissent,* New York: Hawthorn Books, 1967.

FRANCIS X. MEEHAN

PANTHEISM
See **God**

PAPACY
See **Pope**

PARABLE

Jesus taught in parables. But, then, what is a "parable"? The Greek word *parabolē* means a juxtaposition or a comparison of two realities. (The German word for parable, *Gleichness* or "likeness," conveys something of this). A term used in classical rhetoric, the strict parable had only one point of comparison and might be described as an extended simile. The matter is not so simple because in the NT *parabolē* quite often has the wide-ranging meaning of the Hebrew *mashal*. It can be a representation or a type, a simile or a metaphor, a maxim or pithy saying, a symbol or a riddle. It might carry, too, the aura of a "dark saying," implying mystery. The bewildering range of meaning may be gauged from the fact that each proverb in the book of Proverbs—two-line couplets in the main—is a *mashal,* while each lengthy speech of Job is also termed *mashal.* In the gospels, *parabolē* may have the meaning "proverb" (Lk 4:23) or "wisdom saying" (Mk 7:15) or may be an extended comparison (Mk 13:28-29). And when Jn 16:25 refers to "speaking in figure" the word *paroimia* conveys the same meaning as the figurative speech implied by *parabolē* in its broadest sense. While acknowledging the range of meaning, we shall here look only to those stories in our gospels which we today call "parables."

It has been customary to set up a sharp contrast between parablé and allegory. Parable is commonly described as a story that has one point and one point only. It is held to be distinct from allegory, or prolonged metaphor, in which each detail has symbolic meaning (e.g. Eph 6:13-17). The proper distinction is that parable is a specific literary form, while allegory is a device of meaning. What marks off a parable is that it is a story with a particular religious or ethical purpose; it is always thought-provoking and often is a challenge to decisive action. Every parable has two levels of meaning; the second (ethical or religious) level is the one that matters. Allegory, on the other hand, is a component of some parables. An allegorical story can be quite other than parable, but there are parables that are allegorical (e.g. the Prodigal Son). There is a corollary: it had too readily been assumed that anything smacking of allegory was foreign to Jesus: he would have employed only "pure" parables. The truth is that Jesus' intent was ever to challenge attitudes and invite commitment; he was not to be hampered by academic niceties.

By Jesus' day the parable had become a familiar form in rabbinical preaching. (It was not a rabbinical invention as witness Nathan's brilliant parable in 2 Sam 12:1-4—with a hapless David toppling into the parabolic trap, 12:5-7). The parable drew material from daily life and gave it set meanings: vineyard, sons, servants represented Israel, a king or father meant God, a feast indicated the messianic age, and a harvest the judgment. When Jesus chose to speak in parables he was following a convention familiar to his hearers.

Classification

The gospel parables are commonly classified as similitude, parable and exemplary story (with the result that "parable" is inconveniently used in both a broader and narrower sense). The similitude is a brief narrative of a typical or recurrent event from real life: e.g., the Lost Sheep, the Lost Coin (Lk 15:3-7, 8-10), and the Growing Seed (Mk 4:26-29). The parable is a somewhat longer story of a fictitious (yet true-to-life) event: e.g., the Sower (Mk 4:3-8), the Talents (Mt 25:14-30), and the Prodigal Son (Lk 15:11-32). The exemplary story presents an example which illustrates a general principle. There are four of these: the Good Samaritan, the Rich Fool, Dives and Lazarus, the Pharisee and the Tax Collector (Lk 10:29-37; 12:16-21; 16:19-31; 18:9-14).

Setting

Parables as we know them in our gospels may show traces of a twofold, sometimes a threefold, setting: the ministry of Jesus, the life of the early church, and an evangelist's editorial setting. It is never easy, and for the most part impossible, to work back, through the tradition, to an assured setting in the life of Jesus. Still, one may discern characteristic aspects of Jesus' parabolic technique. Even in encounter with his opponents (and a surprising number of his extant parables are addressed to them) he always sought dialogue, aiming to get his listeners to see and adopt his point of view. In his parables Jesus invites his hearers to recognize, in his ministry, God's own activity and to recognize the reason for his association with outcasts and sinners. Through them he issues a call to *metanoia*, a change of heart, and spells out the demands of discipleship.

The fact remains that we know the parables as we find them in our gospels. It is instructive to observe how freely they have been treated within the gospel tradition. These are some indications:

1. The grouping of parables. E.g., concern for the "lost," Lk 15:3-7, 8-10, 11-32; the three seed parables in Mk 4:3-9, 26-29, 30-32.

2. Parables may have different meanings in the gospels. E.g., in Lk 15:3-7 the Lost Sheep is a defense of Jesus' concern for the outcasts of society; in Mt 18:12-14, addressed to a christian community, it is an exhortation to solicitude for erring brothers or sisters.

3. There are differing versions of the same parable: e.g., the Wicked Tenants (Mk 12:1-11; Mt 21:33-43; Lk 20:9-18). More striking are the differences between the Talents and the Pounds (Mt 25:14-30; Lk 19:11-27), and the Wedding Feast and the Great Feast (Mt 22:2-10; Lk 14:15-24).

4. Parables have been fused. E.g., The Wedding Feast (Mt 22:2-10) and the Wedding Garment (Mt 22:11-14).

5. Parables have been giving generalizing conclusions by addition of originally independent sayings of Jesus: e.g., "The last will be first and the first last" (Mt 19:30; 20:16); "Many are called but few

are chosen" (Mt 22:14); a whole string of maxims (Lk 16:9-13) added to the parable of the Astute Steward (16:1-8).

6. An early christian homily attached to some parables: the interpretations of The Sower (Mk 4:13-20, parr.); the interpretation of the Weeds (Mt 13:36-43).

Interpretation

The gospels bear abundant witness to the fact that the first Christians turned to the parables of Jesus as to living words which spoke directly to themselves. Already we are assured that we, too, should hear them as addressed to us. But we must begin by understanding. We should discern, if we can, the original import of a parable; we should look for any sign of adaptation or reinterpretation in the early preaching tradition; we should appreciate the purpose of an evangelist in his choice and presentation of any parable. For, from the first, the parables of Jesus have been "retranslated." It is this process which has shaped them in their present form in our gospels. To hear the gospels through the ongoing retranslations given them in their transmission down the centuries is to grasp how they continue to be Jesus' living word, addressed to every community of every age. For, the whole force of the parables lies in their illustration of our personal world. It becomes clear that the manner in which Christians, from the beginning, have understood and responded to the parables, does provide a valid way of discerning their authentic message. Perhaps this is because no matter how much the early kerygmatic preaching or later christian preachers have adapted or accommodated the parables, nothing could exhaust their essential message. For at their heart stands Jesus himself.

Mark.

No treatment of the gospel parables can avoid trying to come to terms with the implication of Mk 4:10-12. On the face of it, one is told that Jesus deliberately spoke in parables *in order that* his hearers should not understand. This is an incredible notion since this motive is so alien to the purpose of parable and to the character of Jesus. We must look to the evangelist for an explanation. It is already instructive that Matthew (13:10-17) has notably tailored Mark's text to his purpose. He has distinguished between a time when Jesus had spoken openly to "the Jews" and a time when, in reaction to their rejection of him, he reverted to parabolic teaching. Each in his manner, Matthew and Mark are facing up to a problem which exercised the early church: the obduracy of Israel (cf Rom 9-11).

Mark, for his part, seems to take a staunchly deterministic approach: there are those who, divinely enlightened, understand and accept the message of the parables, while "those outside" fatally misunderstand and reject. Mark has capitalized on the mysterious aspect of parable: parables are necessarily "mysterious" for those who will not listen. His verdict reaches beyond Israel. His point is that for all whose "hardness of heart," whose resistance to the good news, places a barrier to the invitation and challenge of Jesus, the parables are riddles to which they had no answer.

Meaning

While it might be gratifying to discern the first historical setting of a parable (in the ministry of Jesus) it is also true that to press too far the academic search for the original flavor could lead one to lose sight of the parable as an art form. Similarly, to seek, pedantically, to confine the meaning of parables to a single point is to impoverish them. The way in which NT Christians understood a parable is a guideline, but not the only one. We may say that a parable ought to remain provocatively open. Jesus surely would want his parables to be set free from the confines of a single *Sitz im Leben* to live

each its own life. The voice in which he first spoke them must remain abidingly alive.

Parables are an art medium. They are stories and, as such, open up whole realms of thought and experience for those who heed them. That is why they are capable of expanding meaning and that is why confining them to one principle of interpretation, historical or otherwise, robs them of their rich potential. As art the parables are not meant to be stagnant but evocative and reproductive. An art forms seeks to capture what is abidingly relevant. That is why the parables have a universal quality and why their happenings are free from time's conditioning. They are existential and immediate because they are aesthetic. In simple terms: they have the timelessness and the power of story.

See **Biblical Criticism, Jesus Christ**

J. Jeremias, *The Parables of Jesus,* New York: Scribner's 1963. D.O. Via, *The Parables. Their Literary and Existentialist Dimension,* Philadelphia: Fortress, 1967. M. I. Boucher, *The Parables,* Wilmington, DE: M. Glazier, 1981. J. Lambrecht, *Once More Astonished: The Parables of Jesus Christ,* New York: Crossroads, 1981.

WILFRID HARRINGTON, OP

PARACLETE
See **Holy Spirit**

PAROUSIA

The Greek word for what is commonly called the Second Coming of Christ in judgment at the end of history.

Scripture

The OT tradition held that God was the Lord of history who directed the course of history to the goal set for it in eternity. When the people deviated from the proper path, the prophets proclaimed a future "Day of the Lord" to indicate a radical intervention of God in the course of Jewish history. Eventually this "Day of the Lord" is extended to all of history as an expression of the final victory of God over the powers of evil. The NT equivalent of the "Day of the Lord" is the coming of the Son of Man (Lk 17:22ff) or the "day of God" (2 Pet 3:12). As a christological title, the term "Son of Man" is drawn from Dan 7:13ff and associates God's judgment of the world and the final victory of God over evil with the figure of Jesus Christ. The usage of the term *parousia* in reference to the Son of Man is found in Mt 16:27; 24:3, 27, 37, 39; 25:31ff; Mk 8:38; 14:62; Lk 9:26; 18:8; 21:27; Jas 5:7, 8; 2 Pet 1:16; 3:4, 12; 1 Jn 2:28. At times Paul uses "revelation" or "unveiling" instead of "parousia" (1 Cor 1:7; 2 Thess 1:7). Signs will precede the parousia (Mt 24:29; Mk 13:24; Lk 21:25-27). Exegetes differ in their views concerning Jesus' expectation of the end. Mk 13:32 may be taken as a biblical warrant for the claim that the precise time of the parousia is not an object of revelation.

Teaching of the Magisterium

The coming of Jesus to judge the living and the dead is an article contained in early creedal formulas (D.S. 6, 10, 13-17, 19). The Fourth Lateran Council says the following: Christ "will come at the end of the world to judge the living and the dead. He will give to all, both the lost and the elect, according to their works" (D.S. 801). In discussing the question of revelation, the Second Vatican Council says of the church that it looks for "the glorious manifestation of our Lord, Jesus Christ" (D.V. I,4). In its "Letter on Certain Questions concerning Eschatology" (May, 1979), the Sacred Congregation for the Doctrine of the Faith reaffirms this statement, making it clear that it understands the parousia of Christ to involve a fullness of salvation which is not identical with the condition of the elect immediately after their personal death. In summary, the official teaching of the magisterium is very limited in scope: it affirms a coming of Christ as judge through which salvation will be brought to its fullness for all of the redeemed. Beyond this, no details are given.

Theological Reflection

It would be a caricature of early Christianity to see the original community as a small, apocalyptic sect that simply waited for the coming of the Lord and the end of history. Two factors speak against such a view: 1) the fact and the nature of the evangelizing mission of the early Christians; 2) the fact that the parousia was a hope and an expectation with no fixed date. The principal theological idea communicated by the concept of the parousia is the doctrine of the final vindication of God's eschatological act in Jesus Christ. The judgment connected with the parousia is the final and decisive realization of God's victory in Christ over the powers of evil. As the final point of history, the judgment may be seen as the manifestation of the wasted possibilities of humanity in the light of the abiding truth of God (H.U. von Balthasar).

Modern theologians are inclined to see the term "second coming" as unfortunate since it seems to distinguish it from a "first coming" (=incarnation) and sets the two over against each other as distinct mysteries. In reality, the parousia emphasizes the saving presence of Christ to history, and the completion on a cosmic scale of the process begun in the incarnation, death and resurrection of Christ. In short, it symbolizes the consummation of history in God. It is in no way contrary to the scriptures or the official teaching of the magisterium when K. Rahner suggests that the parousia is better thought of as the world finally coming to Christ rather than as Christ returning to the world. The parousia is not the return of a Lord who has been absent but the breaking through of a presence that has been continuous throughout history. Modern theology emphasizes that revelation offers us no way of dating the end of history. Concerning the biblical signs of the end, Cardinal Ratzinger, and M. Schmaus express the common view that texts such as Mark 13 and Luke 17 may be read as signs that are characteristic of all periods of history. Even the figure of the anti-Christ is a principle of church history experienced by each age in its own way. What is decisive is not knowing when history will come to an end but being convinced of the future which God offers to the world in Jesus Christ. God will bring creation and history to a fulfilling end through which creation will be transformed into the likeness with its Head, Jesus Christ. It is the teaching of the magisterium that until that has happened, the salvation of no individual is complete.

See Eschatology

———

ZACHARY HAYES, OFM

PASCHAL MYSTERY

This term is repeatedly used by theologians and by the Second Vatican Council as a way of designating the essential aspects of christian redemption. It is an abbreviation for the Easter mystery of the passion, resurrection, and ascension of Jesus Christ. It implies salvation as prefigured in the Hebrew scriptures, the gift of life through Christ, the beginning of the church and its sacramental life. In a narrower sense it refers to the sacraments of baptism and eucharist. The whole christian life is considered to be Paschal because it is through these two sacraments especially that Christians are inserted in the passover of Christ and by which they continue to reenact in their daily lives his saving death and resurrection. The Paschal mystery is what every christian

liturgy celebrates. It is what marks every Sunday as a little Easter or what marks Easter as the great Sunday. The Paschal mystery is the meaning of christian initiation. It is brought to expression in reconciliation with the church. It is the primary image of the sacrament of anointing. It is the purpose of christian ministry. It is the dominant symbol of christian marriage. It is that in which Lent culminates and it is what the Easter triduum memorializes.

The Constitution on the Sacred Liturgy says of Christ: "He achieved his task principally by the Paschal Mystery of the blessed passion, resurrection from the dead, and glorious ascension, where by dying, He destroyed our death and rising, He restored our life" (S.C. 5). But the Paschal event cannot be limited to the death and resurrection of Christ alone. It cannot be understood except in terms of the whole history of salvation, of which it is the climax. In the christian perspective the whole of history leads to it and takes its meaning from it. In that sense Paschal mystery refers to the whole of salvation offered to humankind as an event which converts the whole history of men and women. Here it is possible to distinguish two stages. The first refers to the Paschal event as something which happened in time two thousand years ago. The second refers to the way the Paschal mystery exists in sacramental symbols today. This second way in which the Paschal event is made available to Christians and others takes place through the liturgy and the committed Christian life. Paschal mystery, in sum, means that God has acted to enter the world and this action of God is expressed in several ways. God comes to visibility through specifically christian symbols. They may be historical, cultic, or those of ordinary life.

The word "Paschal" comes from the Greek term, pascha, which in turn is derived from the Hebrew, *pesach*. *Pesach* refers to the annual commemoration of Israel's first passover in Egypt. This passover is the charter event for the Jews because it recalls and marks their people's liberation from bondage. The Jewish pasch is the memorializing of God's covenant with the Israelites by which they were freed from slavery in Egypt. Originally, the feast was a celebration of the season of spring when life comes to the earth again after the death of winter. For the Israelites it took on added meaning beyond that of the revivifying powers of creation. For them it became and remained a festival of redemption. It celebrates the time when God came to them, defeated their enemies, and made them the People of God. It is called passover because God, visiting Egypt on the night the Hebrews were eating the Paschal meal, "passed over" the Hebrew homes. God spared them but brought death to all the other homes in Egypt. The faithful Israelites had marked their homes with the blood of the Paschal lambs.

In passing over Israel, in the sense of not afflicting them with death, God drew them to the promised land. They came under the leadership of God through the Red Sea, through the desert, through the Jordan, to the land of freedom. But the coming to the promised land was more than a geographical relocation. It was a symbol of a new relationship with God. It meant for the Jews then and the Jews today a passage from darkness to light and from death to life. The Jews were the chosen ones, the ones who were redeemed. God had paid the price for them and they belonged to God. Each year at passover the Jews renew this covenant. They make a memorial of the exodus event. But memorial in the Jewish liturgy is a highly symbolic notion. Through their commemoration they believe that they

are present to this redemptive event in their history. It is present to them and they are present to it.

In the phrase, Paschal mystery, the word, mystery, is to be taken in its biblical sense. The scriptural understanding of mystery is not something that cannot be understood because it is obscure or unintelligible. It does not refer to some arcane cult or special knowledge available only to an elite group. There are three levels of meaning to the biblical notion of mystery. It means first of all, the mystery of God, especially the plan of salvation that God has for the world. This is not accessible to human beings and so must be revealed. This mystery is tied to God's wisdom which must be communicated to human beings. For St. Paul, only God is worthy of the name of wisdom since only God knows the pattern of salvation history and only God can bring about this design.

To accomplish this plan God sent God's son, Jesus Christ. Christ is the key to this mystery. This second level of meaning is the Christ-mystery. In his death and resurrection the wisdom of God is realized and revealed. Christ as the Word of God is the revelation of God's mystery and in and through him it is finally and fully made manifest. It continues to be revealed in the way that Christ lives in human beings today. But it is especially in the cross of Christ, in his dying and rising that the meaning of the whole of human history is laid open. And it is on the second level of meaning that the word, Paschal, joins the word, mystery. For Christians, Jesus Christ brings to a new order the passover of the Hebrew scriptures. He is the new covenant with God. The mystery which had been hidden for so many centuries now takes human form. In the christian perspective, Christ is the true pasch. Paul says: "For Christ, our Paschal lamb, has been sacrificed" (1 Cor 5:7). The death of Christ on the cross, which may have occurred at the very time that the Paschal lamb was being sacrificed in the temple (Jn 19:31), has been interpreted as the coming to full reality of all the promises which were connected with the Jewish passover. Through the cross Christians pass from darkness to the light of God, from the death of this world to the resurrection of a future life, from condemnation from sin to freedom of the children of God. In the cross of Christ the glory of God is now made manifest.

The third level of meaning of mystery is the mystery of christian liturgy. Mystery here refers to the sacramental and ritual life of the church. Paschal mystery now has a liturgical expression. It is the mystery of Christ found in cultic form. In the liturgy the death and resurrection are recalled, not as a mere reminder of things past, but in such a way that the saving mystery of Christ is present to the worshippers. The Second Vatican Council said that in the liturgy not only is the Paschal mystery proclaimed, it is actually accomplished. Paschal mystery is actively present in the church's celebrations. The *Constitution on the Sacred Liturgy* states it well: "Thus by baptism men (sic) are plunged into the Paschal mystery of Christ: they die with him, are buried with him, and rise with him ... In like manner, as often as they eat the supper of the Lord they proclaim the death of the Lord until the Lord comes. For that reason, on the very day of the Pentecost, when the Church appeared before the world, 'those who received the word' of Peter 'were baptized.' ... From that time onward the Church has never failed to come together to celebrate the Paschal mystery: reading those things 'which were in all the Scriptures concerning him,' celebrating the Eucharist in which 'the victory and triumph of his death are again made present. . .'" (S.C. 6).

The Paschal mystery should permeate all of christian spirituality. It is to be the mobilizing image of the spiritual life of the church. The recovery of the place of the Paschal mystery in the liturgy will be pointless if there is no human experience of this central christian belief in the worshipper. It is in the human experiences of suffering, pain, and fear of death that this Paschal mystery becomes a reality for most people. Death and resurrection are part of a human passage through life. Death is the climax of passion and suffering. It is the event which calls people to their true humanity. It is in the free and authentic acceptance of human death that the christian mystery of the risen Christ comes alive. A Paschal spirituality is one in which men and women face death honestly and accept it by anticipating that final moment by undergoing the many daily deaths and resurrections. Christian asceticism is nothing other than the personal integration of human death into one's life. What the Paschal mystery offers to Christians and others is that death is not merely biological or animal. There is such an event as *human* death. Christian death is an act of faith in God. Death calls into question the most fundamental beliefs of men and women. It can be a situation of dark despair which people deny and avoid at all costs. It is usually incomprehensible even to the committed believer. But to say yes to human death is to bestow meaning on all death.

This meaning comes from Christ's own death. He freely embraced death to do the will of God and to establish more clearly God's kingdom here on earth. In an act of freedom Christ handed himself over to God. He bestowed a saving significance on human death. The program of christian spirituality is to take on Christ's own internal attitude, his own commitment to God, and his determination to make himself so totally available.

That is the Paschal dimension of spirituality.

The basic pattern of christian living is Paschal. That means that christian life is happening in terms of a transition. It is the movement from dark to light, from captivity to freedom, from dryness to growth, and from alienation to union. This passover, this exodus, responds to the deep human need to be saved from death. Moreover, this understanding of passover gives an enriched meaning to the idea of sacrifice. Sacrifice is not to be seen primarily in negative terms of offering, giving up, self-depreciation. Christian sacrifice is the good christian life. It takes place wherever Christians live out their spirituality based on the Paschal mystery.

Part of this Paschal pattern of spirituality is that Christians live in the times, between the first and second coming of Christ. Christian spirituality and liturgy move back and forth between the two poles of commemoration of the past and future-oriented hope. Both liturgy and spirituality are characterized by a looking back to the death and resurrection of Christ which calls for a response of thanksgiving and praise, and looking forward toward a goal to be achieved which elicits the mood of christian hope. Both aspects of christian spirituality and liturgy center on Jesus Christ, whether giving thanks in the eucharist for the great things he has done for us or waiting in joyful hope for his coming again. The Paschal mystery that permeates christian liturgy and spirituality is briefly and most accurately summed up in the eucharistic acclamation: "Christ has died, Christ is risen, Christ will come again."

See **Liturgy, Passover, Redemption, Sacrifice**

I.H. Dalmais, OP, *Introduction to the Liturgy,* Baltimore: Helicon Press, 1961. Charles Davis, *Liturgy and Doctrine,* New York: Sheed and Ward, 1960.

JAMES L. EMPEREUR, SJ

PASSOVER

The background of this feast is probably pre-Mosaic. It is an offering by semi-nomadic shepherds to secure the welfare of their flocks as the tribe sets out for new pasture grounds. This is in the spring when the young of the sheep and the goats are to be born. The absence of priests, sanctuaries, and altars indicates the antiquity of the feast (see Exod 12:1-20, 40-51; Num 28:16-25; Deut 16:1-8).

Other details correspond to this pastoral setting. Since cooking utensils are kept to a minimum, the animal is roasted, not boiled. The time, i.e., the twilight of the first full spring moon coincides with the return of the shepherds to their camp on the brightest night of the month. The unleavened bread is the usual bread of such shepherds and the bitter herbs are desert plants that serve as spices. The girt loins, sandals, and staff also support the pastoral background. Most significant of all, however, is the blood rite whose purpose is apotropaic. Thus it serves to ward off all dangers to humans and animals, especially the young about to be born. "The destroyer" (see Exod 12:23) personifies all such dangers. The blood smeared on the tent poles is calculated to prevent any mishap.

It is the blood rite that links the tenth plague (the death of the first-born) and the Passover. Israel historicizes the ancient feast by interpreting it as the festival of freedom and redemption par excellence. It is now Yahweh who will go through the land of Egypt at the time of the Exodus and function as the new "destroyer," killing the first-born of both humans and beasts (see Exod 12:12). However, when Yahweh observes the blood on the houses of the Israelites, he will not strike but will "pass over" (Exod 12:13).

The etymology of "passover" is still disputed. Yet its meaning for Israel is exceedingly clear, i.e., "to spare, protect, deliver." This ancient feast of seminomadic shepherds now expresses Israel's relationship with Yahweh. It is no longer the quest for temporary pasture but the final break from bondage to the security of the promise land. The element of change in this feast suited the sense of change in Israel's destiny and provided the sense of hope in the face of all spiritual and physical oppression.

Although Passover is linked to the Feast of Unleavened Bread (see Mk 14:1), they were originally distinct. While Passover did not call for a sanctuary and was celebrated at home, Unleavened Bread was a pilgrimage feast that demanded the attendance of the adult male at the sanctuary (see Exod. 23:15). While Passover was the feast of seminomadic shepherds, Unleavened Bread was the feast of farmers (the beginning of the barley harvest). Since unleavened bread was employed in both feasts and since they took place around the same time of the year, they were eventually joined together. This probably occurred around the time of King Josiah in the second half of the seventh century B.C.E. (see 2 Chr 35:17).

In the NT according to the synoptics Jesus celebrated the Passover supper with his disciples the night before he died (Lk 22:7-14); see also Mt 26:2, 17-19; Mk 14:12-17). According to John, while the meal Jesus shared with his disciples may or may not have been a Passover supper, Jesus died on the eve of the Passover (see Jn 18:28; 19:14). According to this chronology Jesus died at the time the Passover lambs were being slaughtered in the temple. According to Jn 19:36 (that cites the rubric of not breaking the bones of the animal) Jesus is the Passover Lamb whose death brings salvation to the world (see also Jn 1:29, 36). According to Paul (see 1 Cor 5:7) God's action in Jesus is a Passover sacrifice in which a new journey is involved, the one that goes

from death to life. Christians are bidden, therefore, to be fresh dough, unleavened loaves who live out the Passover celebration of Jesus in joy.

See **Jesus Christ**

JOHN F. CRAGHAN

PATRIPASSIANISM

A term used to refer to a form of Modalism or Monarchianism which, because it denies the distinction between Father and Son in the Trinity, maintains that God the Father suffered Christ's passion and death.

PATROLOGY
See **Fathers of the Church**

PEACE

This contemporary theological analysis of peace incorporates biblical insights, ethical norms such as justice, the contributions of the social sciences, empirical data, and an assessment of the signs of the times. It also necessarily inspects the argument that deterrence provides a "peace of a sort," the call for disarmament, and the church's insistence on the centrality of justice as the foundation of true peace in an interdependent world. Finally, this contemporary theological analysis includes some practical ideas for advancing peace and suggests some initial steps which will lead to the development of a theology of peace.

The Biblical Foundation of Peace

For the Christian, the scriptures are foundational to an analysis of peace; three key factors, however, must condition any inspection of OT and NT contributions to the topic of peace, given the complexity of the scriptures. First, the term "peace" has been understood in different ways at various times and in various contexts. For a people of faith, peace implies a right relationship with God, which entails forgiveness, reconcilation, and union. The scriptures also point to an eschatological peace, a final, full realization of God's salvation when all creation will be made whole. While these two meanings predominate in the scriptures, other meanings of peace, such as an individual's sense of well-being, or cessation of armed hostilities are also to be found in the biblical notion of peace. Second, the scriptures reflect many varied historical situations, all different from our own. An awareness of this factor guards against a too facile application of biblical teachings to our own social and political arenas. Third, the scriptures, which speak primarily of God's intervention in history, contain no specific treatise on peace. This topic, therefore, must be seen in light of the overall focus of the scriptures, namely, God's intervention in human affairs and our response to the divine initiative (National Conference of Catholic Bishops, *The Challenge of Peace: God's Promise and Our Response*, C.P. #27-29).

Old Testament. Mindful of these factors, the scriptures nevertheless provide a rich perspective on peace. The OT, whose image of God as a warrior was gradually transformed, particularly after the experience of the exile, understands peace in light of Israel's relation to God, and therefore as a gift from God and as the fruit of God's saving activity. The OT focuses primarily on the unity and harmony of the community, and the restoration of right order among all peoples and within all creation. The right relationship between the people and God was grounded in and expressed by a covenantal union in which God promised to be present to the people, saving them and leading them to freedom; the people, in turn, made a commitment to

be faithful and obedient to God (Lev 26:3-16). Peace, which is a special characterisitic of this covenant (Ezek 37:26), is built upon justice and fidelity to God's law, as the prophets Jeremiah, Isaiah and Ezekiel clearly remind us (Jer 6:14; 8:10-12; Isa 48:18; Ezek 13:16).

Despite the fact that war and injustice continued, God's promise of a final salvation involving all peoples and all creation, an ultimate reign of peace, became an integral part of the hope of the OT. The final stage, the Messianic time, is described as one in which the effects of justice and integrity will be peace (Isa 32:15-20), in which there will be no need for instruments of war (Isa 2:4; Mi 4:3), since righteousness and peace will embrace (Ps 85:10-11), (C.P. #30-38).

New Testament. As Christians, we believe that Jesus is the Messiah, the one through whom all things in heaven and on earth were reconciled to God when Jesus made peace by his death on the cross (Col 1:19-20). Jesus calls for conversion of hearts and proclaims God's kingdom, which has already begun in his presence and person (Mk 1:14-15). In God's reign, the poor are given the kingdom, the gentle inherit the earth, mourners are comforted, those who hunger and thirst for what is right are satisfied, the merciful know mercy, the pure see God, peacemakers are called children of God, and the persecuted know the kingdom (Mt 5:3-10). Jesus' words and actions indicate that forgiveness and love characterize God's reign (see, Mt. 5:33-48; 6:14-15; Lk 6:27-38), but this message costs Jesus his life.

The power of God's reign triumphs, however, as God raises Jesus from the dead (Rom 4:24-25). The NT, a testimony of faith in the risen Jesus, depicts the post-resurrection gift of peace with which Jesus greets his followers as a peace which the world cannot give (Jn 14:27), the fullness of salvation, the reconciliation of the world and God (Rom 5:1-2; Col 1:20), the restoration of the unity and harmony of all creation for which the OT hoped (Eph 2:15-23; Gal 3:28-29).

The NT also testifies to the empowerment of the disciples by Jesus. The community of believers, gifted with the Jesus' own Spirit, are to be ministers of reconciliation (2 Cor 5:19-20), a people who make the peace of God visible through lives characterized by forgiveness and love. Jesus' disciples, calling for reconciliation among all peoples, proclaim God's reign even to the ends of the earth; they live in hope that God's purpose to unite everything and all things under Christ as head, a plan for the fullness of time, will be fulfilled (Eph 1:10) (C.P. #39-54; West German Catholic Bishops, *Out of Justice, Peace,* O.J.P. #31-50).

Peace in the Contemporary Era

Catholic social teaching recognizes that eschatological tension marks contemporary life: the grace of the kingdom of God is already present but the fullness of God's reign has not yet been realized. A certain tension therefore exists between the vision of God's reign and its concrete realization in history. Within this context, the church situates its treatment of peace and war; short of the fullness of the kingdom, peace is possible but neither permanent nor total in a world marred by the presence of sin within the human heart. A true peace, which is always more than the absence of war, flourishes in a social order which is founded on truth, built on justice, enlivened by love and refined in freedom (John XXIII, *Peace on Earth,* #37). The complex struggle to achieve this true peace underlies the church's teaching on just-war, deterrence, disarmament, and global development.

Deterrence as a "Peace of a Sort"

The most complicated aspect of peace and war analysis is the question of deterrence. Is deterrence the best way to maintain peace in the nuclear age, as some theorists contend? Does it provide humanity with a "peace of a sort," an argument which Vatican II admitted into its treatment of the question (G.S. 81). Recent Catholic social thought on the matter takes its cue from Pope John Paul II's 1982 assessment that, given the precarious international situation, deterrence, not as an end in itself but as a step on the way to progressive disarmament, may be judged to be morally acceptable. The Pontiff warns, however, that in order to ensure peace, it is indispensable not to be satisfied with this minimum, which is always susceptible to the real danger of explosion (Message, U.N. Special Session, 1982; 3). John Paul II, however, neither analyzes the type of deterrence strategy at work nor investigates the intention which lies behind the threat of deterrence.

Since the 1982 papal assessment, several major national Catholic bishops' conferences have addressed the question of deterrence. In 1983, The United States bishops rendered a "conditioned moral acceptance" to deterrence, although they insisted that the *raison d'etre* of the strategy must be to prevent use of nuclear weapons, that the quest for nuclear superiority must be rejected, and that deterrence should be used as a step toward progressive disarmament (C.P. #186-89). The bishops, however, still left many aspects of the morality of deterrence unresolved. This fact was not lost on the bishops, who also raised a series of questions in *Challenge of Peace:* May a nation threaten what it may never do? May it possess what it may never use? Who is involved in the threat each superpower makes: government officials or military personnel or the citizenry in whose defense the threat is made (#137)? The bishops recognized that threat is integral to the effectiveness of deterrence; they neither explored the legitimacy of such a threat nor did they judge who is involved in the threat. Recent superpower violations of some of the conditions upon which the bishops based their moral acceptance of deterrence have prompted efforts to review the 1983 position.

The French and West German Catholic bishops also explored the morality of deterrence in 1983. The French bishops argued that "peace is still being served when an aggressor is discouraged and constrained to the beginning of wisdom as a result of an appropriate fear" (*Winning the Peace,* #26). Maintaining that the threat of force is not the use of force and that it is not evident whether the immorality of use renders the threat immoral, the French bishops therefore concluded that deterrence is the lesser of two evils, since abandonment of the deterrent could provoke nuclear blackmail or loss of national life, liberty and identity. The West German bishops, asserting that nuclear deterrence is not a reliable instrument for preventing war in the long run (O.J.P. #140), nevertheless interpreted John Paul II's 1982 assessment as a toleration of deterrence, a position with which they agree, as long as deterrence demonstrably serves to prevent nuclear war (O.J.P. #136-54).

Disarmament: The Road to Peace

Catholic social teaching has unwaveringly denounced the arms race as a grave threat to the establishment of a true global peace. Since Pius XII's 1951 condemnation of the arms race as a disproportionate drain of human and material resources (*Major Addresses of Pius XII,* vol I, p. 143), papal and conciliar statements have labeled the arms race as a treacherous trap, an intolerable scandal, an insanity, a symptom of disorder, a diabolical capacity, a costly madness, a machine running mad, an act of aggression since its high cost starves the poor to death, a tragic con-

tradiction. Queried John Paul II, "Are the children to receive the arms race from us as a necessary inheritance? How are we to explain this unbridled race?" ("The Dignity of the Human Person Is the Basis of Justice and Peace," Address to the United Nations, October 2, 1979). A clear call for an immediate halt to this technological runaway, therefore, has been the consistent position of the Catholic hierarchy on this pressing issue; the church, moreover, has repeatedly argued for a bilateral, gradual, secure, and verifiable dismantlement of the stockpiled nuclear armaments and has supported negotiations aimed at reducing and limiting conventional forces.

The church's position on nuclear disarmament disappoints those who would want to see the church assume a more prophetic stance on this question. Absolute pacifists (those who believe all use of armed force to be morally wrong) usually endorse the call for unilateral disarmament; they argue that trust in weapons of such massive destruction violates the Christian's first priority to trust in God. The hierarchical position, however, places the prevention of nuclear war as its overriding consideration and does not want to risk the possibility that unilateral disarmament might provoke such a war, should an aggressor take advantage of a vulnerable opponent. The United States bishops, however, have encouraged unilateral *initiatives* which might establish a more trusting political climate (C.P. #205-06).

The church clearly sees disarmament as the road to global peace, though it realizes that such a path is long and complicated. The arms race, in contrast, is consistently envisioned as a strategy which fosters only distrust among nations and needlessly squanders human talents and resources—precious commodities desperately needed for human and social development.

Development: A New Name for Peace

Since Pope Paul VI's 1967 encyclical, *On the Development of Peoples (Populorum Progressio),* Catholic social teaching has emphasized the interlocking nature of authentic development and true peace. Authentic development, a complete and integral development which promotes the good of the whole person, of every human being, and society as a whole, eliminates excessive economic, social, and cultural inequities, thereby providing a solid foundation upon which humanity can construct a true peace.

Subsequent papal encyclicals and annual "World Day of Peace" messages have developed this insight by insisting that God has bestowed a precious dignity upon each human being and that grounded in this human nature are certain basic rights, the denial of which thwarts individual human fulfillment and the well-being of society as a whole. These include rights to the fulfillment of materials needs (such as food, clothing, shelter), a guarantee of fundamental freedoms, and the protection of relationships that are essential to participation in the life of society. In his 1987 "World Day of Peace" message, Pope John Paul II explicitly cited certain contemporary practices which prevent human solidarity and development: a xenophobia which closes nations in on themselves, ideologies which foster racial hatred or religious intolerance, and unjust or arbitrary border closings which separate families.

On the international level, development includes the elimination of such problems as North-South inequalities, especially in the area of technology, the external debt of the developing countries, the rise of insurgency and counter-insurgency warfare, and global terrorism.

Catholic social teaching evidences sharp awareness that the human community is interconnected and interdependent. Peace is a value without frontiers; therefore, it cannot be established in a just and lasting fashion except through broader cooperation at the regional, continental, and international levels.

Peacemaking and Education

The responsibility to foster peace is not limited to governments, however, but must also start within each human heart. Education, through family activities, in the local parish, and at all levels of formal learning, is a key but practical ingredient for changing hearts and opening minds.

Family life provides crucial opportunities to impart values which foster peace. The development of nonviolent, cooperative attitudes and skills in children in a home environment which supports affirmation, affection, cooperative chores and games, is an important responsibility which parents can exercise to offset the violence in today's world. Creating time and space for family prayer, vacations, family meetings to resolve domestic conflicts, and corporate projects which engage the political/military establishment (for instance, letter writing to Congressional representatives) are concrete ways in which a family can learn about peace and justice together. Parental example is especially crucial here, since a wife and husband who work for marital harmony provide irreplaceable role models.

The parish community is also an important locus in which creative peace education can take place. Perhaps the greatest challenge to parish ministers is to encourage the congregation to think of justice, the foundation of a true peace, as a "constitutive dimension of the preaching of the Gospel" (*Justice in the World,* introduction) and not as some marginal cause, relevant to only a few "activist" members in the parish. Within the parish setting, the study of scripture, fasting and prayer as a congregation, workshops on nonviolent conflict resolution, and the liturgy itself are just a few of the many channels which are available to a parish community which seeks to become a living "sign of peace" to the wider community.

Formal education on peace, at all levels of learning, remains indispensable for the shaping of a more peaceful world. The classroom can teach younger children about the beauty of the world and the various peoples/cultures within it; it can also impart to them the importance of resolving disputes through negotiation. Education can also introduce high school and college students, by the use of films and eyewitness accounts of war, to the realistic dimensions of the problems of war and peace. At this level, a reverence for life, a sense of responsibility for the ecological well-being of the planet, an awareness of global interdependence, and the challenge of developing imaginative solutions can permeate an interdisciplinary high school or college curriculum.

Toward a "Theology of Peace"

What are some of the characteristics that will shape a future theology of peace? Drawing from biblical studies, systematic theology, moral theology, and the experience and insights of members of the church, a theology of peace must first ground the task of peacemaking solidly in the scriptural vision of God's Kingdom and indicate how such a task is central to the ministry of the church. This ecclesial question is key, since the Catholic Church has committed itself to the role of a "public church" doing "public theology"; it therefore must resist pressures that it embrace a sectarian position on this question. A theology of peace must also incorporate the insights of social and political sciences, identify the specific contributions which a community of faith can make to the work of peace, and relate these to the wider work of peace pursued by other groups and institutions in society. Finally, a theology of peace

must offer a message of hope to a fragmented world desperately in search of peace (See C.P. #24-25).

Conclusion

Peace is both gift and task, requiring the work of human hands and minds and hearts. Short of the fullness of the reign of God, the disciples of Jesus Christ, on pilgrimage in the modern world, work toward shaping a peaceful world which claims justice as its foundation. Working ecumenically, but also with all people of good will, the Catholic Church believes in the bright future and in a God who wills a time for us in which the fullness of God's kingdom is realized and justice and peace eternally embrace.

See **Jesus Christ, Justice, Reign of God, War**

Ronald G. Musto, *The Catholic Peace Tradition,* Maryknoll, NY: Orbis Books, 1986. Vincent A. Yzermans, Ed., *The Major Addresses of Pope Pius XII,* 2 vols. St. Paul, MN: North Central Publishing Company, 1961. Joseph Gremillion, Ed., *The Gospel of Peace and Justice: Catholic Social Teaching since Pope John,* Maryknoll, NY: Orbis Books, 1976. John Paul II, "Development and Solidarity: Two Keys to Peace," *Origins* 16, no. 8, (25 December 1986: pp. 505-11. National Conference of Catholic Bishops, *The Challenge of Peace: God's Promise and Our Response,* Washington, D.C.: United States Catholic Conference, 1983. James V. Schall, Ed., *Out of Justice, Peace* (West German Bishops) and *Winning the Peace* (French Bishops), San Francisco: Ignatius Press, 1984. The United Methodist Council of Bishops, *In Defense of Creation: The Nuclear Crisis and a Just Peace,* Nashville, TN: Graded Press, 1986. Dana W. Wilbanks and Ronald H. Stone, *Presbyterians and Peacemaking: Are We Now Called to Resistance?* New York: The Advisory Council on Church and Society, 1985. Belle Zars, Beth Wilson, and Ariel Phillips, Eds. *Education and the Threat of Nuclear War,* Montpelier, VT: Capital City Press, 1985. James and Kathleen McGinnis, "The Social Mission of the Christian Family," in Judith A Dwyer, Ed., *Questions of Special Urgency: The Church in the Modern World Two Decades after Vatican II,* Washington, D.C.: Georgetown UP, 1986.

JUDITH A. DWYER, SSJ

PELAGIANISM

The views associated with the early fifth century British monk, Pelagius, who appears to have denied the doctrine of original sin and therefore to have attributed to human beings the ability by themselves to choose the good and so to effect their own salvation. Divine intervention served only to illumine and to reward the human effort. Vigorously opposed by St. Augustine, Pelagianism was condemned by the church in the fifth century and then again at the Council of Trent.

PENANCE
See **Reconciliation, Repentance**

PENTECOST

The feast which marks the end of the great fifty days of rejoicing of Easter or the entire fifty-day period from Easter to Pentecost Sunday. The name of the feast is derived from the Greek *Pentecoste* or "Fiftieth (day)," which in turn corresponds to the Hebrew *Shabuoth*, the Feast of Weeks. The Jewish feast was a thanksgiving for the wheat harvest and took place seven weeks after the Feast of Unleavened Bread. By the first century of our era this feast also had an historical association with the giving of the Law on Mount Sinai as well as the covenants with Noah and Abraham.

Christian associations with the feast begin with Acts 2:1-45, the descent of the Holy Spirit in the upper room and the inauguration of apostolic preaching. In the first three centuries the entire fifty-day period was considered a "Great Sunday," a joy-filled period marked by the absence of fasting and kneeling in prayer. As the Easter Vigil became the prime moment for initiation, so also Pentecost Sunday became a baptismal day in some places. Hence the English "Whit Sunday." The fourth century saw the gradual introduction of a special feast of the Ascension, celebrated according to the Lucan chronology forty days after Easter. Thus the original unified period of fifty days began to break up. In addition, there may have been two diverse theological trajectories for Pentecost Sunday as the culmination of the feast in the early church. G. Kretschmar has argued for two traditions: one associated with the Lucan messianic outpouring of the Spirit on Pentecost Sunday and the other (originally Palestinian) focusing on the messianic kingship of Christ, the giver of the New Law. The latter approach was probably responsible for the celebration of the Ascension on Pentecost Sunday, a tradition that disappeared in the fifth century (Talley, pp. 57-66).

By the seventh century the Roman calendar shows an octave after Pentecost, thus further breaking up the original idea of an unbroken fifty days of rejoicing. In Gaul Rogation Days, consisting of fasting and penitential litanies, had also been introduced in the fifth century. In the medieval period each day of the Pentecost octave was associated with one of the seven gifts of the Holy Spirit.

In the 1969 reform of the Roman calendar some attempt has been made to return to the original form of the feast with its period of sustained rejoicing. Hence the Sundays of the Easter season are no longer called Sundays *after* Easter but rather *of* Easter. The feast of the Ascension has been retained, however, as well as the focus on the descent of the Spirit in the lectionary readings for Pentecost Sunday. Despite the unity of the season, the official liturgical color for Pentecost remains red. The octave has been dropped in favor of a kind of "reverse octave" in the period between Ascension Thursday and Pentecost Sunday. At this time the opening prayers of the Roman Sacramentary reflect a particular emphasis on the Holy Spirit.

See **Easter Triduum, Holy Spirit, Liturgy**

Thomas J. Talley, *The Origins of the Liturgical Year*, New York, 1986.

JOHN F. BALDOVIN, SJ

PEOPLE OF GOD

Many have hailed *The Dogmatic Constitution on the Church* (1965) as the most significant achievement of the Second Vatican Council. In this landmark document the council offered a more biblical and dynamic view of the church, emphasizing the paradoxical union of the divine and the human. In chapter two entitled "The People of God" the council focused on the communal nature of the church rather than on the hierarchical and institutional aspects. All—pastors as well as laity—comprise the human side of this community.

The document observes that God "chose the race of Israel as a people unto Himself" (par 9). What is striking, however, is that the OT uses the expression "people of God" only twice. By contrast, it employs the expression "people of Yahweh" seventeen times. When one includes passages whose context demands "people of Yahweh" the number increases to over three hundred. Whereas the council document underlines the ecclesiological dimension of the title, the OT in general stresses the soteriological.

Prior to the emergence of strict monotheism the OT witnesses to the common ancient Near Eastern notion that every people is the people of a particular god. For example, according to Num 21:29 the Moabites are the people of the god Chemosh. Specifically the inhabitants of Moab are the sons and daughters of Chemosh. Even postexilic 2 Chronicles has the officials of King Sennacherib proclaim to the people of Jerusalem: "'Since no other god of any other nation or people has been able to save his people from my hand [Sennacherib] or the hands of my fathers, how much less shall your god save you from my hand!'" (2 Chr 32:15).

It is likely that the Hebrew word for "people" (*'am*) originally meant "paternal uncle." Thus every member of the family and even the extended family constituted the *'am* of a person. When a patriarch died, he was taken to his *'am* (see Gen 25:8; 49:29, 33). What this suggests is that the word *'am* carried the sense of "family" that was expanded to mean "people." However, even here "people" implied a type of super family in which a person was linked to everyone else. Hence every Israelite was a relative of Jacob/Israel (Gen 32:29). Israel's self-perception as the family of Yahweh is probably a remnant of her nomadic past.

If one examines the some three hundred uses of the *'am* of Yahweh in the Hebrew Bible, there are some interesting observations. The expression never occurs in the Wisdom books and only rarely in legal texts. In the 150 times it appears in the narrative texts, only on ten occasions does it mean "the family of Yahweh." It is especially to the prophetic literature (cir. 150 times) and to the Psalter (cir. 50 times) that one must look for the sense of "family of Yahweh." Hence this expression is especially at home in the language of prayer and prophetic proclamation.

One of the special instances in the narrative texts is the Exodus experience. In Exod 5:1 Moses and Aaron approach Pharaoh with the command: "'Let my family [NAB: people] go.'" Because Israel is already Yahweh's family, this God is obliged to intervene to offset the oppression. Thus Yahweh is prompted to act because of a family claim. It is especially in situations of pain and frustration that Yahweh rises up to protect the family interests. Here it is interesting to note that the later priestly tradition envisions Israel becoming Yahweh's family and hence the object of concern only at the time of the Egyptian oppression (see

Exod 6:7).

It should be noted that the expression "family of Yahweh" does not envision Israel's plight only vis-à-vis foreign powers. It also embraces inter-Israelite situations. In one of the rare legal uses Yahweh admonishes Israel's rich to provide for Israel's poor: "'If you lend money to one of your poor neighbors among my family [NAB: people], you shall not act like an extortioner toward him by demanding interest from him'" (Exod 22:24). If the cloak of the poor person is not returned before sunset, Yahweh will heed the cry of the poor and take prompt action.

In the Psalter the lament of the community occupies a central place for this expression. Here Israel has suffered a catastrophe of one sort or another. She feels that she must bring the pain and frustration before her God. For example, in Psalm 60 Israel has suffered a severe military defeat. Unashamed and confident she prays: "O God, you have rejected us and broken our defenses ... you have rocked the country and split it open ... you have made your family [NAB: people] feel hardships" (Ps 60:3-5). In Psalm 44 the author notes Yahweh's graciousness to the fathers but his apparent lack of concern for later generations: "You sold your family [NAB: people] for no great price; you made no profit from the sale of them" (Ps 44:13). It is the sense of family solidarity that urges Israel to omit the facade of false piety and expose her festering discontent.

Isaiah of Jerusalem may serve as an example of the prophetic use of "family of Yahweh." In the opening verses of this eighth-century prophet Yahweh inveighs against his family: "Sons have I raised and reared, but they have disowned me!" (Isa 1:2). Israel's sin is one of sinful ignorance. While the dumb animals are aware of their benefactors, "Israel does not know, my family [NAB: people] has

not understood" (Isa 1:3). For the prophet this sin is not one of slight neglect. It is the egregious malice of not recognizing the head of the family.

The sense of family loyalty is also found in Isaiah's vehement attack on injustice against members of the family. Yahweh functions as a judge who must condemn the actions of the leaders who have disregarded the rights of the less powerful. "The Lord rises to accuse, standing to try his family [NAB: people]" (Isa 3:13). Because the elders and the princes have devoured the poor and confiscated their property, Yahweh has no choice but to pass judgment on such anti-family behavior. "What do you mean by crushing my family [NAB: people], by grinding down the poor, when they look to you?" (Isa 3:15). The poor are always special members of this God's family.

The NT employs the image of God's people by identifying this people with the church. The expression is not found in the gospels but mainly in Paul (see Rom 9:25-26; 2 Cor 6:14-16) and writings associated with Paul (see Tit 2:14; Heb 8:10). These passages develop the status of Christians as the People of God against the background of Israel's rejection of the Good News. A departure from this is 1 Pet 2:10 that does not reflect this polarity. Instead, those who were at one time no people are now God's people.

In summary, the OT understanding of Israel as the family of Yahweh is basically an expression of a theology of grace. It speaks especially to those situations where the oppressed can look to their God as the champion who will defend their rights as family members. It envisions circumstances where the oppressors are both Israelites and non-Israelites. It demands that all those who exercise authority recall that an intimate bond exists between Yahweh and his family. Ultimately the expression is a call to decisive action on behalf of the powerless.

See **Church; God; Bible, Old Testament**

A.R. Hulst. "Am/Goj Volk," *Theologisches Hand-worterbuch vum Alten Testament*. Editors: E. Jenni and C. Westermann. Munich: Kaiser, 1987, Vol. 2, pp. 290-395. N. Lohfink, "The People of God," *Great Themes from the Old Testament.* Chicago: Franciscan Herald Press, 1985, pp. 117-133. R. Meyer and H. Strathmann, *"Laos,"* *Theological Dictionary of the New Testament*, Vol. 4, pp. 29-56. J. Pederson, *Israel: Its Life and Culture*. London: Oxford University Press, 1926, I-II, pp. 54-60.

JOHN F. CRAGHAN

PERSON, DIVINE

The terms "person" or "hypostasis" and "nature" or "substance" have been associated in christian theology since at least the beginning of the third century (Tertullian, Hippolytus of Rome). Person came to be used of what is triply unique and interrelated in the one God: the Father, the Son and the Holy Spirit. Later, person expressed what was unique and unifying in the incarnate Son Jesus Christ, who is simultaneously both wholly divine and wholly human. Hypostasis ranged through all grades of being. It changed from its early meaning of substance (*ousia*) to expressing a specific entity, a concrete example of a nature— Mary or John rather than humanity. Finally it became equivalent to divine person in the Cappadocians and at Chalcedon. With some oversimplifications a general rule may be proposed: nature answers the question "What?"; hypostasis in its intermediate meaning answers "Which?"; a person answers "Who?"

1. The Early Greek and Latin Trajectory of Person

A. *Dramatic Usage.* Person (Greek *prosopon* and Latin *persona,* its near equivalent) first designated an actor's mask in religious drama. The inexorable cosmic order of ancient Greece allowed no ultimate freedom to the personage portrayed, but there was at least an emergence from anonymity, a self-direction, a struggle with fate on the stage. From the outset person conveyed real identity, a characteristic role acted out by addressing and relating to others in a religious setting.

B. *Legal Usage. Persona* was creeping into the language of the courts by the second christian century to denote individuals with rights and duties. Tertullian spoke of God as one divine substance with "three coinhering," which elsewhere he calls "persons." His substance and persons language is pioneering and fluid. Despite his legal training, it is highly unlikely that he meant divine substance on the analogy of a piece of property, and the persons as the titles to its possession. Juridical person signifies a recognizable, responsible human being or corporation.

C. *Literary Usage. Prosopon* for Aristotle applied to a human (but not an animal) face, that expression of inner depths, of individuality, character, and striving for communication. In the Greek OT it conveyed the manifestation of the Lord in judgment, mercy and salvation, as well as intimacy with God and the divine presence in the temple (e.g., Num 6:25-26 and Ps 89:15-16, where in both cases the face and name of God are in parallel; Pss 42:2; 95;2). *Prosopon* occasionally means person in our current sense of an individual in Philo, Josephus and the NT (2 Cor 1:11). Person as effective presence came to denote the speaker in the scriptures for Philo (following Homeric commentators), and many writers from Justin and Tertullian to Augustine (prosopography). In this manner the Hebrew scriptures, especially the Psalms, became for Christians dialogues between the Father and the Son and the Church. This explains how Arians could latch on to the Son saying, "The Lord (Father) created me at the beginning of his work" (Prov 8:22). Consequently,

the scriptures, prayer, and liturgy nourished the third to fifth century christian
efforts to hammer out an agreed language
to share their experience of the triune and
incarnate God. Prosopographical person
was a dialogic and doxological word.

2. Theological and Conciliar Usage

A. Centuries 4-5. The preceding literary
usage helped the Cappadocians develop
their understanding of person as an existence proper and perfect in itself, a
distinct and objective way in which God
is. Their person can be a self present to
other selves. Augustine confessed he
could inject little meaning into *persona,*
but he developed the dimension of relationship inherent in person regarding the
Father, Son and Spirit. Being constricted
by his analogy of Father-Memory, Son-
Understanding and Spirit-Will, which
suggested a single human person, he
arrives at the introspective presence of a
self to itself.

Chalcedon in 451 spoke of "the Lord
Jesus Christ ... acknowledged in two
natures ... coming together in one person
and one hypostasis." Its language is
intuitive and non-technical. The assembled fathers could not have defined their
terms (A. Grillmeier).

B. Centuries 6-14. Boethius (about
480-524) drew on Aristotle to define
person as "an individual substance of a
rational [better, intellectual] nature," an
independent type of being among beings,
whether angelic or human. This obscured
the associated notions of freedom, action
and relationship which are so clear in the
literary scriptural understanding of person. Richard of St. Victor (died 1173)
partially compensated by presenting a
person as "an unshared existence of an
intellectual nature," noting that the "ex-"
meant the person was relational, ecstatic
and reaching out beyond itself without
losing its identity.

Bonaventure (1217-1274), Thomas

Aquinas (c. 1225-1274), and Duns Scotus
(c. 1265-1308) stress the independence
and the dignity of the person, "the peak
of self-existence and consummate in
knowledge" (S. Th. I, q. 29, 3 ad 3).
However, Aquinas deals with the necessary relatedness of persons only when
treating the complex unity of the divine
nature.

C. Centuries 15-20. Since the Scholastics the trinitarian person is identified as a
subsistent relation of opposition: the
Father is paternity, the Son filiation, and
the Spirit spiration. This rarefied but
coherent explanation preserved the full
reality of the shared divine nature, and
the full reality of the three persons as
independent yet interrelated. The East is
more awed by the mystery, and holds
that the relations manifest rather than
constitute the persons in God. They see
the relations not as ones of opposition,
but of radical diversity, reciprocity and
communion (P. Evdokimov). For at least
two reasons christian ontology identifies
person with hypostasis, thereby making
person the constitutive element of entities.
Firstly, all beings must be in some degree
"personal" since they are the product not
of material evolution but of divine
freedom. Secondly, for the East the person of God the Father (not the divine
nature) founds the unity of God by
lovingly and freely begetting the Son and
bringing forth the Spirit.

Thus any nature can exist only in a
hypostasis, as the divine nature does in
the person of the Father. East and West
can agree that being is radically person
(hypostasis), and therefore relational.
Consequently, being is communion—for
the triune God and for humans. The
divine persons exist as, and live out of,
their interrelationships.

The one person of Christ gave rise to
many theories of Scotists and Thomists
about the determining characteristics of
personhood which would allow Jesus to

have two complete natures. These suggestions (independence, integrity, mode of subsistence, etc.) did not cohere with the trinitarian idea of person as a relation (whether of opposition or of mutual revelation and communion). Once again the solution is best seen to lie in the direction of the relationality of the person of Christ. Every human is called forth as an original and unrepeatable relationship to the triune God and to other humans in a distinct human nature, which regulates their potential for communion. The divine person of Christ raises his human nature out of this limitation, and perfects it by personalizing it, by relating his humanity to the Son, the Father, the Spirit, and all creation. In the terms of Bernard J.F. Lonergan, if God has a single divine identity and three divine subjectivities, Jesus Christ has a single divine identity as Son and two subjectivities, the human and the divine.

3. Divine Person Today

A. *Alternative Terminology.* Karl Barth has advocated "mode (or way) of being"; Karl Rahner "three distinct ways of being there (in the economy of salvation) and three different ways of subsistence (immanently)"; John Macquarrie "movements of Being"; Jean Hervé Nicolas "Being God." None of these has anything like the elusiveness and rich allusiveness of "person." It is a living word in daily use which can mobilize the heart and emotions, and which cannot easily be replaced. The foregoing outline of its usage shows that even in theology it is quintessentially relational, and consequently not far from daily speech. By this word the essence of the human, the personal, is drawn into Christ and the triune God. Person shades off into primal nourishing mystery, an all-encompassing reality which is union and communion.

B. *Explanatory Phrases.* The mysterious Father may be called an ultraper-sonal and primordial Being who is above us. The Son is the available personal expressive Being with us. The interpersonal Spirit is unitive Being in and between us (Laurence Cantwell and John Macquarrie). This variation on person brings home how in God person does not denote the same reality which occurs three times, but that which points to what makes the Father, Son and Spirit completely different yet in communion through reciprocal relationships.

C. *Person as Mission.* Hans Urs von Balthasar develops the distinction between an individual and a person on this earth. The individual detaches himself or herself from the collective, and becomes human as human. Only when individuals embrace the particular mission that God has in store they become a person. Each person shares in the mission of Christ through a charism, a unique project from God that establishes a web of relationships and is the core of human personhood. The person of Christ is the Logos, the divine project enabling this man Jesus to carry out all that for which he was sent.

See **Christology, Hypostasis, Nature, Trinity**

H.U. von Balthasar, *Theodramatik 2/2, Die Personen in Christus,* Einsiedeln: Johannes Verlag, 1978. E.J. Fortman, *The Triune God,* Philadelphia: Westminister, 1972. J. Galot, *Who is Christ?,* Chicago: Franciscan Herald, 1981. A. Grillmeier, *The Christ in Christian Tradition,* 1. 2d ed. Atlanta: Knox, 1975. R.W. Jenson, *The Triune Identity,* Philadelphia: Fortress, 1982. A. Milano, *Persona in Teologia,* Naples: Edizioni Dehoniane, 1984. J.D. Zizioulas, *Being as Communion,* Crestwood, N.Y.: St. Vladimir's Seminary, 1985.

BRIAN M. NOLAN

PHILOSOPHY AND THEOLOGY

In christian circles, with which we are here almost exclusively concerned, the history of the relationship between philosophy and theology has been a troubled one. This is most commonly due to misunderstanding; sometimes to the misunderstanding that grows out of simple ignorance, but sometimes also to the more sinister kind of misunderstanding which breeds from exclusivist claims.

From the great centuries-long flourish of first christian writing which we now know as the patristic corpus, a variety of attitudes to philosophy emerge. The truculent Tertullian gave vent to his now famous outburst, "What has Athens to do with Jerusalem?" Augustine is more ambivalent. He sometimes speaks of the Platonists as proto-christians. But he opens his magisterial work on *The Trinity* with a mini-tirade against the arrogance of the philosophers, and he seems to have in mind their pride in the power of reason and the lack of humility, apparent to him at least, in their failure to confess the need for faith. For, as he puts the matter a little more kindly a little later on, when God's revelation is the object of the human quest, the human mind cannot look on light so dazzling unless it has been nourished and strengthened by the justice of faith.

It is, unfortunately, that attitude of suspicion towards philosophy and philosophers, that tendency to link them with the pride of reason rather than the humility of faith—a kind of complaint, one must confess, which was urged in exactly the reverse order by many of the Platonists with whom early christian writers were in contention—it is just that attitude that provides much of the ammunition in those bitter and unchristian arguments about orthodoxy and heterodoxy which have marred christian history from the beginning. It became common to accuse proponents of rival doctrinal views of playing the sophist, worse still, of being victims, willing victims no doubt, of the allurements of the prevailing philosophies.

One cannot travel very far along this particular road without suggesting or enhancing a rather dichotomous distinction between philosophy and theology, in which philosophy represents the pride of human reason and theology the humble acceptance of divine revelation. And this dichotomous distinction is then likely to join and to strengthen the company of similar distinctions: between reason and revelation, between faith and history, between nature and grace; until it becomes very difficult, to say the least, to see God's gracious presence in all of creation, and that immediacy of God to each and every individual, irrespective of race, creed, or even moral status, which was surely the essence of the preaching of Jesus.

Luckily, however, the more eirenic tones of Augustine towards the Platonists also find their precedents in christian writings and they have produced a robust progeny. It was, one would hope, more than a prudent tactical move when one of the first defenders of christianity before its cultured despisers, Justin Martyr in his *Apologies*, asked the Platonists to see the similarities in their own beliefs in a Word or Son of God coming into the world to reveal God's will. And the full flowering of this more open, more human, and perhaps in the end more christian attitude, to one's fellow travelers on the long quest, is found in the fullblooded claim of christian writers such as Clement of Alexandria, to offer a christian *gnosis,* a christian wisdom, a christian philosophy.

For it must become clear even to the novice in the study of those early, formative centuries, that those who took the adversarial view of the relationships between philosophy and that exposition of the christian faith which was later called theology, were guilty of double-misunderstanding. They misunderstood the true religious nature and power of that which they dismissed as philosophy and, more amusingly perhaps, they miscalculated its enormous influence, through a commonly-shared culture, on their own doctrinal expositions of the christian faith. Tertullian, for example, almost certainly shared the prevailing materialist view of reality, and even of spirit, which came from the Stoa.

A careful study of the prevailing religious philosophy (or theology, as it might equally be called) of the first formative centuries of Christianity's existence would well repay the undoubtedly strenuous efforts it would require from most of us. We should have to conduct the study, not as is usually done, with the simplistic intention of proving the superiority of Christianity, for Christianity cannot be proved superior in theory, and not with the aim of illustrating once again the false view that the prevailing philosophy of these centuries was a kind of service industry, providing christian thinkers with shapeless, elastic "concepts" which they could then simultaneously fill with and mould to the distinctive content of the christian faith. The study would have to take seriously the fact, for it is a fact, that the Platonic tradition was as powerful an exposition of a distinctive religious movement as any other which the world has known. It is called the Platonic tradition because of the lasting, architectonic influence of Plato, despite the fact that during the centuries which saw the rise of Christianity, it has come to be called Middle-Platonism, having assimilated elements of Aristotelian and Stoic theology, and from the third century A.D. onwards it is called Neo-Platonism, in order to honor the recreative powers of Plotinus. The result of such study should be an appreciation of the distinctive genius of a powerful religious tradition with its own highly developed philosophical theology and, in addition perhaps, the dawning realization that what is really at issue is not the relationship between philosophy and theology, and

certainly not as the adversarial view presents this, but the far more intriguing and persistent problem of an ecumenism of religious faiths or their mutually damaging hostilities.

It would be impossible to read Plato's dialogues without forming the impression of a powerful religious *élan* coming to expression in an open and artistic "theology": the God who really transcends all human ability to imagine or conceive, and who yet out of overflowing and utterly unqualified goodness creates the world, (the commentary on Plato's *Timaeus* by the Neo-Platonist Porphyry clearly contains the idea of creation out of nothing) who desires only good for all, yet meets the resistance of a certain intransigence in the material world; the answering *eros,* the loving-desire which runs right through the universe and finds its most vivid expression in the aching human heart, the passion which drives men and women to God because it is aroused by the being and goodness, the light and truth which had first come from God into the world. Far from being an exercise in pure theory, a raising of oneself by one's own boot-straps, philosophy to Plato is a "training to die," a love of wisdom as its Greek name states, *eros* reflective. And, like Matthew's "Be ye perfect as your heavenly Father is perfect," the resulting good human life for Plato is *homoiosis theou,* becoming like to God in the measure in which this is possible for humans. And Plato's final conviction is that the one whose loving-desire leads to a life of virtue, and to prayer and worship of God, "is loved by God" (*Laws,* 716), and will pass through death to the presence of God in eternity. Who would regard such a powerful and inspiring religious vision as something to be simply combated? Only someone with a very simplistic or erratic view of relationships between philosophy and theology.

The point that even those early Christians who spoke harshly about the prevailing "philosophy" were profoundly influenced by it, can be best appreciated by a survey of the main theological themes of Middle- and Neo-Platonism. Quite briefly, in pursuit of the common religious need to keep God's transcendence and immanence in balance the Middle-Platonists gradually evolved binitarian structures in which the One, unknown God dealt with a world through an intermediary "level" of divinity. The Stoa had popularized the idea that the divinity was Logos or Word, the creative, dynamic force in the world, and gradually it came to be suggested in the course of the eclectic and scholastic period of Middle-Platonism that the One God, the Father, Zeus, related to the World through Mind or Reason (or Word), that the "ideas" by which all things were created and governed were ideas in this Mind of God (perhaps these were the Platonic Forms). With Plotinus this "binity" in the Godhead became very definitely trinitarian, with trinities in God of Being, Intelligence, Life, or One, Mind and Soul. The Greeks, of course, saw all of this as ways of speaking about one God who was both unknown and yet somehow known. They did not have the same problems of identifying one of these as a personal being present in Jesus, and so the problem of refuting charges of polytheism. The Christians, whose Fourth Gospel said that this Logos or word was incarnate in Jesus, had *that* problem, and their answers are another story. But the influence of non-christian Greek theology on that story is undeniable. A similar influence can be seen in the case of Jewish theology.

The manner in which the Jewish theologian, Philo of Alexandria, contemporary of Paul, appropriated this Middle-Platonic theology in order to present his distinctive faith is extremely instructive for christian historians if only because Philo's procedure proved influential on later christian thinkers. Philo's Jewish faith in a God who could not be apprehended by human vision seemed eminently translatable into the Greek theology of the One or Monad, indeed one "beyond Monad," for whom no creaturely language whatever availed. Yet Philo's God gave origin to the world and was active within it. So God could be known at least through his powers (*dynameis*) and their works or effects (*energeiai*). The two major *dynameis* Philo named as Creator (*ktistes, demiourgos*) and Lord. And the term which denotes that level of divinity which is apprehensible to us, which is manifest as these *dynameis* in their *energeiai*, is Word (*logos*). This Word Philo describes as the first-begotten Son of the uncreated Father, the "second God," the mediator of creation, the "man of God," and in his *Life of Moses* he conveys the impression that this Word was incarnate (or at least *empsychos*) in Moses *par excellence*.

What is visible, then, from a more informed understanding of the formative centuries of christian thought, is not the kind of relationship between philosophy and theology which either adversarial attitudes or simplistic dichotomies might suggest, but, first, a view of philosophy which brings us always to a depth or a height of human experience which is inevitably religious, because the call of an absolute is heard at that height or depth, and, second, an illustration of the way in which, at their best, religious traditions can fertilize each other to their inestimable mutual enrichment. Western Christianity is to this day profoundly Platonic, and Christianity is the vehicle within which the powerful Platonic vision has survived the collapse of its originating civilization.

The story of the relationship of philosophy and theology in the medieval and modern periods has suffered similar distortions and is in need of similar reassessment. The medieval period did indeed produce what Etienne Gilson called *The Christian Philosophy of the Middle Ages* in which men of christian faith, and particularly Thomas Aquinas, took up the new Aristotelianism with all its moral and religious themes and forged for the age an expression of Christian faith of contemporary relevance. But this was not done without struggle; Aquinas suffered official ecclesiastical condemnation both during his life and shortly after For just as there were those like Siger of Brabant and the so-called Latin Averroists who wanted philosophy and theology parted once more, as two different and not necessarily compatible types of truths, there were also those in church office who had forgotten, if they ever knew, that religious visions meet in human history and that their philosophies can merge to their mutual enrichment. And so these officials, mistaking past mergers for revelations dropped whole from heaven, condemned the new mergers as new mistakes and made the permanently pathetic effort to live in the past.

Indeed it was the failure of christian thinkers to continue the necessary task of receiving into and moulding to the christian spirit the best of the emerging philosophical theology of each successive age and place which accounted for the growing alienation of Western society from christian faith *and* the imperious imposition of Western religion-cum-culture in missionary lands, all so damaging to the prospects of Christianity in the modern world.

The modern period in philosophy is thought to have begun in the seventeenth century with Descartes, when new models of scientific reasoning became dominant in Western culture. Dedicated Christians like Kant took up the challenge and sought to give the christian spirit new expression in mutual penetration with the newly emerging natural religious spirit of the age. His ideas were met with impatience and hostility from fellow-Christians, such as many a new, necessary, but at first tentative, philosophic or doctrinal formulation had met before him from the perennial heresy hunters. The ensuing theologies/philosophies of the Age of Reason were decried by Roman Catholics as the bitter fruit of the Reformation, on the grounds that the Protestant Reformers of the sixteenth century, in seeking the causes of christian corporate corruption, had blamed human nature and human reason, and it was no wonder if reason rebelled and sought its autonomy from faith. And Protestants who held that view of corrupt nature and reason joined in the denunciation. The split between philosophy and theology, reason and revelation, nature and grace, was back with a vengeance, and it continues to wreak havoc in christian theology to this day. Even Hegel, the greatest christian theologian of this era, was rejected by the main christian churches, instead of having his manifest goodwill recognized and his monumental efforts at the renewal of christian philosophy/theology adapted and developed, as well it could have been, into the most effective exposition of Christianity for the modern age.

Small wonder, then, if Western philosophy did finally turn against Christianity. When Feuerbach had made one final attempt to show the religion that *The Essence of Christianity* did, after all, center on a divine *man,* Marx simply hammered away at the reactionary nature of religion in social and political terms, its ideological and institutional service to the alienation of human beings from the freedom and dignity which was now possible for all of them; and he considered religion itself simply irrelevant to human prospects. As a result, the modern world, first the West, and more recently the East, has seen for the first time perhaps in human history, the emergence of atheism as a dominant social option.

But two qualifying notes must immediately be added to that, for religious people at least, dismal conclusion. First, it is important to recognize that what Christians see as the main forms of atheism in the modern period of Western philosophy, Marxism and some forms of existentialism, are not in the view of their own major proponents primarily atheistic philosophies at all. They are, on the contrary, first and foremost humanist philosophies to which atheism is quite incidental. Atheism enters in because in their quest for a truly humanist vision, their proponents see the remaining religious philosophies, including Christianity, to be irrelevant. As Sartre put towards the close of his published lecture, *Existentialism and Humanism,* "even if God did exist, that would change nothing."

Secondly, it may become clear to the careful observer of these new and alternative philosophies that have for so many people replaced Christianity in the West, that they have their own concealed absolutes, and that therefore, although being professedly atheistic, they move at the same depth and comprehensiveness as explicitly religious philosophies of life, such as Christianity. The simplest test of this hypothesis is to ask of any of these alternative philosophies whether or not they could endorse warfare. For if, under any conditions, they could endorse warfare, they deal in absolutes and God is the conventional name for any absolute. If it be oil or money or land, it is not less a god for being an idol. And the reason for using war as the indicator of absolutes is this: if I am asked to give my life in the effort to take another's life, then the goal for which I am asked to do this must be an absolute. If it were relative to some part of my time or energy or other

resources which I might be asked to give, then the goal would indeed be a relative value. But I have nothing, literally nothing other than life itself to give or take, and so whatever is offered as the goal for giving or taking life, must be an absolute, a god. The alternative philosophies of this age, then, may well be suspect of concealing substitute absolutes; and if that is the case, the prospects for religious philosophy are alive and well.

And so all is far from lost for Christianity, for christian philosophy, or theology; but the road back to a comprehensive christian philosophy, as sure of its own christian identity as it is open to the correction and enrichment of every religious vision it encounters, even those which are proclaimed atheistic, is likely to be a long one.

See **Revelation, Theology**

W. Jaeger, *The Theology of the Early Greek Philosophers,* Oxford, 1947. E. Gilson, *History of Christian Philosophy of the Middle Ages,* London, 1955. John Dillon, *The Middle Platonists,* London, 1977. J. Lacroix, *The Meaning of Modern Atheism,* NY, 1965.

JAMES P. MACKEY

PHILOSOPHY OF RELIGION

"Philosophy of religion is an ancient branch of inquiry, extending back prior to the time of Socrates" (Cahn and Shatz). "From one point of view, the philosophy of religion is largely an invention of the eighteenth century ... " (Charlesworth). These contrasting statements signify the disagreement over what constitutes philosophy of religion.

In one sense, philosophers always examined topics patently religious, e.g., the One and the many, the efficacy of ritual, the reality of the divine, the origin and the destiny of humanity and the universe, and the relations of religion to morality. But these explorations generally were part of metaphysics or ethics, or preambles for faith (apologetics, fundamental theology).

In another sense, philosophy of religion as the testing of religious claims emerged as a distinct discipline only when the reasonableness of religion became a problem—a characteristic of the eighteenth through twentieth centuries, after the Reformation of the sixteenth century destroyed any semblance of christian unity and the wars of religion of the seventeenth century had shattered the intrinsic cultural authority of christian faith.

The changing status of the "proofs" of God's existence illustrates the shifts. In the eleventh century, St. Anselm of Canterbury wrote what we call the "Ontological Argument for the Existence of God" as part of a prayer. In the thirteenth century, St. Thomas Aquinas rejected Anselm's argument, but developed from Aristotle his "five ways" (from motion, causality, contingency and necessity, the gradations of things, and order), patterns of thinking to lead a person from acknowledging the way things are in the world to acknowledging God. In the seventeenth century Descartes "rediscovered" the ontological argument to prove God's existence philosophically. In the eighteenth century, S. Clarke used arguments like Thomas's "ways" as philosophical proof that God exists, but Hume decisively showed those arguments failed and Kant undercut the ontological argument. But the differences are crucial: what for Anselm was part of a prayer and for Aquinas was *praeambula fidei,* became for Descartes and others independent philosophical proofs, to be disproved by Hume and Kant. In the nineteenth century, the First Vatican Council decreed that God could be known by the light of natural reason through created things (although whether this means "philosophical proof" is unclear). In the twentieth century, N. Malcolm, C. Hartshorne and A. Plantinga have supported versions of the ontological argument, and R. Swinburne has constructed an argument from order. They have convinced few. Whether *all* those who wrote of ways to God are doing philosophy of religion depends upon which way the discipline is defined.

In the twentieth century, philosophers of religion have often attacked or supported "proofs" and discussed the problem of evil. Supporters thought proofs and theodicies could provide rational foundation for religious faith. Their opponents thought that showing the fallacies of proofs and theodicies would show religious faith irrational. These discussions have degenerated into stalemated set pieces, and creative philosophers of religion focus on other topics.

Explorations of the Concept of God. Rather than debate the existence of God, philosophers have tried to make sense of the traditional attributes of God or show that because God, as traditionally understood, would have incompatible attributes, either God cannot exist or the traditional attributes must be rethought. For instance, God is said to be both immutable and omniscient. If omniscience means God knows every truth, then if it is true "Today is Tuesday," God must know it. But if God knows such a time-bound truth, then God's knowledge must change as the truth of "Today is Tuesday" changes; God would not be immutable. But if God does not know such a time-bound truth, then God could not be omniscient, for there would be a truth God didn't know. Philosophers propose numerous traditional and novel ways out of the dilemma, but how one solves this problem affects how one conceives other attributes of God, i.e., infinity, unity, simplicity, timelessness, omnipotence, relation to creation, etc. Process philosophers including Whitehead and Hartshorne have contributed important new arguments and conceptions of divine power, knowledge, and perfection. While some have dismissed these debates as mere word spinning, they can also be seen as needed explorations into the meaning of christian belief and attempts to show that belief in God is not unreasonable.

The Rationality of Religious Belief. Is religious belief beyond-but-not-opposed-to reason, based on reason, or contrary to reason? If religious belief is contrary to reason, then one must be irrational to believe religiously. If religious belief is based on reason, then what are the reasons which ground religious belief? If religious belief is beyond reason, can its (weak) compatibility with reason be shown? Skeptics argue that religious belief is irrational. B. Mitchell, A. Plantinga, R. Swinburne and others have constructed arguments to show that theism is at least as intellectually respectable as humanism or skepticism and is thus compatible with reason. While this debate may seem as sterile as the debate over the existence of God, it has brought forth a new way to approach claims to religious knowledge, "reformed ('Calvinist') epistemology," associated with Plantinga, G. Mavrodes, N. Wolterstorff and others.

The alleged conflict between science and religion is usually explored in this context. Fideists claim that religion cannot be measured by external standards of rationality any more than science can; each is answerable only to internal standards. Hence, there is no conflict; each occupies its own watertight intellectual compartment. Few find this position credible. Others (J. Haught, H. Peukert) have suggested that religion complements science by answering questions beyond the purview of science. This seems more promising, but gives no reason for a person to prefer one form of religious belief (e.g., christian claims) over another (e.g., Buddhist views).

Comparative (Cross-Cultural) Philosophy of Religion

Ethnocentric approaches measuring other religions in terms of one's own and syncretistic approaches reducing all religions to "saying the same thing in different ways" have been rejected. Two more nuanced approaches have emerged. Systems of religious doctrines can be compared and evaluated. W. Christian has shown that religious traditions have doctrines that do conflict with each other, so that if one set of doctrines is true, a conflicting set must be false. Alternatively, forms of religious life, as shown in myth, ritual, and spirituality can be analyzed, compared and contrasted. Here convergences and patterns across religion traditions can be recognized. These may point to unexpected concurrences. The unresolved issue is whether religious doctrines are primary and religious practices and experience secondary or vice versa. Here appeals to religious experience are sometimes made, but cannot help resolve this issue.

Religious Experience

Although religious experience has been impeached as a proof for the existence of God and as a reason for choosing between religions, contemporary debates have shown that it is not to be disparaged as a reason for belief. S. Katz and others have argued that mystical and other religious experiences are partly constituted by their environment. The reformed epistemologists have shown that even though my experience of God is conditioned by my religious expectations, if you cannot show good reason to think that my knowledge-obtaining apparatus is not malfunctioning, then I have a right to believe the reality of the experience and that what the experience delivers is true. Of course, you do not have to accept the truths precipitated from my experience, nor I from yours. We conflict; but each of us has an epistemic right to believe in them (although it has not been shown that such experiences confer on one any moral rights to act in a manner that affects others).

Religion and Morality

Could God command something immoral? Some would argue that would be impossible, but Kierkegaard's reflections on Genesis 22 continue to be relevant to contemporary discussions of whether divine commands must be obeyed. Does morality require a religious foundation? Kant claimed it did, but few find his arguments or recent revisions of them (R. Green) cogent. Many argue that religion provides no grounds for morality generally or vice versa, although belief in life after death may *motivate* one to be moral.

Immortality

Far too many trees have been killed to provide paper for the inconclusive and bewildering discussions of whether a person can witness her own funeral, what criteria could determine whether a resurrected person is the same as the one who died, whether paranormal phenomena provide evidence of life after death, and whether souls are separable from bodies. Philosophers help to show whether various conceptions of post-mortem existence are logically possible, but contribute little else useful.

Miracles

Hume's essay on miracles is classic, arguing their uselessness as evidence for God or the rationality of faith. More recent skeptical philosophers have sought to show that miracles are impossible, but their arguments are not convincing.

Religious Language

Explorations of the status of metaphor and analogy remain central (I. Ramsey, P. Ricoeur, S. McFague, J. Ross, J. Soskice), but as linguistic empiricism wanes and as—"religious" is seen not as a unique type of language, but a context in which all types of language are used, concerns over the meaningfulness of religious claims, often discussed under this rubric, can be found in all the above areas.

J. Charlesworth, *Philosophy of Religion: The Historic Approaches,* New York, 1972. W. Wainwright, *Philosophy of Religion: An Annotated Bibliography of Twentieth Century Writings in English,* New York, 1978. S. Cahn and D. Shatz, *Contemporary Philosophy of Religion,* New York, 1982. R. Audi and W. Wainwright, *Rationality, Religious Belief and Moral Commitment: New Essays in the Philosophy of Religion,* Ithaca, 1986.

T.W. TILLEY

PLATONISM

Platonism refers either to the teachings of the ancient Greek philosopher, Plato (c. 428-347 B.C.), or to various philosophic traditions predominantly shaped by his thought. Follower of Socrates and teacher of Aristotle, Plato preserved the contributions of his master and set the agenda for his student, thus stamping an unparalleled mark on the intellectual formation of Western civilization at its inception. He spent most of his life at Athens and came under the influence of Socrates at an early age. Socrates both amused and angered his fellow Athenians by relentlessly questioning them on the meaning and necessity of virtuous and reflective living. Although Socrates was unsuccessful in his effort to arrive at universal definitions for such virtues as justice, courage and piety, his questioning was designed to encourage pursuit of the most important matters and giving foremost thought to the care of the soul. In this way he attempted to re-orient the concerns of his philosophic predecessors, who had turned away from the city and human affairs in order to study nature, understood as the best, highest, most universal, unchanging, primary cause, and unquestionably non-human. Socrates retained an interest in nature, but directed it specifically to human nature and the nature of good human actions with an eye to the best human being and the best life. His execution in 399 in a politically unstable Athens profoundly affected Plato, who consequently shunned a political career and directed his talents to preserving and developing what Socrates had begun.

The challenge Plato faced was to continue Socrates' "political" task without threatening the citizens or acquiring political power. He responded by establishing the Academy at Athens around 385 and by writing about twenty-eight dialogues, all of them extant and in excellent form. Plato's school of philosophy and higher learning educated future politicians from all over Greece, and remained the center of various expressions of Platonism until its closure by Justinian in 529 A.D. His dialogues, incomparable in their complexity, breadth, brilliance and philosophic-dramatic blend, give center stage to Socrates, who himself wrote nothing for posterity. A dialogue is an imitation of a conversation; the text is an image of speech. Plato's writing grants Socrates' words and life an immortality, and herein lies the dialogue's nobility. But this immortality is bought at great price since a text cannot answer the reader who questions it, and the written words fix live conversations in an eternal mold. Plato's dialogues are an attempt to retrieve the unity of spoken word and speaker; thus he presents not only Socrates' words, but also their limits in his deeds and silence. The *Apology* ends in the silence of condemnation; the *Crito*, in the silence of steadfast decision; the *Phaedo,* in the silence of death. Without Plato's text, Socrates' own silence would be silenced, and his conversations would remain unfinished. The dialogues continue where Socrates

left off as Plato returned to reconsider the non-human cosmos of Socrates' predecessors, but now interpenetrated with the study of the human being, human world, and human understanding. Since the dialogues both record and carry further Socratic speech, it is impossible to know precisely where Socrates ends and Plato begins. While the dialogues break new ground in ethical, political, metaphysical, mathematical, epistemological, aesthetic, literary and textual inquiries, the author remains inseparable from his protagonist because Plato has been "authored" by Socrates. Since he is an image of his teacher, Plato's text must image the teacher's words. The dialogue structure thus implies that no explicit Platonic doctrine is advanced since Plato never writes in his own name. Strictly speaking, he teaches nothing, which means that, generally speaking, so-called "Platonic doctrines" may in fact not be Plato's at all. This, too, is Socratic: philosophy's way is not the handing down of an official set of doctrines from teacher to pupil but rather teacher leading pupil to see for himself. Plato means to teach the way he himself was taught; the dialogues are deliberately pedagogical in form and intent. They are also intentionally obscure. Insofar as Socrates' words were taken in various ways by listeners of various abilities, desires and prejudices, so the textual image of many-sided or "ironic" speech is also fashioned so as to be understood more or less succesfully by various readers. Plato is not adverse to being misunderstood, and the work of many of his followers and commentators, including Christians, betrays a history of misunderstandings.

Socrates' words and Plato's dialogues share a point of departure in *logos,* which refers to speech, to what is revealed or understood in speech, and to human understanding as that which originates speech. Just as a text points back to the spoken word, so the spoken word points back to the speaker and forward to the known, or potentially everything as understandable. *Logos,* then, provides entry into being. Socrates in the *Phaedo* reports that he took refuge in words in order not to be "blinded" by the direct gaze on beings. He began with opinions, but did not end there, and the Platonic dialogue continues the tracing of *logos* through the opinions of the familiar changing world to glimpses of the higher unchanging world. The visible world should image the invisible, but it can also obscure it so that one mistakes the image for the imaged. Such is the life of ignorance lived in the shadows of a cave, an ignorance expressed variously in errors, sophistry, unjust actions, and corrupt politics. *Logos,* then, must be protected from sophists—those who used words to distort and who manipulate truth for the sake of political or personal gain. In human affairs *logos* must be safeguarded since it has a power to shape what should be. The quest for the best city in the *Republic,* Plato's most famous dialogue, resolves into the quest for the best human life—that of the philosopher.

But the ethical and political horizon is left behind by the philosopher in "erotic" pursuit of the highest things and the truly real. This is the unchanging and eternal world of the Forms—the True, the Good, the Beautiful, to name a few—in which the many true, good and beautiful things of the sensible world participate. The ascent from opinion, the city and the sensible world of becoming, to truth, nature and the intelligible world of the Forms involves the overcoming of every obstacle to the philosophic life. The philosopher, however, must return to the city, and the Forms are known only through their manifold participations. There is a strong sense of hierarchy here,

but one that presupposes a place for the lower. Plato's dialogues do not permit a reduction to any one aspect of being, even to the highest. Unity implies diversity and the one implies a many; knowledge arises from and coexists with opinion; the answer needs the question; seriousness is the "sister" of humor; and *logos* is both itself and something other than itself (speech and what is spoken). Presence plays with absence and sameness with difference; being is present through appearances; mathematics interplays with myth and knowledge with desire. The Platonic writings blend poetry with science, citizen with philosopher, contemplation with life. Every one-sided reduction is a simplistic stab at truth that misses the structure of the cosmos and the human world. The soul itself is both one and many: properly constituted, it can be compared to a finely-tuned lyre composed of harmonies of the high and low. Only such a soul will gaze on the Forms.

Every attempt to grasp the unchanging, eternal Forms through and beyond the changing, manifold world is no less noble for being provisional or incomplete. Such is the Platonic dialogue with its suggestive, tentative, free-wheeling and wide-ranging spirit. Just as Plato's writings display and encourage a variety of perspectives so that truth may emerge, so Plato's Academy underwent major shifts from the time of his death until the first century B.C. (Early Platonism). It is obvious that the earlier a major thinker, the more diffuse and powerful his impact, and so we find Plato appearing everywhere in ancient thought in one form or another. The Greek-speaking author of the Book of Wisdom manifests strong Platonic influence, and even identifies the four cardinal virtues of the *Republic* as the fruit of Lady Wisdom (8:7). And Platonic imagery and themes are recast in John's Gospel, including the Prologue's famous doctrine of *Logos,* now reinterpreted as the pre-existent Son of God.

The second major wave of Platonism—the "Middle Platonism" of the second century A.D.—made decisive contributions to christian thought. Some early christian apologists, educated in pagan philosophy, were able to pit such pagan philosophers as Plato against pagan religion. Socrates' death was compared by many apologists to Christ's, and he was thought by St. Justin to have known Christ in part as the pre-existent *Logos.* The compatibility of presumed Platonic teaching with Christianity in such doctrines as the superiority of the unseen and spiritual world, the immateriality and immortality of the human soul, and the "craftsman" of the *Timaeus* as a creator of sorts, led some christian writers, following the Jew Philo, to postulate Plato's familiarity with the OT. Platonism as developed by Plotinus (Neo-Platonism) left a profound mark on the thinking of St. Augustine and through him entered the mainstream of Western christian thought. St. Clement of Alexandria and Origen assured Platonic influence in the East. Although most of Plato's dialogues were unavailable to the medieval world, Plato remained the predominant philosopher, especially through the *Timaeus,* until he was superseded by Aristotle in the thirteenth century. It remained to Marsilio Ficino in the fifteenth century to recover Plato by making a complete translation of his dialogues, thus guaranteeing the Greek philosopher a role in Renaissance thought. Some contemporary Platonic scholars motivated by a desire to return to origins as a response to the intellectual and spiritual impasse of our time, have uncovered important new understandings and themes in the dialogues. These discoveries await theological application.

See **Fathers of the Church, Theology**

LAWRENCE DONOHOO, OP

PLURALISM

While it theoretically could carry a metaphysical connotation and thus refer to a position that reality is manifold (in contradistinction to monism or even dualism), pluralism generally bears a noetic significance and refers to a situation in which a variety of viewpoints, explanations or perspectives are offered as accounting for the same reality. Pluralism is an inalienable characteristic of contemporary society and thought. It is rooted partly in modern philosophy's "turn to the subject," in a greater appreciation of subjectivity as a factor conditioning human knowing. In addition to philosophy, modern historiography has both presumed and corroborated the fact that time and place condition every subject. Thus a variety of subjects are likely to come up with a variety of points of view. Pluralism is also rooted in the development of more effective mass communications systems, resulting in greater awareness of the diversity of points of view among peoples around the world. Political notions such as the freedom of the individual to pursue the truth, freedom of speech and freedom of religion contribute to pluralism, as does the general scientific ethic of free inquiry. While founded upon the existence of a plurality of knowing subjects, pluralism need not entail a radical subjectivism or relativism, in the sense of claiming that all points of view are equally valid. Indeed, some shy away from or condemn pluralism out of fear of such relativism. However, pluralism can be quite compatible with a realist account of knowledge which sees reality—not ideas or the subjective state of the knower—as the term of knowing.

Bernard Lonergan, along with many other theologians, notes that pluralism has profoundly altered the classical ideal of theology which was inherited in part from the scholasticism of the Middle

Ages and especially from the Counter-Reformation tendency to organize theology into a unified and coherent system of truths. The emphasis lay upon the known theological object, not upon the knowing theologian-subject. Uniformity of thought was to some extent the ideal, insofar as it represented the adequate grasp of the same object on the part of a variety of subjects. Within such an outlook, diversity of view often appears to represent error, on the part of either or both of those whose viewpoints diverge. Today there is a growing tendency among theologians to accept pluralism as an ineradicable trait of contemporary theology, to illustrate its affinity to the christian tradition and to elaborate some of its benefits, limitations and implications.

The idea of a unity which encompasses a certain diversity is at the heart of St. Paul's discussion of the church as a body made up of many members, graced with diverse gifts (1 Cor 12-14). Does such unity in diversity apply also to the understanding and expression of the faith? There is no doubt that this is so. The same central christian proclamation takes different, concrete forms when one compares the synoptic gospels to the writings of John and Paul. Such unity in diversity shines forth in the various titles used to profess faith in Jesus and in the various stages within the development of NT Christology. Similarly, the NT offers a variety of models for understanding redemption, ministry and the church, to mention only a few examples. The theological pluralism present within the NT itself represents not the confusion of the tower of Babel but the rich unity of the first Pentecost, in which differences complement one another.

This biblical notion found expression throughout christian tradition, such that a variety of rites, customs and even theological opinions and modes of ex-pression was considered to be quite compatible with unity in faith. Augustine quotes Cyprian as saying "it is allowed to think differently, while keeping the right of communion" (*De baptismo* III, 3, 5). The high scholasticism of the thirteenth century was marked by the theological pluralism stemming from the difference between the more traditional Platonic and the newly rediscovered Aristotelian ways of thinking. Further, the distinction between *fides explicita* and *fides implicita* arose to account for the unity among believers, despite the differences in explicit faith awareness on the part of the learned and the unlearned respectively. Thus, there has always been a certain pluralism within the church.

The Second Vatican Council noted the arrival of a new age in human history in which "a more universal form of culture is gradually taking shape" (G.S. 54). Within such a cultural context, theology must seek out more efficient ways of presenting christian doctrine to contemporary people, "for the deposit and the truths of faith are one thing, the manner of expressing them is quite another" (G.S. 62; see John XXIII, *Gaudet Mater.* A.A.S. 54 [1962], p. 792). In its Decree on Missionary Activity, Vatican II urged each local church to plant the seed of the faith within the rich soil of the customs, wisdom, teaching, philosophy, arts and sciences of its particular people (A.G. 22; for a liturgical application of this see S.C. 40). Several times the Council speaks of a "legitimate variety" which extends even to theological expressions of doctrine (L.G. 13; U.R. 17). Differences need not diminish unity, but indeed contribute to it and make more resplendent the catholicity of the church (L.G. 13; L.G. 23; U.R. 16; O.E. 2). U.R. 4 paraphrases a traditional Latin axiom: "In necessariis unitas, in dubiis libertas, in omnibus caritas," emphasizing the freedom which Christians enjoy for various forms of the spiritual life, for variety in liturgical celebration and in the theological elaboration of revealed truth.

The principal theological rationale for pluralism lay in the difference between any theological expression and the reality intended by that expression. St. Thomas noted that the act of faith terminates not in the expression but in the reality itself (S.Th. II-II, q. 1, a. 2 ad 2). In saying this, he did not forget his own epistemological presupposition that a human knower only knows by means of expressions. In the case of theological knowledge, however, the expression always falls short of the reality. Since no expression is perfect, additional expressions not only are possible but may be beneficial for fuller understanding. To this consideration from theological epistemology may be added a reflection concerning christian eschatology. All of christian life stands between the now of what has been accomplished by Christ's saving deeds and the not-yet of the fulfillment of these deeds at the end of time. This characterizes christian knowledge as well. "Now we see indistinctly, as in a mirror; then we shall see face to face. My knowledge is imperfect now; then I shall know even as I am known" (1 Cor 13:12). Christ sends the Holy Spirit, who "will guide you into all truth" (Jn 16:13). Thus for solid theological reasons one can affirm the insufficiency of current expressions of the faith. Such insufficiency allows for a margin of legitimate diversity among theologians.

But pluralism has limits as well. In recognizing the values of diversity, the church is not handing herself over to doctrinal indifferentism. Legitimate pluralism in theological expression must meet the standards of revelation (as conveyed through scriptures and tradition), of the *sensus fidelium* (as contained in the faith of the People of God as a whole) and of the pastoral magisterium of the church. These three criteria—revelation, the *sensus fidelium* and the magisterium—differentiate legitimate diversity of theological expression from that pluralism which would destroy the doctrinal unity of the church.

The major implication of such a view of pluralism for the overall life of the church lies in its impact upon how one understands the unity of the church. Unity is not and has never been perfect uniformity. While a distinguishing mark of the church, unity always strives toward fuller realization. Such unity is a communion in life and truth. Inevitably tensions and differences arise; through dialogue, education and efforts to seek the complementarity of diverse positions the church progresses toward a deeper communion which is more fully catholic. This is accomplished by the Holy Spirit, who unites the many members into the one Body of Christ.

See **Doctrine, Faith. Unity of the Church**

Yves Congar, *Diversity and Communion,* London: SCM Press, 1984. James D.G. Dunn, *Unity and Diversity in the New Testament,* Philadelphia: Westminster Press, 1977. Bernard Lonergan, *Doctrinal Pluralism,* Milwaukee: Marquette UP, 1971. International Theological Commission, "Unity of the Faith and Theological Pluralism," *The Tablet* 227 (1973), pp. 645-47.

WILLIAM HENN, OFM CAP

PNEUMATOLOGY
See **Holy Spirit**

POLITICAL THEOLOGY

Within a year of the closing of Vatican II Johann Baptist Metz began lecturing and writing on the need for a new political theology. By political theology he did not mean theological reflections on politics, as if it were another topic to be included in the long "theology of ..." lists. Nor was political theology a liberal exercise in reductionism, replacing a properly theological concern with the mystery of God in favor of human moral imperatives. Quite the contrary. From the start political theology insisted on the concrete importance of the transcendence of genuine faith for the redemptive healing and creative transformation of society. This found immediate resonance in Germany, and soon Catholic and Protestant theologians in both Europe and North America began developing political theologies.

Similar to liberation theologies, these political theologies seek to develop mediations of the christian faith which will transform societies and cultures, healing the ravages of widespread social injustice and creating genuinely good social orders. The foundational issues in both types of theology are not primarily hermeneutical— how to relate doctrinal faith and historical criticism. Instead they are the dialectical question of relating the meanings and values of faith to personal and social transformation.

Where liberation theologies arise out of the concerns of those caught in the dehumanizing conditions of massive poverty and oppression, especially in third world countries, political theologies address rather the concerns of those who seek the significance of christian faith in Western post-enlightenment cultures.

Metz insisted that his way was a *new* type of political theology. By that he signaled a hope to set Catholicism on a course which would realize more fully the implications of the orientations which the church had taken at Vatican II. The council had opened up possibilities for a creative and transformative presence of Catholicism in the postmodern world.

For at least the last five centuries, Roman Catholicism had tended to adopt a series of reactionary or restorative stances to political, cultural, and religious developments. The Reformation provoked a counter-reformation; the Enlightenment a counter enlightenment; Modernism an anti-modernism. There were crucial theological issues at stake in each of these developments, which also had profound social and political implications. Vatican II, unlike the previous two councils of Trent and Vatican I, did not adopt a primarily reactive or restorative stance. Indeed, the council set a new pastoral course insofar as it sought to articulate, thanks to the strong theological scholarship which had preceded the council, the important values present in the reformed christian churches, in all other world religions, in the developments of modern science and economies, in the political and religious freedoms and rights of modern democracies.

New political theologies were now in a position, especially within Catholicism, to discern dialectically the genuine advances in modern cultures from the dominative and alienating deformations. The European Catholic reactionary/restorative stances had not really avoided, but often encouraged, an assimilation into church life and praxis of some of the worst aspects of the world it was reacting against. The Counter-Reformation fueled the European wars of religion, showing how Catholicism could be every bit as nationally biased as Protestantism. In reacting against the emergence of empirical sciences, Catholic theologians had consistently failed to recognize how deeply the nominalism and decisionism they decried in the new empirically oriented scientistic cultures were endemic to their theologies as well. In seeking to restore the political fortunes of the European *ancien régime,* the total Catholic negation of modernity had failed to perceive how fully it was infected with the conflictive ideologies constitutive of modern deformations.

That in Germany this conservative restoration was often as alienated as the liberal assimilation it opposed was especially evident to Metz. A major German political theorist, Carl Schmitt, had called in 1922 for a political theology which contained many of the key elements of the Catholic restoration. Schmitt's *Political Theology* completely accepts the two major deformations in all modern political philosophies, whether conservative, liberal, or radical. The deformations are (1) that politics cannot be based upon patterns of non-coercive cooperation, but only on a strongly dominative sovereign capable of deciding between conflictive interest groups; and (2) that knowledge is power to control and through decisive action to impose extrinsic order upon natural and historical realities which are ultimately, indeed ontologically, conflictive and combative in nature. Schmitt's political theology, in the name of restoration, was a completely immanent project with no trace of the transcendence of christian faith. A leading political and legal theorist in Weimar Germany, Schmitt shifted his allegiance to the National Socialists when Hitler came to power.

The new political theology emergent after Vatican II seeks to insure that the reactionary form of political theology will not deform Christianity again. Metz's earlier work with Karl Rahner in a transcendental recovery of Thomas Aquinas had convinced him that the premodern christian and Catholic past had intellectual, moral, and religious achievements crucially important to our own discernment of what is genuine and what is false in modernity. In *Christliche Anthropozentrik* Metz showed how an appropriation of Aquinas would enable a transposition of his treatments of being, God, grace, freedom, and the world from medieval, classical, cosmocentric to modern historical, anthropocentric thought patterns (*Denkformen*).

Divine transcendence, redemptively revealed in the life, death, and resurrection of Jesus, is continued on in the mission of the Spirit within the church. Political theology articulates a twofold response of (1) a *memoria* or remembrance with which the church continually renders present the dead and the past in Christ; and (2) an eschatological, apocalyptic expectation whereby the church is called continually to expect the coming kingdom and so to criticize all efforts at idolatry, whereby particular persons, groups, nations, or empires set themselves up as the lord of history.

Without a lived and intelligent faith, the dialectic of the Enlightenment had tended totally to negate the memories and achievements of what it termed "the dark ages." This total negation has come back to haunt modernity. For it meant that transcendence was effectively dismissed. The massive histories of human suffering and death could not be redeemed by an infinitely loving and intelligent God. Humankind would seek to redeem itself by dismissing the supposedly *other-worldly* concerns of the benighted past. So the eighteenth century saw capitalist individualism enthroned as the lord of history; the nineteenth century put forth a competitor in communist collectivism; overwhelmed with the stresses of international finance and world revolution, the twentieth century has through militarism and virulent nationalism called into question the very possibility of even a *this-worldly* future for humankind.

Contemporary political theologies in Europe and North America articulate this dialectic of the Enlightenment. The purpose is to replace *both* the totalizing negations so characteristic of conservative reactions, *and* the totalizing affirmations so characteristic of liberal assimilation, with dialectics capable of discerning between genuine values and alienating disvalues within both religion and culture, in both the church and the world.

In his classic *City of God* Augustine had attempted an analogous dialectical discernment. There were those who saw the Roman Emperor's acceptance of Christianity as the opportunity to assimilate christian faith totally into Roman culture by making it a christian imperial religion. On the other hand, there were those, such as the Pelagians, who stressed a total rejection of the sins of Roman life in the name of an immanent and unbounded confidence in human nature, by its own God-given powers, to establish a redeemed community of saints over against the sinful world. In the *City of God* Augustine argued that neither assimilation nor negation are adequate, that both neglected the concrete transcendence operative in Jesus' proclamation of the kingdom of God and in the christian sacramental celebration of graced healing as both personal and communal.

In books VI and VII Augustine discusses at length Varro's threefold distinction of theology into what "the Greeks term respectively mythical, physical, and political, and which may be termed in Latin narrative (*fabulosa*), natural, and civil theologies" (VI, 12). Augustine shows how all three forms of Greek and Roman theology are intellectually, morally, and religiously contradictory and false. Augustine does this dialectically, by indicating how christian faith can fulfill far better the narrative, metaphysical, and political or civil functions required for concrete human living in the human journey toward God. The city of God, like the reign of God, is transcendently immanent in genuine christian communities with their eucharistic *memoria* and their eschatological expectations. The empire is demystified by this dialectic.

Augustine, like Athanasius and many other Greek and Latin christian theologians, tended to understand martyrdom, monasticism and asceticism dialectically. The martyrs did not negate life, they are one in the resurrected Christ; monks and nuns did not negate community or koinonia with the church, but renounced an imperial world of domination that continually destroys human cities and states; christian asceticism did not negate the body, rather it refined desire towards mystical union with God.

Contemporary political theologies which seek to reconstruct the subversive memories and dialectical achievements of the past discover the inadequacies and distortions in many modern historical critical reconstructions. The methods of historical scholarship provide invaluable and generally normative advances in our understanding of the past. Political theologies do not in any way reject or diminish their importance; rather they call for a praxis of teaching historical criticism that will be both historical and critical.

Modern historical reconstructions are not exempt from the biases of those doing the reconstructions. To the extent that historical criticism only emphasizes its hermeneutical functions, it can too easily miss or excuse those biases or prejudices. For hermeneutics focuses attention on how there must be what Hans-Georg Gadamer terms a fusion of horizons between interpreter and text, as well as between text and historical context. This can lead exegetes and historians so to attend to the meanings and plausibility structures of text and context that they neglect the dialectical *conflicts* of horizon within and between texts and contexts. So political theologies call for a complementary dialectics which would make explicit the conflict of values in both the past texts as well as in the present reconstructions.

Political theologies call attention, therefore, to the many prejudices or biases which deform both our reconstructions of the past and our personal and social practices in the present. Solidarity with the myriad victims of domination throughout history is not only a moral imperative in our day when dominative power could destroy all life. Nor is such solidarity only a healing religious response to the faith, hope, and love which reveal God's own solidarity with us in the suffering of Christ. It is also a requirement of creative collaboration between christian theology and contemporary natural and human sciences, as well as historical scholarship. The future of the human drama is threatened with extinction because, among other things, the past and present histories of suffering tend to be ignored or repressed.

Contrary to solidarity is the massive alienation of modern individualism. As Hannah Arendt indicated, forms of totalitarian collectivism are only the other side of the same deformation: individuals are herded extrinsically together by all manners of force. Now this individualism, the privatizing of persons into monads only extrinsically related to others, is massively pervasive in modern theologies, and it is one of the major targets of political theologian's critiques. Political theology is not simply another form of social ethics, nor is it another variant of the Social Gospel.

Modern theologies tended to concentrate upon the significance of religious teachings and practices for individuals. Religion is portrayed as a very private, deeply personal matter between individuals and God. So Adolf von Harnack at the beginning of the century, could write that the kingdom of God preached by Jesus comes only to individuals, it is "the rule of a holy God in individual hearts." Harnack shared in the general optimism that modern science and technology would continue to better the human condition. Scientific reason would rule modern societies, while religion would continue to give meaning to individual existence. The pristine preaching of Jesus was primarily practical, but practical only for individuals.

After World War I the distinguished theologian, Reinhold Niebuhr, continued the individualistic orientation, only now with a more pessimistic assessment of the possibilities of progress. In his 1932 *Moral Man and Immoral Society,* although deeply committed to social issues, Niebuhr stressed how the demands of individualistic ethics must be "sharply distinguished" from what can be proscribed for nations and societies. The latter do not, indeed cannot, be expected to abide by the moral and religious values required of individuals.

This moral pessimism regarding society only deepened after World War II, which witnessed the emergence of existentialism into a major philosophical and cultural orientation. The practical import of christian faith was interpreted in various ways as significant for individuals faced with the anxieties of mortality and a modernity in which science had, through nuclear arms, made suicide a planetary possibility. In the later Karl Barth, Rudolf Bultmann, and many other theologians, there was a common tendency to articulate the meaning of christian faith and practice primarily, if not exclusively, in individualistic categories.

Paul Tillich expressed this as the Protestant Principle, whereby christian faith is seen as addressing the ultimate concerns of individuals before God, while the functions of the church are so shot through with ambiguities and fallibility that they cannot be identified with the spiritual kingdom Jesus' preached. The Spiritual Community of the Kingdom impacts upon individuals ultimately concerned about their state of estrangement; but due to the radical ambiguities of history and society, "the essential functions of the church, and therefore certain organizational provisions for their execution, are not of ultimate but of necessary concern." (*Systematic Theology* III,

p. 208, 223 f.). The church as social institution is relegated to expediency, thoroughly cut off from the more profound and genuine existential and theological concerns.

Within Catholicism, this tendency had the result of handing over the church as institution to the canon lawyers, ecclesial bureaucrats, and an arid manualist conceptualism, while more liberal theologians elaborated a symbolism and ecclesiology of the church as mystery which had too little impact on the faithful's concrete experience of church.

For political theologians the consequences of these types of privatizing are that the social and historical mediations of christian faith are more paradoxical than genuinely dialectical. Paradox tends to juxtapose the genuine meanings and values of Christianity, on the one hand, and the many sins, failures, and ambiguities of concrete ecclesial and world history, on the other hand. Paradox does not meet the problems analyzed above as conservative reactions and liberal assimilations. Dialectical analysis does meet those problems to the extent that it shows how such contradictory elements concretely interact and change for either better or worse.

From this perspective Metz claimed that Barth's "dialectical theology" was not really dialectical. Instead the infinitely other God and the kingdom proclaimed by Jesus are only paradoxically juxtaposed in Barth's theology to the concrete processes of history and social life.

While calling for a second reformation emergent out of the churches of the poor in the third world, Metz also seeks to foster cultural and institutional transitions from a Eurocentric Christianity to a genuinely polycentric world Christianity. This, he insists, is not to be a paradoxical leap. Rather the European churches themselves must dialectically appropriate their own histories and thereby make the concrete transitions to a cooperative polycentric world church.

This would, as other political theologians indicate, involve a dialectical retrieval of Catholicity as the universality of christian faith and practice mediated in and through the particularity of local dioceses and parishes. Roman Catholicism is the communion of these many local churches with the local church of Rome and her bishop, the pope. The notion that Catholicism is a monarchy in which the universality of the faith is bureaucratically managed from the Vatican down to the local churches, much as a vertically integrated corporation, is an ultramontanist aberration.

What is at stake is not only the fundamental orientations of christian faith and theology, but also the very possibility of establishing more just and good societies and cultures. For the individualism found in many christian theologies expresses the widespread individualism characteristic of modernity. Faced with two world wars, massive militarism, increasing poverty in the midst of incredible affluence, modern theologians tended either to treat all these issues as moral problems calling for greater individual efforts, or to see them as requiring a total re-formation of creedal symbols and theological concepts. As ecclesial institutions are rent with the controversies spawned by conservative reactions and liberal assimilation, the concrete possibilities for the churches to exercise socially critical functions are diminished. The church does not change the modern world, rather modernity fashions the church into its own image as no more than a voluntary association of like-minded individual believers, who form pressure groups for redressing their various grievances.

This state of affairs is not only a witness to the loss of genuine faith, it also reveals the denigration of modern intelligence and political culture. Seeking to be practical without the healing and creative wisdom of religious faith, modernity is in grave danger of dead-ending. Science severed from wisdom degenerates into an instrumental rationality which is cut off, not only from religious faith but also from any ability, as Alasdair MacIntyre's *After Virtue* demonstrates, to reason morally. The tendencies of various forms of idealism and materialism, of historicism and positivism, to erect insurmountable dichotomies between fact and value, between intelligence and morality, between reason and faith, pose extremely pressing problems. Political theologies seek creative and critical collaboration which will, hopefully, succeed in eventually dismantling those dichotomies, not by collapsing one into the other, but by indicating how they functionally interact both cognitively and practically. Political theology is not simply a call to activism. It is a search for an integrating wisdom capable of being practiced cooperatively in reversing dehumanizing injustices.

Taking seriously the dialectics of theory and praxis in the modern world requires a profound realization of how informed by theory concrete life-practices are, as well as how any and all theorizing is already embedded in ongoing sets or ecologies of social, cultural, intellectual, and moral practices.

Metz had hopes of establishing a Theological Research Institute completely devoted to interdisciplinary collaboration between theology and all the other faculties at the State University of Bielefeld in Germany. That relatively new University was established from the start with institutionalized patterns of interdisciplinary research and teaching. The faculty of the Research Institute would have been ecumenical, and solely engaged in doctoral and post-doctoral interdisciplinary research projects. Unfortunately, the project has not yet received the approval of the Lutheran and Catholic bishops of West Germany.

Several students of Metz published studies aimed at developing some of the methodological and foundational issues of such a project. Helmut Peukert's *Science, Action, and Fundamental Theology* analyzes the modern transitions from theories of science, through theories of human action, to Jürgen Habermas' theory of communicative rationality. Peukert indicates how the latter notion of rationality is intrinsically open to faith and a theology expressive of anamnestic solidarity with the dead as well as the living. Matthew Lamb's *History, Method and Theology* (Atlanta: Scholars Press, 1985[2]) analyzes the transitions from the emergence of historical consciousness, through Wilhelm Dilthey's critique of historical reason, to Bernard Lonergan's praxis grounded transcendental method The latter is able to provide the terms and relations a political theology would need in order to thematize the intrinsic relations between religious, moral, and intellectual praxis. Moreover, Lonergan's work on functional specialties in theology articulates the functional differentiations needed for the two phases of memory and hope in political theology.

While there is as yet no institutionalized practice of intra- and interdisciplinary collaboration by European or North American theologians, their common quest to show how a faith-enlightened understanding and praxis can heal and transform social and political living at the close of the second millennium of Christianity indicates how much political theology is foundational theology.

Johann Baptist Metz, *The Emergent Church*, translated by Peter Mann, New York: Crossroad, 1986[2]. Johann Baptist Metz, *Faith in History and Society: Toward a Practical Fundamental Theology*, New York: Crossroad, 1980. Helmut Peukert, *Science, Action, and Fundamental Theology: Toward a Theology of Communicative Action*, translated by James Bohman, Cambridge: MIT Press, 1985.

John A. Coleman, *An American Strategic Theology*, New York: Paulist Press, 1982. Matthew L. Lamb, *Solidarity with Victims: Towards a Theology of Social Transformation*, New York: Crossroad, 1982. Dermot A. Lane, *Foundations for a Social Theology: Praxis, Process and Salvation*, New York: Paulist Press, 1984.

MATTHEW L. LAMB

POLYGENISM

The view that the human race descended, not from a single biological couple, but from several members of a first human generation. This view is common among paleoanthropologists today, although there is some evidence in favor of a monogenistic origin. In *Humani generis* (1950), Pius XII taught that Catholics were not free to hold polygenism because it is not at all apparent that it can be reconciled with the church's teaching on original sin and its transmission. This teaching was carefully worded so as to place the burden of proof on those who would defend monogenism, but not to rule entirely out of court the possibility of a change in the teaching.
See **Original Sin**

POPE

The pope, the Bishop of Rome, is the principal spiritual leader and supreme pastoral authority within the Roman Catholic Church. The ancient title of pope comes from the Latin *papa*—a term of affection for father. Conveying a sense of spiritual paternity, it originally referred to bishops and, in the East, to priests as well. It was the title of the Patriarch of Alexandria. From the sixth century *papa* began to be applied to the Bishop of Rome and, by the eighth century in the West, this usage was restricted to him.

Other papal titles indicate the unique authority and responsibility of the office.

The *Annuario pontificio* lists the following: Bishop of Rome, Vicar of Jesus Christ, Successor of the Chief of the Apostles, Supreme Pontiff of the Universal Church, Patriarch of the West, Primate of Italy, Archbishop and Metropolitan of the Roman Province, Sovereign of the State of Vatican City, and Servant of the Servants of God. The most theologically significant of these titles, as shall be seen below, refers to the pope as the successor of Peter in the Roman episcopate.

Introduction

The papacy, called by Arnold Toynbee "the greatest of all Western institutions," has been, since the patristic era, the subject of intense theological speculation. This is especially true in today's heightened ecumenical climate, which emphasizes two factors, important in any integrated theological analysis of the papacy. First, the papacy is but one element within the broad framework of Christianity. Catholics believe that the papacy is an essential element in the church, but not that it is the very center of the christian commitment. God, Christ, Spirit, and Kingdom are the focal points of Christianity. The papacy stands in relationship to these fundamental christian truths which determine its unique spiritual mission. Second, the papacy, in addition to its divine dimension, is also an historical reality. Popes, as well as the office itself, are influenced by the broad range of cultural, social, and political factors. The papal office in the early church was not the same as it is today; it developed slowly over the centuries and few institutions have exhibited such a remarkable capacity for adaptation and resiliency.

Biblical Foundations.

Vatican I (1869-70) in the Constitution on the Church, *Pastor aeternus,* defined that Christ the Lord constituted the apostle Peter as chief of all the apostles and visible head of the whole church militant; that Christ himself established by divine right (*ius divinum*) that Peter should have perpetual successors in the primacy over the entire church; and that the Bishop of Rome is the successor of Peter in this same primacy (D.S. 3055, 3058). Three Petrine texts are cited to support this view: Mt 16:17-19 ("You are Peter and upon this rock I shall build my church ..."); Jn 21:15-17 ("Feed my lambs ... Look after my sheep"); and Lk 22:32 ("Strengthen your brothers").

A major theological challenge to the Petrine character of the papacy is the relationship between Peter and the subsequent bishops of Rome. Jesus did not personally appoint successors either to Peter or to the other apostles. Catholic exegetes point out that there is no explicit or direct scriptural evidence that the papacy was instituted as a permanent ecclesial office. Yet the idea of a continuing Petrine ministry is not opposed to scripture and is actually rooted in it. Indeed Peter played a preeminent role in the apostolic community: he was one of the first of the apostles to be called, the first one named in the lists of the apostles, the first witness to the resurrection (1 Cor 15), and the prime spokesman for the church in exercising a vigorous leadership role. Although Peter ministered in fellowship with other apostles and prophets (Eph 2:20), his authority within the early christian community was, after Christ, uniquely superior.

The Roman episcopate increasingly took up and continued many of the functions exercised by Peter among the apostles. This development, guided by the Holy Spirit, was part of the design of God for his church. In that sense the papacy is divinely willed. Several factors contributed to the church's gradual recognition of the connection between Peter and the Bishop of Rome: Rome was the burial place of Peter and Paul, it was the only Apostolic See in the West, and, as capital of the empire, it was the center of political power and commerce. For Ignatius of Antioch (c. 110), Rome was the church "presiding in love," and for Irenaeus (c. 180), the church with "a more imposing foundation." The Church of Rome was accorded special recognition, and its bishops had significant influence in churches throughout the empire, often settling their doctrinal and disciplinary disputes. Orthodox and even heterodox teachers looked to Rome as the guarantor of the true faith. The prestige of the See of Rome grew when the persecutions ended and especially when, in 380, Christianity became the religion of the empire under Theodosius. By the fourth century the popes began to assert explicitly their primatial claims, and the papacy began to function openly as a universal authority. The doctrinal systematization of papal primacy took a major step in the years between Damasus I (366-84) and Leo I (440-61).

The divine institution of the papacy remains a critical ecumenical question. For example, the bilateral conversation in the United States between Lutherans and Catholics (*Dialogue V, 1974*) discussed this issue. The Roman Catholic participants affirmed that the papacy is "divinely instituted" and that it is a sign of unity given by God; yet, for them, the term *"ius divinum,"* because of its historical implications, does not adequately communicate their position. The Lutherans, on the other hand, argued that the papacy is only a product of human law (*ius humanum*): it may be helpful, beneficial, and even desirable at times, but it remains a human institution. They further noted that the distinction between *ius divinum* and *ius humanum* is no longer useful. Despite their differences, however, the participants of both churches agreed on several important points: there is need today for a special ministry to church unity, which ministry they called "Petrine function"; this universal role may be held by one individual without contradicting the biblical evidence; Rome has been the most notable representative of the Petrine ministry; and the papacy and its renewal must be understood in light of Christ and the gospel.

The Primacy of the Pope

Several ecumenical councils—Florence (1438-45), Lateran V (1512-17), Vatican I (1869-70), and Vatican II (1962-65)—issued strong statements on papal primacy. The most detailed of these is the teaching of Vatican I, which defined that Jesus directly and immediately conferred upon Peter not only a primacy of honor but a true and proper primacy of jurisdiction (D.S. 3055). It also affirmed that the pope does not simply have an office of inspection or direction, but rather that he has full and supreme power and ordinary and immediate jurisdiction over every church, every bishop, and every believer (D.S. 3064). The Council asserted further that the pope's authority is truly episcopal; its objects are faith, morals, discipline, and government; and the decisions of the pope as supreme judge are subject to review by no one, not even an ecumenical council (D.S. 3060-3063). Finally, the Council defined that the pope can teach infallibly (D.S. 3073-3074).

The pope's jurisdiction, according to *Pastor aeternus,* is ordinary, immediate, and truly episcopal. The term *ordinary* has a technical, canonical sense referring to power that is not delegated but belongs properly to the office itself; it does not refer to the daily or habitual use of authority, exercised by a bishop in his own see (D.S. 3061). Although the pope can intervene in a diocese at critical moments of conflict, he does not take the place of the bishop in the everyday administration of his diocese. The term *immediate* means that the pope is free to exercise his authority in relation to the entire church directly without having to go through any intermediate person or body. Finally, the term *truly episcopal* emphasizes the genuine sacramental character of the papacy, since the pope, as a bishop, has pastoral authority to sanctify, teach, and rule.

Vatican I defined the universal spiritual jurisdiction of the pope with the Roman Catholic Church. The year 1870 marked the end of the pope's temporal authority over the Papal States, which had existed since the eighth century. Robert Bellarmine argued that the pope as such does not have direct authority in worldly matters, but only indirect temporal jurisdiction. A vestige of this temporal authority remains today in the pope's role as sovereign of the 109 acres of Vatican City.

The awesome list of papal prerogatives affirmed by Vatican I was couched in the language of Roman law rather than biblical categories. The Council did not use the term monarchy; it did, however, describe the pope as the one figure in the church who possesses the fullness of executive, legislative, and judicial authority. If the church is a monarchy, it is only such in an analogical sense; it is a monarchy *sui generis.* It is not an hereditary monarchy whereby the office is passed on from father to son; the process of selecting a pope has always been connected with some kind of election, approbation, or designation. Furthermore, the church is not an absolute monarchy, since the pope is bound by revelation and by defined dogmatic teachings. He cannot, for example, abolish the papacy or episcopate, since they are both of divine origin. Nevertheless, the church may be called a constitutional monarchy, with the pope as the spiritual head within the community of Christians, ministering in accordance with the fundamental affirmations of the faith of that community.

The Pope and the Bishops

Vatican I said very little about the relationship between the pope and the bishops. Vatican II remedied that deficiency with the doctrine of collegiality elaborated in Chapter Three of the Constitution on the Church, *Lumen gentium.* The differences between the two Councils are significant: Vatican I was apologetic, juridical, monarchical, and abstract, whereas Vatican II was dialogic, biblical, collegial, and historical and described ecclesial authority in terms of service rather than dominion. Drawing on the evidence present in scriptural, patristic, and theological studies, Vatican II recognized that a merely juridical conceptualization does not adequately express the full theological reality of church authority. It sought, therefore, to recover the deep pastoral and sacramental character of papal ministry in conjunction with the mission of the episcopal office.

Vatican II taught that the College of Bishops is in continuity with the apostolic college and that the pope succeeds Peter as head of the college. The pope, then, is a fellow bishop, and his primacy is not over the bishops but among the bishops; the College of Bishops does not exist without the pope. In words reminiscent of the 1875 response of the German bishops to Bismarck (D.S. 3112-3117), the Council stated that the bishops are not vicars of the pope but vicars of Christ and that their proper authority is not destroyed by the supreme power of the pope (L.G. 27). The Council, rejecting the idea that the pope is isolated and apart from the bishops, stressed the unity and collaboration that exists between the papal and episcopal offices and said that the entire

College of Bishops has a genuine responsibility for the universal church.

The doctrine of collegiality, based on the rich biblical idea of *communio,* means that the episcopal college, together with its head the Roman Pontiff, "is the subject of supreme and full power in relation to the universal church" (L.G. 22). This one subject of authority can operate in two ways: through a strict collegial act or through a personal act of the pope as head of the college. The pope, of course, as head of the whole church is always free to exercise his authority as he deems appropriate. This explanation of the papal-episcopal relationship protects the rights of both the pope and the college: "Together they represent the entire church joined in the bond of peace, love, and unity" (L.G. 23).

The limits of the papacy remain an important but unresolved question. The plenary power of the pope is restricted by the divine and by natural law, by revelation, dogmatic definitions, and the fundamental structure of the church. Although the pope may be morally bound to consult with others before making any important decision, he is not canonically bound to do so. The pope can also intervene in the affairs of a diocese or receive appeals from the decisions of a particular diocesan bishop. The traditional criteria for such intervention include the good of the church, necessity, urgency, and clear usefulness. Some theologians suggest that the moral norms governing papal actions could and should be made into canonical norms. Such guidelines would have to be accepted by the pope and would not necessarily bind his successors. Yet they would serve as reminders which would encourage collegiality, provide for wider consultation, minimize the potential for the abuse of papal power, and strengthen the bond between the pope and the bishops.

The theology of the papacy in Vatican

II, especially with its emphasis on collegiality, has made the papacy more acceptable to Orthodox and Protestant Christians even though they still have problems with other aspects of the Catholic position. The Orthodox, who hold that all bishops are equal and no one bishop has jurisdictional authority over others, see their own cherished synodal principle embodied, partially at least, in the doctrine of collegiality. They could agree that the Bishop of Rome may be a first among equals (*primus inter pares*) and may enjoy a certain primacy of honor, solicitude, and witness vis-à-vis other churches. Anglicans insist that the papal ministry must be seen in the wider context of *communio*. For them, a universal primate in collegial association with his fellow bishops should foster the distinctive life of the local churches as long as the bond of faith and union is preserved (Anglican-Roman Catholic International Commission, *The Final Report,* 1981). Lutherans suggest three basic principles for the renewal of the papal office: legitimate diversity, collegiality, and subsidiarity (*Dialogue V,* 1974).

The Election of the Pope

Scripture says nothing about the election of the pope; it is a matter of ecclesiastical not divine law. Electoral procedures developed over the centuries. During the first millennium the Bishop of Rome was elected by the local clergy and people. In 1059, Nicholas II (1059-61) designated cardinal bishops as papal electors. In 1179, the Third Lateran Council included cardinal priests and deacons among the electors and demanded a two-thirds majority. The current legislation is found in *Romano pontifici eligendo* issued by Paul VI in 1975. In theory any baptized, male Catholic who is capable of accepting the election and of exercising authority may be elected. If a priest, deacon, or layman

is elected pope, he would have to be consecrated bishop. The true beginning of full papal authority requires both election and consecration. The requirement of consecration indicates the sacramental quality of the papacy and the intimate link between the power of orders and the power of jurisdiction. The present norms also give procedures for the three traditional types of papal elections: acclamation, delegation, and, the most usual, scrutiny (written ballots).

The first pope to take a new name upon election was John II (533-35) whose previous name was Mercury. Since Sergius IV (1009-12), the custom has been followed with only two exceptions: Adrian VI (1522-23) and Marcellus II (1555) kept their baptismal names. Three popes have been honored by the title "Great": Leo I (440-61), Gregory I (590-604), and Nicholas I (858-67). The most popular choices of papal names have been Benedict, Clement, Gregory, John, Innocent, Leo, and Pius. There has never been a Peter II or a John XX. John Paul I was the first pope to choose a double name.

The Loss of the Papacy

The first and most obvious way by which papal authority is lost is by death. Most popes have died from natural causes but many, especially in the early centuries, died as martyrs. Some canonists make insanity the legal equivalent of death, since it renders the pope incapable of exercising his ministry. The second way to lose the papacy is resignation. The clearest example is that of Celestine V (1294) who resigned after a reign of only five months. His reasons were: humility, desire to lead a more perfect life, and physical and mental incapacity to govern the church. It is commonly held that, although the papacy is ordinarily a lifelong position, a pope can legitimately resign. The Code of Canon Law states that for the resignation of the pope to be valid it must be freely made and properly manifested, but it does not have to be accepted by anyone (Canon 332, 2). The third and most controversial loss of the papacy is that of deposition. There are no articles of impeachment in the present law of the church. Tradition, however, reveals that notorious and public heresy are sufficient grounds to deprive a pope of his jurisdiction. But if the pope has supreme power and if "the First See is judged by no one" (Canon 1404), then who carries out the deposition? Some theologians (John of Torquemada and Bellarmine) held for *ipso facto* or divine deposition. For them, an heretical or schismatic pope has, in fact, already separated himself from the church and is no longer a member. Others (Cajetan and Suarez) argued that papal authority does not cease automatically because of heresy or schism but only after the church through the bishops have established the pope's guilt. This does not mean that a general council is superior to the pope: its judgment in this matter does not cause the deposition but merely confirms it.

Conclusion

It is necessary to keep ever in mind that the papacy is above all a spiritual office. Political and juridical explanations do not adequately capture its meaning. The Bishop of Rome has been directly empowered by God to minister to the universal church. The pope is not simply the delegate of the church or even the delegate of the bishops; yet as the visible representative of Christ, he exercises his special responsibility in conjunction with the bishops and the whole church. The Petrine ministry is the concrete expression of unity and the center of communication for the local churches. In his overseeing function of *episkopē*, the pope teaches and safeguards the faith, acts as a witness to the saving presence of Christ among us

in the Spirit, and tries to create an atmosphere of love, peace, and justice. As a stable and permanent office, the papacy encourages collaboration and mutual help between the local churches. Dependent on God's healing grace and guided by the mandates of the gospel, the papal ministry is one of service as the pope and the People of God work together for the full coming of the kingdom.

See **Bishop, Church, Collegiality**

Anglican-Roman Catholic International Commission, *The Final Report,* Washington: USCC, 1982. R.E. Brown, K.P. Donfried, and J. Reumann, Eds., *Peter in the New Testament,* Minneapolis: Augsburg; New York: Paulist, 1973. P.C. Empie and T.A. Murphy, Eds., *Papal Primacy and the Universal Church. Lutherans and Catholics in Dialogue V,* Minneapolis: Augsburg, 1974. P. Granfield, *The Papacy in Transition,* Garden City, N.Y.: Doubleday, and Dublin: Gill and Macmillan, 1980. P. Granfield, *The Limits of the Papacy: Authority and Autonomy in the Church,* New York: Crossroad, 1987. J.M.R. Tillard, *The Bishop of Rome,* Wilmington, Del.: M. Glazier, 1983.

PATRICK GRANFIELD

PRAXIS

Praxis is a notion which has become foundational in many contemporary theologies. Political and liberation theologians first called attention to the need for a restructuring of theology in which praxis would not only be the aim of a theoretical theology already elaborated, but would also be the very foundation of theologizing. The use of the transliterated Greek word, *praxis,* indicates a rather complex set of meanings. Praxis or practice does not mean simply action or activism in opposition to theory. Rather, these theologians call for a "dialectic of theory and praxis" as a transposition of the traditional theological concerns on the relations of faith and reason into a contemporary, as distinct from a modern, context. Tracing the complex set of meanings through the modern, contemporary, and classic contexts indicates the importance of the notion of praxis.

Modern notions of praxis all tend either to connote or explicitly invoke *movement*. The emergence of modern natural sciences in the seventeenth century not only outshines, as Herbert Butterfield remarked, everything since the rise of Christianity. This scientific revolution also gradually, yet inexorably, made *movement* into a master metaphor informing all areas of modern culture and life. It is obvious that all forms of empiricism, positivism, materialism, etc. would reduce everything to matter in motion, to the action and passion constitutive of physical movement.

What is much less evident is how all those political, cultural, philosophical, and religious movements aimed at counteracting the reductionism of empiricism, positivism, and materialism were also influenced by the master metaphor of movement. Various forms of idealism and phenomenology would either concede that only sense intuition can know objective reality, or attempt to claim that concepts and ideas are reality by charting their natural and historical movements. If politics is human movement par excellence, then political science becomes either a form of engineering aimed at predicting or controlling the movements, or a more humanistic theorizing which is as disconnected from concrete political life as the Kantian noumenon was from phenomena. All human sciences and scholarships become bifurcated into (1) those who seek to make their discipline as "scientific" as possible by transposing as many natural scientific techniques of measurement and control as possible; and (2) those who react against this by trying to elaborate more humanistic modes of reflection. This "scientistic" versus "humanistic" rift runs through all human, historical disciplines. Indeed, it transcends all modern ideologies and cultures.

The modern master metaphor of movement informed all understanding of human activity in terms of action-passion or action-reaction patterns. In such a context the call to praxis could mean no more than a call to practicality, to shifting one's stance from passively suffering actions of others to reacting in ways that would, inevitably, make them suffer passively if one's reaction were strong enough to overwhelm their action. At the same time, however, the call to praxis, to the extent that it empowers humans to take responsibility for their own lives gives them experiences of being subjects, and not merely passive objects, of their histories. This experience of empowerment to become responsible subjects does not fit into the categories of action-reaction, nor into any other categories of movement.

This ambiguity is present in most nineteenth- and twentieth-century treatments of praxis and action. Many studies of Karl Marx and Marxists demonstrate how neither Marx himself nor the movement he founded have resolved the ambiguity. Similar ambiguities are found in pragmatism, both as a philosophy and a movement. The ambiguity is far from just a conceptual difficulty. It influenced modern life in countless ways. For if all human activity is basically just another species of movement, then being practical means learning the skills and techniques of control. Modern revolutions for freedom and democracy, for the rights of the poor and oppressed, become less and less genuinely subject-empowering histories, and more and more single movements to install other sets of controllers in the reins of government. As Max Weber saw so clearly, the only way to manage complex modern societies is through ever more refined techniques of bureaucracy. The modern revolutions for freedom in the United States, in France, England, Russia, China, Cuba, etc. end up empowering, not so much the citizens themselves as the governmental and corporate bureaucrats who manage the respective economic, political and cultural movements of the societies.

The contemporary, as distinct from the modern, set of meanings of praxis originated with the recognition of this pervasive presence of technique and an instrumentalist notion of both reason and action. Political theologians turned to the German philosophers and social theorists, especially those in the Frankfurt School of Social Research, who had decisively acknowledged the ambiguities of the liberal democratic and socialist revolutions. Theorists like Max Horkheimer, Ernst Bloch, Kostas Axelos, Hannah Arendt, Jürgen Habermas, and Alasdair MacIntyre began to realize that a retrieval of some elements from the classic work on praxis could be very relevant to modern dilemmas. Aristotle distinguished three general patterns of specifically human activity: the theoretic (*theoria*), the practical (*praxis*), and the productive (*poiesis*) ways of living. These were, for Aristotle, differentiations of human intelligence which corresponded to the intellectual and moral virtues, and to technical skills and artistic craft (*techne*). They also corresponded to three different types of scientific knowledge (*episteme*): theoretical (*theoretike*), practical (*praktike*), and productive (*poietike*) ways of knowing (*Metaphysics* E. 1, K. 7 and *Nicomachean Ethics* VI).

Attention was given to the distinction between praxis and production. Human activity is often a "doing" or "performing" in which the good of the doing or performing is immanent within the activity itself. Conversation among friends, for example, is a good just in the very performance of conversing. Thus praxis is defined as human activities or operations in which the good is immanent within the very performance itself. For

Aristotle politics was such a praxis, and in order for political performance to promote the common good of the *polis* or city, politicians and citizens needed to cultivate intellectual and moral virtues, especially practical wisdom (*phronesis*) and justice. The productive way of life, on the other hand, was very much involved in movement. Artisans and those engaged in "making" or "producing" things learned technical skills, and the goodness of their actions was judged in relation to the objects produced. The skill (*techne*) of a carpenter is judged, not by his/her performance in doing work, but by how well made the table or chair is.

What Aristotle was on to is the difference drawn, for example, between a house and a home. Productive techniques are needed to make a house. But a home is a doing, a performing, a praxis which is a good in itself when it is achieved; and the achievement of the happiness which is a family home requires much more than management techniques: a home requires virtuous parents and children. Similarly, a good *polis* cannot be produced or made the way one constructs its streets and buildings. For a good city or state virtuous citizens are essential. The Greek language can better express the human operations constitutive of praxis since, besides the active and passive voices for verbs it also has a middle voice which expresses how one doing something acts within or on oneself in the very doing.

Political and liberation theologians call attention to this distinction between technique and praxis in order to indicate how, for example, ecclesial communities of worship and action are goods in themselves. Celebrating the eucharist together is not meant to be for something else outside of the eucharistic celebration itself. It is a praxis. The basic ecclesial communities in Latin America, therefore, are ends in themselves. They empower all those who participate to be subjects of worship and christian action. Efforts by some to cast them as marxist cells organized for the overthrow of a government only distorts their genuine praxis into a typically modern instrumentalism.

Generally, all christian discipleship is a praxis. Unfortunately, much of the modern instrumentalist orientation has deformed christian asceticism, prayer, and piety (e.g., the *devotio moderna*), as well as sacramental and ecclesial ministries, into techniques rather than the genuine practices they are meant to be. Ethics was also impoverished by an excessive individualism which treated virtues as techniques rather than as personal and communal empowerments.

To date much more research into both the classic notions, as well as modern complex social patterns, is needed. The distinction between praxis and technique, between communicative action and instrumental reason, is only beginning. Contemporary social theorists such as Jürgen Habermas, tend to make use of this distinction in ways which do not adequately address the dichotomy between "scientistic" and "humanistic" orientations in the human and historical disciplines. To the degree that the natural sciences are conceded to have only an empiricist, positivist, or instrumentalist meaning, the legacy of Max Weber continues to dominate contemporary social theory. There is no romantic escape from the need for empirical sciences and technologies within contemporary societies, including religious institutions. Until those sciences and technologies are understood and appropriated as involving not only skills (*techne*) but also, and more importantly, human operations or practices, including the praxis of theorizing, the modern master metaphor of movement will continue to distort knowledge and policy.

In this regard the methodological work of Bernard Lonergan is especially relevant. For his *Insight* is an invitation to appropriate the human operations or praxis of attending, understanding, judging, and acting. And this invitation to each reader to begin to understand her or his own praxis is developed, not only in regard to the human sciences and historical disciplines, but from the start also in regard to mathematics and the physical sciences. His *Method in Theology* carries the praxis orientation into theology; and his works on Thomas Aquinas indicate how Aquinas further differentiated some of the insights of Aristotle regarding movement and praxis. Thus Lonergan's work provides a context in which to transpose the classic concern with orthodoxy into a contemporary concern for orthopraxis in ways which would do full justice to christian and Catholic faith and practice.

See **Orthopraxis, Virtue**

Clodovis Boff, *Theology and Praxis: Epistemological Foundations,* translated by Robert R. Barr, Maryknoll: Orbis, 1987. Rebecca Chopp, *The Praxis of Suffering: An Interpretation of Liberation and Political Theologies.* Maryknoll: Orbis, 1986. Richard J. Bernstein, *Beyond Objectivism and Relativism: Science, Hermeneutics, and Praxis,* Philadelphia: Univ. of Pennsylvania Press, 1983. Alasdair MacIntyre, *After Virtue: A Study in Moral Theory,* Notre Dame: Univ. of Notre Dame Press, 1984². Hans-Georg Gadamer, *Reason in the Age of Science,* trans. by Frederick G. Lawrence, Cambridge: MIT Press, 1981. David Ingram, *Habermas and the Dialectic of Reason,* New Haven: Yale Univ. Press, 1987.

MATTHEW L. LAMB

PRAYER

This article will: 1) examine the roots of christian prayer, especially in the NT; 2) list significant historical contributions to christian prayer; 3) examine the nature of christian prayer, pointing out references helpful for further study.

Roots of Prayer

In Greek literature as early as the writings of Homer the motive for prayer was the power of the gods: they were stronger and needed to be favorably disposed if the life of mortals was going to be successful. The ancient Greeks felt it was foolish to ignore the gods because no one can resist their will. They had anthropomorphic concepts of the gods, who were never envisioned as omnipotent. For the most part, while invoking some god in every conceivable need, Greek worshipers maintained a respectful distance. They resisted the temptation to set themselves up as rivals by transgressing upon the divine territory in any way. Greek piety did not embrace any thought of mystic union with a god.

In Jewish scripture the poles of prayer are the greatness of God and the needs of mortals. God's greatness evokes hymns of praise, descriptions of his attributes, and expressions of his compassion. The needs of humans found expression in prayers of petition, laments appealing for justice and forgiveness, intercession for those in need, and thanksgivings that celebrated God's help. Psalm 51 is a masterpiece for expressing repentance. The greatest collection of Israel's prayers, the Book of Psalms, served as the hymnal for worship in the Temple of Jerusalem, which itself housed a school of prayer when it was rebuilt after the Babylonian exile. On the verge of the christian era the unknown author of the Wisdom of Solomon wrote a prayer embodying the universal longing for divine wisdom and intimacy (Wis 9:1-18).

Prayer in the NT

Whenever Jesus prayed in public, it was always as trusting son of the Father whose will is the norm for all human existence and activity. In fact, "beloved son" is the name by which God designates Jesus in his two great prayer experiences: the baptism (Mk 1:9-11) and the trans-figuration (Mk 9:2-8). The very word by which Jesus addressed God in Aramaic, *abba* (Father), is preserved in Mark's agony scene (14:36). The gift of the Holy Spirit dwelling within them enables believers to pray with the same intimate "abba" (Rom 8:15; Gal 4:6).

The longest prayer in the NT is that of Jesus to his Father in John's account of the Last Supper (17:1-26). It has been called by various names: the priestly prayer of Jesus, the prayer for unity, even the contemplative version of the Lord's Prayer. Actually it fits no formula and continues to defy all efforts to describe it adequately.

Several truths can be learned from the Lord's Prayer, recorded in two different versions in Mt 6:9-13 and Lk 11:2-4. The most important insight is the primacy of the presence of God in all prayer. The entire first part of the prayer is directed to reminding worshipers that all reality exists for the glory and praise of God and that his fatherly will is the guide and goal of all human striving. Only when his followers have oriented themselves to the transcendent Father does Jesus direct them to petitions for personal needs. And the needs that believers are to ask for are not extravagant. They reflect simplicity of lifestyle and sincerity of heart: food that is necessary at the time; forgiveness that identifies them as followers of Jesus; and protection against the crafty powers of evil.

A prayer that epitomizes the mind and heart of Jesus is that outpouring of his joy in the Holy Spirit when he thanked the Father for hiding the mysterious workings of providence from the wise and revealing it to little ones (Mt 11:25-27; Lk 10:21-22). The joy flows from his gratitude that the Father has handed over "everything" into his hands. As Son he alone knows the Father and alone can give this knowledge, that is, a unique experience of divine intimacy, to humans.

This prayer embodies christian belief in the uniqueness of Jesus as revealer of the divine will and agent in the Father's plan of salvation.

Out of this sense of the universal mediation of Jesus flows the Pauline admonition to pray and to give thanks always, without ceasing in every situation (1 Thess 5:17; Phil 3:17; 4:6; Eph 5:20; 6:18). Such prayer performs the role of keeping believers motivated and dedicated to God's active presence in the world, because they are witnesses to God's universal saving will. The fruit of this quality of prayer is interior peace and loving union with the Lord. It is characterized by the presence of "the fruit of the Spirit" in the lives of believers, namely, love, manifested in qualities like joy, patience, and self-control (Gal 5:22-23). The heart of prayer for Christians is the eucharist, the prayer in which believers remember the self-offering of Jesus on Calvary in response to the will of the Father, making of himself a ransom for humanity (Mk 10:45). The church performs this prayer in obedience to the instruction of Jesus to keep repeating this memorial rite until he comes again (Lk 22:19).

Early christian liturgy was the context for developing the hymns that celebrate the person and mission of Jesus. Paul incorporates the hymn of Christ's self-emptying and his being exalted by God into his letter to the Philippians. The hymn serves to motivate the divided community to practice mutual forbearance. Implied in the image of Christ's receiving the "above-all name" of Lord is a promise that those who are willing to suffer in and with him will also be glorified by the Father (Phil 2:6-11).

The great hymn to the cosmic Christ as image of the invisible God dominates the letter to the Colossians. It celebrates Jesus not only as lord of creation but also as redeemer of the new creation in his position as head of the church (Col 1:15-20). Hymns such as these were decisive in molding faith in Jesus as being at once both pre-existing Word and incarnate Son of God. The liturgical blessing that opens the letter to the Ephesians is a prayer filled with sublime theology. It hails Jesus as effective agent of God's saving blessings on the new and universal Israel predestined to salvation in Christ. His members have received the Holy Spirit as their pledge of eternal glory (Eph 1:3-14).

Some commentators have found baptismal hymns in the First Letter of Peter, but sociological exegesis now sees that letter as reflecting actual conflicts between the beleaguered Christians and hostile social forces opposing their community. Prayers of praise are sung by the heavenly court in the Book of Revelation in the course of the great heavenly liturgy that provides the context for this great apocalyptic prophecy. For the most part its prayers are lists of the divine qualities that move the saints to thanksgiving and awe and praise as they witness the triumph of God's wisdom and power over hostile powers.

Among the evangelists only Luke provides any parables of Jesus about prayer. The two he records encourage perseverance and persistence in begging God's help. The first appears right after the Lord's Prayer. It is the parable of the friend who comes at midnight asking for bread to feed an unexpected guest (11:5-9). The second, often considered as its parallel, is the story of the widow whose persistent cries eventually move the unjust judge to vindicate her claim (18:2-5).

Of all NT writers Paul is the one who provides the most insights about the nature of prayer in the life of christians and the need to pray "in Christ." It is true that his letters contain few actual prayers. Even his "thanksgivings," which telescope the content of his letters in liturgical fashion, are narratives that describe Paul's way of praying rather than his actual prayers. Yet they illustrate that christian prayer is intimately linked to the cross and the glorification of Jesus, which have made his Holy Spirit available to believers as their indwelling teacher of prayer.

David Stanley sums up Paul's vision of prayer in a list of seven qualities: 1) it is a mystery that unfolds only gradually throughout sacred history; 2) it is a result of God's power graciously evoking a response from human weakness; 3) the dialog of prayer leads believers to greater understanding and deeper familiarity with God in Christ; 4) christian prayer is trinitarian in origin, dynamic, and orientation: believers relate to the Father in Christ through the Holy Spirit; 5) this dynamic is the result of faith, love and hope that governs all christian life; 6) by nature it is apostolic, reaching out to all those for whom the Son took on human nature; 7) prayer has an eschatological thrust, carrying believers to be with the risen Lord.

Important Writings on Prayer

Tertullian composed his treatise on prayer about 200 A.D. A more philosophical treatment was written by Origen about 234 A.D. The first of many commentaries on the Lord's Prayer was that of Cyprian a few years later. He did not limit himself to that prayer but included other passages of the Bible. Preparation for baptism provided the occasion for instruction on prayer in the Mystagogical Catechesis, attributed to Cyril of Jerusalem (c. 350-387 A.D.).

The golden age of patristic literature is rich in writings on prayer. This period produced the great religious rules to guide the formation of monks in meditation and in the recitation of the divine hours at specific times during the day. This monastic practice stimulated the influence of the psalms on christian piety. Monasticism as a whole played a decisive

influence on the development of christian prayer. The monks of the East esteemed contemplation, which was the subject of a treatise by Evagrius shortly before 400 A.D. In the West the Benedictines celebrated the divine hours and encouraged commentaries on the psalms. Their cultivation of the liturgy provided the stimulus for the composition of many Latin hymns.

The rise of scholasticism contributed to philosophical reflection on prayer during the Middle Ages. Public and private prayer provided a means to express the total dependence of all things on God. Scholastic theologians produced systematic studies on prayer. They treated such topics as: definition, division, types, degrees, methods, conditions, and benefits of prayer. As usual, Thomas Aquinas provides a model treatment in his *Summa Theologiae* II-II, q. 83. Manuals of prayers were collected for the use of the faithful. Medieval piety was also influential in the construction of artistic places of prayer, such as cathedrals, oratories, and cloister choirs.

After the Reformation Catholic writers in the various schools of spirituality, such as Carmelite, Ignatian, Salesian, Sulpician, and Oratorian, published countless treatises on prayer. These have been frequently reprinted, paraphrased, commented upon, updated, and translated into the languages of other cultures.

Nature of Christian Prayer

The Bible assumes the centrality of prayer in the lives of believers but never provides a definition of it. This gap has been filled by spiritual writers and theologians throughout the christian tradition. In the widest sense, christian prayer is a personal response to the felt presence of God in an effort to intensify that presence as a significant force in human existence. The diversity of definitions of prayer flow from multiple perspectives of the human spirit. All christian schools of spirituality agree on two points: prayer is necessary for salvation, and it is a gift of God in Jesus. The doxology at the end of the eucharistic prayers of the Roman Catholic liturgy reflects this centrality of Christ: "Through him and with him and in him is to thee, almighty Father, all honor and glory."

With the growth of the behavioral sciences the abstract treatments of prayer have become less satisfying for believers who are searching for psychological and anthropomorphic roots of prayer in the depths of the human person. This search has led to phenomenological descriptions of prayer. For psychologists of religion, prayer is a sophisticated form of self-analysis, an imaginative exercise of depth psychology in a mystic mode. It leads to intimate self-knowledge, whether one is dealing with a transcendent other or simply communing with the depths of self. In this approach the emphasis is on technique. Hence the variety of helps proposed to develop methods of prayer: imagery, guided meditation, inner dialog, quietness of spirit, Zen and yoga. Cultural anthropologists develop models of prayer on the basis of key elements: objective, activity, social setting, and aim, all of which are applied to religious groups. As they develop new forms of community such as Focolari, base communities, charismatic groups, contemporary Christians are creating new prayer styles.

Since the specific human mode of communicating is by language, the dynamism of christian prayer can be illustrated by applying to it the analysis of the speech act as conceived by Roman Jakobson, by factors and functions.

In terms of factors: prayer is the *message,* with believers acting as *senders* seeking to communicate with God as *receiver.* The *context* is the history of salvation, the unfolding of God's saving revelation from Abraham until its climax in the incarnate Word, Jesus Christ. The qualities of faith, love and hope establish *contact* and keep this dialog fruitful. The *code* comes from scripture and tradition whose language and images act as signs that believers make use of for praying.

The *expressive* function of the speech act operative in prayer is what classical treatments called the four kinds of prayer: adoration, thanksgiving, petition, and propitiation. These forms act to produce an *evocative* response from God in the *referential* context of the promises found in revelation, especially the words of Jesus to his followers. All the sacramental rites and devotional acts as well as sacred vestments and religious art fulfill the *phatic* function of maintaining contact with God on the part of those who pray. See **Devotion and Devotions, Mysticism, Spirituality, Worship**

"Prière" in *Dictionnaire de Spiritualité,* Paris: Beauchesne, 1986; tome 12, part 2:2196-2347. *Ways of Prayer Series,* Basil Pennington, O.C.S.O., ed., Wilmington, DE: Michael Glazier, 1984. David M. Stanley, S.J., *Boasting in the Lord,* NY: Paulist, 1973. *The Oxford Book of Prayer,* Ed., Bishop George Appleton, NY: Oxford, 1985.

JAMES M. REESE, OSFS

PREACHING

Preaching is the proclamation of the good news of salvation. Derived from the Latin *praedicare* (to announce, declare), the English term encompasses several Greek NT terms: *kerussein* (to herald, proclaim), *evangelizesthai* (to announce the gospel), and *marturein* (to witness). In addition to the liturgical homily (the preeminent form of christian preaching), preaching in the broad sense includes catechesis *(didache/didascalia),* exhortation *(paranesis),* mystagogy (post-baptismal instruction in the mysteries of faith), and various forms of evangelization (broadly, any ministry of the word; more specifically, the initial proclamation of the word of God in a non-christian or non-religious environment).

The christian ministry of preaching is grounded in the ministry of Jesus and the commissioning of the apostolic church. At the core of Jesus' own ministry was his proclamation of the reign of God. Jesus announced the good news of salvation in his presence and his actions as well as in his words. Further he gathered a band of disciples whom he sent to continue this preaching mission "even to the ends of the world" (Lk 9:1-6; 10:1-12; Mt 28:12).

After the death and resurrection of Jesus, the apostolic community proclaimed salvation in his name and in the power of his Spirit. The NT records specifically the post-Easter commissioning of Mary Magdalene (Jn 20:17), the Twelve and their companions (Mt 28:16-20, Mk 16:14-20, Jn 20:19-23), and Paul (Gal 1:11-17) to announce the good news of the resurrection. The central kernel of the apostolic preaching (the kerygma) is reflected in the Acts of the Apostles and the letters of Paul: Jesus who was crucified is risen as Lord and Christ, and all who repent and believe in him will be saved (cf. 1 Cor 15:3-8; Acts 2:22b-24, 3:12b-26, 10:34-43).

In the tradition of Jesus and the Hebrew prophets the apostolic preacher announced the *dabar Yahweh,* the word of God as saving event bringing about what it promises here and now. For Paul, who describes his vocation as a "compulsion to preach" (1 Cor 9:16), the power of preaching is "the power of God" (Rom 1:16; 1 Cor 1:18) active in spite of human weakness (1 Cor 1:25). Conversion, the goal of all preaching, occurs not through "the persuasive force of 'wise' argumentation," but rather through the "convincing power of the Spirit" (1 Cor 2:4).

In the apostolic and post-apostolic eras a variety of preaching ministries was exercised by apostles, prophets, and teachers within diverse local christian communities. The *Didache* (c. 100) gives evidence of charismatic ministries of the word existing side by side with the ministries of local leadership exercised by the bishop (later also by presbyter and deacon) (C.15.1). Even at this point, however, the issue of distinguishing authentic from false prophecy (and teaching) was emerging. Gradually preaching became connected with the teaching office of the church, the prerogative and responsibility of the bishop and his clerical delegates. Some local churches preserved the synagogue practice of allowing anyone gifted with the Spirit to address the congregation while others viewed this as a violation of the church order, as was evident in the controversy between the bishops of Jerusalem, Caesarea, and Alexandria regarding Origen's preaching in the third century.

The earliest evidence of the liturgy of the word including preaching (the homily) as an integral part of christian eucharist is found in the *First Apology* of Justin Martyr (c. 150): "The memoirs of the Apostles or the writings of the Prophets are read. When the reader has finished, the president of the assembly verbally admonishes and invites all to imitate such examples of virtue" (C.67). The *Second Letter of Clement,* described as the earliest existing christian sermon, gives evidence of this style of moral exhortation based on Isaiah 54.

For the most part preachers in this early christian period used an expository method of running commentary on the text(s) of scripture used in the liturgy, followed by an appropriate lesson or application. In the school of Alexandria (notably with Origen, 185-253) allegorical exegesis became the pattern. The style of discourse was free and direct, hence the term "homily" from the Greek *homilia* meaning familiar conversation. Listeners would frequently respond to the homily by applauding or acclaiming the preacher.

In the fourth century preaching became more thematic, catechetical, mystagogical, and rhetorical. Theological homilies on doctrinal themes explained the authentic faith of the church in the face of heresy. Panegyrics and funeral orations provided another form of preaching as the festivals of holy men and women became more a part of the evolving liturgical year. Catechetical homilies were needed to explain Christianity to the increasing numbers seeking entrance into the Lenten catechumenate. Mystagogical catechesis explored the mysteries of faith further for the newly initiated members of the community.

Homiletic theory and skills developed significantly under the influence of Greek rhetoric. Noted rhetorical preachers included the Cappadocians Gregory of Nazianzus (d.c. 390) and Basil the Great (d. 379), as well as John Chrysostom (350-407) in the East and Ambrose (d. 397) and Augustine (d. 430) in the West. Book IV of Augustine's *De doctrina christiana*, the first significant work on homiletics, described the Bible as a kind of sacred rhetoric and explored the differences and similarities between rhetoric and preaching.

By the end of the patristic era, prophecy as the dominant dimension of preaching was replaced by teaching with an emphasis on the unity and authority of the tradition as handed down from bishop to bishop. While the fourth century *Apostolic Constitutions* includes a reference to instruction by lay men (repeating however the prohibition against women speaking publicly as found in the third century *Didascalia*), Pope Leo (440-461) stated clearly that only those of the priestly order may assume "the rank of preacher." The *Statuta Ecclesia Antiqua* (third century France) and the Council of Trullo (691) again describe preaching in terms of authority, rank and permission.

From the sixth to the eighth centuries, the major creative development in preaching was the missionary preaching in Ireland, Scotland, Germany, Denmark and Sweden. Elsewhere the "dark ages" following the barbarian invasions prevailed as preaching was reduced primarily to the sermon (drawn from collections of patristic sermons such as that of Paul the Deacon) in monastery churches. Gregory the Great (Pope Gregory I, d. 604) developed a series of homilies considered to be models of eloquence and read widely in the following centuries. With the Second Synod of Vaison (529) priests were explicitly granted the right to assume the preaching office along with the bishop. If neither bishop nor priest could preach, a deacon was to read a homily by one of the fathers of the church (an acknowledged teacher).

The Carolingian reform in the ninth century brought a renewed emphasis on the importance of preaching, improved clerical education, and valuable collections of sermons by Alcuin and Rabanus Maurus for use by parish priests with limited training and resources. Church councils in Tours (813), Reims (813), and Mainz (847) decreed that bishops should preach homilies and in the vernacular.

The eleventh century saw the development of preaching missions as a means of gathering support for the crusades (and the related unfortunate connection between preaching and indulgences). The reform initiated by Pope Gregory VII at the end of the century challenged all church members to bring their lives into conformity with the gospel and urged secularized parish clergy to return to a genuine evangelical ministry.

Within the "evangelical awakening" of the twelfth to the fourteenth centuries, diverse forms of preaching can be identified: traditional liturgical preaching; sermon occasions similar to contemporary parish missions; instruction given in monasteries and convents; the "preaching" of medieval art, theater, and architecture; the commentaries on scripture of the medieval masters of theology; street preaching; and itinerant preaching bands. The twelfth century was marked by the mystical and scriptural preaching of Bernard of Clairvaux (1090-1153), the emergence of the university sermon which incorporated the logic and dialectic of the classroom, and the development of sermon collections, homiletic manuals, sermon encyclopedias, and technical treatises (the *artes praedicandi*). Still, the near-illiteracy of most parish priests was bemoaned by the Fourth Lateran Council (1215) which initiated reforms in clerical education and life, challenged bishops to preach and promote preaching, and viewed regular annual confession as an opportunity for the pastor to preach to individuals.

Two significant events in this period of renewed evangelical fervor were the rise and temporary papal authorization of lay preaching bands, and the formation of the mendicant orders. The gospel ferment of the age gave rise to groups of lay men and women who wanted to live the *vita apostolica;* i.e., imitate Jesus and the apostles through lives of voluntary poverty and itinerant preaching of penance and reform. Issues of doctrinal orthodoxy, clerical opposition, and obedience to church authority ensued. Alexander III originally authorized the Waldensians in southern France to preach with the permission of their parish priest, though along with the Humiliati in Italy, they were later excommunicated for heresy. Innocent III later authorized the disobedient (but not doctrinally heretical) Humiliati group to preach words of exhortation *(exhortatio),* but not doctrine concerning faith or sacraments *(praedicatio)* since doctrinal preaching presupposed a knowledge of scripture and theology. The Fourth Lateran Council definitively prohibited lay preaching as the unauthorized usurpation of clerical office.

A significant exception to this ruling was found in the formation of the Franciscan Order. Founded as a lay movement dedicated to the imitation of Christ and the apostolate of preaching, the Franciscans had been given permission by Innocent III in 1209 to preach penance everywhere, provided they received the approval of Francis. In 1215, the Dominican Order was founded by the canon regular Dominic de Guzman as a supra-regional "order of preachers" under the direction of the pope rather than a local bishop. The focus of their preaching was converting heretics, hence the need for serious theological study and the decision to embrace the *vita apostolica* with its emphasis on evangelical poverty.

Both the lay preaching movements and the establishment of the new mendicant orders raised questions regarding the source of authority to proclaim the gospel. Alternate claims located the right to preach in 1) the *vita apostolica* (the lay preachers' claim); 2) *missio* or jurisdiction—being sent there by the local bishop or the supra-diocesan pope (the mendicants' argument); 3) rank or office (the justification for the right of medieval abbesses to preach in their cloisters or chapels, also the grounds for the prohibition of lay preaching by the Fourth Lateran Council); and 4) priestly ordination as such (the defense of twelfth-century monks in conflicts with diocesan clergy).

Other developments in preaching in the period preceding the Reformation included the mystical sermon (Meister Eckhart, Johannes Tauler, Henry Suso, and Jean Gerson, among others), street preaching (officially approved by the Council of Vienne in 1312), the evangelical or revival sermon calling for repentance (e.g., Vincent Ferrer, Bernardine of Siena, and John Capistran), and the reform preaching of John Wycliffe and the Lollards, Jan Hus, and Girolamo Savanarola. Nonetheless, the Fifth Lateran Council (1516) lamented that fictitious miracles, false prophecies, and idle tales were being preached in place of the gospel.

At the heart of the Reformers' critique of the church in the sixteenth century was a concern for the preaching of the gospel as the proclamation of God's free and merciful promise in Christ Jesus which can be rightly received only through faith. Protesting against what they perceived as practical abuses and false theological teachings (including a magical notion of sacraments, a cultic view of priesthood, non-biblical preaching, and papal teaching authority), the Reformers emphasized the primacy of the proclaimed word, the priesthood of all the baptized, the pastor as preacher, scripture as the basis for all preaching, and the word of God as the ultimate authority in the church.

While the Council of Trent reaffirmed church doctrine on the sacraments in the face of the Reformers' critique, a special decree concerning preaching (Session V, 1546) reminded bishops that preaching was their principal function and required priests to preach on Sundays and great feast days. The establishment of seminaries for the training of priests and the development of *The Catechism of the Council of Trent* as a doctrinal guide contributed to better theological preparation of priests, though preaching became increasingly doctrinal instruction rather than kerygmatic proclamation.

Brilliant pulpit orators emerged in the seventeenth through nineteenth centuries (including Jacques Bossuet, Francois Fenelon, Henri Lacordaire, and John Henry Newman, among others), but the most significant shift in the Roman Catholic understanding and practice of preaching since the Reformation came in the twentieth century with the kerygmatic movement, the biblical and liturgical renewals, and ultimately the Second Vatican Council.

By 1936 preaching had become, in the estimation of Innsbruck theologian Joseph Jungmann, the "vulgarization of theological tracts" rather than the announcement of "good news." The kerygmatic movement in catechetics and the liturgical renewal sparked a search for a theology of preaching from a Catholic perspective, the major issue being how to explain the efficacy of God's word and the relationship between word and sacrament in the light of the teachings of the Council of Trent. Theologians such as Otto Semmelroth, Yves Congar, Edward Schillebeeckx, Michael Schmaus, and Charles Davis made valuable contributions toward a theology of preaching grounded in a sacramental theology of revelation. Eventually Karl Rahner's explanation of word as symbol and sacraments as the "highest words" of the church forged a breakthrough in the Catholic understanding of the power of the word and the relationship between word and sacrament.

With the Second Vatican Council's Dogmatic Constitution on Divine Revelation, the Catholic church officially proclaimed a theology of revelation centered on the word of God. The council announced that "The Church has always venerated the divine Scriptures just as she venerates the body of the Lord," and that "all the preaching of the Church must be nourished and ruled by sacred scripture" (D.V. 21).

Other council documents reaffirm the primacy of preaching in the mission of Jesus and his followers (S.C. 6), stressing the ecclesial character of preaching and the centrality of preaching in the mission of the church (L.G. 17; A.G. 3). The chief means of evangelization, the primary purpose of missionary activity, is identified as "the preaching of the gospel of Jesus Christ" (A.G. 6). Describing the necessity of preaching as a call to faith and conversion (S.C. 9; cf. Rom 10:14-15) and recognizing the evangelizing, instructional, and exhortatory dimensions of preaching (S.C. 9), the documents reflect the inter-relatedness of all ministries of the word while emphasizing the preeminent place of the liturgical homily.

In a major liturgical reform, the council restored the ancient liturgical homily, emphasizing the intimate connection between word and sacrament and declaring that the homily is "part of the liturgy itself" (S.C. 35,52). Instructions and decrees implementing liturgical reform after the Council note that the homily is an integral part not only of the eucharist, but of the other sacraments as well, highlighting the fact that the homily itself is an act of worship.

As defined by the *Constitution on the Sacred Liturgy,* the sermon is to be a proclamation of God's wonderful works in the history of salvation, that is, the mystery of Christ, which is ever made present and active within us, especially in the celebration of the liturgy" (S.C. 35). The homily (as liturgical preaching is more frequently designated in conciliar and post-conciliar documents), is to draw its content from the scriptural and liturgical texts of the day (S.C. 35), to apply to concrete circumstances of life and particular needs of the hearers (P.O. 4), and to take account of the mystery being celebrated and the seasons and feasts of the liturgical year.

Vatican II highlighted the centrality of preaching in the ministries of bishop (LG. 25; C.D. 12) and priest (P.O. 4; C.D. 28; L.G. 28) while placing a new emphasis on the role of the laity in the prophetic office of the church (A.A. 2; C.D. 35; G.S. 43). While the 1983 Code of Canon Law affirms that by virtue of their baptism and confirmation, lay members of the christian faithful witness to the gospel message by word and by the example of christian life and "can also be called upon to cooperate with the bishop and presbyters in the exercise of the ministry of the word" (canon 759), even in a church or oratory (canon 766), it reserves the homily at eucharist to a priest or deacon (canon 767). Precedents have been set for authorized lay preaching at eucharist with the permission given to the West German bishops by the Congregation for the Clergy (Nov. 20, 1973, renewed in 1977) and the Directory for Masses with Children (Nov. 1, 1973), though theological and canonical questions in this area remain disputed.

Contemporary discussions in both Catholic and ecumenical contexts are probing the theological foundations of preaching: the underlying understanding of revelation and the word of God; the relationship between human experience and the word of God; the impact of various approaches to biblical hermeneutics on proclamation and the relationship between word and sacrament. A renewed emphasis on evangelization and pre-evangelization in a global context raises questions of the enculturation of the gospel, the church's fundamental understanding of the missionary task, the significance of the growth of fundamentalism, and the relationship between word and praxis in the proclamation of the gospel.

The growing phenomenon of lay preaching has prompted further theological reflection on the source of the preaching charism in baptism and confirmation, the value of having the word expressed (and enfleshed) by diverse members of the community, the relationship between the charism to preach and the sacrament of orders, liturgical and canonical understandings of the homily, models of liturgical presidency, and the responsibilities of bishops as "moderators of the entire ministry of the word" (c. 756, #2) to foster preaching and order charisms within a diocese. The theology of ordained ministry is also being redescribed in terms of the primary pastoral responsibility for proclamation of the word.

In recent homiletic literature the impact of developments in narrative theology, liturgical emphasis on the proclamatory nature of the homily, and the insight of literary theorists and biblical scholars that literary form carries theological significance is evident in the shift from didactic modes of proclamation toward other creative forms (e.g., story preaching, inductive preaching, proclamatory preaching). Contemporary communication theory has contributed to the insight that preaching is always at least implicitly dialogical, to further reflection on the role of the congregation in the preaching process, and to exploration of uses of media in a contemporary response to the church's constant mandate to proclaim the gospel "to the ends of the world."

See **Catechesis, Liturgy, Revelation, Word of God**

Y. Brilioth, *A Brief History of Preaching,* Philadelphia: Fortress, 1965. Thomas Carroll, *Preaching the Word* (Message of the Fathers of the Church, Vol. 11), Wilmington: Michael Glazier, Inc., 1983. John Burke, Ed., *A New Look at Preaching,* Wilmington: Michael Glazier, Inc., 1983. Stephen Doyle, *The Gospel in Word and Power,* Wilmington: Michael Glazier, Inc., 1982.

MARY CATHERINE HILKERT, OP

PREAMBLES OF FAITH

A term used to describe knowledge preliminary to or leading to faith. In the Catholic tradition, it is used to refer to the natural knowledge of the existence of God and to historical knowledge of Christ's existence, message, and works sufficiently certain as to make the act of faith in God's revelation in Christ a reasonable human act.

See **Apologetics, Fundamental Theology**

PREDESTINATION

Predestine means literally "to decide or determine beforehand." In theology it refers to an eternal, infallible decree of God by which he brings about all the good in creation, especially the salvation of those who are saved. It translates the Greek *proorizo* which St. Paul first used in speaking of a wisdom which "God *decreed before* the ages for our glorification" (1 Cor 2:7). Later, as he was encouraging the Christians in Rome threatened by persecution, he used it to assure them of God's saving power and love. He spoke of five successive divine saving acts: foreknow, predestine, call, justify, and glorify (see Rom 8:28-30).

Foreknow is used here by Paul in a Semitic sense and refers not so much to cognitive awareness, as to an eternal loving regard (See Rom 11:2 for a similar usage.) Out of this regard God *predestines* what his love intends: from eternity he decides that people should be made like Christ. To implement this decision he *calls* them by grace. The people who accept this call through faith he *justifies,* that is, he forgives their sins, adopts them as his sons and daughters, and thus makes them initially like Christ. When they persevere in a life of love he *glorifies* them by granting them eternal salvation, making them definitively like Christ. Paul does not imply here that those who are predestined and called cannot fall away, for he warns them of this danger (see Rom 11:22). But God is at work on their behalf, and no hostile power is strong enough to separate them from his love (see Rom 8:38-39).

This meaning of *predestine* underwent a change when *foreknow* was understood more in a Greek sense of intellectual knowledge. Thus Clement of Alexandria (died c. 215) wrote that God chose and predestined for membership in the Catholic Church all those who he foresaw throughout history would be just (*Strom.*

7, 17, 107).

A more far-reaching shift took place when St. Augustine (354-430) incorporated predestination into his theology of the omnipotent providence of God. He spoke of God's foreknowing the gifts he decides to confer on those he predestines for salvation: "This and nothing else is the predestination of the saints, God's foreknowledge and preparation of his benefits whereby whoever is liberated is most certainly liberated" (*Gift of Perseverance,* 14, 35). Augustine conceived the whole human race under condemnation to eternal punishment because of the sin of Adam. From this "mass of perdition" God freely chooses to liberate some by his gracious benefits and so predestines them to eternal life. In one place he speaks also of God predestining others to eternal death: "He is also the most just dispenser of punishment to those whom he predestined to eternal death, not only because of the sins which they add of their own will, but also because of original sin even if, being infants, they add nothing of their own" (*The Soul and Its Origin* 4, 11, 16).

However, when the church later approved St. Augustine's teaching on our complete need of grace for salvation, it expressly declined to include his teaching on "the profounder and more difficult questions"(*Indiculus,* Cap. 10, D.S. 249). It is universally agreed that this refers especially to his understanding of predestination.

The Protestant Reformers took the Augustinian position with complete seriousness. John Calvin (1509-1564), in particular, developed his teaching on double predestination under the clear influence of St. Augustine: "Predestination we call the eternal decree of God, by which he has determined in himself, what he would have become of every human individual. For they are not all created with a similar destiny; but eternal life is foreordained for some and eternal damnation for others. Every one, therefore, being created for one or the other of these ends, is, we say, predestined either to life or to death" (*Institutes of the Christian Faith,* III, 21).

If we say that predestination is constituted both by God's eternal knowledge of who accept his grace and by his eternal will that they do so, then we may affirm with Catholic theologians traditionally that predestination is eternal, infallible and gratuitous, but that it does not contradict either God's universal saving will or human freedom. It is eternal, since God knows eternally as present to him who actually accept his grace, and has always willed that they do so. It is infallible, as his knowledge cannot fail, and his will is ever faithful and powerful. It is gratuitous, because it is the ultimate source of human merits and is not caused by them. It does not contradict God's universal saving will, as it flows out of this will which is ineffective only in the case of those who freely resist it. It does not contradict human freedom, as it is in the power of the human will as graced by God to accept his grace while never losing the power to reject it; the Council of Trent taught that the human will is able to resist the very grace that it is as a matter of fact accepting ("Decree on Justification," Chap. 5, D.S. 1525).

See **God, Providence.**

JOHN H. WRIGHT, SJ

PRESBYTER
See **Priest**

PRIEST

Contemporary use of the word "priest" is plagued by a certain confusion. Standard English-language editions of the documents of Vatican II, for example, employ it to translate both *pres-byter* and *sacerdos,* words that carry quite different connotations. The present article will use both "presbyter" and "priest" with the latter serving as an equivalent for the Latin *sacerdos* and the Greek *hiereus.*

The priest is a well known figure in the broader history of religion as well as in the Bible. The blessing of Moses over the tribe of Levi (Deut 33:8-11) indicates that the priesthood in Israel was initially responsible for oracular pronouncements and for the teaching and handing on of the Torah as well as for sacrifice and prayer. Due in part to the growing importance of the synagogue, the priesthood by the time of Jesus had become largely restricted to temple worship with its elaborate sacrificial ritual. This is the situation reflected in the definition of the letter to the Hebrews: "every high priest chosen from among men is appointed to act on their behalf in relation to God, to offer gifts and sacrifices for sins" (Heb 5:1; cf. 8:3).

The language of priesthood, the temple, and sacrifice appears in a radically transformed way in the NT. This is particularly the case in Hebrews where Jesus is described as the great high priest who once and for all entered into the heavenly temple bringing not the blood of animals but his own blood, thus achieving forgiveness and sanctification for all (cf. Heb 9:11-14; 10:1-18). To underline the superiority of this priesthood, it is said to be of the order of Melchizedek (cf. Heb 5:5-10; 7:15-22).

What is central to Hebrews can be found in other forms throughout the NT. Jesus is the temple, the place where God dwells (Jn 2:21); his faith and obedience, his self-giving love constitute a sacrifice pleasing to God (Eph 5:2; 1 Cor 5:7); the words instituting the eucharist include among their many references some that are clearly sacrificial.

Cultic language is also applied to the believing community. To be a Christian is to be in Christ; it involves living according to his Spirit. Such a life is celebrated as an authentic sacrifice, the kind of worship that God finds acceptable (cf. Rom 12:1; Heb 13:15f). Developing a theme long associated with the covenant (Ex 19:6; Isa 61:6), 1 Peter describes all believers as belonging to a "royal priesthood, a holy nation"; they are called to offer spiritual sacrifices to God through Jesus Christ (1 Peter 2:4-10; cf Rev 5:10).

Given this widespread "spiritualized" application of the language of priesthood and sacrifice to Jesus and to believers generally, it is striking that the word priest is nowhere used in the NT of the community leaders. This is surely more than an attempt to distinguish them from the Levitical priesthood. It reflects an awareness of how profoundly all priestly and cultic language has been transformed by the coming of Christ. What might seem to be an exception reinforces the point. In Romans 15:16 Paul describes his preaching of the gospel as a priestly service because it calls people to the kind of life that constitutes authentic sacrifice.

The Greek *presbyteros* means an old man, an elder. In a more technical sense it is used to describe a person holding a position of trust and respect, perhaps even an office. This was the case among the Jews. The book of Numbers attributes the institution of a college of elders by Moses to an intervention of God (Num 11:16ff). After undergoing a relative eclipse under the monarchy, the elders acquired new significance both during and following the exile. In the time of Jesus the Sanhedrin was made up of priests, scribes and elders. A council of elders was ordinarily responsible for the running of each synagogue.

Although possessing a variety of administrative, doctrinal, and juridical functions, Jewish elders were essentially "lay" people, clearly distinct from the priestly caste.

The existence of the presbyter/elder within early Christianity is widely attested to in the NT. In the absence of any precise information, one has to assume that the church simply took over the existing terminology. Without any explanation of their origin elders appear in Acts 11:29f as those to whom Barnabas and Saul brought the donations from the community at Antioch. In the context of the so-called council of Jerusalem they exercise in conjunction with the apostles some kind of teaching authority (cf. Acts 15:2ff).

The presbyter/elder is also found in I Peter, James, and the Pastorals. In I Peter the presbyteral functions are brought together in the image of the shepherd (1 Pet 5:1-4). According to James 5:14f the elders are to be called in to anoint and to pray for the sick. It is clear from the Pastorals that the existence of presbyters has become normative. Although a list of qualifications is given (Tit 1:5ff; 1 Tim 3:1ff), their responsibilities are not spelled out. Particular recognition, however, is due to "those who rule well . . . especially to those who labor in preaching and teaching" (1 Tim 5:17).

There is no single pattern of church structure within the NT, nor is there any common terminology to describe what does exist. The institutionalization process was clearly a complex one that developed slowly and in different ways in the various communities. In all probability the presbyters fulfilled the same tasks as those who elsewhere are called *episcopoi* or bishops. The emphasis everywhere is on oversight or pastoral leadership.

It is only with Ignatius of Antioch

(c. 115) that the traditional threefold division of church office into the episcopate, the presbyterate, and the diaconate is really clear. Each of the churches of Asia Minor reflected in his letters seems to have been led by a single bishop who was supported by a council of presbyters and a number of deacons. In the course of the second century this situation became standard everywhere.

As the communities initially were small and as they all had their own bishop, the liturgical functions of the presbyters were minimal. Time and expansion soon brought a change. Various aspects of the episcopal role were taken over by presbyters. For a long time, however, solemn baptism with its attendant chrismation as well as the reconciliation of sinners were reserved to the bishop.

It is interesting to note that when the language of priesthood began to be used of the christian ministry at the end of the second century, it was applied to the bishop. By the middle of the third century Cyprian employed the terms *episcopus* and *sacerdos* almost interchangeably. It was only later that the word priest became a common way of referring to the presbyter.

Various developments in the thought and practice of the medieval western church led to the situation where the category of priesthood became fundamental for the understanding of the ordained ministry. The separation of orders from jurisdiction focused attention not on pastoral responsibility but on sacramental power. These theoretical developments influenced and were reinforced by the practice of ordaining vast numbers of presbyters whose main religious function was the celebration of Mass. Added to this of course was a widespread loss of the sense of the centrality of preaching to the ministerial office.

The medieval developments provoked

strong reactions at the time of the Reformation. Luther, for example, rejected priestly interpretation of the ministry and insisted on the priority that was to be given to preaching. The Council of Trent, while attempting to deal with abuses in its decrees on reform, basically reiterated the traditional doctrinal positions. The fundamental category to which it had recourse was that of priesthood. In continuity with the old law there is in the church by the institution of Christ "a new, visible and external priesthood, into which the old has been translated" (D.S. 1764). The emphasis is on the "power of consecrating and offering the true body and blood of the Lord and of forgiving and retaining sins" (D.S. 1771).

Vatican II went a long way in *Presbyterorum ordinis,* the decree on the ministry and life of presbyters, to suggest a new orientation. Presbyters, like bishops, although at a surbordinate level (n.2), participate in the threefold office of Christ—priest, prophet, and king or shepherd. Their task is primarily pastoral. They are to exercise a ministry of leadership within the community. Particular emphasis is placed on preaching in all its forms. The sacramental ministry has its center and highpoint in the eucharist. The focus of concern in regard to both word and sacrament is to help the whole community to deepen the quality of its life and its worship.

The document emphasizes the need for collaborative action on the part of presbyters both with their bishop and with the people whom they are meant to serve. Parish and diocesan councils are intended to facilitate cooperation. Senates or councils of presbyters have been created to give form to the renewed sense of the presbyterium.

Ordination to the presbyterate in the Catholic tradition is a sacrament. In addition to officially and publicly designating individuals to their office, it communicates the gifts and graces without which they could not fulfill their responsibilities. It relates them in a special way to the risen Christ so that along with their profound identity with the community they are able in certain aspects of the sacramental sphere to act in the name and in the person of Christ.

In recent years questions have been raised about the wisdom of maintaining celibacy as a necessary condition for the presbyterate, at least as it is exercised in the diocesan clergy. The ordination of women has become in some countries the object of intense debate. Various bilateral dialogues with other christian churches have produced formulations on the ordained ministry that emphasize different aspects of the many-sided responsibilities and relationships involved in it. The decline in vocations and the rising average age of present presbyters have been sources of concern. All of these debates and discussions will inevitably bring modification in our understanding and practice. Whatever these will be, the presbyterate will remain of fundamental importance for the life of the church.

See **Ministry, Orders and Ordination**

B. van Iersel, and R. Murphy, eds. *Office and Ministry in the Church, Concilium* 80, New York, 1972. J. Lécuyer, *et al,* "Decree on the Ministry and Life of Priests," in *Commentary on the Documents of Vatican II,* ed. by H. Vorgrimler, Freiburg, Montreal, 1969, vol IV, pp. 183-297. K. Rahner, ed., *The Identity of the Priest, Concilium* 43, New York, 1969. E. Schillebeeckx, *Ministry,* New York, 1981. J.-M. Tillard, "The Ordained 'Ministry' and the 'Priesthood' of Christ," in *One in Christ,* 14 (1978), 231-46.

DANIEL DONOVAN

PROBABILISM

The term probabilism refers to one of a number of "moral systems" developed in Roman Catholic moral theology, especially in the sixteenth to eighteenth centuries. Probabilism, as a system, had its origin in the work of Bartholomew of Medina, O.P. (1577). The system provides methods for forming conscience, when one is in genuine doubt as to what is required or allowed by the moral law. A crucial question is whether one may follow a probable opinion. Opinion is a state of mind where there is assent to a judgment with some apprehension that its contradictory may be true. A proposition is probable or "provable" when there are arguments for it which support opinion, but not certitude. Doubt is a suspension of assent. Traditional moral doctrine affirmed that one may not act with a conscience in doubt, since this would indicate a willingness to do what is wrong. The doubt, then, has to be removed. Direct evidence, sufficient to support a certain judgment, must first be sought. But sometimes this will not be attainable. In such cases, it is not possible to reach theoretical certitude, but it may be possible to reach practical certitude. This can be done by having recourse to the "reflex principles" provided by the moral systems.

The systems were developed in the juridic style characteristic of the moral theology of the period. The way in which conscience reaches its practical judgment is construed in the manner of a court hearing. Conscience presides like a judge adjudicating a dispute between two litigants, law and liberty. The question to be decided is what falls under law, and what is left to liberty. A basic maxim is: "a doubtful law does not bind." The moral systems determine which side bears the burden of proof, and define the weight of evidence required for a judgment. Reflex principles may not be invoked when it is a question of a goal which has to be attained at all cost, where another's rights are at stake, when there is danger of harm to self or others, and in such matters as the validity of the sacraments. The opinions of recognized theologians are cited

as evidence. Church authority controlled the debate by condemning lists of propositions and placing books on the Index. An extreme position held that, even where evidence for an alternative position was very strong, conscience should always decide for the safest course, that is, avoiding any possible violation of the moral law. This rigorism (Jansenism) was condemned by Pope Alexander VIII in 1690. The other extreme, "Laxism," would accept tenuous evidence as sufficient. This was condemned by Alexander VII in 1665 and Innocent XI in 1679. Three positions were accepted: probabilism, probabiliorism and equiprobabilism. According to probabilism, if solid arguments can be provided in favor of liberty, even though those for the law are stronger, judgment could favor liberty. Probabiliorism holds that, only when the case for liberty certainly outweighs that for the law, can judgment be given for liberty. Equiprobabilism (St. Alphonsus Liguori, 1762), a modified form of probabilism, holds that, if the opinion in favor of law seems certainly more strongly supported, judgment must be for the law. But where the evidence for both sides is of equal weight, and there is question of whether the law exists or not, then judgment may be for liberty. Probabilism was associated with the Jesuits; Probabiliorism with the Dominicans; Equiprobabilism with the Redemptorists. In more recent times, most theologians accepted some kind of probabilism. However, some have criticized the use of juridic categories in moral judgment and have advocated a return to discernment based on prudence, as presented in the works of St. Thomas Aquinas.

It is difficult to understand the intensity and complexity of the debates between the schools, unless the context is appreciated. What was at stake was the fundamental question of how to preserve the enduring values of the gospel, and assist people to live them out in concrete, changing circumstances. Must traditional teaching be simply repeated, despite changing circumstances, or is development possible? The systems represent an historically conditioned endeavor to deal with this perennial question. Despite its legalistic cast, probabilism was ultimately concerned to respect the primacy of the personal conscience.

See Conscience; Freedom; Moral Life, Christian

Henry Davis, SJ, *Moral and Pastoral Theology*, vol. I, London: Sheed & Ward, 1945, pp. 78–115. Bernard Haering, *Free & Faithful in Christ*, vol. 1. *General Moral Theology*, New York: Seabury. Crossroad Book, and London: St. Paul Publications, 1978, pp. 284-294. T. Deman, DTC 13.1:417-619.

BRIAN V. JOHNSTONE, CSSR

PROCESS THEOLOGY

Generically, the term refers to any form of systematic theology which makes extensive use of philosophical categories grounded in the priority of "becoming" over "being." Thus theologies which reflect a cosmic evolutionary perspective (e.g., the thought of Charles Sanders Peirce, Pierre Teilhard de Chardin, etc.) or those which are rooted in the dynamic character of human subjectivity (e.g., various forms of Hegelianism, North American pragmatism or, properly qualified, transcendental Thomism) all manifest the same sensitivity to the fact of change and development, at least within the created order. Specifically, however, the term refers to that type of process-oriented theologizing which takes its inspiration from the work of the philosopher/mathematician Alfred North Whitehead, above all, in *Process and Reality* (1927). Among contemporary Whiteheadians, some (like John Cobb, Lewis Ford, David Griffin, and Schubert Ogden) have followed the lead of Charles Hartshorne in working out the details of Whitehead's

conceptual scheme; others like Bernard Meland and the late Bernard Loomer have sought more immediate empirical confirmation of his basic insights within a broad range of human experiences.

Common to both schools, however, are certain presuppositions about reality derived from Whitehead's "philosophy of organism." The first of these would be that the ultimate units of reality are not substances, but events: what Whitehead calls "actual entities," momentary subjects of experience whose very existence is their process of self-constitution out of data from the surrounding world under the influence of what Whitehead calls the divine "initial aim" for that same self-constitution. Thus every actual entity comes to be in virtue of its own unconscious "decision" to actualize one out of the range of possibilities offered to it by God through the divine initial aim. Once self-constituted, however, the actual entity ceases to be as a subject of experience and becomes instead a "superject"; that is, it thrusts its achieved actuality upon the next generation of actual entities within the societies to which it belongs as a datum in their becoming. The second major presupposition of Whitehead's philosophy, accordingly, is that, while the ultimate units of reality are intangible subjects of experience as described above, the tangible realities of human experience, the "substances" of Aristotelian-Thomistic metaphysics, are "societies," aggregates of actual entities existing for the most part both in space and in time and united with one another in virtue of what Whitehead calls a "common element of form," a pattern of order and intelligibility analogously reproduced in all the members of the society. While individual actual entities come and go, therefore, the societies to whose existence they momentarily contribute endure and are thus perceived as the "substances" of common sense experience.

The advantages of this philosophical conceptuality for the articulation of christian doctrine are focused in the new freedom accorded not only to human beings but likewise to all other finite beings to be active in their own self-constitution. God's power is persuasive, not coercive, since the actual entity makes the ultimate "choice" with respect to its role in the cosmic process. Evil, therefore, comes into existence through the agency of the creature. God "suffers" its effects with the creature in order to bring good out of evil in terms of subsequent initial aims and subsequent "decisions" on the part of future actual entities. The disadvantages of this approach from the perspective of traditional metaphysics converge on the implication that God no longer is in full control of creation, that even God cannot know the future with absolute certainty since the latter is only realized through the moment-by-moment decisions of actual entities.

See **God, Metaphysics**

John Cobb and David Griffin, *Process Theology: An Introductory Exposition,* Philadelphia: Westminster Press, 1976. Norman Pittenger, *Catholic Faith in a Process Perspective,* Maryknoll, NY: Orbis Books, 1981. Marjorie Suchocki, *God-Christ-Church,* New York: Crossroad Pub. Co., 1982). Joseph Bracken, *The Triune Symbol: Persons, Process and Community,* Lanham, MD: UP of America, 1985.

JOSEPH A. BRACKEN, SJ

PROCESSIONS

In the theology of the Trinity, this term refers to the derivation of the Son from the Father and of the Holy Spirit from the Father and the Son. In a stricter sense, the Spirit is said to "proceed" from the Father and the Son, while the Son's procession from the Father is specified as "generation."

See **Trinity**

PROOF FOR EXISTENCE OF GOD

Even though the church Fathers generally held that God's existence could be known through the creation (cf. Rom 1:19; 2:14-15; Acts 14:15-17; 17:24-28), no formal proof was developed. Augustine went far in that direction (*De libro arbitrio* 2, 2-15), but St. Anselm produced the first chiseled argument. Under the influence of Aristotle, whose argument for a Prime Mover is found in *Physics* 6-8 and *Metaphysics* 12, St. Thomas elaborated five ways, or proofs, for showing God's existence in S.Th. I, q. 2, a. 3, Sc.G. I, 13, and elsewhere. Other scholastics proceeded similarly, but with Descartes and the dawn of modern philosophy the Anselmian "ontological proof" again found favor. The Enlightenment employed also a cosmological argument from the order and harmony of the universe. Both proofs were denied by Kant's restriction of pure reason to the realm of the finite, sensible appearances (*phenomena*) that are known according to scientific laws; Kant allowed for reasonable belief in God on the basis of moral experience in the unknowable infinite (*noumenon*). Post-Kantian proofs rely on subjective experience of morality, religious feelings, or intellectual dynamism.

In his believing search for greater understanding Anselm argued that to understand God as the being than which nothing greater can be thought implied his existence. For a being which could not be conceived not to exist is greater than a being which could be conceived not to exist. Existence in the highest degree therefore is included in the very notion of God. Descartes removed Anselm's dynamism while expanding the argument: We have a notion of an infinite, perfect being; if existence were lacking to him, he would not be perfect; hence he must exist; moreover, since we are imperfect and the more perfect cannot proceed from the less perfect, the notion of a perfect being is not caused by us or anything imperfect, but by God. Both trains of argument, from the notion of perfection and from its cause, lead to the affirmation of God's existence. Against the argument Kant observed that existence is not a predicate, i.e., does not belong to the order of concept, or idea; hence the transition from the idea of existence to real existence is invalid. More recent defenders of this approach argue from the mind's dynamic quest for further intelligibility, which projects it toward the real beyond all finite concepts and sees in this reality the ground of the partial intelligibility already attained.

The argument from design, Thomas' fifth way, became popular in a revised version during the Enlightenment when Newton's physics made a great impression on men's minds. Thomas argued that because even unintelligent beings strive toward an end and there is an harmonious order in the universe, revealed in the constant or at least very frequent, recurrent behavior of those beings, they must be directed by the intention of a knowing, intelligent, and ordering Being. The philosophy deriving from the Enlightenment's scientific mechanism imagined God in the role of grand architect or great watchmaker. Kant's contention that the mind's categories order phenomena according to universal law severely weakened the design argument's probative force. The dissolution of the Newtonian synthesis into various incompatible theories of physics, existentialism's emphasis on the individual with all his anxieties, and the problems of evil and innocent suffering have also highlighted the argument's weakness.

Many Thomists still maintain the validity of Thomas' proofs. They dismiss the Kantian critique on the basis of many inconsistencies—for example, how can the *noumeon* be affirmed to be if it is unknowable?—and presuppose the capacity of the mind to attain the real (being) through the senses. If the mind cannot know reality, all thinking would be vain.

Thomas' first way, from motion, summarized Aristotle's argument. On the basis of sensibly perceived motion he argued that whatever is in potency can only be reduced to act by something already in act and that an infinite regress in causes would be impossible (and unintelligible). Hence he concluded to the existence of a Prime Mover. In the argument motion is first envisaged in terms of efficient causality, but given the conclusion of an unmoved Pure Act separate from the world, ultimately final causality is employed to explain the influence of the Prime Mover upon mobile beings: he attracts as loved, or desired (Sc.G. I, 13, 108). Nowhere does Thomas' explicit proof advance beyond Aristotle's except in its succinctness and clarity.

The second way argues simply from the recognition of efficient causality in the world and the impossibility of an infinite regress. Though Aristotle's universe without beginning or end did not demand a first in a series of temporally distinguished efficient causes, Thomists generally argue that not spatial or temporal contiguity is involved but a series of causes essentially ordered to each other as lower to higher. Nonetheless, it is not immediately clear how this second way significantly distinguishes itself from the first way, which started with efficient causality.

The third way proceeds from beings that are generated and subject to corruption, capable of being and not being. Since these beings can be and not be, it is impossible for them to be always. Their being, therefore, needs a cause that did not come to be but always was and is necessary. The argument from contingency was implicit in the previous ways insofar as a final ground of contingent motion or effects was sought. Here contingency was explained in terms of generation and corruption, an Aristotelian subset of motion, and it is not immediately evident why an infinitely extended spatio-temporal universe could not itself be the ultimate ground of individual, transitory beings in a perpetual series of generation and decay.

That Thomas nowhere explicitly goes beyond Aristotle's argument raises the question whether one arrives at anything more than a pure form. Many Thomists point to Thomas' discovery of the essence-existence distinction and argue that an existential aspect is implicit in his proofs: contingency is existential, efficient causality concerns the very existence of beings, and motion reveals an existential potentiality. The insight into the essence-existence distinction is often allowed to be a gift that makes the metaphysician. For Maritain, in a pre-metaphysical (i.e., pre-conceptual) intuition one recognizes the existence of things, one's own existence, and absolute existence; because things exist independently of the self, one feels threatened, aware of death and nothingness; then from threatened existence, spoiled by nothingness, i.e., contingent existence, one grasps the necessity of absolute existence; a second stage of spontaneous reasoning reaches the whole, separate Being, unknown in itself, beyond the totality of which we are a contingent part, yet actuating all beings. Thomas' five ways can then be understood to spell out rationally the content of this insight.

Whereas Cajetanian Thomists insist on being as conceptualizable, transcendental Thomists stress the knowledge of beings attained in a judgment. They generally favor Thomas' fourth way with its Platonic emphasis. Noting various grades of perfection in beings, Thomas argued that the greatest in any genus is the cause of all others in that genus; hence there is a cause of being, goodness, and other perfections in all beings, which is rightly called God. Transcendental Thomists appeal to the mind's active power of synthesis, manifested in a judgment or question, which goes beyond finite realities affirmed to seek their final ground of intelligibility. Since a question presupposes some knowledge, and no finite object or concept can satisfy the mind's desire to know, this spiritual dynamism can reach fulfillment only in the infinite God, source of all existence and knowing. This appeal to the mind's movement recalls Anselm's argument, but in the Thomistic system reference to a sensible reality is always implied; knowledge involves a conversion to the phantasm, or interior sensible image. Furthermore, the potency-act schema underlying the proof demands an infinite Pure Act, whereas some process theologians, who allow for a finite God, approve of the ontological argument.

The difficulties raised against these intellectual proofs are various. For example, insofar as a potential being is oriented to the plenitude of act, its potentiality must be able to attain fulfillment; otherwise it is frustrated, and no argument can be built upon it; but fulfillment, some argue, implies the abolition of potentiality, the very aspect of the being which distinguished it from the pure act to which it was oriented; hence, the potential being must become one with the pure act, yet the pure act cannot increase by the inclusion of the reality of the potential being. (Many Thomists distinguish *potency* from the *subject* in potency which continues even in fullness of act—yet the exact notion of subject, or person (in human beings), has been a cause of controversy among them.) A similar objection considers the finite-infinite relation: how can a finite mind grasp the infinite? And if the finite is oriented to the Infinite, its potentiality will never be satisfied. Some Protestants note that every proof presupposes the contingency of all finite reality to arrive at God, a necessary being; yet the intellectual starting point had to be indubitable, or necessary, if the argument is to be valid; but how can there be a necessity in contingent reality outside of God? That any finite being, or its intellectual equivalent grasped in a concept or formulated in a principle by a finite mind, be deemed strictly necessary and thereby absolutized seems contradictory. Yet without some absolute, or necessary principle, no thought is possible. This is a variant of the epistemological dilemma that man must trust the correctness of his own finite thought while recognizing that finite thought is forever capable of being surpassed.

In the face of such dilemmas many theists employed more subjective approaches. F. Schleiermacher appealed to man's feeling of utter dependence to put him into contact with God. H. Bergson relied on the intuition given in mystical experience to confirm the existence of the loving God directing evolution. R. Otto postulated a special category of the holy, or the noumenous, by which humans perceive with awe the majestic, energizing *mysterium tremendum* of the Wholly Other. M. Blondel analyzed human willing to show the insufficiency of not willing or of willing the finite absolutely; the human person was called to absolute commitment, and all willing in the finite is carried by the Absolute; precisely because commitment must be concrete and absolute, humans are opened to the concrete universal in history, the God-man, who provides the object of absolute commitment in finite form. Kant made room for a rational belief insofar as the moral person, who performs a duty for duty's sake, often suffers greatly thereby, even though such conduct proves the person most worthy of happiness. God is postulated to provide happiness propor-

tionate to duty. (Another variant of the argument: although duty is performed for itself, a person cannot be indifferent to the outcome of all moral actions, viz., the perfect society, where happiness is proportionate to morality, which only God can effect in the next life.) J.H. Newman delicately dissected moral experience in conscience to reveal both a judgment of reason and a magisterial dictate as well as the consequences, the sense of shame and guilt before a personal Lawgiver or peace, joy, gratitude, and hope.

These positions, while revealing other possible ways of experiencing God, do not resolve the metaphysical difficulties and offer no secure basis for further rational language about God. Indeed Kant's view led to agnosticism when the question arose why God does not join happiness to morality now. A new proof, however, relies on the moral experience to resolve objective metaphysical dilemmas. Presupposing a distinction between good and evil, one may describe the experience of the moral "should" as: 1) absolute, since one's entire life may be demanded in fidelity to the moral imperative and the whole world with all its past, present, and future attractions does not ultimately stand against it; 2) suprarational, since no purely rational argument can persuade anyone to give his life—concepts are but finite instruments of discourse and, no matter how numerous, can never attain the absolute; 3) personal, since it involves not only an intelligent, free subject addressed by the moral demand but also a person for whom the demand is made; indeed one does not surrender one's life for an abstract concept; even "justice" receives its significance from its use by and reference to people; 4) free and liberating, since the "should" is not a "must," as our moral failures testify, and the response to the moral demand relativizes all ties that are not in accord with it. These attributes, combined, indicate that morality is ultimately love. While some may deny the validity of such love, asking how finite man and woman can experience a true absolute, their very criticism presupposed the validity of reason. Yet reason finds itself repeatedly in the basic conundrum of absolute-relative, infinite-finite: without an absolute (infinite), thought is relativized and intellectual consistency dissolves, but the relative (finite) mind of the individual cannot grasp the absolute (infinite). Rather than reject reason as absurd, it is possible to let love justify and ground reason. The structures of love and reason exhibit the same infinite-finite, or absolute-relative, polarities. If love is ultimately reality, the structure of thought can be seen as reflecting the structure of reality. This is truth, the correspondence of mind and reality, and the absolute of adherence, which no finite person can claim for himself or herself, is recognized as the God of love. The relation of divine omnipotence and human freedom (necessity and contingency) is revealed as the center of a metaphysics of freedom since it reproduces the same paradox in the order of love that the absolute-relative relation represents in the realm of rational thought. Furthermore, such a proof, in view of the ambiguities of life that easily question love, opens the individual to divine revelation of love in history.

See **God**

J. McDermott, SJ, "A New Approach to God's Existence," *Thom.* 44 (1980), 219-250; "Zwei Unendlichkeiten bei Thomas von Aquin: Gott und Materie," *ThPh* 61 (1986), 176-181, 186-203. J. Maritain, *Approaches to God,* New York: Harper, 1954. A. Plantinga, *The Ontological Argument,* Garden City: Doubleday, 1965. B. Reichenbach, *The Cosmological Argument: A Reassessment,* Springfield: Thomas, 1972. R. Swinburne, *The Existence of God,* Oxford U.P. 1979.

JOHN M. MCDERMOTT, SJ

PROPHECY

In general, prophecy is a phenomenon that only appears within a society that believes in the supernatural. It is a kind of communication from the world of the supernatural to the world of the human. It presumes that these two worlds are quite distinct and separate from each other and require some kind of intermediary to bring them together. Often it is social upheaval, whether economic, political or religious, which precipitates the human need for contact with and direction from supernatural powers. Prophecy is one way of establishing such contact.

Biblical Evidence

The Hebrew word for prophet, *nābî',* can have both a passive and an active meaning, i.e., "one who has been called" and "one who calls." The former meaning focuses on the personal experience of the prophet, while the latter concentrates on the role the prophet plays in the community. The prophet may well experience some kind of ecstacy or possession by a spirit at the time of contact with the supernatural power (Isa 6:1-8; Ezek chap. 1). However, the prophecy itself must be intelligible and relevant if it is to be received within the world of human beings.

Several different views of prophecy can be found within the traditions of biblical Israel. However, it is clear that one view is dominant. It reflects a northern Israelite perspective, hence it has come to be called the Ephraimite tradition. The major focus of this tradition is a summons to fidelity to the covenant established at Sinai. Its principal figure is Moses the mediator of this covenant. Scholars believe that this tradition originated during the period of the judges and was somehow linked with several of the northern shrines. Its influence is found primarily in the Elohist layer of the Pentateuch, the Deuteronomistic History

(Joshua - Kings), and the prophetic writings of Hosea and Jeremiah.

Southern or Judean traditions, on the other hand, have a distinctly Davidic character and emphasize loyalty to the dynasty and its political and religious institutions. Despite this, they have come down to us with a marked Deuteronomistic, hence Ephraimite, quality to them. They were probably edited sometime in the exilic or postexilic period by someone with a Deuteronomistic bias. Postexilic prophetic material shows evidence of both Ephraimite and Judean influence. All of this may explain the predominance of the Ephraimite view of prophecy found in the biblical literature. This does not necessarily mean that its actual historical role was as significant as its interpretive role. Those who recorded the traditions, and who preferred one view of prophecy over another, often portrayed the prophets according to their own view. The sources of our knowledge of biblical prophecy are not unbiased.

Prophetic Traditions

The northern traditions suggest that visionaries and seers also functioned as intermediaries. Using dreams and visions, or some form of divination (interpretation of omens), they sought to discover hidden information about the past, the present or the future. They seem to have disappeared with the rise of the monarchy and their roles taken over by the prophets.

The southern traditions reflect a later development of prophetic activity and a different use of prophetic titles. Although early prophets, *nĕbî'îm,* were seldom part of the sociopolitical structure, as the monarchy became able to provide some degree of social or religious stability the status and function of many prophets changed. No longer did they express the discontent of their constituents on the fringes of society. Being part of the establishment, they were now called upon to speak in favor of the status quo. Their

former critique of society was replaced by their new support of it. This might explain why the Judean traditions use the term *nābî',* for one who is clearly a part of the institution, while *ḥōzeh* refers to one who received some divine revelation directly through a vision.

Prophetic Types

The Book of Deuteronomy contains a clear Ephraimite condemnation of every means of intermediation but prophecy (Deut 18:10f). The passage continues with a promise of a prophet like Moses who will act as mediator between God and the people (v 15). From this promise developed the characterization of Moses as prophet par excellence and model for all succeeding prophets.

Like Moses, the authentic prophet received the word of God directly rather than through some manipulative technique (Jer 1:4). Further, the true Mosaic prophet neither added to nor subtracted from the message received (Jer 1:7). Finally, following the lead of Moses, the prophet functioned within the context of the covenant, interpreting covenantal law (Hosea 10). Every prophet and every prophetic message were judged against Mosaic traditions.

The picture is quite different in the Judean traditions where the prophetic perspective is more Davidic than Mosaic and the concerns flow from the reality of the monarchy and its stability (e.g., Isaiah) rather than from tribal roots and ancient law (e.g., Hosea).

Some prophets functioned at the heart of the society as significant members of the political or religious establishment. Others belonged to marginal groups and addressed the social scene from a less privileged position. (Both Isaiah and Jeremiah seem to have had access to the king to whom they gave counsel, while Amos was an outsider at the shrine of Bethel where he pronounced judgment on the nations.) Their prophetic messages might call for a radical social change or for one that was moderate and gradual. They might press for a return to traditional values and mores or for a steadfast adherence to the status quo. (Isaiah warned against a foreign alliance [Isa 7]; Jeremiah encouraged capitulation to the Babylonians [Jer 38]; Nahum directed his attack against Nineveh, Israel's ancient enemy.) The social context out of which and the religious needs to which the prophet spoke shaped the message that was spoken. The word of prophecy was always a response to a specific situation.

Prophetic Word

Despite the differences in prophetic traditions, the biblical evidence is quite consistent about the origin of prophecy. Its source is to be found in divine revelation (Hos 1:1; Amos 1:1; Isa 1:1; Mic 1:1; Jer 1:2; Ezek 1:3; etc.). The prophets may have been approached by people who were seeking some kind of communication from God, or they themselves may have initiated the appeal, but the prophecy was the word of God and came at God's discretion. It could not be forced and it was not to be distorted.

The prophetic word was always relevant to the historical moment of proclamation. Since it was born out of religious or political crisis, its purpose was to speak to that crisis. It clung to the past to the extent that it was in continuity with the fundamental religious traditions. It predicted the future to the extent that that future would be the consequence of the present. The primary intent of prophecy was to call the people to fidelity to their religious responsibilities here and now.

Most prophecies were either oracles of lament and doom or oracles of promise and salvation. However, the prophets also employed forms that were associated with specific areas in the life of the community. Their legal, wisdom or cultic style may be an indication of their royal,

sapiential or priestly associations, or it may simply mean that such language or expression was part of the common literary stock of the community.

The prophet was embraced by the people when the word of God was comforting and a promise of better things (Isa 40). But when it accused them of infidelity or injustice, when it challenged the very structures of society, the prophet became the object of their wrath (Jer 20). Misunderstanding, rejection, even persecution were the consequences of faithfully proclaiming a revelation from God that the people did not want to hear.

Perhaps the greatest challenge for any community addressed by a prophet figure was to determine the authenticity and reliability of the prophecy. Given the variety of prophetic traditions and conflicting religious and political loyalties, it was difficult to distinguish true prophecy from false prophecy. (The conflict between Jeremiah and Hananiah illustrates this [Jer 27-28]). Different criteria for judging the validity of the message have been advanced: true prophecy never raised false hopes; it always insisted on fidelity to covenantal commitments; its predictions came to pass. The most important criterion was perhaps the most difficult to recognize: true prophecy accurately interpreted the historical moment. Ultimately, there was no way of being certain of the authenticity of any specific prophecy.

The Early Church

The prophetic hopes of "a new heaven and a new earth" (Isa 65:17; 66:22), "a new covenant" (Jer 31:31), and "a new heart" and "new spirit" (Ezek 36:26-27) were founded on a firm conviction of the compassionate love that God bore the people. Moved by divine inspiration, the prophets pointed to a future where these hopes would be fulfilled despite the obstacle that human infidelity placed in the path of fulfillment. Prophecy in the christian tradition must be seen from this perspective.

Jesus was thought to be a prophet (Lk 24:19) and his suffering and death the fulfillment of prophecy (Lk 24:25-27). In fact, the early Christians took great pains to show that most of the major prophetic traditions of Israel were brought to completion in Jesus.

Within the early church, prophecy performed the function of teaching. Since the ultimate revelation was believed to have come in the person and teachings of Jesus, christian prophecy was seen as inspired insight into the "secret and hidden wisdom of God" contained within that revelation (Rom 2:7-13). Ancient Israelite tradition was interpreted in light of the event of Christ and utterances were considered prophetic if they showed an understanding of the mysteries of that event (1 Cor 13:2). Early christian prophecy focused more on understanding Christ than on dealing with broader social reality. It served to establish a firm christian identity so that the challenges of a changing world might be met with a steadfast commitment to the essence of the religious tradition.

Joseph Blenkinsopp, *A History of Prophecy in Israel,* Philadelphia: Westminster, 1978. Walter Brueggemann, *Prophetic Imagination,* Philadelphia: Fortress Press, 1982. Klaus Koch, *The Prophets,* vol. 2, Philadelphia: Fortress Press, 1982. Robert R. Wilson, *Prophecy and Society in Ancient Israel,* Philadelphia: Fortress Press, 1980.

DIANNE BERGANT, CSA

PROSOPON
See **Person**

PROTESTANTISM

The title "Protestant" is used to designate those churches and ecclesial communions of the West that have their origin in the sixteenth-century Reforma-
tion. While the date 1517, and the posting of Martin Luther's ninety-five theses on indulgences on the castle church door in Wittenberg are often given as the start of the Reformation, the division that gave rise to Western churches not in communion with Rome preceded that date by over a century There are several Protestant communities, Waldensian and Moravian, for example, that trace their history to pre-Reformation movements. In these cases, Peter Waldo (d. 1217) and Jan Hus (c. 1396-1415), are counted as founders of these movements-become-churches respectively. Certain biblical, anti-ecclesiastical movements, such as those of John Wycliffe (c. 1329-84) and William Tyndale (1494?-1536) in England laid the groundwork for what would become a massive biblical awakening among dissenting groups in Europe.

Renewal movements in piety and among the laity, like the *devotio moderna* and the Brothers of the Common Life (14th c.) as well as the increasing independence of certain local and national churches like those of Spain, France, England, Austria and Bavaria created a certain ecclesial pluralism relative to the role of the pope and papal influence. The theological pluralism of the century preceding the Reformation, with strong Scotist, Nominalist and Thomist schools in dialogue with a traditional Augustinism created a theological pluralism which some modern theologians in Catholic circles prefer to speak of as a theological confusion. It is difficult to find any of the theological theories espoused by the Reformers that did not have roots in theological thinkers who died in full communion with the Holy See.

The level of theological sophistication of the clergy, where there were parishes with resident clergy, left much to be desired. Clerical discipline, even at the level of bishops and the Roman Curia was much in need of reform, as was freely admitted by the reforming cardinals of the Curia. The Avignon Papacy (1309-1377) left the papal institution in poor reputation, and the influence of the authentic Petrine ministry was obscured by the corruption of the papal court. The proximate cause of Luther's doctrinal reform was the preaching of the indulgence, the proceeds of which were to finance the construction of St. Peter's Basilica in Rome. This indulgence was not allowed to be preached and collected for in many places in Europe, including Luther's own Saxon state. However, Luther, an Augustinian monk, prior of his community, and scripture scholar in the University, responding to the pastoral problems encountered in his confessional, launched what he intended to be a discussion among scholars on the propriety of the manner in which indulgences were being "sold" and the grace of the sacraments, particularly confession, was being preached. The intention of a discreet academic dialogue broke down when the theses were translated into popular German and used as a pamphlet, and when the bishop, Albert of Brandenburg (1490-1545), involved Rome in the discussions.

The debates escalated in Germany and between German scholars, and princes, and Rome between 1517 and 1530 so that by that time there seemed to be little hope of healing the breach. The principal doctrine which was at the root of the concern of Luther and his Evangelical followers was God's free justification of the sinner by grace through faith, without reference to works of the law or merit on the part of the believer. In the judgment of the Evangelical reformers, the sacramental system, the monastic life and works of piety, as well as reliance on the authority of the papacy and the granting of indulgences were all calculated to place too much emphasis on human effort in the face of the free grace of God.

While there were attempts throughout this period to both reconcile the two disputing parties and to silence the dissent, the Roman Catholic position was only clarified at the Council of Trent (1545-63). By that time many of the abuses against which Luther protested were rectified, and a better formulation of Catholic doctrine on justification, grace, sacraments, the role of scripture and the pastoral duties of the bishop were put into place. Although the Roman Catholic reformation, or Counter-Reformation, took several decades to launch and several centuries to complete, it brought to the church a clarity and discipline unknown to the Reformers.

Very soon after the news of Luther's protest became known, the Swiss reformer Ulrich Zwingli (1484-1531) began to preach and eventually to exert leadership in Zurich. While Luther's reforms insisted on continuity with the medieval faith, Zwingli brought a more critical renaissance mind to the reforming task. The differences between Luther and the Swiss Reformer were sharpest in their understanding of Christ's presence in the Lord's Supper. While Luther was critical of the Roman Mass, and particularly of the theological and pastoral abuses of his time, he insisted on a strong theology of the real presence and of the centrality of word and sacrament in the life of the church. Zwingli affirmed a spiritual and symbolic presence in the eucharist. After the Marburg discussion of 1529 there was a parting of the ways between the Evangelicals (Lutherans) and those who would come to be called Reformed.

While Zwingli was killed in battle soon thereafter, the Swiss Reformation was continued under the leadership of Geneva, with John Calvin (1509-64) as its chief theologian and architect of church order. While Luther left the ordering of the church, once it was clear that the episcopacy in Germany would not be with his reforms, to the secular princes,

Calvin worked very closely with the laity to establish structures of collegiality which provided for full participation of clergy and laity in an ordered approach to church and civil government.

Calvin's theology, with its emphasis on the sovereignty of God, carried the doctrine of justification to its logical Augustinian conclusion in predestination. The Calvinist Reformation became the established religion in Scotland under the leadership of John Knox (c. 1513-72) and in Holland. Luther's Evangelical theology eventually became the established faith of northern Germany and Scandinavia, with the episcopal form of church order prevailing throughout Scandinavia, and the Swedes maintain to this day the continuity of the historic episcopate from the ancient church.

The Church of England, the mother Church of the Anglican Communion, does not consider itself Protestant, properly speaking. However, its schism with Rome dates from the Reformation period and its theology was influenced, in part, by the Reformers from the continent. While the Elizabethan settlement (1559) was not intended to set a course outside of communion with Rome, the action of the Holy See finalized the break. While the criticisms of the papacy in the Church of England, and especially among the continental Reformers, were never answered formally in the Council of Trent, gradual Roman reforms began to bring the papacy back into a leadership and eventual reforming role within those churches remaining in communion with it.

Indeed, by the First Council of the Vatican (1870) the role of the papacy and its esteem were so developed that the scope and role of the exercise of infallibility by the pope on behalf of the Church universal could be so limited that Reformation critiques, enshrined in the Lutheran Confessions for example, were

no longer applicable. Further developments in the theology of the church, enunciated in the Second Vatican Council (1961-65), have set the papacy into a much wider ecclesiological context so that many of the reforms envisioned by the Protestant and Anglican reformers may now be realizable.

In addition to the Evangelical (Lutheran), Reformed (Calvinist), and Anglican traditions to emerge from the sixteenth century, there were also the multiple movements often grouped under the title "radical" or left wing Reformation. These movements are most clearly associated with those groups claiming a separated existence from the state churches, Protestant and Catholic, calling for baptism of adult believers alone (Anabaptists), and resisting compromise with the ethics of the state on behalf of the ethical call to purity, the ethics of the Kingdom. The most notable surviving community of these often persecuted groups is the Mennonites, with their various strains, including the Amish, the observers of strict separation and simplicity of life. The theologian of this group of churches is Menno Simon, from whom they derive their name.

Sixteenth-century Protestantism, after reconciliation within the Catholic communion became impossible, and Catholicism, turning to its own internal renewal in the Counter-Reformation, both gave themselves over to a period of orthodox formulation and consolidation of their church life within state supported religion. Except for the radical reformers and the dissenting Calvinist Puritans in England, the majority of European Christians continued to take the traditional relations of the church and state for granted, including persecution of those of other confessions.

The concerns for doctrinal purity and polemic against the other, be they Protestant or Catholic, continued through the seventeenth and eighteenth centuries. New religious movements and orders within Catholicism and pietistic and missionary developments within Protestantism brought parallel renewal within the divided faith families of the West.

The earliest Protestant settlers in the Americas brought with them a desire to be free of the religious pressures and persecutions of Europe. Puritans in New England, Scotch-Irish Presbyterians in the Middle Atlantic colonies, Quakers in Pennsylvania, and many without a high religious commitment became the core of Protestant America. The Anglican revival movement under the leadership of John and Charles Wesley (1703-91, 1707-88) provided a style of piety, leadership and mission particularly well suited to the colonies and eventually the frontier. Due to the unwillingness of the Bishop of London to provide proper Anglican ordination for John Wesley's missionaries, American Methodists evolved from a missionary movement into a church (1784).

In New England, where the dissident English Puritans had established themselves in their own form of state church after 1620, various dissenters eventually appeared. Of these, the Baptists, led by Roger Williams (1604-1683), developed an understanding of gathered local church, with covenanted adult believers, affirming separation of church from state and freedom of conscience under the scripture. In the colony that came to be called Pennsylvania, under the leadership of William Penn (1644-1718), the Quakers came to take a particularly important role. The Quakers, because of their special devotion to the Holy Spirit, disavowing any formal or sacramental worship, or any clergy, had been generally persecuted in England and the other colonies.

Because of their reliance on lay leadership, revivalism throughout the eighteenth and nineteenth century, and a simplified theology without great demands on clergy formation, Methodists and Baptists have become the predominant Protestant forms in the United States. World-wide Anglicanism and Lutheranism would be the largest Protestant communions. Due to the civil tensions and eventual war in the United States, Methodists, Baptists, Presbyterians divided along North-South political lines. In the twentieth century the Methodist and Presbyterians have reunited, though there are many smaller Wesleyan and Holiness bodies who owe their origin to these nineteenth-century controversies.

While there have been Lutherans in the United States since colonial times, the influx of immigrants in the late nineteenth and early twentieth century swelled Lutheran ranks as it did those of the Catholic Church. The nineteenth century showed a great rise in Protestant energy in the United States. In addition to the classical churches of the Reformation (the indigenous Methodist, Baptist and Holiness communions) the Christian Churches, now represented by the Churches of Christ and Disciples of Christ, were formed to unite divided Protestant Christians and restore NT Christianity. The Pentecostal Churches, the fastest growing communities in the world today, owe their origins to the 1906 Azusa Street revival (Los Angeles).

The nineteenth century saw strong Protestant collaboration in mission, evangelism, religious education, philanthropic service and social concern. As deep as were the divisions over slavery in the mid-nineteenth century, so did divisions over biblical interpretation become among early twentieth-century American Protestants. The extremes of these differences show themselves as Fundamentalism and Modernism, though between these two poles are a host of polarizing positions. In 1908 the traditional Protestant Churches, sometimes called mainline or liberal, formed an ecumenical body, the Federal Council of Churches. The conservative churches, and conservative to fundamental members within the traditional churches, formed the National Association of Evangelicals in 1943. In 1950 the Orthodox and Lutheran Churches, and many cooperative Protestant agencies joined with the Federal Council to form the National Council of Churches of Christ in the United States.

Since the Decree on Ecumenism of the Second Vatican Council, Roman Catholics view themselves as in real, but imperfect, communion with these separated Christians of the West. The task Catholicism puts before itself relative to these sisters and brothers is: 1) inner renewal so as to become more faithful to the evangelical witness of the gospel, 2) to engage in dialogue for the purpose of restoring full communion with these churches, and 3) to work in common mission and witness in the world. Liturgical, social justice and biblical renewal are all related intimately to christian insights shared from the Reformation churches.

In the United States the National Conference of Catholic Bishops, through its Committee on Ecumenical and Interreligious Affairs, is in dialogue with five Protestant Church traditions: Lutheran, Episcopal (Anglican), Methodist, Baptist, Presbyterian/Reformed. Through the Commission on Faith and Order of the National Council of Churches, it is in dialogue with Moravian, Anabaptist, Pentecostal, Holiness, and other groups. The Vatican Secretariate for Promoting Christian Unity is in dialogue with the same worldwide families, in addition to Pentecostals, Disciples of Christ/Christian Church, and Conservative Evangelicals. The Secretariate also relates to the churches of the World Council of Churches through its Commission of Faith and Order and many other units of that council. While the goals of each of these dialogues is different depending on the ecclesiological self-understandings of the partners, the Catholic Church is committed to deepening the communion that already exists, and overcoming the historical barriers of theology and church order that separate us from full union in Christ.

In the few years that have elapsed since the Council, remarkable achievements have already been attained by the theologians at work on behalf of the church. Statements on such diverse areas as justification by faith, baptism, eucharist, ordained ministry, papal primacy, infallibility, scripture, marriage, tradition and a host of pastoral and ethical issues have been presented to the churches for their response, reception and action. The pastoral implementation and ecclesial reception of these results is now before the Catholic Church in an unprecedented way.

Paul Minus, *The Catholic Rediscovery of Protestantism*, Paulist, 1967. Peter Manns, *Martin Luther*, Crossroads, 1983. Arthur Carl Piepkorn, *Profiles in Belief*, Harper and Row, 1977. Jaroslav Pelikan, *The Christian Tradition: A History of the Development of Doctrine*, vol. 4, Reformation of Church and Dogma, U. of Chicago, 1984. Q. Lucas Visher and Harding Meyer, *Growth in Agreement: Statements of Ecumenical Conversations on a World Level*, Paulist, 1982.

JEFFREY GROS, FSC

PROVIDENCE

Providence means literally "foresight," and when used of God means, in the most general sense, the divine care of the world, God's guidance of history and human affairs toward the achievement of his purpose. The English word "providence" translates the Latin *providentia* and the Greek *pronoia*. The term itself is not strictly biblical, but was a technical expression of Stoic and Neo-Platonic philosophy used to designate the rule of divine reason or *logos* over all events.

However, it does occur in the deutero-canonical Book of the Wisdom of Solomon (14:2; 17:2), written in Greek and manifesting some influence from Greek philosophy. It came thus to be defined as "the divine plan of the order of things to the end according to which God governs the world."

Although the term "providence" is not itself biblical, the idea of a wise, loving and powerful God who is everywhere at work in the world pervades the entire Bible. It is found in the story of creation (Gen 1-2), underlies the whole history of Israel, from the call and election of Abraham and his offspring (Gen 12:1-3), through the events of the Exodus (Ex 10:1-3 etc.) and the giving of the Covenant (Ex 24:1-8), the establishment of the monarchy (1 Sam 9:16), to the Babylonian exile (2 Kgs 23:27) and the return (Jer 29:10). In the teaching of Jesus, God is our Father who cares for us (Mt 10:29-31), answers our prayers (Lk 11:9-13), forgives us our sins if we forgive one another (Mt 6:14-15), asks us to live as his children (Mt 5:16), and calls us to eternal life (Jn 6:40). But for the NT, the greatest expression of God's love and concern is the sending of his Son Jesus as our redeemer (Jn 3:16; Rom 8:3-4).

In Stoic and Neo-Platonic philosophy, the doctrine of providence emphasized the power and wisdom of God rather than the motivation or purpose that inspired God to act. Thus it differed from the biblical teaching by focusing on power rather than on love, on an impersonal force rather than on personal care and concern. Frequently enough, they viewed creation as a necessary emanation of God. Early christian writers took over the term "providence" to express the biblical sense of God's fatherly love and care. For example, around 181 A.D. Theophilus of Antioch wrote: "If I call God Providence, I refer only to his goodness" (*To Autolycus* 1, 3). But grad-ually it came to have connotations deriving from its use in Stoicism, and to emphasize a plan executed by the power of God, rather than God's loving care and concern. This Stoic influence brought with it two main problems: the problem of human freedom and the problem of evil.

The tendency toward a Stoicized view of providence came to forceful expression in St. Augustine (354—430). In *The City of God* (C.G. 413—426), written to explain the fall of the Roman Empire, St. Augustine asserts: "Divine Providence alone explains the establishment of human kingdoms. Those who speak of fate, but mean by fate the will and power of God, should keep their conception but change their expression" (C.G. 5, 1). Later he cites the Stoic poet Seneca: "Fate leads the willing and drags the unwilling on." He explains that "fate" means the will of "the Father and Lord of the World," and adds his agreement with the verse understood in this way (C.G. 8). He acknowledges the necessity that this lays upon human activity, but seeks to avoid a denial of human freedom: "We who profess belief in the supreme and true God confess, likewise, his will, his supreme power, his foreknowledge. Nor are we dismayed by the difficulty that what we choose to do freely is done of necessity, because he whose foreknowledge cannot be deceived foreknew that we would choose to do it" (C.G. 9).

St. Augustine viewed all suffering in the world as a result of human sin. This led him to place a hitherto unheard of emphasis on the fall of Adam and Eve. By their sin the whole human race became a *"massa in radice damnata,"* a lump of clay damned in its root. From this lump God mercifully chooses to make some vessels destined for eternal life, the rest he justly lets go to eternal damnation (*Admonition and Grace* 7, 16). Augustine even speaks of God predestining some to eternal death simply on account of original sin (*The Soul and Its Origin* 4, 11, 16). However, God is so powerful that he would never let evil enter creation if he were not able to draw good from it (*Enchiridion of Faith, Hope and Love* 11), at least the manifestation of his justice.

All this compelled Augustine to reinterpret the teaching that God wills to save everyone (1 Tim 2:4). He said it means either that God wills to save all those who are saved, or that God wills to save some from every class of human beings, but not that he truly wills the salvation of each human being; for being all powerful, the will of God always accomplishes what he truly wills (*Enchiridion* 27).

The root difficulty many have with Augustine's view of providence is that, for him as for the Stoics, God's action is ultimately understood as irresistible power. It is not that he doubts the love of God, but that love operates only within a sphere established by power, rather than the other way around. A favorite quotation of Augustine is: "Whatever the Lord pleases he does in heaven and on earth" (Ps 135:6; see *Admonition* 14,45). Within this context of power everything else must be given meaning.

However, St. John Damascene (c. 645—c. 749) suggested another way of conceiving the providence of God, one more in keeping with the biblical view, when he distinguishes between the antecedent and the consequent will of God (*The Orthodox Faith* 2, 29). The antecedent will intends and makes possible salvation for everyone; the consequent will condemns those who remain unrepentant. This enables us to speak of an antecedent and a consequent plan of God's providence. The antecedent plan provides for all the possibilities of the world. It includes what God wants to happen as well as what he is willing to let happen in view of human freedom. It includes the total initiative of divine grace. It determines how each event can somehow be made to further his love, if only humans are willing. The consequent plan is that aspect of the antecedent plan which God actually puts into execution in view of human free choices. It contains God's response to human freedom by divine judgment, and includes rewards and punishments.

This conceives the full plan of God's providence as a kind of "contingency planning." God has indeed a purpose that cannot fail: the communication of his goodness in eternal life to a society of created persons, the heavenly Jerusalem. His plan to achieve this purpose provides means that in the whole human race cannot fail: the light and attraction of grace, which, however, do not coerce or necessitate any individual's choice. For just as God provides infallibly that the whole human race not die of hunger (though some may freely choose to starve to death), by giving both the desire for food and the abundance of the earth, so he provides that the City of God be built (though some may freely choose to exclude themselves) both by inspiring the human heart with love and light, and by providing situations in which choice is to be exercised. There is a basic infallibility in this plan prior to any particular exercise of free choice, though the actual membership of the City of God is not thereby determined. All are welcome; no one is antecedently excluded, and some will certainly respond positively, as in the case of hunger for food.

Thomas Aquinas (1225—1274) spoke of providence as the order of the world to its end as this order pre-exists in the mind of God causing it (S.Th. 1, 22, 1). He too presupposed "contingency planning" in his understanding of this order. For when he advanced his reason for affirming that the will of God is always accomplished he did not argue from the omnipotence of God, as Augustine had, but from the universality of the divine will: "Since, then, the will of God is the universal cause of all things, it is impossible that the divine will not achieve its effect. Hence, what seems to depart from the divine will according to one order, falls back into it according to another; as a sinner, who as far as in him lies, departs from the divine will by sinning, falls back into the order of the divine will by being punished through God's justice" (S.Th. 1, 19, 6). This reference to different "orders" of the divine will points to the many varied possibilities opened up by the antecedent plan of divine providence for human choice. For each of these choices God has a response in keeping with his gracious purpose.

For Thomas (in contrast to Augustine), infallible divine knowledge does not lay necessity on human choice, since God does not *foresee* what is to happen as something future to him, but as transcendent *sees* all things in their presentiality, though they may be future to us who exist in time. Knowledge of what is present can be infallibly certain without imposing necessity on what is known, as can be seen even in human knowing (S.Th. 1, 14, 13).

Thomas basically accepted Augustine's solution to the problem of evil (S. Th. 1, 48, 5). However, recent thinkers have been reluctant to see *all* human suffering as a consequence of sin, whether original sin or the personal sin of oneself or another. Natural disasters seem quite unrelated to human sinfulness, and seem rather part of the very structure of a world that operates through statistical laws to make possible the emergence and the exercise of human freedom. We should say rather that some things happen which God does not directly intend (though he intends their possibility in willing to make a universe where emergent freedom is a reality), whether these be sins and

their effects or natural contingent events, and that God is present in them as in every other situation to draw good from them, if only we are willing: "We know that in everything God works for good with those who love him" (Rom 8:28).

See **Freedom**

Eric Fuchs, "Providence and Politics: A Reflection on the Contemporary Relevance of the Political Ethics of John Calvin," *Louvain Studies* (1985, no. 3) 10: 231-43. Mary Ann Fatula, "Trusting in the Providence of God," *Review for Religious* (Jan-Feb 1985) 14: 26-32. Terrence Tilley, "The Use and Abuse of Theology," *Horizons* (Fall 1984) 11: 304-19. Thomas Bernnard, "God's Providence and Human Politics," *Bible Today* (Jul 1985) 21: 248-51. James Walsh and P. G. Walsh, *Divine Providence and Human Suffering* (Wilmington, Del: M. Glazier, 1985).

JOHN H. WRIGHT, SJ

PSYCHOLOGY

The turn to the human subject in contemporary theology has led to increasing dialogue between theology and psychology. Psychology for its part as the study of human behavior and experience has concerned itself recently with more nuanced interpretations of the religious subject and the diversity of religious experience. In fact, the field of psychology and religion of which the dialogue between theology and psychology is a subset is emerging as a promising area of scholarship. Awareness of the pluralism of modern society suggests that one perhaps speak more appropriately of theologies rather than theology and likewise psychologies rather than psychology. Psychologies range from strictly empirical studies based on carefully constructed research instruments and statistical analyses to the dynamic or depth interpretations of human experience and motivation emerging from clinical work and the application of various psychodynamic principles. In what follows, the field of psychology and religion will be surveyed with the goal of underlining the significant ways in which psychology has interacted with religion and theology. A growing convergence of certain psychological and theological perspectives on the human person will be seen to point in the direction of future fruitful collaboration and interdisciplinary work.

In the opening decades of this century psychologists in the United States began to apply their principles to religious experience and so gave birth to the psychology of religion. In an intellectual climate where the explanatory power of science was being applied to one area after another, early pioneers tried to make psychological sense of religious phenomena such as conversions and mysticism. These pioneers, representatives of a psychology which studied personal and social adaptation and adjustment were by and large sympathetic to religion and were curious as to how religion functioned in individual lives and how psychology might contribute to more effective religious education.

G. Stanley Hall (1846-1924) at Clark University was a major motivating force in the early days of the movement. His study of adolescence included the role of religion in adolescence and noted the phenomenon of conversion at that life stage. Edwin Diller Starbuck (1866-1947) expanded on Hall's work and produced a classic study of conversion based on information gathered through questionnaires (*The Psychology of Religion: An Empirical Study of the Growth of Religious Consciousness,* New York Scribner's, 1899). His goal was to see into the laws and processes of religious development. In addition to his efforts at a psychological description of religious phenomena, he worked at a psychologically-informed approach to religious education and character education. Like Starbuck, George Albert Coe (1862-1951) shared an abiding interest in both religious education and the psychology of religion (*The Psychology of Religion.* Chicago: Univ. of Chicago Press, 1916). While Coe recognized the value of psychological study of the part processes (e.g., perception, intellection, emotion, etc.) which make up a complex religious experience, he also noted the "something more" present in religious experience which was not simply the sum total of the parts. His attention to religious phenomena was wide-ranging and included probing explorations of the psychology of prayer.

The most notable of the early pioneers is William James (1842-1910) whose classic *The Varieties of Religious Experience* (Gifford Lectures 1901-1902) embodies a spirit of inquiry often overlooked in subsequent years but of perennial value. For James believing was a viable option which made easy and felicitous what was in any case necessary. As he explored diverse religious phenomena, his concern was to draw attention to the fruits of religion, the good results it brought to countless people. His method in studying religion was predominantly experiential and biographical. The typology of religious experience which he presented was simply a pointer to the tremendous variety in religious experience. He contrasted the religious experience of the "healthy-minded" whose religious growth was a gradual process with that of the sick souls who needed to be born again through a conversion experience. James noted that in conversion previously peripheral ideas move to center stage within the stream of consciousness. These ideas then constitute a "hot place" in consciousness, a new center of energy, and they provide a new framework for organizing a multitude of experiences.

Unfortunately the openness of James to the richness of religious phenomena was not matched by the following generation of psychologists who were concerned more with controlled observation and replication. Thus, after a promising start, the psychology of religion in America went into a marked decline until fairly recent times. The pioneer period was not without some major limitations inasmuch as it focused almost exclusively on individual religious experience, in particular, on mysticism and conversion, and neglected the corporate dimensions of religious life. Contemporary efforts which match James's spirit of openness allow for the multidimensionality of religion.

On the continent, Sigmund Freud (1856-1939) began to apply the principles of his new science of psychoanalysis in interpreting religious phenomena. Whereas James and other pioneers had concerned themselves with the fruits of religion, Freud was interested in the origins of religion and religious ideas. In what would be in effect a programmatic essay, "Obsessive Actions and Religious Practices" (1907), Freud suggested that religious rituals were ultimately grounded in unperceived motives and desires. He sometimes approached religious ideas as illusions springing from the infantile desires of the believer for protection from the harshness of reality. But Freud really saw them as delusions and as pathological. Religion represented a transitional stage that humanity was passing though on its way to full maturity. His approach to religious phenomena was reductionistic. The notion of God had its roots in the young boy's experience with his natural father and humanity's experience with a primal tyrant who was both loved and feared. Although Freud's formulations were correctly perceived as hostile to religion, contemporary psychology of religion builds on some of his formulations and sees them as helpful in purging religious practice of idolatry.

In line with Freud's focus on what lies beneath the surface of a person's psycho-

logical makeup, the dynamic unconscious, Anton Boisen (1876-1965), founder of the clinical pastoral education movement, began to focus on the integrative function of religion (*The Exploration of the Inner World,* Chicago: Willet, Clark, & Co., 1936). Out of his personal experience of psychotic breaks, Boisen learned that severe mental illness represented the breakdown of a worldview and an experience of profound alienation for which religion offered the possibility of reconstruction and reconciliation. His study of living human documents, detailed case histories, continues to influence the pastoral counseling movement and the contemporary approach to the psychology of religion. In his thinking Boisen was guided in part by the psychology of Carl Gustav Jung (1875-1961) who saw religion as beneficial to humanity because of its symbol system which kept humanity in touch with the unconscious (*Modern Man in Search of a Soul,* New York: Harcourt, Brace & World, 1933). Jung detailed a process of individuation which occurred in adulthood and led a person to befriend the unconscious and discover the true self. For Jung Christ was a symbol of this full self and the passion of Jesus a model of the individuation process.

The work of Erik H. Erikson (1902-) and others has further rejuvenated the psychoanalytic psychology of religion and made it a more suitable dialogue partner for theology. Erikson's *Young Man Luther: A Study in Psychoanalysis and History* (New York: Norton, 1958) is a landmark in the history of the psychology of religion. In it Erikson applied his theory of psychosocial development to a major religious figure and noted how a religious person comes to discover who he or she is in the light of a transcendent Other. Building on Freud's theory of psychosexual development, Erikson described the psychosocial crises people typically face as they live out their life course and interact with an expanding social milieu. In the very first of these crises, the crisis in infancy, the individual is introduced through the hands of a benevolent caretaker to an experience of the sacred. Erikson's theory sees the value of religion in framing various crises individuals face and in ultimately guiding the search for relatedness to its transcendent end.

Positive appreciation for religion's role in life came also from a number of humanistic psychologies (Allport, Maslow, Rogers). Gordon Allport (1897-1967) wrote in some detail about a religious sentiment and differentiated immature religion which he saw as magical, wish-fulfilling, and self-centered from a mature religion that was dynamic and critical (*The Individual and His Religion,* New York: Macmillan, 1950). His typology of religion as extrinsic (immature) and intrinsic (mature) has generated a sizeable body of empirical research in which the types of religion were correlated with various attitudes such as prejudice. Abraham Maslow (1908-1970) studied self-actualizing people and the "peak-experiences" which they enjoyed. For him peak-experience, which he identified with mystical experience, was the primary element in religion. Through such experience one gained a vision of transcendent reality.

In the 1960's renewed interest in the psychology of religion led to the appearance of works which are more comprehensive treatments of religious phenomena. Erwin Goodenough (1893-1965) noted that William James had really studied only the varieties of *Protestant* religious experience. Goodenough's work (*The Psychology of Religious Experiences,* New York: Basic Books, 1965), extends the typology of religious experience in a truly ecumenical direction. Included in his range of types of religious experience are: legalism, supralegalism, orthodoxy, supraorthodoxy, aestheticism, symbolism, sacramentalism, church, conversion, and mysticism. Paul W. Pruyser, who continues to write on the psychology of religion (*A Dynamic Psychology of Religion,* New York: Harper & Row, 1968; and "Forms and Functions of the Imagination in Religion," *Bulletin of the Menninger Clinic,* 49 (1985), 353-370), takes some different tacks in the psychological understanding of religious phenomena in his works. Unlike other writers who organized their studies around central religious categories such as prayer, mysticism, and conversion, Pruyser uses properly psychological categories. This gives his work a perspectival integrity where the perspective of religion or theology on religious phenomena is not confused with a psychological perspective on the same material. Pruyser addresses a set of psychological items found in religion such as perceptual, intellectual, and emotional processes, linguistic functions, thought organization, and relations to self, persons, and things.

Pruyser would also be ranked with those who are currently involved in a new phase in the psychoanalytic psychology of religion (Meissner, Rizzuto, McDargh) which is based on recent developments within psychoanalysis itself. This new phase follows the leads of object relations theorists within psychoanalysis who put primary emphasis on the human need for relatedness rather than the older Freudian emphasis on drive satisfaction. In particular, the formulations of D.W. Winnicott (*Playing and Reality,* London: Tavistock, 1971) have led to a reevaluation of the place and value of illusion in human development and provided a conceptual framework for studying and interpreting the products of the religious imagination and locating religious experience psychically. This new approach has already increased the understanding of narcissistic distortions in religious imagery. It provides a nuanced interpretation of religious phenomena and should prove an engaging partner in the dialogue with theology. Future work from this psychoanalytic perspective will entail a further specification of how the religious imagination is tutored to imagine properly about transcendent reality.

Complementing this new psychoanalytic work are some ongoing research projects on moral development (Lawrence Kohlberg, "Education for Justice: A Modern Statement of the Platonic View," in *Moral Education: Five Lectures,* Cambridge: Harvard U.P., 1970, p. 57-83; and Carol Gilligan, *In a Different Voice: Psychological Theory and Women's Development,* Cambridge: Harvard U.P., 1982) and faith development (James W. Fowler, *Stages of Faith: The Psychology of Human Development and the Quest for Meaning,* San Francisco: Harper & Row, 1981; and Lucy Bregman, *Through the Landscape of Faith,* Philadelphia: Westminster, 1986). This research has been influenced by Jean Piaget's understanding of cognitive development (genetic epistemology) and attempts to uncover fairly predictable turning points in the evolution of moral decision-making and of faith's imaging of the ultimate environment which surrounds humanity. Other continuing contributions to the understanding of religious phenomena are coming from the areas of social psychology of religion (Michael Argyle and Benjamin Beit-Hallahmi, *The Social Psychology of Religion,* London: Routledge & Kegan Paul, 1975) and family systems theory (Edwin H. Friedman, *Generation to Generation: Family Process in Church and Synagogue,* New York: Guilford, 1985). Both areas suggest interpretations of religious phenomena which take into account the social context and changing relationships within religious groups.

This review of the psychology of religion sets in relief the fact that there are really diverse psychologies of religion. Each represents an attempt to dissect religious phenomena with the conceptual tools of a particular psychological theory. The aims and motivation which sustain psychologists of religion in their quest for understanding would be quite various. Sometimes the motives have been hostile to religion. But, even when positive motives had been at work, the invasion of the sacred domain by a secular psychologist was not always regarded kindly by religionists. The varying attitudes of professional religionists to psychology and the psychology of religion in particular become clearer as the various theological uses of psychology and the dialogue between theology and psychology are briefly considered.

The attitudes of theologians to the contributions of psychology can be divided into two basic sets of concerns (John McDargh. "Theological Uses of Psychology; Retrospective and Prospective," Horizons, 12 (1985), 247-264). The first of these sets especially characterizes Catholic reactions to psychology and centered around a fear that psychology would undercut the dignity of the human person and obscure, if not conceptually eliminate, the human person's fundamental orientation to the transcendent. At issue here were often two divergent images of the human person, one emerging out of a theological anthropology emphasizing human freedom and graced existence and the other the product of scientific formulation emphasizing determinism and reductionism (as in Freudian psychoanalysis). An additional problem in Catholic circles was the commitment to a neo-scholastic faculty psychology. The development of a more nuanced psychology which goes beyond determinism and reductionism and a growing openness on the part of theology to psychology's power to help illuminate the human situation has removed a certain amount of fear and set up the conditions for dialogue between Catholic theology and psychology.

The second set of concerns more characteristic of Protestant reactions to psychology focused on the possible diminishment of the divine and elimination of any discontinuity between the sacred and human orders. These concerns were of varying intensity in line with the relative liberalism or conservatism of different theologians. Although one cannot speak of any uniform openness developing in the different theological positions, some dialogue with psychology has been initiated along with appropriation of some psychological interpretation of the current cultural situation. In fact, Peter Homans, a major spokesperson for the dialogue, issued a call for a psychology which would provide interpretation of contemporary images of the transcendent, which is precisely the psychology of religion emerging in psychoanalytic circles (*Theology after Freud,* Indianapolis: Bobbs-Merrill, 1970).

A general use of psychology and the psychology of religion has occurred in much pastoral counseling across denominational lines. Likewise spiritual direction and religious education are often informed by developmental models drawn from psychology. Recently David Tracy's revised critical correlational methodology has provided guidance in bringing together a theological perspective and psychological perspective on the human situation in a mutually critical way (*Blessed Rage for Order: The New Pluralism in Theology,* New York: Seabury, 1975). As a generally adversarial relationship between theology and psychology continues to diminish, the prospect of theology's enrichment by psychology and psychology's enrichment by

theology is enhanced.

See **Experience, Religious**

Sigmund Freud. (1907). *Obsessive Actions and Religious Practices.* In *Standard Edition of the Complete Psychological Works of Sigmund Freud.* Ed. By James Strachey. Vol. 9. London: Hogarth Press, 1959. pp. 115-127. William James. *The Varieties of Religious Experience.* New York: Collier, 1961. Abraham H. Maslow. *Religion, Values, and Peak-Experiences.* New York: Penguin 1964. W.W. Meissner. *Psychoanalysis and Religious Experience.* New Haven: Yale University Press, 1983. Ana-Maria Rizzuto. *The Birth of the Living God: A Psychoanalytic Study.* Chicago: University of Chicago Press, 1979.

RAYMOND STUDZINSKI, OSB

PURGATORY

The doctrine of purgatory expresses the belief that those who are basically just at the time of death but still burdened with temporal punishment due to sins already forgiven must undergo purgation after death. These departed ones can be aided by the prayers and good works of those living on earth. This state of purgation is understood to be an intermediate condition between individual death and entrance into heaven.

Scripture

While there is no scriptural evidence that contradicts the doctrine, the scriptural basis for the doctrine remains unclear. In support of the doctrine theology has commonly referred to 2 Macc 12:38-46 which speaks of prayer for those who have fallen in battle. Three NT texts have been commonly cited: Mt 5:26, Mt 12:32, and 1 Cor 3:11-15. While the doctrine may not be taught directly in these texts, some support may be found in them since they allow for the possibility that some sins are forgiven in this world and some in the next.

History of Doctrine

History provides abundant evidence for the christian practice of praying for the dead from the earliest centuries. This practice is seen by many to imply a belief in the need for purgation after death. Precisely how and where this purgation was to take place is ambiguous in the tradition. That language about purgation is common in the Fathers is clear. But it is not clear that purgatory was thought of as a particular place until the late twelfth century (cfr. J. Le Goff, *The Birth of Purgatory,* Chicago, 1984). The idea that purgation after death is carried out in a specific place between heaven and hell and for a time proportionate to the number and quality of sins in this life was soon systematized by the university theologians of the thirteenth century and popularized by authors such as Caesar of Heisterbach and Stephen of Bourbon. The connection between purgatory, penance, confession, indulgences and the "power of the keys" is highly developed in late medieval theology. Over the centuries, the doctrine of purgatory has been a point of controversy between Roman Catholics and the Eastern Orthodox as well as between Roman Catholics and Protestants. The difference between the East and the West reflects a deeper difference in the theological understanding of salvation. Because its doctrine of salvation was drawn up largely in legal metaphors, the West emphasized the penal nature of purgation. In harmony with its own more contemplative spirituality, the Eastern Fathers were inclined to see purification in terms of maturation and growth in the contemplation of God (cf. R. McBrien, *Catholicism,* Minneapolis, 1981, p. 1143f.). In harmony with their doctrine of salvation by grace alone, the Protestant Reformers of the sixteenth century denied the meaningfulness of prayer for the dead, thus rejecting what both the East and the West had held in common until that point.

Teaching of the Magisterium

The doctrine is affirmed by the Second Council of Lyons (1274) and the Council of Florence (1439), both of which dealt with the relations between the East and the West, and the Council of Trent (1563), which dealt with the problems raised by the Reformation in the West (D.S. 856-8, 1304, 1580, 1820). In recent times, it is presupposed by the Second Vatican Council in its Dogmatic Constitution on the Church (L.G. 51). It has been reaffirmed by Pope Paul VI in his *Credo of the People of God* (1968) and by the "Letter on Certain Questions Concerning Eschatology" (1979) from the Congregation for the Doctrine of the Faith. The teaching of the Council of Trent may be summarized in the following points: 1) purgatory exists; 2) those detained there may be aided by the prayers and good works of the faithful, particularly by the sacrifice of the altar. Beyond this, the Council commands the bishops to take care that a sound doctrine about purgatory be maintained by the faithful. The more difficult questions that do not contribute to piety are to be avoided from the instruction of the people. Everything that savors of idle curiosity, superstition, or money-making is prohibited.

Theological Reflection

The limited nature of the official teaching leaves much room for theological reflection on the mystery of purgation. Some contemporary theologians see purgation to be an aspect of the encounter with God at the moment of death. For some, this is seen to take place in its fullness in the experience of death (L. Boros, G. Greshake, G. Lohfink); for others, the purgation involved in the person's ultimate decision in death works itself out in phases through all the dimensions of the person's human nature (K. Rahner, M. Schmaus). For Cardinal Ratzinger it is impossible to describe the moment of this encounter in temporal categories. It is neither long nor short in terms of physical time. Its true measure is to be taken in terms of the depth of the resistance in the human person that must be broken down or "burned" away in the encounter with the divine. These modern interpretations see purgation in terms of maturation more than in terms of paying a debt. In this sense, they are more in harmony with the Eastern tradition than with the late medieval theology of the West. In their general orientation, they stand within the framework of theological possibilities set out by the church's official teaching, though particular aspects of the theories may be problematic.

ZACHARY HAYES, OFM

Q

QUIETISM

A tendency in some mystical writings so to stress the element of passivity in the spiritual life that all activity, whether of prayer, asceticism, or concern for one's own salvation, is rejected or undervalued.

R

RATIONALISM

"What has Athens to do with Jerusalem?" The characteristically forthright exclamation of the third-century apologist, Tertullian, foreshadowed many similar reactions in the course of christian history. Tertullian was convinced that the use of the rational categories of Greek philosophy in christian theology necessarily compromised the supernatural content of divine revelation. And although Tertullian's attempt to dissociate christian faith and theology from Greek philosophy was repudiated by the mainline tradition, the question to which he gave such an uncompromising response has nevertheless remained at the interface of such perennially controversial issues as the evidence for the act of faith, the possibility of a christian philosophy, and the relations between nature and grace and reason and revelation. Moreover, despite the repudiation of the radical disjunction between faith and philosophy, Christianity, most notably in the modern age, has been confronted with the consequences which were anticipated in Tertullian's dismissive exclamation. In the most general sense, Rationalism designates the disposition which submits the objects of religious faith and the data of revelation to the tribunal of unaided human reason. Rationalism, therefore, excludes the supernatural or "mysterious" components of religious faith. Or, in another variation, it extracts the rational core from what it sees as a primitive or mythical religious matrix. It follows, of course, that Rationalism also subjects all claims based on authority or tradition to the critical scrutiny of reason.

The maxim, "faith in search of understanding," constituted the horizon within which classical theology developed. It was only in the turbulent intellectual and spiritual climate of the late-medieval period that critical questions were raised concerning the primacy of faith and the supernatural character of revelation. The first noteworthy breach in the theological consensus occurred in the thirteenth century when the rationalist system of the Muslim thinker, Averroes, was sympathetically received by christian theologians. Averroes' Rationalism was appropriated by the Parisian master, Siger of Brabant, who drew a sharp dividing line between philosophy and theology. Although Siger acknowledged that there were "two truths," his speculation was weighted in favor of the natural and rationally comprehensible truths of philosophy. In the following centuries, the complex and varied cultural ferment of the Renaissance gave further impetus to the growth of the rationalist mentality. The Renaissance humanists, for instance, rebelled against what they saw as the excessively dogmatic and "Scholastic" formulations of christian doctrine.

Through their concentration on textual and philological criticism, their antipathy towards speculative theology, and their advocacy of simpler and more accessible expression of belief and devotion, the humanists eroded the supernatural dimension of faith. Numerous strands in Renaissance culture highlighted human autonomy and self-sufficiency and thus presented a further challenge to the traditional conception of the subordinate role of reason in the act of faith. The Reformation, on the other hand, with its emphasis on faith and religious experience, its denigration of reason and philosophy, and its reliance on scripture presented a profile which seemed to exclude the rationalist disposition. Paradoxically, however, the Reformers' defense of the rights of conscience and their insistence on individual interpretation of the Bible contributed substantially to the rise of modern Rationalism.

The wide cultural penetration of the mathematical and scientific methods in the seventeenth century was the most important influence in the emergence of modern Rationalism. Thus, while René Descartes deliberately excluded revelation from the purview of his rational system, his critical spirit, methodic doubt, and emphasis on mathematical clarity inspired numerous successors in their destructive criticisms of the religious tradition. Having submitted the Bible to the tribunal of natural reason, the Jewish philosopher, Baruch Spinoza, concluded that the rational core of religion coincided with his own naturalistic and pantheistic philosophy. In the name of critical reason, the advanced thinkers of the eighteen-century Enlightenment likewise subjected the christian tradition to a radical critique. The titles of the works of John Locke (The Reasonableness of Christianity) and Immanuel Kant (Religion within the Bounds of Reason Alone) testify to their conviction that Christian-

ity had been deprived of its supernatural credentials. From the perspective of enlightened reason, the revealed doctrines of the Trinity and Incarnation were accorded only a symbolic value, and christian theology was reduced to the level of a vague and naturalistic deism. In another key, enlightened reason relegated faith and revelation to a pre-rational or mythological stage of human development. The theme of historical development played an even more crucial role in the influential nineteenth-century systems of Auguste Comte and G.W.F. Hegel. For his part, Comte was convinced that modern scientific rationality, or what he called Positive Philosophy, was the culmination of an historical process in which human consciousness had progressively emancipated itself from theology and metaphysics. Hegel, on the other hand, subsumed christian revelation and theology in an all-embracing and transparently rational system of absolute knowledge.

For the most part, modern and contemporary manifestations of Rationalism have been variations on Enlightenment, Comtean and Hegelian themes. Even in its agnostic and atheistic forms, however, modern Rationalism has not severed all links with the inheritance of christian revelation and theology. But the fact that many contemporary Christians of different denominations have followed Tertullian in his call for a dissociation of faith and reason testifies to the gravity of the challenge which Rationalism presents to Christianity.

See Faith, Philosophy, Theology

GERALD HANRATTY

RECAPITULATION

A translation of the Greek term, ana-cephalaiosis, this term was suggested by Eph 1:10 where God is said to have "summed up all things" in Christ. It refers to Christ's redemptive work as a process of fulfilling all OT prophecies and types, of bringing back into unity all that sin had disrupted and scattered, and of realizing God's original plan for humanity. It was a particularly powerful motif in the thought of St. Irenaeus.

See **Redemption**

RECEPTION

Reception as a theological concept refers to the process through which an ecclesiastical community incorporates into its own life a particular decision, teaching, or practice. Today the term is used in two distinct but related contexts. The "classical" or historical sense of the term refers to the acceptance by local churches of particular ecclesiastical or conciliar decisions. A more contemporary, ecumenical use of the term refers to the acceptance by one church of a theological consensus arrived at with another church, and ultimately, the recognition of the other church's faith and ecclesial life as authentically christian.

The process of reception is constitutive for the life of faith and for the church itself which exists from the reception of the apostolic preaching, the word of God, and Jesus himself. Behind the Latin words *receptio* and *recipere* lie the NT Greek words *lambanein* ("to receive") and *dechesthai* ("to accept") and their derivatives. In Paul the idea of reception appears in the context of tradition, for he several times uses the Greek equivalents for the technical rabbinic terms for the process of handing on (*paradidonai*) and receiving (*paralambanein*) the tradition (1 Cor 11:23; 15:1). The same dynamic of receiving can be seen in the formation of the NT canon, for those christian writings accepted by the early communities as expressions of the apostolic faith were henceforth recognized as sacred scripture. Still later the process can be seen in the receiving of liturgical practices, church laws, and customs of one church by others. In the sixth century the Roman liturgy was received in Germany. In the tenth century Rome and ultimately the entire western church received from Germany the Mainz Pontifical. Thus reception as a reality in the life of the church has a broad application.

In its classical sense, however, the term reception is generally used more restrictively to refer to the process through which ecclesiastical decrees and decisions, particularly those of the great ecumenical councils, were discussed, interpreted, and received by local churches or later councils. The eventual acceptance, after considerable opposition, of the doctrinal decrees of the council of Nicaea (325) is an obvious example. But the process could also lead to a rejection. The church today does not make the claim of Boniface VIII in the bull *Unam Sanctam* (1302) "that it is absolutely necessary for the salvation of all men that they submit to the Roman pontiff" (D.S. 875). Nor did it receive the decree *Haec Sancta* (1415) of the Council of Constance which espoused the conciliarist teaching on the supremacy of a general assembly of bishops over a pope, though the validity and intention of this decree is still debated by theologians.

It is important to note that the practice of reception emerged as an ecclesiological reality during the first millennium when the church was understood as a communion of churches. It becomes more difficult to explain the process against the background of the late medieval or post-Tridentine church, for the excessively hierarchical concept of church which developed so emphasized the role of ecclesiastical authority that the notion of reception was virtually rejected.

In an ecumenical context a new element

enters the process of reception, for now what is involved is the rediscovery of a common faith through a reception process between churches separated from each other by differences of history, doctrine, and structure. In the years following Vatican II, the appearance of the various bilateral and multilateral consensus statements, formulated to express agreement in faith, has made reception a crucial issue in the search for christian unity. If both the classical and the ecumenical concepts of reception are understood as part of a broader reality in the life of the church a number of conclusions can be drawn.

1. Reception is a process involving the whole church; it cannot be reduced to a juridical determination, either of authority or on the part of the faithful. In the ancient church ecclesiastical decisions or teachings became normative for the later church only when they were received by the faithful. Vatican II, with its emphasis on the traditional "sense of the faith" (L.G. 12) or "assent of the Church"(L.G. 25), teaches that the whole church is involved in grasping christian truth. Not all initiatives on the part of authority have been received by the faithful. In the fifteenth century the failure of church authorities to translate the agreements reached between the Eastern churches and the Latin West at the Council of Florence into terms intelligible to the clergy and faithful of both traditions resulted in the failure of this attempt at reconciliation. Some theologians have raised the question as to whether or not *Humanae Vitae*, Pope Paul VI's encyclical on artificial contraception, has been genuinely received by the faithful, and thus, by implication, the question of what kind of authority the encyclical itself possesses. On the other hand, reception does not constitute a decision as legitimate. Yves Congar has emphasized that reception "does not confer validity,

but affirms, acknowledges and attests that this matter is for the good of the Church."

2. Reception also involves formal decision on the part of church authorities. Sometimes it is the role of the bishops in council to initiate a process of reception through formal conciliar decisions, as they did in formulating the creed proclaimed by Nicaea. For a council itself to be ecumenical it must be received by the pope. Sometimes the authority of the bishops serves to give formal approval to a process of reception already underway, thus bringing the process to a juridical close. For example, the long disputed practice of private, frequent confession, introduced to the European continent by the Irish missionaries in the sixth and seventh centuries, ultimately was accepted and became the official practice when the Fourth Lateran Council (1215) decreed that every Christian who committed a serious sin should confess it within the year. Thus church authorites have a role to play in the process of reception, but they do not exercise that role simply by making juridical decisions. Their role is to articulate what is the faith of the church.

3. Reception cannot be reduced to the acceptance of doctrinal formulations; it involves the recognition of a common faith and ecclesial life. This is especially important in an ecumenical context. Forms of worship, life, and practice emerge out of a living tradition which bears the faith experience of a community. To accept a liturgical practice from another community or to arrive at a theological consensus on those issues which had previously divided two churches is to discover a common faith.

4. The norm for receiving a practice or doctrinal formulation is not agreement with one's own ecclesial position but rather agreement with the apostolic tradition. Therefore entering into an

ecumenical process of reception implies for a church a willingness to renew whatever might be deficient in its own tradition or ecclesial life.

See **Doctrine, Faith, Magisterium**

Yves Congar, "Reception as an Ecclesiological Reality," in *Election and Consensus in the Church,* Concilium vol. 77, Eds. Giuseppe Alberigo and Anton Weiler, New York: Herder and Herder, 1972, pp. 43-68. Anton Houtepen, "Reception, Tradition, Communion," in *Ecumenical Perspectives on Baptism, Eucharist and Ministry,* Ed. Max Thurian, Geneva: World Council of Churches, 1983, pp. 141-60. Edward J. Kilmartin, "Reception in History: An Ecclesiological Phenomenon and Its Significance," JES 21, 1984: pp. 34-54. Ulrich Kuhn, "Reception—an imperative and an opportunity," in *Ecumenical Perspectives on Baptism, Eucharist and Ministry,* pp. 163-74. Lukas Vischer, " The Process of 'Reception' in the Ecumenical Movement," *Mid-Stream* 23, 1984: pp. 221-33.

THOMAS P. RAUSCH, SJ

RECONCILIATION

Introduction

Reconciliation is a complex biblical term which includes God's invitation and our response to ongoing conversion within a community of faith. The terms "confession" and "sacrament of penance" have historically served as synonyms for reconciliation but have usually been understood in a more restricted way. (Reconciliation and penance will be used as interchangeable terms in this article.) Reconciliation has usually reflected the pastoral practice and theological understanding of the sacraments of initiation in each historical period. Through initiation, the Christian receives forgiveness of sin and is incorporated into the church and its mission. It is within this baptismal context that Vatican II's description of penance is to be understood: "By baptism men are brought into the People of God. By the sacrament of penance sinners are reconciled to God and the Church"(P.O. 5). Once again applying the ancient axiom. "The law of worship established the law of belief" (D.S. 246) the Council

reasserted the traditional twofold character of the Lenten season as both baptismal and penitential (S.C. 109-110) and ideally suited to recall the social as well as the personal consequences of sin.

Reconciliation to God and the church is worked out in the human situation. This complex situation includes both pastoral practice and the particular social context in which Christians find themselves. Like the sacraments of initiation, penance also carries with it certain assumptions about the nature of sin and redemption, about models of the church and its mission. The actual pastoral practice in a given historical epoch may accurately reflect these assumptions, for better or worse, while contradicting some of the theories about penance itself. In both the sixth and twentieth centuries, for example, fairly sophisticated theological understandings of penance did not seem to affect the declining use of the sacrament by Christians. A more recent concern for both the historian and theologian of penance is the social context in which the sacrament is celebrated and theories are developed. Celtic penance of the sixth century, for example, is firmly rooted in the social and cultural life of that people and its import easily misunderstood apart from that context.

The Reforms of Vatican II

Vatican II's call for a renewal of penance (S.C. 72) and the post-conciliar attempts to implement this renewal provide an excellent starting point for examining the historical and theological developments of the sacrament. Seen within the large conciliar concerns about the church as sacrament and people of God and its mission to the world, the Council asked for more than ritual revision. This is apparent if the statements of Trent and Vatican II are compared. In a polemical stand against the Reformers, Trent described, in juridical language, the situation of sinners after baptism as standing "before this tribunal in the role of the accused, in order that they might be freed by the sentence of the priest, and this not once, but so often as they admit their sins and have recourse thereto as penitents" (D.S. 1671). As expressed in the biblical language of pardon and reconciliation, the emphasis and scope of Vatican II are different: "Those who approach the sacrament of penance obtain pardon from the mercy of God for offenses committed against Him. They are at the same time reconciled with the Church, which they have wounded by their sins, and which by charity, example, and prayer seeks their conversion" (L.G. 11).

In 1973, when the new Rite of Penance was promulgated, this theme of conversion was reasserted: "Thus the people of God becomes in the world a sign of conversion to God. All this the Church expresses in its life and celebrates in the liturgy when the faithful confess that they are sinners and ask pardon of God and of their brothers and sisters. This happens in penitential services, in the proclamation of the word of God, in prayer, and in the penitential aspects of the eucharistic celebration" (par. 4). While insisting on the personal nature of sin, this conciliar theology of penance also acknowledges the ecclesial and the social dimensions of both sins and conversion (Rite of Penance 5). In ritualizing this theology, the new Rite provides for the proclamation of the word of God and prayerful dialogue between the priest and penitent, for communal celebrations with individual confession and absolution, and in certain situations, with general confession and absolution. Penitential celebrations without absolution were also encouraged to deepen the spirit of penance within the christian community and to assist children and catechumens in preparing for the sacrament.

Despite this renewal in theological understanding and ritual expression of the sacrament, two underlying pastoral phenomena emerged in the next decade: a steady decline in individual confession and a widespread use of communal penance, especially when general absolution was given. In 1983, the canons on penance (959-997) in the new Code of Canon Law and the discussion of penance at the Synod of Bishops represented responses to this pastoral situation. While simplifying certain canonical procedures (e.g., faculties for confessors), the canons in the new Code on general absolution (961-63) may be interpreted as a retrenchment from a more flexible pastoral approach indicated in rescripts and norms given after Vatican II. The discussions at the Synod of Bishops also mirrored the tensions between a pastoral desire to shape the theology and celebration of penance to the contemporary situation and institutional concerns about the abuse of general absolution and the decline of private confession.

The current state of the sacrament summarizes some of the perennial tensions that have persisted in the development of the history and theology of penance. First, when the theoretical or practical relation between the sacraments of initiation and penance is weakened or lost, there are inevitable problems and distortions. Secondly, the ecclesial and personal dimensions of penance and reconciliation must not simply be juxtaposed but be in dialogue with one another. Thirdly, continuing evangelization and adequate ministries are necessary for the fruitful celebration of communal and individual penance within the church. Finally, the practice and theory of penance should be mutually corrective and clarifying. With these observations in mind, we can proceed to an overview of some of the major historical and theological developments of penance and reconciliation.

The New Testament Communities

To appreciate the attitudes of the NT communities toward penance, three important contexts should be kept in mind: (1) the eschatological intensity of the earliest christian communities: (2) the churches' sense of mission and witness to the world as a sinless messianic community: (3) the gift of salvation as experienced in reconciliation with God and the forgiveness of sins. A typical example of this early kerygma is found in the post-resurrection words of Jesus to the disciples: "Thus it is written that the Messiah must suffer and rise from the dead on the third day. In his name, penance for the remission of sins is to be preached to all nations, beginning at Jerusalem. You are witnesses of this" (Lk 24:46-48). Paul reiterates this same theme of reconciliation to the churches of his time (2 Cor 5:14-21).

The lessening of this eschatological intensity coupled with the long term problems of living the gospel life provide the background for the pastoral approach of NT communities toward post-baptismal sins. A general principle seems to be that sinners are to be corrected and helped, sin is to be prevented, and obdurate sinners are to be excluded until they reform. While the eschatological perspective implies high expectations in the moral life of Christians (e.g., 1 Jn 3:9; 1 Pet 1:14-16), even the earliest communities are aware of the need for ongoing forgiveness of the baptized (Mk 2:10, as a possible example). Mutual confession and forgiveness is considered a normal part of christian living (e.g., Mt 5:23-24; Jas 5:16).

But this pastoral compassion is balanced by a keen awareness of the corporative nature of the church and its mission. The sin of the individual also affects the life and work of the church

(e.g., 1 Cor 5:6; 2 Cor 2:5). If the pastoral correction of the sinner is not effective, then that person is excluded from the community ("to hand over to Satan") until there are signs of repentance (e.g., 1 Cor 5:3-5; 1 Tm 1:19-20). (A similar process of correction or eventual exclusion is found in the Qumran community.) This conviction about being either under the reign of Satan or that of Christ forms a background for understanding the key texts of "binding and loosing" (Mt 18:18) and the forgiveness of sins (Jn 20:22-23). Against any rigorist tendencies in the NT communities, the church of Christ continues to exercise his correction and healing of sinners so that they may remain under the reign of Christ.

The NT communities, however, are aware of attitudes on the part of baptized sinners that may block their eventual repentance: "For when men have once been enlightened and have tasted the heavenly gift and become sharers in the Holy Spirit, when they have tasted the good word of God and powers of the age to come, and then have fallen away, it is impossible to make them repent again, since they are crucifying the Son of God for themselves and holding him up to contempt" (Heb 6:4-6). To set one's self persistently against the reign of Christ and his saving power is the ultimate blasphemy that seems to be reflected in the biblical phrase, "blasphemy against the Holy Spirit" (Mk 3:29; Lk 12:10). It would be misleading, however, to deduce from these references any doctrine of irremissible or unforgiveable sins in the practice of the church.

Canonical Penance

Because the early church valued the unearned forgiveness of sin (*aphesis*) in baptism and took the initiation commitment of an adult so seriously, the question of continuing conversion and repentance after baptism (*metanoia*) required pastoral and theological clarification. In the second century Hermas reluctantly speaks of one further possibility of repentance after baptism, though his teaching was influenced by his conviction of the imminent destruction of the world. The principle of a single repentance after baptism must be understood within the context of an ecclesial and public process that dealt with certain sins. These sins exclude the sinner from the christian community because they are an obstacle to the mission of the church as much as they are offensive to God (e.g., apostasy).

Several characteristics emerge from this canonical process of reconciliation. First, the process always involves excommunication, at least in the form of exclusion from the eucharist. This ecclesial dimension distinguishes the process from later developments in the sacramental celebration of penance. Second, serious sins which, if they were known, would require ecclesial penance are the proper object of this repentance. The process addresses more the effects of sin rather than the later preoccupation with the nature of sinful acts. There is no private sacramental penance, as we know it, even though the public character of canonical penance may vary. Prayer, fasting, almsgiving, and the reception of the eucharist seem to have been the normal remedies for the daily sins of Christians. Third, the penitential process generally resembles the catechumenal transformation of baptismal candidates in requiring an ongoing view of conversion and an active reintegration into the liturgical life of the community. Finally, reconciliation with the church does not necessarily mean an end to the penitential practices of the process.

Historically, canonical penance gradually becomes a moribund practice in the Western Church by the sixth century. This is due not only to the corresponding disintegration of the catechumenal proc-

ess but also to a growing pastoral rigorism about admission to canonical penance. Because of the unrepeatable character and the harsh nature of this penance, there is a tendency to delay its reception until the moment of death.

Irish Tax Penance

For reasons that are not totally clear, the Irish church seems to have early on taken shape as a monastic church. One of the practical results of this unique situation was that monastic spirituality and practices quickly influenced general pastoral practice. Another anomaly that may be tied to this monastic context is that canonical penance never seems to have become a pastoral practice in the Irish church.

Irish monks, like their Eastern counterparts, were accustomed to personal confession of their state of soul to another monk or to their abbot and sometimes, to communal confession in a monastic chapter of faults. The monk was assigned a penance for the specific sins confessed. After completion of penance, he returned for the abbot's absolution. Eventually the hearing of such confessions was reserved to priests, although sinners were still urged to confess to a fellow monk or lay spiritual director if a priest were not available. A unique Irish and Anglo-Saxon literature of penitential books gradually developed to assist the confessor in judging the severity of penance to be assigned for each sin confessed. These books were influenced, in part, by Celtic civil law as well as by monastic spirituality.

This monastic form of penance was eventually extended to the lay people to whom the monks ministered. After confessing the specific nature and number of their sins, the penitent received a penance determined by the gravity of sins confessed. Upon receiving assurance that the penance would be performed (in contrast to an earlier form in which the penitent had to return after performing the penance), the confessor then gave a declaratory absolution (in contrast to the usually deprecatory formula of canonical penance). This new form of penance was eventually brought to the continent by the Irish monks and, although initially rejected, quickly replaced the vestiges of canonical penance.

There are some striking differences between canonical and tax penance. First, the canonical form is generally unrepeatable while the Irish form is not. Second, the ecclesial nature of sin and reconciliation is much more sharply emphasized in canonical than in Irish penance. Third, the canonical form encourages a long-term view of conversion while Irish penance subtly fosters a short-range conception. Fourth, the penitential acts and the reception of personal absolution in the Irish practice are emphasized in contrast to the communal liturgical intercession and ecclesial reconciliation of canonical penance. Finally, and most importantly, the role of the minister of reconciliation is transformed from the patristic notion of "medicus" (doctor/healer) to that of "judex" (judge). On the other hand, Irish tax penance was rooted in the social and cultural heritage of the people and probably was more effective pastorally than the available forms of canonical penance would have been. Like its civil and monastic precedents, Irish penance was a form of social control as well as a spiritual discipline.

Theologies of Penance

Although the practice of canonical and Irish tax penance carried with it implicit theologies of penance, some of which were theoretically developed, it is with the advent of the early middle ages that the theological and canonical dimensions of penance were articulated. With the formalization of penance as one of the seven sacraments, its particular theology was developed in more systematic fashion within the larger medieval sacramental system of matter and form. Rather than proceed historically from this point, it would be to the advantage of the reader to follow certain themes which will provide an overview of these theological developments, spanning the medieval and contemporary periods. The three themes to be discussed are (1) the acts of the penitent; (2) the role of the confessor; (3) the celebration and reception of the sacrament.

Acts of the Penitent

In Irish tax penance the penitential satisfaction performed by the Christian was emphasized, but the confession itself, with its accompanying shame, was viewed as having particular expiatory value. The absolution of the confessor was linked to the willingness of the penitent to confess and to perform the penitential sentence imposed. In the more systematic theologies of penance until the thirteenth century theologians were unanimous in their belief that the sincere sorrow of the penitent obtained the forgiveness of sins before confession, provided that the penitent wished to receive the sacrament. But this raised the question: does the sorrow of the penitent or the absolution of the priest effect the forgiveness of sin in the sacrament?

The eventual classical solution of Thomas Aquinas is that the acts of the penitent (contrition, confession, satisfaction) are the matter of the sacrament while the absolution of the priest is the form. When the penitent lacks a sufficiently profound contrition, the sacrament perfects this imperfect contrition as long as the penitent does not place an obstacle. But Thomas balances this teaching with a reminder to the confessor that he may not absolve without some sign of contrition.

Within contemporary theology, the acts of the penitent, appreciated as part of the ongoing appropriation of initiation, and the ministry of the church, seen as a continuing reconciliation of its members for the work of the gospel, still form a unity whose richness has not been exhausted. The current awareness of the social as well as the personal dimension of both sin and responsible witness to the gospel suggests directions for better understanding the social, psychological, and ecclesial nature of conversion, and therefore contrition, within the sacrament. This awareness has been further sharpened by the theological and liturgical revaluing of the word of God as enabling the christian community and individual to continue in the way of penance.

Role of the Confessor

As already noted, two privileged terms summarize the role of the minister of penance: *medicus* (healer/doctor) and *judex* (judge) The term of "healer/doctor," while first applied to Christ, was eventually used to describe the ecclesial ministry of reconciliation by the fathers of the church. (Thus, the *Apostolic Constitutions* described the bishop as a "compassionate physician.") The notion of "judge" began to assume prominence with Irish tax penance, even though the traditional term of "doctor" is still used to describe the confessor. By the eighth century, there is a juxtaposition of the two terms which accurately reflects the pastoral practice and theology. Because the confessor, in Irish tax penance, must know the details of the serious sins confessed before assigning the penance, the role of "doctor" will gradually be reinterpreted according to the role of "judge." At the Council of Trent, the line of reasoning that results from this juxtaposition is that just as the sick must show their wounds to a doctor in order to receive a prescription, so sinners must reveal the specific nature and number of serious sins so that the judge may give sentence (e.g., C.T. VII: 347-49).

The dual description of the confessor as "doctor/judge" also summarizes, then, the doctrine of the integrity of confession, i.e., the obligation of the penitent to tell the species and number of serious sins and the corresponding obligation of the confessor to assist the penitent in fulfilling this obligation. When the Council of Trent reiterates this teaching (D.S. 1707), it must be appreciated within the perennial concern of the sacrament—ongoing conversion. That integrity of confession has always been understood as a means (and not an end in itself) to this goal of conversion is obvious not only from the discussion at Trent but from the traditional reminder to confessors that they were excused from pursuing the matter of integrity when it might be harmful either to themselves or to the penitent. No wonder then that in the *summae confessorum* (the medieval compendia for confessors that succeeded the penitentials) there are usually "two keys" proposed as necessary for the confessor: that of discretion (attached to the "doctor" image) and that of power (related to the "judge" image).

In contemporary theology the role of the minister of reconciliation has been revalued within the traditional context of sharing God's word with penitents, praying with penitents, and imaging Christ in their respectful care and concern for them. Just as those responsible for catechumenal formation of candidates for initiation are expected to enter the process of conversion with them, so the minister of reconciliation is invited to assume, not the role of a functionary, but of sharer in the penance that heals.

The Celebration and Reception of the Sacrament

The post-conciliar ritual of penance and reconciliation firmly resituated the liturgical celebration of the sacrament within its traditional ecclesial context: "The celebration of this sacrament is thus always an act in which the Church proclaims its faith, gives thanks to God for the freedom with which Christ has made us free, and offers its life as a spiritual sacrifice in praise of God's glory, as it hastens to meet the Lord Jesus"(no. 7). This ecclesial emphasis sets the tone both for the personal and communal expressions of reconciliation.

What is particularly striking in all the post-conciliar ritual celebrations of reconciliation is the restoration of the liturgy of the word of God. Ongoing evangelization is a key to honest sacramental celebration as both the fathers of Trent and Vatican II recognized. The goal of this evangelization within reconciliation is "that the word of God may be more deeply understood and heartfelt assent may be given to it," as the new order of penance urges (no. 24). Equally important is the new order's note that the penitent may share in the selection of a scriptural text (no. 43) and that penitents themselves may read the text (no. 17).

Communal celebrations of reconciliation witness "more clearly the ecclesial nature of penance" (no. 22). Linked to this is the conviction that just as christians share in injustice, they must help each other in doing penance (no. 5). These celebrations are a pastoral opportunity to challenge the christian community's awareness of the social dimension of both sin and witness so that they work more closely together "for justice and peace in the world" (no. 5).

Throughout the history of reconciliation, the fruitful participation of ministers and recipients in the honest celebration of penance has been a constant concern. There is no better way to close this survey of reconciliation than to return to the starting point of initiation and its demand for unceasing conversion. The new order of penance describes this conversion, as fostered by the sacrament, in the words of Paul VI: "This is a profound change of the whole person by which one begins to consider, judge, and arrange his life according to the holiness and love of God, made manifest in his Son in the last days and given to us in abundance" (no. 6a). The celebration and reception of the sacrament rests firmly on the promise of this profound change.

See Absolution; Baptism; Catechumen; Confession; Conversion; Initiation, Christian; Moral Life, Christian; Sin

The Rites of the Catholic Church, New York: 1976. C. Vogel, Le Pécheur et la Pénitence dans l'Eglise Ancienne, Paris: 1963. C. Vogel. Le Pécheur et la Pénitence au Moyen-Age, Paris: 1969. K. Rahner, Theological Investigations, vols XV, II, III, X; P. Anciaux, La Théologie du Sacrement de la Pénitence au XIIe siècle, Louvain: 1949; T. Tentler, Sin and Confession on the Eve of the Reformation Princeton, N.J.: 1977. The Rite of Penance: Commentaries 3 vols. I: Understanding the Document, ed. R. Keifer and F. McManus; III: Background and Directions, ed. N. Mitchell, Washington, D.C.: The Liturgical Conference, 1975, 1978.

REGIS A. DUFFY, OFM

REDACTION CRITICISM
See Biblical Criticism

REDEMPTION

Redemption is a central category of christian theology, for it explicates the christian proclamation of Jesus as the Christ, as our Redeemer and Savior. The English word "redemption" literally means a buying back. The term "redemption" is closely related but distinct from three other terms. "Atonement," which is often used to express a kind of propitiation of God by Jesus, literally means at-one-ment, a bringing together of parties divided against each other. "Reconciliation" refers to the bringing together of parties that have been estranged and separated from one other. Strained relations of discord and hostility are brought back to harmony and peace. "Salvation" refers to a healing, a bringing to health or a making whole and well. All terms refer to a transition from one state or status to another.

The term "redemption" is best understood as a liberation from one state to another: from bondage to liberation. Redemption is the act or process by which the change takes place. Throughout the centuries, christian theology has used a variety of categories to describe each of these states and the transition between them. The one: the enslavement of humans to sin, death, the law, flesh, the devil, oppression, the powers of the world and of darkness. The other: forgiveness, eternal life, freedom, transformation, divine sonship, liberation, new birth, life and light. Christian conceptions of the process of redemption have likewise varied. The undeviating affirmation that the redemption of humanity has taken place through Christ has been made in concepts, symbols, and stories exhibiting a vast diversity in understanding that process.

Sometimes these theories are classified into two groups: the "objective" and "subjective" theories of redemption. The objective theory supposedly implies that the change in the relation between humans and God depends primarily upon a change in God, as for example, the so-called doctrine of propitiation. The subjective theory supposedly implies that the change involves primarily a change in humans and their life-practice, as for example, the so-called "moral influence view." These designations, as the history of theological conceptions of redemption demonstrates, are misleading, for they overlook the complexity and diversity of views.

Although redemption is central to christian faith, its conception and understanding has never been an immediate and direct object of ecclesial or conciliar definition. Indirectly, conciliar statements the christology, justification, or the eucharist imply specific understandings of

redemption, but do not explicitly define it. Nevertheless, redemption remains a pivotal conception around which much turns: the understanding of sin and grace, the church and sacraments, creation and eschatology, Christ and his mission. Around the concept of redemption circle a cluster of religious notions that converge upon the meaning of making good, new, or free, delivering from death, mortality, and sin, and renewing of self and society.

Because of the centrality of redemption to christian faith and to the diverse clusters of associated ideas, Christianity is often referred to as a religion of salvation or redemption. A number of the world religions are often classified as such because they emphasize salvation from a state of perdition, doom, mortality that is achieved by a savior or by the individual. Various typologies of religions as redemptive have been attempted, but their diversity and pluralism show such typologies to be highly inadequate. The diversity of conceptions within Christianity itself from the time its scriptures were written until the present show that even Christianity cannot be brought simply under one label.

Hebrew Scriptures

The Hebrew scriptures use two terms to describe redemption. One term "to purchase" or "to ransom" (Heb. *padah*) is a neutral commercial term. It refers to the purchase of a person from slavery (Exod 21:7-11; Lev 19:20, and Job 6:23). The other term "redeemer" (Heb *go'el*," from the verb *ga'al*) is prevalent in the Jerusalem tradition and stems from family law. It refers primarily to the redeeming of relatives from slavery, the redemption of property from foreign owners, and the removal of someone from diaster and distress. It also includes the redemption of inheritance and of tithes. This conception emphasizes the reestablishment of a previous relation (Ps 77, 15). It emphasizes Yahweh's loyalty to his people. "Let the redeemed the Lord say so, whom he has redeemed from trouble" (Ps 107, 2).

The Deuteronomic tradition uses the term *padah* as a central concept in the narration of Exodus. Yahweh has led Israel out Egypt and has thereby redeemed his people from servitude. The Exodus, the liberation of Israel from Egypt, is a central historical event by which the Hebrew scriptures understand redemption. The redemption of Israel from Egypt becomes for the prophet Micah, for example, the paradigmatic event that establishes the relation between Yahweh and his people. Yahweh's act of redemption has established a relationship of community. Whereas *padah* is used in the Deuteronomic tradition, *go'el* is used in a special tradition that denotes the familial tradition. Yahweh stands in the closest relation to Israel whom he has redeemed. Hence Yahweh is the redeemer of his people.

Second Isaiah describes the eschatological event as a redemption. Israel will be redeemed from the servitude of Babylon. "And the ransomed of the Lord, shall return, and come to Zion with singing; everlasting joy shall be upon their heads" (Isa 51:11). In Second Isaiah the term "the redeemer" (*go'el*) becomes almost a standard expression for Yahweh's fidelity in the eschatological salvation, in which the first and second exodus are related. In redeeming his people in the first exodus, Yahweh has established Israel; the second exodus is the definitive eschatological redemption of Israel from its enemies.

In short, the Hebrew scriptures speak of the redemption of the individual from a situation of need. The event of Exodus is the primal event for an understanding of redemption, especially Yahweh's definitive eschatological redemption.

Christian Scriptures

The NT writings interpret Jesus' proclamation, life, ministry, death and resurrection. Each of the NT writings is contextual, that is, each is written to particular communities and deals with specific issues. In explicating the meaning of redemption, these writings incorporate previous oral and written traditions that are likewise distinctive interpretations of Jesus and his activity. NT statements about redemption emerge within various levels of tradition and redaction. Consequently, the relation between these levels of tradition and the historical Jesus is a central problem of the interpretation of redemption.

The Historical Jesus. The major question of what can modern scholarship know about the historical Jesus becomes in regard to redemption: whether or how did the historical Jesus understand his activity as redemptive? This question revolves around the interpretation of his proclamation of the kingdom of God and his understanding of his life and death.

Jesus proclaimed God's coming and saving reign and this proclamation was central to his ministry. The earthly Jesus clearly did not understand God's reign as a moral or spiritual reign of God in the hearts of individuals, but rather as God's rule over all creation. Unclear, however, is the nature of Jesus' own expectation. Is God's rule already breaking in, imminent, or future? A general consensus is that an adequate interpretation of his use of symbol and language of kingdom must include all three dimensions.

Redemption is both present and future. It is present and breaking in in Jesus' preaching and actions. His exorcisms and acts of healing are not only signs of God's rule, but constitute a real redeeming presence which liberates from the powers of evil, sin, and sickness. Although God's rule is already breaking in, its definitive establishment is outstanding.

A soteriology is implicit within Jesus' life-practice and proclamation. His life-practice displayed his concern for the poor, outcasts, and sinners. His exorcisms, healing, and forgiveness are his saving deeds for these groups. In Jesus God turns to all, especially the lost of Israel, and brings forgiveness and redemption. The proclamation of God's reign is a proclamation of the nearness and breaking in of a kingdom of wholeness. It is a proclamation of forgiveness, for the forgiveness of sins was a part of the coming of God's rule.

A much more difficult question in Jesus' understanding of his death is whether he understood his death as salvific. As an exegetical and historical question, the issue remains controverted today. Texts within the eucharist accounts have been attributed to the earthly Jesus by some scholars. These same texts have been attributed by others to the early christian communities and their attempt to interpret theologically the significance of Jesus' death. As a historical question the issue remains debated.

Nevertheless, a unity and continuity exist between Jesus' public activity and his fate on the cross. His fate on the cross should be seen not in isolation from his freely chosen public activity. It is this activity that leads to the description of Jesus' existence as a "proexistence." This term, used by twentieth-century theologians such as Barth, Bonhoeffer, and Schillebeeckx, is a fit description of the life activity of the earthly Jesus. This proexistence of Jesus symbolizes that solidarity with God and humans that finds it culmination in his death on the cross. It raises the issue of how Jesus' life and death is not only a real symbol of God's salvific grace, but as such effects human redemption. This theological question underlies the earliest attempts within Christianity as well as current attempts to understand Jesus as redeemer.

Pre-Gospel Tradition: Q. The kerygmatic center of Q (the source common to Matthew and Luke) primarily connects salvation with the coming Son of Man. Nevertheless, Q applied the traditional statements of the violent fate of prophets to Jesus. In dying, Jesus shared the destiny of God's messengers and prophets. This understanding of Jesus' death as the fate of an eschatological prophet or as the suffering and dying of a just and righteous person represents one of the earliest attempts to interpret Jesus's death that provided the basis for what would be later explicitly articulated in different conceptual categories.

Paul. In the pre-Pauline traditions, one of the earliest references to redemption is Rom 3:24b-25a: "through the redemption which is in Christ Jesus, whom God put forward as an expiation by his blood, to be received by faith." The meaning of this text is most controverted. Earlier interpretations suggested that the Greek term *hilasterion* can refer to the lid of the sacred box that was sprinkled with blood on Yom Kippur as a part of the ritual by which God's forgiveness was granted. It refers to expiation rather than propitation. Whereas propitiation means the turning away of wrath, expiation means the taking away of sin. The text does not suggest that Christ placates God's wrath, but that God puts forward Christ for the remission of sin.

Today, the text is interpreted against the background of 4 Maccabees 17:22 in which the death of the seven brothers is viewed as an offering. The similarities between the death of Jesus and the death of the Jewish martyrs is striking. Like them, he was innocent, but was put to death by a hostile government. Likewise as with the martyrs, it was believed that God had vindicated Jesus. In addition, there was the idea that the undeserved death of exceptionally worthy persons can effect expiation. This idea, current in hellenistic Judaism, provided the framework by which Christians could view Jesus' death as meaningful. In this context, Romans 3:25 means that God regarded Christ's crucifixion as a means of expiation for all humans.

In Paul's writings the term for redemption (*apolytrosis*) is not as significant as the terms justification, reconciliation, and salvation. Paul's conception of redemption combines elements of pre-Pauline material (1 Cor 15:3) with his own theological conceptions of justification and reconciliation. Paul understands sin as a cosmic power. The human situation is one of subjection and enslavement to the powers of the law and death. Redemption therefore does not simply blot out the punishment of sin, but it frees and liberates humans from the cosmic power of law, sin and death. Although present, redemption is also future and it embraces not only humans, but the whole creation.

Paul's view of redemption has its center in the justification of the sinner through faith. This center is intrinsically related to his message of freedom: the redemption of human reality from the cosmic power of this aeon. The liberation from the powers of the world, from the law and from sin and guilt all taken together constitute Paul's comprehensive understanding of redemption.

Mark. In Mark's account of the Last Supper, the verse "This is my blood of the covenant, which is poured out for many" (Mk 14:24) expresses the notion of a vicarious death for others. Mark's gospel itself develops the central emphasis on the cross of Jesus insofar as it presents christian discipleship as the following of Jesus in suffering and the cross.

Luke. Luke, however, does not focus on the death of Jesus but rather upon the whole way of Jesus. The whole complex of Jesus' life is redemptive: his ministry, healing, preaching, death, resurrection, and exaltation. In Luke's gospel, "salvation" denotes deliverance from such evils as sickness, infirmity, or sin. Jesus' turning to the poor, infirm and lost is redemptive. "The Son of Man has come to seek and save the lost" (Lk 19:10). The death of Jesus is comprehended as an event within the whole drama of God's salvific plan that is being realized in Jesus. Luke presents Jesus as the suffering Messiah, but gives more salvific significance to the resurrection of Jesus because through the resurrection Jesus became the "leader of life."

John's Gospel The Johannine view of redemption does not so much emphasize Jesus' death as expiation as it emphasizes his incarnation and exaltation as the saving events. Jesus brings life as the revealer sent by the Father and returned to the Father. John's gospel understands redemption within a dualistic context. The world is constituted by darkness, deception, and death. Jesus is the light, the truth, and life. Jesus is the revealer and bringer of divine life. Redemption consists in participating in Jesus unity with God. In this conception, Jesus' death is not a sacrifice for sin, but an event of the ascent of the Son to the Father that reveals his identity. The death expresses God's love and reorients human life. In a world of darkness, the believer has the choice of living in disbelief and darkness or the light.

Hebrews. The Epistle to the Hebrews refers to Christ's death as a sacrifice, but contrasts it with the levitical sacrifices. Sin is a defilement and the blood of Jesus is a cleansing from the defilement of sin. Christ is the heavenly priest who has offered himself as a sacrifice once and for all. The church is the wandering people of God on their way to their heavenly rest.

Revelation. In the Book of Revelation John uses apocalyptic and prophetic imagery to describe redemption as liberation from bondage and slavery. Those who have been redeemed through the death of Jesus Christ have a new dignity. This dignity is expressed with the titles "kingdom" and "priests," which in antiquity refer to political and sacral authority. The author's use of political imagery is strong and he maintains that final redemption and salvation is only realized when the state of dominion on earth is radically changed, when Satan and the Roman Empire as a concrete demonic manifestation no longer rule but God and the Lamb reign on earth.

Summary. The references to redemption within the various NT writings spell out the meaning of redemption in a myriad of symbols, images, and terms. They are cultic, legal, medical, cosmic, social and political. Redemption is achieved through Jesus's life, death, and resurrection and yet redemption remains to be achieved.

History of Theology

Early Christianity. The history of christian theology within the first millennium exhibits diverse conceptions of redemption. Many of the traditional NT categories are continued and developed. Nevertheless, different traditions with distinct categories develop in the East and the West. Three developments are significant.

Christ as Pedagogical Paradigm. In the Apostolic Fathers, a key understanding of redemption is as *paideia.* Redemption is presented as a new teaching, a new direction, a new example through Christ. Through the example of his life-praxis and preaching, Christ opens the way to a new knowledge, imitation, and community with him. Through Christ humans are brought from darkness to light and from ignorance to knowledge. Whereas in the first century, the focus was the saving teaching and illumination of the earthly Jesus, the second century shifted the emphasis to the Logos.

Irenaeus' doctrine of recapitulation expands this notion in two ways: First, it views redemption as a historical process that moves toward a culmination. Redemption does not simply affect the transformation of an individual's life, but affects the history of the human race. Second, it expands the role of Christ as paradigm through a notion of "corporate identity or solidarity." In placing the understanding of redemption within the narrative context of salvation history, Irenaeus uses the image of recapitulation to dramatize the solidarity between Christ and the human race. Irenaeus' notion of recapitulation does not yet represent the "physical theory" of redemption, but moves in its direction.

Anthropological. Another tradition, called the Greek or physical theory relates redemption to human mortality. Corruption and death are the primary effects of the human sinful state. The very act of Christ becoming human entails an elevation, transformation, and sanctification of human nature. Christ's redemption effects "incorruption" and "immortality." In connection with the Platonic doctrine of universals, this tradition views human nature as a concrete universal in which all humans participate. Human nature is deified by the incarnation, for by becoming human Christ restored the divine image in humans and therefore effected their deification. Some, like Clement of Alexandria, refer to the Logos deifying humans by teaching (Protrep. XI, 114; Strom VI, 15, 125).

Mythic and Political Imagery. A third tradition interpreted Jesus' redemption with imagery of a political battle between two hostile forces. On a cosmic scale God and Satan were engaged in a battle over the human race. The chief consequence of the fall was to place humans under the power of the devil. This tradition envisioned redemption as the emancipation of humans from the devil's power. The devil's right to retain humankind in bondage was maintained. This tradition drew on the imagery of the bait and the hook of Christ's body as the bait by which the devil was caught like a mouse in a trap (Augustine, *De trin.* 13, 19). In some versions, God offered Jesus as a ransom to the devil. The devil accepted Jesus, but could not hold him. Hence the devil was tricked. In a more refined form, the devil is overcome because satisfaction has been given to God who has pardoned humans.

Medieval Christianity. Anselm. In distinction from patristic approaches to soteriology, Anselm of Canterbury's *Cur Deus Homo* established the prevailing pattern for medieval conceptions of redemption. Anselm disowned any account of redemption as a ransoming from the devil. Instead he developed a theory of satisfaction within the intellectual horizon of feudal legal categories and the penitential practice of the medieval church.

Anselm understands the problem of sin and redemption quite differently from the patristic period. He shifts the emphasis on the necessity of the incarnation from the deification of humans to an emphasis upon a supererogatory satisfaction for human sin. For example, Athanasius maintained that sin could be removed through penance, that incarnation was necessary for morality (*De Incarnatione verbi* 7). Anselm argues that it is not enough for humans to cease from sin. They must offer satisfaction for the sins that they have already committed. They can offer as satisfaction only what they do not already owe to God, a work of supererogation. But humans cannot do that since they owe their Creator everything. Therefore, only Jesus, born without sin, can offer such a work of supererogation. Jesus offers his life as satisfaction. Because Jesus is also God his life has infinite worth and effects human redemption. Anselm's theory requires as a meta-physical necessity for redemption that Jesus be both divine and sinless.

Anselm's conception has been significant and influential. Unfortunately, the influence has had significant negative effects. First, Anselm rightly criticized the mythological imagery of ransom and the need to liberate humans from the power of the devil. But his critique and theory, however correct, led to an over-emphasis upon a legalistic conception of redemption as satisfaction and to a neglect of the meaning and truth exhibited in the traditional metaphors, images, and mythic drama.

Second, his theory of redemption as satisfaction was developed within a specific societal-political context. Interpretations outside of this context often misunderstand the theory. Honor in Anselm's context does not refer simply to a virtue or a personal feeling of value, but honor is a societal concept, related to the acknowledged legal feudal order. In this context honor is the respect before mutual obligations of justice. Anselm does not offer an individualized conception of redemption as internal renewal nor does he question the justice of the societal order of his time. Instead, using the categories of that order, he sees redemption as the restoration of the order of creation that has become distorted.

Abelard. Abelard advances a theory of redemption in which Christ's revealing the love of God in his teaching and example leads to a response of love. In his commentary upon Romans (Rom 3:25) Abelard rejects any idea of redemption from the claims of the devil. In Christ the love of God was made manifest in that Christ assumed our nature and remained faithful unto death. That supreme love redeems humans. It liberates them not only from the servitude of sins but gives them the freedom of children of God. Christ's faith and love arouse faith and love in humans and become the ground of forgiveness.

Thomas. Abelard's theory of redemption would find more advocates within modern theology; whereas Anselm's conception prevailed within medieval theology, but not without two significant modifications. First, the subject of the work of redemption was decidedly human nature, that is, the human will of Jesus as united with the divinity. This emphasis upon the human subject as the agent of redemption corresponds to a tendency within Anselm's work that he did not develop. Christ's dying represented a free, active, and meritorious deed. The second modification was to soften Anselm's affirmation of the logical necessity of the incarnation. Both modifications are present in Thomas Aquinas.

Thomas emphasizes the mystery of the love of God for humans. All the activities and mysteries of Jesus' whole life are redemptive: incarnation, life, ministry, passion, death and resurrection. In elucidating the specific efficacy of Jesus' death, Thomas appropriates traditional categories (satisfaction, sacrifice, and redemption), but modifies them with the notion of a liberating love. These modifications are especially evident in his conceptions of satisfaction and merit as well as his emphasis on Jesus' humanity as a free instrument of God.

Thomas replaces the metaphysical necessity of satisfaction with one of convenience. The suffering and passion of the earthly Jesus is redemptive, but for the sake of a certain convenience the suffering and death were necessary. The death on the cross is a sign of love expressing Jesus' faith and obedience in love. Thomas also modifies the very concept of satisfaction. In a proper sense satisfaction is given when one gives to the offended that which the person loves equally or more than he hates the insult. Through suffering, Christ gave God something greater than any satisfaction.

Thomas brings into the center of his conception of redemption Christ's active personal love that embraced his whole life and was especially manifest in the passion of his crucifixion. Because of the superabundance of his love, Jesus merited redemption for those united with him in love.

For Thomas, God is the principal cause of human redemption, but Christ's human nature is its instrumental cause. A modern reader with a technological conception of instrument might misunderstand Thomas as devaluating Jesus' human nature. Instead, instrument should be understood as a sacrament or sign or exemplary symbol. Thomas not only underscores Christ's human freedom and autonomy, but also points to his human nature as an instrument of salvation as exemplary cause affecting humans. In Thomas, merit and efficiency are subordinate to instrumentality.

Reformation. The Reformation understanding of redemption placed much more emphasis on the representational or substitutional role of Christ in contrast to the medieval emphasis on satisfaction.

Luther. Martin Luther's understanding of redemption underscored Jesus' role as the representative of all humanity. Jesus represents humanity not so much in the offering of satisfaction as in enduring, as the crucified one, God's wrath against sin. In distinction from Anselm, Luther emphasizes that in suffering and dying, Christ has willingly borne the divine punishment for sin. Although Luther continues to use the words satisfaction and reparation, his central category is representation: Jesus has really taken the place of the guilty and has suffered the deserved punishment on their behalf. Christ is depicted as the one has become cursed and has suffered for all.

In explicating the vicarious nature of Jesus' penal suffering, Luther employed the term "happy exchange." An exchange takes place: Christ bears our sin; we in exchange share in his righteousness. Luther's position is thus far removed from the medieval position that saw a meritorious act of the human nature of Christ that would be equivalent to a justification by good works. The cross and death of Jesus reveals both God's wrath and love as well as God's justice and mercy.

Calvin. Whereas Anselm appropriated medieval feudal law to explicate his conception of redemption, John Calvin appropriated criminal law. Whereas in Anselm humans have failed to render what is due to God, in Calvin's conception humans are guilty before God's judgment seat and have to bear the punishment for disobedience. For Anselm, Christ renders what humans owe; for Calvin, Christ bears the punishment in place of humans. God has given humans the law. Humans have defied God by breaking the law. Consequently, they have been condemned by a righteous God. Christ has redeemed humans because he "was made a substitute and a surety in the place of transgressors and even submitted as a criminal to sustain and suffer all the punishment which would have been inflicted upon them." (*Institutes*, 2:16:10).

Grotius. The use of legal categories was modified by Grotius in a very influential way. The model was not so much that of a court of law condemning a criminal or a debtor but rather that of the head of a government responsible for establishing law, order, and justice. Punishment is for the sake of the proper ordering of society.

Modern Theology. Within the modern age, especially the Enlightenment, traditional notions of vicarious satisfaction and representation underwent a severe criticism. In the nineteenth century, modern theology attempted to rethink the meaning of redemption without bypassing the Enlightenment's critique, but taking it into account. The modern theological endeavor emphasizes the role of Christ in relation to the human self and the christian community.

Nineteenth-Century Liberal Theology. Friedrich Schleiermacher, known as the father of modern theology, sought to overcome both the traditional emphasis upon vicarious satisfaction and penal substitution and the moralism of the Enlightenment. His understanding of religion as neither metaphysical nor moral led him to define sin as that which prevents a proper relationship between self, world, and God. Sin arrests the development of the human consciousness of God. Jesus, with his sinless perfection, affects his disciples so that they are drawn under the power and influence of his sinless perfection. Due to the power and presence of God in him, Jesus is the historical and productive ideal, the historical archetype that creates something new. Redemption is not some act that Jesus does. Instead it is what Jesus is and its impact and power upon the christian community.

Schleiermacher's achievement is the double linkage: not only between the work and the being of Christ, but also between the work of Christ and the christian community. The being and work of Christ are one. The redemptive activity of Christ is connected with the presence of God in Christ and his formative activity upon christian community. Christ's redemptive activity needs to be understood in relation to his God-consciousness and its impact upon the christian community.

Schleiermacher's conception influenced the liberal theology of Albrecht Ritschl, and Horace Bushnell in the United States, and Johann Adam Moehler's conception of the unity between Christ and the christian community. The tradition was developed by Ritschl with his elucidation of Jesus' faithfulness to his calling and of the christian vocation. Ritschl's emphasis on practice and the kingdom of God strongly influenced the Social Gospel movement.

Schleiermacher's conception is dependent upon Romanticism with its emphasis upon individuality, personality, and the creative genius of great persons. The impact upon the community of Jesus' creative personality and life rather than his death is at the center of his redemptive activity. The traditional notion of satisfaction and substitution gives way to an emphasis upon the human self and the consciousness of God. The eschatological and political dimensions of redemption as described in the scriptures and the early church also lose their valence in this anthropocentric interpretation of redemption.

Twentieth-Century Conceptions of Redemption. The emphasis on the human self continues in the twentieth century, but the human self is understood as a much more fragile and ambiguous self. Consequently the existential and transcendental approaches continue and develop elements of modern conceptions of redemption with important modifications. At the same time a reaction to modern anthropological approaches leads to a more trinitarian conception of redemption. And the rediscovery of the eschatological dimension of the christian gospel as well as heightened experiences of oppression lead to new understandings of redemption within liberation and political theologies.

Existential and Transcendental Approaches

The existential and transcendental approaches use personalistic and existential categories to conceptualize redemption. They also link redemption strongly with the doctrine of grace and sanctification. God's redemption and grace primarily justify and sanctify human subjectivity.

From Inauthenticity to Faith. Rudolf Bultmann appropriates Martin Heidegger's categories of self-understanding and authenticity. Consequently, the biblical understanding of sin is explicated as the inauthenticity of human existence, whereas faith represents authentic existence. The way from inauthenticity to authenticity, from sin to faith, is possible only as grace and as faith in a saving event that is the act of God in Christ's death and resurrection. The Jesus-event is the saving word through the Word, by being proclaimed as God's saving act that is encountered as kerygma.

From Estrangement to Centeredness. Paul Tillich uses a modern philosophical category of estrangement to explicate sin, which is the personal act of turning away from God, the self, and the world. Estrangement expresses this state in which humans are foreign even to themselves for they are not what they should be. Jesus is the New Being and not simply an ideal archetype of human essence above the conditions of existence. He participates in human finitude, the consequence of estrangement and the tragic dimension of human existence. It is in the cross that Christ's participation in existential estrangement becomes manifest. Manifestation means more than becoming known or becoming communicated; it is an effective expression or actualization of God's taking upon himself the consequences of human guilt so that atonement is actualized through the cross of Christ.

From Guilt to Freedom. Karl Rahner argues that classic christology often does not adequately express the soteriological significance of the Christ-event and that the horizon of modern Western individualism does not readily grasp the "assumption" of the whole human race in an individual, the individual human reality of Jesus. The tendency is to view Jesus as performing the redemptive activity rather than being the salvific event. While he is especially critical of traditional notions of expiation and satisfaction, Rahner emphasizes the grace of God's universal salvific will. The death on the cross does not so much effect a change in God's relation to humanity as it manifests Jesus' acceptance of God's will. His acceptance is a real symbol that signifies divine grace. Rahner thereby shifts traditonal emphasis on the "pro nobis" from Christ to God.

For Rahner, the human situation— freedom, toil, ignorance, sickness, pain, and death—is characterized by guilt. Jesus is the absolute savior. The question is the connection between the death of Christ as God's grace and human freedom as liberated. Jesus' death and resurrection possess causality of a quasisacramental and real-symbolic nature. That which is signed and symbolized, the death and resurrection, causes what it signifies in and through the sign. God's offer is entered into in free obedience and surrender to God.

Restoration of Vision. H. Richard Niebuhr suggests that redemption has traditionally been understood with the aid of legal symbols and the correlative vocabulary of those symbols: commandment, obedience, transgression, and repentance. Instead he suggests the alternative symbol of the human as the maker and realizer of ideals. In this understanding human wretchedness is self-contradictoriness. Sin is not so much lawbreaking as vice. It is the perverse direction of human will, *hamartia,* missing the mark, rather than transgression of the law. Salvation is the restoration of the vision of God to humans, and the actualization of the power to live in the likeness of the vision. Christ as the responsible model, has the dual role: representing God to humanity and humanity to God.

From Passivity to Self-Affirmation. Feminist theology has criticized traditional theologies of sin and grace as well as the meaning of redemption. Traditionally human sin was conceived in terms of pride and power. Redemption was the result of loving self-sacrificial obedience. The grace of redemption makes possible such sacrificial love and obedience. Feminist analysis of the experience of women indicates that not desire for power but powerlessness, not pride but a lack of self-affirmation, characterizes the existential dilemma of women. Consequently, redemption and its grace should be not conceptualized primarily in categories of self-sacrifice and obediential love, but rather as the re-imaging of relations and empowering to a self-identity within human relations.

Each of these five existential interpretations of redemption shows how redemption involves a transition from one state to another state. Their contribution is to show the meaning of sin and redemption for human existence. Their weakness is that the eschatological dimensions of christian redemption relating to God and to society do not receive sufficient attention.

Trinitarian Conceptions of Redemption

Attempts to think of conceptions of redemption primarily in terms of the activity of God as triune represent an effort to counterbalance the anthropocentric interpretations of redemption.

Reconciliation and Redemption. Karl Barth made eschatology rather than Christology the locus for the doctrine of redemption. In his trinitarian approach to systematic theology, Barth distinguishes between reconciliation and redemption. The life and death of Jesus Christ accomplish the reconciliation of the world with God that is manifest in the resurrection. Reconciliation and redemption are thereby distinguished. Barth underscores the four *pro-nobis* elements of the reconciliation: Christ is the judge; he is judged in our place; the judgment was his death; and he establishes and reveals the righteousness of God. In Christ as the judge, humans meet a savior who acts to overcome wrong and to establish righteousness and bring salvation. Jesus took the place of humans as sinner and is put to death in our place. Barth's exposition of atonement is critical of traditional conceptions. Atonement is neither satisfaction offered to the wrath of God nor does substitution prevent our sufferings. It is not God's wrath that is satisfied but God's love that works itself out through the victory over sin. Barth's conception has used not only juridical and forensic terms primarily, but the modern emphasis upon human subjectivity has been transferred to God so that God is seen as absolute subject. By distinguishing reconciliation and redemption, Barth underscores the need for the redemptive Spirit to work in the church and society to effect the work of redemption.

Event within God. Eberhard Jüngel proposes that the death of Jesus establishes a new relationship to God. It discloses the being of God in its divine vitality. God bears Jesus' death and by taking it on conquers. God demonstrates in the death and resurrection of Jesus that the divine reality is a living unity of life and death. In this way the doctrine of the trinity is a doctrine of soteriology. The victory over death in the resurrection of Jesus constitutes not only God's overcoming of death on the cross but also God's identification with the dead Jesus. God's identification with Jesus in his death is a turning around of death.

Jürgen Moltmann's trinitarian understanding of God exhibits the dialectic of the identification of the cross and suffering with hope and the resurrection. This dialectic of suffering and hope in cross and resurrection is located in the Trinity which incorporates the suffering of history in itself. By relating suffering to the Trinity, suffering is not only placed in the

radical ground of all being, but the answer to suffering, the righteousness of God is fulfilled by the resurrection of Christ and the sending of the Spirit as the history of God's love in suffering for the whole world.

Dramaturgical Event. In a sharp criticism of Karl Rahner's stress on God's unchanging salvific will, von Balthasar seeks to develop an understanding that appropriates the classical substitution theory with some modification. The redemptive death of Jesus on the cross is a double paradox. Jesus is handed over so that the sin of the world might vent its wrath on him. Upon the cross Jesus experiences the darkness of the state of sin in a most radical manner because his experience takes place in the relation of the divine hypostases. The handing over by God the Father of Jesus is made possible through the Son's loving obedience. Jesus' crucifixion, therefore, is both an abandonment and a manifestation of God's love. It is not just a manifestation of God's love but it is an event that relates to the inner-Trinity, so that one can speak of Jesus' death as relating to God the Father and effecting human redemption.

Redemption in Political and Liberation Theology

At the turn of the century various movements, for example, religious socialism, the Social Gospel, and the Ritschlian School sought to emphasize the social dimension of redemption. The resource for these attempts lies primarily in their emphasis upon the social nature of Kingdom language. These movements emphasized the political and social images of redemption within the tradition. The scriptures explicitly testify to a political and social dimension of redemption. Redemption for Israel extends not only to forgiveness of Israel's sin, but includes a political and societal dimension. The discovery that the historical context of

NT eschatology was apocalypticism, however, led to a criticism of the understanding of eschatology and redemption within these movements.

In the 1960's the emergence of political and liberation theologies has sought to take into account historical criticism and yet to appropriate eschatology and apocalypticism anew. In this appropriation political and liberation theologies have commonly sought to explore the social and political dimensions of redemption. Yet they have done so in diverse ways.

Metz. Johann Baptist Metz underscores the apocalyptic character of eschatology. His view provides an eschatological reservation and critique of all political parties and programs. It reveals that the christian conception of history is not simply an immanent progressive evolution to higher and higher stages of history. The christian understanding of redemption asserts that the human history of suffering is at the same time a history of guilt. This history of suffering is a history of victims and unmasks the ideology of emancipatory progress. Arguing that no theoretical solution can mediate between suffering, history, and redemption, Metz argues for an understanding of redemption that is a narrative and commemorative solidarity with Jesus.

Latin American Theologians. Latin American liberation theologians criticize the understanding of redemption within political theology, represented by Metz's advocacy of apocalypticism and Moltmann's inner-Trinitarianism. They argue that where love, peace, and justice take place on earth, there is already the beginning, incomplete and imperfect, of the final eschatological peace and love, an "*identification* without total *identity*" between the redemptive salvation and political liberation.

Various models can express this identification that is not a total identity: 1) a unity in duality, as for example the Chalcedonian model of two natures but one person; 2) a sacramental model according to which the divine salvific will is signified and made present with human historical reality in an incomplete and partial mode; 3) an anthropological model that uses the language of body and soul to express the relation of redemptive salvation and liberation, so that redemptive salvation always transcends historical and political liberation just as spirit transcends body. Yet they constitute a unity in duality within a single history just as spirit and body constitute the unity of the human being.

Schillebeeckx. The mediating approach of Edward Schillebeeckx stands between the more apocalyptic model of redemption within Metz's political theology and the more incarnational-integrational model of Latin American liberation theology. His emphasis upon Jesus' *abba* experience and life-praxis and his refusal to attribute a salvific role to Jesus' death, considered alone and in itself, places him close to nineteenth-century liberal conceptions of redemption. Nevertheless, he explores the meaning of Jesus' death on the cross within the early christian kerygma. Within this context he criticizes the political ineffectiveness of Metz's purely formal "eschatological proviso" and seeks to relate christian redemption to human wholeness and integrity. A theological and practical exposition of the christian proclamation of redemption points to the limitations of emancipatory processes insufficiently attentive to the limits of self-liberation and to individual freedom within modern society.

Systematic Theology

Diversity and Ambiguity. The diversity within traditional Christianity on the meaning of redemption represents not so much a deficit as an abundance. The diversity of images, symbols, and categories of redemption cannot be reduced to a unified system or point without omitting important elements of the meaning of redemption. Commemorative narratives about the history of suffering and the redemptive history of Jesus and the christian community also cannot be reduced to a single notion of redemption. Consequently, the task of a theology of redemption is first of all to underscore the diversity of these symbols, images, and categories as well as the irreducibility of the narratives of suffering and redemption.

How Christians understand redemption affects their conceptions not only of God and Christ, but also of the human self and the world. The tradition has used metaphors such as sacrifice, expiation, propitiation, ransom, trickery, exchange, satisfaction, merit, instrumental causality, substitution, moral influence, etc. Each of these categories represents not only distinct understandings of redemption, but they also affect how the christian community understands itself, its mission, and its role in the world.

The interpretation of symbols must attend not only to their diversity but also to their ambiguity, The more profoundly religious a symbol is, the more profoundly ambiguous it can be. The cross of Jesus as a symbol of self-sacrificial love has been one of the most powerful symbols of Christianity. As a symbol, it challenges Christians to self-transcendence in their faith and commitment. But as a symbol it can also be repressive if it is proclaimed to oppressed groups and individuals. Just as the symbol of cross has its meaning in the context of the life history and practice of Jesus, so too its appropriation and application needs to be guided by this life-practice.

Representation and Redemption. Modern discussions about the redemptive nature of Jesus' life, death, and resurrection move between "subjective" and "objective" conceptions as two extremes.

Subjective approaches criticize notions of representation and substitution as well as satisfaction and propitiation. Guilt and sin are individual and cannot be transferred. Redemption is both an effect and cause of personal influence. Objective approaches criticize the subjective theories for their individualism and their inability to grasp the social nature of sin, guilt, and human nature. Such contrasts and extremes falsify the understanding of redemption. Although the historical tradition spoke of Jesus' suffering and death as redemptive, it went beyond it in three ways. It related Jesus' suffering and death to his life, the community, and God.

First: language about the redemptive meaning of Jesus' suffering and death makes no sense unless it takes into account to what extent his suffering and death is to be seen as a consequence of his proclamation, ministry, and life-practice. His life practice manifests a double solidarity with God and with humans: Jesus as pro-existence and *pro nobis.* Only within the context of the life of Jesus does the expression of the solidarity of his death display its meaning.

Second: the death has to be connected with the emergence of the christian community as a response to the life of Jesus and to his death. Jesus' redemptive role includes the power of his Spirit in the community. It is important to avoid an individualistic conception of sin and guilt. Human existence is social and political. As social, human selves are formed within and through social interaction, humans incur responsibility that extends to others. Everyone is integral to the community in which she or he lives and works. Jesus has therefore a representational significance within the human community.

Third: Jesus' death has to be related to God's gracious love, manifest in creation, reconciliation and redemption. Jesus' pro-existence is at the same a manifestation of God's *pro nobis.* The christian belief in God's raising up of Jesus brings to the fore the identity of God and Jesus. It is not just that Jesus' identity and solidarity come to expression in his death, but it is equally true that the christian belief in Jesus' death and resurrection brings to expression Jesus' identity.

Redemption and Suffering. Redemption included not only liberation from guilt, but also liberation from suffering. The experience and history of suffering is a current reality so that any proclamation of redemption has to take into account the history of suffering. One cannot simply eliminate suffering through interiority, through denial, or by theory; suffering has to be overcome in practice. In classic terms redemption involves a liberation from spiritual powers, from death, etc.; therefore an adequate conception of redemption needs to take into account not only this more comprehensive understanding of redemption, but also the singular influence and importance of both. To play off individual suffering against political suffering or political suffering against personal suffering is to betray the meaning of redemption. A redemption that is not universal and inclusive, both personal and political, is not redemption at all because of its fragmentary and partial nature.

Redemption and Community. A survey of the diverse historical models of redemption indicates a tension between inclusivity and exclusivity. An example might be the tendency within neo-scholastic theories of redemption to focus upon the death of Christ as salvific to the exclusion of all else. Such an exclusion stands in sharp contrast to Thomas' emphasis upon the whole life of Jesus as redemptive. The full range of the christian tradition and images of redemption indicates that redemption should not be reduced to a single event. It is God's action not only in Jesus but also in the community and in history that is redemp-tive. Redemption concerns not only the relationship between Jesus' life and his death, but also that between Jesus and the community. The community's existence, purpose, and function need to be seen as a part of God's redemptive task. The distinctions between redemption and sanctification, between redemption and full salvation fail to fully articulate the redemptive role of the community and its task. This task involves not only a redemptive mission to society and to the political world; it is a task involving the members of the community, whose very identity and selves are formed within the community and its relation to society.

Redemption and Emancipation. The christian belief in redemption asserts that no specific group or agent within history can realize salvation. The christian affirmation that redemption is an act of God and Christ means that the agent of redemption cannot be identified with any particular social or political group within history. But at the same time, this christian belief proclaims that this redemption is a power affecting society and the world. This same belief calls the christian community to its task as a community affirming God as a redeeming God.

The relationship between social and political emancipatory tendencies and the christian doctrine of redemption has to be maintained in a dialectic tension. The use of apocalyptic models of redemption to critique all historical mediation of redemption and salvation leads to a passive inactivism. The use of duality-in-unity models leads to the danger that the identification might be reduced to total unity. Consequently, it becomes necessary to use the apocalyptic eschatological symbols as corrective to counterbalance duality—in unity models. Christian proclamation has to affirm this tension and dialectic in practice.

Redemption and Eschatology. The christian belief in redemption is a belief in a historical and eschatological vision. It has been expressed in images of a reconciliation of persons with themselves, with society, with nature, and with God as the ultimate cause and ground of all reality. This eschatological vision of redemption is not a vision of reality in comparison to which the present world is only a shadow within a cave. Instead it is a vision of a redemption that has begun in Jesus with his proclamation of a gracious God and with his healing and exorcisms. It is a vision of a total redemption of life and death as the christian belief in Jesus' death and resurrection proclaims. It is a vision entrusted to the christian community as task.

See Christology, Eschatology, Grace, Justification, Reign of God, Sacrifice, Sin

Gustaf Aulen, Christus Victor: An Historical Study of the Three Types of the Idea of Atonement, New York: Macmillan, 1969. F.W. Dillistone, The Christian Understanding of Atonement, Philadelphia: Westminster, 1968. Edward Schillebeeckx, Christ. The Experience of Jesus as Lord, New York: Seabury, 1977. Günther Wenz, Geschichte der Versöhjnungslehre in der evangelischen Theologie der Neuzeit, Two volumes, Munich: Kaiser, 1986. Dieter Wiederkehr, Belief in Redemption: Explorations in Doctrine from the New Testament to Today, Atlanta: John Knox, 1979. Sam K. Williams, Jesus' Death as Saving Event: The Background and Origin of a Concept, Missoula, Montana: Scholars Press, 1975.

FRANCIS SCHÜSSLER FIORENZA

REGENERATION

Meaning "rebirth," this term refers to the renewal of life accomplished through the grace of Christ, which in Jn 3:5 is described as being "born again."

See Grace, Justification.

REIGN OF GOD

The coming of God's reign was used by Jesus of Nazareth as the keynote of his mission. In the Synoptic Gospels it remains a central theological symbol through which major dimensions of Jesus' teaching and ministry are to be understood.

While the centrality of this metaphor is recognized by practically every interpreter of the NT, its precise meaning is the subject of much debate. The notion of "God's reign" was not invented by Jesus or the early church; it has deep roots within the theology and history of Israel. To gain some idea of its meaning in the NT, therefore, we should begin by tracing the origin of this concept within the Hebrew Scriptures.

I. Old Testament and Jewish Background of the "Reign of God"

While the specific term "kingdom" or "reign" of God is a NT formulation, the notions underlying this concept of God's ultimate sovereignty have deep roots within biblical history and the Hebrew Scriptures. The full concert of motifs that will merge in the NT metaphor are to be found only in post-exilic Judaism but most of the basic elements reach back to the earlier stages of Israel's history. It should not be assumed, however, that the notion of God's Reign underwent a smooth evolutionary development. In this, as in most matters, OT thought is pluralistic and non-systematic in its expression.

A number of strands of OT theology underlie the "Reign of God" motif:

1) God's Salvific Power in the History of Israel. God's reign or sovereignty over Israel is experienced first and foremost in Israel's own history of salvation. The events of deliverance from slavery in Egypt, protection and guidance during the wilderness wandering, the forging of the covenant, the gift of the land, protection from surrounding enemies, the establishment and continuation of the monarchy, the return from exile—all of these and more were viewed as acts of God's salvific power on behalf of Israel. There are many metaphors used to

express such salvific acts: God is seen as Shepherd (Psalm 23), as *Go'el* or redeemer (Is 44:6), as Father (Jer 3:19), as Mother (Is 49:15), as Warrior (Ex 15:3) and so on. Within this array of images that of "king" takes its place.

It is difficult to determine if the explicit use of "king," or the more frequent active designation of God's "reign" or "rule," predates the period of the monarchy. (Because the biblical uses of this metaphor emphasize the dynamic character of God's relationship as "king" [*melek* in Hebrew; *basileus* in Greek] the preferred translation of the Hebrew word *malkut* [kingdom] and the Greek *basileia* [kingdom] is that of "reign" or "rule" rather than the more static term "kingdom.") But preparation for this use is surely found in the constant acknowledgements of God's saving power on behalf of Israel and the allegiance Israel owed God because of this. This is, in fact, a fundamental motif of the entire Pentateuch. The famous creed in Deuteronomy 26 is typical: "A wandering Aramean was my father; and he went down into Egypt and sojourned there, few in number; and there he became a nation, great, mighty, and populous. And the Egyptians treated us harshly, and afflicted us, and laid upon us hard bondage. Then we cried to the Lord, the God of our fathers, and the Lord heard our voice, and saw our affliction, our toil, and our oppression; and the Lord brought us out of Egypt with a mightly hand and an outstretched arm, with great terror, with signs and wonders; and he brought us into this place and gave us this land, a land flowing with milk and honey" (Deut 26:5b-9). Much of Deuteronomistic theology centers on the active memory of God's saving deeds on behalf of the people.

Use of the kingly metaphor is found in the famous "canticle of sea" (Exod 15:1-18) which praises the warrior God who delivered Israel from the Egyptians: "I will sing to the Lord, for he has triumphed gloriously; the horse and his rider he has thrown into the sea. The Lord is my strength and my song, and he has become my salvation; this is my God, and I will praise him, my father's God, and I will exalt him. The Lord is a man of war; the Lord is his name..." (Exod 15:1-3).

At its conclusion the hymn moves explicitly to speak of God's "reign," an idea implicit in the entire recital of God's protective power; "Thou wilt bring them in, and plant them on thy own mountain, the place, O Lord, which thou hast made for thy abode, the sanctuary, O Lord, which thy hands have established. The Lord will reign for ever and ever" (Exod 15:17-18). This text probably dates from the period of the monarchy, although it is coupled to what is one of the oldest traditions in the Pentateuch (see the song of Miriam in Exod 15:21 which praises God as delivering warrior).

2) God as Creator and Cosmic Ruler. Some have suggested that another source for the later notion of Yahweh as ruler is to be found in ancient Near Eastern mythologies which exerted their influence on Israel by way of Canaanite culture. These creation myths depicted God exercising royal power in the primeval struggle to create the world and in the continual cycle of fertility and renewal that sustained creation. Such myths were celebrated in cult where the primeval combat between good and evil and the renewal of the fertility of the earth were reenacted. The gods would be acclaimed as kings because of their exercise of sovereignty and protection over the life of the people.

It is difficult to determine the exact extent to which such myths influenced the worship of Israel, but it is probable that Israel was not immune to its surrounding culture. What is clear is that especially in Israel's cult are the notions of Yahweh as cosmic king to be found. The enthronement psalms are the most forceful example of this. Psalm 93 merges creation motifs with acclamation of Yahweh as king: "The Lord reigns; he is robed in majesty; the Lord is robed, he is girded with strength. Yea, the world is established; it shall never be moved; thy throne is established from of old; thou art from everlasting" (Ps 93:1-2).

Cosmic motifs are also found in Psalm 96: "O sing to the Lord a new song, sing to the Lord, all the earth. . . Say among the nations, 'The Lord reigns! Yea, the world is established, it shall never be moved. . .'" (Ps 96:1, 10).

Similarly Psalm 97 presents Yahweh as reigning from a cosmic throneroom and moving all the earth to offer awed homage: "The Lord reigns; let the earth rejoice; let the many coastlands be glad! Clouds and thick darkness are round about him; righteousness and justice are the foundation of his throne. Fire goes before him, and burns up his adversaries round about. His lightnings lighten the world; the earth sees and trembles. The mountains melt like wax before the Lord, before the Lord of all the earth" (Ps 97:1-5).

The same motif is found in Psalms 98 and 99: "The Lord reigns; let the peoples tremble! He sits enthroned upon the cherubim; let the earth quake!" (Ps 99:1).

The Psalms are a distillation of many currents of OT thought and that is the case here. Besides the introduction of cosmic and creation motifs, the Psalms also blend in two other aspects of God's sovereignty or reign: 1) the extension of God's rule to all nations; 2) and the motif already discussed above—God's saving actions on behalf of Israel. Psalm 97, for example, stresses that Yahweh is "Lord of all the earth" and acclaims ". . . thou, O Lord, art most high over all the earth; thou art exalted far above all gods," a universal sovereignty that is echoed in creation itself ("The heavens proclaim God's righteousness") and in God's

particular deliverance of Israel (". . . God preserves the lives of the saints; God delivers them from the hand of the wicked"). A similar blend is found in Psalm 47: "For the Lord, the Most High, is terrible, a great king over all the earth. God subdued peoples under us, and nations under our feet. God chose our heritage for us, the pride of Jacob whom he loves." Psalm 136 is a recital of God's kingly deeds that moves from God's cosmic lordship and rule over creation through the story of the exodus deliverance to the donation of the land— the whole span of motifs subsumed under the notion of God's reign.

Such a blend is implicit in much of the theology of the OT but comes to its most exuberant expression in Israel's cult. Here is most clearly seen how foundational and expansive are the OT roots for the later metaphor of "The Reign of God."

3) *The Experience of the Monarchy.* While some explicit use of the metaphor of Yahweh as king may have preceded the establishment of the monarchy in Israel, there is no doubt that a major impulse to the use of this symbol came with Israel's own experience of centralized government. The adopting of a monarchical system came slowly and with some reluctance. Israel's more independent tribal or clan system ultimately gave way to a centralized monarchy under the pressures of outside threat, particularly from the threat of the coastal Philistines to the west attempting to retrieve the hill country absorbed by the Israelite tribes, but also from the perennial incursions of desert marauders from the east and southeast.

Although the monarchy would eventually be established under Saul and David, the Bible still contains wry comment on the dangers of centralized rule. The curious fable in Judg 9:8-15 about the olive tree, the fig and the vine all reluctant to rule and then allowing the useless brambles to be the ruler seems to imply that only the unproductive and the useless are willing to be king. In 1 Samuel 8 this anti-monarchical strain comes to the surface. The failure of the judges leads the elders to ask Samuel to appoint a king over them (1 Sam 8:1-6). Yahweh's response interprets this request as a rejection of his own reign over Israel: "Hearken to the voice of the people in all that they say to you; for they have not rejected you, but they have rejected me from being king over them. According to the deeds which they have done to me, from the day I brought them up out of Egypt even to this day, forsaking me and serving other gods, so they are also doing to you" (1 Sam 8:7-8).

Samuel is then instructed to tell the people "the ways of the king who shall reign over them," which leads to a catalogue of the abuses of centralized authority which exploits the people for the aggrandizement of the king (see 1 Sam 8:10-18). Despite such warnings the people persist in asking for a king and Yahweh concedes. The process of selecting Saul then begins.

Such wry warnings and reluctance about the monarchy help temper the divine sanctions ultimately ascribed to the Davidic monarchy. While the King is given God's blessing and is promised divine protection and even an enduring dynasty, this authority was clearly understood to be limited by God's own sovereignty. Yahweh's ultimate reign over Israel is not relinquished in the presence of an earthly king. The earthly king is empowered by God and through coronation becomes "son of God" (see Ps 2:7). As God's "son" the king is both imbued with divine authority and responsible to act in God's name and in the manner of God's own saving and compassionate care for Israel.

The encounters of David and Nathan illustrate well both the scope and limits of monarchy in Israel. The prophet's oracle brings divine sanction to the monarchy which is now established, not reluctantly, but in order to protect Israel: "And I will appoint a place for my people Israel, and will plant them, that they may dwell in their own place, and be disturbed no more; and violent people shall afflict them no more, as formerly, from the time that I appointed judges over my people Israel; and I will give you rest from all your enemies" (2 Sam 7:10-11).

David and his offspring will be the means by which God establishes an everlasting dynasty: "When your days are fulfilled and you lie down with your ancestors, I will raise up your offspring after you, who shall come forth from your body, and I will establish his kingdom. He shall build a house for my name, and I will establish the throne of his kingdom for ever. I will be his father, and he shall be my son" (2 Sam 7:12-14).

But the limits of the earthly king's authority are immediately set: "When he commits iniquity, I will chasten him with the rod of men, with the stripes of the sons of men..." (2 Sam 7:14). That chastisement quickly comes in David's own sin in having Uriah killed so that the king could take his wife. The prophet Nathan becomes the oracle of judgment just as he had been the oracle of blessing (see 2 Sam 12:1-15).

This exalted role for the king stood in obvious contrast to the actual history of the monarchy. Even David, who is presented in ideal terms, failed and exploited the weak. Solomon's wisdom was tainted by his idolatries. And the subsequent history of the kings is a seemingly endless parade of failures and compromises, leading to weakness and division, and ultimately to the demise of the north and exile for the south. The prophetic critique of the injustices perpetrated by the monarchy and the eventual failure and destruction of the monarchy set the stage for the final element leading to the post-exilic theology of the reign of God.

4) *Eschatological Hope for God's Rule.* Disillusionment with monarchy would give shape to a renewed theology of God's definitive reign over Israel. The destruction of the Northern Kingdom and the Babylonian exile were viewed by the prophets as judgments against the sins of Israel. Likewise, return from exile was seen as an act of God's forgiveness, a powerful act of salvation that itself was an exercise of God's reign over Israel. Deutero-Isaiah presents Cyrus, the King of Persia who allowed the exiles to return, as an instrument of Yahweh: "Thus says the Lord, your Redeemer ... who says of Jerusalem, 'She shall be inhabited,' and of the cities of Judah, 'They shall be built, and I will raise up their ruins' ... who says of Cyrus, 'He is my shepherd, and he shall fulfill all of my purpose'; and of the temple, 'Your foundation shall be laid.'" (Isa 44:24, 26-28).

The return to Israel is seen as act of God's powerful reign: "Sing aloud, O daughter of Zion; shout, O Israel! ... The Lord has taken away the judgments against you, he has cast out your enemies. The King of Israel, the Lord, is in your midst; you shall fear evil no more. On that day it shall be said to Jerusalem: 'Do not fear, O Zion; let not your hands grow weak.'" (Zeph 3:14-16).

Israel's hopes for restoration also fuel its vision of final salvation. At this point the notion of Yahweh's reign takes on eschatological tones, an aspect of capital importance for the NT use of the metaphor. Jeremiah foresees a new Davidic ruler, the messiah who will restore the fortunes of Judah: "Behold, the days are coming, says the Lord, when I will raise up for David a righteous Branch, and he shall reign as king and deal wisely, and shall execute justice and righteousness in the land. In his days Judah will be saved

and Israel will dwell securely. And this is the name by which he will be called: 'The Lord is our righteousness'" (Jer 23:5-6).

Deutero-Isaiah speaks in exultant and expansive terms of Yahweh's liberation of Israel from exile and of a future hope for salvation: "Thus says the Lord, your Redeemer, the Holy One of Israel: 'For your sake I will send to Babylon and break down all the bars, and the shouting of the Chaldeans will be turned to lamentations. I am the Lord, your Holy One, the Creator of Israel, your King. Thus says the Lord, who makes a way in the sea, a path in the mighty waters, who brings forth chariot and horse, army and warrior... Remember not the former things, nor consider the things of old. Behold, I am doing a new thing; now it springs forth, do you not perceive it? I will make a way in the wilderness and rivers in the desert. The wild beasts will honor me, the jackals and the ostriches; for I give water in the wilderness, rivers in the desert, to give drink to my chosen people, the people whom I formed for myself that they might declare my praise'" (Isa 43:14-21).

The famous text of Isa 52:7-10 breathes a similar eschatological tone: "How beautiful upon the mountains are the feet of him who brings good tidings, who publishes peace, who brings good tidings of good, who publishes salvation, who says to Zion, 'Your God reigns.'... Break forth together into singing you waste places of Jerusalem; for the Lord has comforted his people, he has redeemed Jerusalem. The Lord has bared his holy arm before the eyes of all the nations; and all the ends of the earth shall see the salvation of our God."

While the return to Jerusalem is the immediate referent for these songs of praise, their scope extends to God's final, eschatological salvation. Subsequent post-exilic history added more force to this projection of future hopes. Israel's political fortunes continued to wane, ruled first by Alexander, then by the Ptolemaic and then the even more repressive Seleucid dynasties. A brief respite of freedom under the Hasmoneans fell apart because of internal corruption and division as well as pressure from the Romans—who eventually seize power over Israel. Frustrated hopes for freedom and peace gave further impetus to the eschatological dimension of God's rule. What had not and could not be achieved by human effort would be finally accomplished by God's own intervention.

This aspect of the reign of God is attested in apocalyptic works like Daniel ("And in the days of those kings the God of heaven will set up a kingdom which shall never be destroyed, nor shall its sovereignty be left to another people. It shall break in pieces all these kingdoms and bring them to an end, and it shall stand for ever." Dan 2:44) and in non-biblical works such as the *Assumption of Moses* and *The Testament of the Twelve Patriarchs*. Radical reform movements such as Qumran withdrew from the corrupt environment of Hasmonean Jerusalem and its Temple system to await the final days which would be the definitive combat between good and evil and end with the establishment of God's reign.

Conclusion: God's reign or rule in the OT catches up major dimensions of biblical theology. It is a metaphor expressing God's sovereignty over every aspect of Israel's life. God's saving acts in history, God's creation and sustaining of the world, God's lordship over the nations, God's promise of ultimate salvation and peace—all of these are expressed in the metaphor of God's reign. The experience of monarchy provided the existential referent for such a theology: like the ideal king God was the cohesive and identifying force of the people, protecting them from destruction, sanction-

ing justice and befriending the weak and defenseless. At the same time, the historical failure of the monarchy projected Israel's hopes to the eschaton: in the final days Israel's impotent attempts to establish peace and justice would be swept aside and God's own reign would come.

How that was to be accomplished was not always clear nor was it projected in a single consistent way. Some traditions such as *The Psalms of Solomon* have a decisively this-worldly focus while others are more eschatological in tone (e.g., *The Testament of the Twelve Patriarchs*). Some traditions envisaged a Davidic messiah, others a priestly ruler (in the Qumran materials both expectations seem present) who would be the means by which the rule of God would be established. In other traditions God acts directly. The Zealot movement apparently believed that direct political and military action on their part against the Roman occupation would precipitate God's reign. For later rabbinic traditions, the acceptance of God's reign was equivalent to acceptance of the yoke of the Torah. In all cases Israel's hopes for salvation were firmly grounded in their memory of God's continuing fidelity to his people Jesus' own interpretation of this metaphor, while not unrelated to apocalyptic and rabbinic thought, has its own characteristics.

II. *The Reign of God in the New Testament*

The term the "reign of God" occurs more than 150 times in the NT, almost two thirds of these in the Synoptic Gospels (this includes Matthew's use of a similar term, the "kingdom of heaven"; the word "heaven" is probably a euphemism for "God" so that the metaphor has little difference in meaning). There is little doubt that the coming of God's reign was a keynote of Jesus' own ministry. Both Mark and Matthew cite this as an inaugural summary of Jesus' preaching: "Now after John was arrested, Jesus came into Galilee, preaching the gospel of God, and saying, 'The time is fulfilled, and the kingdom of God is at hand; repent, and believe in the gospel'" (Mk 1:14; similarly Mt 4:17). Although Luke formulates the beginning of Jesus' ministry in a different fashion, he, too, stresses the importance of this motif early in the gospel: "I must preach the good news of the kingdom of God to the other cities also; for I was sent for this purpose" (Lk 4:43). The reign of God is also a consistent subject of Jesus' parables and is linked to his healings and exorcisms (Mt 12:28; Lk 11:20). Claims to kingship seem to have been a contention of Jesus' trials before the Sanhedrin and Pilate and may reflect the use of this metaphor in his preaching. And all four of the gospels identify Jesus as the Davidic messiah.

In spite of the frequent reference to the "reign of God" there is no clear definition of its meaning in the ministry of Jesus or as it is used by the later NT traditions. This may be due in part to the very nature of this motif. As Norman Perrin and others have insisted it is less a "concept" or idea than it is a "symbol" whose meaning is rich and not capable of being exhausted by this or that definition or formulation. Speaking of the reign of God as a symbol rather than a clear cut concept does not imply it is without content or that attempts to decipher its meaning are invalid. Rather, the meaning of the coming "reign of God" for Jesus must be culled from the overall character of his ministry. It is to that task we now turn.

a) *The Reign of God as experience of salvation.* All of the gospels present Jesus as God's messiah, as the one who effects salvation. In the Synoptic Gospels this is interpreted as an experience of God's reign. Jesus calls Israel to repentance and

to acceptance of the approaching reign of God (Mk 1:14-15); such conversion opens one to an experience of new life. In the past the poor and the defenseless had been exploited by the kings and ruling classes; such would not be the case under God's reign. The reign of God would be "good news for the poor" (Mt 11:5; Lk 4:18).

The Gospels of Matthew and Luke explicitly link Jesus' exorcisms and healings with the experience of the Kingdom; it is implicit in the gospel of Mark as well: ". . . if it is by the Spirit of God that I cast out demons, then the kingdom of God has come upon you" (Mt 12:28; see Lk 11:20). The healings and exorcisms are stories of salvation. The sick and disabled are not only physically cured but, equally important, are given access to the community (e.g., Mk 2:1-12). Leprosy, a disease symbolic of mortality itself in the Bible, is cleansed (Mk 1:40-45). The Gadarene demoniac who dwells in the tombs, wails incessantly, is self-destructive and isolated from family and clan, is, through the power of Jesus, liberated from his demons, restored to his family and empowered to become a missionary of the gospel to the Decapolis (Mk 5:1-20). The woman bent double is not only cured of her infirmity but, over the protests of the synagogue manager, has her dignity as a "Daughter of Abraham" affirmed (Lk 13:10-17).

To the healings and exorcisms can be aligned the reports of Jesus' association with marginal people: "Behold a glutton and a drunkard, a friend of tax collectors and sinners!" (Mt 11:19; Lk 15:1). Jesus' relationships with social and religious outcasts are a type of "healing" in that he draws such people into the circle of acceptance and dissolves their alienation. A similar case could be made about Jesus' significant association with women (e.g., Lk 8:1-3) and occasional Samaritans

(Lk 17:11-19) and Gentiles (Mk 7:24-30; Mt 8:5-13). As with the healing stories such actions proclaim the inclusive and salvific nature of God's impending reign.

These stories define the reign of God as an experience of salvation. The community of Israel is restored on a just and inclusive basis. This aspect of the reign of God as defined by Jesus' ministry of salvation has obvious links with OT expectations. The gospel of Matthew evokes Isaiah 29:18-19 and 35:5-6 when Jesus lists the "deeds of the Christ" for John's emissaries: "Go and tell John what you hear and see: the blind receive their sight and the lame walk, lepers are cleansed and the deaf hear, and the dead are raised up, and the poor have good news preached to them" (Mt 11:4-5). The programmatic text of Isaiah 61 (enriched by Isa 58:6) fulfills a similar function in Luke's presentation of Jesus in the synagogue of Nazareth (see Lk 4:18-19). Jesus, as the Davidic Messiah, ushers in the longed for reign of God, a reign characterized by forgiveness and reconciliation, by universal justice and peace. To establish that reign means the transformation not only of the human heart but of the oppressive social structures that dehumanize and exclude the poor and defenseless from participation in the family of Israel.

Jesus' teaching and parables, along with his actions, proclaim this same message. The parables have been the focus of enormous interest in the past few decades; much of their message is related to Jesus' proclamation of the reign of God. Some recent interpreters resist boiling down the meaning of the parables to certain key ideas or motifs. The parables are a word event in themselves, inviting transformation of one's world through insertion into the new world created by the story or parable. While an overly analytical approach to the parables should be avoided, it is still legitimate,

however, to translate the meaning of the parables into discursive language. The evangelists reinterpreted and developed the parables, highlighting motifs important to their own theological perspective, but the link of the parables to the proclamation of the reign of God is attributable to Jesus himself.

The parables stress that the reign of God comes as "grace," that is, salvation is a gift of God to which one must respond (Mt 20:1-16, the householder who hires laborers and pays them as he will). That grace comes as gratuitous forgiveness (Lk 15:11-31; 7:41-43; Mt 18:23-35). Because salvation is rooted in God the establishment of God's reign is sure, even when its effects seem uncertain or hidden (Mk 4:3-9; 4:26-29; 4:30-32). The offer of salvation provokes crisis because it compels humans to change their lives and respond to grace (Mt 13:44; 13:45-46). Coupled with this are parables of judgment: failure to be alert for the coming of God's reign or to adequately respond to it leads to condemnation and death (Mt 13:47-50; 25:1-13; 31-46).

Much of this same teaching is found in Jesus' sayings. Here, too, there is proclamation of salvation as a gift of God (Mt 5:3-10), a consequent call for repentance (Mt 18:3), for response to the reality of God's reign expressed in mutual forgiveness (Mt 6:12, 14-15; 5:43-48) and justice (Mt 25:31-46). One must "enter into" the reign of God, an expression that connotes the necessity of the transformation and commitment demanded by the urgent reality of the reign (Mt 5:20; 7:21; 18:3; 19:23, 24; Mk 9:47; 10:23-25; Lk 18:25; Jn 3:5).

b) *The Reign of God as eschatological event.* The "timing" of the coming reign of God is perhaps the most controverted aspect in all discussions of this subject. Since the publication of Johannes Weiss's *Jesus' Proclamation of the Kingdom of God* in 1892 biblical scholarship has had to confront the strongly eschatological nature of Jesus' preaching. As noted above, the longing for God's definitive salvation of Israel had already taken root in OT theology in the post-exilic period, especially in the wake of the failure of the monarchy.

The problematic aspect of Jesus' message is that the longed-for end time is declared to be imminently present in Jesus' own ministry. The reign of God is *"at hand"*(Mk 1:14-15). The disciples are promised that they will not taste death until the reign of God has come in power (Mk 9:1; Mt. 10:23). Material like this led Weiss, A. Schweizer and others to conclude that Jesus himself expected the imminent arrival of the endtime.

But that "imminence" verges on presence in some sayings: e.g., ". . . if it is by the Spirit of God that I cast out demons, then the reign of God *has come upon you*" (Mt 12:28; Lk 11:20); "The reign of God is not coming with signs to be observed; nor will they say, 'Lo, here it is!' or 'There!' for behold, the reign of God is *in the midst of you*" (Lk 17:20; see also Lk 10:7, 11). In sayings like these the reign of God is identified with Jesus' own ministry; the experience of salvation proclaimed by Jesus and enacted in his liberating healings and exorcisms *is* the eschatological reign of God now present. This present aspect led C.H. Dodd (*The Parables of the Kingdom*) to formulate his notion of "realized eschatology."

However, the problem is further complicated by other sayings and parables which seem to present the reign of God as still future event. In the Lord's prayer, Jesus prays for the *coming* of the reign of God (see Luke 11:2-4; Mt 6:10). Judgment parables such as Mt 13:24-30 (see also 13:36-43 and 24-25) project the consummation of the reign of God as future event. So, too, does the whole complex of Son of Man material; in the so-called apocalyptic discourses of the Synoptic

Gospels, only the future coming of that exalted figure, beyond a series of crises within history and subsequent to the completion of the community's mission, will usher in the eschatological reign of God (see Mk 13:5-37).

Neither Weiss's or Dodd's solutions have proved convincing. Inevitably some dialectical approach seems necessary. Jesus, as a first century Jew, did view the reign of God as an urgent eschatological event. That reign could be identified with no particular political expression or point in time; Jesus proclaimed the definitive reign of God, the ultimate experience of salvation, that transcended every human effort to achieve peace and justice. At the same time, however, Jesus did have a peculiar sense of his own authority, as one sent by God to proclaim and effect salvation. In his own words and actions the experience of God's reign was present and accessible even if the consummation of that reign was yet to come. Thus there is an "already now but not yet" character to Jesus' proclamation of the reign of God. The compromise nature of such a solution is lessened if one keeps in mind that the biblical notion of the reign of God cannot be reduced to temporal and spatial categories. While salvation deals with genuine human pain and hope—and therefore is inevitably tied into political and social aspirations—it is not to be confused with some Camelot-type realm. The reign of God is "qualitative" as much as it is "quantitative"; in the experience of healing and reconciliation effected through the grace of God one anticipates and is already immersed in the eschatological reign of God. While the future coming of the reign of God means a profound transformation of all human reality and is a transcendent experience beyond space and time, the inbreaking of that transcendent reality through the mission of Jesus enables people to respond to God's offer of salvation and to be affected by it now, within history.

c) *The Reign of God as Theological Revelation.* Discussion of the reign of God as salvific and eschatological must also be connected with its fundamentally "theological" character; that is, the reign of God metaphor is ultimately an expression of Israel's *longing to experience God.* Because all human institutions proved impotent and because Israel hungered for peace, it looked to the coming of God as its only hope for salvation. This returns us to the starting point of our discussion; the "reign" metaphor is validated in God's sovereignty over the life of all humanity and all creation.

The gospels testify to Jesus' vivid sense of God's presence. His own piety, expressed in his characteristic address of God as *abba* (Mk 14:36), reflects a deep conviction about God's intimate presence. His teaching also emphasizes the closeness of God to creation and even more so to the human person (Mt 6:25-33; 10:25-29), particularly to the weak and insignificant whose angels behold the face of God (Mt 18:10). Several of Jesus' parables, such as the Lost Sheep (Lk 15:3-7) the Lost Coin (Lk 15:8-10), and the Lost Son (Lk 15:11-32), as well as saying something about the importance of the "little ones" (Mt 18:10), extend that providence to the individual, a peculiar emphasis of Jesus' ministry born out in his call of isolated tax collectors and disabled beggars to the company of his disciples (e.g., Mk 2:13-17; 10:46-52). God's own compassion and gracious forgiveness become the model for love of enemies and reconciliation within the community (Mt 5:43-48; 18:21-35). The disciples are to be "perfect" or "complete" (*teleios*) as God is "perfect" (Mt 5:48; Lk's parallel, 6:36, uses the term "merciful").

In short, if the reign of God is "at hand" one must ask what kind of a God and what will be the nature of God's reign? Here all of the various facets of this metaphor converge. The proclamation of Jesus reveals that God is a saving God whose coming will effect personal and social transformation. A God whose reign will mean "good news," particularly for those who have experienced oppression (Lk 6:20-23). A God whose coming will, therefore, call for decisive response and whose appearance will create crisis and provoke judgment for those whose way of life is not in accord with the reality of that reign.

III. Interpretation of the Reign of God

As with all biblical concepts and symbols, the "reign of God" proclaimed by Jesus became subject to reinterpretation by subsequent generations. This is already apparent in the NT itself. Resurrection faith concentrated on the unique identity and role of Jesus within the history of salvation. Each of the Synoptic Gospels adds its own emphasis and perspective in its presentation of Jesus and his mission. But the slogan—"Jesus preached the reign of God and the early church preached Jesus"—is not entirely accurate. The Synoptics proclaim Jesus, but a Jesus who proclaims the reign of God. There is, therefore, a credible sense of continuity between what one can deduce about the teaching of the historical Jesus and the post-Easter portrayals of Jesus' teaching and ministry in the gospels.

The gospel of John refers to the reign of God only twice (see Jn 3:3,5); apparently other symbols, such as "eternal life," function in place of the "reign" metaphor. Paul refers to the "reign of God" some 10 times, usually with a strong eschatological sense. Those who are "unjust" will not "inherit the reign of God" (see 1 Cor 6:9, 10; 15:50; Gal 5:21). In 1 Cor 15:24 Paul depicts and eschatological scenario in which Christ hands over the "reign to God the Father after destroying every rule and every authority and power." But Paul can also refer to the reign of God in a manner that suggests it is also a present reality: "For the reign of God is not food and drink but righteousness and peace and joy in the Holy Spirit" (Rom 14:17; see also 1 Cor 4:20).

The Apocalypse uses the metaphor of "throne" and "reign" as major symbols of its entire theology. The Roman Empire is depicted as a dehumanizing and demonic rule that is opposed to and will be destroyed by the Lordship of the Risen Christ. This apocalyptic combat is future but the reign of the triumphant Lamb will be over a "new heavens and new earth" (Rev 21). In the climactic chapter 19 when the vassals of Rome mourn its loss, the heavenly court offers homage to Christ who is exalted as "King of kings and Lord of lords" (Rev 19:16).

Therefore in most of the subsequent NT uses of this metaphor some of the tension between present and future already found in Jesus' proclamation remains.

Throughout Christian history various interpretations of the "reign of God" have held sway. Key issues have been whether and in what way the church is to be considered coextensive with the reality of God's reign. Augustine, for example, identified the reign of God with the church triumphant. Some later medieval theology would identify the reign of God with the historical church on earth. Interpretation of this symbol is also closely bound with one's understanding of eschatology. For those who see God's salvation as mainly future and other worldly, the reign of God is primarily an individual and spiritual experience. For those who see God's salvific power at work in the present, the reign of God is more closely tied to social and political reform.

Renewed contact with the eschato-logical tone of Jesus' and early christian thought offers an opportunity to restore this key metaphor to more of its biblical force. The "reign of God" is not an abstract, individualistic, ethical concept as some nineteenth century theologians presumed. Nor, as liberation theologians have rightly insisted, can it be divorced from social and political transformation. The key to proper interpretation of this symbol is to maintain in tension the full scope of its biblical elements: it is a metaphor expressing the impact of God's gracious and decisive act of salvation; it reveals the quality of human existence defined in the person and ministry of Jesus; it is a corporate experience to be revealed in fullness at the end of human history and yet, already now, in the light of faith, impinges on human action and human institutions. So defined the metaphor of God's coming reign found in the NT has profound continuity with its OT roots; the fundamental difference is the decisive impetus and peculiar character given to this symbol by Jesus Christ.

See **Eschatology, Parable**

Bruce Chilton (ed.), *The Kingdom of God* (Issues in Religion and Theology 5), Philadelphia: Fortress, 1984. G. Klein, "The Biblical Understanding of 'The Kingdom of God'," *Interpretation* 26 (1972) 387-418. Norman Perrin, *Jesus and the Language of the Kingdom: Symbol and Metaphor in New Testament Interpretation*, Philadelphia: Fortress, 1976. Rudolf Schnackenburg, *God's Rule and Kingdom*, New York: Herder & Herder, 1963. Johannes Weiss, *Jesus' Proclamation of the Kingdom of God*, Philadelphia: Fortress, 1971.

DONALD SENIOR, CP

RELICS

Relics are best understood theologically in terms of the place they occupy in christian memories and hope. Although the latter have first and foremost to do with what God's grace accomplished once and for all in Jesus of Nazareth, they do not stop there. As witnessed by the Acts of the Apostles, they include as well what the grace of forgiveness won on Calvary brought about in and through others such as Peter (2:14-37), Stephen (6:8-60) Paul (9:1-20), and Lydia (16:14-15, 40).

Less than forty years after their deaths in Rome, the memory of both Peter and Paul is evoked in an effort to restore peace to the church in Corinth (*1 Clement* V:1-7). At the beginning of the second century, Polycarp of Smyrna—for the benefit of others—shares letters that Ignatius, Bishop of Antioch, had written— at least some on the way to martyrdom in Rome (*Letter to the Philippians* XIII:2).

Through what they taught and wrote as well as through their example, saints influenced their contemporaries as well as succeeding generations. It was, however, only through their bodies that saints were able to do this. Those bodies—even after the saints had left this world— remained the instruments through which the invisible world of things divine had been glimpsed. This memory provided grounds for Christians to venerate the mortal remains of the saints (*relics* in the strict sense). So likewise did a twofold hope: a) that the saints would rise again in resurrection; and b) that the saints even after death would continue to do for others by the help of God's grace the great things they had done while on earth. By extension the term *relics* came to refer to objects that had come in contact with a saint's mortal remains.

A very early witness to the cult of martyrs and respect for their relics is found in a letter of the church of Smyrna, *The Martyrdom of Polycarp* (A.D. 156 c.). Attitudes and practices of this kind spread. They are desribed at length by Augustine in his *City of God.* The Second Council of Nicea (787) censured those who rejected relics and required that churches not be consecrated without relics (*Conciliorum Oecumenicorum*

Decreta, ed., G Alberigo, Freiburg, Herder, 1962, pp. 113, 121).

Through the centuries relics became the occasion of the most serious kind of abuses: e.g., misplaced piety at least bordering on polytheism and idolatry, superstition, and avarice. The Reformers of the sixteenth century objected to relics on these grounds with Luther denouncing as worst of all "...the claim that relics effect indulgences and the forgiveness of sins..." (*Smalcald Articles* II, 2, 23).

At the urging of Cardinal Guise of Lorraine, who was concerned with Calvinism, the Council of Trent defended relics and mandated reforms aimed at correcting abuses (D.S. 1822, 5).

In words that are relevant to (though not explicitly applied to) the veneration of relics, the Second Vatican Council teaches that every authentic witness of love offered to the saints in heaven terminates in Christ, the crown of all the saints, and through him in God (L.G. 50).

Peter Brown, *The Cult of the Saints,* Chicago: University of Chicago Press, 1981. J. Pelikan, *The Spirit of Eastern Christendom,* Chicago: University of Chicago Press. 1974, and esp. "Images of the Invisible" 91-145.

CARL J. PETER

RELIGIONS

Recognition of religions other than one's own has existed from the beginning of the great world civilizations. The foreign religion was usually reduced to allegory, euhemerism, or some natural cause. The study of the world religions begins when one observes with seriousness religious pluralism; the study has foundation when religious experiences and expressions are made intelligible to those outside the tradition; the study flourishes when significant meaning is grasped by the outsider. The passage from observation to intelligibility and finally to meaning rests upon the assumption that one can ultimately come to understand the religious experiences of another from the perspective of that person.

History of the Study of the Religions

The first phase of this study began with the natural philosophers of ancient Greece and ended with the rationalist and romantic philosophers of the eighteenth century. The heightened curiosity of the ancient Greek thinkers focused on the stories of the gods, namely, the myths and rituals of their neighbors. One tendency of the philosophers was to reduce the pluriformity of myth and cult to a single primal principle of nature; others advanced allegory or even psychological need as basis for pluriformity. These same reasons were drawn upon well into the christian medieval period. The Greeks, however, did discover a key in the comparative method by explaining foreign gods with attitudes from their own culture and cult.

Hebrew and christian scripture took a more defensive and exclusive stance toward the myths and rituals of others. The major concern during this formative period was to preserve a people, a nation, the followers of Jesus, and other religious groups were competitors to such goals. The christian apologists were the first to move beyond cultural provincialism. While gathering massive data on ancient religions and cults, they appropriated the philosophical reductionism of the ancient Greeks. Two tendencies developed among the early Fathers of the Church: the Latin Fathers adopted biblical notions of exclusivity, while the Greek Fathers, although still apologetic, drew upon the Greek notion of *logos spermatikos*—the seminal word—as foundational for the sharing of truth in the world of Greek, Jew, or Christian. Later thinkers utilized this notion as the basis for the development-fulfillment theory in explaining the relationships between religions and the ever emerging new religions in history.

Even Islam in relating itself to Judaism, Christianity, and the other traditions of Semitic and Arabic origin saw itself as the development and fulfillment of the earlier traditions. For Muslims the seminal word is the literal word, namely, the *Qur'an*. The first history of world religions may have been written by a Muslim, Shahrastani, in 1153 C.E., titled *Religious Parties and Schools of Philosophy*. Some descriptions of the religions of northern Europe began to appear in the eleventh and twelfth centuries. Roger Bacon in the thirteenth century did a major work (although not published until the eighteenth century) classifying and describing all religions known to him. Neither the contact of the church with Islam nor the encounter between christian and Arabic philosophers contributed to a mutual understanding of these traditions. Christian thinkers were without sufficient materials to move beyond apologetical motivation and method. The christian missionary effort from the thirteenth century onward was far more enlightened as it amassed a new body of information. Some few descriptive studies did appear in this first phase of study; the comparative method and classification of religions were indicators of future study.

The second phase in the study of world religions began in the eighteenth century with the first knowledge of the so-called primitive (primal) religions reaching Europe. A new wave of christian missionaries became the early ethnologists and amateur anthropologists. The subject of scholarly concern was still myth and ritual of all that was foreign, but the primitive world raised the new question of religious origins. Philosophy of religions, as a discipline, emerges, and David Hume (1711-1776) writes *Dialogues Concerning Natural Religions* in which he argues that polytheism is the first stage of religious civilization. Three major intellectual influences impacted on the modern study of religions: evolution, empiricism, and interiority. Darwin's 1859 *Origin of the Species* influenced early scholars of religion. The positivism of nineteenth century philosophy resulted in a rigid empiricism and equally severe historicism whereby the human mind in its speculation was limited to empirical data. Yet, the German pietism of Friedrich Schleiermacher (1768-1844) and Ludwig Feuerbach (1804-1872) rejected the naturalists' approach to religion by focusing on subjectivity and the absolute dependence on the Infinite in human experience. New materials, discoveries, and competencies contributed in advancing the study of religions from mid-nineteenth century onward: a period of language competency began with Indo-European philology and comparative linguistics; ethnological data collected by missionaries continued with schools of researchers going out to tribes of Australia, Polynesia, Africa, North and South America; archaeological discoveries abounded in Egypt, the Hittite civilization of the Middle East, the Harappa and Mohenjo-Daro civilization of the Indus river valley; translations of the religious classics of the world began with Indian texts (*Rig-Veda*) and Persian texts (*Avesta*) available to western scholars for the first time; Max Muller began a gigantic translation project with the *Sacred Books of the East*.

The modern study of world religions advanced with the emergence of the humanistic disciplines of anthropology, history, psychology, sociology, and phenomenology. Underlying the new disciplines was the study of language and literature, in this case new languages and new literatures. The study of world religions became not only multi-disciplinary but also multi-methodological and multi-cultural. In university circles, area studies were introduced, namely, Japanese or Chinese studies within which religion is one component, or Indian,

Persian, and Arabic studies within which the religions of these civilizations form a major component. Study of the religions developed into a field of studies more than a discrete or single discipline.

Early anthropological approaches, drawing upon ethnography of primal cultures and initially focusing on myth and ritual, became more concerned with religious origins or religious development. Theories of animism (E. Tylor), pre-animism (R.R. Marett and K.T. Preuss), the high sky-god (A. Lang), primitive monotheism (W. Schmidt), pre-logical mentality (L. Levy-Bruhl) were responses to ancient religious origins. These theories, each with some partial validity, appropriated the comparative method, and through the observation of parallel phenomena constructed typologies. Bronislaw Malinowski (1884-1942), through rigorous field method requiring the scholar to be a "participant observer," brought refinement to anthropological method. Malinowski also went beyond questions of religious origins and development and focused upon religion as a total way of life and attempted to capture in his study the experience of that life.

Modern anthropology of religion is frequently divided between the social anthropologists (A.R. Radcliffe-Brown, E.E. Evans-Pritchard) who perceive religion sustaining and legitimating the social order, and the structural anthropologists (C. Levi-Strauss, and G. Dumezil in comparative literature) who perceive religion ordering environment and experiences. Social anthropologists seek out the function of social and religious institutions and facts; structuralists search for either the unconscious or conscious foundations of behavior and phenomenon. Clifford Geertz, Mary Douglas, Victor Turner are representative of the most contemporary anthropological approach to the study of religion which is to view religious phenomenon as symbol and a particular religion as a symbolic world or symbol system. Anthropology supports the premise that religion supplies the resources to deal with a suffering human condition.

Social scientists still look to Emile Durkheim (1853-1917) and Max Weber (1864-1920) as significant social theorists of religion. Durkheim's 1912 book, *The Elementary Forms of Religious Life,* based religious origins on a theory of totemism which ultimately judged religion as a projection of social experience. The psychological, evolutionary, and comparative influences are evident in his work, but he is especially recognized as one who saw the theoretical development of dual realities as a methodological aid to understanding, e.g., sacred and secular, society and culture, state-religion. With Max Weber came a shift of interest by sociology of religion to religious behavior and especially modernization and secularization processes. Weber more than his predecessors brought to this study non-European and non-christian interests with materials from Jewish, Indian, and Chinese cultures. Utilizing the comparative method, Weber developed a series of typologies for the study of religious groups and their relationships to social, political and economic order. Joachim Wach (1898-1955) wrote the first systematic study of the sociology of religion. His concern was the whole of religious experience as it interacts with social experience. Contemporary sociologists view religion either as derivative of social experience or religion as legitimating social life. Wach kept society and religion in reciprocal relationship in order to analyze their functional character. Recent scholars (R. Bellah, P. Berger, T. Luckmann) have shifted the interest in religion study to the social construction of reality.

Sigmund Freud (1856-1939) not only introduced psychoanalytic method to the study of religion but also the unconscious as the seat of repressive and subliminal infantile conflicts and the source of neurotic projection. Although his writing on the origin and development of religion drew heavily on totemism, his notion of psychological projectionism is taken up by scores of social scientists. Carl Jung (1875-1961) took a more optimistic stance toward the riches of the collective unconscious which he saw filled with archetypes or patterns of universal behavior. He moved the subject of religion study to religious behavior, and dream analysis was his special methodology. In 1902 William James published *The Varieties of Religious Experience,* a book which not only proposed new psychological typologies (healthy-minded and sick-minded) but also established that religion is *sui generis* and need not be reduced through social scientific study. Although James' study is one of the first accounts of mysticism by a social scientist, it identifies religious experience in ordinary human life. Analysis of the religious personality continues among more contemporary scholars. The range of methodologies is most significant among recent scholars whose analysis may entail psychohistory (E. Erikson), a personalist/humanist focus (A. Maslow, E. Fromm), or behaviorist (B.F. Skinner), structuralist (J. Piaget), and developmentalist frameworks (L. Kohlberg, G.W. Allport).

Max Muller (1823-1900) coined the notion of a science of religion (*Religionswissenschaft*). He viewed the study of religion as an autonomous discipline. Although a linguist professionally, he is considered the father of the comparative study of religion, who once observed that he who knows one religion knows none. Cornelis P. Tiele (1830-1902) attempted the first systematic typology of religions. Like scholars to follow he was both a generalist in religious phenomena and a specialist in a more particular area, in this case the traditions of Iran. P.D. Chantepie de la Saussaye (1848-1920) in writing a manual of religion was one of the first to use the phrase the phenomenology of religion. He distinguished the historical study from the phenomenological study of religious phenomena, the former preceding in time the latter. Upon this foundation a host of scholars advance the study: W. Brede Kristensen, F. Heiler, C.J. Bleecker, R. Pettazoni. They contribute to the historical and phenomenological study of religion as a cross-cultural and inter-religious task. Special mention needs to be made of several monumental figures. Rudolph Otto published *Das Heilige* (The Idea of the Holy) in 1917, and in the following two decades this classic went into twenty-five editions. His work, on the one hand, is considered by some to be a psychological study of humankind's deepest feelings in face of the totally other and, on the other hand, judged by others to reflect a phenomenological analysis of the structures of high religious experience, namely, the *tremendum et fascinans.* Otto was to influence G. Van der Leeuw who in 1933 wrote a monumental phenomenological study of religion, *Religion in Essence and Manifestation.* It is here that Husserl's philosophical vocabulary of phenomenology is employed: *epoche* (the suspension of the scholar's value judgements) and eidetic vision (an intuitive grasp of the meaning of the phenomenon). The method has been vigorously debated with the apparent resolution that historical analysis, along with phenomenological and structural analysis, is required for a more integral understanding of religion. From this point onwards empathy (*Einfuhlung*) for one's materials characterizes the researcher. Mircea Eliade (1907-1986) in his original work *Patterns in Comparative Religion* and in essays to follow employs a structural approach based in symbolism as a methodological framework. Wilfred

Cantwell Smith, an Islamicist with historical, comparativist, and linguistic interest, has argued for a personalist understanding of the religious traditions. He clearly distinguishes between the understanding of historical tradition and the faith of a living community. W.C. Smith has made the meaning of faith and the role of the believer in the study of religions a leading question today. The scholars cited above have characteristically been specialists in some one religious tradition other than their own while attempting to make statements pertaining to religions in general and in global history.

Classifications and Types of Studies

Early studies have indicated that no single system of classification is adequate. Geographical classifications were at one time popular: middle-eastern (Judaism, ancient Greek and Latin cults, Christianity, Islam), subcontinent of India (Hinduism, early Buddhism, Jainism, Sikhism); far-eastern (Confucianism, Taoism, Shinto, Mahayana Buddhism). Ethnographic classifications were also common with early linguists (for example, religions of the Oceanic, African, American, Mediterranean, Semitic, Indo-European peoples). Philosophical and theological classifications were utilized until recent times (monotheistic-polytheistic religions; supernatural-natural religions; historical-ahistorical religions; religions of the divine, of nature, or of magic). Early scholars came up with morphological categories corresponding to evolutionary forms: animism, pre-animism, polytheism, primitive monotheism. Phenomenological classifications have been the most lasting and some have extended to our own time. For example W. B. Kristensen in *The Meaning of Religion* classifies religions according to cosmology, anthropology, cultic acts, and cultic times, places, and images. Van der Leeuw, another phenomenologist, broadly categorizes religious phenomena according to the object of religion, the subject of religion, and object and subject in their reciprocal relationships. Wach draws distinctions between theoretical expressions (symbol, myth, doctrine), practical expressions (acts, cult), and social expression (community, church, covenant, and authority). Classification and categorization usually reflect the time and place of origination and methodological assumptions.

Recent studies have been more modest than the pioneers of earlier generations. Socio-historical studies are limited to one or a group of religious traditions; anthropological or literary studies are limited to one or a group of myths and rituals. The most challenging studies have been from a symbolic perspective: Eliade working with a cluster of symbols; Geertz establishing an operative symbol system; W.C. Smith focusing on faith symbols; Wach speaking of the distinctive and characteristic element(s) of one or more religious traditions. The greatest body of research in our day on the religions of the world are highly specific studies on a single topic limited by time, place, and resources. It should be noted that thorough or integral study must reflect three levels of analysis: the socio-historical; the experiential-mystical; the philosophical-theological. Too often one or another is absent. Joachin Wach once observed that method is heuristic as new data and new approaches surface. Although no one scholar can attempt an integral study of one religion or many, scholars are convinced that an integral study, multi-disciplinary and multi-methodological, is possible, in a global society.

Current Issues

In recent times there has been an increase in the diversification of the methodological discussion. It remains to be seen whether different approaches are complementary or opposed. This is especially critical when philosophical and theological questions arise. Although there has been significant work in comparative world philosophy, a tendency to ignore strictly theological questions is evident. Although philosophical and theological data must be part of this body of understanding, neither discipline can supply categories for understanding nor can truth claims be resolved in religion study. In fact the study of world religions has been too dominated by western categories with the result that such study may not be significant to the Asian, African, or Islamic worlds. A small but significant group of international scholars have tried to establish dialogue between theology and the study of world religions. The christian community can point especially to R.C. Zaehner, R. Panikkar, W.C. Smith, and J.B. Cobb, Jr., while M. Buber, D.T. Suzuki, S. Radhakrishnan, and S.H. Nasr are representative of other world traditions. Some challenging topics of discussion are: theology of religions; revelatory uniqueness and universality; perennial philosophy; interreligious dialogue; the religious experience of one individual in several traditions; future of mission activity and its theology; and finally Marxist and secularist aspects of religion. Feminist studies are taking place in many world religions. The interest of the Roman Catholic community in some of these issues has been evident with the openness of the Vatican Council II and its document *Nostra Aetate* which explicitly recognized the truth in the religions of the world.

Knowledge of religions is a global study. In the past western scholars have focused mainly on non-christian traditions. The impact of western scholars in the nonwestern world has come under serious scrutiny. Non-western and non-christian scholars of religion in our time have begun a study of the west and christianity, a focus frequently ignored by western scholars in the past. The christian experience has been the academic focus primarily for theologians and historians; yet the broader study including the social scientist, phenomenologist, and the religionist is commencing. Although historical study of religions has been substantive, we have no truly world history of religions. The provincialism of our historical sense has not helped us to grasp the global experience of religions. No religious tradition has developed in isolation, but historical development has always been in relation to other religious traditions and in relation to other cultural worlds. We need better to understand how other religious traditions continually form us and reform us as we form and reform them. To take religious pluralism with seriousness has been a major challenge to modern intellectual life. It is the major challenge to face the traditions themselves in the coming century.

See **Experience, Religious**

Mircea Eliade, *A History of Religious Ideas,* Vol. 1 *From the Stone Age to the Eleusinian Mysteries,* trans. Willard R. Trask. Chicago: The University of Chicago Press, 1978. Mircea Eliade, Vol. 2 *From Gautama Buddha to the Triumph of Christianity,* trans. Willard R. Trask. Chicago: The University of Chicago Press, 1982. Mircea Eliade, Vol. 3, *From Muhammad to the Age of Reforms,* trans. Alf Hiltebeitel & Diane Apostolos-Cappadona. Chicago: The University of Chicago Press, 1985. Frederick J. Streng, Series Editor. *The Religious Life of Man Series.* Belmont, California: Wadsworth Publishing Company. Jacques Waardenburg, *Classical Approaches to the Study of Religion: Aims, Methods, and Theories of Research.* 2 volumes. The Hague & Paris: Mouton, 1973. Frank Whaling, editor, *Contemporary Approaches to the Study of Religion, Vol. 1, The Humanities,* Vol. 2, *The Social Sciences.* Berlin, New York, Amsterdam: Mouton, Vol. 1, 1983, Vol. 2, 1985.

WILLIAM CENKNER

RELIGIOUS LIFE

All conscious christian living originates in the call of Jesus Christ to "Come follow me," and takes its characteristic direction from the exhortation to "Go and do likewise." All Christians hear a call, have a vocation to both seek God and make God known in our world. This call is described in chapter five of Vatican II's *Dogmatic Constitution on the Church (Lumen Gentium)* as the universal call to holiness. Given to all by God's grace, it is manifested in each person's life. "Every person should walk unhesitatingly according to his [her] own personal gifts and duties in the path of a living faith which arouses hope and works through charity" (no. 41).

Although this statement is of relatively recent origin, it reflects a conviction as old as Christianity itself. The NT reveals communities of disciples who heeded the call of Jesus and found their lives to be transformed. Filled with an outpouring of the spirit, empowered with new courage, they themselves proclaimed the good news of salvation. Joining together in communities of faith and belonging, they enfleshed God's love in their love for one another.

While many of the early disciples gave themselves over to a life of proclamation, many more continued in their previous states of life. transformed as these were by God's good news. As different needs arose within the early communities, the gifts of different persons were recognized and called forth for the sake of the community. The naming of the seven deacons in Acts 6:1-7 refers to this process; and Paul lists various gifts of the Spirit (1 Cor 12:1-11, 28-31), stressing that they are for the upbuilding of all. A wonderful outpouring of God's Spirit, manifested in an abundance of gifts, facilitated the continuation of proclamation and provided for the needs of all within the community. Eventually, certain ways of life began to be recognized as specific and somewhat stable groupings. Among these were the widows who served the communities and who remained celibate. These were the "real" widows, over 60 years of age, wife of only one husband, known for their service and their saintliness. They were to be "enrolled" (1 Tim 5:9), recognized by all as having a special service within the community.

Voluntary celibacy and acknowledgement by the community, already present with regard to widows and virgins who chose a life of celibacy, were to remain two major characteristics of religious life as the forms of that life were to develop through the centuries. By the end of the second century, widows and virgins were clearly recognized and were praised within the christian community for their dedication and the witness which they gave. By the fourth century, they were consecrated in a public ceremony and placed under the direction of their bishop.

Removal from the world in order to search more intensely for God inspired the eremitical movements of the East in the third and fourth centuries. As disciples gathered around those who had gone into the desert, monasticism came into being. Sts. Anthony, Pachomius, and Basil are credited with establishing communities who gathered together around a "master," who knew some form of common life and who, eventually, followed a Rule of Life. The monastic movement also found a home in the West, due in no small part to the encouragement of Sts. Athanasius and Jerome. In the West, however, monasticism took on a particular character when ordained clergy were organized into religious communities. St. Augustine, while Bishop of Hippo (396), organized his clergy into a common life which included renunciation of property and obedience.

Non-clerical monasticism also found a place in the West through the efforts of Sts. Martin of Tours, John Cassian and Caesarius. It received its broadest and most definitive form in Benedictine monasticism (c. 480-547). Meant for lay and clerics alike, Benedict's rule established a monastic structure which centered upon the importance of the abbot as spiritual leader and temporal administrator, incorporated Caesarius' idea of stability, both for abbots (who were elected for life) and for monks (who were to remain attached to a specific monastery for life). The Benedictine monastery became a self-sustaining world, providing for the needs of the community through its own work (*labora*), and praising God in its prayer (*ora*). Benedictinism dominated religious life in the western church for centuries. Its phenomenal growth and prominence led at times to a vitiation of its original impetus. Several reform movements, such as those of Cluny, Citeaux, and Clairvaux, sought a return to the founding insights.

The eremitical life reappeared in the Camaldolese and Carthusian orders, while the clerical religious continued as the Canons Regular; but the most significant development in religious life in the Middle Ages was that of the formation of the mendicant orders of the Franciscans and the Dominicans. Members of these orders were not bound to one monastery but to the order as a whole . This meant that they were much more able to move about and to have more communication with the world at large. The Dominicans stressed the activity of preaching and were decidedly apostolic in character even as they maintained the rule of Mass and the recitation of the Holy Office. The Jesuits, in the mid-sixteenth century, extended the apostolic concept to include worldwide missionary activity. Multiple expressions of religious life have flourished in the last few centuries. The nineteenth century witnessed the establishment of an abundance of religious congregations devoted to apostolic activities such as education, health care, and missionary activity. Secular institutes, which do not require common life and which stress service in the world, were officially approved as a recognized form of religious life by Pius XII in 1947.

Traditionally, religious life has been understood as a striving for perfection according to the evangelical counsels. These counsels, viewed as gospel directives toward a more perfect life, were considered desirable but not morally binding on all Christians. Longstanding and widely accepted interpretations of texts such as 1 Corinthians 7 and Matthew 19 led the church to hold voluntary chastity in special honor and to view those who chose it as seeking a "higher way." In addition, voluntary poverty was understood in light of the Matthean version of the story of the rich young man who, if he would be "perfect," should "go sell what you possess and give to the poor, and you shall have treasure in heaven; and come follow me" (Mt 19:21). Obedience, finally, was imitation of Christ who "humbled himself" and was "obedient unto death" (Phil 2:5-8).

Following of these counsels was expressed in the profession of vows. Voluntary celibacy, first praised in widows and virgins, has remained at the heart of religious life. Poverty and obedience, although generally recognized as fundamental, were universally accepted only in the thirteenth century. Other vows, such as that of stability or service to the pope, have also been professed by members of specific religious communities. By profession of vows, men and women bind themselves to a specific religious community and to the pursuit of the ideals expressed in the vows.

Three other elements have remained relatively constant in religious life: separation from the world, common life, acceptance by the larger church. Removal from the distractions and temptations of the world in order to devote oneself fully to the search for perfect holiness was most graphically expressed in the eremitical tradition, but has remained a common theme in all forms of religious life. One fled "the world, the flesh, and the devil" when one entered the convent or the cloister. Common life, inspired by accounts of the early christian communities (cf. Acts 2:42-47; 4:32-37; 5:17-40), was viewed as witness to the communitarian nature of Christianity and as the arena for the practice of perfect charity. The official recognition of secular institutes marks a broadening of the church's understanding in this regard.

Acknowledgement of religious orders and congregations by the official church has also been deemed fundamental to religious life. This acknowledgement, generally expressed through approval of the rules and constitutions of the various communities, has witnessed to the care of the church for its religious as well as to the need for unity within the church. This requirement has not been uncontroversial. The struggles among Franciscans in the thirteenth century and the suppression of the Jesuits in the eighteenth are only two of many examples of difficulties in getting and keeping official approbation. As with all living and developing realities, experience has often outpaced definition and conflict has ensued.

The presence and importance of women in the history of religious life in the church is frequently overlooked, even though the vast majority of religious are women, and great numbers of women have consistently chosen religious life as their response to Jesus' call. There were feminine counterparts to the earliest monks. Mary, sister of Pachomius, established a monastery for women, while Paula and her daughter Eustochium founded convents for women during the time of Jerome. Melania founded one near Jerusalem, and the mother and sister of Basil entered another one. The fourth century witnessed the formation of women's convents in the west; Augustine provided guidelines for a rule for at least one of these. Women quickly adopted the Benedictine rule, and abbesses frequently exercised jurisdiction as broadly as did abbots.

The middle ages witnessed the establishment of a feminine counterpart to the Franciscans by Clare of Assisi, and the foundation of convents for nuns following the Dominican rule. In the thirteenth century, the Beguines came into existence in Belgium, Germany, and Holland. Although never officially approved by the church, their lives of prayer and works of charity were prophetic of future developments in religious life.

Endemic to women's religious life was the imposition of strict enclosure. Introduced by Caesarius of Arles in the sixth century, reinforced by Boniface VIII in the thirteenth, it was made even more stringent by the Council of Trent in the sixteenth. The equation of women's religious life with cloister led to great difficulties when other forms were envisioned. In 1545, St. Angela Merici established the Company of St. Ursula as a community of women dedicated to service and the education of young women. The Company was soon made to conform to accepted standards of religious life for women. When Mary Ward founded the Institute of the Blessed Virgin Mary and sought to adopt the Jesuit rule and live without cloister, she was condemned. The Institute was suppressed in 1631. When St. Vincent de Paul founded the Daughters of Charity in 1634 and envisioned a life of service without cloister, he too met with great difficulties.

In the nineteenth century, numerous congregations with specific apostolic goals such as education, nursing, care of orphans, and missionary work were established. These congregations struggled to find the balance between demands of enclosure and service of God's people. The official approval of apostolic religious communities in the early twentieth century was the culmination of struggles endured by women such as the Beguines, Angela Merici, and Mary Ward.

No event has affected religious life as radically as that of the Second Vatican Council (1962-1965). The Council speaks explicitly about religious life in two documents, *The Dogmatic Constitution on the Church (Lumen Gentium)*, and *The Decree on the Appropriate Renewal of the Religious Life (Perfectae Caritatis)*. In *Lumen Gentium*, the chapter devoted to religious life follows upon the section which deals with the universal call to holiness, and places religious life within that context. This is significant for it reflects an understanding of religious life as part of the church's grace and mission, but not as "higher" or "more perfect." The choice of religious life is not a "better" choice than any other.

Lumen Gentium (chapter 6) points out that religious life is not an intermediate state between clerical and lay, but rather a way of life open to both (no. 43). Religious life is described as a gift of the Holy Spirit to the church, assisting it in carrying out its mission, particularly in terms of the revelation it gives of Christ in his saving mission. This life is seen to be a genuinely human one, and religious are "neither strangers nor useless citizens of the earthly city" (no. 44). Religious are praised as gift and are urged to perseverance and increasing excellence in their vocation (no. 47). *Perfectae Caritatis* established the principles for the renewal of religious life and insisted that such renewal must be both internal and external: "(1) a continuous return to the sources of all Christian life and to the original inspiration behind any given community and (2) an adjustment of the community to the changed conditions of the times" (no. 2).

Religious communities took the call to renewal to heart and entered into processes aimed at returning to sources and adapting to the times. The return to sources led to the rediscovery of the charism of founders and foundresses and to the testing of contemporary life in light of those inspirations. It also encouraged study of theology, especially study of scripture. This study profoundly enriched the spirituality of many religious, leading them to view their lives in terms of the life and ministry of Jesus and to recognize their apostolate as participation in his mission.

Examination of the conditions of the times, as well as an increased emphasis on competent professional preparation, has encouraged many religious to reach beyond the confines of traditional apostolates to new forms of ministry. Lifestyles, clothing, fixed schedules, forms of common prayer, demands of enclosure were measured against the call to ministry and were adapted in service of that ministry.

Two other teachings of Vatican II were of prime importance in the renewal of religious life: the definition of the church as the people of God, and the concern for the world which was stressed in *The Pastoral Constitution on the Church (Gaudium et Spes)*. A vision of church as people of God tends to diminish somewhat the importance of hierarchical stratification as well as the divisions between lay/religious/clergy. While distinctions do not cease to exist, their meaning resides in their service of the unity and enrichment of all God's people. All members of the people of God are called to assume responsibility for the mission of the church. For religious this has meant a new appreciation for, and a less restricted collaboration with, those previously viewed as "seculars." It has also been felt by many as a call to assume responsibility for/in the church.

Gaudium et Spes declares that "The joys and the hopes, the griefs and the anxieties of the men [women] of this age, especially those who are poor or in any way afflicted, these too are the joys and hopes, the griefs and anxieties of the followers of Christ" (no. 1). This declaration has been profoundly significant to religious, especially to religious of the Americas within the turbulent times of the past decades. Combined with renewed theological and scriptural studies, the sharing in the world's joys and sorrows—particularly among the poor and the afflicted—has led many religious to strong, active commitments to justice and peace and to an understanding of such commitment as integral to their religious vocation.

The renewal called for by Vatican II was not achieved without difficulty. It has not yet been completed, nor has it served to resolve all the questions. Urgent, concrete ones remain. Among these, the adaptation of the ministries of congregations in light of smaller numbers and the care of aging members with dwindling congregational resources are crucial. Equally urgent are those of the connection or distinction between work for justice and political involvement, and the relationship between religious congregations of adults, who have their own national identities, and the hierarchy of the church, particularly the Roman hierarchy.

Religious life in the church has known the same developments and evolution as the church itself. Sometimes an impetus for change and reformation, sometimes a source of consternation, it has nonetheless remained a constant manifestation of the presence of God's grace, the call to follow, the exhortation to do likewise. At varying times in history, different aspects of that call and exhortation have been stressed, occasionally to the point of imbalance; yet religious life continues to remind the church of the call to love and serve God and one another in myriad ways with one's whole being.

See **Monasticism, Religious Orders**

Walter Abbott, SJ, ed., *The Documents of Vatican II*, New York: 1966. Louis Bouyer, *The Meaning of the Monastic Life*, Trans K. Pond. New York: 1955. Jean Leclerq, *The Life of Perfection*, Trans., L.J. Doyle. Collegeville, MN: 1961. Ernst McDonnell, *The Beguines and Beghards in Medieval Culture*, New Brunswick, NJ: 1954. Rosemary R. Reuther, "Mothers of the Church: Ascetic Women in the Late Patristic Age," *Women of Spirit: Female Leaders in the Jewish and Christian Traditions*, Eds., R. Reuther and E. McLaughlin. New York: 1979, pp. 71-98.

JULIANA CASEY, IHM

RELIGIOUS ORDERS

Religious life, as witness to search for God and service to God's people, is gift to the church. The multiplicity and diversity of the forms of this life are sign of the richness of God's gift and evidence of the continuing inspiration of the Spirit in the hearts of men and women.

It is helpful to begin an overview of the development of the many and varied forms of religious institutes with a clarification of some basic distinctions. Three types of religious institutes are generally distinguished: religious orders whose members profess solemn vows and live a common life, religious congregations whose members profess simple vows and also live a common life, secular institutes whose members commit themselves to observance of the evangelical counsel of poverty, chastity and obedience but do not necessarily live a common life. In addition, the church recognizes societies of common life whose members live together but do not necessarily commit themselves by means of sacred vows.

Further distinctions are made between apostolic and monastic institutes. Apos-

tolic institutes stress the mission of religious life and are less bound by rules of stability or cloister. While engaged in a whole-hearted search for God, members of these institutes serve in various ministries for the sake of the church. Monastic institutes, on the other hand, have as their aim the praise and worship of God. Members generally belong to one monastery for life and pray the office of the church in common. They too serve God's people, either through public ministry or through less visible but no less important prayer and sacrifice. Religious institutes are either diocesan or of pontifical right. Diocesan institutes function in relation to the local diocesan authority, while pontifical institutes relate to Rome, particularly to the Congregation of Religious and Secular Institutes.

All religious institutes, whether order or congregation, monastic or apostolic, diocesan or pontifical, are marked by the permanent commitment of their members to a life characterized by the following of the evangelical counsels of poverty, voluntary celibacy, and obedience. Each institute has a rule or constitution which interprets these counsels for the particular group, which gives form to its life, and which guides the members in their search for God and struggle for perfect charity. Many of the distinctions are historical in origin and no longer point to radical differences between religious institutes. The distinction between simple and solemn vows, for example, is not made in the most recent Code of Canon Law.

A brief historical overview shows that different forms of religious life have predominated at various times in the church's history. Religious orders originated in the groups which formed around the men and women anchorites of the third and fourth centuries. Members of these groups separated themselves from the world, lived in common, and followed a rule of life. Monastic orders flourished and reached their most complete expression in Benedictine monasticism (sixth century) with its stress on stability and the creation of a society independent from the world. The monastic form of religious life became the most important one in the church and remained so throughout much of the Middle Ages. All women religious in the west were under the Benedictine rule from the eighth until the twelfth centuries.

The establishment of the mendicant orders (Franciscans and Dominicans) in the early thirteenth century marked a significant new development in religious life. Members belonged to the whole order rather than to a specific monastery, and were thus more free to move about. The Dominican vision was decidedly apostolic in nature, and stressed the preaching of the gospel. Others orders were established which followed the model of the Franciscans and Dominicans and religious life began to move back into the world in order to serve both the gospel and the people. These orders, however, retained the rule of conventual Mass and Divine Office and maintained strict enclosure for the women's convents.

Clerical religious institutes, begun in the fourth century by St. Augustine, received new impetus after the Council of Trent. Known as the Canons Regular, they wore no distinctive garb, did not pray the office in common, and devoted themselves to priestly ministry. The largest, the Jesuits, broadened the apostolic focus to include the whole world as arena for their mission.

While monastic and contemplative orders continued and instituted significant reforms at crucial moments in their history, apostolic congregations have flourished in the past few centuries, particularly among women. The vision of groups joined together in common commitment whose members engaged in some form of active ministry appeared several times in history. Actualization of this vision was frequently thwarted by a limited understanding of religious life on the part of church authorities. Eventually, however, active apostolic congregations became a reality for women as well as men. These congregations, uninhibited by strict enclosure, have devoted themselves to various types of service such as education, health care, care for the abandoned and the homeless. The nineteenth century witnessed a phenomenal growth in apostolic religious congregations which were characterized by dedication to ministry. Most of these groups focused upon particular works such as education or health care and eventually became identified with them. Great men and women saw needs among the people they served and established communities dedicated to ameliorating these needs. Others were inspired with a strong sense of mission and founded communities to preach the gospel among those who did not know of it. Many religious congregations came to the Americas in this way, and many others were founded to continue the mission of the church in the new lands.

The most recent development in forms of religious life is that of the secular institute. It has antecedents in the lifestyles of the Beguines of the twelfth century and the visions of Angela Merici, Mary Ward, and Catherine Macauley. These institutes, whose members are bound together by common commitment to the gospel and an articulated vision of life, do not seek separation from the world but rather to transform the world from within. Their official approval by Pius XII in 1947 marked the latest in a continually expanding understanding of religious orders.

All types of religious institutes exist today, and all continue to be gift to the church. Vatican II, with its call for the renewal of religious life, has led religious orders to rediscover their original charisms and to recommit themselves to the service of the gospel. Religious institutes in the United States are marked by strong commitment to justice and peace, dedication to ministry and increasingly diverse types of service. Orders which in past times remained somewhat self-sufficient now collaborate in service, communities who were previously exclusively devoted to one particular ministry have reached out to serve new needs as these needs have arisen.

Finally, the universal call to holiness which echoed from the Vatican Council has also affected religious institutes in profound ways. One of the most significant ways has been that of the rediscovery of the importance of the ministry of the laity. Ministry in the church is no longer viewed as the exclusive prerogative of priests and religious, but is rather the call to all persons. As a consequence, many who would have previously joined religious institutes in order to serve the church now do so as lay persons. The numbers of men and women religious have declined even as the church has witnessed a rise in the richness of lay ministries among its people.

See **Monasticism, Religious Life, Religious Orders**

Walter Abbott, SJ, ed., *The Documents of Vatican II*, New York: 1966. Louis Bouyer, *The Meaning of the Monastic Life*, Trans K. Pond. New York: 1955. Jean Leclerq, *The Life of Perfection*, Trans., L.J. Doyle. Collegeville, MN: 1961. Ernst McDonnell, *The Beguines and Beghards in Medieval Culture*, New Brunswick, NJ: 1954. Rosemary R. Reuther, "Mothers of the Church: Ascetic Women in the Late Patristic Age," *Women of Spirit: Female Leaders in the Jewish and Christian Traditions*, Eds., R. Reuther and E. McLaughlin. New York: 1979, pp. 71-98.

JULIANA CASEY, IHM

REPARATION
See **Satisfaction, Redemption**

REPENTANCE

The beginning of the christian vocation is marked by a call to repentance. Like the call to conversion, repentance is one of the central themes found in both the OT and NT and in the life of the church. The term is always linked to the promise of forgiveness and the assurance of God's mercy. The penitential rites which have been developed historically to mediate the event of repentance in the believer's life have changed dramatically, but in Roman Catholicism the sacraments of baptism and of reconciliation have played an important part in the church's call for continual penance and for the need to reconcile one's life with God.

The fact that humanity has turned away from God in sin is the background to the biblical call to repentance. In the OT, the term *shub* (to turn about) is frequently used to demand that humanity must turn away from evil and return back to God who offers forgiveness. The turning about that is required is a radical reorientation of one's whole being and conduct, and such a conversion implies an interior aspect of repentance, which is rendered in the Septuagint by the Greek term *metanoia*.

As awareness of the depth of human sinfulness increased, various penitential practices were developed to implore the forgiveness of God for both personal and collective evils. Divine pardon was beseeched through ascetical practices and penitential prayers, such as fasting (Judg 20:26; 1 Kgs 21:8); the tearing of clothes and the putting on of sack-cloth (1 Kgs 20:31; 2 Kgs 6:30; Isa 22:12); and rolling in ashes (Isa 58:5). The collective confession of sin was frequently made (Judg 10:10; 1 Sam 7:6), and gradually recourse was made to the intercession of a prophet (Exod 32:30; Jer 14:1-15:4). After the exile the prophets, fearful of the superficiality of external practices, appealed to their people to repent through an interior change of heart. The national conversion of Israel was accomplished, in part, through the preaching of these prophets and the lengthy experience of exile. It was especially after the exile that the sense of repentance was so firmly rooted in the heart of Israel that the entire spirituality of the nation was affected.

In the NT, the first recorded word of Jesus in his public ministry was: "The time has come and the reign of God is near; repent, and believe this good news" (Mk 1:15). *Metanoia* and *epistrophe* are the two Greek words used to express the total interior conversion and radical turning around that was demanded by Jesus' call to repentance. For Jesus, the disposition of genuine repentance was only possible when one took on the attitude of a child (Mt 18:3) and turned away from the dispositions of self-righteousness and presumption (Lk 18:10-14). The repentance that Jesus preached was good news to be received with joy. Though he did not make any allusion to pentitential liturgies, Jesus did require baptism for the forgiveness of sins and a faith in his gospel that would reconcile humanity with God.

After his resurrection, Jesus sent his followers to preach repentance and to baptize all nations for the remission sin. The early Christians willingly accepted their mission, but many within the community believed that the act of repentance or conversion, sealed by baptism, was accomplished once and for always. Thus, the view developed that it was impossible to renew the grace received in baptism (Heb 6:1-6), although it was recognized that the baptized were capable of falling once again into sin. In the first three centuries there was a keen debate whether baptized believers who committed the capital sins of apostasy, impurity and bloodshed were admissible to reconciliation in this life. Almost without exception, all the great christian writers of the second and early third centuries (e.g., Hippolytus, Tertullian and Origen) sided with the rigorists and refused reconciliation. However, after the Decian persecution (ca. 250 A.D.) the ban against reconciliation was removed for the apostates and other offenders, and at the Nicene Council it was decreed that every sort of offense should find the door of reconciliation.

It did not take long for the early christian communities to develop for its members penitential practices to mediate publicly the call to repentance. In the first three centuries the procedure for penance comprised (1) a confession of sin to the bishop or priest, (2) a public course of penance or exomologesis, and (3) a reconciliation or absolution, usually public. Such a rite was allowed only once in the Christian's lifetime, so many waited until the time of death before taking part in it. The fourth and fifth centuries were confronted with different situations, and as a result new practices were initiated in various parts of the christian world. For example, in the Asian provinces the system of graded penance developed for a time, and the terms of satisfaction for sin were often lengthy and rigorous. On the other hand, at Constantinople and other neighboring churches a priest penitentiary heard confessions, assigned penances and granted reconciliation privately. Generally though, the practice remained that repentance through sacramental reconciliation was permitted only once after baptism, and so most Christians put off the reception of the sacrament until the death bed.

By the seventh century the church's penitential practice had taken a different course. Sacramental reconciliation was permitted more than once after baptism, and the rite itself shifted more to private penance. The movement to private penance was occasioned by the influx of the British and Irish practices into continental

Europe. The beginnings of the Celtic system that surrounded repentance could already be discerned in the sixth-century *Praefatio de penitentia* of Gildas and in the records of the synods of Llandewi-Brefi. These documents indicate that the confession of sins was private, as was the performance of the penance by the penitent. Gradually, penitential books were written (e.g., Finian of Clonard and Columbanus), which listed the penalties or penances that were appropriate for particular offenses. These books, and the penitential practices which gave rise to them, made their way to the continent and informed the standard sacramental practice of the church. As these practices took hold, there emerged over the next few centuries the duty to confess one's sins at least once a year. Eventually in 1215, at the Fourth Lateran Council, it was decided that all the faithful who had reached the age of discretion must confess their sins to their priest at least once in the year. Finally, at the Council of Trent in the sixteenth century, the sacrament of penance or reconciliation was defined for the Catholic church, and the proper elements of sacramental confession included the aspects of sorrow, confession of sins and atonement.

In the contemporary era the call to repentance has been viewed more developmentally. The church as the people of God is on a journey, a pilgrimage that necessitates the daily withdrawal from sin and a gradual, but radical, turning back to God through repentance. The need for repentance is not restricted to the sacramental rites of the church, as necessary as they are, but emphasis is also placed on the acquisition of the virtues of humility and of hope and the need for contrition in the christian life. With the development of the theological notion of a fundamental option that underlies moral acts, many theologians today stress not merely acts of repentance

but also, and maybe more fundamentally, the basic orientation of one's life as repentant. In addition, many bishops at the Rome Synod in 1983, which was held to discuss penance and reconciliation in the mission of the church, called for a return to the order of penitents that was practiced in the penitential discipline of the ancient church. Reinstitution of such a discipline, it was argued, would provide opportunities for catechesis for all members of the faith community and engage the entire membership as a whole in the celebration of repentance.

As a life-long disposition or orientation of christian life and as realized in concrete acts, repentance remains one of the most fundamental aspects of the christian vocation. Because sin manifests its continual presence in both individual lives and in the structures of society, the call to repentance requires personal and societal conversion. Commitment to justice, especially on behalf of the poor, has recently become one of the central themes that illuminates the meaning of christian repentance. Filled with hope and joy, the Christian ventures to renew the face of the earth through acts of charity and penance, always with the expectation of the fullness of the coming reign of God.

See **Asceticism, Baptism, Mercy, Reconciliation, Sin**

Bernard Häring, *Free & Faithful in Christ: Vol. 1,* New York: The Seabury Press, and London: St. Paul Publications, 1978. "Repentance-Conversion," in *Dictionary of Biblical Theology,* ed. Xavier Léon-Dufour, trans P. Joseph Cahill, London: Geoffrey Chapman, 1969, 430-434. Karl Hermann Schelkle, *Theology of the New Testament: Morality,* trans., William A. Jurgens, Collegeville, Minnesota: The Liturgical Press, 1973. Rudolf Schnackenburg, *The Moral Teaching of the New Testament,* trans J. Holland-Smith and W.J. O'Hara, New York: Herder and Herder, and London: Burns and Oates, 1965. Oscar D. Watkins, *A History of Penance,* 2 vols., New York: Burt Franklin, 1961.

JAMES J. WALTER

RESERVATION, EUCHARISTIC

The keeping, for various purposes, of the consecrated bread (rarely, the wine) after the eucharistic liturgy.

Originally, the sacrament was reserved for the communion of those unable to celebrate the eucharist with the church. Justin notes (1 Apol. 65, 67) that at Rome c. 150 the deacons took the eucharist to those who were absent. Communion of the ill and viaticum for the dying with the reserved sacrament are attested from the third century. It was also the custom then for Christians to keep the sacrament in their homes for communion on weekdays when the eucharist was not celebrated. Later, hermits and monks would do the same in their isolated cells, and some early monastic groups communicated regularly in the sacrament kept from the weekly eucharistic liturgy. Another early practice was to send the reserved sacrament from one church to another to symbolize unity in faith.

In the Middle Ages, there were other uses of the reserved sacrament. At Rome and in other episcopal churches in the West, the *fermentum,* a consecrated particle, was sent to surrounding presbyteral churches to be placed in the cup during their eucharistic liturgies as a sign of the communion of local churches with their bishop, Or the *sancta,* a particle reserved from one liturgy to the next in the same church, joined all the liturgies into one eucharist. Since Good Friday was a day without Mass, communion was distributed from the reserved sacrament in what came to be called a liturgy of the presanctified. Later, the consecrated bread was often "entombed" during the rites of Good Friday, and watch was kept until the "Resurrection" of the host on Easter morning. Abuses were not unknown: consecrated bread was buried with corpses, sealed in altars at their consecration, or carried habitually on journeys not only for communion

of the sick but as a kind of amulet to ward off infidels and brigands.

During the first millennium, the mode of eucharistic reservation moved from the simple to the increasingly elaborate, from outside to the inside of the churches. The sacrament, once kept at home or on one's person in small wooden or ivory boxes, or in little baskets or folded in chrismals of cloth or leather, became the sacrament kept by clerics in the sacristy or in the church itself. The sacrament could be reserved in an ambry, a cupboard in the wall of the church to hold the pyx, a box containing the hosts. Or the pyx might be kept directly on the altar or suspended above it inside a container often shaped like a dove over which hung a veil and canopy. Though medieval rituals describe the communion of the sick with bread and wine, it is not clear how the wine was reserved. Some European churches reserved hosts which had been intincted in eucharistic wine.

All of these developments parallel and reflect other phenomena: the distancing of the people from participation in a liturgy more and more taken over by clerics, the increasingly rare communion of lay persons, the shift from appreciating the eucharistic elements as holy food to revering them with awe as holy objects, and a growing taste for popular devotions into which the sacrament might be drawn.

Largely in reaction to controversies about the real presence of Christ in the eucharist begun in the ninth century and sparked anew by Berengarius of Tours in the eleventh, the western church stressed the reality of that presence during Mass and also its permanent and lasting reality in the reserved sacrament, a belief implied in the very fact of reservation.

Though some older liturgical uses of the reserved sacrament disappeared by the twelfth century, the original purposes remained: to communicate the sick and the dying. More and more, however, reservation was deemed important for two other reasons: for the communion of the faithful (admittedly rare for individuals) who, though present for mass, were commonly communicated after or apart from mass; for adoration by all either privately or in developing forms of public cult.

The place and manner of reservation mirrored this shifting emphasis. Reservation within the church was customary though not exclusive by the twelfth century. Reservation on the altar, however, became more and more common, first in veiled vessels of various kinds, then in forerunners of the tabernacle. In the Low Countries and Germany, freestanding, elaborate sacrament houses, often tower-shaped, appeared in the late Middle Ages, their locked grills permitting the sacrament to be seen while holding it secure. Burning one or more lights continuously near the place of reservation was common by the thirteenth century.

Just before the Council of Trent (1545-63), the altar tabernacle as we know it appeared in Italy and quickly became the norm. The Roman Ritual of 1614 prescribed it for the Latin church. Though other modes of reservation continued in parts of Europe, the altar tabernacle became common and was universal in the U.S. until the liturgical movement preceding Vatican II.

Roman documents and liturgical norms for eucharist reservation since Vatican II:

1. Reassert the practice and benefits of eucharistic reservation.

2. State that the primary and original reason for reservation is for viaticum; the secondary reasons are the giving of communion and the adoration of Christ present in the sacrament. The former led to the latter.

3. Provide that the communion of the sick and dying may be in either the bread or the wine or both. At least temporary reservation of the wine is allowed for this purpose.

4. Strongly discourage the abuse of communicating the faithful from the reserved sacrament during Mass. However, reservation for communion during non-eucharistic services of word, prayer, and communion led by deacons and designated lay person is allowed. This usage is growing today as the number of priests declines.

5. Recognize that the action of the eucharistic liturgy and the reserved sacrament are intimately connected since the second flows from and leads back to the first. But the dynamic presence of Christ in the action of the Mass may be clearer if it is not confused with his permanent presence in the reserved sacrament. Therefore the sacrament should not be reserved from the beginning of Mass on an altar where the eucharist is celebrated, nor may the Mass be celebrated in the same place where there is exposition of the sacrament for public adoration.

6. Presume that reservation is within the church and enjoin that it be in a preeminent place. The place should be suitable for private adoration and prayer. Reservation should not be on the principal altar where Mass is celebrated with the people. Thus a chapel apart from the main body of the church is recommended. Reservation may be on an altar or in some part of the church other than an altar.

7. Require reservation in a solid, unbreakable tabernacle—a single one in each church. It should be veiled, and a lamp must burn continuously near it.

The reserved sacrament, therefore, is a sign coming from the eucharistic liturgy; it is holy food for the communion of believers; it leads those who worship Christ present in it back to the liturgy and to communion with Christ and his church.

See **Adoration, Eucharistic**

A. King, *Eucharistic Reservation in the Western Church*, London, 1965. Instruction *Eucharisticum mysterium* (1967); *Holy Communion and Worship of the Eucharist outside Mass* (1973); *Code of Canon Law* (1983) cc. 934-944.

ALLAN BOULEY, OSB

RESTORATION OF ALL THINGS

This term, which is sometimes used in the sense of "recapitulation," more narrowly is used of the view of Origen that in the final Kingdom of God all, including the evil demons and those condemned to hell, will be reconciled to God. As a denial of the eternity of hell, it was condemned by the Synod of Constantinople in 543.

See **Hell**

THE RESURRECTION OF CHRIST

Christianity began with a very specific message: the crucified Jesus had been raised from the dead (1 Cor 15:3-5; Acts 2:22-24) to become the effective Savior (Rom 4:25) and ever-present living Lord of the world (Rom 10:9; 14:9; 1 Cor 12:3; 16:22; Phil 2:8-11). The entire NT was written in the light of this new faith. Redemption from sin and the risen life to come depended on Jesus' personal resurrection (1 Cor 15:14, 17), a reality on which all early Christians agreed (1 Cor 15:11; Acts 2:32) and which structured their very account of God (1 Cor 15:15; Gal 1:1). They recognized that if they were wrong about Jesus' rising from the dead, they would be the "most pitiable" of all people (1 Cor 15:19) and could only grieve like all those "who have no hope" (1 Thess 4:13).

Today, as always, faith in Jesus' resurrection stands at the heart of the Christian creed: "On the third day he rose again." Easter remains *the* feast of the church's year. The eucharistic acclamations express the central belief that salvation comes through the resurrection of the crucified Christ: "Dying you destroyed our death. Rising you restored our life. Lord Jesus, come in glory."

The Background

A clear and explicit hope for a general resurrection (at least for the just) emerges late in the OT. Rather than alleging some outside source (for example, Persian religion), most scholars now recognize that this resurrection hope results from Israel's long experience of God's limitless power and utter fidelity. As omnipotent Creator, the God of life and justice will raise the persecuted righteous (Dan 12:1-4) and, in particular, those who accept martyrdom rather than disobey the divine law (2 Macc 7). At times this hope envisages a return to a full life in a renewed world (Isa 26:7-21; see 65:16-25; 66:22). The Wisdom of Solomon uses the Greek language of the "soul" when speaking of life after death for the just who suffer now (3:1-4; 7-8; 5:15-6:21). But so far from claiming for them a "natural" immortality of their souls alone, Wisdom thinks of God's gift of eternal life for their whole being.

Jesus himself experienced and served the final rule of God as already breaking into our world and soon to be consummated. His preaching presupposed that the dead would rise to be judged on their fitness to enter the divine kingdom (Lk 11:31-32; Mk 9:43, 48). The resurrection of the patriarchs was implied in the imagery Jesus used for the final feast of the nations (Mt 8:11). His beatitudes not only spoke to our earthly existence but also looked to a happy, fulfilled life to come "in heaven" (Lk 8:20-23).

The resurrection of the dead turned up for debate with the Sadducees, who unlike the Pharisees and others in first-century Palestine did not accept this hope (Mk 12:18-27). In his response Jesus insisted that resurrected existence will be no mere return to the conditions of this world but a new life to come through the power and fidelity of the God of the living (Mk 12:24-27).

The three predictions of his death and resurrection attributed to Jesus (Mk 8:31; 9:31; 10:33-34) include material added by Christians in the light of the events themselves. Yet there seems to be a historical core, at least in the case of the second and simplest of these predictions. Jesus applied to himself the theme of the righteous sufferer: after a violent death he would be speedily vindicated by God. He faced death with the confidence that he would share with his companions in the coming kingdom (Mk 14:25).

The Apostolic Message

Shortly after his crucifixion and burial Jesus' followers began to proclaim that he had been raised from the dead and was to be acknowledged as Messiah (or "the Christ"), divine Lord and Son of God (Acts 2:36; Phil 2:9-11; Rom 1:3-4). According to contemporary Jewish belief, someone crucified was thought to be cursed by God (Deut 21:23; Gal 3:13; 1 Cor 1:23). The Temple Roll from Qumran also witnessed to that conviction (64:12). A crucified Messiah, even more a crucified and resurrected Messiah, was unthinkable and absurd. Yet the first Christians and then Paul announced Jesus to be just that.

Various attempts have been made to reduce the resurrection claim. Jesus "rose" because people honored him and imitated his style of life. The "resurrection" indicated merely a radical change in the disciples themselves, not a new beginning for Jesus himself. Such theories, however, must suppose that the early Christians, while appearing to assert some new fact *about Jesus* (his personal resurrection from death to a transformed, definitive life), were really using a deceptive form of discourse and speaking only about themselves. This position is quite implausible.

When St. Paul, for example, quoted a frequently used, early christian formulation about "Jesus Christ and God the Father, who raised him from the dead" (Gal 1:1; see 1 Thess 1:10; 1 Cor 6:14, etc.), ordinary linguistic conventions indicate that this confession made some factual claim about what happened to Jesus himself after his death. A new event, distinct from and subsequent to the crucifixion brought Jesus from the condition of death to that of a new and lasting life.

How did the disciples know about this event? Unlike the apocryphal Gospel of Peter (9:35-43) which dates from the second century, the NT never alleges that anyone witnessed the actual resurrection itself. Rather it names (a) the appearances of the risen Christ to individuals and to groups (1 Cor 15:5-8; Lk 24:34; Mk 16:7; Acts 10:40f.; 13:30f.; Jn 20:11-18) and (b) the discovery of the empty tomb (Mk 16:1-8; Jn 20:1-2) as the two dramatic causes which indicated that his resurrection had happened. The appearances were the primary way the disciples came to know that Jesus had been raised to new life. The discovery of the empty tomb served as a secondary, negative sign confirming his resurrection.

(a) There is a notable "ordinariness" about the Easter appearances as reported very briefly by Paul (1 Cor 15:5-8) and narrated by the gospels. Unlike other communications from God, they do not take place during ecstasy (Acts 10:9ff.; 2 Cor 12:2-4; Rev 1:10ff.), nor in a dream (Mt 1:20; 2:12f.; 19f.; 22), nor by night (Acts 16:9; 18:9; 23:11; 27:23). The appearances occur under "normal" circumstances and without the traits of apocalyptic glory which we find elsewhere (Mk 9:2-8; Mt 28:3f.). The one exception comes in the way Acts describes Paul's experience on the Damascus Road when he sees "a light from heaven, brighter than the sun" (Acts 26:13; see 9:3; 22:6, 9). But there is no mention of this phenomenon when Paul himself refers to his encounter with the risen Christ (1 Cor 9:1; 15:8; Gal 1:12; 16).

These Easter appearances, if "ordinary," were also special experiences, reserved to a small group of several hundred witnesses at the very beginnings of Christianity. Those disciples who had been with Jesus during his ministry recognized the risen Christ as being identical with the master whom they had known and followed: "It is the Lord" (Jn 21:7). No later group or individual believer, not even Paul, could duplicate this aspect of those first post-resurrection meetings with Christ. Peter, Mary Magdalene and other disciples served as bridge persons who linked the period of Jesus' ministry with the post-Easter situation. In that way their experience of the risen Lord was unique and unrepeatable. Yet more should be added about their "once only" experience and its aftermath.

Peter, Paul and other apostolic witnesses who meet the risen Christ have the mission to testify to that experience and found the church. These witnesses have seen for themselves and believed. In proclaiming the good news and gathering together those who have not seen and yet are ready to believe, these original witnesses do not need to rely on the experience and testimony of others. Their function for Christianity differs from that of any subsequent believers, inasmuch as they alone have the once-and-for-all task of inaugurating the mission and founding the church. Others will bear the responsibility to continue that mission and keep the church in existence. But the coming-into-being of the church and its mission cannot be duplicated. The way in which that unique function implies some difference between their respective experiences is expressed by John's classic distinction between those who have seen and believed and those who are "blessed" because they "have not seen and yet

believe" (Jn 20:29, see 1 Pet 1:8).

St. Paul also draws attention to some real differences between the fundamental post-resurrection encounters and all later experiences of the risen Lord. "Last of all," he recalls, Christ "appeared also to me" (1 Cor 15:8). This episode constituted Paul's apostolic calling and the basis for his mission (1 Cor 9:1; Gal 1:11ff.). Other Christians share with him life "in Christ," and have various experiences/gifts of the Holy Spirit (Gal 3:2ff.; 1 Cor 12-14). But they did not and do not experience that fundamental meeting with the risen Lord which made Paul a founding father of the church. He never remarks to his readers: "Christ has appeared" or "Christ will appear to you." He invites others to believe and live out their faith, but not to repeat his special, apostolic experience of the risen Lord.

This is not to say that Christians other than the resurrection witnesses were thought to have no experiential access whatsoever to the risen Jesus. He remained present through word and sacrament (Lk 24:30ff.), in the community (Mt 18:20), in his body (1 Cor 12:27), through persons who suffer (Mt 25:31-46) and through his Spirit (2 Cor 3:17). Nevertheless, the risen Lord did not appear to all those other Christians and make them normative witnesses to his resurrection and authoritative founders of the christian church.

(b) The discovery of the empty tomb was a secondary, confirmatory cause when the first disciples came to know that Jesus was risen from the dead. There is very good evidence that the church of the Holy Sepulchre in Jerusalem does in fact contain Jesus' grave. Moreover, the story of women finding Jesus' tomb to be open and empty (Mk 16:1-8 and parallels) seems unique to Christianity. But is the story reliable?

Here it does no harm to recall that very many critical exegetes and historians defend the empty tomb story. There is a reasonable case to be made for their conclusion.

As regards the fate of Jesus' body, both the tradition behind the synoptic gospels (Matthew, Mark and Luke) and that which entered John's gospel testified to one (Mary Magdalene) or more women finding Jesus' grave to be open and empty. Early polemic against the message of his resurrection supposed that the tomb was known to be empty. Naturally the opponents of the christian movement explained away the missing body as a plain case of theft (Mt 28:11-15). But we have no early evidence that anyone, either Christian or non-Christian, ever alleged that Jesus' tomb still contained his remains. Furthermore, the place of women in the story of the empty tomb speaks for its historical reliability. If this story had been a legend created by early Christians, they would have attributed the discovery of the empty tomb to male disciples rather than women, who in that culture did not count as valid witnesses. Legend-makers do not usually invent positively unhelpful and counterproductive material.

If we are satisfied about the historical case for the empty tomb, the further challenge then is to explore and appreciate what this discovery could and does mean. How would it improve our Easter faith and theology if we understood something of the empty tomb's significance?

First of all, the emptiness of Jesus' grave reflects the holiness of what it once held, the corpse of the incarnate Son of God who lived for others and died to bring a new covenant of love for all people. This "Holy One" could not "see corruption" (Acts 2:27). Then the very emptiness of the tomb can suggest and symbolize the fullness of the new and everlasting life into which Jesus has gone.

Finally, the empty tomb expresses something vital about the nature of redemption, namely that redemption is much more than a mere escape from our scene of suffering and death. Rather it means the transformation of this material, bodily world with its whole history of sin and suffering. The first Easter began the work of finally bringing our universe home to its ultimate destiny. God did not discard Jesus' earthly corpse, but mysteriously raised and transfigured it so as to reveal what lies ahead for human beings and their world. In short, that empty tomb in Jerusalem is God's radical sign that redemption is not an escape to a better world but an extraordinary transformation of this world.

The History of Christianity

In the history of the church Jesus' own victory over death was soon developed as the basis for christian hope in resurrection (Clement of Rome and Tertullian). By means of their baptism and the eucharist Christians experienced Christ's passage through death to a new life being actualized and realized liturgically in their midst and to their advantage. It was above all the Easter vigil service which offered (and offers) Christians their richest redemptive experience of Christ's "Passover" (see the witness of Melito of Sardis, Cyril of Jerusalem, Gregory of Nazianzus, Etheria, Augustine and others).

In the Christological debates of the fourth and fifth centuries, often Jesus' resurrection was discussed only in connection with the incarnation, and sometimes not at all. The Council of Chalcedon (A.D. 451) provided the classic formulations about Christ's one person and two natures, but had nothing to say about his crucifixion and resurrection. In the centuries which followed, an all-absorbing theology of the incarnation often monopolized attention. In the Middle Ages theologians at times were content to speculate about the nature of the risen body rather than reflect on the saving power of the risen Christ. In modern times apologists for Christianity not uncommonly presented the resurrection as a mere proof for Jesus' claims, "the greatest of all miracles" which demonstrated his divinity. This was to ignore a key truth eventually highlighted by Vatican II's Dogmatic Constitution on Divine Revelation, *Dei Verbum:* the climax of God's self-revelation came with the crucified Christ's resurrection from the dead and the sending of the Holy Spirit (n. 5).

As much as ever, Easter faith remains a reasonable and free decision supported by the power of grace. We depend on the testimony of those who witnessed to their post-crucifixion encounters with the living Lord. We see what faith in that message has brought in the story of the christian church. Facing our own personal experiences of death, absurdity and hatred, we can find through faith in the risen Jesus new life, meaning and love. In our case too the words of 1 Peter can come true: "Without having seen him you love him; though you do not now see him you believe in him and rejoice with unutterable and exalted joy" (1:8).

See **Christology**

Reginald H. Fuller, *The Formation of the Resurrection Narratives,* New York, 1971. Xavier Léon-Dufour, *Resurrection and the Message of Easter,* New York, 1975. Gerald O'Collins, SJ, *What are they saying about the Resurrection?,* New York, 1978. *Jesus Risen,* Mahwah, New Jersey, 1987. Pheme Perkins, *Resurrection,* New York, 1984.

GERALD O'COLLINS, SJ

REVELATION

The Idea of Revelation

Although the idea of revelation does not appear formally within the Bible, and in fact does not become a central theme of theology until after the Enlightenment, "revelation" (from the Latin *revelare,* "to remove the veil") is a dominant theme in biblically based religious traditions. However, today it is also one of the most controversial ideas in theological discussion.

In the history of Christian theology "revelation" has often been understood as an inner "illumination" or as a divine teaching and instruction. At times this understanding has led to what has been called a "propositional" theory of revelation. That is, "revelation" has been taken to be the communication of information capable of being expressed in sentences or propositions. However, the propositional understanding has become questionable in modern theology, and the central model for understanding revelation has shifted to a more "personal" one. Revelation is now understood fundamentally as God's *self*-revelation. It is first of all the gift of God's own being, and only secondly is it the illuminative or propositional unfolding of the foundational event of a divine self-giving. Revelation is not primarily the uncovering of hidden truths of information otherwise inaccessible to reason and ordinary experience. Such a "gnostic" idea, tempting though it has been since early in the history of Christianity, trivializes the idea of revelation, making it appeal more to curiosity than to our need for transformation and hope. Instead revelation means God's self-unveiling and self-gift.

As Karl Rahner has often insisted, revelation is fundamentally the communication of the mystery of God to the world. This divine self-communication influences the world at every phase of its coming-to-be, and not just within the confines of the biblical world alone. Revelation is the ongoing outpouring of God's creative, formative love into the entire world. In this sense it has a "general" character, and it is even constitutive of all things. Thus the idea of revelation in contemporary theology tends to converge with the biblical theme of creation. Creation itself is already the self-revelation of God.

However, biblical faith has influenced theologians to speak also of "revelation in history," "historical revelation," or "special revelation," in addition to God's universal or "general" self-revelation. In the history of Israel and in the person of Jesus of Nazareth, Christians believe that God who is present to the world everywhere and at all times manifests the divine essence in a definitively redemptive way.

While Christians celebrate the apparently "exceptional" divine self-disclosure in Christ, the notion of a "special" revelation in history is today the source of much controversy. To some the idea of a unique revelation by a universal God to a specific people in a limited historical setting seems arbitrary and unreasonable. And the apparently absolutist claims of revelation seem to be in conflict with the inevitable relativity of any culture's outlook on the world. The consensus of much recent theology (Jewish, Protestant and Catholic), however, is that the idea of revelation in history does not imply a magical intrusion of privileged information untouched by the vicissitudes of history, as is often imagined in popular piety. Special revelation does not suspend the limited and historically contingent character of all human consciousness. Instead it may be understood as the manifestation of the divine mystery to the whole world from within the limitations of a particular people's existence.

The idea of a special historical revelation is also problematic to many who dwell within the broad "religious context" of human experience. Although they are quite willing to agree that all people are touched by the *mystery* that surrounds our existence, they see no need to posit a special and decisive historical revelation of this mystery. And they are sometimes suspicious of the apparent pretentiousness

of those who do. (See, for example, Karl Jaspers and Rudolf Bultmann, *Myth and Christianity,* trans. by N. Guterman, New York: Noonday Press, Inc. 1958.) This is a serious objection, and theology today must take it into account, for a strong temptation to triumphalism can indeed accompany a naive doctrine of special revelation. Although there are strong warnings against such self-importance in the scriptures, a theology of revelation today has to be especially sensitive to the accusations of special privilege.

In order to obviate such arrogance many contemporary theologians emphasize that the primary meaning of revelation is God's gift of self to the *world.* Such a formula prohibits our restricting this gift to a specific people or to a specific church community. Revelation in its fundamental meaning is universal. If we still continue to speak of a special historical revelation we do not mean that it is special in the sense that the people to whom it is communicated are thereby superior to other human beings. Nor do we mean that they are any more valued by God. Even though it inevitably bears the mark of particularity, a feature that is inseparable from the christian doctrine of the incarnation, the idea of God's revelation in history means something much deeper, more universal and less pretentious than these suspicions seem to warrant.

The self-revealing God is given to faith not as a possession but in the mode of *promise.* The sense of a divine revelation occurred first to people whose destinies were uncertain but whose lives were nonetheless filled with expectation. Today as well, any meaningful conviction of revelation can occur only to those who share this same sense of promise and the hope that adheres to it. Hence the most important reason for our accepting the notion of revelation is not to evoke a sense of privilege, but to give strong expression to faith's perennial impression of the always surprising initiative or "prevenience" of God, that is, to the conviction that we are not ourselves the authors of the promise we live by. The notion of revelation is indispensable in any theology grounded in faith's experience of a mystery of promise that is by its very nature always new, surprising and unpredictable.

St. Thomas Aquinas understood revelation as the "saving act by which God provides us with the truths necessary for our salvation." This "cognitive" interpretation with its accent on propositional "truths" greatly influenced subsequent scholastic theology as well as ideas on revelation operative at the Council of Trent and the First Vatican Council. The former was intent on preserving (in opposition to the Reformers) the "objective" character of revelation as existing independently of the believer's faith. And the First Vatican Council insisted (against rationalism and fideism) that some revelatory truths are accessible to reason and can be found in the natural order, while others come to us through the prophets, apostolic witnesses and the church. It is important to keep in mind that these councils were not concerned so much with providing a fully developed theology of revelation as they were with combating what they considered to be doctrinal errors. It is not surprising, therefore, that in their polemics they carried on a rather "cognitive" approach to revelation.

The Second Vatican Council, however, represents a renewal of revelation theology that began in the last century and continues today. Its "Dogmatic Constitution on Divine Revelation" reflects the contemporary shift toward emphasizing the promissory nature of revelation and the notion of God's self-communication. Its treatment of revelation is more biblical, more attuned to the theme of salvation history, more personalistic and less "propositional" than previous Catholic documents on the subject had been. Of particular importance is the document's emphasis on the importance of the revelatory word of the Scriptures for theology and christian life. Although it still holds to the view that "sacred tradition and sacred Scripture" together constitute "one sacred deposit" of the word of God, there is a distinct emphasis on the importance of the Bible as a source of revelation. The Second Vatican Council no longer views revelation simply in terms of propositional "truths" that support dogmatic positions. Though the document on revelation is little more than an outline, its tone and perspective are a radical departure from official dogmatic formulations of the past. And it challenges us to think of revelation not as a collection of timeless formulas, but as an always enlivening embodiment of God's word that can illuminate and transform each new situation in a special way.

The Meaning of Revelation

Any attempt to express the meaning of revelation must do so in terms of the issues that concern us at this particular time in our history. Otherwise the idea of revelation will be irrelevant and uninteresting. It is important therefore that we first bring our questions and uncertainties out into the open. In order to do so we must first become aware of what Paul Tillich calls our "situation," which is the context out of which our questions arise. It is obviously impossible for us to cover every aspect of our situation here, but we can at least delineate six major areas: the cosmos, history, society, religion, the self and reason. The following will attempt briefly to "correlate" the idea of revelation with some of the questions that arise from our reflecting on these six areas of our situation.

The Cosmos and Revelation. Because of developments in modern science we now know that we are living in a world-in-process. Our universe is "unfinished." Most scientists are convinced that the cosmos has only slowly and arduously "evolved" to its present state. Over a twenty billion year period matter has struggled to become alive, and life to become conscious. Conscious of this emergent cosmos, we can hardly help asking where it is going and whether it has any purpose to it.

This evolving universe is the "situation" out of which many educated persons today raise their most urgent questions. The most obvious of these is whether there is any final meaning to the cosmic process of which our lives seem to be such a transient and insignificant episode. Is there any purpose to the universe? This question is inseparable from our own individual concern for significance (which we shall look at below). For if the universe as a whole is finally no more than a senseless movement of matter, it would seem that our own individual claims of significance are rather tenuous also.

Is the universe alone? Have the galaxies struggled in absolutely solitary silence throughout the ages of their evolution? Has evolution been completely unaccompanied by any principle of care and concern? Has life on earth labored along for two or three billion years in lonesome struggle eventually to produce the human species only by accident?

Modern cosmic pessimism will answer "yes" to these questions. According to much modern thought the absolute indifference of the universe is the basis from which all honest thinking must begin. Followers of the biblical tradition, however, believe that they have heard a "word" speaking out to us in our apparent lostness, a light shining in the darkness, a divine voice telling us we are not alone

and that the cosmos has from the beginning been delivered from its apparent companionlessness. The breaking through of this word into the silence of the universe may be called "revelation."

This word is communicated essentially in the form of *promise*. The awareness of a self-giving God is "revealed" to faith as a *promise* of ultimate fulfillment. Centuries ago, according to the biblical story, a man who came to be known as Abraham felt the promise of a deeply fulfilling future summoning him to leave his ancestral home and venture forth into the unknown. His sons and daughters conveyed in their own life situations a sense of the promise felt by their father. The hope for a great future has been passed on from generation to generation down to the present. The names of Abraham, Isaac, Jacob, Joseph, Moses, Joshua and the great judges, kings and prophets of Israel all call to mind for believers to this day that a word of promise has broken the apparent silence of the universe. Reading the biblical accounts of their lives and struggles puts us in touch with the promise and the hope that through them broke into our world. For the Christian the person of Jesus of Nazareth constitutes the decisive breaking in of the promise of fulfillment felt long ago by Abraham. The event of Jesus the Christ, and especially the accounts of his resurrection appearances, may be understood as essentially *promissory* in nature, opening up what lies in store for the universe as a whole (Jürgen Moltmann, *Theology of Hope,* NY: Harper & Row, 1967, pp. 139-229).

From the moment of its creation the universe has "felt" the outpouring of God's own being into itself, arousing it to reach out toward ever more intense modes of fulfillment. This divine self-donation is known as "universal" or "general" revelation. And the calling of Abraham, Moses and the prophets may be seen as special instances of the breaking in of God's promise to the universe within the context of a particular people's existence. From the point of view of cosmology the particularity, contingency and relativity of the promissory address to Israel are no more scandalous than the fact that at an earlier time in cosmic evolution life itself came about as a unique event within a particular, contingent and relative situation. By its very nature the introduction of unprecedented novelty into the cosmic process at any point has to be a unique, particular event. Therefore, locating the special call of Israel or the church in terms of the whole sweep of cosmic evolution may help soften the "scandal of particularity" involved in the special call of God to a particular, culturally limited people to bear witness to the absolute mystery of a divine promise to the cosmos.

If we situate the idea of revelation in the context of an evolutionary universe, revelation may be understood as the full unfolding and blossoming forth of the universe itself. It is the coming to a head of the struggles of all the cosmic epochs for a significance that might validate their labored journeying. According to Paul's *Letter to the Romans:* "...the creation waits with eager longing for the revealing of the sons of God.... We know that the whole creation has been groaning in travail together until now..." (Rom 8:19, 22) From one point of view revelation is the "interruptive" utterance of a word of promise into what otherwise may be seen as a cosmic void. But in terms of the cosmos-in-evolution it is legitimate to see revelation as the flowering fulfillment of the universe itself. Revelation is, in one sense at least, the very purpose of the evolving universe.

History and Revelation. We may think of *history* as a second aspect of our situation, quite distinct (though, of course, not separate) from the cosmos. In one sense history is the content of revelation, and in another it is the context of revelation. Hence we may think of "revelation *of* history" as well as "revelation *in* history."

Revelation of History. Is there any meaning to history? Because history is made up cumulatively of the actions and experiences of persons endowed with the elusive quality of freedom, its intelligibility is not easily comprehended. Once we humans acquired the distinct feeling that our historical existence has "exiled" us to some degree from the regularities and rhythms of nature, we became restless to find exactly where we do fit in. What pattern or order, if any, does history have that can give us a sure sense of where and who we are? The "fall" of the human species from the predictabilities of nature into the "terrors" of history has been a most adventurous development in the total unfolding of the universe. But it has certainly been a troubling one as well, as we are far from grasping its significance in a clear way.

Interestingly, biblical religion itself has been partly responsible for sparking the disturbing impulse to move beyond purely natural existence out into the uncertainty of history. In fact, it seems that biblical religion opened up the horizon of "history" in an unprecedented way. It did so especially because of the promissory nature of its revelation. Sensitive to this promise, our biblical ancestors moved decisively into history as the central context of their lives and aspirations. History is itself a gift made possible by a revelatory promise. Therefore, instead of our speaking only of God's revelation *in* history, it is just as appropriate for us to speak here of God's revelation *of* history. History is the result, and not just the medium of revelation. History is itself what is revealed or "unveiled." History as such is the horizon of human existence and action bequeathed to us by a revelatory promise.

The emergence of the Hebrew religion was a very unsettling occurrence. In the call of Abraham to leave the home of his ancestors, in Moses' leading his followers away from acquiescence in slavery, in the prophetic and apocalyptic vision of a new age, in Jesus' idealizing of homelessness, in the evangelists' turning our attention toward the Risen Lord and in Paul's relentless call to freedom, we have a disturbing chronicle of discontent at the idea that we can find our fulfillment in nature apart from history. According to the Bible our fulfillment as human beings begins by our embarking upon a journey into the unknown future opened up by a promise that pulls us away from the familiarity of a purely natural existence. This call into history has been painful as well as promising, and it is always tempting to turn back toward the "paradise" of non-historical existence.

The uncertainty of the future into which history is taking us would be unbearable unless we are guided by some vision of fulfillment. The quest for revelation may therefore be understood, in the present context at least, as the seeking of a resolution to the uncertainty that confronts us as we peer into the unknown outcome of historical events. The import of the biblical revelation is that we may trust in the promise of an unimaginably fulfilling future without which the move into history would be too terrifying for us. History without promise is intolerable. It is no wonder that so many avenues of escape are devised by those who see history as holding no promise. Gnostic movements of the body, the spirit and the mind are inevitable temptations whenever history is denuded of the expectancy of fulfillment that brought it about in the first place. Escapist movements are quite intelligible whenever history is seen as bereft of a fulfilling future.

Revelation, therefore, may be understood as the promise of an ultimate meaning to history. History's final meaning is pointed to in the Bible (and in a special way in Jesus' teaching) by images and parables of the "Kingdom of God." The Bible does not specify in any completely clear way what this meaning is. But by way of our communally dwelling within the biblical imagery surrounding this and other biblical portrayals of human destiny, the promise of history may take root in our consciousness and continue to keep the horizon of ultimate meaning open for us today. Revelation *is* promise, and without our response of hope neither revelation nor history's meaning can take hold of us in our present situation.

Revelation In History. However, we must have some grounds for believing in the promise of an ultimately fulfilling future. Faith can never be completely without reasons. It must have a foundation based in human experience itself. Concrete deeds and events in our history are needed to vindicate our hope for fulfillment.

It is in this connection that we may speak more strictly of revelation *in* history. For as we look with our tradition into the past we can discern innumerable instances of God's fidelity to the promise that is revelation. This fidelity is embodied prototypically in the biblical account of the *covenant* of Yahweh with Israel, where God is portrayed as pledging everlasting faithfulness (e.g. Exodus 19-24). The theme of divine fidelity is the dominant theme in biblical religion, and revelation is the story of the mighty acts of a God who remains faithful in spite of our lack of trust. For Christians the Christ-event is the decisive manifestation of this divine promise and fidelity.

Discernment of the revelatory nature of the Christ-event and other instances of God's fidelity requires that we belong to the inner life of a faith community that perceives its very identity as having been founded by the story of divine acts of fidelity to the promise. To those who participate in this "inner history" such occurrences as the call of Abraham, the Exodus from Egypt, the tortured lives of the prophets, the redemption of Israel and Judah from captivity, the events surrounding the life and death of Jesus, including the acts of the apostles and the establishment of the church, all have a revelatory significance that would not inevitably be obvious to scientific historians. Participation in the shared memory of a people and its own foundational story relates us to these occurrences in an intimate way that could hardly be possible through a purely detached or "external" chronicling of the same events in the manner of scientific history. The conviction that we belong to a history whose meaning is promise could hardly take shape outside the life of a community whose very existence is based on that promise.

Richard Niebuhr has articulated the difference between "inner" and "outer" history and its importance for understanding the idea of revelation. Though his well-known distinction of inner and outer history should not be stretched too far, it is quite useful for understanding how we may encounter any possible revelation in history. Niebuhr gives us a simple analogy to help us comprehend the duality of internal and external history. Consider the case of a blind man who undergoes an operation and, as a result, receives back his sight. Then try to imagine how his own account of this momentous healing event would differ from that of the doctors who operated upon him. The medical account will be couched in the idiom of a decidedly external reporting. On the other hand, the account given by the blind man, instead of being clinically "objective," will be filled with language of deep feeling, gratitude and emotional involvement. It will be an "inner history," giving us a perspective which the doctors are not able to provide. And the inner history provided by the man whose sight has been restored will give us an intimacy with the event that even the most careful clinical language could never come close to providing.

Similarly the revelatory and healing significance of the promissory events in the life of Israel and the church may not be obvious from the perspective of a purely external recital. An external report cannot state exactly why we may perceive these events as a basis for our hope here and now. Scientific history can shed much interesting light on the historical circumstances surrounding the great events upon which hope is founded, and critical historical work can even become a necessary ingredient in a community's recalling of its foundational moments. But only a participation in the "inner life" of a community puts us in a position to "confess" these events as moments of divine fidelity to the covenantal promise that comprise God's relation to our life as a people formed by these events. In order to be grasped by the reality of a possible revelation in history, we must be prepared to risk involvement in the life of a community founded by the memory of an inner history often inaccessible to a purely "objective" recording (Niebuhr, pp. 44ff). For Christians it is the function of the church to provide the context for this intimacy with revelation. By partaking of the church's mysteries of "word" and "sacrament," and by dwelling in the images and teachings given in the scriptures and tradition, the believer is brought into encounter with the events grounding christian hope.

Society and Revelation. Closely related to the historical context is the human struggle to bring about the "right" social order. Reflection on the "impossible" situation of creating workable and humane social and economic configurations may also lead us to the point where we can be open to a revelatory word that addresses us in the complexities of our social existence.

The idea of revelation becomes meaningful to faith especially in those situations which according to human reckoning are characterized by what we may call "impossibility." Its proximity to situations of apparent impossibility has characterized the biblical promise in all the major "stories of God." So when we think of the notion of revelation today, we are called to understand it in terms of the divine promise of a way out of dilemmas that seem resistant to any possible solution we can imagine. An attitude of trust in God's fidelity must accompany our awareness of the seemingly irredeemable social, political and economic quandaries in which we find ourselves embroiled today. It is doubtful that revelation in its essentially surprising and unpredictable freshness could be experienced palpably except in such situations of apparent impossibility. And it is quite a simple matter to become aware of the "impossible" deadends to which our human attempts to establish the "right" social orders on the basis of our own purely human ideals have always led us. When we realize the frustration to which our best-intentioned social programs bring us, we are perhaps once again in a position to hearken to a revelatory response to our situation.

If we are looking for a *specific* answer to our social quest, however, we will not find it in revelation. The revelatory "answer" will inevitably be quite disappointing to us if we expect it to fall within the general class of "solutions" that have been proposed by professional experts. If we look to it for a specific social program, we will end up hopelessly trivializing the biblical response to our quest. Without doing it great violence we cannot look

into the Bible for *the* perfect answer to our own socio-economic problems. Such a fundamentalism is unworthy of any genuine faith in revelation. For the revelatory response lies on a different plane from the one shaped by our usual social expectations and planning. It is once again only in the sphere of hope and promise that we may authentically seek a response to the injustice and suffering (including the forgotten suffering) inflicted by our social structures.

Revelation and the Kingdom of God. In the Bible, the theme of the "Kingdom of God" once again stands forth most obviously as the primary symbol of the goal of our social searching. From the perspective of the social dimension of our situation we may understand the quest for revelation in terms of the long human quest for the Kingdom of God. And the content of the biblical imagery of the Kingdom may be at least partially grasped in terms of two other prominent biblical themes: *justice* and *liberation*. These themes become more and more transparent as we move through Israel's history into the mind of Jesus and the early christian church.

Justice (in Hebrew, *s͗daqah*, implying foremost Yahweh's gracious fidelity to the covenantal promise) is a *revelatory* aspect of our social relationships, and without it the God of revelation remains hidden from us. Our own practice of justice is a necessary condition for God's becoming manifest in our historical and social existence. Therefore, in order for us to experience today the revelation of God we must also experience and practice justice in the social dimension of our existence. To the extent that justice does not yet reign, revelation remains obscured.

And yet, the revelation of God's justice has, at least to faith, entered irreversibly into our world. It is present in the mode of promise, and it abides wherever there is genuine hope. This hope, however, is not content with a quietistic complacency any more than it is impatient with the absence of immediate achievement of utopian dreams. It is an active hope, energized by the conviction of the reality of a promise-keeping God. It is a transformative hope, intent to alter any social situations, political structures and economic conditions that impede the pouring out of God's justice here and now. Such a hope has to be involved with social planning, though with the constant reservation that our human plans are likely to be short-sighted, onesided and in need of criticism in accordance with a wider vision of justice. Social planning is not to be repudiated as such. The biblical ideal of justice requires only that we avoid a planning that does not provide for the poor and that forgets about the suffering of the past and present. Social planning has often been characterized by a neglect of the poor, the disenfranchised, the weak, the stranger and of forgotten sufferings of the past, of all those elements that do not "fit." But any social vision that leaves these out is destined to be only a fragment. The "Kingdom of God" is an image of communal human fulfillment with God that challenges us continually to widen our social understanding so as to include all of these incongruities, even when it does not seem economically feasible to do so. The very comprehensiveness of this image of the Kingdom, of course, makes it seem unbelievable from the perspective of our customary styles of social thinking. Yet the biblical promise demands nothing less than the expanding of our social vision and our sense of justice so as to include all those elements that we normally leave out.

Another aspect of the Kingdom of God is the theme of liberation. Intimately associated with "justice," the theme of liberation is central to the biblical vision of God and of society. The Exodus event,

the liberation of an oppressed people from the threats of slavery and annihilation, is the central event through which Israel came to understand the nature of God. It is inappropriate therefore, in the biblical context at least, to think of God without simultaneously thinking of liberation. Loving and liberating justice is God's essence, and it is out of this essence that the revelatory promise is given to society and its history. In the biblical context this liberating justice does not refer only to a salvation beyond history, but also to a salvation of history and a deliverance within history. Typically the promise of deliverance is felt first and becomes most intensely alive in the lives of those whom our social institutions have marginalized and made to feel as though they do not belong. It is to such as these that Jesus' proclamation of the Good News of freedom and justice was delivered first and foremost. Social outcasts, oppressed and rejected people have been the constant mediators of revelation. For it is through their hope in and acceptance of a promise of liberation that a space was opened up for our own history and future to make its appearance. The debt we owe to the poor for allowing the promise of liberation to open up for us the sphere of our historical existence is inestimable.

For centuries christian theology has been able to some extent to overlook the themes of promise, justice and liberation that permeate the biblical texts. An overemphasis on the metaphysical aspects of God as understood especially in terms of Greek philosophy has sometimes obscured the liberating themes in the Bible and their implications for our social existence here and now. But recent developments in biblical studies and theology render it impossible any longer to suppress these themes, and particularly in any attempt to get to the heart of what is meant by revelation. In the context of our social situation, revelation means the promise of justice for and liberation of all whose basic needs have not been met and whose human dignity has not yet been recognized. An encounter with the God of revelation takes place primarily in those situations through which the sense of a promise of liberating justice breaks through into our history.

Religion and Revelation. The religious intuitions of the human species suggest that the most comprehensive situation in which we dwell is neither history nor society nor the cosmos, but *mystery.* Religions invite us into the dimension of mystery by way of symbols and stories, as well as by ritualistic actions that give bodily and dramatic expression to the meaning inherent in symbols and myths. It is precisely in symbolic expression that the dimension of mystery seems to dwell and "reveal" itself to us.

Broadly speaking, a symbol is anything through which we are given a glimpse of something else. By saying one thing directly a symbol or symbolic expression says something else indirectly. The indirect or symbolic meaning, however, is never quite clear. The symbol points us to the meaning, and the meaning needs the symbol in order to communicate itself to us, but it can never be fully translated into non-symbolic propositions. There is a fullness of meaning in any original symbolic expression that can never be adequately translated into a series of direct statements.

It is easy to see why religions employ symbols as their primary language. Mystery and symbols naturally go together. The horizon of mystery to which religious expression points discloses itself to the religious person or community by way of symbols (and their mythic and ritualistic embodiments). For this reason we can say that *revelation universally has the character of symbolic communication (Dulles, pp. 131-54).* In a very general

sense "revelation" means the breaking through of the dimension of mystery into our ordinary awareness. And it is especially through the intrinsically revelatory medium of symbols that this unconcealment of mystery occurs. In this sense revelation occurs in many ways in all the religions.

We cannot form any clear idea of the mystery that religious symbols reveal. For symbols hide from us the very reality that simultaneously comes to expression in them. They conceal what they reveal. They pull us into the realm of the mystery they represent, but in doing so they still leave us in the darkness of unclarity. But in surrendering to them we find that they remain an endless source of meaning for us. Our thinking must return again and again to the realm of the symbolic in order to receive nourishment, indeed to find anything of importance to think about at all. An appreciation of the "symbolic life" is a necessary condition for the reception of revelation. (See Paul Ricoeur, *The Symbolism of Evil,* trans. by E. Buchanan, Boston: Beacon Press, 1967.)

Mystery and Special Revelation. In terms of the perennial human search for adequate symbolic representations of the universally intuited dimension of mystery we may now gain further understanding of what is meant by a "special" historical revelation. For Christians too are part of the long human adventure into mystery. They believe, however, that the ultimate mystery that beckons all of us is made decisively manifest for them in the person of Jesus the Christ. To christian faith Jesus is the definitive symbolic revelation of the ultimate mystery of the universe. This special symbolic representation of mystery occurs, of course, within the larger biblical narrative context reciting the "mighty acts" of God in all of nature and history. But in Jesus christian faith perceives what has been called a "final" revelation of the mystery of the universe. To understand what mystery is essentially, believers are invited to look at this man and his liberating words and works. In John's Gospel, Philip asks Jesus to show the disciples the mysterious "Father" who has been announced by Jesus. And the Fourth Gospel portrays Jesus as responding to this request by pointing to himself: "Have I been with you so long, and yet you do not know me, Philip? He who has seen me has seen the Father." (Jn 14:9) To see Jesus, and to participate in the Jesus-story, is to enter into the mystery that he calls "Father." Religiously speaking Jesus is for christian faith the manifestation of the heart of the mystery that surrounds us. His person, life, words, deeds, death and resurrection are *symbolically* revelatory of an ultimate reality.

However, Christians are not obliged to hold that mystery is in every detail disclosed by way of the experience of Israel and the person or teaching of Jesus, or in the scriptures, or in tradition. A close reading of these sources of the christian idea of God will itself show that none of them has imposed such a restriction on christian faith. Instead the classic sources of theology have always maintained that the inexhaustible mystery of God remains hidden even while it is being revealed. If this is the case, if God is truly a hidden God, then there is no reason why aspects of God that remain hidden from us in our experience of specifically christian history and symbolism cannot become genuinely transparent to others in their own religious existence, and to us in our association with other religions and traditions.

What then can the christian belief in "special revelation" possibly mean when it is articulated in terms of the penumbra of mystery that constitutes the widest context of our existence and which is testified to universally in human religious experience and symbolism? "Special revelation" means the specific "face" this mystery takes to those who participate in the *christian* story. We have said that wherever mystery becomes manifest there is revelation. This is what is meant by the theological notion of "general revelation." As Paul Tillich has put it, revelation is the "manifestation of the mystery of Being." And all religion is revelatory in this sense. But to the christian there is a "special," "decisive," or "final" character to the revelation of God in Jesus as the Christ. Thus a central question for the theology of revelation today is that of how to reconcile emphasis on the definitiveness of Christ with our acknowledgement of the continual openness to the general revelation of mystery given universally to our universe, to human existence and especially to religious experience? In the writings of the NT and in christian tradition we are told, often in so many words, that the fullness of revelation occurs in Jesus the Christ. Can a Christian honestly engage in open conversation with other religions while clinging to this particularity (and apparent relativity) of belief? Can one openly and honestly encounter the mystery of the universe in other traditions without surrendering the claim of the universal significance of Christ?

One way of responding to this contemporary theological problem is to think out more fully the implications of belief in "the universal significance of Christ." This expression entails, among other things, that we need never fear being open to the truth, no matter how foreign it appears in terms of our present understanding. If Christ is universal in his presence and significance, the christian need never fear that an openness to the truth will be impaired by this belief. For if the name and universality of "Christ" stands for anything, it means openness to and tolerance of otherness. Living in Christ would then promote an openness to dialogue and a vulnerability to the interpretation of human experience by those of other traditions. Christian faith allows no construal of revelation as an imprisoning body of truths that restricts us from exploring the vast universe of nature, culture and religion. Revelation is not meant to draw an impenetrable circle of safety around our consciousness. And the experience of a "special revelation" in terms of the figure of "Christ" may actually provide the liberating images that can lead our consciousness toward an adventurous exploration of the inexhaustible mystery that manifests itself everywhere, and especially in the world's religious traditions. Special revelation therefore would not mean simply a content for us narrowly to look *at* or to focus on, but instead a specific symbolism *with* which and *out of* which we are able to look as we face the mystery of the universe.

The Self and Revelation. It has often been observed that a longing for significance is the deeply interior desire that dominates our lives. The social world in which we are each embedded and in which our personalities are shaped provides us with all sorts of opportunities to gain a sense of significance before others. Indeed society is in part a "system of heroics" constantly holding out to us criteria of self-worth. (The expression "system of heroics" is employed by Ernest Becker as a central concept in *The Denial of Death* New York: The Free Press, 1973.) Parental, familial, political, academic, athletic, artistic, ecclesiastical and many other dimensions of our social environment give us all the opportunities we need to convince others of our importance.

The longing to be accepted is part of our human nature. And yet the degree of significance provided by our immediate environments with their various criteria of worth does not always satisfy this longing. The need for approval rises up

again and again from out of a deep inner loneliness. And the quest for some relief from this loneliness continues. Beneath the surface of our social involvements there lurks a personal loneliness that may grow more and more burdensome even as we win the esteem of others. Can one find personal significance in the depths of this loneliness?

The quest for revelation, as interpreted from the perspective of individual selfhood, may be understood as the quest for this significance. It is the longing for a "word" that might convince us that there is an answer to our quest for significance. Christians have believed, ever since the time of the first disciples, that such a word is graciously offered to us in the life, person, and teachings of Jesus. It is a word spoken not only to the universe, society and history, but also to the hidden selfhood of each one of us. Throughout the christian centuries the interpreters of this word have emphasized that such a revelation can take root in our universe and in society and its history only if it is first implanted in the life of the individual. It is indeed a word of promise addressed to all, but it has to be received concretely by individuals who then share the promise with others.

The christian faith maintains that in Christ the promise of divine companionship is offered to each person. The early followers of Jesus found in him the definitive and unsurpassable disclosure of a divine friendship signifying the intrinsic importance of each individual. Jesus' mission was to tear through the obscuring veil of social and religious systems in order to bring to light a love that places no criteria of worth on the individual. His gestures and teachings relativize the reigning criteria of worth. He wants people to realize that they cannot *earn* their sense of significance, no matter how hard they try, since they are *already* accepted as important. Their quest for "identity" by proving themselves worthy through rigid conformity to religious, ethical or any other "conditions of worth" is futile. For their significance as persons intimately cared for by an unsurpassable love is *already* established. This identity is sufficient, and no social achievements will make them any more intrinsically valuable than they already are.

Jesus' actions and parables consistently make this point. And his reference to God as "Abba," a name of intimacy and deep affection, already contains the nucleus of the christian revelation that an unconditional love has already been offered to us. Of course accepting this acceptance, an attitude that Paul Tillich identifies as the heart of christian faith, may be more difficult than trying to earn it. For such a trust requires a humble admission on our part that we cannot earn our significance by our own efforts. Perhaps we can now see once again why the revelation of God enters into history especially throught the sensitivities of the poor, the sinners, the desperate who are in the "impossible" situation of no longer being able to prove themselves worthy of anything. Such individuals can only open themselves to the promise of acceptance in spite of their social insignificance.

The otherness and the "contradiction" traditionally associated with the idea of revelation are nowhere more obvious than in the shocking disclosure by Jesus of a love whose bestowal is not contingent upon our social, moral or spiritual achievements. This idea clashes so radically with ordinary experience that believers tend to see it as a revelatory "interruption" of normality. If we take it seriously, the belief that our value does not depend on our achievements can completely overturn our usual way of looking at the world and at ourselves. And it can have even revolutionary implications for society's self-understanding. Its truly startling nature makes it an acceptable candidate for claiming the status of "revelation." Jesus must have known this. Perhaps that is why he insisted that one must become like a little child in order to accept it.

Reason and Revelation. Revelation, in the words of Wolfhart Pannenberg, is the "arrival of the future." And the God of the Bible always addresses us out of the inexhaustible "newness" of the future. This means that our present religious consciousness must assume the distinctive attitude of radical openness to the future if it is to be properly receptive of revelation. Such an attitude is called *hope*. But can hope in God's promise of an ultimately fulfilling future legitimately be called a *realistic* attitude? Can we *reasonably* maintain that God speaks to us in history out of an open-ended future of promise?

In theological discussions today the very plausibility of the notion of revelation is often at issue. And much of the present controversy occurs as a result of our not knowing quite how to deal with the modern spirit of scientific, psychological and social criticism that places the idea of revelation in question. This "critical consciousness' demands quite properly that we "face reality." But it holds that our ideas and convictions are in touch with reality only if they are "verifiable" or "falsifiable" according to publicly accessible methods of knowing. Hence it is suspicious of such "esoteric" ideas as those of which special revelation appears to be composed.

The methods of reason, and especially scientific reason, possess an apparent neutrality and public accountability that would seem to make them apt measuring rods for the veracity of all our ideas. The allegedly impersonal methods of logic and science seem to allow for a minimum of subjective involvement and flights of individual fancy. And by eliminating as far as possible the coefficient of personality from the knowing process, these methods are said to open our consciousness to the real world without distortively subjective filters. It is little wonder that critical consciousness has enshrined reason and scientific method, with their ideals of detachment and disinterestedness, as the only valid ways of determining the truth-status of our ideas.

Such methods of confirming the validity of many propositions are unquestionably appropriate. However, there is an understanding of "reality" operative in the realm of revelatory promise and hope that may not be subject to the demands of critical consciousness as it is usually understood. Criticism, after all, usually operates in the realm of the predictable or the "probable," in the area of what is reasonably acceptable according to science and common human experience. It can accept as valid only that for which there are already analogies or precedents that "objective" science and reason can discern. And scientific method works by taking large numbers of *similar* occurrences and generalizing from them. A completely novel, unpredictable or unique occurrence would not constitute sufficient basis for such scientific generalizing, and so it would not be subject to critical methods of inquiry. Science is incapable of dealing with the radically new, the unpredictable or the "improbable." Hence the notion of revelation, which biblical religion cannot separate from what is considered improbable in terms of scientific standards of credibility, seems to contradict critical consciousness. To those for whom criticism is the only criterion of "truth," therefore, revelation will inevitably be problematic.

Moreover, critical consciousness is oriented essentially toward what is verifiable in the present or in the past. Scientific method can confirm only those hypotheses for which there is a sufficient amount of data available from the records left by the past or capable of being experimentally observed in the present. But the "data" upon which the "hypothesis" of revelation is based are to a large degree unavailable by definition to scientific investigation. For the realm from which christian faith senses the appearance of revelation is the *future*. Revelation as the "arrival of the future" is given essentially in the form of promise. This promise contains a foretaste of the future; but the future is not yet fully present, and so it remains beyond the limits of what is critically verifiable or publicly accessible.

We can agree of course with reason's wholesome demand that we be true to the real and try to avoid illusions. And we can also adhere to criticism's demand that we test our private aspirations in the context of a community and its sense of reality. But a trust in revelation may realize these demands by way of following a vision and "praxis" of shared hope. Christian faith holds that our abiding within a community founded on hope in God's promise, and living a life that is actively and cooperatively involved in transforming history in accordance with the biblical ideals of justice and liberation, is the most "realistic" posture we can take in the world. Such an approach is realistic precisely because the realm of the "really real" or of "ultimate reality" is located in the dimension of futurity. The past is gone, and the present is only fleetingly "now" before it disappears into the past. The temporal dimension that is the most trustworthy and "faithful" in bringing freshness and new life into the present is the future. To christian faith the future is the domain of the "really real." Therefore, facing reality means facing toward the future. And it is only through shared images of hope that we can turn our consciousness toward this future. The God of the Bible, according to much contemporary theological reflection, is one whose very essence is futurity. Therefore, approaching the question of the reality of God's self-revelation requires that we ask also about how we would open ourselves most completely to the realm of the divine which Karl Rahner has called the Absolute Future. How can we face this Future if it is not verifiable in the same way as objects of science and ordinary experience?

It seems that only *hope* can orient us toward the "really real,' if indeed the fullness of reality lies in the future. For hope is an openness to the breaking in of what is completely unpredictable and unanticipated from the point of view of what is considered to be possible by ordinary standards of expectation. To avoid any misunderstanding here, hope should be distinguished from wishing. Wishing is a mode of desire that takes its bearing entirely from the present. It tends to imagine that the future will turn out the way I would like, on the basis of what pleases me now. Wishing, associated with what Sigmund Freud called the "pleasure principle," can give rise only to fantasies and illusions. But hoping renounces such illusions and opens itself to a future that may turn out to be quite different from the one I wish for. Hoping is open to the radically new and "improbable" in a way that wishing is not. Hoping, therefore, can be considered a realistic, indeed the most realistic, stance our consciousness can take. Hoping is faith's way of accepting what Freud called the "reality principle." And if revelation means the arrival of the future into the present, then our acceptance of revelation is consistent with the critical demand that we face reality. (On the distinction between wishing and hoping see H.A. Williams, *True Resurrection,* New York: Harper Colophon Books, 1972, pp. 178f.)

Revelation, though, does not mean the acceptance of notions that are contrary to reason or to science. Much of the modern protest against the notion of revelation stems from a fear that revelation intends to provide *information* that potentially conflicts with reason or science. And since reason and science carry so much weight today, any alternative source of information will be suspect. But revelation is not informative in the sense of adding cumulatively to any list of "facts." Hence it does not compete with nor conflict with reason or science. In any case, only items in the same class or category can contradict one another. Reason and science could hardly contradict revelation unless we contrivedly thrust revelation into the category of scientifically informational discourse. Such a reduction is in fact still being attempted today by "scientific creationism" which reads the biblical account of cosmic origins and God's activity as though they were alternative scientific reports. However, situating the biblical stories in the (actually quite modern) category of science, a style of understanding completely unknown to the biblical authors themselves, both belittles the legitimate achievements of science and diminishes the notion of revelation. Revelation does not give us information that may be placed side by side with scientific understanding. As Tillich puts it, revelation is not the uncovering of information at all, but rather the unfolding of a relationship. Revelation mediates to us the mystery of God's love and promise for the world, not data that we might easily gather by our own rational and scientific efforts. Science can provide helpful assistance in our attempts to understand the circumstances within which the mystery of God is disclosed. But it would be a serious misunderstanding of revelation to place its content in the same realm of ideas as those discussed by scientists. Revelation offers us a content that is much more relational and

foundational than any we can receive through ordinary ways of collecting information. And so it will appear as unreasonable or scientifically unrealistic only if we erroneously read this content as though is were a body of competing information about the world or history. Revelation is too important to be consigned to the same category as the disciplines which fill in the empty spaces of human ignorance. Instead revelation, especially as a disclosure of mystery, may be interpreted by faith as opening up and continually extending the horizon within which human consciousness is set free to pursue its various disciplinary objectives.
See **History, Hope, Promise**

Avery Dulles, *Models of Revelation* (Garden City, New York: Doubleday & Co., 1983). H. Richard Niebuhr, *The Meaning of Revelation* (New York: Macmillan, 1941). Richard McBrien, *Catholicism,* Vol I. (Minneapolis: Winston Press, 1980), pp. 201-43. Vatican Council II, *Dogmatic Constitution on Divine Revelation* (*Dei Verbum*), 1965.

JOHN F. HAUGHT

RIGHTEOUSNESS
See **Justice, Justification**

RIGHTS, HUMAN

While christian concern with what are now termed human rights issues may be traced from the birth of Christianity, it is basically since the Second World War that the phenomena of human rights have appeared consistently as items on the agenda of the churches throughout the world. In the sphere of practical involvement, violations of human rights have been denounced, causes espoused, and submissions made to individual governments, the United Nations and other responsible agencies. Concurrent with this activity, attempts have been made by individual theologians, church commissions and ecumenical groups to penetrate the rhetoric of human rights and formulate theological perspectives so that the participation of Christians in support of human rights and responsibilities might be the more consistent and mature.

Although the language of human rights and duties became prominent in the eighteenth century in Europe and America, their conception belongs to every age and culture. Human rights address situations where power is being exercised in such a manner as to control human beings by manipulation or coercion so that they are unable to affirm their dignity and humanity fully. Such an exercise of power may derive from an individual, group, nation or government and creates a conflictual situation. Human rights are basically protective devices and affirmations in law and morality which are designed to shield human beings from random violence and neglect, and from systemic exercises of destructive power. They are mechanisms to control the use of power by an individual, group or nation in relation to other human beings, and to promote the conditions necessary for the individual alone or with others, to affirm his or her humanity. Thus Francisco de Vitoria (1485-1546) and Bartolomé de las Casas (1474-1566), for example, argued for the rights of the Indians against the oppressive use of power by Spain in its colonizing activity, while the same appeal is made for similar reasons in respect to the Indians of the Amazon region today. The appeal to human rights is as universal as the denial of human dignity.

Historically, human rights language emerged in the philosophical writing of the seventeenth century in the work of Hugo Grotius, Thomas Hobbes and John Locke, and first came to prominence when the fathers of the French and American Revolutions attempted to create a society where their hard-won freedoms would not be impugned, thus according each citizen equality and the opportunity to participate in decision-making. That certain fundamental rights belong to human beings as such, and can therefore be called "human rights" without qualification, found popular expression in the American *Declaration of Independence* (1776) and in the French *Declaration of the Rights of Man and the Citizen* (1789). This insight, however, was an application in a new context of a much older principle.

In the Middle Ages a ruler or "prince" (in most of the treatises) possessed theoretically absolute sovereignty over his territory and could legislate for his own immediate interests and those of his most powerful subjects. Anyone who was oppressed through such legislation had no one to whom to appeal. In practice this absolute sovereignty was limited by the authority of the Church which claimed the right to declare any of the prince's laws invalid if it did not conform to an absolute standard of justice, but such ecclesiastical authority fell into decline so that this mechanism to control the abuse of power became ineffective. In the period of the Renaissance and the Reformation, subjects themselves began to question their duty to obey "princes" who used power to manipulate and subjugate them, thus diverging from what was perceived through reason to be a higher moral value phrased as either natural law or divine law. While subjects were still enjoined by the Reformers to respect the rulers, this was not an unqualified injunction. Such respect was conditional upon the ruler's duty to practice justice, and not oppress or dehumanize men and women, thus contravening divine justice. Some Reformers, e.g., John Knox, phrased the right to resist tyrannous rulers, and to depose them, thus stressing that all human beings are subject to the sovereignty of God and not simply to the enactments of rulers.

With the creation of the "Commonwealth" in England and other patterns of society in Europe not based on the prince-subject relationship, a greater definition of the rights and obligations of citizens toward one another proved necessary. Once again the dominant concern centered on the need to ensure protection and freedom from the use of power in a destructive manner by individuals or groups in society in relation to other individuals or groups. Just as in the earlier phases of the development of the notion of "rights," a profoundly theological insight provided the basis for the concept of human rights. The notion of "natural rights" advanced by John Locke among others in this period, had as its foundation the conception of *men* being God's property; thus, they might not dispose of each other, or even of themselves, entirely as they wished. *Men* therefore possessed duties towards each other, which ensured that the dignity of the other was not impaired. At this time there was little attention paid to the rights of women. Some such notion of a human dignity antecedent to laws and Constitutions is evident in the phrases "We hold these truths to be self-evident, that all men are created equal; that they are endowed by their Creator with certain unalienable rights" (United States *Declaration of Independence*); and "the natural, inalienable, and sacred rights of man" (French *Declaration of the Rights of Man and the Citizen*).

This conception of rights, of the ability of human beings to challenge the use of power which oppresses them even when that power is exercised by their government, forms the classical conception of civil and political rights. Such rights with their corollary in the duty to insure that one's own exercise of power is not oppressive to others are normally phrased in negative terms, e.g. freedom from torture, and are generally justiciable, appearing under such rubrics as "protection from," "guaranteed freedom from." Positive rights, or "freedom to," partake of the same characteristics as the negative rights insofar as they conceive of circumstances arising when power will be exercised in ways which prevent the exercise of such rights as free speech. These classical, or civil and political, rights are sometimes called the first "generation" of rights.

The second generation of rights, associated with Karl Marx and socialism, relate to the fundamental conditions necessary before the individual is enabled to exercise his or her freedoms. In point of fact, Marx himself never ceased to advocate "the free development of individualities" in a society of associated, and not antagonistically opposed individuals (*Grundrisse*). However, the second generation of rights emphasizes, as Marx did, the importance of health care, employment, housing and education as essential to the development of human beings, through which they become enabled to exercise their classical rights. These rights, generally called social and economic rights, are seen to be "aspirations," and in some circumstances they are difficult to conceive as justiciable.

Since the 1960's a third generation of rights has been emerging. Associated with "developing nations," these rights lay claim to the basic needs for living— water, food, shelter—without which human beings can claim no other rights. It is possible to perceive this as a claim arising out of a use of power which at times oppresses some people through the exploitation of their natural resources, or as the failure to use power which might transfer or harness resources so that people might have the right to life. Like the second generation of rights, the rights of this third generation appear to be aspirations, and less open to justiciability.

Human rights, though pointing to values which are antecedent to law, are normally enshrined in the legal provisions of nations—in bills of rights or constitutions. How a state treated its citizens was regarded until recently as a matter for its own sovereign determination, and not a legitimate concern of anyone outside its own frontiers. Since the Second World War, with its precursors in International Humanitarian Law, however, there has arisen through international treaties and agencies an *International Code of Human Rights,* enshrined above all in the U.N. Declaration of Human Rights and its two Covenants (1966) and Protocols, and in regional Covenants and Conventions, e.g., the European Convention of Human Rights (1953). With their machinery for ensuring implementation, an international standard transcending national boundaries makes human rights violations and aspirations the legitimate concern of each citizen and nation in the world.

The three generations of human rights arise in the context where power is used to oppress people and where a constructive mode of the exercise of power is seen to be essential to enhance the human dignity of people. Within the human rights community of discourse, however, there are a number of important disputed questions. A number of human rights lawyers and commentators are prepared to recognize as human rights only those rights which are justiciable. Out of a legal positivist tradition they stress that a claim for human rights can only be made in a context where it can be met by appropriate legislation and action. Thus even though the *International Code* notes second and sometimes third generation rights, it is perceived that they may have the force of moral claims but are not human rights as such. In this way, this tradition of thought would reserve the term "human rights" to the classical civil and political rights. A second issue of current debate is the extent to which it is possible to speak of the "rights of peoples" or minorities. The *International Code,* while it affirms the right to self-determination of peoples, is basically phrased in terms of rights pertaining to individuals. Persons belonging to this or that minority may be denied their rights because of their membership in a minority group, but redress can only be sought on the basis of an individual's application. The major way in which this tension is being faced is through the articulation of freedom from genocide, and the affirmation of the rights of indigenous peoples, e.g., Amazonian Indians, Aborigines, Canadian Indians and Eskimos.

The language and affirmation of human rights finds its basis in a number of philosophical and religious traditions. Although human rights have often been perceived as a secular phenomenon by the Churches, e.g., the nineteenth century Roman Catholic encyclicals, theological insights have played an important role in the phrasing of the nature of human rights and responsibilities. While some concept of human dignity is evident in most philosophies from Socrates through the Enlightenment to contemporary thinkers, and though philosophers have asserted that human rights can be discerned through the use of reason, the concept of human dignity in the Judaeo-Christian tradition stresses the understanding that human beings are made in the image of God. Human beings in this tradition are declared to be created and sustained by and in relationship with God and thus are to be considered as selves in relation to God. God is portrayed throughout this tradition as treating men and women with respect. Because of this relationship with and love of God, every human being is a subject of reverence to other people. Despite the fact that this relationship with God has been broken through sin, the image of God has not

been eliminated from human beings. Because of the remnant of God's image in them, men and women are declared to possess no small dignity.

The event and death of Jesus Christ are seen to demonstrate that God has a purpose for human beings. This remnant and this purpose, conferred by God, carry the implication that people are to be honored and treated as sacred. Theologians of all Christian traditions have clearly affirmed human dignity based on the image of God in each person and the purpose of God demonstrated in Jesus Christ. From this human dignity there can be derogation. Men and women are to be treated as God intends them to be. Christian theology, then, grounds human dignity in its doctrine of God. Human beings have dignity because God created human beings in his own image, and then restored that image by living, dying and rising in Christ. Human life is seen to be essentially social because human beings have been created in the image of God who is Trinity and who combines both unity and relationship in self. But human life is flawed. Christian thinking about human rights emphasizes not only the dignity and social nature of humanity but also the fact that that dignity and social relationship is constantly violated through a failure to accept the "otherness" of the other, and a desire to exercise power only in one's own interests. Thus in any theological discussion of human rights the doctrine of sin has an important place beside the doctrine of God. From the christian understanding, the need to affirm human rights arises because of human sin. Human rights are a mechanism to control the mode of exercise of power which dehumanizes persons. If power were always exercised in a positive and constructive mode there would be no necessity for human rights language or legislation. Human rights emerge from the matrix of a situation where persons are being controlled or oppressed by other persons—from a situation of sin.

Throughout the centuries, the christian churches have both affirmed and violated human rights. While theological principles have provided a rationale for human rights alongside insights from a variety of philosophies and religious traditions, it is primarily since the 1960's that the different christian traditions have undertaken a theological analysis of human rights.

In the nineteenth century, the Roman Catholic Church clearly rejected the liberal concept of human rights on the grounds that the individual was being elevated to such a position that social cohesion and the common good were being undermined. The popes further argued that implicit in the demand for freedom of expression and religious liberty was a relativism in regard to truth. While individual theologians and thinkers in the church continued to argue for a decisive commitment to human rights, it was primarily at the Second Vatican Council and subsequently that a specific Roman Catholic contribution to the theological reflection on human rights appeared. The document which draws on and sums up all this work is from the Pontifical Commission *Justitia et Pax* and is entitled *The Church and Human Rights.* Drawing on *Gaudium et Spes,* and the encyclical *Pacem in Terris,* the document begins by affirming the inseparability of "rights" and "duties." After outlining the history of the relationship between the Roman Catholic Church and human rights, a doctrinal approach is taken, essentially Thomistic in methodology. The report affirms that the teaching of the magisterium on fundamental human rights is based in the inherent requirements of human nature itself on the level of reason and within the sphere of natural law. The fundamental human rights, akin to those enunciated in

the *International Code,* which are said to have been deduced from reason, and which have been affirmed in the teaching of the magisterium, are listed, along with the appropriate church statement. In this both classical civil and political rights are noted alongside social and cultural rights—thus holding together individual rights in tension with "the common good."

With this foundation, the report goes on to consider the central themes and supporting arguments "on the plane of faith and of a specifically Christian outlook." The theological "loci" which are then examined are the concepts of the incarnation, imago Dei, liberation and the church. Humankind is created in the image of God, and because of this, "everyone has imprinted on his conscience the moral sense which moves him to act according to the laws laid down by the Creator." The Incarnation, however, throws a new light on the concept of man and of his dignity suggested by natural reason. The Incarnation, the report goes on to stress, reveals man to himself, in that Jesus is the perfect man. Jesus is seen to have sanctified all humanity, through his life, death and resurrection, directing humankind to the love of neighbor. The truths revealed by Jesus about humankind are both the foundation of the Church's teaching on human nature, and the impetus for the mission of promoting the "human" throughout the world. The theme of the church's mission in the field of human rights is further emphasized by the ecclesiology enunciated in the document, viz. the church is described in terms of being the continuation of the presence of Christ in the world and in history. Since the work of Christ is that of liberation, so the task of the church is to help liberate humankind.

This approach does not explicitly face up to the question as to why human rights have not been affirmed by the church, nor why specific human rights only become apparent at certain times in history, e.g., the right not to be enslaved in the seventeenth century, or the right of women to participate in all spheres of human activity in the nineteenth and twentieth centuries. But a strong stress on human sin and on the eschatological nature of the church as journeying towards the truth—themes evident in the Second Vatican Council and in the encyclicals of Pope John Paul II (especially *Redemptor Hominis*) has helped to confront the particularity of human rights as protections from the use of power which dehumanizes human beings.

Since the Second Vatican Council and the contemporary theological affirmation of human rights, movements have emerged in the Roman Catholic Church appealing for a bill of rights within the church, because of the ways in which some manifestations of power are perceived as "oppressive." In this appeal it is stressed that the Roman Catholic Church needs to take seriously those values in its internal life as a sign of God's care for human beings.

Concurrent with this exploration by the Roman Catholic Church of the theological perspectives on human rights, other christian traditions have embarked on similar ventures using different methodologies. The World Alliance of Reformed Churches through an examination of scriptures came to conclusions similar to recent Roman Catholic studies, though a stronger stress was placed on God's covenants—especially the New Covenant in Jesus Christ and the liberating power and exercise of power of Jesus Christ. The Lutheran World Federation, employing an "ideal type" approach, stressed that human rights point to human sin, and that human rights are to be located in three types of rights, freedom, equality and participation, which are seen to be analogous to the values of the kingdom. Subsequent to

those three studies, an ecumenical study in the context of the World Council of Churches has been initiated which draws on the previous work of these international commissions, but which is exploring the concept of "power" from a theological perspective.

It has become apparent once again, however, that the major problem to be faced in respect to human rights is not the enunciation or rationalization of human rights but their implementation, and since the Second World War the christian churches have been active in seeking to protect human beings from destructive uses of power, and to promote the development of the human, thus affirming that "in Christ there is neither Jew nor Greek, male nor female" (Gal 3:28).

See **Anthropology, Christian; Feminist Theology; Justice; Sin**

Karl Barth, *Protestant Theology in the Nineteenth Century*, London: SCM, 1972. Ian Brownlie, Ed., *Basic Documents on Human Rights*, Oxford: Clarendon Press, 1981, 2nd ed. David Cairns, *The Image of God in Man*, London: Collins, 1973. Zechariah Chafee Jr., ed., *Documents on Fundamental Human Rights*, New York: Athaeneum, 1963. Alan D. Falconer, *Understanding Human Rights*, Dublin: 1980. Walter Laquer and Barry Rubin, Ed., *The Human Rights Reader*, New York: Meridian, 1979. Eckehart Lorenz, Ed., *How Christian are Human Rights?*, Geneva: Lutheran World Federation, 1981. Allan Miller, Ed., *A Christian Declaration on Human Rights*, Grand Rapids: Eerdmans, 1977. Paul Sieghart, *The Lawful Rights of Mankind*, London: Oxford U.P., 1985. Gustave Thils, *Droits de l'Homme et Perspectives Chrétienne*, Louvain-la-Neuve, 1981. *Lutheran Perspectives on Human Rights*, Geneva: Lutheran World Federation, 1977.

ALAN D. FALCONER

RITES

The word "rite" is used in a variety of ways. It may refer to the order of service for celebrating a particular sacrament (Rite of Marriage) or other liturgical event (Rite of Blessing of Oils). It may be used for an extensive ritual process which includes a number of such rites (Rite of

Christian Initiation of Adults). Finally, it may be used in a comprehensive sense to designate the worship of a particular church (Roman Rite). It is this last sense that is the focus of this article.

In its *Decree on the Eastern Catholic Churches* Vatican Council II recognized that the Holy Catholic Church is made up of groups of faithful which form particular churches or rites (O.E. 2). When one speaks of a rite in this manner, one is referring not just to the collected orders of liturgical service, but to a whole world of meaning that includes a spiritual and theological tradition.

The rites of Eastern and Western Christianity emerged in close association with developments and conflicts that took place within the history of the church. In the East, the cities of Antioch and Alexandria emerged as centers of power and influence for the early christian communities. As such, they served as points from which the various Eastern rites developed. Jerusalem also exerted a strong influence and Constantinople eventually became an additional center because of its significance as capital of the empire. The story of the emergence of rites associated with each of these places is a complex one which includes theological controversies, geographical, social and political factors, and the influence of diverse cultures. A rich diversity of Eastern rites was the outcome of the process.

The Byzantine Rite which came from Constantinople but was a development of the Antiochene tradition as influenced by Jerusalem eventually became the most popular of the Eastern rites. It is presently used by all Orthodox Churches and by some Eastern Catholics. Also in existence at present are a number of other Eastern rites (e.g., Maronite, Armenian, Coptic) which can trace their origins back to these centers.

The places associated with the development of rites in the Western christian tradition are North Africa, Rome, Gaul, Spain, and Milan. Jungmann identifies two liturgical families in the early Western tradition: the Roman-African and the Gallic. He subdivides the latter into four chief forms: the Gallican, the Celtic, the Old Spanish, and the Milanese or Ambrosian. Unfortunately, the lack of sufficient liturgical sources from the early period leaves the story of the origin of these rites an obscure one.

More sources are available from the period which extends from the end of the sixth century to the close of the eleventh, and they disclose the complex story of the development of what eventually came to be known as the Roman Rite. During this period the Roman liturgy was given shape, was transported into the Frankish kingdom by pilgrims and rulers where it intermingled with the ancient Gallican liturgy so that it became a Romano-Frankish or Romano-German liturgy and returned as such to Rome. It was a modified form of this hybrid liturgy that would later be designated to serve as the basis for the Roman Rite mandated for the Roman Catholic Church after the Council of Trent. The conflicts that appeared within Western Christianity during the sixteenth century and resulted in divisions within that tradition also led to the eventual formation of new rites (e.g., Lutheran, Reformed, Anglican).

In the years between the Council of Trent and the Second Vatican Council, the Roman Rite was characterized by uniformity. The reform of the liturgy mandated by Vatican II was directed toward restoring the classical simplicity which had characterized the Roman Rite before its hybridization. In light of the diversity of cultures within which local churches are established, that same council recognized the need for diversity within the liturgy of the Roman Rite as long as its substantial unity was maintained (S.C. 37-40). In the years since the council some efforts have been made to implement this goal of having a Roman Rite which is particularized in diverse local churches. The task is a complex one and much of the work is yet to be accomplished.

See **Liturgy, Worship**

Joseph A. Jungmann, SJ, *The Mass of the Roman Rite: Its Origin and Development,* 2 vols., trans., F.A. Brunner, New York: Benziger, 1951. Hans-Joachim Schulz, *The Byzantine Liturgy: Symbolic Structure and Faith Expression,* trans, Matthew J. O'Connell, New York: Pueblo, 1986. Cyrille Vogel, *Medieval Liturgy: An Introduction to the Sources,* trans., William Storey and Niels Rasmussen, OP, Washington, D.C.: The Pastoral Press, 1986. Herman Wegman, *Christian Worship in East and West: A Study Guide to Liturgical History,* trans., G.W. Lathrop, New York: Pueblo, 1985.

MARGARET MARY KELLEHER, OSU

RITUAL

The term "ritual" has at least two meanings. It can be used to refer to a book, a collection of rites other than the eucharist or liturgy of the hours, which are under the presidency of a priest rather than a bishop. The Roman Ritual, in use prior to the liturgical reforms initiated by the Second Vatican Council is the most recent and well known example. Ritual, however, has a more generic meaning as a particular form of action and this is the sense of the word that is operative in this article.

Interest in the nature of ritual emerged during the post-conciliar reform of the rites of the church as people became more sensitive to the fact that liturgy is a form of ritual action. Liturgical scholars who realized that insights into the nature and dynamics of ritual would illumine their understanding of liturgical action began to turn to a variety of disciplines in which ritual has been a subject of study.

Cultural anthropology has been a particularly rich source of information because of the attention given in this field to ritual within its social context. Victor Turner was one of the leading figures in the study of ritual until his death in 1983 and the following explanation of ritual is based on his work.

Ritual can be understood as a social, symbolic process which has the potential for communicating , creating, criticizing, and even transforming meaning. To say that ritual is a social process is to indicate that it is the product or creation of a society which is itself in process. Ritual emerges gradually from within the dynamics of the social process, the interplay between two different needs, the need for structure or social order and the need to experience the more basic human bonding that is prior to any order. Within any society there are times of crisis and periods of transition, and ritual can play a significant role in the emergence or resolution of such phases. New elements of a ritual may be born in the midst of these dynamics.

To say that ritual is a symbolic process is to suggest that the basic units of rituals are symbols. A ritual is a dynamic system of symbols, a process constituted by symbols and their significations. A ritual symbol can be any object, activity, relationship, word, gesture, or spatial arrangement which serves as a unit in the ritual process. Some symbols serve as dominant ones within a particular ritual and within an entire ritual system. These are the core or key symbols which carry the central beliefs and values that give the group its corporate identity. Among the important characteristics of dominant symbols is their multivocality, their ability to carry and condense a variety of meanings.

The close relationship between ritual and the social process becomes evident in the fact that dominant ritual symbols can gain or lose meaning as they participate in the social process. The history of any dominant ritual symbol will disclose something of the story of the society to which it belongs.

The processual nature of ritual also appears in the fact that every ritual has a rhythm. This can be seen both in the various stages through which a ritual progresses and in the dynamic interaction that takes place between and among people and symbols within any particular phase of the ritual action.

Relationships established in the course of this interaction play a significant role in mediating whatever meanings are effected by the ritual. In one ritual the dynamics may be such that the group may be strengthened in its bonds around corporate beliefs and values. At another time, ritual may be the occasion for engaging in some critical reflection on these same beliefs and values. Rituals are not merely expressive of a society's corporate identity. They can also play a significant role in contributing to the ongoing creation and transformation of that identity.

Although there is much to explore in the social dynamics of ritual, those who wish to understand how ritual symbols operate in human persons must move beyond the boundaries of anthropology into other fields. Although many psychologists have treated ritual as a pathological phenomenon, Erik Erikson, by contrast, has made a significant contribution by suggesting that ritualization is a necessary dimension of healthy human development. There is a need for further dialogue between the psychological and social approaches to the study of ritual. Neurobiology may contribute to the dialogue, for some scholars are suggesting that research being carried out on the human brain may disclose a biological foundation for ritual behavior and an explanation of how ritual symbols work. Ritual can be studied from many vantage points, all of which can be illuminating for the person who is attempting to understand liturgy as a form of ritual action.

See **Liturgy**

Eric Erikson, *Toys and Reasons: Stages in the Ritualization of Experience*, New York: W.W. Norton and Co., 1977. Ronald L. Grimes, *Beginnings in Ritual Studies*, Lanham: U. Press of America, 1982. Victor Turner, *Dramas, Fields, and Metaphors: Symbolic Action in Human Society*, Ithaca: Cornell U. Press, 1974; *The Ritual Process: Structure and Anti-Structure*, Ithaca: Cornell U. Press, 1969; *On the Edge of the Bush: Anthropology as Experience*, Ed., Edith L.B. Turner, Tucson: The U. of Arizona Press, 1985.

MARGARET MARY KELLEHER, OSU

ROSARY
Prayer Form

This extra-liturgical Marian devotion in its entirety consists of the recitation of fifteen decades of Hail Marys with each decade or set of ten Hail Marys preceded by the Our Father, and followed by a doxology, as well as accompanied by a meditation upon a mystery of our redemption by Mary's Son. The complete rosary comprises fifteen mysteries: five joyful contemplating the beginnings of our salvation in the Incarnation, namely, the annunciation, the visitation, the nativity, the presentation, and the finding of the child in the temple; five sorrowful mysteries focusing our prayerful attention upon the redemptive sufferings and death of Christ, i.e., the agony in the garden, the scourging, the crowning with thorns, the carrying of the cross, and the crucifixion; and, the five glorious mysteries fastening our gaze of faith, hope, and love upon the glorification of Jesus and Mary, and the completion of the paschal mystery in the sending of the Holy Spirit on Pentecost, which are the resurrection, the ascension, the descent of the Holy Spirit, the assumption, and the coronation of Mary.

The usual practice has been for the faithful to recite one cycle of the mysteries of the rosary, which is the requirement of the Catholic Church to gain a plenary indulgence through this devotion on any particular day. Its traditional form was established by Pope St. Pius V in 1569, and has been called the "Dominican Rosary," a digest of the main events of salvation history in the lives of Jesus and Mary as well as a compendium of the principal liturgical seasons of the church's year.

Historical Development

The rosary finds its chief liturgical source in the psalter or OT book of 150 psalms as distributed in the Liturgy of the Hours or Divine Office. In an effort to make the spiritual riches of the liturgy accessible to all the faithful, a "psalter of the laity" emerged during the early Middle Ages. The Irish monks, who divided the psalter into three sets of fifty psalms each, brought this custom to the European continent in their missionary efforts. Lay brothers in the monasteries were required to say fifty psalms or fifty Our Fathers for a deceased monk, and this practice of substituting the Lord's Prayer for a psalm spread among the laity. To count these prayers strings of beads were used, the origin of rosary beads.

Devotion to Mary followed a similar pattern. A psalter of 150 Hail Marys began to take shape, and towards the end of the twelfth century this prayer (i.e., the first part of what we say today—the greetings of the angel at the annunciation and of Elizabeth at the visitation) came to be one of the prayers that all the faithful should know and understand along with the Our Father and the Creed. Meditation upon the mysteries developed by the addition to each psalm of a phrase referring to Jesus and Mary. Eventually the psalms were omitted, and the phrases became brief lives of the Son and his mother from the annunciation to their glorification. Between 1410 and 1439

Dominic of Prussia, a Carthusian, helped to make the practice popular by joining fifty Hail Marys with fifty such phrases. The name "rosary" thus began since a *rosarium* (a rose garden) was used to designate this collection of fifty points of meditation. The rose, a symbol of joy, was fittingly applied to Mary, "cause of our joy" in bringing us Christ. Another Carthusian, Henry of Kalkar, divided the Hail Marys into decades with an Our Father between each decade.

Although the essential elements of the rosary were in place by the first part of the fifteenth century, it had to be simplified before it became a truly popular prayer form. In 1483, *Our Dear Lady's Psalter,* a book on the rosary by a Dominican, mentions fifteen mysteries, the same as today except that the fourteenth (fourth glorious) combined the coronation with the assumption, and the fifteenth was the last judgment. In 1470, Blessed Alan de la Roche, a Dominican, founded the Confraternity of the Psalter of Jesus and Mary, forerunner of the Rosary Confraternity through which it became a devotion of the universal church. Pope St. Pius V's Bull of 1569, *Consueverunt Romani Pontifices* (frequently referred to as the *magna carta* of the rosary),established it in the church only after many centuries of significant development of the devotion. He completed it as a close connection of mental and vocal prayer, and made its meditative aspect a necessary condition for gaining the indulgence attached to the devotion.

In *Marialis Cultus,* an apostolic exhortation issued in 1974 for the right ordering and development of marian devotion, Pope Paul VI emphasizes the contemplative aspect of the rosary (cf. 47). He calls it the "soul of the devotion, but also refers to the recitation of the vocal prayers as being helpful to meditation upon the mysteries when the rosary is recited with a "quiet rhythm and a lingering pace"(47). The pope also reflects upon the effectiveness of this private devotion both as a preparation for the celebration of the same mysteries of our redemption in the eucharistic liturgy and as a continuation of its special graces in our lives (cf. 48). Thus he proposes a profound harmony between the rosary and the liturgy when it is contemplatively recited outside celebration.

W.A. Hinnebusch, "Rosary," in *New Catholic Encyclopedia*, vol. 12, pp. 667-670. F.M. William, *The Rosary: Its History and Meaning*, tr.E. Kaiser, N.Y., 1953.

F.M. JELLY, OP

S

SABELLIANISM

Sabellianism was one name for an early heresy falling under the general category of modalism. Some early Christians had considerable difficulty in reconciling the fact that they believed in only one God with the reality that they also believed in the divinity of Christ. An unacceptable attempt to resolve this dilemma was known as monarchianism. One form of monarchianism was subordinationist, teaching that Christ was divine only in some secondary sense since only the Father was fully divine.

Another form of monarchianism was labeled, in general, modalism. This held that what we call the persons of the Trinity were merely the titles human beings attached to different manifestations (*modi*) of the one God. Father, Son and Spirit as "persons" had no foundation in the divine reality. This form of modalism was sometimes called "Patripassionism" in the West. If the "Son" died on the cross, then so did the "Father" (*Patris passio*). Sabellianism was an alternate term for this type of modalism. Little is known of the historical Sabellius; he was condemned in Rome in the early third century.

ROBERT B. ENO, SS

SACRAMENT

The word "sacrament" translates the Latin *sacramentum* and the Greek *mys-terion* signifying one of the seven central liturgical rites of the church through which participants experience the paschal mystery of Christ, are formed into the body of Christ and grow in the life of grace. The evidence of the Greek term in descriptions of cultic rites (Mithras, Isis and Osiris), which insured new birth and vitality after death, and in philosophy (Plato), where tangible things are symbols of heavenly reality and the initiated learn secret teachings which bring them wisdom, shows the importance of this notion in pre-christian writings.

Scripture

Mysterion is found in the scriptures but its meaning is much broader than the seven rites noted above. The few evidences of "mystery" in the OT (e.g., Wisdom, and Daniel) refer to God's saving action enacted in history which gives wisdom to save (Wis 6:22); the wisdom revealed looks toward an eschatological *mysterion* that God will reveal (Dan 2:28, 47). In the synoptics *mysterion* refers to "the secrets of the kingdom of heaven" (Mt 13:11, Mk 4:11, Lk 8:10) which Jesus reveals through parables. In St. Paul's writings *mysterion* often refers to Christ (1 Cor 2:7-10, Rom 16:25-26, Col 1:26-27, 4:3, Eph 1:9-10, 3:3-12, 1 Tim 3:16) who reveals the divine will to save all people, who himself is the mystery through whom all things are restored, and who dwells in those who believe. Christ crucified is the supreme manifestation of God's wisdom (1 Cor 2:1f., Col 2:2). While the rites of baptism and eucharist are known in the NT era (Acts 2:41, 1 Cor 11:17-34) and their usage is reflected in NT texts (e.g., as background in the Last Supper accounts or John 6), neither of them is called a sacrament at this time.

Patristic Age

The first indication of reflection on sacraments is in the writings of the Apostolic Fathers in the polemic against the Gnostics and Manichees. The christian defense of the goodness of nature and of sensible things begins with the fact that they are used in celebrations which purify and sanctify the participants. Justin Martyr (d.165) describes the reality of both baptism and eucharist but he does not use the word sacrament. The baptized are called "reborn" and "enlightened." "Through the word of prayer that comes from [Christ], the food over which the eucharist has been spoken becomes the flesh and blood of the incarnate Jesus in order to nourish and transform our flesh and blood" (*Apology* I, 61,66). Tertullian (d.220) introduces the term sacrament into christian language when speaking about christian initiation. He understands the word to mean that which makes holy, the consecration itself, that which is consecrated and that to whom one is consecrated. In addition for Tertullian *sacramentum* means a sacred action, object or means. Examples of these are the persons in God, the economy of salvation, Christ's life, death and resurrection, and figures for Christ in the OT. With regard to sacramental rites, Tertullian distinguishes a two-fold reality in their visible dimension: element and word. He understands "word" to be the word of God which has a determinative role in sacraments as do the things used in their celebration. Under the influence of neoplatonism some authors begin to speak of the visible dimension as a "symbol" of the divine operating in sacraments.

Some of the clearest examples of the way patristic authors dealt with sacraments are found in the fourth and fifth century catechetical instructions delivered to candidates for christian initiation. The catecheses ascribed to St. Cyril of Jerusalem (d.387), St. Ambrose (d.397), St. John Chrysostom (d.407) and Theodore of Mopsuestia (d.428) describe the various rites of initiation and elaborate on their meaning. While a certain fluidity of terminology exists, some terms used at this time influence later theological reflection. These include *typos* and *aletheia* signifying symbol and reality. What occurs in water baptism by way of symbolic imitation of Christ insures the reality of salvation enacted in the rite. Sacramental signs make present an aspect of Christ's incarnate life, death and resurrection so participants can share in those saving mysteries. Baptism symbolizes Christ's sufferings and makes them present through the use of the symbol water. Neoplatonic thought influences these authors to explain that what happened to Christ in his paschal mystery happens to the initiates "in likeness," that is, in as real a way as these events happened to Christ (see Cyril's *Mystagogic Catechesis II* n. 7). While no systematic doctrine of sacraments has yet evolved, these catecheses evidence the important role which commentary on the rites plays in understanding what sacraments are.

St. Augustine (d.430) reflects a fluid notion of sacrament and mystery, which words he allies closely with the terms *figura, allegoria, prophetia, symbolum,* etc. For him OT sacraments are the rituals of circumcision, sacrifices, offerings, the Temple altars, pasch, anointing etc. NT sacraments include baptism, eucharist, the paschal mystery, imposition of hands, ordination, the Lord's prayer, symbol of faith, feasts etc. All sacraments pertain to the *magnum sacramentum-mysterium*, Christ and the church. Augustine does not develop a systematic treatment of sacramental doctrine but he leaves a terminology and understanding about sacraments which later theologians will develop. He calls sacrament a sacred sign, a *signaculum,* a visible word. He states that "one joins the word to the material element and behold the sacrament, that is, a kind of visible work" (*In Johannem* 80, 3; P.L. 35,1840). Sacraments are sacred signs (*City of God* 10, 5; P.L. 41,282); "when signs refer themselves to divine reality they are called sacraments" (*Epistle* 138,7: P.L. 33,527). Sacraments are likenesses of what they signify. For example: water washes the body and signifies a cleansing of the soul. We are buried with Christ in the waters of baptism.

Augustine introduces the term *res* in connection with *sacramentum* to distinguish between the sacrament of Christ's body and the reality or effect of the sacrament when received. By reality or *res* Augustine means the ultimate effect of the eucharist, that is, the grace of union with Christ. In the eleventh century this notion will be referred to and expanded when theologians debate questions of eucharistic presence (see below regarding Berengarius). For Augustine sacraments are effective because Christ and the Holy Spirit act through them. He regards the role of the ordained minister in sacraments as essential but subordinate. Augustine maintains that baptism and certain other sacraments have permanent effects: later theology will call this the sacramental character. For Augustine a sacrament is a celebration in which the things commemorated, the passion of Christ, are applied. He teaches that sacraments are instituted by Christ after the resurrection.

Sixth to Twelfth Centuries

Augustine's thought clearly influences the terminology and interpretation of Isidore of Seville (d.636) who states that there are three sacraments: baptism, chrism and eucharist. He contends that beneath the covering of bodily things used in these sacred actions "the divine power works secretly the salvation proper to these same sacraments"; these are fruitful when administered in the church by the Holy Spirit who works the effects of sacraments (*Etymologiae* 1.6 c.19, n.39; P.L. 82,255).

In the following centuries the Carolingian reform sought to unify liturgical practices in the Western Church and to insure a codification in all areas of church life. A problem that emerges at this time was how to describe sacraments in a way that preserved their reality as both symbolic and real at the same time. The controversies over eucharistic presence in the ninth century exemplify this issue. Paschasius Radbertus (d.860) authored the first systematic treatment on the eucharist, *De Corpore et Sanguine Domini.* He stressed the identification of the eucharist with the historical body of Christ in such a realistic way that his realism eclipsed an understanding of the symbolic nature of the sacrament. To counteract this Ratramnus (d.868) wrote a treatise stressing the real and sacramental presence of Christ in the eucharist which was not to be identified physically or literally with his historical body. This debate informs an understanding of the writing of Berengar of Tours (d.1088) who appealed to what he maintained was authentic Augustinian thought to describe a sacrament as a *sacrum signum.* He compared the water of baptism to the bread and wine of the eucharist. Just as water symbolizes the cleansing graces of Christ, so the bread and wine merely symbolize the body and blood of Christ. Unfortunately by this time the notion of symbol had lost its meaning as something real, and the language of substance was used to describe what was real. Notions of substance and symbol were now irreconcilable. Hence Berengar was accused of heresy because he did not affirm the reality of Christ's sacramental presence in the language of substance. From this time on theologians search for a satisfactory explanation of how sacraments are both signs and realities at the same time.

Theologians also continue to distinguish sacraments from other sacred rites and to determine their number. Peter Damian (d.1072) states that there are twelve sacraments: baptism, chrismation, anointing of the sick, anointing of a bishop, a king, canons, monks and hermits, the dedication of a church, penance, consecration of virgins and matrimony. Peter Abelard (d.1142) distinguishes between major and minor sacraments: the spiritual are the major sacraments, the minor are not. He lists five sacraments: baptism, chrismation, eucharist, anointing, and matrimony. St. Bernard (d.1153) knows eleven, including the washing of the feet. Even with this tendency to enumerate what are sacraments, properly speaking the liturgy used the notion of sacrament in a wide sense; for example, the sacramentaries at this time described Lent as the "venerable sacrament."

New definitions of sacrament developed. The Augustinian formula *sacrum signum* was adjusted by Lanfranc of Canterbury (d.1089), Ivo of Chartres (d.1116) and Peter Abelard to *sacrae rei signum,* i.e., a sacrament is a sacred sign because it is the sign of a sacred reality. Hugh of St. Victor (d.1141) maintained that the key to interpreting sacraments was God's interventions in history, especially in creation and the incarnation. Within this broad vision of sacramentality Hugh notes the things that are sacraments in the strict sense since not every sign of a sacred thing is a sacrament. He writes

that a sacrament "is a corporeal or material element set before the external senses, representing by similitude, signifying by institution and containing by sanctification, some invisible and spiritual grace" (*De Sacramentis Christianae Fidei* P. IX c.2; P.L. 176, 317b). Hence water is appropriately used in baptism, bread and wine in the eucharist, oil for the anointing of the sick, etc. The restriction of the number of sacraments to seven was still unknown at this point. Hugh himself counted such rites as the use of holy water or blessed ashes, the consecration of monks and burial as "receptacles of grace." He contextualized his treatment of sacraments by speaking about the incarnation and the church as the body of Christ.

Berengar's denial of Christ's true presence in the eucharist led to the formulation in the twelfth century of the expression *res et sacramentum.* Augustine had introduced the term *res* to sacramental language (see above) to signify the grace of union with Christ as the ultimate effect of eucharistic participation. Berengar affirmed that the eucharist was the sign of Christ's body and the efficacious symbol of spiritual nourishment and union with Christ. However he denied that Christ's true body was present in the sacrament. Berengar held that there were two elements in the sacrament: the external sign or symbol *(sacramentum)* and the ultimate effect, the grace of spiritual nourishment and charity *(res).* In order to preserve the symbolism of the eucharist and to safeguard the reality of Christ's presence in the eucharist, eleventh-century theologians such as Lanfranc of Canterbury and Guitmund of Aversa searched for a third element to describe the sacramental action. A definitive formulation was established by Hugh of St. Victor and Peter Lombard in the twelfth century and endorsed by Pope Innocent III at the beginning of the thirteenth century. These theologians added *sacramentum et res* to the *sacramentum tantum* and the *res tantum*. Innocent III stated that the form of the eucharist was bread and wine (a sacrament and not the reality), the truth is of the body and blood (both sacrament and reality) and the power is of unity and charity (reality). When Innocent spoke of the *sacramentum tantum* he meant the permanent sacrament and not the words of consecration. However in later years the expression *sacramentum tantum* was applied to the sacramental rite which has for its immediate effect the *res et sacramentum* and for its ultimate effect the *res tantum* or sacramental grace.

During this period a synthesis emerges about sacraments that integrated the church as the means of salvation into Christology within the scope of a universal salvation history. Here sacraments are regarded as instituted by Christ since they are part of the divine plan of salvation (the Pauline mystery of salvation for all). Sacraments receive their precise determination from the various stages of Christ's life and ministry and they attain their purpose in the church. Sacraments thus are understood as high points of the saving revelation of God in the church's present experience of Christ's redemption through the operation of the Holy Spirit. Hence sacraments continue to be understood as self-expressions of the church and as part of how the divine economy of salvation is experienced in the present.

The notion of sacrament as a remedy for sin was a dominant theme in the twelfth century and is a determinative way of understanding the economy of the sacraments in the twelfth and thirteenth centuries. Peter Lombard (d.1160) begins his treatment of sacraments in the *Book of the Sentences* by comparing God's institution of the sacraments to the Good Samaritan (Lk 10:30) who brought assistance to the wounded man. Lombard stands squarely in the Augustinian tradition and uses Augustinian terms and phrases to describe sacraments. He maintains that every sacrament is a sign but that not every sign is a sacrament; a sacrament bears resemblance to the thing of which it is a sign. He states that "a sacrament is properly so called because it is a sign of the grace of God and the expression of invisible grace, so that it bears its image and is its cause" (*Book of the Sentences* 1, IV, d.1,n.2). Thus it is Lombard who introduces the notion of cause and causality into the definition of sacrament. Other twelfth-century theologians such as Hugh of St. Victor and William of Auxerre maintained that sacraments contain grace (*vasa gratiae*, a vessel of grace, *vasa spiritualia*, a spiritual vessel, *vasa medicinalia*, a vessel that heals), in the sense that God himself operates through sacraments. Lombard specifies causality as essential to an understanding of sacraments by adding this notion to the common axiom that a sacrament is *invisibilis gratiae visibilis forma*, that is, a sacrament is the visible form of an invisible grace, and that a sacrament *efficit quod figurat*, that is, a sacrament produces [the effect] which it represents.

In addition Lombard determined that there are seven "sacraments of the New Law . . . baptism, confirmation, the bread of blessing, that is, the eucharist, penance, extreme unction, orders, marriage" (*Sentences* d.2,c.1). This designation of seven sacraments confirms what others had pointed to: that seven was a significant number for completion, totality and inclusiveness (for example, the seven days of creation in Genesis). Seven is appropriate for the number of sacraments since it is the sum of three, the symbol for the divine, and four, a symbol of cosmic perfection (or the three persons in God and the four seasons). Thus seven sacraments demonstrate God's saving presence at all times.

Lombard's definitions of sacrament will be subjected to the scrutiny of the prevailing metaphysics of the schools. The parts that deal with the "sign-cause" and the "reality signified and caused" will occupy the attention of scholastic theologians. What will result is a hylomorphic interpretation of sacramental sign which attributes the function of "matter" to the sensible things used in the celebration, and the function of "form" to the words that accompany the application of matter to the subject of the sacrament. Here the form specifies the significance of the matter used. This interpretation has its advantages, especially since it points out what is essential for a sacrament to be valid and licit. The question of sacramental validity in the twelfth century was essentially a discussion of sacramental objectivity; as such it was the concern of both canonists and theologians. While it was only in the fourteenth century that the terms valid/invalid appear in connection with the sacraments, and at first only in connection with marriage, the beginnings of this kind of language is evidenced in Lombard.

Although the theology of this period does not neglect the importance of faith and other human actions as determinative for sacramental efficaciousness, in practice their role will be reduced to conditions without which the sacraments do not occur. Even though Lombard raised the question of causality this notion did not find a completely satisfying or universally accepted explanation at the time (although Aquinas' theory of instrumental causality described below is most influential). What is agreed upon is the fact that christian sacraments are "efficacious ex opere operato, (this technical term "by the work done" means that sacraments are effective by means of the sacramental rite itself not because of the worthiness of

minister or participant) and not just ex opere operantis (this technical term "by the work of the doer" means that the effectiveness of sacraments depends on the moral rectitude of minister or participant; when it first evolved in the thirteenth century this term was applied to rites of the OT in contrast with those of the NT).

With regard to Lombard's assertion about what is signified and effected in sacraments, that is grace and the experience of salvation, a notable gamut of opinions will evolve. One difficulty with such attempts at codification is that the dynamism of the biblical understanding of justification suffers in the process. Lombard is true to Augustinian thought when he speaks about the involvement of the minister in sacraments. Lombard stresses the importance of the minister's "right intention" when celebrating sacraments. It is from Lombard's works that the formula emerged, "the intention of doing what the church does."

Thirteenth to Sixteenth Centuries

With Thomas Aquinas Catholic teaching on the notion of sacrament advances far beyond anything that had yet been achieved. For Aquinas the function of sacraments is to initiate, restore, preserve or intensify the life of grace in believers. Sacraments incorporate the Christian into the body of Christ and confer the Spirit promised by the risen Christ. Aquinas is very much influenced by the work of Augustine, Dionysius, Hugh of St. Victor and Peter Lombard. St. Paul's reference to being buried with Christ in baptism and walking in newness of life through Christ's resurrection (Rom 6:3-5) forms an essential foundation for Aquinas' teaching. He describes a sacrament as the sign (following Augustine) of the Incarnate Word, his passion and resurrection, which sanctifies the participant. God accomplishes this through the humanity of Jesus manifest in the sacramental sign itself. The effects of sacraments are not only remedies for sin, they produce new life, the life of Christ, in the church. Aquinas' treatment of sacraments in the *Summa* follows upon his treatment of the "mysteries of the incarnate Word" since "it is from this same Incarnate Word that these derive their efficacy." Aquinas deals with sacraments in the *Summa* 3a, questions 60-65; these concern: what a sacrament is (60), the necessity of sacraments (61), grace as the effect of sacraments (62), character as the other effect (63), the causes of sacraments (64) and the number of sacraments (65).

By stating that a sacrament is a sign which actually causes what it signifies Aquinas shows his dependence on Lombard. Aquinas assigns sacraments to the general category of signs (S.Th. q.60,a.1c); "'sacrament' is properly applied ... to that which is a sign of a sacred reality inasmuch as it has the property of sanctifying men" (q.60, a.2 a). With regard to the function a sacrament has in sanctification Aquinas argues that it is the "actual cause" of sanctification because it is an experience of Christ's passion, it is the "form" of sanctification because it endows the participant with grace and virtues, and it is the "ultimate end" which sanctification is to achieve, that is, eternal life. Aquinas shows his reliance on the liturgy of sacraments when he states that "as a sign a sacrament has a threefold function. It is at once commemorative of that which has gone before, namely the passion of Christ, demonstrative of that which is brought about in us through the passion of Christ, namely grace, and prognostic, i.e. a foretelling of future glory" (q. 60, a.3 c).

When Aquinas describes how sacraments as signs cause grace he breaks new ground. Two tendencies were commonly held before him. The position held by Dominicans before Thomas is termed "efficient, dispositive causality." According to this theory a sacrament causes a "disposition" to grace because it places the symbolic reality in the recipient, causing a real change or disposition which, in virtue of God's supernatural providence, carries grace with it, unless there is an impediment of ill will. The other theory, often called the Franciscan school, is a *pactus divinus* (that is, a divine covenant) theory wherein God communicates directly but does so only at the occasion of the administration of the sacrament. Following Bonaventure, Duns Scotus opposes dispositive causality. He speaks of sacramental efficaciousness as a consequence of a passive will of God and the disposition of God with regard to the external action of the minister. He also opposes instrumental causality because grace comes not from a sacrament but from God himself. This approach uses terms such as *pactus divinus* (divine covenant), *ordinatio* (ordination) and *dispositio divina* (a divine ordering of things) to describe what will later be called "moral casuality."

When Aquinas describes how sacraments as signs cause grace he distinguishes between two kinds of efficient causes, principal and instrumental. Since only God can produce the effect of sanctification in virtue of his form, he alone can be called a principal cause. Thus sacraments are instrumental causes; they work only in virtue of the impetus given them by the principal agent, God (S.Th. q. 62 a. 1 c). Through the use of material things (e.g. water) sacraments produce effects on that which it touches (washing) and in the soul of the person washed (grace). Sacraments do this by the power from Christ's passion (q. 62, a.6c).

Sacraments produce two effects: they are remedies for sin and "bring the soul to its fullness in things pertaining to the worship of God in terms of the Christian life as a ritual expression of this" (q. 63, a. 1 c). This deputation to worship derived from initiation and orders is evidenced by a "spiritual character" (q. 63, a.1 c). For Aquinas sacramental character "consists in a certain participation in Christ's priesthood present in his faithful ... Just as Christ has the full power of a spiritual priesthood so his faithful are brought into configuration to him in that they share in a certain spiritual power relating to the sacraments and the things pertaining to divine worship" (q. 63, a.5 c). For Aquinas this character is spiritual, is granted in baptism, confirmation and orders and "remains indelibly in the soul." This understanding of character leads him to consider the minister as instrument in sacraments through which God works as principal agent (q. 64, a.1 c). This distinction enables Aquinas to follow Augustine's position that even evil ministers can confer sacraments; they can do so because they act in virtue of the power of God. Thus he is faithful to the prevailing doctrine of *opus operatum* (the value of the sacrament comes from the fact that the sacramental rite is "done" independent of the dispositions of the minister) (q. 64, a. 5 c). Aquinas betrays a certain negative understanding when naming the seven sacraments because he maintains that each is a remedy against sin in its own way (q. 65, a.1 c). He argues that it is appropriate that there are seven sacraments because each deals with a facet of human life; taken together the seven comprise all of human existence.

The Council of Florence (1438-1445) gives the first authoritative statement of the church on the sacraments. As a declaration concerning essential elements of the sacraments it is taken almost verbatim from Aquinas. The Reformers of the sixteenth century attacked abuses in sacramental doctrine and liturgical practice. This polemic is most clear in Luther's *On the Babylonian Captivity of the Church* (1520). He was skeptical about five of the rites considered sacraments; he held that baptism and eucharist were sacraments because of the NT evidence. He also kept penance as a useful rite although he did not regard it as a sacrament strictly speaking. (There is also a certain fluidity in his understanding of the sacramentality of holy orders.) The Reformers' writings on sacraments reflected the deeper issues of justification (the relationship between faith and sacrament) and the place of the Word of God in the church (the conflict between word and sacrament.) In the heat of the Reformation debates the Reformers preferred to choose faith and the word over the Romans' sacramental practice.

The Council of Trent (1545-63) clarified sacramental questions in the seventh session (1547), gave a doctrinal statement on the eucharist in the thirteenth (1551), debated eucharistic doctrine and practice in the twenty-first and twenty-second sessions (1562), discussed orders at the twenty-third session (1563) and reformed marriage legislation at the twenty-fourth session (1563). The Council fathers did not intend to formulate a systematic doctrinal summary on sacraments; instead they dealt with individual areas of concern brought about because of the Reformers' criticisms. Hence the statement of Trent can be said to be clarifications on controverted matters, not a systematic treatment of sacraments. Certain abuses in sacraments were eliminated by the council and a codification of liturgical rubrics and texts resulted from Trent (e.g., the 1570 Roman Missal). However the council did not bridge the distance between Protestants and Catholics on sacramental issues.

Sixteenth to Nineteenth Century

While much post-Tridentine theology followed the council's teaching with commentaries and catechisms, some works of the period dealt with issues raised by the Reformers. An example is Melchior Cano's *De Sacramentis* in which he dealt with the faith-sacrament question debated at the council. Cano (d.1560) affirmed that the sacraments are undoubtedly necessary but in the same measure in which an explicit faith, expressed in sensible signs, is necessary for a person to be saved. Robert Bellarmine (d.1621) addressed this same issue in *De Controversiis Christianae Fidei* and spoke of the necessity of faith for the efficaciousness of sacraments. Suarez's (d.1617) work *Commentaria ac Disputationes in III partem D. Thomae* represented a kind of manual that noted the Reformers' objections and then presented the analysis and comment of the scholastics. Such works influenced manuals of theology that dealt with issues raised by the Reformers about sacraments: the number seven, their efficaciousness *opus operatum,* institution by Christ, their matter and form and the role of the ordained minister. An apologetic approach to Catholic sacramental teaching and practice prevailed.

In the nineteenth century works on sacraments began to appear that reflected the revival of interest in scripture, patristics, and in the history of theology. *Symbolik* by John Adam Moehler (d.1838) helped in the revival of theology at Tübingen. Matthias Scheeben (d.1888) in his classic *Die Mysterien des Christentums* proposed a theory of sacraments based on sacramental character. He argued that an ecclesial consciousness was essential to understanding the medieval term *res et sacramentum.* This approach helped to overcome some of the individualism associated with sacraments since the Middle Ages.

Twentieth Century

The twentieth century liturgical movement was undoubtedly the main stimulus

within the church for the contemporary renewal of sacramental practice and for a revived understanding of sacraments. The work of liturgical scholars in the late nineteenth and early twentieth centuries was responsible for a reawakening of the importance of liturgy as public worship which by its nature required the active participation of the participants. Official church endorsement of the movement came in the early 1900's with the writings of Pope Pius X (e.g., on the reception of the eucharist and the revival of Gregorian chant for popular participation).

The contribution of Benedictine monasticism to this movement is exemplified in the publication of important works on sacramental teaching and in the celebration of the liturgy. Lambert Beauduin's *La Piété de l'Église* (Belgium, 1914) and Ildefons Herwegen's *Ecclesia Orans* (Germany, 1918) demonstrate the relationship between liturgy and sacramental doctrine. Herwegen was instrumental in fostering the serious scholarship reflected in the periodical *Jahrbuch für Liturgiewissenschaft* which contained probing and insightful articles by Odo Casel. Casel's work (part of which was translated into English in 1962 as *The Mystery of Christian Worship*) centered on the mystery of God present and active in the liturgy. He rediscovered the notion of liturgical memorial that is central to understanding Jewish liturgy and christian sacraments (part of which had at least been noted by Thomas Aquinas when he referred to sacraments as commemorative, demonstrative and prefigurative signs). Casel revived much of the patristic teaching about the cultic dimension of sacraments and was influenced by the way the Fathers interpreted sacraments based on the liturgical rites. This approach was ground-breaking compared with the tradition of manual theology that preceded him. For Casel the liturgy makes present the unique, unrepeatable mystery of Christ, realized historically in the past and sacramentally represented in the liturgical commemoration. The liturgy makes these mysteries manifest so that the church may make contact with them and be saved by doing so. The essential point Casel reiterated was that Christians experience the mysteries of Christ anew in liturgy and sacraments; they do not simply gain graces from Christ. Casel is more concerned with an inner attitude toward liturgical participation than exterior demonstrations of involvement, although the latter was not ignored. While Casel's work did not pass without criticism and correction (namely his overemphasis on parallels between Greek mystery religions and christian cult, and the lack of a stronger ecclesial sense in liturgical commemoration) his work was seminal and influential.

Although independent of the liturgical movement on the continent, the work of another Benedictine proved also to be influential at this time, that of Anscar Vonier of Buckfast in *A Key to the Doctrine of the Eucharist* (1925). He wanted to illumine the most central aspects of Aquinas' thought on eucharist, especially those which involved the liturgical dimension of sacraments. The first chapters of the work deal with faith, sacramental signification, and the liturgical setting of eucharist, topics which had largely been ignored since Trent in Catholic writing. The central portion of the book deals with the scholastic teaching about sacraments as emphasized and outlined in the teaching of Trent. Vonier's contribution was to present and interpret the teaching of Aquinas himself, not his commentators. The final section of the book deals with the eucharistic liturgy and the eucharistic banquet, topics that were unfamiliar in eucharistic theology at the time. Thus Vonier restored to eucharistic doctrine some of the richness not reflected in post-Tridentine theology.

What surfaced in this period was a strong ecclesial foundation for liturgy and sacraments. The patristic adage: "in the sacraments the church generates its children, but it is also itself generated" was restored to its rightful position after centuries when teaching on sacraments was codified theologically, juridically and rubrically. Analyzing sacraments from the liturgical perspective led to an increased awareness of their Christological and Trinitarian foundation. The grace of God comes through, with and in Christ; the self-offering of the church is in union with the unique offering of Christ to the Father. The sanctifying action of God is realized in sacraments through Christ, who in turn gives the participants his Holy Spirit.

This Christological approach to sacraments is emphasized by Edward Schillebeeckx' important work *De sacramentele Heilseconomie* (1952). Schillebeeckx presents an understanding of sacraments that combines traditional approaches with insights from contemporary anthropology and phenomenology. For him salvation is a personal act of encounter between the human person and God through Christ; grace is a personal encounter with God. Schillebeeckx roots this in his understanding of Christ whose paschal mystery is metahistorical and transtemporal in the sense that this mystery is experienced in the liturgy of sacraments. He asserts the unique and once-for-all character of Christ's act of redemption and complements it by stating that this mystery is always offered through sacraments to the church. Christ is thus understood to be the central sacrament, manifesting God's love to the world. The seven sacraments are specifications and manifestations of this original sacrament. The phenomenon of encounter becomes operative in this approach since the church encounters God through Christ; individual sacraments are occasions for this encounter to take place. Schillebeeckx emphasizes the role of active faith in sacraments without which they cannot be fruitful. He parallels his Christological treatment with an ecclesial understanding, which emphasizes that a sacrament is valid only when it is ecclesial.

The ecclesial foundation of sacraments is emphasized in Karl Rahner's work *Kirche und Sakramente* (1961). Like Schillebeeckx before him, Rahner approaches traditional sacramental categories from a new perspective; he argues that the church is the fundamental sacrament and that it is through the church that one participates in Christ's redemption. He argues that one can adequately understand the sacramentality of individual sacraments only on the basis of the sacramentality of the church. This ecclesial foundation grounds Rahner's interpretation of the teaching that Christ instituted the seven sacraments. Rahner held contemporary NT exegesis makes it impossible to say that Jesus instituted seven specific sacramental rites (such an approach had made the NT the source of proof-texts for institution.) Sacraments were instituted by Christ in the sense that over generations the church reflected on its practice and determined seven rites as uniquely sacraments.

More recent theologians (for example Raymond Vaillancourt and Kenan Osborne) have elaborated on the contributions of both Schillebeeckx and Rahner. That Christ is the original sacrament *(ursakrament)* and the church is the ground sacrament *(grundsakrament)* of the seven ecclesial acts is commonly understood today. The language of encounter and phenomenology also characterizes contemporary reflection on the dynamism of sacraments. Such an approach signals a shift from emphasizing Christ's presence in sacraments to the community's transformation through sacraments; it also marks a shift from, emphasizing sacraments as things to sacraments as event.

Another recent avenue of approach to sacraments is symbolism. That sacraments are essentially symbolic actions that affect participants on many levels with their ambiguity and polyvalence is an important component in some contemporary theories (e.g., Louis-Marie Chauvet and David Power). The rediscovery of the polyvalent nature of the symbolic elements used in sacraments and the ambiguity of sacramental (performative) language has influenced sacramental theologians to relate the understanding of sacrament to philosophical and psychological studies of symbol. Symbol language has reentered Catholic theology about sacraments in the sense that sacraments are respected as real, symbolic encounters. In sacraments God reveals and grants salvation through Christ's paschal mystery in symbolic acts and words; at the same time the church worships God through Christ empowered by the Holy Spirit by means of active participation in gestural speech and symbolic action.

The development of secularization theologies helped move theological reflection about grace and sacraments away from a cultic understanding to one wherein sacraments are viewed as strong moments of God's self-disclosure which occur throughout human life. This approach, influenced by Rahner's incarnational approach to theology, holds that human nature has been redeemed and grace is always available to redeemed creation through Christ. In this perspective sacraments are not the exclusive channels of God's grace; yet they are central moments and privileged means of encountering God through Christ. Such an approach returns to the wide context of how God acts in creation, in the incarnation and in the paschal mystery as the appropriate context for experiencing and interpreting sacraments as unique signs of God's grace and favor.

Another critique of a cultic notion of sacrament comes from liberation theologians (Juan Luis Segundo) who try to determine the life relation of sacramental participation. They argue that a too facile celebration of sacraments can numb consciences to the social and political realities of living the christian life. The challenge which engagement in sacraments entails is to live the justice and peace of God's kingdom which is experienced in sacraments. The liberative power of sacraments is thus to be channeled into a way of living life that reveals the liberative power of the gospel of justice and peace.

Inquiry into the human phenomenon involved in individual sacraments (e.g. initiation, reconciliation, taking on a new identity) has led some theologians to emphasize sacraments as rites of passage (derived from the seminal work of Arnold van Gennep). While exact parallels between some sacraments and rites of passage is often hard to establish (e.g. confirmation) this avenue of inquiry is useful in emphasizing the life situations which sacraments articulate.

The fact that some Christians no longer participate regularly in sacraments because they see little or no value in them has led theologians to reflect on this pastoral phenomenon and to attempt to articulate the importance of sacraments (Raymond Vaillancourt, Henri Denis and Raymond Didier). The relationship of evangelization and sacramental practice is thus raised as is the relationship between sacramental celebration and a vibrant experience of church life. This also raises the delicate question of prerequisite faith for admission to sacraments (especially initiation). Some pastoral approaches (e.g. Christianne Brusselmans) find the method employed in the

Rite of Christian Initiation for Adults (catechumenate, immediate ecclesial preparation, celebration and mystagogia) a model to follow in other sacraments.

The post-Vatican II proliferation of official bilateral and multilateral dialogues on the sacraments has ushered in a new era of speaking about sacraments in ways that are often grounded in the tradition and yet which had been neglected in the post-Reformation era. For example, the revival of the term *Anamnesis* as a way of describing the memorial experienced in sacraments has occurred largely because of this ecumenical impetus. Among others, Max Thurian saw this as a way of transcending the terms of disagreement over the eucharist between Protestant and Roman Catholic Churches.

This ecumenical context has also heightened awareness of the importance which the Word plays in a common understanding of sacraments. The restoration of the Word to a position of prominence in the revised sacramental rites has led theologians to reflect on the full meaning of the fact that Catholic and Protestant congregations share the same Word in worship. Karl Rahner argues that sharing in the Word is to share in what sacraments are at their foundation, signs of God's self-communication and self-revelation. This avenue opens up new possibilities for ecumenical dialogue about how sacramental acts specify the Word and how common appreciation of the Word can lead to a common appreciation of sacraments.

The traditional maxim *lex orandi, lex credendi* (the law of prayer establishes the law of belief) has been revived in contemporary systematic study of sacraments so that the liturgy becomes a major source of theological reflection. That there should be a reciprocal relationship between liturgy and theology where each influences the other, but with the liturgy being given a position of clear predominance and emphasis is more commonly accepted by sacramental theologians today. This also includes an understanding of the liturgy that goes beyond the texts and prayer used in sacraments, to include gesture, symbol, singing, and silence. Many liturgists (e.g., Mary Collins) argue that the tools of social science should be utilized to interpret the data collected from observation on sacramental celebration (e.g. sociology, anthropology) in order to develop an adequate method to deal with sacraments. Contemporary writing on Spirit Christology and the role of the Holy Spirit in sacraments (e.g. Edward Kilmartin) has helped overcome the absence of such an emphasis in conventional understandings of sacraments. The clear reference to the Spirit in almost all sacramental formulas and the example of the Eastern tradition in understanding sacraments as the work of the Holy Spirit helps Western theology today to address this lack in its interpretation of sacrament.

While a completely satisfactory approach to the study of sacraments has yet to emerge in the postconciliar church, the evidence of this last century, particularly the rapid development of such studies since Vatican II, attests to a growing maturity in the liturgical celebration of and theological reflection on sacraments.

See **Anamnesis, Church, Liturgical Movement, Liturgy, Memorial**

Edward Kilmartin, "A Modern Approach to the Word of God and Sacraments of Christ: Perspectives and Principles," in *The Sacraments: God's Love and Mercy Actualized,* by Francis Eigo. Villanova: Villanova U.P., 1979, pp. 59-109. Bernard Leeming, *Principles of Sacramental Theology,* New York and London: Longmans, 1956. David Power, *Unsearchable Riches, The Symbolic Nature of Liturgy,* New York: Pueblo Pub. Co., 1984. Edward Schillebeeckx, *Christ The Sacrament of the Encounter With God,* London and New York: Sheed and Ward, 1963. (Reprinted 1986) Raymond Vaillancourt, *Toward A Renewal of Sacramental Theology,* Trans., Matthew O'Connell, Collegeville: Liturgical Press, 1979.

KEVIN W. IRWIN

SACRAMENTALS

Sacramentals are sacred signs which bear a resemblance to the sacraments in so far as they signify the effects, especially of a spiritual kind, which are obtained through the church. Vatican II's *Sacrosanctum Concilium*) addresses the revisions of sacramentals in the same chapter that it directs a revision of sacraments. Passage of time may have obscured the nature and purpose of sacramentals, so they are to be adapted to the needs of the time. Sacramentals differ from sacraments in the sense that their number is not limited, they are instituted by the church, and they achieve their effect not as sacraments do by being placed (*ex opere operato*) but by the intercession of the church (*ex opere operantis ecclesiae*). Sacramentals include a variety of signs, objects and prayers, e.g., sign of the cross, statue, medal, blessed ashes, holy water, palms, grace at meals, Stations of the Cross, blessings, exorcisms.

Sacramentals are no longer thought as as things or actions but as sacred signs, according to the redefinition in the *Constitution on the Liturgy* (S.C. 60) The 1983 Code of Canon Law has been simplified, reducing in number the many canons on sacramentals in the 1917 code. Although the Apostolic See retains the authority to determine which sacramentals are legitimate as well as their rites and formulae, much more latitude is provided for. Now lay persons are ministers of some sacramentals, e.g., parents blessing their children, laity distributing ashes. Non-Catholics can be recipients of blessings. Objects which are blessed are to be treated with reverence; when no longer of use they are to be destroyed without profanation.

See **Sacraments**

(Code of Canon Law) 1166-1172; (Sacrosanctum Concilium 60-63; 79.)

JOSEPH L. CUNNINGHAM

SACRIFICE

Sacrifice and its partial synonym, offering, is found in one form or another in almost all cultures and religions. Where present it usually "stands at the center of a dynamic process in which the divine [or spiritual] and the human come into contact." Where rejected, as in Buddhism, gnosticism and most Greek religious philosophy, and where spiritualized in whole or in part as in Christianity, Judaism and Hinduism, the very rejection or spiritualization becomes a formative influence. Its plurality of meanings and connotations resist general definitions such as: "Sacrifices and offerings are alienations of human goods by way of destruction (sacrifice) or simple renunciation (offering) vis-a-vis the [invisible] power[s], according to purposes and in function of needs or concerns which differ from culture to culture" (di Nola). This problem of definition is compounded by the secular use of the word sacrifice in western culture to describe "some sort of renunciation, usually destruction, of something valuable in order that something more valuable may be obtained" (Yerkes). Its modern secular connotations associated with deprivation now make extremely difficult a true understanding of the ancient biblical and classical views of sacrifice as something usually positive, desirable and joyful.

The most common suggestions from the history of religions for an "essential idea" or "primary element" of sacrifice were: (1) gift to the deity, (2) homage to the deity, (3) expiation, (4) communion with the deity, (5) life transmitted to the deity and then conferred upon the worshipers. Although full agreement was never reached, the single most helpful category for understanding sacrifice in the Judaeo-Christian tradition has proven to be the gift idea which, by c. A.D. 50, had reached a mature theoretical expression in Philo.

Old Testament Sacrifice

Critical scholarship shows that the sacrificial code (Lev 1-7; also Num 28-29) is the result of a highly complex development. It reflects more an idealized post-exilic priestly theology than an objective description. In the context of this development the undeniably fierce prophetic criticism (Isa 1:11-17; Jer 6:20; 7:21-26; Amos 5:21-25; Hos 6:6; 9:4; Mic 6:6-8; Mal 1:10-14; 2:13) actually presumes the validity of the cult.

There are two main types of OT sacrifice. Overall the most frequent was the whole burnt offering or holocaust (cf. Lev 1; Gen 8:20-21; 22:1-14; 1 Kgs 18:20-38). It expressed homage, adoration, thanksgiving, etc., and was the major context for the development of the "theology" of divine acceptance: i.e., that sacrifices are useless unless accepted by God, who accepts only from those with the proper dispositions. But by NT times, the second major type, the sin offering (cf. Lev 3, 16), with its attendant "theology" of atonement, so dominated Jewish religious consciousness that a necessary connection between sacrifice, especially, blood sacrifice, and atonement/forgiveness seems to have developed: "Without the shedding of blood there is no forgiveness of sins" (Heb 9:22; cf. Mt 26:28).

The process of atonement came to be perceived, from within the OT itself, as ultimately not a human action but as a creature-directed action of God with a positive function of making persons or objects "acceptable" to Yahweh, and a negative or apotropaic function of averting the course of evil set in motion by sin or transgression. Gen 9:4, Deut 12:23 and esp. Lev 17:11 provide a glimmer of insight into this process: "It is the blood [on the altar] that makes atonement by reason of the life [in the blood]." The LXX, in mistranslating the final phrase as "instead of the soul/life," provided ground for the theologically aberrant penal substitution theory in later Christian theology.

Spiritualization, which was the key element in this development (with remarkable parallels elsewhere, especially in Hinduism), also resists easy definition. All of its common synonyms such as dematerializing, sublimating, humanizing, deepening, ethicizing, rationalizing, interiorizing, symbolizing, are inadequate or misleading, esp. "dematerializing," which suggests the narrow stereotype of ranking religions according to their degree of development beyond a material cult. It cannot do justice to the creational thinking of Judaism and the incarnational thinking of Christianity. Within those contexts, spiritualization broadly includes all those movements which attempt to emphasize the inner, spiritual or ethical significance of sacrifice over against the *merely* material or *merely* external. The specific *christian concept of sacrifice* is intimately connected with the process of spiritualization which began deep in the OT, reached a high-point in post-biblical, early rabbinic Judaism, and culminated in its "christologization."

New Testament Thought

The NT says very little about sacrifice in the proper sense, doubtless because the early Christians associated it with Judaism and paganism. But there is, especially in the Pauline writings, a strikingly rich use of spiritualized (i.e., christologized) sacrificial language and imagery. Some of these texts refer directly to the *sacrifice of Christ:* he is the paschal lamb (1 Cor 5:7) or sin offering (2 Cor 5:21; Gal 3:13), or they simply speak of his redemptive activity in sacrificial language (2 Cor 5:14-15; Rom 5:6-11; 8:23; Gal 2:20; Eph 5:2, 25; Col 1:24; 1 Tim 2:5-6; Tit 2:13-14; 1 Jn 3:16; see also Hebrews and the eucharistic words of institution). A second category of texts speaks of the *Christians,* individually or in community, *as the new*

temple, i.e., the place where the sacrifices of the new law are offered (1 Cor 3:6-17; 6:15, 19; 2 Cor 6:16). These supply the interpretative framework for the many texts which speak of the indwelling of the Spirit or the body of Christ (Rom 5:5; 8:9, 11, 15-16; 1 Thess 4:8; 1 Cor 2:10-16; 12:12-31; 2 Cor 1:22; 1 Tim 3:15; 2 Tim 2:20-22; Tit 2:14; Eph 1:22; 2:16, 19-22; 3:6; 4:4, 11-16; 5:23-24; 1 Pet 2:4-10). A third category speaks implicitly or directly of the *sacrifice of the Christian.* When texts such as Rom 8:36; 2 Cor 4:10-11; Gal 2:20; Phil 2:17, 25; 4:18; (cf. Col 1:24; 2 Tim 4:6) are examined in their full context and in connection with the five texts which seem to say something about the nature of christian sacrificial activity (Rom 12:1; 15:15-16; 1 Pet 2:4-10; Heb 10:19-25; 12:18—13:16) there remains no doubt that the NT writers, especially Paul, see the active, lived christian life in sacrificial images. Moreover, the *only* christian activity referred to as sacrificial is not liturgical or cultic but ethical, charitable, or actively apostolic.

Thus we can distinguish three phases of spiritualization (see Daly, pp. 135-140). (1) Even as early as the tenth century Yahwist, and providing the basis for the covenant theology of the prophets and Deuteronomist, there developed an awareness of the necessity of proper dispositions for material sacrifice to be acceptable to God and thus have its effect. (2) Under the pressures of the exilic and diaspora separations from the Jerusalem temple, where alone material sacrifice could be offered, the effective, dynamic center of sacrifice shifted from the external ceremony to the *dispositions* of the worshiper. Sacrifice *in obedience to the Law* is what occasioned atonement (hence the motto: "obedience, not sacrifice"). This enabled the Qumran sectarians and other Jews to develop a sacrificial soteriology without actual material sacrifice. (3) A specifically christian *incarna-*

tional spiritualization or *christologization* of sacrifice which (a) incarnates the *material* elements of sacrifice in the *bodily* (cf. Rom 12:1) life and works of christian life and which (b) identifies (not merely imitates) the dispositions of sacrifice with Christ's self-giving love.

This alone is the true basis for the christian use of sacrificial language and imagery in Christology, liturgiology, sacramentology, soteriology, atonement theory, spirituality, asceticism, etc. Taken *strictly,* or in the general sense defined in our opening paragraph, (which was not, of course, what Trent had in mind with its defensive *"verum et proprium sacrificium"* [D.S. 1751]), *Christianity has no sacrifice.*

Nevertheless, Christ's redemptive work and our participation in it is clearly described in the NT as "sacrificial," and Christians through the ages have, as did Paul, imaged their lives in sacrificial terms. Christian theology cannot ignore these facts. However, in view of the contemporary widespread negative connotations of "sacrifice" which tend to obscure its central Christian reality as an act of christic self-giving love and service, one has to question the homiletic and pastoral wisdom of using sacrifical words and images indiscriminately.

See **Christology**

R.J. Daly, *The Origins of the Christian Doctrine of Sacrifice* [1978]v . A.M. di Nola in *Encyclopedia delle Religion* [1973] 5.651). R.K. Yerkes, *Sacrifice in Greek and Roman Religions and Early Judaism* [1952] 2.

ROBERT J. DALY, SJ

SAINTS

In the christian scriptures the word "saint" (Gr. *hagios*) is used to describe the faithful ones who lived before the time of Christ (Mt 27:52), the members of the New Covenant "in Christ Jesus" (Phil 1:1), and more commonly, as a synonym for the christian faithful as, for instance, in the opening greetings of Paul to the church of Rome (Rom 1:7); Corinth (1 Cor 1:2: 2 Cor 1:1); Ephesus (Eph 1:1), etc.

Quite early in the history of the church the word *saint* took on a more technically precise meaning. The saint was one who (a) was in heaven with the Lord, who (b) could intercede for the needs of the earthly church and respond to those needs, and (c) merited public honor and cultic recognition by the church. As early as the first half of the third century we have Origen's testimony in *On Prayer* (11.2) that the intercessory prayers addressed to the saints are powerful and valid. The value of that intercession was cogently stated by Augustine in his extended discussion of the miracles of the saints in *The City of God* (xxii. 8ff.).

The role of the saint in early Christianity was tied intimately to the reality of persecution and the prestige of the martyrs. Indeed, until the peace of Constantine in the fourth century one can safely generalize that the cult of the saint was the cult of the martyr. When the period of the persecutions drew to a close, the popularity of the saint did not diminish. It became common to think of the ascetics as the new martyrs who, in the words of Athanasius writing about the ascetic Saint Anthony, withdrew "to his cell, and was there daily being martyred by his conscience, and doing battle in the contests of the faith" (*The Life of Anthony*. Cap. 47).

It is difficult to overstate the influence of the cult of the saints and their relics in the first millennium of the church's history. That cult had an enormous impact on everything from church architecture and the development of the liturgy to the production and dissemination of christian literary works. Besides *The Life of Anthony* already mentioned, Jerome wrote lives of ascetics like Paul the

Hermit, Hilarion, and Malchus, while Gerontius (?) wrote an influential life of the female ascetic Melania the Younger. The Life of Martin of Tours (*Vita Martini*) by Sulpicius Severus, written in the early fifth century, was an immensely popular and influential work in Europe well into the period of the Renaissance.

Along with these early *vitae* a whole literature on the saints developed which we now recognize under the generic name of hagiography. There were compilations of miracles made at shrine sites; *legenda* (i.e. treatises read aloud at liturgical services); accounts of miracles performed as a saint's relics were installed in a shrine or moved to another place; etc. Inevitably, fact, fiction, pious elaborations, and folklore became part and parcel of this literary tradition. The detection of historical strata under this material was a daunting task, not undertaken with anything approaching sophistication until the seventeenth century with the work of the Bollandists and Maurists.

Although the social role of the living holy person and the venerated saint in early Christianity is a very complex one, as Peter Brown and others have shown, there are two basic theological themes in this tradition which deserve mention.

The saints, especially after their death and through the power of their relics, were a source of religious power. Early Christianity shared with the pagan world the basic assumption that the Sacred could break through into the world of the mundane. The church saw in the manifestations of the sacred power of the saints a convincing proof of the triumph of Christ over the power of the demonic which they saw as embedded in paganism. St. Bede cites a letter in his history of England in which Pope Gregory the Great instructs the missionary Mellitus to build christian shrines over pagan temples precisely as an apologetic tool to show the pagans of Britain that the relics of the saints overcome the power of the pagan deities. Gregory's instructions explicitly articulate what was a common assumption of the church.

Secondly, the saint served as a paradigmatic figure for those who wished to follow the life of Christ. In the *Confessions,* for instance, Augustine pays tribute to the power of Anthony's life of asceticism as he, and his friends, sought to discover a way of ascetic living in pursuit of God. The church set forth the saints as models of religious behavior and as reliable guides for those who undertook the spiritual path. One *topos* that runs through the entire corpus of hagiography is the saint as *imitator Christi*. In that sense the hagiographical tradition set forth models for those who wished to follow Christ within their own chosen style of life. The saint modeled Christ as an ideal of the monk, the ascetic, the monarch, the missionary, etc.

How did the saint get recognized as a saint in the church? The process by which a saint was canonized (i.e. listed in the *canon* of those worthy of cultic veneration in the church) has a long history. Well into the early Middle Ages the saint was proclaimed either by public acclamation or through episcopal decree. The first saint canonized by a Roman pontiff seems to be Saint Uldaricus proclaimed a saint by Pope Benedict VI in 973 A.D. In 1234 Pope Gregory IX restricted all canonizations to the papacy itself. In the Tridentine period Pope Sixtus V established the Sacred Congregation of Rites (1588) as the papal agency for canonizations. The procedures for canonization were minutely described by Prospero Lambertini (later Pope Benedict XIV) in 1727; his volumes on the canonization process are at the core of present day practice. Both the reforms of the late Pope Paul VI and the new code of canon law have further modified the canonization procedures which, today, fall under the competence of the Sacred Congregation for the Causes of the Saints.

The present-day canonization process is a rigorously bureaucratic one that examines possible candidates for sainthood to determine if they lived lives of heroic virtue or died as martyrs *in odium fidei* and if there is evidence of miraculous intervention through their intercession. The process of inquiry does not normally begin until fifty years after the death of the candidate. The first level of the process involves beatification which permits the person to receive limited cultus (e.g. in a specific religious order or in a particular diocese or country) and, finally, canonization which authorizes liturgical cultus for the universal church. There has been persistent criticism of the present procedures because they tend to favor those with more immediate access to the bureaucratic process itself. One empirical indication of the validity of this criticism is the disproportionate number of European clerics and religious who are canonized in the contemporary church.

Apart from the historical and juridical considerations already discussed we might further inquire into the place of the saints in theology. The theological foundations of sainthood have received short shrift in the theological tradition partially, one suspects, because of the perceived notion that the saints are part of the "popular" tradition of Catholicism rather than central to the Catholic doctrinal tradition. Upon closer examination, however, it seems clear that the notion of sanctity is closely linked to a number of central Catholic doctrines. Both the Second Vatican Council's *Dogmatic Constitution on the Church* (L.G. 50) and the *Constitution on the Sacred Liturgy* (S.C. 8) discuss the saints in terms of their eschatological

significance. The saints are already with the Lord and, in recalling their memory and evoking their assistance in our worship, we affirm in faith our own belief in the salvific plan of Christ and, simultaneously, state our conviction that the church is not merely an earthly aggregation, but part of that larger reality which traditional theology has called "The Communion of Saints." In that sense, and from that perspective, the deepest theological meaning of the saints best expresses itself in the venerable liturgical formulations of the eucharistic prayers where we beg to be worthy "to share eternal life with Mary the Virgin Mother of God, with the apostles, and with all the saints who have done your will throughout the ages."

We are bound to the saints, however, not only through our communion with them in worship, but also because the greatest of them at least are the "classics" of our collective memory, our tradition. They encapsulate the best of an age while showing us new aspects of gospel fidelity. The saints, in short, are our most conspicuous pedagogues. What do they teach us?

In the first instance the lives of the saints manifest the inherent values of the gospel tradition. In every age the saints demonstrate existentially that in times that are decadent, ridden with confusion or ennui, or in periods of doubt, it is not only possible to live out the gospel, but that the gospel can be enfleshed in an extraordinary manner. In that lived tradition the saint witnesses to the truth of Christ (and hence, is a *martyr* in the most profound and widest sense of the term) and, at the same time, renders prophetic judgment on the age. The saint transforms the abstract claims of preaching, teaching, and theology into lived realities.

The saint not only witnesses to the

perennial values of the gospel but dialectically, opens up new possibilities hitherto unimagined or unexplored. Karl Rahner once wrote that the saint is the person who shows an age that it is possible to live as a Christian even in *this* manner. In our times, fraught with confusion and suspicion, it is useful and salutary to remember an important lesson from the tradition of the saints: the greatest of them, like Francis of Assisi, Teresa of Avila, Ignatius of Loyola, now safely enshrined in our common tradition, were all subject to official diffidence and/or popular suspicion as they tried to articulate with their very lives new forms of living for the truth of the gospel.

The call to holiness is universal. While recent scholarship emphasizes the social class of canonized saints (historically, the preponderance of canonized lay saints comes either from the aristocratic or educated classes), the proclaimed ideal is that sainthood, and its official recognition, cuts across class and ecclesiastical office. This ideal is pertinent for the current theological interest in those who are marginalized in the church. Women, to cite a conspicuous example, are barred from most high offices in the church because of their exclusion from Holy Orders. Nonetheless, many women in the history of the church have exercised a charismatic authority because of their recognized holiness. Thus, a Clare of Assisi or a Catherine of Siena could exercise a prophetic power in the highest circles of church life due to the power of their spiritual life. The recent interest of feminist scholars in the tradition of the saints testifies to the yet largely unexplored hagiographical tradition from a theological perspective. But even here we should remember that until this century women made up only twenty percent of canonized saints.

In the new *Code of Canon Law* only two canons (1186 and 1187) deal explicitly with the saints. Canon 1186 enunciates the legitimacy of the cult of the Blessed Virgin and the other saints while the following canon restricts such public veneration to those persons officially recognized by ecclesiastical authority as worthy of such honors. The juridical narrowness of the *Code* does not exhaust the interest of most Catholics in the place of the saints in the working out of the christian life. Apart from a renewed interest in the cult of the Virgin and the saints as a manifestation of popular religion by the liberation theologians, most Catholics look to the saints, whether canonized or not, because the saintly person provides the model for christian living appropriate for our age. The continuing influence of the late Dorothy Day or Thomas Merton (neither canonized) reflects a common desire to see how one can combine a deep spirituality with a thirst for social justice in a setting congenial to the contemporary experience. At this level of inquiry, christian orthodoxy need not be a controlling factor as the persistent interest in a paradigmatic saintly personality like the late Mohandas Gandhi amply demonstrates. Just as one distinguishes the saint as a generic term for those who are "in Christ" from those who are publicly recognized in the church as worthy of liturgical recognition, so also one can distinguish yet another category: those saintly persons who, without any official recognition, can make a claim on us either as models to be imitated or resources to be studied.

A satisfactory systematic theology of the saints has yet to be written but the raw materials for such a study are there. There has been an explosion of historical studies in the last decade on the place of the saints in the christian tradition along with a continuing flood of critically edited hagiographical texts. This abundance of material parallels the development and maturation of the study of the role of narrative in theology. More recently, there has been an increased call for serious study of the many ways in which the *imitatio Christi* has been enfleshed in the various manifestations of the christian tradition. This shift has resulted in a serious theological examination of art, architecture, popular piety, *belles lettres*, etc. in its relationship to the theological tradition.

David Tracy's *The Analogical Imagination* (1981) provides one important way in which a systematic theology of the saints might be constructed. Tracy argues that the primary task of the systematic theologian is to explicate the christian "classics" in such a way that they have a contemporary resonance. The classic is that extraordinary epiphany of a religious truth that not only sums up a given age or a particular religious truth, but also one that has a pertinence and a depth to give later generations new and fresh insights. The classic, in short, possesses its own history but makes claims on those later generations who encounter it. Classics, clearly, do not mean only classic texts. Tracy makes it quite explicit that he also refers to persons; indeed, the classic, *par excellence,* is Jesus the Christ.

The saints are also "classics." The greatest of them—Francis of Assisi comes immediately to mind—not only exemplifies the depths of Christomimesis as reflected in a certain age, but an encounter with that life reveals to us both the perennial value of the gospel and its value for us in a way that the saints themselves may not have fully articulated. A theology based on the exemplary value of the saints would have to take into account both the historical character of the saint's life (Franciscan poverty both means and does not mean the same thing today) and the "narrative quality" of that life as it comes to us in this time.

The saintly personality has been studied in this century from the aspect of psychology (William James), the philosophy of religion (Henri Bergson), and sociology (Pitirim Sorokin; Pierre Delooz). The historical literature continues apace. It is now the task of the theologian to give a coherent account of those great figures of our tradition who, in the words of John Henry Newman, are "the proper and true evidence of the God of Christianity."

Peter Brown, *The Cult of the Saints*, Chicago, 1981. Lawrence Cunningham, *The Meaning of Saints*, San Francisco, 1981. Pierre Delooz, *Sociologie et Canonisations*, Liege and The Hague, 1969. Donald Weinstein, *et. al., Saints and Society,* Chicago, 1982. Stephen Wilson ed., *Saints and Their Cults,* Cambridge, 1983 (With an abundant annotated bibliography).

LAWRENCE CUNNINGHAM

SALVATION
See **Redemption**

SALVATION HISTORY

The term *Heilsgeschichte* (variously translated as "history of salvation," "redemptive history," "holy history," or "salvation history") first became prominent in nineteenth-century German Protestantism through the work of J.C. von Hofmann (1810-1877) and the Erlangen school. Some influence undoubtedly came from the covenant-based theology of J. Cocceius (1603-1669), and from the strong interest in biblical history evinced by J.A. Bengel (1687-1752) and his followers. For Hofmann, salvation history is about our communion with God, revealed in Scripture and mediated by Christ, which takes place in clear, progressive, historical stages, culminating in the establishment of the Kingdom of God. Outside the theological mainstream of the day, concern for salvation history as such faded in the latter half of the nineteenth century as the history of religions approach grew. The term received renewed interest only after World War I.

Most commonly, salvation history is used in a special sense to refer to those events which the Bible narrates as manifesting God's deeds for the salvation of the world. A general outline of such a history would begin with the exodus (Exod 14-15:21; Deut 5:15; 6:20-23; Josh 24:6-7, 16-17; Isa 51:10; Hos 11:1; 13:4-5; Mic 6:4; Psalms, *passim*). The divine purpose is revealed in the covenant (Exod 19:1-6) whereby Israel became God's own people, settled in the land earlier promised to the patriarchs (Deut 4:1; 6:18-19, 23; 34:4; Josh 1:2-6). Israel also came to recognize divine guidance in the events surrounding the lives of the patriarchs (Gen 12-50). Creation, too, and humanity's first encounter with sin and punishment (Gen 1-11) illustrated God's saving design from the beginning.

With the establishment of the monarchy and God's covenant with the Davidic dynasty (2 Sam 7; 23:5; 1 Chr 17), a new era begins. But the Deuteronomistic history indicates how failure to live up to the covenant led to punishment, exile and loss of national independence (1 Sam 12:13-15; 1 Kgs 2:4; 16:25-26). During this same period the prophets were urging justice and morality and threatening punishment for sin (Amos 6; Hosea 10; Isaiah 5). They advised trust in God's guidance of events rather than in political alliances (Isa 7:4-17). Most especially, they gave Israel a transformed vision of her future: the old covenant would be replaced by a new and lasting one (Jer 31:31-34; Ezek 37:26-28); a new Davidic kingdom would be established with justice and peace for all (Isa 9:5-7; 11:1-5; Amos 9:11-12); even images of a new paradise appear (Hos 2:20-21; Amos 9:13; Isa 11:6-9). Apocalyptic literature envisions the final stage of this history when evil is punished and justice is established forever.

The NT era opens with Jesus proclaiming the fulfillment of OT prophecies (Lk 4:16-21; Mt 13:17). He announces that the Kingdom of God is near (Mk 1:15), that in fact it is present in his works (Mt 12:28; Lk 10:17-19; Jn 12:31-32), but requires repentance and return to God (Mk 1:15). There is a paradox here: salvation has come in Jesus (Jn 5:25-27; Heb 2:10-18), yet its final realization is in the Parousia, Jesus' return at the end of history in judgment (Mt 24:29-31; 25:31-46; Acts 3:20-21).

Central to various theologies of the NT are "salvation history" perspectives. Lukan theology divides all time from the creation to the judgment into three epochs: that of the Law and the Prophets which is preparation for the Christ, the time of Jesus' earthly ministry, and the era of the church which continues the work of Jesus (Lk 16:16; Acts 10:37-42). Pauline theology also has three ages: Adam to Moses, a time of sin; Moses to Christ, the period of the Law; and Christ to the end (Rom 4:15; 5:13; 10:4). Embracing this entire history is the hidden plan of the Father, revealed in the gospel, by which every creature would be reconciled to him through Christ, forming that kingdom which Christ will turn over to the Father (Eph 1:9-10; 1 Cor 14:24-25, 28). Johannine theology stresses more the uniqueness of Jesus' earthly ministry as the time of eschatological salvation (Jn 6:47; 8:51) and source of the church's life and institutions. But the historical aspect is not lost sight of since the "hour" of Jesus' glorification is the culmination of a long period of preparation which looks forward to a final judgment (6:39-40, 44).

Despite such an orderly outline, however, there are problems with the way the term has been applied. Some have viewed the biblical data objectively as being, to a greater or lesser degree, a particular history within the general history of the world (Lowith, Blank, Sharbert). But this tends to ignore discrepancies and disjunctures in the biblical record of events and would mask divergent theological viewpoints. It would be wrong to view the biblical evidence as one, long, unbroken continuum of the realization of salvation (Barr). In addition, because such a view emphasized the unfolding nature of this revelation and particularly the fulfillment of promises, earlier stages of this revelation (the OT) could appear to be superseded, invalidated, and useless in terms of Christ. Others would stress the history as confessed by the biblical authors, a "kerygmatic" approach (von Rad, Cullman). But this could be viewed as eliminating the need for objective history altogether. Nor should it be understood that the salvific aspect of events was always immediately or thoroughly perceived by the participants. It was only with difficulty and after the passage of time, for instance, that the authentic prophet could be distinguished from the false. Some opposed the concept of "salvation history" to that of "historicity," the existential moment of decision which was open to faith alone and could not be prepared for (Bultmann). Others stressed the wholeness and finality of all history as it progressed toward an eschatological consummation (Moltmann, Pannenberg). It would also be argued that the uniqueness of the salvation offered in Christ (the "kairos") could not be contained or even verified historically (Hesse, Klein, Gunneweg). Finally, by the very nature of the term itself, it removes from its purview much of the wisdom literature and many of the psalms, hymns and legal material which lack the historical context of the other biblical books.

In the debate about the term, therefore, it has moved between its special biblical sense and the broader theological context where it affirms that salvation takes place in history and that all history is salvific. There is no way in which secular history can be isolated from salvation history in this sense that there is no moment when one's historical existence is not also affected by grace. God's salvific will, therefore, is directed toward redeeming the sinful condition of humanity, and also brings about those events in various times and places which will offer grace. It means that salvation will be brought about within the historical context of human activity itself, and has past, present, and future phases. This offer of salvation, however, is hidden in secular history, and must be made clear through the interpretive works of God and especially through Christ (Rahner). Thus is derived the notion of salvation history in its special sense—the history of Israel as interpreted authoritatively by the word of God in Scripture. Modern reflection on salvation history is also linked with theological and philosophical conceptions about the meaning of the whole of history, which have Augustine as their remote ancestor, and G.W.F. Hegel as their most influential recent exponent.

A.J. Ehlen, "Old Testament Theology as *Heilsgeschichte*," *CTM* 35 (1964) 517-44. H.G. Reventlow, *Problems of Old Testament Theology in the Twentieth Century*, Philadelphia: Fortress, 1985, 87-110. K. Berger, A. Darlap, K. Rahner, "Salvation. III. History of Salvation ('Salvation History'), *Sacramentum Mundi* 5 (1970) 411-25. H. Kistner, E.L Peterman, J.E. Fallon, "Salvation History (Heilsgeschichte)," *NCE* 12 (1967) 998-1001.

THOMAS P. McCREESH, OP

SANCTIFICATION

In christian theology this term designates a condition of holiness or the process of being brought to that state. Holiness in turn is understood in terms of its meanings in the OT and NT. There it refers to the infinite difference which characterizes God as distinct and separate from any creature. It applies as well to created beings, whose holiness derives from some closeness of the holy God; e.g., the heavens are called holy because Yahweh dwells there (Deut 26:15); the Spirit's indwelling sanctifies and makes the Christian a holy temple (1 Cor 3:16-17). God's agency is to be looked to for the sanctification of the Thessalonians in all things (1 Thess 5:23). The Corinthians are told that Christ Jesus has been made their wisdom from God, *justice* (uprightness), *sanctification,* and redemption (1 Cor 1:30). 1 Peter (1:1-2) is addressed to those who were chosen in accord with the foreknowledge of God the Father in the sanctification of the Spirit for the obedience . . . of Christ Jesus' blood. Converts who were once among those who will not possess God's Kingdom are told that they have been *washed* (Baptism), *sanctified,* and justified (1 Cor 6:9-11) in the name of Christ Jesus our Lord and in the Spirit of our God. But sanctification has consequences with regard to conduct: one whose members are Christ's and a temple of the Holy Spirit is to avoid fornication (1 Cor 6:12-20). Children of *obedience* conformed to the Holy One who called them; Christians are to be holy because their God is holy (1 Pet 13-16). Sanctification, then, involves being made and in that sense becoming less unlike God in one's being and behavior.

This decrease in dissimilarity has been understood in different ways through the centuries. With its attachment to John's Gospel, Eastern Christianity has chosen very frequently to confess what God did for human beings through Jesus Christ in the Holy Spirit by making use of the theme of *deification.* One who is made holy in the mysteries by the Holy Spirit becomes less unlike God ("deified") because of the indwelling Trinity. Western theologians like Augustine and Thomas Aquinas took a similar approach when they stressed that grace and glory bring human beings a participation in God's holiness and eternity. But for various reasons the theme of *divine forgiveness* attained greater prominence in the West; in other words greater emphasis was placed on the divine mercy and compassion expressed in the forgiveness of sins. Correspondingly one who is made holy by grace becomes less unlike God because sins are forgiven.

To illustrate this Western approach to sanctification, it may help to recall the dispute between Augustine and Pelagius in the fifth century. The underlying issue was whether historical human beings could ever overcome their alienation from God without the grace of justification. The Pauline influence on both is obvious. Augustine's answer was in the negative. In his view, divine grace is necessary: not merely to obtain the forgiveness of past sin but to avoid sinning in the future; not only to enlighten the mind to know God's commandments but also to inspire the will to love what God loves; not merely to facilitate but to enable free choice to carry out what God expects of it (D.S. 225-7). Augustine spoke explicitly of the grace of justification. But when he explains why that grace is needed, it is immediately clear that he is speaking of sanctification as well in the biblical sense of becoming less unlike God through the remission and avoidance of sin.

In the Middle Ages the theology of sanctification developed when use was made of the Aristotelian notions of potency, act, and nature. Becoming or being made less unlike God despite the even greater difference insisted on by the Fourth Lateran Council (D.S. 806) involved: (a) being touched by *habitual* or sanctifying grace in the depths of one's spiritual *nature* (soul); (b) having faith as a theological virtue in one's mind (intellectual *potency*) together with hope and charity as corresponding virtues in one's will (affective *potency*); and receiving *actual* graces to give one spontaneous inclinations to think and will as God wishes. In all of this the indwelling of the Trinity was asserted to be sure. But the Aristotelian terminology had not envisioned a mystery of creaturely sanctification by the infinitely-distant God's being present and giving self as Father, Son, and Spirit. That sort of terminology was better able to describe the kinds of *created* graces mentioned above.

The Reformers insisted on justification by faith alone and saw sanctification as radically incomplete in this life because concupiscence remains in the baptized and by its very presence is sinful. This keeps *any* human action or work from being altogether sinless. The grounds for works-righteousness are thus removed and sinful human beings are warranted in looking to Christ alone for forgiveness and sanctification. Also having to do with sanctification was the *Augsburg Confession's* objection to the claim that "... the monastic life earned righteousness and godliness ... " and that " ...more merit could be obtained by monastic life than by all other states of life instituted by God ... " (27:11-13). Similarly Luther protested against monastic " ... services, invented by men, which claim to be superior to the ordinary Christian life and to the offices and callings established by God" (*Smalkald Articles* II, 3, 2).

In this regard the Council of Trent taught that the process by which one is brought by God's grace to justification leads as well to sanctification and inner renewal through the reception of grace and other gifts (D.S. 1528). Concupiscence, to be sure, remains in the baptized; it comes from and leads to sin but by its mere presence is not sin in the true and proper sense of the term (D.S. 1515). Those made holy by baptism do *not* sin at least venially in every act (D.S. 1575). At the same time venial sin is said to be not only compatible with being justified; it is the lot even of God's holy ones in this life (D.S. 1537, 1573).

For its part the Second Vatican Council taught that Christ's disciples, called by God not because of their works but by his grace and justified in the Lord Jesus, are God's children in the baptism of faith, partake of the divine nature, and so are truly sanctified (L.G. 40). To be sure, the religious state of life reminds God's people of the eschatological truth that it has here no lasting city (L.G. 44). Still there is a universal call to holiness. Indeed all Christians in the conditions, duties, and circumstances of their life and through these will sanctify themselves if they receive all things with faith from the hand of God and cooperate with the divine will, thus showing forth in that temporal service the love with which God has loved the world (L.G. 41).

In contemporary Roman Catholic theology there has been a development with regard to the proper understanding of the universal divine salvific will in Christ. By not a few (e.g., Karl Rahner), the latter has been taken to imply that in all who enter this redeemed world there is as a constituent of the historical reality of each an invitation to union with the Triune God. This clearly involves a call of all to sanctification.

See **Good Works, Indulgences, Justification, Merit**

F.E. Greenspahn, *The Human Condition in the Jewish and Christian Traditions*, Hoboken: Ktav, 1986. *The Dogmatic Constitution on the Church* in *Vatican II: The Conciliar and Post Conciliar Documents*, Ed. A. Flannery, Dublin: Dominican Pub., and Newport: Costello Publ., 1984.

CARL J. PETER

SATAN
See **Demons**

SATISFACTION

An act performed to make amends for some wrong or injury inflicted. It is used in the theology of redemption to explain Christ's suffering and death as reparation for the violation of God's honor by sin. In sacramental theology, it refers to acts performed by the penitent in compensation for and as a temporal punishment for his sins.

See **Reconciliaton, Redemption**

SCHISM

Schism is a willful separation from unity or ecclesiastical communion. It may also refer to the state of separation or the christian group constituted in such a state, for example the Greek schism. A schismatic is one who causes schism whether he be a fomenter, one who bears responsibility for it, or one who adheres to it by conviction or simply as a matter of fact (Congar).

The word comes from the Greek through its use in the NT, passed on to ecclesiastical Latin and then into modern languages. In a proper sense its signifies a gap or a tear. In a figurative sense it refers to dissent, divergence of opinion. In the NT, its use by Paul gives it its ecclesiastical use. It appears three times in the first letter to the Corinthians where it refers to the troubles occupying the church at Corinth: "I beg you, brothers, in the name of the Lord Jesus Christ, to agree in what you say. Let there be no factions; rather be united in mind and judgment" (1:10; cf. 11:18; 12:25). Paul does not speak of schism strictly speaking here because he does not speak of sects or ecclesiastical groups separated from the communion but speaks rather of parts within the communion who hold differing interpretations of Christianity.

The development and variations in the meaning of schism are due to two main factors: the manner in which one con-ceives of the unity of the church and the actual schisms in the church at a given time and in a determined place. The Apostolic Fathers had a very rich sense of the unity of the church but the notion of schism had not developed the technical meaning it would have later. Schism was simply envisioned as a rupture of unity within the framework of the local church and the act of schism was understood in relation to the legitimate, local authority. Gradually, within a theology of church as communion, schism comes to be seen as a rupture in the communion at the level of church understood as a community of human beings gathered through the exercise of the means of salvation, especially the eucharist of which the bishop is the chief minister. For this reason, in the patristic period, one often designated the act of schism as setting altar against altar (Ignatius of Antioch, Cyprian). A schism was first committed in relation to the altar and the bishop within the context of the local church. However, since the communion is universal inasmuch as the bishops are in communion with one another, a person in communion with his bishop is so with the whole church and can participate everywhere at the same altar.

The notion of schism develops simultaneously with the directions of ecclesiology. In the Roman Catholic Church, with progressive centralization of the church in the Roman See and the development of a monarchic form of ecclesiology of the universal church, schism came to be understood in terms of a rupture of communion with the pope. The most significant modification of the meaning of schism occurred in the Counter-Reformation. Until this time, provided that grave differences in matters of faith were not involved and provided that a breach with legitimate authority did not occur, the sacramental, hierarchical organism of the church remained intact and hence the dissenting portion of the church was still regarded as in communion. An imbalance occurred when the church was understood primarily in its visible, hierarchically constituted, societal dimension under the supreme authority of the bishop of Rome and when the church was identified simply with the Roman Catholic Church. At this point, schism came to signify separation from the church itself.

The Second Vatican Council returned to an ecclesiology of communion and centered again on the notion of the church as mystery. In this understanding the church of Christ is not perceived as confined within the limits of the Roman Catholic Church which is its fullest manifestation. Other churches and ecclesial bodies participate in the reality of the church as mystery in varying degrees (L.G. 8, U.R. 3). This recognition that those not in full communion with the Roman See still participate in some way in the mystery of the church calls for a re-examination of the meaning of schism as passed on from the theology of church of the Counter-Reformation. Schism now must be viewed from two perspectives. Canonically, it signifies a breach in jurisdictional relations with the See of Rome (CIC, c. 751). But theologically, schism is understood to place an obstacle to the full and manifest realization of unity in faith and participation in the church as the one, unique, sacramental and hierarchical reality. Schism is an obstacle to the manifestation of the unity of church in sacraments and especially in the eucharist, the sacrament of unity. But this does not deny that "some, even very many, of the most significant elements and endowments which together go to build up and give life to the church itself, can exist outside the visible boundaries of the church" (U.R. 3).

In the contemporary ecumenical climate, Roman Catholic theology believes that it is possible within history to achieve a truly universal unity which is both spiritual and visible. It does not reserve the achievement of this unity to an ultimate eschatological fulfillment. This is because the Kingdom of God has already begun and moves forward in history to its full manifestation. So even though there are divisions, differences and tensions, the church is gifted with a unity in faith, sacramental life, communion and a unity which is universal in extension. It is a unity which proceeds from the Father, through Christ and by the Holy Spirit who, as Principle of love binds all together in a universal communion of persons. Within this communion of persons the initiatives of each and all are respected but are also recognized as limited and in need of being complemented by the initiatives of others. These developments occur within the unity of the church which seeks to prevent such initiatives from becoming irreconcilable differences. All such initiatives and movements must unfold within the communion itself as part of the whole.

The healing of schisms is at the center of the ecumenical movement. This healing takes different forms. For some Protestant communities, it takes the form of mutual agreements in the practice of intercommunion, pulpit sharing and other aspects of worship without necessarily achieving full agreement on matters of doctrine. Others, who fall under the general category of "Catholic" seek unanimity of faith and agreement with regard to the hierarchical sacramental structure first before engaging in full sacramental communion.

As a matter of ecumenical sensitivity, terms such as schism and schismatic are not used because persons who belong to these churches and ecclesial bodies have been born into them and have received their religious formation within these communities. They cannot be held responsible for historical division. Furthermore, both sides of the division must bear responsibility for it. Finally, in a renewed ecclesiology of the church emphasis must be placed on those elements which the churches hold in common as the foundation upon which a fuller visible unity can be achieved.

See **Church, Unity of the Church**

Yves Congar, "Schisme," *Dictionnaire de theologie catholique,* vol. 14, c. 1286-1312, Eds. A. Vacant, E. Mangenot, Msgr. E. Amann, Paris: Libraire Letauzey, 1943; "Signification theologique et spirituelle du schisme," *Le schisme,* Editions Xavier Mappus: Lyons, 1967; *L'eglise, une, sainte, catholique et apostolique,* Paris: Cerf, 1970, pp. 70-84. Christophe Dumont, "Schism," in *Sacramentum Mundi,* vol. 6, pp. 6-8.

TIMOTHY MACDONALD, SA

SCHOLASTICISM

The term "scholasticism" has taken a large number of unconnected meanings, many of them belonging more to the history of theological polemic than to theology proper. Indeed, the notion of a unitary scholasticism is originally polemical, having arisen from Renaissance and Reformation controversies over the value of medieval works "from the schools," as well as sixteenth century efforts at philosophical historiography. In the last two centuries, the term has been rehabilitated, but also further confused. It has referred variously to sets of themes or doctrines, to methods, to religious influences, and to historical or institutional periodizations, not to speak of the many possible combinations (historico-doctrinal, historico-methodological). A review of three influential definitions will show the difficulties caused by these confused meanings.

At the middle of the nineteenth century, "scholasticism" often meant in academic circles both medieval philosophy or theology and the later forms of church learning derived from them. Thus, in 1845, a French academic body announced a competition for a work on "scholastic [i.e., medieval] philosophy," with special attention to its intimate bond with theology. The winning essay, by Hauréau, was published as *De la philosophie scolastique* (1859) and then, after revision, as *Histoire de la philosophie scolastique* (1872). In the latter work, Hauréau argues a double definition of scholasticism. On the one hand, it is "the philosophy taught in the schools of the Middle Ages from their establishment [by Alcuin] to their decline [with Ockham]" (I:36). On the other hand, Hauréau argues that this historical period is thematically unified by the question of universals—and, indeed, by the formulation of that question in Porphyry's *Isagoge* (I:46-50).

Hauréau's historico-thematic definition has several defects, leaving aside problems of periodization. First, the definition oversimplifies the history of medieval thought by reducing everything to the dispute over universals, which was never the only or even the most important issue. Second, the definition does not advert to the deep importance of "scholastic" philosophy for theology or, thus, its growing place in the church *after* Ockham. On this score, the emphatically religious definitions offered by Picavet in response to Hauréau would be more adequate.

A much more rigorous attempt at a definition was undertaken by De Wulf at the turn of the century. In a series of preliminary essays and then in his *Introduction à la philosophie scolastique* (1903), De Wulf argues that none of the prevailing definitions of scholasticism is defensible. The common notions about it are vague and often pejorative; they also conflate philosophy and theology. The learned definitions are usually extrinsic, De Wulf continues, relying on such things as setting in the schools, terminology and method, historical period, or relation to ancient philosophy and other disciplines. The few intrinsic or doctrinal definitions available to him De Wulf finds incomplete. He suggests that a complete intrinsic definition would set forth the "fundamental doctrines" of the "system" of scholasticism in metaphysics, theodicy, physics, psychology, moral philosophy, and logic (tr. Coffey, 142-143). Historically, De Wulf finds this system most clearly expressed in certain medieval authors. "There is a philosophical synthesis common to a group of the leading doctors of the West. That synthesis does not sterilize originality of thought in the case of any one of them. It is predominant in the Middle Ages" (46). For De Wulf, the autonomous philosophical synthesis is related to theology only as pedagogical preparation or as methodological inspiration (67-68).

De Wulf's proposed definition has always been controversial and it remains liable to serious objection. First, it overstates the doctrinal unity of medieval philosophy, imposing a certain Thomism as if it were the standard doctrine. Second, De Wulf's definition exaggerates the autonomy of philosophy in relation to theology, mistaking a formal and procedural distinction for a fundamental separation. Third, De Wulf presupposes modern (indeed, almost Hegelian) notions about the propositional character of philosophical "systems" and their historiography. His conceptions of theology and philosophy as sciences are radically at odds with the medieval conceptions he proposes to expound.

A third and more adequate definition of scholasticism was offered by Grabmann in his history of scholastic method (1909). After reviewing a number of proposed definitions, including De Wulf's, Grabmann turns to the medieval texts themselves, beginning with Anselm of Canterbury's two (Augustinian) mottos, "faith seeking understanding" (*fides quaerens*

intellectum) and "I believe, that I may understand" (*credo, ut intelligam*) (I:33-36). Grabmann concludes the survey with his own definition (I:36-37): Scholastic method applies reason or philosophy to the truths of revelation in order to gain the greatest possible understanding of the content of faith. It strives for a "systematic" and "organic" representation of the whole of saving truth, while seeking to resolve any of reason's objections against it. The techniques and forms of scholastic disputation or commentary were developed gradually just to embody this effort.

Grabmann's definition marks an enormous advance in historical fidelity. But it also abandons the attempt to find a doctrinal definition spanning all scholasticisms from the ninth century to the nineteenth. Grabmann understands scholasticism as a project of reflection based on certain assumptions about the nature of reason, about the interpretation of historically specific authoritative texts, and about the grounds of rational pedagogy. He does not see it as a set of solutions or as a single system. Of course, what Grabmann gains in historical accuracy he must lose in speculative simplicity. There is also a danger in the concentration on method. It is true that a certain set of procedures developed in the twelfth and thirteenth centuries, though these procedures were neither static nor uniform. But it is not the case that these procedures were understood in the same way or that they rested on the same notions about truth or reason.

The dispute over the nature of scholasticism did not end with Grabmann, despite his large and well earned influence. Ehrle, for example, returns almost entirely to the emphasis in Picavet, holding that the "characteristic" of scholasticism is an "inner, harmonious relation" between Aristotelianism and Christian revelation (1-2). As late as 1950,

Balić was still urging an integral scholasticism, at once philosophical and theological, as well as a plurality of scholastic views. Moreover, the dispute was linked around 1927 with the new controversy over the possibility of "Christian philosophy." This controversy rehearsed much of the same dialectic, though with different interlocutors: Gilson, Maritain, Bréhier, Van Steenberghen. The debate over "Christian philosophy" continues.

It is not clear whether the debate over "scholasticism" continues or, in fact, if it should. The term "scholasticism" has outlived whatever usefulness it may once have had in serious discussion. Historically, it would be better to speak more narrowly and, so far as possible, according to the language of texts under study. At the very least, we should distinguish medieval "scholasticisms" from Tridentine or nineteenth century ones and should not prejudge the issue of doctrinal or methodological uniformity within or across periods. Substantively, it would be better to avoid "scholasticism" and similar generalities altogether. These terms reduce and reify complex sets of conceptual affiliations and oppositions. There is no one thing, no set of concepts or procedures, to be denoted by the term "scholasticism" or any similar term. The term has posited a conceptual unity that does not exist except as the projection of polemic.

See **Neo-Scholasticism**

Barthélemy Hauréau, *Histoire de la philosophie scolastique,* 2 vols., Paris: Durand et Pedone-Lauriel, 1872. François Picavet, "La valeur de la scolastique," in *Ier Congrès International de Philosophie ... ,* Paris: Armand Colin, 1902, 4:239-257. Maurice De Wulf, *Scholasticism Old and New: An Introduction to Scholastic Philosophy Medieval and Modern,* tr., Peter Coffey, Dublin: M.H. Gill, and London: Longmans, Green, 1910. Martin Grabmann, *Die Geschichte der Scholastischen Methode,* 2 vols., Freiburg i. B.: Herder, 1909-11. Franz Ehrle, *Die Scholastik und ihre Aufgaben in unserer Zeit,* 2 ed. by Franz Pelster, Freiburg i. B.: Herder, 1933. Carolus Balić, "De programmate congressus," in *Scholastica ratione historico-critica instauranda ...,* Rome: Antonianum, 1951, pp. 15-22.

MARK D. JORDAN

SCIENCE AND RELIGION

Whether it is possible sincerely to profess the christian faith while at the same time accepting what science teaches is a question that poses an ancient problem, the relationship between reason and religious belief, in a specifically modern context. From the venerable principle that truth is one and God is its author, together with the fact that by its derivation "science" means knowledge, it would seem to follow that sacred and secular science, knowledge of God and knowledge of what God has created, cannot in the long run be incompatible. Contemporary usage, however, restricts the meaning of "science" to the natural and especially the physical sciences as they have developed since the seventeenth century; and science, so defined, is thought of more often than not as quite separate from and more or less at odds with christian belief. Like much conventional wisdom, this view needs to be examined, and it can best be understood in light of its origins.

Historians differ as to whether natural science in its modern form arose because of Christianity or in spite of it. Until recently the majority opinion has been the one epitomized in the classic title *A History of the Warfare of Science with Theology in Christendom.* On this interpretation there is an inherent and irresolvable antagonism between the tenets of any religion that claims to base its life and doctrine on revealed truth, and the methods and results of a mode of inquiry that can acknowledge no authority except human intelligence. Inevitably, therefore, the conflict that erupted with Galileo's trial and condemnation has recurred, notably when Darwin published his theory of evolution, and inevitably the loser in this as in many other battles has been christian teaching. "Extinguished theologians," said one of Darwin's champions, "lie about the cradle of every science."

Partly in reaction to one-sided and simplistic versions of the thesis, it has been argued that, on the contrary, christian theology provided the soil in which one fundamental precondition of all scientific investigation could and did take root, namely the conviction that an orderliness and regularity can be discovered in the natural world. Medieval theologians, according to this argument, had worked out a doctrine of creation according to which the very existence of the universe depends entirely and at every moment upon the free decision of an infinitely intelligent God, a God neither arbitrary nor impersonal but conceived, as A.N. Whitehead put it, "as with the personal energy of Jehovah and with the rationality of a Greek philosopher." By the intelligibility of its orderly patterns, such a universe can be expected to reflect the orderly intelligence of the God who creates it; equally, its being a created rather than a self-sufficient universe means that all its regularities exist only *de facto*—contingently rather than necessarily. There is nothing that *must* be as it is, everything *might* be otherwise, and so the intelligibilities of nature cannot be deduced in advance. They have to be discovered. Presently, the founders of modern science set out to discover them.

This more recent argument may go some way towards explaining why science as the term is now used first appeared in christian Europe rather than in India or China, although just how much the appearance owed to Europe's Christianity remains a matter of scholarly debate. Less debatable and perhaps more significant is the fact that in 1600, despite

the religious upheavals of the previous century, European culture *was* still identifiably christian, whereas by 1700 it was not. For, in large measure, this momentous change was a result of the "scientific revolution," so called, which in Herbert Butterfield's well known words "outshines everything since the rise of Christianity and reduces the Renaissance and Reformation to the rank of mere episodes, mere internal displacements, within the system of medieval Christendom." Even if christian doctrine did pave the way for modern science, it was not long before modern science was heading in a direction of its own.

The case of Galileo has long been a stock example from which to argue that in so far as the revolution in science was also a revolt against something, Christianity is what is was against. Recent historical studies tend to avoid such black-and-white generalizations, but the episode remains an instructive one. The point at issue—whether the sun revolves around the earth or, as Copernicus had recently proposed, *vice versa*—seems straightforward enough. In fact, it was bound up with a knotty question that is even now a topic of lively debate: what exactly *is* scientific knowing? Galileo was not condemned for advocating Copernican cosmology on the ground that it explained astronomical observations more adequately than any other hypothesis. On that ground Copernicus himself had been content to argue: not Galileo. The new heliocentric system was not, in his judgment, the best available hypothesis; it simply was true—necessarily and therefore demonstrably true in the strict logical sense. Things could not possibly be otherwise; that the sun moves and not the earth was a flat impossibility. But there were good arguments against Copernicus which Galileo failed to refute, while the "demonstrations" he advanced to prove this allegedly necessary truth by reasoning from observations of tides and sunspots were not only unconvincing; they were not demonstrations. He was right, to be sure; but not for the reasons he claimed he was.

As for the theological side of the matter, Galileo's somewhat intransigent stance raised (not for the first time, or the last) the difficult question of how the Bible is to be understood. Does its religious meaning bear on other matters as well, on astronomy for instance? If not, where is the line to be drawn? If so, what about cases where biblical statements apparently contradict knowledge derived from other sources? Such questions were the more intractable in that by the time of Galileo christian scripture had long been combined with other texts that were deemed authoritative, to produce an impressively unified and all-encompassing worldview. Although three or four verses of the Bible, traditionally interpreted, did play a part in the controversy, it was not from these alone that Galileo's ecclesiastical opponents drew their conclusions. It was from the scriptural texts as threads in a tapestry into which had also been woven the wisdom of saints and sages and philosophers, Aristotle in particular. In some sense the conflict Galileo was involved in was less a contest between science and religion than an episode in the early modern rejection of authority as such: the authority of christian revelation, certainly, but with it the authority of Aristotle's physics, Ptolemy's astronomy, Galen's medicine, and the like.

In place of such inherited lore, it is often said that modern science took its stand on observation and experiment. But this too is an oversimplified account. Like most revolutions, the revolution in science was not a completely fresh beginning; Galileo's ideas on motion, for example, have been shown by recent scholarship to be heavily indebted to the work of his scholastic predecessors. Whatever the early modern experimenters may have claimed, they were not starting from scratch, and the philosophical tradition they brought to their work is as important as its results. Thus, while the authority against which Galileo and his successors set themselves most deliberately and explicitly was that of Aristotle, they were in fact maintaining a very Aristotelian notion of what science consists in when they insisted that scientific knowledge is knowledge of what cannot happen otherwise than it does and that the "laws of nature" which they formulated are true of necessity. But Aristotle himself considered that only mathematics, properly speaking, embodied his logical ideal of scientific knowledge, since all terrestrial changes (which belonged to the subject-matter of "physics" as he used the word) were more or less contingent and might happen differently; whereas Newton followed Galileo and Laplace followed Newton in holding that their new science of physics studied what necessarily and invariably happens, and that physical laws, once discovered, were unconditionally true.

Conceiving scientific knowledge in this way carries important consequences for religion in general and Christianity in particular, and it was not long before they were drawn. If the world runs the way it does because it cannot run otherwise—if it is a self-contained web of "cause" and "effect"—then clearly the doctrine of creation, at least in the form Thomas Aquinas, for example, gave it, has to go. And go it did. For Thomas, "creation" refers neither to an event nor to a change but to a relation. God alone exists necessarily; anything that God chooses to create exists, but only as a matter of contingent fact and in relation to God: it *is* inasmuch as God creates it, and its existence would otherwise be inexplicable. But for such a universe as

Newton was thought to have established, a law-abiding concatenation of particles moving in mathematically regular paths, no explanation is needed, except perhaps to account for how the whole business got started in the first place. In that case, however, creation could only be thought of as one particular event, which happened at some particular time, when God as it were wound up the celestial clockwork and set it ticking.

Such was the doctrine of the eighteenth-century Deists. For some of them, no doubt, it served to express genuine awe in the face of nature's marvelously ordered intricacy. Nevertheless it was a doctrine that did not open onto any further mystery; it had nothing to say about sin or redemption; and it was in any case a compromise. Although Newton himself seems to have held that occasionally the divine watchmaker needs to adjust the mechanism in order to keep the orbits of the planets lined up, Laplace, who ironed out this and a few other wrinkles that remained when Newtonian physics was applied to the solar system, could dispense with the deistic compromise entirely. Asked by Napoleon what part God played in his celestial mechanics, Laplace reportedly answered that he had no need for such a hypothesis. His universe rolled along quite nicely on its own.

So it was that however sincerely Kepler might refer to one of his astronomical works as "a sacred sermon, a veritable hymn to God the Creator," however solemnly the charter of the Royal Society for the Promotion of Natural Knowledge might charge its members with pursuing their work to the glory of God, science gradually repainted the picture of the universe that had informed Western minds and hearts for centuries—and, deliberately or otherwise, painted God out. Laplace added two of the finishing touches. He made explicit the determinism that the Newtonian world-machine implies, and he advanced a conception of probability that persisted well into the twentieth century. The two are closely connected, for the possibility that there are some events which occur randomly or by chance is antithetical to the idea of a universe completely governed by laws such as Newton's. Laplace accordingly denied the reality of any occurrence which, in itself, is more or less probable and so not wholly determined. He did allow that there may be, for the time being, degrees of probability in scientific knowledge *about* reality; but all this meant was that what statistical investigations disclose is not the nature of the world but merely the limitations of human knowing. Statistics could never be more than a cloak for ignorance.

The enormous success of the scientific enterprise in the eighteenth and nineteenth centuries gave it a prestige that remains, only a little tarnished, today. Other disciplines tend to be gauged according to their conformity with the procedures that work so well in physical science, and conversely the status of real knowledge is often withheld from the results of any inquiry that does not so conform. Ethics, politics, psychology, aesthetics, philosophy, economics—all have been faced with the choice of approximating to, or else distancing themselves from, the "hard" sciences. Theology has by and large adopted the latter policy, which admits of several variations. To borrow the metaphor of the warfare school, these might be classified as border skirmishes, retreats, uneasy truces, and surrenders.

Border-skirmishing is probably the least satisfactory response; basically it revives the strategy of the Deists by searching for aspects of the natural world that have not been explained scientifically—at least not yet—and assigning to them a supernatural cause. This has been called the "God of the gaps" approach. It attempts to find room with an otherwise scientific worldview for the activity of a God who is directly responsible, if not for "all that is, seen and unseen," at least for some of it now and then—for the origin of biological species, or the origin of the human soul, or for some other special class of occasions. Such tactics are doubly hazardous. On the one hand, since science progresses it may well fill tomorrow what seem like gaps today, while on the other hand a God who acts occasionally and interstitially, as one of many agents in the cosmos, is something less than God.

The strategy of retreat avoids this potential difficulty by accepting Kant's somewhat disingenuous claim to have established the boundaries of objective knowledge—by which he meant Newtonian science—in order to make room for faith. All "objective" reality must be surrendered into the hands of the scientists, while theology takes refuge in an altogether separate and permanently unassailable citadel. So long as it does not venture outside its proper realm, the interior, "subjective" realm of personal encounter or artistic spontaneity or both, Christianity can hope to enjoy freedom from the tyranny of unbreakable laws of causality. Such a partition of reality often goes along with a more or less justifiable criticism of the natural sciences: what is taken to be their disengaged, manipulative, "objectivizing" concern with technological power is set over against the existential meaning and value of human life. But the cost to theology of maintaining so stark a contrast is heavy: the doctrine of creation must be sacrificed entirely, along with any relation of the natural world to God.

Much the same kind of contrast, though without the implied or explicit disparagement of science, is typical of many uneasy truces. Most of these apply a separate-but-equal principle by arguing that science and religion are different, even disparate; however, for this reason they need not be antagonistic. Each is a distinct paradigm or horizon or language-game, an internally consistent way of thinking about and living in the world. One of them is characterized by reasoning that is conceptual, often logical, and sometimes mathematical; the other, by multifariously meaningful symbols and poetic narratives that engage affectivity as well as imagination; both, however, are valid ways of bestowing coherence and structure on the world. *Détente* on such terms, however, is more easily proclaimed than adhered to, for there is an intrinsic human exigence for unity that is not satisfied with separate, juxtaposed "worlds of discourse." How these worlds are related is a question that can and does arise, and to dismiss it unanswered as meaningless is to stifle a desire for understanding that animates theology as well as science.

Finally there is capitulation, which can be more or less complete. In order to recover the plausibility it has been losing for the last three hundred years, Christianity has not infrequently accommodated itself to what have presented themselves as scientific viewpoints. The "process theologies," for example, are built on a philosophy of organism that endeavored to take seriously the most sophisticated developments in evolutionary biology and especially in early twentieth-century physics. But the result substitutes for the (allegedly incoherent) God of classical theism, a God who is neither ultimate reality, nor one "with whom is no variableness or shadow of turning" (Jas 1:17), but a changing and changeable being, affected by every development in the universe, whose memory of human beings is the only salvation they can hope for. Somewhat closer to traditional Christianity is the work of Teilhard de Chardin, which draws more on biology than on physics to present a magnificent panorama of the universe moving through evolution towards an omega point that Teilhard identifies with Christ. What remains unclear is whether this Christ can be identified either with Jesus of Nazareth or with 'the only Son of God, eternally begotten of the Father." Both of these examples retain some notion of theology as reasoned discourse about God and about all things in relation to God. A more thorough capitulation would entirely replace theology in the classical sense with religious studies—the history, phenomenology, psychology, and sociology of religion—conceived as empirical disciplines that can emulate natural science in so far as they restrict their aim to explaining the data on human religiousness.

These four are not the only strategies that can be adopted—there is also extreme fundamentalism and what remains of orthodox scholasticism—but they do at least indicate the main lines followed in the twentieth century by christian theologians endeavoring to address questions that have arisen since the scientific revolution. And despite considerable variety they would seem to be in agreement in two respects. The first is that the natural sciences are largely if not wholly to blame for the fundamental religious crisis of modern times: loss of transcendence. It is not so much that God is dead as that he is irrelevant to the culture of the present time. The great, perennial human questions about the best way to live and what there is to live for have not disappeared, but it is widely felt they can be answered without going beyond the world of space and time—the world which some suppose the sciences have mastered, if not entirely, at least far enough to bestow on men and women the power to achieve virtually any ends they choose. Paradoxically, they can expect

no help in their choosing from either the natural or the human sciences, because the very idea of ends, of orientation or finality or purposiveness intrinsic to the natural order yet also pointing beyond it, was expelled from modern scientific thinking from the first. When Hobbes extended from planets to persons the mechanistic philosophy he thought was inseparable from science, he quite consistently denied that there is any *summum bonum* or Greatest Good to be pursued, either in this world or beyond it. His own view of human living turned instead on the avoidance of a Greatest Evil: death. Much the same stand was later taken by those Darwinists who saw mere survival as the basis of social as well as biological development; by Marx, who collapsed all human affairs into the workings of inviolable economic necessity; by Freud, who conceived human personality in terms of a quasi-mechanical accumulation and discharge of psychic energy. If these philosophies are, as they claim to be, scientifically based, then science is indeed a source of *malaise*.

Are they so based? The second point on which theology's usual strategies for dealing with modern science tend to agree is one they share with these typically modern ways of construing the world—namely, that modern science is what its proponents and popularizers have said it is. But as no less estimable a scientist than Einstein observed—and the observation applies to himself—anyone who would find out what science is should pay attention to what scientists do, not what they say. The history of science provides ample confirmation of what he meant. Side by side with the undeniable achievements that have followed the scientific revolution there is a story *about* those achievements, which has done much to shape popular attitudes and ideas but which does not stand up under scrutiny. Galileo claimed to have discovered necessary truths, but in point of fact natural science as it has been practiced since his time is concerned not with necessity but only with verifiable possibility, expressed in hypotheses which can be confirmed by observation and experiment. Again, Newton imagined that the moving bodies of which he thought the universe is comprised move in an "absolute" space and time, to which all observed extensions and durations are relative, but since Einstein it has come to be accepted that space and time themselves are variable, not absolute, and contemporary physicists aim at understanding entities which simply cannot be pictured. Again, Laplace's assertion of determinism and his disparagement of statistics have both been superseded, tentatively by Darwin's "chance variations," more recently and decisively by the indeterminacy or randomness that quantum physics finds in the nature of subatomic events.

It may be doubted whether theological border skirmishes into the "new physics" will be any more successful than similar maneuvers in the past. But twentieth-century developments in science do put its relations with theology in a new light. The mechanist determinism of the previous two hundred years has been exploded in principle, though in fact it can be expected to linger on, partly because it has seeped into the unstated philosophies that inform academic disciplines other than the natural sciences, but partly too because it lends support to the individualistic ethos of modern times: there is no need to take responsibility for a determined universe. By contrast, the indeterminate universe that actually exists is *ipso facto* a mysterious universe. Its very intelligibility is such as to allow for the fact of human freedom and moreover for the fact of God's existence as the ground of that intelligibility. This is a rather sweeping claim, however, which cannot be made good until two very basic problems have been dealt with.

First, there is a problem of education. "Scientism" has been defined as science out of bounds, and the whole of the present article has meant to suggest that extra-scientific views on questions that belong properly to philosophy—what is and is not real, what does and does not constitute objectivity, what can and cannot be known—have been blended with strictly scientific explanations of observable data since the seventeenth century. It has been these views, far more than science as such, which have provoked most of the warfare with christian theology. Unfortunately, the same views also makes their presence felt not only in the way science is taught but in other fields as well. Not that they are explicitly stated. It is more a matter of tending to equate "learning science" with storing up concepts suitable, as Bacon put it, for constraining nature to yield up her secrets; of making terms like "prove" and "theory" carry inappropriate epistemological freight; of taking on trust inherited accounts of the history of science that contemporary historians have abandoned.

Conversely, in the second place, there is a problem of theological method. It is clear that what passes for natural science has been a principal source of modern worldviews. Yet it can also be argued that "scientific worldview" is a contradiction in terms, unless "world" is defined as the sum of everything that is intrinsically conditioned by space and time. But such a definition begs the question, for about anything that is not so conditioned, science, as science, has nothing to say. If scientists declare that there *is* nothing else, or that what science cannot pronounce on cannot be known at all, they are speaking as amateur philosophers. But it is one thing to assert the existence of such transcendent realities—meaning, value, love, grace, not to mention God—

and another to show how it is convincingly and objectively possible to discuss them. Religious studies can offer little help; while there is ample data on human religiousness and its expression in different cultures and epochs, there is no data on God. It follows that if the only meaningful statements are those of an empirical science, there can be meaningful statements about religion, but not about a Creator who transcends his creation, much less about a Savior who redeems it. What is it, then, that Christians are doing when they make such statements about the God they worship? That is the question of theological method.

It was said at the outset that the question about the relationship between science and religion transposes a very fundamental question into a new context. If at present there are no definitive answers, that is partly an index of the range and complexity of the issues involved. But it also indicates that in its new context the question calls not only for new answers but for a new kind of answers. That they will be philosophical answers, broadly speaking, has been suggested here. More concretely, they will be answers drawn from the actual practice of scientists as scientists, of religious persons as religious, and of theologians as both.

See **Theology**

Ian G. Barbour, *Issues in Science and Religion,* Englewood Cliffs, NJ: Prentice-Hall, Inc. 1966. Patrick H. Byrne, "God and the Statistical Universe," *Zygon* 16 (1981), pp. 345-363. M.B. Foster, "The Christian Doctrine of Creation and the Rise of Modern Natural Science," *Mind* 43 (1934), pp. 446-468. Holmes Rolston, *Science and Religion: A Critical Survey,* New York: Random House, 1987. A.R. Peacocke, *Creation and the World of Science,* Oxford Press, 1979. A.R. Peacocke, *Science and the Christian Experiment,* Oxford Univ. Press, 1971.

CHARLES C. HEFLING, JR.

SEMI-PELAGIANISM

An attempt at a middle position on the theology of grace between an extreme Augustinianism and Pelagianism, it argued that a person could make the first step towards God which God must then confirm and bring to completion by his grace. It was condemned by the second Council of Orange in 529.

See **Grace**

SENSES OF SCRIPTURE

The Bible is "Word of God"—what does that mean? Only humans can communicate *in words*. This being so, when one designates a divine communication "word of God," one is asserting that God does truly communicate with humankind, but one asserts, too, that revelation by word of God is divine revelation which has been given human expression by humans. To grasp the meaning of the word of God we must discern the meaning of the text in and through which word of God is conveyed. It is obviously necessary to establish the literal meaning—the basic sense of scripture. The question remains: Does scripture convey meaning or meanings beyond the literal? The question has resonated down the centuries. It will suffice to note a response of the recent past.

The Literal Sense

There is agreement on the priority of the literal sense. Here the term is taken to indicate that meaning of the words of scripture intended by the biblical author. This meaning is to be determined by the historico-critical method of exegesis, complemented, as we have come to appreciate, by literary criticism. What we are looking at here is a theory of scriptural senses beyond the literal.

More-Than-Literal Senses

The contention is that, in the Bible, beyond the literal sense, there is present—to an extent not easily determined— a deeper literal sense, contained in the letter, but foreseen and intended only by the Holy Spirit. We may speak of a *fuller sense:* that fuller and deeper significance of a text which is intended by the divine author and which is discerned in the light of further revelation, particularly in the light of the NT. While the fuller sense is concerned with words, the *typical sense* arises when the persons or events or things designated in the primary sense typify persons and events and things of a higher order and when this significance is divinely intended. For example, we hear from the NT that Melchizedek is a type of Christ (Heb 7:1-3), that the crossing of the Red Sea is a type of baptism (1 Cor 10:1-2) and that the brazen serpent raised up by Moses is a type of Jesus on the cross (Jn 4:14-15).

This typical sense is firmly based on a primary literal sense, for the significant facts or "types," which are the object of the typical sense, find their place in the Bible and are known only through the text. Abraham sacrificing his son and the manna feeding the people in the desert are types of Calvary and the eucharist only insofar as these events are recorded by the writer and under the form in which he has recorded them. A biblical type is founded not alone on a historical reality but also on a literary existence. It may happen that the literary existence is the only real one: Jonah is a literary, not a historical, figure (cf. Mt 12:38-41). The essential factor is that the typical sense must be sought and found in the words of scripture.

The Fuller Sense

In the twentieth century and, for practical purposes, in the 1950's and 1960's, the pursuit of a secondary sense of scripture took a particular turn in Roman Catholic circles: a pursuit of the *sensus plenior* or "fuller sense." More than any other, R.E. Brown has contributed to the study. He makes the point that NT exegesis of the OT might be characterized, in general, as more-than-literal exegesis.

He proposes a definition of the *sensus plenior:* "The Sensus Plenior is the deeper meaning, intended by God but not clearly intended by the human author, that is seen to exist in the words of scripture when they are studied in the light of further revelation or of development in the understanding of revelation." One may acknowledge fuller senses within each Testament (and not only within an OT-NT relationship); and fuller senses may be uncovered through development in post-biblical understanding of revelation.

There are two especially important kinds of fuller sense. The first is more restricted and is connected with the OT passages which have been classically identified as prophecies referring to Christ and to the christian dispensation; the theory of Sensus Plenior permits the Christian to retain at once the literal OT sense and the christian prophetic sense of these passages. The second form, the general Sensus Plenior, pertains to the field of biblical theology: it is the fuller meaning uncovered when a text has been placed in a wider biblical context. Two criteria have been proposed: (1) The Sensus Plenior must be homogeneous with the literal sense, developing what the author wanted to say; (2) authoritative interpretation of the words of scripture— even in later authentic tradition of the church. Yet, when all is said and done, it is not without significance that the proponents of a fuller sense have seldom appealed to it in practical exegesis but have kept it for discussion on the theoretical level. Perhaps the prime contribution of the discussion is as a reminder that historical-critical exegesis of a scriptural text does not exhaust its meaning.

The Text

Nowadays one hears little of more-than-literal senses. It is evident that a fuller sense theory had a close connection with a neo-scholastic theory of scriptural inspiration which is now abandoned. What prevails today is a more elastic and more realistic understanding of inspiration. In a specifically christian sense scriptural inspiration means that the Bible is experienced by the faith community as animated by the Spirit of Christ and as communicating the truth and power of the Spirit—and this means acknowledging the patent presence of the Spirit of God in the OT. An equally important factor is the role of those who receive the written word—the degree to which the church and the individual are able to recognize the Spirit in the writings.

Perhaps more decisively, the latest trend in biblical interpretation is to concentrate on the *text*. That is to say, it is recognized that biblical criticism is, necessarily, literary criticism—the Bible *is* literature. Yet, the realization that a text has a life of its own does not justify arbitrary interpretation; a text cannot be made to say just anything one may wish it to say. In this connection the contention (in some structuralist theory) that a text is quite independent of its author (as though it mattered not at all who wrote it) is surely misguided. Any given writing has a historical setting and is culturally conditioned. What is true is that a text— and we are dealing with classic texts— may have a meaning beyond that which the author had in mind, a meaning, or meanings, perceived by the reader. It should be clear that one is not thinking of arbitrary meanings but of meanings which the text can sustain.

It would seem that in a reasonable concern to discover the intention of an author (but who can hope to pin down the intent of an ancient writer?) we had tended to neglect the one tangible factor: the text. For it has to be admitted that preoccupation with tradition and author did tend to get in the way of the text. Concern with the "senses of Scripture" has to be a paramount interest of biblical studies. How we discern that meaning or those meanings will be best served not by clinging to theories of the past but through openness to approaches and perspectives that may lead to fresh understanding of the Word.

See **Biblical Criticism, Holy Spirit**

R.E. Brown, "Hermeneutics," JBC, 610-623. W. Harrington, *The Path of Biblical Theology,* Dublin: Gill and Macmillan, 1973, pp. 282-313.

WILFRID HARRINGTON, OP

SENSUS PLENIOR
See **Senses of Scripture**

SEXUALITY

In 1975, the Sacred Congregation for the Doctrine of the Faith issued a *Declaration on Certain Questions Concerning Sexual Ethics* in which sexuality is acknowledged "as one of the factors which give to each individual's life the principal traits that distinguish it." The *Declaration* continues by affirming that, in fact, "it is from sex that the human person receives the characteristics which, on the biological, psychological and spiritual levels, make that person a man or a woman, and thereby largely condition his or her progress towards maturity and insertion into society" (#1). Given the immense influence which it exerts upon an individual's character and growth, it is important and logical that Christians should attempt to understand sexuality within the context of their calling both as human beings and as Christians.

The Meaning of Sexuality

In no way is the significance of sexuality arbitrarily determined. Christians discover, rather, that its meaning is derived essentially from the spiritual meaning of their lives as human beings. As a people of faith, Christians realize that humanity has been loved into being; created out of love, we are made for love. We live because God loves us, and to the extent that we live with his life inside us, we are enabled to love even as he has first loved us. In its truest form christian living is, as James Nelson suggests, an extension of the Incarnation, a continuation of Christ's embodiment of God's love for us. Thus by professing to be Christians, we commit ourselves to giving an affirmative response to God's expectation that love will become flesh in our attitudes and actions.

Sexuality plays a crucial role in the ability to answer our call to love, for it is sexuality which reveals both our incompleteness and our relatedness, and in our sexuality we find the biological, emotional and psychological grounding of our capacity to love. Sexuality, in fact, is nothing less, says Nelson, than "God's ingenious way of calling us into communion with others through our need to reach out and touch and embrace—emotionally, intellectually, physically." As such, sexuality is simply essential both to our human existence and to our becoming fully human.

Because our lives are to be spent in loving others, sexual expression, whatever else it may involve, must be for Christians an externalization of love; it must be love-in-action. Explicit physical sexual relationships are meant to be embodiments of love, but they neither exhaust the possible ways of loving, nor are they always appropriate. We must be loving always, and we cannot avoid being sexual in our relationships, but we simply are not always engaged in, or desirous of explicit genital or physical sexual unions. There is something special about the physical love-expression of human sexuality, and its distinctiveness must be discovered and preserved.

Biblical Data

Our understanding of the special character of human sexuality is rooted deep within the Judeo-christian tradition. As Christians, we have received from Christ the radical charge that we are to love one another even as he has first loved us (Jn 15:12). We are called, then, not just to love, but to a special kind of love, and there is no dimension of human living which is exempt from the challenge of Christ's command. Thus within the specific area of physical sexual expression, it is expected that the love which such activity must embody and reflect will be a manifestation of the kind and quality of love shown us by Christ, whose love is itself nothing less than a revelation of the Father's love for us.

God's selfless and unconditional love is eminently revealed in the history of his creative and faithful covenant with us, and it is this covenant which serves as the model for the creative and faithful love that is the necessary and desired context for human expressions of physical sexuality. To say that God's creative and faithful love serves as the norm for physical love-expressions of sexuality is to say that when it fully reflects its ideal, or when it embodies its full richness, human sexual love is both open to procreation and intent upon permanence. Sexual expression is meant to communicate both life and love, and to do so within the embrace of a commitment to exclusive and permanent fidelity in imitation of God's life-giving and faithful covenant with his people.

Sexual love's characteristics of procreativity and unitive fidelity are highlighted in the creation stories of Genesis. Man and woman are simultaneously created in God's image and likeness, and after having been blessed by God, they are given the mission of being fruitful, of multiplying and of filling the earth (Gen 1:27-28). An older account of creation (Gen 2:18-25) portrays God as first creating man, but becoming concerned over man's loneliness, God fashions him a companion. Woman is bone of man's bone and flesh of his flesh; each reflects the face of God, and each is drawn to fulfillment in relationship with the other. "This is why a man leaves his father and mother and joins himself to his wife, and they become one body" (v. 24). In marriage, a man and woman are so empowered to become one that they belong to each other only and forever.

The Genesis accounts suggest several themes: man and woman equally embody the glory of God; sexuality is a good gift of God's creation, and in no way is it a cause for shame; the differentiation of the sexes establishes humanity's procreative possibility, and in the complementary nature of the two sexes, human beings are offered the best opportunity for the realization of their fulfillment.

So uniquely precious is the marital relationship of man and woman that some of the Jewish prophets (Hosea, chaps. 1-3, and Ezekiel, chap. 16) see it as a living symbol of God's union with his people. Later, the NT affirms that the marital relationship is a reflection of the union of Christ with the church (Eph 5:31-32). It is realized, finally, that God's covenant with humanity and a man and woman's marital commitment are so much alike that the two realities are reciprocally illuminative: God is as close to us as a husband and wife are to each other, and a husband and wife are to be as loving and faithful to each other as God is to his people.

With God's creative and faithful love as the model for human love, scripture endorses heterosexual, monogamous, permanent and procreative marital relationships as the normative context for physical sexual expression. In this matter, Christians are responding to the promptings and exhortations of a personal God whose manner of loving we are called to incarnate. Within marriage, the pleasures of sexuality are to be enjoyed mutually by spouses who must resist any inclination to use sex as a weapon (1 Cor 7:3-5). Being numbered, moreover, among God's covenantal people means that our bodies are members of the body of Christ and temples of the Holy Spirit; they are to be used, therefore, only for the glory of God (1 Cor 6:15-20) in a way that is "holy and honorable, not giving way to selfish lust like the pagans who do not know God" (1 Thess 4:5). God's people are cautioned that no one "who actually indulges in fornication or impurity or promiscuity— which is worshipping a false god—can inherit anything of God's kingdom" (Eph 5:5). Scripture, in general, offers numerous specific condemnations of deviations from the norm of loving and life-giving marital expressions of sexuality; prohibited are: adultery (Lev 20:10; Gen 39:9; Sir 23:16-21; Exod 20:14; Deut 5:18; Mk 7:22; Mt 5:28; 15:19; 1 Cor 6:9); fornication (Sir 42:10; Deut 22:13-21; Lev 19:29); *porneia* or "sexual immorality" (Mk 7:21; Mt 15:19; 1 Cor 5:9-11; 7:2; 2 Cor 12:21; Gal 15:19); and homosexual acts (Lev 18:22; 20:13; Rom 1:27; 1 Cor 6:9).

Theological Tradition

As Christianity spread beyond the boundaries of Israel, it was influenced by several intellectual currents running at the time. Platonism, Stoicism and the dualistic teachings of Gnosticism and Manicheism all left their impressions upon the christian outlook toward sexuality. By way, primarily, of Augustine (354-430) Christianity absorbed some of the Manichean suspicion concerning the human body and sexuality. But such an attitude is scarcely compatible with the essential christian beliefs that there is one Creator of all realities, that this Creator is good beyond measure, and that, therefore, there is nothing that has been created which is evil in itself. For Christianity, then, there develops a built-in uncomfortableness with any view that regards the body and sexuality as evil, and throughout its theological history, Christians have been trying to understand more precisely the relationship that exists between the human spirit and the human body.

In its attempts to understand the nature of the human person, Christianity has been greatly influenced by Thomas Aquinas (c. 1225-1274) who introduced much of the western world to the thinking of Aristotle. Aristotelianism and Thomism affirm that there is an essential interplay of body and spirit in the human person. The individual, therefore, is not simply a spirit enslaved in a body; rather a person is an embodied spirit, an ensouled body. Both body and spirit are essential to the person. In this context, when the question was asked about the meaning and purpose of sexuality, the latter was rather immediately and primarily identified with its biological or physical dimension. The question thus became: What is the purpose of this biological process or faculty called sexuality? In this way, the question was reduced to the same level as such questions: What is the faculty of sight for? What is the faculty of speech for? The answers were considered to be obvious. Sight is for seeing, speech is for talking, sex is for procreating. Since procreation was thus regarded as the basic purpose of sexuality, it was seen as necessary that children should be properly prepared for and provided with a suitable atmosphere for growth. Hence, sexual expression was directly associated with the institution of marriage as the proper context for sexual expression leading ultimately to the birth and nurturing of children.

Using one's sexual faculty to provide for the continuation of the human race was seen as an expression of the natural order of things. It constituted a part of the so-called natural law. Deliberately to exclude this purpose from the use of one's sexual faculty was regarded as a violation of the natural law. The idea of the natural law has been an undeniably influential factor shaping the understanding of sexuality in traditional Roman Catholic thinking and teaching. Recognizing the finality or purpose of the sexual faculty is seen as a critical reference point for sexual morality. It is respect for this finality or purpose which ensures moral goodness, provided, of course, that the desire for, and openness to, procreation is shared with someone to whom the individual is committed in a marital union. According to the 1975 *Declaration on Certain Questions Concerning Sexual Ethics,* the objective standard to be used in evaluating sexual expression is this: My action must "preserve the full sense of mutual self-giving and human procreation in the context of true love" (#5). This is also the teaching of the *Pastoral Constitution on the Church in the Modern World* (G.S. 51).

The medievalists were encouraged in their view that procreation constitutes the natural purpose or finality of sexual expression, because it is this finality of sexuality which the human species shares in common with other animal species. To observe the natural law in the area of sexuality means, therefore, that when we express ourselves fully in a physical sexual way, we must do so in a manner that allows for the possibility of procreating. As the medievalists saw it, this meant that there must be insemination or the depositing of semen in the vagina.

On the basis of this biological understanding of the requirement of the natural law, two categories of sin or evil are distinguished. Sins *against* nature are those where the natural process of insemination does not occur (masturbation, sodomy, fellatio, cunnilingus, contraception and bestiality); such acts are essentially non-procreative. In addition to these acts, there are others which constitute sins *according to* nature; here, insemination, the natural biological function of the sex act, occurs, but the distinctively human aspects of sexuality are violated (fornication, adultery, rape and incest). Because the generative power of sexual activity is more universal in that it is common to humanity and other species, procreation came to be seen as the primary purpose of sexuality, while the fostering of a mutual relationship of love, a power reserved to human beings, was relegated to the status of a secondary purpose of sexual expression.

Critics of the natural-law emphasis regarding sexuality say that it has produced a morality of "physicalism" whereby individual acts are ethically evaluated simply on the basis of the physical structure of the acts themselves, without sufficient reference to the persons performing them. In addition, the natural law perspective is confronted with the charge of "biologism" in that it perceives human sexuality too much in terms of the physical processes involved, with not enough attention being paid to the affective and psychological dimensions of sex which are just as real as the biological.

Vatican II's *Gaudium et Spes* affirms that coital expressions of conjugal love have substantial value independent of procreation. Marital acts of love are called "noble" and "worthy," and in their truly human expression, they "signify and promote that mutual self-giving by which spouses enrich each other with a joyful and a thankful will" (49). At the same time, however, conjugal love is related to the procreation and education of children, who are, indeed, the "ultimate crown" (48) of this love. Moreover, precisely as "the supreme gift of marriage," children "contribute very substantially to the welfare of their parents" (50).

In elaborating further upon the place of children in married life, *Gaudium et Spes* urges that, "while not making the other purposes of matrimony of less account. ... parents should regard as their proper mission the task of transmitting human life and educating those to whom it has been transmitted" (50). On this point, however, the document steadfastly refuses to employ the traditional terminology of a "hierarchy of goals or ends" whereby the procreation and education of children is referred to as the primary purpose of conjugal sexuality, while the expression and fostering of love between spouses is designated as the secondary purpose of marital sex.

According to the official legislative history of the Council, various amendments to this text were proposed, calling for a reassertion of the idea of a "hierarchy of ends," that is, the distinction between primary and secondary purpose or goals. However, all of these amendments, one of which stated explicitly that "conjugal love is ordained to the primary end of marriage, which is offspring," were rejected. Thus conjugal sexuality is seen as having dual purposes, but the Council Fathers broke tradition in refusing to rank these purposes first and second.

Two Dimensions of Sexuality

Historically, sexual morality has, perhaps, too facilely implied that all sex prior to marriage is exploitative, while within marriage no sex is such. In truth, however, exploitation in sex is possible both inside of and outside of marriage precisely to the extent that sex becomes impersonal and, consequently, inhuman. If the peculiar personal and human dimensions of sexuality are to be maintained, we must, at the very least, appreciate the fact that in human beings, sexuality is far more deeply rooted and more pervasive than genital expression. Putting it simply, if there is more to the human person than biology, then there is more to sexuality than genital pleasure.

Genitality is only one dimension of human sexuality; failure to realize this, reduces sexuality to genitality and sexual fulfillment is subsequently equated with genital orgasm. What needs emphasizing today is the fact that while the genitals are important symbols of our sexuality, they are not its only focus. There is a whole other dimension to human sexuality, namely, the social or affective dimension which shows itself in the human capacity to relate to others with emotional warmth, compassion, and tenderness. All of these human qualities are rooted in sexuality and are true expressions of it, but they are not specifically genital in nature or focus.

Surely, when we act as loving individuals, we are acting as sexual beings, but we are not necessarily involved genitally. In fact, in some loving relationships there is never any question of genital involvement, while in other relationships the genital expression of love may be more or less important and imperative. It is not unusual to find that to the extent that the affective dimension of sexuality is undeveloped and unappreciated, preoccupation with the genital or physical aspects of sexuality increases significantly. This often leads to behavior which is destructive and/or futile, because although physical sexual needs surely are real, they are not the highest human needs, and if these latter human needs go unrecognized and remain unmet, no satisfaction of our physical sexual needs is likely to result in a sense of human fulfillment.

Psychologists make much of the fact that it is not unusual for people to attempt to address their needs for human sexual fulfillment, self-acceptance and a sense of belonging by satisfying their desire for sexual pleasure by means of relationships involving genital contact. The need, however, for affirmation and for relationships of real intimacy is much more fundamental and more powerful

than the need for genital expression itself, and it is not as easily fulfilled. Experience often enough proves that genital relationships provide no guarantee for the realization of intimacy; no less does experience bear witness to the fact that intimacy is possible without genital expression. It seems that when the higher, greater, or more powerful human needs are being met, our lower needs are more manageable, even as their fulfillment is more gratifying. One key, then, to keeping the physical or genital dimension of a relationship in proper perspective is to develop the affective dimension of sexuality. It is, indeed, possible to live fully and happily without the pleasing experience of genital sexuality, but it is not possible to do so without developed affective sexual relationships.

Sexuality, Chastity and Love

Many theologians today are proposing a sexual morality that makes sense in terms of personal relationships. More and more, it is acknowledged that sex does not create a relationship; rather, it expresses a relationship that already exists. The question being asked is whether or not the physical sexual relationship corresponds to the depth of intellectual, emotional and interpersonal commitment that is shared by two people. Bishop John A. T. Robinson has made the suggestion that chastity is honesty in sex; it implies, in other words, that we have "physical relationships that *truthfully express* the degree of personal commitment" that is shared with another. What this means is that two people, in their physical sexual relationship, should not transcend, or go beyond, the degree of activity that is appropriate for the commitment that actually exists between them.

The criterion of honesty is not verified by what two people tell each other about the level of their mutual commitment, but rather by whether or not their physical sexual expression exceeds or goes beyond their overall level of mutual commitment, regardless of what, or how much, they tell each other.

Once chastity is described as honesty in sex, it becomes necessary to distinguish between chastity and virginity. There are obviously people who give up their virginity but who in no way abandon their lives of chastity. Such people are spouses whose physical relationships give honest testimony to the deep commitment and love which they share. Chastity is for all people and not just for those who are single. Spouses are, ideally, chaste non-virgins. At the same time, however, it is possible to be an unchaste virgin, which simply means that a person may retain his or her physical virginity but still be involved in a relationship that is not honest in terms of physical sexual expression. Thus the question of chastity should arise in a relationship before the question of virginity because often chastity is forgotten long before virginity is lost.

Donald Goergen identifies chastity as a virtue that accepts a person's striving for pleasure and "attempts to put that striving in the service of other human and Christian values." More specifically, he says that chastity moderates one's sexuality and enables a person to place genitality's intense physical pleasure at the service of love. It must be said, of course, that while genital sexual expression is properly limited to those relationships which embody a living love, it would be quite another thing to say that relationships of love are limited to those in which physical or genital sexual expression would be appropriate. Such a stance, in fact, could never be maintained, because the reality of love is far more inclusive or more comprehensive than the reality of genital sex. In other words, even though it is argued that genital sexual expressions should be limited or confined to relationships in which love has come to life, love is certainly not confined or limited to expressions of physical or genital sexuality. Thus, while it is true that love is always a necessary condition for expression of genital sexuality, love is not always a sufficient condition for these expressions; rather a special form of love, namely, pledged or committed love, must provide the setting for genital sexuality.

Moreover, while genital expression should reflect the level of personal commitment between two people, love itself may very well decide sometimes that such expression would be inappropriate, precisely because it would be unloving, and must, therefore, be curtailed or sacrificed. Thus, for example, husbands and wives may refrain from sexual intercourse with their spouses out of consideration for their physical or emotional well-being. Such sensitivity reflects one of the key insights of the christian tradition, namely, that true love is distinct from physical sex. Genital sex is not the primary language or ultimate proof of love; rather, the greatest proof of love is caring for others even to the point of self-sacrifice (Jn 15:13). In one way or another, the lover must die to self so as to live for the beloved.

Conclusion

Once it is clear that the meaning of human sexual expression is not adequately defined in terms of the natural law with its emphasis on procreation, a fuller and more personal understanding of sexuality emerges, one which makes clear who we are, not only biologically, but also psychologically, socially, affectively and theologically. Sexuality plays an essential role in the task we face of becoming fully human. It is also a crucial factor in the mission we enjoy as Christians, namely, the offering of God's love to all people. For it is our nature as sexual beings that enables us to be lovers, but it is a special kind of love which must be the context for our expressions of genital sexuality.

Any human relationship which deserves to be called loving involves concern and caring for the other, but in order for genital intimacy to be a proper part of a relationship, not only must the people involved be open to procreation, but also each must assume unconditional responsibility for the other. The promise and decision to live not only with, but also for, one's beloved are a crucial part of the truth that is proclaimed in the act of sexual intercourse. The body-giving of physical intercourse is an in-the-flesh expression of the self-giving which is the essence of love. For this reason, the act cannot honestly be entered into casually.

Sexual intercourse is an act of self-revelation and self-giving which is so complete that it bears the potential of creating another life. As such, the act is too awe-inspiring to be risked with anyone who is not appreciative of both one's beauty and one's faults. The only time genital intimacy tells the whole truth of the beauty and power of human sexuality is when it signifies that a man and woman have united themselves as one and are willing to have their mutual love find fulfillment in the creation of new life.

James T. Burtchaell, *For Better, For Worse: Sober Thoughts on Passionate Promises,* Paulist Press, 1985. Lisa Sowle Cahill, *Between the Sexes. Foundations for a Christian Ethics of Sexuality,* Fortress Press and Paulist Press, 1985. Donald Goergen, *The Sexual Celibate,* Seabury Press, 1974. James B. Nelson, *Embodiment, An Approach to Sexuality and Christian Theology,* Augsburg Publishing House, 1978.

VINCENT J. GENOVESI, SJ

SIMUL IUSTUS ET PECCATOR

The phrase means "at once justified and a sinner." It became a sort of slogan of the Reformation doctrine of justification, and in its strictest meaning it implies that a Christian, although justified in Christ, remains in himself a sinner. If this means that justification is merely an external or forensic declaration of God, without altering the very being of the Christian before God, it is rejected by the church. But it can be used in a Catholic sense if it means the total dependence of the Christian's status before God on grace and the fact that the Christian is never utterly without sin.

See **Grace, Justification**

SIN

This article is concerned with sin as a personal act. Thus it does not treat of original sin. It is divided into the following major parts: (1) the reality and central meaning of sin; (2) the distinction between mortal and venial sin; (3) the way of sin to death.

1. The Reality and Central Meaning of Sin

A. Biblical Teaching. The basic features of sin are dramatically portrayed in the story of the "fall" in Gen 3:1-24. A known precept of God is deliberately violated (Gen 3:3-6). At the heart of the outward act of disobedience is an inner act of disrespect, one motivated partially by suspicion regarding God's loving concern for human persons, partially by irritation over the limits imposed by God's precept, and partially by a desire for the immediate good promised by the performance of the sinful act. The act of rebellion has harmful consequences for the sinners themselves (Gen 3:7) and damages their relation with God and with each other (Gen 3:8-24). Faced with their sinful deed, the sinners try to defend themselves by specious rationalizations (Gen 3:8-13), but these are of no help in preventing the disastrous effects of their sin (Gen 3:14-24).

In wanting "to be like gods," our

progenitors, here typifying each of us. wanted to substitute themselves for God in deciding between good and evil. In setting themselves up as the arbiters of good and evil they refused to recognize God as the one on whom they and all else depended, thereby perverting the relationship between God and humankind.

This notion of sin as a perverse revolt against God is central to OT thought. Sin is rebellion against the Lord (Num 14:9; Deut 28:15), a contemptuous spurning of God (2 Sam 12:10; Isa 1:4; 43:24; Mic 4:6). Viewed from the perspective of divine wisdom, sin is branded a "foolishness" (Deut 32:6; Isa 29:11; Prov 1:7). Seen from the perspective of God's holiness, it is declared an "abomination" (Lev 16:16; 18:26; Judg 20:6). Seen from the perspective of the covenant between God and his people, sin is recognized as an act of unfaithfulness and adultery (Isa 24:5; 48:8; Jer 3:20; 9:1; Ezek 16:59; Hos 3:1). While it is true that once the covenant is established, sin does violence to it, one must not conclude that sin is limited to covenant violations. The chosen people's idolatry was sinful even before the establishment of the covenant (Ezek 20:7-8), and the prophets denounced vehemently the sins of pagan nations who had no special covenant relationship with God (Amos 1:3-2:3). Moreover, St. Paul taught that pagans living outside the covenant knew enough of God by virtue of the "law" written in their hearts to sin truly by their willingness to engage in immoral acts (Rom 1:18-22; 2:14-16).

Aside from a few passages which reflect a primitive view of sin as the violation, however unintended, of a "taboo" (1 Sam 6:6-7), the OT consistently teaches that sin is rooted in human freedom and consists in an abuse of the gift of free choice (Sir 15:11-20), that it springs from the "heart" of a person, and as such is an act involving a personal, inner, and enduring wrong (1 Sam 16:7; Jer 4:4; Ezek

11:19; Ps 51). And this teaching of the OT is fully ratified in the NT (see, e.g., Mk 7:20-23).

A rich vocabulary is used in both Testaments to describe the reality and evil of sin. In the OT three of the most commonly used words to designate sin are *hāttā'*, *pesha'*, and *'awōn*. *Hāttā'*, which literally means "missing the mark," stresses sin as a willful rejection of the known will of God. *Pesha'*, meaning "rebellion," shows how in sinning human persons reject God and his love. *'Awōn*, meaning "iniquity" or "guilt," refers to the way in which sin twists and distorts the sinner's inner being. Among the terms used in the NT to refer to sin we find *hamartia* and *hamartēma*, *anomia*, *adikia*, *pseudos* and *skotos*. *Hamartia* and *hamartēma* are like the OT *hāttā'*, and designate sin as a freely chosen deed casting aside God's loving norms for human life. *Anomia*, literally meaning "lawlessness" and frequently used in the singular, stresses that sin consists in a spirit of rebellion and contempt for God and his law. *Adikia*, "injustice," emphasizes that sin is a refusal to accept God and his reign revealed in Christ and to live in the justice that God has given; *pseudos*, "falsehood," and *skotos*, "darkness," reveal sin as an opposition to the truth of God, to Jesus Christ, who is the way, the truth, and the life, to one's fellow men, and to the truth of being a human person.

The OT teaching on sin is masterfully summarized in Psalm 51, the *Miserere*, which is rightly considered as a brief compendium of OT thought on the reality and evil of sin. The initial verses of this Psalm, in which David prays for forgiveness for his sin of adultery with Bathsheba, draw together the OT view of sin in a fascinating way: "Have mercy on me, O God, according to your unfailing love; according to your great compassion *blot out my transgressions (pesha')*. Wash away all my iniquity (*'awōn*), and cleanse me from my sin (*hāttāt*). For I know my transgressions (*pesha'*), and my sin (*hāttā't*) is always before me. Against you, you only, have I sinned (*hātā'*), and done what is evil (*ra'*) in your sight" (Ps 51:1-4). Note that here David identifies his sin by all three of the major OT terms. In committing adultery he had rebelled against God's precepts, deviated from the path they marked out and made himself wicked and hateful to the Lord. Note, too, the acknowledgment that sin is a terrible evil precisely because it offends God ("against you, you only, have I sinned"). In saying this David is in no way denying that his sin of adultery was a terrible injustice to Bathsheba's husband; rather, he is stressing that sin is essentially a base affront to God, the arbiter of good and evil and the one whose holy will and loving plan for mankind—a will and plan concerned only with the authentic good of human persons (see Deut 6:24)—is the norm for human action. Finally, in this prayer of repentance David begs the Lord to create in him a new heart, to heal him of his sin (Ps 51:10). In so praying he stresses another major biblical teaching on sin, namely that only God can forgive sin and bring the sinner back to life.

While sin is regarded essentially as an offense against God, sin does not hurt or harm God in his inner being, for God as the wholly transcendent One can in no way be harmed by the actions of his creatures. Rather sin harms the sinner (Job 35:6; Isa 59:1-2; Jer 7:8, 19). Nonetheless, sin does wound God in his "image," i.e., in the human person he has made to share in his life. As a refusal on the part of sinners to let themselves be loved by God, sin, in a certain sense, harms the "God who suffers from not being loved, whom love has, so to speak, rendered 'vulnerable'" (S. Lyonnet, "Sin" in *Dictionary of Biblical Theology,* ed. X. Leon-Dufour. Rev. ed., New York:

Seabury, 1973, pp. 550-555).

All these OT themes on sin are taken up and deepened in the NT. The deeper understanding of sin as separation from God stems from the deeper understanding in the NT of the loving intimacy that God wills to share with humankind. The Father so loves us that he sends his only-begotten Son to be with us and for us, actively seeking to reconcile sinners with himself. Thus sin is seen as a refusal of the Father's love (Lk 15), a refusal rooted in the heart. At its core, sin is a free, self-determining choice to reject God's offer of grace and friendship. Just as light and darkness have nothing in common, so neither do the life offered us in Christ and the Spirit and the iniquity of sin (2 Cor 6:34). Jesus and the devil, belief and unbelief, God and idols are absolutely opposed; so too are uprightness and iniquity (2 Cor 6:15-16).

There is a distinct tendency in the NT to shift the focus from individual sinful acts (the plural *hamartiai, hamartēmata*) to sin itself (the singular *hē hamartia, hē adikia*). This is particularly manifest in the Johannine and Pauline literature. Sin (in the singular) is lawlessness (*hē anomia;* 1 Jn 3:4) and unrighteousness (*hē adikia;* 1 Jn 5:17). The sinner is from the devil (1 Jn 3:8) and is the slave of sin (Jn 8:34). Sin endures in the sinner and is opposed to the truth (1 Jn 3:6-9). Paul treats sin not only as a state or condition but as the common human condition. Without excusing anyone—for sin is a deliberate, willful act—he presents a world in which sin reigns and is overcome only by the reign of Christ and complete submission to him (Rom 5–8). He sees sin as a power that has entered into human persons by their voluntary submission to it, reigning in their "flesh" as a kind of pseudo-law. In short, in the NT sin is much more the unitary reality of one's single state of alienation from God than the multiple reality of an individual's many wicked deeds. Sins are sins because they give rise to and prolong life apart from God. The good news, the *eu-angelion,* is that God has himself come to visit his people, to call them to repentance, to reconcile them to himself. This he does in the saving death-resurrection of Jesus, a saving act in which all can share by dying to sin in baptism and rising, in baptism, to a new kind of life made possible by God's only-begotten Son's redemptive deed and by the gift of the Spirit, who will be with this re-created people, leading them along a path of righteousness and honor.

B. *Theological Understanding.* One way to develop a theological understanding of sin is to begin with some famous definitions of sin offered by St. Augustine and to comment on them with the help of insights provided by St. Thomas Aquinas, other theologians, and the teaching of the church. While Augustine offered many descriptions and "definitions" of sin, two have become classic. The first defines sin as "anything done, said, or desired against the eternal law" (factum, dictum, vel concupitum contra legem aeternam) (*Contra Faustum,* 22.27). The second defines sin as a "turning away from God and turning toward the creature"(aversio a Deo, conversio ad creaturam) (*De libero arbitrio,* 2.53).

The first definition, with its emphasis on sin as a willed violation of the eternal law, is not regarded too favorably by some contemporary writers who prefer to define sin as a rupturing of a personal relationship with God. Their fear is that this Augustinian definition provides, or at least can be interpreted as providing, a "legalistic" notion of sin as the infraction of some externally and arbitrarily imposed norm. But if we keep in mind the traditional Catholic understanding of law as a wise and loving order of human persons to the goods—and the Good— perfective of them, we can see the good sense of this definition. The teaching of

Vatican Council II is relevant here. Recapitulating the tradition rooted in scriptures and in the thought of theologians such as Augustine and Aquinas, Vatican Council II taught that "the highest norm of human life is the divine law—eternal, objective, and universal—whereby God orders, directs, and governs the entire universe and all the ways of the human community by a plan conceived in wisdom and love." Continuing, the Council said, "Man has been made by God to participate in this law, with the result that, under the gentle disposition of divine providence, he can come to perceive ever increasingly the unchanging truth" (D.H. 3; cf. also G.S. 16-17).

This passage makes it clear that there is an objective moral order, one that finds its ultimate expression in the divine and eternal law. It likewise holds that human persons have the capacity, given to them by God himself, to know the demands of this law, this "truth" about what they are to do if they are to be the beings God wills them to be. Although this passage does not use the expression "natural law," its authors evidently considered the "natural law" to be the participation by human persons in God's loving plan for the human community, for at the end of the passage they added a note explicitly referring to three important texts of St. Thomas. In one of these texts Aquinas said: "The eternal law is unchanging truth, and everyone somehow knows this truth, at least the common principles of the natural law, even though in other matters some people share more and some less in the knowledge of the truth" (S.Th. I-II, 93, 2; the other texts are 91, 1, and 93, 1). In short, the eternal law is the wise and loving plan of God for the good of human persons, and so great is God's respect for them that he has made them able to share actively in his loving plan so that they are not only ruled and measured by it but are capable inwardly of shaping their choices and actions by ruling them in accord with their intelligent participation in God's law (see S.Th. I-II, 91, 2).

With "eternal law" understood in this way, we can see how sin is a morally evil act, i.e., a freely chosen act known to be contrary to the eternal law as made manifest in our conscience (see D.H. 3; G.S. 16). As evil, the freely chosen sinful act is deprived of the goodness that it can and ought to have (St. Thomas, *De Malo,* 7, 3). As an evil or deprivation of the moral order, the sinful act blocks the fulfillment of human persons on every level of existence, inwardly harming and twisting the person (see G.S. 27), destroying human community, and rupturing the relationship God wills to exist between himself and humankind (see G.S. 13).

Understood as a freely chosen act of self-determination opposed to the eternal law, sin is an act deprived of the openness it ought to have to the full good of human persons, the good to which they are directed by the eternal law. Sin, in other words, is a deliberate act known to violate the basic norm of human activity, namely, that such activity, "in accord with the divine plan and will, should harmonize with the authentic good of the human race, and allow men as individuals and as members of society to pursue their total vocation and fulfill it" (G.S. 35).

God's eternal law, his wise and loving design for leading human persons to fulfillment and happiness, is known, in some measure at least, even to the unbeliever, for its basic requirements are, as St. Paul taught, written in their hearts (see Rom 1:18-22). Less metaphorically put, they are, as Vatican Council II declared, made known to humankind through the mediation of conscience (see D.H. 3; G.S. 16-17). Thus one who knowingly acts in opposition to the truth made known in conscience always deviates from the loving plan of the eternal

law and thus offends God (see S.Th. I-II, 71, 2, ad 4; 71, 6), and it is precisely from the perspective of its nature as an offense against God that sin is considered in theology (see S.Th. I-II, 71, 6 ad 5).

Because the sinful act is opposed not only to the eternal law as the "highest norm of hman life" but also to good human reason (our personal participation in the eternal law), some theologians during the seventeenth century suggested that nonbelievers, in acting immorally, might be guilty only of what they termed "philosophical sin," i.e., an offense against good human reason, and not of "theological sin," an offense against God. Pope Alexander VIII strongly condemned this view (D.S. 2291), and for good reason, for it drives a wedge between nature and grace and ignores the existential situation of human beings who are summoned inwardly by God to a life of love, a life possible only if they are willing to act in accord with the truth mediated to them through conscience. Thus, St. Thomas taught that even unbaptized persons are capable, by virtue of their power of self-determining free choice and with the help of God's grace, to accept God and his law of love or to repudiate him and his law, in their first fully human act of self-determination (see S.Th. I-II, 89, 6).

But for believers, God's eternal law is made manifest not only through the mediation of conscience but also through the revealed truth proclaimed by the church and accepted in faith. Believers know, or ought to know, that their freely chosen immoral acts not only violate God's loving plan for human persons but also repudiate his offer of life and the surpassing gifts of love that he has bestowed upon them. Thus sin, as an offense against God, takes on a special heinousness for believers; it is an act of ungrateful infidelity, as the prophets, especially Hosea, make clear. By sinning,

Christians exchange the life and freedom won for them by Christ for renewed death and slavery (see Romans 6 and Galatians 5). Moreover, since the Christian is irrevocably, by virtue of baptism, a member of Christ's body, the church, there is an ecclesial aspect to every sin of a Christian; sin violates the Christian's responsibility to Christ and to the Church (see Rom 14:7-8; Gal 5:13-6:10).

Further dimensions of sin and its evil come to light in considering the second Augustinian definition of sin as a "turning away from God and a turning toward a creature." This definition brings out the truth that in sin there is a twofold aspect, one positive, the turning toward a creature, and the other negative or, more precisely, privative, the turning away from God. Before commenting on these aspects of sin, however, it is necessary to offer some words in criticism of this definition. Because of the strong Neo-platonic influence upon him, Augustine did not, it seems, properly appreciate the inherent worth of created goods and the role they have to play, in God's plan, in fulfilling human persons. Unlike Aquinas, who regarded such created goods as life, knowledge, beauty, harmonious relationships with others and with God and the like as "ends" or "points" of human existence—subordinate, of course, to the uncreated good that God is—(see S.Th. I-II, 94, 2), Augustine looked upon such goods as mere "means" to the final end, God. God alone, the highest and incommutable good, was, for Augustine, to be "enjoyed"; all created goods, even those inwardly perfective of human persons, were to be "used." Augustine's thought here needs to be corrected, and the truth of his definition can be better grasped if we speak of sin as a turning away from God and an *inordinate* or *unmeasured* turning toward a creature.

The turning away from God is, as noted already, the "privative" aspect of

sin, the aspect that makes the sinful choice to be evil, i.e., deprived of the goodness it can and ought to have. This same privative element was identified in the prior Augustinian definition of sin as the violation of God's eternal law; here it is more theologically identified as an aversion from God himself. The turning toward the creature is the positive element; it designates the "good" that entices and attracts the sinner. There is, in this definition of sin, a richness of meaning. No one does evil for the sake of evil (see, e.g., S.Th. I-II, 72, 1). Rather, in doing what we know to be wrong and opposed to God's law, we seek to participate in some appealing good. As St. Thomas notes, the aversion from God and setting aside of his law is not precisely what we are setting out to do in sinning. This private aspect is not the aim or point of our intentional action; rather our intent is to participate in some appealing good. Thus, the sinner need not "intend," in the precise sense of that term, to offend God and turn aside from him (S.Th. I-II, 72, 1; 73, 1; 75, 1-2; 78, 1). The sinner may only be wishing to enjoy himself (see S.Th. I-II, 71, 2, ad 3; 77). But the point is that the sinner knows he is seeking some created good in a way that cannot be reconciled with a love for God. The sinner's choice could and ought to conform to the requirements of God's law, the law that directs us to love him above all else and to love our neighbor as ourselves. The sinner recognizes that this choice to pursue a particular good in a particular way here and now necessarily requires him to close his heart, his person, to this love. Because of this recognition, he realizes that his pursuit of this particular good here and now means putting love for it ahead of his love for God. In this way, the sinner turns from God, to whom he ought to cling in his inmost being, and puts in God's place some created good (see S.Th. I-II, 71, 6; 79, 2).

Reflection on these Augustinian definitions of sin has disclosed some of its significance as a contemptuous rebellion against God. But in order to grasp its reality and terrible evil more fully, some words about the inner core of sin and its social dimensions are necessary.

The core of the sinful act is the free choice of self-determination whereby the sinner gives to himself a moral identity. As the scriptures make clear, sin flows from the heart, i.e., from the inner core of a person as a free and responsible being. Through the acts we choose to do we give to ourselves our identity as persons of a certain kind, and in sinning we give to ourselves the identity of sinners, e.g., of murderers, adulterers, liars, cheaters, etc. The external behavior proceeds from our free choice, and while the external behavior passes away, the being that we give to ourselves through the free choice to engage in this behavior remains within us as part of our identity. As St. Thomas notes, human action is immanent, not transitive; that is, it abides within the agent, either to fulfill and perfect the agent, if it is morally upright and in accord with the loving plan of God, or to damage and harm the agent, if it is morally wicked and sinful (see, e.g., S.Th. I-II, 57, 4). Because the inner core of sin is a self-determining choice that abides within the person, the reality of sin, traditionally termed the "guilt" or "stain" of sin, remains within the sinner.

In short, one makes oneself to be what one is by the choices that one makes. In every sinful choice, one makes oneself to be a sinner and guilty in the sight of the Lord (see S.Th. I-II, 86, all articles; 87, 6). This perduring of sin within the sinner is what is meant by the "state" of sin or condition of sinfulness. But there is no need to think of a state or condition of sin distinct from the sin itself, for this state is simply the abidingness of the sinful choice within us. Jesus summons us to recognize

our sinfulness and to have a change of heart, a *metanoia,* a conversion, which consists in a new self-determining choice whereby, in response to and with the help of God's healing grace, we give to ourselves the identity of repentant sinners, of persons who have been reconciled to God.

Sin, in other words, is not simply deviation in isolated pieces of external behavior. It is evil in the existential domain and extends to all that exists by or is affected by sinful choices. Thus, sin persists in the being of the person who sins, and one morally evil commitment can lead to many moral wicked acts. In addition, the sinful choices of individuals, when tolerated and accepted by the society in which they live, soon become the practices of the society. They become embedded in its law and customs, in its way of life, in its way of mediating reality to its people. Thus it is right to consider sin as social as well as personal. But it must be kept in mind that every social sin originates in and is perpetuated by individual persons' sinful choices. Particular persons are responsible, for instance, for initiating and maintaining such social evils as the oppression of minorities, the existence of unjust wars, the manipulation of communications, etc. (see, e.g., John Paul II, *Reconciliatio et Poenitentia,* n. 16).

Finally, while sin is the result of the abuse by created persons of their gift of freedom, "deep within its human reality there are factors at work which place it beyond the merely human in the border area where man's conscience, will, and sensitivity are in contact with the dark forces which, according to St. Paul, are active in the world almost to the point of ruling it" (*Reconciliatio,* n. 14; see Rom 7:7-25, Eph 2:2; 6:12). It is for this reason that only God, the one from whom we turn away in choosing to sin and the one whose loving law we freely choose to set aside, can rescue us from this dread evil;

and, in his mercy, he has chosen to do so by sending us his only-begotten Son who, by fully accepting our humanity and by his redemptive death-resurrection, has conquered sin and its power over us.

2. The Distinction between Mortal and Venial Sin

The biblical and theological understanding of sin previously set forth is properly applicable only to what the Catholic tradition has come to call mortal or deadly or grave sin (although, as will be seen, restricting the definition of sin as "anything done, said, or desired against the eternal law" to mortal sin raises some difficulties). This understanding, in other words, is fully realized only in the sort of sin in which human persons cleave inordinately to some created good, putting this good in the place that God ought to have in their hearts. This is the sort of sin in which the human person is dead to divine life, to friendship with God; it is the sort of sin whereby human persons truly rebel against the Lord and, by their own self-determining choice, oppose themselves to his love and his law.

But do human persons so oppose themselves to God in every immoral act? Common sense and the Catholic tradition maintain that some immoral acts are not "mortally" sinful, i.e, so opposed to the love and law of God that they destroy divine friendship. Such immoral acts are called "venial" sins.

A. Biblical and Ecclesial Sources for the Distinction. Although the scriptures do not formally distinguish between mortal and venial sins, both Testaments clearly bear witness to the distinction. The OT required an expiatory offering for sins of human weakness and inadvertence (see Lev 4-5). It taught, however, that other sins were crimes against the covenant community and its God. These could not be atoned for by an expiatory offering; they were punished by death or by cutting the sinner off from the community (see Lev 7:25; 17:8-10, 14; 19:7-8). In the NT Jesus distinguishes between the "beam" in the hypocrite's eye and the "mote" in the eye of the hypocrite's brother (Mt 7:5), and it is obvious that he regards the sin of the hypocrite greater than that of the one the hypocrite criticizes. Moreover, in the prayer he taught his disciples, he asks them to beg forgiveness for their daily "debts" or transgressions (Mt 6:12; Lk 11:4), while he threatens others with hell's fire for their sins (Mt 23:33). The epistles distinguish between the daily sin of which even the regenerated can be guilty and those offenses which exclude one from the kingdom (contrast Jas 3:2; 1 Jn 1:8 with 1 Cor 6:9-10; Gal 5:19-21), and they likewise speak of sins that lead to death (Rom 6:16) and call for excommunication from the community (1 Cor 5:13). Moreover, in a passage with a long patristic and medieval tradition, reflected in the writings of Jerome, Augustine, Aquinas, Bonaventure, and others, regarded as a firm biblical basis for the distinction between mortal and venial sins, St. Paul said that people build differently on the foundation that is Jesus Christ. Some build with gold, silver, and jewels, whereas others build with wood, hay, and straw. On judgment day each one's work will be tested; one whose building burns because of its poor material can be saved, but only through fire. Others, however, have utterly destroyed God's temple by severing themselves from Jesus; these will be destroyed, not saved (1 Cor 3:10-17).

Not only do the scriptures provide a basis for distinguishing between "mortal" and "venial" sins, the church's teaching is clear on this matter. The Council of Orange (529 A.D.), rejecting Pelagian doctrine, taught that even the upright Christian is guilty of sin (D.S. 228-230). The Council of Trent in the sixteenth century taught that not all sins deprive one of God's grace; some are venial (D.S. 1537); the same Council required Catholics to seek the forgiveness of God and the church through sacramental confession for all mortal sins of which they are aware, whereas ecclesial confession of venial sins, while recommended, was not required (D.S. 1679-1681). This teaching of Trent was reaffirmed by the 1983 Synod of Bishops and by Pope John Paul II in his Apostolic Exhortation, *Poenitentia et Reconciliatio* (n. 17).

B. The Classical Theological Understanding of This Distinction. The classical theological understanding of the difference between mortal and venial sin has best been set forth by St. Thomas Aquinas. With the Fathers he stressed that mortal sin is irreparable by human power—only God can save us from this spiritual death. Venial sin, on the other hand, is reparable from a source of healing within the person. What accounts for this difference? According to Aquinas the principle of our moral-spiritual life is ordered to our final end, God. If this principle is destroyed, one has no inner source to draw on to repair the harm one has done. Mortal sin destroys this principle, i.e., our inner ordering to God, and it is therefore irreparable, bringing death to the person as a moral-spiritual being, although God can conquer this death by his re-creative power. But this principle, he taught (summarizing, in doing so, the thought of the Fathers and medieval theologians), is not destroyed by sins that involve a disorder only with respect to something subordinate to the final end. Since the power of God is still present within a person who sins in this way, the person can repent of venial sins by reshaping his life in accord with this principle. Such sins are like bodily diseases which can be overcome by the body's inherent vitality (S.Th. I-II, 88, 1). In sinning mortally, in other words, a person fully turns away from God toward

a creature; in sinning venially, one does not turn away from God, although there is some disordered attachment to a created good.

Thomas further held that venial sin, which can be called "sin" only in a derivative sense, is "not against the law [*contra legem*] since one who sins venially does not do what the law forbids or fail to do what it requires by a precept; but such a sinner behaves apart from the law [*praeter legem*] by not keeping to the reasonable mode which the law points out" (S.Th. I-II, 88, 1, ad 1). While a venial sin, he maintained, is not referred to God and his glory, neither is it directed to a different ultimate end (S.Th. I-II, 88, 1, ad 2; see 88, 2; 89, 3). Aquinas says this in viewing sin according to the definition of sin as "anything done, said, or desired against the eternal law"; he obviously holds that this definition applies properly only to mortal sin.

His position here seems questionable. While it is true that only mortal sin fully turns away from God, our last end, it is difficult to understand why venial sins are simply "apart from the law" (*praeter legem*) and not "against the law" (*contra legem*). The immorality involved in filching a newspaper from a rack is surely against the precept forbidding theft. Still the main thrust of his thought here is clear. Venial sin, while morally evil, does not entail acting in a way that cuts one off from the ultimate end (God) to which we are directed by God's eternal law.

Aquinas maintained that three conditions are necessary if a sin is to be mortal, i.e., opposed to the love that God pours into our hearts. These are grave matter, sufficient reflection, and full consent (S.Th. I-II, 88, 2, 6). Sins venial by reason of insufficient reflection or full consent do not have a determinate kind. That is, offenses which are of themselves grave, for instance, blasphemy or adultery, can be venial (pardonable, reparable) if they proceed from a person who is confused or ignorant about what he is doing or whose choice is not adequately free. Such sins are venial in their "cause," i.e., in the person responsible for them. Other sins, he taught, are venial by reason of their "object" or subject matter, in contrast to others that are of themselves gravely or mortally sinful. His position, which summarizes well the thought of his predecessors, subsequent tradition, and the teaching and pastoral practice of the church, is that some kinds of human acts are known to be incompatible with the love that should exist between humans and God and within human society. For instance, blasphemy and idolatry are simply irreconcilable with love for God, while murder, adultery, and the like are completely opposed to love for our neighbor. Such acts, when freely chosen with adequate knowledge about what one is doing, are mortally sinful. Other kinds of acts entail some moral disorder but are not destructive of love for God or neighbor, e.g., aimlessly chatting, telling a lie that does not harm anyone. These are the matter or object of venial sin (S.Th. I-II, 88, 2).

Grave matter is here identified with actions deliberately opposed to love of God and neighbor. This appears to be a sound criterion. Yet there does seem to be a problem here, namely, why some moral evils do not constitute grave matter. Charity, after all, is love of divine goodness; but every morally evil act seems to be incompatible with this love and opposed to it. In addition, charity is love of one's neighbor and a willingness to serve the neighbor's need. A small lie to my wife, e.g. telling her I have mailed a letter she asked me to when I forgot (intending to mail it as soon as I can), seems to violate this love. The problem here is similar to the one we saw previously, when venial sin was described as a morally evil deed that was "apart from the law" and not "against the law." In short, although this position, namely, that some moral evils constitute "light" matter insofar as they are compatible with love of God and neighbor and thus occasion only venial or pardonable sin whereas others constitute "grave" matter because of their incompatibility with such love and thus give rise to mortal sin seems quite reasonable, some perplexities remain about this criterion.

C. Fundamental Option and This Distinction. Several contemporary theologians (K. Rahner, J. Fuchs, J. Glaser, et al.) distinguish between categorical freedom, the sort exercised in ordinary acts of free choice (e.g., my choice to write this article), and fundamental or transcendental freedom, which is the disposition of the whole person to God, either in a relationship of love or in one of separation and alienation. Fundamental freedom, on this view, is exercised at the very core of the human person and is, therefore, the locus of self-determination and hence of grave moral responsiblity. The object of this fundamental option is not any particular alternative to be adopted by ordinary free choice (e.g., to smoke this cigarette or not; to commit adultery or not); rather it is the relationship of the whole person to God (or to something conceived as ultimate, such as the entire moral order).

Applying this theory to the distinction between mortal and venial sin and between grave and light matter, proponents of fundamental option argue that grave matter is the sort of thing likely to be an occasion for making or reversing one's fundamental option. Actions not likely to change one's fundamental disposition toward or against God are light matter. "Grave" and "light" can be used to designate not only morally evil acts, but also morally upright acts. Some morally good acts are of graver import than others. While grave matter, for instance, killing an innocent person or committing adultery, provides the occasion for reversing one's fundamental orientation to God, it does not necessarily follow that a particular act of this kind destroys one's basic commitment to love God, although there is definitely the possibility that it may. In other words, for the proponents of this view grave matter is a sign that the exercise of one's fundamental option is entailed. Still, it remains possible that one could freely choose to engage in an act involving grave matter and still not act against one's fundamental option. In short, what makes a sin "mortal" is a fundamental option against God and his love, not the matter of the act, even if the matter is grave and the act is freely chosen (an exercise of categorical freedom). Thus, advocates of this position frequently distinguish three basic kinds of sins: venial sins, in which light matter only is involved or in which only a peripheral kind of freedom is exercised; grave sins, which entail serious matter freely chosen; and mortal sins, which require a change in one's fundamental option, i.e., in one's core of transcendental freedom.

This summary makes it clear that proponents of fundamental option recognize that one can change one's stance before God in particular acts of free choice. Moreover, with Aquinas they recognize that the transition from being a friend of God to being one who is opposed to his love is a matter of profound importance and that a basic commitment for God is "not easily lost" (see *De Veritate,* 27, 9, ad 1). This position also seems right in looking at our moral-spiritual life as a unified whole, not as a series of disparate and isolated acts, so that a person is not flipping back and forth from a state of sinfulness to one of friendship with God.

Nonetheless, there are serious problems with this account of the difference between mortal and venial sin. First of all, the theory of fundamental option shifts the locus of self-determination from the free choices that we make every day (e.g., my choice to lie to my wife, to commit adultery, to write this essay) to an inferred act of total self-disposition deep within the person which remains vague and inaccessible to consciousness (J.M. Boyle, Jr., "Freedom, the Human Person, and Human Action," in *Principles of Catholic Moral Life,* ed., William E. May. Chicago: Franciscan Herald Press, 1981, pp. 237-266;). Does our entire moral-spiritual life depend upon an option of which we may not be consciously aware in a way that it does not depend upon very specific free choices of which we are acutely conscious, e.g., a person's free, deliberate, and considered choice to kill another? This seems unlikely. Rather, we make or break ourselves as moral persons in and through the free choices we make in our daily lives. We become liars, adulterers, cheaters, etc. by freely choosing to lie, commit adultery, etc. As noted earlier, at the core of our actions as moral beings is a free, self-determining choice, and this choice abides in us until a contradictory kind of choice is made.

In addition, proponents of this position admit that some acts are so gravely evil that freely choosing them is likely to change a good fundamental option. But at the same time, most proponents also claim that in some and perhaps many cases immoral acts involving grave matter (e.g., killing an innocent person, committing adultery) can be done with sufficient reflection and full consent without subverting a good fundamental option. This seems odd, and it can lead to serious self-deception (see Grisez, 385-386).

These objections are weighty and in my opinion lead to the conclusion that the effort of proponents of fundamental option to explain the difference between mortal and venial sin is erroneous.

D. Fundamental Commitments, the Christian Way of Life, and Mortal Sin. Despite the criticism just given, proponents of fundamental option are, it seems, correct in holding that the difference between grave and light matter is to be found in the depth to which different kinds of immoral acts disrupt the existential being of the person. Aquinas and the traditional account of the difference between mortal and venial sin seem correct in holding that certain sorts of choices entail intelligible subject matter known to be completely incompatible with love of God and neighbor, whereas others entail matter which, although immoral and incompatible with a perfected love of God and neighbor, is reconcilable with such love.

Moreover, while a fundamental option at the core of one's being whereby one disposes oneself totally for or against God seems mysterious and inaccessible to consciousness, it is true that certain kinds of free choices, ones that can rightly be called commitments, do orient a person in a definite direction and establish a person in a definite way of life—e.g., the choice to become a Christian, the choice to marry, the choice to become a priest or religious or doctor or research scholar, the choice to join the Mafia or the Nazis or a drug ring. These, it is to be noted, are specific exercises of free choice of which a person is consciously aware. Thus it seems reasonable to conclude that there is a basic option for the Christian, namely, the option to become a Christian through baptism (and to ratify the baptismal commitment in confirmation). This fundamental option, the act of living faith, is a definite choice, of which a person is quite conscious. The church teaches definitively that faith is the source of all justification and the beginning of our salvation, that it is God's gift and that it is accepted by a free human act (D.S. 1528-1532; D.V. 5; D.H. 2-3). It further teaches that this definite choice commits one to a life of good works (D.S. 1532-1539; L.G. 35; D.H. 5, 10).

In addition, some morally evil acts have been regarded by the church from the very beginning as incompatible with the specific requirements of faith, with the way of life to which one is committed in dying and rising to life with Christ in baptism. Such acts involve grave matter, and the free choice, knowingly made, to engage in them, is a choice absolutely incompatible with the life to which one's act of faith commits oneself. The act of living faith, in other words, has definite specifications, not only with respect to what one is to believe but also with respect to what one is to do and to refrain from doing. The church has consistently taught that certain specific kinds of acts constitute grave matter and, if freely and knowingly chosen, are mortal sins (fornication, adultery, killing of the innocent, etc., in addition to acts directly contrary to faith) (see John Paul II, *Reconciliatio et Poenitentia,* n. 17; see also Grisez, 393-396).

In conclusion, mortal sin is the sort of sin that involves grave matter, that is, matter judged by the church to be incompatible with the life to which one commits oneself by living faith. In addition mortal sin requires sufficient reflection and full consent, i.e, an adequately free human choice. Venial sin, while immoral, is sin venial either by reason of its matter, which is judged compatible with the life to which living faith commits a person, or by reason of defects of knowledge and freedom in the sinner.

3. The Way of Sin to Death

St. Paul spoke of a "law" that he found in his "members," one opposed to the "law" that he found in his "mind" (Rom 7:22-23). This "law" of his members inclined him to act in ways that he knew were wrong. The church and theologians have seen in this passage of St. Paul, in which he voices a universal human experience, biblical warrant for the reality of concupiscence. Concupiscence, which derives from original sin and inclines toward sin (Council of Trent, D.S. 1515), remains even in those who have, through baptism, died to sin and risen to the new kind of life, a life of holiness, made possible by Christ's redemptive act. Although it is not itself sin—since sin requires consent to what is evil—concupiscence exists within us as a source of sin and an inclination toward evil. As a result of original sin and the concupiscence resulting therefrom, we find ourselves in a condition of disintegration and experience terrible tension within ourselves, being drawn toward the good by the native thrust of our will and by the loving plan of God written in our hearts, and being inclined toward evil by concupiscence (see Vatican Council II, G.S. 13).

In addition to concupiscence, we are by nature passionate and emotional beings as well as intelligent and willing beings. Our passions, as both the scriptures (Jas 1:13-14) and human experience bear witness, can at times make alternatives that we know are not in accord with God's loving plan very appealing to us. Thus temptations arise, and powerful forces within us (passions and the disintegrating influence of concupiscence) incline us to consent to what we know to be wrong.

Moreover, as noted previously, the sins of individuals, when accepted by society, become a part of a society's way of life. The "world" shaped by sin (see Rom 5:12; 1 Jn 5:16; Jn 1:29) obscures values, provides bad example, and quite frequently pushes us toward sin by bad example plus pressure.

Finally, in addition to sources within us and in the world in which we live, the devil, the father of lies, prowls about like a roaring lion seeking whom he may devour (1 Pet 5:8). He and his legions are, the scriptures and the church instruct us, at work seeking to lead us into evil.

Still, the only cause of sin is our own free will, our own choice deliberately to set aside the loving plan of God and to choose to do what we know to be evil. Once we yield to temptation we are subject to further temptation as we seek to integrate our life with the sinful self we have made ourselves to be. The effort to do this leads to rationalizations and dishonesty. Once we sin personally, we are strongly inclined to distort our relationship with God by self-righteousness or, at times, by flight.

While venial sin is sin only in an analogous sense, it can prepare the way for mortal sin. It makes us aware of sinful possibilities which might otherwise have remained unknown; it puts us in situations difficult to escape without mortal sin; and it puts before us objectives we are tempted to pursue by mortal sin (see S.Th. I-II, 88, 3; G. Grisez, *The Way Of The Lord Jesus Christ, Vol. 1, Christian Moral Principles.* Chicago: Franciscan Herald Press, 1983. pp. 311-458).

Traditionally, too, theologians have spoken of "capital" sins or vices. Since the time of Gregory the Great seven have been commonly listed: vainglory (pride), covetousness (avarice), lust, gluttony, anger, envy, and sloth. They are called capital because they are sources (heads, *capita*) for other sins. Some capital sins are sinful attitudes that compete with love for God and neighbor, seemingly offering ways to fulfill ourselves other than by wholehearted dedication to God and neighbor. Thus pride is a disposition to find fulfillment in status and the respect of others; lust and gluttony are dispositions to fulfillment in immediate sensible gratifications; avarice, a disposition to fulfillment in possessions (S.Th. I-II, 84, 4; II-II, 118, 7; 148, 5; 155, 4; 162, 8). Others are attitudes whereby we seek to rationalize our sinfulness. Thus sloth disposes us to put off reform in our spiritual and moral life, resisting the effort needed to give up sinful attachments (S.Th. II-II, 35); envy makes us opposed to the good of others, whose goodness makes undesirable demands upon ourselves (S.Th. II-II, 36). As a capital sin, anger is a disposition to wipe out especially whatever poses a threat to our sinful self (S.Th. 158, 2, 6, 7).

Catholic faith proclaims that every sin, because of God's surpassing love, can be forgiven during this life (D.S. 349). Still, the scriptures do speak of sins that cannot be forgiven in the sense that they constitute a terrible offense against the truth and the light, against the Holy Spirit (Mt 12:31-32; 1 Jn 5:16). In speaking of sin in this way, the scriptures are referring to a sin more radical than most mortal sins, for it is sin whose nature blocks forgiveness. From the time of Augustine theologians have provided a list of sins against the Holy Spirit, proceeding from initial impenitence through obduracy, presumption, despair, rejection of known truth, envy of the grace that others enjoy, to final impenitence (see S.Th. II-II, 14, 1-4). And final impenitence leads to hell, the eternal separation from God begun in this life through our free self-determining choice to turn from God and his law of love and to cleave inordinately to some created good that, in effect, we put in his place.

In sum, through our willingness to do what we know is wicked in the sight of the Lord, we dig a pit between ourselves and God. Through rationalization we dig this pit deeper until we are deaf to his call,

blind to the light and the truth that he sends into the world. The gospel is the good news that God himself has come to save us from sin, to be with us and for us, to be our Immanuel. Only by a self-determining act of *metanoia,* of penance, made possible by the saving death-resurrection of Jesus, can we climb out of this pit and rise to a life of holiness, a life of constant conversion and growth in the way of truth and light. But in this struggle we can take heart and hope confidently in God, for with St. Paul we can say that "nothing, neither death nor life, no angel, no prince, nothing that exists, nothing still to come, not any power, or height or depth, nor any created thing, can ever come between us and the love of God made visible in Christ Jesus our Lord" (Rom 8:38-39).

J. Fuchs, *Human Values and Christian Morality,* Dublin: Gill, 1970, pp. 91-99. J. Gaffney, *Sin Reconsidered.* New York: Paulist, 1983. G. Grisez, *The Way Of The Lord Jesus Christ, Vol. 1, Christian Moral Principles.* Chicago: Franciscan Herald Press, 1983. John Paul II, Apostolic Exhortation *Reconciliatio et Poenitentia,* December 2, 1984, in *Origins* (December 20, 1984) 14.27, 433-458. T. O'Connell, *Principles For A Catholic Morality,* New York: Seabury, 1978. G. Quell, G. Bertram, G. Stahlin, and W. Grundmann, "Hamartanō," in *Theological Dictionary Of The New Testament,* ed. G. Kittel, trans. G. Bromiley. Grand Rapids: Eerdmans, 1964, 1.267-316. K. Rahner, "Theology of Freedom," *Theological Investigations,* Vol. 6, *Concerning Vatican Council II,* trans. K-H. and B. Kruger, Baltimore: Helicon, 1966, 190-195.

WILLIAM E. MAY

SITUATION ETHICS

Situation ethics is a term used for a wide range of ethical methodologies which stress the uniqueness of the situation in which a moral decision is made and diminish or reject the role of general principles. The topic has been the subject of debate in both Roman Catholic moral theology and Protestant ethics since the 1940's. A European variety of situation ethics had its philosophical base in the rejection of a view of the world as an ordered system founded on timeless being. In the absence of such a system, individuals must shape their own personal meaning. Similarly, in forming an ethical response, one must fall back on immediate experience in the particular situation. A type of situation ethics developed in Roman Catholicism as a protest against what was deemed a rigid, impersonal legalism. It was condemned by Pius XII in 1952.

In the officially accepted account of the moral order, there is an objective, unchanging order of being, reflected in human nature, such that universal moral principles can be discovered and known with certainty. Under these general principles all particular obligations can be subsumed. A moral judgment is made by applying the principles to particular cases. Universal negative norms absolutely exclude certain choices. Thus, there are intrinsically disordered acts that, when chosen freely and with due knowledge, inevitably infect the will with moral evil. General principles may need to be more precisely defined to cover conflict cases, but may not be set aside. For example, the notion of "stealing" needs to be defined precisely so as to indicate that where one, in extreme need, takes the goods of another who is not reduced to similar need, this is not "stealing" as prohibited by the general norm. In the 1950's Karl Rahner proposed an "existential ethic" according to which the general norms are by no means excluded, but need to be brought to a unique focus for the individual in a particular moment. A concrete obligation is not only an application of general law but also the unique call to self-realization of the particular person.

In contemporary debate, different terms are used, but the problem of the relation between general principles and the particular act remains. Many points of tension are evident. In criticism of the static, "classicist" world view, many urge a historical consciousness. Reacting against an unduly "physicalist" interpretation of human nature, some have developed a more tightly reasoned ethic of basic human goods while others have questioned the natural law itself. Many contemporary authors argue that the moral quality of an act cannot be determined in abstract or general propositions, but only when account is taken of the intention of the subject and all the concrete circumstances, especially the consequences. This approach, with its key notion of "proportionate reason," has been developed by Catholic theologians such as Louis Janssens, Bruno Schueller, and Richard McCormick. Some would deny that there are "intrinsically evil acts" in the sense explained above. Official Roman Catholic teaching has, however, retained the concept of intrinsically disordered acts, particularly in statements on sexual ethics.

There have been many different varieties of situationism in Protestantism. The popularizer of the term, Joseph Fletcher, argued that love was the only absolute. The most loving thing was to be determined by a kind of utilitarian calculus. Karl Barth focused on the objective command of God given in each moment. Rudolph Bultmann held that the Christian can, in love, perceive the neighbor's need with a kind of intuition. Paul Tillich understood moral judgment as founded on an intuitive grasp of the potentialities of being. Paul Lehmann, H. Richard Niebuhr and, more recently, James M. Gustafson have been described as contextualist. A radical situationism would imply a fragmentation of the moral life into isolated segments, and a dissociation of individual choice from community bonds. Contextualists are particularly concerned to preserve the community dimension. The whole debate is highly complex and sometimes confused. For example, it is not always sufficiently clear whether the issue is the way in which personal moral judgment ought to be made or the processes by which community norms ought to be validated.

See **Moral Life, Christian**

Charles E. Curran and Richard A. McCormick, S.J. Eds., *Readings in Moral Theology,* no. 1, *Moral Norms and Catholic Tradition,* New York: Paulist Press, 1979. James M. Gustafson, *Protestant and Roman Catholic Ethics,* Chicago: U. of Chicago Press, 1978.

BRIAN V. JOHNSTONE, CSSR

SOCIOLOGY

All social scientists study people in interaction with other people. However, while political scientists focus on power relations, economists on wealth, anthropologists on culture, and social psychologists on personality, sociologists examine intergroup and intragroup relations of all kinds.

Sociology is the study of human life in groups—their origins, development and changes. Roles, norms and values held by group members are major units of analysis. As people interact with one another in the process of living, they invent ways of propagating themselves and learning how to survive, ways of providing food, clothing and shelter, of organizing for effective action and dividing the labor, of accumulating and dispersing wealth, of healing the body afflicted by illness, resting and relaxing after strenuous effort, of responding to ultimate reality, and of passing all their accumulated experience along to newcomers. These inventions eventually become institutionalized customs which, through language, the most basic institution, are specified by names. The names of these institutions are familiar to us: family, community, the economy, government, health care, recreation, religion,

education. Different groups of people develop different styles for fulfilling such similar basic functions as procreation, education, government, curing and worship. In time, these styles of behavior generate cultures that define a moral whole that is quite resistant to change, even though in practice it exploits some of the people. Why this happens is related to having power, access to wealth, and differing human appearance and beliefs about what is sacred and secular.

Sociologists examine the complex of formal and informal ways of organizing that people have developed down through history and across societies with their attendant normative patterns, in order to describe the range of ways the variety of cultures provide for doing similar functions. They seek to account for the existing structures, to determine how social change occurs, to discover what actually changes, to try to predict what direction social change may take in the future, how it is resisted and facilitated in the present and how it actually occurred in the past.

By looking comparatively at the same structures in different regions of the world, or in the same region in different time frames, the sociologist can determine what type of family structure is likely to occur within different economic, political and other social settings. Comparative analysis also reveals social class systems, ethnic and sex relations, and social movements in patterns that are characterized as social problems when some groups and individuals are exploited by other groups controlling access to resources needed for survival, or exerting oppressive governance over those defined as inferior, or dangerous, or as less human by the standards of one group evaluating the organization or practices of another. In this context, what people believe to be true or false, good or evil, has a powerful influence on behavior.

Those who have access to media of communication also have an advantage of power in determining what is named to be good and right because they have a means to introduce and reinforce the symbols that interpret human experience and through which people share the thoughts and feelings they have about life. The study of language and communications media is a major factor in sociology today. The comparative study of religions reveals varying conceptions of deity, of evil, of explanations of life, death and the purpose of life. Different modes of worship, prayer and ethical norms actually practiced in the group life of one society can be demonstrated to color its vision of other groups whose customs and meanings it does not share. By examining the institution of church at different eras in the same society, the sociologist can point out how definitions of what is right and good have changed and can account for some of these changes by examining the related systems of education, government, economy and ideology.

There are certain basic principles that sociologists discover. One of these is that large changes in the size of the population are a basic determinant of organizational and institutional change. This means that the society regroups when it becomes very large. It has to do so to provide adequately for members. Formal structures for producing food and other basic necessities become more differentiated. The division of labor becomes more complex; anonymity becomes a reality. New ways of communicating become necessary and old forms of community die out or are destroyed. If the population declines again in size, the reverse process occurs. In small communities, face-to-face communication in small groups orients members to what needs to be done for human survival and development; in very large collectivities, more

formal methods are invented. Thus, education is done within the extended family in old tribal groups, often nomadic in form. However, complex school systems with access to textbooks or mass media communication are invented and initiated in sedentary groups with formal educational systems, medical centers, government bureaucracies, complex financial and productive systems and churches.

When populations become too large for the resources available in a given location, migrations occur, local or inter-hemispherical, depending on the degree of need or inventiveness. War of one group on another is another way the struggle for scarce goods has been resolved. Slavery, war, and unjust work relations are some exploitative inventions for addressing problems of human need. Labor unions, co-operative organizations, and international trade are some participative ways. People create ethical systems to define the quality of preferred solutions of problems of human survival and development. These systems are related to their conceptions of human nature, human rights and access to human resources. Often these conceptions are rooted in religious belief systems and ritual practices.

How the normative is defined to provide rationale for behavior is a basic function that sociologists study. Determining what is right and just is an aspect of religion that sociologists examine.

Within the discipline of sociology, a range of theories are operative to account for the stability and change in social structures. Functionalists assume that, if a structure exists in a society, it must be fulfilling some needed function. They focus on how current institutions came into existence and why they continue to exist in a given society. Conflict theorists try to account for social change on the basis of conflict of interest groups and assume that people act in their own self-interests. They focus on classes struggling for control over and access to scarce goods. Symbolic interactionists, concluding that the variety of human patterns for living indicate the enormous creativity of human beings to invent modes of survival and development, focus on the meaning which the myths, symbols, and patterns of behavior have for the actors in the groups where they exist. This task continually reveals new insights into human behavior, human aspirations and potential. Sociobiologists begin with the premise that genetic survival subsumes all meaningful, as well as all natural, patterns of interaction: hence the sociological task is to show the genetic intent. Even religion, or more especially religion in this context, is explained through its *quid pro quo* functions. Sociobiology is a new form of social Darwinism and brings us back to the origin of sociology in the work of Auguste Comte who invented the term to introduce a new discipline needed in the mid-nineteenth century to account for the major institutional changes occurring in Europe at that time as a result of the bourgeois revolutions in France, Italy, Germany, England, and incipiently in Eastern Europe. Religion plays a major role in sociological explanation from Comte down through Talcott Parsons. The Second Vatican Council of the Catholic Church formally recognized the need of taking sociological explanation into account in examining the role of religion and the church in modern society. It is essential for understanding the emergence of liberation theology in the late 1960's which initiated theological reflection from the human experience of the oppressed poor rather than from abstracted absolutes, thereby making history and current definitions of the prevailing social situation by reflective groups of people essential elements of theological development.

Roger Brown, *Social Psychology, second edition,* New York: Free Press, Macmillan, 1987. Randall Collins, and Michael Makowsky, *The Discovery of Society,* fourth ed., New York: Random House, 1987. Anthony Giddens, *Sociology: a Brief Critical Introduction,* second edition, New York: Harcourt Brace Jovanovich, 1987. Phillip E. Hammond, ed., *The Sacred in a Secular Age,* Berkeley: Univ. of California Press, 1985. Patrick H. McNamara, *Religion North American Style,* second edition, Belmont, Cal.: Wadsworth Pub. Co., 1984. Talcott Parsons, *The Social System* Glencoe, Ill., Free Press, 1951. Talcott Parsons, *The System of Modern Societies,* Englewood Cliffs, N.J. Prentice-Hall, 1971. Theda Skocpol, *States and Social Revolutions: a Comparative Analysis of France, Russia, and China,* New York: Cambridge Univ. Press, 1979.

MARIE AUGUSTA NEAL, SND

SOLA FIDE

The phrase, "by faith alone," was often used at the Reformation to refer to justification which man can only receive by faith and cannot earn by his good works. Put that simply, it is a truth which Catholics also hold. If it is used to imply that the grace of justification does not make a Christian able to perform good works and to merit salvation, then it contradicts Catholic teaching.

See **Faith, Good Works, Grace, Justification**

SOLA GRATIA

The phrase "by grace alone" refers to the utter primacy of God's grace in the justification and salvation of the sinner, a position on which Catholics and Protestants can agree. At times, it is used to imply a purely forensic interpretation of justification and the inability of the Christian to merit salvation, and in these senses it is not accepted by the church.

See **Good Works, Grace, Justification, Sanctification**

SOLA SCRIPTURA

Another Reformation slogan, the phrase "by Scripture alone" is often used

to deny the role of Tradition in God's revelation and of the magisterium in the interpretation of revelation. As such, the principle is rejected by the Catholic Church, which however, at the Second Vatican Council left open the question of the material sufficiency of Scripture.
See **Magisterium, Revelation, Tradition**

SOTERIOLOGY
See **Redemption**

SOUL
See **Anthropology, Christian**

SPIRATION

A term used in the theology of the Trinity to refer to the procession of the Spirit from the Father and the Son.
See **Trinity**

SPIRITUALITY

The term spirituality refers to both a lived experience and an academic discipline. For Christians, it means one's entire life as understood, felt, imagined, and decided upon in relationship to God, in Christ Jesus, empowered by the Spirit. It also indicates the interdisciplinary study of this religious experience, including the attempt to promote its mature development.

The word spirituality, as it refers to experience, has an interesting history. Originally a christian term—from Paul's letters—it was an exclusively Roman Catholic term until the late nineteenth century. It retained its original reference to life according to the Holy Spirit, yet gradually came to mean that life as the special concern of "souls seeking perfection" rather than as the common experience of all Christians. Seeking perfection became a matter of the individual, interior practice of special spiritual exercises requiring careful guidance by experts. Emphasis was on affectivity and obedience to authority; critical reflection was suspect. The contemporary theological shift toward a recovery of sources in scripture, history, and liturgy has demonstrated how distorted the previous understanding had become. The last section of this article will elaborate on the current use of this term.

Until the high Middle Ages all theology was spiritual theology; that is, it was reflection upon the experience of faith expressed in scripture, liturgy, private prayer, and pastoral experience. Thomas Aquinas' divisions of his *Summa Theologiae* effectively set the divisions of all theology until Vatican II: dogma, moral, and christology. In the eighteenth and nineteenth centuries two subdivisions of moral theology developed: ascetical and mystical theology. Using first principles from dogma and a scholastic vocabulary, ascetical theology studied the life of perfection up to the beginning of passive mystical experience. Mystical theology examined that life from the beginning of infused contemplation to its climax in the union with God possible outside of the beatific vision. Throughout history, many valuable documents on the spiritual life were written outside of formal theology in various literary genres. For example, there are monastic rules, scripture commentaries, sermons, poems, autobiographies. Some of these were written by professional theologians, but many of them were done by nonprofessionals. The contemporary field of spirituality as interpretation and communication of religious experience, as experience, is still emerging as a discipline.

I. History of Spirituality

Paul's Letters. Paul understands his life and that of every Christian as life "in Christ." Faith in God's action in raising Christ incorporates us into Christ who pours out his Spirit, enabling us to recognize God as "Abba." Thus, Paul's religious experience is one of seeing the risen Lord, feeling empowered by the Spirit to witness to God's re-creation of all women and men in Christ: Jew and Greek, slave and free.

For Paul, the experience of day-to-day life in Christ centers on bearing one another's burdens, which is fulfilling the whole law; giving and receiving the Spirit's gifts which build up the body of Christ; offering ourselves as living sacrifices of praise and thanksgiving for God's overwhelming love for us in Christ—the love that nothing can ever separate us from. Eating the meal of unity and love, remembering Christ Jesus, renews our faith in God's re-creating action in Christ, the new Adam, and in us.

In the beginning of Paul's life in Christ his experience of the risen Christ led him to concentrate on proclaiming the power of the resurrection. Later, his experience of struggle and failure in his ministry led him to appreciate more deeply the mystery of Christ's passion. Thus, his mature experience was one of ever deeper participation in the paschal mystery, of loving trust even unto death so that the power of God manifest in Jesus' weakness might be manifest also in Paul's weakness and in ours.

Mark's Gospel. Concerns and questions of the community influence the focus of every gospel. The faith-experience of Mark's community centers on Jesus as the suffering servant Messiah because these disciples of Jesus are persecuted and ask: Why is this happening to me? The gospel replies that the disciple is one who follows the master's path of faithful love, giving one's last breath as Jesus did.

Mark's gospel portrays the original disciples as fearful and very slow to learn that the servant of God must love even unto death, thus teaching the community that they, too, will receive Jesus' patient mercy as they grow in faith, even as Peter and the earlier disciples did.

Luke's Gospel. Luke's community is a missionary church that is learning to expand its boundaries of sharing and concern. Only slowly and painfully are they realizing that life in Christ calls them to care for more than just their own family and friends. As Jesus was impelled by the Spirit to bring the good news of God's covenantal love to the poor and oppressed, so they are called to lives of complete generosity and service to all. Those in positions of authority are reminded, particularly, of their responsibility to follow Jesus' path of serving, not being served.

Matthew's Gospel. Matthew's community experiences its identity as deeply committed to Mosaic teaching with Jesus as the expositor, yet wrenched by outsiders challenging this identity. They long to clarify and reaffirm their bonds with Israel's tradition, law, and experience of righteousness. Their meditation, therefore, is upon Jesus, the personification of wisdom, whose interpretation of the law is the embodiment of Israel's righteousness: mercy, forgiveness, trust in the midst of persecution—the Beatitudes. Living according to this teaching is to cooperate with God in bringing into being God's new covenant, that is God's reign of peace and justice, in a community called *ekklesia,* "church."

John's Gospel. This community experiences unity as well as alienation. More than any other gospel community, its members realize the depth of Jesus' unity with God and their own indwelling in God through rebirth as God's daughters and sons, as friends and sisters/brothers of Jesus, as those in whom the new Paraclete lives and continues to teach the meaning of Jesus' words. Their alienation stems from being rejected by the wider Jewish community of their experience and their need to respond to the challenges raised by this rejection.

At the heart of the apostolic spirituality of the fourth gospel is the experience of being sent even as Jesus was sent from the Father. Over and over, this gospel echoes the phrase "as...me, so...you." In their own way, the disciples experience the *same* relationship Jesus has to his Father, the same work as Jesus, the same Spirit, the same joy, the same life!

Spirituality of the Hebrew Bible. For Paul and the communities of the gospels, all understanding of their religious experience comes through interpretation of the Jewish scripture in light of their unique experience of Jesus, the Christ. Christians, valuing their Jewish roots, must respect the contemporary and continuing integrity of revelation in the Hebrew Bible on its own terms. For this interpretation it is best to turn to Jewish theology. For example, Abraham Joshua Heschel's theology of God's *pathos* examines Israel's tradition regarding Torah, prophets and wisdom from the perspective of its central religious experience: God's search for humanity.

Early Christianity. Liturgical and theological texts indicate that Christians understood their lives as personal participation in the mystery of Christ begun in faith, sealed by baptism into the death and resurrection of Jesus Christ, nourished by sharing in the Lord's Supper which celebrated his saving presence and action in their lives, and expressed by universal love that bore witness to life in the Spirit and drew others to faith. This common faith was experienced within the diversity of the later Roman empire's history: persecution of Christians, and

then rule by a christian emperor; eastern and western centers of culture and theology; profound theological disputes; assimilation and rejection of the dominant culture.

Christian spirituality is composed of a constellation of elements (e.g., God-images, community, prayer, ministry, asceticism) that receive different emphases at various times or for different persons. Rearranging one element of the constellation affects all the others. Early christian history exemplifies this principle.

By centering on the Sunday eucharist celebrated in house churches or in larger communities made up of rich and poor, educated and illiterate, women and men, early christian spirituality reinforced certain feelings, insights, and convictions. Love, acceptance, reconciliation, hope, and the challenge to honest love and generosity were dominant feelings. Understanding the various senses of scripture—literal, allegorical, moral, and eschatological—was fostered through informed preaching. Conviction deepened that community is the primary place where one meets the risen Lord.

Initial emphasis on martyrdom affected all later interpretation of christian experience. Whereas Paul sees ministry as the imitation of Christ, early martyrs understand their experience as the closest imitation of Jesus. Praising martyrdom, then, reinforced Greek culture's tendency to deny the body and the world. When martyrdom was no longer possible, complete self-denial was sought in asceticism and early monasticism.

Asceticism arose as a counter-cultural movement among Christians against the christian church that was too identified with Alexandrian, Antiochene, Byzantine and Roman institutions. Primarily a lay movement, it had two sides: solitary, that tended toward excessive contempt for the flesh; and communal, which stressed simple prayer that relished scripture and promoted the necessary attitudes for the interpretation of scripture: deep charity, and purity of conscience. Some theologians (e.g., Augustine) lived in community precisely in order to foster their study and ministry of teaching. Wise ascetics (e.g., Benedict) attracted persons seeking spiritual guidance. Benedict's rule, and before him Basil's, set the tone for the monasticism (and its offspring mendicancy) of east and west.

Sayings of the desert fathers and mothers manifest a profound realization that tradition is not a set formula but a continuity of life lived according to the gospel. Desert wisdom is perennial yet, naturally, mirrors the authoritarian, patriarchal and matriarchal society from which it comes.

Christian culture's absorption of ancient learning promoted an influential model and method of spirituality. Philosophical contemplation which centered on the mind became the ideal. Its method involved subjection of the passions to reason.

As Peter Brown explains in *Christian Spirituality* (1985), the ideal of virginity, practiced equally by women and men, enjoyed a moral and cultural supremacy in Christianity that was unchallenged until the Reformation. For men and women in ancient mediterranean society, sexual abstinence was a social act with negative and positive connotations foreign to modern post-puritans. For early Christians, virginity meant fighting against tensions of unfulfilled sexuality; but, even more significantly, it meant struggling against the force of social convention which swept a person into his or her "natural" social role as a married person, enjoying sexual intercourse in order to perpetuate family kinship. Positively, in virginity one committed oneself to different grounds of social cohesion: to "true" joining out of free choice, in faith, in order to "mediate" between the divine

and the human. This high theory was not always practiced, yet its symbolic power cannot be underestimated. Gradually, this theory modified the Platonic universe of soul withdrawn from body, so that the emphasis became one of the withdrawal of the body-self from society's claims regarding the primacy of family and kin. This made the inclusive gospel vision of society more possible if not more actual.

Medieval Spirituality. This period was innovative, for example in styles of religious life and art, but it was not revolutionary because it remained firmly rooted in traditions from the previous era.

Popular spirituality could be distinguished from professional. Mass conversions, low levels of general education, and pastoral neglect promoted religious experience characterized by a cult of relics, magic under the guise of sacraments, pilgrimages simply for the sake of travel, and thinly veiled paganism. Professional spirituality was informed by study and guidance. This distinction does not intend to overlook the uneducated saints nor self-righteous monks and nuns.

Professional religious life flourished in a variety of forms. While women and men continued to withdraw into solitude, there also emerged an urban ministry of clerics devoted to including laity in cathedral liturgy. Monks tended to see monastic life as the only place in which the image of God could truly be restored to humanity in this life. In contrast, there arose mendicant women and men (e.g., Francis, Dominic) convinced that genuine evangelical life was possible outside the monastic structure. Believing that anyone could preach who was called by God's spirit, they wandered the countryside calling all to conversion, using metaphors appealing to the new merchant class. Living in poverty, they alternated periods of solitude with preaching that focused on the humanity of Jesus in the incarnation and passion. The Beguines were another type of lay group. Independent from men's authority, these women often lived at home in voluntary poverty and chastity. With no formal church supervisors, they combined work, common prayer, and life in the world. Eventually these women were forced into the cloister, and mendicant preaching was clericalized.

The constellation of elements in medieval spirituality was moved, for some, by the image of God and of Jesus as mother. Noting how this popular medieval image was embedded in people's experience of ministry and in their culture clarifies the notion of spirituality as a constellation of interrelated elements.

Although Julian of Norwich may be best known for her theology of God's motherhood, she is not original since feminine God images are present in the Bible and in early christian writing. The significance of her contribution must be evaluated in light of the fact that the most developed theology of the motherhood of God and the nurturing qualities of Christ occurred in the writing of medieval Cistercian monks. Thus, as an idea it had more significance historically for men than for women.

Carolyn Walker Bynum's research (1984) demonstrates that many Cistercian abbots, needing to supplement their experience of religious authority with what they considered feminine characteristics—gentleness, tenderness, availability—projected those qualities onto Christ, their model of monk and abbot. In the process of infusing authority with love, these men romanticized motherhood, repeated female stereotypes, and imaged Christ as a nursing mother even while they maintained their distance from and even hostility toward actual women.

Medieval spirituality interprets its experience of being human as one of being the image and likeness of God. Here it continues patristic themes: grace as divinization; intellect, memory, and will as

reflections of the Trinity (e.g., *The Cloud of Unknowing*); the image of God as given from the beginning yet tarnished by sin, and asceticism as the way to develop the true likeness to God (e.g., *The Imitation of Christ*). For medieval women and men, such as Clare and Francis of Assisi, for example, one becomes one's true self through conformity to the model of true humanity: Jesus Christ.

In the midst of the wars and religious divisions of late western medieval history, significant women heeded the voices of their inner religious experience which urged them to redirect political affairs. Catherine of Siena, for example, advised the pope, and Joan of Arc led armies. They demonstrate the inseparability of religious and "worldly" experience.

Medieval eastern spirituality is well represented in Gregory of Palamas (1296-1359). He integrated *hesychasm*, eastern Christianity's ancient tradition of contemplative monasticism, into a doctrinal synthesis. In his anthropology, the whole person is called now to enjoy the first fruits of final deification. This includes social and political implications. In his theology of union with God, Gregory teaches that we participate in God's existence, God's "energies," yet God's essence remains unattainable and beyond all participation. Gregory wants to emphasize the immediacy and intimacy of the union while preserving the ultimate transcendence of God.

A central feature of *hesychasm* is prayer of the heart; that is, prayer of the whole person, including the body. Its aim is to be conscious of the grace of baptism that is already given but hidden by sin. Its method was influenced by Islam's joining of the holy name to the rhythm of breathing. Its wider context is the eastern understanding of active and contemplative life. These terms refer to interior development not to external situation. Active refers to the redirection (not suppression) of passions and contemplative refers to silence of heart. An enclosed nun, therefore, could be in the active life-stage while a doctor committed to her patients could be in the contemplative life if she had silence of heart. Prayer of the heart is a way of constant prayer possible to all persons, not just to monks or nuns.

Russian spirituality, which retained its medieval perspective into the nineteenth century, includes these characteristics. God is experienced in nature and history. Icons (religious images) and beautiful liturgy are powerful means of drawing believers and unbelievers into the mystery of God's saving presence. Christ is imaged as pantocrator rather than as humble or suffering; Mary's motherhood is emphasized rather than her virginity; beauty is embodied in angels. Asceticism is imaged as labor, as constant effort rather than as war. The Jesus-prayer, for example, is appreciated as a way to pray constantly. Russian religious ethics stress charity toward the destitute and poor.

Having given only modest attention to the east, this article makes a sharp turn back to the west where it remains.

The Reformation. Protestant experience of aspects of medieval tradition led to a new understanding of spirituality. Monasticism was no longer desirable as the special place to experience God; rather, God was free to be present intensely in all of life. Celibacy was no longer the privileged state of life in which to achieve union with God; instead, marriage was valued, and in some cases became almost an obligation for clergy. In this move women lost the advantages of convent life, among them independence from patriarchal marriage and the opportunity for higher education; instead they received a new role-expectation: the pastor's wife. Reformation Catholics and Protestants each tended to respond to issues by emphasizing the opposite posi-

tion and assuming the other's view had no merit. Contemporary Catholics, on the other hand, can appreciate Luther's insights and notice relationship to the great Spanish mystics that neither Luther nor Teresa and John consciously intended.

For Luther, speech about God is speech about absence; God is met only in the cross of Christ, that is, in lonely despair where there are no signs of transcendence, no conceptual neatness, no mystical assurances. Teresa of Jesus and John of the Cross would agree with Luther's conviction that one cannot contain or control God. Luther and authentic Catholic contemplative tradition object to the perversion of contemplation into a mysticism which imprisons God in a set of human experiences. John of the Cross, especially, teaches the inevitability of the dark night in which human desire is transformed and one's human projections onto God are eventually surrendered to allow authentic union with God in Christ. John, Teresa and Luther would agree also that knowledge of God is possible only on God's terms: when humans yield their self-assertive will and allow God to take the initiative in undeserved love. This affinity between Luther and the great Carmelite reformers does not, however, discount their differences regarding grace, church and human nature.

Carmelite reform, initiated by Teresa of Jesus and extended to the friars through John of the Cross, intended to make religious life a community of loving friends, living in poverty and solitude in order to be completely disposed to God's action for the sake of the needs of the church. Teresa's astute interpretation of her own process of religious development, explained in her *Life* and *The Interior Castle* and other writings, eventually made her a doctor of prayer for the universal church. While describing years of struggle with her own personality and cultural conditioning in order to surrender to God, Teresa communicates her experience of deepening prayer through the image of four waters. Her efforts at self-knowledge and honest love (drawing water from the well) yield a greater capacity for receiving God's love (a water wheel eases the effort); fidelity in the desert of love's purification allows the full force of God's acceptance and love to inundate her (the river) with unusual gifts of intimacy and leadership in the church (rain).

Ignatius of Loyola also distilled his religious experience into guidelines for spiritual growth. His *Spiritual Exercises* are an adaptable, imaginative method of meditation and contemplation of scripture designed to assimilate one to the mysteries of Christ as a contemplative in apostolic action.

Modern Spirituality. As the Reformation affected later Catholic spirituality through Spanish writers, so from the seventeenth century onward French spirituality was very influential.

The seedbed was not so much monasteries or universities as the parlour of Madame Acarie, later known as the Carmelite Mary of the Incarnation. Her discussion group included Benedict of Canfield and Pierre de Berulle. They absorbed the Platonic perspective of Pseudo-Denys the Areopagite, a medieval writer incorrectly identified for centuries as a disciple of Paul, and reshaped it to support their own understanding of spirituality. Canfield's *Exercise of the Will of God* stressed holiness as accessible to all. Its central theme is the mysticism of "nothingness" by which a person experiences the self-emptying of Jesus Christ in his passion. Berulle also teaches participation in the mysteries of Christ. In his *Grandeurs de Jesus* the goal of christian life is to reproduce on earth the adoration and servitude of Christ in heaven.

This era was also influenced by the exceptional personality of Francis de Sales. A bishop best known for his warmth and sensitivity as a spiritual director, his *Introduction to the Devout Life* is a classic treatment of laity's pursuit of holiness in everyday life. Through his friend Jeanne de Chantal, foundress of the Visitation Order, de Sales' theory and practice of spiritual direction became a lasting influence.

Jansenism, a complex and controversial combination of theological, political, and economic issues, was named for Cornelius Jansen whose rigorist presentation of Augustine's theology of grace had longlasting effects. Jansen maintained that grace is irresistible; in confession a penitent should never be given the benefit of the doubt through casuistry; one should sometimes give up holy communion as an act of devotion or through mortification; moral life must be strict. Although Blaise Pascal is associated with this movement, he is not Jansenist in any narrow sense.

Discovery of new lands generated a missionary spirituality characterized by the desire to announce the mystery of Christ as his ambassador by means of an evangelical life of fidelity and unswerving charity. Inspired by the mystique of Isaac Jogues and other missionary martyrs, it was encouraged by the pope's establishment of the Congregation for the Propagation of the Faith.

A distinct theological discipline called mystical theology also arose. Its aim was doctrinal and scientific study of the journey of the soul to contemplative union with God. All steps of the spiritual life were conceived as preparation for this union. Manuals of mystical theology attempted scientific classification of these steps, asking, for example, whether "spiritual marriage" is a state higher than "transforming union." This discipline offered a type of unified, speculative structure of all spirituality.

Nineteenth- and twentieth-century spirituality was, like all previous spirituality, a creative response to God's presence discerned in events and ideas Response to the Enlightenment, secularism, atheism, and political revolution ranged from anti-intellectualism in theology and piety on the one hand, to redemptive identification with modern struggles of faith in Therese of Lisieux and attempts to reconcile science and religion in Pierre Teilhard de Chardin. Concern to restore biblical prayer, share monastic riches with the laity, and reunite spirituality and theology motivated the liturgical movement. Religious revival took the form of parish "missions" which paralleled Protestant methods of evangelization in some ways. Response to industrialism included the social spirituality taught in papal encyclicals, Dorothy Day's spirituality of the Catholic Worker movement, and the founding of the Little Brothers and Sisters of Jesus who, inspired by Charles de Foucauld, live a ministry of evangelical presence as poor workers among workers. Devotion to Mary tended to compensate for Jansenist rigorism and patriarchal religion by promoting Mary as the kind, approachable mediatrix of all grace.

Theological and pastoral trends that shifted Catholic emphasis from "the soul" to the person, from dogma to history, from logic to method, from first principles to experience, culminated in the renewal of Vatican II.

II. Spirituality in the Life of the Church Since Vatican II

All the documents of Vatican II reflect concern for renewed spirituality. Some of their implications for the life of the church were expected while others were quite unanticipated.

The Constitution on the Sacred Liturgy announces that the primary goal of the entire council is to intensify christian spirituality, that is "the daily growth of Catholics in Christian living" (S.C. 1). This is the primary reason for renewing the liturgy, especially the eucharist. Enabling Christians to participate knowingly, actively, and fruitfully (S.C. 11) will draw them into authentic religious experience, namely conscious participation in the mysteries of Christ's life, ministry, death, and resurrection.

Dramatic consequences followed. Catholics shifted from an experience of going to watch "the priest say Mass" in Latin to one of being drawn into an experience of active listening to scripture (D.V. 21) read in their own language, and responding in song, procession, antiphonal prayer, and participation in the eucharistic meal of unity, remembering Jesus' saving teaching and action. Personal faith became more demanding because this style of participation made it harder simply "to go through the motions" of attendance. In addition, renewed liturgy set up expectations that one would receive adequate understanding of scripture and a call to conversion, warm welcome from an inclusive community, and faithful witness to Jesus' ministry to the poor and marginalized. When these expectations were not met, Christians became dissatisfied and responded in various ways.

Post-Vatican II Catholicism has, for many reasons, become less and less a eucharistic community. Women's alienation from the liturgy's predominantly masculine God-language and male clericalism, for example, has caused some to turn away from the Roman Catholic eucharist. Availability of fewer priests and the lack of consideration of alternatives such as the ordination of women or married men has led to the phenomenon of thousands of christian communities living far from the council's vision of the eucharist as the "outstanding means for Christians to express in their lives and manifest to others the mystery of Christ and the nature of the Church" (S.C. 1).

Two themes in the Dogmatic Constitution on the Church significantly affected spirituality: the universal call to holiness, and the call to the same holiness cultivated in various duties of life. First, "all the faithful of whatever rank ... are called to the fullness of the Christian life and to the perfection of charity" (L.G. 40). Because the document continues to assume the traditional perspective of higher and lower "rank" in which bishops, priests, and religious were assumed to be called to a special holiness, this document, in effect, extended this same call to "ordinary lay people." They heard it and responded enthusiastically to grass roots movements for spiritual renewal, such as Cursillo, Marriage Encounter, and the charismatic movement. One program to rejuvenate parish spirituality, for example, involved four thousand parishes within five years. Emphasizing the council's biblical definition of holiness as mercy, kindness, humility, and other fruits of the Spirit, these movements often manifest an egalitarian style of ministry implied in the second theme from the document on the church.

Although the documents of Vatican II retain the view of different ranks (e.g. clergy and laity), and states of life (lay and religious), the hierarchical attitude perpetuated by this language was undermined by also teaching that the "same holiness is cultivated in various duties of life" (L.G. 41), and the whole church "is missionary by her very nature" (A.G. 2). Inspired by this more egalitarian vision, laity, sisters, brothers, and priests made a Cursillo, for example, in which they both received and gave spiritual ministry, or joined a charismatic prayer group in which the Spirit's gifts of leadership were sometimes recognized in women rather than in priests.

The notion of every Christian participating in the church's "mission" was gradually translated into language of universal "ministry." Under the impact of returning to the scripture as "the pure and perennial source of the spiritual life" (D.V. 21), Catholics discovered the NT experience of the ministry of reconciliation exercised by every person through mutually supportive gifts. Although the documents of Vatican II speak of "ministry" only when referring to the clergy, within twenty years the dominant practical understanding of "ministry" became one that is based upon the experience of spiritual gifts and not upon ordination to the priesthood. Moreover, there is widespread declericalization of ministries, such as spiritual direction and retreats, areas once assumed to be the prerogative of priests.

Reversing a long tradition of viewing "the world" as inimical to the church, as a sphere divided from "the sacred" and to be converted and taught, the document on the Church in the Modern World affirms the value of the world and confesses that the church could learn from the world and should be receptively reading "the signs of the times." Christian spirituality, therefore, becomes more authentically biblical, discerning God's presence in the midst of the events of history as well as in the movements of one's inner spirit.

Not only is the secular world affirmed as having something to teach the church, but also Protestants, eastern Orthodox, Jews and all non-christian religions are approached with respectful attention to what they can contribute to Catholic spirituality. "Each branch of the human family possesses ... some part of the spiritual treasure entrusted by God to humanity..." (G.S. 86). The church's task is to uncover, cherish, and ennoble all that is true, good, and beautiful in the human community (G.S. 96).

This openness to receive from persons outside the Catholic community encouraged not only unprecedented outreach in interreligious dialogue, but also new openness to diversity within Catholic spirituality. Black, Mexican, Filipino, Puerto Rican and other cultures celebrate and develop their unique religious experience in liturgy, education, and action for justice. In some places in the United States they constitute the majority of Catholics, while in other places they are regarded as marginal because the NT principle of genuine diversity in unity is not yet familiar or acceptable to many Catholics. Openness to diversity and critical evaluation of the past has, in fact, created not only possibilities for enrichment and shared gifts, but also divisiveness and polarity. In summary, the perspective of Vatican II has generated either a holistic spirituality which adheres to God at the center of everything and seeks to cooperate with God in bringing God's reign into every sphere of life; or, for some, a defensive spirituality that values certitude more than understanding.

Thomas Merton is a paradigm of spirituality in the life of the church of Vatican II. Long before the Council, Merton gradually perceived the direction of God's spirit in his life moving him from a desire to flee the world in order to find God in the sacred sphere of the monastery to a realization that his former perspective was an illusion. "Finding God" was, rather, a matter of entering fully into himself and into every dimension of the world of human friendship, of action for justice, of humanity praising and seeking God in non-christian religions. Catholic spirituality since Vatican II has moved steadily in these directions, rejoicing in the Spirit's gifts and facing the inevitable questions and discomfort associated with new pathways.

III. The State of the Issues in Spirituality Today

Spirituality, in the 1980s, is an immature discipline. It is past the initial stage in which scholars develop some common vocabulary, basic categories, and journals for publication. Yet it has not reached the mature point at which it has the generalized theory which would enable it to be a developed discipline fully recognized in academic circles. Spirituality is in the fascinating intermediate stage in which it creates its new identity while remaining linked to its family of origin.

A primary issue, then, is the nature or identity of the discipline itself. Here one of the most significant contributions comes from Sandra M. Schneiders. What follows is her explanation of the contemporary understanding of the term "spirituality," and the basic characteristics of the discipline.

While striving to avoid christian exclusiveness and denominational narrowness, virtually everyone discussing spirituality today is talking about self-transcendence which gives integrity and meaning to life by situating the person within the horizon of ultimacy. A distinction can be made, at this point, between self-transcendence understood in a philosophical or religious sense. The *philosophical meaning* is based on a distinction between the material and the spiritual, the spiritual being understood as that capacity for self-transcendence through knowledge and love which characterizes the human being as a person. Thus, in the philosophical sense of the term, all humans are essentially "spiritual" and actualize that dimension of selfhood through the establishment of human relationships. The *religious meaning* of spirituality is based on the conception of what constitutes the proper and highest actualization of the human capacity for self-transcendence in personal relationships, namely, relationship with God. Spirituality, then, in its religious sense, refers to the relationship between the individual and God pursued in the life of faith, hope, and love. The *christian meaning* is a particular specification of the religious meaning, indicating actualization of the capacity for self-transcendence that is constituted by the gift of the Holy Spirit which gives a relationship to God in Christ within the believing community. Christian spirituality, therefore, is trinitarian, christological, ecclesial religious experience.

When spirituality is understood as Schneiders suggests, certain features will characterize the emerging discipline which purports to study spirituality. First, this discipline will be *descriptive and analytic* rather than prescriptive and evaluative. Whether the researcher is studying discernment, action for social justice, God-images or any other of the hundreds of other topics which are attracting scholars today, the first task will be to understand the phenomenon on its own terms, that is, as it is or was actually experienced by Christians. Second, an *interdisciplinary approach* is essential. Very diverse phenomena fall within the field of spirituality and each demands its appropriate method. At times it may be historical, at other times it may be psychological or literary or theological. No single method is sufficient to deal with the documents, events, or persons that comprise the "data" of this field. Third, spirituality is now committed to an *ecumenical and even cross-cultural* approach. Part of understanding any phenomenon is seeing how it fits into the larger picture of the human quest for meaning and integration, of which the christian quest is only one actualization. Fourth, spirituality is *inclusive or holistic* in its approach. It is not "the soul" who seeks integration in holiness of life but the whole person, body and spirit, mind and will and emotions, individual and social, male and female. Fifth, spirituality seems to be a necessarily *"participant" discipline*. The researcher must know the spiritual quest by personal experience if he or she is to understand the phenomena of spirituality. One might be studying a spirituality quite different from one's own, but without some analogous experience one could hardly be expected to comprehend the activities and passivities of the spiritual life. Sixth, spirituality studies not principles to be applied nor general classes or typical cases but *concrete individuals:* persons, works, events. Consequently the researcher in spirituality is necessarily involved in what Ricoeur (*Interpretation Theory,* 1976) has called the "science of the individual" in which interpretation plays the key role and validation of interpretation through a dialectic of explanation and understanding rather than verification of repeatable scientific results is the objective. Lastly, spirituality, like psychology, has a *triple objective* that cannot be neatly simplified. One studies spirituality to understand it; but one also studies it in order to foster one's own spirituality and to foster the spirituality of others. The relative importance of each of these objectives differs from scholar to scholar and project to project but it is not possible to state once and for all that spirituality is either a theoretical or a practical discipline. It is both, although the emphasis varies at different moments in each project.

The methods and content of recent books and journals in spirituality demonstrate at least five significant trends in this field: sustained attention to feminist issues; concern for the link between prayer and social justice; reliance on classical sources for answers to current questions; recognition of the value of developmental psychology and its understanding of "the self"; and agreement that experience is the most appropriate starting point.

The presence of one trend often includes several others, as Mary Jo Weaver's summary of feminist spirituality demonstrates (pp. 211-12). Feminist spirituality is both old and new, alive to ancient rhythms of the goddess while willing to experiment with spontaneous feminist rituals. It is rooted in the tradition—sometimes eager to claim connections with the eucharistic celebration of the christian church—and yet opposed to its expression of exclusive male power. Roman Catholic feminist spirituality is clearly political, in the sense that it is predicated on a world view that finds the sacred in what used to be called the secular, and yet may have something much in common with mystical prayer: perhaps God/ess (Rosemary R. Ruether's term for the fullness of divinity, combining masculine and feminine words for the divine) can only be experienced in a combination of active service on behalf of the marginalized and lively, daring participation in moments of divine disclosure deep within the soul.

Roman Catholic feminist spirituality, Weaver maintains, recapitulates the questions of feminist historians by interrogating the tradition of female sanctity in Catholicism. By an exclusive focus on Teresa of Avila as a mystic without corresponding attention to her uphill struggle for personal integration and power, the tradition obscured an important part of her value for feminist interpreters. Similarly, past visions of female sanctity emphasized Catherine of Siena's obedience to the pope or disparagement of female weakness to the neglect of her independence and personal power as a reformer and spiritual director. By choosing to look differently at these saints, feminist researchers remind us that nuns and laywomen have always encountered opposition in the church when they embodied visions that were at odds with the option of complementarity (i.e. women complete men by serving and supporting their roles) and cloister presented to them by patriarchal males allegedly speaking for God. In looking at Julian of Norwich, we are reminded of

how much we need feminist theologians and critical interpreters of the tradition in addition to visionaries. Most of all, in gathering the many versions of Mary together to intuit the possibilities of a composite symbol, feminists convey some sense of the need for solidarity and the power of collective action.

In short, Weaver's summary of feminist spirituality exemplifies the five themes mentioned above. She assumes the importance of classical sources and a starting point in experience as well as the centrality of the issues of self-development and social justice.

The issue of "the self" is the focal issue in contemporary spirituality's examination of the relationship between psychology and religion and between grace and nature. Because this theme is so important, the rest of this article will examine Thomas Merton's and Ann Ulanov's positions on the relationship between human and religious development. For them, development is a matter of recognizing and receiving one's true self.

Contemplation, for Merton, fulfills our deepest human capacities, yet it does not come without some work on our part. We must develop certain human intellectual and affective capacities in order to facilitate contemplation. For example, reason must sift critically all spiritual experiences in order to judge which ones really correspond to genuine faith. Imagination, originality, freshness of response—qualities dulled by industrial society—need to be reinvigorated in order to promote contemplative experience. Most of all, one must "return to the heart," to love, to one's deepest center which includes and goes far beyond the consciousness reached by studies in psychology. For contemplation, in Merton's eyes, is life itself, fully awake to oneness with God. The intuition of our "real self" brings this awareness of profound union with God and with all persons and things.

Merton's model of spiritual development, therefore, is basically a pattern of discovery. As we discover our true self we also discover the true God on whom we depend, and this discovery is a matter of choices, of ever greater freedom, and of awareness or discernment. All of these are interdependent. Merton—true to the contemporary discipline of spirituality which begins by examining concrete individual experience through a "participant" mode—describes the process in first person terms. I discover my true self by conscious choices to love, by choices which deliver me from self-seeking. This deliverance is the core of freedom, because the most important aspect of freedom is the liberation from whatever tends to keep alive the illusion (the false self) that opposes God's reality living in me. As long as I perceive no greater subjective reality in me than my false self, I have no freedom. When I am delivered from self-seeking then I am free to seek God on whom I am dependent and who is present at the heart of my true self. My discovery or knowledge of God is paradoxically a knowledge not of God as the object of scrutiny, but of myself as utterly dependent on God's saving and merciful knowledge of me. Ultimately, Merton declares, you discover there is no duality between your true self and God. To a friend Merton once confided, "You have to see your will and God's will dualistically for a long time. You have to experience duality for a long time until you see it's not there."

Although Merton, a contemplative monk, views the self primarily from a theological point of view, his discussion necessarily has implications for psychological issues. For example, the "true self" is a reality below the level of ego consciousness, but this does not make ego consciousness irrelevant. The ego contributes to contemplation by actively opening to deeper levels of awareness and by facing the fact that it is an illusion to consider itself the whole self. Typical of Catholic theology of nature and grace, Merton views the self as innately and naturally self-transcending and would, therefore, expect to find evidence of transcendence in psychological theories of the self. On the other side of the issue, psychologically sophisticated study of Merton's spirituality of the self could serve as data for what some contemporary theologians are calling an "empirical theology of grace."

Ann Ulanov, a Jungian analyst and christian theologian, also explores the nature of religious experience through sustained reflection upon the nature of the self. Unlike Merton who uses the patristic language of true/false self, Ulanov uses a feminist revision of the Jungian language of the self which has feminine qualities. Both Ulanov and Merton, however, come to similar conclusions about what constitutes a mature relationship to God, as we shall see below; and the similarities are noticeable despite the different language because both authors stay close to precisely the same focus: experience of the self.

Ulanov's model of religious development, for men as well as women, is constituted by receptivity to all of ourselves. She recommends special sensitivity to the way both feminine experience and feminine elements of being are analogous to religious experience, that is, to God's action in our lives.

Both men and women benefit from meditation upon the way their religious experience is analogous to feminine experience (i.e., the concrete experience possible only to females: birthing). Like a mother, the religious person must await God's movement and follow God's transforming lead, must both participate vigorously in the opening to new life and receive submissively the action and "tempo" of the other.

Religious experience is also analogous to certain elements of being that are actually found in both men's and women's lives but are called "feminine" and are symbolized through feminine images because our primary experience of them begins with women: our mothers. One example of a feminine element of being is a sense of being-at-the-core-of-oneself. This involves a capacity to be at rest, sensing one's "self" as somehow found, given, and reflected, instead of achieved, or manufactured. The origins of this experience can be seen in the activity of a mother acting as a mirror for her infant, reflecting back in her responses the child's being-there. This experience also involves vulnerability but not lack of individual reality and worth. It means vulnerability because the essential "I am" is discovered through our dependence on another person reflecting back to us the fact that "we are." However, a successful dependence yields not a fixation but a full-bodied sense of individual being rooted at the core, a center existing for oneself. Clearly, Ulanov points out, this sense of "I am" created by togetherness is at the heart of religious experience.

In summary, Merton and Ulanov are examples of the trend in contemporary spirituality to recognize the primacy of the issue of the self. They exemplify also the advantages of spirituality's method of staying close to experience in all explanations and testing past assumptions against one's critical reflection upon experience. This allows some basic agreements between different positions to stand out. For example, because both Merton and Ulanov focus on careful description of the phenomenon of relationship to God as it is experienced by Christians, Merton's description of contemplation using traditional patristic language of the true/false self can be seen to have striking parallels with Ulanov's psychological description. Merton describes his discovery of his true self as one that is embedded in his discovery and acceptance of radical adult dependence upon God. This bears a strong resemblance to the feminine quality of being-at-the-core described in Ulanov's discussion of religious experience.

Other aspects of this issue of the self will, no doubt, constitute the agenda for spirituality in the future. As scholars examine the implications of psychoanalysis, for example, they are asking how God-representations formed at early stages of development can be revised at more mature stages. As feminists question the validity of psychological models based on exclu-sively male observations of mother/child relationships, for another example, they ask whether that relationship is more accurately described as mutuality rather than as fusion or mirroring understood only as receptivity. Responses to these questions could make a significant difference for understanding the nature of religious experience.

The agenda for spirituality also includes very practical sides of this issue of the self. For example, could a more adequate theory of the self resolve the tension some Christians experience between contemplative solitude and social service? Spirituality must also address the dangers of inviting people who have a formless or poorly differentiated self to simplify their prayer or devote themselves to religious ministry. Without explicit attention to the work of identity formation, in the former situation, what is an inner condition of lack can be mistaken for the boundlessness of mystical union; in the latter case, a person might fuse with the ideology of a worthy cause and become authoritarian or a religious fanatic.

In summary, a synthesis of these trends sets the future agenda for christian spirituality: a discipline that is rooted in experience, attentive to the issue of the self, nourished by history, and concerned for social justice especially by promoting genuine mutuality and equality between women and men.

See **Anthropology, Christian; Asceticism; Celibacy; Laity; Monasticism; Mystical Theology; Mysticism; Paschal Mystery; Prayer; Religious Life; Religious Orders**

Louis Bouyer, Jean Leclercq, and Francois Vandenbroucke, *A History of Christian Spirituality,* 3 vols., New York: Seabury, 1977; 1982. Carolyn Walker Bynum, *Jesus as Mother,* Berkeley: U of California, 1984. Bernard, McGinn, John Meyendorff, and Jean Leclerq. *Christian Spirituality: Origins to the Twelfth Century,* New York: Crossroad, 1985. Sandra M. Schneiders, "Theology and Spirituality: Strangers, Rivals, or Partners?", *Horizons* 13/1 (Spring 1986). Mary Jo Weaver, *New Catholic Women,* San Francisco: Harper and Row, 1985.

JOANN WOLSKI CONN

SUBORDINATIONISM

A view of Christ which maintains that he is not equal in substantial being with God the Father but is in some fashion subordinate to him. This view as articulated in Arianism was repudiated by the Council of Nicaea.

See **Jesus Christ, Trinity**

SUBSIDIARITY

A principle prominent in Catholic social teaching according to which all social bodies exist for the sake of the person, so that what individuals are able to do, societies should not assume, and what smaller societies can do, larger societies should not take over. That negative delimitation is balanced by the positive assertion that what individuals or smaller societies are not able to do should be done for them by society. The principle has been applied to civil society by every pope since Pius XI. That it should also apply in the church, with due respect for its hierarchical order, was stated by Pius XII and Paul VI, under whom it was also accepted as a principle for the reform of canon law.

SUBSTANCE AND ACCIDENT

These two philosophical terms are correlatives, i.e., each one is understood by reference to the other. *Substance* means that which is apt to exist in itself and not in another, i.e., not as part of another being. *Accident* means that which is apt to exist not in itself but only in another. Substance is the concrete individual thing in the real order, the ultimate subject of all its attributes in the real order and of all its predications in our language about it.

The doctrine of substance and accident was introduced by Aristotle to explain or render intelligible two main features of reality as we experience it. *First,* we notice in reality many different individual things, each of which is the subject or bearer of several different attributes or properties, that are predicated of it when we speak about it in language. *Substance* expresses the unifying core of the thing that is the ultimate subject or bearer of all its attributes, of all that is predicated about it, and which itself cannot be predicated of anything else. It exists *in itself,* not in any other being as part of it. Aristotle called this the *hypokeimenon,* that which lies under all its attributes, and this came down to us in Latin as *substantia,* that which stands under its attributes. He also distinguished two meanings of substance: the primary one he called *first substance,* which means the concrete individual thing in the real order; *secondary substance* refers to the common nature abstracted from many concrete individuals and expressed in a universal concept applicable to all, e.g., "man." We will be concerned only with first substance here.

The attributes or properties of the individual being which do not constitute its essence but belong to it as non-essential modifications of its being are called *accidents*, i.e., that which *happens to* or *belongs to* a substance, but is not identical with it. Note that these accidents are not complete being or "things" on their own, but can exist only *in* some substance, as modes *of* something, so that their definition must include some subject in which they inhere. In fact neither substance nor accident are complete beings on their own. Every accident needs some substance in which to inhere, and most substances (at least all the ones in our experience) need *some* accidents to complete them, though the latter can change over time. The later technical term for such incomplete correlative components of a real being is that they are *metaphysical co-principles* combining to make one complete being. Though *really distinct* from one another (i.e., objectively non-identical, irreducible in the real order), they are *not separable* from each other (a serious distortion of the classical doctrine that came in after St. Thomas, with William of Ockham and the Nominalist School, and which opened the door to serious later misunderstandings).

The classical *definitions* resulting from the above analysis are as follows: *substance* is that which is apt to exist *in itself* and not in another; *accident* is that which is apt to exist not in itself *but only in another*.

The *second feature* of reality which the doctrine is designed to explain is that the same individual being undergoes a process of change in which it retains its individual identity throughout the series of changing states or attributes, e.g. John is now angry, then happy; now cold, then hot, etc. Here substance is needed as a *principle of continuity* in terms of which the being retains its individual identity through the series of changing accidents across time. In its first role substance is a center of unity for many accidents possessed *simultaneously* in time; here in its second role, substance serves as the center of unity for many *successive* accidents across time.

In this second case it is even clearer why a substance and its accidents must be *really distinct* from one another (though not able to exist separately): in a change process old accidents go and new ones come; now if each were identical with the substance it would have to be present wherever the substance is found, which means it could never come or go, thus rendering impossible the very fact of change. That there are in fact substances which retain their identity through changes is evident from our experience, especially of our own selves: if we deny this, it makes unintelligible my experience of *memory* of my past actions as *mine,* my *moral responsibility* for my past actions as worthy of praise or blame now ("I did this and I am sorry for it.").

Substance and Accident as Potency and Act

Since a given substance is able to acquire a certain set of new accidents across time and not others, it must have in it a *natural capacity or aptitude* to acquire these and no others (e.g., a plant can put out new leaves, but it cannot learn mathematics), which Aristotle called a *potentiality.* The concrete subject which has the potentiality is called *a potency,* and the actual accident which it now has is called its *act.* The potency is said to be *in act* toward the accident it now has, and *in potency* toward any future or possible accidents it does not now possess. Thus the potentiality of any nature explains why it can undergo such and such a set of changes but no others. It is at once an *opening* toward the future, as being a natural aptitude for all its possible accidental modifications, and a *closure,* closing it off from any modifications beyond its natural capacity.

Application to God

Since everything real in any way must be either a substance or an accident, existing either in itself or in another, God must be the supreme substance in an analogous way appropriate to his own nature, such that his substance is identical to his act of existing, which is not true of any created substance, since it receives its act of existence from God. Also, since God as infinite fullness of all perfection cannot change to acquire some new perfection he did not have before, and cannot be composed in his being, he must be pure substance with not really distinct accidents, *pure Act* with no potency.

Kinds of Accidents: the Categories of Being

Substance and the various basic or irreducible kinds of accidents make up the primary *categories of being and predication* (i.e., categories of reality and of our language about it). Aristotle listed *nine* ultimate *categories of accidents*: (1) quantity; (2) quality; (3) action; (4) passion (i.e., being acted upon); (5) relation; (6) position of body (standing, sitting); (7) dress (wearing a hat, armed, etc.); (8) time; (9) place. Since position can be reduced to relations between parts of the body, and dress, time and place, can be reduced to relations to something extrinsic to the substance's own real being, the nine categories of linguistic predication can be reduced to *five* irreducible categories of *real accidents*, i.e., the first five in the above list.

Another important distinction between kinds of accidents is that between accidents that are *contingent* or mutable, i.e., can come and go, and those that are *essential properties*, not identical with the substance but flowing naturally and necessarily from its essence, so that they always accompany the substance, e.g., the various operative faculties of human nature: senses, intellect and will.

Medieval Thought: St. Thomas

The Aristotelian doctrine, introduced into the medieval West through Latin translations in the late twelfth and early thirteenth centuries, was taken up and made a central piece in most medieval metaphysical systems, especially by St. Thomas Aquinas, with minor refinements and more precision. Thus St. Thomas highlights what was certainly implicit in Aristotle, that substance, as identical with active nature, is not inert or static (a misunderstanding introduced later by Locke) but has a dynamic relationship to its accidental operations. "Every substance exists for the sake of its operations" (*Summa contra Gentes*, I, 45); ". . . indeed operation is the ultimate perfection of each thing" (III, 113). Thus the proper technical description of an accidental change is that in it *the substance itself changes* (is really affected by the change) but *not substantially,* i.e., does not lose its essential identity. As Aristotle has already explained, if the change does go so deep as to break down the essential unity of the substance itself we have another kind of change, called a *substantial change,* which requires a deeper composition within the substance itself, that of substantial form and primary matter.

Another important precision of St. Thomas is that the substance of all created beings, since it signifies the same as their essence, is not identical with its act of existence but receives it as a potency receives its proper act, whereas the substance of God is identical with his act of existence.

Modern Philosophy

The substance/ accident doctrine was passed down to modern Western philosophy through Descartes, but underwent significant modifications at the hands of several thinkers. The first was *Descartes* himself, who redefined substance as "a thing which so exists that it needs no other thing for existence" (*Principles of Philosophy*, I, 51), except God, of course, he added, for created substance. This apparently small change from the classical *in itself* to the Cartesian *by itself* is in fact a serious distortion of the classical understanding, leading to the notion of a substance as an *isolated, unrelated* monad, sufficient to itself. It was precisely this Cartesian definition and not the classical one that was the starting point for the rejection of substance by Whitehead and Process philosophy in general, on the quite sound grounds that all real entities are intrinsically related.

The second misunderstanding was due to *John Locke,* the English empiricist. Exaggerating the real distinction of accident from substance, he concluded that accidental qualities were the direct objects of our knowledge, known to us absolutely by themselves, and hence that the substance, which he agreed was necessary to support them, was a mere substratum unknown and unknowable to us. This led to the conception of substance as an *inert, static, unknowable "X",* soon to be rejected as useless by later thinkers. This is a far cry from the classical notion of substance as a dynamic center of action manifesting itself in and through its accidents, known only as modes *of* their supporting substance.

The third misunderstanding was that of *David Hume,* the radical English empiricist. For him, if substance were to be really distinct from its accidents, it must be *separable* from them, so that each could exist without the other. Since it is impossible to find such a naked substance in our experience (or even imagine one), he rejected the whole idea of substance as a myth of the metaphysicians. All we perceive is a flow of sense impressions of qualities, "accidents" with no separable underlying something uniting them. Quite true, if real distinction implies separability, which both Aristotle and St. Thomas would have roundly rejected.

The fourth major change in the understanding of substance was the work of *Immanuel Kant.* For him, since things in themselves are unknowable, substance becomes no longer a basic structure of real things in themselves but rather an *a priori* form of our thought which we impose on the flow of sense appearances in order to render them intelligible. It is not therefore a structure of the thing but of our thought about the appearances of the thing.

Later modern and contemporary thinkers have rejected some or all of these modern reinterpretations of the classical notion of the substance and accident composition, often for good reasons. But as a result they often reject the notion of substance entirely, seemingly unaware that there is an older classical notion of substance as dynamic, really related to other substances by its actions, and inseparable from its accidents (and vice versa), though not reducible to any of them. Thus a number of contemporary thinkers, such as John Macmurray (*The Self as Agent*), while rejecting the "traditional notion of substance," accept the notion of man as "agent," expressing himself through his ongoing actions. This is precisely the classical notion of substance as *active nature*. In fact, in the classical doctrine the notions of essence, nature and substance all refer to the same reality: *essence* answers the question *what* something is; *nature* signifies the same essence as *center of action; substance* signifies the same nature or essence as *principle of unity* of its various attributes.

Application to Theology

Substance is important for talking with precision about person and nature in the Incarnate Son of God, as we have already mentioned above, and also in the Trinity of Divine Persons with the same nature or substance. The notion of accident is also important for understanding the ontological status of the various supernatural graces and gifts conferred upon us by God. Although these gifts (e.g. sanctifying grace conferred by the sacraments, actual graces, the gifts of the Holy Spirit, even the final gift of the beatific vision in heaven) are of the supernatural order, raising us to a new participation in the divine life itself, still they all remain ontologically in the *accidental order* of being. Since they are gifts given to enrich *me,* I must remain the same substantial self in order to be thus enriched, rather than turn into some essentially different person.

But the most important application is to the transformation of bread and wine into the body and blood of Jesus Christ in the sacrament of the Holy Eucharist. This process has been traditionally expressed in the church's teaching as *transubstantiation* Unlike the ordinary changes we know in our experience, what remains after the words of consecration are pronounced is not the substance of bread and wine, while the accidents or surface appearance change, but the reverse: the whole substance of the bread and wine, including both form and matter, disappear, to be replaced by the whole substance of Christ's body and blood, while the outward appearances or accidental properties of the bread and wine remain the same—the only known case of such a change. The accidents are now

directly supported by the power of God in place of the support of their natural substance. But such a change obviously could not take place, even by a miracle, unless the substance and accidents of the bread and wine were somehow really distinct. Otherwise to change one would be to change the other too. It should be noted, however, that the church does not commit herself in her dogmatic definition to any one strictly philosophical explanation of the mystery, not even to the technical doctrine of substance and accident. It contents itself with speaking of the reality of the bread and wine disappearing while the appearance (*species*) of the bread and wine remain. Still, the notions of substance and accident are indispensable for theological discussion.

See **Eucharist, Jesus Christ**

B.F. Brown, *Accidental Being: A Study in the Metaphysics of St. Thomas,* Lanham, MD: U Press of America, 1985. D Connell, "Substance and Subject," *Philosophical Studies* (Maynooth), 26 (1979), pp. 7-29. L. De Raeymaeker, *Philosophy of Being,* St. Louis: Herder, 1956. M. Loux, *Substance and Attribute,* Boston: Reidel, 1978. R.E. McCall, *The Reality of Substance,* Washington: Cath. U of America, 1956. "Substance" and "Accident" in *New Cath. Encyclopedia,* New York: McGraw-Hill, 1967. *Proceedings of Amer. Cath. Phil. Assoc.,* 61 (1987) on theme of Substance. L. Rumble, "Science, Substance and Sacrament," *Homiletic and Pastoral Rev.,* 59 (1959), pp. 638-48. J. Felt, "Whitehead's Misconception of Aristotle's Substance," *Process Studies,* 14 (1985), pp. 224-46.

NORRIS CLARK, SJ

SUFFERING

Suffering is the disruption of inner human harmony caused by physical, mental, spiritual, and emotional forces experienced as isolating and threatening our very existence. As the deprivation of human good, suffering is inseparable from the mystery of evil. However, suffering and evil are not caused by God, the author of all good (Genesis 1), but are inherent in the universe's natural processes and in the uniqueness of human freedom, in the misuse of free will that is the moral evil of sin. The reasons for and meaning of the suffering apparently inseparable from human life have been the subject of questioning throughout history

An early Hebrew view interpreted suffering as God's punishment upon the sin which has wounded humankind since its beginning (Gen 3:16-19). A sense of national solidarity influenced other writers to understand suffering as divine retribution for personal and communal sin; the evil deeds of one person could draw down suffering upon family members, the nation, and future generations (Num 12:1-15; Deut 8:28; 2 Sam 24:10-17). As a corrective to this view the post-exilic prophet Ezekiel proposed a theology of individual retribution: suffering is punishment only for one's own sin (Ezek 31:29-30).

Yet the suffering of innocent people gave the lie even to Ezechiel's modified theory. Psalmists voiced the cry of the innocent over the injustice of sinners prospering (Ps 6:4; 34:17; 88:47), and the author of Job finally could counsel only silence before the inscrutable wisdom of God (Job 42:1-6). Other post-exilic scriptures found the answer to human suffering in a conception of God's eschatological justice which would mete out eternal reward for the good and punishment for the wicked (Dan 12:1-3; 2 Macc 7:9, 11, 23).

The exile experience also led several of the prophets to see suffering as a means of individual and national conversion (Isa 25:8; 35:4-10; Jer 31:15-20). Isaiah's "Servant Songs" (Isa 42:1-4; 49:1-7; 50:4-11; 52:13-53:12) further interpreted Israel's suffering during the exile as a vicarious atonement for the sins of the nations.

This last insight aided NT authors to understand the significance of Jesus' death as a vicarious atonement for the sin of the entire human race (1 Pet 2:24; Rom 3:25). His suffering and death are the means of reconciling the whole universe to God (Col 1:20-21), and union with his passion is the indispensable way of sharing in his glorious victory over sin and death itself (Rom 6:5; 7:4; 8:17). A christian outlook thus finds the meaning of suffering in Jesus' own redemptive death and resurrection.

The destructive impact of sin leaves its inevitable wounds of suffering not only in the sinner but also in the innocent victims of sin. But Jesus, God's living word of mercy, has plunged himself into the depths of human suffering. From within this chasm which evokes primarily bitterness and rage from the human race, he has uttered with his life a human *yes* of unconditional love and absolute self-giving. The infinite force of this love has broken through even into his body, transforming him into the risen, life-giving Lord of the universe (2 Cor 3:17-18). A christian response to the tragedy of sin and suffering thus arises from personal experience of the power of Jesus' resurrection to heal the alienating, self-centered forces in every human heart.

Post-Reformation theology had stressed the need to endure patiently the personal sufferings of mind and body viewed as crosses sent by God to test and purify us spiritually. But modern atheism has argued forcefully against the existence of a God who could cause or even permit the magnitude of world-wide social suffering which contemporary news media make it impossible to ignore.

In light of these developments, the theology of Vatican II focuses christian attention today on the meaninglessness of human suffering viewed apart from Jesus' healing death and resurrection (G.S. 21, 22). Christians are called to alleviate suffering actively, especially as it results from unjust social and political structures, and, wherever possible, to eradicate its causes (A.A. 8, 13; A.G.

5, 12).

The christian proclamation of the risen Lord thus centers on the power of his Spirit enabling us to live a wholly new kind of existence, a life of communion and compassion instead of isolation and oppression. The very nature of this new life in the risen Christ forbids Christians to be indifferent to any suffering, especially when its causes are personal and social sin. Christians are called to say with their lives, "I fill up in my own body what is lacking in the suffering of Christ" (Col 1:24). For in the suffering of the innocent, Christ himself now suffers; and in the labor to heal the causes of suffering, Christ himself now labors.

A christian understanding of human suffering is aided also by increased awareness of the inseparable interplay between spirit and body, between spiritual, mental and emotional deprivation, and bodily illness. Contemporary advances in the medical, social, and theological sciences have helped to direct christian attention to the need for healing the wounds caused by suffering in the human soul and psyche.

The modern rediscovery of the healing power of spirituality, the restorative power of the sacraments and prayer, and the help offered by psychological counseling and medical and economic aid can do much to lessen the weight of suffering. A holistic life style that encourages inner peace, emotional autonomy, creative activity, and loving, supportive relationships also fosters human well-being. Yet suffering, co-existent in all of its forms with life itself, invites the Christian to a life-long process not only of personal healing but also of commitment to the healing of others.

When available help still leaves us powerless before a specific suffering, we confront a mystery which pushes us to the very brink of the mystery of human existence. In these situations, often the only recourse open to us is the prayer of the powerless one begging God for relief and for the heart to surrender ourselves in union with Jesus' own passion (Ps 107:6, 13, 19, 28; Lk 22:42-43). In yielding ourselves to this path, we may hope to experience God's own closeness to the brokenhearted (Ps 34:18; 147:3) and, in the midst of suffering that cannot be alleviated, to grow more compassionate, wiser, stronger.

The lives of those who suffer in this way unveil to the world the inherent beauty and dignity of the human person. They reveal as well to the eyes of faith a God who has responded to our human suffering by plunging into its depths with us, a God who now invites us to labor together for the world's healing. They disclose to us a God whose love has robbed even the most unspeakable tragedy of its power to destroy us; a God, finally, whose love is strong enough to transform even our deaths into an unimaginable future where he himself will wipe every tear from our eyes (Rom 8:28-39; Rev 21:4).

See **Eschatology, Evil, Jesus Christ, Redemption**

Ladislaus Boros, *Pain and Providence,* New York: Seabury Crossroad, 1966. Flavian Dougherty, C.P., Ed., *The Meaning of Human Suffering,* New York: Human Sciences Press, 1982. Monika Hellwig, *Jesus, The Compassion of God,* Wilmington, DE: Michael Glazier, 1985. John Paul II, "Apostolic Letter on the Christian Significance of Human Suffering," in James Walsh, S.J., and P.G. Walsh, Eds., *Divine Providence and Human Suffering,* Wilmington, DE: Michael Glazier, 1985. Dorothee Soelle, *Suffering,* trans. by Everett R. Kalin, Philadelphia: Fortress Press, 1975.

MARY ANN FATULA, OP

SUNDAY

For Christians, Sunday is a "little Easter," a celebration of life in the Risen Lord by his people of the new creation. The theology of the christian Sunday has a rich history of meanings. Communal worship celebrating the paschal mystery of the Lord marked the christian Sunday from early times. A variety of names for the Lord's Day, as well as changing devotional practices point to the relationship of cultural and theological meanings. Throughout the diversity of cultures, places, and centuries, the celebration of the paschal mystery has remained central to the holiness of the christian Sunday.

Names for the Christian Sunday

In the primitive church, a favorite name for Sunday was the "eighth day." This name was linked to the Jewish enumeration of the days of the week. The seventh day was the Sabbath, the day on which "God rested," the day that climaxed the week. The Jewish scriptures used the term "eighth day" as a symbol of the Day of the Lord which would usher in a new creation forever (Eccl 11:2). Christians believed that the death and resurrection of Jesus Christ was the completion, perfection, and fulfilled promise of the new creation. Sunday, the "eighth day," replaced the Jewish Sabbath as the primary day of the week. It was both fulfillment of what the Sabbath tradition hoped for, and beginning of the new creation whose fulfillment was still to come at the end time. Sunday, the little Easter, was both last and first day of the week, an end that was at the same time a new beginning.

The evangelists are careful in stating that is was "on the first day of the week" that the resurrection of the Lord occurred (Mk 16:2; Mt 28:1; Lk 24:1; Jn 20:1). Paul and Luke both point to the gathering of the christian community on the first day of the week (Acts 20:7; 1 Cor 16:2). This first day of the week was called "the Lord's Day" by the end of the first century (Apoc 1:10). This name and its importance consists in the meaning of the word "Lord" in context of the time and place in history. In the Jewish scriptures, the day of the Lord referred to the day of God's final judgment ushering in the kingdom. Through his death and resurrection, Jesus Christ is Lord (Acts 2:36). The divine power is revealed in and through Christ the Lord. From this point on, the celebration of the Lord's Day will be marked by the Lord's Supper, or the Lord's Meal. Christ is Lord of all creation, and all will be reconciled in him.

By the second century, another meaning is embodied in the title of the Lord's day. Since the end of the first century, the title "lord" was applied to the Roman emperor meaning he was a divine being. Nero was the first emperor to have himself called "lord." The emperor worship demanded of the people at this time meant that they acclaimed Nero or the residing emperor as a divine being. When Christians named Sunday the Lord's Day, they were making a profession of faith in Jesus Christ. This profession of faith meant they could not name Nero or any other emperor "lord."

The Roman sun's day, or Sunday, was given a christian meaning as early as the second century. Christians called Christ their "sun," for he rose in renewed splendor on Easter. As Easter was the celebration of light and life in the year, so Sunday, a little Easter, celebrated the everlasting light and life of Christ for the world.

Celebrating the Day of the Lord

It is clear from the NT that celebration of the Lord's Supper or Lord's Meal was central to the new creation renewed on the Lord's Day. For Jewish Christians, the tradition of the Sabbath provided foundations for the meaning of the christian Lord's Day. Sabbath was a time for prohibition from "work" so that the experience of entering "God's rest" could renew the face of the earth. Remembering to delight in the Lord was a means of renewal for persons and community so that God's presence could be mediated to all. Those Jews who would not take time to remember were "foolish servants" whose works were no longer those of God.

Christians "kept the Sabbath" in spirit when they remembered that all days are potentially holy in Christ. The eschatological age, or end time, had come through the death and resurrection of Jesus Christ. Doing everything in the name of the Lord Jesus Christ is a way to know and be renewed by a "perpetual Sabbath." Refraining from physical work on Sunday was not essential for early Christians. Refraining from works of evil was the way to keep the Sabbath, and everyday, holy. In this way, Christians proclaimed that Jesus Christ remains Lord of the Sabbath. His works of healing, consoling, and teaching on the Sabbath show the real meaning of God's law of love which knows no rest. This sentiment is already evident in the reflections of writers of the second century, like Justin Martyr: "The new law demands that you (Christians) observe a perpetual sabbath, whereas you (Jews) consider yourselves pious when you refrain from work on one day out of the week. . . . If there is any perjurer or thief among you, let him mend his ways . . . in this way he will have kept a true and peaceful sabbath of God" (Dialogue with Trypho 12).

In the christian churches of the second century, it is clear that the Jewish Sabbath has been given Christocentric interpretations. The eschatological sabbath has begun in Christ. There is a diversity of practice among gentile and Jewish Christians around the observance or non-observance of the sabbath. But there is christian unity in the clear observance of Sunday as the high point of the week, the fulfillment of the Sabbath. The Sabbath is a symbol of the first creation, while the Lord's Day is fulfillment and new creation. "Do you not know that the two days are sisters?" writes Gregory of Nyssa (De Castigatione).

From the fourth through the twentieth centuries, there remains a consistency in the centrality of the eucharist for the celebration of the Lord's Day. In time, there would be a breakdown of the early connection between worship and living that worship by doing good and avoiding evil.

Keeping the Lord's Day Holy

In 321, Emperor Constantine promulgated the first laws that explicitly forbade public work on Sunday, with the exception of farming. There is no comparable church legislation at this time, for leisure became a pastoral problem when Sunday rest was dictated. The games and festivals of the culture were not acceptable forms of activity for Christians. Particularly, it was the less wealthy and less educated people who would have little possibility for using the imposed leisure in a creative or renewing way.

The Synod of Laodicea, c.370, produced the first written ecclesiastical law about the rest appropriate to the christian Sunday. The synod prescribes worship and abstaining from physical work as far as possible (Council of Laodicea, canon 29). The third Council of Orleans, c.538, clearly legislated absence from work so that the peasants could attend prayer and instruction (Third Council of Orleans, Mansi, IX, c. 19). By the seventh century there is a tendency to use a literal interpretation of "rest" to mean rest from physical work. "On the Lord's Day, let no one presume to do servile works, because this is forbidden by the law, as sacred scripture testifies everywhere." (Mansi, XI, Appendix, cc.47-48.)

From the eighth through the twentieth centuries, there arose varieties of interpretations about the nature of Sunday rest, and what constituted "servile work." Thomas Aquinas was among the minority who retained a sense of the early church meaning of "rest" as delight in the Lord. For Thomas, the meaning of Sunday "rest" included resting from evil acts so that delight in the Lord could be experienced. Any work that served God or others was a way of keeping the Sunday holy. (S.Th., II-II, q. 122, a.4)

Theological opinions abounded over the issue of what makes work "servile work," work which may not occur on Sunday. Cajetan, Suarez, Alphonsus Liguori, and many others discussed the degrees and kinds of servile work. Sabbatarian movements of the sixteenth through nineteenth centuries employ strict observance of "physical rest." Early twentieth-century manuals of moral theology continue to state the obligation to hear Mass and refrain from servile work, listing the conditions that make nonobservance a venial or mortal sin.

The liturgical movement of the nineteenth and twentieth centuries has returned the more integral and traditional meanings of "keeping the Lord's Day." The centrality of the paschal mystery for the christian Sunday, a little Easter, is clearly focused both in the *Constitution on the Sacred Liturgy*, 106, and in the revised *Code of Canon Law,* c.1246, 1247.

The earliest celebration of the christian Sunday stressed the holiness of all life in Christ. The celebration of the eucharist invites the community into the new creation in Christ. Sunday is a day to delight in, and to foster, this new creation in which there are no destructive divisions of sexes, races, or creeds, for Christ will be all in all.

Willy Rordorf, *Sunday* (London: SCM, 1968).

SHAWN MADIGAN

SUPERNATURAL

In theology "supernatural" has little to do with the "eerie" of ghost literature. Both as an adjective and as a noun, it represents a concept quite precisely defined in terms of certain relationships. The relationships exist within the scholastic hierarchy of natures; principally (in ascending order) mineral, vegetable, animal, human, angelic, divine. Anything found in a lower nature which is proper only to some higher nature is relatively supernatural. Anything found in a lower nature which is proper only to the divine nature is absolutely supernatural.

The notion was elaborated to deal with certain facts of revelation, notably: (1) the Incarnation, where a human nature becomes the way of being of a divine Person; (2) sanctifying grace, where a human person becomes oriented to God as personal end and lover; and (3) the light of glory, where a human being becomes actually united to God in beatific vision. The word has been familiar in theology since Scotus Erigena (c. 850) and has had its full technical sense since the *De bono* of Philip the Chancellor (c. 1225).

It played an important role in Aquinas' synthesis of Catholic doctrine on grace. The infinite openness, the hungers, the eros of the human spirit can not be satisfied with anything less than God perfectly and eternally possessed. "Thou hast made us for thyself, O Lord, and our heart is restless until it rest in thee" (Augustine). But actual perfect union with God in total personal love is inconceivable to unaided reason. The mystery, then, the apparent intrinsic contradiction of humanity as known by reason alone, is that human nature seems built to overreach itself. To this mystery Christianity provides God's answer: God's gift of the love which is God's self (1 Jn 4:8; Rom 5:5). Beyond human imagining, beyond human control, it meets all human needs in a superabundant way, granting a share in the divine nature. God gives grace (2) through the Incarnate Word (1) in order to bring about that eternal union (3).

This thirteenth-century synthesis gave an intelligible coherence to basic facts of christian revelation. Later well-meaning efforts to improve the coherence on the basis of logic alone led rather to a breakdown of the synthesis and a distortion of the notion of the supernatural. Theologians argued that possession of a super-nature, with its end in God, entitatively distinct from the human nature with which one is born, implied that human nature had its own end distinct from the vision of God. This led to a conception of the supernatural not so much as God's freely granted fulfilment of the infinite aspiration placed by God in every human heart, but rather as a superstructure imposed on top of nature, invisibly, silently achieving its own end by its own means, while nature went on at its lower level pursuing lower and natural ends through the normal activities of life. Instead of grace building on nature, grace paralleled nature at a higher level. The experiential integrating reality of God's gift of love was often overlooked.

In this two-tiered human universe, the human goodness of actions might be measured by their natural end, but supernatural goodness and merit were measured by the quantity of grace from which they proceeded. "Elevating grace" gave actions a value not proportioned to any recognizable excellence they had in themselves or to the actual motives for which they were performed. Even mechanical repetitions of rituals and instances of mindless obedience could come to be esteemed above deeds of honesty, justice, patience, fidelity and love. This was a perversion, but many theologians promulgated it under the impression it was the doctrine of St. Thomas.

The term "supernatural" began appearing in official church teaching documents in 1567 (condemnations of Baius, followed by chapters and canons of Vatican I [1869-70] and the encyclical *Humani Generis* [1950]). Though their wording occasionally seems to presuppose the two-tiered universe, careful reading shows that they do not impose it and that their language is not intended to be taken technically. Their concern is to preserve the basic doctrine of the gratuity of God's gifts of grace. Their focus is the essential christian notion that God has done something for us that we could never have done for ourselves; that God promises us something we could never have attained for ourselves; and that God will bring his gifts to fruition and fulfill all his promises. "Gratuitous" in those documents has its root meaning of "freely, spontaneously, lovingly given." It must not be taken with contemporary connotations of "without point, a decorative, incidental, idle afterthought." The reality indicated by "the supernatural" is the basic motive of christian gratitude. The word categorizes the basic inspiration for christian reliance on God and humble attribution of all success to God's grace.

The distinction of nature and supernatural, for all its dangers, remains theologically useful as a set of conceptual epistemological correlatives. It points up: (1) God's transcendence; (2) the gratuity of God's self-offering; (3) the unexpected, unimaginable reality of the Incarnation; and (4) the need in the concrete of a christian humanism which goes beyond the merely human.

See **Grace, Nature**

QUENTIN QUESNELL

SYMBOL

Symbols are produced by the imagination. From the Greek etymology (*sym-*

ballein), symbols are understood to indicate more than one meaning, "thrown together" in such a way that one meaning implies or entails others. To use an example from early Greek life two halves of the same broken coin, exchanged at a sale of land, indicated the binding of two individuals in a contract. Each half implied the other with its financial and political responsibilities. A contemporary working definition of symbol could be developed from these preliminary linguistic notions. A symbol is a complex of gestures, sounds, images, and/or words that evoke, invite, and persuade participation in that to which they refer.

This definition places symbols at one end of a spectrum of human communicative devices that extends from the most conventional signs (mathematical symbols, symbolic logic, stop signs) to the most polyvalent images of psychological, moral, and religious values (dream symbols, narratives of guilt and innocence, the law of Moses, and the cross of Christ).

At the other end of the scale, signs unambiguously point to a single referent. They give information or offer directions. They appear through social agreement, and committees often construct them. The international signs regulating automobile traffic and pedestrians are an example.

Symbols, such as darkness and light, water or oil, emerge from the drama of human experience and enjoy cross-cultural power. Comparison of such symbols across temporal and geographical distances indicates similarities, even identities, that cannot be explained by oral, literary, or ritual influences. Some would claim that the similarities have their origin in a common psychological unconscious shared by all human beings. Symbols constantly convey a surplus of meaning. Their versatility as carriers of meaning makes it impossible to say that they have a one-to-one correspondence with their referents. Water is not only cool, refreshing, and life-giving but also destructive, thirst-provoking, cleansing and scalding. With their roots in our biological life, symbols direct our thoughts, desires, and actions, making pre-reflective demands on our psyches.

In what follows, we shall briefly describe (1) the status of symbols in the process of knowing; (2) some theological dimensions of symbols; (3) the contemporary suspicion of symbols; and (4) the importance of symbols to various aspects of contemporary theology.

Symbols in the Process of Knowing

The "images" of all five senses are necessary at every level of human consciousness. Images are the operative content of the perceptual flow. They are exploratory in that they provide the basis for understanding and lead toward reflective attitudes in consciousness. They can also be carefully developed signals, abstracting some particular import of the sensible flow of consciousness, isolating it for clarity and distinctness as in scientific language. In this sense, some sensitive awareness and response anticipating and leading toward what we do not know is a permanent feature of human life. Human beings are symbolic creatures.

Images also engage our feelings, arresting or promoting our affective development. Sexual identity, dreams, personal and public policy are guided by or determined through symbols. Moreover, artists intensify the particular images of their experience in a non-conceptual patterning of the sensible world. They present their works of art for our affective, intellectual and moral identification. Artistic artifacts call for personal engagement and public action. The continuing enactment of audiences' lives through their participation in Shakespeare's *Hamlet*, Balanchine's dances, or Britten's *War Requiem* establishes these works of art as classic in western society. They become symbols not only of a particular person or of a limited society, but of human culture in general.

Symbols work the way metaphors do in poetry. The tensive juxtaposition of unlike elements that seems to make no clear literal sense (Bob is a leopard) is a strategy to awaken hearers into understanding the world in a new way. By deliberately placing humanity and animality in a single sentence, the author prods listeners into letting go of old classifications and appropriating different views. Likenesses appear between the terms of the metaphor. When Juliet says: "Come, night; come, Romeo; come, thou day in night," (*Romeo and Juliet,* III, ii, 17), the juxtaposition of her lover, night and day governs her understanding of each element. It opens a new way of seeing Romeo and conversely a new view of night. There is an innovative meaning made available in the impertinent likenesses she elaborates. Such implicit comparisons are never exhaustible. Paraphrases by interpreters of the passage are infinite. By entertaining the delights of language, affect, moral possibilities, and actions evoked by the metaphors, listeners redirect their lives toward new worlds of romantic love, night and day, and an evaluation of lovers.

Drawn by the pleasure of new insight, participants in symbols actualize, however briefly, the world disclosed by the metaphoric juxtapositions. They become what they imagine. As a result, symbols are not only crucial for the development and decline of the self, but also significant for the establishment of communal experience. Symbols can lead us towards self-transcendence, but they can also fixate the confusions of self-destruction and social bias. So pornography symbolizes not only an individual fixation of pleasure at the level of sight, but also exemplifies and supports social ruptures entailing dominance and submission.

Symbols can have powerful public effect issuing in new familial structures, new metaphors for economic exchange, and differing governmental polities. One need only point to the Liberty Tree of the American Revolution or the red flag of the Bolsheviks to see such symbols consolidating, legitimating and developing powerful groups in their various social milieux.

Theological Dimensions of Symbol
Due to the effective power and primordial importance of symbols, it is not surprising that they become apt vehicles for religious meanings. However, religious value is not added to the symbol as though propositional doctrines were aggregated to an already established clear statement. Rather religious symbols, working the way metaphors do, awaken in participants an encounter with an ultimate Other at the limits of human existence. The symbols of suffering, guilt, death, hatred, peace, justice, love, and joy can disclose the Uncanny Mystery (Otto), Ultimate Concern (Tillich), the Holy Mystery (Rahner), the Totally Unconditioned (Lonergan), and Transcendence (Berger). The fragile contingency of human life is experienced as unowed, transcended for the moment by an ecstatic freedom. These experiences of symbol are described as gracious, as a gift of the Other to the participant.

Christian symbolism emerges within Jewish eschatological typologies. The menorah (seven-branched candlestick) and the shophar (ram's horn) foreshadow the end-times, the perfect temple and its worship. Christ's story of the eschatological vineyard (Mt 21:33-41) echoes Isaiah's use of the same image (5:1-7). Christians quickly spoke of the promise of OT symbols being fulfilled in Christ, as in the books of Hebrews and Revelation. Early Greek writers, such as the authors of *The Odes of Solomon* and the

Didache, Ignatius of Antioch, Justin Martyr, and Clement of Alexandria used symbols as a primary mode of catechesis for the rites of initiation, as an explanation of membership in the church, and for the meaning of salvation in Christ.

Early thinkers built upon the Pauline notion of *mysterion* (mystery) (Rom 16:25-26; Eph 3:1-6), as the secret plan of God hidden from eternity and now revealed in Christ, and the Johannine structure of *semeion* (sign) (e.g. Jn 2:11; 4:54), in which Christ's actions and works revealed a new exodus and the arrival of the heavenly wisdom. They combined these images and NT categories with neo-Platonic thought on the symbolic unity of all reality and developed a theology in which OT history prefigured NT events and natural events disclosed heavenly messages.

Augustine organized the use of such symbolism through his training in classical rhetoric in *On Christian Doctrine*. He elaborated a notion of signs as a way of understanding the scriptures. The combination of natural symbolism (such as smoke indicating fire), intellectual symbols (words conveying meaning), and religious rituals (bread and wine disclosing the unseen) furthered the theological discussion and created philosophical difficulties. Ps-Dionysius established an elaborate neo-Plotinian hierarchy of being in which each lower symbolic level anticipated the higher and in which humanity, by participating in various stages of illumination, became gradually deified, leaving behind the senses for the mystical darkness of divine unity. His work was assumed to have been written by Dionysius of Athens (Acts 17:34) and became generally known and highly influential in the western church through the translations of John Scotus Erigena.

Building upon these thinkers and later controversies concerning the eucharist in the ninth and tenth centuries, theologians of the Middle Ages sought a systematic set of terms and relations to organize the symbols of nature, religious history and contemporary action. What were the roles of the major christian artifacts within the cultural context as a whole? How did they relate to the continuing presence of salvation for the believer?

The medieval west particularly attempted to rationalize scriptural interpretation through the use of four senses (literal, moral, allegorical, and anagogic) and to understand the nature of sacramental efficacy (instrumental causality). The School of St. Victor in Paris, especially in Hugh of St. Victor on the sacraments and in Andrew of St. Victor on literal exegesis, organized the Augustinian position. The school of Chartres, especially Thierry of Chartres, studied the relationship between Platonic thought on nature and OT symbolism surrounding creation. The writings of Joachim of Fiore correlated typologies of historical events not only from the OT and NT to the present, but also from the present to the future, giving to each symbol a prophetic and apocalyptic dimension in the immediate political situation.

Thomas Aquinas attempted to provide a theory about all the concerns and questions of medieval symbolic life. By combining the Augustinian notion of signs with Aristotelian causality, he offered an understanding of the effectiveness of the sacraments. He described the signifying power of the sacraments as related to past, present, and future and he articulated a participative dimension to sacramental life from baptism to the beatific vision. The natural symbolism of the sacraments was the substrate for their supernatural transforming power; the verbal power of the sacramental symbols represented the saving history of Christ; and their natural signification was the instrumental cause of the believers' participation in God.

The theological developments concerning symbolism in the Middle Ages were based upon the doctrinal conviction that the incarnation of God in Christ disclosed that nature and history could bear divine meanings. The visible could give evidence of the invisible; the part provide proof of the whole; and the known could lead to the unknown. The scriptures, the sacraments, even the church itself were an extension of this incarnational principle.

But the principle of cultural embodiment did not always contain an internal corrective. The proliferation of visual symbols in civic and religious life at the end of the Middle Ages (pageants, feasts, processions, relics, eucharistic miracles, etc.) often obscured the central christian symbols. The scriptures were little read, barely understood and poorly preached; the eucharist was for spectators; marriage rituals were for the wealthy; penance only once a year; and anointing for the dying. Theologians and ecclesiastics did not always find it easy to maintain intellectual and magisterial order among the symbols of popular piety. Nor did the dialectical negativity of Ps-Dionysius and late-medieval mystics always forestall complete superstitious identification of symbols with the reality indicated.

With the rise of the Reformation, the growth of rationalism, and the development of science, symbols lost their privileged place in social discourse. The radical reformers of the sixteenth century whitewashed church paintings, smashed statues and stained-glass windows, and abbreviated sacramental services. Seventeenth-century civil conflicts among religious interpretations so offended the peacefully minded that they began to develop a tolerant rational religion, a mediating voice among the strife-mongering confessional traditions. Rational religion, or deism as it came to be called, had little use for the opacity and poly-semantic power of symbols. Early modern science demoted the role of symbols even more, exalting experiment, rational argument, and conceptual clarity to prime importance. The explorations by western European empire-builders began to compare religious and social symbols in different cultures discovering their similarities. Symbols became human products relative to particular religious traditions, specific cultural contexts, and particular geographies and histories.

However, beginning in the late eighteenth and early nineteenth centuries with the developments of romanticism, poets and thinkers as diverse as Wordsworth, Coleridge and Shelley in England; Chateaubriand in France; Schleiermacher, Tieck, and Schelling in Germany; and Bushnell and Emerson in the United States developed historical arguments, poetic evocations, educational manifestos, novels, and philosophical and theological treatises arguing for the cognitive, moral, aesthetic, philosophical and religious role of symbols in human affairs. Victorian poets and thinkers such as Arnold, Newman, Pater, von Hugel, Mallarmé, and Valery stressed the ways in which symbols could focus the dimensions of religious ultimacy through aesthetic experience.

Catholic modernists such as Loisy and Tyrrell were influenced by these nineteenth-century developments. Using the notion of symbol to explain the origins of the church from the gospels, the relationship of Christianity to other religions, and the nature of the church as a sacrament, they developed explanations of revelation, faith, church, and the sacraments parallel, or sometimes in opposition, to public positions of the church. Their methodological naiveté and pseudonymous political writings provoked ecclesiastical judgment. The encyclicals *Lamentabili* and *Pascendi* (1907) condemned their theology and created a situation of fear and disquiet that has persisted in Catholic life.

Only as Maritain, Rahner, Lonergan, and Schillebeeckx have rehabilitated the notion of symbol through revised readings of Aquinas has it been possible to refer again to symbol in Catholic theology. By reestablishing the role of signs in Aquinas' theology of the sacraments, by interpreting the notion of symbol in an ontological sense, and by relating artistic creation and theology, these thinkers have connected nineteenth-century romantic insights with the Catholic medieval tradition in philosophy and theology.

The Contemporary Suspicion of Symbols

Contemporary suspicion about the functions of symbols in human affairs has not primarily been ecclesiastical, but philosophical and cultural. (1) If poets can make symbols, then how do we know that they reveal anything but human history and subjectivity? (2) If they have their origins in the human psyche, then do they tell us anything but the disturbed characteristics of our own psychic history? (3) If symbols are the primary mode of human expression, do we ever reach a non-metaphoric, non-symbolic statement about reality? And finally, (4) if symbols are socially constitutive, how do we keep them from demonically destroying society?

Each question has its philosophical and social background. The first has its origins in philosophy from Kant to Nietzsche on the nature of human cognition and the ability of knowing to contact extralinguistic reality. Freud's critiques of the human psyche dominate the second question. His assertions about the Oedipus complex, about the intrinsic relationship between pleasure and death, about the libidinous origins of art, about religion as an illusion, and about the primal "splitting up" of human identity have made all symbols suspicious. The third question has been raised by com-

mentators from Nietzsche to Derrida in their insistence upon the polysemantic metaphoricity of all language and the inability of "getting behind" to conceptual and metaphysical understandings of "being." Symbols refer to each other rather than to reality. Finally, the experience of the Jewish Holocaust and its support in Nazi propaganda, as well as other genocides of this era and political oppressions, have made it impossible not to question the meaning behind social, political, and economic symbols. How does one judge the difference between social symbols that lead toward the transformation of society for the good and those that lead toward evil?

The Importance of the Notion of Symbol for Theology

Although many fundamental questions about the nature of symbols need to be resolved, a number of contemporary theologians believe that the epistemological, psychological, sociological, anthropological, and ontological dimensions of symbols have been sufficiently resolved to warrant the reestablishment of symbol at the center of their investigations. Indeed, they believe that christian theological language can contribute to the critique of social and cultural concerns that is inherent in twentieth-century questions about the validity of symbols. Knowing that the natural sciences themselves have discovered their own indebtedness to symbolic models in their investigative procedures, some theologians would argue that religious symbols can transform all socio-cultural systems.

The literary and oral forms of symbols (lyrics, stories, laws, visions, etc.) now form the basis for theologies of revelation. Recognizing that divine revelation comes to us first through the scriptural texts, authors analyze the modes of divine communication (Schoeckel, Ricoeur, Dulles). Biblical scholars study the interpretive theories of literary critics, utilizing their results in the analysis of the narrative form of the gospels, the parables, and the visionary structures of prophecies and apocalypses (Funk, Crossan, Via, Marin).

Christological studies investigate the development from the primarily literary and symbolic genres of NT and patristic expressions to the doctrinal and conceptual languages of Nicaea (325) and Chalcedon (451) (Lonergan, Rahner, Grillmeier). Theologians develop categories around Christ as the supreme symbol, representing God's ways with men and women (Tillich, Tracy).

When the Second Vatican Council called the church itself a sacrament (L.G. 1), it confirmed earlier thinking and prompted further reflections. Seeing symbol and sacrament as analogous, both signifying and causal, ecclesiologists included symbol in their theological grammar. The nature of a missionary church (Buehlmann), the re-presentational character of the church and its revealing, transforming power (Rahner, Dulles) benefited from the analysis of symbolic activity. The social and historical mediation of ecclesial symbols has been stressed by others (Komonchak).

The analysis and performance of the sacraments themselves have been influenced by the recovery of symbolism as a primary category in christian life. Whether it is understanding the interpersonal dynamics (Schillebeeckx), the philosophical underpinnings (Rahner), the anthropological transitions (Kavanaugh, Collins), social and political influences (Segundo, Power), or pastoral practices (Searle), the notion of symbol is pervasive.

Knowing that societies are changed more by symbols than by concepts, liberation theology or theologies of emancipation have focused upon the transformative dimension of symbols. Metz's critique of Rahner, Lamb's interpretation of Lonergan, Power's use of Ricoeur, and Fiorenza's and Duffy's indebtedness to the Frankfurt school of critical theory have all contributed to contemporary concerns for the transformation of society through critical symbols. Symbols not only reflect social systems; they change them. Contemporary theologians are aware that through christian symbols they cannot simply scold the world for not living up to its ideals, but they must also propose alternate symbolic modes of expression that can heal human pain and redirect human desires. Only in that way can they establish the christian tradition as the inculturation of the Incarnate One.

See **Imagination, Religious**

E. Cassirer, *The Philosophy of Symbolic Forms,* New Haven, Ct., 1955, 3 vols. M. Eliade, *Images and Symbols,* New York 1961. S. Happel, "Sacrament: Symbol of Conversion," *Creativity and Method: Essays in Honor of Bernard Lonergan,* ed. Matthew Lamb, Milwaukee, 1981, 275-290. S. Langer, *Philosophy in a New Key: A Study in the Symbolism of Reason, Rite and Art,* Cambridge, Mass., 1969. Lonergan, *Method in Theology,* London, 1972, esp. 57-99. D. Power, *Unsearchable Riches: The Symbolic Nature of Liturgy,* New York, 1984. K. Rahner, "The Theology of the Symbol," *Theological Investigations,* IV, Baltimore, 1966, 221-252. P. Ricoeur, *The Rule of Metaphor: Multidisciplinary Studies of the Creation of Meaning in Language,* Toronto, 1977. E. Schillebeeckx, *Christ the Sacrament of the Encounter with God,* New York, 1963. P Tillich, "Theology and Symbolism," *Religious Symbolism,* ed. F.E. Johnson, New York, 1955. D. Tracy, *The Analogical Imagination: Christian Theology and the Culture of Pluralism,* New York, 1981.

STEPHEN HAPPEL

SYNOD OF BISHOPS

On September 15, 1965, in the *motu proprio* "Apostolica sollicitudo," Paul VI called for the establishment of a "permanent consultative body of Bishops for the Universal Church subject directly and immediately to Our authority and to be known as the Synod of Bishops." This body, representing the entire Catholic episcopate, perpetual in character, and exercising its function occasionally, is to assist in maintaining the close communion and collaboration between the pope and the bishops. While described as a participation in the "solicitude for the Universal Church" proper to the bishop of Rome, this body of bishops could also exercise deliberative power, if such powers were to be granted it by the Holy See.

The institution of the synod was included in the final draft of the conciliar decree *Christus Dominus*. There it is placed within the context of the universal dimension of the episcopal ministry. Thus paragraph 5 affirms: "This council, as it will be representative of the whole Catholic episcopate, will bear testimony to the participation of bishops in hierarchical communion in care of the universal church."

Since its establishment the synod has been summoned eight times. There have been six " ordinary synods" dealing with various topics: the unfinished business of the council (1967), priestly ministry and world justice (1971), evangelization (1974), catechesis (1977), the christian family (1980), and penance and reconciliation (1983). A synod to be held in 1987 will focus on the laity. There have also been two extraordinary synods. In 1969 one such synod addressed the issue of collegiality and the relationship of episcopal conferences to the Holy See. In 1985 an extraordinary synod was held in order to celebrate and affirm the Second Vatican Council on the twentieth anniversary of its conclusion.

While it is clear that the synod has become a part of the church's life, a question remains as to its significance. The uncertainty surrounding the synod reflects the conciliar ambiguity on the relationship between papal primacy and episcopal collegiality. There are some who maintain that the synod is clearly an extension of papal primacy, that its function is simply advisory to the supreme pontiff in his universal ministry. There are others who contend that the synod is a true exercise of the collegial dimension of the episcopal office. An analysis of what the synods have as a matter of fact produced reinforces the ambiguity. *Familiaris consortio,* a papal document issued after the 1980 synod, seems to reflect almost none of the concerns brought to the synod by the bishops. On the other hand, the synod of 1969 strengthened the role of bishops' conferences, while the synod of 1974 provided an opportunity for bishops of the younger churches to speak their mind on mission and evangelization. Many of their concerns were taken over by Paul VI in *Evangelii nuntiandi.*

The synod is a recent form of "lived collegiality." It remains for the church to reflect more deeply on its significance and to provide for more effective structures and procedures.

See **Collegiality, Pope**

Jan Grootaers and Joseph Selling, *The 1980 Synod of Bishops "On the Role of the Family",* Leuven, 1983.

WILLIAM MCCONVILLE, OFM

T

TEMPTATION

Temptation is commonly understood as an inducement to sin, to wrongdoing. In a sense it is a normal part of the human condition, a natural consequence of human freedom and choice. Indeed, it would be impossible to avoid all the allurements of evil that ordinary life contains. The occasion of temptation may be any stimulus that provokes a response of attraction to moral evil, but the ultimate source is the inclination to sin that seems to be so much part of fallen human nature, the residual effect of what is called original sin. It is not a sin in itself, any more than temptation is, but it is a bias in the direction of sinful selfishness that requires constant effort and God's grace to control. This basic weakness is common to all human beings, but it is aggravated by the particular nature of each person, involving temperament, character, habits of response, etc.

Although the experience of temptation for an individual is unique on each occasion, so that no two temptations are exactly the same, nevertheless it is common for people to have a certain sameness or pattern in the temptations they experience. The character traits that influence a person's habitual reaction to stimuli vary from person to person, so that experiences or situations that are a continuous source of temptation to one individual may leave another totally unmoved.

The pattern of a person's response to temptation, whether in one or more areas, affects his capacity for coping with later temptations. Repeated resistance to temptation builds up good habits, while continuous capitulation becomes a bad habit which will weaken the ability to resist on later occasions. Hence it is important to form good habits to strengthen one's moral character in the battle with temptation. But the human personality is not simply a random collection of reactions and habits. These are formed by and reflect the person's basic orientation or fundamental option, in the light of which all other choices are made. In the battle with temptation, therefore, it is important to remember this unity of the person, so that it is not enough to fight off temptations against chastity unless one is also striving for control in other areas such as laziness, dishonesty, insensitivity, coarseness, aggression. A tendency to dishonesty in dealing with others can mean that one may be dishonest with oneself in recognizing or dallying with temptations against chastity. Any positive development in the spiritual depths of one's basic option is bound to be helpful in specific areas of morality, and therefore in one's ability to cope with temptation.

There are degrees of temptation insofar as one is more or less affected or the temptation is to greater or less evil. Thus there can be a temptation which one is just barely aware of and not strongly drawn to, or one that engages the subject totally, with a whole spectrum of intermediate degrees. Temptations are described as light or grave depending on whether the subject is strongly drawn to choose a serious evil, or the evil is slight or attracts only slightly. In practice it is not very helpful to get into such hair-splitting, but common experience accepts that there is a spectrum of gravity ranging from slight to serious.

Prudence dictates that if there is a moral obligation to do good and avoid evil, this extends to resisting temptation. Temptation is a threat to one's option for good and one's life of union with God. In general one must do what one can to avoid giving in. Moral theologians have discussed the kinds of resistance required. The minimum would seem to be with-holding consent, but common experience and the church's condemnation of quiet-ism would seem to indicate that this is not sufficient in practice. To be effective, the resistance needs to be positive, though not necessarily direct. In many cases an indirect approach is better, diverting attention to something else at the time of temptation, or more overall effort in living the christian life.

The story of the Fall in the third chapter of Genesis is an excellent description of the moral experience of temptation ending in capitulation. There are many such descriptions throughout the Bible. But the biblical texts also use the word temptation (Hebrew *massâ*) in the sense of to try, to prove, to put to the test. The Bible presents temptation as a situation in which one experiences a challenge to chose between fidelity and infidelity to God. God "tempts" us when he tests our fidelity to the covenant, and we in turn "tempt" God when we test him to reward or punish us. The psalmist often calls upon God to test him, to show that he really trusts in God's power to save. The

Wisdom books warn the people to expect temptation. Job is the classical example of the man put to the test or tempted by God. At first he protests at the treatment he receives, but then admits that God has every right to try him, indeed that it is only to be expected that man be tempted. Finally, he accepts that he has no right to question God.

The NT presents the christian life as a constant struggle with temptation to sin, and Jesus warns his followers against giving in to it. For Paul, temptation is basic to spiritual growth. From within there are the sinful desires of the heart, the lusts of the flesh, pride and arrogance. Other trials or temptations come from without, through those who would destroy christian faith in people who have accepted it. The Apocalypse presents in dramatic symbolic form the church's continual battle against the temptations of Satan, and the final victory of God who will reward those who have stood up to the test. In all of the biblical texts there is the assurance that God's help is always available in the struggle. The NT assures us that in Jesus who overcame sin and death we have the guarantee of our hope of victory.

See **Moral Life, Christian; Sin; Virtue**

SEÁN FAGAN, SM

TEN COMMANDMENTS

The expression "Ten Commandments" is a translation of the Hebrew "ten words" found in Exod 34:28; Deut 4:13; 10:4. Traditionally they are known as the Decalogue. According to the Deuteronomy texts the expression applies to the commandments found in Deut 5:7-21 which speak of the two tablets of stone (see Deut 5:22). The expression is secondary in Exod 34:28 since the number of commandments in Exod 34:14-26 is twelve, not ten. Finally the expression refers to the commandments given in the theophany on Mount Sinai (see Exod 20:3-17).

The Bible contains incomplete texts or summaries of the Ten Commandments (see Lev 19:3-4, 11-13; Ps 15:3-5; Hos 4:2). The Ten Commandments developed from such series and with the exception of the ones dealing exclusively with duties toward Yahweh reflect ancient tribal wisdom. Thus the young were expected to learn them from their elders who sought to provide for the good of the tribe. Such series were regarded as an enumeration of death sins. Thus they focus on those crimes that are so serious that they compromise and endanger the community itself.

The legal form of the Ten Commandments is significant. It is a series of apodictic laws, i.e., laws that impose an obligation directly on a person. They command the person to perform (or refrain from performing) a particular action that the legislator considers desirable (or harmful). These apodictic laws have two forms: (a) third person, e.g., "No one shall be put to death on the testimony of only one witness" (Deut 17:6) and (b) second person, e.g., "You shall not have intercourse with your father's wife" (Lev 18:8). Although apodictic laws are rather exceptional in the ancient Near East, they are characteristic of Israel. Moreover, the second person forms, inasmuch as they express the basic religious attitude of an entire people, are unique to Israel.

These second person singular forms offer a dimension of intimacy. Here Yahweh speaks directly to the individual. Consequently, although murder and adultery were already forbidden in the ancient Near East, the biblical commandments are really new laws. According to the introduction (see Exod 20:2; Deut 5:6), Yahweh identifies himself as one who has liberated slaves who now constitute his covenant people. Yahweh assumes and surpasses the position of the tribal elders. Israel is called upon to obey, not only because these regulations are for the good of the tribe, but also because Yahweh has intervened decisively in their lives.

The prominence of the Ten Commandments can be observed in the present arrangement of the Book of Exodus. At a first stage the fear experienced by the people at Sinai (Exod 20:18) was the direct result of God's appearance in Exodus 19, specifically the storm theophany (Exod 19:16b-17, 19). Hence the people deputed Moses to hear the entire revelation (Exod 20:19). At a second stage because of the importance of the Ten Commandments the people listened to this basic law (Exod 20:1-17). However, this listening then led to their fear that, in turn, led to Moses' receiving the rest of the legislation, i.e., the Covenant Code in Exod 20:22-23:19. This second stage highlighted the significance of the Ten Commandments since, unlike the Covenant Code, God revealed them directly to the entire people.

There are differences in the Ten Commandments as found in Exod 20:3-17 and Deut 5:7-21. For example, the motivation for keeping the sabbath in Exod 20:11 is creation, whereas in Deut 5:15 it is the Exodus. To the list of those not to work on the Sabbath (Exod 20:10) Deut 5:14 adds the ox and ass. To the commandment of honoring one's parents (Exod 20:12) Deut 5:16 adds: "as the Lord, your God, has commanded you." The most striking difference is the order of not coveting the house and wife of one's neighbor. According to Exod 20:17 it is: "You shall not covet your neighbor's house. You shall not covet your neighbor's wife." According to Deut 5:21 it is: "You shall not covet your neighbor's wife. You shall not desire (a different verb) your neighbor's house."

Various faith communities have adopted either the enumeration of Exodus or the enumeration of Deuteronomy. Roman Catholics and Lutherans follow Deuteronomy while the Jews, Eastern Orthodox Christians, and Protestants other than the Lutherans follow Exodus. These communities preserve the number "ten" in a variety of ways. For the Jews the first commandment is the introduction, "I, the Lord, am your God" etc. Their second commandment is the prohibition of false gods *and* images. Their tenth commandment is the prohibition of coveting the house *and* wife of one's neighbor. For Eastern Orthodox Christians and Protestants other than Lutherans the first commandment is the prohibition of false gods. Their second commandment is the prohibition of false images. Their tenth commandment is the prohibition of coveting the house *and* wife of one's neighbor. For Roman Catholics and Lutherans the first commandment is the prohibition of false gods. The prohibition of false images is either included in this first commandment or suppressed in the enumeration. Their second commandment is the vain use of God's name. Their ninth commandment is the prohibition of coveting the wife of one's neighbor. Their tenth commandment is the prohibition of coveting the house of one's neighbor.

See **Bible, Old Testament; Moral Life, Christian;**

JOHN F. CRAGHAN

THEISM

Though the term is etymologically derived from the Greek (*theos:* god), "theism" was first employed by the Cambridge Platonist Ralph Cudworth in *Intellectual System of the Universe* (1678). Through the Enlightenment it remained indistinguishable in content from deism until the nineteenth century.

I. Kant distinguished theism from deism insofar as the latter develops a theology through purely transcendental concepts and arrives only at a cause of the world, whereas the former develops a natural theology through concepts drawn from man's psychological, moral constitution and applied by analogy to the Supreme Being; God is thus conceived as cause, or author, of the world through understanding and freedom.

Definitions of theism vary greatly. It may best be grasped by contrasting it with other -isms. Against atheism it affirms the existence of God. As opposed to polytheism and henotheism, the worship of one god among many, theism maintains the existence of only one God. In contrast to pantheism, which identifies the universe as god, theism insists on a God separate from the universe and utterly transcendent. Whereas deism imagines a distant God who caused the world to exist and then left it to develop according to its own inherent laws, theism postulates a personal God, ruling the world with his providence, whose immanence is as real as his transcendence. Theism can refer to a purely philosophical system, as held, e.g., during the Enlightenment by such thinkers as Voltaire and Kant, or to an historical religion. Judaism, Christianity, and Islam are clearly enumerated among theistic religions, as are certain late movements of Hinduism, like the Bhakti sects, and several mahayana versions of Buddhism.

However well polytheism may account for the diverse forces of the universe and the conflicting tensions within people by attributing them to distinct deities, polytheism suffices neither philosophically, morally, nor psychologically. Before plurality, the mind seeks the underlying unity; competing wills can frustrate or render arbitrary the course of justice; psychologically, man, who must deal with a potentially unlimited number of divine forces in conflict, can never unify his life in total dedication but is condemned to fear or schizophrenia. The Homeric epics spoke vaguely of a fate (*moira*) or destiny (*heimarmene*) behind the gods, but this somewhat impersonal, but all-powerful, reality threatened to deprive the gods of their influence upon human affairs.

Henotheism fails to explain adequately why any particular deity is alone to be worshiped if its favor may be restricted and its power overthrown by another. Israel passed through a henotheistic stage to recognize, at least by the time of Second Isaiah, Yahweh as the one God over all the earth.

Pantheism, while answering the philosophical desire for ultimate unity, fails to account sufficiently for diversity, especially in peoples' consciousness of free action with responsibility for decisions. Although pantheism may arise out of a romantic yearning for unity with the all or its doctrine may conquer a debilitating fear of being condemned or separated from the ground of being, it can also lead to resignation before evil, a denial of its reality, or a presumptuous justification of it. By attributing everything of value to the deity, or Nature, the special place, responsibility, and value of humankind in the universe may easily be lost.

Although Aristotle's Prime Mover, unconcerned with the world, offers a partial anticipation, deism seems to have been a special product of the Enlightenment with its mechanistic physical laws, as if the universe only needed a shove to be set into motion. The trust in conceptual reason made it apparently easy to juxtapose God and the universe insofar as they were represented by distinct concepts. Such a view not only ignores God's infinite omnipotence but also deprives human freedom of room for action.

Modern atheism, in many ways a reaction against deism, leaves people incapable of orienting themselves in the universe. Insofar as no positive infinity is acknowledged, the human mind, which transcends all finite realities and concepts, is confronted with the inexhaustible infinity of matter, or nonbeing. Some atheists, like Sartre, postulate the primacy of nonbeing over (conceptualizable) being and conclude to the absurdity of existence. Others maintain a faith in science and its laws, thus subordinating human freedom to science, even though modern physics has been forced to acknowledge indeterminacy and various unresolved conundrums. Marxists project a future, perfect society of justice wherein man's/woman's actual judgments about injustice are proleptically grounded. But they are confronted with a double dilemma: 1) how can any finite stage of society be considered final and perfect in a world process continually surpassing itself? 2) if the perfect society is fated to come about, human freedom seems incapable of substantially influencing the process; but if human freedom can exercise a substantial influence, its renegation of duty would frustrate the intended goal and the process of history will be rendered absurd.

A merely philosophical theism founders on the problem of evil. Certainly a philosopher cannot explain sin; for as what *should not* be, sin cannot be understood in terms of causes, a rationally developed series of what *must* be; for if what should not be must be, an immoral universe necessarily results from which God must be banished or for which God must be blamed. Other questions arise. In a world where the innocent suffer, why does God not intervene? If he cannot, he is not God; if he wills not to, he does not love and is not worthy of our devotion. Furthermore, if we consult our own hearts, we must acknowledge the weakness of the witness that they bear to love. Who can assure humankind that love and the God of love exist? Who can restore the unity in love that the fall caused? No finite part of humanity can claim the total dedication of love so as to ground the renewed unity of love among all people. The person therefore must look to history for a proof that love exists, and that proof must allow him/her to respond in love for his/her salvation. The diversity that the person experiences within himself/herself, reflecting the fractured state of humanity, calls for unity. Thus the questions posed to theism open man and woman to a readiness to accept Christ and the church's message.

See **Agnosticism; Atheism; Evil, The Problem of; God; Monotheism**

E. Gilson, *God and Philosophy,* New Haven: Yale, 1941. J. McDermott, S.J. "The Loving Father and the Tormented Child," *Thought* 53 (1978), 70-82.

JOHN M. MCDERMOTT, SJ

THEOCRACY
See **Church and State**

THEODICY
See **Evil, Problem of**

THEOLOGICAL NOTES

Theological notes are short qualifying phrases often used in manuals of Catholic theology prior to the Second Vatican Council indicating the degree of authoritativeness of a particular theological proposition. Parallel to theological notes, which assign a positive value to propositions, are theological censures—notations indicating various degrees of error of particular propositions.

The negative gradation appears earlier in church history, already discernible in condemnations of Franciscans in the late thirteenth and early fourteenth centuries. The errors of Peter John Olivi were variously characterized as faulty in judgment, heretical, dangerous, presumptuous, against the saints and philosophers

and rash. John XXII condemned the errors of the Fraticelli in 1317 as "partly heretical, partly unhealthy and partly fabulous." Such differentiations continued in later condemnations, from those of Wycliffe, Hus and Luther right up to the twentieth century.

The positive gradation of propositions according to theological notes appears later. Renaissance humanism, with its interest in classical thought and, later, Counter-Reformation polemical needs, incited not simply a return to the sources of christian belief, but also a concern to evaluate the various sources. This movement gave rise to "positive theology" as distinct from "speculative theology," that is, a theology interested in listening to the historical sources through which the faith is handed on (*auditus fidei*) as distinct from systematizing the doctrine of the faith in a way which is coherent and intelligible to contemporary thinkers (*intellectus fidei*). The *De locis theologicis* of Melchior Cano (1509-1560) set the standard for this approach to evaluating the tradition. Cano maintained that theology rests on two basic sources of knowledge—authority and reason. These two fan out into ten separate "loci" which, far from being equal in weight, may be listed in the following order of importance 1) scripture; 2) verbal tradition; 3) the Catholic Church as a whole; 4) the ecumenical councils; 5) the Roman Church; 6) the Fathers of the Church; 7) scholastic theologians and canonists; 8) natural knowledge known by reason; 9) the philosophers and 10) history. Cano further proceeded to classify theological truths. Some pertained to faith directly (all which God in speech or in writing handed on to the church); some indirectly (all conclusions about which the church could fashion a defined teaching) and some as appendices to the faith.

There never seems to have been a wholly uniform system of theological notation. Perhaps the most complete systematization appears in Sixtus Cartechini's *De valore notarum theologicarum* (1951). Of his ten categories, the following are the most important (the examples are those provided by Cartechini): 1) *Dogma fidei*, also called *de fide, de fide catholica* and *de fide divina et catholica*, refers to a truth which is revealed by God and taught by the ordinary or extraordinary teaching office of the church (e.g., the inerrancy of the Bible). When such a truth is solemnly defined by the pope or by a council it may also take the notation *de fide definita* (e.g., the doctrine of the Immaculate Conception). 2) *De fide ecclesiastica definita* refers to a solemnly defined truth which is not contained in revelation (e.g., that the eucharist is validly received under one species). 3) *De fide divina* notes truths contained in revelation which have not been defined by the church (e.g., that Christ merited his glorious resurrection). 4) *Proxima fidei* refers to truths unanimously considered to be revealed (e.g., monogenism). 5) *Theologice certum* indicates a conclusion derived from the application of reason to revealed truth (e.g., that the existence of God can be demonstrated). Cartechini's remaining five categories are 6) *Doctrina catholica* (a truth perennially taught but not as revealed—e.g., that the human biblical authors are true but secondary authors); 7) *certum, commune et certum, moraliter certum*—e.g., that sacraments are true causes; 8) *securum* or *tutum*—e.g., what is taught by one of the Vatican congregations; 9) *communius* or *communissimum*—a very common opinion such as that sin is removed by the infusion of grace; and 10) *probabilius, probabile*—a more or less probable explanation such as Bainism or Molinism.

These categories clearly are based upon degrees of authority and, at the same time, imply degrees of certainty. A *de fide definita* truth has the highest level of authority and certainty; a *probabile* opinion has the lowest. Corresponding to these categories, Cartechini indicates gradations of errors and of required degrees of assent.

As it stands, the approach to christian truth represented by theological notes has fallen out of favor in post-Vatican II theology. It emphasizes the degrees of authority of various propositions, giving the impression that theology is an activity of systematizing propositions and expanding the body of truths by deducing new propositions. Such an outlook contrasts sharply with the overall understanding of revelation expressed in Vatican II's Constitution on Divine Revelation.

The system of theological notes, however, does resonate well with several contemporary themes pertaining to doctrine. It shares some kinship with the hermeneutical effort to more adequately assess the degrees of authority behind the various teachings of the christian tradition. It stands as a reminder that an element of authority remains inextricably bound to truth which is revealed and, hence, received. Furthermore, the notion that differing degrees of assent are called for by different types of teaching touches on the question of religious freedom vis-a-vis revealed truth and the possibility of dissent. Finally, the effort to order truths according to their formal authority as represented in the system of theological notes finds a parallel in contemporary efforts to order truths according to their material content—a movement seen in discussions of the hierarchy of truths and short formulas of the faith.

See **Doctrine, Hierarchy of Truths, Theology**

Sixtus Cartechini, *De valore notarum theologicarum*, Rome: Typis Pontificiae Universitatis Gregorianae, 1951. E.J. Fortman, "Notes, Theological," *New Catholic Encyclopedia*, vol. X, New York: McGraw-Hill, 1967, pp. 523-24. Albert Lang,

Die Loci Theologici des Melchior Cano und die Methode des dogmatischen Beweises, München: Verlag Kösel & Pustet, 1925.

WILLIAM HENN, OFM CAP

THEOLOGY

1. Meaning of the Term

The term "theology" (from the Greek *theos,* "God" and *logos,* "meaning") is of ancient provenance but bears a variety of differing but related meanings. For pagan antiquity it meant a mythological explanation of the ultimate mysteries of the world (Plato: *Republic* 379a). Stoic thought sought more for reasoned knowledge but of the "divine" dimension of things consisting of the logos structure immanent in the world. Aristotle uses it as a synonym for what he more properly calls "first philosophy" or metaphysics (*Meta.* 1026 a 19-22), a usage he later abandons when metaphysics is understood to deal with being as such rather than with the immaterial unmoved mover. The early Greek Fathers used *theologia* in correlation to *oikonomia;* the former referring to the inner mysteries of the Godhead, the later to God's plan for the world manifest in the Christ event. In fact, not until Abelard in the twelfth century will the word be used explicitly in our sense of signifying an intellectual discipline, i.e., an ordered body of knowledge about God.

2. Historical Background

An alteration began, most effectively displayed in the work of Anselm of Canterbury (+ 1109) with the introduction of dialectics as a method proper to theology. This replaced the earlier procedure of relying almost entirely on authority wherein theology was limited by and large to expositions of and commentary upon recognized authorities. Dialectics engaged the subject matter of classical sources, contrasting opinions one with another on the basis of intrinsic coherence and illuminative power. By the next century (the thirteenth) another radical change occurred with the reintroduction of Aristotle into the West. Dialectics now gave way to the logic of Aristotle's *Organon* and more significantly to his philosophy proper. This enabled theology to assume the status of a unitary science either in the strict deductive sense of Aristotle's *episteme* (Thomas Aquinas) or in the broader sense of a salvific practical science of the love of God (Bonaventure). In either case a realist metaphysics was the instrument of seeking to understand what faith confessed. All of this was to change with the Enlightenment (seventeenth and eighteenth centuries), which undercut any understanding of theology as a unitary science. Henceforward theology became, as it remains today, increasingly an aggregate of multiple, highly specialized disciplines: exegesis, church history, patristics, dogmatics, ethics or moral theology, pastoral theology, spirituality, comparative religion, etc.

The issue of all this is that theology today finds itself in a state of crisis, called upon to define itself anew. Metaphysical thinking, prominent in the neo-scholastic period (late nineteenth and twentieth centuries), has long since given way first to existential thinking (Bultmann and Rahner) and subsequently to historical thinking (Pannenberg and Metz). Theology no longer traces an objective dynamism from the cosmos to its Transcendent Cause but turns to the subject and the immanence of thought in an avowed anthropological emphasis; the latter in turn has tended towards a radical historicality and a focus upon praxis. Catholic theology attempted a new beginning in an endeavor to engage modern thought, which had become by and large inimical to Catholic thought of the past. This movement known as neo-scholasticism, whose charter was laid down by Pius XI's encyclical entitled *Aeterni Patris* in 1879, was concerned however more with refuting modern thought than with meeting it on its own terms. Central to the project was a distinction between positive theology and speculative or scholastic theology. So conceived, theology's first task was to take an inventory of the revealed data— i.e., truths conveyed at God's initiative that were unavailable to pure reason and so accepted by faith in an uninterpreted manner. These were the truths found in scripture, creeds, councils, liturgy, the Fathers, etc. Positive theology was thus *fides ex auditu* in a systematic or scientific state. Without being an historical science, it made use of the historical method. Subsequent to this was the work of speculative theology concerned with grasping the inner intelligibility of such truth, but especially with deducing new conclusions from the truths formally revealed. The light under which such a project proceeded was known as "virtual" revelation. In time it became clear that the motive of adhesion to such conclusions was reason itself, making theology a rational or logical science. Gradually an altered view of theology came to the fore as a corrective to this rationalized version. Henceforward it was recognized that formally revealed truths were themselves historically and culturally conditioned, and theology's role was one of interpreting the multiple dimensions of truth conveyed by God—an activity of reason, but under the formal rather than merely virtual light of revelation. The distinction between faith and theology became one of mere assent to God revealing in contrast to a discursive understanding.

One of the more suggestive issues of this line of development was Karl Rahner's distinction between transcendental revelation which was nonobjective and preconceptual, and categorical revelation

that was precisely objectification and conceptual thematization of the former. Such thematic expression of the unthematic devolved to theology as one of its prime functions. Rahner was able to show, for example, that the canonical texts were able to *communicate* in an objective way truths that were not expressly *stated* in so many words. Edward Schillebeeckx refers to this phenomenon as a "prophetic expandability" characteristic of the text itself. Thus theology assumed the methodological role of hermeneutics first suggested in the nineteenth century by Dilthey and Schleiermacher.

3. Theology and Revelation

Contemporary theology by and large views itself today as a reflection on religious experience, meaning by the latter not some special sphere of human engagement but a depth dimension to ordinary human experiences (L. Gilkey). These, initiated by God himself, amount to disclosure experience which is to say they constitute the phenomenon of revelation. Such experiences need to be correlated to past experiences of the christian community which have become sedimented institutionally as tradition. The starting point of theology then is a dipolar one: the texts of the past which enshrine original christian experience and our contemporary experience. Significant in this is the understanding that experience is always interpreted experience, not by way of an interpretation that is subsequent to the experience, but one ingredient in the very experience itself, due to interpretive schemas developed out of past experience and brought to the new experience. Understood here is that tradition mediates meaning but must itself be open to newness of meaning.

a) *Priority of the Past*. Traditionally theology has been understood as the understanding of and elaboration upon the content of revelation, the latter mediated by its normative articulation into sacred scripture and tradition. These were the sources of belief expressing divinely communicated truth reducible ultimately to concepts and propositions. Faith was assent to such truth revealed in the past, and theology assumed the task of unfolding the meaning resident therein. The concern of the former was truth (in the act of judgment) while the concern of the latter was meaning (in the act of understanding). Theology was thus a cognitive act elicited by the intellect (and thus formally speaking a rational act) but under the light of faith, seeking conceptual clarity and synthesis, and exercised on the symbols, especially the conceptual ones, in which God's revelation in the past was articulated. Anselm's description of theology thus became the classic one: *fides quaerens intellectum* ("faith seeking understanding").

b) *Priority of the Present.* Radical changes in the understanding of revelation—originating in the nineteenth century work of Schleiermacher but culminating in the thought of the early twentieth century—meant a corresponding alteration in the perceived task and nature of theology. Karl Barth launched the neo-orthodoxy movement with a portrayal of revelation as an existential event, whereby God constituted himself precisely as a God for mankind (*Deus pro nobis*), an event whose existentiality enabled it to transcend temporal passage. Revelation thus became God's present address to believers in the act of faith occurring at the moment of proclamation. Theology now became the task of mediating the Word of God by way of explaining the human language appropriated by God in bringing about the phenomenon of faith (in contrast to mere religion as a product of mankind's inefficacious striving after God). The theological task remains basically an exegetical one, bridging the gap between God's Word and the proclamatory act, largely by way of laying bare the meaning of human language when it is appropriated by God for a revelatory purpose. Theology thus functions analogically, not however by assuming a correspondence between creature and God (*analogia entis*) but rather by acknowledging such between the graced and justified believer and God in the very act of faith (*analogia gratiae*).

However, once revelation is conceived as coming to pass within consciousness, it was a short step to putting the focus on experience as the sphere in which the revelatory act occurred—contrary to Barth's own deepest convictions that theology begins with the Word of God that interprets us rather than with our own experiences which we seek to interpret. Nonetheless, theology now became a reflection upon christian experience, and the symbols in which such experience came to expression. Such experiences were viewed as encounters with God and thereby gained a revelatory character; they were, in short, disclosure experiences. Theology ceased to be an unfolding of doctrines already adhered to in faith but now concerned itself with creative interpretations, symbolically, of such experience. Behind this altered state of affairs lay a new theory of truth. No longer was it a matter of correspondence to the content of an objective revelation mediated conceptually and propositionally (*adequatio rei et intellectus*). Now revealed truth became a matter of what Heidegger referred to as *aletheia*, i.e., God's presencing of himself to men and women in an act of unconcealing and of unveiling himself in the existential experience of faith. Because the locus of such encounter was human consciousness, theology markedly ran the risk of being privatized, of subjectivism and even of fideism. This was evidenced, for example, in Barth's recourse to a meta-history of God with mankind (*Urgeschichte*), and in Bultmann's kerygmatic theology advocating a commitment to God's summons to human authenticity as the genuine, demythologized message of the NT.

c) *Priority of the Future.* A counter reaction to this ahistoricism quickly came to birth with the contention that human consciousness is indigenously historical with the consequence that not only is revelation history, but that more radically history is revelation. Theology thus became the study of history as, in its universality, it constituted revelation. History can be conceived as having a universal meaning in spite of the fact that it has yet to run its course and faces an open future, in virtue of Christ's resurrection understood as an anticipation of what will be the end of history. Here, theology becomes a study of God as the power of the future impacting upon the present (W. Pannenberg), or as the promise of a future to come (J. Moltmann). Theology, so conceived, views the hallmark of the Christian, not so much as faith, but rather as hope, with a switch of emphasis from the individual to society.

4. Theology and the Bible

From the beginning of the post-apostolic period to the end of the high Medieval period, theology was exercised upon the Bible as its book. Indeed, until the early thirteenth century, the occupant of the chair of theology in the newly emerging universities was known as *Magister Sacrae Paginae* ("master of the sacred page"). Theology at this time was well nigh exclusively biblical much as it had been inherited from the Fathers, in spite of some absorption of Hellenization from Plato, the stoics and especially neo-Platonism. This began to change when Alexander of Hales (+1245) inaugurated the practice of using the *Sentences* of Peter Lombard (+1160) as the official textbook for the study of theology. Yet even at this time theological students dealt with the Lombard only after completing a survey course covering all of the books of the Bible. Scotus (+1308) was the first major theologian to initiate his theological work with a commentary on the *Sentences* before completing commentaries on the books of the Bible. Still and all, this marked the beginning of a disastrous separation of biblical exegesis and theology. Exegesis assumed a more and more positivistic character and the schemas of theology became more rationalistic and alien to biblical exegesis. Today all this has changed with scripture looked upon not as a deposit of truths but as a culturally conditioned witness and interpretation of God's proffer of salvation in the historical Christ-event. Scripture, as a privileged interpretation of this originating event by the first disciples, has regained its status as a *norma non normanda*. Tradition is not an autonomous source of revelation alongside scripture expressing truths not to be found in the bible, but "the history of the effects of Scripture" (B. van Iersel). The teaching of the church likewise is not the introduction of new revelation but the interpretation of scripture which is authoritative in virtue of the activity of the Holy Spirit. This closer alliance between biblical studies and theology leaves exegesis with its own proper task—the recovery of the text in its original setting and the meanings it held for its authors. But this function is no longer neutral and naively objective but demands a faith commitment and some preunderstanding on the part of the investigator that is brought to the text. It now functions as a privileged moment in the larger hermeneutical task which acknowledges that the text yields up its fullest meaning only in the perspective of an ongoing tradition. It is theology that unleashes by various methodologies that fuller meaning.

5. Status as Science

With the reintroduction of Aristotle into the West from the mid-twelfth century on, theology was able to exhibit something of the character of science on analogy with what Aristotle calls *episteme* in the *Posterior Analytics,* meaning demonstrated knowledge in contrast to opinion (*doxa*). The way here was led by Thomas Aquinas (+1274) whose dominant operating conception was *sacra doctrina* meaning "holy teaching" (*doctrina* from the Latin verb *docere* maintaining the force not so much of a noun as of a participle). Such holy teaching induced in human intelligence, as a first terminative effect, the *habitus* of faith as a perduring disposition of assent to God revealing. Such belief, however, of itself gave rise spontaneously to the need to understand, issuing in a discursive act which Thomas called *theologia* as a reasoned mode of understanding *secundum revelationem* ("according to revelation"). Theology, then, as a second terminus of sacred doctrine expressed its discursive function as only one of its several roles. Theology thus was not faith but human argumentative thought undergone, however, always in subordination to faith. In this sense it corresponded analogously to what Aristotle called science. Its distinctiveness consisted in the formal light (the *formale quo*) under which it proceeded, which was not revelation (the *formale quo* of faith) but *revelabilitas* meaning the precise intelligibility that things possessed in the mind of God himself. This express subordination to faith led Aquinas to designate theology as a "subalternated science" (S.Th., I q. 1a.2), which never proceeded *ad probandum fidei* ("as probative of faith") but solely *ad manifestationem fidei* ("as clarifying the intelligible relationships between the truths held by

faith). Theology was thus demonstrative knowledge only insofar as the search for understanding arose from and remained within the ambiance of the light of faith, i.e., in virtue of the intrinsic intelligibility of the first principles of faith which were appealed to in lieu of the intuitive intelligibility of the first principles of natural reason as the origin of Aristotle's science.

There remained a third terminus to the *sacra doctrina,* one of which for theology as science was the inchoation, namely the beatific vision of God in the eternal life to come towards which theology tended in this life. This explained Thomas' understanding of theological knowledge as oriented by a dynamic of its own towards mystical knowledge in this life. Without losing its deliberative and discursive character, and the critical function grounded therein, theology of the wayfarer tended to ever greater docility towards the prompting of the Holy Spirit, with a corresponding greater reliance upon doxological language.

Contemporaneous with this development, however, there remained a resistance to it coming from the entrenched Augustinianism with its preference for neo-Platonic categories over Aristotelian ones. Here the finite creaturely world was not garrulous of God by way of its own inner intelligibility and goodness. Rather, the cosmos and even scripture itself functioned only *symbolically* in bringing the human intelligence before God. Theology was thus grace from God, i.e. the gracious indwelling of God's Word in the finite intellect. Theological knowing was less a matter of abstraction (one which functioned within the ambit of analogy both in natural and, differently, in supernatural knowing) than of divine illumination. For Bonaventure (+1274) at any rate, perhaps its most illustrious spokesman, this was a refraction into the human soul of God's uncreated contemplation of the eternal ideas. These latter were the Platonic pure forms viewed in christian Platonism as subsisting only in the mode of exemplar ideas in the divine mind. Theologians defending this Augustinian position could not allow that Aristotle's epistemology could ever arrive at the God of christian revelation, and indeed could not absolve its use by the followers of Aquinas of an idolatrous character. For Scotus, metaphysical ideas were applicable to God not in himself (and so analogously) but solely in virtue of the univocal character of being which could be predicated finitely of the creature and infinitely of God. Theology thereby forfeited its strict character as science (cf. *Opus Oxon,* prol., q. 3 & 4) attaining to God himself not as knowable but only as capable of being loved in accord with the injunctions of the gospel. Much of the motivation for this changed attitude was the ecclesiastical censure of Aquinas' Aristotelianism in 1277, first at Paris and then eleven days later at Oxford. The final stage was reached with William of Ockham (+1334) who opened the way to nominalism by insisting that our concepts and distinctions of reason were not applicable at all to God in his reality but only to our attempts at knowing him. This gradual devaluation of reason culminated eventually in fideism, which in turn gave theology a positivistic character and fostered a critical approach to the sources of theology; theology was no longer a unitary science but gave way instead to an aggregate of auxiliary sciences.

6. Theological Pluralism

A significant contemporary factor is theological pluralism, not to be confused with pluralism of faith or beliefs. This is not the mere fact of there being a multiplicity of diverse theologies, but the recognition that there is an inherent heterogeneity to the theological endeavor itself. Most of all, this consists in a pluralism of methods, attributable to the differing philosophies utilized instrumentally by different theologians, but even more radically to an abandonment of any presuppositions about uniformity of meaning on the part of the theological sources themselves. Underlying this is a growing awareness since Kant of the historicity of man and of all human knowledge with the corresponding relativizing of all theological systems. Without succumbing to relativism, no theologian can any longer ignore the limitations inherent in his own method. Ingredient in this new awareness, too, is the factual transition from the classical culture of antiquity considered as one, universal, and normative, to the empirical culture of modernity as experience-based and so ever altering (B. Lonergan). Empirical culture is avowedly pluralistic in that it views ideas and conceptual systems as products of human understanding that develop over time and differently in different places and cultures; meaning is gained by insight into data that constantly changes so that what is attained cognitively is always only an approximation to truth (which is not a denial that certain truths are permanently true). Making common cause with this is a tendency to see faith as being freed from the constraints of rational structures and entering into an alliance rather with history; if reason tends to transcend time and so to unify, the flux of history tends to fragment. Other factors are: the "anthropocentric turn" in which the subjectivity of the believer becomes a valid starting point for theological reflection and in which concern for the categories of being give way to those of consciousness with a resulting subjectivity, but one that avoids an arbitrary subjectivism; the revised notion of revelation as God's self-communication in present address to humankind; the encroachment into theology of a complexus of non-philosophical disciplines, above all the various social sciences; and perhaps most of all an understanding of theology as hermeneutics, meaning not merely a technique for interpreting texts, but a mode of understanding in which one is able to hear in a text a meaning not available to earlier generations of believers, due to new questions brought to the text from present experience. Such theological pluralism seems irreversible and irremedial, and moreover is one that crosses confessional lines. Its deepest source is awareness of the finitude of all human knowing. If on the one hand it has opened the way to bewilderment, producing a crisis of theological identity and making constructive theology difficult, on the other hand it recalls to theology that its goal remains Mystery that is incomprehensible and ineffable.

7. Crisis of Language

Underlying the present crisis in theology is the vexing problem of language. The problem has been radicalized to where the question no longer is one of the validity and truth of our assertions about God, but rather whether such language can have any meaning whatsoever. This has come to the fore in the so-called "linguistic turn" wherein the language of philosophy and theology is seen as operating on a second level of meaning; it is no longer speech about reality but speech about speech. Since our language has an empirical origin, referring to entities of the spatio-temporal world, there seems no way in which it can refer to a realm which is by definition transcendent to the empirical order. Some theologians, relying upon linguistic philosophy, have contended that the application of our words to God is a case of equivocation in which our words lose all meaning and leave God as unknown even if believed in; theology thus adopts an agnostic stance and is a pure *theologia negativa*. At the

very opposite end of the spectrum others, sympathetic to process philosophy, see predication about the divine as rather univocation, in which our words retain the meaning they have when used of finite realities except that they signify God in an infinite mode. The presupposition here, however, is that God constitutes part of the cosmos and transcends it only relatively. The majority of christian theologians assume a medium position allowing that language about deity does have a genuine cognitive character but one that remains indirect, oblique, and relational. The modes of discourse about deity are multiple and varied in kind, and complementary. Generally speaking, this reduces to three distinct uses of language: myth, symbol, and analogy. Mythological language is an attempt to speak objectively about what cannot be objectified; it cannot be taken literally yet is, in its own evocative and alogical way, a vehicle of truth for what cannot be represented in literal speech. Symbolic language functions on a dual level of meaning; an immediately intended literal meaning points suggestively to another meaning which the former conveys without stating. The difference between myth and symbol is that in the latter the speaker clearly recognizes the difference between the symbol and the symbolized. Its most common occurrence is perhaps the metaphor, as e.g., calling Jesus the "good shepherd." Analogy, by contrast, is literal speech rather than the figurative speech used in myth and symbol—without, however, signifying univocally; it uses concepts rather than images. The analogical concept "designates" God without "representing" him., i.e., the objective contents of the concept are creaturely only, they are not transferred to God but simply supply a vector from which he can be named. Theories on the nature and functioning of analogy are multiple and varied. In a very general sort of way these reduce to two: one rooted in a metaphysics of being; the other in an ontology of existence. Both surmise a proportionate likeness between God and world that prevails within a greater difference, indeed what Kierkegaard calls "an infinite qualitative difference." The former finds the correspondence in the objective order of reality (e.g., Aquinas); the latter locates it in encounter with the other as subject in which the awareness of God is illumined by human personal encounter (a position hinted at but left undeveloped by Bultmann). More common today, however, is the language of models and paradigms which uses analogies not in a normative way but purely as descriptive and as functioning heuristically, affording a means of exploring the meaning of the unknown in a tentative way. Thus, several models complement one another and each is readily abandoned when a new and preferred model offers itself. Mention must be made also of the language of narration wherein discourse in the sense of argument is eschewed in favor of simply retelling the christian stories, whether in the literal and historical sense they be true (e.g., the account of Jesus' death) or mythic (e.g., the parables of Jesus). Such narratives are not literal reiterations but creative recasting of the stories in contemporary contexts. Ordinarily they are recounted without interpretation; rather, they intend to build up in the listener an experience of God's offer of salvation and to invite the believer to confess or to imitate in one's own life the message conveyed—a message which is self-authenticating in its very telling.

8. Theory and Praxis

Once theology became preeminently (though not exclusively) a hermeneutic project, it was inevitable that different understandings of the hermeneutic problem would come to the fore. One of the more richly exploited at present construes the hermeneutical circle as the relationship, not between past (tradition) and present (experience), nor between part and whole, but between theory and praxis. The figure of Karl Marx looms large here, especially in his commentary on the eleventh thesis of Feuerbach, where he insists that the purpose of philosophy is not to know the world but to change it. The congeniality of this for christian thought—whose central truth is that of God becoming incarnate as the man Jesus for the salvation of the world—is obvious. Henceforward, theology cannot be disengaged from involvement in worldly affairs and left in a realm of theory. Its role is not simply that of interpreting the world, but of transforming it in response to God's initiatives in setting up the Kingdom which has already been inaugurated in this life. Praxis here, it should be noted, is not mere practice; it is not the mere implementation of what has already been worked out in theory. Neither is it to be confused with the notion of pragmatism in American philosophy. Praxis is rather the dialectical relationship between theory and concrete practical life. Human behavior thus assumes a cognitive character of its own insofar as, arising out of and directed by thought and analysis, it qualifies such theorizing by altering the very reality reflected upon in the first place. Some contemporary theologians (e.g., J.B. Metz, Matthew Lamb, Dermot Lane) prefer to afford priority to praxis over theory, viewing the latter as arising from reflection upon praxis. A caution needed here, perhaps, is that praxis no matter how dedicated to a given cause, cannot of itself offer criteria for truth. Praxis can supply the motivation and context for christian thinking that is transformative and emancipatory in kind, but it cannot formally determine that critical thinking on the second-order level which seeks meaning and truth. Allied to this "turn to praxis" is the advent on the theological scene of the "critical social theory" of knowledge associated with the Frankfurt School represented most influentially by Jürgen Habermas, in which knowledge is largely the product of society and so never entirely free of distortions. Praxis recognizes these distortions as oppressive, and as the origin of suffering in the world. E. Schillebeeckx has made rich use of the category of "contrast experiences" wherein God is revealed as the source sustaining humanity in the face of human failure and global suffering. Theology thus becomes less a reinterpretation of tradition than a hermeneutics of christian praxis as it aligns itself against all forms of oppression and suffering. Its function is that of a "critical negativity," knowing and opposing everything that is humanly undesirable without claiming a definitive knowledge of what is positively desirable for the fulfilment of humanity. This inaugurates a movement towards emancipation but one seemingly lacking positive content. Such positively is supplied when critical theory becomes critical theology, i.e., when the critique bases itself on the promises of God by remembering and re-experiencing (in praxis, then) the life, death and resurrection of Jesus. This supplies a positive orientation towards the historical actualization of what is truly human.

9. Divisions of Theology

In its broadest sense theology is understood today as comprising a complexus of sciences: exegesis, church history, liturgy, moral theology, pastoral theology, etc. But theology proper, retaining a generic unity, has come to be regarded commonly as three subdisciplines: fundamental, systematic, and practical theology. David Tracy (The Analogical Imagination, 1981) taking theology as public discourse, differentiates these on the basis of the publics addressed: respectively academy, church, and society. Fundamental theology engages in critical inquiry, examining truth claims on the basis of rational argument, bracketing religious commitment. Systematic theology tends to assume truth claims, acknowledges fidelity to a religious confession, and proceeds ordinarily as a hermeneutic of a religious tradition it takes to be disclosive of truth. Practical theology concerns itself with practice informed by theory on the social, political, cultural and pastoral level on the basis of personal involvement in and commitment to ethical goals not exclusive to any one religious tradition. One instance of practical theology is pastoral theology dealing with church ministry in the concrete circumstances of actual life. Another development is the emergence of foundational theology (which some theologians prefer to call philosophical or historical theology) as a replacement for an earlier fundamental theology which functioned as a natural theology and an apologetics, seeking respectively the rational grounds for the existence of a Transcendent Cause and of the credibility of revelation. Both remain legitimate pursuits but are now understood as conducted within the ambiance of revealed theology in which from the very beginning revelation is understood as illumining the meaning of human existence. Foundational theology, by contrast, functions analogously to philosophy in its critical role. It seeks to uncover the basic categories with which a systematic theology can be developed. It takes cognizance of the truth that knowledge of reality is available only on the basis of the structure of the particular being who questions it (Heidegger's Dasein). Historicity is thus taken, not as an accidental factor, but as an essential constituent of human beingness, with exploration focusing on the relationship between christian symbols and common human experience. Such theology is unavoidably pluralistic both in its religious presuppositions and its philosophical under-pinnings. Obviously, there is available a wide spectrum of epistemological options ranging from strict empiricism and linguistic analysis (Wittgenstein) to neoclassic metaphysics (Whitehead). Generally discernible is the refusal of commitment to any one metaphysical system; not infrequently this is radicalized into an anti-metaphysical bias. David Tracy (*Blessed Rage for Order,* 1975) has singled out five contemporary viable "models" of foundational theology: orthodox, liberal, neo-orthodox, radical and revisionist.

10. Prevailing Theological Methods

An index of this pluralism appears in the following selective and non-taxative survey of what would appear to be eight presently dominant theological methods in which theology is viewed respectively: a) as itself a method, b) as existentialism, c) as transcendental anthropology, d) as hermeneutics, e) as eschatology, f) as linguistic analysis, g) as process thought, and h) as liberation praxis.

a) *Theology as Itself a Method.* Bernard Lonergan has argued that theology is less a discipline with its own nature than a method of thought isomorphic with the other humane sciences, a method that is rooted in the invariant structure of human consciousness as a dynamism of self-transcendence that moves in a fourfold way from experience to understanding, thence to judgment, and finally to decision. Experience is of data, understanding seeks meaning, judgment affirms truth, and decision commits the subject to values. In correspondence with this, theology is constituted by eight functional specialities ranged in two groups of four: the first is an ascending movement from research to interpretation, thence to history, and finally to dialectics; the second is a descending movement from

foundations to dogmatics, thence to systematics, and finally to communications. This altered notion of theology has been made necessary by the transition from the classical culture of antiquity to the empirical culture of modernity. Here genuine objectivity lies not in naive realism but in the subjectivity of the believer structuring a world of meaning for the self. Theology is thus, in effect, reflection upon religious experience which attends not to propositions which embody objective revealed truths, but to the acts of theologians striving to understand and respond to God's revealing act. Implicit in this view is a theory of meaning as achieved by way of intentionality; a position common to those who share the transcendental method. Central to this, in turn, is a focus on the act of conversion: intellectual, moral, and religious. Theology is thus truly integral only when entered upon by the theologian who has undergone conversion; faith itself, as grounding theology, is a knowledge born of the love of God. Intellectual conversion, though critically mediated, means ultimately an acceptance of the "turn to the subject," and is the decisive factor in deciding upon the merits of viewpoints and positions which are contrasted, one with another, in dialectics. Among the reservations to which this theory must respond, the most common perhaps is the charge of "decisionism."

b) *Theology as Existentialism.* Influential from the early twentieth century onward is a concept of theology that arises, in reaction against the humanism of liberal theologies (especially that of Schleiermacher) from conceiving of divine revelation as present event, as God's present address to humanity. Karl Barth (+1968) attempted to recoup the relevance of Christianity against the atheist thought of L. Feuerbach (+1872) especially, by an appeal to the existential thought of S. Kierkegaard (+1855), while Rudolf Bultmann (+1976) turned to the existential phenomenology of the early Heidegger to counter the charges against Christianity coming from the advocates of higher historical criticism. Barth's dialectical theology (so-called because every statement about God needed to be balanced by a counter-statement) so emphasized the sovereignty of the Word of God that all natural theology as a propaedeutic to revealed theology was deemed idolatry. The Word exists in a threefold state: as revealed (Christ), as written (scripture), and as proclaimed. Exegesis therefore preceded theology as dogmatics, and the role of the latter was not apologetic but purely that of witnessing. Yet it did so critically, retaining a public and ecclesial character in, as it were, calling the preacher to order. Theology's concern is not with science, nor with philosophy, nor even with historical criticism but with preaching. It remains an autonomous discipline and need not seek to harmonize its findings with what comes from secular disciplines. Our speech about God retains its character as truth, not in virtue of anything naturally common between our world and God (*analogia entis*) but solely in virtue of a commonality established by God's grace (*analogia gratiae*). It is this depreciation of the natural and the rational, the radical alienation from the secular world, and the almost absolute hiatus between God and man, that remains the most glaring weakness in this conception of theology and has earned for it the charge of fideism. R. Bultmann offers a somewhat different view of how theology parallels existential thought in confronting us with existence in the present. This conviction was precipitated by his own skepticism concerning the historicity of the NT. The categories of the christian scriptures could recoup their relevancy if presented in terms of the "existentials" of Heidegger's philosophy. The message of the NT was a *kerygma* ("good news") addressed by God to humanity but one embedded in the outdated language of mythology. The task of theology is thus precisely this translation or reinterpretation, in short a task that Bultmann calls "demythologization." Once freed from its mythological framework, the *kerygma* confronts us with what is God's summons to authenticity of life. This opens up the possibilities that are inherent in the structure of our very existence which the categories of Heidegger can bring to light and accent their contemporaneity. Paul Tillich (+1965) is a similar advocate of existential theology, most graphically so in calling for a method of "correlation," i.e. the attempt to correlate the human existential situation with the revealed message of Christianity. The former poses questions to which the latter supplies answers—not in the sense that the answers can be derived from the questions, but not in the sense either (contra Barth) that the questions arise only out of the answers. Rather, theology mediates dialectically between the believer's own ideas about God (which enable one to understand God's revelation) and that revelation itself. Tillich thus is at least open to the move beyond existential categories into ontological ones, and is less negative about the possibility of natural theology. Friedrich Gogarten, by contrast, understands theology as having broken free once and for all from metaphysics with Luther's *sola fide*. Theology is rather concerned with the origin of faith in the existential interpretation of history which discloses to us the historical structure of our own existence. The question which all existential theologies leave us with, however, is whether they have not escaped the demands of genuine history which is the true hallmark of Christianity, and sought instead the safe harbor of an ahistorical emphasis upon the present that safeguards christian truth claims from historical criticism. In its extreme form, this could amount to a crypto-supernaturalism.

c) *Theology as Transcendental Anthropology.* Understandably, the main differentiating factor in theological methods is the epistemological one. The neo-scholastic revival, dominated by Jacques Maritain and Etienne Gilson, attempted to rescue realism, in which the intelligence is understood as grasping extra-mental reality as it is in itself thereby avoiding the perils of subjectivism. Against this, however, the phenomenalism of Kant for whom the object of perception was a product of that very act itself, continued to prevail. An attempt to counter this was made by Joseph Maréchal (+1949) who, starting from Kant's own position, introduced a system of critical realism. He contended that what was given as conscious phenomenon, led in the light of transcendental analysis, to the conclusion that relation to the absolute and unconditional was constitutive for that phenomenal object itself. In brief, ideas of God do not function only in a regulative way as for Kant but attain to the real or noumenal order. This gave origin to a new theological method which came eventually to be identified as Transcendental Thomism, attempting to uncover the a priori conditions for the very possibility of knowledge, in this case a knowledge of God. What came to light is that a real relation to God is co-posited in every act of knowledge *by the subject,* on the basis of an a priori, nonobjective, preconceptual, innate but conscious pregrasp of God as the very structure of consciousness. In such a method, we do not conclude to God (in a method of deduction) but rather begin with him (in a method of reduction). This dynamism to God is not from the object known to its transcendent cause, but from the subject knowing to what constitutes the infinite horizon of its knowing. This

pregrasp of the Absolute, not as object but as horizon, is an a priori structure of human existence as such, yet it exists only as mediated a posteriori in the categorical apprehension of finite existents. Scripture and church doctrines, as well as theology itself, are thus thematizations in culturally determined images and concepts of this nonobjective and preconceptual awareness of God. Moreover, Karl Rahner (perhaps the most influential practitioner of this transcendental Thomism) makes clear that this pregrasp (*Vorgriff*) of God is not indigenous to man's nature but is an existential and universal structure thereof, due entirely to grace and constituting a "supernatural existential" in which men and women stand open to the God of a possible revelation. Such revelation, should it occur is simultaneously transcendental as God's unthematic but universal offer of himself to be known and loved, and categorical as its mediation thematically in time and space, i.e. in the events of history. This grounds a distinction between the former as faith and the latter as beliefs. Ingredient in this theory of knowing is an understanding that the finite cannot be known as finite without presupposing a prior awareness of the infinite: knowledge of limitation is unintelligible apart from a primordial awareness of something that can undergo limitation. Human knowing is thus always a driving through the finite objects of knowledge in a striving for the absolute. Man is then a question never answered (Rahner), an unrestricted desire to know and love (Lonergan), transcendentally oriented towards God as a known unknown, as "Holy Mystery." Theology accordingly *is* anthropology; less the science of God then the study of humanity as it stands before God. This claim perhaps should be qualified to mean that since the question about God is always man's own question, every statement about God is unavoidably at the same time a statement about man himself. Reservations on this "method of mediation" have been expressed, especially on its anthropomorphism, which runs the risk of measuring the mysteries of revelation by the meaning they bear for humankind. It is precisely in opposition to this that Hans Urs von Balthasar has strongly argued for the option of conceiving theology as aesthetics, (a theo-aesthetics, followed subsequently by a theo-dramatic and a theo-logic) in which God's concrete action in history, in its own splendor (*Herrlichkeit*), interprets itself to man in ways impossible to surmise from the latter's own existence.

d) *Theology as Hermeneutics.* As the science of interpretation, hermeneutics is first given a theological function in the work of W. Dilthey and F. Schleiermacher who view it as the attempt to understand a biblical text by reconstructing the conditions in which the text originated, and thereby entering into the mind and intentions of the author. The early Heidegger furthered this with the claim, through a phenomenological analysis of consciousness, that the human existent was an active constitutor of its world of meaning. The later Heidegger altered the vector of this process, viewing the human subject more passively as the "shepherd of being," as the place (the *Da*) where the being-process (*Sein*) occurs in Being's giving of itself to *Dasein* by way of language as the voice of Being. Hans-Georg Gadamer completed and qualified Heidegger's project by stressing the estrangement prevailing between a past text and the present understanding of the interpreter, making necessary a "fusing of the horizons" through the creation of a new horizon of understanding and language bridging the hiatus. Bultmann and his disciples, notably Ernst Fuchs and Gerhard Ebeling, appropriated this thinking as a method for theology, largely on the premise of a correspondence between the linguistic component and what theology meant by the Word of God. The latter is clearly given an event-like character; reality emerges and expresses itself as language—enabling one to understand that the resurrection of Christ, for example, reoccurs in its proclamation, in the sense that its meaning becomes actual and interprets (rather than being interpreted by) human existence. All of this transpires only in faith, and, issues ultimately in tradition. Theology is thus hermeneutics insofar as it is an interpretation, or reinterpretation, of the Word of God that always surmounts every past event or scriptural account. The text thus mediates an encounter with the subject matter of the text which comes to newness of expression through the text today. One hears in the text what was previously unheard, as new possibilities for present and future existence are opened up. Contemporary theology has dealt at length with the so-called "hermeneutical circle"—e.g., the past can only be understood in the light of the present, but the present can only be understood in the light of the past. Catholic theologians were quick to adapt the hermeneutical method to their own purposes, with perhaps a greater stress upon the identity of faith in its reinterpretative understanding. Actually, Catholic theology had for some time been concerning itself with hermeneutical principles under the rubric of "development of dogma." The overriding danger in the hermeneutical method in general is clearly the temptation to collapse christian faith into pure historicism, as well as a tendency to hypostasize language.

e) *Theology as Eschatology.* As hermeneutics, recent theology has developed from a hermeneutic of existence (in Bultmann's separation of meaning and event) to hermeneutics as language-event (in the merging of meaning and fact by

Gadamer and Fuchs) and finally to a hermeneutic of history (in which revelation appears not only in history but precisely as history in the thought of Wolfhart Pannenberg and Jürgen Moltmann). This last option arose as a reaction against the ahistoricism of the first two positions. In this latter stage, meaning is ingredient in events themselves insofar as they anticipate the end of history and so its final meaning. History, however, is revelation only as it is universal, and since the end of history has not yet occurred, its final meaning appears only proleptically in the resurrection of Jesus of Nazareth (Pannenberg). All our knowledge is thus provisional in the sense that it remains subject to revision in the light of subsequent events. Still, meaning is immanent in events themselves so that historical happenings bear within themselves their own interpretation. Meaning, and so truth which cannot be bracketed off as if autonomous from meaning, emerges from context, i.e., it is contextual in the relationship of part to whole, of historical event to the consummation of history (as opposed to Lonergan's theory of meaning as intentional). Here, the truths of faith are viewed by the theologian as hypotheses, falsifiable in principle but able to be maintained in a provisional way as long as testing does not dictate that they be abandoned. Thus, the future remains open and so this theory avoids Hegel's absolutizing of history as a totality already completed and simply unfolding itself in time. Revelation is at once definitive and provisional, situating the believer between the "already" and the "not yet." At work here is an idiosyncratic reversal of time in which the present comes to us, not out of the past, but out of the future. This ontological priority of the future means that God lies not "above," nor "within," but "ahead"; his actions in history thus assume the character of promises to which the preeminent christian response is hope rather than faith. Thus, one views "the world as history, history as history of the end, faith as hope and theology as eschatology" (J.-B. Metz: "Le Eglise et la monde," *Theologie d'aujourd'hui et de demain,* 1967, p. 140). One feature of this method is its endeavor to deprivatize theology (explicit in Metz's move beyond Rahner), issuing in political theology, meaning not an option for any political ideology, but a recovery of a communal dimension to theology bespeaking an impact on the structures of present society. Another characteristic of this historical method is an implied compromise on the Reformational principle of *sola scriptura;* the NT, remaining normative, is not something directly inspired by God, but rather a witness to his acting that can be grasped only within a living and developing tradition. What this eschatological method avoids is an authoritarian confessionalism (e.g., Barth) on one hand, and subjective decisionism (e.g., Lonergan) on the other. It is not entirely free itself of the charge of relativism and of reducing faith to historical knowledge.

f) *Theology as Linguistic Analysis.* Though the so-called "God is dead" phenomenon of the 1960's has long since faded from view, the problem of which it was a sympton continues to exercise theologians. The underlying problem involved a switch from the question of truth to that of meaning, from a concern about reality to concern about language. No longer was the grounding question, "Does God exist?" but "Does language about God convey any meaning whatsoever?" The root of this more radical question was that if language arises from empirical experience of the spatio-temporal world, how can it refer to divinity that is by definition transcendent to the world. An early answer of Logical Positivism simply classified all speech about the divine as "non-sense," i.e.

devoid of meaning. Ludwig Wittgenstein's subsequent analysis of ordinary language recognized that such speech did have meaning within the context of the way language was used by those who shared common convictions or beliefs, based on a simple agreement as to how words could and could not be used. Theology now became a language game, a set of rules governing proper speech in matters religious. The question of truth was thus bracketed, i.e., left in the domain of faith, something beyond public verification. Theology's concern is here meaning and the focus of meaning is the proposition or statement; theology's function is therefore the analysis of the meaning of religious language. The import of this is that theology, like philosophy and unlike the natural and empirical sciences, does not convey information; it does not seek to explain but simply to describe (Wittgenstein), and even here is less a description of reality than of the way in which we relate linguistically to the world. So conceived, theology is a matter of language skills, favoring a performative theory of truth and eschewing general theories of interpretation such as those available from hermeneutics. Clearly this view of theology exhibits a decided reticence towards all metaphysical schemas of being or of history. This issues in an undercutting of all attempts at seeking grounds for belief. Religious belief is a given linguistic phenomenon, not available for public discourse (there are some things about which we must remain silent, says Wittgenstein), which theology can clarify but not adjudicate. Later reflection abandoned the theory of verification (only that which can be empirically verified can be considered true) in favor of a principle of falsification (something may be hypothetically held as true until it has been falsified). In this way the truths of faith are the hypotheses of theology.

g) *Theology as Process Thought*. A decidedly new theological method has recently become manifest on the Anglo-American scene consisting of an adaptation of Alfred North Whitehead's philosophy of organism to christian belief by such thinkers as Charles Hartshorne, John Cobb, Norman Pittenger, Lewis Ford, Shubert Ogden, Langdon Gilkey, and others. Central to this endeavor is a conviction of the ontological primacy of becoming over being, in which God himself "becomes" in creative interaction with the world. In this Neo-Classical Metaphysics, the ultimate category is not God (who is but one actual entity among the others), but Creativity which is not itself actual otherwise than as instantiated in the God, world relation of mutual dependency. God is conceived as dipolar in nature, at once eternal and infinite but non-actual in a "primordial nature" constituting the mental pole of his being, and at the same time temporal and finite but actual in a "consequent nature" constituting the physical pole of his being. The deity lures the world forward by presenting it with initial aims which it can actualize in a self-creative process; then actualizes itself by way of prehending the actual values the world makes available to it. All values are in a process of constant perishing as regards themselves and are preserved only as absorbed into and transformed within the divine being. The attributes of God in his present state of becoming, though immeasurably greater than the perfections achieved passingly in the world, are formally speaking univocal with them. Language can thus refer to God in his own being. God here appears as a cosmic deity who does not create the world and is dependent upon it. The God of process theology appears less as a personal saving deity than as an explanatory principle of the universe. Other conflicts with traditional Christianity lie in a relativizing of Christ and his resurrection, which lose all claim to qualitative uniqueness. An approximation in Catholic thought, but in some respects only, to this method and the conclusions it delivers, appears in Teilhard de Chardin's re-presentation of Christianity in terms of universal evolution.

h) *Theology as Liberation Praxis.* Another theological method has developed especially in Latin America giving rise to what has come to be called liberation theology, worked out in the thought of Gustav Gutiérrez, Juan Luis Segundo, and Leonardo Boff, among others. It owes much to the political theology developed in Germany especially by Jürgen Moltmann, Johann Baptist Metz and Dorothee Sölle. Though both view the relationship between theory and praxis as a dialectical one, they agree on the primacy of orthopraxis over orthodoxy. The two theologies cannot be exactly equated, however, Political theology arose as a reaction against the privatizing of faith and religion by theologies employing the methodologies of existentialism and transcendentalism, which latter were seeking solutions to the secularism of the Enlightenment by withdrawing faith into the sphere of the personal and the private. As a corrective, political theology relocates christian truth as a transforming dynamism in the social realm which is the new context for the experience of transcendence. It is not a theology of politics in the sense of an "applied" theology (indeed, it resists identity with any and every political ideology) but rather the conviction that all theological thinking is of its very nature oriented to action. Its procedures are hermeneutical, but one wherein the hermeneutical circle is not that of the relationship of past to present but rather of theory to practice. An apocalyptic element surfaces here in the rejection of an evolutionary context for Christianity, in the refusal of a "developmentalism," in

favor of an imminent expectation, and one that is temporally understood, of God's action in the world. Hope comes to the fore here as the distinctive christian virtue looking to the consummation of history, however, as God's eschatological act; the temptation towards a teleological view is overcome by the "dangerous memory" of Christ's cross. Christian love is less something interpersonal than a social concern about justice for others. Faith is the freedom to be critical of existing society and the church is the institution that makes this socio-critical freedom possible. Liberation theology, while cognate with this, is not to be identified with it. Its starting point is not a reaction to the Enlightenment separation of religion and culture but to the concrete experience of oppression— political, racial, economic, and sexual— inimical to the gospel. Thus black theology and feminist theology are further instances of liberation theology. This *point de départ* is less academic, more real and concrete; it establishes theology as critical reflection on christian praxis in face of such oppression. A common concern with Marxism is manifest in the goal of seeking to change the world rather than merely to know it. This explains the priority of praxis in a world that can be changed, and the view of salvation as a social event, moreover one that is conceived in the category of liberation rather than such more traditional categories as redemption. In keeping with this, sin is less a personal category than a social one, i.e., it is the sedimentation of evil in the institutions of society. Emphasis falls upon a liberative interpretation of the life and preaching of the historical Jesus. L. Boff (*Jesus Christ Liberator,* 1978, p. 43 f.) draws attention to five options which characterize the methodology at work here: a greater concern for anthropological concerns than for ecclesiastical ones; a utopian vision in place of contentment with the prevailing state of affairs; a critical method rather than a dogmatic one; an emphasis on the social rather than the personal; and a primacy to orthopraxis over orthodoxy. The major reservation to liberation theology is the fear that it makes the goal of the church's mission an immanent socio-political one, minimizing its eschatological and transcendent character. Nonetheless, the Vatican Congregation for the Doctrine of the Faith in its two instructions on liberation theology (*Origins*, Sept. 13, 1984 and April 17, 1986) echo the words of Pope John Paul II to the bishops of Brazil that, purged of certain adulterating elements, the movement is "not only opportune but useful and necessary."

11. Additional Factors

Recent theology carries forward a suggestion made at Vatican Council II (U.R. 2) into a theory of the hierarchy of truths of christian doctrine, representing an alternative to a former concern with "theological notes." Order among revealed truths is determined on the basis of proximity to the foundational truth who is Jesus the Christ. This allows differentiating primary truths (Trinity, Incarnation, Redemption, etc.) from subordinate truths concerned with the means of salvation (church, sacraments, apostolic succession, etc.). Another characteristic is the distinguishing of theology from the new discipline of religious studies on the grounds that theology must concern itself with truth claims and cannot limit itself to the phenomenon of meaning, as well as the fact that it retains some form of relationship to church. Another factor is the transfer of theology from a seminary to a university setting with the regaining of free inquiry. Also operative today is a sense of "local theology" in which attention is given to the process of inculturation or of contextualization wherein widely differing geographic and cultural contexts (e.g., Europe, North America, Latin America, Africa, Asia) shape differently the reflective act, raising new questions and altering old answers. Allied with this is a new global consciousness opening theology to a dialogue with world religions. Theology thus has become more catholic, more ecumenical, less certain, more oriented towards the world and the future though always with the eschatological proviso, i.e., the truth that God alone gives final meaning to history beyond our capabilities and expectations, and so not derivable from history itself.

Claude Greffre, *A New Age in Theology*, trans. by Robert Schillen with Francis McDonagh and Theodore L. Westow. New York, Paramus, Toronto: Paulist Press, 1974. *Communio: International Catholic Review; Approaches to the Study of Theology*, entire issue, VI/1, Spring, 1979. Wolfhart Pannenberg, *Theology and the Philosophy of Science*, trans. by Francis McDonagh, Philadelphia: Westminster Press, 1976. Fergus Kerr, *Theology After Wittgenstein*, Oxford: Basil Blackwell, 1986.

WILLIAM J. HILL, OP

THEOLOGY, HISTORY OF

"Theology," in Anselm's classic formulation, is "faith seeking understanding." "Faith" may be regarded as a stance of the whole person towards God, characterized by radical trust, hope, love, and commitment. In the christian view, faith is a response to "revelation," i.e., to a divine initiative recognized to be present and operative in a mysterious way within the concrete history of the human race. When human reason attends to this divine self-communication, it can discover important truths about God and the created world, and about the relationship between them. The intellectual effort to appreciate, understand, and order these truths—an activity of reason in obedience to revelation—is precisely what is meant by "theology."

Since christian faith regards divine revelation as a reality achieved and mediated in certain unrepeatable events, theology must always be oriented towards historical realities (an attitude of "listening" to the historically given "Word of God"). At the same time, the effort to understand these divinely given truths involves the use of all the resources of human reason, e.g., the insights and modes of thought of philosophy, and there is always a rational component in theology which may even take the form of speculation. The intellectual enterprise of theology, therefore, is characterized by a certain polarity, which can be expressed in a series of familiar oppositions: revelation and reason, authority and rational argument, scripture and philosophy, "positive" and speculative. In the history of theology, one can notice an alternation of emphasis on one side or the other of this polarity.

Earliest Period: the Primitive Church

The very earliest period of christian theology is the time of the "primitive church," when most of the NT writings were produced. Although these texts have become the primary source for all later theology, they do not contain any kind of systematic, speculative treatment of the mystery of Christ. They bear witness to the events which gave rise to christian faith, above all to the person of Jesus the crucified and risen one. In general, the first believers interpreted the event of Jesus against the background of Jewish faith. Jesus was regarded as Messiah (*Christos* in Greek), and texts of the Hebrew scriptures, especially the Prophets, were interpreted as predicting and foreshadowing him. Initially there was a strong eschatological awareness and an expectation of the imminent return of Jesus which would bring about the consummation of the world and its history. When the event of Jesus' return did not take place, the church had to

develop a somewhat different view of God's plan for history. The most prominent example is the theology of history found in Luke's two-volume work. The most profound, difficult, yet rewarding texts in the NT canon are the letters of St. Paul. In later centuries, it was especially his Letter to the Romans which had an important influence on many great thinkers.

The Patristic Period

As Christianity emerged from the matrix of Judaism and gradually became a religion of the Roman Empire, theology underwent a transformation involving the creative use of Hellenistic thought forms to express the truths of the faith. There are indications of this shift in the NT itself, but the decisive turn to the world of Greco-Roman culture came with the works of the Apologists in the early and middle second century. This led toward the rich and intense theological activity of the following four centuries (the period of the Fathers).

Theology as a self-conscious intellectual project really began only as individuals educated in the heritage of Greece (especially its philosophy) set themselves to articulate and defend the truths of christian faith. The first attempts at using Greek philosophical terms to talk about Christ were apologetic in intent. That is, they wished so to understand the message of Christianity that it could be commended to the mentality of educated people of good will in the dominant culture. In order to do this, there was need of "bridge" concepts which could bring the mystery of Christ into some intelligible correlation with the thought-world of Hellenistic culture. A good example of this is found in the thought of Justin Martyr, who made use of the Stoic term *logos*.

In the late second century, Irenaeus elaborated and defended the essential christian beliefs against the speculative and mythological distortion of Gnosticism. He appealed to the bishops as reliable possessors of the authentic apostolic teaching, summed up in the Church's "rule of faith." He also achieved a profound speculative understanding of Christ as the "recapitulation" of the whole human race.

In the third century, Origen was a figure of outstanding importance for the development of theology. Like Clement, his predecessor as director of the famous Catechetical School of Alexandria, he sought after a christian "knowledge" (*gnosis*) which went beyond simple faith. An indefatigable scholar, Origen edited the text of the Bible and wrote many exegetical works. He was also the first truly systematic speculative thinker of the christian tradition. Influenced by Greek philosophy, especially Plato, he constructed a coherent edifice of thought in which he interpreted the traditional beliefs of the church in an original way. His influence upon succeeding thinkers in the East was strong and lasting, even though some of his ideas were later condemned by the church as heretical.

The fourth and fifth centuries were a time of decisive importance for the formation of the basic doctrines of the church on the Trinity, the divine-human mystery of Christ, and grace. A number of great theologians contributed to this process by defending and clarifying disputed points of christian faith. Especially worthy of mention are Athanasius, the champion of the faith of Nicaea against Arianism; the "Cappadocians" (Gregory of Nyssa, Basil, Gregory of Nazianzus) who helped clarify the full divinity of the Holy Spirit and worked out the terminology for distinguishing the threeness and oneness of God; and Cyril of Alexandria, who affirmed the truth of the Incarnation against the Nestorian tendency to separate the man Jesus from the God who dwelt within him.

Augustine of Hippo was perhaps the greatest of the Fathers, whose theological writings synthesized many of the riches of the patristic period. He was deeply religious and highly speculative at the same time, and a master of rhetoric. In controversy with the Donatists, he worked out an understanding of church and sacraments which became normative for the Western Church. In controversy with Pelagius, he elaborated a theology of sin and grace which entered lastingly into the consciousness of the church. His great work on the Trinity was a masterpiece of creative meditation on an inexhaustible mystery. Augustine's works were a rich legacy for the medieval period, and his influence has continued to be all-pervasive in western theology down to the present day.

The Medieval Period

Early medieval theology began with the revival of learning under the leadership of Alcuin in Charlemagne's time. The method of this monastic style of theology was the meditation and interpretation of the sacred text: first and foremost of the Bible, and secondarily of the patristic texts which had survived the collapse of Roman civilization and the chaos of the dark centuries. This theology was motivated not by a speculative interest but rather by the desire for union with God through loving attention to the truth revealed by him. It thus showed a concentration on the historical pole of theology, i.e., the authority of divine revelation as contained in the Bible and the Fathers.

In the eleventh century, Anselm of Canterbury showed the beginnings of a new way of treating the material of scripture and tradition. The form of his work was that of a pious meditation, sometimes in the form of a prayer. But his mind searched out the intrinsic intelligibility of what he believed, as he attempted to discover *rationes necessariae* for such mysteries as the Trinity and the Incarnation. His thought was metaphysical, though not dependent on Aristotle, and dialectical, though not yet expressed in the later technical form of the *Quaestio.* Because of this rigorous rational character of his theology, Anselm is regarded as the Father of Scholasticism.

In the twelfth century, the dialectical use of human reason became increasingly important in theology. Abelard, especially in his work *Sic et Non,* helped to elaborate what eventually became the standard method of scholastic theology, the *Quaestio.* As this was employed later by Thomas Aquinas and others, it followed a more or less standard methodical format. A question would be proposed; evidence both pro and con would be cited (scripture texts, opinions of the Fathers, philosophical arguments); then the problem would be resolved through rational argument, often by means of the finely drawn distinctions; finally, responses would be given to each of the contrary opinions or arguments, so as to defend the position taken.

A further development of great importance for scholastic theology was the translation of Aristotle's works from Arabic and Greek in the late twelfth and early thirteenth centuries. This ancient Greek philosopher was quickly recognized to be not only a master of logical reasoning but also a teacher of the most sophisticated and comprehensive knowledge of the real world. This human wisdom, quite independent of revelation and the church's tradition, was fascinating, even seductive, for many of the best minds of the thirteenth century.

It was Albert the Great and his brilliant student Thomas Aquinas who deliberately took Aristotle's philosophy as a new resource for christian theology. In effect, Aristotle's doctrine, especially his metaphysics, became a speculative framework for thinking systematically about the christian view of reality. In his great works, the *Summa Theologica,* Thomas synthesized the human, rational wisdom of Aristotle (subject, of course, to some corrections) with the divine, revealed truths of the christian tradition.

The influence of Thomas Aquinas stamped Catholic thought with a characteristic concern to give full value to human reason, while still subordinating it to divine revelation. His confident use of reason reflected his conviction of the integrity and intrinsic intelligibility of the created world, as well as the harmony between truths knowable by human reason and the higher truths knowable only through divine revelation.

Looking at scholasticism as a whole, one must recognize that it was a great work of human reason, taking up the data of revelation (scripture and the Fathers) as then known and understood, and integrating them with the newest and best human wisdom available to them (especially as formulated in Aristotle's philosophy). It thus showed a remarkable balance between the two poles of history and speculation, authority and human reason.

There were, however, undeniable weaknesses and dangers in the whole scholastic method. The enthusiasm for rational arguments and logical distinctions could lead away from sufficient attention to the "positive" basis of theology, i.e., scripture and the Fathers. Moreover, medieval thinkers in general lacked a true historical sense in dealing with texts. The dialectical method could and did lead to excessive and useless subtlety. Finally, the formation of "schools" led, in later generations, to a narrow formalism in maintaining the technical terms and special doctrines of particular schools.

These faults showed up especially in the period following the great creative work of the thirteenth century. The fourteenth and fifteenth centuries are generally regarded as a time of decadence for scholastic theology. The important intellectual movement of nominalism, stemming from William of Ockham, had a significant effect on theology in this period. By attributing the existing order of reality to the absolute and unrestricted freedom of God, this mentality seemed to deny the intrinsic intelligibility of things. In effect, nominalism withdrew almost all the data of faith from the realm of reason. The consequences were a split between religion and rational knowledge, a distrust of reason, and often enough a kind of fideism. The Thomistic synthesis of faith and reason had been lost.

Sixteenth Century: Reformation and Council of Trent

The new humanism of the Renaissance had already begun to turn away from scholasticism and towards the texts of christian antiquity, newly edited, for a fresh appreciation of Christianity, when Martin Luther initiated the great religious upheaval of the sixteenth century. Luther's concern for the personal certainty of salvation led him to a creative rediscovery of the meaning of some key biblical texts, and on the basis of this new understanding he was led gradually to a radical and comprehensive critique of existing forms of church life and thought. In his return to scripture as the unique source of christian truth, he rejected vehemently the decadent scholasticism which he knew, and even went so far at times as to denigrate reason itself. His style of thought was spiritual, personal, almost "existential" in a modern sense, as well as biblical. In all this, he initiated a style of theology in striking contrast to the calm, objective, rational method of Thomas Aquinas.

A more systematic theologian of the Reformation was John Calvin, who developed the basic principles of Protestantism in a distinctive way that would influence large areas of Europe and, eventually, North America. His *Institutes (Institutio Christianae Religionis)* has become a classic work of the Western theological tradition.

The Catholic response to Luther and the other Reformers was slow in coming. There were several decades of bitter polemics between Catholic and Protestant writers, with little mutual understanding. Finally, the moderate and careful theological work of the Council of Trent reaffirmed and explained authentic Catholic doctrine in scholastic terms, in such a way as to reject clearly the teachings of Luther and the other Reformers. This restatement of Catholic faith would serve, then, as the unquestioned basis for Catholic life and theology for centuries to follow.

An obvious consequence of the Reformation struggles and the Catholic response at Trent was that Catholic theology was bound to be defensive and conservative in the following period. Inevitably, too, there were many controversial writings aimed against the errors of the Protestants. The most notable such controversialist was the Jesuit Robert Bellarmine.

Thomistic thought was kept alive and enriched during the sixteenth and seventeenth centuries especially by the work of the great Dominican school of theology at Salamanca, founded by Francisco de Vitoria. His student Melchior Cano devoted explicit methodological attention to the positive sources of Catholic speculative theology in his influential work, *De Locis Theologicis.* Later representatives of this school were Banez and Medina, who both published commentaries on Thomas' *Summa Theologica.* These theologians were part of a notable series of gifted commentators on Thomas which includes the names of Capreolus, Cajetan, and John of St. Thomas. Scholastic thought found vital expression also in the more eclectic theologians of the Jesuit school, especially in the outstanding figure of Suarez.

Seventeenth Century: Historical Scholarship

The seventeenth century also saw the beginning of scholarly historical study of the Fathers and of church history. Most prominent in this work were the Benedictine monks of the Congregation of St. Maur in France (the Maurists), who carried out solid and valuable patristic research. The most famous of these were Mabillon and Montfaucon. Their work continued in the eighteenth century, and was paralleled by the research done then in Germany at the Benedictine Abbey of Sankt Blasien under the leadership of Martin Gerbert. Outstanding scholars such as Maffei and Muratori were also active in Italy at the same time. In the long run, this historical work would greatly enrich Catholic theology, even though for a long time it appeared to have little relation to current scholastic thought.

Eighteenth Century: The Enlightenment

Theology entered into a new epoch in the eighteenth century under the impact of the dominant intellectual culture of the Enlightenment. The glorification of reason was accompanied by a profound distrust of tradition and authority, as well as a disbelief in the supernatural. Deistic rationalism and naturalism rejected the belief in a divine revelation containing truths beyond human reason. Christianity was valued, at most, as embodying the principles of the universal natural religion of reason. Such a radical challenge to the very basis and presuppositions of christian theology was bound to have an effect on the work of theologians.

Among some Protestant churchmen and theologians during the latter half of the eighteenth century, there was a drastic reinterpretation of the content of christian faith along rationalistic lines. The pastoral concern to relate the church's beliefs to people's moral life led to a soft-pedaling if not outright denial of those doctrines which seemed irrelevant, e.g., not only original sin but even the divinity of Christ and the Trinity. Such an attitude to the Church's traditional beliefs was supported by the new methods of biblical criticism, represented by Ernesti, Michaelis, and Semler, which were uncovering the thoroughly human character and historical relativity of both the Bible and later church tradition

Catholic theologians in this same period were somewhat slower to respond to the Zeitgeist and reluctant to cast away any of the dogmatic substance of their tradition. Their thought was still formulated largely in the fixed categories of a sterile scholasticism, insufficiently oriented to the sources of theology, which operated within the limits set by its own conceptuality. There was, however, a growing awareness of the inadequacy of scholasticism for the needs of the times. Catholic theology needed a new speculative framework and new intellectual resources for restating the abiding truth of this tradition, but finding this new form of thought would be a slow, difficult, and ambiguous process.

Nineteenth Century

The nineteenth century was a time of rich and intense theological activity, as christian believers attempted to understand and defend their faith in a quite new intellectual setting. A few of the problems and needs of theology in this period can be mentioned. The Enlightenment denial of revelation had to be countered in some way, so as to vindicate the most basic christian conviction that God has spoken in history. Then, the new methods of critical-historical study of the Bible and the history of dogma raised serious problems for theology. Furthermore, as already noted, theology needed to turn to new intellectual resources for the rational, speculative interpretation of its material, and it was natural to look to contemporary philosophers such as Schelling and Hegel. Finally, theology had to deal with the human phenomenon of religion which had now become the object of much study and philosophical analysis. In all these problem areas, faith and reason were in new forms of tension, and the age-old polarity between the historical and the speculative took on new urgency.

On the Protestant side, the towering figure was Schleiermacher, whose influence upon all subsequent Protestant theology has been enormous. Inspired by the mentality of German Romanticism, he initiated a new way of grounding theology in the immediacy of religious feeling. His early work, *Speeches on Religion,* has become a modern classic of theological literature. His great life-work was *The Christian Faith,* in which he treated all the traditional doctrines of Christianity from his novel methodological viewpoint.

On the Catholic side, the early decades of the century saw some remarkable theological initiatives in Germany—departing from the fossilized scholasticism of the preceding century, but also going beyond the shallow rationalism of the Enlightenment. The most original and influential of the new movements in Catholic theology was the "Catholic Tübingen School." The initiator and seminal thinker of this tradition was J.S. Drey, whose major publication was a three-volume Apologetics. His most brilliant and famous student was Johann Adam Möhler, who is still remembered for his Romantic study of the church (*The Unity in the Church*) and his great controversial work *Symbolism.* Other members of this group were the moral theologian Hirscher, the church historian

Hefele, and the dogmatic theologians Staudenmaier and Kuhn. The dominant concern of this style of theology was to synthesize the historical and the speculative. As a group, they were remarkably open to the results of the new historical studies of the Bible and church history, but at the same time they entered into serious confrontation with the dominant philosophical currents of the age (Kant, Fichte, Schelling, Hegel). In general, their goal was to discover a rationally intelligible system in the seemingly disparate and accidental data of history (in particular, of the history of Christianity). The early works of this tradition were strongly influenced by the thought-world of German Romanticism.

In England, John Henry Newman was a lone figure of striking originality in his efforts to do justice to the historical dimension of the church and of church beliefs. His theory of the development of doctrine shows some affinities with the thought of Drey and Möhler, although he had not read their works.

The openness to contemporary culture and the sense of history which had characterized much Catholic theology in the first half of the nineteenth century gradually gave way to a quite different mentality in the later decades. A new enthusiasm for the theology of the great scholastic thinkers now became widespread and eventually dominant, eclipsing the viewpoint of the Catholic Tübingen School and other liberal thinkers. This "neo-scholasticism" was advocated especially by Kleutgen, Clemens, Schrader, and Schäzler. It was strongly promoted by the papacy in the encyclical *Aeterni Patris* (1879), which established Thomas Aquinas as the normative teacher of Catholic theology and directed Catholic scholars to the recovery of his thought.

The triumph of neo-scholasticism was related to the Catholic Church's very difficult defensive situation in the modern world. In the face of the rationalism, naturalism, and historical relativism of the nineteenth century, the church retreated into a solid fortress of medieval thought which seemed uniquely suited to express the perennial truths of Catholic faith. Hence, any subsequent efforts within the church to think the meaning of the faith in non-scholastic terms were inevitably regarded by church authorities as heretical departures from the normative truth of revelation. This had a dampening effect on creative theological work during the period between *Aeterni Patris* and the Second Vatican Council.

The urgent problems raised by modernity did not, however, go away. Towards the end of the nineteenth century and in the opening years of the twentieth century, a number of Catholic thinkers attempted to face honestly the new critical-historical understanding of the Bible, the new cultural mentality of post-Enlightenment Europe, and the pastoral need to re-think Catholic beliefs in relation to modern spiritual experience. Most prominent among these were Blondel, von Hügel, Loisy, and Tyrrell. For the most part, they did not succeed in articulating an understanding of the faith which church authorities could recognize as orthodox. In the end, the pope condemned a number of ideas which were grouped together under the term "Modernism," and both Loisy and Tyrrell were excommunicated (although neither Blondel nor von Hügel were singled out for condemnation).

Twentieth Century: Renewal of Catholic Theology

The renewal of Catholic theology in the twentieth century was prepared by a number of concurrent movements in the church: biblical and patristic studies, the liturgical movement, the ecumenical movement. In France, the slogan *ressourcement* was coined to characterize the movement back to the sources of christian faith in the Bible and the patristic authors. The Dominicans Chenu and Congar, and the Jesuits de Lubac and Danielou did valuable work in historical theology during the 1930's and 1940's.

In Germany, Karl Rahner was undoubtedly the single most influential figure in recent Catholic theology. Working within the general ambience of neo-scholasticism, he developed a theological anthropology inspired by modern thought which enabled him to reformulate the meaning of all the church's doctrines in a profound new way.

In the Netherlands, Edward Schillebeeckx's early work in sacramental theology (*Christ the Sacrament of Encounter with God*) shed a new light on the whole scholastic treatise concerning the sacraments, and helped to renew the sacramental life of the church.

The watershed event for recent Catholic theology was the Second Vatican Council. At this meeting of the world's Catholic bishops, new currents of thought found their way into the official documents of the church. The absolute hegemony of neo-scholastic thought was broken, and there was a new openness in the Catholic Church for a variety of theological approaches. Moreover, the pastoral thrust of the Council oriented Catholic theologians to the values and needs of the larger world, in an ecumenical openness to other christian churches and other religions.

This survey will end with a brief look at the post-conciliar situation in Catholic theology. First of all, there is no longer one normative Catholic theology, but rather a pluralism of theological methods. Secondly, the problem of history has become acute, in a way that can no longer be avoided. A good example of a dogmatic theologian facing this challenge honestly is Schillebeeckx in his more recent works (*Jesus, Christ, Ministry,*

The Church with a Human Face). Third-ly, theology is becoming increasingly ecumenical, trying to take into account the varied experiences and intellectual traditions of all the branches of Christianity (and even of non-christian religions). Finally, many theologians have a new concern to let their thought be relevant to the struggle for justice and peace (political theology, liberation theology).

It is perhaps inevitable, in a situation of so much ferment and variety, that there is also considerable disagreement and confusion among Catholic theologians. There are differences of both method and substance which cannot be mediated without getting to the most fundamental presuppositions of the respective thinkers. When the differences seem to bear on essentials of Catholic faith, this pluralism can be painful.

These pains accompany the Catholic Church's resolute openness to the modern world which was affirmed at the Second Vatican Council. Faith seeking understanding today has a difficult task, but the rewards of finding a truly contemporary understanding that is faithful to revealed truth are correspondingly great. Theology is, therefore, significantly in the service of the faith of present-day believers.

See Scholasticism; Trent, Council of

Karl Barth, *Protestant Theology in the Nineteenth Century: its Background and History*, Valley Forge, PA: Judson Press, 1973. Yves M.-J. Congar, *A History of Theology*, Garden City, NY: Doubleday, 1968. Martin Grabmann, *Die Geschichte der katholischen Theologie seit dem Ausgang der Väterzeit*, Freiburg im Breisgau: Herder & Co., 1933. John Macquarrie, *Twentieth-Century Religious Thought: the Frontiers of Philosophy and Theology, 1900-1980*, New York: Scribner, 1981. Mark Schoof, *A Survey of Catholic Theology, 1800-1970*, New York: Paulist Newman Press, and Dublin: Gill and Macmillan, 1970.

WAYNE L. FEHR

THOMISM

Beginning with the thirteenth century, there have been many dozens of "Thomisms," all of them claiming in varying degrees to represent or extend the thought of Thomas Aquinas. With so many and such contradictory claims upon the term, it is best to give a historical outline of the stages in the reading of Aquinas's text through the eighteenth century. Developments from the nineteenth century on are treated under the heading neo-Thomism.

Within a few years of Aquinas's death, his texts and teachings had already attracted advocates, especially within the Dominican order. Some had been his students, but many others were simply readers who had been persuaded by his works. Of course, this first generation of "Thomists" was not unanimous in doctrine or teaching. There were those who wanted to defend Thomas from attack by reflective exegesis, and there were those who wanted to extend his doctrine while correcting what they judged to be errors in it. For both, the characteristically Thomist positions were those picked out by controversy either with rival accounts or with the official condemnations of 1277. These included such general questions as the being/essence distinction, the soul as form of the body, and the importance of sensation for understanding, together with such particular issues as the indemonstrability of the world's temporal beginning. Partly because of the pressure of controversy, Dominican legislation became increasingly insistent in securing Thomas's doctrinal authority. In 1279, the General Chapter prohibited any attacks on his teaching; in 1286, it ordered that every friar was to promote it as at least defensible. By 1309, all teaching within the order was to be done according to Thomistic doctrine. Thomas's authority was finally secured by his canonization in 1324.

Still, this authority was largely for Dominicans. Church-wide Thomism was not so much a medieval as a Renaissance movement. One of the very greatest Thomist exegetes, John Capreolus (d. 1444), marks the end of the medieval reception. The years just after his death, at the middle of the fifteenth century, saw in Italy a new generation of exegetes, powerful reform movements within the Dominican order, and the rise of important Thomists at the papal court—evident not least in Thomas's being honored there liturgically as one of the great doctors of the Latin Church. Much of the talent came from the reforming Dominican schools in northern Italy, which produced in quick succession two great expositors, Thomas de Vio Cardinal "Cajetan" (1468-1498) and Francesco Silvestri "Ferrarensis" (1474-1528). Just a few years later, there was a renewal of Thomism at Salamanca, usually counted as beginning with the assumption of the chair in metaphysics by Francisco de Vitoria (1486-1546). Vitoria undertook a series of commentaries on the *Summa* and hastened its substitution for the *Sentences* commentary as the basic text of theological instruction. He was also responsible for redirecting the study of Thomas's moral, legal, and political doctrines. In this one can see the influence of his teacher at Paris, Peter Crockaert (fl. 1510-1525), who was both Thomist and humanist. Vitoria inaugurated a line of distinguished Spanish Thomists—chief among them Melchior Cano (1509-1560), Domingo Soto (1494-1560), and Domingo Bañez (1528-1604)—who would both rework Thomism and help to promote it as the most authoritative tradition in the church, largely through their influence at and after the Council of Trent. Thomism is most often noted in Trent's documents on the sacraments and on grace, but the sixteenth century rereading of Thomas was comprehensive. It cannot be summarized, any more than Thomas can. But it should be noted that the logical and epistemological concerns of early modernity affected Tridentine Thomism in various ways, sometimes by forcing false dichotomies, at other times by changing the presuppositions about the nature and limits of philosophical or theological discourse. These changed presuppositions find sharp expression in Cano's *De locis theologicis*.

Trent marks the universalization of Thomistic terminology and teaching, though it did not impose Thomas on all points of controversy. The newly established Jesuit order quickly contributed its share of eminent interpreters of Thomas, among them Francisco Toledo (1533-1596) and Robert Bellarmine (1542-1621). Francisco Suarez (1548-1617) cannot be regarded as a Thomist; he represents, indeed, one of the great Scholastic alternatives to Thomism and became one focus of the disagreements between Dominicans and Jesuits. Most of the religious orders followed Thomas more closely, always excepting the Oratorians. Two of the great works of Thomistic commentary were produced by teams of Discalced Carmelites at Alcalá de Henares (the "Complutenses") and Salamanca (the "Salmanticenses"). The faculty at Alcalá produced the philosophical curriculum known as the *Cursus artium*, which went from four volumes in the first edition (1624-1628) to seven volumes after the fourth. Much more ambitious were the Carmelite elaborations of matter from Thomas's *Summa*, published as *Cursus theologicus* (1631-1712) and the *Cursus theologiae moralis* (1665-1724). By the eighteenth century, much of the energy had gone out of Thomism, which felt itself under pressure from modern philosophies and the anti-Aristotelian results of modern science. But Thomism was by no means extinguished, especially among the Dominicans. The Master

General, J.T. Boxadors, reiterated the early legislation about Thomas' authority (1757, 1777) and his exhortations to new study were answered. For example, Salvatore Rosselli's *Summa philosophica* (1777), dedicated to Boxadors, was to prove influential for the leaders of the nineteenth century neo-Thomistic renewal.

See **Theology**

Frederick J. Roensch, *Early Thomistic School*, Dubuque, IA: Priory Press, 1964. Martin Grabmann, *Mittelalterliches Geistesleben*, 3, Munich Max Hueber, 1956). Paul Oskar Kristeller, "Thomism and the Italian Thought of the Renaissance," in *Medieval Aspects of Renaissance Learning*, Ed. and trans., Edward P. Mahoney, Durham, NC: Duke U Press, 1974, pp. 29-91. Carlo Giacon, *La seconda scolastica: I grandi commentatori di san Tommaso*, Milan: Fratelli Bocca, 1944-1946.

MARK D. JORDAN

TOLERANCE

See **Church and State, Religious Freedom**

TRADITION

The Question

The word "tradition" derives from the Latin, *traditio,* corresponding to the Greek *paradosis:* both mean "transmission. The basic meaning refers to the transmission in the church, of beliefs, doctrines, rituals, and entities such as the scriptures. The vocabulary that designates this transmission has been diversified, allowing for the perception of a number of aspects of tradition seen as a historical and theological question. As to its object, the word "tradition" refers to what is transmitted, an object or content; or to how it is transmitted, a process: it is *passive* or *active.* As to its source, it can be *apostolic* or *post-apostolic,* having its origin in the time of the apostles or later. As to its form, it is said to be *written* or *unwritten:* this can have two meanings,

for "written" may be understood of any writing or designate only the writing of holy scripture. As to its function in the church, tradition can act both as memory of the past and as anticipation of the future: it is then *preservative* or *constitutive* of doctrine. As to its relation to society, it is *public* or *private.* As to its extension in space, it is *universal, regional,* or *local.* As to its binding character, it is *normative* or *non-normative.* Another distinction has come to light more recently: as to its time, tradition is *scriptural* or *post-scriptural,* referring to scripture as an embodiment of the earliest transmission of the gospel, or to the transmission of christian doctrine after the canon of scripture was finalized.

History

When Christians gave up their early expectation of a prompt return of Christ in glory, it became imperative, in the second century, to agree on the sources of authentic teaching. From being chiefly prophetic, the christian faith became predominantly historical. The Church Fathers (from Irenaeus, in *Against the Heretics,* to Vincent of Lerins, in the *Commonitorium*) drew on a stoic philosophical model to determine that binding christian tradition should have the three marks of "antiquity, universality, and consensus" (in keeping with Cicero's description of truth in the *Tusculana oratio,* I, xv, 35). In application of this principle, the early church was able to identify the canon of the NT against the gnostics' claims to secret traditions: it comprises the gospels, epistles, and other writings generally received in the churches' liturgical usage as deriving from apostolic times and transmitting the apostles' preaching. Against Marcion, it accepted the OT in the Septuagint Greek version as the tradition of Christianity's preparation in Judaism.

Irenaeus located the post-scriptural

tradition in the consensus of the churches that were directly founded by apostles. However, on the basis of the lists of successive bishops that he was acquainted with, he could only claim the church in Rome to be such: this church goes back, as was already recognized in the *Letter of Clement to the Corinthians* (c. 95), to the preaching of both Peter and Paul. This gave the church in Rome a *potentior principalitas,* "a more powerful origin." The early tradition, often called the "rule of faith," was summarized in the creeds or "symbols" used at baptism. Tertullian defended it, against recent heretics, with the legal argument of a prescription of long ownership. For the *Gelasian decree* (a private document of the end of the sixth century), tradition is at the service of the one foundation, Jesus Christ; the status of post-scriptural tradition derives from its documents having been "regularly received," notably in the decrees of the great councils. Thus "reception" was determinative in regard to the authentic transmission of doctrine.

The trinitarian and christological controversies resulted in the adoption of conciliar creeds as further embodiments of the authentic tradition: the creeds of *Nicaea* (325), *Constantinople I* (381), and *Chalcedon* (451) were taken to be fundamental for the later transmission of doctrine. Chalcedon even forbade making new creeds and adding new articles to the creeds already received. The normativity of the creeds enhanced the exemplary value of the patristic liturgies as the liturgical context for the confession of faith, of the corresponding theologies as explaining the origin and interpretation of the creeds, and of the threefold hierarchical church-structure (bishops, priests, deacons and, in many places, deaconesses), as being entrusted with the further transmission of what each age has received from the previous age. Thus the patristic period became, in a unique

sense, normative for later times. In this, however, lay the basis for the medieval split between the Latin and the Greek Churches, as each side interpreted the normative tradition in the light of what it knew best in the patristic era: the Greek Fathers, and especially the Cappadocians, for the Greek or Eastern tradition, the Latin Fathers, dominated by St. Augustine, for the Latin or Western tradition.

At the end of the patristic period, the later ecumenical councils formulated this notion of normative tradition in no uncertain terms. For the fifth council (Constantinople II, 553), "we rightly confess the doctrines that have been transmitted to us by the divine scriptures and the teaching of the holy fathers, and by the definitions of the one and selfsame faith made by the four holy councils" (canon 14). For the seventh council (Nicaea II, 787), anyone who "rejects the ecclesial tradition, written or unwritten" (canon 4) must be anathematized. The eighth council (Constantinople IV, 869-870, but never recognized as ecumenical in the East), professed to "obey and keep the rules which have been transmitted to the holy catholic and apostolic church by the illustrious apostles, by the universal and local councils of the Orthodox, and by any inspired father and doctor of the church" (canon 1).

The western Middle Ages brought no new basic element to the theology of tradition. Yet they had a major impact in four areas. (1) The estrangement between the eastern and the western traditions grew into a schism (1054). (2) The *Filioque* was added to the Latin creed, first in Spain (Council of Toledo III, 589), next in Charlemagne's empire (Council of Frankfurt, 794), finally in the whole Latin Church (accepted by Pope Benedict VIII in 1014). (3) Canon law gained importance for the normative enforcement of tradition in the West, thus strengthening the power of those who watch over the application of laws, namely the bishops, advised by canon-lawyers: whence the notion of the *magisterium* or normative teaching office. (4) The *magisterium* in the West became more centralized in the bishop of Rome, who is alone able, for Thomas Aquinas, to "determine new articles of faith."

The Reformation brought the notion of tradition into question, as it asserted, historically, that many medieval traditions do not derive from the apostles, and, theologically, that only scriptural traditions are normative. The formal principle of "Scripture alone," endorsed by the reformers, balanced the material principle of "justification by faith" in safeguarding the doctrine of redemption by "Christ alone." At its fourth session (1546), the Council of Trent responded by endorsing as normatively traditional: the Nicene-Constantinopolitan creed (with the *Filioque*), the scriptures in the Vulgate edition, with the interpretation of it which "Mother Church has held and holds" in keeping with "the unanimous consensus of the fathers" (D.S. 1507). It also justified tradition by the need for preserving "the purity of the gospel," and defined it as "the truth and discipline" of the gospel, "contained in written books and unwritten traditions." These traditions, deriving from Christ himself or from the Holy Spirit through the apostles, "have come down to us as though by hand," relate "to faith and to mores," and have been passed on "in continuous succession." Such traditions must be "received and venerated with equal piety and reverence" (D.S. 1501).

Importance of Tradition for the Church

The Counter-Reformation reflected on the place of tradition in the life of the church: tradition provides the source and determines the nature of theological arguments (the *loci theologici* of Melchior Cano, 16th c.); it is integral to the life of

all societies, and it may even hold the key to the origin of language, religion, and politics (special theses of "traditionalism," 19th c.). As a process, it is not static, but dynamic, identical with the experience of the Holy Spirit in the church (school of Tübingen, 19th c.). This gives tradition an orientation to the future. It implies that doctrine, in the course of its transmission, progresses, passing through an organic development that may be compared both to the unfolding of an idea in the mind and to the growth of a seed into a tree (John Henry Newman, 19th c.). At the same time, the counter-Reformation generally, though not universally, took the Council of Trent to mean that scripture and tradition are two complementary sources of christian doctrine, each containing a part of the divine revelation. This tended to oppose sharply the Catholic concept of tradition to the Protestant notion of "Scripture alone" as the only source of faith.

The problem of tradition was raised in several ways in Russian Orthodoxy. When, in the sixteenth century, icon-painters started illustrating theological theories rather than symbolizing the presence of the divine, the Council of Moscow of 1551 outlawed such innovations: just as the traditional icons express and transmit traditional doctrine, new styles would promote new, and therefore erroneous, doctrines, thus changing the very nature of christian life and piety. Yet is the church forever bound to obsolete social customs that have no doctrinal implications? When, in the seventeenth century, Peter the Great imposed structural and liturgical reforms on the church, the *Old Believers* denied to the tsar and the church the right to alter old customs, on the ground of a naive belief in their apostolic origin.

In France, the Jansenist controversy (17-18th c.) brought attention to the magisterium's responsibility to transmit doctrine in its integrity. Can the bishop of Rome demand assent that the "five propositions" on grace, condemned by Innocent X in 1653, were effectively present in the book of Cornelius Jansen, *Augustinus?* Is there a real distinction between "fact" and "right," (*le fait et le droit*), when it comes to determining doctrine? Can a "respectful silence" on the part of dissenting Catholics be legitimate? These kinds of questions came to a head at Vatican I (1870): the constitution *Dei Filius* examined the relations between human reason and divine revelation, while the constitution *Aeterni Patris* determined four conditions under which the bishop of Rome is said to speak *ex cathedra,* that is, infallibly, proclaiming doctrines that are "irreformable."

Vatican II

The discussions around *Modernism* in the early twentieth century brought up some problems relating to tradition: Can dogmas have symbolic religious value in the absence of historical value? Must christian facts (history) and christian beliefs (dogma) coincide? Should history and dogma verify each other? Granted that there is indeed more in action (*praxis*) than in what is said or written about it, what is the function of christian action in the tradition of doctrine? The Catholic conception of tradition was seen, with Maurice Blondel, to lie between "extrinsicism" (the external seal of divine or church authority is sufficient) and "historicism" (no dogma is acceptable unless it be in harmony with scientific history): thus, tradition, as transmission of doctrine "by word, writing, and action," enfolds scripture, but extends also to the living church today, still guided by the Spirit.

Meanwhile, the question of tradition was raised, for Protestantism, between the two wars, by the rivalry between the two lines of the ecumenical movement: *Life and Work* held that "doctrine divides, but action unites," thus proposing to disregard doctrinal tradition; *Faith and Order* considered that doctrinal agreement is a key to final unity among Christians. By bringing a degree of commonalty to most of the Protestant Churches, the ecumenical movement also made them aware of the distinctiveness and richness of their separate traditions in liturgy, piety, preaching, and theology. The problem was studied after World War II in several contexts, especially in the American *Consultation on Church Union* at Oberlin (1963), and in the *Faith and Order Conference* at Montreal (1963). A pragmatic consensus emerged, which distinguished between Tradition (capital "T") as the process of transmission, tradition (small "t," singular) as the content of what is transmitted, and traditions (small "t," plural) as the distinctive inheritance of separate churches or movements. Theologians remarked that Tradition as transmission of doctrine has a kerygmatic, a liturgical, and a historical dimension. But some argued, in light of the principle of "Scripture alone," for limiting the normative period of tradition to the time of the apostles (Oscar Cullmann).

In the 1940's and '50's, discussion of several points in the Catholic concept of tradition prepared the ground for Vatican II. Ecumenical studies inspired comparison of the Catholic concept with the *consensus quinquesaecularis* in Lutheranism, and with the Anglican distinction, found among the Caroline divines, between "fundamentals" and "non-fundamentals." The methods of modern biblical exegesis underlined the existence of diverse, perhaps mutually incompatible, traditions within scripture. Sociological studies showed the role of traditions in shaping and preserving societies. In studying the Council of Trent, scholars disagreed as to the meaning of "and" (*et*), which, in the decree of 1546, ties together the scriptures *and* the traditions: Does it mean the same as the words of the original draft which it replaced (*partim... partim*)? Does this expression mean "partly... partly," or is it equivalent to "and"? Does "and" imply that revelation is partly in each, or totally in both, or partly in one and totally in the other?

The constitution *Dei Verbum* was promulgated at Vatican II on Nov. 18. 1965. It was a work of a "mixed commission" (half the members taken from the Theological Commission of the council, the other half from the Secretariat for Christian Unity) established by John XXIII on Nov. 21, 1962, after many bishops had severely criticized a proposed schema on *The Sources of Revelation.* This schema wanted the council to endorse the Counter-Reformation idea that tradition and scripture are two separate, partial, and complementary sources of revelation. By the same token, it would have imposed one interpretation of the Tridentine decree, over against other historically possible interpretations. In six chapters, the council describes: (1) Revelation; (2) the transmission of Revelation; (3) the inspiration and interpretation of scripture; (4) the OT; (5) the NT; (6) the use of scripture in the church. Above all, Vatican II wanted to restore the reading of scripture as a major element in Catholic piety and theology. While it did not end debate, it effectively favored a non-dualistic view of tradition and scripture. Tradition, itself, it described as both process and content. For the first time in a council, it connected tradition and progress in doctrine, this being understood as a deepening insight into the divine truth. Vatican II affirmed that "authentic interpretation of God's Word in Scripture or Tradition" has been entrusted only to the magisterium; yet it also subordinated the magisterium to the word of God which it serves.

Contemporary Debates

Post-Vatican II discussion has centered on three kinds of problems. First, the nature and process of the "reception" of doctrine by the *consensus fidelium* have been seen to require more investigation. Second, the acculturation of Christianity in Africa and Asia has brought into question the completeness of tradition in its European and American settings: Can the cultures of Africa and Asia, in spite of their non-Judeo-Christian backgrounds, positively contribute to the christian tradition? Third, this problem has brought up another set of questions: Are non-christian religious traditions objective ways of salvation? Can there be a christian "theology of paganism?" Is the OT still a valid way of salvation for Jews? Are there many "Old Testaments," each non-christian religion acting as a providential way of salvation in a given culture? Are there many divine revelations, or is the revelation in Jesus Christ unique and exclusive? Is this revelation somehow inclusive of the teaching of non-christian prophets? No consensus is yet discernible on any of these points.

See **Church, Development of Doctrine, Revelation, Scripture**

Günter Biemer, *Newman on Tradition,* New York: Herder and Herder, 1966. Yves Congar, *Tradition and Traditions,* London: Burns and Oates, 1966. Josef Geiselmann, *The Meaning of Tradition,* New York: Herder and Herder, 1966. R.P.C. Hanson, *Tradition in the Early Church,* London: SCM Press, 1962. Joseph Kelly, Ed., *Perspectives on Scripture and Tradition,* Notre Dame, Ind.: Fides, 1976. J.P. Mackey, *Tradition and Change in the Church,* Dayton: Pflaum, 1968. John Henry Newman, *An Essay on the Development of Christian Doctrine,* [1845], New York: Doubleday, 1960. George H. Tavard, *Holy Writ or Holy Church,* New York: Harper, 1959; *The Seventeenth-century Tradition,* Leiden: Brill, 1978; *Dogmatic Constitution on Divine Revelation of Vatican Council II,* New York: Paulist, 1966. Jan Walgrave, *Unfolding Revelation,* Philadelphia: Westminster, 1972.

GEORGE H. TAVARD

TRADITIONALISM

As a generalized current of thought, traditionalism was quite widespread in nineteenth century theology. Beginning with the Romantic reaction against the individualism, rationalism and mechanism of Enlightenment thought, traditionalism remained a force in Catholic theology until shortly before Vatican I. Among its earlier representatives were de Maistre, de Bonald, de Lamennais and Bautain in France and the Tübingen theologians, Drey and Mohler, in Germany. At the middle of the century Ventura and Bonnetty were among its leaders in Italy and France and the theological faculty at Louvain had become one of its strongholds.

Rome issued several condemnations against traditionalist theologians during the second third of the century. The Roman Congregations, often influenced by their scholastic theologians, were troubled by the traditionalists' hostility to scholasticism and by their distrust of its Aristotelian discursive reason. Traditionalists believed that modern epistemology had discredited Aristotle's discursive reason. It was no longer useful in apologetics, since it could neither give convincing proofs of God's existence nor establish anything about his nature. It could neither prove the immortality of the soul nor provide the grounding for a christian ethics.

Knowledge of the moral and religious truths required for social life had been given to the human race through a primitive divine revelation. Unless that revelation were received through an implicit act of faith, the human mind could not acquire the intuitive knowledge of the first principles on which discursive reasoning depends. Human beings would be incapable of rational speech, and they could not understand the basic moral principles on which social life is founded. Therefore it is the revelation, received through faith, which distinguishes human beings from brutes. For, without it, human beings would be incapable of speech, morality or social life.

Our present knowledge of God's primitive revelation has been handed down to us through the language and tradition of the society into which we have been born and in which we live. For the only way in which revelation can reach us is through the speech of the elders who educate us in society. And so the mind's own power to reason is posterior by nature to faith, speech and tradition. Since this is so, there can be no basis for the individual reason of Enlightenment philosophy with its boasted independence of faith and tradition.

A number of traditionalists identified God's primitive revelation with the mind's intuitive grasp of God's own being or of the divine ideas proposed in the philosophy of St. Augustine. Others associated it with the intuitive grasp of the Absolute which post-Kantian idealism attributed to its higher form of reason or *Vernunft*. This meant that some traditionalists belonged to the nineteenth century stream of Augustinianism called ontologism, while others belonged to one or other of the German schools of theology influenced by post-Kantian idealism. Still others, such as de Bonald, Bonnetty and Ventura eschewed any connection with other movements. These were the pure traditionalists, who conceived primitive revelation to be a unique and supernatural divine activity.

Rome's objection to traditionalism was twofold. First, the traditionalists' primitive revelation, to say the least, confused, if it did not actually deny, the proper distinction between faith and reason. Second, by denying natural reason's ability either to prove God's existence and the immortality of the soul or to establish the foundations of individual and social ethics, the traditionalists had failed to give natural reason its proper due. By doing that, they had blurred the necessary distinction between the natural and the supernatural orders.

When Vatican I defined natural reason's ability, at least in principle, to establish God's existence and to determine his attributes, and when the Council further defined that revelation was necessary, not because of any deficiency in human reason, but purely because the supernatural mysteries exceeded its range, strict, or extreme, traditionalism could no longer be held. Many traditionalists, however, including a number of the bishops present at Vatican I, favored a more moderate traditionalism. In their view, although natural reason, could prove God's existence and establish the foundations of morality, revelation, transmitted by tradition, was morally necessary for it to do so. The bishops at Vatican I consciously excluded this moderate form of traditionalism from their condemnation. Nevertheless, in the changed climate after Vatican I, traditionalism ceased to be an important force in Catholic theology.

See **Faith, Revelation, Tradition**

Roger Aubert, *Le Problème de l'Acte de Foi,* Louvain: Warny 1950. Wayne L. Fehr, *The Birth of the Catholic Tübingen School: The Dogmatics of Johann Sebastian Drey,* Chico, CA: The Scholars Press, 1981. Joseph R. Geiselmann, *Die Katolische Tübinger Schule,* Freiburg: Herder, 1964. Thomas F. O'Meara, O.P., *Romantic Idealism and Roman Catholicism: Schelling and the Theologians,* Notre Dame: U of Notre Dame Press, 1982. Paul Poupard, *L'Abbé Louis Bautain,* Paris, Desclée 1961.

GERALD A. MCCOOL, SJ

TRANSCENDENTALS

In general, transcendentals are concepts whose meaning and reference are utterly unrestricted. Virtually everyone who has studied the matter agrees that a complete list of transcendentals should include "being," "unity," "truth," and "goodness." There are sharp disagreements, however, regarding the total number of transcendentals, their genesis, and their epistemic status.

Number

Pre-modern thinkers assume the epistemic objectivity of the transcendentals, and thus their discussion of transcendentals proceeds as a frankly metaphysical treatment of being and its properties precisely as being. For the scholastics, for example, being is "transcendental" in the sense of "transcategorical." It extends both across and beyond the ten categories of Aristotelian metaphysics, and it excludes nothing save pure nothingness. Unity, truth, and goodness are "convertible" with being and one another. That is to say, they are properties of being that are only notionally distinct from being itself and one another. Unity is being, viewed as intrinsically undivided; truth is being, viewed as intrinsically knowable; and goodness is being, viewed as intrinsically desirable. Some in the scholastic tradition argue that beauty must be counted a distinct transcendental. Others reject this claim, contending either that beauty is at most an attribute of material being rather than being as such, or that beauty, properly understood, reduces to goodness. Again, some maintain that such properties as reality, particularity, duration, and similarity are distinct transcendentals; while others hold either that they are not transcendentals at all or that at least they are not distinct from the others.

Genesis

A hallmark of modern thought is its concern to avoid simply assuming the epistemic objectivity of mental contents and, on the contrary, to inquire explicitly about both their epistemic objectivity and, as an antecedent factor, their genesis in consciousness. Three different and highly influential modern understandings of the transcendental concepts may be illustrated by comparing three modern thinkers on these two issues in turn.

For Joseph Owens, standing in the broad tradition of neoscholasticism, the contents of the transcendental concepts are radically acquired, empirical, *a posteriori*. The first moment in their genesis is one's intellectual (and, more narrowly, judgmental) intuition of some material thing's actual existence. Next, through negative judgments of separation, one eliminates from this intuited content every feature that characterizes it as the existence of a *material* thing, thus arriving at the concept, "being as such." Finally, one articulates the remaining transcendental concepts by envisaging "being as such" under various aspects.

By contrast, for Immanuel Kant and his successors, and again for Bernard Lonergan and others in the "transcendental realist" tradition stemming from Joseph Maréchal, the contents of the transcendental concepts are radically innate and "transcendental" in the sense of "*a priori* conditions of the possibility of the human subject's functioning." More exactly, Kant argues that "unity," "truth," and "goodness" are nothing other than his "categories of quantity," concepts expressing three features of the basic pattern according to which one connects logical subject and predicate whenever one makes particular judgments. These features are prefigured by an immanent structure of the human subject, the *a priori* faculty of understanding, and thus they as well are *a priori*. The concepts expressing them arise through deduction in "transcendental logic."

Lonergan, on the other hand, maintains that "unity," "truth," and "goodness" are concepts expressing three intrinsic features of the total goal of human intending, the exhaustive goal toward which one is striving at least operationally whenever one asks particular questions. These features are prefigured by an immanent structure of the human subject, the *a priori* desire to know and to love, and thus they as well are *a priori*. The concepts expressing them arise through objectification in "transcendental methodology."

Epistemic Objectivity

Are the transcendental concepts epistemically objective? The answer one gives to this question reflects both one's account of the genesis of the transcendentals in consciousness and one's very notion of epistemic objectivity. For Owens, the answer is affirmative, because the transcendental concepts express what one apprehends in part through intellectual (and, more exactly, judgmental) intuition, and for a concept to be epistemically objective is for it to express a content that one apprehends in just that way. For Kant, the answer is negative, because one has no intellectual intuition at all, yet for a concept to be epistemically objective is for it to express a content that one apprehends through intellectual intuition. For Lonergan, the answer is affirmative, because the transcendental concepts express *a priori* features of the total goal of one's desire to know and to love, and for a concept to be epistemically objective is for it to express something of just that goal.

See **Metaphysics**

Joseph Owens, *An Elementary Christian Metaphysics,* Milwaukee: Bruce, 1963. Immanuel Kant, *Critique of Pure Reason,* B 33, 45, 66-75, 92-93, 113-15, 295-315. Bernard Lonergan, *Method in Theology,* New York: Herder & Herder, and London: Darton, Longman & Todd, 1972.

MICHAEL VERTIN

TRANSUBSTANTIATION
See **Eucharist**

TRENT, COUNCIL OF

Except for a brief period at Bologna in the Papal States, the nineteenth ecumenical council met at Trent, an Italian city under the jurisdiction of the Holy Roman Empire. The Council declared its task to involve both the doctrine and the discipline of the church: the clarification of dogmas at issue in Reformation controversies; the correction of abuses long denounced but now dramatically attacked by Protestant reformers. Chronically delayed and suspended due to vacillation in papal and international politics, its twenty-five sessions were held during three phases: 13 December 1545—16 February 1548; 1 May 1551—28 April 1552; 18 January 1562—4 December 1563. The supposed delay, however, between Luther's emergence in 1517 and the meeting of the Council reflects the fact that measures other than a Council were deemed preferable by many, and that all those directly affected by a Council (Pope, Protestants, curia, Emperor, bishops, Catholic and Protestant princes) envisioned it as a serious potential threat to themselves. Despite political and theological crises which repeatedly threatened to destroy the Council and its work, it issued decrees on the comprehensive range of questions with such clarity and force that the Council of Trent came to epitomize the entire Catholic Reform and symbolized for generations the cohesiveness of Roman Catholic theology and ecclesial administration. Thus, it surprises many to discover that the decrees of Trent were not completely accepted in vast segments of the Roman Church. The doctrinal decrees were officially accepted by all Catholic rulers and governments. But the disciplinary decrees were approved in their entirety only in Poland, Portugal, the Italian states, and the Hapsburg hereditary lands. In France and the Holy Roman Empire, they may have inspired reform but were not accorded official status. The Spanish Church with its world-wide missions had been reformed long before the Council and received its decrees only subject to royal prerogatives.

In matters of dogma, the most significant decrees of Trent concerned the doctrine of original sin; justification and the related questions of divine grace, human will, faith and good works; the number and nature of the sacraments, especially the real presence in and the transubstantiation of the Eucharist; the status of matrimony as a sacrament; the sacrificial nature of the Mass; purgatory and indulgences; and the status of both scripture and tradition as sources of revelation. The Council did not directly pronounce on the nature of the church or the relative authority of the bishops, councils, and the pope.

The theological masterpiece of the council was the decree on justification, which walked the narrow line between Pelagianism and deterministic Protestantism. On the one hand, it attempted to define a Catholic position against various Protestant views, while on the other it avoided a decision among competing Catholic schools (Thomists, Scotists, etc.) Thus, its subtle complexity did not preclude further controversy, some of it violent, within the Roman Church (e.g., the Jesuit-Dominican dispute *de auxiliis,* the Jansenist-Jesuit dispute). Essentially, it upheld the necessity of divine grace for all stages of justification, including that of human co-operation with grace. Yet, against Luther it held that co-operation by the human will is necessary. Also against Luther, it declared that justification not only remits sins but sanctifies the person. While faith is the "foundation and root" of justification, hope and charity are also requisite. The human person can acquire merit by virtuous deeds. But certainty of one's election is always impossible, for this is known only to God. Depending as does all else on God's initiative, eternal life is thus a gift, not a reward.

In matters of discipline, Trent generally struck compromises between Roman conservative and more radical Spanish, French, and German proposals. The chief example was the debate whether bishops held their office directly from God or mediately from the pope, a controversy that almost wrecked the Council. Trent mandated major reforms of abuses, but upheld the essential legitimacy of such practices as prayer to the saints, the veneration of relics, the merit of vows, communion under one species, and the granting of indulgences. Its most consistent concern was to reinstate the authority of bishops over their sees and to cut away the undergrowth of dispensations which had exempted from their authority such groups as cathedral chapters, lay patrons, and religious orders. Trent's crowning glory was the mandate for seminaries to educate the hitherto haphazardly trained diocesan priests.

The Council left to the pope further tasks accomplished soon thereafter: editions of a standard catechism for pastors, a standard breviary, a definitive Roman Missal, a text of the Vulgate, an Index of Forbidden Books; and the reform of the Roman Curia.

Trent dramatized the fact that Catholicism was entering a new age; while some abuses continued and some reform lagged, the Council both reflected and reinforced the new vigor of the church. So solid was its accomplishment that another council was not deemed necessary for over 300 years. While unquestionably deferential to papal authority, it left open important questions about authority in the church. Thus, the ensuing age was not one of unfettered papal control, particularly after 1600. (It was, for example, commonly taught in French seminaries until 1870 that a council was superior to the pope.) While the Council of Trent formalized many points of difference from Protestant beliefs, which was essential at the time, it does not always pose an insuperable obstacle to contemporary ecumenical efforts.

Canons and decrees of the Council in a critical edition in *Conciliorum Oecumenicorum Decreta,* G. Alberigo, ed., New York, 1963, pp. 633-775. and in convenient translation in *Canons and Decrees of the Council of Trent,* H.J. Schroeder, ed., St. Louis, 1941; repr. Rockford, IL, 1981. All other acts, letters, etc. pertaining to the Council in the ongoing multi-volume *Concilium Tridentinum,* Goerresgesellschaft, ed., Freiburg, 1963. Classic early histories of the Council by the antagonistic Paolo Sarpi and the apologetic Cardinal Sforza Pallavicino. Modern histories by Hubert Jedin, *A History of the Council of Trent,* 2 vols. (to 1547 only; later volumes are unpublished or untranslated from German), St. Louis, 1957ff. Hubert Jedin, *Papal Legate at the Council of Trent: Cardinal Seripando,* St. Louis, 1947, (covers the entire Council). Joseph Lecler, et. al., *Latran Vet Trente,* Paris, 1975, and *Trente,* Paris, 1981.

JAMES MICHAEL WEISS

TRINITY

A commonplace of contemporary trinitarian theology is the priority it grants to the narrative and symbolic discourse of christian worship and proclamation over the leaner, conceptual discourse of theological theory itself. Theology continues to employ conceptual forms of thought in probing the meaning of Trinity, but recently deepened appreciation of the more spontaneous discourse of lived christian praxis—both biblical and ongoing in the life of the church—suggests a more conscious subordination of trinitarian theory to what might be called the "semantic aim" of christian proclamation and worship.

Narratives and symbols express cognitive meanings and refer to reality just as more "literal" forms of discourse do. They perform this semantic function indirectly and in a more complex way, involving not only an interplay of multiple meanings but an interplay of cognition with human affection and aspiration.

Symbols are often said to make the realities to which they refer present. This is so because they orchestrate the participant's experience of the reality which they disclose, however ineffably. In religion such forms of discourse are so closely bound to the faith experience to which they give access that they are the primary and indispensable carriers of living religious tradition. Theological reflection which is truly "faith seeking understanding" participates in the rich semantic aim of the primary discourse, tentatively providing sharper focus and, as needed, critical discrimination. What is important, though, is that theology take the "surplus of meaning" of this primary discourse as its starting point and that it return again and again from the autonomous conceptual structures, which it rightly employs, to the primary discourse for its heuristic stimulation and its corroboration.

In between this primary christian discourse and theology there is the genre of doctrine. As teaching is a function of proclamation, so doctrine overlaps and participates in the function of the primary discourse. Doctrine is an attempt to communicate clearly the cognitive and moral discernments of the christian faith experience. As such, it diminishes the tensive interaction which constitutes the discourse of worship and proclamation and overlaps theology, mixing the conceptual thought forms of theology with the ordinary language of common sense. Through the centuries the word "doctrine" has commonly been associated with officially sanctioned church teaching entailing various levels of intended binding authority. Since the nineteenth century the word "dogma" has come to designate doctrinal definitions of the highest level of church teaching authority. Although the church's dogmas commonly have used the conceptually refined language of theology, it is generally acknowledged

that the intention of the dogmas is not to canonize theological systems of thought, which are historically relative. Karl Rahner has helpfully suggested that a dogma is "a *linguistic* ruling on terminology which must not be mistaken for the thing itself or respectively must not be confused with a statement which can be made only by starting from the thing itself" (*Theological Investigations* 5, p. 54). A dogmatic definition might well be viewed, then, as a kind of "grammatical rule" of christian discourse the intent of which is to preserve from aberration the implicit "grammar" or semantic structure of the originary discourses of doctrine and theology.

The meanings of these terminological distinctions between primary discourse, doctrine, dogmas, and theology overlap even as they are defined here. They certainly were not sharply delineated from one another in the history of the church. However their discrimination is essential if we are to make sense of the history and meaning of Trinity in our current context.

In this article the term "Trinity" shall refer primarily to the divine Mystery Itself as the divine Mystery is experienced and expressed in the primary discourse of christian worship and proclamation. The interweaving doctrinal, theological, and even dogmatic articulations of the Trinity will be surveyed and interpreted in light of their respective relations to the primary meaning.

I. The Biblical Experience of God
A) The Old Testament

The basic Hebrew experience of God has been aptly and succinctly described in terms of a "proper name" and an "identifying description" (Robert Jenson, *The Triune Identity*). Israel experienced her God as the "one who" encountered her in the saving events of her history. The encounter was conceived according to the model of a personal self-introduction by means of a proper name, "Yahweh," and an identifying description which was always a saving event of Israel's history accomplished by Yahweh, e.g., "I am Yahweh, your God, who brought you out of the land of Egypt" (Exod 20:2). The sequence of saving events which came to constitute Israel's history (*Heilsgeschichte*) eventually extended from the first saving act of creation to the final Day of Yahweh.

This distinctively Israelite mode of experiencing God accentuates the personal aspect of the divine Mystery as the "one encountering" via the mediation of historical events. Similarly, as "Lord of all history," God's unity and transcendence of history are preserved. God's active agency in history was evocatively expressed in such stabilized, yet dynamic, metaphors as "Spirit of God," "Word of God," "Wisdom of God," etc., without jeopardizing God's unity and transcendence. At times these metaphors were used to express poetically a radical sense of God's immanence to creation; e.g., Psalm 51 suggests an identity between the divine Spirit and the human spirit renewed through repentance; some of the Wisdom songs suggest an identification of the Wisdom of God with the immanent ultimate meaning of creation (Job 28, Prov 8, Sir 24, Wis 7). By the time of Christ these Jewish symbols of divine immanence were often represented with a high degree of autonomy vis-à-vis God, but scholars are in increasing agreement that this does not imply that they had come to represent distinct realities. They represented the agency within creation of Yahweh the one transcendent Lord of all.

B) The New Testament

Father. The God to whom the whole NT witnesses is this same Yahweh, but now the identifying description is the historical event of Jesus culminating in the communal experience of Easter. For various reasons the sacred proper name of Yahweh had become reserved for special occasions and was replaced in ordinary usage by other appellatives and other more generic names of divinity. It is clear, nevertheless, that the God of NT witness is this same Yahweh whom Jesus called Father (*Abba*) and who is now decisively reidentified as "him who raised Jesus our Lord from the dead" (Rom 4:24; see also Rom 8:11, 1 Pet 1:21, etc.). What is new for the understanding of God in this NT witness is the sometimes subtle but ever present identification of Jesus with the divinity of "the one" who raised him. The Spirit of God is the same Spirit of prophetic and later judaism (see above, but now usually spoken of in reference to God's saving event in Jesus.

In attempting to understand the NT witness it is important that we not anachronistically read back later doctrinal and theological formulations and apply such adjectives as "adoptionistic," "primitive," "undeveloped," "elemental," "merely functional," etc., to the NT teaching. The presumption here is that the rich originary discourse of the NT witness says *more* and not less than the understandably more abstract language of later theology and even doctrine. The clarifications provided by these latter forms of discourse can be better appreciated when considered within the contexts of their later formulation.

The Son. The NT identifies "God" with the Father whose reign Jesus proclaimed and 'who raised him from the dead." Nevertheless, the ascription of divinity to Jesus is pervasive in the NT if we do not limit the evidence to texts which explicitly call Jesus "God" (*theos*). Raymond Brown (*Jesus God and Man*) identifies three clear such instances (Heb 1:8-9, Jn 1:1, Jn 20:28) and five probable instances (Rom 9:5, Tit 2:13, Jn 1:18, 1 Jn 5:20, 2 Pet 1:1) in which Jesus is called God. If we grant, that the language of metaphor, symbol, hymn, narrative, etc., is not "merely functional" and is capable of predicating meaning of reality, the force of the NT witness to Jesus' divinity becomes more evident. This is especially so in the frequent application to Jesus of the OT metaphors of divine immanence. Jesus is identified in hymns (Col 1:15-20, Heb 1:1-4, Jn 1:1-14) and gospel *logia* (Matthew) with the very Wisdom of God which in the sapiential poetry of the OT was the divine presence immanently grounding the meaning of creation (see above). The divinity of Wisdom is most clearly affirmed in Wisdom 7 and 8 which like the other sapiential poems provides imagery which is echoed in the NT hymns.

Similarly, Paul's metaphorical description (1 Cor 15:35-53) of the resurrection body, which he obviously associates with his experience of the risen Lord, as incorruptible (*en aphtharsia*), glorious (*en doxē*), and powerful (*en dynamei*) is a subtle yet sure ascription to the risen Jesus of characteristics associated with divinity in Hellenistic-Jewish religion at that time. This Pauline text reflects both the experiential and the eschatological nature of the earliest christian discernment of Jesus' divinity.

The image of sonship only gradually came to convey a firm sense of Jesus' divine status in the NT. Indeed, there is broad consensus among exegetes that Jesus, during his earthly life, addressed God as Father (*Abba*) with a degree of intimacy not typical of Jewish tradition, and that this reflected a profoundly personal and unique experience of God by Jesus, undoubtedly underlying his urgent call to proclaim the inbreaking of the reign of God. Nevertheless, the title "Son of God" initially was confessed of Jesus in light of his Easter exaltation, celebrated as the fulfillment of the royal messianic psalms (e.g., Ps 2 and Ps 110). Its initial connotation was messianic and in a sense "adoptive" in that it was associated with the moment of royal enthronement (e.g., Rom 1:3f). The messianic character of this title is illustrated by its frequent coupling with the messianic *christos* (e.g., "the Christ, the Son of God"). On the other hand, the tendency of this title to take on subtle divine connotation within the Easter experience of the early church is already suggested by Rom 1:4: "appointed Son of God in power (*en dynamei*) through resurrection from the dead." In the Gospel of John the "Son" imagery combines with the preexistent Wisdom imagery to provide the most explicit NT confession of Jesus' divinity. That the Word (*logos*) of Jn 1 is Wisdom can be seen in the obvious resonances with the sapiential poetry and is corroborated by parallel usage of *sophia* and *logos* in the judaism of the time. This Johannine Word/Son which "was God" (Jn 1:1), "was with the Father in the beginning," and "came down from heaven," was to become the dominant model for construing the divinity of the Son in christian theology.

The acclamation of Jesus as "Lord" (*Kyrios*) within the worship of Greek speaking communities which used the Septuagint version of the OT is another example of powerful yet subtle attribution to the risen Jesus of divine status. *Kyrios* was used widely in the Greek OT as a divine appellative. Its double appearance in Ps 110:1, "The Lord said to my Lord ... ," in the context of liturgical celebration of Jesus' Easter exaltation (see above) was a natural poetic suggestion of Jesus' divine status. That this acclamation went beyond poetic suggestion to worshipful confession is evident in the early hymn in Philippians 2: " ... God highly exalted him ... So that at Jesus' name every knee must bend ... and every tongue proclaim to the glory of God the Father: Jesus Christ is Lord!" (9-11). Likewise, in such Pauline texts as 1 Cor 8:6 and 1 Cor

12:5-6 the Lordship of Jesus is placed in parallel with the divinity of the one God. While more ambiguous in its ascription of divinity to Jesus than the Word/Son imagery of John, the NT confession of Jesus' Lordship does retain a stronger sense of the intrinsic role which Jesus' concrete history and resurrection played in the NT experience of God. This is of no minor importance to a contemporary trinitarian theology concerned with a fuller retrieval of the NT witness.

Holy Spirit. The divine status of the "Spirit of God" can similarly be seen as pervasive in the scriptures if one appreciates the metaphorical structure and semantic aim of the OT and NT pneumatology in its original context. The OT Spirit of God (*rûach YHWH*) was the very reality of God in the creature empowering with life (e.g., Ps 104:29-30), prophecy (e.g., Mic 3:8), just discernment (e.g., Isa 28:5-6), holiness (e.g., Ps 51:12-13), and an eschatological kingdom of ineffable justice, peace and freedom (e.g., Isa 11) etc. The metaphorical identification of the divine Spirit with the immanent creaturely agency in these texts is striking; e.g., the converted human spirit is poetically identified with the Spirit of God.

The Holy Spirit of the NT is this same Spirit of God now identified as the Spirit of Christ in the light of the Easter experience. Rom 8:9 illustrates this connection clearly: "You are not in the flesh but in the *spirit* since the *Spirit of God* dwells in you. Anyone who does not have the *Spirit of Christ,* does not belong to him." The first use of "spirit" in this text—spirit (*pneuma*) as opposed to flesh (*sarx*)—is common in the Pauline and Johannine NT writings. In this case spirit refers to the condition of divine empowerment as opposed to the creature living on its own by its own creaturely resources (flesh). The derivation of such pneumatic empowerment from the Easter experience is evidenced in 1 Cor 15:35-53 where Paul metaphorically identifies the risen Lord as "life-giving spirit" and sums up his description of the resurrection body with the expression "spiritual body" (*sōma pneumatikon*). In this context "spiritual" carries the connotation of divine status as did the preceding adjectives "incorruptible," "glorious," "powerful" (see above). As the text of Rom 8:9 indicates, this spiritual empowerment is due to the Spirit of God (=Spirit of Christ) dwelling in us. Paul attributes to the indwelling Spirit the empowerment: to love (Rom 5:5), to call God "Father" (Rom 8:15), to pray (Rom 8:26), to be free (2 Cor 3:17), to prophesy (1 Cor 12:10), etc., Paul's metaphorical identification-in-difference of the Spirit with the risen Lord ought not be judged in the light of later trinitarian dogma as an unfortunate confusion due to its early stage of development. Rather it is a vital link to be retrieved in modern trinitarian reflection, with due respect to the later dogma's emphasis on differentiation.

John likewise uses the spirit/flesh antithesis (Jn 3:1-10; 6:63). The dominant form of divine empowerment which John attributes to the indwelling Spirit is "new life." This new life is not simply ascribed to the Spirit but actually *identified with the Spirit* (4:10; 7:39; 20:22).

A distinctive aspect of the Johannine pneumatology is the use of the term Paraclete (*paraklētos*) to denote the Spirit in certain functions which, as it were, compensate for the absence within the christian community of the physical, earthly presence of Jesus who was by implication the first paraclete; e.g., the Paraclete abides with the disciples of Jesus teaching and guiding them, reminding them of the teachings of Jesus, and witnessing to and for them. The Paraclete imagery, which for the most part is restricted to Jn 14-16, is the high point of the biblical personification of the Spirit. The Paraclete is clearly differentiated from the Father and the Son and is spoken of as "proceeding" from the Father (15:26) and as being "sent" either by the Father (14:26) or by the Son from the Father (15:26; 16:7). This language will heavily influence the later formulation of trinitarian doctrine. It should be noted that the word "proceeds" (*ekporeuesthai*), which the later Greek theology and doctrine would apply to the eternal inner life of God, is judged by current biblical scholarship to refer in its original Johannine context to the temporal gift of the Paraclete associated with the Son's return to the Father. Although the Paraclete is differentiated from the Son as "another paraclete" (14:16), a similar metaphorically tensive identification exists between the Johannine Paraclete and the risen Jesus as in the Pauline pneumatology between the risen Lord and the Spirit. This subtle identification-in-difference is captured by Raymond Brown's succinct summation: "It is our contention that John presents the Paraclete as the Holy Spirit in a special role, namely, as the personal presence of Jesus in the Christian while Jesus is with the Father" (*The Gospel according to John XIII-XXI*, p. 1139).

C) The Trinitarian Structure of NT Experience

The very passages which express the powerful NT testimony to the divinity of the Father, Son, and Spirit likewise reveal the emergence, especially in early worship and proclamation, of a threefold pattern in the christian experience of God. As Jesus taught them, the early christians prayed to God as Father. This prayer was made in solidarity with Jesus who was most properly the Son and whose special relationship with God was shared by his followers. At times Jesus the Son was the object of worship in the context of recognition of his divine exalted status (e.g., 2 Pet 3:18; Rev 1:5-6). The Spirit of God is never the specific object of worship in the NT. This was not due to vagueness or doubt about the divinity of the Spirit but to the spontaneous experiential realization that the Spirit was the very divine presence immanently empowering them to pray, to prophesy, to love, to live. Numerous NT triadic formulae of diverse literary genre and formulation suggest the gradual linguistic stereotyping of this experiential pattern in the direction of the classic christian doxological and confessional forms: "To the Father, through the Son, in the Holy Spirit" and "From the Father, through the Son, in the Holy Spirit." The variety of greeting and benediction formulae in the Pauline epistles reveal this pattern even when they are not explicitly triadic. The great commissioning text of Mt 28:19 (" . . . baptizing them in the name of the Father and of the Son and of the Holy Spirit") along with the overtly triadic pattern of the accounts of Jesus' baptism in the Jordan, demonstrate the intimate connection already in NT times between the triadic pattern of experience and christian baptism. This liturgical connection will be the primary carrier of trinitarian faith into the post-NT period.

It is important to recognize the essential continuity between this triadic NT experience of God and the OT experience of Yahweh. God the Father is Yahweh, "the one who has done things." *Jesus* is the new, distinctive event which God has wrought as an act of final and decisive identification—i.e., Jesus in his concrete life, death, and destiny as discerned in Easter faith. The eschatological identification of Jesus' Easter destiny with the decisive reign of God, which Jesus proclaimed, and hence ineffably with the very reality of God is the very heart of the distinctive NT experience of God. The more protologically oriented imagery of Wisdom/Word, which, as we have seen, affirms Jesus' divinity and universal significance, must always presuppose and never fully replace the eschatological. The eschatological imagery emphasizes the temporality of the NT experience of God and preserves the important tension between the "already" and the "not yet" of the final saving event. Protological imagery alone would tend toward the a-temporality of myth and the denigration of Jesus' concrete humanity. 1 John reacts to such misreadings of the Johannine Christology—already in NT times—by more sharply focusing the "high" Johannine Christological imagery on the concrete humanity of Jesus. Finally, in the NT experience the Spirit is the very divine immanent presence realizing now in anticipation the eschatological event realized in Jesus. As such, the Spirit is never the explicit object of NT worship, nor is the Spirit ever represented in NT discourse as interacting in an interpersonal way with the Father and the Son, except as the immanent ground of human prayer to God; e.g., Rom 8:15; Gal 4:6.

II. Post-NT Theological and Doctrinal Development

This NT experiential trinitarian pattern continued on into the liturgical life of the second century christian communities and is reflected without marked change in the earliest post-NT extant literature. A major shift of context, however, took place in the mid-second century as the christian proclamation encountered the Greek interpretation of deity.

A) The Interface with Greek Thought

Christians (the "apologists") conversant with the then dominant philosophy of middle-Platonism seized the opportunity to proclaim and elucidate the christian message in a thought form which was meaningful to the educated classes of the widespread Hellenistic society. This movement, which Catholic theology has generally evaluated positively, will have an enormous impact on the development of christian theology. God in middle-Pla-

tonic thought was monotheistic and transcended the world, and like the Judeo-christian God was the absolute ground of all that is. Unlike the God of christian proclamation, this God of Greek philosophy was not experienced via historical encounter but was inferred as the ultimate and absolute ground or principle (*archē*) of the perishable world. The experience of the perishability of the temporal-material world was deep within the Hellenic psyche. The God whose existence they inferred was radically different from this world: imperishable, a-temporal, immaterial, unchangeable, impassible, etc. The radical otherness, transcendence, and ineffability of this absolute principle was so extreme by the mid-second century, that they had to postulate intermediary principles between the absolute principle and the finite world.

Confident that the God they preached was the Father of Jesus Christ and the salvation they proclaimed was that of Jesus, the apologists adapted much of the Hellenic world-view for their purpose. The Father was the (*archē*,) a personal rather than abstract absolute origin of all things. To the Father were attributed, on the one hand, the personal characteristics of the biblical God and, on the other hand the negative attributes of the absolute *archē:* unoriginated, unchangeable, immovable, impassible, etc. The Son was the divine *logos* which bridged the abyss between God and the world. This *logos* doctrine, while intended to be in continuity with the Johannine doctrine, was decidedly more Hellenic in character. The stoic distinction between the immanent word (*logos endiathetos*) and the expressed word (*logos prophorikos*) was employed either implicitly or explicitly by the various apologists. Originally the immanent Word was present in the mind of God as an idea is present in a human mind. In preparation for creation the Word was uttered forth and begotten as

Son. This Son/Word was God's agent in creation and was present from the beginning to reveal truth universally. In Jesus the Word became human. Whereas the Johannine Word/Wisdom imagery focused on expressing the universal significance of the Jesus-event, making *Jesus* the referent of the discourse, the *logos* doctrine of the apologists shifts the emphasis to the Son "in the beginning," and at times gives scant attention to Jesus, the incarnate *logos*. This new emphasis on the preexistent Word apparently occasioned some confusion for the understanding of the Spirit. References to the Spirit became notoriously sparse in the writings of the apologists, and the references, when explicit, are often vaguely related to the Word. Theophilus, the first writer to use the term "triad" of God, identified the triad as God, Word, and *Wisdom,* reflecting the shift that had taken place from the NT Johannine *logos* theology.

This creative adaptation of the Hellenic philosophical context for the defense and proclamation of the christian message expresses well the universality inherent in the christian understanding of God and the capacity of the gospel to speak effectively to the soteriological concerns of a distinctive cultural context. However, it raises important questions for our assessment today of its impact upon the development of the christian doctrine of God. Protestant scholars to this day are disturbed by the troubled juxtaposition of two ultimately conflicting notions of God: the concrete living God disclosed in revelation, and the timeless absolute of middle-Platonism. Traditionally, catholic theology has more positively evaluated the philosophical notion of God, tempering its negations with a more positive ontology, yet recognizing both religiously and philosophically the limits and indirectness of all reference to God. Today both protestant and catholic theologians,

remaining consistent with their traditions but in light of our contemporary historical consciousness, are assessing more carefully the historical impact of the Hellenic view of deity on christian thought and life. To what extent did the Hellenic concern for the timelessness, immateriality, and radical otherness of the divine inform the context in which the church formulated its understanding of the God experienced in the triadic discourse of its worship, proclamation and biblical texts?

B) The Emergence of Theological Terminology

Until the third century, the "three" of the divine Triad in church life and theology were referred to concretely, i.e., as "the Father," "the Son," "the Holy Spirit." There existed as yet no generic term for the three. This changed in the third century with Tertullian and Hippolytus in the west and Origen in the east.

The West. The reinforcement of Hebraic monotheism with the strong monotheism of the Hellenic *archē* had a profound impact upon western christianity. By the third century the temptation was extreme "monarchianism" (i.e., stress on the unity of God) in the various forms of "modalism" i.e., the tendency to diminish the distinction between the "three" of the divine triad by considering them merely as temporary modes or aspects of, or even mere names for the one *archē*. Both Hippolytus and Tertullian reacted to this extreme monarchianism by stressing the "economy" of the divine life. Irenaeus had already used the word "economy" (*oeconomia* = organization, distribution) in reference to the unfolding of God's plan in the history of salvation. Tertullian uses it to refer to *God's own self-distribution* in connection with the saving history. It becomes here a trinitarian term expressing the unity between God's inner life and salvation history. It is this "economy ... which distributes the unity into trinity (*trinitas*)"

(Praxeas 2.4). This is the first known use of the term "trinity." Tertullian uses the term "person"(*persona*) as a generic term for the three of the divine economy. *Persona,* like the Greek term *prosopon* used by Hippolytus, was an everyday word for the human individual connoting specifically the aspect of distinctive *individuality* established by one's social role.

Tertullian emphasized equally the unity of the three persons by stating that they are of "one substance." Scholars debate as to how literally Tertullian intended the subtle stoic materialistic connotation associated with his use of the word "substance." What is generally agreed upon is the enormous impact of Tertullian on the terminology of subsequent Latin trinitarian theology—e.g., person, "of one substance," economy, trinity. Another subtle but important Tertullian usage, that will differentiate the style of western from eastern theology, is his tendency to identify the name "God" with the divine substance: "God is the name for the substance, that is, the divinity" (Hermogenem 3). In the east as in the NT "God" is always equated with the Father.

The East. Origen appropriated the philosophy of middle-Platonism more systematically than the apologists and Tertullian had. The Father is the absolute, unoriginated origin (*archē*). The Son is his Word (*logos*) mediating between the Father's absolute unity and the multiplicity of creation. However, the Son's generation from the Father is *eternal:* "There never was a time when the Son was not." This concept of "eternal generation" was an adaptation of the middle-Platonic doctrine that the whole world of spiritual beings was eternal. The Son is eternally derived (or generated) from the very being of God and hence is of the Father's essence, but second to the Father. Origen was vague about the status of the Spirit, although he does say

that the Spirit "is ever with the Father and the Son; like the Father and the Son it always was, is, and will be." Likewise, the Spirit is "associated in honor and dignity with the Father and the Son." Origen, like Tertullian coined a generic term for the "three" of the divine triad. The Father, the Son, and the Holy Spirit are "three *hypostaseis*" (=individuals). This term does not as such connote personhood in the modern sense of the term but distinct individuality.

Origen's major contribution to the formulation of the trinitarian doctrine is the notion of eternal generation. His generic term for the "three" (*hypostasis*) will be adopted and refined in the fourth century. The troublesome legacy of Origen's trinitarian thought is the implied inferiority or subordination of the Spirit to the Son and of the Son to the Father (subordinationism). This will be corrected in the fourth century.

D) The Trinitarian "Problem" and the Dogmatic Settlement

The problem inherent in the christian adaptation and appropriation of the Hellenic notion of deity and the related tendency of *logos* Christology to prescind from Jesus in the direction of the preexistent Son all come to a head with Arius at the turn of the fourth century. The church will wrestle with these issues theologically and dogmatically, first as they relate to the divinity of the Son and then to the divinity of the Spirit.

Arius. Arius took the implications of the Hellenic idea of God quite seriously. If to be divine is to be the absolute *archē*—i.e., to be unoriginated, utterly underived in any sense—then only the Father is God. The Son as *originating* from the Father before time is indeed our Savior, but precisely as originating from, or being begotten of, the Father, the Son does not possess the essence of divinity, i.e., absolute unoriginatedness. The Son is the first of creation, produced from nothing by an act of the Father's will. Recent scholarship has shown a strong *soteriological* concern in Arius' theology (R. Gregg & D. Groh, *Early Arianism*). To be our Savior and the model of our growth in virtue and holiness the Son must have been capable of change and moral choice, and hence not divine. This soteriological concern, if indeed important for Arius, would simply demonstrate the concern for salvation underlying the whole fourth century trinitarian struggle. A major argument against Arius will be that a created redeemer could not have redeemed us. The trinitarian debates, while heavily political and often involving abstruse speculation about the ineffable reality of God, were at root concerned with salvation.

Nicaea. The Council of Nicaea (325) directly condemned the position of Arius. The creed of Nicaea states that the Son is "begotten, not created, one-in-being (*homoousion*) with the Father." Further, the council condemns those who say, "'There was a time when he did not exist' and . . . 'He was made from nothing,' . . . alleging that the Son of God is mutable or subject to change . . ."

Clearly the intention of the council was to affirm apodictically the full divinity of the Son. It is difficult to sort out contextual factors from the essential intention of the definition. The Hellenic stress on divine immutability and concern about the Son as pre-existent were certainly contextual factors shred by the Arians and the council. The council did significantly qualify the excessively abstract Hellenic identification of the deity with "unoriginatedness" by affirming that the Son is both fully divine and "begotten." However ineffably, then, the divinity is both unoriginate and begotten.

Athanasius and the Cappadocians. Initially the acceptance of the Nicaean settlement was fragile. The following fifty years were filled with confusion and often bitter dispute over the implications of *homoousios*. In what sense is God one? How is God yet three?

Athanasius led the response to the first question. At the time the word *homoousios* could have meant "of like essence" or "of the same essence." Athanasius argued that the Son was of the same essence as the Father—not simply sharing the same generic essence as human beings share the same essential humanity but rather the same *identical* essence. He then argued that as the Son was of the same essence as the Father, so the Spirit was of the same essence (*homoousion*) as the Son. By this time the status of the Spirit had become theologically vague and was being challenged by the semi-Arian "Tropici."

The Cappadocians, Basil, Gregory of Nazianzus, and Gregory of Nyssa, followed up on Athanasius' insistence on the identity of essence of the "three," but their primary concern was to respond to the second question above: "How is God yet three?"

Basil never did explicitly apply *homoousion* to the Spirit. Whether for reasons of tactful irenicism or of theological subtlety, he affirmed the divinity of the Spirit in a way that would have a lasting impact. Basil fostered a shift in the doxological formula within his church of Caesarea. In place of the traditional doxology, "*to* the Father, *through* the Son, *in* the Holy Spirit," he encouraged that praise be directed "to the Father, *with* the Son *and* the Holy Spirit." His own response to criticism that he was innovating tends to confirm the rather limited pre-history of the practice that he was encouraging. His brother, Gregory of Nyssa, was probably the person responsible for having the "innovation" inserted into the revised creed of 1 Constantinople (381) in the form "the Holy Spirit . . . who with the Father and the Son is adored and glorified." Positively, this change powerfully affirms the divinity of the Spirit. A negative result—certainly unintended by Basil—is that by making the Spirit the object of worship it lessens the experiential sense of the Spirit as immanent *source* of worship. It tends to place the divine Mystery entirely over-against the worshipper, diminishing the sense of envelopment implied in the NT experiential pattern.

If the "three," then, possess one identical essence, how are they three? The Cappadocians cumulatively formulated the answer to this question in terms of origin and mutual relations. They took the ambiguous word *hypostasis,* which could be used either as a synonym for "essence"(*ousia*) or as connoting a distinct individual reality. They employed it in this latter sense and applied it as a generic term for the "three." In what sense are they distinct? The biblical evidence provides a distinguishing characteristic (*idiotētes*) for each of the "three." The Father is distinguished as "ungenerated" (This is consonant with the early christian equation of the Father with God, and further with the Greek appreciation of God as "unoriginated origin" or *archē*). The Son is distinguished as "generated," and the Spirit as "proceeding." These distinguishing characteristics connote mutual relatedness or more specifically mutually interrelated "modes of coming to be" (*tropoi hyparxeos*). In every other respect the "three" are identical. The Son is eternally begotten of the Father and is really distinct from the Father *only* in that the Son is generated and the Father is the generator. Likewise, the Spirit proceeds "out of the Father and receives from the Son," differing from each of the others *only* as the one proceeding. The Trinity, then, is one absolutely simple, concrete, individual, infinite essence (*ousia*) subsisting *without multiplication* in three really distinct modes, characterized respectively as ungenerated, generated, and proceeding, in the order just

delineated.

The Cappadocians were acutely aware of the inadequacy of these formal terms to express the ineffable divine Mystery, but they were convinced that the biblical language followed this logic. Nyssa's argument from the identity of the divine activity to the identity of the divine essence illustrates this. According to the NT, every divine action in creation is done by all three together: the divine action "has its origin in the Father, proceeds through the Son, and reaches completion in the Holy Spirit." Thus none of the hypostases possesses a separate operation of its own, but one identical power is exercised by them all. (N.B.: For the Cappadocians the prepositional pattern "from, through, in" is still operative here!) Another point illustrated by this example is that whenever the Cappadocians attempted to speak of the divine Mystery Itself (theology), they always spoke in terms of salvation history (economy).

The Trinitarian Dogma. In effect the Council of Constantinople (381) canonized the basic logic of trinitarian predication provided by the Cappadocians. The Niceno-Constantinopolitan creed, reflecting Basil's doxological innovation, is essentially a reaffirmation of the doctrine of Nicaea with further elaboration on the status and role of the Holy Spirit. The creed itself does not explicitly apply the word *homoousion* to the Spirit and the actual documents of the council have been lost. However, conveniently for us, two synods were held the following year, one in Constantinople and the other in Rome, and confirmed the teaching of the council, providing us with Greek and Latin formulations respectively. According to the respective formulations God is one power and substance (*ousia, substantia*), in three distinct persons (*hypostaseis, personae*), and both the Son and the Spirit are of one identical substance (*homoousion, unius substantiae*) with the Father. While the terms in the two languages have different nuances, their intention here is basically the same. The dogma of Constantinople (381) has subsequently been received as binding on all churches of east and west, e.g., at Chalcedon (451).

Later councils and synods will make additions to this dogma of 381 but these additions are usually viewed as refinements or explicitations of the original dogma. For example the definition by the Council of Florence (1442) of the co-inherence (*perichorēsis, circuminsessio*) or mutual indwelling of the divine persons is an explicitation of the true identity of substance. The so-called Florentine principle, "In God all is one where there is no opposition of relation" (1442), was already operative in the logic of Athanasius and the Cappadocians assumed by Constantinople (381), before it was explicitated by Anselm.

E) Subsequent Theology—East and West

The subsequent theological history of the Trinity is long and detailed. Since it follows two separate trajectories—east and west—we shall briefly focus on a dominant figure in each tradition as we generally characterize the history.

The West. Augustine's pervasive influence on western trinitarian theology is generally recognized. Unfortunately Augustine's access to the nuanced reflections of the Cappadocians was limited, but it is quite clear that he completely accepted the trinitarian dogma and took as a major task to reflect upon and teach this "rule of faith" that the Trinity is God, one identical substance, subsisting in three persons. This formulation reflects the distinctive style of Augustine's theology: God is identified with the divine substance, and the one substance is considered before the three persons. In itself the linguistic alteration of identifying

"God" with the divine substance rather than with the Father was not problematic. It was in accord with the logic of the dogma and was occasionally done even by the Cappadocians. The problem is that this attenuates the sense of modal differentiation which is implied when the one identical essence is identified in order with each of the three distinct modes of being (without being multiplied). For the Cappadocians the divine substance is "modified" with each modal differentiation. In other words, the hypostasis characterized by "generation" is not simply a relation *within* the divine essence, rather it *is* the divine essence in an eternally distinct mode. Overlooking this modal differentiation leads to more abstract results when one applies the principle that "In God all is one where there is no opposition of relation." This is nowhere clearer in Augustine than in his frequent use of what later will be called "appropriation."

Augustine always insists—as the Cappadocians did—that when God acts in creation he acts as one principle and that we appropriate the activity to one or other of the persons as it is symbolically fitting. The reasons for this are that the Bible seems to do it this way and further that opposition of relation is not involved, hence the activity should be predicated to the Trinity as one. An important difference here from the Cappadocians is that for them the modal pattern was preserved. God's creation, for example, was one divine action but it was accomplished from the Father, through the Son, and in the Holy Spirit. The difference in effect is more than verbal, for with mere "appropriation" there is a weakening of the linkage to the trinitarian experiential pattern. In Augustine's hands this was offset by constant appeal to biblical language and the experiential pattern of his own interiority.

Augustine's emphasis on the Spirit's

proceeding from the Father *and* the Son (*filioque*), acting as one principle, is similarly based jointly upon biblical citations and the application in an abstract way of the principle demanding unity where relation is not applicable. Once again Augustine beautifully elaborates this abstractly derived notion into his doctrine of the Spirit as the "bond of love" in the Trinity.

Augustine's trinitarian theology is best known for its numerous trinitarian analogies. A point often overlooked is the intensely experiential pattern reflected in some of these analogies. Many of the analogies are rather tenuous examples of how three things may in a sense also be one. However, when Augustine reflects on his personal appropriation of his own being (*esse*), his knowing (*nosse*) of this being, and his freedom (*velle*) in this being, it is evident that the analogy—which is still an analogy—is closest to the ineffable Trinity.

It is only in the Middle Ages that some of these analogies are systematically developed into theories—still analogical—of the Trinity, e.g., Richard of St. Victor (lover, beloved, love), and Thomas Aquinas (mind, self-knowledge, self-love). In the hands of these great medieval theologians, the distinction between immanent and economic Trinity—already present in Augustine and the eastern Fathers—is becoming stronger, but a vital connection is always retained between the two. The later western tradition will tend more to separate the consideration of God's inner life from the economy of salvation by using as the starting point of its reflection the formal statements of the dogma rather than the narratives of salvation history.

The East. Trinitarian theology in the east was spared the extreme formalization, which gradually occurred in the west, by reason of the fact that eastern trinitarianism remained in closer contact with liturgical and monastic spirituality. Nevertheless, it inherited the same "transcendentalizing" tendency of the Hellenic view of deity as a-temporal and immutable.

Gregory Palamas (1296-1359) represents this tradition well. As a hesychast monk (Hesychasm was a mystical monastic spirituality which strongly emphasized the experiential presence of God in prayer.), he reacted to the extreme intellectualism of western trinitarian theology. Palamas' primary concern was to affirm the *reality of communion with God*. He rejects as inadequate the western notion of "created grace" in favor of the richer "divinization" (*theōsis*) of the early Greek Fathers. In a real sense the Christian "becomes divine." To account for this, Palamas distinguishes between the divine "essence" (which is absolutely transcendent and unchangeable), the three "hypostases," and the "uncreated energies." The uncreated energies constitute God's radically immanent activity and presence in the creature. This attempt to do justice to God's immanence as "divinization" is receiving attention in contemporary theology. It is noteworthy though, that, for Palamas, the second and third hypostases were so identified with God's transcendent, incommunicable essence that they could not have been conceived as the immanent divine energies which they were in the NT.

F) Current Trinitarian Theology

There are several points of wide consensus in contemporary trinitarian theology. First, the separation of the immanent from the economic Trinity is unacceptable. What we know of the divine Mystery in Itself, we know through its unfolding in the history of salvation, hence the return to biblical discourse as a starting point. Second, the trinitarian term "person," if retained, should be used with care to avoid suggesting a multiplicity of operations (e.g., intellect, will) within

God contrary to the dogma. Third, the trinitarian biblical discourse and our own "historical consciousness" demand a more careful consideration of the implications of this doctrine for divine immanence in creation and the "difference" that this makes for God.

Karl Rahner. The trinitarian theology of Karl Rahner, though not heavily biblical in its provenance, has contributed significantly to the addressing of these concerns. The primary focus of Rahner's theology is the immanence of grace as a true "divinization." He speaks of a real "self-communication" of God in which the divine reality becomes "the innermost constitutive element" of the creature. This self-communication of God, or this "becoming" of God in history, takes place in the incarnation and in grace. It entails a threefold modal differentiation in God, in that it is a real becoming of God in the otherness of created history. Rahner prefers modal language reminiscent of the Cappadocians to the "person" language of the west for the reason expressed above. The one infinite divine essence initially identified with the unoriginated "mode of subsistence" which we call Father is fully expressed in the humanity and person of Jesus in a second "mode of subsistence" which we call logos or Son, and is given in grace as the "mode of subsistence" which we call Holy Spirit. Having thus so strongly affirmed the immanence of the Trinity to history, Rahner then seems conversely to affirm the immanence of the historical divine self-enactment to the Trinity when he proclaims repeatedly: "The economic Trinity *is* the immanent Trinity and the immanent Trinity *is* the economic Trinity." The first part of the slogan he affirms and corroborates explicitly with the argument that God's self-communication was not a true self-communication unless the divine Mystery presented Itself as it is eternally. It is not clear how strictly Rahner intends the converse to be taken. On the one hand, on the rare occasions when he speaks of the Trinity in abstraction from the economy to deal with a question like the pre-existence of the *logos,* he says such things as, " ... the second (mode of subsistence) is exactly identical with God's *ability* to express himself in history," suggesting that God *actually* becomes triune only in history. On the other hand, he insists repeatedly on the absolute immutability of God in himself, at times speaking as if the processions within God were distinct from the missions in history.

The Agenda for Trinitarian Theology. We might formulate the essential task facing trinitarian theology as the catalytical unlocking of the meaning inherent in the primary discourse of the tradition in the context of our historically conscious modern world. "Historical consciousness" involves more than a sense of the past. It takes seriously the history in which we live and our responsibility for it. We value freedom as the capacity creatively to imagine finer possibilities and to be drawn into a new future. We cherish this temporal structure of the "becoming of our being," although with people of every age we experience its fragility and perpetual perishing. Our historically conscious culture is in sharp contrast to the classical culture within which the doctrine of God was formulated. Catholic theology in the past several decades has become well aware of this cultural shift and is only beginning to appropriate its implications for the doctrine of God. This involves profoundly difficult philosophical problems.

Is God absolutely immutable? Scholars generally agree that the "steadfastness" of will which the Bible ascribes to God is different from the unchangeability of God which is universally predicated of God since the interface with Hellenic culture. For Gregory of Nyssa, Augustine, and Aquinas it is clear that unchange-ability is virtually identifiable with God's nature as infinite plenitude of being ("I am"). How can the infinite plenitude of being become? Assuming with these great theologians that "infinity of being" is a valid limit-concept referring to a reality beyond our comprehension, might not an ineffable "becoming" be possible for the Infinite without entailing an increase of its perfection or a multiplicity of infinity, and hence contradiction? Is not such ineffable capacity to become already suggested in the modal terminology of the Cappadocians where the "three" are characterized as "modes of coming to be" (*tropoi hyparxeos*), although the Cappadocians themselves would predicate un-changeability even of these modes?

Another related philosophical problem revolves around necessity and freedom. Necessity to be is implied in the absolute plenitude of God's being. God could *not* not be, since the divine essence is "to be." On the other hand, christian theology has always viewed God as free, but this freedom extends only to possible creation and not to God's own being, as if the divine being were completely determined by necessity. God certainly could not choose not to be, but if freedom is as primordial to God's being as the christian claim "God is love" suggests, might it not be that the "modes" of God's being are rooted in God's eternal freedom?

Then there is the relationship between the infinite and the finite. Rahner often paraphrases Hegel to the effect that the truly infinite cannot be thought of only as the opposite of the finite; it must also transcend this opposition, and be the unity of itself and the other to which it gives rise. For the finite to exist "outside" the infinite would deny the infinity of the infinite. Rahner, of course, holds that God creates freely, but if God does create, a radical participatory immanence of some degree must be involved.

Finally there is time and eternity. In Greek thought eternity was timeless. Augustine, whose description of time is classic, views time primarily in terms of its perishability and contrasts it sharply to God's eternity, which is God's very substance and hence simply *is*. However, in view of our historical consciousness of time as "becoming" and as "possibility to be," and further, of God's immanence to this becoming, might we not conceive of eternity as the ineffable fullness of time in God's everlasting future? This is described in various ways by theologians. White-headian process theologians speak of God "prehending" time. Rahner even says "it is *in* time, as its own mature fruit, that 'eternity' comes about." Wolfhart Pannenberg views God's eternity as *future* vis-à-vis time. For him biblical escha-tology entailed precisely this shift to the futurity of God's absolute future. The reign of God which Jesus proclaimed was this divine future and hence God's very being. In the christian experience of Easter Jesus was discerned as *identified* with this reign.

These preliminary reflections on the relative as well as absolute, or immanent as well as transcendent aspects of God's essence, are intended to free the originary trinitarian discourse of proclamation and worship to bespeak for our time the divine relativity as well as absoluteness in accordance with its full biblical intention.

Three possibilities open up, corre-sponding to each of the divine "three": first, we can retrieve the biblical identi-fication of the Son, the Word, with the concrete life and person of *Jesus*. Rahner speaks of Jesus' history as "the history of God," as the "divine drama of God-in-process," and says that God "has done himself" in Jesus. The incarnation is not the extension of a procession which took place in the primal past of God's eternity but an event of divine *free* self-determi-nation, unfolding historically in the mode of full divine self-expression in the life and person of Jesus, climaxing in the resurrectional identification of Jesus with God's reign. Jesus did not "become" divine; his life and destiny were a "becoming" of God in time for eternity.

Second, the biblical identification of our life in grace with the very Spirit of God, which was grasped in the early eastern theology of divinization, can again take on its original vivid sense of divine immanence. The Spirit does not simply cause our holiness or love but *constitutes* it within us. The Spirit is God's full infinity of being in the "mode of coming to be" in the creature.

Third, a proper sense of divine temporality might enable us to grasp how the deepest intention of the philosophical notion of God relates to the biblical God. As the apologists realized, the biblical God was the *archē*, the "unoriginated origin," from whom are all things. What biblical eschatology, culminating in the life and destiny of Jesus, adds is that the same *archē* is also the *eschaton* to whom are all things. The Cappadocians in different formulations associated two distinct distinguishing characteristics (*idiotētes*) with the first divine "mode": unoriginateness and paternity. Later theologians debated as to which of these was truly constitutive of the first hypostasis. If we allow freedom to be equiprimordial with God's necessity, we might say that God is necessarily *unoriginate* (the philosophical notion of God), but eternally has chosen to be "for us" as *Father,* and to have a future including our history through Jesus, his Son, in his Holy Spirit (the NT God).

Recent concern within feminist theology with the patriarchal structure of the trinitarian symbolism is sometimes addressed by noting the feminine gender and imagery associated with Spirit (*rûach*) in the OT and in early Syrian Christianity. Retrieval of this feminine dimension would be noteworthy, especially if it is true that religious experience which stresses transcendence tends toward symbolization in the form of archetypal fatherhood, and that which stresses immanence toward symbolization in terms of archetypal motherhood. Whatever form linguistic sensitization may take to open us to the "feminine" in God and diminish the possibility that our very experience of the divine reinforce the evils of sexism, its purpose would be greatly enhanced by the liberation of the inner divine symbols of immanence from captivity within a divine nature conceived as exclusively absolute.

Conclusion. Rahner has been criticized for preferring the abstract term "mode of subsistence" to "person" in his trinitarian theology. It is said we do not relate to abstractions as we do to persons. This criticism misses the point as to the purpose of theology and its relation to the primary trinitarian discourse which informs our christian experience. Trinitarian "person" itself is an abstract theological term introduced, as we have seen, in the third century to connote distinct individuation. Neither of these terms is at home in worship or proclamation. These abstract terms, as theological, serve to guide our understanding and preserve the integrity of our experience of the one God, "in whom we live move and have our being," and whom we address as Father when we pray *with* Jesus *in* their Spirit.

See **Christology, God, Holy Spirit**

Jean Ladrière, "Le discours théologique et le symbol," *Revue des sciences religieuses* 49, 1-2, Strasbourg, 1975, pp. 116-41. J.D.G. Dunn, *Christology in the Making,* Philadelphia: Westminster Press, 1980. Michael Fahey & John Meyendorff, *Trinitarian Theology East and West,* Brookline, MA: Holy Cross Orthodox Press, 1977. Walter Kasper, *The God of Jesus Christ,* New York: Crossroad, London: S.C.M., 1984. Karl Rahner, *Foundations of Christian Faith,* New York: Seabury Press, London: Darton, Longman & Todd, 1978.

EDMUND J. DOBBIN, OSA

TRUTH

In the primary sense of the word, truth is a property of one's knowledge. In secondary senses, truth is a property of being and, again, a property of one's communicative expressions. Thus we may speak of cognitional truth, metaphysical truth, and communicational truth.

Cognitional Truth

In general, truth in the primary sense is the epistemic validity or epistemological objectivity of one's knowledge, the property by virtue of which one's knowledge, precisely as knowledge, is genuine, authentic, successful. The developmental or non-dialectical opposite of truth in this sense is cognitional non-truth, the simple absence of epistemic validity, the hallmark of ignorance. The radical or dialectical opposite is cognitional untruth or falsity, the presence of epistemic invalidity, the hallmark of cognitional error. There are as many specific accounts of cognitional truth as there are different specific accounts of human knowledge itself. Let us consider six, notable for both their systematic significance and their historical influence.

The first two accounts of cognitional truth share the view that in principle human knowing is fundamentally nothing other than sensory and/or intellectual intuition and that a knowledge claim is true precisely insofar as it mirrors, reflects, represents the contents of intuition. That is, truth is a matter of the *unmediated correspondence* of a knowledge claim and an intuited reality. Now, for thinkers in the traditions of Epicurus or Plato, the requisite intuitions often do occur and thus truth is a possible achievement. For thinkers in the traditions of Hume or Kant, by contrast, the requisite intuitions never occur and thus the achievement of truth is but an empty hope.

The third and fourth accounts of cog-

nitional truth assert in common that in principle the key element of human knowing is conceptual understanding and that a knowledge claim is true exactly insofar as it logically entails or is entailed by certain other knowledge claims. That is to say, truth is a matter of the *logical coherence* of a knowledge claim with a set of privileged knowledge claims. Now, in the traditions of Leibnitz or Hegel the privileged knowledge claims are envisioned as those arising from rational reflection; in the logical positivist tradition, those maintained by contemporary empirical science. In these traditions, therefore, the set of privileged claims against which all others are to be tested for logical coherence is clearly specifiable; and a definitive advance in truth thus is seen as possible. In the tradition of Marx, on the other hand, the privileged claims are envisioned as nothing less than all the claims that could be made by someone who understood the entire universe in its every part and every aspect. Until such exhaustive understanding actually emerges, however, the set of privileged claims cannot be clearly specified; and thus the truth of any given claim can be held as only probable at best, never definitive.

According to a fifth account, professed by persons in the tradition of Peirce, James, and Dewey, human knowing is at root just useful thinking and a knowledge claim is true just to the extent that it facilitates the attainment of some concrete goal. That is to say, truth is a matter of *practical effectiveness* of a knowledge claim in relation to the solution of some problem or the performance of some task.

On a sixth account, proposed by those in the tradition of Aquinas, Maréchal, and Lonergan, human knowing culminates in the process of judgmental affirmation. First, the conscious subject arrives at some hypothetical knowledge claim. Next, she comes authentically to grasp that knowledge claim as fulfilling the criteria of rational affirmation that constitute in part the dynamic structure of her very subjectivity. Finally, she posits, asserts, affirms the knowledge claim; and in and through that affirmation she achieves knowledge of the real. On this view, it follows that truth is a matter of the *mediated correspondence* of a knowledge claim and a judgmentally affirmed reality—a correspondence mediated by the subject's act of rational affirmation.

Metaphysical Truth

While "truth" in its primary sense denotes a property of one's knowledge, in a secondary sense it denotes a property of what one's knowledge is of, namely, of what exists or occurs, reality, being. Metaphysical or transcendental truth is the intrinsic knowability of being as such, just as transcendental unity is its intrinsic undividedness and transcendental goodness is its intrinsic desirability. On this mode of conception and speech, which is common especially but not solely in the scholastic tradition, transcendental truth, unity, and goodness are "convertible" with one another. Each of these properties is only notionally distinct from being itself and from the other transcendental properties. Thus transcendental truth is nothing other than being itself, considered under the aspect of its inherent aptness for being known. The non-dialectical opposite of truth in this sense is transcendental non-truth, the simple intrinsic unknowability of what merely is not, a distinguishing trait of pure non-being. The dialectical opposite is transcendental untruth or falsity, the intrinsic absurdity of what could and ought to be but is not, a distinguishing trait of moral deficiency.

Communicational Truth

Besides denoting the epistemic validity of one's knowledge and the intrinsic knowability of being, "truth" can also denote a property of one's communicative expressions, the words, deeds, or products by which one purports to inform other persons of something. Communicational truth is the fidelity to one's own knowledge that one intends for those expressions by which one both purports and aims to inform. The non-dialectical opposite of truth in this sense is communicational non-truth, the simple absence of intended fidelity to one's own knowledge, the characteristic feature of those expressions by which one does not purport to inform. The dialectical opposite is communicational untruth or mendacity, the presence of intended infidelity to one's own knowledge, the characteristic feature of those expressions by which one purports to inform but aims to deceive.

Bernard Lonergan, *Insight: A Study of Human Understanding*, New York/London: Philosophical Library/Longmans Green, 1957; *Collection: Papers by Bernard Lonergan*, New York/London: Herder & Herder/Darton, Longman & Todd, 1967; *Method in Theology*, New York/London: Herder & Herder/Darton, Longman & Todd, 1972; *A Second Collection*, Philadelphia: Westminster, 1974.

MICHAEL VERTIN

U

ULTRAMONTANISM

Ultramontanism describes the theological movement which placed a strong emphasis on the authority of the papacy in matters of doctrine and ecclesiastical government. Different expressions of ultramontanism also looked to the papacy either as a means of promoting a liberal Catholic renewal in postrevolutionary Europe or as an indispensable element in preserving a conservative European political order. Though the term itself ("beyond the mountains") indicates the orientation towards Rome which characterized this theological outlook, strong advocates of the ultramontane cause were found in France, Germany, and England.

While voices which called for a strong papacy were present in the church even in medieval times, ultramontanism is more precisely seen as a movement in the Roman Catholic Church in the seventeenth, eighteenth, and nineteenth centuries. In the seventeenth and eighteenth centuries it was largely a reaction against the teachings of Gallicanism and Jansenism.

It was in the nineteenth century that ultramontane thought became a dominant factor in the Catholic Church. The century began with a renewed respect for the pope after Pius VII's defiance of Napoleon. Many held the conviction that only in a strong papacy could the clergy and the church find protection against arbitrary laws of civil governments.

Ultramontanism became a major theological development in nineteenth-century France, largely as a result of two quite different interests. On the one hand, a call for a strong papal authority came from liberal French Catholics who wished to break with the Bourbon restoration after the Congress of Vienna (1814-15) and saw a clear acceptance of liberal ideas as the most fruitful means of promoting a Catholic revival. The leaders of this group, Felicité de Lamennais, Count Charles Montalembert, and the Dominican Henri Lacordaire, saw in the papacy a potentially strong ally in promoting their ideas. On the other hand, a similar call for a strong papacy came from those who looked to Rome as the principal bulwark against the liberal forces which were thought to be threatening the established order of christian Europe. Most prominent among this group was Joseph de Maistre. His best seller *Du Pape* (1818) was a major factor in achieving acceptance of the ultramontane outlook.

Segments of German Catholicism also promoted ultramontane views. The scholastic revival associated with the diocese of Mainz looked to Roman authority as the most effective means of combating the secularism and rationalism of the day. Ultramontane ideas found strong if not universal support among English

Roman Catholics under the leadership of Nicholas Wiseman, archbishop of Westminster in 1850, and his successor in 1865, Henry Edward Manning.

During the pontificate of Pius IX (1846-1848) many factors at Rome also served to promote the advance of ultramontane views. The personal appeal of the pope and his lengthy pontificate, the appointment of bishops of ultramontane outlook, the establishment of national seminaries in Rome, the support of religious (many of whom had headquarters at Rome), the proclamation by the pope of the dogma of the Immaculate Conception (1854)—all served to advance the ultramontane spirit and doctrine. The Jesuits, re-established in 1814, had an important role in this development.

Vatican I (1869-70) represents the victorious climax of the nineteenth-century ultramontane movement. The majority of the bishops at the council were sympathetic to the tenets of a moderate ultramontane doctrine, though some advocated an understanding of the papacy which tended to isolate the papacy from the bishops. A small but significant minority of bishops emphasized the relationship between the papacy and the episcopacy and served to temper the excesses of extreme views. The efforts of the minority had a moderating effect on the council's final statement, the constitution *Pastor aeternus*. But it was the broader ultramontane attempt to make the papacy the spiritual basis of Western European christian civilization and the bulwark against the secularizing trends coming from the Enlightenment and French Revolution which provides the context and an interpretive key for the ecclesiology of Vatican I.

The teaching of Vatican II, on the church as communion, on collegiality, and on the church's role in the modern world, puts many of the issues of nineteenth-century ultramontanism in a new context and sees them in a new light. *See* **Pope, Vatican I,**

R. Aubert, *Le pontificat de Pie IX (1846-1878)*, rev. ed., Paris, 1963.

FREDERICK J. CWIEKOWSKI, SS

UNCTION, EXTREME
See **Anointing of the Sick**

UNITY OF THE CHURCH

The NT offers a wide variety of images to describe the church: remnant, God's field, temple of God, building, house of God, city, spouse, and especially People of God and body of Christ. The principal term of reference for each image is God from whom the church derives its unity and uniqueness. The one, unique God is the principle and source of the unity and uniqueness of the church.

The Fathers presented the church as the one people of God—Father, Son and Holy Spirit. This trinitarian basis for the unity of the church is established by the saving act of the one God (1 Cor 8:6), in the revelation of the one crucified, risen and glorified Christ (Rom 14:7f), by the movement of the one Spirit of God and of Christ (Eph 2:18). By his death and resurrection Christ redeemed humankind, sent his Spirit upon it and formed human beings mystically into members of his own body. In this body, particularly through the sacraments of Baptism and Eucharist, Christians are united to the glorified Christ in such a way that the trinitarian life is communicated to them. Incorporation into the body of Christ takes place at baptism: "In this sacred rite, fellowship in Christ's death and resurrection is symbolized and brought about..." (L.G. 7). Hence all the baptized live in intimate, vital union with Christ. They are also united to one another: "As all the members of the human body, though they are many, form one body, so also the faithful in Christ (cf. 1 Cor 12:12)" (L.G. 7). All are one in Christ.

Ultimately this unity will be fulfilled eschatologically when "God will be all in all" (1 Cor 15:28). Meanwhile in its earthly pilgrimage, the church is in a condition of the already given but not-yet-fully-realized communion in God and with one another. The church possesses the first fruits of unity but it is only the beginning of a definitive reality. In its earthly condition, then, the church is characterized by a duality, a dialectical structure which corresponds to its "already-not-yet" character. This can be expressed in terms of *sacramentum et res:* the exterior, sensible mediation and the reality of grace. The full expression of the unity of the church includes both a unity of grace as an interior reality and a unity of means to attain grace or communion. In the earthly condition of the church this means that there can be, and in fact there is, a distinction between the two.

The Acts of the Apostles described the community of disciples as "devoted to the apostles' instruction and the communal life, to the breaking of bread and the prayers" (2:42). This unanimity points to three essential elements of unity: faith, worship and service. The principal element of unity is faith based on a covenant relationship with God through Christ by the Spirit, in which God first discloses himself to us and his plan of salvation for us. In an interior way, God is the Source or Principle and the Goal of faith. In an external sense, within the present economy, faith includes external mediations: prophets, apostles, scripture, the teaching of the church. These mediations communicate and condition faith. Further they have normative value, especially the scriptures as word of God, for believers. Faith, then, is central to the unity of the

church because all hold the same truths, and share in the same witness of scripture, of the apostles and of the mission of teaching which continues in the church. Faith, then, is both the principle of unity for the church in its realization of a participation in divine life as common to all believers, and it is also the means binding the church to its Source from which it receives its existence.

The second element in ecclesial unity is worship as expressed in the sacramental life of the church. The sacraments enable the believer to enter into the total, definitive, unique and historical event through which God has achieved salvation. The eucharist itself is the sacrament of unity whose spiritual effect is the unity of the mystical body. In the eucharist, "the nourishment given to us is the Word of God Himself, the celestial nourishment, the eschatological bread for those whom God unites to Himself in a divinizing communion of life" (Congar). The unity of all in Christ is accomplished here: "Because the loaf of bread is one, we, many though we are, are one body, for we all partake of the one loaf" (1 Cor 10:17). Through our participation in Christ's loving act of obedience to the Father, we receive an increase of love which unites us to the Father and one another. In the eucharist we celebrate the fact that Christ "is the sign of God's redemptive love extended toward all mankind, and of the response of all mankind to that redemptive love" (Dulles).

The third element in the unity of the church flows from the Holy Spirit who through Christ unites by love all Christians and distributes to each diverse gifts for the upbuilding of the church. This love brings multiplicity to unity in that it unites a great number of persons in the same quest, causes them to cooperate in all kinds of services, and enables them to participate in the same Root and Source of life. On the one hand it gathers diversity into unity and on the other it realizes the force of unity in diversity. Since the Holy Spirit enables Christians to participate in the life of God who is Love, they also become committed to mutual service (Congar).

Among the external mediations which communicate and direct faith are the authoritative structures of the church built on the mission of Christ to the apostles. The college of bishops both expresses the unity of the church and safeguards it through direction and teaching. Collegiality characterizes the college of bishops in that it expresses the communion of bishops in the unanimity of faith. Dispersed in their particular churches, the bishops form a communion together under the authority of the pope. "United in one college or body for the instruction and direction of the universal church, the bishops sharing in the solicitude of all the churches exercise this their episcopal function ... in communion with the Supreme Pontiff and subject to his authority" (C.D. 3). *Lumen Gentium* speaks of the bishop as a manifest symbol of charity and the unity of the mystical body. In such a community under the ministry of a bishop, "Christ is present through whose power and influence the one, holy, catholic and apostolic church is constituted" (26). The pope as successor to Peter is the visible head of the universal church entrusted with the common good of the universal church and the particular good of all the churches (C.D. 2). The bishops in communion with the pope guide the faithful and safeguard the unity of faith, worship and service in the one body of Christ.

The dialectical understanding of the church as already given but not yet fully realized is most especially evidenced in our time in the disunity of the christian churches. As Hans Küng writes: "The Church *is* one and therefore *should* be one." This unity given to the church from the divine initiative seeks to be expressed concretely in the life of the churches. It is an eschatological imperative which draws Christians to seek its fullest, visible expression in history. This impetus of the Spirit has brought about the flowering of the ecumenical movement in the twentieth century and the active participation of the Roman Catholic Church especially since Vatican II and the promulgation of the Decree on Ecumenism in 1964. Ecumenical activity has flourished on the regional, national and international levels and significant progress has been attained in the realm of theological agreements, study and cooperative social action. Especially significant is the area of theological consensus and agreement accomplished through a host of dialogues and multi-lateral conversations on such topics as eucharist, ministry, baptism, marriage, and authority in the church.

See **Church, Ecumenism, Schism**

Yves Congar, *L'eglise, une, sainte, catholique et apostolique,* vol. 15 of *Mysterium Salutis,* Paris: Les Editions du Cerf, 1970. Congar, *I Believe in the Holy Spirit,* vol. II, New York: Seabury, 1983. Avery Dulles, *Models of the Church,* Garden City, N.Y.: Doubleday, 1974. *A Church to Believe In,* New York, Crossroads, 1982. Hans Küng, *The Church,* New York: Sheed and Ward, 1967. Karl Rahner *et al, Sacramentum Mundi,* vol. I, New York: Herder and Herder, 1968, the section on the church pp. 313-357.

TIMOTHY MACDONALD, SA

V

VALIDITY

The notion of sacramental "validity" is primarily a juridical concept which was gradually introduced into theological discourse and only became a standard term in magisterial vocabulary during the pontificate of Benedict XIV (1740-58). The validity of a sacrament refers to the minimal requirements necessary for church recognition of an action or celebration as a true sacrament. In addition to such essential conditions for validity, there are many additional canonical requirements for "liceity," or licitness, that is, for the celebration of the sacrament to be fully lawful as well as valid. The principal factors that affect the validity of sacraments are the matter and form, the person and intention of the minister, and the capability and intention of the recipient.

Scholastic theologians distinguished the matter and form of each of the seven sacraments. For baptism, the matter is water; the form is the trinitarian formula. For confirmation, the matter is the anointing with chrism; the form (in the Latin rite) is the words, "Be sealed with the gift of the Holy Spirit." The matter of the eucharist is wheat bread and grape wine (grape juice is valid but illicit without proper authorization); the form is the words of consecration. The matter of the sacrament of penance consists of the penitent's contrition, confession, and satisfaction and the form is the words of absolution. The oil of the sick or, in emergency, any oil made from plants, is valid matter for the anointing of the sick, and the form is the words that accompany the anointings. For holy orders, the matter is the imposition of hands by the bishop and the form is a small part of the consecratory prayer. For marriage both matter and form is the consent of the two parties.

Only bishops may validly confer the sacrament of holy orders; any bishop validly confirms. Only a priest (bishop or presbyter) can celebrate the eucharist or anoint the sick, and only priests with the faculty given by law or delegation can validly absolve penitents or confirm the baptized. (Eastern rite priests may confirm in virtue of their ordination.) The ministers of the sacrament of marriage are the parties themselves. The minimal intention necessary on the part of the minister for the validity of any sacrament is "to do what the Church does" when it celebrates the rite in question. Any person with this intention can validly baptize.

Those capable of baptism are any persons not yet baptized. Only the baptized are capable of receiving the other sacraments. Baptism, confirmation, and the three grades of holy orders can only be received once. Only males may be ordained under the present discipline. For marriage, both parties must be free of canonical impediments.

The intention and disposition of the penitent can also affect the validity of certain sacraments received by persons with the use of reason. For example, for the validity of general absolution, those in serious sin must be suitably disposed (have sorrow for sin and a purpose of amendment) and also intend to confess individually the serious sins which at present cannot be so confessed (canon 962, § 1). For marriage the intention of the parties is a *sine qua non* because it is their free consent that makes the marriage (canon 1057, § 1).

The church also has the power to establish other requirements for the validity of sacraments, such as the requirement of the canonical form for any marriage of a Catholic. Only the supreme authority of the church—the pope or an ecumenical council—can establish criteria for the validity of sacraments (canon 841).

See **Sacrament**

John A. Gurrieri, "Sacramental Validity: The Origins and Use of a Vocabulary," *The Jurist* 41 (1981): pp. 21-58. John Huels, *One Table, Many Laws: Essays in Catholic Eucharistic Practice,* chap. 3, Collegeville: Liturgical Press, 1986.

JOHN M. HUELS, OSM

VATICAN COUNCIL I

The First Vatican Council was solemnly convened on December 8, 1869, by Pope Pius IX, who had previously announced the holding of the council on June 29, 1867, and exactly a year later had issued the formal bull of convocation. Of the approximately 1050 prelates entitled to participate in the Council, some eight hundred—cardinals, patriarchs, archbishops, bishops, abbots, and superiors general of religious communities—were actually present; these official members were assisted by numerous theological consultants and ecclesiastical officials.

Preliminary planning for the council began in 1865 with the appointment of a Central Preparatory Commission. Subsequently, five subordinate commissions were established: Faith and Dogma, Ecclesiastical Discipline, Religious Communities, Eastern Churches and Missions, and Politico-ecclesiastical Affairs. These commissions were responsible for drafting the documents that the council-members would consider. Although fifty-one documents on a wide range of topics were prepared by these commissions, only six were actually considered on the floor of the council, and only two of these were eventually adopted and then only after extensive revision.

The public announcement of the forthcoming council created considerable discussion, particularly on the question of "papal infallibility." Further stimulus for contention was provided on February 6, 1869, when the quasi-official Roman Jesuit publication, *Civiltà Cattolica,* expressed its hope that "the Council will be very short" and that "the dogmatic infallibility of the Sovereign Pontiff" would be defined without debate, "by acclamation." The *Civiltà* article quickly became "a sign of battle" in two important respects.

First, within the Roman Catholic Church, the impression was given that the council was supposed to rubber-stamp the documents drafted by the preparatory commissions which were largely staffed by members of the Roman Curia; such an assumption annoyed many bishops, who felt that their responsibility at the council was to be "official judges" of doctrine. Secondly, the *Civiltà* article antagonized European governments, which were upset by the possibility of a change in the legal provisions governing church-state relationships in their countries; some European governments seriously considered intervening in the affairs of the Council, but eventually decided against any direct intervention. Moreover, at the time the Council met, the previously extensive Papal States had been reduced to Rome and its immediate environs, which were protected by French forces; without that protection, it was feared that the Council might be disrupted; such fears were later realized and the Council had to be suspended.

By the time of the Council's opening session, lines were already drawn between those favoring and those opposing a definition of "papal infallibility." During the early days of the Council, it became evident that the pro-infallibilists, numbering approximately three-fourths of the bishops, constituted a majority; the anti-infallibilists, consisting of approximately one-fifth of the bishops, formed a minority. Attempting to mediate between these two groupings was a small "third party" whose efforts at compromise ultimately proved ineffective.

However, it would be inaccurate to characterize Vatican I simply in terms of a conflict between pro-infallibilists and anti-infallibilists, for the views of the prelates at the council were more nuanced than a simple polarization suggests. On the one hand, the majority-bishops, while favoring a definition of "papal infallibility," differed in their interpretations of it. On the other hand, the minority was not so much an "opposition party," as a group of individuals who opposed the proclamation of "papal infallibility" for a variety of reasons, some theological, others non-theological.

Among the non-theological concerns was the fear of some bishops that the proposed doctrine would harm delicately balanced church-state relations, or would provoke governmental interference in their dioceses or even in the Council itself. Also, some prelates felt that a definition of "papal infallibility" would place the church in the position of championing autocratic absolutism and of rejecting the rising tide of democracy. In addition, many bishops from countries where Catholics were a minority felt that this doctrine would jeopardize their relationships with non-Catholics. Such factors fed the opposition of the minority-bishops, a number of whom had been manifestly "pro-papal" prior to the council.

In addition to such practical objections there were serious theological issues. First, many bishops felt that the doctrine could not be defined with sufficient precision and clarity, and so thought it best to leave the issue a matter of theological opinion. Also, some objected that "papal infallibility" was being treated as an isolated issue without adequate connection with the infallibility of the church. In addition, the proposed definition seemed irreconcilable with a number of historical incidents when previous popes had been mistaken in their official teaching; failure to address these historical difficulties led some to fear that a definition of infallibility would be tantamount to a whitewashing of past papal abuses and a carte blanche for future papal absolutism, thus preventing the church from undertaking needed reforms. Finally, the behavior of a few majority-extremists at the council led many to share Newman's feeling that "a grave dogmatic question was being treated like a move in ecclesiastical politics."

This political maneuvering of a few pro-infallibilists first became evident in handling the initial item of business, the election of members to four conciliar commissions: Faith, Ecclesiastical Discipline, Religious Communities, and Eastern Churches and Missions. The majority was successful in its efforts to exclude bishops known to be anti-infallibilists from these commissions. As an unfortunate result, the conciliar commissions responsible for redacting the Council's documents were not representative of the spectrum of viewpoint of the members of the Council.

Nonetheless, the first phase of deliberations, from December 28 to January 10, made it equally clear that the Council members had no intention of simply rubber-stamping the documents prepared by the pre-conciliar commissions. After a discussion which surfaced numerous amendments, the draft on "Catholic Teaching" was returned to the Commission on Faith for revision. Similarly, after lengthly discussion, from January 14 to February 22, the drafts on episcopal responsibilities, clerical life, and a universal catechism, were also returned for revision.

To allow the commissions sufficient time to make the extensive revisions requested, the Council was recessed for nearly a month. On March 18, discussion resumed on the revised text on "Catholic Faith," which now consisted of four (out of an original nine) chapters: Creation, Revelation, Faith, Relationship between Faith and Reason. After further discussion and emendation, the Council unanimously approved the revised text as the constitution, *Dei Filius,* in the solemn session of April 24, 1870.

From April 29 through May 4, the Council again considered the universal catechism; although this revised text was ready for a final vote, it was never taken; further action on the catechism was preempted by the decision to consider the question of "papal infallibility." This decision, though arousing the strenuous protests of the minority, represented the desire of some five hundred bishops, who in early January had signed petitions requesting that the topic be placed on the Council's agenda; in contrast, counterpetitions against such a definition had obtained the signatures of only some 136 of the minority.

The document proposed for discussion was called the "First Constitution on the Church of Christ," because the Council, after treating the question of papal primacy, intended to treat other aspects of the church in a second constitution, which was prepared but, due to the suspension of the Council, never discussed. The "First Constitution," customarily designated *Pastor Aeternus,* consisted of four chapters: the Petrine institution of the primacy, its perpetuity and continuation through the bishops of Rome, the nature and powers of the primacy, and the infallibile magisterium of the Roman Pontiff.

For the next two months, from May 14 through July 16, the Council fathers discussed the proposed constitution in over 120 speeches, about sixty percent favoring, and about forty percent objecting to, the proposed definition. The anti-infallibilist speeches emphasized the definition's inopportuneness, by citing the many social-political difficulties, historical problems, and theological questions involved. The pro-infallibilist speeches in response considered infallibility as a matter of biblical revelation and apostolic tradition, and advocate the definition as a necessary defense of the spiritual power of the Petrine primacy at a time when the temporal power of the pope was threatened.

The final text of *Pastor Aeternus* reflects "a moderate infallibilism." On the one hand, it did not adopt the exaggerated view that all papal pronouncements should be considered infallible; on the other hand, it rejected both Conciliarism and Gallicanism, two positions that once were historically important, though not widely held at the time of Vatican I. The heated debate on infallibility thus seems to have had one beneficial effect: the definition was moderate enough to win the subsequent acceptance of the minority-bishops, as well as that of the overwhelming majority of Roman Catholics.

Unfortunately, this moderate tone was not evident in the final days of the Council. When it became certain that the definition was going to be approved, some sixty of the minority-bishops left

Rome under protest rather than attend the fourth solemn session of July 18, 1870, at which *Pastor Aeternus* was approved by 533 votes in favor and 2 in opposition; the two bishops casting negative votes (Edward Fitzgerald, Bishop of Little Rock, and Luigi Riccio of Caiazzo, Italy) immediately indicated their acceptance.

Due to the outbreak of the Franco-Prussian War the following day, most of the bishops immediately left Rome. There were three more sparsely attended meetings of the Council in late summer. After the occupation of Rome by Italian forces on September 20, there were no further sessions, and on October 20, Pius IX suspended the Council "until a more opportune and favorable time." Though consideration was given to transfer the council to another city, Vatican I never reconvened.

After the Council, interpretations of "papal infallibility" ranged across a spectrum, from those which maximalized its meaning to those which interpreted it very restrictively. While this spectrum of interpretations made *Pastor Aeternus* generally acceptable, several thousand Roman Catholics in Germany, Austria, and Switzerland, under the leadership of a number of university-professors led a protest movement that subsequently resulted in the formation of the Old Catholic Church.

Almost a century later, the teaching of Vatican I on infallibility was amplified by Vatican II, which taught that not only the pope, but also the college of bishops, could exercise the infallibility of the church.

Cuthbert Butler, The Vatican Council 1869-1870, based on Bishop Ullathorne's Letters, London: Longmans, Green, 1930; abr.: Westminster, MD: Newman, 1962. Frederick Cwiekowski, *The English Bishops and the First Vatican Council*, Bibliothèque de la Revue d'Histoire Ecclésiastique 52, Louvain: Publications Universitaires, 1971. John Tracy Ellis, "The Church Faces the Modern World: The First Vatican Council," *The General Council*, ed., by William McDonald, Washington: Catholic University of America, 1962, pp. 113-145. John T. Ford, "Infallibility: From Vatican 1 to the Present,"

Journal of Ecumenical Studies 8 (1971) 768-791. James Hennesey, *The First Council of the Vatican: the American Experience*, New York: Herder and Herder, 1963.

JOHN T. FORD

VATICAN COUNCIL II

The Second Vatican Council, the twenty-first ecumenical council in the history of the church, met in four sessions from October 9, 1962 to December 8, 1965. It was attended by more bishops from more countries and produced a larger set of documents than any previous council, and it has had a greater impact upon the life of the Catholic Church than any event since the Protestant Reformation.

Preparation

Although both Pius XI and Pius XII had entertained the idea of reopening the First Vatican Council, it was Pope John XXIII, who started the Catholic world by announcing on January 25, 1959 that he intended to convoke an ecumenical council. Rather than a reconvening of Vatican I, the Council was to be an entirely new assembly which the pope hoped would provide the church an opportunity to undertake an examination of its own life and activity with three purposes in mind: spiritual renewal in the light of the Gospel, updating (*"aggiornamento"*) to meet the demands of the modern age, and the promotion of the reunion of all Christians.

The preparation for the Council began with an invitation extended to all the bishops of the world, to the heads of clerical religious orders, to Catholic universities and faculties, and to the members of the Roman Curia that they submit their ideas for a conciliar agenda. This consultation was by far the most extensive ever carried out in the church's history, and it resulted in the submission of over 9300 proposals. This material was then sorted out, indexed, and distributed to ten preparatory commissions which Pope John appointed in June, 1960, to prepare draft-documents to be submitted for the Council's consideration.

These commissions met between November 1960 and June 1962. They produced over seventy documents, reducible when collated to some twenty texts. Each of these was then reviewed by a Central Preparatory Commission, revised in the light of its comments, and then submitted for the pope's approval. In the summer of 1962, several of these documents were sent out to the bishops of the world as the texts that would be discussed when the Council opened in the fall.

The First Session

The Council met in four sessions (October to December, 1962; September to December, 1963, September to November, 1964, September to December, 1965). It is not possible here to give even a brief summary of the Council's history, but something must be said about the first session, which was the most dramatic and the most important; its decisions were to give the essential direction to the Council's entire work. Four moments were particularly significant. The first was Pope John's opening address, in which he urged that the Council take a pastoral direction. It was not principally to be concerned with repeating what was already secure Catholic doctrine, nor to propose condemnations of errors. The bishops were urged not to indulge in an attitude of gloom towards the modern world but to consider whether God was not introducing a new moment in human history. They should distinguish between the substance of the faith and the way in which it has been stated and concern themselves with the question how the ancient faith might best be expressed in the new situations of the day.

The second key moment came when, on the first working-session, the bishops refused to vote immediately on the membership of their own conciliar commissions. This was seen at the time as an expression of a widespread disagreement with the tone and substance of many of the prepared drafts. The bishops insisted on taking the time to get to know one another, so that they could elect to the conciliar commissions members who would not simply repeat the emphases of the prepared texts.

The third significant moment was the conciliar debate on the draft document on the liturgy, which revealed that a majority of the bishops would ratify the pope's call for renewal. The mind of the Council was further revealed when the debate on the draft "On the Sources of Revelation" began. This doctrinal text was very severely criticized by many of the bishops, and in a final vote on the text, over 60% of them asked that it be withdrawn. Although this was an insufficient number to remand the text, Pope John intervened and ordered that the text be thoroughly revised. This fourth dramatic moment illustrated the intention of the majority of the bishops to embark on a course which represented in several ways a departure from the attitudes and strategies which had characterized the Roman Catholicism of the previous 150 years.

Pope John XXIII died in June 1963. He was succeeded by Pope Paul VI, one of whose first acts was to announce that the Council would continue and that it should follow the directions outlined by Pope John and confirmed at the first session. It was during the three sessions presided over by Pope Paul that the essential work of the Council was accomplished, but rather than tell their history, it will be more helpful to offer a brief description of the Council's achievement.

The Documents

The Second Vatican Council produced sixteen documents: four Constitutions: on the Sacred Liturgy, on the Church, on

Divine Revelation, and on the Church in the Modern World; nine Decrees: on the Instruments of Social Communication, on the Oriental Catholic Churches, on Ecumenism, on the Pastoral Role of Bishops in the Church, on the Renewal of Religious Life, on Priestly Formation, on the Apostolate of the Laity, on the Church's Missionary Activity, and on the Ministry and Life of Presbyters; and three Declarations: on Christian Education, on the Church's Relationship to Non-Christian Religions, and on Religious Freedom. As is clear from their titles, this body of material was far-ranging in its scope; and it represents by far the largest set of documents ever produced by an ecumenical council.

The centerpiece of the Council's work is the Dogmatic Constitution on the Church (*Lumen gentium*); and it will be used here as a framework within which briefly to introduce the major achievements of the Council. *Lumen gentium* departs significantly from the dominant official ecclesiology of the recent past, which was marked by an emphasis on the institutional dimensions of the church. It begins with a view of the church as Mystery, as the community of men and women called together into a participation in the life of the Triune God. This communion in God produces the communion among the members of the church which makes them the People of God, the Body of Christ, and the Temple of the Spirit. There are not two churches, but one in which the divine and the human dimensions create a distinct social phenomenon, the church of Christ, which "subsists in" the Roman Catholic Church, although many of the most important elements which constitute it and give it life are also acknowledged to exist outside its boundaries (L.G. 8; see U.R. 3).

Lumen gentium went on to speak of the church as the People of God in which the Mystery is realized in the historical period between Christ's Ascension and the Parousia. The whole church is this People, and the Council stresses the fundamental equality in dignity and activity which underlies the distinctions it makes between the hierarchy, the laity and the religious One is fully incorporated into this church society by possession of the Spirit of Christ and communion in the faith, the sacraments, and discipline and structure. This church is catholic in the sense that it reaches out to all peoples and cultures, seeking to bring them under the Lordship of Christ and to enrich the universal church by the mutual sharing of all the cultural resources of the various peoples. Here and elsewhere the Council placed great stress on the theology of the local church, that is, on the principle that the mystery of the church is always realized in local communities, in parishes, dioceses, larger geographical and cultural areas. This perspective is particularly evident in the Decree on the Church's Missionary Activity (*Ad gentes*).

The theological and spiritual perspectives of the first two chapters of *Lumen gentium* are explored at greater length in the Dogmatic Constitution on Divine Revelation (*Dei verbum* and the Constitution on the Sacred Liturgy (*Sacrosanctum Concilium*). *Dei verbum* discusses revelation as God's self-communication in word and act, reaching its perfection in Jesus Christ. This redemptive revelation is handed on through the Scriptures and the Tradition. The Council, in discussing these two mediations of revelation, stressed the central role of the Scriptures and confirmed the validity of modern critical scholarship. It also insisted on the role of Tradition, understood as the living process by which the Scriptures are received and interpreted in the full life of the church.

Sacrosanctum Concilium, after a theological introduction which stated the constitutive role of the liturgy and particularly of the eucharist, set down the principles for a thoroughgoing review and reform of the church's liturgical life. The rites of the church were to be renewed so that they would more clearly symbolize the mystery of salvation, of which they are the instruments and would enable a fuller active participation of all the members of the church.

After its discussions of the church as Mystery and People of God, *Lumen gentium* turned to the differentiations of the church's members. Chapter III was on the hierarchy, particularly on the episcopate. Its purpose was to balance Vatican I's emphasis on the papacy by inserting that ministry of unity into the larger context of the episcopal college. The sacramental character of the episcopate was taught, as well as the responsibility of the bishop over his particular church and for the welfare of the universal church. Vatican I's doctrine on the magisterium was repeated but interpreted more fully than had been possible in 1870. Two concluding chapters discussed the priesthood and decided upon the restoration of the diaconate as a permanent ministry. The material in this chapter was filled out in the Decrees on the Pastoral Office of the Bishop (*Christus Dominus*), on the Ministry and Life of Presbyters (*Presbyterorum ordinis*), and on Priestly Formation (*Optatam totius*).

Chapter IV of *Lumen gentium* was devoted to the laity. It proposed a "typological description" of the layperson as a Christian with full rights to participate in the life and mission of the church, but who lives out his christian life in the secular world. The laity are the presence of the church in the world, where they have the task of bringing Christ's word and grace to everyday problems. In turn they bring the insights their secular life permits as their contribution to the buildingup of the church. The principles

briefly outlined in this chapter are taken up more fully in the Decree on the Apostolate of the Laity (*Apostolicam actuositatem*).

The chapter on religious in the church gives an exposition of the three vows with which religious take up the challenge of the evangelical counsels and exhorts religious to carry out their own responsibility for the life and mission of the church. The Decree on the Adaptation and Renewal of the Religious Life (*Perfectae caritatis*) lays down principles for reform and renewal.

In its sixth and seventh chapters, *Lumen gentium* returns to consideration of the whole church, stressing the universal call to holiness and the communion of the church on earth with the church triumphant in the Kingdom. The last chapter of the Constitution is devoted to the Blessed Virgin Mary and makes her role as both member and symbol of the church the interpretative key to Marian theology.

The deeper and richer ecclesiology of *Lumen gentium* had enormous implications for ecumenical relationships between the Catholic Church and other christian churches and communities. These the Council explored both in *Lumen gentium* and in the Decree on Ecumenism (*Unitatis redintegratio*), the Decree on the Eastern Catholic Churches (*Orientalium Ecclesiarum*), and the Declaration on the Church's Relationship to Non-Christian Religions (*Nostra aetate*). These texts represent an enthusiastic commitment of the church to the effort to replace suspicion and hostility among churches and religions with an attitude of dialogue and collaboration.

The Council also devoted two documents to the situation of the church in the modern world. *Gaudium et Spes,* the Pastoral Constitution on the Church in the Modern World, presents the church as sharing in the joys and hopes, grief and anguish of contemporaries, with whom it shares the responsibility of contributing to the making of history. The first part of the text offers theological reflections on the relationship between church and world, stressing particularly that each has something to give the other. These principles are then applied in the second part to contemporary questions on marriage and family, culture, economic, social, and political life, and on peace and war.

The Declaration on Religious Freedom (*Dignitatis humanae*) provided an opportunity for the Council to address the question of church and state. The Council defended the right of the human person to freedom of religion and opposed governmental intervention in its exercise. In this document and in *Gaudium et Spes,* the Council proposed a far more open attitude towards the modern world than had been characteristic of Roman Catholicism for the previous 150 years.

The Impact of the Council

This very brief summary of most of the conciliar documents cannot convey by itself a sense of the Council's impact on the life of the church. The Council itself, as an event, had a tremendous effect. It was the first experience in the living memory of the church of a collegial exercise of supreme authority in the church. A church which had often prided itself on its immutability was seen undertaking a thorough self-examination and self-criticism. Many of the typical modern Roman Catholic attitudes and strategies were reviewed and challenged in the light both of the gospel and of contemporary needs.

This phenomenon was to continue in the years after the Council. The most obvious changes took place in the liturgy, as Pope Paul VI not only insisted that the Council's call for reform be fully implemented but that it be taken even further than the Council had required. Reforms were also authorized in almost every other area of church life as well: relations between clergy and laity, pope and bishops, bishops and priests, Rome and the local churches, Catholics and non-Catholics, etc. The officially directed reforms were often accompanied by powerful movements from below, some of which were in continuity with the Council and in harmony with the official reforms, some of which represented far more radical changes than the Council had anticipated or mandated.

The Council was received differently in different geographical and cultural areas, but it is no exaggeration to say that there was no church in the world that was left unaffected by the conciliar reforms. This was itself a vindication of the Council's emphasis on the local church and on the participation and co-responsibility of all Christians in its life. In some areas the changes were so rapid and deep enough that it was not uncommon for people to speak of a "crisis" in the church, and what was widely considered the "decomposition of Catholicism" began to receive greatly varying interpretations.

Twenty years after the Council closed, a vigorous debate is in course on both the meaning of the Council and the value of what has happened since. Broadly speaking, three interpretations vie for acceptance. A progressive view considers the Council as the long-overdue moment at which an irrelevant church finally faced the challenges of modernity. A traditionalist view agrees that the Council brought about major changes, but it sees in what the progressives praise an unfortunate capitulation of the church to principles and movements it had correctly opposed since the French Revolution. These two views agree in assigning the Council epochal significance, although they utterly disagree in their assessments of the shift.

Between these two equally exaggerated

extremes, the real struggle is for a midd e-position. Some see the Council as "merely" reformist, not intending many of the developments which ensued, responsibil-ity for which should be laid at the feet of progressives who ignored the Council's letter in favor of their own idea of its "spirit." They believe that the solution to post-conciliar confusion lies in a return to both the letter and the true spirit of the Council. Others argue that whatever the Council members intended themselves, many of the "reforms" which they endorsed had in fact quite revolutionary implications for everyday attitudes, strategies, and habits of modern Roman Catholicism. They point particularly to the Council's more open attitude towards the modern world, its call for self-exami-nation, and its promotion of the local realization of the church. For such interpreters, the Council itself is responsible for many of the great changes in the church since. Its texts need to be located historically and sociologically against the backdrops of modern Roman Catholic-ism. The 1985 Synod of Bishops, called to celebrate the twentieth anniversary of the Council's close, provided a forum for this debate about the Council.

The discussion shows no signs of abat-ing. What a council really is, how sig-nificant and valuable its work is for the church, is something only determined in the process of its reception by the whole church. Twenty years is too short a time within which to make any final assess-ments of the Second Vatican Council. Many elements in the Council's teaching have been widely implemented and grate-fully received by the church; others have yet to be sufficiently honored in practice. But it is already clear that Vatican II represents a turning-point in the modern history of the Catholic Church, a moment in the church's existential self-realization that has only begun to reveal its truth and power.

Vatican Ii Revisited by Those Who Were There, ed. A. Stacpoole, Minneapolis: Winston Press, 1986. *The Reception of Vatican II*, ed. G. Alberigo, J.-P. Jossua, and J.A. Komonchak, Washington: Cath-olic University of America Press, 1987. *Synod 1985—An Evaluation*, ed. G. Alberigo and J. Provost, *Concilium* 188; Edinburgh: T. & T. Clarke, 1986. *Vatican II: Open Questions and New Horizons* ed. G.M. Fagin, Wilmington: Glazier, 1984. *Vatican II and Its Documents: An American Reappraisal*, ed. T.E. O'Connell, Wilmington: Glazier, 1986.

JOSEPH A. KOMONCHAK

VENIAL SIN
See **Sin**

VIRGIN BIRTH
Usage of Terms

"Virgin Birth" is ordinarily used to designate the miraculous conception of Christ in the womb of Mary apart from the procreative power of the marital act. And so it is more precisely called the "virginal conception" as is done through-out this article. According to the tradi-tional formula, the total mystery of Mary's virginity has been contemplated in three principal aspects, namely, *ante partum* or virginal conception, *in* or *durante partu*, i.e., her virginal parturition which maintains that her virginity re-mained intact while giving birth to Christ, and *post partum* or perpetual virginity, the belief that Mary was a virgin through-out her entire life. Each one of the three aspects will be considered separately in the context of the special theological problems that it poses today, and the concluding section of this article reflects upon the significance of Mary's virginity for the contemporary church.

Virginal Conception

The NT basis for the traditional chris-tian faith concerning the virginity of Mary in conceiving Christ is found in Mt 1:18-25 and Lk 1:26-38. Both evangelists were primarily interested in its Christological significance since the virginal conception emphasizes the central mystery of christian faith that Christ has only one Father in heaven, and so is true God, while having one mother on earth, and so is true man. Sometimes it is called the "pneumatological conception" because both inspired writers revealed the mystery as taking place through the power of the Holy Spirit. This has shaped the formulation of faith in the creeds from the earliest days of the church: " ... by the power of the Holy Spirit he was born of the Virgin Mary, and became man." The witness to belief in the virginal conception among the Fathers of the Church is as early as the Apostolic Father, St. Ignatius of Antioch, who was martyred c. 110. The patristic testimony to it is constant, which reflects not only the teaching of the church but the belief of all the faithful.

There seems to be no doubt that Matthew, Luke, and the Fathers of the Church understood the virginal conception literally, i.e., as an historical fact or reality with a profound Christological meaning, and not just as a theologoumenon or Christologoumenon, i.e., as purely a symbol that is not also factual. Even Roman Catholic scripture scholars question whether or not its historicity can be derived from the NT texts in their literal sense. Generally speaking, however, they do appear to accept its facticity on the basis of the Catholic Tradition. Those scholars who argue in favor of finding the traditional teaching and belief regarding the virginal conception of Christ by Mary and the Holy Spirit in the infancy narratives, raise the question of where the evangelists obtained the idea if it were not from God's revealing word. They assert that there is no basis for holding it originated with the pagan myths of parthenogenesis which were quite different from the pneumatological conception, i.e., by the power of the Holy Spirit. The "virgin" of pagan mythology

is inseminated by the "gods" and does not come to be with child by a God who transcends sexual differences and can cause human life to begin without depending upon conjugal intercourse. Another argument contrary to the interpretation of the biblical revelation of the virginal conception as a Christologoumenon is that, if Joseph were the natural father of Christ, this fact would have been clearly affirmed especially in the predominantly Jewish setting of Matthew's Gospel where paternity was so important to support any claims based upon one's genealogy. And Matthew's genealogy called Jesus Christ, "the son of David, the son of Abraham" (1:1), in the fulfillment of prophecies in the OT.

Regardless of how we might resolve the source of our faith in the matter, the American Bishops, in their pastoral letter, *Behold Your Mother: Woman of Faith,* have taught in favor of a literal meaning of the virginal conception: "The Virgin birth is not merely a symbolical way of describing God's intervention in human history, not just a literary device to convey the divine preexistence of the Word. Nor is the Virgin birth a human construct, as if Christians feared that the divinity of Jesus would be compromised by his having a human father. What really matters here is the manner in which God in fact chose to 'send his Son in the fullness of time.' We know what God has done not only from the text of the Bible, taken in isolation, but from the Bible as read, interpreted, and understood by the living Church, guided by the Holy Spirit. Catholic belief in the Virgin Birth rests not on the Scriptures alone, but on the constant and consistent faith of the Church" (n. 44).

Virginal Parturition

That Mary remained a virgin in giving birth to Christ is indicated in the infancy narrative of Mt 1 25. This is significant for his purpose since he sees in her the fulfillment of the ancient prophecy in Isaiah 7:14 that the "virgin" will both conceive and *bear* the child. Obviously modern scripture scholars of the OT do not thus interpret its literal sense, but the evangelist was inspired to perceive the fuller meaning of the virginal conception and parturition in the prophecy. Generally speaking the Fathers of the Western Church taught this aspect of Mary's virginity in terms of a preservation of her bodily integrity and her exemption from experiencing the ordinary pangs of childbirth. The Eastern Fathers emphasized Mary's experience of joy and freedom from pain in giving birth to Christ. Both East and West did not reach a general agreement on the doctrine until the period between 375-425. The concern of many earlier christian writers, particularly of Tertullian, was that it seemed to favor the heresy of the Gnostic Docetists, who denied that Jesus truly took human flesh and blood from Mary. St. Augustine sums up the patristic witness that developed during his time by simply stating: "She conceives and is a virgin; she gives birth and is a virgin" (P.L. 38, 1319). In 449 Pope St. Leo the Great taught in a letter to Flavian, the Archbishop of Constantinople, in preparation for the council of Chalcedon two years later: "... she [Mary] brought him forth without the loss of virginity, even as she conceived him without its loss ... [Jesus Christ was] born from the Virgin's womb because it was a miraculous birth..." (D.S. 291, 294). The unanimous acceptance of this teaching by the ecumenical council at Chalcedon indicates its universal doctrinal status by that time.

During recent years there has been some theological discussion about the precise conceptual content of the virginal parturition. Is it a matter of Catholic faith that the teachings of the Fathers about Mary's bodily integrity must be interpreted literally? In a book which appeared about ten years before Vatican II, Albert Mitterer expressed his opinion that a denial of the opening of Mary's womb and its ordinary consequences is a virtual rejection of the realism of her motherhood of Jesus. If this be so, what content remains in the traditional teaching? Karl Rahner attempted to meet the problem posed by Mitterer's opinion. He does not accept Mitterer's theory that Mary had to experience birth pangs to be the real mother of Jesus, and so the virginal parturition means nothing more than an application of her perpetual virginity to the act of bringing him forth. Rather Rahner was convinced that divine revelation does not address such genetic details, and proposed that Mary's virginal parturition means that she, who is the immaculate mother of the Word made flesh, was free from sin and concupiscence, and so each aspect of her childbearing must have been essentially distinct as a graced human experience from those who are subject to the consequences of sin. His authority seems to be in accord with the way the Fathers of the Eastern Church expressed their belief in the mystery. Rahner's approach is in conformity with the instruction of the Holy Office (now the Congregation for the Doctrine of the Faith), issued on July 27, 1960, which cautioned against the unfitting way of discussing the question on a biological level instead of the theological. At the same time he does propose an interpretation that preserves the spiritual significance of the doctrine.

Perpetual Virginity

Although the Fathers and theologians of the Middle Ages, including Martin Luther, used Ezek 44:2 (the "gate" of Mary's womb shall remain shut since the Lord, the God of Israel, has entered by it) as the biblical basis for Mary's perpetual virginity, there is certainly no clear reference to the doctrine in Sacred Scripture. In the Tradition the teaching that Mary remained a virgin throughout her life became prominent during the latter part of the fourth century, but considerable testimony had been given it for some time before, e.g., by Clement of Alexandria, Origen, Hilary of Poitiers, and Basil the Great. Athanasius during the latter half of the fourth century portrayed Mary as the model of virgins in the church. Epiphanius introduced "ever-virgin" into the Eastern version of the Nicene Creed, a title for Mary which became very popular. The usage of the threefold formula, *ante, durante (in), post,* became standard with Augustine. In its Marian teaching, Vatican II makes use of the liturgical expression found in Eucharistic Prayer I, "of the glorious ever Virgin Mary, Mother of Jesus Christ our Lord and God" (cf. L.G. 52), which continually confirms the Catholic Tradition of doctrine and faith in the matter.

The belief that Mary had vowed to remain a virgin her entire life at a very early age prior to the Annunciation, which has never been proposed by the church as a matter of divine faith, is being questioned by many today. Such a belief, although tenable in itself, does cause undue difficulties concerning the betrothal between Mary and Joseph which, according to the religious customs of the times, would seem to have been a commitment to bearing children together. St. Thomas Aquinas did not consider that Mary had made a *vow* of virginity to God before the revelation that she received at the annunciation, since only then did she come to learn the will of God for her (cf. S.Th. III, q. 28, a. 4). It appears much more likely that her commitment of perpetual virginity came about as a result of total consecration to her Son and his mission.

The apparent denial of this doctrine by the NT reference to the "brothers of the Lord" calls for an explanation that goes beyond saying that they were just cousins of Christ. This cannot stand the test of textual criticism since the Greek of the NT did have a special word for "cousin" and did not have to use "brother" or "sister" to designate this kinship. Jerome himself discarded this theory later in his life. A reasonable hypothesis is that the "brothers" were sons of Joseph's sister who were brought up with Jesus after their own father died. Although their relationship was really that of first cousins, they could, therefore, be readily called his "brothers" as we would do in a similar situation today.

Contemporary Significance

Because the doctrine of Mary's virginity as an historical reality is a matter of faith in the Roman Catholic Church by reason of her ordinary universal magisterium, its spiritual significance should be stressed, especially in our time. This completely accords with the theological reasons of fittingness for it found in the Tradition, particularly in Augustine and Aquinas who did not hesitate to articulate the inspiring symbolic meaning of the doctrine. Her perpetual virginity was viewed by such outstanding christian scholars and saints as a type of the church's virginal motherhood which begets and nourishes the life of Christ in the world through her spiritual ministries of word and sacrament. It has traditionally been an inspiring example for those in the church who are called to a life of consecrated virginity and celibacy for the sake of the Kingdom, so that they might be more available both for the contemplation of God and for ministry to his people. The witness of these men and women has been called eschatological in pointing to the primacy of the kingdom fulfilled in heaven where there is no marriage. Karl Barth saw in Mary's virginal conception of Christ a testimony to the complete gratuitousness of the Incarnation and so a deepening of the great christian dogma of grace. All such interpretations of Mary's virginity preclude any negative attitude towards the sexual expression of love in marriage.

See **Mary**

R.E. Brown et al, *Mary in the New Testament* N.Y., Phila., Toronto, 1978. F.M. Jelly, O.P. "Mary's Virginity in the Symbols and Councils," *Marian Studies* 21 (1970), pp. 69-93; *Madonna. Mary in the Catholic Tradition,* Huntington, IN, 1986, pp. 78-89. J. McHugh, *The Mother of Jesus in the New Testament,* N.Y., 1975. K. Rahner, "*Virginitas in partu:* A Contribution to the Problem of the Development of Dogma and of Tradition.," *Theological Investigations* IV, trans., K. Smyth, Baltimore and London, 1966, pp. 134-162.

F.M. JELLY, OP

VIRTUE

Possibly no term in the history of moral thought has stimulated more interest, reflection and speculation than that of virtue. Its importance for moral living has been uncontested, but the precise definition of virtue, its relation to other elements of moral experience, and the number and unity of the virtues have varied widely over the centuries according to different conceptions of the moral life.

There is no Hebrew term in the OT that conveys the general meaning of virtue. While the authors of the Hebrew scriptures were certainly aware of many human virtues, it was not until the OT was translated into Greek (Septuagint) that the word *arete* (virtue or excellence) was used (e.g., Wis 4:1 and 5:13). The term is also infrequently used in the NT (Phil 4:8; 1 Pet 2:9; 2 Pet 1:3; 1:5), but possibly the reason for this is because the NT authors may have thought that the word was too anthropocentric and stressed human achievement and merit. Whenever the word is used, however, it does denote moral goodness.

Though the word virtue is used infrequently in the NT, it is more commonplace to find lists of virtues that describe moral existence in the early years of the christian community, especially in the Pauline

corpus and in the Pastoral Epistles (e.g., Gal 5:22-23; Rom 1:29-31). Both Greek and Jewish influence are found in these lists, but clearly their authors viewed the virtues as having their origin in the effect of the Holy Spirit and not in human effort. In these texts it is faith and love which become the key virtues which transform all the others that are borrowed from Jewish and pagan sources.

It was the Greeks who articulated philosophically the nature and definition of virtue. Socrates, Plato, Aristotle, the Stoics, and the Neo-Platonists have all made their mark on the theory of virtue and the necessity of virtue for proper moral living. Because these philosophers almost always conceived the acquisition of moral virtue as directed toward public life within the community, their writings have had an enormous impact upon the moral thought and development of Western political societies.

For Aristotle, virtue is intimately related to human happiness or eudaemonia as the final end of humanity. Within his teleological view of human nature, Aristotle argued that the moral virtues do not arise in us naturally but are acquired and then perfected by consistently exercising them through a habit (*ethos*). Thus, persons become virtuous by doing virtuous acts in their relations with others and by performing these actions as the virtuous person would perform them. Simply considered, Aristotle defined virtue (*arete*) as a state of character (*hexis*) concerned with choice, lying in a mean intermediate between two extremes (vices).

In the patristic period one finds frequent reference to various virtues by which the christian moral life ought to be lived. The *Didache* (chaps. 1-6), or *Teaching of the Twelve Apostles,* is a fine example of one of the earliest attempts to describe the virtuous life (way of life) among Christians. The *Tutor (Paeda-*

gogus) of Clement of Alexandria provides a series of detailed instructions on the christian moral life, including a primitive definition of virtue as "a state of the soul rendered harmonious by reason in respect to the whole life" (Book One, chap.13). The apologists also spoke frequently of the virtues (e.g., Aristides, Theophilus of Antioch and Minucius Felix), but it was probably Lactantius, following the pagan Cicero, who first formulated a general concept of christian virtue and linked it to the willing of the good.

The most significant development of the concept of virtue in early Christianity came in the fifth century with Augustine of Hippo. His far-reaching mind tackled several of the more theoretical issues involved in the definition, nature and unity of the virtues. Two definitions of virtue seem to exist side by side in his writings. On the one hand, he defined virtue as a fixed disposition of the soul, making connatural the response to what is morally right, and, on the other hand, he defined it as the art of living rightly and in a proper manner. What is probably more important, though, was Augustine's understanding of the unity and inter-connection of the virtues in the christian life. He accepted the four cardinal virtues of the Greeks, viz., prudence, justice, fortitude and temperance, but he gave pride of place to the christian virtues of faith, hope and especially charity. For him, it was charity which animates and unifies all the virtues, and it was God who gives true virtue by which we are enabled to serve God and one another in love. As his argument against Julian makes clear (Contra Julianum Eclanum), Augustine held that the necessary condition for true virtue to exist depended not merely on the agent performing the morally right action but more importantly on the agent's intention to perform the action for the right reason. Thus, the key element in virtue for Augustine was not right

action (officium) but the end (finis) for which an action is done. Augustine was convinced that charity (the end or purpose for which actions should be performed) was so central to the nature and unity of the virtues that he seemed to discount the possibility of non-Christians ever attaining true virtue, since their intention of the end for which any action would be done could never be motivated by the love of God.

The scholastic period saw the flourishing of systematic treatises on the virtues. The two main influences on the thought of the scholastic authors were Augustine and Aristotle. It was particularly through the commentaries on Boethius that Aristotle's concept of virtue as a fixed disposition of the soul was introduced. By applying the Aristotelian notion of habit to the virtues, the scholastics were now able to distinguish clearly the natural virtues from the supernatural virtues of faith, hope and charity.

Thomas Aquinas in the thirteenth century stood at the apex of scholastic thinking on the virtues. With the complete text of Aristotle's Ethics now available, St. Thomas constructed a synthesis of christian and pagan sources on virtue that many believe has been unsurpassed in the history of Christianity.

Aquinas's systematic treatise on the virtues in his Summa Theologiae pre-supposed his theological anthropology and his neo-platonic understanding that all things come from God (exitus) and are oriented back to God (reditus). This exitus-reditus schema implied that humanity could acquire the means (naturally and supernaturally) by which a return to God was possible. For Aquinas, virtue, as a good operative habit (habitus) productive of the good, is one of the several means by which we might return to God. Though Aquinas maintained that the intellect and will as powers of the soul are naturally oriented to the true and good, and thus we possess the virtues inchoately, these powers are in need of perfection so that they can be disposed regularly and easily to truth and goodness. Thus, the subject of the virtues is the perfection of some power or faculty of the soul, and their object is the production of some goodness.

The theological and philosophical background to Aquinas's discussion of the relation and distinction between the natural and infused (supernatural) virtues was clearly his understanding of the relationship and distinction between nature and grace. Viewed abstractly, by nature, i.e., without grace, the powers of the human soul and good moral actions are directed to a natural finality or goodness. Aquinas argued, though, that this natural aptness is insufficient in itself and thus the acquisition of the cardinal virtues is required for those who would live the moral life well. However, for these powers and actions to be directed toward a supernatural destiny, and thus to intend God as their ultimate end, the divine gift of grace must be infused. Just as grace perfects nature, so the infusion of the theological virtues of faith, hope and charity perfects and gives a supernatural finality to the actions which were performed under the acquired virtues of prudence, justice, temperance and fortitude. Thus, the natural or acquired virtues and the supernatural virtues do not differ in the respect of being habits, for both are considered as habits by Aquinas, but they differ in the finality or kind of goodness to which they regularly dispose us, in the kind of merit that is gained, and in the degree of perfection that is reached by the powers of the soul.

Jonathan Edwards, the Calvinist theologian of the Great Awakening in the eighteenth century, perhaps has been the most influential commentator on the nature of virtue among Protestant authors in North America and maybe elsewhere.

Edwards' own Calvinist heritage, together with influences from the moral sense school of philosophy and neo-platonism, led him to reflect in a distinctive way on the nature of authentic virtue for christian moral living. For him, natural humanity, motivated by self-love, is capable only of achieving inferior virtue, not true virtue. The origin of true virtue, or moral beauty, is a gift from God in grace, and Edwards assigned three interrelated aspects to its nature: (1) it is primarily concerned with the affections or will; (2) it involves a cognitive aspect which corrects the possibility of disordered or misdirected affections; and (3) it possesses symmetry and proportion. By weaving together the aesthetic and the moral into a singular fabric, Edwards gave a unique texture to how virtue was to be understood and practiced.

Following the tradition established by Augustine and Aquinas, theologians within the Catholic tradition, in particular, have emphasized the different kinds of virtues. The cardinal or "hinge" (cardo) virtues of prudence, justice, temperance and fortitude and the theological virtues of faith, hope and charity are frequently mentioned. One should also note the eschatological virtues of gratitude, humility, vigilance, serenity and joy that are given to the believer by the Holy Spirit. These lists of virtues suggest at least two things: (1) that different virtues are needed to perfect the various powers and appetites of the moral subject; and (2) that there is a diversity of goods or values to be sought after in the moral life, and each set of values requires a distinct aptness or ready disposition to achieve them. For example, prudence and faith dispose reason to seek values of an intellectual nature; and the virtues of justice, hope and charity facilitate the will to achieve moral values on a regular basis. Though the Catholic tradition has carefully coordinated the natural, supernatural and eschatological virtues in the moral subject, such distinctions have been based on an anthropology that viewed nature and supernature abstractly as distinct and integral levels of human activity with their own respective ends. If the moral subject and the virtuous life are viewed less abstractly, and therefore more historically, it is possible to argue that there has always been only one historical order in which the divine-human interaction has taken place. Thus, in every authentic human act the virtue of charity is involved in fact, disposing the moral subject and all truly good acts to the only destiny possible—love of God through the neighbor.

The fact that there are many virtues and multiple goods towards which the virtues lead us could be cause for doubting that there is any unity to the virtues in particular and to the moral life in general. The claim that the virtues are somehow one, and thus that the life of virtue is unified, was the position of Socrates, Plato, Plotinus, Augustine and Aquinas. For Augustine, charity unified the virtues, and for Aquinas it was prudence and charity. Recently, however, some theologians have come to question this ancient claim by pointing to the possibilities that tragedy, as an inevitable part of the human condition, can force a conflict between two virtues or that virtue can lead, not to happiness, but to the greatest suffering. Most contemporary theologians, though, continue to argue for the unity of the virtues, but the methods for doing so differ. In the Catholic tradition, some scholars unify the virtues by continuing to coordinate and interrelate the different finalities of nature (natural virtues) and supernature (infused virtues), while others unify the virtuous life by arguing that every true moral act intends, at least implicitly but really, God as its object. In the latter view, transcendental method is used to demonstrate that char-

ity is the font of all the virtues by how it can inform, unify and direct all aspects of the moral subject and moral action towards life with God.

Contemporary literature in both philosophy and theology indicates an intense interest in an analysis of virtue. Such interest signals a return in moral theory and practice to a focus on the kind of person the moral subject is rather than focusing on the kind of actions the moral agent performs. The person as moral subject and as moral agent is the same, but it is possible to distinguish these two aspects in moral theory. The two aspects of the moral person are certainly interrelated, for the kinds of actions which one does are dependent on the intentions, dispositions and virtues of the the agent. Conversely, by performing good acts over a period of time, the person becomes a certain kind of moral subject who now possesses distinctive traits or virtues.

The emphasis on the person as moral subject has resulted recently in a proliferation of literature on the importance of narrative or story for the formation of moral character. Alasdair MacIntyre and Stanley Hauerwas have been major proponents of this view arguing for the primacy of character and narrative in philosophical and theological ethics. For Hauerwas, in particular, character can be defined as the qualification of self-agency by the moral subject's beliefs and intentions. Because he argues that all moral theory and practice are narrative-based, Hauerwas maintains that the origin of the Christian's beliefs and intentions that qualify moral agency is the specific story or narrative of the christian community as this is appropriated by the believer. Though Hauerwas has chosen to focus more on the general notion of character and its formation within the christian community than on specific virtues, nonetheless his writings have indicated one way of unifying the moral life and the virtues through the use of narrative.

Since the 1940's many Catholic theologians have sought to overcome the split that occurred in the sixteenth century between moral theology and the other theological disciplines, e.g., dogmatic and ascetical theology. These efforts bore their greatest fruits both at the Second Vatican Council (1962-65) and in its aftermath when theologians turned their attention to the necessity to ground moral theology in the scriptures and in the spiritual life of the believer. With the development of the notion of a fundamental option which underlies moral choice and action, more attention has been focused on the need for continual conversion of the person. Conversion, as the gradual turning away from sin and the turning towards God in faith and love, requires a life of virtue that incarnates and manifests the fundamental option in daily actions. But christian virtue, as the ready disposition to act on behalf of values for the well-being of others, can never be acquired, and the process of conversion can never be undertaken, in isolation. Both require a community of believers who commit themselves in love to one another and who sustain each other's efforts. Likewise, virtue and conversion are never merely private realities in individuals' lives, but they also have a necessary and inevitable public end whereby the converted and virtuous person acts to convert the structures of society into mediations of social justice and love.

Because persons develop over a long period of time and journey through many different stages toward adult moral maturity, many Catholic theologians, such as Bernard Häring, Bernard Lonergan and those who have followed them, not only have emphasized the primacy of the moral subject over action in moral theory, but also have stressed the importance of viewing the moral life in general and the acquisition of virtue in particular within a developmental perspective. The psychological theories of Erik Erikson, Jean Piaget and Lawrence Kohlberg have been used in articulating this emphasis on the developmental nature of the moral subject. These theologians have retained the unity and interconnection among the many virtues, but they have also recognized, not unlike Augustine and Aquinas, that the virtuous life is undertaken over a lifetime with the grace and assistance of the Holy Spirit.

See Anthropology, Christian; Conversion; Faith; Grace; Holy Spirit; Hope; Love; Moral Life, Christian

Thomas Aquinas, STh 1a 2ae, qq. 49-67. Aristotle, *Nicomachean Ethics,* in *The Basic Works of Aristotle,* Ed. and trans., Richard McKeon, New York: Random House, 1941. Stanley Hauerwas, *A Community of Character: Toward a Constructive Christian Social Ethic,* Notre Dame: IN: U of Notre Dame Press, 1981. John P. Langan, "Augustine on the Unity and the Interconnection of the Virtues," *Harvard Theological Review* 72 (January-April, 1979). pp. 81-95. Alasdair MacIntyre, *After Virtue: A Study in Moral Theory,* Notre Dame, IN: U of Notre Dame Press, 1981. Karl Hermann Schelkle, *Theology of the New Testament: Morality,* trans., William A. Jurgens, Collegeville, Minnesota: Liturgical Press, 1973. A. Michel, "Vertu," *DTC.* T.C. O'Brien, "Virtue," *New Catholic Encyclopedia,* 1967.

JAMES J. WALTER

VISIONS

Clarification of Concepts.

Visions are often referred to as apparitions, e.g., of Christ as the Sacred Heart to St. Margaret Mary or of Mary to St. Bernadette of Lourdes. The visionaries or seers behold an object that is not naturally visible to human beings. An authentic supernatural vision is different from illusions or hallucinations resulting from pathological conditions or diabolical interventions. Such a vision is a charism *(gratia gratis data)* given to a person or group, e.g., the three children to whom Our Lady appeared at Fatima, primarily for the spiritual good of others and not their own sanctification, even though visionaries frequently show signs of growth in holiness through their extraordinary experiences. And so visions are distinct from the divine enlightenment bestowed upon mystics, e.g., Sts. John of the Cross, Teresa of Avila and Catherine of Siena.

According to Sts. Augustine, Thomas Aquinas, John of the Cross, and Teresa of Avila, visions are corporeal, imaginative, and intellectual. Corporeal visions are often called apparitions in which the eyes of the seer perceive an object that would normally be imperceptible to the sense of sight. It may derive from an external reality or a power directly impressing an image upon the sense of seeing. God may cause the phenomenon directly or through the mediation of another, e.g., an angelic power. Imaginative visions result from the supernatural impression of an image or phantasm upon the internal sense apart from the external sense of sight. It may take place during sleep or waking hours when this kind of vision is ordinarily accompanied by ecstasy or rapture. When one receives the charism of an intellectual vision, which is considered the highest type, that person is given a simple intuitive understanding, often of some supernatural truth or divine mystery. God causes this kind of vision without any impressed species in the internal sense of the imagination or the external sense of sight. And, since God alone can directly act upon the human spirit without doing violence to a person's freedom, an intellectual vision takes place without the mediated agency of any creature such as an angel.

Theological and Ecclesial Implications

Although visions or apparitions are also part of public revelation in the divine disclosure of the deposit of faith which concluded with the witness of the apostles to Christ in the church, this article is concerned with those visions that may be connected with private revelation that does not make any substantial addition to that deposit in Tradition. Even after the proper ecclesiastical authorities have approved certain visions or apparitions, e.g., at Lourdes and Fatima, still they are proposed by the church as worthy of "pious belief" and do not become the object of divine Catholic faith. This official approval is the result of a very careful investigation of the alleged apparition. Only five of the marian apparitions have received such approval, namely, Guadalupe (1531), to St. Catherine Laboure in Paris (1830), La Salette (1846), Lourdes (1858), and Fatima (1917). This, however, does not mean that all other alleged apparitions have been disapproved or condemned as inauthentic. Others, besides any that may have been clearly dismissed, can still be deemed as credible, depending upon the evidence.

The most significant criterion of the church in assessing the authenticity of a vision is whether or not the message or private revelation associated with it is faithful to the message of the gospel or public revelation. The messages attributed to the Blessed Mother at her various approved apparitions in one way or another call for prayer and penance which is at the very heart of her Son's gospel. At Lourdes in 1858, just four years following the solemn definiton of the dogma of the Immaculate Conception as a truth revealed by God, Mary identified herself to Bernadette, the visionary, by saying, "I am the Immaculate Conception."

Another very important sign that an apparition may be authentic is the nature of the spiritual effects which the message and experience seem to have upon the seers and those who are attracted to believe in the vision. Of course, the miraculous bodily healing that frequently takes place through devotions at the shrines of the apparitions are indications that they have come from God. But one must look more deeply into the spiritual healing that occurs in those persons who are miraculously cured as well as at the "miracles" of grace among the countless others who are drawn closer to Christ and his church through their pious belief in the apparition and its message.

Regarding the marian apparitions in particular, Vatican II (cf. L.G. 66 and 67) calls us to a balanced attitude towards their place in our devotional life. We should avoid both a vain credulity and a narrow-minded skepticism in such matters as visions or apparitions and private revelations, the messages of which always remain essentially "private" no matter how widespread they become. We are not, therefore, to allow them to draw us away from the central mysteries and practices of our christian faith which would be contrary to any authentic apparition. At the same time, the opposite extreme of a negative attitude towards those who use well the spiritual fruits produced through these private revelations is to be overcome in the church, especially by the ministries of pastors and theologians. Even more, although we may remain devout believers without accepting the authenticity of a particular vision, if we are completely skeptical about the very possibility of such supernatural happenings, then our own faith is suspect. For belief in the possibility of such supernatural happenings is based upon faith in Christianity as a supernatural, historical, and revealed religion. We cannot deny, it seems that God could will to continue freely to make divine self-disclosures for the sake of rendering public revelation more meaningful at any given time in the salvation history of the post-apostolic Pilgrim Church.

See **Revelation, Deposit of Faith**

J. Aumann, "Visions" in *New Catholic Encyclopedia*, vol. 14, p. 717. Thomas Aquinas, S.Th. II-II,

qq. 171-175. K.V. Truhlar, "Visions" in *Encyclopedia of Theology—The Concise Sacramentum Mundi*, Ec., K. Rahner, N.Y.: The Seabury Press, 1975, pp. 1806-1807.

F.M. JELLY, OP

VOCATION

In traditional christian usage, vocation refers to a divine call to undertake a particular activity or embrace a particular "stage of life" on behalf of God or the community. Popularly, the term often became attached more or less exclusively to a calling to priesthood or religious life, although theologians were careful to treat marriage and the single state outside of religious community also as genuine vocations. They also stressed that, prior to a call to a particular state of life, there is a universal vocation to salvation and holiness; since Vatican II, out of sensitivity to ecumenical concerns, some writers have described this universal vocation as a call to "self-actualization," "self-transcendence," "freedom," "openness to others and to God."

Vocation in Scriptures

The OT is replete with the stories of individuals whom God called upon to fulfill the divine plan. God sent Abram out of Ur (Gen 12); sent Moses to Pharaoh (Exod 3); chose Joshua to lead the people into the Promised Land (Josh 1); selected first Saul (1 Sam 8) then David (1 Sam 16) as king. God called Isaiah and Jeremiah to be his prophets; their calls were deemed predestined "from the womb" (Isa 49:1, Jer 1:5). Israel itself was corporately called to be God's covenant partner, to acknowledge him as God and to be God's people (Gen 17, Deut 11).

NT writers describe Jesus as coming to call sinners (Mt 9:13) to repentance and faith (Mk 1:15). He also called particular individuals to discipleship (Mt 10:1; Mk 3:13; 6:7), teaching them specially (Mk

4:33) and bestowing on them authority to imitate his ministry of healing and exoricism(Lk 9:1).

The early church continued to experience certain individuals, notably Paul (Gal 1:15) and Barnabas (Acts 13:2), as divinely called to particular ministries. It also interpreted conversion to Christ as a call (1 Cor 7:17) whereby God joined Christians to his Son (1 Cor 1:9), destined them for peace (1 Cor 7:15), liberty (Gal 5:13), holiness (1 Thess 4:7) and eternal life (1 Tm 6:12), lived out amongst all "the saints" (1 Cor 1:2), so they might share the glory of the Kingdom (1 Thess 2:12). The NT asserts that Christians have been called out of darkness to God's own light (1 Pet 2:9) and so must live lives worthy of their call (Eph 4:1).

Patristic Period

The post-NT church witnessed the transition from a plurality of ministries to a relatively uniform and fixed structure of official ministry. Though the actual process of selecting candidates for such ministry is unclear, the community and its leaders called their *episcopoi* ("He who governs all should be selected by all."—Gregory the Great; "It comes from divine authority that a bishop be chosen in the presence of all the people before the eyes of all, and that he be approved as worthy and fit by public judgment and testimony."—Cyprian); and those chosen had to accept the office freely. Occasionally monks, like Gregory of Nazianzus (330-390), were made bishops by popular acclaim against their will; and Ambrose was only a catechumen when the crowds in Milan made him bishop. Though the selection was the community's task, this selection was understood as an expression of divine call.

At the same time, with Anthony of Egypt (250-356) and more properly with Pachomius (290-346), an intensely ascetical way of life, embracing the "evangelical counsels"—poverty, chastity and obedience—emerged for the laity. Anthony's own religious experience became paradigmatic for the movement: he heard the gospel words ("If you would be perfect, sell what you have, give to the poor ... and come follow me,"—Mk 10:21), determined that these words were addressed specifically to him, and complied. Both this "religious life" and martyrdom grew out of early Christianity's eschatological orientation; with the peace of the church (312), the way of the counsels (particularly virginity) came to be regarded as an unbloody or "white" martyrdom, now continuous and perpetual.

The Fathers generally held that this life of the evangelical counsels was open to all, and could be urged upon all Christians (See Chrysostom, "On Virginity"; Ambrose "Concerning Virgins"; Augustine "On Holy Virginity"). Those aspiring to live the counsels did not need any extraordinary religious experience beyond a desire to follow Christ. Though regarded as a more perfect way of christian life, no individual was morally bound to embrace the counsels (See Basil, "On Virginity"; Chrysostom, "On Virginity"; Cyprian, "On the Habit of Virginity"; Ambrose, "On Widows"). However, once an individual had decided upon this way of life, the Fathers urged as little delay as possible (Basil, *Monastic Constitutions;* Chrysostom, *Homily 27 on Matthew;* Gregory the Great, *Pentecost Homily*) lest temptations or worldly concerns deter the individual from the decision.

Medieval Church

In the patristic era, religious life had been governed by the rules written by Pachomius, Basil, Cassian, and, quintessentially, Benedict. As religious life became more formally organized, the question of vocation increasingly assumed a legal cast. (Indeed the concept of a permanent "state of life" derived from

Roman civil law; a person incurred obligations from which dispensation were required.)

The Gregorian reforms (G. 1025?-1085), and Gratian's twelfth-century organization of canon law raised questions about the nature of the vows and the status of the vowed individual in the church. It was at this time that the distinction between "secular" and "religious" clergy first appeared. Monks, religious clergy and virgins now were seen as forming a common state (von Hertling).

The new vigor of the mendicant orders promoted the practice of, and reflection upon, religious life and the vows. But Scholastic speculation on the christian states of life suffered from its attempt to express patristic spirituality in Aristotelian philosophical categories. Gradually Scholastic theology articulated more clearly the distinction between the life of the counsels, as an *ecclesial* vocation (that is, as having the church as its source), and priesthood, as a *divine* vocation (instituted by Christ) to administer the sacraments. The first mention of the three vows of poverty, chastity and obedience is in the twelfth-century *Rule for the Hermits of St. Augustine*; and it was Innocent III (1202) who termed those vows "essential to monastic life."

St. Thomas Aquinas

For Thomas, the "states" are those ways of christian life within which the individual can realize the "particular perfection" proper to each state. And so each Christian, living in the "state" of supernatural grace, realizes perfection by obeying the command of loving God and neighbor. The individual in the religious life realizes a higher perfection by accepting the counsel to renounce all so as to live for God alone. Episcopacy is also a state of perfection, realized in the pastoral responsibilities bishops undertake. "Hence one is said to be properly in the state of perfection not because he performs a perfect act of charity, but because he has obligated himself forever, and with some solemnity, to those things that pertain to perfection" (S.Th., I-II, 184, a.4).

For Thomas, vocation to religious life had both an external source (scripture, the example of Jesus and the apostles) and an internal one (the impulse of grace). The external call predisposes the individual to hear Christ's words; but that external call is not efficacious without an internal grace or call. This internal grace is only given to those whom God has predestined for the life of the counsels. At the same time, no one is bound under pain of sin to embrace religious life since vows are counsels, not commands.

Luther and Calvin

The Protestant Reformers stressed that the call of God was most particularly answered by performing the duties of ordinary secular life. In place of evangelical counsels, the Reformers sought to inculcate the virtues of business and family life. Calvin declared that "every man's mode of life . . . is a kind of station assigned him by the Lord, that he may not be always driven about at random" (*Institutes* bk III, ch X, sect 6). One is bound to walk in this path as God had determined it. Such an approach raises the importance of all "mundane" activity; but it also curbs ambition and social mobility, for, "free from the impulse of rashness, [the Christian] will not attempt more than his calling justifies, knowing that it is unlawful to overleap the prescribed bounds" (ibid).

Luther reversed the usual Scholastic arrangement of the life of counsels as higher than the life of fulfilling the precepts. Instead, Luther argued, ". . . because God's command is there, even [housework] must be praised as a service of God far surpassing the holiness and asceticism of all monks and nuns. For here there is no command of God. But there God's command is fulfilled, that one should honor father and mother and help in the care of the home" (*Works,* Erlanger ed., vol V, p. 102).

Generally, Luther agrees with Calvin on the sacred value of faithfully performing secular tasks. Since such duties are only vocations in the strict sense if undertaken as genuine service to others, Luther must encounter difficulty in assessing the purity of that internal disposition. Furthermore, Luther's distinction of law and gospel raises the problem of how grace could operate through law in the various secular vocations.

Catholic Reformation

After the Council of Trent, much of the Catholic reformation effort focused on abuses among the clergy and religious. Spiritual writers increasingly attacked what came to be termed the "external vocation theory," which held that the call was general and external and hence requiring neither special internal signs of divine call, nor any serious discernment on the part of the individual. There grew up a universal condemnation of the practice (praised by Aquinas, among others) of sending children to the priesthood as an oblation for parents. Instead these writers, following the lead of St. Alphonsus Liguori, asserted that only those who knew themselves truly called by God should be ordained. This special internal call was now deemed to constitute vocation properly speaking; without it there was no licit ordination. At the same time, a called individual has a grave obligation to respond to such a call; ignoring such a call certainly risked rejecting the graces of God and could imperil one's salvation.

This new theory (later termed "attraction theory") went on to articulate the signs whereby one could detect the presence of such a predestining call to priesthood: sanctity of life, purity of intention, sufficient education and ability to dis-

charge the duties of ministry. Bishops were to be charged with the responsibility of investigating those signs, and declaring if God has called the candidate to priesthood. One final element introduced to the theory was the presence in the soul of a strong and relatively permanent attraction to ordination, admitting of no serious doubt that such was God's will for the individual. Catholic writers continued to stress the voluntary nature of religious life, due to its ecclesial source and its nature as response to counsels rather than obligating precepts.

Lahitton

In 1909, a French canon, Joseph Lahitton rejected this internal attraction theory as too mystical and unverifiable. In particular he claimed that someone could demand ordination on the grounds that he would risk damnation if he failed to follow God's will—as revealed in his attraction to priesthood; and the church would be obliged in justice to ordain him. But, Lahitton objected, no one has a right to ordination. Further, he asked, what of those priests who never felt such an internal call; were they not really ordained?

Lahitton instead maintained that vocation has a material element (the presence of the aptitudes and right intentions the older theory rightly demanded) and a formal element (the call of the ordaining prelate). Thus only those whom a legitimate ecclesial superior calls to priesthood in fact have a vocation. Hence merely having the material element bestows no "right" to ordination; only a hierarchical act of ecclesial authority does that. And such an act bestows valid and licit ordination, without regard to any quasi-mystical attraction or religious experience of locution or internal movement of the Holy Spirit.

A papal commission, under Cardinal Secretary of State Merry del Val investigated Lahitton's book and in 1912 gave it qualified support. It agreed that no one had a right to ordination, and that those validly ordained could be assured that they had thereby received a vocation from God.

Thomistic Revival

Lahitton's objections to the popular theology of vocation forced theologians to reexamine their assumptions about divine call and the role of the church in vocation. Coordinate with a general revival of interest in Thomism, a number of theologians in the 1930's and '40's returned to Thomas to mine anew his approach to vocation. Generally they agree that vocation consists of both the external call of the scriptures and an interior grace by which God moves a particular individual to respond to that call. The question then debated was the nature of this grace: was it efficacious antecedent to the individual's response, or consequent upon one's free acceptance of the call? (Such a discusson in fact was a replay of the debates of the Dominicans and Jesuits of the seventeenth and eighteenth centuries on the relationship of predestination and free will.) Most theologians agreed that church authority discerns and confirms the presence of that grace and the authenticity of the response. These authorities increasingly made use of medical and psychological tools as part of this investigation.

Vatican II

The Second Vatican Council urged religious communities to renew their foundational charisms; but it paid greatest attention not to religious life but to the laity. The council grounded its meditation on the laity in the supreme reality of the nature of christian baptism. It held that all Christians have a vocation to serve the church's mission in the world; and they have this, not by derivation or concession of the hierarchy, nor by particular religious experience, but by virtue of their baptism. The council left behind all

the discussion about the nature of auxiliary grace, in order to assert that vocation was not the province of the few in the life of religious vows or in orders, but the duty of all who belong to Christ.

Personalism

In the aftermath of Vatican II, greater ecumenical sensitivity made spiritual writers aware that their notion of vocation had ignored most of the world. Did God only speak to Christians? If God called to non-Christians, was God's only word to them, "convert—become Christian"? If there is a universal vocation to salvation, how does God address that call to most of humanity? Through the ontological structures of their self-transcendence (Rahner)? Through their own religions (Kung)? If God does not demand that all be christian, then does God demand a particular way of life for any given individual?

Personalism maintains that the traditional notion of the "will of God" or a specific plan for one's life violates human freedom, now seen as the chief characteristic of human life. Rather than having such a plan, God instead ratifies all good choices and works all of them together for the Kingdom. Everyone has a vocation to refer all creation back to God in praise and thanksgiving; but then to embrace one's freedom, live Kingdom values of justice and truth, and God will endorse all that is good, and reshape all that is inadequate, for the coming Kingdom.

Contemporary State of the Question

The present discussion of vocation has frequently been subsumed under the larger question of the nature of ministry: the uniqueness of ordained ministries, their relationship to lay ministries, to religious life, and to the mission of the church. But the general theological presumptions on which that discussion is based is well expressed by the bishops meeting at Puebla in 1979: "According to God's plan, all of us Christians are to find fulfillment as human beings. This is our *human vocation.* We are also to find fulfillment as Christians, living out our baptism and its summons to be holy (communion and cooperation with God), to be active members of the community, and to bear witness to the Kingdom (communion and cooperation with others.) This is our *christian vocation.* Finally, we must discover the concrete vocation (as lay person, consecrated religious, or hierarchical minister) that will enable us to make our specific contribution to the construction of the Kingdom. This is our *specific christian vocation.* In this way we will carry out our evangelizing mission in a full and organic way." (*Evangelization in the Latin American Church: Communion and Participation,* final document of Bishops' Conference at Puebla, Mexico, 1979; #854).

See **Baptism, Laity, Orders and Ordination, Religious Life**

Ludwig von Hertling. "Die Profession der Kleriker und die Entstehung der drei Gelubde," *Zeitschrift fur katholische, Theologie* 56 (1932), p. 173.

PAUL D. HOLLAND, SJ

VOLUNTARISM

The view which, in reference either to God or to human beings, gives priority to the will over the intellect or reason. In God, of course, intellect and will are not distinct, but it makes a difference how one relates them. An exaggerated stress on the divine will makes it idle to attempt to seek the intelligibility of God's work in creation or redemption. Applied to moral theology, voluntarism implies that things are good or bad because commanded or forbidden by God rather than their being commanded or forbidden because they are good or bad. Applied to a theory of law, voluntarism considers laws binding because of the will of the legislator rather than because of their coherence with reason.

See **Freedom, God**

W

WAR

The Catholic tradition on war is a long and complex one, evolving from Augustine to recent statements by John Paul II. Central to this tradition is the presumption which binds all Christians: we should do no harm to our neighbors; how we treat our enemy is the key test of whether we love our neighbor; we should consider the possibility of taking even one human life with the utmost hesitation. The tradition admits, however, that it is possible to move from these presumptions to the idea of a justifiable use of force, provided that certain demands of justice are met. It does so because Catholic theology recognizes that only in the Kingdom of God will peace and justice be fully realized. In history, efforts to pursue both peace and justice can, at times, be in tension, given the reality of sin and the inordinate quest for power or material gain which result from sin. The struggle for justice, which is the foundation of a true peace, may therefore necessitate some restricted use of force in order to achieve an order in which human dignity and human rights may flourish.

Origin of the Just-War Theory

Augustine, keenly aware of the fact and the consequences of sin, was the first to articulate certain principles which came to be part of the "just-war theory" which has evolved in Catholic theology. Augustine saw war as both the result of sin and as a tragic remedy for sin in the life of political societies. War arose from disordered ambitions, but it could also be used in some cases at least to restrain evil and protect the innocent. Faced with an attack on the innocent, the presumption that we do no harm even to our enemy yielded to the command of love and the need to restrain an enemy who would injure the innocent. While the just-war argument has taken several forms in the history of Catholic theology, this Augustinian insight remains its central premise.

Thomas Aquinas, Francisco de Vitoria and Francisco Suarez, among others, made subsequent additions to the just-war theory, as the scope and horror of warfare continued to increase. Their writings emphasize that just-war teaching attempts to prevent war but recognizes that in certain very restricted circumstances, the presumption in favor of peace and against war must be overridden. If war cannot rationally be avoided, the theory seeks to restrict and reduce its horror by providing a set of rigorous conditions which must be met if the decision to go to war is to be morally permissible.

Just-War Criteria

Conditions for the justified taking up of arms (known as *jus ad bellum* criteria) require a just cause, declaration of war by competent authority, right intention which seeks the restoration of peace, the exhaustion of all peaceful alternatives, the probability of success and an assessment of proportionality, that is, a decision that the good expected by taking up arms outweighs the damages to be inflicted and the costs incurred by war.

Just-war teaching also provides conditions which must be met during combat. These *jus in bello* criteria include the principles of discrimination and proportionality. Discrimination protects the immunity of noncombatants from direct military attack by restricting direct targeting to combatants, military installations and factories whose products are directly related to the war effort. The *jus in bello* principle of proportionality demands an assessment of the good and evil consequences which can reasonably be foreseen as resulting from specific actions in warfare.

Twentieth-Century Developments

Two important developments in the twentieth century regarding Catholic teaching on war are Pius XII's restriction of "just cause" to self-defense (1944), thereby removing the right to punish an offense and the right to recover something as justifiable reasons for going to war, and the treatment of modern war as a "question of special urgency" at Vatican II. The Council presented nine key points in its teaching on war which remain crucial for all subsequent Catholic teaching: (1) the reaffirmation of the traditional right of a nation to engage in legitimate defense once every means of peaceful settlement has been exhausted; (2) the reaffirmation of the role of legitimate authority to protect the welfare of the people entrusted to its care, coupled with the exhortation that authority give awesome thought to its responsibility before God and the human race; (3) the recognition that every military and political use of war potential is not necessarily just and that there can be unjust conduct in war; (4) the outright condemnation of total warfare; (5) the unequivocal and unhesitating condemnation of "any act of war aimed indiscriminately at the destruction of cities or of extensive areas along with the population as a crime against God and the human community"; (6) the realization that acts of war involving weapons capable of "massive and indiscriminate destruction" far exceed the bounds of legitimate defense; (7) the recognition of the right to conscientious objection against certain unjust actions within war; (8) the recognition of nonviolence as a legitimate Catholic stance; (9) the call to undertake an evaluation of war with an entirely new attitude, given the destructive capacity of modern warfare. While the Council does not explicitly use the just-war theory, the logic of that construct clearly underlies its teaching.

Recent Papal Teaching

Since the Council, Popes Paul VI and John Paul II have emphasized the horror of modern warfare, especially with the development of ever more sophisticated atomic, biological, and chemical weapons. The price of war which is paid in human lives, in suffering, in the devastation of the social fabric, in the loss of necessary tranquility, and in the growth of mistrust and hatred, necessitate eradicating the roots of war, the deepest of which lie within the human heart. A conversion of hearts and attitudes is essential if humanity is to eliminate both a greed which fosters aggression and unjust conditions which drive people to take up arms. Postconciliar papal teaching also clearly condemns the arms race, highlights the economic impact of war, and calls for the development of new structures of international government which will adjudicate disputes before they erupt into war.

Despite this emphasis on the enormous physical and psychological damage which war can produce, the papal teaching continues, nevertheless, to recognize that war has not been rooted out of human affairs so long as its danger remains and no competent and sufficiently powerful authority at the international level exists. Catholic theology, therefore, continues to recognize that peoples have a right and even a duty to protect their existence and freedom against aggression and that, at times, this will necessitate the use of even deadly force. Papal teaching has also refrained from condemning all uses of atomic, biological, and chemical weapons as intrinsically evil, although the thrust of pontifical statements is clearly a plea for no use of these weapons which differ so qualitatively from conventional arms.

Additional Developments in Catholic Theology

The Council's wake has also witnessed pastoral letters and statements by several national episcopal conferences on the topic of modern war, especially in light of the growing nuclear arsenal. Catholic bishops in Austria, Belgium, East Germany, France, Great Britain, Hungary, Ireland, Japan, the Netherlands, Scotland, the United States, and West Germany have addressed this issue—a number which testifies not only to the Council's decision to strengthen the role of regional and national bishops' conferences, but also to a growing sense of responsibility and concern for the safety of the human community on the part of the bishops. While these various letters and statements condemn certain uses of nuclear weapons, and, in some cases, press beyond conciliar and papal teaching, (for example, when the United States' bishops condemn first use of nuclear weapons), none revoke the traditional right of a nation to defend itself against aggression.

The debate among scholars concerning the justified use of nuclear weapons continues, although there appears to be a growing conviction among American Catholic theorists that, on the basis of just-war criteria, any use of nuclear weapons is morally irresponsible (Charles Curran, Judith Dwyer, J. Bryan Hehir, David Hollenbach, Richard A. McCormick, Francis X. Winters). There is also a strong consensus that insurgency, counter-insurgency and terrorist warfare warrant more sustained, scholarly analysis.

Conclusion

Catholic teaching on warfare captures the tension of human existence: we already live in the grace of the Kingdom of God, but this kingdom is not yet fully realized. The Christian therefore lives "between the times" in an already present but not yet fully realized Kingdom. Short of the fullness of this Kingdom, a true peace, which is the fruit of justice, remains possible but neither permanent nor total.

See **Pacifism, Peace**

James T. Johnson, *Ideology, Reason, and the Limitation of War*, Princeton: Princeton U Press, 1975; *Just War Tradition and the Limitation of War*, Princeton: Princeton U Press, 1981; *Can Modern War Be Just?*, New Haven: Yale U Press, 1984. Leroy Brandt Walters, "Five Classic Just-War Theories: A Study in the Thought of Thomas Aquinas, Vitoria, Suarez, Gentilii, and Grotius," (Ph.D. dissertation, Yale U, 1971. Pius XII, "Christmas Message 1944," *Acta Apostolicae Sedis* 37 (1945): 18. "The Church in the Modern World," (G.S.), Joseph Gremillion, Ed., *The Gospel of Peace and Justice: Catholic Social Teaching Since Pope John*, Maryknoll: Orbis Book, 1976. Judith A. Dwyer, Ed., *Questions of Special Urgency: The Church in the Modern World Two Decades After Vatican II*, Washington, D.C.: Georgetown U Press, 1986. Agostino Casaroli, "The Vatican's Position on Issues of War and Peace," *Origins* 13, no. 26 (December 8, 1983): pp. 433-40. National Conference of Catholic Bishops (U.S.A.), *The Challenge of Peace: God's Promise and Our Response*, Washington, D.C.: United States Catholic Conference, 1983. Judith A. Dwyer, Ed., *The Catholic Bishops and Nuclear War: A Critique and Analysis of the Challenge of Peace*, Washington, D.C.: Georgetown U Press, 1984. James V. Schall, S.J., Ed., *Out of Justice, Peace*, (Joint Pastoral Letter of the West German Bishops) *Winning the Peace* (Joint Pastoral Letter of the French Bishops), San Francisco: Ignatius Press, 1984. Mark Heirman, "Bishops' Conferences on War and Peace in 1983," *Cross Currents* 33 (Fall, 1983): pp. 275-88.

JUDITH A. DWYER, SSJ

WORD OF GOD

Biblical and theological statements about the word of God begin from the observation that this word is not simply external utterance or solely intellectual discourse, but the efficacious self-communication of God to the world and to humanity. The Hebrew word *dābār* of the OT means not only "spoken word," but also "event, affair, act." The word contains the power and dynamism of God's creative function (Gen 1; Ps 33:6). The word also conserves creation (Ps 147:15, 18; Job 38:34; 39:27). God's word also connotes his redemptive activity, as he "speaks" to each of the patriarchs to prepare a people, as he speaks "mouth to mouth" with Moses to form that people of the covenant (Num 12:8; cf. Sir 45:5), and as he gives his "ten words" (decalogue) as commandments for ethical guidance (Exod 20:1). In this context the word of God is another expression for revelation, not as abstract information, but as a dynamic encounter.

With the prophets the word of God becomes central, calling the prophets (Amos 3:8; Isa 40:6-8), transforming them (Jer 20:7-9; Ezek 2:8—3:3), and acting through them so that their words bear the power to achieve what they speak (Jer 1:9-10). In this context, the word of God as revelation becomes associated with preaching as the vehicle for that encounter. This enduring power of the word of God giving substance to the preaching of the prophet is what Second Isaiah calls "the good tidings" or "gospel" (40:9). Without being personified, the word of God takes on quasi-substantial dimension as if it existed independently (Isa 55:10-11). In fact the definitive statement of radical monotheism by Second Isaiah is made possible because God's word is the only word which is living and powerful enough to affect history (45:21).

In the last stages of OT history the word of God became associated with other terms that were indeed personifications. Wisdom is attributed divine roles, being with God at creation (Prov 8:22-31) and achieving the work of revelation and redemption in history (Wis 10-12), and this wisdom "came forth from the mouth of the Most High" (Sir 24:3) just as God's "all-powerful word leaped from heaven" (Wis 18:15). Sirach 24:23-25 indicates what became prevalent in later rabbinic writings, the identification of wisdom with the law, which is itself personified, and which is also paralleled with the word of God (Isa 2:3).

In the NT the qualities of the word of God as living and effective are maintained, but they are deepened and focused on the person of Jesus himself. The word is related to Jesus as he extends the prophetic vocation in his own life (Mt 12:41; Mk 6:4). His proclamation is often referred to as the word of God (Lk 5:1). His preaching is seen as powerful and efficacious, often translated into signs and wonders (Mt 8:16), and accompanied by the Spirit who enables the teaching of Jesus to now become the "good news" (Lk 4:18). However, the fullest statement of the NT on the word of God comes with the deepening of the process of personification and the appreciation of Jesus as the very word of God incarnate (Jn 1:14). John's use of the Greek term *logos* draws more from the Hebrew *dābār* than it does from the Hellenistic philosophical understanding of the term as intellectual abstraction. Jesus is "word of life" and the dynamic self-disclosure of God is most fully experienced in what "we have seen with our eyes" and "touched with our hands," the human reality of Jesus (1 Jn 1:1).

Furthermore, this Jesus as word of God incarnate is risen and present. The "good news" is no longer the preaching *of* Jesus but the preaching *about* Jesus, and, indeed, the preaching which renders Jesus present, creating, revealing and redeeming (Heb 1:1). Thus, the presence of Jesus as Lord gives rise to the church in which a principal function is proclamation "in words not taught by human wisdom but taught by the Spirit" (1 Cor 2:13). Christian preaching is a living and effective power "able to save souls" (Jas 1:21), an imperishable seed of new life which abides (1 Pet 1:23). All of later theology maintains the relationship of God's word to the word preached in the church, but as the NT era drew to a completion, the word of God came to be given special prominence as the written word. The "good news" came to be seen in the written works of the four evangelists and in the Bible as a whole.

The era of the Fathers of the Church shows their concern to reaffirm the dynamic power of the word of God and the relationship of preaching to the Bible and to the developing theology of sacraments and ministry, so that all these elements render Jesus the word of God active in his church. The *Didache* reminds its readers: "Where the Lordship (of God) is proclaimed, the Lord is present" (4:1). Augustine links preaching to the Bible: "A man speaks more or less wisely in proportion as he has made more or less progress in the Holy Scriptures" (*De Doctrina Christiana* 4:5). Caesarius of Arles declared that "the word of God is not to be treated as inferior to the body of Christ" (*Sermon* 78:2). For the Fathers, in fact, liturgy becomes the fitting place where Jesus as the word of God is fully encountered, first in the scriptural flesh and blood of the *logos* and then in celebration of that word in the bread and wine of the eucharist.

Succeeding theology through to the Middle Ages, while not losing sight of the efficacy of the preaching of the word of God, nevertheless devoted more and more emphasis to the sacramental dimensions of the church. Also of gradual develop-

ment during this long period of theology was another concern which had roots in the apostolic and patristic churches, namely the discernment of the truth content of the word of God and the maintenance of orthodoxy in the face of an expanding church and the threat of heresies. This was accompanied by the evolution of a specific teaching ministry. While these developments were not originally incompatible with the appreciation of the word of God as living and efficacious, they did pose the threat of reducing that word simply to intellectual concepts or to doctrine about God rather than God's self-disclosure.

The delicate weave of all these elements that characterized scholastic theology at its height came unraveled in the next centuries. The overemphasis that grew on sacraments and on philosophical systematization of doctrine led the Protestant Reformers with some variation to develop the principle of "Scripture alone" as source of the word of God, and to attack the teaching authority of a hierarchy as an obstacle to the authentic word of God. The Council of Trent concerned itself with a defense of sacramental theology and also insisted that the truth of the gospel is found in written books and in unwritten traditions. While Trent itself left open the relationship between scriptures and tradition, subsequent Catholic theology treated tradition as if it were a second source independent of scripture. The centuries after the Reformation and Trent were thus centuries of polarization, with Protestants stressing the preaching of the word of God, especially from its biblical roots and especially with its interior power within the individual, and Roman Catholics maintaining the conceptual and doctrinal dimensions of the word of God and stressing tradition, a teaching authority and sacraments over the biblical source of the word.

Since Vatican II the polarization between Protestants and Catholics has lessened. The council promulgated a document on revelation entitled *Dei Verbum* ("The Word of God"), returning to the biblical presentation of the word of God as God's self-disclosure, culminating in Jesus himself, and experienced in the proclamation of the word by the Church. It thus moved Catholicism away from its overemphasis on the word of God as intellectual doctrine. It also rejected the notion of scripture and tradition as two separate sources of the word of God, but saw tradition rather as the faith of the living church which surrounds, preserves and transmits the scriptures and makes them come alive. The council refined its perception of a teaching authority; such ministers do not simply parrot the biblical text, but their teaching must be consistent with what is found in the written text. *Dei Verbum* also returned to the early church teaching that the best proclamation of the word of God is found in liturgy. It thus restored prominence to the preaching of the word while not diminishing sacramental theology.

Current theology is still striving to adequately explain the interrelationship between these varied elements that constitute church and that enable it to proclaim the word of God in every age. In addition, theology is challenged by a further question which actually had roots in the Age of Enlightenment. This age, with its strong emphasis on science and reason, posed the question of how the word of God could exist in any human words. Both recent Protestant and Catholic responses to this question have maintained the transcendence of God's word over human words, though some (e.g., Tillich and Rahner) have been more optimistic about the capacity of the human to be graced by the divine, while others (e.g., Barth) see God's word as judgment on any human word. Finally, concern to maintain the transcendence of God's word has had the healthy effect of emphasizing development of doctrine and the appreciation of hermeneutical presuppositions related to spoken and written human words, but has also had the unhealthy effect of a rising fundamentalism which equates the human words of the Bible with the transcendent word of God.

See **Development of Doctrine, Fundamentalism, Hermeneutics, Magisterium, Revelation, Tradition, Truth**

Dei Verbum, in *The Documents of Vatican II,* Ed., Walter M. Abbott, S.J., New York/London: Herder and Herder/Geoffrey Chapman, 1966, pp. 111-128. Frederick E. Crowe, S.J., *Theology of the Christian Word,* New York: Paulist Press, 1978. Raymond E. Brown, "The Human Word of the Almighty God," *The Critical Meaning of the Bible,* New York/London: Paulist Press/Geoffrey Chapman, 1981, pp. 1-22.

ANTHONY J. TAMBASCO

WORK

1. Introduction

Theology must consider work in light of creation, incarnation, sin, redemption and eschatology, and not, as often happens, merely in terms of one or other of these mysteries. It must understand the social, historical and economic factors that make work so elevating or degrading. Difficulties begin immediately, however, because there is no accepted definition of work. Language is fluid: e.g., liturgy is the "work of the people," and we "work on our golf game" and "play a managerial role."

The primary analogue of work is agrarian-artisan activity: using bodily energy to change the physical world in order to provide for basic needs. Contemporary work, however, also includes such variations as intellectual research and the provision of social services. A brief look at our tradition will show that the theology of work has evolved and continues to do so.

2. The Tradition

As we might expect, the Bible has no one view of work. Work includes God's activity in creation and the slave's labor in the fields. The same word is used for effort, toil, service and worship. Work is acknowledged and affirmed in both Testaments, but also criticized.

a. Hebrew Scriptures.

The earth is the Lord's. Like a manual laborer, God "makes," "forms," "builds" and "plants"; and God has to "rest" from this work (Gen 2:2ff). After the seventh day, God does not stop working (Isa 5:12; Ps 28:5). "The firmament proclaims God's handiwork" (Ps 19:2). While theologians have contrasted this "anthropomorphic" picture to the power of God's word (Gen 1:3ff; Ps 33:6), such theological bias is gradually changing.

In the main, human work is taken for granted as merely a normal human activity. Saul plowed, David was a shepherd, and the rabbis were gainfully employed. The decalogue allows six days of work, but commands a day free from work for humans and their animals (Exod 20:8-11). And while manual work deadens the mind, it maintains God's handiwork and is necessary for the community (Sir 38:1-9, 24-34). God inspires the temple builder and instructs the farmer (Exod 35:20—36:2; Isa 28:23-29). In medicine "God's creative work continues without cease" (Sir 38:1-9).

The Hebrew evaluation of work is mixed. The "image of God" has dominion over creation (Sir 17:3f; Ps 8:7), but idols are fashioned by human crafts (Isa 44:9ff). By God's blessing, honest toil yields abundant fruit and leads to wealth, while idleness produces disgraceful poverty (Pss 65, 127, 128; Isa 65:20-23; Deut 28:11f; Prov 10:4f, 12:11). "To cultivate and care for" the garden is the task given by God before the Fall, and hence work should not be understood as a punishment for sin (Gen 2:15). After the Fall, however, work is laid under a curse which has cosmic as well as human bearing: the world will not yield, and human toil is marked by sweat (Gen 3:17-19; 4:12).

b. New Testament.

In the gospels, ordinary work is usually mentioned only in illustrations. Some exegetes hold that the life and the sayings of Jesus undercut the value of work. Though subsequent tradition has made much of Jesus' work as an artisan or carpenter, only Mark 6:3 mentions it, and there it is part of an attack that keeps Jesus from working miracles. Jesus is no where pictured as actually doing manual labor, but rather as an itinerant preacher. John stresses Jesus' work, but that work is the gospel: "My Father works even until now, and I work" (Jn 5:17). Jesus exhorts his followers to "work not for perishable food," since only the bread which comes down from heaven" gives life (Jn 6).

The disciples leave their work to fish for human beings. Trust in God is contrasted with worrying about livelihood (Mt 6:19-34; Lk 12:13-41). Doing the work of God is to have faith (Jn 6:29). We are "co-workers with God" who plants and builds the faith of the community, and we are co-workers of one another in that same activity (1 Cor 3:5ff; Rom 16:3-12; Col 1:28f; Mk 16:20). The NT found no special religious significance in the mundane tasks of life. Unlike our current usage, the NT idea of vocation does not refer to our earthly occupations.

Subsequent centuries commonly cited Paul's example, his judgments, and his motivation for work: first, Paul himself continued to work; second, Paul rebuked those whose expectation of an imminent Parousia led to idleness: no work, no eat; third, Paul's motives for his own work were independence and almsgiving, and he encouraged others to work because then they will mind their own business, avoid trouble, and keep a quiet spirit (1 Thess 2 9; 4:11f; 2 Thess 3:7-12;

Eph 4:28).

The Epistles assume that ordinary work is simply part of life, and they do not see any intrinsic worth in manual labor. The "house rules," oriented to domestic slaves, provide both commonplace injunctions to be faithful and obedient to one's superiors as well as christian counsel to suffer injustice. These virtues are transformed by doing all willingly as imitators and "slaves of Christ" (Eph 6:5-9; Col 3:17-25; 1 Pet 2:18-24). Patience and indifference in work are fitting because this world will be utterly consumed in the fiery Coming of Christ (2 Pet 3:10-13; 1 Cor 7:29-31).

c. Post-Biblical Tradition. A crucial difference between the Greek and Latin "Fathers" can be roughly indicated. For the former, the curse of the Fall and the subsequent redemption include all of creation. The Latin theologians, however, tend to restrict the Fall and redemption to rational beings, and therefore the perfection of the universe is not directly part of salvation. As a consequence, Western asceticism often stressed flight from the world; work had value only through "good intentions" or insofar as it contributed to spiritual development. By contrast, the Greek tradition held that being the "image of God" implies participating in God's action to restore the universe itself—a theme resumed in recent church documents.

None of the early teachers of the church developed a systematic treatise on work. They were interested, not in the good produced nor in self-realization through work, but chiefly in the virtues that accompany work. Through work, persons 1) become self-sufficient, and thus are no burden to others; 2) avoid idleness, the devil's workshop; 3) imitate Christ and Paul; 4) chastise the flesh; 5) gain humility and simplicity; 6) practice obedience and submission; 7) earn enough to help the needy; 8) exercise self-dis-

cipline; 9) do penance; 10) experience a leveling equality.

Overall, the danger of wealth, possessions and preoccupation with this world were clearer to the tradition than any fulfillment in working or any benefits of a variety of goods. The monastic movement, however, counteracted a Greco-Roman association of work with slavery by showing that labor could freely be performed. The monks modeled a balanced life of manual labor, intellectual life, and prayer.

The Middle Ages saw the rise of trade and the guilds, and the nature of work began rapidly to change. A strong sense of an earthly common good prevailed; God was thought to fit an individual for a specific task needed by the community. At the same time, living conditions for many, if not most people were horrible, and the working family suffered considerably. The theology of work often appealed to trust in providence, christian resignation, and *theologia crucis*.

d. Modern Era. In the West, Luther redirected theology by shifting the idea of vocation from the monastery to the marketplace. Calvinism inspired a new form of inner worldly asceticism, which developed into the Protestant work ethic. Wesley preached, "Gain all you can; save all you can; give all you can." This new ethos emphasized thrift and the rewards of hard work as a sign of divine favor; and, though unintended by the reformers, eventually there ensued a spirit of unrestricted acquisition for its own sake.

The emergence of mechanized industry disrupted the life of the worker. Human work became regulated by the tempo of the machine, by clock time, and by the control of the manager. No longer were human rhythms determinative. Social theorists began to analyze this new world of work. Adam Smith noted that as work became repetitious, it turned human beings into mindless automatons. Karl

Marx protested that the worker's value had become merely a manufacturing cost, no different from raw materials and machines. Profit from the labor of the many ended up as private property of a few, rather than contributing to everyone's life.

e. *Social Encyclicals.* To address these changes in labor, the social encyclicals were written. Leo XIII's *Rerum Novarum* (1891) is the foundational document. Recognizing that the lot of the working class is often "a yoke little better than slavery," it proposes that the common good requires a partnership between unequal workers and management (1, 6, 26, 28). For Leo, in our exile on earth, work has value both for securing our basic needs and as a "compulsory and painful expiation of his sin" (9, 27, 33, 62).

Pius XI's *Quadragesimo Anno* (1931) describes work as the natural activity of applying our forces to nature for developing our powers. It insists that "labor cannot be bought and sold like any piece of merchandise" (pp. 28, 38, 41). Pius developed the principle of subsidiarity, and demanded the recognition of the social and individual nature of work (pp. 35, 40). According to John XXIII's *Mater et Magistra* (1961), work is endowed with dignity and is "an expression of the human person" wherein persons perfect themselves and engage in "a true human fellowship." The principle of subsidiarity encourages freedom and responsibility in the work place (18, 51-55, 81-83, 91-92, 145, 256).

Gaudium et Spes initiates a massive change in the theology of work. It revives the biblical notion that God works, and notes that through their work Christians are unfolding the Creator's own work. Human labor, which includes services, is primary in economic life. Work humanizes and orders nature, and it joins workers in service and charity. Workers are partners in perfecting God's creation; indeed, work associates them with the redemptive work of Christ who gives work its eminent dignity. Work must suit the needs of workers, enabling them to develop themselves and to participate actively in running an enterprise (34, 67-68).

For Paul VI's *Populorum Progressio* (1967), development cannot be limited to economic growth, and every life is a vocation of self-fulfillment. Because of selfishness in work and a lack of solidarity, "The world is sick." Still work is "willed and blessed by God," and through it we complete God's work. Indeed "everyone who works is a creator," and labor is "the mission of sharing in the creation of the supernatural world" (14-15, 27-28, 66). John Paul II's *Laborem Exercens* (1981) strongly emphasizes the "self-realization" or subjective dimension of work. Work has intrinsic significance beyond anything it produces. "By means of work man participates in the activity of God" and thus imitates "Christ, the Man of Work." Moreover, "Man in a way collaborates with the Son of God for the redemption of humanity" (26-27).

3. Contemporary Theology of Work

Attempts at a systematic theology of work are relatively new. Modern economic activity is exceedingly varied and complex, and a theology of work must strive to transcend partial images of work—neither the traditional picture of agriculture and handicrafts nor the modern images of creative technology suffice. Furthermore, theology must constantly appreciate how sinfulness can and does pervert all that is good.

a. *Worldly Spirituality.* Most of us spend a large part of our day at work. But, as Teilhard observed, Western spirituality too readily ignored the intrinsic meaning of our work. Grace today must be understood in its earthly forms; we are not angels passing time in a foreign land. God invites us to enter into God's development of the material universe of which we are a part. We can cooperate with the God who works as creator, sustainer, judge, redeemer, etc. Thus "offering up the day" is not sufficient; effective engagement in the world is also invited and required by God. God's love has an objective focus, namely, perfection of creation. The world itself is consecrated through a faith-filled transformation of the world.

The sanctification of the world is achieved by forming it within Christ's covenantal love. "All things have been created through and unto Him" (Col 1:16). We are to do the works that Jesus did, even greater than these (Jn 14:10-12; 15:5). We are not merely stewards working for an absent landlord. Our God is working (in God's transcendent, primary-cause fashion), and inviting us to join in that work. In personalist terms, we share or participate in God's action.

b. Self-Realization. Along with the religious vision of work as cooperating with God, the most fundamental difference between a modern theology of work and its predecessors is the view that work can be a form of self-realization. Work is central to our *existence,* not peripheral to it. That is, work is *one* of the ways that we stand out from nature and realize our humanity. Work is not merely a means to subsistence. It helps constitute the human, and thus is on a par with contemplation.

What we do forms who we are, including our basic beliefs and attitudes. Our human nature is only a rough sketch, a beginning of full person that has to flesh itself out through activity. Work contributes to the development and maturation of our talents. Artists not only express their inchoate intuitions through their activity; they also develop their abilities in realizing those intuitions. Similarly, through work we may realize potentials that otherwise would go undeveloped. Like praying or thinking,

working is itself valuable, over and above its product. Because work can be a form of self-realization, unemployment can be dehumanizing.

Work, of course, is not fully humanizing, and almost every form of work threatens to alienate some human capacities. Even when it is challenging, work usually develops only some human potentials. Moreover, work today typically is motivated by a functional and monetary attitude, and these quickly steal from the intrinsic value of work. Fortunately, since the work mindset is only a semi-autonomous region of the personality, a worker can often endure alienated work without becoming wholly dehumanized.

Ascetical discussion of the virtues that work promotes should reckon with the fact that different kinds of work promote different virtues. Some work is free from close supervision, has substantial content and complexity, is non-routinized, provides for self-development and expression, and involves interaction and cooperation with others. Thus it promotes the personal virtues of independence, responsibility, and interpersonal sensitivities. By contrast, "working class" jobs are often beyond the worker's control and even understanding, and the work is supervised, routine, and relatively mindless. For these workers, there is little scope for personal growth, initiative, imagination and interpersonal connections; rather this kind of work promotes virtues such as obedience, attention to external order, and endurance. Thus when the self-developmental aspects of work are praised, one should carefully note which virtues are being instilled. Often the virtues of work affirmed by the rich or middle class are impossible to the poor.

c. Products and Services. Human beings have a drive for an intensity and a fullness of life that, at least in its more spiritual forms, is inexhaustible. This drive begets a vast and complex array of spiritual and material goods. Its "object" may be an artistic idea, a plot of soil, or the output of a machine. Its "object" may also be a service—some assistance we offer to others. Work is an activity devoted to perfecting reality, to maintaining it, or to keeping it from getting worse.

Without denying the primacy of the worker, it can be said that these goods have a value beyond that of the worker who produces them. An object produced for selfish reasons or through alienating work still has value in itself and for persons. In the usual case, we work to fulfill some human need, beginning with the basic life-needs and extending almost indefinitely. The paradox is that as we satisfy our needs with ever more goods, we create still more needs to be satisfied. This crescendo should not be hastily condemned. To be sure, created goods often are more a distraction than an invitation to union with God and neighbor. But a proper christian critique of "materialism" and "consumerism" should not obscure the challenge to make the world responsive to remarkably diverse persons and revelatory of God's richness and largess. In any case, those who have an abundance of available goods should be wary of preaching the virtues of simplicity to the poor.

d. Social Existence. Civilization is the gradual sedimentation of human creativity in time and space. Our work develops social existence beyond the provision of basic goods. The noblest social goal of work is to provide the basis for a culture in which all can realize their fullest human potential. Socialism has more clearly than capitalism preserved the medieval insight that work is a social activity. Workers enter an historical process of giving and taking, producing and consuming the community's goods. They realize their social nature not only through personal encounters, but also through weaving the social fabric out of these human activities and products. In the contemporary world, one's neighbor is not just the stranger one meets, but all who live in the global village. Thus charity must become political, effectively using the wealth and power that derive from work to aid the unmet stranger. If the first consideration about work is the worker, the second is what it does to and for and with humanity.

e. Finitude. Through work, we are forced to face our finitude. Not only must we try to subdue reality, but we also must learn to "let it be." Recent theologies of work have often stressed masculine control to the neglect of a "feminine" emphasis on nurturance and relationships. The world has its own worth and dynamisms which resist our control. Work's promise of power, appropriation, and personal satisfaction needs to be complemented with the dynamics of receptivity, belonging, care, and self-giving.

All of us experience futility in our work when our projects end in some failure. Much work merely repairs the deterioration which comes from nature's law of entropy and from human use and abuse. Much work is activity that we *have* to do in order to survive. Further, widely varying talents and social factors make it hard for many workers to believe they are making any "significant contribution."

Responding to the finitude and failures of our earthly work, the ascetical tradition concentrated on the interior attitude of the worker. Work can point up the fragility of this world's vanity, and it can stem the lust for power. This tradition properly grasped that work's ultimate value is that it flows from us and fits us for God's Kingdom. Failure in work reminds us that we neither are nor need try to be God. The failures and inevitable disappointments involved in work serve to clear a space for looking to the transcendent dimensions of our graced life.

The ascetical perspective emphasized that the work of the janitor may be as good or better than that of the president, since what we do is not as important as how, religiously, we do it. Though this ascetical view often did not grasp either that work can be meaningful in itself or that it can be socially enriching, it did and does speak to our finitude.

f. Redemptive and Penitential. Since the 1950's, theologians have been developing a positive view of work. They recognized that it is hard to see work as a kind of penance for sin when it is satisfying, successful, challenging, self-expressive, psychologically maturing, and communally engaging. On the other hand, it is hard to see work as either cooperating with God or as self-fulfilling when in fact it is deadeningly dull and painful. For many of us, work is exhausting toil done out of necessity. For many of us, it is painfully clear that the earth is cursed and we earn our bread by the sweat of our brow.

Hence the penitential view of work has been and can continue to be part of the theology of work. Work may be seen as a participation with Christ in his entrance into and crucifixion by a flawed world (Rom 5:17-19; Lk 9:23; L.E. 27). The ascetical tradition points out that the more difficult or painful or monotonous a work is, the more it may force us to focus on "higher things" or to submit to a fitting discipline or penance. Still, liberation theology reminds us not to yield to suffering too quickly. Faith leads to a justice which strives to overcome the alienating material and social structures of the world.

g. Eschatological Ambivalence. A theology of work needs the critique of the eschaton. Work's forms range from the enormously uplifting to the utterly dehumanizing, from constraining necessity to joyful expansiveness. Work can be so engaging as to make people forget God,

or so estranging as to have the same effect. All worldly tasks are too small for the human spirit, yet many jobs can become idols demanding the sacrifice of persons.

Advocates for theologies of work modeled on either creation or the cross must carefully consider the effects of these views. Creation-centered theologies of work often overlook or minimize real toil, especially the spirit-draining toil of the many. On the other hand, these theologies set forth a positive standard for reforming that toil. A cross-oriented theology of work often ignores human and worldly fulfillments, and it may discourage reform of working conditions. On the other hand, it reminds us that this world is not and never will be heaven; it both enables those who endure miserable work and requires those who enjoy fulfilling work to look beyond their work: work is not *the* meaning of life.

An eschatological view points up the religious ambiguity of work. Without some continuity between this world and the next, our efforts to develop ourselves and the world would be intrinsically pointless. On the other hand, this world is not the Kingdom. Going beyond Vatican II's ambiguous solution to this problem (G.S. 39), John Paul II encourages a Christian to "know the place that his work has not only in earthly progress but also in the development of the kingdom of God" (L.E. 27). Here is a modern version of Paul's vision of recapitulation. Christ recapitulates the whole of evolving reality in his mystical body. The travail of the whole of creation is brought together in Christ (Rom 8:18-21; Col 1:15-20).

See **Anthropology, Christian; Economics**

Goeran Agrell, *Work, Toil and Sustenance,* Lund: Verbum, 1976. Gregory Baum, Ed., *Work and Religion,* New York: Seabury 1980. Richard Gillett, *The Human Enterprise,* Kansas City: Leaven Press, 1985. Gideon Gossen, *The Theology of Work,* Dublin: Mercier, 1974. Edwin Kaiser, *Theology of*

Work, Westminster, MD: Newman, 1966. Alan Richardson, *The Biblical Doctrine of Work,* London: SCM, 1963. Dorothee Soelle, *To Work and To Love,* Philadelphia: Fortress, 1986.

EDWARD COLLINS VACEK, SJ

WORLD

See **Creation**

WORSHIP

Worship is a complex phenomenon which is difficult to capture within a definition. It has been described as a response of adoration evoked in one who has encountered the presence of God. It has also been depicted as the grateful rejoicing of those who have experienced God's action in their lives. At times it has been equated with the formal services or rites of a particular religion, and it has also been set out as a way of life.

The notion of worship as expression is basic to all of these descriptions. Worship expresses and mediates the divine-human relationship. Underlying any understanding of worship is a prior understanding of God and human subjectivity. The possibility of worship implies both human subjects who desire a relationship with God and a God who fulfills that desire. Ultimately, whatever particular expressions it may take, worship is the outcome of God's gracious self-gift.

Christian worship has its foundation in Jesus Christ, the one in whom we find both God's self-disclosure and a paradigm for a life of worship. Persons who are brought into relationship with God through Jesus Christ are also made participants in Christ's worship because they share in his life. *Koinōnia* is the term used in the NT to denote the shared life which is constitutive of christian identity and which makes christian worship possible. It is a gift received by all those who are baptized into the christian community.

The gift of *koinōnia* is one which calls forth a response. The *koinōnia* received must become one which is lived, one which is manifested in a variety of ways. From the earliest days of the church, participating in the Lord's Supper was recognized as a manifestation and intensification of the community's shared life in Christ (1 Cor 10:16-17). Paul made it clear to the Corinthians that participating in the life of their Lord and authentic remembering of his life and death in the Lord's Supper had to be accompanied by sharing in the attitude of self-giving which had dominated his life. He called upon various christian communities to express their *koinōnia* by contributing to a common fund for the poor of Jerusalem (Rom 15:25-27). Christian worship is not to be self-serving or individualistic. The gifts of all are to be placed in the service of building up the church (1 Cor 14:26-27).

Liturgy is the formal public worship of christian assemblies. It is a form of ecclesial ritual action in which Christians gather to remember, express, and reappropriate their identity as co-worshippers with Christ. Christian liturgical worship emerged from within the traditions of Jewish worship but finds its particular identity from its rootedness in the paschal mystery. This mystery provides a focus for the rhythm of the church's feasts and seasons and has a central place in the celebration of the sacraments and the liturgy of the hours.

To say that liturgical worship is a form of ecclesial action is to emphasize the assembly's role as subject of the liturgy because of its union with Christ, the ultimate subject. As *Sacrosanctum Concilium* states: "In the liturgy the whole public worship is performed by the Mystical Body of Jesus Christ, that is, by the Head and his members" (#7). Although each worshipping assembly is bound in *koinōnia* with all the other assemblies which constitute the church, liturgy is actually performed by local assemblies gathered in particular places. Therefore, the historical, social, and cultural context of each assembly will affect its worship.

Identifying liturgical worship as a form of ritual action calls attention to the fact that it is a symbolic process. Liturgical worship is a dynamic symbolic activity in which space, objects, actions, words, time, and relationships all play a significant role in the shaping of meaning. In liturgy, worship is symbolically expressed or mediated.

However, christian worship is not restricted to liturgy. The symbolic actions of liturgical worship are intended to mediate lives of worship, lives of remembrance and hope, of praise and thanksgiving, lives of service grounded in the shared life which is the experience of those who have communion in God's Spirit through Jesus Christ.

See **Assembly, God, Jesus Christ, Liturgy, Paschal Mystery**

John E. Burkhart, *Worship,* Philadelphia: Westminster Press, 1982. Ferdinand Hahn, *The Worship of the Early Church,* Philadelphia: Fortress Press, 1973. Frank C. Senn, *Christian Worship and Its Cultural Setting,* Philadelphia: Fortress Press, 1983. W. Stahlin, "Koinonia and Worship," *Studia Liturgica* 1 (1962) pp. 220-227. Evelyn Underhill, *Worship,* New York: Crossroad, 1936, repr. 1982. Herman Wegman *Christian Worship in East and West: A Study Guide to Liturgical History,* trans., G.W. Lathrop, New York: Pueblo, 1985. James F. White, *Introduction to Christian Worship,* Nashville: Abingdon Press, 1980.

MARGARET MARY KELLEHER, OSU

Contributors

Francis H. Agnew, C.M., Kenrick Seminary, St. Louis, Missouri.

D.S. Amalorpavadass, University of Mysore and Acharya-Guru of Anjali Ashram, Mysore, India.

Diane Apostolos-Cappadona, Georgetown University, Washington, D.C.

Gerard Austin, O.P., The Catholic University of America, Washington, D.C.

John F. Baldovin, S.J., Jesuit School of Theology at Berkeley, California.

Bernard Batto, DePauw University, Greencastle, Indiana.

Christopher T. Begg, The Catholic University of America, Washington, D.C.

Dianne Bergant, C.S.A., Catholic Theological Union, Chicago, Illinois.

John Borelli, Bishops' Committee for Ecumenical and Interreligious Affairs, Washington, D.C.

Allan Bouley, O.S.B., St. John's University, Collegeville, Minnesota.

Joseph Boyle, St. Michael's College, Toronto, Ontario.

Joseph A. Bracken, S.J., Xavier University, Cincinnati, Ohio.

David B. Burrell, C.S.C., University of Notre Dame, Indiana.

Denis Carroll, Blackrock, Dublin.

Juliana Casey, Mundelein Seminary, University of St. Mary on the Lake, Mundelein, Illinois.

William Cenkner, The Catholic University of America, Washington, D.C.

W. Norris Clarke, S.J., Fordham University, Bronx, New York.

Ardis B. Collins, Loyola University of Chicago, Illinois.

John J. Collins, University of Notre Dame, Indiana.

Mary Collins, O.S.B., The Catholic University of America, Washington, D.C.

Joann Wolski Conn, Neumann College, Aston, Pennsylvania.

Mary Shawn Copeland, O.P., St. Norbert College, De Pere, Wisconsin.

John F. Craghan, St. Norbert College, De Pere, Wisconsin.

John W. Crossin, O.S.F.S., De Sales School of Theology, Washington, D.C.

Agnes Cunningham, S.S.C.M., Mundelein Seminary, University of St. Mary of the Lake, Mundelein, Illinois.

Joseph L. Cunningham, St. Vincent de Paul Regional Seminary, Boynton Beach, Florida.

Lawrence S. Cunningham, Florida State University, Tallahassee, Florida.

Frederick J. Cwiekowski, S.S., St. Mary's Seminary and University, Baltimore, Maryland.

Gabriel Daly, O.S.A., Augustinian House of Studies, Dublin.

Robert Daly, S.J., Boston College, Chestnut Hill, Massachusetts.

Carl A. Dehne, S.J., Loyola University of Chicago, Illinois.

William Dinges, The Catholic University of America, Washington, D.C.

Edmund J. Dobbin, O.S.A., Washington Theological Union, Silver Spring, Maryland.

Lawrence J. Donohoo, O.P., Providence College, Providence, Rhode Island.

Daniel Donovan, St. Michael's College, Toronto, Ontario.

Catherine Dooley, O.P., The Catholic University of America, Washington, D.C.

Regis Duffy, O.F.M., Washington Theological Union, Silver Spring, Maryland.

Avery Dulles, S.J., The Catholic University of America, Washington, D.C.

Judith A. Dwyer, S.S.J., Weston School of Theology, Cambridge, Massachusetts.

John Eagleson, Editorial Director, Meyer-Stone Books.

James L. Empereur, S.J., Jesuit School of Theology at Berkeley, California.

Robert B. Eno, S.S., The Catholic University of America, Washington, D.C.

John L. Esposito, College of the Holy Cross, Worcester, Massachusetts.

Seán Fagan, S.M., Secretary General of the Society of Mary, Rome.

Michael A. Fahey, S.J., St. Michael's College, Toronto, Ontario.

Alan D. Falconer, Irish School of Ecumenics, Dublin.

Robert Faricy, S.J., Pontifical Gregorian University, Rome.

Edward G. Farrugia, S.J., Pontifical Oriental Institute, Rome.

Mary Ann Fatula, O.P., Ohio Dominican College, Columbus, Ohio.

Wayne L. Fehr, University of Notre Dame, Indiana.

Francis Schüssler Fiorenza, Harvard University, Cambridge, Massachusetts.

Robert M. Friday, The Catholic University of America, Washington, D.C.

John T. Ford, C.S.C., The Catholic University of America, Washington, D.C.

Stephen Funk, The Catholic University of America, Washington, D.C.

Vincent J. Genovesi, S.J., St. Joseph's University, Philadelphia, Pennsylvania.

Philip Gleeson, O.P., Dominican House of Studies, Dublin.

Donald J. Goergen, O.P., Aquinas Institute, St. Louis, Missouri.

David Granfield, O.S.B., The Catholic University of America, Washington, D.C.

Patrick Granfield, O.S.B., The Catholic University of America, Washington, D.C.

Daniel P. Grigassy, O.F.M., Christ the King Seminary, Buffalo, New York.

Jeffrey Gros, F.S.C., Commission on Faith and Order, National Council of Churches of
    Christ in the USA, New York.

Charles W. Gusmer, Immaculate Conception Seminary, Seton Hall University, South
    Orange, New Jersey.

Roger Haight, S.J., Regis College, Toronto School of Theology, Ontario.

Gerald Hanratty, University College, Dublin.

Stephen Happel, The Catholic University of America, Washington, D.C.

Daniel J. Harrington, S.J., Weston School of Theology, Cambridge, Massachusetts.

Wilfrid Harrington, O.P., Milltown Institute of Theology and Philosophy and the
    Dominican House of Studies, Dublin.

John F. Haught, Georgetown University, Washington, D.C.

Zachary Hayes, O.F.M., Catholic Theological Union, Chicago, Illinois.

Charles C. Hefling, Jr., Boston College, Chestnut Hill, Massachusetts.

Monika K. Hellwig, Georgetown University, Washington, D.C.

William Henn, O.F.M. Cap., Capuchin College, Washington, D.C.

James Hennesey, S.J., Canisius College, Buffalo, New York.

Mark Henninger, S.J., Loyola University of Chicago, Illinois.

Mary Catherine Hilkert, O.P., Aquinas Institute, St Louis, Missouri.

Edmund Hill, O.P., St. Augustine's Seminary, Roma, Lesotho.

William J. Hill, O.P., The Catholic University of America, Washington, D.C.

Eugene Hillman, C.S.Sp., University of Nairobi, Kenya.

Paul D. Holland, S.J., South Bend, Indiana.

John Huels, Catholic Theological Union, Chicago, Illinois.

Robert P. Imbelli, Boston College, Chestnut Hill, Massachusetts.

Kevin W. Irwin, The Catholic University of America, Washington, D.C.

Werner G. Jeanrond, University of Dublin, Trinity College, Dublin.

Frederick M. Jelly, O.P., Mount St. Mary's Seminary, Emmitsburg, Maryland.

Joseph Jensen, O.S.B., The Catholic University of America, Washington, D.C.

Brian V. Johnstone, C.S.S.R., The Catholic University of America, Washington, D.C.

Mark D. Jordan, University of Notre Dame, Indiana.

Georgia M. Keightley, Loyola College in Maryland, Baltimore, Maryland.

Margaret Mary Kelleher, O.S.U., The Catholic University of America, Washington, D.C.

Anthony J. Kelly, C.S.S.R., Yarra Theological Union/Melbourne College of Divinity, Australia.

Joseph A. Komonchak, The Catholic University of America, Washington, D.C.

Matthew L. Lamb, Boston College, Chestnut Hill, Massachusetts.

Philip Land, S.J., Center for Concern, Washington, D.C.

Dermot A. Lane, Mater Dei Institute of Education, and the Seminary of Holy Cross College, Dublin.

John Langan, S.J., Woodstock Theological Center, Georgetown University, Washington, D.C.

Ernest E. Larkin, O.Carm., Phoenix, Arizona.

F. Lawrence, Boston College, Chestnut Hill, Massachusetts.

John Linnan, C.S.V., Catholic Theological Union, Chicago, Illinois.

William P. Loewe, The Catholic University of America, Washington, D.C.

James Lopresti, S.J., St. Ignatius Loyola Parish, New York, New York.

John E. Lynch, C.S.P., The Catholic University of America, Washington, D.C.

Timothy MacDonald, S.A., St. Francis of Assisi Novitiate, Garrison, New York.

James P. Mackey, University of Edinburgh, Scotland.

Shawn Madigan, College of St. Catherine, St. Paul, Minnesota.

Berard L. Marthaler, O.F.M.Conv., The Catholic University of America, Washington, D.C.

William E. May, The Catholic University of America, Washington, D.C.

William McConville, O.F.M., Washington Theological Union, Silver Spring, Maryland.

Gerald A. McCool, S.J., Fordham University, Bronx, New York.

Thomas McCreesh, O.P., Dominican House of Studies, Washington, D.C.

John M. McDermott, S.J., Fordham University, Bronx, New York.

Enda McDonagh, St. Patrick's College, Maynooth, Ireland.

Patrick McGoldrick, St. Patrick's College, Maynooth, Ireland.

John H. McKenna, C.M., St. John's University, Jamaica, New York.

Martin McNamara, M.S.C., Sacred Heart Missionaries, Galway, Ireland.

Vincent MacNamara, Trinity College, Dublin.

Louis McNeil, Glenmary Research Center, Atlanta, Georgia.

Francis X. Meehan, Immaculata College, Immaculata, Pennsylvania.

Raymond Moloney, S.J., Milltown Institute, Dublin.

Marie Augusta Neal, S.N.D. de Namur, Emmanuel College, Boston, Massachusetts.

Brian M. Nolan, All Hallows Missionary College, Dublin.

James C. Notebaart, St. Dominic's Major Seminary, Lusaka, Zambia.

Irene M. Nowell, O.S.B., Mount St. Scholastica, Atchison, Kansas.

Michael O'Carroll, C.S.Sp., Blackrock College, Dublin.

Gerald O'Collins, S.J., Gregorian University, Rome.

John O'Donnell, S.J., Gregorian University, Rome.

Leo J. O'Donovan, S.J., Loyola College in Maryland, Baltimore, Maryland.

Thomas F. O'Meara, O.P., University of Notre Dame, Indiana.

Ladislas Örsy, S.J., The Catholic University of America, Washington, D.C.

Kenan B. Osborne, O.F.M., Franciscan School of Theology, Graduate Theological Union, Berkeley, California.

Gilbert Ostdiek, Catholic Theological Union, Chicago, Illinois.

John T. Pawlikowski, O.S.M., Catholic Theological Union, Chicago, Illinois.

M. Basil Pennington, O.C.S.O., Abbey of Our Lady of St. Joseph, Spencer, Massachusetts.

Pheme Perkins, Boston College, Chestnut Hill, Massachusetts.

Carl J. Peter, The Catholic University of America, Washington, D.C.

Quentin Quesnell, Smith College, Northampton, Massachusetts.

Boniface Ramsey, O.P., Sacred Heart Parish, Jersey City, New Jersey.

Thomas P. Rausch, S.J., Loyola Marymount University in Los Angeles, California.

James M. Reese, O.S.F.S., St. John's University, Jamaica, New York.

Nancy C. Ring, Le Moyne College, Syracuse, New York.

Rosemary Ruether, Garrett-Evangelical Theological Seminary, Evanston, Illinois.

John R. Sachs, S.J., Weston School of Theology, Cambridge, Massachusetts.

T. Howland Sanks, S.J., Jesuit School of Theology at Berkeley, California.

Michael J. Scanlon, O.S.A., Washington Theological Union, Silver Spring, Maryland.

Thomas F. Schindler, S.S., St. Mary's Seminary and University, Baltimore, Maryland.

Donald Senior, C.P., Catholic Theological Union, Chicago, Illinois.

Gerard Sloyan, Temple University, Philadelphia, Pennsylvania.

Raymond Studzinski, O.S.B., The Catholic University of America, Washington, D.C.

Carroll Stuhlmueller, C.P., Catholic Theological Union, Chicago, Illinois.

Francis A. Sullivan, S.J., Gregorian University, Rome.

Lionel Swain, West Sussex, England.

Anthony J. Tambasco, Georgetown University, Washington, D.C.

George H. Tavard, A.A., Methodist Theological School in Ohio, Delaware, Ohio.

David M. Thomas, Regis College, Denver, Colorado.

J.M.R. Tillard, O.P., Dominican House of Studies, Ottawa.

Terrence Tilley, St. Michael's College, Winooski, Vermont.

Denys Turner, University of Bristol, England.

Julia Upton, R.S.M., St. John's University, Jamaica, New York.

Edward Collins Vacek, S.J., Weston School of Theology, Cambridge, Massachusetts.

Michael Vertin, St. Michael's College, Toronto, Ontario.

James J. Walter, Loyola University of Chicago, Illinois.

Thomas E. Wangler, Boston College, Chestnut Hill, Massachusetts.

James Michael Weiss, Boston College, Chestnut Hill, Massachusetts.

John Welch, O.Carm., Washington Theological Union, Silver Spring, Maryland.

James A. Wiseman, O.S.B., The Catholic University of America, Washington, D.C.

Richard Woods, O.P., Loyola University of Chicago, Illinois.

John H. Wright, S.J., Woodstock Theological Center, Georgetown University, Washington, D.C.

Gordon C. Zahn, University of Massachusetts—Boston.